Again,

for Joan and Debra.

And for David, Dan, Jennifer and Steve,

Robin and Tom, Sara, Peter and Vivianne,

Rick and Marie, and all their children

that are and may be. And for Kristin, Ben,

and Henry.

TENTH EDITION

LITERATURE
THE HUMAN EXPERIENCE

TENTH EDITION

LITERATURE
THE HUMAN EXPERIENCE

RICHARD ABCARIAN

AND

MARVIN KLOTZ
California State University, Northridge, Emeriti

SAMUEL COHEN
University of Missouri

BEDFORD/ST. MARTIN'S
Boston ◆ New York

For Bedford/St. Martin's

Senior Executive Editor: Stephen A. Scipione
Developmental Editor: Amy Hurd Gershman
Production Editor: Katherine Caruana
Production Supervisor: Jennifer Peterson
Marketing Manager: Adrienne Petsick
Editorial Assistant: Kate Mayhew
Copyeditor: Mary Lou Wilshaw-Watts
Senior Art Director: Anna Palchik
Text Design: Joan O'Connor
Cover Design: Donna Lee Dennison
Cover Art: Tonya Engel, *Best Actress.* Courtesy of Morgan Gaynin, Inc.
Composition: Glyph International
Printing and Binding: Quebecor World Taunton

President: Joan E. Feinberg
Editorial Director: Denise B. Wydra
Editor in Chief: Karen S. Henry
Director of Marketing: Karen R. Soeltz
Director of Editing, Design, and Production: Marcia Cohen
Assistant Director of Editing, Design, and Production: Elise S. Kaiser
Managing Editor: Elizabeth M. Schaaf

Library of Congress Control Number: 2009927954

For information, write: Bedford/St. Martin's, 75 Arlington Street, Boston, MA 02116
(617-399-4000)

ISBN-10: 0–312–55644–6
ISBN-13: 978–0–312–55644–0

Acknowledgments

PREFACE FOR INSTRUCTORS

We all suffer alone in the real world; true empathy's impossible. But if a piece of fiction can allow us imaginatively to identify with a character's pain, we might then also more easily conceive of others identifying with our own. This is nourishing, redemptive; we become less alone inside. It might just be that simple.

—David Foster Wallace

Introductions can be awkward. People who don't know each other are asked to make a connection in what might be a highly artificial setting. Introductions can go well: people can hit it off, finding a connection based on common life experiences or ways of looking at things, and may even form lifelong friendships. Sometimes, though, introductions go badly, and those possible areas of commonality are never discovered. This is a shame.

As with life, so too with literature. In the constructed setting of the classroom, we teachers want our students to hit if off with literature. We don't want awkward silences and stiff formality. We want students to connect to the literature we admire and enjoy—to find common ground with it, to see how it meets and illuminates the themes and concerns of their own lives. As teachers, we hope that our efforts will not merely acquaint students with literature but also make it a lifelong companion, to be relied on for inspiration, insight, and wisdom.

As the authors of this volume, we hope and expect that your students will hit it off with much of the literature on these pages. Our new coauthor, Samuel Cohen, has brought with him a host of selections by young and emerging writers (including many whose works grace that recent genre students find so beguiling: creative nonfiction). He has also introduced innovations to the book's pedagogy, such as compact clusters of literary works that encourage critical comparative thinking and creative writing topics that give students opportunities to see literature—and life—from a writer's point of view. In its tenth edition, *Literature: The Human Experience* has grown slimmer but still contains multitudes. It remains a complete resource for introducing students to literature and helping them connect it to their own lives.

A THEMATIC ORGANIZATION THAT CONNECTS LITERATURE TO LIFE

We believe that students are most immediately engaged by works in which they can see themselves. The ability of students to connect their experiences to those they read about does not mean they should be assigned nothing but

vii

literature about students or Americans or Westerners or young people from anywhere; it does mean that the human experience, in its dazzling variety, can be represented in art and responded to no matter the different circumstances of reader and writer. In gathering these works, we tried to meet students where they live and take them to places they have never seen. The best way to do this is to concentrate on different themes drawn from human experience and to ask students to read different treatments of these themes from divergent perspectives. The anthology is organized into five thematic sections: "Innocence and Experience," "Conformity and Rebellion," "Culture and Identity," "Love and Hate," and "The Presence of Death." Each section opens with a short introductory essay and questions that invite students to reflect on their own experiences with the chapter's theme.

To provide the utmost flexibility for teaching, the thematic structure is augmented by two subordinate organizations. Embedded in each thematic section, the stories, poems, plays, and nonfiction are grouped by genre; and within each genre, selections are arranged chronologically by author's birth date. (The date following the title indicates the selection's first appearance in a book; a designation in parentheses indicates the date of either composition or appearance in a publication other than a book. We have not attempted to date traditional ballads.) The dates, together with an appendix containing biographical notes on the authors, provide students with a brief historical context for each work. So whether you teach literature thematically or generically or historically—or some combination of the three—the organization of *Literature: The Human Experience* accommodates your approach.

SUPPORT FOR READING AND WRITING ABOUT LITERATURE

Two introductory chapters, "Responding to Literature" and "Writing about Literature," give students the tools to think about and appreciate what they read and to put those thoughts into words. In these chapters, we discuss the formal elements of each genre and provide descriptions and samples of various forms of written response and documentation. Throughout the thematic sections, study questions challenge students to analyze works, to make connections between them, and to write about them in a variety of ways. At the end of the book, the "Glossary of Literary Terms" and the "Glossary of Critical Approaches" provide additional resources for students learning about how to approach literature.

NEW TO THIS EDITION

While retaining most of the classic and signature works that have long characterized this anthology, the tenth edition also includes an especially engaging selection of contemporary literature that your students will be eager to experience.

PROVOCATIVE NEW FICTION—More than half of the nineteen new stories are by renowned younger writers, such as Aimee Bender, Jonathan Lethem,

Hari Kunzru, and Jhumpa Lahiri. Moreover, many of the new stories explore the perspectives, adventures, and dilemmas of youthful characters.

RECENT POETRY BY POETS TO WATCH—Of the fifty-eight new poems, many are by contemporary poets who are as well regarded as they are rarely anthologized in textbooks: poets such as Joshua Clover, Mark Halliday, Kay Ryan, Tomaž Šalamun, and Mary Ruefle.

SHORT PLAYS BY ACCLAIMED CONTEMPORARY PLAYWRIGHTS—The two new brief, teachable dramatic works are David Henry Hwang's *Trying to Find Chinatown* and a play sequence from Suzan-Lori Parks's *365 Days/365 Plays*.

A FRESH GATHERING OF NONFICTION—Almost all of the fifteen new essays date from the past few years and represent some of the most stimulating work in this increasingly important genre—from prizewinning essays by David Sedaris, Toi Derricotte, and Ellen Levy to short examples of creative nonfiction from the much-admired online journal *Brevity*.

Also new to the tenth edition:

LIVELY "CONNECTIONS" CLUSTERS PROMOTE ENGAGED CRITICAL READING AND WRITING—The thematic sections are punctuated with twenty-four short units that pair or cluster literary works—often classic with contemporary. While promoting comparative critical thinking with their accompanying questions and writing assignments, these compact clusters provide engaging reading for students. For example, "Connecting Stories: Superantiheroes" features work by Harlan Ellison and Jonathan Lethem about alienated and peculiar superheroes. In "Connecting Poems: Self-Declarations," five poets with memorable first-person voices (and a penchant for cataloging) own up to their heritages. In "Connecting Nonfiction: Demystifying Love" two essayists take a hard look at romance—one from a biological and the other from a cultural perspective.

A NEW CASEBOOK CONNECTS WRITING AND REVISION—A new casebook presents Raymond Carver's eye-opening revisions of two of his best-known stories. This author-in-depth casebook joins three other casebooks, each representing a different approach to thinking about literature: a critical casebook on Sophocles' play *Oedipus Rex*, a contextual casebook on Martin Luther King Jr.'s "Letter from Birmingham Jail," and a visual casebook that pairs full-color paintings with poems about them.

MORE HELP FOR READING AND WRITING—The introductory chapters emphasize the importance of making connections and explain how relating to what we read can help us understand literature, ourselves, and each other and can guide us more easily through the writing process. Practical models of how to work with literature include a new annotated poem and a new example of plot summary.

ADDITIONAL RESOURCES FOR TEACHING AND LEARNING

Re: Writing for Literature is the best collection of Web resources for literature and composition classrooms. Free, open, and easy to access at **bedfordstmartins .com/rewritinglit,** students will find tutorials for close reading, links to author biographies, quizzes on literary works, and a glossary of literary terms. Model documents, writing exercises, grammar help, and resources for finding and citing sources provide invaluable writing help. The site features the *VirtuaLit Interactive Poetry Tutorial* offering in-depth readings with coverage of literary elements, cultural contexts, and critical approaches for Elizabeth Bishop's "The Fish," Theodore Roethke's "My Papa's Waltz," and Andrew Marvell's "To His Coy Mistress."

LiterActive is a CD-ROM that offers tutorials, a multimedia library, and research and documentation advice and exercises to help students read, think, research, and write about literature. To order this CD-ROM with student copies of the book, use package ISBN-10: 0-312-41333-5, ISBN-13: 978-0-312-41333-0.

Re: Writing Plus gathers Bedford/St. Martin's premium digital content into one collection for literature and composition. Explore our newest resource, Video Central, a growing collection of over fifty brief videos for the literature and writing classroom. To order *Literature: The Human Experience,* Tenth Edition, with *Re:Writing Plus,* use package ISBN-10: 0-312-48849-1, ISBN-13: 978-0-312-48849-9.

Editor's Notes for Teaching **Literature: The Human Experience** offers teaching ideas for each selection in the anthology as well as additional thematic connections and writing topics. *Editor's Notes* is available online at **bedfordstmartins.com/experience_literature/catalog.**

Literary reprints of classic works are available in the Case Studies in Contemporary Criticism series, the Bedford Cultural Editions series, the Bedford Shakespeare series, and the Bedford Series in History and Culture. Volumes can be shrink-wrapped with *Literature: The Human Experience* for instructors who wish to teach longer works in conjunction with the anthology. To learn more, visit **bedfordstmartins.com/literaryreprints.**

TradeUp adds value and choice to your students' learning experiences. Package their Bedford/St. Martin's textbook with one of a thousand titles from Macmillan publishers—at a discount of 50 percent off the regular price.

Video and DVD library selections of plays and stories included in the anthology are available from Bedford/St. Martin's to qualified adopters.

ACKNOWLEDGMENTS

We would like to thank the professors who generously took time to share their ideas about the previous edition of this anthology. They are Fred Allen, George Fox University; Andrew Block, ECPI College of Technology; Bridgett Boulton,

Truckee Meadows Community College; Pamela Callan, Limestone College; Patricia Cockram, Lehman College CUNY; Ana Douglass, Truckee Meadows Community College; Noreen Lois Duncan, Mercer County Community College; Mary M. Evans, Hudson Valley Community College; Vivian A. Hagood, Tulsa Community College; Timothy G. Kiogora, Eastern Kentucky University; Caroline Lewis, Georgia College & State University; Maria Makowiecka, Bergen Community College; Rene A. Martin, Miami-Dade College; Timothy B. Messick, Mohawk Valley Community College; Ray Nowak, Axia College of University of Phoenix Online; Biljana Obradovic, Xavier University of Louisiana; Nancy O'Donnell, Monroe Community College; Joseph Powell, Central Washington University; Michael L. Richmond, NOVA Southeastern University; Ilknur Sancak-Marusa, West Chester University; Stephen Schaffrath, Slippery Rock University; Steven Schneider, Rockland Community College; Tannie Shannon, Sam Houston State University; Robert Vettese, Southern Maine Community College; Monica Wagner, Lutheran High School; Frederick White, Slippery Rock University.

We wish to thank Karissa Lagos, whose precocious writing skills provided us with a superb research paper. We also wish to thank Anita Zubère, who helped untangle some knotty lines of poetry; Roy Merrens for explaining some of the arcane features of the urban London landscape; and Bainbridge Scott, whose knowledge of music made our task easier. Our thanks also go to Mary Lawless for her thoughtful contributions to the introductory chapters on reading and writing and to Sara Eaton Gaunt for her smart and detailed updates to the biographical notes.

Experienced and wise people at Bedford/St. Martin's have guided this book along the way. We thank the president, Joan Feinberg, and the editorial director, Denise Wydra, for supporting this tenth edition. As well, we are grateful to Sandy Schecter and Douglas Hernandez for procuring permissions, Mary Lou Wilshaw-Watts for copyediting, and Elizabeth Schaaf and Katherine Caruana for shepherding the book through production. We thank Donna Dennison for creating the design of an engaging new cover, Joan O'Connor for redesigning the interior pages, and Adrienne Petsick for providing expert marketing advice. We thank editor in chief Karen Henry for her encouraging and nurturing leadership. For the work of reconceiving the book for its new edition and with its new author, senior executive editor Steve Scipione is owed enormous thanks, as is associate editor Amy Hurd Gershman, for her vision, hard work, and endless patience and good humor. This book would simply not be what it is without their contributions—it would not exist at all. Some of this labor (there's certainly enough to go around) must surely be credited to editorial assistant Kate Mayhew: to her, many thanks as well.

Richard Abcarian
Marvin Klotz
Samuel Cohen

CONTENTS

CONNECTING POEMS: REVISITING FAIRY TALES 169

CONNECTING POEMS: VOICES OF EXPERIENCE 176

DRAMA   182

NONFICTION   261

CONNECTING NONFICTION: ADVICE TO GRADUATES   278

CONFORMITY AND REBELLION   288

QUESTIONS FOR THINKING AND WRITING   290

CONNECTING POEMS: REVOLUTIONARY THINKING   424

CONNECTING POEMS: REMEMBERING FATHERS   943

APPENDICES   1341

ALTERNATE CONTENTS

Arranged by genre and alphabetically by the author's last name

FICTION

POETRY

ART

DOCUMENTS

EXCERPTS FROM LONGER WORKS

ARISTOTLE

D. W. LUCAS

INTRODUCTION

RESPONDING TO LITERATURE

There is no Frigate like a Book
To take us Lands away
Nor any Coursers like a Page
Of prancing poetry—

This Traverse may the poorest take
Without oppress of Toll—
How frugal is the Chariot
That bears the Human soul.
    —Emily Dickinson (ca. 1873)

WHY WE READ LITERATURE

The epigraph from poet Emily Dickinson promotes reading as an escape, a way for us to take a vacation from our lives. If we think about our experiences with literature—and with movies and TV shows—that probably sounds about right. Most of us have enjoyed forgetting about the cares of the world with a page-turning thriller or a tear-jerking melodrama. But literature can also help us get closer to life, to understand it in a new way when we get back from our literary journey. We understand what Dickinson means because we can connect to it— we think about our experiences as readers and that helps us understand the poem while, at the same time, the poem clarifies something about how reading makes us feel. The best literature helps us to understand ourselves, each other, and our world in new ways and to make connections that had never occurred to us or that we might have sensed but were unable to express.

Of course, you may not feel this way about reading the kind of literature you expect to find in a textbook. It may be that opening a textbook signals to you that the fun is over. And certainly reading and responding to serious literature requires concentrated attention and is not relaxing in the way that kicking back and watching a TV show might be. But many things you enjoy may require energetic engagement—for example, playing sports or video games. And you have been responding critically to literature all your life. The cartoons you watched as a child; the cartoons you may watch now; the movies, TV dramas, and sitcoms you enjoy have all marked your life. Inevitably, when you encounter any kind of literature, you distinguish good from evil, right from wrong. The writers convey cultural ideas about the nature of love, of duty, of heroism—sometimes broadly, sometimes with subtlety—and you agree or disagree, are moved or not. You may not now be moved by the same literature that entranced you when you were a child, or you may have come to appreciate that literature in a fuller, more nuanced way. But you may be surprised, when you turn your attention to "serious" literature, to find how much these works have in common with the books and movies you have turned to for entertainment. Some "popular" authors—John Le Carré, Dorothy Sayers, P. D. James, and others—who write spy novels and detective fiction are routinely read in college courses that celebrate literature. Their exciting and suspenseful novels are often made into films, but so, too, are the classic works of William Shakespeare, Jane Austen, Charles Dickens, Henry James, William Faulkner, and Ernest Hemingway.

Serious literature, no less than popular literature, embodies thrilling adventure. Serious literature is replete with monsters (consider the Old English epic *Beowulf*), ghosts (at the outset of Shakespeare's *Hamlet* and in the middle of *Macbeth*), witches, supernatural spirits, magical transformations, unspeakably brutal wars, terrible murders, and bloody vengeance. Given the close ties between popular and serious literature, scholars, teachers, and readers frequently debate what should be included in textbooks like this one, what literature best represents the "literary canon." Here things get a bit murky. *Canon* is derived from the Latin word meaning "measuring line or rule" and is used ecclesiastically to signify "sacred writings admitted to the catalog according to the rule." Early theologians decided which books were the authentic word of God and which were not. But, much like today's literary scholars, they did not always agree. Although it attempts to establish the body of literature that humans need to study and master, the literary canon changes frequently in response to political and social changes. Further, a literary canon is bound to reflect the cultural tradition that produces it. The literary canon of China will differ markedly from the literary canon of the United States. And both will change with the eruptions of history and the demands of fashion.

For example, although American literary history is replete with women writers, they have often been undervalued by the literary canon's guardians. But a century of political struggle—which led, first, to enfranchising women as voters and, later, to a feminist movement that demanded equality for women and their works—has allowed some women authors to gain traction in the canon, forever changing it. Writers like Kate Chopin and Charlotte Perkins Gilman are now routinely included in university courses and women writers are broadly represented in this anthology. Further, the political struggles of Native American, African American, Latin American, and Asian American citizens have drawn considerable attention to a large and diverse body of writing that was often overlooked by Eurocentric critics. Skillful literary artists from these groups are also represented here.

You might reasonably ask, What difference does broadening the literary canon make? If you love books and movies, then you know how influential they can be and you'll probably agree that what we read makes a tremendous difference to the world we live in. You learn a great deal about your society from reading—what it values, what it condemns, how it expects you to behave, what constitutes success both economically and morally, what it sees as the very nature of good and evil. If your reading were limited to, say, Eurocentric works and you were embedded in a non-European social group, you would not discover yourself or your peers in the books you read. Thus, schools and anthologies that project a narrow literary canon would present a world foreign to your experience. The resulting sense of anomie—a rootless lack of purpose, identity, and values—could be terribly damaging. At the same time, ignorance of your neighbors' lifestyles could also seriously impair your life by giving you a skewed, incomplete vision of the world. Conversely, reading widely could help you avoid the baleful consequences of racism, hypernationalism, and ignorance.

The stories, poems, plays, and essays in this textbook have been selected from a diverse array of important authors, some of them very popular, others often most appreciated by scholars. Some of these writers have been read and studied in schools and colleges for centuries while others, especially from historically underrepresented groups like Native Americans and women, may be entirely new to you. We have brought together this exciting collection of authors and thinkers in a way that we hope allows you to find surprising commonalities— among these very different writers and between them and you. The units are organized around universal themes—love and death but also relationships with parents or attitudes toward authority—and are designed to help you connect your own life and the things you are reading to the many literary traditions that join us to each other, to our collective history, and to the world at large. The literature in this volume will take you out of your comfort zone to "lands away" while giving you new tools for understanding yourself and your immediate world. The only "toll" required is an open mind and a watchful eye.

READING ACTIVELY

Read attentively! Don't read passively! Don't let the author con you. Keep a pencil in your hand and interact with the page. Mark words you don't recognize and look them up in the dictionary (you might want to do this when you've finished the piece). When you feel a protest rising in your throat, mark your feeling in the margin. When you find a line that tickles you, mark that also. If you feel the author has generated an insight, state it in the margin. If the story reminds you of something in your own life or in another work of art—if you make any kind of connection—write that down, too. We might sum up this advice by urging you to read *interactively*—to engage in a conversation with the author or even with the story's characters.

READING AND THINKING CRITICALLY

In a well-ordered universe, you would enjoy all your reading—and your delight would derive from your complete understanding of what you read. But if you have already reached this happy condition, you would have no need of a course such as this. You would know how literature "worked." You would recognize its historical sources, all the allusions, all the verbal wit, all the moral energy. You would be an authoritative judge of the success or failure of each piece you read. Alas, none of us will ever reach that exalted plane. We all keep on learning and acquiring new tools that allow us to pry the lids off new containers of wit and wisdom. When we ask you to read critically, we ask that you use that complex set of experiences that define you as a human being to analyze the work you encounter. Primarily, you need to bring sensitivity to language as well as a sense of the cultural imperatives among which you live.

When you become a critical reader, you learn to address your biases, enlarge your universe, and test your comfortable convictions. Thus, when you adopt a critical position toward a piece of literature, you need to test and question that position. To read a work critically, ask, What perspective does the author have that led him or her to write this work? What social, cultural, or historical conditions influenced the production of the work of literature? What other ways might the author have presented the ideas or subjects of the work? Are the author's values different from your own? How do your views and experiences affect whether you like or dislike the work?

As you begin writing about a work and developing a working thesis, test the evidence you use. Does any evidence in the story point to conclusions other than the ones you draw? Review the work and your notes on it to be certain you have not overlooked or misinterpreted details that might contradict your thesis. Scrutinize your argument to determine whether your readers will find your thesis persuasive and your supporting evidence convincing.

For example, read Peter Meinke's "Advice to My Son" (p. 177). On a first look at the poem's imagery, it might seem to readers familiar with Christian practice that the bread and wine mentioned in the last three lines allude to Holy Communion. But review the entire poem for evidence of this interpretation. The speaker's paradoxical advice on how best to live in a dangerous world counsels a combination of prudence ("plant squash and spinach, turnips and tomatoes") and intense pleasure ("the peony and the rose," "marry a pretty girl"). It concludes with an admonition to "always serve bread with your wine." The body of the poem strongly suggests that "bread" represents a prudent attention to the mundane requirements of living, while "wine" represents physical pleasure. Temper your pursuit of pleasure by serving bread when wine is served; but enjoy life passionately by always serving wine. Carefully scrutinizing your evidence and reasons in this way—and setting aside arguments not supported by the work—will strengthen your thesis and make it more convincing.

READING FICTION

Fiction creates imaginary worlds by telling stories written in *prose* (ordinary, unrhymed language), about realistic characters, set in physical environments, and with sustained attention to descriptive detail.

Works of fiction *narrate*, or tell, stories. Of course, narrative is not specific to fiction or to any other literary genre: telling stories pervades almost every aspect of our daily lives. We learn very early on how to recognize and tell stories, and we rely heavily on narrative to organize and make sense of our experience. For example, when we study history, we mostly study stories of various events.

Likewise, an astronomer's account of the universe's origins may take the shape of a narrative. Even in our sleep, we tell ourselves stories in the form of dreams. It is impossible to imagine our lives without these narratives; in fact, every culture uses them to order and make sense of lived experience. Narrative fiction is not meant to recount actual events, of course, though it may refer to real events or real persons. Rather than relate actual experiences, fiction uses narrative to shape imaginary ones.

Works of fiction, however, cannot be reduced to a listing of their narrative events any more than paintings can be replaced by diagrams. Such summaries diminish a work's realism, which is produced by careful description of characters, settings, and actions, as well as its depths of meaning. For example, the emotional impact of James Joyce's "Araby" cannot be captured by summarizing its simple plot. Without suspending critical judgment, readers of fiction have to be willing to suspend disbelief, that is, to enter the imaginary world of the novel or short story.

The Methods of Fiction

In order to examine the methods of fiction—tone, setting, plot, theme, characterization, point of view, and irony—let us look more closely at James Joyce's "Araby" (p. 92).

TONE One of the things most readers first respond to in a short story is its *tone*. Because it is like a mood, tone is difficult to talk about. It can be defined as an author's implicit attitude toward the characters, places, and events in the story and toward the reader of the work. Tone depends for its substance on delicate emotional responses to language and situation. Notice how a distinct tone is established in the language of the opening lines of "Araby":

> North Richmond Street, being blind, was a quiet street except at the hour when the Christian Brothers' School set the boys free. An uninhabited house of two storeys stood at the blind end, detached from its neighbours in a square ground. The other houses of the street, conscious of decent lives within them, gazed at one another with brown imperturbable faces.

Is this scene cheerful? Vital and active? Should we expect this story to celebrate the joys of growing up in Dublin? Negative responses to these questions arise from the tone of the opening description. Notice, for example, that the dead-end street is "blind"; that the school is said to "set the boys free," which makes it sound like a prison; that the uninhabited house is "detached from its neighbours"; and that the other houses, personified, gaze at one another with "brown imperturbable faces"—*brown* being a nondescript color and *imperturbable* reinforcing the still, lifeless, somber quality of the passage as a whole.

PLOT Through the series of events that make up a story's *plot*, an author presents us with a carefully created fictional world. In "Araby," the plot, or the arrangement of a connected sequence of narrative events, can be simply stated. A young boy who lives in a drab but respectable neighborhood develops a crush on his playmate's sister. She asks him if he intends to go to a charity fair that she cannot attend. He resolves to go and purchase a gift for her. He is tormented by the late and drunken arrival of his uncle, who has promised him the money he needs. When the boy finally arrives at the bazaar, he is disappointed by the difference between his expectation and the actuality of the almost deserted fair. He perceives some minor events, overhears some minor conversation, and the climax occurs when he confronts the darkened fair and the banal expression of sexual attraction between two gentlemen and a young woman. This sequence of events prompts the boy to see himself "as a creature driven and derided by vanity."

CHARACTERIZATION   One of the obvious differences between short stories and novels is that story writers develop characters rapidly and limit the number of developed characters. Many stories have only one fleshed-out, or *round,* character; the other characters are frequently two-dimensional, or *flat.* Rarely does a short story have more than three developed characters.

One feature that distinguishes "Araby" is its *characterization,* or the process by which the characters are rendered to make them seem real to the reader. Characterization, however, cannot easily be separated from the other elements of fiction; that is, it depends heavily on tone, plot, theme, setting, and so on. It is part of the boy's character, for example, that he lives in a brown imperturbable house on North Richmond Street, that he does the things he does (which constitute the plot of the story), and that he learns about what he does (which is the theme). Much of this characterization in "Araby" emerges from Joyce's rich *style,* or the way he uses language and images. Consider how the boy's character is revealed in the following paragraph:

> Her image accompanied me even in places the most hostile to romance. On Saturday evenings when my aunt went marketing I had to go to carry some of the parcels. We walked through the flaring streets, jostled by drunken men and bargaining women, amid the curses of labourers, the shrill litanies of shop-boys who stood on guard by the barrels of pigs' cheeks, the nasal chanting of street-singers, who sang a *come-all-you* about O'Donovan Rossa, or a ballad about the troubles in our native land. These noises converged in a single sensation of life for me: I imagined that I bore my chalice safely through a throng of foes. Her name sprang to my lips at moments in strange prayers and praises which I myself did not understand. My eyes were often full of tears (I could not tell why) and at times a flood from my heart seemed to pour itself out into my bosom. I thought little of the future. I did not know whether I would ever speak to her or not or, if I spoke to her, how I could tell her of my confused adoration. But my body was like a harp and her words and gestures were like fingers running upon the wires.

In this passage, character is revealed through *diction,* or choice of words. By using the words *litanies, prayers,* and *adoration,* the narrator draws heavily from the distinctive vocabulary of the Roman Catholic Church. (The reference to the harp also reinforces the religious tone of the passage.) *Chalice* and *throng of foes* are related to this tradition as well; a chalice is a cup for the consecrated wine of the Eucharist, and throngs of foes often confronted the Christian martyrs whose deeds are immortalized in religious literature. At the same time, however, these last two phrases call up the world of chivalric romance, which is alluded to in the first line of the paragraph. The narrator's diction casts his awakening sexuality in the mold of high romance on the one hand and Christian devotion on the other. This sense of holy chivalry (reinforced by the earlier reference to the priest who owned a chivalric novel) stands in sharp contrast to the humdrum experience of carrying groceries home from the market.

SETTING   Unlike novels, short stories usually work themselves out in a restricted geographical *setting*—in a single place and within a short period of time. Any consideration of setting should include the historical time when a story takes place and the social situation set in the story, as well as the physical location of the events. In "Araby," the dreary details of Dublin are significantly described in the story's very first lines.

POINT OF VIEW   A character's or narrator's diction raises important questions about who is narrating the story. What is the narrator like? Is he reliable or unreliable? How can we judge? These questions help us distinguish another element of fiction, *point of view*. "Araby" is a first-person narrative; that is, the story is told from the perspective of a narrator who speaks in the first person. Most of the time, first-person narrators use the singular (*I, my*); in "A Rose for Emily" (p. 000), however, Faulkner's narrator uses the first person plural (*we, our*).

Third-person point of view—in which the narrator does not appear as a character in the story—is the most common perspective used to tell stories. Using third-person point of view, a narrator tells a story from the outside, referring to the characters as *she, he,* and *they*. A narrator who knows everything, can tell us what the characters are thinking, and can move around in space and time at will is an *omniscient narrator*. Alternatively, a narrator who chooses to focus on the thoughts, feelings, and actions of a single character is called a *limited omniscient narrator*. Generally, the brevity of the short story makes the first-person or limited omniscient narrations the most frequently used points of view for these works, while the lengthy and comparatively complex narrative of novels is more suited to the omniscient point of view.

A less frequently employed point of view is that of the second person, in which the author addresses the action to a character identified as *you*. For example, "You ask the clerk for change; he gives you four quarters. You go outside and wait for the bus." Although it evokes a rare intimacy with the reader, second-person point of view is difficult to sustain even in a short story.

IRONY   Authors' decisions about point of view create powerful narrative effects. Throughout "Araby," we sense a gap between the boy's sensibility and that of the more mature narrator, who refers at various times to his "innumerable follies" and "foolish blood." That is, we see the events of "Araby" from the boy's perspective, even though the language is that of an adult. The gap between the boy's knowledge and the narrator's creates *irony*.

There may be more than one level of irony at work in a story. When the narrator calls himself "a creature driven and derided by vanity," whose eyes "burned with anguish and anger," this overstatement is known as *verbal irony*. Some critics have maintained that the romanticized language of the story's conclusion itself invites an ironical reading—that is, we readers may know something about the narrator that he does not know himself—that he idealizes disenchantment as fervently as the boy idealized romance and religion. In short, Joyce may be using *dramatic irony,* encouraging the reader to see things about the first-person narrator that he does not see about himself. Both kinds of irony hinge on differing levels of knowledge and the author's skillful manipulation of narrative perspective.

THEME   *Theme* is an underlying idea, a statement that a work makes about its subject. This tiny stretch of experience out of the boy's life introduces him to an awareness of the differences between imagination and reality, between his romantic infatuation and the vulgar reality all about him. The theme of "Araby" emerges from the drab setting and mundane events of the story as a general statement about an intensely idealized and childish love, the shattering recognition of the false sentimentality that occasions it, and the enveloping vulgarity of adult life. By detailing a few events from one boy's life, the story illuminates the painful loss of innocence we all endure. In this case, the *protagonist,* or main character, experiences what Joyce called an *epiphany,* or sudden flash of recognition, that signals the awareness of a set of moral complexities in a world that once seemed uncomplicated and predictable.

We often speak of tone, setting, plot, theme, characterization, and point of view as separate aspects of a story in order to break down a complex narrative into more manageable parts. But this analytic process of identifying various elements is something we have done to the story: the story (if it is a good one) is an integrated whole. The more closely we examine the separate elements, the clearer it becomes that each is integrally related to the others.

In "Araby," Joyce employs the methods of fiction to create a world based on 1895 Dublin and Irish middle-class society. The success or failure of the story depends on Joyce's ability to render that world convincingly and our willingness to enter it imaginatively. We must not refuse to engage that world because the characters do not act as we would have them act or because the events never actually happened. Novelist Henry James urged that readers allow the author to have his or her *donnée,* or "given." When we grant this, the act of reading fiction provides us with much more pleasure and emotional insight.

Exploring Fiction

Here are some questions to ask as you set out to read or write about fiction. Your answers to these questions will help you brainstorm and develop the ideas that form your response to a story.

1. What is the tone of the story? Read the first several paragraphs to see how the tone is established. Does the tone change with the events in the story or remain fixed? How does the tone contribute to the effect of the story?

2. What is the plot of the story? Does the sequence of events that make up the plot emerge logically from the nature of the characters and circumstances? Or does the plot rely on coincidence and arbitrary events?

3. Who are the principal characters in the story? (There are rarely more than three in a short story; the other characters are often portrayed sketchily, sometimes even as stereotypes.) What functions do the minor characters serve? Do any characters change during the course of the story? How and why?

4. What is the setting of the story? Does it play an important role, or is it simply the place and time where things happen? How would some other setting affect the story?

5. From what point of view is the narrator telling the story? Do you trust him or her? If a first-person narrator who participates in the action is telling the story, what significant changes would occur if the narrator were omniscient? Keep in mind that first-person narrators do not know what other characters think but that omniscient third-person narrators know everything about the lives of the characters.

6. What is the theme of the story? All the elements of fiction—tone, setting, plot, characterization, point of view, irony, imagery—have been marshaled to project a theme, the moral proposition the author wishes to advance. Does the title reinforce or point to the theme? Can you locate any particular places in the story where the theme is addressed?

7. Do you find ambiguities in the story? That is, can you interpret some element of the story in more than one way? Does that ambiguity result in confusion, or does it add to the complexity of the story?

8. Does the story seem to support or conflict with your own political and moral positions?

9. When was the story written? Draw on your knowledge of history and contemporary events as you read the story. Does the story clarify, enhance, or contradict your understanding of history?

10. Can you connect the story to anything else you have read or seen? To events in your own life? Does the story clarify or contradict your prior assessments of these other works or events?

READING POETRY

Reading poetry is unlike the other reading you do. To appreciate the sounds and meaning of a poem, it is best to start by reading it aloud. Some poems are straightforward, requiring little analysis; others are more dense and complex. Try reading the poem "When I Heard the Learn'd Astronomer" (1865) by Walt Whitman out loud.

When I heard the learn'd astronomer,
When the proofs, the figures, were ranged in columns before me,
When I was shown the charts and diagrams, to add, divide, and measure them,
When I sitting heard the astronomer where he lectured with much
    applause in the lecture-room,
How soon unaccountable I became tired and sick,
Till rising and gliding out I wander'd off by myself,
In the mystical moist night-air, and from time to time,
Look'd up in perfect silence at the stars.

Whitman's distinction between mind (intellectual knowledge) and heart (emotion and feelings) is an old but a useful one. Compelled to analyze, dissect, categorize, and classify, the poem's narrator finally yearns for the simple pleasure of unanalytical enjoyment—to look up "in perfect silence at the stars." You may very well enjoy a poem without recognizing its patterns of imagery or the intricate way its author weaves together the past and the present. But understanding the elements of poetry will allow you to use analysis to enhance your emotional response to a poem—and thereby deepen the pleasure a poem can give you.

Poems have to be read with great intensity but without any sense of urgency. Reading with a relaxed but complete mindfulness, try to slow down, pay attention, and allow the language of the poem to work.

Word Choice

Once you have listened to the poem, what should you pay attention to next? Start with the words that make up the poem. *Where* a poem takes the reader is inseparable from *how* it takes the reader. Poets pay especially close attention to *diction,* or their choice of words; every word in a poem counts. In your everyday reading, you encounter unfamiliar words and phrases, and figure out their meanings from the contexts in which they occur. Reading poetry requires even more scrupulous attention to unusual words and phrases. Here, again, making connections will help you get the most out of your reading. Look for words or images that repeat or change as a poem continues. Finding patterns can be the first step in developing an interpretive reading of a poem.

Critics often describe poetry as "heightened language," meaning that the poet strives for precision and richness in the words he or she uses. For the poet, "precision" and "richness" are not contradictory. Words have dictionary, or *denotative,* meanings as well as associative, or *connotative,* meanings; they also have histories and relationships with other words. The English language is rich in synonyms—words whose denotative meanings are roughly the same but whose connotations vary widely (*excite, stimulate, titillate, inflame; poor, impoverished, indigent, destitute*). Many words are identical in sound and often in spelling but differ in meaning (*forepaws, four paws; lie* ["recline"], *lie* ["fib"]). The meanings of words have changed over time, and the poet may deliberately select a word whose older meaning adds a dimension to the poem.

Henry Reed's "Naming of Parts" (p. 417) develops a contrast between the instructions a group of soldiers are receiving on how to operate a rifle (in order to cause death) and the lovely world of nature (representing life and beauty). In the fourth stanza, bees are described as "assaulting and fumbling the flowers." *Fumbling*, with its meaning of awkwardness and nervous uncertainty, may at first strike us as a puzzling word. Yet anyone who has watched a bee pollinating a flower will find the word denotatively effective. In addition, *fumbling* describes the actions of human beings caught up in sexual passion—a connotation appropriate to the poet's purposes, since pollination is a kind of sexual process. Furthermore, the meanings of *fumbling* contrast powerfully with the cold, mechanical precision of the death-dealing instruments the recruits are learning to use. The next line of the poem exhibits yet another resource of words: "They call it easing the Spring." The line repeats almost exactly a phrase used two lines earlier, except *Spring* is now capitalized. While *Spring* retains its first meaning as part of the bolt action of the rifle, the capitalization makes it the season of the year when flowers are pollinated and the world of nature is reborn. With a typographical change, Reed is able to evoke in a single word the contrast (the cold steel of a rifle and the fecund beauty of nature) that gives the poem its structure and meaning.

Figurative Language

Figurative language is the general term we use to describe the many devices of language that allow us to speak nonliterally in order to achieve some special effect. Figurative language makes a comparison between the thing being written about and something else that allows the reader to better picture or understand it. When Robert Burns compares his love to a red rose in his poem "A Red, Red Rose" (p. 920), and Keats, in "On First Looking into Chapman's Homer" (p. 141), speaks of reading as travel "in the realms of gold," they abandon literal language because the emotional energy of their thoughts can be expressed more effectively in figurative language.

Figurative language allows us—and the poet—to use *imagery* to transcend both the confinement of the literal and the vagueness of the abstract. The world is revealed to us through our senses—sight, sound, taste, touch, and smell. Through imagery, the poet creates a recognizable world by drawing on this fund of common experiences. Bad poetry is often bad because the imagery is stale ("golden sunset," "the smiling sun," "the rolling sea") or so skimpy that the poem dissolves into vague and meaningless abstraction.

The difference between good and bad poetry often turns on the skill with which imagery (or other figurative language) is used. When Robert Frost in his poem "Birches" (p. 150) compares life to "a pathless wood" (l. 44), the image strikes us as natural and appropriate (life sometimes feels like a path or road, and we find it easy to accept the author's use of a wood or forest as a metaphor for a state of moral bewilderment).

Consider these familiar old sayings: "The grass is always greener on the other side of the fence"; "A bird in the hand is worth two in the bush"; "The early bird catches the worm." Although these sayings make literal sense (the grass you see from a distance looks greener than the grass under your feet), their meaning to a native speaker of English is clearly not literal. When we use them, we are making general and highly abstract observations about human attitudes and behavior. Yet these generalizations and abstractions are embodied in concrete imagery. Try to explain what any of these expressions mean and you will quickly discover that you are using many more words and much vaguer language than the expression itself uses. This is precisely what happens when you try to paraphrase or put into your own words the language of a poem. Like poetry, these sayings rely on the figurative use of language.

Because poetry is an intense and heightened use of language, it relies on more frequent and original use of figurative language than does ordinary speech. One of the most common figurative devices, *metaphor,* in which one thing is compared to something else, occurs frequently in everyday language. "School is a rat race," or "That issue is a minefield for the mayor," we say, and the meaning is vividly clear. When W. H. Auden, commenting on the death of William Butler Yeats, says, "Let the Irish vessel lie/Emptied of his poetry," he pays a complex tribute to the great Irish poet with a metaphor that compels readers to confront not only the loss of a man but also the loss of his poetic voice.

Simile is closely related to metaphor. But where metaphor says that one thing *is* another, simile says that one thing *is like* another, as in Burns's "O My Luve's like a red, red rose" and Frost's "life is too much like a pathless wood." The distinction between simile and metaphor, while easy enough to make technically, is often difficult to distinguish in terms of effect. Frost establishes a comparison between life and a pathless wood and keeps the two even more fully separated by adding the qualifier "too much." Burns's simile maintains the same separation and, in addition, because it occurs in the opening line of the poem, eliminates any possible confusion the reader might experience if the line were "O My Luve is a red, red rose." You can test the difference in effect by changing a metaphor into a simile or a simile into a metaphor to see if the meaning is in any way altered.

Personification, another device of figurative language, attributes human qualities to things or ideas. Personification can make an abstract thing more understandable in terms of human form, emotion, or action. For example, when John Donne, in his poem "Death, Be Not Proud" (p. 1184), exclaims "Death, thou shalt die," he transforms the abstraction death into a human adversary (while also creating a memorable paradox).

Allusion to other literary works, persons, places, or events enables poets to call up associations and contexts that complicate and enrich their poems. Whether these allusions are obvious or subtle, they draw on knowledge shared by the poet and the reader. In T. S. Eliot's dense and difficult "The Love Song of J. Alfred Prufrock" (p. 646), the speaker says at one point, "I have seen my head (grown slightly bald) brought in upon a platter." A reader familiar with the New Testament might recognize this allusion to John the Baptist's decapitation and better understand Prufrock's sense of spiritual desolation. The association Eliot makes brings an added, intensified layer of meaning to the work.

A *symbol,* in its broadest sense, is anything that stands for something else. In this sense, most words are symbolic: the word *tree* stands for an object in the real world. When we speak of a symbol in a literary work, however, we mean something more precise. In poetry, a symbol is an object or event that suggests more than itself. It is one of the most common and powerful devices available to the poet, for it allows him or her to convey economically and simply a wide range of meanings.

It is useful to distinguish between two kinds of symbols: *public symbols* and *contextual symbols*. Public symbols are those objects or events that history has invested with rich meanings and associations—for example, national flags or religious objects such as a cross. Yeats uses such a symbol in his poem "Sailing to Byzantium" (p. 1191), drawing on the celebrated and enduring art of the ancient Byzantine Empire as a symbol of timelessness.

In contrast to public symbols, contextual symbols are objects or events that are symbolic by virtue of the poet's handling of them in a particular work— that is, by virtue of the context. Consider, for example, the opening lines of Robert Frost's "After Apple-Picking" (p. 1193).

> My long two-pointed ladder's sticking through a tree
> Toward heaven still,
> And there's a barrel that I didn't fill
> Beside it, and there may be two or three
> Apples I didn't pick upon some bough.

The apple tree is a literal tree, but it also symbolizes the speaker's life, with a wide range of possible meanings (do the few unpicked apples symbolize the dreams that even the fullest life cannot satisfy?). Contextual symbols tend to present more interpretive difficulties than public symbols do because recognizing them depends on a sensitivity to everything else in the poem.

The Music of Poetry

A number of terms describe the various sound patterns that project the *music* of poetry. Of these, *rhyme*—the repetition of the final stressed vowel sound and any sounds following—is the best known: *brow, now; debate, relate;* and so on. *Alliteration*, or the repetition of a consonant sound, usually at the beginning of words in close proximity, is also common: "*besiege thy brow.*" Alliteration is frequently used to underscore key words and ideas.

Rhythm, created by the relationship between stressed and unstressed syllables, is another way poets can convey meaning. The pattern formed when the lines of a poem follow a recurrent or similar rhythm is the poem's *meter*. The smallest repeated unit in this pattern is called a *foot*. Looking, for example, at the first line of one of Shakespeare's sonnets, we see that the foot consists of an *iamb*—an unstressed syllable followed by a stressed one:

When forty winters shall besiege thy brow.

Because the line consists of five iambs, or sets of unstressed syllables followed by stressed ones, it is called *iambic pentameter*. (If the line had four iambic feet, it would be in iambic tetrameter; if six, iambic hexameter; and so on.)

   Other metrical feet include the *trochee, anapest, dactyl,* and *spondee* (all of which are defined in the "Glossary of Literary Terms"); but such terms are the tools of literary study and not its object. Perhaps the most important thing to remember about meter is that it should not be mistaken for the actual rhythm of the poem. Instead, it is best thought of as a kind of ideal rhythm that the poem can play against. Meter suggests certain patterns that invite expectations that may or may not be satisfied. Much of the poet's art consists of crafting variations of sound and rhythm to create specific effects.

   Some of these effects are illustrated nicely in the following passage from Alexander Pope's "An Essay on Criticism," in which the definitions of bad and good verse are ingeniously supported by the music of the lines.

> These[1] equal syllables alone require,
> Though oft the ear the open vowels tire;
> While expletives their feeble aid do join;
> And ten low words oft creep in one dull line;
> While they ring round the same unvaried chimes,
> With sure returns of still expected rhymes;
> Where'er you find "the cooling western breeze,"
> In the next line, it "whispers through the trees";
> If crystal streams "with pleasing murmurs creep,"
> The reader's threatened (not in vain) with "sleep";
> Then, at the last and only couplet fraught
> With some unmeaning thing they call a thought,
> A needless Alexandrine[2] ends the song
> That, like a wounded snake, drags its slow length along.
>
>   . . . . .
>
> True ease in writing comes from art, not chance,
> As those move easiest who have learned to dance.
> 'Tis not enough no harshness gives offense,
> The sound must seem an echo to the sense:
> Soft is the strain when Zephyr gently blows,
> And the smooth stream in smoother numbers flows;
> But when loud surges lash the sounding shore,
> The hoarse, rough verse should like the torrent roar:
> When Ajax[3] strives some rock's vast weight to throw,
> The line too labors, and the words move slow;
> Not so, when swift Camilla[4] scours the plain,
> Flies o'er the unbending corn, and skims along the main.

---

[1] Bad poets.
[2] Twelve-syllable line or a line with six rhythmic feet. As in Pope's example, alexandrines often follow lines of pentameter, or lines with five metrical feet.
[3] A Greek warrior celebrated for his strength.
[4] A swift-footed queen in Virgil's *Aeneid.*

When the speaker condemns the use of ten monosyllables, the line contains ten monosyllables: "And ten low words oft creep in one dull line." When he speaks of the wind, the line is rich in hissing sounds that imitate that wind. When he speaks of Ajax striving, clusters of consonants and stressed syllables combine to slow the line; when he speaks of Camilla's swiftness, the final consonants and initial sounds form liaisons that can be pronounced swiftly.

Consider also the following opening lines of Wilfred Owen's poem "Dulce et Decorum Est" (p. 435) (from *Dulce et decorum est pro patria mori*—it is sweet and fitting to die for one's country—a quotation from the Roman writer Horace). The lines describe a company of battle-weary World War I soldiers trudging toward their camp and rest:

> Bent double, like old beggars under sacks,
> Knock-kneed, coughing like hags, we cursed through sludge.

These lines are dominated by harsh, explosive, and alliterating consonant sounds (*b, d, c, g*) that manage to reinforce the ungainly and indecorous images in these lines. In particular, the first two syllables of each line are heavily stressed, which serves to slow the reading. While the poem ultimately develops a prevailing meter, the irregular rhythms of these opening lines imitate a weary, stumbling march.

Analysis of this sort can illuminate and enrich our understanding of poetry, but it does not exhaust the significance of a poem. As Dylan Thomas once remarked,

> You can tear a poem apart to see what makes it technically tick and say to yourself when the works are laid out before you—the vowels, the consonants, the rhymes, and rhythms—"Yes, this is it. This is why the poem moves me so. It is because of the craftsmanship." But you're back where you began. The best craftsmanship always leaves holes and gaps in the works of the poem so that something that is not in the poem can creep, crawl, flash, or thunder in.

A truly fine poem not only repays attention to its formal features but also points beyond its technique to something more sensuous and less domesticated.

Exploring Poetry

Here are some questions to ask when you face the task of reading and writing about poetry.

1. Who is the speaker? What does the poem reveal about the speaker's character? Do you think you can trust this speaker? In some poems the speaker may be nothing more than a voice meditating on a theme, while in others the speaker takes on a specific personality. For example, the speaker in Shelley's "Ozymandias" (p. 1185) is a voice meditating on the transitoriness of all things; except for the views expressed in the poem, we know nothing about the speaker's character. The same might be said of the speaker in Hopkins's "Spring and Fall" (p. 145), but with this important exception: we know that he is older than Margaret and therefore has a wisdom she does not.

2. Is the speaker addressing a particular person? If so, who is that person, and why is the speaker interested in him or her? Many poems, like "Ozymandias," are addressed to no one in particular and therefore to anyone, any reader. Others, such as Donne's "A Valediction: Forbidding Mourning" (p. 914), while addressed to a specific person, reveal nothing about that person because the focus of the poem is on the speaker's feelings and attitudes. In a dramatic monologue (see "Glossary of Literary Terms"), the speaker usually addresses a silent auditor. The identity of the auditor will be important to the poem.

3. Does the poem have a setting? Is the poem occasioned by a particular event? The answer to these questions will often be no for lyric poems, such as Frost's "Fire and Ice" (p. 922). It will always be yes if the poem is a dramatic monologue, such as Browning's "My Last Duchess" (p. 142), or a poem that tells or implies a story, such as Tennyson's "Ulysses" (p. 399).

4. Is the theme of the poem stated directly or indirectly? Some poems, such as Owen's "Dulce et Decorum Est" (p. 435), use language in a fairly straightforward and literal way and state the theme, often in the final lines. Others may conclude with a statement of the theme that is more difficult to apprehend because it is made with figurative language and symbols. This difference will be readily apparent if you compare the final lines of the Owen poem with, say, the final stanzas of Stevens's "Sunday Morning" (p. 406).

5. From what perspective (or point of view) is the speaker describing specific events? Is the speaker recounting events of the past or events that are occurring in the present? If past events are being recalled, what present meaning do they have for the speaker? These questions are particularly appropriate to the works in the section "Innocence and Experience," many of which contrast an early innocence with adult experience.

6. Does a close examination of the figurative language of the poem (see p. 13 and "Glossary of Literary Terms") reveal any patterns? Yeats's "Sailing to Byzantium" (p. 1191) may begin to open up to you once you recognize the pattern of bird imagery. Likewise, Thomas's attitude toward his childhood in "Fern Hill" (p. 155) will be clearer if you detect the pattern of biblical imagery that associates childhood with Adam and Eve before the Fall.

7. What is the structure of the poem? Since narrative poems—those that tell stories—reveal a high degree of selectivity, it is useful to ask why the poet has focused on particular details and left out others. Analyzing the structure of a nonnarrative or lyric poem can be more difficult because it does not contain an obvious series of chronologically related events. The structure of Thomas's "Fern Hill," for example, is based in part on a description of perhaps a day and a half in the speaker's life as a child. But more significant in terms of its structure is the speaker's realization that the immortality he felt as a child was merely a stage in the inexorable movement of life toward death. The structure of the poem, therefore, will be revealed through an analysis of patterns of images (biblical, color, day and night, dark and light) that embody the theme. To take another example, Marvell's "To His Coy Mistress" (p. 950) is divided into three verse paragraphs, the opening words of each ("Had we," "But," "Now therefore") suggesting a logically constructed argument.

8. What do sound and meter (see "Glossary of Literary Terms") contribute to the poem? Alexander Pope said that in good poetry, "The sound must seem an echo to the sense"—a statement that is sometimes easier to agree with than to demonstrate. For sample analyses of the music of poetry, see the section on music (p. 15).

9. What was your response to the poem on first reading? Did your response change after study of the poem or class discussions about it?

ANNOTATING WHILE YOU READ

Be a serious and aggressive reader. Don't let your eyes wander languidly over the assigned texts. Keep a pencil in hand, and interact with the text; pin it to the mat by writing observations, questions, even complaints in the margins of your book. (Use sticky notes or note cards if you are reading library books.) Each of the discussions of the four literary genres concludes with a series of questions that you might bring to the reading of any text. Attempt to answer those questions as you read—and note your responses as you do. Look at the considerations we raise for readers of poetry (pp. 17–18). Take some chances; be honest, but engage with the piece as if you had an argument with it. Point out what you find difficult, what you think you understand, what you confidently understand. We asked some students to apply this annotating technique to Shakespeare's Sonnet 29, a moderately difficult poem. Here is a composite of what they produced:

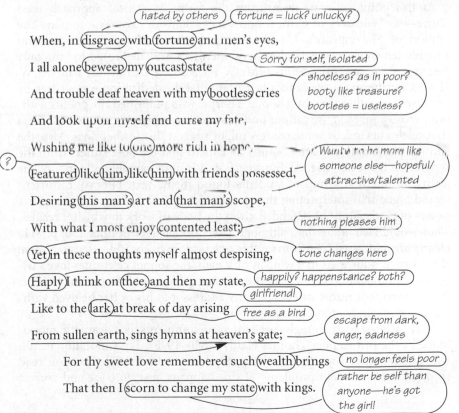

All in all, the annotations to this sonnet are quite good. The students grasped the poet's design, largely overcame the difficulties created by somewhat archaic language, and recognized the poet's aim to both flatter his love and express the saving grace that love provides.

But curious things happen with language. The deconstructionist critics (see "Glossary of Critical Approaches," p. 1343) have argued that because each reader brings a different set of experiences and assumptions to texts, it is difficult (some say impossible) to confidently understand any text. Put another way, different readers will interpret the same text in vastly different ways. For example, some readers, at the crucial moment when the poet remarks, "Haply I think on thee" (l. 10), might interpret the pronoun not as an allusion to a friend or lover but as an allusion to God. In this interpretation the sonnet resolves, not with the saving grace of a love that sets all things right, but with the ineffable saving grace of God that, with the promise of heaven, makes human pain and misery insignificant. Is such a religious reading of the poem simply wrong? And if so, what evidence could we use to show that it is wrong? Are the students who agree that the poet's girlfriend is the agent of his lifted spirits quite right? These are difficult questions, not the least because Shakespeare's sonnets seriously trouble scholars to this day.

At this point (moving away from the formalist critical approach used above—see "Glossary of Critical Approaches"), history comes into play. The edition of Shakespeare's 154 sonnets, published without his permission roughly ten to eleven years after he wrote them, was dedicated to "the only Begetter of These Insuing Sonnets Mr. W. H." Alas, we are not sure who Mr. W. H. was. Furthermore, we cannot be certain that the dedication was written by Shakespeare, rather than by Thomas Thorpe, who published the poems without permission. Next, we cannot find among Shakespeare's sonnets any others that celebrate God, as some readers might suggest this sonnet does. Also, the sonnets just before and after Sonnet 29 lament that the poet suffers from the separation from his "friend." But that friend is quite possibly a man, not the girlfriend our first group of students found in the text. Literary historians would argue that interpreting this sonnet as a poem praising the restorative power of God cannot be defended given the body of work in which it resides. They would also argue that, although later sonnets (see Sonnet 130, p. 911) clearly are addressed to a woman, this one is more likely addressed to a man. But whether addressed to a woman or a man, the sonnet celebrates love's triumph over the mundane human despair that afflicts us all from time to time. And the modern reader can confidently address it to his or her beloved without being misunderstood.

Here, printed with enough space for your comments, is a dramatic monologue by the British poet Thomas Hardy (1840–1928). Try annotating it. You will discover that your first notions may have to be modified as you read through the poem. No problem—if this happens, just go back and correct your initial responses. Then compare your annotations to the composite annotations on page 22.

The Man He Killed

"Had he and I but met

By some old ancient inn,

We should have sat us down to wet

Right many a nipperkin!

"But ranged as infantry,

And staring face to face,

I shot at him as he at me,

And killed him in his place.

"I shot him dead because—

Because he was my foe,

Just so: my foe of course he was:

That's clear enough; although

"He thought he'd 'list, perhaps,

Off-hand-like—just as I—,

Was out of work—had sold his traps—

No other reason why.

"Yes; quaint and curious war is!

You shoot a fellow down

You'd treat, if met where any bar is,

Or help to half-a-crown."

The Man He Killed

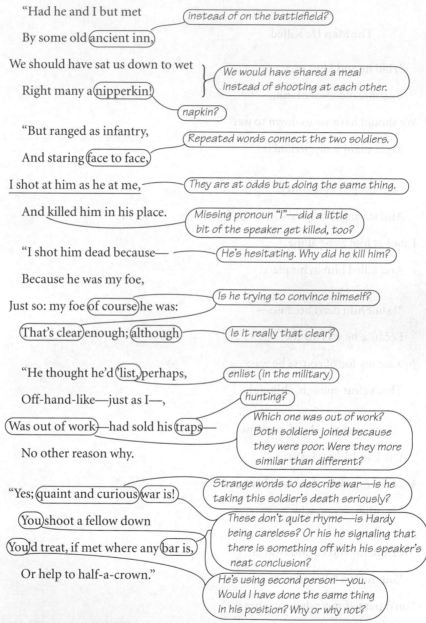

"Had he and I but met   *instead of on the battlefield?*

By some old (ancient inn,)

We should have sat us down to wet   *We would have shared a meal
instead of shooting at each other.*

Right many a (nipperkin!)

                                         napkin?

"But ranged as infantry,   *Repeated words connect the two soldiers.*

And staring (face to face,)

I shot at him as he at me,—   *They are at odds but doing the same thing.*

And killed him in his place.   *Missing pronoun "I"—did a little
bit of the speaker get killed, too?*

"I shot him dead because—   *He's hesitating. Why did he kill him?*

Because he was my foe,

Just so: my foe (of course) he was: *Is he trying to convince himself?*

(That's clear) enough; (although)   *Is it really that clear?*

"He thought he'd (list,) perhaps,   *enlist (in the military)*

Off-hand-like—just as I—,   *hunting?*

(Was out of work)—had sold his (traps)—   *Which one was out of work?
Both soldiers joined because
they were poor. Were they more
similar than different?*

No other reason why.

"Yes; (quaint and curious) war is!   *Strange words to describe war—is he
taking this soldier's death seriously?*

(You) shoot a fellow down   *These don't quite rhyme—is Hardy
being careless? Or his he signaling that
there is something off with his speaker's
neat conclusion?*

(You'd treat, if met where any (bar is,)

Or help to half-a-crown."   *He's using second person—you.
Would I have done the same thing
in his position? Why or why not?*

READING DRAMA

Drama is fundamentally different from other literary forms. Unlike fiction, for example, most plays are designed to be performed in public and not read in private. The public nature of drama is reflected in the words we use to discuss it. The word *drama* itself is derived from the Greek word for "action, deed, or performance," and *theater* derives from the Greek word for "sight or contemplation." By their nature, plays are more spectacular than poems or works of fiction. Directors and their staffs pay great attention to costumes, set design, lights, and stage movement; the reader, who doesn't experience these elements, must imagine the action on the basis of words alone. Dramatists use words as starting points for, rather than realizations of, their artistic visions.

Although plays typically lack narration and description—they are designed to show, not tell—they can be considered in terms of setting, plot, theme, characterization, and irony. Indeed, these notions are even more important in drama than in fiction, where narrative style and point of view carry great weight, or in poetry, where diction and imagery are central.

As much as possible, the way to read a play is to imagine that you are its director. In this role you must visualize yourself creating the set and the lighting. You will envision people dressed so that their clothes give support to their words. You will think about timing (how long between events and speeches) and blocking (how the characters move as they interact on stage). Perhaps the best way to confront the literature of the stage, to respond most fully to what is there, is to attempt to produce some scenes either in class or after class. If possible, attend the plays or the rehearsals of plays in production on campus. Nothing will provide better insight into the complexities of the theater than attending a rehearsal where the problems are encountered and solved.

As you read any of the opening speeches of any of the plays in this anthology, imagine yourself the director and make decisions. How should the lines be spoken (quietly, angrily, haltingly)? What should the characters do as they speak (remain stationary, look in some direction, traverse the stage)? How should the stage be lit (partially, brightly, in some color that contributes to the mood of the dialogue and action)? What should the characters who are not speaking do? What possibilities exist for conveying appropriate signals solely through gesture and facial expression—signals not contained in the words you read?

Stages and Staging

Although staging is more important to spectators than to readers, some knowledge of staging history can enrich your reading of a play. For example, it helps to know that in the Greek theater of Dionysius in Athens (below), there was no scene shifting. In *Oedipus Rex* (p. 183), which was staged in an open air amphitheater seating about 14,000 people, actors entered from the *skene,* or a fixed-stage house, which might have had painted panels to suggest a scene. Important events, especially violent ones, occur offstage, and the audience learns of these events from a messenger, who comes onstage to describe them. This convention was partly a matter of taste, but the conditions of the Greek stage also prevented Sophocles from moving the action to another scene. Later dramatists, writing for a more flexible stage and a more intimate theater, exploited the dramatic possibilities of such violence.

The Dionysius Theatre in Athens

The vast outdoor theater imposed restrictions on acting style. Facial expressions played no role in the actor's craft; in fact, the actors wore large masks, which were probably equipped with some sort of megaphone to amplify speech. As a result, it was difficult to modulate speech to create subtle effects, and the speeches were probably delivered in formal, declamatory style. In addition to these limitations, the Athenian government made available only three principal actors, all male, as the cast (excluding the *chorus,* a group of citizens that commented on the action and characters) for each play. Consequently, there were never more than three players onstage at once, and the roles were designed so that each actor could take several parts, each signified by a different mask.

Shakespeare's stage was altogether different from Sophocles'. Although both theaters were open-air, the enclosure around the Elizabethan stage was much smaller than the Greek amphitheater, and the theater's capacity was limited to between 2,000 and 3,000 spectators. As in classical drama, men played all the roles, but they no longer wore masks. The stage protruded into the audience, allowing for more intimacy and a greater range of speech, gesture, and expression. Even so, and despite Hamlet's advice to the troupe "to hold as 't were, the mirror up to nature," Shakespearean tragedy did not lend itself to a modern realistic style. Those great speeches are written in verse; they are frequently meant to augment the meager set design with verbal imagery; and they are much denser in texture, image, and import than is ordinary speech. Most of the important action was played out on the uncurtained main platform, jutting into the audience and surrounded on three sides by spectators. The swiftly moving scenes followed each other without interruption, doubtless using different areas of the stage to signify different

Interior of the Swan Theatre, London, 1596

locations. There was some sort of terrace or balcony one story above the main stage, and there was an area at the back of the main protruding stage that could be curtained off when not in use. Although Shakespeare's plays are usually divided into five separate acts in printed versions, they were played straight through, without intermission, much like a modern motion picture. These characteristics distinguish the Shakespearean stage from the familiar realism of most contemporary theater.

Much current theater uses a *box stage*—essentially a box with one wall removed so that the audience can see into the playing area. The box stage lends itself to realistic settings. It can easily be furnished to look like a room; or, if outdoor scenes are required, painted backdrops and angled sets provide perspective. Shortly after the introduction of the box stage, the possibilities for scenic design produced great set designers and increasingly sophisticated stage machinery. These new possibilities, in turn, freed the dramatist from the physical limitations imposed by earlier stages.

By the late nineteenth century, the versatility of the box stage enabled playwrights such as Henrik Ibsen to write detailed stage settings for the various locations in which the drama unfolds. Further, the furnishing of the stage in Ibsen's plays sometimes functions symbolically to visually reinforce the claustrophobic quality of the bourgeois life depicted in his plays. Later dramatists have relied on realistic settings to convey meaning and to serve symbolic functions. The modern production may take place in a theater that is simply a large empty room (with provisions for technical flexibility in the matter of lighting)

Hypothetical reconstruction of the interior of the Globe Theatre in the days of Shakespeare

A seventeenth-century French box stage

that can be rearranged to suit the requirements of specific productions. This ideal of a "theater space" that can be freely manipulated has become increasingly attractive since it frees the dramatist and the performance from limitations built into permanent stage design.

The Elements of Drama

CHARACTERS Plays usually consist of narratives with plots, settings, themes, characters, and irony, and most plays have no narrators as such. In Greek drama, the chorus functions as a kind of narrator. In Shakespearean drama, the *soliloquy,* in which an actor speaks thoughts aloud, allows the audience to hear what a character is thinking. But in most plays, the story unfolds before your eyes without the intervention of an authorial voice or point of view.

Without a narrator to tell us what a character is thinking, we usually infer a character's thoughts by his or her actions and demeanor, and by *dialogue,* or the words a character speaks to others. *Characterization,* in plays as in fiction, is a process by which the author establishes the personality of a character, revealed through what the particular character does and says, and by what other characters say. The main character, the hero or *protagonist,* is the center of our attention. He or she is often opposed by another major character, the *antagonist,* whose opposition creates the central conflict of the drama. The protagonist and the antagonist, as well as other characters of major significance in the drama, have a vital interest in the outcome of the action, and grow and develop as the action progresses and are therefore described as *rounded* characters. Those characters who are peripheral to the action, who often supply the kind of exposition a third-person narrator does in fiction, are minor, or *flat,* characters.

DRAMATIC IRONY *Dramatic irony* allows the audience to know more than the characters do about their own circumstances by letting the audience hear more than the characters hear. Shakespeare's *Othello* (p. 958) provides an excellent illustration of the uses of dramatic irony. At the end of act II, Cassio, who has lost his position as Othello's lieutenant, asks Iago for advice on how to regain favor. Iago, who, unknown to Cassio, had engineered Cassio's disgrace, advises him to ask Desdemona, Othello's adored wife, to intervene. Actually this is good advice; ordinarily the tactic would succeed, so much does Othello love his wife and wish to please her. But Iago explains, in a soliloquy to the audience, that he is laying groundwork for the ruin of all the objects of his envy and hatred—Cassio, Desdemona, and Othello:

> . . . for while this honest fool
> Plies Desdemona to repair his fortunes,
> And she for him pleads strongly to the Moor,
> I'll pour this pestilence into his ear
> That she repeals him for her body's lust;
> And, by how much she strives to do him good,

> She shall undo her credit with the Moor.
> So will I turn her virtue into pitch,
> And out of her goodness make the net
> That shall enmesh them all.

Of course, Desdemona, Cassio, and Othello are ignorant of Iago's enmity. Worse, all of them consider Iago a loyal friend. But the audience knows Iago's design, and that knowledge provides the chilling dramatic irony of act III, scene 3.

When Cassio asks for Desdemona's help, she immediately consents, declaring, "I'll intermingle every thing he does / With Cassio's suit." At this, the audience, knowing what it does, grows a little uneasy. As Iago and Othello come onstage, Cassio, understandably ill at ease, leaves at the approach of the commander who has stripped him of his rank, thus providing Iago with a magnificent tactical advantage. And as Cassio leaves, Iago utters an exclamation and four simple words:

> Ha! I like not that.

These words do not mean much to either Othello or Desdemona. But they are for the audience the intensely anticipated first drop of poison. Othello hasn't heard clearly:

> What dost thou say?

Maybe it will all pass, and Iago's clever design will fail. But what a hiss of held breath the audience expels when Iago replies:

> Nothing, my lord: or if—I know not what.

And Othello is hooked:

> Was not that Cassio parted from my wife?

The bait taken, Iago begins to play his line:

> Cassio, my lord? No, sure, I cannot think it,
> That he would steal away so guilty-like,
> Seeing you coming.

And from this point on in the scene, Iago cleverly and cautiously leads Othello. He assumes the role of Cassio's great friend—reluctant to say anything that might cast suspicion on him. But he is also the "friend" of Othello and cannot keep silent in his suspicions. So "honest" Iago, apparently full of sympathy and kindness, skillfully brings the trusting Othello to emotional chaos. And every word they exchange is doubly meaningful to the audience, which perceives Othello led on the descent into a horrible jealousy by his "friend." The scene ends with Othello visibly shaken and convinced of Desdemona's faithlessness and Cassio's disloyalty:

> Damn her, lewd minx! O, damn her!
> Come, go with me apart; I will withdraw.
> To furnish me with some swift means of death
> For the fair devil. Now art thou my lieutenant.

To which Iago replies:

> I am your own for ever.

All the emotional tautness in the audience results from irony, from knowing what the victims do not know. But dramatic irony is the special tool of the dramatist, well suited to produce an electric tension in a live audience that watches and overhears the action onstage.

PLOT AND CONFLICT Plays often portray oppositions between characters or groups or even between two aspects of a character's personality. This opposition often takes the form of a *conflict* that drives the plot. In *Othello*, for example, a variety of conflicts shapes the action of the play. Most obviously, Iago's scheming puts Othello in conflict with Cassio, and turns him against Desdemona. But conflicts can be less literal: Othello and Desdemona's marriage puts them at odds with Venetian society, raising larger questions about race and culture. And conflicts can be within a single character: Othello's jealousy triggers conflicting emotions about himself and about his wife.

Understanding the methods of drama can help us analyze a play and its various effects. But such analysis only gestures at the emotional experience produced by successful drama. More than other forms of literature, plays give physical expression to the social and psychological conflicts that define us individually and collectively. As in *Othello*, a play may torment its audience by imposing on admirable characters unfair circumstances that will result in tragic deaths. Or, as in Susan Glaspell's *Trifles* (p. 1050), a play may mock prevalent attitudes and compel an audience to reexamine its values. By giving expression to human impulses and conflicts, plays enact our most persistent concerns with the greatest possible intensity.

A traditional and still useful way of looking at the plot of a play is to see it in five parts: exposition, rising action, climax, falling action, and denouement. *Exposition* provides the audience with information about background matters important to the play. The first part of the plot also includes *rising action,* as the plot progresses toward complexity and conflict, which reaches a crisis, or *climax,* of some sort. This is the turning point of the play, when the protagonist must act decisively or make a critical choice from which there is no turning back. This in turn leads to the *falling action,* as the protagonist confronts the inexorable consequences of his or her act or decision. The play ends with the *denouement* (French for "untying or unraveling"), with the conflict resolved or the mystery solved. Although this template cannot be applied to every play, it comes close enough in describing the structure of many plays to make it a useful tool for analyzing much drama.

Exploring Drama

Here are some more specific questions to ask when you begin to read or write about drama. Write out your answers to check your understanding of a play or to begin collecting ideas for an essay assignment.

1. How does the play begin? Is the exposition presented dramatically as characters interact, novelistically through long speeches that convey a lot of information, or through some device such as a messenger who delivers long letters or lengthy reports?

2. How does the information conveyed in exposition (which may occur at various moments throughout the play) establish the basis for dramatic irony? Does the audience know more than the characters do? How does that irony create tension in the audience?

3. Who are the principal characters, and how are the distinctive qualities of each dramatically conveyed? How do they change as the play proceeds? Are they sympathetic? What function do the minor characters serve? (An essay that thoughtfully assesses the role of minor characters can often succeed better than an attempt to analyze major figures who may be too complex to deal with in a thousand words.)

4. Where is the play set? Why does it matter that it is set there? Does the setting play a significant role in the drama, or is it merely a place, any place?

5. What is the central conflict in the play—between characters, between groups, or even between two parts of a character's personality? How is it resolved? Is the resolution satisfying?

6. To appreciate the play fully, do you need to know the historical circumstances out of which the play emerged, or something of the life of the author? If so, how does the information enhance your understanding?

7. Since plays are usually written to be performed rather than read, what visual and auditory elements of the play are significant to your response? If you are reading a text, place yourself in the position of the director and the actors to respond to this aspect of drama.

8. What is the play's theme? How does the dramatic action embody that theme?

9. Has the play been made into a film? In the adaptation, what has been added and what has been deleted? How does this production compare with your reading of the play?

READING NONFICTION

Essays differ from fiction in that they generally do not create imaginary worlds inhabited by fictional characters. We know, for example, through media accounts and the testimony of his friends, that Martin Luther King Jr. was indeed jailed in Birmingham, Alabama, where he wrote his famous argument for social justice, "Letter from Birmingham Jail" (p. 529). And, although we cannot independently verify that George Orwell actually shot an elephant (p. 788), his work exhibits the formal nonfictional qualities of the essay rather than the imagined world of the short story.

Writers turn to the essay form when they wish to confront their readers directly with an idea, a problem (often with a proposed solution), an illuminating experience, an important definition, or some flaw (or virtue) in the social system. Usually, the essay is relatively short, and almost always embodies the writer's personal viewpoint. And although the essay may share many elements with other literary forms, it generally speaks with the voice of a real person about the real world. The term *essay* derives from the French verb *essayer*—"try, attempt." That verb, in turn, derives from the Latin verb *exigere*—"weigh out, examine."

While the French term calls attention to the personal perspective that characterizes the essay, the Latin verb suggests another dimension. The essay not only examines personal experiences but also explores and clarifies ideas by arguing for or against a position. Essays like Joan Didion's "On Morality" (p. 264) do both, using personal experience as a way of getting at larger questions about right and wrong.

As you read an essay, you need to ask yourself, What is the central argument or idea? Sometimes the answer is obvious, sometimes less so. Didion argues clearly that it is impossible to rigidly define *right* and *wrong*, but you have to read her whole essay carefully to grasp the limits of its moral relativism and its subtle warning about how "concern" can turn into "coercion."

Some essays address the inner lives of their readers. John Donne's "Meditation XVII" (p. 1315), for example, does not attack or justify anything. Rather, it reminds us to be aware of our mortality and thereby to alter our interactions with or perceptions of the people around us.

Types of Nonfiction

If you have taken a composition course, you may have read and written narrative, descriptive, expository, and argumentative essays. While reviewing the characteristics of each of these types, keep in mind that in the real world, authors of essays are more interested in effectiveness than in purity of form, and frequently combine features of different formal types.

NARRATIVE NONFICTION Narrative essays recount a sequence of related events and are often autobiographical. But those events are chosen because they suggest or illustrate some larger insight or problem. In "Shooting an Elephant" (p. 788), for example, George Orwell narrates an episode from his life that led him to an important insight about imperialism. In Maxine Hong Kingston's "No Name Woman" (p. 1065) the narrator's reflections on the significance of her aunt's suicide in China many years ago, a tragic family secret that still haunts her, powerfully illustrates the deep connection between past and present and the troubling idea that family and culture can oppress. In these narrative essays, the writers discover in their own experiences the evidence for generalizations about themselves and their societies.

DESCRIPTIVE NONFICTION   Descriptive essays depict sensory observations in words. They evoke in the reader's imagination the sights and sounds, perhaps even the smells, that transport the reader to such places as Joan Didion's Death Valley or George Orwell's Burma. Sometimes, the writer is satisfied simply to create a lifelike evocation of some engaging object or landscape, but Didion uses her description as a vehicle for expressing ideas about morality. The descriptive essay, like the narrative essay, often addresses complex issues that trouble our lives, but it does so by appealing primarily to sensory awareness—sight, sound, touch, taste, smell—rather than to intellect. The power of description is so great that narrative and expository essays often use lengthy descriptive passages to communicate forcefully.

EXPOSITORY NONFICTION   Expository essays attempt to explain and eluci-date, to organize and provide information. Often they embody an extended definition of a complex conception such as love or patriotism; other times, they describe a process—how to do something. This book's coverage of essays, for example, is clearly not narrative because it doesn't depend for its form on a chronological sequence of meaningful events. It is not descriptive in the pure sense of that type because it does not depend on conveying sensory impres-sions. It is, in fact, expository. It acquaints its readers with the techniques and types of essays and provides some tips to help students read essays both analyt-ically and pleasurably. Many of these approaches involve making some kind of connection. You may recognize a number of rhetorical strategies from writing courses you may have taken. We *classify* essays by type; we *compare and contrast* them; we use *definition;* we give *examples* to make a point; we imply that there is a *cause-and-effect* relationship between what readers bring to an essay and the pleasure they derive from it. Similarly, the essayists represented in this book use a variety of such rhetorical strategies to achieve their aims.

ARGUMENTATIVE NONFICTION   Although Orwell's "Shooting an Ele-phant" can be categorized as a narrative essay, we might reasonably assert that it is also argumentative because it is designed to convince readers that imperialism is as destructive to the oppressors as to the oppressed. The argumentative essay wishes to persuade its readers. Thus, it usually deals with controversial ideas, mar-shals arguments and evidence to support a view, and anticipates and answers opposing arguments. Martin Luther King Jr. accomplishes all these ends in his "Letter from Birmingham Jail" (p. 529). So does Jonathan Swift in "A Modest Pro-posal" (p. 497), with an approach complicated by his reliance on irony and satire.

Analyzing Nonfiction

THE THESIS   The best way to begin analyzing an essay is to ask, What is the point of this piece of writing; what is the author trying to show, attack, defend, or prove? If you can answer that question satisfactorily and succinctly, then the analysis of the essay's elements (i.e., its rhetorical strategies, its structure, style, tone, and language) becomes easier. E. L. Doctorow's "Why We Are Infidels?" (p. 513), for example, projects a clear thesis. On the other hand, a much more complex and ambitious essay, such as Virginia Woolf's "What If Shakespeare Had Had a Sister?" (p. 775), does not yield up its thesis quite so easily. We might say that Woolf's examination of the historical record leads her to argue that women did not write during the Elizabethan period because literary talent could not flourish in a social system that made women the ill-educated property of men. This formulation of the essay's thesis, as you will see when you read the essay, leaves a good deal out—notably the exhortation to action with which Woolf concludes the piece.

STRUCTURE AND DETAIL   Read carefully the first and last paragraphs of a number of essays. Note the writers' strategy for engaging you at the outset with an irresistible proposition:

> In Moulmein, in lower Burma, I was hated by large numbers of people—the only time in my life that I have been important enough for this to happen to me.

> If I speak in the tongues of men and of angels, but have not love, I am a noisy gong or a clanging cymbal.

> I was saved from sin when I was going on thirteen.

These opening sentences are startling, hooking readers so that they will eagerly read on to find out what it was that made the writer so hated in Burma, why love is so important, how Langston Hughes was saved from sin. You will find that the opening lines of most well-wrought essays instantly capture your attention.

Endings, too, are critical. And if you examine the concluding lines of any of the essays in this collection, you will find forceful assertions that sharply focus the matter that precedes them. Essayists, unsurprisingly, systematically use gripping beginnings and forceful endings.

What come between those beginnings and endings are often abstract issues—the nature of love, the inevitability of death, the evils of imperialism. Though such abstractions do significantly influence our lives, as subject matter for reading they seem impersonal and distant. Reading about great ideas becomes a sort of academic task, relegated to some intellectual sphere, separate from the pain and passion of our own humanity. The accomplished essay writer, however, entices us to confront such issues by converting abstract ideas into concrete and illustrative detail.

For example, George Orwell points out early in "Shooting an Elephant" that "anti-European feeling was very bitter" in British-controlled Burma. But he immediately moves from the abstraction of "anti-European feeling" to "if a European woman went through the bazaars alone somebody would probably spit betel juice over her dress" and "when a nimble Burman tripped me up on the football field and the referee (another Burman) looked the other way, the crowd yelled with hideous laughter." The tiny bits of hateful experience, because they are physical and concrete, powerfully reinforce the abstract assertion about "anti-European feeling" that lies at the center of Orwell's essay, and the narrative account of the speaker's behavior in front of the mob culminates in an illuminating insight: "I perceived in this moment that when the white man turns tyrant it is his own freedom that he destroys." The large generalization emerges from deeply felt personal experience.

STYLE AND TONE The word *style* refers to all the writing skills that contribute to the effect of any piece of literature. And *tone*—the attitude conveyed by the language a writer chooses—is a particularly significant aspect of writing style. As an illustration of the effect of tone, consider these opening lines of two essays—Martin Luther King Jr.'s "Letter from Birmingham Jail" and Langston Hughes's "Salvation":

> While confined here in the Birmingham city jail, I came across your recent statement calling my present activities "unwise and untimely." Seldom do I pause to answer criticism of my work and ideas. If I sought to answer all the criticisms that cross my desk, my secretaries would have little time for anything other than such correspondence in the course of the day, and I would have no time for constructive work. But since I feel that you are men of genuine good will and that your criticisms are sincerely set forth, I want to try to answer your statement in what I hope will be patient and reasonable terms.

> I was saved from sin when I was going on thirteen. But not really saved. It happened like this. There was a big revival at my Auntie Reed's church. Every night for weeks there had been much preaching, singing, praying, and shouting, and some very hardened sinners had been brought to Christ, and the membership of the church had grown by leaps and bounds. Then just before the revival ended, they held a special meeting for children, "to bring the young lambs to the fold."

Both first-person accounts use provocative openings, immediately hooking the reader. King's tone, however, is formal; his grave rhythm ("Seldom do I pause") and diction ("If I sought to answer") recall a certain kind of well-known oratory. Consider his mature and studied word choices: *confined, statement, correspondence, constructive, sincerely, patient, reasonable.*

Hughes's tone, in his first-person account, is personal and informal. He uses colloquial diction ("It happened like this," "leaps and bounds") and a sardonic wit ("some very hardened sinners had been brought to Christ"). Although a reminiscing adult describes the event, the writer creates the voice of a child by using simple grammar and a child's vocabulary.

The tone a writer creates contributes substantially to the message he or she conveys. Jonathan Swift might have written a sound, academic essay about the economic diseases of Ireland and how to cure them—but his invention of the speaker of "A Modest Proposal," who ironically and sardonically proposes the establishment of a human-baby meat-exporting industry, jars the readers in ways no scholarly essay could. The reflective tone of Joan Didion's "On Morality" reinforces the ambivalence of her attitude toward right and wrong and provides an example of the kind of careful consideration she is encouraging. The high seriousness of Donne's tone in "Meditation XVII" perfectly suits his contemplation of the relationship among the living, the dying, and the dead.

Style is a more difficult quality to define than tone is. Dictionaries define *style* as both "a manner of expression in language" and "excellence in expression." Certainly it is easier to distinguish between various *manners* of expression than it is to describe just what constitutes *excellence* in expression. For example, the manners of expression of John Donne in "Meditation XVII" and of Judith Ortiz Cofer in "American History" clearly differ. The first muses about death, God, alienation, and community in a style characterized by formality and complex extended images. The second uses the conversational style of a memoirist to evoke a particular moment in her life that has larger resonance in the story of twentieth-century America. Although Cofer considers some of the same broad themes as Donne does, her perspective, focus, and conclusions are entirely different, and this difference is reflected in the tone and style of the piece.

Despite their vast differences, we can describe the excellence of each style. Donne, an Anglican priest, meditates on the community of all living humans and the promise of eternal life in the face of physical death. He evokes a remarkable image when he states that "all mankind is of one author." Not so remarkable, you might argue; God is often called the "author of mankind." But why? This image is powerful not just because it is an apt metaphor but because it is an apt metaphor that famously appears in the opening lines of the Gospel according to John in the Bible, the "holy book" to Donne and other, which tells us that "[i]n the beginning was the Word, . . . and the Word was God." Donne develops this idea, further insisting on the intimate relationship among all people because humankind "is one volume." Then he extends this metaphor by arguing that "when one man dies, one chapter is not torn out of the book, but translated into a better language." The vivid image is further extended. "God," Donne tells us, "employs several translators; some pieces are translated by age, some by sickness, some by war, some by justice." By alluding to the actual making of a book by the bookbinder, Donne elaborates on the central image and reestablishes the idea of community: "God's hand is in every translation, and his hand shall bind up all our scattered leaves again for that library where every book shall lie open to one another." Donne alludes to the Bible repeatedly throughout the essay, adding layers to the significance of the "holy book" image and further demonstrating his own faith by showing the depths of his biblical knowledge. The complexity and aptness of Donne's figurative characterization of death is a remarkable stylistic achievement, and one need not share his beliefs to be impressed by his mastery of his medium.

By contrast, Judith Ortiz Cofer's very specific examination of some apparently irreparable rifts in the "human volume" opens with a reference to

Ripley's Believe It or Not, hardly an exhaulted cultural allusion and one whose words suggest anything but faith. While Donne argues—in language that you might find alienating—that we are all connected by God, Cofer attempts a more earthly connection, using everyday language and popular references that she expects contemporary American readers to recognize and grasp immediately. For readers her age, the Kennedy assassination became the ultimate where-were-you-when-you-heard moment, and the emotional resonance of the reference is as historically specific as Donne's references are not. While Donne's imagery seems intended to convey timeless religious truths, Cofer's brings to mind worldly divisions: even their shared grief over President Kennedy cannot bridge the various cultural divides between the young narrator and her neighbors. Her Catholicism implicitly separates her from white Protestant America and connects her to the martyred Kennedy, yet teenage heartache is more meaningful to the narrator than the death of Kennedy or any comfort or meaning that faith might provide. Indeed, looking toward heaven for answers is registered as a kind of denial in Cofer's essay: even as the girl looks up into the falling snow, she cannot keep from her mind the knowledge that it will get dirty the minute it touches her urban backyard. The "veil" of snow evokes nuns or even the Virgin Mary's traditional cloak, but Cofer tells us, once one looks around and sees the whole picture, one cannot avoid noticing the dirt of urban life turning that white snow grey. Although these essays have some surprising connections—like many essayists, both authors are struggling with questions about their mortality and their place in the world—their larger points, and thus their styles, are starkly different. Particularly in their uses of allusion—the kinds of works they refer to and why—the two pieces could hardly have less in common. Yet what they do share is that the style of each is ideally suited to its subject matter and position, that it reinforces some larger truth about each piece. These writers exhibit distinctive manners of expression and distinctive varieties of excellence; in short, they have distinctive styles.

Your principal concern, when reading an essay, must always be to discover the essay's central thesis. What does the writer wish you to understand about his or her experience, the world, or yourself? Once you have understood the essay's thesis, you can enhance your understanding by examining the means the author used to convey it and, perhaps, recognize techniques that will enhance the quality of your own writing. To that end, you ought to examine the essay's structure and the rhetorical strategies that shape it. How does it begin and end? What type is it—narrative, descriptive, expository, argumentative? How do rhetorical strategies—definition, cause and effect, classification, exemplification, comparison and contrast—function to serve the author's purposes? Then analyze the sources of the essay's effectiveness by closely analyzing the language of the essay. Watch writers energize abstract ideas with details and moving experience; consider the uses of figurative language—the metaphors and similes that create both physical and emotional landscapes in the prose; respond to the tone of voice and the stylistic choices that create it. When you have done all this successfully, when you have discovered not only *what* the author has said but also *how* the author moved you to his or her point of view—then you will have understood the essay.

Exploring Nonfiction

Here are some questions to ask when you face the task of reading and writing about essays.

1. What is the author's thesis (or unifying idea)? What evidence or arguments does the author advance to support the thesis? Is the thesis convincing? If not, why not? Does the author rely on any basic but unstated assumptions?

2. What is the author's tone? Select for analysis a passage you consider illustrative of the author's tone. Does the author maintain that tone consistently throughout the essay?

3. How would you characterize the author's style? For example, are the syntax, length of sentences, and diction elevated and formal or familiar and informal?

4. What rhetorical strategies does the author use? For example, can you identify the effective use of narration, description, classification, comparison and contrast, analogy, cause and effect, or definition? Note that one of these rhetorical strategies may constitute the unifying idea of the essay or the means of structuring it.

5. What are the major divisions in the essay? How are they set off? Are the transitions between the divisions effective and easy to follow?

6. Analyze the author's opening paragraph. Does it effectively gain the reader's attention? Does it clearly state the essay's thesis? If it does not, at what point do the author's thesis and purpose become clear?

WRITING ABOUT LITERATURE

If reading literature offers a way to listen to the surprisingly alive voices of the past, writing about literature affords the opportunity to respond to these voices. Depending on how complicated the piece is or how foreign its world is to your own experiences, your initial responses might just be a jumble of vague impressions. Classroom discussion can help to clarify your thoughts, but the best ideas do not usually come together until you sit down and write. The act of composition often generates a line of thinking. Writing about literature is an invitation to organize your impressions and to check those impressions against the work that prompted them. When you accept this invitation, you undertake a process that helps make sense of the literary work and helps you understand your reactions to it.

RESPONDING TO YOUR READING

As you know from experience, complete essays do not pop into your head immediately after you read a work of literature. The process starts with an impression here, a fragment there, or a question about something that catches your attention.

Imagine this scenario. Your teacher asks you to write an essay about one of the works you've read, and you don't have a clue about where to start. Consider the following very short poem, "The Span of Life" (1936), by Robert Frost:

> The old dog barks backward without getting up.
> I can remember when he was a pup.

Take five minutes to write a response to the poem. Don't worry about style or grammatical correctness—just start writing anything that comes to mind.

You may be able to write very little at first. What is there to say? The poem— plain and clear—seems to need no explanation; its words are familiar, and the dog image unambiguous. How could someone write even a short essay about this piece? Is this a joke?

But looking at it again closely, we may come to a few more observations. First, the title seems awfully grand for this tiny poem. Somehow, these two lines and sixteen words are to make a poetic statement about the nature of life itself. Perhaps we had better look at the lines and words carefully. As a first step, let's scan the poem:

The old dog barks backward without getting up.

I can remember when he was a pup.

Speak the poem aloud. Note that the first half of line 1 seems to move slowly, while line 2 seems to prance. That series of four stressed syllables in line 1 "slows" the line. Further, it seems that the words are hard to say quickly—perhaps because the last letter of each stressed syllable has to be finished before you can speak the first letter of the following word: "old dog barks backward without." The *meter* and the sound patterns that describe the dog, old and tired as he is, contribute to the lethargy described in line 1. But is this poem about a mere dog's life or, perhaps, life in general?

In the second line, the lilting *anapestic meter* dances across the page. (An *anapest* is a metrical foot consisting of two unaccented syllables followed by an accented syllable. See *Meter* in the "Glossary of Literary Terms.") The final *n* of "can" slides easily into the initial *r* of "remember"; the easy movements between words and in the sound sequences that follow all contribute to the quickness of the line. (Don't take our word for it; say the words aloud!) Thus, the joyful playfulness of a puppy, suggested by the bounding anapestic meter, is reinforced by the sound patterns embodied in the words chosen to evoke the old dog's youth. Since the title of the poem invites the reader to generalize, we could assume that human life spans, like the old dog's, move from the energetic exuberance of youth to the fatigued immobility of advanced age.

Now the title makes sense—and the *poetic* quality of the sixteen-word *couplet* (two consecutive rhyming lines) emerges from the rhythm and the sounds that reinforce the meaning of the words.

Reread your five minute exploratory writing. Did you note any of these matters? Did you wonder about the poem's title? Do you have an alternative reading to suggest? After this discussion, could you now write a short essay on Frost's poem? These first jottings do not require that you bring any special knowledge to this poem, just that you attend to what's there on the page—a puzzling title, an unusual variation of metrical patterns, and the sounds that embody the poem.

Writing about literature challenges you to teach yourself. Every element in a literary work has been deliberately put there by the author—the description of the setting, the events that form the plot, the dialogue, the imagery. E. M. Forster, a literary critic and novelist, had one of his characters say, "only connect." This notion is a good one to follow when trying to write an essay that analyzes literature. Does what you are reading remind you of anything in your own life? Of anything else you have read? When you slow down and read even more carefully, you will notice connections between words and images that can help you find the key to interpreting the work of literature at hand. Readers experience a mysterious intellectual and emotional event as a result of the writer's purposeful manipulation of language. When you write about what you've read, you confront not only your response to a work but also the elements within the work that cause your response.

Think about a short story or novel that you have read or a movie you have seen recently. Did you like or dislike the story? Try to list the reasons for your general reaction and evaluation: the characters were interesting or dull and lifeless; the ending satisfied expectations or, perhaps, was surprising; the story was easy to understand; it offered new insights about people, or places, or a different society; you couldn't wait to see what would happen next (or found the story so boring that you had trouble finishing it). Your personal impressions, as you jot them down, represent your response to the work.

When you write about literature, you begin with your response to the work. Then you need to consider the writer's purpose. This is not easy; in fact, some critics argue that the reader can never fully recover the writer's purpose. But you can explore the text, try to discover how the plot, setting, characterizations—the very words (sometimes symbolic)—all conspire to generate the theme, and, finally, work on your feelings so that you have some response.

To write about literature is, in one way or another, an attempt to discover and describe how the writer's art created the reader's response. In other words, whatever your assignment, the fundamental task is to answer two questions: How do I respond to this piece? How has the author brought about my response?

Keeping a Journal

Your instructor may require you to keep a journal—a day-by-day account of your reactions to and reflections on your reading. Even if a journal is not required, you might want to keep one for a variety of reasons. From a purely practical perspective, writing in a journal regularly is excellent practice at conquering the blank page and generating ideas. You need not construct grammatical sentences, write cohesive paragraphs, develop your ideas, or even make sense. In a journal you are free to comment on only one aspect of a work or on a personal recollection that something in the work triggered. You are recording your reactions, ideas, feelings, questions. Jotting down personal connections— for example, if a character reminds you of a friend or teacher—can be helpful even if they don't make it in into your essay. If you are conscientious about keeping your journal, you may come to find writing in it a pleasant activity.

A journal's helpfulness extends beyond its use as a place for reflection. When the time comes to write a full-length essay for your class, the journal can provide many possible topics. Use your journal to express in writing the pleasure (or pain) of each reading assignment. Jot down hard words (which you should then, of course, look up in your dictionary). Note your reactions to characters—that some are nasty, others too saintly, some realistically rendered, still others unbelievable. Some of your journal entries may be confessions of confusion, posing open-ended questions about a reading.

You may want to write about the personal feelings and recollections triggered by a work. Dylan Thomas's "Fern Hill" might remind you of feelings you experienced during a particular period of your childhood. Exploring your own childhood feelings and comparing them with those expressed in Thomas's poem could lead to a fascinating essay—for example, about how poets give memorable and vivid expression to experiences we've all had. Or you might jot down, after reading Kate Chopin's "The Storm," your disapproval of the story's central event—marital infidelity. You might then reread the story to discover whether it seems to disapprove of infidelity or whether you have imposed on it your own moral values. Thinking critically about such reactions might generate an essay that examines the conflict between your own moral values and those embodied in a particular work.

Finally, remember that—unless your instructor has specific guidelines for journal keeping—your journal will be the one place where you can write as much or as little as you please, as often or as infrequently as you wish, with care and deliberation or careless speed. Its only purpose is to serve your needs. But if you write fairly regularly, you will probably be surprised not only at how much easier the act of writing becomes but also at how many ideas suddenly pop into your head in the act of writing. Henry Adams was surely right when he observed, "The habit of expression leads to the search for something to express."

Exploring and Planning

ASKING GOOD QUESTIONS   Often the best ideas for paper topics begin as questions or as responses that can be turned into questions. In reading James Joyce's "Araby," for example, you may notice that the narrator makes a big deal out of carrying the groceries home. This observation can be converted into a question: Why the big deal about carrying the groceries home? Or, to focus the question a bit, Why and how does the boy idealize these everyday situations? Note that these questions do not lead to a single irrefutable answer. When you write responses to literature, your goal is to pose a good question, answer it clearly, and support the answer with evidence from the work.

While it is important to clear up basic questions—for example, what a word or phrase means, or who did what, or how the characters are related to one another—successful papers usually take up questions that are less easily settled. For example, you would probably not want to ask whether it was a mistake for Shakespeare's Othello to trust Iago, or whether the tragedy could have been avoided if he had acted otherwise. Questions such as these do not lend themselves to sustained discussion. Questions of personal taste are not immediately useful for the same reason; if you say you like a particular work, there is little anyone can say to the contrary. Sometimes such assertions can be usefully converted, especially if you begin to ask why you like or dislike a work. In general, however, you should strive to explore open-ended interpretative and thematic questions rather than rehash the facts or declare personal preferences.

ESTABLISHING A WORKING THESIS   Early in the writing process, as you gather ideas about what to write, you should formulate a tentative *working thesis* that states your topic and the point or comment you wish to make about the topic.

Although your working thesis will probably change as you collect information, articulating it will help you focus your thoughts and further research. Make your working thesis as specific as possible to limit your topic and keep the scope of the essay manageable. Consider the audience appeal of your working thesis as well.

A *thesis* states the main point you'll make in your final essay. In your opening paragraph, a clear thesis statement should both indicate the position you intend to take and prepare your reader for what follows. The thesis statement should be accompanied by some indication of the *scope* of your argument—the several issues you intend to explore.

For example, generating ideas for an essay about *Othello*, you may be struck by a line uttered by Othello when he is speaking before the Duke in Act I: "Rude I am in my speech, / and little blessed with the soft phrase of peace." Despite this line, you notice that Othello's speech is admirably measured and eloquent. Is he being falsely modest? Is he tailoring his rhetoric to his noble audience? Is there a genuine note of insecurity being sounded? Whatever your preliminary answer, it is the beginning of your working thesis. The next step is to re-examine Othello's speeches to see if you can find evidence to support and refine the claim of your working thesis.

GATHERING INFORMATION   Once you have chosen your topic and articulated a working thesis, you need to consider what additional information you will need to explore the issue. This may mean identifying examples from the text of the literary work you are analyzing to support your thesis or gathering information from other sources. The library is likely to be the principal source of additional information, though online research is becoming increasingly more reliable.

If you use an electronic source, it is often a simple matter to print online information. If you use print sources in a library, you will need to make a photocopy or take notes. In any case, be sure to indicate on your printout or your note cards the exact publication and location information for all your sources so that you can properly document your sources in the final essay. Even if you are using just one source, you will need to provide information crediting that source in your list of works cited. For more information about crediting sources and creating a Works Cited page, see p. 75.

ORGANIZING INFORMATION   Writing an essay would be a much quicker and more straightforward process if you could somehow magically know what you wanted to write about before you began your research and then whipped up a succinct thesis followed by a structured outline in which arguments I, II, and III were supported by points A, B, and C. In the real world, writers research a preliminary topic and then impose order on the information they have amassed. Think about how best to group or organize your points so that they will be persuasive to your readers.

One general approach to organizing an essay requires you to complete this statement: "The purpose of this essay is X. To demonstrate X, I will argue A, B, and C," substituting your thesis and the arguments that support it for X, A, B, and C. In an essay on *Othello,* for example, you might write, "The purpose of this essay is to argue that Othello's fall is a logical consequence of his situation and his character. To demonstrate this thesis, I will examine his age and race, his military life, and his inexperience with European women."

Once you've nailed down the thesis and scope of the essay, you can, in your draft, add layers to support your claim:

> Many writers have argued that the rapid fall of the noble Moor
>
> Othello is unbelievable. But consider his situation. He is a black man
>
> in a white country; he is much older than his beautiful wife. As a military
>
> man, he self-consciously lacks social grace. And his inexperience with
>
> European women contributes to the emotional insecurity that finally
>
> destroys him.

Where you cite other writers' arguments—as in the first sentence—you must offer documentation for your sources.

The next several paragraphs would follow the organization set up by the opening. First might be a paragraph on Othello's race and age and the attitudes toward him established in act I, followed by a paragraph on Othello's self-conscious unfamiliarity with the behavior of European women. The next paragraph might argue that he sees himself as unappealing to women from his adopted city. Each of these assertions should be supported with dialogue from the play. A conclusion would follow: Othello was never quite as noble as some have suggested and, under the circumstances, was doomed from the start.

One of the intellectual hurdles you'll face as a student of literature is learning to distinguish between a *summary* that recounts events and details and an *analysis* that interprets what events and details might mean. Of course an analysis should provide enough plot summary so that your reader has the context to understand what you are talking about. In fact, if you are confused about the plot of a literary work—what happened, in what order?—then writing a summary may help to clear up your confusion. Moreover, writing a summary is often a first step to writing an analysis and offering an interpretation. As you describe what happens in a work of literature, you begin to ask questions about why those events happened. In choosing the details and events to include in your summary, you are making decisions about which details and events are worth attending to when you try to ascribe meaning to them in the context of analysis and interpretation.

The following summary of Shakespeare's *Othello* reduces the play to its major plot elements. Notice that it does not interpret the play, focusing on particular details and explaining what they mean. (Notice also that it is narrated in the present tense, a conventional practice when you summarize.) This is in contrast to the later analysis of *Othello* in this chapter that answers questions of why things happened in the play and what these events might mean to us as readers.

A Summary of *Othello*

Set in Venice and then Cyprus, *Othello* opens with a scene of the villainous Iago and his henchman Roderigo hatching a vengeful plot against Iago's commanding general Othello, who has passed him over to promote the handsome Michael Cassio to be his Lieutenant. Iago first tries to undermine Othello by anonymously revealing to the father of Othello's new wife that his daughter is now married to a person of a different race (Othello is a Moor—an African). The father, a nobleman named Brabantio, is appalled that his daughter, Desdemona, is married to a Moor, but when he takes his argument to the Duke of Venice, the Duke, who desires Othello's services to protect Venice from an invasion from Cyprus, judges that Othello and Desdemona truly love each other, and approves their wedding. Thwarted in his first attempts at vengeance, Iago contrives to draw Cassio into a drunken street brawl that leads to Othello stripping Cassio of his new rank. Iago then advances his vengeance by leading Othello to believe Desdemona has betrayed him with Cassio. Exploiting his loving wife Emilia, Iago uses a handkerchief that Emilia obtains from Desdemona to fool Othello into believing Desdemona is involved with Cassio. Succumbing to Iago's lies, Othello grows mad with jealousy and asks Iago to help him kill Cassio and Desdemona. Iago continues to weave a series of lies and schemes that ultimately trick Othello into murdering his guiltless wife Desdemona. Believing himself a cuckold, Othello ignores Desdemona's protestations of innocence and strangles her in her bed. Then he discovers through Emilia how he has been duped by Iago. Confronted with Iago's betrayal and the enormity of his own crime against an innocent woman who loved him, Othello chooses to commit suicide rather than try to exculpate himself and live knowing his folly. Iago's vengeance is complete, but his crimes, which include the murder of Roderigo and Emilia, have come to light and he is arrested. Still he vows neither to repent nor ever to speak again of his crimes, even in the face of torture and death.

DRAFTING THE ESSAY

It is important to start writing even if you are unsure about the exact shape or direction of your argument since frequently your ideas develop and become more focused as you proceed. In working through a draft essay on *Othello*, you may initially find yourself interested in, on the one hand, how eloquent you found Othello's address to the court of the Duke of Venice and, on the other hand, his self-characterization as plain-spoken, even ill-spoken. Does Othello really believe he is a "rude" speaker? Is he perhaps manipulating his audience? But as you write your first draft and your thoughts evolve, you may find yourself moving from a thesis that Othello has crafty control of his language to something quite different. Keep writing and stay flexible. A first draft does not have to be perfect. It's a stage for making discoveries and clarifying your ideas.

Refining Your Opening

Once the draft is done and you have a clear idea of your thesis and the passages in the work that best support it, you can begin to shape and refine the essay. In doing so, pay special attention to the introductory paragraph, which should introduce the topic and lead directly to a clear, arguable thesis. While there is no surefire formula for a first paragraph, some strategies are better than others. Avoid the following types of opening sentences:

> Ever since the dawn of time, people have been fascinated by the fall of great men.

> Insecurity is a feeling that can prove harmful in even the most accomplished people.

This kind of throat-clearing generalization is common and even helpful at the draft stage, but it gets the essay off to a slow start. If the working thesis is that Othello is undone not only by treachery but also because of the insecurities that lurk beneath his formidable bearing, a direct approach is more effective:

> In Othello's first speech at the court of the Duke, he presents himself as simple soldier awkwardly attempting to explain how he won the hand of the beautiful Desdemona. In fact his "rude" words are highly eloquent, and a reader may judge that the proud general is using false

modesty to advance his case. Such a judgment ignores a more central issue than Othello's pride and eloquence. His words hint at the insecurities—as a military man short on civilian social graces, an older man with a young wife, a black African in a white European culture—that will cloud his judgment and ultimately prove his undoing.

Note that this opening paragraph introduces the topic and moves directly toward an explicit and arguable claim. By doing so, it lets the reader—and the writer—know where the essay is going. That is, once a clear thesis is in place, both writer and reader can use it as a road map for the rest of the essay.

Supporting Your Thesis

The body of the essay will be devoted to supporting the thesis. The best way to establish a claim is to cite and analyze carefully selected passages from the text that relate directly to it. The following paragraph focuses on lines that support our sample claim directly:

As indicated by the preceding examples, numerous passages reveal Othello's various insecurities. But in the following passage, his language manifests them all:

> Haply, for I am black,
>
> And have not those soft parts of conversation
>
> That chamberers have, or for I am decline'd,
>
> Into the vale of years—yet that's not much— (3.3 263–266)

Here Othello catalogs his self-perceived flaws: His African-ness ("for I am black"), his rough manners ("I . . . have not those soft parts of conversation"), and his age ("decline'd / Into the vale of years"). He is now tormented by the very qualities and achievements that once set him proudly apart from others in European culture.

The first part of the paragraph tells the reader what to look for in the cited lines, and the subsequent analysis underscores their relevance to the overall argument clearly and convincingly.

If you offer a claim, support it with an analysis of the relevant passages, and consider different interpretations of those passages, you have completed the main task in much writing about literature. Concluding paragraphs can move toward closure by reviewing the claim and its significance, which you should be careful not to overstate. In the essay on *Othello,* for example, it would not be effective to conclude with a sweeping claim that the Moor's insecurities represent Shakespeare's indictment of European culture in his era. Your readers will find your claims more convincing if you do not exaggerate their importance.

REVISING THE ESSAY

After you've completed your draft, it is time to look at the essay more critically, paying special attention to revision. Revision involves taking a fresh look at your essay's thesis and support, as well as its organization and language. Reading your essay aloud, or asking someone else to read it, will help you catch many problems. Revision is most effective if begun well before the paper is due. Start writing early so that you have time to review your decisions, ask for feedback from others, and revise accordingly. Because you cannot always anticipate audience reaction, a preliminary reading of your writing by a friend, a teaching assistant, a tutor, or an instructor can highlight the areas that need attention or additional revision.

The basic guidelines for good style are not mysterious; in fact, you use them every day in conversation. In conversation and in writing, we all rely heavily on cooperation to make sense of exchanges, and a polished practical style makes cooperation easier. Writers develop such a style by acknowledging that readers expect the same things that listeners expect in conversation: clarity, relevance, and proportion. If you listen to someone who is not clear, who cannot stay on the topic, or who offers too much or too little information, you will quickly lose interest in the conversation. Writers, too, need to be clear, stay on the topic, and give information appropriately. In fact, this attention to audience and appropriateness may be even more important in writing than in conversation because writing does not permit the nonverbal communication and immediate feedback that are part of conversation. As writers, we have to anticipate the absent reader's response; in effect, we have to imagine both halves of a virtual conversation.

Begin by evaluating your essay's thesis. Is it clear? Vagueness or tentativeness here may mean problems later in the essay, so make sure your thesis is crystal clear. Second, is the evidence you present relevant to each major point? While it is tempting and sometimes productive to go off on tangents while drafting a paper, in the final essay if the evidence doesn't fit the claim, tinker with the claim, or go back to the early exploratory writing you did and to your sources to look for better evidence. Are there any points that need to be clarified? Check all your quotations, paraphrases, and summaries for their citations and for accuracy.

Next, can you tighten the organization of your draft? Are your claims and evidence unified? Put yourself in your reader's place, and clarify ambiguities. Each detail or piece of evidence in a paragraph should relate back to the claim it supports in the topic sentence of that paragraph. At the same time, avoid oversupporting some points with too much discussion or detail.

Finally, ask yourself if the general proportions of your essay are suitable. A five-page paper should not use three of those pages to introduce the topic or recount a work's plot. If the essay is too short, the trouble might be an unarguable thesis or insufficient evidence. If it is running too long, eliminate or compress the parts that do not bear directly on the main claim, or limit the claim to something more manageable.

Editing Your Draft

After you have evaluated and revised your draft and determined the format for your paper, you are ready to edit it carefully, paying close attention to each sentence and paragraph. These guidelines will help you focus on some common trouble spots.

SELECTING STRONG VERBS   Careful selection of lively, active verbs will make your writing more interesting to your audience. Consider the main verb in the following sentence:

> Three conflicts, all of which play crucial roles in the plot, are evident in
> Othello.

The core assertion of this sentence is that "[t]hree conflicts . . . are evident." Notice that nothing actually happens in this sentence. To stir things up, borrow the verb *play* from another part of the sentence:

> Three conflicts play crucial roles in the plot of Othello.

The revision is better, but the sentence can be made even more concise using *drive:*

> Three conflicts drive the plot of Othello.

The revised sentence more clearly gets to the point, an effect that is rarely lost on an audience. It also permits a more direct move to the topic—namely, the conflicts. Finally, in an economical seven words rather than a verbose fifteen, it neither belabors nor omits anything of importance in the first sentence.

Writing that relies too heavily on *be* verbs often produces wordiness and unnecessary abstraction:

> There was opposition to interracial marriage among most of the citizens of
> Venice.

Deleting the *be* verb (*was*) and converting the abstract noun *opposition* into a verb make the sentence more active:

> Most Venetians opposed interracial marriage.

This clearer sentence lets the verb do the major work. Of course, a good verb does not always present itself as an abstract noun in an early draft. Sometimes you'll need to consult a thesaurus or a dictionary to find just the right word.

Search your draft for weak verbs and insignificant words and for sentences that begin *There is, There are, It is.* Often, a few words later, a *that, which,* or *who* will appear. Overuse of *There is* and *There are* produces sentences where the action is buried. Edit these sentences by deleting the weak verb constructions and replacing them with strong, precise verbs. For example, change "*There is* a destiny *that* controls the fate of Sam" to "Destiny controls Sam's fate."

Finally, check your draft for passive constructions (the ball *was thrown*), and replace them when possible with active verbs. Passive sentences are often wordy and dull the action of a sentence. For example, change "The essay was read by the class" to "The class read the essay."

ELIMINATING UNNECESSARY MODIFIERS When choosing or revising a verb, you are also choosing the sentence elements that necessarily accompany it. These other sentence elements are called *complements* because they complete the meaning of the verb. In the following sentences the complements are underlined:

> Iago betrays Othello.

> The boy idealized his situation.

Iago cannot just betray; he has to betray something. Likewise, *his situation* completes the meaning of the verb *idealized.* Almost everything else added to these sentences will be *modifiers*—additional elements that will modify, rather than complete, the meaning of the sentences. A writer can add any number of modifiers to a sentence:

> Iago betrayed Othello cold-bloodedly, with a malignity beyond measure,
> a malignity that Coleridge characterized as "motiveless."

From a grammatical standpoint, these modifiers are optional; without them the sentence still expresses a complete thought. Unnecessary modifiers can make your writing heavy and murky:

> Basically, the Greeks invented a rather innovative and distinctive form of
> government known as democracy.

Eliminating the modifiers and making a few other snips result in the following:

> The Greeks invented democracy.

The clearer sentence does not lose much in the way of content. Of course, being able to eliminate modifiers does not mean that you should; sometimes modifiers are the most significant parts of a sentence. You can always use modifiers for nuance or emphasis, but you must ruthlessly trim unnecessary modifiers from wordy, unclear sentences.

GRAMMATICAL CONNECTIONS Make sure your sentences and paragraphs are firmly linked by using explicit transitional phrases such as *however, although, likewise, for example, therefore,* and so on. Note in this sample opening paragraph how the underlined transitional phrases indicate the relationships between the sentences:

> In his speech before the Duke's court, Othello speaks disarmingly to the assembled nobles. He flatteringly describes his audience as being potent, grave, and reverend. He modestly describes himself as being a blunt-spoken soldier hardly qualified to talk of anything but the wars that he has seen and fought. <u>However</u>, Othello's modesty is belied by the deeds of which he speaks. <u>In particular</u> he boldly admits to having won both the love of Desdemona and many battles, dating from when he was but a child. The court is looking for a conqueror, and in his guise of modesty Othello presents himself as that man.

The appearance of *however* halfway through the paragraph signals the contrast between Othello's professed modesty and his powerful deeds. The transitional phrase *in particular* in the next sentence signals that we are narrowing the preceding point and focusing our discussion. Experienced readers look for such transitional phrases that suggest an interpretive path through an argument.

Note that the third sentence of the paragraph repeats a key word from the second one (*describes*); so does the first and fourth sentence (*speaks*). The repetition helps keep the spotlight on Othello's rhetoric, an important notion in the paragraph. (Note also the repetition of *modesty.*) By repeating key terms, sometimes with slight variation, you can powerfully illuminate the main idea of a paragraph.

After checking for explicit connections within paragraphs, make sure that the progression of ideas from one paragraph to another is clear. Here again, transitional phrases are useful. A simple transition such as *nevertheless, furthermore,* or *on the other hand* is often adequate. Sometimes the entire opening sentence of a paragraph may provide the transition, including key words, pronouns, or other references to the previous paragraph.

Proofreading Your Draft

Print out, type, or (if your instructor allows it) neatly write in ink the final copy of your essay for submission to your instructor, taking care to follow any special instructions about format that you have been given. Don't rush; be meticulous. When you have finished, proofread the final copy carefully, looking for spelling or punctuation errors, omitted words, disagreement between subjects and verbs or between pronouns and antecedents, and typographical errors that will detract from the essay you have worked hard to write.

For additional advice on checking your use of sources and documenting in your final essay, see "Some Matters of Form and Documentation" (p. 73). Finally, use "A Checklist for Writing about Literature" (p. 77) to help with a quick review of your final draft.

SOME COMMON WRITING ASSIGNMENTS

A writing assignment for a literature course may require any of a variety of kinds of writing. You might be called on to compare and contrast literary works, to analyze the language of a work, to discuss the interaction of a work's parts, to discuss a work's theme, or to articulate your own responses to the work. Sometimes an instructor may ask simply that you write an essay on one of the pieces you have read. This type of assignment requires you to create your own boundaries—to find a specific focus that both suits the piece you choose and is manageable within a paper of the assigned length. Sometimes you may be asked to simply summarize a complex literary work. The summary of *Othello* (p. 958) would be adequate if the assignment was this straightforward. Other times, you may be asked to respond creatively, to come up with original work that reimagines a poem or story from your own point of view and in your own words. However, in many literature courses, assigned essays tend to fall into one of three modes—explication, analysis, and comparison and contrast—or some combination of these. Familiarity with these three kinds of writing about literature will help you not only with full-length essay assignments but also with exams and other in-class writing.

Explication

In an explication essay, you examine a work in much detail. Line by line, stanza by stanza, scene by scene, you explain each part as fully as you can and show how the author's techniques produce your response. An explication is essentially a demonstration of your thorough understanding of a work.

Here is a sample essay that explicates a relatively difficult poem, Dylan Thomas's "Do Not Go Gentle into That Good Night" (p. 1217).

> Dylan Thomas's villanelle "Do Not Go Gentle into That Good Night"
>
> is addressed to his aged father. The poem is remarkable in a number of
>
> ways, most notably in that contrary to most common poetic treatments of

the inevitability of death, which argue for serenity or celebrate the peace that death provides, this poem urges resistance and rage in the face of death. It justifies that unusual attitude by describing the rage and resistance to death of four kinds of men, who each can summon up the image of a complete and satisfying life that is denied to him by death.

The first tercet of the intricately rhymed villanelle opens with an arresting line. The adjective *gentle* appears where we would expect the adverb *gently*. The strange diction suggests that *gentle* may describe both the going (i.e., gently dying) and the person (i.e., gentleman) who confronts death. Further, the speaker characterizes "night," here clearly a figure for death, as "good." Yet in the next line, the speaker urges that the aged should violently resist death, characterized as the "close of day" and "the dying of the light." In effect, the first three lines argue that however good death may be, the aged should refuse to die gently, should passionately rave and rage against death.

In the second tercet, the speaker turns to a description of the way the first of four types of men confronts death (which is figuratively defined throughout the poem as "that good night" and "the dying of the light"). These are the "wise men," the scholars, the philosophers, those who understand the inevitability of death, men who "know dark is right." But they do not acquiesce in death "because their words had forked no lightning," because their published wisdom failed to bring them to that sense of completeness and fulfillment that can accept death. Therefore, wise as they are, they reject the theoretical "rightness" of death and refuse to "go gentle."

The second sort of men—"good men," the moralists, the social reformers, those who attempt to better the world through action as the wise men attempt to better it through "words"—also rage against death. Their deeds are, after all, "frail." With sea imagery, the speaker suggests that these men might have accomplished fine and fertile things—their deeds "might have danced in a green bay." But with the "last wave" gone, they see only the frailty, the impermanence of their acts, and so they, too, rage against the death that deprives them of the opportunity to leave a meaningful legacy.

The "wild men," the poets who "sang" the loveliness and vitality of nature, also learn as they approach death that the sensuous joys of human existence wane. As the life-giving sun moves toward dusk, as death approaches, their singing turns to grieving, and they refuse to surrender gently, to leave willingly the warmth, pleasure, and beauty that life can give.

Finally, with a pun suggestive of death, the "grave men," those who go through life with such high seriousness as never to experience gaiety and pleasure, see all the joyous possibilities that they were blind to in life. And they, too, rage against the dying of a light that they had never properly seen before.

The speaker then calls on his aged father to join these men raging against death. Only in this final stanza do we discover that the entire poem is addressed to the speaker's father and that, despite the general-ized statements about old age and the focus on types of men, the poem is a personal lyric. The edge of death becomes a "sad height," the summit of wisdom and experience old age attains includes the sad knowledge of life's failure to satisfy the vision we all pursue. The depth and complexity of the speaker's sadness is startlingly given in the second line, when he calls on his father to both curse and bless him. These opposites richly suggest several related possibilities: "Curse me for not living up to your expectations. Curse me for remaining alive as you die. Bless me with forgiveness for my failings. Bless me for teaching you to rage against death." And the curses and blessings are contained in the "fierce tears"—fierce because you will burn and rave and rage against death. As the poem closes by bringing together the two powerful refrains, the speaker himself seems to rage because his father's death will cut off a relationship that is incomplete.

This explication deals with the entire poem by coming to grips with each element in it.

You can learn a great deal about the technique of drama by selecting a short, self-contained scene and writing a careful description of it. The length of plays will probably require that you focus on a single segment—a scene, for example—rather than the entire play. This method of explication will force you to confront every speech and stage direction and to come to some conclusion regarding its function. Why is the set furnished as it is? Why does a character speak the words he or she does or remain silent? What do we learn of characters from the interchanges among them? Assume that everything that occurs in the play, whether on the printed page or on the stage, is put there for a purpose. Seek to discover the purpose, and you will, at the same time, discover the peculiar nature of drama.

Fiction, too, can be treated effectively in a formal explication. As with drama, it will be necessary to limit the text: you will not be able to explicate a ten-page story in a 1,000-word essay. Choose a key passage—a half page that reflects the form and content of the overall story, if possible. Often the first half page of a story, where the author, like the playwright, must supply information to the reader, will make a fine text for an explication. Although the explication will deal principally with only an excerpt, feel free to range across the story and show how the introductory material foreshadows what is to come. Or perhaps you can explicate the climax of the story—the half page that most pointedly establishes the story's theme—and subject it to a close line-by-line reading that illuminates the whole story.

Analysis

Breaking a literary work down into its elements is only the first step in literary analysis. When you are assigned an analysis essay, you are expected to focus on one of the elements that contributes to the complex compound of a work. This process requires you to extricate the element you plan to explore from the other elements that you can identify, to study this element—not only in isolation but also in relation to the other elements and the work as a whole—and, using the insights you have gained from your special perspective, to make an informed statement about it.

This process may sound complicated, but if you approach it methodically, each stage follows naturally from the stage that precedes it. If, for example, you are to write an analysis essay on characterization in *Othello*, you would begin by thinking about each character in the play. You would then select the character whose development you would like to explore and reread carefully those speeches that help to establish his or her substance. Exploring a character's development in this way involves a good deal of explication: in order to identify the "building blocks" that Shakespeare uses to create a three-dimensional role, you must comb very carefully through that character's speeches and actions. You must also be sensitive to the ways in which other characters respond to these speeches and actions. When you have completed this investigation, you will probably have a good understanding of why you intuitively responded to the character as you did when you first read the play. You will also probably be prepared to make a statement about the character's development: "From a realistic perspective, it is hard to believe that a man of Othello's position could be so gullible; however, Shakespeare develops the role with such craft that we accept the Moor as flesh and blood." At this point, you have moved from the broad *subject* of "characterization in *Othello*" to a *thesis,* a statement that you must prove. As you formulate your thesis, think of it as a position that you intend to *argue* for with a reader you need to persuade. This approach is useful in any essay that requires a thesis, where you move beyond simple explication and commit yourself to a stand. Note that our sample thesis is *argumentative* on two counts; "characterization in *Othello*" is not remotely argumentative. Further, you have more than enough material to write a well-documented essay of 1,000 words supporting your proposition; you cannot write a well-documented 1,000-word essay on the general subject of characterization in *Othello* without being superficial.

You may be one among the many writers who have trouble finding a starting point. For example, you have been assigned an analysis essay on a very broad subject, such as imagery in love poetry. A few poems come to mind, but you don't know where to begin. You read these poems and underline all the images that you can find. You look at these images over and over, finding no relation among them. You read some more poems, again underlining the images, but you still do not have even the germ of a thesis.

The technique of *freewriting* might help to overcome your block. You have read and reread the poems you intend to write about. Now, put the assignment temporarily out of your mind, and start writing about one or two of the poems without organizing your ideas, without trying to reach a point. Write down what you like about a poem, what you dislike about it, what sort of person the speaker is, which images seemed striking to you—anything at all about the work. If you do this for perhaps ten minutes, you will probably discover that you are voicing opinions. Pick one that interests you or seems the most promising to explore.

The basic form of the analysis assignment has a few variations. Your instructor might narrow the subject in a specific assignment: analyze the development of Othello's character in act I. This sort of assignment limits the amount of text you will have to study, but the process from this point on is no different from the process you would employ to address a broader subject. Sometimes instructors will supply you with a thesis, and you will have to work backward from the thesis to find supporting material. Again, careful analysis of the text is required. The problem you will have to address when writing an analytical essay remains the same regardless of the literary genre you are asked to discuss. You must find an arguable thesis that deals with the sources of your response to the work.

Suppose your instructor has made the following assignment: write an analysis of Harlan Ellison's story "'Repent, Harlequin!' Said the Ticktockman," in which you discuss the theme of the story in terms of the characters and the setting. Now consider the following opening (taken from a student paper):

> "'Repent, Harlequin!' Said the Ticktockman" is a story depicting a society in which time governs one's life. The setting is the United States, the time approximately A.D. 2400 somewhere in the heart of the country. Business deals, work shifts, and school lessons are started and finished with exacting precision. Tardiness is intolerable as this would hinder the system. In a society of order, precision, and punctuality, there is no room for likes, dislikes, scruples, or morals. Thus, personalities in people no longer exist. As these "personless" people know no good or bad, they very happily follow in the course of activities that their society has dictated.

At the outset, can you locate a thesis statement? The only sentences that would seem to qualify are the last three in the paragraph. But notice that, although those sentences are not unreasonable responses to the story, they do not establish a thesis that is *responsive to the assignment*. Because the assignment calls for a discussion of theme in terms of character and setting, a thesis statement should argue how character and setting embody the theme. Here is another opening paragraph on the same assignment (also taken from a student paper):

> Harlan Ellison's "'Repent, Harlequin!' Said the Ticktockman" opens with a quotation from Thoreau's essay "Civil Disobedience," which establishes the story's theme. Thoreau's observations about three varieties of men--those who serve the state as machines, those who serve it with their heads, and those who serve it with their consciences—are dramatized in Ellison's story, which takes place about 400 years in the future in a setting characterized by machinelike order. The interaction

among the three characters, each of whom represents one of Thoreau's

types, results in a telling restatement of his observation that "heroes,

patriots, martyrs, reformers in the great sense, and men . . . necessarily

resist [the state] and . . . are commonly treated as enemies by it."

Compare these two opening paragraphs sentence by sentence for their responsiveness to the assignment. The first sentence of the first opening does not refer to the theme of the story (or to its setting or characterization). In the second sentence, the discussion of the setting ignores the most important aspect—that the story is set in a machine- and time-dominated future. The last three sentences deal obliquely with character, but they are imprecise and do not establish a thesis. The second opening, on the other hand, immediately states the theme of the story. It goes on to emphasize the relevant aspects of the futuristic setting and then refers to the three characters who animate the story in terms of their reactions to the setting. The last sentence addresses the assignment directly and also serves as a thesis statement for the paper. It states the proposition that will be developed and supported in the rest of the paper. The reader of the second opening will expect the next paragraph of the paper to discuss the setting of the story and subsequent paragraphs to discuss the response to the setting of the three principal characters.

The middles of essays are largely determined by their opening paragraphs. However long the middle of any essay may be, each of its paragraphs ought to be responsive to some explicit statement made at the beginning of the essay. Note that it is practically impossible to predict what the paragraph following the first opening will address. Here is the first half of that next paragraph as the first student wrote it:

The Harlequin is a man in the society with no sense of time. His

having a personality enables him to have a sense of moral values and a

mind of his own. The Harlequin thinks that it is obscene and wrong to

let time totally govern the lives of people. So he sets out to disrupt the

time schedule with ridiculous antics such as showering people with jelly

beans to try to break up the military fashion in which they are used to

doing things.

The paragraph then goes on to discuss the Ticktockman, the capture and brainwashing of the Harlequin, and the resulting lateness of the Ticktockman.

Note that nothing in the opening of this student's paper prepared readers for the introduction of the Harlequin. In fact, the opening concluded rather inaccurately that the people within the story "happily follow in the course of activities that their society has dictated." Hence, the description of the Harlequin in the second paragraph is wholly unexpected. Further, because the student has not dealt with the theme of the story (as the assignment asked), the comments about the Harlequin's antics remain disconnected from any clear purpose. They are essentially devoted to what teachers constantly warn against: a mere plot summary. The student has obviously begun to write before analyzing the story sufficiently to understand its theme. With further thought, the student would have perceived that the central thematic issue is resistance to an oppressive state—the issue stated in the epigraph from Thoreau. On the other hand, because the second opening makes that thematic point clearly, we can expect it to be followed by a discussion of the environment (that is, the setting) in which the action occurs. Here is such a paragraph taken from the second student's paper:

> Ellison creates a society that reflects one possible future
>
> development of the modern American passion for productivity and
>
> efficiency. The setting is in perfect keeping with the time-conscious
>
> people who inhabit the city. It is pictured as a neat, colorless, and
>
> mechanized city. No mention is made of nature: grass, flowers, trees,
>
> and birds do not appear. The buildings are in a "Mondrian arrangement,"
>
> stark and geometrical. The cold steel sidewalks, slowstrips, and
>
> expresstrips move with precision. Like a chorus line, people move in
>
> unison to board the movers without a wasted motion. Doors close silently
>
> and lock themselves automatically. An ideal efficiency so dominates the
>
> social system that any "wasted time" is deducted from the life of an
>
> inefficient citizen.

Once the setting has been established, the writer turns to the characters, linking those characters to thematic considerations, beginning with a short transitional paragraph that shapes the remainder of the middle of the essay:

> Into this smoothly functioning but coldly mechanized society,
>
> Ellison introduces three characters: Pretty Alice, one of Thoreau's
>
> machinelike creatures; the Ticktockman, one of those who "serve the state
>
> chiefly with their heads, and, as they rarely make any moral distinctions,
>
> they are as likely to serve the Devil, without intending it, as God"; and

Everett C. Marm, the Harlequin, whose conscience forces him to resist the oppressive state.

Following a logical organization, the essay then includes a paragraph devoted to each of the three characters:

Pretty Alice is, probably, very pretty. (Everett didn't fall in love with her brains.) In the brief section in which we meet her, we find her hopelessly ordinary in her attitudes. She is upset that Marm finds it necessary to go about "annoying people." She finds him ridiculous and wishes only that he would stay home, as other people do. Clearly, she has no understanding of what Everett is struggling against. Though her anger finally leads her to betray him, Everett himself can't believe that she has done so. His own loyal and understanding nature colors his view of her so thoroughly that he cannot imagine the treachery that must have been so simple and satisfying for Pretty Alice, whose only desire is to be like everybody else.

The Ticktockman is more complex. He sees himself as a servant of the state, and he performs his duties with resolution and competence. He skillfully supports a System he has never questioned. The System exists; it must be good. His conscience is simply not involved in the performance of his duty. He is one of those who follow orders and expect others to follow orders. As a result, the behavior of the Harlequin is more than just an irritant or a rebellion against authority. It is unnerving. The Ticktockman wishes to understand that behavior, and with Everett's time-card in his hand, he muses that he has the name of "*what* he is, not *who* he is. . . . Before I can exercise proper revocation, I have to know *who* this *what* is." And when he confronts Everett, he does not just liquidate him. He insists that Everett repent. He tries to convince Everett that the System is sound, and when he cannot win the argument, he dutifully

reconditions Everett, since he is, after all, more interested in justifying
the System than in destroying its enemies. It is easy to see this man
as a competent servant of the devil who thinks he is serving God.

But only Everett C. Marm truly serves the state because his
conscience requires him to resist. He is certainly not physically heroic. His
very name suggests weak conformity. Though he loves his Pretty Alice, he
cannot resign from the rebellious campaign on which his conscience
insists. So without violence, and mainly with the weapon of laughter, he
attacks the mechanical precision of the System and succeeds in breaking it
down simply by making people late. He is himself, as Pretty Alice points
out, always late, and the delays that his antics produce seriously threaten
the well-being of the smooth but mindless System he hates. He is captured
and refuses, even then, to submit, and so his personality is destroyed by
the authorities that fear him. The Ticktockman is too strong for him.

An appropriate ending emerges naturally from this student's treatment of
the assignment. Having established that the story presents characters who deal
in different ways with the oppressive quality of life in a time- and machine-
obsessed society, the student concludes with a comment on the author's criticisms of such a society:

Harlequin is defeated, but Ellison, finally, leaves us with an
optimistic note. The idea of rebellion against the System will linger in the
minds of others. There will be more Harlequins and more disruption of this
System. Many rebels will be defeated, but any System that suppresses
individualism will give birth to resistance. And Harlequin's defeat is by no
means total. The story ends with the Ticktockman himself arriving for
work three minutes late.

Comparison and Contrast

An essay in comparison and contrast shows how two works are similar to and
different from one another. It almost always starts with a recognition of similarities, often of subject matter. Sometimes you may be asked to connect what

you have read with something in your own life, creating an original comparison, for example, between Peter Meinke's "Advice to My Son" (p. 177) and advice you have been given by an adult in your own life. Most comparison-and-contrast assignments involve two works of the same genre. While it is possible to compare *any* two works, the best comparison-and-contrast essays emerge from the analysis of two works similar enough to illuminate each other. Two works about love, or death, or conformity, or innocence, or identity give you something to begin with. The groupings in this book will suggest some ways you might read certain works together. For example, both Emily Dickinson's "Apparently with no surprise" (p. 1189) and Robert Frost's "Design" (p. 1196) are about death, and they both use remarkably similar events as the occasion for their poems. Starting with these similarities, you would soon find yourself noting the contrasts (in tone, for example, and theme) between nineteenth-century and twentieth-century views of the nature of God.

Before you begin writing a comparison-and-contrast essay, it is especially important to have clearly in mind the points of comparison and contrast you wish to discuss and the order in which you can most effectively discuss them. You will need to give careful thought to the best way to organize your paper, jotting down the plan your comparison will follow. As a general rule, it is best to avoid dividing the essay into separate discussions of each work. That method tends to produce two separate, loosely joined analysis essays. The successful comparison-and-contrast essay treats some point of similarity or contrast between the two works, then moves on to succeeding points, and ends with an evaluation of the comparative merits of the works.

Like any essay that goes beyond simple explication, a comparison-and-contrast essay requires a strong thesis statement. However, a comparison-and-contrast thesis is generally not difficult to formulate: you must identify the works under consideration and state clearly your reasons for making the comparison.

Here is a student paper that compares and contrasts Dylan Thomas's "Do Not Go Gentle into That Good Night" with the poetic response it triggered from a poet with different views:

Dylan Thomas's "Do Not Go Gentle into That Good Night" and

Catherine Davis's "After a Time" demand comparison: Davis's poem was

written in deliberate response to Thomas's. Davis assumes the reader's

familiarity with "Do Not Go Gentle," which she uses to articulate her

contrasting ideas. "After a Time," although it is a literary work in its own

right, might even be thought of as serious parody—perhaps the greatest

compliment one writer can pay another.

"Do Not Go Gentle into That Good Night" was written by a young man of thirty-eight who addresses it to his old and ailing father. Perhaps because Thomas had very little of his own self-destructive life left as he was composing this piece, he seems to have more insight into the subject of death than most people his age. He advocates raging and fighting against it, not giving in and accepting it.

"After a Time" was written by Davis at about the same age and is addressed to no one in particular. Davis has a different philosophy about death. She "answers" Thomas's poem and presents her differing views using the same poetic form—a villanelle. Evidently, she felt it necessary to present a contrasting point of view eight years after Thomas's death.

While "Do Not Go Gentle" protests and rages against death, Davis's poem suggests a quiet resignation and acquiescence. She seems to feel that raging against death is useless and profitless. She argues that we will eventually become tame, anyway, after the raging is done.

Thomas talks about different types of men and why they rage against death. "Wise men" desire immortality. They rage against death occurring before they've made their mark on history. "Good men" lament the frailty of their deeds. Given more time, they might have accomplished great things. "Wild men" regret their constant hedonistic pursuits. With more time they could prove their worth. "Grave men" are quite the opposite and regret they never took time for the pleasures in life. Now it is too late. They rage against death because they are not ready for it.

His father's death is painful to Thomas because he sees himself lying in that bed; his father's dying reminds him of his own inevitable death. The passion of the last stanza, in which the poet asks his father to bless and curse him, suggests that he has doubts about his relationship with his father. He may feel that he has not been a good enough son. He put off doing things with and for his father because he always felt there would be time later. Now time has run out and he feels cheated.

Catherine Davis advocates a calm submission, a peaceful acquiescence. She feels raging is useless and says that those of us who rage will finally "go tame / When what we have we can no longer use." When she says "One more thing lost is one thing less to lose," the reader can come to terms with the loss of different aspects of the mind and body, such as strength, eyesight, hearing, and intellect. Once one of these is lost, it's one thing less to worry about losing. After a time, everything will be lost, and we'll accept that, too, because we'll be ready for it.

Thomas's imagery is vivid and powerful. His various men not only rage and rave, they *burn*. Their words "forked no lightning," their deeds might have "danced in a green bay," they "sang the sun in flight," and they see that "blind eyes could blaze like meteors." Davis's images are quiet and generally abstract, without much sensory suggestiveness, as in "things lost," a "reassuring ruse," and "all losses are the same." Her most powerful image—"And we go stripped at last the way we came"—makes its point with none of the excitement of Thomas's rage. And yet, I prefer the quiet intelligence of Davis to the high energy of Thomas.

"And we go stripped at last the way we came" can give strange comfort and solace to those of us who always envied those in high places. People are not all created equal at birth, not by a long shot. But we will all be equal when we die. All wealth, power, and trappings will be left behind, and we will all ultimately be equal. So why rage? It won't do us any good.

THE RESEARCH PAPER

Research papers depend on secondary sources (the primary source is, of course, the work, the historical event, or the literary theory you are studying). Research assignments send you to the library, to the Web, or to any source of information that bears on your project. Whether you are researching to discover the varied responses to a work, to gain some insight into the author's life and times, or to identify relevant critical principles, you will synthesize what you have read *about* the work into a well-organized paper and provide *proper documentation*. But a research paper is not a mindless recitation of what your secondary sources have said. Nor does it require you to suspend your own critical judgment. By the time you settle into writing your paper, you will have learned some things you didn't know before. You have earned—and ought to exercise—the right to make some judgments. An assigned research topic will probably ask you to come to some conclusions. If you choose your own topic, you must discover in your research support for a clear, focused thesis before you begin to write.

Here is a sample student research paper that illustrates the technique. The marginal notes call attention to some of the details that make this a successful effort. In general, notice that the author has done research, but the paper is not weighed down with it. The opening paragraph provides a historical context for the subject of the paper, Kate Chopin's short story "The Storm" (p. 805). The writer has a point of view about the story, or thesis, stated in the second paragraph. While that thesis is developed throughout, the writer makes interesting observations on such matters as the relationship of other Chopin works to the story, the names of characters, local color, and a notable change in American moral attitudes. Note how the writer concludes with two paragraphs that resolve the issues raised in the opening two paragraphs.

The sample paper employs the Modern Language Association's (MLA) standard documentation and footnote form. The section that follows the research paper provides further samples that will help you manage formal matters and documentation. It concludes with a checklist that you might want to consult both before you begin writing your paper and before you submit your final draft.

AN ANNOTATED STUDENT RESEARCH PAPER

Lagos 1

Krissa Lagos

Professor Richard Abcarian

English 255

Sex and Sensibility

in Kate Chopin's "The Storm"

Kate Chopin's openly erotic depictions of marital
infidelity in her literary works separate her from all other
American female writers of her time. The adulterous affair of a
strong independent woman depicted in her novel *The Awakening*
(1899) created a public scandal. And, though she "never flouted
convention as strongly as did her fictitious heroine, she did
exhibit an individuality and strength remarkable for upper-
middle-class women of the time" (Moon). Her honest and direct
portrayal of the sexuality of her female characters was rejected
until well into the 1900s, when the minds of readers caught
up to her advanced thinking (Skaggs 5). Works such as "The
Storm"—once shunned (especially by the male community)
because of their focus on sexual exploration—are now celebrated
as serious literature. In fact, when Chopin wrote "The Storm"
in 1898, she knew that no magazine would ever publish such
an uninhibited and uncritical account of an adulterous
encounter, and so never attempted to have it published
(Toth 206).

Writer's name
and page
number.

Use MLA
standard style
or follow
instructor's
criteria.

Center title.

First paragraph
establishes
context.

Documents an
Internet source
with no page
number (see
Works Cited).

Documents a
book in Works
Cited and gives
page number.

Lagos 2

States the
elements of the
paper's thesis.

In "The Storm," Chopin utilizes the irony characteristic of her writing to give the story a light, easy feel. She also uses diction and imagery to draw the reader into the emotions of her characters. She ignores the usual implications of unfaithfulness to a spouse, and instead focuses on the pleasure inspired by the instant gratification of physical desire.

Provides
important
context for the
story's events.

"The Storm" is in fact a sequel to another short story, "At the 'Cadian Ball." In the first tale, which takes place in Louisiana, a favorite setting for Chopin,[1] a farmer named Bobinôt is captivated with spirited, Spanish-blooded Calixta. Calixta, however, has her eyes on a handsome local planter, Alcée Laballière, who is charmed by her attractive features and openly sexual attitude. At the end of the night, however, Clarisse, a woman who is Alcée's social equal (and also happens to be his cousin), suddenly appears and agrees to marry him. Calixta, deserted by Alcée, is "deemed lucky to get anyone, even stodgy Bobinôt" (Ewell 77).

Discusses the
significance of
setting.

By setting "The Storm" in Louisiana, Chopin is able to take advantage of the unstable, muggy weather of the region to help build up to the story's climax. The events of the tale occur because of the weather: the storm strands Bobinôt and his son Bibi at a store while wife and mother Calixta is at home, and Alcée is driven into Bobinôt and Calixta's house by the approaching rain. More subtle events, nearly all of which

Uses concrete
examples to
bolster
assertions.

carry sensual undercurrents, are also inspired by the weather conditions.

For instance, when Calixta is first mentioned, she is sewing, and Chopin immediately introduces an indirect sexual undertone to her movements: ". . . she felt very warm and often stopped to mop her face on which the perspiration gathered in beads. She unfastened her white sacque at the throat" (Chopin, "The Storm" 805). Except for what follows, there would be no reason at all to interpret this minor event. However, when Alcée arrives, the loosened collar eventually leads to more than one would imagine possible. First, Calixta is driven into his arms by the lightning crashing all around the house. Alcée attempts to ease her fears while at the same time fighting the desire for her that has been reawakened by contact with her body. Her unbuttoned collar is part of what defeats his battle against his desires:

> He pushed her hair back from her face that was
> warm and steaming. Her lips were as red and moist
> as pomegranate seed. Her white neck and a glimpse
> of her full firm bosom disturbed him powerfully. As
> she glanced up at him the fear in her liquid blue
> eyes had given place to a drowsy gleam that
> unconsciously betrayed a sensuous desire. (Chopin,
> "The Storm" 807)

Obviously the sole reason for Calixta and Alcée succumbing to their passions is not that she unbuttoned her shirt collar. However, the accumulation of this and other details—their shared climax with the storm, the correspondence between them lying contented afterward while the storm departs softly—make

Ellipses indicate omission in a direct quote.

Identifies the specific work from the Works Cited list when there is more than one work by the same author.

Shows how Chopin uses details to advance the plot.

this story a powerful work of art. Chopin crafts her sentences to enhance her narrative's power.

The French Louisiana setting of "The Storm" is typical of many of her writings (Ewell 52). The detailed local color is reflected by the French names of the characters. Calixta, Bobinôt, and Bibi speak the 'Cadian dialect of Louisiana, which in Calixta's case occasionally includes a small smattering of French (Ewell 77). Alcée, in contrast, speaks impeccable English, reflective of his better education. Chopin inserts a significant detail at the beginning of the story when Bobinôt purchases "a can of shrimps, of which Calixta was very fond" (Chopin, "The Storm" 805). The small gesture reveals Bobinôt's affectionate appreciation of his wife.

Discusses Chopin's view of the rights of women.

In "The Storm," Chopin conveys the theme of autonomy, something familiar to her female characters, especially in "The Story of an Hour."[2] Both Calixta and Clarisse are happiest in "The Storm" when they are separated from their husbands and free to do as they wish.

> As for Clarisse, she was charmed upon receiving her husband's letter. She and the babies were doing well. The society was agreeable; many of her old friends seemed to restore the pleasant liberty of her maiden days. Devoted as she was to her husband, their intimate conjugal life was something which she was more than willing to forego for a while. (Chopin, "The Storm" 809)

Lagos 5

Therefore Clarisse, though far from the actual storm, benefits from its effects. She feels unfettered, pleased at being given space for the first time since she has been married to Alcée. For Calixta, the short time she spends with Alcée during the storm is enough to make her lift "her pretty chin in the air" and laugh with delight (Chopin, "The Storm" 808).

In "At the 'Cadian Ball," the two couples are paired together at the end of the night due to Alcée's notion of honor and propriety (Ewell 77). As Chopin explains in "The Storm," he never intended to marry Calixta, but he did want more from her than what he took in the story's prequel at the ball: "If she was not an immaculate dove in those days, she was still inviolate; a passionate creature whose very defenselessness had made her defense, against which his honor forbade him to prevail" (Chopin, "The Storm" 807). When the ball ended, only Calixta was left unsatisfied, but by the time "The Storm" takes place, only Bobinôt is still utterly content.

The fact that Calixta is now married somehow frees Alcée from his previous restraints, and he is able to satisfy his craving for her at last. As a result, Alcée is also more content with his wife away, which leads him to write the letter to her urging her to prolong her stay in Biloxi. Bobinôt is the most easily pleased of all. He reaches home cringing at what his wife will say to Bibi and him when she notices how dirty they are. Luckily for the father and son, she is still glowing from her brief interlude with Alcée, and "they laughed much and so loud that anyone might have heard them as far away as Laballière's" (Chopin, "The Storm" 808).

> Earlier story is used to establish Alcée's character.

Chopin's irony shines through "The Storm" in many parts of the story. One of these moments occurs when she addresses the issue of natural right while Calixta and Alcée are making love: "Her firm, elastic flesh that was knowing for the first time its birthright, was like a creamy lily that the sun invites to contribute its breath and perfume to the undying life of the world" (Chopin, "The Storm" 807). Chopin goes further than condoning the affair between Calixta and Alcée by describing it as something completely natural, an event that was meant to occur.

What would have been most shocking to audiences in the nineteenth century was the fact that when the storm ended, there were no repercussions. Alcée "turned and smiled" at Calixta "with a beaming face" and rode away, Calixta showed "nothing but satisfaction" when her husband and son returned home, Bobinôt and Bibi "began to relax and enjoy themselves" when they saw that Calixta was in good spirits, and Clarisse stayed in Biloxi, enjoying herself. For such severe sins to be committed and go unpunished was unheard of in Chopin's time, and "even today some readers find that conclusion unforgivable" (Skaggs 62).

In truth, this very conclusion elevates "The Storm" to the high level it resides on. Through adultery, deception, and self-indulgence, the characters achieve happiness, a surprise ending that Chopin adopted from Guy de Maupassant.[3] This ironic twist makes the story a unique departure from the norm, even today, and "The Storm" ends on a comic note, the reader left as contented as the story's characters.

Asserts the proven thesis stated in the second paragraph.

Notes

[1]Chopin set many of her stories in the Cane River country of Louisiana; her husband, Oscar, was raised in Louisiana, and they lived there together for twelve years (Toth 92).

[2]In Chopin's "The Story of an Hour," the main character discovers that she prizes individual freedom over all else—even the life and love of her husband.

[3]Guy de Maupassant (1850–1893) was a French writer whose short stories often featured surprise endings.

Works Cited

Abcarian, Richard, Marvin Klotz, and Samuel Cohen, eds.
    Literature: The Human Experience. 10th ed. Boston:
    Bedford. 2010. Print.

Chopin, Kate. "At the 'Cadian Ball." *The Complete Works of Kate
    Chopin.* Ed. Per Seyersted. Baton Rouge: Louisiana State
    UP, 1969. 219-27. Print.

---. "The Storm." Abcarian, Klotz, and Cohen 805-09. Print.

Ewell, Barbara C. *Kate Chopin.* New York: Ungar, 1986. Print.

Moon, Jennifer. "ClassicNote on Kate Chopin." *GradeSaver.*
    ClassicNotes by GradeSaver. GradeSaver LLC, n.d. Web.
    30 Mar. 2000.

Skaggs, Peggy. *Kate Chopin.* New York: Twayne, 1985. Print.

Toth, Emily. *Unveiling Kate Chopin.* Jackson: UP of Mississippi,
    1999. Print.

SOME MATTERS OF FORM AND DOCUMENTATION

After you have worked hard to draft, revise, and edit an essay, check to be sure you have documented your sources accurately and fairly. A consistent, well-documented essay allows readers to focus on your argument rather than on your document.

Titles

When included in the body of your essay, the first word and all main words of titles are capitalized. Ordinarily (unless they are the first or last word), articles (*a, an,* and *the*), prepositions (*in, on, of, with, about,* and so on), conjunctions (*and, but, or,* and so on), and the *to* in an infinitive ("A Good Man Is Hard to Find") are not capitalized.

The titles of short stories, poems, articles, essays, songs, episodes of television programs, and parts of larger collections are enclosed in quotation marks.

The titles of plays, books, movies, periodicals, operas, television series, recordings, paintings, and newspapers are italicized. If your word-processing program does not produce italic type that is easily distinguishable from non-italic type, use underlining.

The title you give your essay is neither placed in quotation marks nor underlined. However, the title of a literary work used as a part of your title would be either placed in quotation marks or italicized, depending on the type of work it is.

Quotations

Quotation marks indicate that you are transcribing someone else's words; those words must, therefore, be *exactly* as they appear in your source.

As a general rule, quotations of not more than four lines of prose or two lines of poetry are placed between quotation marks and incorporated into your own text:

> Near the end of "Young Goodman Brown," the narrator asks, "Had Goodman Brown fallen asleep in the forest and only dreamed a wild dream of a witch-meeting?" (90).

If you are quoting two or three lines of verse in your text, indicate the division between lines with a slash. Leave a space before and after the slash:

> Prufrock hears the dilettantish talk in a room where "the women come and go / Talking of Michelangelo."

Longer quotations are indented ten spaces from the left margin and are double-spaced. They are not enclosed in quotation marks, since the indention signals a quotation.

BRACKETS AND ELLIPSES If you insert anything into a quotation—even a word—the inserted material must be placed within brackets. If you wish to omit some material from a passage in quotation marks, the omission must be indicated with ellipsis points—three equally spaced periods. When an ellipsis occurs between complete sentences or at the end of a sentence, a fourth period, indicating the end of the sentence, should be inserted.

Here is an example of a full quotation from an original source:

> As one critic puts it, "Richard Wright, like Dostoevsky before him, sends his hero underground to discover the truth about the upper world, a world that has forced him to confess to a crime he has not committed."

Here is the quotation with insertion and omissions:

> As one critic puts it, "Richard Wright . . . sends his hero [Fred Daniels] underground to discover the truth about the upper world. . . ."

Use a full line of spaced periods to indicate the omission of a line or more of poetry:

> For I have known them all already, known them all—
>
> Have known the evenings, mornings, afternoons,
>
> I have measured out my life with coffee spoons;
>
> . . . .
>
> And I have known the eyes already, known them all—
>
> The eyes that fix you in a formulated phrase.

QUOTATION MARKS AND OTHER PUNCTUATION Periods and commas are placed *inside* quotation marks:

> In "The Lesson," the narrator describes Miss Moore as someone "who always looked like she was going to church, though she never did."

Other punctuation marks such as colons or semicolons go outside the concluding quotation marks unless they are part of the material being quoted.

> Bartleby repeatedly insists that he "would prefer not to"; eventually these words become haunting.

For poetry quotations, provide the line number or numbers in parentheses immediately following the quotation:

> With ironic detachment, Prufrock declares that he is "no prophet" (83).

Documentation

You must acknowledge sources for the ideas you paraphrase or summarize and material you quote. Such acknowledgments are extremely important, for even an unintentional failure to give formal credit to others for their words or ideas can leave you open to an accusation of *plagiarism*—that is, the presentation of someone else's ideas as your own.

In the body of your essay, use parenthetical citations to document those works that you quote, paraphrase, or summarize. A list of your sources should be the last page of your essay, the Works Cited page. If you use other kinds of sources not listed here, consult the *MLA Handbook for Writers of Research Papers*, seventh edition (2009), or online at <www.mla.org/style>.

This whimsical paragraph demonstrates the use of parenthetical citations.

> Leslie Fiedler's view of the relationship between Jim and Huck (669-70) uses a method often discussed by other critics (Abcarian, Klotz, and Cohen 7-10). Cooper's 1971 study (180) raises similar issues, although such methods are not useful when dealing with such a line as "North Richmond Street, being blind, was a quiet street except at the hour when the Christian Brothers' School set the boys free" (Joyce, "Araby" 92). But when Joyce refers to the weather (*Dubliners* 224), the issue becomes clouded.

The first citation gives only the page reference, which is all that is necessary because the author's name is given in the text and only one work by that author appears in the list of works cited. The second citation gives the editors' names and thus identifies the work being cited. It then indicates the appropriate pages. The third citation, because the author's name is mentioned in the text, gives only a page reference. The fourth citation must provide the author's name *and* the work cited, because two works by the same author appear in the list of works cited. The last citation, because it refers to an author with two works in the list of works cited, gives the name of the work and the page where the reference can be found.

In short, your parenthetical acknowledgment should contain (1) the *minimum* information required to lead the reader to the appropriate work in the list of works cited and (2) the location within the work to which you refer.

Citations give credit whenever it is due and enable your reader to go directly to your sources as quickly and easily as possible.

Works Cited

Abcarian, Richard, Marvin Klotz, and Samuel Cohen, eds. *Literature: The Human Experience*. 10th ed. Boston: Bedford. 2010. Print.

Cooper, Wendy. *Hair, Sex, Society, Symbolism*. New York: Stein, 1971. Print.

Fiedler, Leslie. "Come Back to the Raft Ag'in, Huck Honey." *Partisan Review* 15 (1948): 664–71. Print.

Joyce, James. "Araby." Abcarian, Klotz, and Cohen 92–6.

---. *Dubliners*. Eds. Robert Scholes and A. Walton Litz. New York: Penguin, 1976. Print.

The first of these citations is for this book. Note that the first editor's name is presented surname first, but the second and subsequent names are presented with the surname last. The second entry illustrates the form for citing a book with one author. The third gives the form for an article published in a periodical (note that the title of the article is in quotes and the title of the journal is italicized). The fourth entry shows how to cite a work included in an anthology. The fifth citation, because it is by the same author as the fourth, begins with three hyphens in place of the author's name.

DOCUMENTING INTERNET SOURCES   The Internet is still a relatively new research tool and, until recently, there were few standards governing the citation of electronic sources. It is increasingly common to employ at least some online tools while conducting research. The form suggested below will probably serve for most citations to online books, articles, online databases, and other kinds of sites. Keep in mind, however, that if it does not, you will have to decide for yourself the best way to include additional information. The most important thing is that you accurately cite every single source you consult whether that source is a Web site or a more traditional source like a book or an encyclopedia.

1. Author's name
2. Title of the work in quotation marks
3. Title of the Web site (italicized)
4. Sponsor or publisher
5. Date of publication or most recent update

6. Medium of publication

7. Date of access

> O'Rourke, Megan. "A Pessimist in Flower." *Slate*. Washington Post.
>
> Newsweek Interactive Co. LLC, 18 Jan. 2007. Web. 9 Mar. 2009

A CHECKLIST FOR WRITING ABOUT LITERATURE

1. Is my essay clearly responsive to the assignment?

2. Does my essay put forward a clearly defined thesis at the outset?

3. Does each paragraph have an identifiable topic sentence?

4. Have I marshaled my paragraphs logically and provided appropriate transitions?

5. Do I support my assertions with evidence?

6. Have I used direct quotations appropriately, and have I transcribed them accurately?

7. Do I document the sources of other people's ideas and the direct quotations I use? Is the documentation in appropriate form?

8. Have I written syntactically correct sentences (no run-ons and no fragments except by design)?

9. Have I eliminated as many passive constructions and forms of the verb *to be* as possible?

10. Have I avoided long sequences (say, three or more) of prepositional phrases?

11. Can I feel good about this essay? Does it embody serious thinking in attractive form (free of typos and other errors)? Can I put my name on the essay with pride?

INNOCENCE AND EXPERIENCE

Pedro, 1974, by Fernando Botero.

Humans strive to give order and meaning to their lives, to reduce the mystery and unpredictability that constantly threaten them. Life is infinitely more complex and surprising than we imagine, and the categories we establish to give it order and meaning are, for the most part, "momentary stays against confusion." At any time, the equilibrium of our lives, the comfortable image of ourselves and the world around us, may be disrupted by something new, forcing us into painful reevaluation. These disruptions create pain, anxiety, and terror but also wisdom and awareness.

The works in this section deal generally with the movement of a central character from moral simplicities and certainties into a more complex and problematic world. Though these works frequently deal with awareness, even wisdom, their central figures rarely act decisively. The main character or protagonist is more often a passive figure who learns the difference between the ideal world he or she imagines and the injurious real world. If the protagonist survives the ordeal, he or she often becomes a better human—better able to wrest some satisfaction from a bleak and threatening world. Many of the works here deal with the passage from childhood to adulthood, a time of simplicities and certainties that give way to the complexities and uncertainties of adult life.

Almost universally, innocence is associated with childhood and youth, as experience is with age. We teach the young about an ideal world, without explaining that it has not yet been and may never be achieved. As innocents, children are terribly vulnerable to falsehood, to intrusive sexuality, and to the machinations of the wicked, who often triumph.

But the terms *innocence* and *experience* range widely in meaning, and that range is reflected here. Innocence may be social—the innocence of Brown in Nathaniel Hawthorne's "Young Goodman Brown." Or innocence may be seen as the child's ignorance of his or her own mortality, as in Gerard Manley Hopkins's "Spring and Fall" and Dylan Thomas's "Fern Hill." In such works as Nathaniel Hawthorne's "Young Goodman Brown" and Robert Browning's "My Last Duchess," one discovers the tragic consequences of an innocence that is blind.

The contrast between what we thought in our youth and what we have come to know, painfully, as adults stands as an emblem of the passage from innocence to experience. Yet all of us remain, to one degree or another, innocent throughout life, since we never—except with death—stop learning from experience. Looked at in this way, experience is the ceaseless assault life makes on our innocence, moving us to a greater wisdom about ourselves and the world around us.

QUESTIONS FOR THINKING AND WRITING

As you read the selections in this section, consider the following questions. You may want to write out your thoughts informally in a journal or notebook as a way of preparing to respond to the selections, or you may wish to make one of these questions the basis for a formal essay.

1. Innocence is often associated with childhood; responsibility, with adulthood. Were you happier or more contented as a preteen than you are now? Why? Which particular aspects of your childhood do you remember with pleasure? Which with pain? Do you look forward to the future with pleasurable anticipation or with dread? Why?

2. Do you know any adults who seem to be innocents? On what do you base your judgment? Do you know any preteens who seem to be particularly "adult" in their behavior (beyond politeness and good manners—they may, for example, have to cope with severe family difficulties)? On what do you base your judgment?

3. Have you spent your life under the authority of others, such as parents, teachers, and employers? How do you deal with authorities you resent? Do you look forward to exercising authority over others (your own children, your own students, employees under your supervision)? How will your experiences affect your behavior as an authority figure?

4. How does the growth from innocence to experience affect one's sexual behavior? Social behavior? Political behavior?

FICTION

NATHANIEL HAWTHORNE   (1804–1864)

YOUNG GOODMAN BROWN   1846

Young Goodman[1] Brown came forth at sunset into the street at Salem village; but put his head back, after crossing the threshold, to exchange a parting kiss with his young wife. And Faith, as the wife was aptly named, thrust her own pretty head into the street, letting the wind play with the pink ribbons of her cap while she called to Goodman Brown.

"Dearest heart," whispered she, softly and rather sadly, when her lips were close to his ear, "prithee put off your journey until sunrise and sleep in your own bed to-night. A lone woman is troubled with such dreams and such thoughts that she's afeared of herself sometimes. Pray tarry with me this night, dear husband, of all nights in the year."

"My love and my Faith," replied young Goodman Brown, "of all nights in the year, this one night must I tarry away from thee. My journey, as thou callest it, forth and back again, must needs be done 'twixt now and sunrise. What, my sweet, pretty wife, dost thou doubt me already, and we but three months married?"

"Then God bless you!" said Faith, with the pink ribbons; "and may you find all well when you come back."

"Amen!" cried Goodman Brown. "Say thy prayers, dear Faith, and go to bed at dusk, and no harm will come to thee."   5

So they parted; and the young man pursued his way until, being about to turn the corner by the meeting-house, he looked back and saw the head of Faith still peeping after him with a melancholy air, in spite of her pink ribbons.

"Poor little Faith!" thought he, for his heart smote him. "What a wretch am I to leave her on such an errand! She talks of dreams, too. Methought as she spoke there was trouble in her face, as if a dream had warned her what work is to be done to-night. But no, no; 'twould kill her to think it. Well, she's a blessed angel on earth; and after this one night I'll cling to her skirts and follow her to heaven."

---

[1] Equivalent to *Mr.*, a title given to a man below the rank of gentleman.

With this excellent resolve for the future, Goodman Brown felt himself justified in making more haste on his present evil purpose. He had taken a dreary
road, darkened by all the gloomiest trees of the forest, which barely stood aside
to let the narrow path creep through, and closed immediately behind. It was all
as lonely as could be; and there is this peculiarity in such a solitude, that the
traveller knows not who may be concealed by the innumerable trunks and the
thick boughs overhead; so that with lonely footsteps he may yet be passing
through an unseen multitude.

"There may be a devilish Indian behind every tree," said Goodman Brown to
himself; and he glanced fearfully behind him as he added, "What if the devil
himself should be at my very elbow!"

His head being turned back, he passed a crook of the road, and, looking for-   10
ward again, beheld the figure of a man, in grave and decent attire, seated at the
foot of an old tree. He arose at Goodman Brown's approach and walked
onward side by side with him.

"You are late, Goodman Brown," said he. "The clock of the Old South[2] was
striking as I came through Boston, and that is full fifteen minutes agone."

"Faith kept me back a while," replied the young man, with a tremor in his
voice, caused by the sudden appearance of his companion, though not wholly
unexpected.

It was now deep dusk in the forest, and deepest in that part of it where these
two were journeying. As nearly as could be discerned, the second traveller was
about fifty years old, apparently in the same rank of life as Goodman Brown,
and bearing a considerable resemblance to him, though perhaps more in
expression than features. Still they might have been taken for father and son.
And yet, though the elder person was as simply clad as the younger, and as
simple in manner too, he had an indescribable air of one who knew the world,
and who would not have felt abashed at the governor's dinner table or in King
William's[3] court, were it possible that his affairs should call him thither. But the
only thing about him that could be fixed upon as remarkable was his staff,
which bore the likeness of a great black snake, so curiously wrought that it
might almost be seen to twist and wriggle itself like a living serpent. This, of
course, must have been an ocular deception, assisted by the uncertain light.

"Come, Goodman Brown," cried his fellow-traveller, "this is a dull pace for
the beginning of a journey. Take my staff, if you are so soon weary."

"Friend," said the other, exchanging his slow pace for a full stop, "having   15
kept covenant by meeting thee here, it is my purpose now to return whence I
came. I have scruples touching the matter thou wot'st of."

"Sayest thou so?" replied he of the serpent, smiling apart. "Let us walk on,
nevertheless, reasoning as we go; and if I convince thee not thou shalt turn
back. We are but a little way in the forest yet."

---

[2] A church in Boston.
[3] Ruler of England from 1689 to 1702.

"Too far! too far!" exclaimed the goodman, unconsciously resuming his walk. "My father never went into the woods on such an errand, nor his father before him. We have been a race of honest men and good Christians since the days of the martyrs;[4] and shall I be the first of the name of Brown that ever took this path and kept—"

"Such company, thou wouldst say," observed the elder person, interpreting his pause. "Well said, Goodman Brown! I have been as well acquainted with your family as with ever a one among the Puritans; and that's no trifle to say. I helped your grandfather, the constable, when he lashed the Quaker woman so smartly through the streets of Salem; and it was I that brought your father a pitch-pine knot, kindled at my own hearth, to set fire to an Indian village, in King Philip's war.[5] They were my good friends, both; and many a pleasant walk have we had along this path, and returned merrily after midnight. I would fain be friends with you for their sake."

"If it be as thou sayest," replied Goodman Brown, "I marvel they never spoke of these matters; or, verily, I marvel not, seeing that the least rumor of the sort would have driven them from New England. We are a people of prayer, and good works to boot, and abide no such wickedness."

"Wickedness or not," said the traveller, with the twisted staff, "I have a very 20 general acquaintance here in New England. The deacons of many a church have drunk the communion wine with me; the selectmen of divers towns make me their chairman; and a majority of the Great and General Court[6] are firm supporters of my interest. The governor and I, too—But these are state secrets."

"Can this be so?" cried Goodman Brown, with a stare of amazement at his undisturbed companion. "Howbeit, I have nothing to do with the governor and council; they have their own ways, and are no rule for a simple husband-man[7] like me. But, were I to go on with thee, how should I meet the eye of that good old man, our minister, at Salem village? Oh, his voice would make me tremble both Sabbath day and lecture day."

Thus far the elder traveller had listened with due gravity; but now burst into a fit of irrepressible mirth, shaking himself so violently that his snake-like staff actually seemed to wriggle in sympathy.

"Ha! ha! ha!" shouted he again and again; then composing himself, "Well, go on, Goodman Brown, go on; but, prithee, don't kill me with laughing."

"Well, then, to end the matter at once," said Goodman Brown, considerably nettled, "there is my wife, Faith. It would break her dear little heart; and I'd rather break my own."

---

[4] A reference to the persecution of Protestants in England (1553–1558) by the Catholic monarch Mary Tudor.

[5] War waged (1675–1676) against the colonists of New England by the Indian chief Metacomet, also known as "King Philip."

[6] The Puritan legislature.

[7] An ordinary person.

"Nay, if that be the case," answered the other, "e'en go thy ways, Goodman   25
Brown. I would not for twenty old women like the one hobbling before us that
Faith should come to any harm."

As he spoke he pointed his staff at a female figure on the path, in whom Goodman Brown recognized a very pious and exemplary dame, who had taught him
his catechism in youth, and was still his moral and spiritual adviser, jointly with
the minister and Deacon Gookin.

"A marvel, truly, that Goody[8] Cloyse should be so far in the wilderness at
nightfall," said he. "But with your leave, friend, I shall take a cut through the
woods until we have left this Christian woman behind. Being a stranger to you,
she might ask whom I was consorting with and whither I was going."

"Be it so," said his fellow-traveller. "Betake you to the woods, and let me keep
the path."

Accordingly the young man turned aside, but took care to watch his companion, who advanced softly along the road until he had come within a staff's
length of the old dame. She, meanwhile, was making the best of her way, with
singular speed for so aged a woman, and mumbling some indistinct words—a
prayer, doubtless—as she went. The traveller put forth his staff and touched
her withered neck with what seemed the serpent's tail.

"The devil!" screamed the pious old lady.   30

"Then Goody Cloyse knows her old friend?" observed the traveller, confronting her and leaning on his writhing stick.

"Ah, forsooth, and is it your worship indeed?" cried the good dame. "Yea,
truly is it, and in the very image of my old gossip, Goodman Brown, the grandfather of the silly fellow that now is. But—would your worship believe it?—my
broomstick hath strangely disappeared, stolen, as I suspect, by that unhanged
witch, Goody Cory, and that, too, when I was all anointed with the juice of
smallage and cinquefoil and wolf's bane"[9]—

"Mingled with fine wheat and the fat of a new-born babe," said the shape of
old Goodman Brown.

"Ah, your worship knows the recipe," cried the old lady, cackling aloud. "So,
as I was saying, being all ready for the meeting, and no horse to ride on, I made
up my mind to foot it; for they tell me there is a nice young man to be taken
into communion to-night. But now your good worship will lend me your arm,
and we shall be there in a twinkling."

"That can hardly be," answered her friend. "I may not spare you my arm,   35
Goody Cloyse; but here is my staff, if you will."

So saying, he threw it down at her feet, where, perhaps, it assumed life, being
one of the rods which its owner had formerly lent to the Egyptian magi.[10] Of
this fact, however, Goodman Brown could not take cognizance. He had cast

---

[8] A polite title for a wife of humble rank.
[9] All these plants were associated with magic and witchcraft.
[10] Allusion to the biblical magicians who turned their rods into serpents (Exodus 7:11–12).

up his eyes in astonishment, and, looking down again, beheld neither Goody Cloyse nor the serpentine staff, but his fellow-traveller alone, who waited for him as calmly as if nothing had happened.

"That old woman taught me my catechism," said the young man; and there was a world of meaning in this simple comment.

They continued to walk onward, while the elder traveller exhorted his companion to make good speed and persevere in the path, discoursing so aptly that his arguments seemed rather to spring up in the bosom of his auditor than to be suggested by himself. As they went, he plucked a branch of maple to serve for a walking stick, and began to strip it of the twigs and little boughs, which were wet with evening dew. The moment his fingers touched them they became strangely withered and dried up as with a week's sunshine. Thus the pair proceeded, at a good free pace, until suddenly, in a gloomy hollow of the road, Goodman Brown sat himself down on the stump of a tree and refused to go any farther.

"Friend," said he, stubbornly, "my mind is made up. Not another step will I budge on this errand. What if a wretched old woman do choose to go to the devil when I thought she was going to heaven: is that any reason why I should quit my dear Faith and go after her?"

"You will think better of this by and by," said his acquaintance, composedly. 40 "Sit here and rest yourself a while; and when you feel like moving again, there is my staff to help you along."

Without more words, he threw his companion the maple stick, and was as speedily out of sight as if he had vanished into the deepening gloom. The young man sat a few moments by the roadside, applauding himself greatly, and thinking with how clear a conscience he should meet the minister in his morning walk, nor shrink from the eye of good old Deacon Gookin. And what calm sleep would be his that very night, which was to have been spent so wickedly, but so purely and sweetly now, in the arms of Faith! Amidst these pleasant and praiseworthy meditations, Goodman Brown heard the tramp of horses along the road, and deemed it advisable to conceal himself within the verge of the forest, conscious of the guilty purpose that had brought him thither, though now so happily turned from it.

On came the hoof tramps and the voices of the riders, two grave old voices, conversing soberly as they drew near. These mingled sounds appeared to pass along the road, within a few yards of the young man's hiding-place; but, owing doubtless to the depth of the gloom at that particular spot, neither the travellers nor their steeds were visible. Though their figures brushed the small boughs by the wayside, it could not be seen that they intercepted, even for a moment, the faint gleam from the strip of bright sky athwart which they must have passed. Goodman Brown alternately crouched and stood on tiptoe, pulling aside the branches and thrusting forth his head as far as he durst without discerning so much as a shadow. It vexed him the more, because he could have sworn, were such a thing possible, that he recognized the voices of the minister and Deacon Gookin, jogging along quietly, as they were wont to do, when bound to some ordination or ecclesiastical council. While yet within hearing, one of the riders stopped to pluck a switch.

"Of the two, reverend sir," said the voice like the deacon's, "I had rather miss an ordination dinner than to-night's meeting. They tell me that some of our community are to be here from Falmouth[11] and beyond, and others from Connecticut and Rhode Island, besides several of the Indian powwows,[12] who, after their fashion, know almost as much deviltry as the best of us. Moreover, there is a goodly young woman to be taken into communion."

"Mighty well, Deacon Gookin!" replied the solemn old tones of the minister. "Spur up, or we shall be late. Nothing can be done, you know, until I get on the ground."

The hoofs clattered again; and the voices, talking so strangely in the empty air, passed on through the forest, where no church had ever been gathered, nor solitary Christian prayed. Whither, then, could these holy men be journeying so deep into the heathen wilderness? Young Goodman Brown caught hold of a tree for support, being ready to sink down on the ground, faint and overburdened with the heavy sickness of his heart. He looked up to the sky, doubting whether there really was a heaven above him. Yet there was the blue arch, and the stars brightening in it.

"With heaven above and Faith below, I will yet stand firm against the devil!" cried Goodman Brown.

While he still gazed upward into the deep arch of the firmament and had lifted his hands to pray, a cloud, though no wind was stirring, hurried across the zenith and hid the brightening stars. The blue sky was still visible, except directly overhead, where this black mass of cloud was sweeping swiftly northward. Aloft in the air, as if from the depths of the cloud, came a confused and doubtful sound of voices. Once the listener fancied that he could distinguish the accents of towns-people of his own, men and women, both pious and ungodly, many of whom he had met at the communion table, and had seen others rioting at the tavern. The next moment, so indistinct were the sounds, he doubted whether he had heard aught but the murmur of the old forest, whispering without a wind. Then came a stronger swell of those familiar tones, heard daily in the sunshine at Salem village, but never until now from a cloud of night. There was one voice, of a young woman, uttering lamentations, yet with an uncertain sorrow, and entreating for some favor, which, perhaps, it would grieve her to obtain; and all the unseen multitude, both saints and sinners, seemed to encourage her onward.

"Faith!" shouted Goodman Brown, in a voice of agony and desperation; and the echoes of the forest mocked him, crying, "Faith! Faith!" as if bewildered wretches were seeking her all through the wilderness.

The cry of grief, rage, and terror was yet piercing the night, when the unhappy husband held his breath for a response. There was a scream, drowned

[11] A town near Salem, Massachusetts.
[12] Medicine men.

immediately in a louder murmur of voices, fading into far-off laughter, as the dark cloud swept away, leaving the clear and silent sky above Goodman Brown. But something fluttered lightly down through the air and caught on the branch of a tree. The young man seized it, and beheld a pink ribbon.

"My Faith is gone!" cried he, after one stupefied moment. "There is no good 50 on earth; and sin is but a name. Come, devil; for to thee is this world given."

And, maddened with despair, so that he laughed loud and long, did Goodman Brown grasp his staff and set forth again, at such a rate that he seemed to fly along the forest path rather than to walk or run. The road grew wilder and drearier and more faintly traced, and vanished at length, leaving him in the heart of the dark wilderness, still rushing onward with the instinct that guides mortal man to evil. The whole forest was peopled with frightful sounds—the creaking of the trees, the howling of wild beasts, and the yell of Indians; while sometimes the wind tolled like a distant church bell, and sometimes gave a broad roar around the traveller, as if all Nature were laughing him to scorn. But he was himself the chief horror of the scene, and shrank not from its other horrors.

"Ha! ha! ha!" roared Goodman Brown when the wind laughed at him. "Let us hear which will laugh loudest. Think not to frighten me with your deviltry. Come witch, come wizard, come Indian powwow, come devil himself, and here comes Goodman Brown. You may as well fear him as he fears you."

In truth, all through the haunted forest there could be nothing more frightful than the figure of Goodman Brown. On he flew among the black pines, brandishing his staff with frenzied gestures, now giving vent to an inspiration of horrid blasphemy, and now shouting forth such laughter as set all the echoes of the forest laughing like demons around him. The fiend in his own shape is less hideous than when he rages in the breast of man. Thus sped the demoniac on his course, until, quivering among the trees, he saw a red light before him, as when the felled trunks and branches of a clearing have been set on fire, and throw up their lurid blaze against the sky, at the hour of midnight. He paused, in a lull of the tempest that had driven him onward, and heard the swell of what seemed a hymn, rolling solemnly from a distance with the weight of many voices. He knew the tune; it was a familiar one in the choir of the village meeting-house. The verse died heavily away, and was lengthened by a chorus, not of human voices, but of all the sounds of the benighted wilderness pealing in awful harmony together. Goodman Brown cried out, and his cry was lost to his own ear by its unison with the cry of the desert.

In the interval of silence he stole forward until the light glared full upon his eyes. At one extremity of an open space, hemmed in by the dark wall of the forest, arose a rock, bearing some rude, natural resemblance either to an altar or a pulpit, and surrounded by four blazing pines, their tops aflame, their stems untouched, like candles at an evening meeting. The mass of foliage that had overgrown the summit of the rock was all on fire, blazing high into the night and fitfully illuminating the whole field. Each pendent twig and leafy festoon was in a blaze. As the red light arose and fell, a numerous congregation alternately shone forth, then disappeared in shadow, and again grew, as it were, out of the darkness, peopling the heart of the solitary woods at once.

"A grave and dark-clad company," quoth Goodman Brown.   55

In truth they were such. Among them, quivering to and fro between gloom and splendor, appeared faces that would be seen next day at the council board of the province, and others which, Sabbath after Sabbath, looked devoutly heavenward, and benignantly over the crowded pews, from the holiest pulpits in the land. Some affirm that the lady of the governor was there. At least there were high dames well known to her, and wives of honored husbands, and widows, a great multitude, and ancient maidens, all of excellent repute, and fair young girls, who trembled lest their mothers should espy them. Either the sudden gleams of light flashing over the obscure field bedazzled Goodman Brown, or he recognized a score of the church members of Salem village famous for their especial sanctity. Good old Deacon Gookin had arrived, and waited at the skirts of that venerable saint, his revered pastor. But, irreverently consorting with these grave, reputable, and pious people, these elders of the church, these chaste dames and dewy virgins, there were men of dissolute lives and women of spotted fame, wretches given over to all mean and filthy vice, and suspected even of horrid crimes. It was strange to see that the good shrank not from the wicked, nor were the sinners abashed by the saints. Scattered also among their pale-faced enemies were the Indian priests, or powwows, who had often scared their native forest with more hideous incantations than any known to English witchcraft.

"But where is Faith?" thought Goodman Brown; and, as hope came into his heart, he trembled.

Another verse of the hymn arose, a slow and mournful strain, such as the pious love, but joined to words which expressed all that our nature can conceive of sin, and darkly hinted at far more. Unfathomable to mere mortals is the lore of fiends. Verse after verse was sung; and still the chorus of the desert swelled between like the deepest tone of a mighty organ; and with the final peal of that dreadful anthem there came a sound, as if the roaring wind, the rushing streams, the howling beasts, and every other voice of the unconcerted wilderness were mingling and according with the voice of guilty man in homage to the prince of all. The four blazing pines threw up a loftier flame, and obscurely discovered shapes and visages of horror on the smoke wreaths above the impious assembly. At the same moment the fire on the rock shot redly forth and formed a glowing arch above its base, where now appeared a figure. With reverence be it spoken, the figure bore no slight similitude, both in garb and manner, to some grave divine of the New England churches.

"Bring forth the converts!" cried a voice that echoed through the field and rolled into the forest.

At the word, Goodman Brown stepped forth from the shadow of the trees   60
and approached the congregation, with whom he felt a loathful brotherhood by the sympathy of all that was wicked in his heart. He could have well-nigh

sworn that the shape of his own dead father beckoned him to advance, looking downward from a smoke wreath, while a woman, with dim features of despair, threw out her hand to warn him back. Was it his mother? But he had no power to retreat one step, nor to resist, even in thought, when the minister and good old Deacon Gookin seized his arms and led him to the blazing rock. Thither came also the slender form of a veiled female, led between Goody Cloyse, that pious teacher of the catechism, and Martha Carrier,[13] who had received the devil's promise to be queen of hell. A rampant hag was she. And there stood the proselytes beneath the canopy of fire.

"Welcome, my children," said the dark figure, "to the communion of your race. Ye have found thus young your nature and your destiny. My children, look behind you!"

They turned; and flashing forth, as it were, in a sheet of flame, the fiend worshippers were seen; the smile of welcome gleamed darkly on every visage.

"There," resumed the sable form, "are all whom ye have reverenced from youth. Ye deemed them holier than yourselves, and shrank from your own sin, contrasting it with their lives of righteousness and prayerful aspirations heavenward. Yet here are they all in my worshipping assembly. This night it shall be granted you to know their secret deeds: how hoary-bearded elders of the church have whispered wanton words to the young maids of their households; how many a woman, eager for widows' weeds, has given her husband a drink at bedtime and let him sleep his last sleep in her bosom; how beardless youths have made haste to inherit their fathers' wealth; and how fair damsels—blush not, sweet ones—have dug little graves in the garden, and bidden me, the sole guest, to an infant's funeral. By the sympathy of your human hearts for sin ye shall scent out all the places—whether in church, bed-chamber, street, field, or forest—where crime has been committed, and shall exult to behold the whole earth one stain of guilt, one mighty blood spot. Far more than this. It shall be yours to penetrate, in every bosom, the deep mystery of sin, the fountain of all wicked arts, and which inexhaustibly supplies more evil impulses than human power—than my power at its utmost—can make manifest in deeds. And now, my children, look upon each other."

They did so; and, by the blaze of the hell-kindled torches, the wretched man beheld his Faith, and the wife her husband, trembling before that unhallowed altar.

"Lo, there ye stand, my children," said the figure, in a deep and solemn tone, almost sad with its despairing awfulness, as if his once angelic nature could yet mourn for our miserable race. "Depending upon one another's hearts, ye had still hoped that virtue were not all a dream. Now are ye undeceived. Evil is the nature of mankind. Evil must be your only happiness. Welcome again, my children, to the communion of your race."

"Welcome," repeated the fiend worshippers, in one cry of despair and triumph.

---

[13] One of the women hanged in Salem in 1697 for witchcraft.

And there they stood, the only pair, as it seemed, who were yet hesitating on the verge of wickedness in this dark world. A basin was hollowed, naturally, in the rock. Did it contain water, reddened by the lurid light? or was it blood? or, perchance, a liquid flame? Herein did the shape of evil dip his hand and prepare to lay the mark of baptism upon their foreheads, that they might be partakers of the mystery of sin, more conscious of the secret guilt of others, both in deed and thought, than they could now be of their own. The husband cast one look at his pale wife, and Faith at him. What polluted wretches would the next glance show them to each other, shuddering alike at what they disclosed and what they saw!

"Faith! Faith!" cried the husband, "look up to heaven, and resist the wicked one."

Whether Faith obeyed he knew not. Hardly had he spoken when he found himself amid calm night and solitude, listening to a roar of the wind which died heavily away through the forest. He staggered against the rock, and felt it chill and damp; while a hanging twig, that had been all on fire, besprinkled his cheek with the coldest dew.

The next morning young Goodman Brown came slowly into the street of 70 Salem village, staring around him like a bewildered man. The good old minister was taking a walk along the graveyard to get an appetite for breakfast and meditate his sermon, and bestowed a blessing, as he passed, on Goodman Brown. He shrank from the venerable saint as if to avoid an anathema. Old Deacon Gookin was at domestic worship, and the holy words of his prayer were heard through the open window. "What God doth the wizard pray to?" quoth Goodman Brown. Goody Cloyse, that excellent old Christian, stood in the early sunshine at her own lattice, catechizing a little girl who had brought her a pint of morning's milk. Goodman Brown snatched away the child as from the grasp of the fiend himself. Turning the corner by the meeting-house, he spied the head of Faith, with the pink ribbons, gazing anxiously forth, and bursting into such joy at sight of him that she skipped along the street and almost kissed her husband before the whole village. But Goodman Brown looked sternly and sadly into her face, and passed on without a greeting.

Had Goodman Brown fallen asleep in the forest and only dreamed a wild dream of a witch-meeting?

Be it so if you will; but, alas! it was a dream of evil omen for young Goodman Brown. A stern, a sad, a darkly meditative, a distrustful, if not a desperate man did he become from the night of that fearful dream. On the Sabbath day, when the congregation were singing a holy psalm, he could not listen because an anthem of sin rushed loudly upon his ear and drowned all the blessed strain. When the minister spoke from the pulpit with power and fervid eloquence, and, with his hand on the open Bible, of the sacred truths of our religion, and of saint-like lives and triumphant deaths, and of future bliss or misery unutterable, then did Goodman Brown turn pale, dreading lest the roof should thunder down upon the gray blasphemer and his hearers. Often, awakening suddenly at midnight, he shrank from the bosom of Faith; and at morning or eventide, when the family knelt down at prayer, he scowled and muttered to himself, and gazed sternly at his wife, and turned away. And when he had lived long, and was borne to his grave a hoary corpse, followed by Faith, an aged woman, and children and grandchildren, a goodly procession, besides neighbors not a few, they carved no hopeful verse upon his tombstone, for his dying hour was gloom.

FOR ANALYSIS

1. At the end of the story, the narrator asks, "Had Goodman Brown fallen asleep in the forest and only dreamed a wild dream of a witch-meeting?" Why, instead of answering the question, does he say, "Be it so if you will"?

2. Examine the seemingly supernatural events Brown experiences as he penetrates ever deeper into the forest. Can the reader determine whether those events are really taking place? If not, what purpose does the ambiguity serve?

3. What attitude does this story express toward the church of Puritan New England?

4. What elements of the story can be described as **allegorical** or **symbolic**?

5. What is the "guilty purpose" (para. 41) that has drawn Brown to the forest?

MAKING CONNECTIONS

1. Both this story and Melville's "Bartleby, the Scrivener" (p. 291) deal with protagonists who withdraw from life. What similarities and differences do you find in the reasons for their withdrawal, the ways in which they withdraw, and the consequences of their withdrawal?

2. Both Hawthorne's "Young Goodman Brown" and Ellison's "'Repent, Harlequin!' Said the Ticktockman" (p. 372) rely on fantasy. What advantages does the use of fantasy give the authors?

WRITING TOPICS

1. Write an essay in which you argue for or against the proposition that the "truth" Brown discovers during the night in the forest justifies his gloom and withdrawal.

2. Write out a paraphrase of Satan's sermon.

JAMES JOYCE   (1882–1941)

ARABY   1914

Nrth Richmond Street, being blind, was a quiet street except at the hour
when the Christian Brothers' School set the boys free. An uninhabited
house of two storeys stood at the blind end, detached from its neighbours in a
square ground. The other houses of the street, conscious of decent lives within
them, gazed at one another with brown imperturbable faces.

The former tenant of our house, a priest, had died in the back drawing-
room. Air, musty from having been long enclosed, hung in all the rooms, and
the waste room behind the kitchen was littered with old useless papers. Among
these I found a few paper-covered books, the pages of which were curled and
damp: *The Abbot,* by Walter Scott, *The Devout Communicant* and *The Memoirs
of Vidocq.* I liked the last best because its leaves were yellow. The wild garden
behind the house contained a central apple-tree and a few straggling bushes
under one of which I found the late tenant's rusty bicycle pump. He had been a
very charitable priest; in his will he had left all his money to institutions and
the furniture of his house to his sister.

When the short days of winter came dusk fell before we had well eaten our
dinners. When we met in the street the houses had grown sombre. The space of
sky above us was the colour of ever-changing violet and towards it the lamps of
the street lifted their feeble lanterns. The cold air stung us and we played till
our bodies glowed. Our shouts echoed in the silent street. The career of our
play brought us through the dark muddy lanes behind the houses where we
ran the gauntlet of the rough tribes from the cottages, to the back doors of the
dark dripping gardens where odours arose from the ashpits, to the dark odor-
ous stables where a coachman smoothed and combed the horse or shook
music from the buckled harness. When we returned to the street, light from the
kitchen windows had filled the areas. If my uncle was seen turning the corner
we hid in the shadow until we had seen him safely housed. Or if Mangan's sister came out on the doorstep to call her brother in to his tea we watched her
from our shadow peer up and down the street. We waited to see whether she
would remain or go in and, if she remained, we left our shadow and walked up
to Mangan's steps resignedly. She was waiting for us, her figure defined by the
light from the half-opened door. Her brother always teased her before he
obeyed and I stood by the railings looking at her. Her dress swung as she
moved her body and the soft rope of her hair tossed from side to side.

Every morning I lay on the floor in the front parlour watching her door. The
blind was pulled down to within an inch of the sash so that I could not be seen.
When she came out on the doorstep my heart leaped. I ran to the hall, seized
my books and followed her. I kept her brown figure always in my eye and,

when we came near the point at which our ways diverged, I quickened my pace and passed her. This happened morning after morning. I had never spoken to her, except for a few casual words, and yet her name was like a summons to all my foolish blood.

Her image accompanied me even in places the most hostile to romance. On 5 Saturday evenings when my aunt went marketing I had to go to carry some of the parcels. We walked through the flaring streets, jostled by drunken men and bargaining women, amid the curses of labourers, the shrill litanies of shop-boys who stood on guard by the barrels of pigs' cheeks, the nasal chanting of street-singers, who sang a *come-all-you*[1] about O'Donovan Rossa, or a ballad about the troubles in our native land. These noises converged in a single sensation of life for me: I imagined that I bore my chalice safely through a throng of foes. Her name sprang to my lips at moments in strange prayers and praises which I myself did not understand. My eyes were often full of tears (I could not tell why) and at times a flood from my heart seemed to pour itself out into my bosom. I thought little of the future. I did not know whether I would ever speak to her or not or, if I spoke to her, how I could tell her of my confused adoration. But my body was like a harp and her words and gestures were like fingers running upon the wires.

One evening I went into the back drawing-room in which the priest had died. It was a dark rainy evening and there was no sound in the house. Through one of the broken panes I heard the rain impinge upon the earth, the fine incessant needles of water playing in the sodden beds. Some distant lamp or lighted window gleamed below me. I was thankful that I could see so little. All my senses seemed to desire to veil themselves and, feeling that I was about to slip from them, I pressed the palms of my hands together until they trembled, murmuring: *"O love! O love!"* many times.

At last she spoke to me. When she addressed the first words to me I was so confused that I did not know what to answer. She asked me was I going to *Araby*. I forgot whether I answered yes or no. It would be a splendid bazaar, she said she would love to go.

"And why can't you?" I asked.

While she spoke she turned a silver bracelet round and round her wrist. She could not go, she said, because there would be a retreat that week in her convent. Her brother and two other boys were fighting for their caps and I was alone at the railings. She held one of the spikes, bowing her head towards me. The light from the lamp opposite our door caught the white curve of her neck, lit up her hair that rested there and, falling, lit up the hand upon the railing. It fell over one side of her dress and caught the white border of a petticoat, just visible as she stood at ease.

"It's well for you," she said. 10

"If I go," I said, "I will bring you something."

---

[1] A street ballad beginning with these words. This one is about Jeremiah Donovan, a nineteenth-century Irish nationalist popularly known as O'Donovan Rossa.

What innumerable follies laid waste my waking and sleeping thoughts after that evening! I wished to annihilate the tedious intervening days. I chafed against the work of school. At night in my bedroom and by day in the class-room her image came between me and the page I strove to read. The syllables of the word *Araby* were called to me through the silence in which my soul lux-uriated and cast an Eastern enchantment over me. I asked for leave to go to the bazaar on Saturday night. My aunt was surprised and hoped it was not some Freemason affair. I answered few questions in class. I watched my master's face pass from amiability to sternness; he hoped I was not beginning to idle. I could not call my wandering thoughts together. I had hardly any patience with the serious work of life which, now that it stood between me and my desire, seemed to me child's play, ugly monotonous child's play.

On Saturday morning I reminded my uncle that I wished to go to the bazaar in the evening. He was fussing at the hallstand, looking for the hat-brush, and answered me curtly:

"Yes, boy, I know."

As he was in the hall I could not go into the front parlour and lie at the win- 15
dow. I left the house in bad humour and walked slowly towards the school. The air was pitilessly raw and already my heart misgave me.

When I came home to dinner my uncle had not yet been home. Still it was early. I sat staring at the clock for some time and, when its ticking began to irritate me, I left the room. I mounted the staircase and gained the upper part of the house. The high cold empty gloomy rooms liberated me and I went from room to room singing. From the front window I saw my companions playing below in the street. Their cries reached me weakened and indistinct and, leaning my forehead against the cool glass, I looked over at the dark house where she lived. I may have stood there for an hour, seeing nothing but the brown-clad figure cast by my imagination, touched discreetly by the lamplight at the curved neck, at the hand upon the railings and at the border below the dress.

When I came downstairs again I found Mrs. Mercer sitting at the fire. She was an old garrulous woman, a pawnbroker's widow, who collected used stamps for some pious purpose. I had to endure the gossip of the tea-table. The meal was prolonged beyond an hour and still my uncle did not come. Mrs. Mercer stood up to go: she was sorry she couldn't wait any longer, but it was after eight o'clock and she did not like to be out late, as the night air was bad for her. When she had gone I began to walk up and down the room, clenching my fists. My aunt said:

"I'm afraid you may put off your bazaar for this night of Our Lord."

At nine o'clock I heard my uncle's latchkey in the hall door. I heard him talking to himself and heard the hallstand rocking when it had received the weight of his overcoat. I could interpret these signs. When he was midway through his dinner I asked him to give me the money to go to the bazaar. He had forgotten.

"The people are in bed and after their first sleep now," he said.   20

I did not smile. My aunt said to him energetically:

"Can't you give him the money and let him go? You've kept him late enough as it is."

My uncle said he was very sorry he had forgotten. He said he believed in the old saying: "All work and no play makes Jack a dull boy." He asked me where I was going and, when I had told him a second time he asked me did I know *The Arab's Farewell to His Steed.* When I left the kitchen he was about to recite the opening lines of the piece to my aunt.

I held a florin tightly in my hand as I strode down Buckingham Street towards the station. The sight of the streets thronged with buyers and glaring with gas recalled to me the purpose of my journey. I took my seat in a third-class carriage of a deserted train. After an intolerable delay the train moved out of the station slowly. It crept onward among ruinous houses and over the twinkling river. At Westland Row Station a crowd of people pressed to the carriage doors; but the porters moved them back, saying that it was a special train for the bazaar. I remained alone in the bare carriage. In a few minutes the train drew up beside an improvised wooden platform. I passed out on to the road and saw by the lighted dial of a clock that it was ten minutes to ten. In front of me was a large building which displayed the magical name.

I could not find any sixpenny entrance and, fearing that the bazaar would be   25 closed, I passed in quickly through a turnstile, handing a shilling to a weary-looking man. I found myself in a big hall girdled at half its height by a gallery. Nearly all the stalls were closed and the greater part of the hall was in darkness. I recognised a silence like that which pervades a church after a service. I walked into the centre of the bazaar timidly. A few people were gathered about the stalls which were still open. Before a curtain, over which the words *Café Chantant* were written in coloured lamps, two men were counting money on a salver. I listened to the fall of the coins.

Remembering with difficulty why I had come I went over to one of the stalls and examined porcelain vases and flowered tea-sets. At the door of the stall a young lady was talking and laughing with two young gentlemen. I remarked their English accents and listened vaguely to their conversation.

"O, I never said such a thing!"

"O, but you did!"

"O, but I didn't!"

"Didn't she say that?"   30

"Yes. I heard her."

"O, there's a . . . fib!"

Observing me the young lady came over and asked me did I wish to buy anything. The tone of her voice was not encouraging; she seemed to have spoken to me out of a sense of duty. I looked humbly at the great jars that stood like Eastern guards at either side of the dark entrance to the stall and murmured:

"No, thank you."

The young lady changed the position of one of the vases and went back to 35
the two young men. They began to talk of the same subject. Once or twice the
young lady glanced at me over her shoulder.

I lingered before her stall, though I knew my stay was useless, to make my
interest in her wares seem the more real. Then I turned away slowly and
walked down the middle of the bazaar. I allowed the two pennies to fall against
the sixpence in my pocket. I heard a voice call from one end of the gallery that
the light was out. The upper part of the hall was now completely dark.

Gazing up into the darkness I saw myself as a creature driven and derided by
vanity; and my eyes burned with anguish and anger.

FOR ANALYSIS

1. Reread the opening paragraph. How does it set the tone for the story?

2. What does the **tone** of this story, particularly its lack of humor, tell us about the
kind of significance the adult narrator attaches to this childhood experience?

3. What does Mangan's sister represent to the narrator?

4. Why does the dialogue the narrator overhears at the bazaar trigger the climax of
the story and the insight described in the final paragraph?

5. Carefully examine the language of paragraph 5. What stylistic devices allow the
narrator to transform a simple shopping trip into a chivalric romance?

MAKING CONNECTIONS

1. Compare the use of the first-person **point of view** in this story with the first-
person point of view in Bambara's "The Lesson" (p. 110) and Cisneros's "The House
on Mango Street" (p. 119).

2. Describe an experience that led you to realize that you were not acting out of the
selfless motives you had thought you were.

WRITING TOPICS

1. Write a page describing a romantic infatuation you experienced when you were
younger that blinded you to the reality of the person you adored.

2. Analyze the imagery of light and vision in this story.

FLANNERY O'CONNOR   (1925–1964)

A GOOD MAN IS HARD TO FIND   1953

The grandmother didn't want to go to Florida. She wanted to visit some of her connections in east Tennessee and she was seizing at every chance to change Bailey's mind. Bailey was the son she lived with, her only boy. He was sitting on the edge of his chair at the table, bent over the orange sports section of the *Journal.* "Now look here, Bailey," she said, "see here, read this," and she stood with one hand on her thin hip and the other rattling the newspaper at his bald head. "Here this fellow that calls himself The Misfit is aloose from the Federal Pen and headed toward Florida and you read here what it says he did to these people. Just you read it. I wouldn't take my children in any direction with a criminal like that aloose in it. I couldn't answer to my conscience if I did."

Bailey didn't look up from his reading so she wheeled around then and faced the children's mother, a young woman in slacks, whose face was as broad and innocent as a cabbage and was tied around with a green headkerchief that had two points on the top like a rabbit's ears. She was sitting on the sofa, feeding the baby his apricots out of a jar. "The children have been to Florida before," the old lady said. "You all ought to take them somewhere else for a change so they would see different parts of the world and be broad. They never have been to east Tennessee."

The children's mother didn't seem to hear her but the eight-year-old boy, John Wesley, a stocky child with glasses, said, "If you don't want to go to Florida, why dontcha stay at home?" He and the little girl, June Star, were reading the funny papers on the floor.

"She wouldn't stay at home to be queen for a day," June Star said without raising her yellow head.

"Yes and what would you do if this fellow, The Misfit, caught you?" the 5 grandmother asked.

"I'd smack his face," John Wesley said.

"She wouldn't stay at home for a million bucks," June Star said. "Afraid she'd miss something. She has to go everywhere we go."

"All right, Miss," the grandmother said. "Just remember that the next time you want me to curl your hair."

June Star said her hair was naturally curly.

The next morning the grandmother was the first one in the car, ready to go. 10 She had her big black valise that looked like the head of a hippopotamus in one corner, and underneath it she was hiding a basket with Pitty Sing, the cat, in it. She didn't intend for the cat to be left alone in the house for three days because he would miss her too much and she was afraid he might brush against one of the gas burners and accidentally asphyxiate himself. Her son, Bailey, didn't like to arrive at a motel with a cat.

She sat in the middle of the back seat with John Wesley and June Star on either side of her. Bailey and the children's mother and the baby sat in front and they left Atlanta at eight forty-five with the mileage on the car at 55890. The grandmother wrote this down because she thought it would be interesting to say how many miles they had been when they got back. It took them twenty minutes to reach the outskirts of the city.

The old lady settled herself comfortably, removing her white cotton gloves and putting them up with her purse on the shelf in front of the back window. The children's mother still had on slacks and still had her head tied up in a green kerchief, but the grandmother had on a navy blue straw sailor hat with a bunch of white violets on the brim and a navy blue dress with a small white dot in the print. Her collars and cuffs were white organdy trimmed with lace and at her neckline she had pinned a purple spray of cloth violets containing a sachet. In case of an accident, anyone seeing her dead on the highway would know at once that she was a lady.

She said she thought it was going to be a good day for driving, neither too hot nor too cold, and she cautioned Bailey that the speed limit was fifty-five miles an hour and that the patrolmen hid themselves behind billboards and small clumps of trees and sped out after you before you had a chance to slow down. She pointed out interesting details of the scenery: Stone Mountain; the blue granite that in some places came up to both sides of the highway; the brilliant red clay banks slightly streaked with purple; and the various crops that made rows of green lace-work on the ground. The trees were full of silver-white sunlight and the meanest of them sparkled. The children were reading comic magazines and their mother had gone back to sleep.

"Let's go through Georgia fast so we won't have to look at it much," John Wesley said.

"If I were a little boy," said the grandmother, "I wouldn't talk about my   15 native state that way. Tennessee has the mountains and Georgia has the hills."

"Tennessee is just a hillbilly dumping ground," John Wesley said, "and Georgia is a lousy state too."

"You said it," June Star said.

"In my time," said the grandmother, folding her thin veined fingers, "children were more respectful of their native states and their parents and everything else. People did right then. Oh look at the cute little pickaninny!" she said and pointed to a Negro child standing in the door of a shack. "Wouldn't that make a picture, now?" she asked and they all turned and looked at the little Negro out of the back window. He waved.

"He didn't have any britches on," June Star said.

"He probably didn't have any," the grandmother explained. "Little niggers in   20 the country don't have things like we do. If I could paint, I'd paint that picture," she said.

The children exchanged comic books.

The grandmother offered to hold the baby and the children's mother passed him over the front seat to her. She set him on her knee and bounced him and told him about the things they were passing. She rolled her eyes and screwed up her mouth and stuck her leathery thin face into his smooth bland one. Occasionally he gave her a faraway smile. They passed a large cotton field with five or six graves fenced in the middle of it, like a small island. "Look at the graveyard!" the grandmother said, pointing it out. "That was the old family burying ground. That belonged to the plantation."

"Where's the plantation?" John Wesley asked.

"Gone With the Wind," said the grandmother. "Ha. Ha."

When the children finished all the comic books they had brought, they 25 opened the lunch and ate it. The grandmother ate a peanut butter sandwich and an olive and would not let the children throw the box and the paper napkins out the window. When there was nothing else to do they played a game by choosing a cloud and making the other two guess what shape it suggested. John Wesley took one the shape of a cow and June Star guessed a cow and John Wesley said, no, an automobile, and June Star said he didn't play fair, and they began to slap each other over the grandmother.

The grandmother said she would tell them a story if they would keep quiet. When she told a story, she rolled her eyes and waved her head and was very dramatic. She said once when she was a maiden lady she had been courted by a Mr. Edgar Atkins Teagarden from Jasper, Georgia. She said he was a very good-looking man and a gentleman and that he brought her a watermelon every Saturday afternoon with his initials cut in it, E.A.T. Well, one Saturday, she said, Mr. Teagarden brought the watermelon and there was nobody at home and he left it on the front porch and returned in his buggy to Jasper, but she never got the watermelon, she said, because a nigger boy ate it when he saw the initials, E.A.T.! This story tickled John Wesley's funny bone and he giggled and giggled but June Star didn't think it was any good. She said she wouldn't marry a man that just brought her a watermelon on Saturday. The grandmother said she would have done well to marry Mr. Teagarden because he was a gentleman and had bought Coca-Cola stock when it first came out and that he had died only a few years ago, a very wealthy man.

They stopped at The Tower for barbecued sandwiches. The Tower was a part stucco and part wood filling station and dance hall set in a clearing outside of Timothy. A fat man named Red Sammy Butts ran it and there were signs stuck here and there on the building and for miles up and down the highway saying, TRY RED SAMMY'S FAMOUS BARBECUE. NONE LIKE FAMOUS RED SAMMY'S! RED SAM! THE FAT BOY WITH THE HAPPY LAUGH. A VETERAN! RED SAMMY'S YOUR MAN!

Red Sammy was lying on the bare ground outside The Tower with his head under a truck while a gray monkey about a foot high, chained to a small chinaberry tree, chattered nearby. The monkey sprang back into the tree and got on the highest limb as soon as he saw the children jump out of the car and run toward him.

Inside, The Tower was a long dark room with a counter at one end and tables at the other and dancing space in the middle. They all sat down at a board table next to the nickelodeon and Red Sam's wife, a tall burnt-brown woman with hair and eyes lighter than her skin, came and took their order. The children's mother put a dime in the machine and played "The Tennessee Waltz," and the grandmother said that tune always made her want to dance. She asked Bailey if he would like to dance but he only glared at her. He didn't have a naturally sunny disposition like she did and trips made him nervous. The grandmother's brown eyes were very bright. She swayed her head from side to side and pretended she was dancing in her chair. June Star said play something she could tap to so the children's mother put in another dime and played a fast number and June Star stepped out onto the dance floor and did her tap routine.

"Ain't she cute?" Red Sam's wife said, leaning over the counter. "Would you 30 like to come be my little girl?"

"No I certainly wouldn't," June Star said. "I wouldn't live in a broken-down place like this for a million bucks!" and she ran back to the table.

"Ain't she cute?" the woman repeated, stretching her mouth politely.

"Aren't you ashamed?" hissed the grandmother.

Red Sam came in and told his wife to quit lounging on the counter and hurry up with these people's order. His khaki trousers reached just to his hip bones and his stomach hung over them like a sack of meal swaying under his shirt. He came over and sat down at a table nearby and let out a combination sigh and yodel. "You can't win," he said. "You can't win," and he wiped his sweating red face off with a gray handkerchief. "These days you don't know who to trust," he said. "Ain't that the truth?"

"People are certainly not nice like they used to be," said the grandmother. 35

"Two fellers come in here last week," Red Sammy said, "driving a Chrysler. It was a old beat-up car but it was a good one and these boys looked all right to me. Said they worked at the mill and you know I let them fellers charge the gas they bought? Now why did I do that?"

"Because you're a good man!" the grandmother said at once.

"Yes'm, I suppose so," Red Sam said as if he were struck with this answer.

His wife brought the orders, carrying the five plates all at once without a tray, two in each hand and one balanced on her arm. "It isn't a soul in this green world of God's that you can trust," she said. "And I don't count nobody out of that, not nobody," she repeated, looking at Red Sammy.

"Did you read about that criminal, The Misfit, that's escaped?" asked the 40 grandmother.

"I wouldn't be a bit surprised if he didn't attack this place right here," said the woman. "If he hears about it being here, I wouldn't be none surprised to see him. If he hears it's two cent in the cash register, I wouldn't be a tall surprised if he. . . ."

"That'll do," Red Sam said. "Go bring these people their Co'-Colas," and the woman went off to get the rest of the order.

"A good man is hard to find," Red Sammy said. "Everything is getting terrible. I remember the day you could go off and leave your screen door unlatched. Not no more."

He and the grandmother discussed better times. The old lady said that in her opinion Europe was entirely to blame for the way things were now. She said the way Europe acted you would think we were made of money and Red Sam said it was no use talking about it, she was exactly right. The children ran outside into the white sunlight and looked at the monkey in the lacy chinaberry tree. He was busy catching fleas on himself and biting each one carefully between his teeth as if it were a delicacy.

They drove off again into the hot afternoon. The grandmother took cat naps 45 and woke up every few minutes with her own snoring. Outside of Toombsboro she woke up and recalled an old plantation that she had visited in this neighborhood once when she was a young lady. She said the house had six white columns across the front and that there was an avenue of oaks leading up to it and two little wooden trellis arbors on either side in front where you sat down with your suitor after a stroll in the garden. She recalled exactly which road to turn off to get to it. She knew that Bailey would not be willing to lose any time looking at an old house, but the more she talked about it, the more she wanted to see it once again and find out if the little twin arbors were still standing. "There was a secret panel in this house," she said craftily, not telling the truth but wishing that she were, "and the story went that all the family silver was hidden in it when Sherman[1] came through but it was never found. . . ."

"Hey!" John Wesley said. "Let's go see it! We'll find it! We'll poke all the woodwork and find it! Who lives there? Where do you turn off at? Hey Pop, can't we turn off there?"

"We never have seen a house with a secret panel!" June Star shrieked. "Let's go to the house with the secret panel! Hey Pop, can't we go see the house with the secret panel!"

"It's not far from here, I know," the grandmother said. "It won't take over twenty minutes."

Bailey was looking straight ahead. His jaw was as rigid as a horseshoe. "No," he said.

The children began to yell and scream that they wanted to see the house 50 with the secret panel. John Wesley kicked the back of the front seat and June Star hung over her mother's shoulder and whined desperately into her ear that they never had any fun even on their vacation, that they could never do what THEY wanted to do. The baby began to scream and John Wesley kicked the back of the seat so hard that his father could feel the blows in his kidney.

---

[1] William Tecumseh Sherman (1820–1891) was a notorious Union Army General during the American Civil War.

"All right!" he shouted and drew the car to a stop at the side of the road. "Will you all shut up? Will you all just shut up for one second? If you don't shut up, we won't go anywhere."

"It would be very educational for them," the grandmother murmured.

"All right," Bailey said, "but get this: this is the only time we're going to stop for anything like this. This is the one and only time."

"The dirt road that you have to turn down is about a mile back," the grandmother directed. "I marked it when we passed."

"A dirt road," Bailey groaned.   55

After they had turned around and were headed toward the dirt road, the grandmother recalled other points about the house, the beautiful glass over the front doorway and the candle-lamp in the hall. John Wesley said that the secret panel was probably in the fireplace.

"You can't go inside this house," Bailey said. "You don't know who lives there."

"While you all talk to the people in front, I'll run around behind and get in a window," John Wesley suggested.

"We'll all stay in the car," his mother said.

They turned onto the dirt road and the car raced roughly along in a swirl of   60
pink dust. The grandmother recalled the times when there were no paved roads and thirty miles was a day's journey. The dirt road was hilly and there were sudden washes in it and sharp curves on dangerous embankments. All at once they would be on a hill, looking down over the blue tops of trees for miles around, then the next minute, they would be in a red depression with the dust-coated trees looking down on them.

"This place had better turn up in a minute," Bailey said, "or I'm going to turn around."

The road looked as if no one had traveled on it for months.

"It's not much farther," the grandmother said and just as she said it, a horrible thought came to her. The thought was so embarrassing that she turned red in the face and her eyes dilated and her feet jumped up, upsetting her valise in the corner. The instant the valise moved, the newspaper top she had over the basket under it rose with a snarl and Pitty Sing, the cat, sprang onto Bailey's shoulder.

The children were thrown to the floor and their mother, clutching the baby, was thrown out the door onto the ground; the old lady was thrown into the front seat. The car turned over once and landed right-side-up in a gulch off the side of the road. Bailey remained in the driver's seat with the cat—gray-striped with a broad white face and an orange nose—clinging to his neck like a caterpillar.

As soon as the children saw they could move their arms and legs, they   65
scrambled out of the car, shouting, "We've had an ACCIDENT!" The grandmother was curled up under the dashboard, hoping she was injured so that Bailey's wrath would not come down on her all at once. The horrible thought she had before the accident was that the house she had remembered so vividly was not in Georgia but in Tennessee.

Bailey removed the cat from his neck with both hands and flung it out the window against the side of a pine tree. Then he got out of the car and started looking for the children's mother. She was sitting against the side of the red gutted ditch, holding the screaming baby, but she only had a cut down her face and a broken shoulder. "We've had an ACCIDENT!" the children screamed in a frenzy of delight.

"But nobody's killed," June Star said with disappointment as the grandmother limped out of the car, her hat still pinned to her head but the broken front brim standing up at a jaunty angle and the violet spray hanging off the side. They all sat down in the ditch, except the children, to recover from the shock. They were all shaking.

"Maybe a car will come along," said the children's mother hoarsely.

"I believe I have injured an organ," said the grandmother, pressing her side, but no one answered her. Bailey's teeth were clattering. He had on a yellow sport shirt with bright blue parrots designed in it and his face was as yellow as the shirt. The grandmother decided that she would not mention that the house was in Tennessee.

The road was about ten feet above and they could see only the tops of the 70 trees on the other side of it. Behind the ditch they were sitting in there were more woods, tall and dark and deep. In a few minutes they saw a car some distance away on top of a hill, coming slowly as if the occupants were watching them. The grandmother stood up and waved both arms dramatically to attract their attention. The car continued to come on slowly, disappeared around a bend and appeared again, moving even slower, on top of the hill they had gone over. It was a big black battered hearse-like automobile. There were three men in it.

It came to a stop just over them and for some minutes, the driver looked down with a steady expressionless gaze to where they were sitting, and didn't speak. Then he turned his head and muttered something to the other two and they got out. One was a fat boy in black trousers and a red sweat shirt with a silver stallion embossed on the front of it. He moved around on the right side of them and stood staring, his mouth partly open in a kind of loose grin. The other had on khaki pants and a blue striped coat and a gray hat pulled down very low, hiding most of his face. He came around slowly on the left side. Neither spoke.

The driver got out of the car and stood by the side of it, looking down at them. He was an older man than the other two. His hair was just beginning to gray and he wore silver-rimmed spectacles that gave him a scholarly look. He had a long creased face and didn't have on any shirt or undershirt. He had on blue jeans that were too tight for him and was holding a black hat and a gun. The two boys also had guns.

"We've had an ACCIDENT!" the children screamed.

The grandmother had the peculiar feeling that the bespectacled man was someone she knew. His face was as familiar to her as if she had known him all her life but she could not recall who he was. He moved away from the car and began to come down the embankment, placing his feet carefully so that he wouldn't slip. He had on tan and white shoes and no socks, and his ankles were red and thin. "Good afternoon," he said. "I see you all had you a little spill."

"We turned over twice!" said the grandmother. 75

"Oncet," he corrected. "We seen it happen. Try their car and see will it run, Hiram," he said quietly to the boy with the gray hat.

"What you got that gun for?" John Wesley asked. "Whatcha gonna do with that gun?"

"Lady," the man said to the children's mother, "would you mind calling them children to sit down by you? Children make me nervous. I want all you all to sit down right together there where you're at."

"What are you telling US what to do for?" June Star asked.

Behind them the line of woods gaped like a dark open mouth. "Come here," 80 said their mother.

"Look here now," Bailey said suddenly, "we're in a predicament! We're in. . . ."

The grandmother shrieked. She scrambled to her feet and stood staring. "You're The Misfit!" she said. "I recognized you at once!"

"Yes'm," the man said, smiling slightly as if he were pleased in spite of himself to be known, "but it would have been better for all of you, lady, if you hadn't of reckernized me."

Bailey turned his head sharply and said something to his mother that shocked even the children. The old lady began to cry and The Misfit reddened.

"Lady," he said, "don't you get upset. Sometimes a man says things he don't 85 mean. I don't reckon he meant to talk to you thataway."

"You wouldn't shoot a lady, would you?" the grandmother said and removed a clean handkerchief from her cuff and began to slap at her eyes with it.

The Misfit pointed the toe of his shoe into the ground and made a little hole and then covered it up again. "I would hate to have to," he said.

"Listen," the grandmother almost screamed, "I know you're a good man. You don't look a bit like you have common blood. I know you must come from nice people!"

"Yes mam," he said, "finest people in the world." When he smiled he showed a row of strong white teeth. "God never made a finer woman than my mother and my daddy's heart was pure gold," he said. The boy with the red sweat shirt had come around behind them and was standing with his gun at his hip. The Misfit squatted down on the ground. "Watch them children, Bobby Lee," he said. "You know they make me nervous." He looked at the six of them huddled together in front of him and he seemed to be embarrassed as if he couldn't think of anything to say. "Ain't a cloud in the sky," he remarked, looking up at it. "Don't see no sun but don't see no cloud neither."

"Yes, it's a beautiful day," said the grandmother. "Listen," she said, "you 90 shouldn't call yourself The Misfit because I know you're a good man at heart. I can just look at you and tell."

"Hush!" Bailey yelled. "Hush! Everybody shut up and let me handle this!" He was squatting in the position of a runner about to sprint forward but he didn't move.

"I pre-chate that, lady," The Misfit said and drew a little circle in the ground with the butt of his gun.

"It'll take a half a hour to fix this here car," Hiram called, looking over the raised hood of it.

"Well, first you and Bobby Lee get him and that little boy to step over yonder with you," The Misfit said, pointing to Bailey and John Wesley. "The boys want to ast you something," he said to Bailey. "Would you mind stepping back in them woods there with them?"

"Listen," Bailey began, "we're in a terrible predicament! Nobody realizes   95 what this is," and his voice cracked. His eyes were as blue and intense as the parrots in his shirt and he remained perfectly still.

The grandmother reached up to adjust her hat brim as if she were going to the woods with him but it came off in her hand. She stood staring at it and after a second she let it fall to the ground. Hiram pulled Bailey up by the arm as if he were assisting an old man. John Wesley caught hold of his father's hand and Bobby Lee followed. They went off toward the woods and just as they reached the dark edge, Bailey turned and supporting himself against a gray naked pine trunk, he shouted, "I'll be back in a minute, Mamma, wait on me!"

"Come back this instant!" his mother shrilled but they all disappeared into the woods.

"Bailey Boy!" the grandmother called in a tragic voice but she found she was looking at The Misfit squatting on the ground in front of her. "I just know you're a good man," she said desperately. "You're not a bit common!"

"Nome, I ain't a good man," The Misfit said after a second as if he had considered her statement carefully, "but I ain't the worst in the world neither. My daddy said I was a different breed of dog from my brothers and sisters. 'You know,' Daddy said, 'it's some that can live their whole life out without asking about it and it's others has to know why it is, and this boy is one of the latters. He's going to be into everything!'" He put on his black hat and looked up suddenly and then away deep into the woods as if he were embarrassed again. "I'm sorry I don't have on a shirt before you ladies," he said, hunching his shoulders slightly. "We buried our clothes that we had on when we escaped and we're just making do until we can get better. We borrowed these from some folks we met," he explained.

"That's perfectly all right," the grandmother said. "Maybe Bailey has an   100 extra shirt in his suitcase."

"I'll look and see terrectly," The Misfit said.

"Where are they taking him?" the children's mother screamed.

"Daddy was a card himself," The Misfit said. "You couldn't put anything over on him. He never got in trouble with the Authorities though. Just had the knack of handling them."

"You could be honest too if you'd only try," said the grandmother. "Think how wonderful it would be to settle down and live a comfortable life and not have to think about somebody chasing you all the time."

The Misfit kept scratching in the ground with the butt of his gun as if he were thinking about it. "Yes'm, somebody is always after you," he murmured. 105

The grandmother noticed how thin his shoulder blades were just behind his hat because she was standing up looking down on him. "Do you ever pray?" she asked.

He shook his head. All she saw was the black hat wiggle between his shoulder blades. "Nome," he said.

There was a pistol shot from the woods, followed closely by another. Then silence. The old lady's head jerked around. She could hear the wind move through the tree tops like a long satisfied insuck of breath. "Bailey Boy!" she called.

"I was a gospel singer for a while," The Misfit said. "I been most everything. Been in the arm service, both land and sea, at home and abroad, been twict married, been an undertaker, been with the railroads, plowed Mother Earth, been in a tornado, seen a man burnt alive oncet," and he looked up at the children's mother and the little girl who were sitting close together, their faces white and their eyes glassy; "I even seen a woman flogged," he said.

"Pray, pray," the grandmother began, "pray, pray. . . ." 110

"I never was a bad boy that I remember of," The Misfit said in an almost dreamy voice, "but somewheres along the line I done something wrong and got sent to the penitentiary. I was buried alive," and he looked up and held her attention to him by a steady stare.

"That's when you should have started to pray," she said. "What did you do to get sent to the penitentiary that first time?"

"Turn to the right, it was a wall," The Misfit said, looking up again at the cloudless sky. "Turn to the left, it was a wall. Look up it was a ceiling, look down it was a floor. I forget what I done, lady. I set there and set there, trying to remember what it was I done and I ain't recalled it to this day. Oncet in a while, I would think it was coming to me, but it never come."

"Maybe they put you in by mistake," the old lady said vaguely.

"Nome," he said. "It wasn't no mistake. They had the papers on me." 115

"You must have stolen something," she said.

The Misfit sneered slightly. "Nobody had nothing I wanted," he said. "It was a head-doctor at the penitentiary said what I had done was kill my daddy but I known that for a lie. My daddy died in nineteen ought nineteen of the epidemic flu and I never had a thing to do with it. He was buried in the Mount Hopewell Baptist churchyard and you can see for yourself."

"If you would pray," the old lady said, "Jesus would help you."

"That's right," The Misfit said.

"Well then, why don't you pray?" she asked trembling with delight suddenly. 120

"I don't want no hep," he said. "I'm doing all right by myself."

Bobby Lee and Hiram came ambling back from the woods. Bobby Lee was dragging a yellow shirt with bright blue parrots in it.

"Throw me that shirt, Bobby Lee," The Misfit said. The shirt came flying at him and landed on his shoulder and he put it on. The grandmother couldn't name what the shirt reminded her of. "No, lady," The Misfit said while he was buttoning it up, "I found out the crime don't matter. You can do one thing or you can do another, kill a man or take a tire off his car, because sooner or later you're going to forget what it was you done and just be punished for it."

The children's mother had begun to make heaving noises as if she couldn't get her breath. "Lady," he asked, "would you and that little girl like to step off yonder with Bobby Lee and Hiram and join your husband?"

"Yes, thank you," the mother said faintly. Her left arm dangled helplessly and she was holding the baby, who had gone to sleep, in the other. "Hep that lady up, Hiram," The Misfit said as she struggled to climb out of the ditch, "and Bobby Lee, you hold onto that little girl's hand." 125

"I don't want to hold hands with him," June Star said. "He reminds me of a pig."

The fat boy blushed and laughed and caught her by the arm and pulled her off into the woods after Hiram and her mother.

Alone with The Misfit, the grandmother found that she had lost her voice. There was not a cloud in the sky nor any sun. There was nothing around her but woods. She wanted to tell him that he must pray. She opened and closed her mouth several times before anything came out. Finally she found herself saying, "Jesus, Jesus," meaning Jesus will help you, but the way she was saying it, it sounded as if she might be cursing.

"Yes'm," The Misfit said as if he agreed. "Jesus thown everything off balance. It was the same case with Him as with me except He hadn't committed any crime and they could prove I had committed one because they had the papers on me. Of course," he said, "they never shown me my papers. That's why I sign myself now. I said long ago, you get your signature and sign everything you do and keep a copy of it. Then you'll know what you done and you can hold up the crime to the punishment and see do they match and in the end you'll have something to prove you ain't been treated right. I call myself The Misfit," he said, "because I can't make what all I done wrong fit what all I gone through in punishment."

There was a piercing scream from the woods, followed closely by a pistol report. "Does it seem right to you, lady, that one is punished a heap and another ain't punished at all?" 130

"Jesus!" the old lady cried. "You've got good blood! I know you wouldn't shoot a lady! I know you come from nice people! Pray! Jesus, you ought not to shoot a lady. I'll give you all the money I've got!"

"Lady," The Misfit said, looking beyond her far into the woods, "there never was a body that give the undertaker a tip."

There were two more pistol reports and the grandmother raised her head like a parched old turkey hen crying for water and called, "Bailey Boy, Bailey Boy!" as if her heart would break.

"Jesus was the only One that ever raised the dead," The Misfit continued, "and He shouldn't have done it. He thown everything off balance. If He did

what He said, then it's nothing for you to do but thow away everything and follow Him, and if He didn't, then it's nothing for you to do but enjoy the few
minutes you got left the best way you can—by killing somebody or burning
down his house or doing some other meanness to him. No pleasure but meanness," he said and his voice had become almost a snarl.

"Maybe He didn't raise the dead," the old lady mumbled, not knowing what 135
she was saying and feeling so dizzy that she sank down in the ditch with her
legs twisted under her.

"I wasn't there so I can't say He didn't," The Misfit said. "I wisht I had of
been there," he said, hitting the ground with his fist. "It ain't right I wasn't there
because if I had of been there I would of known. Listen lady," he said in a high
voice, "if I had of been there I would of known and I wouldn't be like I am
now." His voice seemed about to crack and the grandmother's head cleared for
an instant. She saw the man's face twisted close to her own as if he were going
to cry and she murmured, "Why you're one of my babies. You're one of my
own children!" She reached out and touched him on the shoulder. The Misfit
sprang back as if a snake had bitten him and shot her three times through the
chest. Then he put his gun down on the ground and took off his glasses and
began to clean them.

Hiram and Bobby Lee returned from the woods and stood over the ditch,
looking down at the grandmother who half sat and half lay in a puddle of
blood with her legs crossed under her like a child's and her face smiling up at
the cloudless sky.

Without his glasses, The Misfit's eyes were red-rimmed and pale and
defenseless-looking. "Take her off and thow her where you thown the others,"
he said, picking up the cat that was rubbing itself against his leg.

"She was a talker, wasn't she?" Bobby Lee said, sliding down the ditch with a
yodel.

"She would of been a good woman," The Misfit said, "if it had been some- 140
body there to shoot her every minute of her life."

"Some fun!" Bobby Lee said.

"Shut up, Bobby Lee," The Misfit said. "It's no real pleasure in life."

FOR ANALYSIS

1. From whose **point of view** is the story told—that is, through whose eyes do we see
events unfold? What is the effect of O'Connor's choice of narrator?

2. How would you describe the **tone** of this story? Is it uniform, or does it vary? How?
Why do you think O'Connor uses tone the way she does?

MAKING CONNECTIONS

1. Hawthorne's "Young Goodman Brown" (p. 81) and "A Good Man Is Hard to Find"
are both in part about religious belief, though they are of course very different stories.
In what do the main characters—Brown, The Misfit, and the grandmother—believe,
and not believe?

2. An important line in Toni Cade Bambara's "The Lesson" (p. 110) comes near the end: " 'Anybody else learn anything today?' " (para. 52). "The Lesson" is more obviously a story of education, but in what way is "A Good Man Is Hard to Find" also one? What character learns a lesson in the story? What is the lesson? "The Lesson" ends with the narrator reflecting on the impact of her lesson. What is the impact of the lesson in O'Connor's story?

WRITING TOPICS

1. Compare and contrast The Misfit and the grandmother. Do they come to seem more different or more alike over the course of the story? In what ways?

2. The story's last line is The Misfit's: he says, "It's no real pleasure in life" (para. 142). While "A Good Man Is Hard to Find" is a sad, violent story, there is pleasure in reading it. Write about some of these pleasures. How do you reconcile them with the story's darkness?

TONI CADE BAMBARA (1939-1995)

THE LESSON 1972

Back in the days when everyone was old and stupid or young and foolish and me and Sugar were the only ones just right, this lady moved on our block with nappy hair and proper speech and no makeup. And quite naturally we laughed at her, laughed the way we did at the junk man who went about his business like he was some big-time president and his sorry-ass horse his secretary. And we kinda hated her too, hated the way we did the winos who cluttered up our parks and pissed on our handball walls and stank up our hallways and stairs so you couldn't halfway play hide-and-seek without a goddamn gas mask. Miss Moore was her name. The only woman on the block with no first name. And she was black as hell, cept for her feet, which were fish-white and spooky. And she was always planning these boring-ass things for us to do, us being my cousin, mostly, who lived on the block cause we all moved North the same time and to the same apartment then spread out gradual to breathe. And our parents would yank our heads into some kinda shape and crisp up our clothes so we'd be presentable for travel with Miss Moore, who always looked like she was going to church, though she never did. Which is just one of the things the grownups talked about when they talked behind her back like a dog. But when she came calling with some sachet she'd sewed up or some gingerbread she'd made or some book, why then they'd all be too embarrassed to turn her down and we'd get handed over all spruced up. She'd been to college and said it was only right that she should take responsibility for the young ones' education, and she not even related by marriage or blood. So they'd go for it. Specially Aunt Gretchen. She was the main gofer in the family. You got some old dumb shit foolishness you want somebody to go for, you send for Aunt Gretchen. She been screwed into the go-along for so long, it's a blood-deep natural thing with her. Which is how she got saddled with me and Sugar and Junior in the first place while our mothers were in a la-de-da apartment up the block having a good ole time.

So this one day Miss Moore rounds us all up at the mailbox and it's puredee hot and she's knockin herself out about arithmetic. And school suppose to let up in summer I heard, but she don't never let up. And the starch in my pinafore scratching the shit outta me and I'm really hating this nappy-head bitch and her goddamn college degree. I'd much rather go to the pool or to the show where it's cool. So me and Sugar leaning on the mailbox being surly, which is a Miss Moore word. And Flyboy checking out what everybody brought for lunch. And Fat Butt already wasting his peanut-butter-and-jelly sandwich like the pig he is. And Junebug punchin on Q.T.'s arm for potato chips. And Rosie Giraffe shifting from one hip to the other waiting for somebody to step on her foot or ask her if she from Georgia so she can kick ass, preferably Mercedes'. And Miss Moore asking us do we know what money is, like we a bunch of retards. I mean real money, she say, like it's only poker chips or monopoly papers we lay on the grocer. So right away I'm tired of this and say so. And would much rather snatch Sugar and go to the Sunset and terrorize the West Indian kids and take their hair ribbons and their money too. And Miss Moore files that remark away for next week's lesson on brotherhood, I can tell. And finally I say we oughta get to the subway cause it's cooler and besides we might meet some cute boys. Sugar done swiped her mama's lipstick, so we ready.

So we heading down the street and she's boring us silly about what things cost and what our parents make and how much goes for rent and how money ain't divided up right in this country. And then she gets to the part about we all poor and live in the slums, which I don't feature. And I'm ready to speak on that, but she steps out in the street and hails two cabs just like that. Then she hustles half the crew in with her and hands me a five-dollar bill and tells me to calculate 10 percent tip for the driver. And we're off. Me and Sugar and Junebug and Flyboy hangin out the window and hollering to everybody, putting lipstick on each other cause Flyboy a faggot anyway, and making farts with our sweaty armpits. But I'm mostly trying to figure how to spend this money. But they all fascinated with the meter ticking and Junebug starts laying bets as to how much it'll read when Flyboy can't hold his breath no more. Then Sugar lays bets as to how much it'll be when we get there. So I'm stuck. Don't nobody want to go for my plan, which is to jump out at the next light and run off to the first bar-b-que we can find. Then the driver tells us to get the hell out cause we there already. And the meter reads eighty-five cents. And I'm stalling to figure out the tip and Sugar say give him a dime. And I decide he don't need it bad as I do, so later for him. But then he tries to take off with Junebug foot still in the door so we talk about his mama something ferocious. Then we check out that we on Fifth Avenue and everybody dressed up in stockings. One lady in a fur coat, hot as it is. White folks crazy.

"This is the place," Miss Moore say, presenting it to us in the voice she uses at the museum. "Let's look in the windows before we go in."

"Can we steal?" Sugar asks very serious like she's getting the ground rules ₅ squared away before she plays. "I beg your pardon," say Miss Moore, and we fall out. So she leads us around the windows of the toy store and me and Sugar screamin, "This is mine, that's mine, I gotta have that, that was made for me, I was born for that," till Big Butt drowns us out.

"Hey, I'm goin to buy that there."

"That there? You don't even know what it is, stupid."

"I do so," he say punchin on Rosie Giraffe. "It's a microscope."

"Whatcha gonna do with a microscope, fool?"

"Look at things." ₁₀

"Like what, Ronald?" ask Miss Moore. And Big Butt ain't got the first notion. So here go Miss Moore gabbing about the thousands of bacteria in a drop of water and the somethinorother in a speck of blood and the million and one living things in the air around us is invisible to the naked eye. And what she say that for? Junebug go to town on that "naked" and we rolling. Then Miss Moore ask what it cost. So we all jam into the window smudgin it up and the price tag say $300. So then she ask how long'd take for Big Butt and Junebug to save up their allowances. "Too long," I say. "Yeh," adds Sugar, "outgrown it by that time." And Miss Moore say no, you never outgrow learning instruments. "Why, even medical students and interns and," blah, blah, blah. And we ready to choke Big Butt for bringing it up in the first damn place.

"This here costs four hundred eighty dollars," say Rosie Giraffe. So we pile up all over her to see what she pointin out. My eyes tell me it's a chunk of glass cracked with something heavy, and different-color inks dripped into the splits, then the whole thing put into a oven or something. But for $480 it don't make sense.

"That's a paperweight made of semi-precious stones fused together under tremendous pressure," she explains slowly, with her hands doing the mining and all the factory work.

"So what's a paperweight?" asks Rosie Giraffe.

"To weigh paper with, dumbbell," say Flyboy, the wise man from the East.   15

"Not exactly," say Miss Moore, which is what she say when you warm or way off too. "It's to weigh paper down so it won't scatter and make your desk untidy." So right away me and Sugar curtsy to each other and then to Mercedes who is more the tidy type.

"We don't keep paper on top of the desk in my class," say Junebug, figuring Miss Moore crazy or lyin one.

"At home, then," she say. "Don't you have a calendar and pencil case and a blotter and a letter-opener on your desk at home where you do your home-work?" And she know damn well what our homes look like cause she nosys around in them every chance she gets.

"I don't even have a desk," say Junebug. "Do we?"

"No. And I don't get no homework neither," says Big Butt.   20

"And I don't even have a home," say Flyboy like he do at school to keep the white folks off his back and sorry for him. Send this poor kid to camp posters, is his specialty.

"I do," says Mercedes. "I have a box of stationery on my desk and a picture of my cat. My godmother bought the stationery and the desk. There's a big rose on each sheet and the envelopes smell like roses."

"Who wants to know about your smelly-ass stationery," say Rosie Giraffe fore I can get my two cents in.

"It's important to have a work area all your own so that . . ."

"Will you look at this sailboat, please," say Flyboy, cuttin her off and pointin   25
to the thing like it was his. So once again we tumble all over each other to gaze at this magnificent thing in the toy store which is just big enough to maybe sail two kittens across the pond if you strap them to the posts tight. We all start

reciting the price tag like we in assembly. "Handcrafted sailboat of fiberglass at one thousand one hundred ninety-five dollars."

"Unbelievable," I hear myself say and am really stunned. I read it again for myself just in case the group recitation put me in a trance. Same thing. For some reason this pisses me off. We look at Miss Moore and she lookin at us, waiting for I dunno what.

"Who'd pay all that when you can buy a sailboat set for a quarter at Pop's, a tube of glue for a dime, and a ball of string for eight cents? It must have a motor and a whole lot else besides," I say. "My sailboat cost me about fifty cents."

"But will it take water?" say Mercedes with her smart ass.

"Took mine to Alley Pond Park once," say Flyboy. "String broke. Lost it. Pity."

"Sailed mine in Central Park and it keeled over and sank. Had to ask my 30 father for another dollar."

"And you got the strap," laugh Big Butt. "The jerk didn't even have a string on it. My old man wailed on his behind."

Little Q.T. was staring hard at the sailboat and you could see he wanted it bad. But he too little and somebody'd just take it from him. So what the hell. "This boat for kids, Miss Moore?"

"Parents silly to buy something like that just to get all broke up," say Rosie Giraffe.

"That much money it should last forever," I figure.

"My father'd buy it for me if I wanted it." 35

"Your father, my ass," say Rosie Giraffe getting a chance to finally push Mercedes.

"Must be rich people shop here," say Q.T.

"You are a very bright boy," say Flyboy. "What was your first clue?" And he rap him on the head with the back of his knuckles, since Q.T. the only one he could get away with. Though Q.T. liable to come up behind you years later and get his licks in when you half expect it.

"What I want to know is," I says to Miss Moore though I never talk to her, I wouldn't give the bitch that satisfaction, "is how much a real boat costs? I figure a thousand'd get you a yacht any day."

"Why don't you check that out," she says, "and report back to the group?" 40 Which really pains my ass. If you gonna mess up a perfectly good swim day least you could do is have some answers. "Let's go in," she say like she got something up her sleeve. Only she don't lead the way. So me and Sugar turn the corner to where the entrance is, but when we get there I kinda hang back. Not that I'm scared, what's there to be afraid of, just a toy store. But I feel funny, shame. But what I got to be shamed about? Got as much right to go in as anybody. But somehow I can't seem to get hold of the door, so I step away for Sugar to lead. But she hangs back too. And I look at her and she looks at me and this is ridiculous. I mean, damn, I have never ever been shy about doing nothing or going nowhere. But then Mercedes steps up and then Rosie Giraffe and Big Butt crowd in behind and shove, and next thing we all stuffed into the doorway with only Mercedes squeezing past us, smoothing out her jumper and walking right down the aisle. Then the rest of us tumble in like a glued-together jigsaw done all wrong. And people lookin at us. And it's like the time me and Sugar crashed into the Catholic church on a dare. But once we got in there and everything so hushed and holy and the candles and the bowin and the handkerchiefs on all the drooping heads, I just couldn't go through with the plan. Which was for me to run up to the altar and do a tap dance while Sugar played the nose flute and messed around in the holy water. And Sugar kept givin me the elbow. Then later teased me so bad I tied her up in the shower and turned it on and locked her in. And she'd be there till this day if Aunt Gretchen hadn't finally figured I was lyin about the boarder takin a shower.

Same thing in the store. We all walkin on tiptoe and hardly touchin the games and puzzles and things. And I watched Miss Moore who is steady watchin us like she waitin for a sign. Like Mama Drewery watches the sky and sniffs the air and takes note of just how much slant is in the bird formation. Then me and Sugar bump smack into each other, so busy gazing at the toys, 'specially the sailboat. But we don't laugh and go into our fat-lady bump-stomach routine. We just stare at that price tag. Then Sugar run a finger over the whole boat. And I'm jealous and want to hit her. Maybe not her, but I sure want to punch somebody in the mouth.

"Watcha bring us here for, Miss Moore?"

"You sound angry, Sylvia. Are you mad about something?" Givin me one of them grins like she tellin a grown-up joke that never turns out to be funny. And she's lookin very closely at me like maybe she planning to do my portrait from memory. I'm mad, but I won't give her that satisfaction. So I slouch around the store bein very bored and say, "Let's go."

Me and Sugar at the back of the train watchin the tracks whizzin by large then small then gettin gobbled up in the dark. I'm thinkin about this tricky toy I saw in the store. A clown that somersaults on a bar then does chin-ups just cause you yank lightly at his leg. Cost $35. I could see me askin my mother for a $35 birthday clown. "You wanna who that costs what?" she'd say, cocking her head to the side to get a better view of the hole in my head. Thirty-five dollars could buy new bunk beds for Junior and Gretchen's boy. Thirty-five dollars and the whole household could go visit Granddaddy Nelson in the country. Thirty-five dollars would pay for the rent and the piano bill too. Who are these people that spend that much for performing clowns and $1000 for toy sailboats? What kinda work they do and how they live and how come we ain't in on it? Where we are is who we are, Miss Moore always pointin out. But it don't necessarily have to be that way, she always adds then waits for somebody to say that poor people have to wake up and demand their share of the pie and don't none of us know what kind of pie she talking about in the first damn place. But she ain't so smart cause I still got her four dollars from the taxi and she sure ain't gettin it. Messin up my day with this shit. Sugar nudges me in my pocket and winks.

Miss Moore lines us up in front of the mailbox where we started from, seem 45 like years ago, and I got a headache for thinkin so hard. And we lean all over each other so we can hold up under the draggy-ass lecture she always finishes us off with at the end before we thank her for borin us to tears. But she just looks at us like she readin tea leaves. Finally she say, "Well, what did you think of F. A. O. Schwarz?"

Rosie Giraffe mumbles, "White folks crazy."

"I'd like to go there again when I get my birthday money," says Mercedes, and we shove her out the pack so she has to lean on the mailbox by herself.

"I'd like a shower. Tiring day," say Flyboy.

Then Sugar surprises me by sayin, "You know, Miss Moore, I don't think all of us here put together eat in a year what that sailboat costs." And Miss Moore lights up like somebody goosed her. "And?" she say, urging Sugar on. Only I'm standin on her foot so she don't continue.

"Imagine for a minute what kind of society it is in which some people can 50 spend on a toy what it would cost to feed a family of six or seven. What do you think?"

"I think," say Sugar pushing me off her feet like she never done before, cause I whip her ass in a minute, "that this is not much of a democracy if you ask me. Equal chance to pursue happiness means an equal crack at the dough, don't it?" Miss Moore is besides herself and I am disgusted with Sugar's treachery. So I stand on her foot one more time to see if she'll shove me. She shuts up, and Miss Moore looks at me, sorrowfully I'm thinkin. And somethin weird is goin on, I can feel it in my chest.

"Anybody else learn anything today?" lookin dead at me. I walk away and Sugar has to run to catch up and don't even seem to notice when I shrug her arm off my shoulder.

"Well, we got four dollars anyway," she says.

"Uh hunh."

"We could go to Hascombs and get half a chocolate layer and then go to the 55 Sunset and still have plenty money for potato chips and ice cream sodas."

"Un hunh."

"Race you to Hascombs," she say.

We start down the block and she gets ahead which is O.K. by me cause I'm going to the West End and then over to the Drive to think this day through. She can run if she want to and even run faster. But ain't nobody gonna beat me at nuthin.

For Analysis

1. What are Sylvia's outstanding traits? How are they reflected in her language and in her description of her neighborhood?

2. How is Sylvia's character revealed through her relationship with Sugar?

3. Describe the lesson Miss Moore tries to teach the children by taking them to visit F.A.O. Schwarz.

4. How is Sylvia's assessment of Miss Moore at the beginning of the story borne out by the ending?

5. What evidence is there that Sylvia has been changed by the visit to F.A.O. Schwarz?

MAKING CONNECTIONS

1. Compare and contrast the use of the **first-person narrator** in this story with that in Cisneros's "The House on Mango Street" (p. 119).

2. In "On Morality" (p. 264) Joan Didion argues that "we have no way of knowing—beyond that fundamental loyalty to the social code—what is 'right' and what is 'wrong,' what is 'good' and what 'evil'." Sylvia's sense of right and wrong is awakened in "The Lesson." Though the phenomena Didion writes about are of a very different sort, can we use her essay to help us think about Sylvia's sense of right and wrong? Where does it come from? Is there a social code of economic inequality? Do you think it is right or wrong?

WRITING TOPICS

1. Write an essay arguing for or against the proposition that the story ends optimistically.

2. In your opinion, is Sylvia a reliable or unreliable narrator?

JAMAICA KINCAID (B. 1949)

GIRL (1983)

W ash the white clothes on Monday and put them on the stone heap;
wash the color clothes on Tuesday and put them on the clothesline to
dry; don't walk barehead in the hot sun; cook pumpkin fritters in very hot
sweet oil; soak your little clothes right after you take them off; when buying
cotton to make yourself a nice blouse, be sure that it doesn't have gum on it,
because that way it won't hold up well after a wash; soak salt fish overnight
before you cook it; is it true that you sing benna[1] in Sunday school?; always eat
your food in such a way that it won't turn someone else's stomach; on Sundays
try to walk like a lady and not like the slut you are so bent on becoming; don't
sing benna in Sunday school; you mustn't speak to wharf-rat boys, not even to   10
give directions; don't eat fruits on the street—flies will follow you; *but I don't
sing benna on Sundays at all and never in Sunday school;* this is how to sew on a
button; this is how to make a button-hole for the button you have just sewed
on; this is how to hem a dress when you see the hem coming down and so to
prevent yourself from looking like the slut I know you are so bent on becoming; this is how you iron your father's khaki shirt so that it doesn't have a
crease; this is how you iron your father's khaki pants so that they don't have a
crease; this is how you grow okra—far from the house, because okra tree har-
bors red ants; when you are growing dasheen,[2] make sure it gets plenty of
water or else it makes your throat itch when you are eating it; this is how you   20
sweep a corner; this is how you sweep a whole house; this is how you sweep a
yard; this is how you smile to someone you don't like too much; this is how
you set a table for dinner with an important guest; this is how you smile to
someone you don't like at all; this is how you smile to someone you like completely; this is how you set a table for tea; this is how you set a table for dinner;
this is how you set a table for lunch; this is how you set a table for breakfast;
this is how to behave in the presence of men who don't know you very well,
and this way they won't recognize immediately the slut I have warned you
against becoming; be sure to wash every day, even if it is with your own spit;
don't squat down to play marbles—you are not a boy, you know; don't pick   30
people's flowers—you might catch something; don't throw stones at black-
birds, because it might not be a blackbird at all; this is how to make a bread
pudding; this is how to make doukona;[3] this is how to make pepper pot; this is
how to make a good medicine for a cold; this is how to make a good medicine

[1] Calypso music.
[2] Taro root.
[3] Spicy plantain pudding.

to throw away a child before it even becomes a child; this is how to catch a fish; this is how to throw back a fish you don't like, and that way something bad won't fall on you; this is how to bully a man; this is how a man bullies you; this is how to love a man, and if this doesn't work there are other ways, and if they don't work don't feel too bad about giving up; this is how to spit up in the air if you feel like it, and this is how to move quick so that it doesn't fall on you; this is how to make ends meet; always squeeze bread to make sure it's fresh; *but what if the baker won't let me feel the bread?*; you mean to say that after all you are really going to be the kind of woman who the baker won't let near the bread?

40

FOR ANALYSIS

1. What does the title of this piece suggest?

2. Who is the speaker? To whom is she speaking?

3. What kind of "girl" is the advice intended to produce?

4. What is the speaker's biggest fear?

5. Are the girl's two responses spoken aloud to the speaker, or are they only the girl's thoughts? Explain.

6. What do the girl's two responses suggest about her relationship to the speaker?

MAKING CONNECTIONS

1. Compare the girl in this story with Sylvia, the narrator of Bambara's "The Lesson" (p. 110).

2. Describe the speaker in this story, and then compare the speaker with the father in Meinke's poem "Advice to My Son" (p. 177). How do they differ? Do they share any qualities?

WRITING TOPICS

1. List the advice you received from your parents and other elders, and write a paragraph in imitation of Kincaid's piece.

2. Examine the details that constitute the advice in this story. What kind of society and culture do these details seem to suggest?

THE HOUSE ON MANGO STREET 1983

We didn't always live on Mango Street. Before that we lived on Loomis on the third floor, and before that we lived on Keeler. Before Keeler it was Paulina, and before that I can't remember. But what I remember most is moving a lot. Each time it seemed there'd be one more of us. By the time we got to Mango Street we were six—Mama, Papa, Carlos, Kiki, my sister Nenny, and me.

The house on Mango Street is ours and we don't have to pay rent to anybody or share the yard with the people downstairs or be careful not to make too much noise and there isn't a landlord banging on the ceiling with a broom. But even so, it's not the house we'd thought we'd get.

We had to leave the flat on Loomis quick. The water pipes broke and the landlord wouldn't fix them because the house was too old. We had to leave fast. We were using the washroom next door and carrying water over in empty milk gallons. That's why Mama and Papa looked for a house, and that's why we moved into the house on Mango Street, far away, on the other side of town.

They always told us that one day we would move into a house, a real house that would be ours for always so we wouldn't have to move each year. And our house would have running water and pipes that worked. And inside it would have real stairs, not hallway stairs, but stairs inside like the houses on T.V. And we'd have a basement and at least three washrooms so when we took a bath we didn't have to tell everybody. Our house would be white with trees around it, a great big yard and grass growing without a fence. This was the house Papa talked about when he held a lottery ticket and this was the house Mama dreamed up in the stories she told us before we went to bed.

But the house on Mango Street is not the way they told it at all. It's small and red with tight little steps in front and windows so small you'd think they were holding their breath. Bricks are crumbling in places, and the front door is so swollen you have to push hard to get in. There is no front yard, only four little elms the city planted by the curb. Out back is a small garage for the car we don't own yet and a small yard that looks smaller between the two buildings on either side. There are stairs in our house, but they're ordinary hallway stairs, and the house has only one washroom, very small. Everybody has to share a bedroom—Mama and Papa, Carlos and Kiki, me and Nenny.

Once when we were living on Loomis, a nun from my school passed by and saw me playing out front. The laundromat downstairs had been boarded up because it had been robbed two days before and the owner had painted on the wood YES WE'RE OPEN so as not to lose business.

Where do you live? she asked.

There, I said pointing up to the third floor.

You live *there*?

There. I had to look to where she pointed—the third floor, the paint peeling, 10 wooden bars Papa had nailed on the windows so we wouldn't fall out. You live *there*? The way she said it made me feel like nothing. *There.* I lived *there*. I nodded.

I knew then I had to have a house. A real house. One I could point to. But this isn't it. The house on Mango Street isn't it. For the time being, Mama said. Temporary, said Papa. But I know how those things go.

FOR ANALYSIS

1. Why did the family have to leave the flat on Loomis Street so fast?

2. What effect does Cisneros achieve by using the present tense in paragraphs 2 and 5?

3. What is the significance of the nun's comment on the speaker's house (para. 9)?

4. Describe the speaker's feelings about the move to Mango Street.

5. Would you describe the narrator's family as healthy and happy? Explain.

6. How would you characterize the **tone** of the final paragraph?

MAKING CONNECTIONS

1. Compare the **symbolism** of the house in this story with that of the quilt in Alice Walker's "Everyday Use" (p. 590).

2. Compare the significance for the **narrator** of the house on Mango Street to the significance of the farm for the speaker in Dylan Thomas's "Fern Hill" (p. 155).

WRITING TOPICS

1. Write a personal essay that is organized, like Cisneros's story, around some place or object (home, neighborhood, toy) or person (parent, sibling, friend, teacher) that symbolizes important emotions and meanings for your life.

2. Describe the effects of moving to different homes during your childhood.

3. The narrator yearns for what she calls "[a] real house. One I could point to." Write an essay describing your own experience of living in what you did not consider a "real house."

AIMEE BENDER (B. 1969)

TIGER MENDING 2004

My sister got the job. She's the overachiever, and she went to med school for two years before she decided she wanted to be a gifted seamstress. (What? they said, on the day she left. A surgeon! they told her. You could be a tremendous surgeon! But she said she didn't like the late hours, she got too tired around midnight.) She has small-motor skills better than a machine; she'll fix your handkerchief so well you can't even see the stitches, like she became one with the handkerchief. I once split my lip, jumping from the tree, and she sewed it up, with ice and a needle she'd run through the fire. I never even had a scar, just the thinnest white line.

So of course, when the two women came through the sewing school, they spotted her first. She was working on her final exam, a lime-colored ball gown with tiny diamonds sewn into the collar, and she was fully absorbed in it, constructing infinitesimal loops, while they hovered with their severe hair and heady tree smell—like bamboo, my sister said—watching her work. My sister's so steady she didn't even flinch, but everyone else in class seized upon the distraction, staring at the two Amazonian women, both six feet tall and strikingly beautiful. When I met them later I felt like I'd landed straight inside a magazine ad. At the time, I was working at Burger King, as a block manager (there were two on the block), and I took any distraction offered me and used it to the hilt. Once, a guy came in and ordered a Big Mac, and for two days I told that story to every customer, and it's not a good story. There's so rarely any intrigue in this shabberdash world of burger warming, you take what you can get.

But my sister was born with supernatural focus, and the two women watched her and her alone. Who can compete? My sister's won all the contests she's ever been in not because she's such an outrageous competitor, but because she's so focused in this gentle way. Why not win? Sometimes it's all you need to run the fastest, or to play the clearest piano, or to ace the standardized test, pausing at each question until it has slid through your mind to exit as a penciled-in circle.

In low, sweet voices, the women asked my sister if she'd like to see Asia. She finally looked up from her work. Is there a sewing job there? They nodded. She said she'd love to see Asia, she'd never left America. They said, Well, it's a highly unusual job. May I bring my sister? she asked. She's never traveled either.

The two women glanced at each other. What does your sister do? 5

She's the manager of the Burger King down on Fourth.

Their disapproval was faint but palpable, especially in the upper lip.

She would simply keep you company?

121

What we are offering you is a position of tremendous privilege. Aren't you interested in hearing about it first?

My sister nodded lightly. It sounds very interesting, she said. But I cannot travel without my sister.

This is true. My sister, the one with that incredible focus, has a terrible fear of airplanes. Terrible. Incapacitating. The only way she can relax on a flight is if I am there, because I am always, always having some kind of crisis, and she focuses in and fixes me and forgets her own concerns. I become her ripped hemline. In general, I call her every night, and we talk for an hour, which is forty-five minutes of me, and fifteen minutes of her stirring her tea, which she steeps with the kind of Zen patience that would make Buddhists sit up in envy, and then breathe through their envy, and then move past their envy. I'm really really lucky she's my sister. Otherwise, no one like her would give someone like me the time of day.

The two Amazonian women, lousy with confidence, with their ridiculous cheekbones, in these long yellow print dresses, said OK. They observed my sister's hands quiet in her lap.

Do you get along with animals? They asked and she said, Yes. She loved every animal. Do you have allergies to cats? they asked, and she said, No. She was allergic only to pine nuts. The slightly taller one reached into her dress pocket, a pocket so well hidden inside the fabric it was like she was reaching into the ether of space, and from it her hand returned with an airplane ticket.

We are very happy to have found you, they said. The additional ticket will arrive tomorrow.

My sister smiled. I know her; she was probably terrified to see that ticket, and also she really wanted to return to the diamond loops. She probably wasn't even that curious about the new job yet. She was and is stubbornly, mind-numbingly, interested in the present moment.

When we were kids, I used to come home and she'd be at the living room window. It was the best window in the apartment, looking out, in the far distance, on the tip of a mountain. For years I tried to get her to play with me, but she was unplayable. She'd stare out that window, never moving, for hours. By night, when she'd returned, I'd usually injured myself in some way or other, and I'd ask her about it as she tended to me; she said the reason she could pay acute attention was because of the window. It empties me out, she'd said, which scared me. No, she'd said, to my frightened face, and she'd sat on the edge of my bed and ran a washcloth over my forehead. It's good, she'd said. It makes room for other things.

Me? I'd asked, with hope, and she'd nodded. You.

We had no parents, by that point. They'd died at the hands of surgeons, which is the real reason my sister stopped medical school.

That night, after she took the job, she called me up and told me to quit my job, which was what I'd been praying for for months—that somehow I'd get a magical phone call telling me to quit my job because I was going on an exciting vacation. I threw down my BK apron, packed, and prepared as long an account of my life complaints as I could. On the plane, I asked my sister what we were doing, what her job was, but she refolded her tray table and said nothing. Asia, I said. What country? She stared out the porthole. It was the pilot who told us, as we buckled our seat belts; we were heading to Kuala Lumpur, straight into the heart of Malaysia.

Wait, where's Malaysia again? I whispered, and my sister drew a map on the 20 napkin beneath her ginger ale.

During the flight, I drank Bloody Marys while my sister embroidered a doily. Even the other passengers seemed soothed by watching her work. I whispered all my problems into her ear and she returned them back to me in slow sentences that did the work of a lullaby. My eyes grew heavy. During the descent, she gave the doily to the man across the aisle, worried about his ailing son, and the needlework was so elegant it made him feel better just holding it. That's the thing with handmade items. They still have the person's mark on them, and when you hold them, you feel less alone. This is why everyone who eats a Whopper leaves a little more depressed than they were when they came in. Nobody cooked that burger.

When we arrived, a friendly driver took us to a cheerful green hotel, where we found a note on the bed telling my sister to be ready at 6 A.M. sharp. It didn't say I could come, but bright and early the next morning, scrubbed and fed, we faced the two Amazons in the lobby, who looked scornfully at me and my unsteady hands—I sort of pick at my hair a lot—and asked my sister why I was there. Can't she watch? She asked, and they said they weren't sure. She, they said, might be too anxious.

I swear I won't touch anything, I said.

This is a private operation, they said.

My sister breathed. I work best when she's nearby, she said. Please. 25

And like usual it was the way she said it. In that gentle voice that had a back to it. They opened the car door.

Thank you, my sister said.

They blindfolded us, for reasons of security, and we drove for more than an hour, down winding, screeching roads, parking finally in a place that smelled like garlic and fruit. In front of a stone mansion, two more women dressed in printed robes waved as we removed our blindfolds. These two were short. Delicate. Calm. They led us into the living room, and we hadn't been there for ten minutes when we heard the moaning.

A bad moaning sound. A real bad, real mournful moaning, coming from the north, outside, that reminded me of the worst loneliness, the worst long lonely night. The Amazonian with the short shining cap of hair nodded. 30

Those are the tigers, she said.

What tigers? I said.

Shh, she said. I will call her Sloane, for no other reason than it's a good name for an intimidating person.

Sloane said, Shh. Quiet now. She took my sister by the shoulders and led her to a wide window that looked out on the land. As if she knew, instinctively, how wise it was to place my sister at a window.

Watch, Sloane whispered.

I stood behind. The two women from the front walked into view and settled 35 on the ground near some clumps of ferns. They waited. They were very still-minded, like my sister, that stillness of mind. That ability I will never have, to sit still. That ability to have the hands forget they are hands. They closed their eyes, and the moaning I'd heard before got louder, and then in the distance, I mean waaaay off, the moaning grew even louder, almost unbearable to hear, and limping from the side lumbered two enormous tigers. Wailing as if they were dying. As they got closer, you could see that their backs were split open, sort of peeled, as if someone had torn them in two. The fur was matted, and the stripes hung loose, like packing tape, ripped off their bodies. The women did not seem to move, but two glittering needles worked their way out of their knuckles, climbing up out of their hands, and one of the tigers stepped closer. I thought I'd lose it; he was easily four times her size, and she was small, a tiger's snack, but he lumped over, in his giantness, and fell into her lap. Let his heavy striped head sink to the ground. She smoothed the stripe back over, and the moment she pierced his fur with the needle, those big cat eyes dripped over with tears.

It was very powerful. It brought me to tears, too. Those expert hands, as steady as if they were holding a pair of pants, while the tiger's enormous head hung to the ground. My sister didn't move, but I cried and cried, seeing those giant broken animals resting in the laps of the small precise women. It is so often surprising, who rescues you at your lowest moment. When our parents died in surgery, the jerk at the liquor store suddenly became the nicest man alive, and gave us free cranberry juice for a year.

What happened to them? I asked Sloane. Why are they like that?

She lifted her chin slightly. We do not know, but they emerge from the forests, peeling. More and more of them. Always torn at the central stripe.

Do they ever eat people?

Not so far, she said. But they do not respond will to fidgeting, she said, 40 watching me clear out my thumbnail with my other thumbnail.

Well, I'm not doing it.

You have not been asked.

They are so sad, said my sister.

Well, wouldn't you be? If you were a tiger, peeling? Sloane put a hand on my sister's shoulder. When mending was done, all four—women and beasts—sat in the sun for at least half an hour, tigers chests heaving, women's hands clutched in their fur. They day grew warm. In the distance, the moaning began again, and two more tigers limped up while the first two stretched out and slept. The women sewed the next two, and the next. One had a bloody rip across its white belly.

After a few hours of work, the women put their needles away, the tigers 45 raised themselves up, and without any lick or acknowledgment, walked off deep into that place where tigers live. The women returned to the house.

Inside, they smelled so deeply and earthily of cat that they were almost unrec-
ognizable. They also seemed lighter, nearly giddy. It was lunchtime. They joined
us at the table, where Sloane served an amazing soup of curry and prawns.

It is an honor, said Sloane, to mend the tigers.

I see, said my sister.

You will need very little training, since your skill level is already so high.

But my sister seemed frightened, in a way I hadn't seen before. She didn't eat
much of her soup, and she returned her eyes to the window, to the tangles of
fluttering leaves.

I would have to go find out, she said finally, when the chef entered with a 50
tray of mango tartlets.

Find out what?

Why they peel, she said. She hung her head, as if she was ashamed of her
interest.

You are a mender, said Sloane, gently. Not a zoologist.

I support my sister's interest in the source, I said.   55

Sloane flinched every time I opened my mouth.

The source, my sister echoed.

The world has changed, said Sloane, passing a mango tartlet to me, reluctantly, which I ate, pronto.

It was unlike my sister, to need the cause. She was fine, usually, with just how
things were. But she whispered to me, as we roamed outside looking for clues,
of which we found none; she whispered that she felt something dangerous in
the peeling, and she felt she would have to know about it in order to sew the
tigers suitably. I am not worried about the sewing, she said. I am worried about
the gesture I place inside the thread.

I nodded. I am a good fighter, is all. I don't care about thread gestures, but I
am willing to throw a punch at some tiger asshole if need be.

We spent the rest of the day outside, but there were no tigers to be seen— 60
where they lived was somewhere far, far off, and the journey they took to arrive
here must have been the worst time of their lives, ripped open like that, suddenly prey to vultures and other predators, when they were usually the ones to
instill fear.

We spent that night at the mansion, in feather beds so soft I found them
impossible to sleep in. Come morning, Sloane had my sister join the two
women outside, and I cried again, watching the big tiger head at her feet while
she sewed with her usual stillness. The three together were unusually productive, and sewn tigers piled up around them. But instead of that giddiness that
showed up in the other women, my sister grew heavier that afternoon, and said
she was sure she was doing something wrong. Oh no, said Sloane, serving us
tea. You were remarkable.

I am missing something, said my sister. I am missing something important.

Sloane retired for a nap, but I snuck out. I had been warned, but really, they
were treating me like shit anyway. I walked a long distance, but I'm a sturdy
walker, and I trusted where my feet went, and I did not like the sight of my sister

staring into her teacup. I did not like the feeling it gave me, of worrying. Before I left, I sat her in front of the window and told her to empty herself, and her eyes were grateful in a way I was used to feeling in my own face but was not accustomed to seeing in hers.

I walked for hours, and the wet air clung to my shirt and hair. I took a nap inside some ferns. The sun was setting, and I would've walked all night, but when I reached a cluster of trees something felt different. There was no wailing yet, but I could feel the stirring before the wailing, which is almost worse. I swear I could hear the dread. I climbed up a tree and waited.

I don't know what I expected—people, I guess. People with knives, cutting in. I did not expect to see the tigers themselves, jumpy, agitated, yawning their mouths beyond wide, the wildness in their eyes, and finally the yawning so large and insistent that they split their own back in two. They all did it, one after the other—as if they wanted to peel the fur off their backs, and then, amazed at what they'd done, the wailing began.

One by one, they left the trees and began their slow journey to be mended. It left me with the oddest, most unsettled feeling.

I walked back when it was night, under a half-moon, and found my sister still at the window.

They do it to themselves, I whispered to her, and she took my hand. Her face lightened. Thank you, she said. She tried to hug me, but I pulled away. No, I said, and in the morning, I left for the airport.

FOR ANALYSIS

1. What words would you use to describe the **narrator?** Is she serious or sarcastic? Purposeful or scattered? How is she different from her sister?

2. What is bothering the narrator's sister at the end of the story? Why does the narrator's discovery in the forest make her sister feel better but cause the narrator to leave?

MAKING CONNECTIONS

1. "Tiger Mending" is about the desire not simply to experience the world but to find out why things are the way they are. Kincaid's "Girl" (p. 117) is about how the world is and how to behave in it. While "Girl" has no characters who show evidence of wanting to know why things are the way they are; it could be said that the story itself is curious in this way. Compare the two stories in terms of how they ask Why? and how (or whether) they answer this question.

WRITING TOPICS

1. At the end of the story the narrator says she is "left . . . with the oddest, most unsettled feeling" (para. 66). How do you feel at the end of the story? Like the narrator, or different? Describe the feeling the story leaves you with, and explain how you think the story achieves this effect.

2. Write a brief essay exploring the meaning of the tigers' stripes. Why do you think Bender chooses them as the thing that needs repairing?

CONNECTING STORIES: LEARNING ON THE JOB

In American culture, what you "do" for work is an important part of your adult life and a major component of your identity. Your experience at work (the time you spend doing work and how you think about work), then, is central to your sense of self. The two stories in this unit explore the intimate connections between people's jobs and who they are. As you read these stories, think about how these things are determined. Why do the **protagonists** in these two stories have the jobs they have? What kind of social backgrounds do they have? What kind of possible futures? What impact might the choices they make in the stories have on their futures? And what are they learning about all of this while they are on the job?

JOHN UPDIKE   (1932–2009)

A & P   1961

In walks these three girls in nothing but bathing suits. I'm in the third check-out slot, with my back to the door, so I don't see them until they're over by the bread. The one that caught my eye first was the one in the plaid green two-piece. She was a chunky kid, with a good tan and a sweet broad soft-looking can with those two crescents of white just under it, where the sun never seems to hit, at the top of the backs of her legs. I stood there with my hand on a box of HiHo crackers trying to remember if I rang it up or not. I ring it up again and the customer starts giving me hell. She's one of these cash-register-watchers, a witch about fifty with rouge on her cheekbones and no eyebrows, and I know it made her day to trip me up. She'd been watching cash registers for fifty years and probably never seen a mistake before.

By the time I got her feathers smoothed and her goodies into a bag—she gives me a little snort in passing, if she'd been born at the right time they would have burned her over in Salem—by the time I get her on her way the girls had circled around the bread and were coming back, without a pushcart, back my way along the counters, in the aisle between the checkouts and the Special bins. They didn't even have shoes on. There was this chunky one, with the two-piece—it was bright green and the seams on the bra were still sharp and her belly was still pretty pale so I guessed she just got it (the suit)—there was this one, with one of those chubby berry-faces, the lips all bunched together under her nose, this one, and a tall one, with black hair that hadn't quite frizzed right, and one of these sunburns right across under the eyes, and a chin that was too long—you know, the kind of girl other girls think is very "striking" and "attractive" but never quite makes it, as they very well know, which is why they like her so much—and then the third one, that wasn't quite so tall. She was the queen. She kind of led them, the other two peeking around and making their shoulders round. She didn't look around, not this queen, she just walked straight on slowly, on these long white prima-donna legs. She came down a little hard on her heels, as if she didn't walk in her bare feet that much, putting down her heels and then letting the weight move along to her toes as if she was testing the floor with every step, putting a little deliberate extra action into it. You never know for sure how girls' minds work (do you really think it's a mind in there or just a little buzz like a bee in a glass jar?) but you got the idea she had talked the other two into coming in here with her, and now she was showing them how to do it, walk slow and hold yourself straight.

She had on a kind of dirty-pink—beige maybe, I don't know—bathing suit with a little nubble all over it, and what got me, the straps were down. They were off her shoulders looped loose around the cool tops of her arms, and I guess as a result the suit had slipped a little on her, so all around the top of the cloth there was this shining rim. If it hadn't been there you wouldn't have known there could have been anything whiter than those shoulders. With the straps pushed off, there was nothing between the top of the suit and the top of her head except just *her*, this clean bare plane of the top of her chest down from the shoulder bones like a dented sheet of metal tilted in the light. I mean, it was more than pretty.

She had sort of oaky hair that the sun and salt had bleached, done up in a bun that was unravelling, and a kind of prim face. Walking into the A & P with your straps down, I suppose it's the only kind of face you *can* have. She held her head so high her neck, coming up out of those white shoulders, looked kind of stretched, but I didn't mind. The longer her neck was, the more of her there was.

She must have felt in the corner of her eye me and over my shoulder Stokesie 5 in the second slot watching, but she didn't tip. Not this queen. She kept her eyes moving across the racks, and stopped, and turned so slow it made my stomach rub the inside of my apron, and buzzed to the other two, who kind of huddled against her for relief, and then they all three of them went up the cat-and-dog-food-breakfast-cereal-macaroni-rice-raisins-seasonings-spreads-spaghetti-soft-drinks-crackers-and-cookies aisle. From the third slot I look straight up this aisle to the meat counter, and I watched them all the way. The fat one with the tan sort of fumbled with the cookies, but on second thought she put the package back. The sheep pushing their carts down the aisle—the girls were walking against the usual traffic (not that we have one-way signs or anything)—were pretty hilarious. You could see them, when Queenie's white shoulders dawned on them, kind of jerk, or hop, or hiccup, but their eyes snapped back to their own baskets and on they pushed. I bet you could set off dynamite in an A & P and the people would by and large keep reaching and checking oatmeal off their lists and muttering "Let me see, there was a third thing, began with A, asparagus, no, ah, yes, applesauce!" or whatever it is they do mutter. But there was no doubt, this jiggled them. A few houseslaves in pin curlers even looked around after pushing their carts past to make sure what they had seen was correct.

You know, it's one thing to have a girl in a bathing suit down on the beach, where what with the glare nobody can look at each other much anyway, and another thing in the cool of the A & P, under the fluorescent lights, against all those stacked packages, with her feet paddling along naked over our checkerboard green-and-cream rubber-tile floor.

"Oh Daddy," Stokesie said beside me. "I feel so faint."

"Darling," I said. "Hold me tight." Stokesie's married, with two babies chalked up on his fuselage already, but as far as I can tell that's the only difference. He's twenty-two, and I was nineteen this April.

"Is it done?" he asks, the responsible married man finding his voice. I forgot to say he thinks he's going to be manager some sunny day, maybe in 1990 when it's called the Great Alexandrov and Petrooshki Tea Company or something.

What he meant was, our town is five miles from a beach, with a big summer 10 colony out on the Point, but we're right in the middle of town, and the women generally put on a shirt or shorts or something before they get out of the car into the street. And anyway these are usually women with six children and varicose veins mapping their legs and nobody, including them, could care less. As I say, we're right in the middle of town, and if you stand at our front doors you see two banks and the Congregational church and the newspaper store and three real-estate offices and about twenty-seven old freeloaders tearing up Central Street because the sewer broke again. It's not as if we're on the Cape; we're north of Boston and there's people in this town haven't seen the ocean for twenty years.

The girls had reached the meat counter and were asking McMahon something. He pointed, they pointed, and they shuffled out of sight behind a pyramid of Diet Delight peaches. All that was left for us to see was old McMahon patting his mouth and looking after them sizing up their joints. Poor kids, I began to feel sorry for them, they couldn't help it.

Now here comes the sad part of the story, at least my family says it's sad, but I don't think it's so sad myself. The store's pretty empty, it being Thursday afternoon, so there was nothing much to do except lean on the register and wait for the girls to show up again. The whole store was like a pinball machine and I didn't know which tunnel they'd come out of. After a while they come around out of the far aisle, around the light bulbs, records at discount of the Caribbean Six or Tony Martin Sings or some such gunk you wonder they waste the wax on, sixpacks of candy bars, and plastic toys done up in cellophane that fall apart when a kid looks at them anyway. Around they come, Queenie still leading the way, and holding a little gray jar in her hand. Slots Three through Seven are unmanned and I could see her wondering between Stokes and me, but Stokesie with his usual luck draws an old party in baggy gray pants who stumbles up with four giant cans of pineapple juice (what do these bums *do* with all that pineapple juice? I've often asked myself) so the girls come to me. Queenie puts down the jar and I take it into my fingers icy cold. Kingfish Fancy Herring Snacks in Pure Sour Cream: 49¢. Now her hands are empty, not a ring or a bracelet, bare as God made them, and I wonder where the money's coming from. Still with that prim look she lifts a folded dollar bill out of the hollow at the center of her nubbled pink top. The jar went heavy in my hand. Really, I thought that was so cute.

Then everybody's luck begins to run out. Lengel comes in from haggling with a truck full of cabbages on the lot and is about to scuttle into that door marked MANAGER behind which he hides all day when the girls touch his eye. Lengel's pretty dreary, teaches Sunday school and the rest, but he doesn't miss that much. He comes over and says, "Girls, this isn't the beach."

Queenie blushes, though maybe it's just a brush of sunburn I was noticing for the first time, now that she was so close. "My mother asked me to pick up a jar of herring snacks." Her voice kind of startled me, the way voices do when you see the people first, coming out so flat and dumb yet kind of tony, too, the way it ticked over "pick up" and "snacks." All of a sudden I slid right down her voice into her living room. Her father and the other men were standing around in ice-cream coats and bow ties and the women were in sandals picking up herring snacks on toothpicks off a big glass plate and they were all holding drinks the color of water with olives and sprigs of mint in them. When my parents have somebody over they get lemonade and if it's a real racy affair Schlitz in tall glasses with "They'll Do It Every Time" cartoons stencilled on.

"That's all right," Lengel said. "But this isn't the beach." His repeating this 15 struck me as funny, as if it had just occurred to him, and he had been thinking all these years the A & P was a great big sand dune and he was the head lifeguard. He didn't like my smiling—as I say he doesn't miss much—but he concentrates on giving the girls that sad Sunday-school–superintendent stare.

Queenie's blush is no sunburn now, and the plump one in plaid, that I liked better from the back—a really sweet can—pipes up, "We weren't doing any shopping. We just came in for the one thing."

"That makes no difference," Lengel tells her, and I could see from the way his eyes went that he hadn't noticed she was wearing a two-piece before. "We want you decently dressed when you come in here."

"We *are* decent," Queenie says suddenly, her lower lip pushing, getting sore now that she remembers her place, a place from which the crowd that runs the A & P must look pretty crummy. Fancy Herring Snacks flashed in her very blue eyes.

"Girls, I don't want to argue with you. After this come in here with your shoulders covered. It's our policy." He turns his back. That's policy for you. Policy is what the kingpins want. What the others want is juvenile delinquency.

All this while, the customers had been showing up with their carts but, you 20 know, sheep, seeing a scene, they had all bunched up on Stokesie, who shook open a paper bag as gently as peeling a peach, not wanting to miss a word. I could feel in the silence everybody getting nervous, most of all Lengel, who asks me, "Sammy, have you rung up their purchase?"

I thought and said "No" but it wasn't about that I was thinking. I go through the punches, 4, 9, groc, tot—it's more complicated than you think, and after you do it often enough, it begins to make a little song, that you hear words to, in my case "Hello (*bing*) there, you (*gung*) hap-py *pee*-pul (*splat*)!"—the *splat* being the drawer flying out. I uncrease the bill, tenderly as you may imagine, it just having come from between the two smoothest scoops of vanilla I had ever known were there, and pass a half and a penny into her narrow pink palm, and nestle the herrings in a bag and twist its neck and hand it over, all the time thinking.

The girls, and who'd blame them, are in a hurry to get out, so I say "I quit" to Lengel enough for them to hear, hoping they'll stop and watch me, their unsuspected hero. They keep right on going, into the electric eye; the door flies open and they flicker across the lot to their car, Queenie and Plaid and Big Tall Goony-Goony (not that as raw material she was so bad), leaving me with Lengel and a kink in his eyebrow.

"Did you say something, Sammy?"

"I said I quit."

"I thought you did." 25

"You didn't have to embarrass them."

"It was they who were embarrassing us."

I started to say something that came out "Fiddle-de-doo." It's a saying of my grandmother's, and I know she would have been pleased.

"I don't think you know what you're saying," Lengel said.

"I know you don't," I said. "But I do." I pull the bow at the back of my apron 30 and start shrugging it off my shoulders. A couple customers that had been heading for my slot begin to knock against each other, like scared pigs in a chute.

Lengel sighs and begins to look very patient and old and gray. He's been a friend of my parents for years. "Sammy, you don't want to do this to your Mom and Dad," he tells me. It's true, I don't. But it seems to me that once you begin a gesture it's fatal not to go through with it. I fold the apron, "Sammy" stitched in red on the pocket, and put it on the counter, and drop the bow tie on top of it. The bow tie is theirs, if you've ever wondered. "You'll feel this for the rest of your life," Lengel says, and I know that's true, too, but remembering how he made that pretty girl blush makes me so scrunchy inside I punch the No Sale tab and the machine whirs "pee-pul" and the drawer splats out. One advantage to this scene taking place in summer, I can follow this up with a clean exit, there's no fumbling around getting your coat and galoshes, I just saunter into the electric eye in my white shirt that my mother ironed the night before, and the door heaves itself open, and outside the sunshine is skating around on the asphalt.

I look around for my girls, but they're gone, of course. There wasn't anybody but some young married screaming with her children about some candy they didn't get by the door of a powder-blue Falcon station wagon. Looking back in the big windows, over the bags of peat moss and aluminum lawn furniture stacked on the pavement, I could see Lengel in my place in the slot, checking the sheep through. His face was dark gray and his back stiff, as if he'd just had an injection of iron, and my stomach kind of fell as I felt how hard the world was going to be to me hereafter.

FOR ANALYSIS

1. Describe Sammy's voice as he tells the story. How does Updike's choice to have him narrate help us get a sense of Sammy as a character? Is he understandable? Is he likable? Can readers sympathize with him?

2. What about "Queenie" is most attractive to Sammy? Is it just her appearance? What else figures in?

WRITING TOPIC

Retell the story with Lengel as **narrator,** showing how that change might affect **point of view,** voice, and meaning.

VIRGIL SUÁREZ   (B.1962)

A PERFECT HOTSPOT   1992

This idea of selling ice cream during the summer seems ridiculous, pointless. I'd much rather be close to water. The waves. Where I can hear them tumble in and then roll out, and see the tiny bubbles left behind on the sand pop one by one. Or feel the undercurrents warm this time of year. Swimming. Watching the girls in bikinis with sand stuck to the backs of their thighs walk up and down the boardwalk. At this time of the morning, the surfers are out riding the waves.

Instead I'm inside an ice cream truck with my father, selling, cruising the streets. The pumps suck oil out of the ground rapidly with the creaking sounds of iron biting iron in a fenced lot at the end of the street. They look like giant rocking horses. Father turns at the corner, then, suddenly, he points to another ice cream truck.

"There's the competition," he says. "If the economy doesn't improve soon, these streets'll be full of them."

He's smoking, and the smoke floats back my way and chokes me. I can't stand it. Some of the guys on the swim team smoke. I don't understand how they can smoke and do their best when it's time for competition. I wouldn't smoke. To do so would be like cheating myself out of winning.

All morning he's been instructing me on how to sell ice cream.   5

"Tonio," he says now, "come empty your pockets."

I walk to the front of the truck, stick my hands deep into my pockets and grab a handful of coins—what we've made in change all morning. The coins fall, overlap, and multiply against the sides of the grease-smudged, change box. I turn my pockets inside-out until the last coin falls. He picks out the pieces of lint and paper from the coins.

When he begins to explain the truck's quirks, "the little problems," as he calls the water leaks, burning oil, and dirty carburetor, I return to the back of the truck and sit down on top of the wood counter next to the window.

"Be always on the lookout for babies," father says. "The ones in pampers. They pop out of nowhere. Check your mirrors all the time."

A CAUTION CHILDREN cardboard sign hangs from the rearview mirror. ₁₀
Running over children is a deep fear that seems to haunt him.

All I need, I keep reminding myself, is to pass the CPR course, get certified,
and look for a job as a beach lifeguard.

"Stop!" a kid screams, slamming the screen door of his house open. He runs
to the grassy part next to the sidewalk. Father stops the truck. The kid's hand
comes up over the edge of the window with a dollar bill forked between his
little fingers.

"What do you want?" I say.

"A Froze Toe," he says, jumping up and down, dirt rings visible on his neck.
He wets the corners of his mouth with his cherry, Kool-aid-stained tongue. I
reach inside the freezer and bring out a bar. On its wrapper is the picture of an
orange foot with a blue bubble gum ball on the big toe.

"See what else he wants," father says. "Make sure they always leave the dollar." ₁₅
The kid takes his ice cream, and he smiles.

"What else?" I ask him.

He shrugs his shoulders, shakes his head, and bites the wrapper off. The
piece of paper falls on the grass. I give him his change; he walks back to his
house.

"Should always make sure they leave all the money they bring," father says.
"They get it to spend it. That's the only way you'll make a profit. Don't steal
their money, but exchange it for merchandise." His ears stick out from underneath his L.A. Dodgers cap. The short hair on the back of his head stands out.

I grin up at the rearview mirror, but he isn't looking. ₂₀

"Want to split a Pepsi, Tonio?" he says.

"I'm not thirsty."

"Get me some water then."

The cold mist inside the freezer crawls up my hand. After he drinks and
returns the bottle, I place it back with the ice cream.

"Close the freezer," he says, "before all the cold gets out and they melt." ₂₅

If the cold were out I'd be at the natatorium doing laps.

On another street, a group of kids jumps and skips around a short man. The
smallest of the kids hangs from the man's thigh. The man signals my father to
stop, then walks up to the window. The kids scream excitedly.

"Want this one, daddy," one of the girls says.

"This one!" a boy says.

The smallest kid jumps, pointing his finger at the display my father has ₃₀
made with all the toys and candies.

"No, Jose," the man says, taking the kid by the wrist. "No candy."

The kid turns to look up at his father, not fully understanding, and then
looks at me. His little lips tremble.

"Give me six Popsicles," the man says.

"I don't want no Pop—"

"Popsicles or nothing, I don't have money to buy you what you want." ₃₅

"A Blue Ghost. I want a Blue Ghost."

"No, I said,"

The smallest kid cries.

"Be quiet, Jose, or I'm going to tell the man to go away."

I put the six Popsicles on the counter.   40

"How much?" the man asks. The skin around his eyes is a darker brown than that of his nose and cheeks.

"A dollar-fifty," I say.

He digs inside his pockets and produces two wrinkled green balls which he throws on the counter. The two dollar bills roll. I unfold the bills, smooth them, and give them to father, who returns the man his change through the front window.

The man gives each kid a Popsicle, then walks away with his hands in his pockets. Jose, still crying, grabs his as he follows his father back to their house.

"He doesn't want to spend his beer money," father says, driving away from   45
the curb.

After that, we have no more customers for hours. Ever since he brought the truck home two years ago, father has changed. Ice creams have become his world. According to father, appearance and cleanliness isn't important as long as the truck passes the Health Department inspection in order to obtain the sales license. The inside of the truck is a mess: paint flakes off, rust hides between crevices, the freezer lids hold layer upon layer of dirt and melted ice cream. Here I'll have to spend the rest of my summer, I think, among the strewn Doritos, Munchos, and the rest of the merchandise.

The outside of the truck had been painted by father's friend, Gaspar, before mother died. I remember how Gaspar drank beer after beer while he painted the crown over the K in KING OF ICE CREAM and assured mother, who never missed one of my swim meets and who always encouraged me to become the best swimmer I could be, that I was going to make it all right in the end.

Father lives this way, I know, out of loneliness. He misses mother as much as I do.

I count the passing of time by how many ice creams I sell. It isn't anything like swimming laps. Doing laps involves the idea of setting and breaking new limits.

"How much do you think we have?" my father asks. The visor of his cap tilts   50
upward.

"I don't know." I hate the metallic smell money leaves on my fingers.

"Any idea?"

"No."

"A couple of months on your own and you'll be able to guess approximately how much you make."

A couple of months, I think, and I'll be back in high school. Captain of the   55
varsity swim team. A customer waits down the street.

"Make the kill fast," father says.

A barefooted woman holding a child to her breast comes to the window. She has dirty fingernails, short and uneven, as if she bites them all the time. Make the kill fast, I think.

Ice creams on the counter, I tell her, "Two dollars."

She removes the money out of her brassiere and hands it to me, then she walks away. She has yellow blisters on the back of each heel.

After that, he begins to tell me the story of the wild dog. When he was a kid, 60 a wild bitch came down from the hills and started killing my grandfather's chickens. "Seeing the scattered feathers," father says, "made your grandfather so angry I thought his face would burst because it'd turned so red."

"Anyway," he continues, "the wild dog kept on killing chickens."

Not only my grandfather's, but other farmers' as well. The other farmers were scared because they thought the wild dog was a witch. One morning, my grandfather got my father out of bed early and took him up to the hills behind the house with a jar of poison. A farmer had found the bitch's litter. My grandfather left my father in charge of anointing the poison all over the puppies fur so that when the mother came back, if he hadn't shot it by then, she'd die the minute she licked her young. My father didn't want to do it, but my grandfather left him in command while he went after the wild dog to shoot it. The dog disappeared and the puppies licked each other to death.

When he finishes telling me the story, father looks at the rearview mirror and grins, then he drives on. He turns up the volume in the music box and now *Raindrops Keep Falling on My Head* blares out of the speakers. The old people'll complain, he says, because the loud music hurts their eardrums, but the louder the music, the more people'll hear it, and more ice creams'll get sold.

Farther ahead, another kid stops us. The kid has his tongue out. His eyes seem to be too small for his big face. Though he seems old, he still drools. He claps his small hands quickly.

"Does he have money?" father asks. 65

"Can't see."

The kid walks over to the truck and hangs from the edge of the window.

"Get him away from the truck," father says, then to the kid, "Hey, move away!"

"Come on," I tell the kid, "you might fall and hurt yourself."

"Wan icleam," the kid says. 70

"We'll be back in a little while," father tells him.

"Wan icleam!" He doesn't let go. "Wan icleam!"

"Move back!" father shouts. "Tonio, get him away from the truck."

I try to unstick the kid's pudgy fingers from the metal edge of the window, but he won't let go. His saliva falls on my hands.

"Wan icleam!" 75

I reach over to one of the shelves to get a penny candy for him so that I can bait him into letting go, but father catches me.

"Don't you dare," he says.

He opens the door and comes around the back to the kid, pulling him away from the truck to the sidewalk where he sets the kid down, and returns.

"Can't give your merchandise away," he says. "You can't make a profit that way, Tonio."

The kid runs after us shouting, waving his arms. I grab a handful of candies 80 and throw them out the window to the sidewalk, where they fall on the grass and scatter.

The sun sets slowly, and, descending, it spreads Popsicle orange on the sky. Darkness creeps on the other side of the city.

If I don't get a job as a lifeguard, I think, then I'm going to travel southeast and visit the islands.

"How are the ice creams doing?" father asks. "Are they softening?"

I check by squeezing a bar and say, "I think we should call it a day."

"Tonio," he says. He turns off the music, makes a left turn to the main street, 85 and heads home. "Why didn't you help me with that kid? You could have moved him. What will happen when you're here by yourself?"

"Couldn't do it."

"Here," he says, giving me the change box. "Take it inside when we get home."

"I'll get it when we get there."

He puts the blue box back down on top of the stand he built over the motor. Cars speed by. The air smells heavy with exhaust and chemical fumes. In the distance, columns of smoke rise from factory smokestacks.

He turns into the driveway, drives the truck all the way to the front of the 90 garage, and parks underneath the long branches of the avocado tree.

"Take the box inside," he says, turning off the motor. He steps down from the truck and connects the freezer to the extension cord coming out of the kitchen window.

I want to tell him that I won't come out tomorrow.

"Come on, Tonio. Bring the box in."

"You do it," I say.

"What's the matter, son?" 95

"I'd rather you do it."

"Like you'd rather throw all my merchandise out of the window," he says, growing red in the face. "I saw you."

He walks toward me, and I sense another argument coming. Father stops in front of me and gives me a wry smile. "Dreamers like you," he says, "learn the hard way."

He turns around, picks up the change box, and says, "I'm putting the truck up for sale. From now on you're on your own, you hear. I'm not forcing you to do something you don't want to."

I don't like the expressionless look on his face when usually, whenever he got 100 angry at me, his face would get red and sweaty.

He unlocks the kitchen door and enters the house.

I jump out of the truck, lock the door, and walk around our clapboard house to the patio. Any moment now, I think, father'll start slamming doors inside and throwing things around. He'll curse. I lean against the wall and feel the glass of the window behind me when it starts to tremble.

FOR ANALYSIS

1. Why do you think Suárez chose "A Perfect Hotspot" as the title of this story? To which meaning or meanings of *hotspot* do you think he is alluding?

2. How does Suárez use the physical details of the **setting** to further the narrative? How do they compare to the imagined details of the places Tonio would rather be?

WRITING TOPIC

Early in the story, Tonio reflects on the smokers on his swim team, thinking, "To do so would be like cheating myself out of winning" (para. 4). Later, he remembers the man who painted the truck years ago telling Tonio's mother that Tonio "was going to make it all right in the end" (para. 47). Write a couple of paragraphs responding to the idea that the "A Perfect Hotspot" is about winning in the end in a larger sense.

MAKING CONNECTIONS

1. "Dreamers like you," Tonio's father tells him in "A Perfect Hotspot," "learn the hard way" (para. 98). How is Tonio a dreamer? How is Sammy in "A & P" also a dreamer? In what ways do the stories hint at the hard lessons each character will learn?

2. How are the two jobs and workplaces in these stories described? What do these two first-person narratives reveal about the boys who work these jobs? What do they see? What do they not see?

3. After Sammy quits his job over Lengel's treatment of the girls, Lengel says, "It was they who were embarrassing us" (para. 27). Who, in this statement and in this story, is Them, and who is Us? Is there a similar Us and Them, present or implied, in "A Perfect Hotspot"?

POETRY

WILLIAM BLAKE (1757–1827)

THE CHIMNEY SWEEPER 1789

When my mother died I was very young,
And my Father sold me while yet my tongue
Could scarcely cry " 'weep! 'weep! 'weep! 'weep!"
So your chimneys I sweep, and in soot I sleep.

There's little Tom Dacre, who cried when his head,
That curled like a lamb's back, was shaved: so I said,
"Hush, Tom! never mind it, for when your head's bare
You know that the soot cannot spoil your white hair."

And so he was quiet and that very night
As Tom was a-sleeping, he had such a sight!   10
That thousands of sweepers, Dick, Joe, Ned, and Jack,
Were all of them locked up in coffins of black.

And by came an Angel who had a bright key,
And he opened the coffins and set them all free;
Then down a green plain leaping, laughing, they run,
And wash in a river, and shine in the Sun.

Then naked and white, all their bags left behind,
They rise upon clouds and sport in the wind;
And the Angel told Tom, if he'd be a good boy,
He'd have God for his father, and never want joy.   20

And so Tom awoke; and we rose in the dark,
And got with our bags and our brushes to work.
Though the morning was cold, Tom was happy and warm;
So if all do their duty they need not fear harm.

THE LAMB 1789

Little Lamb, who made thee?
  Dost thou know who made thee?
Gave thee life, and bid thee feed
By the stream and o'er the mead;
Gave thee clothing of delight,
Softest clothing, wooly, bright;
Gave thee such a tender voice,
Making all the vales rejoice?
  Little Lamb, who made thee?
  Dost thou know who made thee?   10

Little Lamb, I'll tell thee,
  Little Lamb, I'll tell thee:
He is callèd by thy name,
For he calls himself a Lamb.
He is meek, and he is mild;
He became a little child.
I a child, and thou a lamb,
We are callèd by his name.
  Little Lamb, God bless thee!
  Little Lamb, God bless thee!   20

THE GARDEN OF LOVE 1793

I went to the Garden of Love,
And saw what I never had seen:
A Chapel was built in the midst,
Where I used to play on the green.

And the gates of this Chapel were shut,
And "Thou shalt not" writ over the door;
So I turn'd to the Garden of Love,
That so many sweet flowers bore,

And I saw it was filled with graves,
And tomb-stones where flowers should be: 10
And Priests in black gowns were walking their rounds,
And binding with briars my joys & desires.

FOR ANALYSIS

1. What meanings does the word *love* have in this poem?
2. What is Blake's judgment on established religion?
3. Explain the meaning of *Chapel* (l. 3) and *briars* (l. 12).

WRITING TOPIC

Read the definition of **irony** in "Glossary of Literary Terms." Write an essay in which you distinguish between the types of irony used in "The Chimney Sweeper" and "The Garden of Love."

LONDON   1794

I wander through each chartered[1] street,
Near where the chartered Thames does flow
And mark in every face I meet
Marks of weakness, marks of woe.

In every cry of every man,
In every infant's cry of fear,
In every voice; in every ban,
The mind-forged manacles I hear:

How the chimney-sweeper's cry
Every blackening church appalls,   10
And the hapless soldier's sigh
Runs in blood down palace-walls.

But most, through midnight streets I hear
How the youthful harlot's curse
Blasts the new-born infant's tear,
And blights with plagues the marriage-hearse.

THE TYGER   1794

Tyger! Tyger! burning bright
In the forests of the night,
What immortal hand or eye
Could frame thy fearful symmetry?

London
   [1] Preempted by the state and leased out under royal patent.

In what distant deeps or skies
Burnt the fire of thine eyes?
On what wings dare he aspire?
What the hand dare seize the fire?

And what shoulder, & what art,
Could twist the sinews of thy heart?
And when thy heart began to beat,   10
What dread hand? & what dread feet?

What the hammer? what the chain?
In what furnace was thy brain?
What the anvil? what dread grasp
Dare its deadly terrors clasp?

When the stars threw down their spears,
And water'd heaven with their tears,
Did he smile his work to see?
Did he who made the Lamb make thee?   20

Tyger! Tyger! burning bright
In the forests of the night,
What immortal hand or eye
Dare frame thy fearful symmetry?

JOHN KEATS   (1795–1821)

ON FIRST LOOKING INTO CHAPMAN'S HOMER[1]   1816

Much have I travelled in the realms of gold,
And many goodly states and kingdoms seen:
Round many western islands have I been
Which bards in fealty to Apollo[2] hold.
Oft of one wide expanse had I been told
That deep-browed Homer ruled as his demesne;°   realm
Yet did I never breathe its pure serene°   clear air
Till I heard Chapman speak out loud and bold:

On First Looking into Chapman's Homer
[1] George Chapman published translations of *The Iliad* (1611) and *The Odyssey* (1616).
[2] The god of poetry.

Then felt I like some watcher of the skies
When a new planet swims into his ken;   10
Or like stout Cortez[3] when with eagle eyes
He stared at the Pacific—and all his men
Looked at each other with a wild surmise—
    Silent, upon a peak in Darien.

ROBERT BROWNING   (1812–1889)

MY LAST DUCHESS   1842

FERRARA

That's my last Duchess painted on the wall,
Looking as if she were alive. I call
That piece a wonder, now: Frà Pandolf's[1] hands
Worked busily a day, and there she stands.
Will't please you sit and look at her? I said
"Frà Pandolf" by design, for never read
Strangers like you that pictured countenance,
The depth and passion of its earnest glance,
But to myself they turned (since none puts by
The curtain I have drawn for you, but I)   10
And seemed as they would ask me, if they durst,
How such a glance came there; so, not the first
Are you to turn and ask thus. Sir, 'twas not
Her husband's presence only, called that spot
Of joy into the Duchess' cheek: perhaps
Frà Pandolf chanced to say "Her mantle laps
Over my lady's wrist too much," or "Paint
Must never hope to reproduce the faint
Half-flush that dies along her throat": such stuff
Was courtesy, she thought, and cause enough   20
For calling up that spot of joy. She had
A heart—how shall I say?—too soon made glad,

On First Looking into Chapman's Homer
   [3] Keats mistakenly attributes the discovery of the Pacific Ocean by Europeans to Hernando Cortés
(1485–1547), the Spanish conqueror of Mexico. Vasco Núñez de Balboa (1475–1519) first saw the
Pacific from a mountain located in eastern Panama.

My Last Duchess
   [1] Frà Pandolf and Claus of Innsbruck (who is mentioned in the last line) are fictitious artists.

Too easily impressed; she liked whate'er
She looked on, and her looks went everywhere.
Sir, 'twas all one! My favor at her breast,
The dropping of the daylight in the West,
The bough of cherries some officious fool
Broke in the orchard for her, the white mule
She rode with round the terrace—all and each
Would draw from her alike the approving speech,   30
Or blush, at least. She thanked men—good! but thanked
Somehow—I know not how—as if she ranked
My gift of a nine-hundred-years-old name
With anybody's gift. Who'd stoop to blame
This sort of trifling? Even had you skill
In speech—which I have not—to make your will
Quite clear to such an one, and say, "Just this
Or that in you disgusts me; here you miss,
Or there exceed the mark"—and if she let
Herself be lessoned° so, nor plainly set   taught 40
Her wits to yours, forsooth, and made excuse,
—E'en then would be some stooping; and I choose
Never to stoop. Oh sir, she smiled, no doubt,
Whene'er I passed her; but who passed without
Much the same smile? This grew; I gave commands;
Then all smiles stopped together. There she stands
As if alive. Will't please you rise? We'll meet
The company below, then. I repeat,
The Count your master's known munificence°   generosity
Is ample warrant that no just pretense   50
Of mine for dowry will be disallowed;
Though his fair daughter's self, as I avowed
At starting, is my object. Nay, we'll go
Together down, sir. Notice Neptune, though,
Taming a sea-horse, thought a rarity,
Which Claus of Innsbruck cast in bronze for me!

FOR ANALYSIS

1. To whom is the duke speaking, and what is the occasion?

2. What does a comparison between the duke's feelings about his artwork and his feelings about his last duchess reveal about his character?

3. Does this poem rely on **irony**? Explain.

WRITING TOPIC

Write an essay in which you argue that the reader either is or is not meant to sympathize with the duke's characterization of his wife.

EMILY DICKINSON   (1830–1886)

I FELT A FUNERAL, IN MY BRAIN   1861

I felt a Funeral, in my Brain,
And Mourners to and fro
Kept treading—treading—till it seemed
That Sense was breaking through—

And when they all were seated,
A Service, like a Drum—
Kept beating—beating—till I thought
My Mind was going numb—

And then I heard them lift a Box
And creak across my Soul   10
With those same Boots of Lead, again,
Then Space—began to toll,

As all the Heavens were a Bell,
And Being, but an Ear,
And I, and Silence, some strange Race
Wrecked, solitary, here—

And then a Plank in Reason, broke,
And I dropped down, and down—
And hit a World, at every plunge,
And Finished knowing—then—   20

THOMAS HARDY   (1840–1928)

THE RUINED MAID   1902

"O 'Melia, my dear, this does everything crown!
Who could have supposed I should meet you in Town?
And whence such fair garments, such prosperi-ty?"
"O didn't you know I'd been ruined?" said she.

"You left us in tatters, without shoes or socks,
Tired of digging potatoes, and spudding up docks;°   digging herbs
And now you've gay bracelets and bright feathers three!"
"Yes: that's how we dress when we're ruined," said she.

"At home in the barton° you said 'thee' and 'thou,'   farmyard
And 'thik oon,' and 'theäs oon,' and 't'other'; but now   10
Your talking quite fits 'ee for high compa-ny!"
"Some polish is gained with one's ruin," said she.

"Your hands were like paws then, your face blue and bleak
But now I'm bewitched by your delicate cheek,
And your little gloves fit as on any la-dy!"
"We never do work when we're ruined," said she.

"You used to call home-life a hag-ridden dream,
And you'd sigh, and you'd sock; but at present you seem
To know not of megrims° or melancho-ly!"   sick headaches
"True. One's pretty lively when ruined," said she.   20

"I wish I had feathers, a fine sweeping gown,
And a delicate face, and could strut about Town!"
"My dear — a raw country girl, such as you be,
Cannot quite expect that. You ain't ruined," said she.

GERARD MANLEY HOPKINS   (1844–1889)

SPRING AND FALL   1880

TO A YOUNG CHILD

Márgarét, áre you gríeving
Over Goldengrove unleaving?°   losing leaves
Leáves, líke the things of man, you
With your fresh thoughts care for, can you?
Áh! ás the heart grows older
It will come to such sights colder
By and by, nor sparc a sigh
Though worlds of wanwood leafmeal[1] lie;
And yet you wíll weep and know why.
Now no matter, child, the name: 10
Sórrow's spríngs áre the same.
Nor mouth had, no nor mind, expressed
What heart heard of, ghost° guessed: soul
It ís the blight man was born for,
It is Margaret you mourn for.

Spring and Fall
[1] Pale woods littered with mouldering leaves.

FOR ANALYSIS

1. In this poem Margaret grieves over the passing of spring and the coming of fall. What does the coming of fall symbolize?

2. Why, when Margaret grows older, will she not sigh over the coming of fall?

3. What are "Sórrow's spríngs" (l. 11)?

A. E. HOUSMAN   (1859–1936)

TERENCE, THIS IS STUPID STUFF[1]   1896

"Terence, this is stupid stuff:
You eat your victuals fast enough;
There can't be much amiss, 'tis clear,
To see the rate you drink your beer.
But oh, good Lord, the verse you make,
It gives a chap the bellyache.
The cow, the old cow, she is dead;
It sleeps well, the hornéd head:
We poor lads, 'tis our turn now
To hear such tunes as killed the cow.   10
Pretty friendship 'tis to rhyme
Your friends to death before their time
Moping melancholy mad:
Come, pipe a tune to dance to, lad."

Why, if 'tis dancing you would be,
There's brisker pipes than poetry.
Say, for what were hopyards meant,
Or why was Burton built on Trent?[2]
Oh many a peer of England brews
Livelier liquor than the Muse,   20
And malt does more than Milton can
To justify God's ways to man.[3]
Ale, man, ale's the stuff to drink
For fellows whom it hurts to think:

---

[1] Housman originally titled the volume in which this poem appeared *The Poems of Terence Hearsay.* Terence was a Roman satiric playwright.

[2] The river Trent provides water for the town's brewing industry.

[3] In the invocation to *Paradise Lost,* Milton declares that his epic will "justify the ways of God to men."

Look into the pewter pot
To see the world as the world's not.
And faith, 'tis pleasant till 'tis past:
The mischief is that 'twill not last.
Oh I have been to Ludlow fair
And left my necktie God knows where,   30
And carried halfway home, or near,
Pints and quarts of Ludlow beer:
Then the world seemed none so bad,
And I myself a sterling lad;
And down in lovely muck I've lain,
Happy till I woke again.
Then I saw the morning sky:
Heigho, the tale was all a lie;
The world, it was the old world yet,
I was I, my things were wet,   40
And nothing now remained to do
But begin the game anew.

    Therefore, since the world has still
Much good, but much less good than ill,
And while the sun and moon endure
Luck's a chance, but trouble's sure,
I'd face it as a wise man would,
And train for ill and not for good.
'Tis true the stuff I bring for sale
Is not so brisk a brew as ale: 50
Out of a stem that scored the hand
I wrung it in a weary land.
But take it: if the smack is sour,
The better for the embittered hour;
It should do good to heart and head
When your soul is in my soul's stead;
And I will friend you, if I may,
In the dark and cloudy day.

    There was a king reigned in the East:
There, when kings will sit to feast,   60
They get their fill before they think
With poisoned meat and poisoned drink.
He gathered all that springs to birth
From the many-venomed earth;
First a little, thence to more,
He sampled all her killing store;

And easy, smiling, seasoned sound,
Sate the king when healths went round.
They put arsenic in his meat
And stared aghast to watch him eat;   70
They poured strychnine in his cup
And shook to see him drink it up:
They shook, they stared as white's their shirt:
Them it was their poison hurt.
—I tell the tale that I heard told.
Mithridates, he died old.[4]

FOR ANALYSIS

1. What does the speaker of the first fourteen lines object to in Terence's poetry?

2. What is Terence's response to the criticism of his verse? What function of true poetry is implied by his comparison of bad poetry with liquor?

WRITING TOPIC

How does the story of Mithridates (ll. 59–76) illustrate the theme of the poem?

WHEN I WAS ONE-AND-TWENTY 1896

When I was one-and-twenty
    I heard a wise man say,
"Give crowns and pounds and guineas
    But not your heart away;
Give pearls away and rubies
    But keep your fancy free."
But I was one-and-twenty,
    No use to talk to me.

When I was one-and-twenty
    I heard him say again,
"The heart out of the bosom
    Was never given in vain;
'Tis paid with sighs a plenty
    And sold for endless rue."
And I am two-and-twenty,
    And oh, 'tis true, 'tis true.   10

Terence, This Is Stupid Stuff
[4] Mithridates, the King of Pontus (in Asia Minor), reputedly immunized himself against poisons by administering to himself gradually increasing doses.

WILLIAM BUTLER YEATS   (1865–1939)

LEDA AND THE SWAN[1]   1928

A sudden blow: the great wings beating still
Above the staggering girl, her thighs caressed
By the dark webs, her nape caught in his bill,
He holds her helpless breast upon his breast.

How can those terrified vague fingers push
The feathered glory from her loosening thighs?
And how can body, laid in that white rush,
But feel the strange heart beating where it lies?

A shudder in the loins engenders there
The broken wall, the burning roof and tower   10
And Agamemnon dead.
                           Being so caught up,
So mastered by the brute blood of the air,
Did she put on his knowledge with his power
Before the indifferent beak could let her drop?

ROBERT FROST   (1874–1963)

THE ROAD NOT TAKEN   1915

Two roads diverged in a yellow wood,
And sorry I could not travel both
And be one traveler, long I stood
And looked down one as far as I could
To where it bent in the undergrowth;

Then took the other, as just as fair,
And having perhaps the better claim,
Because it was grassy and wanted wear;

Leda and the Swan
   [1] In Greek myth, Zeus, in the form of a swan, rapes Leda. As a consequence, Helen and Clytemnestra
are born. Each sister marries the king of a city-state: Helen marries Menelaus, and Clytemnestra
marries Agamemnon. Helen, the most beautiful woman on earth, elopes with Paris, a prince of Troy, an
act that precipitates the Trojan War in which Agamemnon commands the combined Greek armies. The
war ends with the destruction of Troy. Agamemnon, when he returns to his home, is murdered by his
unfaithful wife.

Though as for that the passing there
Had worn them really about the same,   10

And both that morning equally lay
In leaves no step had trodden black.
Oh, I kept the first for another day!
Yet knowing how way leads on to way,
I doubted if I should ever come back.

I shall be telling this with a sigh
Somewhere ages and ages hence:
Two roads diverged in a wood, and I —
I took the one less traveled by,
And that has made all the difference.   20

BIRCHES   1916

When I see birches bend to left and right
Across the lines of straighter darker trees,
I like to think some boy's been swinging them.
But swinging doesn't bend them down to stay
As ice-storms do. Often you must have seen them
Loaded with ice a sunny winter morning
After a rain. They click upon themselves
As the breeze rises, and turn many-colored
As the stir cracks and crazes their enamel.
Soon the sun's warmth makes them shed crystal shells   10
Shattering and avalanching on the snow-crust—
Such heaps of broken glass to sweep away
You'd think the inner dome of heaven had fallen.
They are dragged to the withered bracken by the load,
And they seem not to break; though once they are bowed
So low for long, they never right themselves:
You may see their trunks arching in the woods
Years afterwards, trailing their leaves on the ground
Like girls on hands and knees that throw their hair
Before them over their heads to dry in the sun.   20
But I was going to say when Truth broke in
With all her matter-of-fact about the ice-storm
I should prefer to have some boy bend them
As he went out and in to fetch the cows—
Some boy too far from town to learn baseball,

Whose only play was what he found himself,
Summer or winter, and could play alone.
One by one he subdued his father's trees
By riding them down over and over again
Until he took the stiffness out of them, 30
And not one but hung limp, not one was left
For him to conquer. He learned all there was
To learn about not launching out too soon
And so not carrying the tree away
Clear to the ground. He always kept his poise
To the top branches, climbing carefully
With the same pains you use to fill a cup
Up to the brim, and even above the brim.
Then he flung outward, feet first, with a swish,
Kicking his way down through the air to the ground. 40
So was I once myself a swinger of birches.
And so I dream of going back to be.
It's when I'm weary of considerations,
And life is too much like a pathless wood
Where your face burns and tickles with the cobwebs
Broken across it, and one eye is weeping
From a twig's having lashed across it open.
I'd like to get away from earth awhile
And then come back to it and begin over.
May no fate willfully misunderstand me 50
And half grant what I wish and snatch me away
Not to return. Earth's the right place for love:
I don't know where it's likely to go better.
I'd like to go by climbing a birch tree,
And climb black branches up a snow-white trunk
Toward heaven, till the tree could bear no more,
But dipped its top and set me down again
That would be good both going and coming back.
One could do worse than be a swinger of birches.

E. E. CUMMINGS (1894–1962)

IN JUST- 1923

in Just-
spring   when the world is mud-
luscious the little
lame balloonman

whistles   far   and wee

and eddieandbill come
running from marbles and
piracies and it's
spring

when the world is puddle-wonderful   10

the queer
old balloonman whistles
far   and   wee
and bettyandisbel come dancing

from hop-scotch and jump-rope and

it's
spring
and
    the

        goat-footed   20

balloonMan   whistles
far
and
wee

STEVIE SMITH   (1902–1971)

NOT WAVING BUT DROWNING   1957

Nobody heard him, the dead man,
But still he lay moaning:
I was much further out than you thought
And not waving but drowning.

Poor chap, he always loved larking
And now he's dead
It must have been too cold for him his heart gave way,
They said.

Oh, no no no, it was too cold always
(Still the dead one lay moaning)   10

I was much too far out all my life
And not waving but drowning.

FOR ANALYSIS

1. Explain the **paradox** in the first and last stanzas, where the speaker describes some-one dead as moaning. Who do you suppose the *you* of line 3 is? The *They* of line 8?

2. Explain the meaning of line 7. Can it be interpreted in more than one way?

3. Explain the meanings of *drowning*.

4. The only thing we learn about the dead man is that "he always loved larking" (l. 5). Why is this detail significant? What kind of man do you think he was?

5. Does the speaker know more about the dead man than the man's friends do? Explain.

WRITING TOPICS

1. Write an essay describing how you or someone you know suffered the experience of "not waving but drowning."

2. Write an essay describing how you came to the realization that someone close to you was not the person you thought he or she was.

TO CARRY THE CHILD   1966

To carry the child into adult life
Is good? I say it is not,
To carry the child into adult life
Is to be handicapped.

The child in adult life is defenceless
And if he is grown-up, knows it,
And the grown-up looks at the childish part
And despises it.

The child, too, despises the clever grown-up,
The man-of-the-world, the frozen,   10
For the child has the tears alive on his cheek
And the man has none of them.

As the child has colours, and the man sees no
Colours or anything,
Being easy only in things of the mind,
The child is easy in feeling.

Easy in feeling, easily excessive
And in excess powerful,
For instance, if you do not speak to the child
He will make trouble.   20

You would say a man had the upper hand
Of the child, if a child survive,
But I say the child has fingers of strength
To strangle the man alive.

Oh! it is not happy, it is never happy,
To carry the child into adulthood,
Let the children lie down before full growth
And die in their infanthood
And be guilty of no man's blood.

But oh the poor child, the poor child, what can he do,   30
Trapped in a grown-up carapace,
But peer outside of his prison room
With the eye of an anarchist?

COUNTEE CULLEN   (1903–1946)

INCIDENT   1925

Once riding in old Baltimore,
    Heart-filled, head-filled with glee,
I saw a Baltimorean
    Keep looking straight at me.

Now I was eight and very small,
    And he was no whit bigger,
And so I smiled, but he poked out
    His tongue and called me, "Nigger."

I saw the whole of Baltimore
    From May until December:
Of all the things that happened there   10
    That's all that I remember.

DYLAN THOMAS   (1914–1953)

FERN HILL   1946

Now as I was young and easy under the apple boughs
About the lilting house and happy as the grass was green,
    The night above the dingle° starry,   *small wooded valley*
        Time let me hail and climb
    Golden in the heydays of his eyes,
And honored among wagons I was prince of the apple towns
And once below a time I lordly had the trees and leaves
        Trail with daisies and barley
    Down the rivers of the windfall light.

And as I was green and carefree, famous among the barns   10
About the happy yard and singing as the farm was home,
    In the sun that is young once only,
        Time let me play and be
    Golden in the mercy of his means,
And green and golden I was huntsman and herdsman, the calves
Sang to my horn, the foxes on the hills barked clear and cold,
        And the sabbath rang slowly
    In the pebbles of the holy streams.

All the sun long it was running, it was lovely, the hay
Fields high as the house, the tunes from the chimneys, it was air   20
    And playing, lovely and watery
        And fire green as grass.
    And nightly under the simple stars
As I rode to sleep the owls were bearing the farm away,
All the moon long I heard, blessed among stables, the nightjars[1]
    Flying with the ricks, and the horses
        Flashing into the dark.

And then to awake, and the farm, like a wanderer white
With the dew, come back, the cock on his shoulder: it was all
    Shining, it was Adam and maiden,   30
        The sky gathered again
    And the sun grew round that very day.
So it must have been after the birth of the simple light
In the first, spinning place, the spellbound horses walking warm
    Out of the whinnying green stable
        On to the fields of praise.

[1] Nightjars are harsh-sounding nocturnal birds.

And honored among foxes and pheasants by the gay house
Under the new made clouds and happy as the heart was long,
    In the sun born over and over,
        I ran my heedless ways,   40
        My wishes raced through the house high hay
And nothing I cared, at my sky blue trades, that time allows
In all his tuneful turning so few and such morning songs
    Before the children green and golden
        Follow him out of grace.

Nothing I cared, in the lamb white days, that time would take me
Up to the swallow thronged loft by the shadow of my hand,
    In the moon that is always rising,
        Nor that riding to sleep
        I should hear him fly with the high fields   50
And wake to the farm forever fled from the childless land.
Oh as I was young and easy in the mercy of his means,
        Time held me green and dying
    Though I sang in my chains like the sea.

FOR ANALYSIS

1. What emotional impact does the color imagery in the poem provide?

2. Trace the behavior of "time" in the poem.

3. Fairy tales often begin with the words "once upon a time." Why does Thomas alter that formula in line 7?

4. Explain the **paradox** in line 53.

WRITING TOPICS

1. Lines 17–18, 30, and 45–46 incorporate religious language and biblical **allusion.** How do those allusions clarify the poet's vision of his childhood?

2. Compare this poem with either Hopkins's "Spring and Fall" (p. 145) or Housman's "When I Was One-and-Twenty" (p. 148).

RUTH STONE   (B. 1915)

METAPHORS OF THE TREE   2002

The play yard with its automobile tire
hanging from the one tree, like a lynching.

The tree wrapped around itself in multiple muscles;
a clump of trees come together under the bark,
twisting up; a corporate tree, the only tree in the yard.

The tree with its thousand subsidiaries
cluster-blooming, testing the air, expanding;
its product underground, growing chemicals;
pulling the guts from the soil, involved with the fungus.

The tree, tilting its leaves to capture bullets of light; inhaling,   10
exhaling; its many thousand stomata breathing, creating the air.

Then the absent tree when the play yard is paved with asphalt;
a blank space where the tree was, a space that the birds pass over,
where the wind does not pause.

FOR ANALYSIS

1. What effect does the **simile** connecting the tire to a "lynching" (l. 2) have on the **tone** of the poem?

2. For each of the **stanzas,** ask yourself, In moral terms, is this a positive or a negative metaphor for a tree? Explain your answers.

3. Is the conclusion expected or shocking? Explain.

WRITING TOPIC

Explain the theme of this poem. Keep in mind that while the poet uses many metaphors to describe the tree, the tree is both literal (it grows in a yard and is then cut down) and, as the title suggests, metaphoric (it represents both threats and promises).

LAWRENCE FERLINGHETTI   (B. 1919)

CONSTANTLY RISKING ABSURDITY   1958

Constantly risking absurdity
          and death
   whenever he performs
         above the heads
            of his audience
the poet like an acrobat
       climbs on rime
         to a high wire of his own making
and balancing on eyebeams
      above a sea of faces   10
   paces his way
      to the other side of day

performing entrechats[1]
and sleight-of-foot tricks
and other high theatrics
and all without mistaking
any thing
for what it may not be

For he's the super realist
who must perforce perceive   20
taut truth
before the taking of each stance or step
in his supposed advance
toward that still higher perch
where Beauty stands and waits
with gravity
to start her death-defying leap

And he
a little charleychaplin[2] man
who may or may not catch   30
her fair eternal form
spreadeagled in the empty air
of existence

PHILIP LARKIN   (1922–1985)

A STUDY OF READING HABITS   1960

When getting my nose in a book
Cured most things short of school,
It was worth ruining my eyes
To know I could still keep cool,
And deal out the old right hook
To dirty dogs twice my size.

Constantly Risking Absurdity
[1] In ballet, a leap straight upward in which the legs are repeatedly crossed or heels struck together.
[2] Charles Spencer Chaplin (1889–1977) was cinema's most celebrated comedian of the silent-film era. His trademark was the mustachioed Little Tramp, whose pathos and comedy were accompanied by extraordinary acrobatic skills.

Later, with inch-thick specs,
Evil was just my lark:
Me and my cloak and fangs
Had ripping times in the dark.   10
The women I clubbed with sex!
I broke them up like meringues.

Don't read much now: the dude
Who lets the girl down before
The hero arrives, the chap
Who's yellow and keeps the store,
Seem far too familiar. Get stewed:
Books are a load of crap.

FOR ANALYSIS

1. What sort of books did the speaker read as a schoolchild (stanza 1)?

2. How might reading cure "most things short of school" (l. 2)?

3. Describe the change in the speaker's reading habits revealed in the second stanza.

4. Explain why the speaker asserts that he doesn't read much now (l. 13). What experiences led him to the conclusion that "[b]ooks are a load of crap" (l. 18)?

WRITING TOPIC

Describe the poem's metrical pattern and its **rhyme** scheme. See **ballad** in the "Glossary of Literary Terms" (p. 1431), read some ballads in this book, and argue for or against the proposition that this poem is a modern ballad.

THIS BE THE VERSE   1974

They fuck you up, your mum and dad.
    They may not mean to, but they do.
They fill you with the faults they had
    And add some extra, just for you.

But they were fucked up in their turn
    By fools in old-style hats and coats,
Who half the time were soppy-stern
    And half at one another's throats.

Man hands on misery to man.
    It deepens like a coastal shelf.   10
Get out as early as you can,
    And don't have any kids yourself.

AUDRE LORDE (1934–1992)

HANGING FIRE 1978

I am fourteen
and my skin has betrayed me
the boy I cannot live without
still sucks his thumb
in secret
how come my knees are
always so ashy
what if I die
before morning
and momma's in the bedroom   10
with the door closed.

I have to learn how to dance
in time for the next party
my room is too small for me
suppose I die before graduation
they will sing sad melodies
but finally
tell the truth about me
There is nothing I want to do
and too much   20
that has to be done
and momma's in the bedroom
with the door closed.

Nobody even stops to think
about my side of it
 I should have been on Math Team
my marks were better than his
why do I have to be
the one
wearing braces
I have nothing to wear tomorrow   30
will I live long enough
to grow up
and momma's in the bedroom
with the door closed.

FOR ANALYSIS

1. How do you think the speaker's skin has "betrayed" her (l. 2)?

2. What does the expression *hang fire* mean? In what ways is the speaker hanging fire?

MAKING CONNECTIONS

Compare the speaker's repeated statements about her fear of death in "Hanging Fire" to the wounded child in Hanan Mikha'il 'Ashrawi's "From the Diary of an Almost Four-Year-Old" (p. 163). What is different about the attitudes expressed—toward life, toward death, toward growing up—in these two poems?

WRITING TOPICS

1. Look up the origins of the phrase used in the poem's title. Where does it come from? Is there anything about this original meaning that might add to the poem's meaning?

2. Analyze the structure of the poem—how it is divided into parts, how certain lines and images and feelings are repeated. How does the structure enrich the poem's meanings?

STEPHEN DOBYNS   (B. 1941)

DO THEY HAVE A REASON?   2000

Life begins, you make some friends,
what futures you plan for one another.
No failures here, no one sent to prison.
When you first start out, you can't imagine
you won't succeed, even if the road's unclear
and your parents call you dumb, your brother
pulls your cars, somehow you'll make it work,
even if what you want is to rob a bank,
to be a first-rate crook, but mostly we start out
idealistic—doctors, astrophysicists—or maybe   10
we have a taste for fame and money—actors,
stockbrokers—but always something at the top
and always several: Maybe I'll be this or that,
we say. And mostly our friends encourage us
just so we'll encourage them. Sure you'll be
a surgeon, they say, you got the hands. So we
loll about the riverbank with our first cigars
and watch the ducks float by. It's summer
and third grade is dead forever. We lean back
on our elbows and blow some smoke. I'll be   20

an astronaut, you say, and own a fleet of trucks.
You bet, says your cousin, and I'll play ball.
And he's the guy who dies a drunk at thirty-five.
Think of the moment when you at last catch on.
Some kids get it right away, others not so quick.
One day you experience a click in your head
as the world turns from one place to another.
Does the sky change color, the river get colder?
Like when you stroll into the local diner after school
for a Coke and a hot pretzel, a place you visit
every day to meet your pals, but today your pals   30
are having fun someplace else, and there instead
are half a dozen kids you've never seen before:
sixth graders for certain. They snatch your pack,
toss your stuff around, one tears your shirt,
another rips your books. What's their reason?
They don't need a reason. When the world
you love is changed for another, it's like that.

LOUISE GLÜCK   (B. 1943)

THE SCHOOL CHILDREN   1975

The children go forward with their little satchels.
And all morning the mothers have labored
to gather the late apples, red and gold,
like words of another language.

And on the other shore
are those who wait behind great desks
to receive these offerings.

How orderly they are—the nails
on which the children hang
their overcoats of blue or yellow wool.   10

And the teachers shall instruct them in silence
and the mothers shall scour the orchards for a way out,
drawing to themselves the gray limbs of the fruit trees
bearing so little ammunition.

HANAN MIKHA'IL 'ASHRAWI (B. 1946)

FROM THE DIARY OF AN
ALMOST-FOUR-YEAR-OLD   1988

Tomorrow, the bandages
will come off. I wonder
will I see half an orange,
half an apple, half my
mother's face
with my one remaining eye?

I did not see the bullet
but felt its pain
exploding in my head.
His image did not   10
vanish, the soldier
with a big gun, unsteady
hands, and a look in
his eyes
I could not understand.

If I can see him so clearly
with my eyes closed,
it could be that inside our heads
we each have one spare set
of eyes   20
to make up for the ones we lose.

Next month, on my birthday,
I'll have a brand new glass eye,
maybe things will look round
and fat in the middle—
I've gazed through all my marbles,
they made the world look strange.

I hear a nine-month-old
has also lost an eye,
I wonder if my soldier   30
shot her too—a soldier
looking for little girls who
look him in the eye—
I'm old enough, almost four,
I've seen enough of life,

but she's just a baby
who didn't know any better.

FOR ANALYSIS

1. How was the speaker injured?

2. What words in this poem would not ordinarily be part of the vocabulary of an average four-year-old? Does the use of such language detract from the poem's impact? Explain.

3. Discuss the effect of the words "a look in / his eyes / I could not understand" (ll. 13–15).

4. Discuss the various meanings of "look him in the eye" (l. 33).

5. The speaker contrasts her almost four years of experience with the innocence of a nine-month-old baby. What impact does this have?

WRITING TOPIC

Armed conflict often creates "collateral damage." Define the term. Under what circumstances is such damage morally justified or plainly immoral?

KATHERINE MCALPINE   (B. 1948)

PLUS C'EST LA MÊME CHOSE[1]   1994

LINES WRITTEN UPON CHAPERONING THE
SEVENTH GRADE DANCE

When did these little girls turn into women?
Lip-glossed and groomed, alarmingly possessed
of polish, poise and, in some cases, breasts,
they're clustered at one corner of the gym in
elaborate indifference to the boys,
who, at the other end, convene with cables,
adjusting speakers, tuners and turntables
to make the optimum amount of noise.
If nobody plans to dance, what's this dance for?
Finally the boys all gather in formation,   10
tentatively begin a group migration
across the fearsome distance of the floor—
and then retreat, noticing no one's there.
The girls have gone, en masse, to fix their hair.

Plus C'est la Même Chose
   [1] The title comes from the French expression *Plus ça change, plus c'est la même chose,* which means "The more things change, the more they remain the same."

FOR ANALYSIS

1. What is the **tone** of this sonnet? Point to specific elements to support your response.

2. Explain the title.

3. Explain the appropriateness of "elaborate indifference" (l. 5), "gather in formation" (l. 10), and "migration" (l. 11).

WRITING TOPIC

Write an essay in which you use one of the following as a thesis statement: (1) the poem embodies a traditional, sexist view of gender differences, or (2) the poem describes, without making a judgment, the culturally determined differences between males and females. If you disagree with both of these statements, formulate your own.

RITA DOVE (B. 1952)

LAMENTATIONS 1995

Throw open the shutters
to your darkened residences
can you hear the pipes playing,
their hunger shaking the olive branches?
To hear them sighing and not answer
is to deny this world, descend rung
by rung into no loss and no desire.
Listen: empty yet full, silken
air and brute tongue,
they are saying.   10
To refuse to be born is one thing—
but once you are here,
you'd do well to stop crying
and suck the good milk in.

SANDRA CISNEROS (B. 1954)

MY WICKED WICKED WAYS 1987

This is my father.
See? He is young.
He looks like Errol Flynn.[1]

My Wicked Wicked Ways
  [1] Errol Flynn (1909–1959) was a handsome leading man in many Hollywood movies during the 1930s and 1940s.

He is wearing a hat
that tips over one eye,
a suit that fits him good,
and baggy pants.

He is also wearing
those awful shoes,
the two-toned ones   10
my mother hates.

Here is my mother.
She is not crying.
She cannot look into the lens
because the sun is bright.
The woman,
the one my father knows,
is not here.
She does not come till later.

My mother will get very mad.   20
Her face will turn red
and she will throw one shoe.
My father will say nothing.
After a while everyone
will forget it.
Years and years will pass.
My mother will stop mentioning it.

This is me she is carrying.
I am a baby.
She does not know   30
I will turn out bad.

FOR ANALYSIS

1. Why does the speaker tell us that her mother "is not crying" (l. 13)?
2. What will the speaker's mother "get very mad" about (l. 20)?
3. What is the connection between the last four lines and the rest of the poem?

WRITING TOPIC

Discuss the meaning of the final line of the poem. What does the speaker mean by
bad?

JOHN BREHM (B. 1955)

AT THE POETRY READING 1998

I can't keep my eyes off the poet's
wife's legs—they're so much more
beautiful than anything he might
be saying, though I'm no longer
in a position really to judge,
having stopped listening sometime ago.
He's from the Iowa Writers' Workshop
and can therefore get along fine
without my attention. He started in
reading poems about his childhood—   10
barns, cornsnakes, gradeschool, flowers,
that sort of stuff—the loss of
innocence he keeps talking about
between poems, which I can relate to,
especially under these circumstances.
Now he's on to science, a poem
about hydrogen, I think, he's trying
to imagine himself turning into hydrogen.
Maybe he'll succeed. I'm imagining
myself sliding up his wife's fluid,   20
rhythmic, lusciously curved, black-
stockinged legs, imagining them arched
around my shoulders, wrapped around my back.
My God, why doesn't he write poems about her!
He will, no doubt, once she leaves him,
leaves him for another poet, perhaps,
the observant, uninnocent one, who knows
a poem when it sits down in a room with him.

EVELYN LAU (B. 1971)

SOLIPSISM 1994

I spend days at the gym enclosed by four mirrors,
a silver pole balanced on my shoulders.
I slide keys out of the machines, slot them lower
to lift my weights with increased strain,
to pump the last reps in my personal program.

I watch on television a show that is being taped
in the studio across the hall. It is shown simultaneously
in the green room but will not be broadcast publicly
until next week. I feel very special
yet out of step with the rest of the viewing world.   10

In aerobics class we lie on our backs and pump our hips
repetitively towards the ceiling. Soon lovers will come
to smother us with their bodies, pumping equally.
Now there are only our midriffs rising and lowering,
our shapes contained in lycra and cotton.

I break cold medication out of its blister wrap
in the green room, I swallow sedatives in soothing colours.
The makeup person touches my face with gentle fingers.
She covers me in a smock the colour of roses
and together we watch the changes in the mirror.   20

The faces around me are glazed with perspiration,
their bodies are lovely and plain by turns.
I take my position at the exercise bar between two bodies.
I resume the process of making myself perfect
as they both are, yet not like them, uniquely myself.

I see my body in four funhouse mirrors.
It is shaped exactly like an upended couch.
The gym is a marvel of bodies in motion,
lineups are polite at the popular machines,
active minds are occupied with weight goals, diet instructions.   30

The audience would wave if the camera glanced their way.
It would stampede to the nearest exit in case of fire
or planted bomb, crushing members of its own sex and race.
I am very calm. I have rehearsed my instructions,
not once do I stray from the script or structure.

Journalists declare there are weather and wars
happening outside the fitness-club doors,
but I hear only music and the splash of water fountains.
I only notice how others have tied back their hair.
Rarely do I look outside, for something other or more.   40

FOR ANALYSIS

1. Look up *solipsism* in the dictionary. Is it an appropriate title for this poem? Explain.

2. Consider the first three lines of the last stanza. How do they relate to the central issue of this poem?

3. How might you define *perfect* as it is used in line 24? Can the speaker make herself perfect in the fitness club? Explain.

WRITING TOPICS

1. Describe the circumstances that would allow you to feel that nothing exists or is real but yourself.

2. Using someone you know—or know of—as a model, describe the behavior of a solipsistic person. Do you believe that solipsism is a desirable or an undesirable trait? Explain.

CONNECTING POEMS: REVISITING FAIRY TALES

For centuries, fairy tales were often dark and violent stories that served as warnings to children. More recently, however, they have been tamed, stripped of violence and sexual undertones, and have adopted a new focus on magical worlds and happy endings—seemingly unrealistic views of the human experience. Despite this shift, fairy tales continue to encompass some of the most significant cultural assumptions—fears, beliefs, and ideas about how the world is and should be. The poems in this unit revisit fairy tales that are likely to be familiar to you. As you read the poems, keep the two kinds of fairy tales in mind. Do the poems remain faithful to their innocent models? Do they describe a magical world? Do they end happily? Or do they focus on the darker side of experience? Are they realistic? How does the language in which they are written—the kinds of words and images and tone they use—reflect their relationship to fairy tales?

ANNE SEXTON   (1928-1974)

CINDERELLA   1971

You always read about it:
the plumber with twelve children
who wins the Irish Sweepstakes.
From toilets to riches.
That story.

Or the nursemaid,
some luscious sweet from Denmark
who captures the oldest son's heart.
From diapers to Dior.
That story.   10

Or a milkman who serves the wealthy,
eggs, cream, butter, yogurt, milk,
the white truck like an ambulance
who goes into real estate
and makes a pile.
From homogenized to martinis at lunch.

Or the charwoman
who is on the bus when it cracks up
and collects enough from the insurance.
From mops to Bonwit Teller.   20
That story.

Once
the wife of a rich man was on her deathbed
and she said to her daughter Cinderella:
Be devout. Be good. Then I will smile
down from heaven in the seam of a cloud.
The man took another wife who had
two daughters, pretty enough
but with hearts like blackjacks.
Cinderella was their maid.   30
She slept on the sooty hearth each night
and walked around looking like Al Jolson.
Her father brought presents home from town,
jewels and gowns for the other women
but the twig of a tree for Cinderella.
She planted that twig on her mother's grave
and it grew to a tree where a white dove sat.
Whenever she wished for anything the dove
would drop it like an egg upon the ground.
The bird is important, my dears, so heed him.   40

Next came the ball, as you all know.
It was a marriage market.
The prince was looking for a wife.
All but Cinderella were preparing
and gussying up for the big event.
Cinderella begged to go too.

Her stepmother threw a dish of lentils
into the cinders and said: Pick them
up in an hour and you shall go.
The white dove brought all his friends;   50
all the warm wings of the fatherland came,
and picked up the lentils in a jiffy.
No, Cinderella, said the stepmother,
you have no clothes and cannot dance.
That's the way with stepmothers.

Cinderella went to the tree at the grave
and cried forth like a gospel singer:
Mama! Mama! My turtledove,
send me to the prince's ball!
The bird dropped down a golden dress   60
and delicate little gold slippers.
Rather a large package for a simple bird.
So she went. Which is no surprise.
Her stepmother and sisters didn't
recognize her without her cinder face
and the prince took her hand on the spot
and danced with no other the whole day.

As nightfall came she thought she'd better
get home. The prince walked her home
and she disappeared into the pigeon house   70
and although the prince took an axe and broke
it open she was gone. Back to her cinders.
These events repeated themselves for three days.
However on the third day the prince
covered the palace steps with cobbler's wax
and Cinderella's gold shoe stuck upon it.

Now he would find whom the shoe fit
and find his strange dancing girl for keeps.
He went to their house and the two sisters
were delighted because they had lovely feet.   80
The eldest went into a room to try the slipper on
but her big toe got in the way so she simply
sliced it off and put on the slipper.
The prince rode away with her until the white dove
told him to look at the blood pouring forth.

That is the way with amputations.
They don't just heal up like a wish.

The other sister cut off her heel
but the blood told as blood will.
The prince was getting tired.   90
He began to feel like a shoe salesman
but he gave it one last try.
This time Cinderella fit into the shoe
like a love letter into its envelope.

At the wedding ceremony
the two sisters came to curry favor
and the white dove pecked their eyes out.
Two hollow spots were left
like soup spoons.

Cinderella and the prince   100
lived, they say, happily ever after,
like two dolls in a museum case
never bothered by diapers or dust,
never arguing over the timing of an egg,
never telling the same story twice,
never getting a middle-aged spread,
their darling smiles pasted on for eternity.
Regular Bobbsey Twins.[1]
That story.

FOR ANALYSIS

1. Where does one usually find the first four "stories" mentioned in the poem? Why do such stories interest readers?

2. Do you remember your feelings as a child in response to the story of Cinderella— particularly Cinderella's success? How are those feelings modified by the last stanza?

WRITING TOPIC

The language and formal structure of this poem resemble prose. Through examination of the image patterns and individual lines, describe the qualities that make the piece a poem.

Cinderella
[1] The ever-cheerful central figures in a series of children's books.

BRUCE BENNETT (B. 1940)

THE TRUE STORY OF SNOW WHITE 1989

Almost before the princess had grown cold
Upon the floor beside the bitten fruit,
The Queen gave orders to her men to shoot
The dwarfs, and thereby clinched her iron hold
Upon the state. Her mirror learned to lie,
And no one dared speak ill of her for fear
She might through her devices overhear.
So, in this manner, many years passed by,
And now today not even children weep
When someone whispers how, for her beauty's sake,   10
A child was harried once into a grove
And doomed, because her heart was full of love,
To lie forever in unlovely sleep
Which not a prince on earth has power to break.

FOR ANALYSIS

1. Describe the **allusion** at the center of this poem, and explain how it contributes to
the poem's force.

2. Note that the poem is a **sonnet.** Explain how this choice of form contributes an
ironic element that reinforces the poem's grim message.

3. Why would the mirror learn "to lie" (l. 5)? What "devices" (l. 7) might frighten the
Queen's subjects?

WRITING TOPIC

Compare and contrast this sonnet (see "Glossary of Literary Terms" on p. 1439) with two
others from the text, and characterize each. How do they differ, and how do they resemble each other? Are they personal lyrics, political statements, or psychological insights?

MARILYN HACKER (D. 1942)

CONTE 1981

(CINDERELLA, SOMETIME AFTER THE AFFAIR

OF THE GLASS/FUR SLIPPER)

First of all, I'm bored. It's not
what you'd think. Every day, meetings
I can't attend, I sit and sit and stick

my fingers with petit-point needles. Ladies
ignore me, or tell me all their petty secrets
(petty because *they* can't attend meetings)
about this man or that. Even his mistress—
you would have assumed he had a mistress—
gritted her teeth and had me come to lunch
and whined about the way she was mistreated.
And I suppose she's right, she was mistreated.   10
The plumbing is appalling, but I won't
go into that. He is forever brooding
on lost choices he might have made; before
three days had passed, I'd heard, midnight to dawn,
about the solitary life he craved.
Why *not* throw it all up, live on the coast
and fish, no, no, impossible with wives!
Why *not* throw it all up, live on the coast,
or cut my hair, teach (what?) little girls   20
and live at home with you? I schooled myself
for this, despised *you* for going to meetings,
reading instead of scrubbing, getting fat
(scorn of someone who burns off bread and puddings).
I made enduring tedium my virtue.
I'll have to keep my virtue. I could envy
you, but I'm sick of envy. Please allow
me now, at least, to call you sisters. Yours, C.

FOR ANALYSIS

1. This poem turns out to be a letter. To whom do you think it was written?

2. How does the original fairy tale of Cinderella end? When does this poem's narrative take place? Does it end the same way?

3. A *conte* is a short tale of adventure. Is this poem a short tale of adventure? Why do you think Hacker chose that word for the title?

WRITING TOPIC

Write two of your own letters from one character in a well-known story to another. Make sure the characters you choose are from one story in which things have turned out as expected, and another in which they have not.

HAZEL TELLS LAVERNE   1976

last night
im cleanin out my
howard johnsons ladies room
when all of a sudden
up pops this frog
musta come from the sewer
swimmin aroun an tryin ta
climb up the sida the bowl
so i goes ta flushm down
but sohelpmegod he starts talkin   10
bout a golden ball
an how i can be a princess
me a princess
well my mouth drops
all the way to the floor
an he says
kiss me just kiss me
once on the nose
well i screams
ya little green pervert   20
an i hitsm with my mop
an has ta flush
the toilet down three times
me
a princess

FOR ANALYSIS

1. How would you describe Hazel?

2. What does Hazel's language tell us about her?

3. Would the use of punctuation change the poem in any way?

WRITING TOPIC

Write an analysis of this poem's humor.

MAKING CONNECTIONS

1. Compare the endings of Sexton's "Cinderella" (p. 169) and Hacker's "Conte"
(p. 173) to the ending of the original story, in terms of both events and **tone.** Is either
happy?

2. Each of the original fairy tales on which the selections in this unit are based feature royalty. How do the poems handle the element of royalty? What does royalty mean in the originals? What does it mean in these poems?

3. In what ways is each of these poems about the dream of a better life? What do the poems say about those dreams?

CONNECTING POEMS: VOICES OF EXPERIENCE

The poems in this unit explore the role parents, or parental figures, play in guiding children through the innocence of childhood into the world of experience. The poems also address the contradictions and inconsistencies inherent in this role and in the world of human experience. As you read, pay attention not only to the ways the experienced try to guide the innocent—and the difficulties they have doing it—but also to the texture of their voices. How have the poets personalized these voices? How does the way they speak relate to what they have to say? What do the innocent have to say about the advice they are being given, and how does the way the poets have them express their thoughts relate to the how we hear them?

LANGSTON HUGHES (1902–1967)

MOTHER TO SON 1926

Well, son, I'll tell you:
Life for me ain't been no crystal stair.
It's had tacks in it,
And splinters,
And boards torn up,
And places with no carpet on the floor—
Bare.
But all the time
I'se been a-climbin' on,
And reachin' landin's,   10
And turnin' corners,
And sometimes goin' in the dark
Where there ain't been no light.
So boy, don't you turn back.
Don't you set down on the steps
'Cause you finds it's kinder hard.
Don't you fall now—

For I'se still goin', honey,
I'se still climbin',
And life for me ain't been no crystal stair.   20

FOR ANALYSIS

1. What are the two kinds of stairs in this poem? What do they stand for?

2. Analyze the structure of the poem. What are the functions of the various instances of repetition?

WRITING TOPIC

Write a poem, "Son to Mother," in response to Hughes's poem. It should be about the same topic but have a different point of view, perhaps with a different **tone** or sense.

PETER MEINKE   (B. 1932)

ADVICE TO MY SON   1965

—FOR TIM

The trick is, to live your days
as if each one may be your last
(for they go fast, and young men lose their lives
in strange and unimaginable ways)
but at the same time, plan long range
(for they go slow: if you survive
the shattered windshield and the bursting shell
you will arrive
at our approximation here below
of heaven or hell).   10

To be specific, between the peony and the rose
plant squash and spinach, turnips and tomatoes;
beauty is nectar
and nectar, in a desert, saves—
but the stomach craves stronger sustenance
than the honied vine.
Therefore, marry a pretty girl
after seeing her mother;
speak truth to one man,
work with another;   20
and always serve bread with your wine.

But, son,
always serve wine.

FOR ANALYSIS

1. Explain how the advice of lines 17–21 is logically related to the preceding lines.
2. What do the final two lines tell the reader about the speaker?

WRITING TOPIC

The advice of the first stanza seems contradictory. In what ways does the second stanza attempt to resolve the contradiction or explain the "trick" (l. 1)? What do the various plants and the bread and wine symbolize?

ROBERT MEZEY   (B. 1935)

MY MOTHER   1970

My mother writes from Trenton,
a comedian to the bone
but underneath, serious
and all heart. "Honey," she says,
"be a mensch[1] and Mary too,
it's no good to worry, you
are doing the best you can
your Dad and everyone
thinks you turned out very well
as long as you pay your bills   10
nobody can say a word
you can tell them to drop dead
so save a dollar it can't
hurt—remember Frank you went
to highschool with? he still lives
with his wife's mother, his wife
works while he writes his books and
did he ever sell a one
the four kids run around naked
36 and he's never had,   20
you'll forgive my expression
even a pot to piss in
or a window to throw it,
such a smart boy he couldn't
read the footprints on the wall

My Mother
[1] A person of integrity and honor.

honey you think you know all
the answers you don't, please try
to put some money away
believe me it wouldn't hurt
artist shmartist life's too short   30
for that kind of, forgive me,
horseshit, I know what you want
better than you, all that counts
is to make a good living
and the best of everything,
as Sholem Aleichem[2] said
he was a great writer did
you ever read his books dear,
you should make what he makes a year
anyway he says some place   40
Poverty is no disgrace
but it's no honor either
that's what I say,
                    love,
                       Mother"

MOLLY PEACOCK   (B. 1947)

OUR ROOM   1984

I tell the children in school sometimes
why I hate alcoholics: my father was one.
"Alcohol" and "disease" I use, and shun
the word "drunk" or even "drinking," since one time
the kids burst out laughing when I told them.
I felt as though they were laughing at me
I waited for them, wounded, remembering how I imagined they'd howl at me
when I was in grade 5. Acting drunk
is a guaranteed screamer, especially   10
for boys. I'm quiet when I sort the junk
of my childhood for them, quiet so we
will all be quiet, and they can ask what
questions they have to and tell about what
happened to them, too. The classroom becomes
oddly lonely when we talk about our homes.

My Mother
  [2] Pen name of the Jewish author Sholem Naumovich Rabinovich.

FOR ANALYSIS

1. The implication of line 6 is that the children were laughing not at the speaker but at something else. What might that have been?

2. Describe the speaker's attitude toward her classmates.

3. Explain the title.

WRITING TOPIC

Have you ever experienced shame about your family? Describe what caused the shame, your feelings at the time, and your present feelings about it.

GARY SOTO (B. 1952)

BEHIND GRANDMA'S HOUSE   1985

At ten I wanted fame. I had a comb
And two Coke bottles, a tube of Bryl-creem.
I borrowed a dog, one with
Mismatched eyes and a happy tongue,
And wanted to prove I was tough
In the alley, kicking over trash cans,
A dull chime of tuna cans falling.
I hurled light bulbs like grenades
And men teachers held their heads,
Fingers of blood lengthening   10
On the ground. I flicked rocks at cats,
Their goofy faces spurred with foxtails.
I kicked fences. I shooed pigeons.
I broke a branch from a flowering peach
And frightened ants with a stream of piss.
I said "Shit," "Fuck you," and "No way
Daddy-O" to an imaginary priest
Until grandma came into the alley,
Her apron flapping in a breeze,
Her hair mussed, and said, "Let me help you,"   20
And punched me between the eyes.

FOR ANALYSIS

1. What word appears more than any other in this poem? What might it mean that it appears so often?

2. Who gets "the last word" in this poem? Of what does this "last word" consist?

3. What is the actual last word in the poem? Is there a pun involved?

WRITING TOPIC

Describe the effect of the poem's account of the speaker's actions. What feeling comes across from the **rhythms** and sounds and images? What moral judgment do you make of the actions they describe? Do these two sets of reactions go together? If not, what is the effect of their being seemingly mismatched?

MAKING CONNECTIONS

1. Compare the **tone** of the advice given in Meinke's "Advice to My Son" (p. 177) with that given in Mezey's "My Mother" (p. 178).

2. While only one of these poems is explicitly about school, all are in some way about education. How is each of these about teaching and learning? Is there only one way to teach?

3. The voices of experience in two of these poems are explicitly ethnic. What effects do the poems get from quoting, directly or indirectly, the ethnic dialects of their experienced voices?

DRAMA

CASE STUDY

CRITICAL RESPONSES
TO *OEDIPUS REX*

Sophocles' *Oedipus* (sometimes *Rex*, sometimes *Tyrannus*, depending on the translator) is the most celebrated of the relatively few ancient Greek tragedies that have survived. Its role in literary history makes it a particularly interesting candidate for in-depth study. We gather here a few texts, ancient and modern, designed to excite further investigation and to introduce you to certain nagging problems in literary theory and interpretation.

In preparation for this case study, first read the definition of *tragedy* in the "Glossary of Literary Terms" (p. 1440); then read the short biography of Sophocles in "Biographical Notes on the Authors" (p. 1418).

The Oedipus story was well known to Sophocles' audience—in fact, it was well known even before Homer told it in *The Odyssey* some 300 years before the dramatist created his play. (A compilation of the Oedipus folklore is included here for your consideration.) Hence, the outcome of the drama did not surprise its audience, and suggestions that the play is a detective story are certainly misleading. Oedipus, as detective, finally understands the twisted sequence of events that bring him down—but the audience knows from the outset that Oedipus is the cause of the plague afflicting Thebes. The ancient Greek audience would be similar to a modern Western audience watching a play based on the life of Jesus or on Moses leading his people out of Egypt. That audience knows that Jesus will be crucified, that the Red Sea will part, even if the characters within the drama do not. *Dramatic irony* occurs when the audience knows things a character does not and, consequently, hears things differently. Remarkably little has been written about how dramatic irony might have affected the sensibilities of the contemporary audience as it watched the inexorable degradation of this noble man.

Sophocles' *Oedipus Rex* raises a serious question. In *The Poetics*, which we excerpt (p. 226), Aristotle, as literary theorist, asserts that a tragic hero falls because of some flaw *(hamartia)* in his character. Generations of commentators such as D. W. Lucas, whose essay we include (p. 239), have been struggling to identify just what flaw brought Oedipus down. Would any action on his part serve to avert the fate that the oracles had proclaimed? Strangely, one of the most pervasive suggestions has been that Oedipus is guilty of *hubris*—overweening pride—for attempting to avert the will of the gods who had predicted that he would murder his father and marry his mother.

In *The Poetics* (ca. 340 B.C.), Aristotle rather casually reveals the assumptions embedded in the politics of his time. He asserts that the protagonist of a tragedy must be a noble man—and the tragedy will be his fall from his noble position. Note that Western literary history mirrors this political perspective: Shakespeare's tragedies (like those of other European writers prior to the nineteenth century) feature kings, princes, and military heroes. Not until the political upheavals that culminated in the French Revolution did writers employ common men and women as proper subjects of tragedy. Although Arthur Miller might conceivably have written something like *Oedipus Rex*, it would be utterly inconceivable for Sophocles to have written something like *Death of a Salesman*.

Francis Fergusson and David Wiles both reflect further on the political aspects of *Oedipus Rex*. Sigmund Freud, on the other hand, borrowed the story of the play, and the name of its eponymous protagonist, for his theory of psychological development. The debate about the meaning of this play attests both to its enduring power and to its resistance to being pinned down.

SOPHOCLES   (496?–406 B.C.)
OEDIPUS REX[1]   CA. 429 B.C.

PERSONS REPRESENTED

Oedipus	Messenger
A Priest	Shepherd of Laïos
Creon	Second Messenger
Teiresias	Chorus of Theban Elders
Iocastê	

Scene
Before the palace of Oedipus, King of Thebes. A central door and two lateral doors open onto a platform which runs the length of the facade. On the platform, right and left, are altars; and three steps lead down into the "orchestra," or chorus-ground. At the beginning of the action these steps are crowded by suppliants who have brought branches and chaplets of olive leaves and who lie in various attitudes of despair. Oedipus enters.

---

[1] An English version by Dudley Fitts and Robert Fitzgerald.

PROLOGUE

Oedipus. My children, generations of the living
  In the line of Kadmos,[2] nursed at his ancient hearth:
  Why have you strewn yourselves before these altars
  In supplication, with your boughs and garlands?
  The breath of incense rises from the city
  With a sound of prayer and lamentation.
                        Children,
  I would not have you speak through messengers,
  And therefore I have come myself to hear you—
  I, Oedipus, who bear the famous name.
  [*To a Priest.*] You, there, since you are eldest in the company,   10
  Speak for them all, tell me what preys upon you,
  Whether you come in dread, or crave some blessing:
  Tell me, and never doubt that I will help you
  In every way I can; I should be heartless
  Were I not moved to find you suppliant here.
Priest. Great Oedipus, O powerful King of Thebes!
  You see how all the ages of our people
  Cling to your altar steps: here are boys
  Who can barely stand alone, and here are priests
  By weight of age, as I am a priest of God,   20
  And young men chosen from those yet unmarried;
  As for the others, all that multitude,
  They wait with olive chaplets in the squares,
  At the two shrines of Pallas,[3] and where Apollo[4]
  Speaks in the glowing embers.
                     Your own eyes
  Must tell you: Thebes is in her extremity
  And can not lift her head from the surge of death.
  A rust consumes the buds and fruits of the earth;
  The herds are sick; children die unborn,
  And labor is vain. The god of plague and pyre   30
  Raids like detestable lightning through the city,
  And all the house of Kadmos is laid waste,
  All emptied, and all darkened: Death alone
  Battens upon the misery of Thebes.

  You are not one of the immortal gods, we know;
  Yet we have come to you to make our prayer

---

[2] The legendary founder of Thebes.   [3] Athena, goddess of wisdom.   [4] God of sunlight, medicine, and prophecy.

As to the man of all men best in adversity
And wisest in the ways of God. You saved us
From the Sphinx,[5] that flinty singer, and the tribute
We paid to her so long; yet you were never   40
Better informed than we, nor could we teach you:
It was some god breathed in you to set us free.

Therefore, O mighty King, we turn to you:
Find us our safety, find us a remedy,
Whether by counsel of the gods or men.
A king of wisdom tested in the past
Can act in a time of troubles, and act well.
Noblest of men, restore
Life to your city! Think how all men call you
Liberator for your triumph long ago;   50
Ah, when your years of kingship are remembered,
Let them not say *We rose, but later fell—*
Keep the State from going down in the storm!
Once, years ago, with happy augury,
You brought us fortune; be the same again!
No man questions your power to rule the land:
But rule over men, not over a dead city!
Ships are only hulls, citadels are nothing,
When no life moves in the empty passageways.

Oedipus. Poor children! You may be sure I know   60
All that you longed for in your coming here.
I know that you are deathly sick; and yet,
Sick as you are, not one is as sick as I.
Each of you suffers in himself alone
His anguish, not another's; but my spirit
Groans for the city, for myself, for you.

I was not sleeping, you are not waking me.
No, I have been in tears for a long while
And in my restless thought walked many ways.
In all my search, I found one helpful course,   70
And that I have taken: I have sent Creon,
Son of Menoikeus, brother of the Queen,
To Delphi, Apollo's place of revelation,
To learn there, if he can,

---

[5] A winged monster, with a woman's head and breasts and a lion's body, that destroyed those who
failed to answer her riddle: "What walks on four feet in the morning, two at noon, and three in the
evening?" When the young Oedipus correctly answered, "Man" ("three" alluding to a cane in old age),
the Sphinx killed herself, and the plague ended.

What act or pledge of mine may save the city.
I have counted the days, and now, this very day,
I am troubled, for he has overstayed his time.
What is he doing? He has been gone too long.
Yet whenever he comes back, I should do ill
To scant whatever hint the god may give.   80
Priest. It is a timely promise. At this instant
    They tell me Creon is here.
Oedipus.   O Lord Apollo!
    May his news be fair as his face is radiant!
Priest. It could not be otherwise: he is crowned with bay,
    The chaplet is thick with berries.
Oedipus.   We shall soon know;
    He is near enough to hear us now.

[*Enter Creon.*]

                        O Prince:
    Brother: son of Menoikeus:
    What answer do you bring us from the god?
Creon. It is favorable. I can tell you, great afflictions
    Will turn out well, if they are taken well.   90
Oedipus. What was the oracle? These vague words
    Leave me still hanging between hope and fear.
Creon. Is it your pleasure to hear me with all these
    Gathered around us? I am prepared to speak,
    But should we not go in?
Oedipus.   Let them all hear it.
    It is for them I suffer, more than for myself.
Creon. Then I will tell you what I heard at Delphi.

    In plain words
    The god commands us to expel from the land of Thebes
    An old defilement that it seems we shelter.   100
    It is a deathly thing, beyond expiation.
    We must not let it feed upon us longer.
Oedipus. What defilement? How shall we rid ourselves of it?
Creon. By exile or death, blood for blood. It was
    Murder that brought the plague-wind on the city.
Oedipus. Murder of whom? Surely the god has named him?
Creon. My lord: long ago Laïos was our king,
    Before you came to govern us.
Oedipus.   I know;
    I learned of him from others; I never saw him.

Creon. He was murdered; and Apollo commands us now   110
  To take revenge upon whoever killed him.
Oedipus. Upon whom? Where are they? Where shall we find a clue
  To solve that crime, after so many years?
Creon. Here in this land, he said.
                              If we make enquiry,
  We may touch things that otherwise escape us.
Oedipus. Tell me: Was Laïos murdered in his house,
  Or in the fields, or in some foreign country?
Creon. He said he planned to make a pilgrimage.
  He did not come home again.
Oedipus.   And was there no one,
  No witness, no companion, to tell what happened?   120
Creon. They were all killed but one, and he got away
  So frightened that he could remember one thing only.
Oedipus. What was that one thing? One may be the key
  To everything, if we resolve to use it.
Creon. He said that a band of highwaymen attacked them,
  Outnumbered them, and overwhelmed the King.
Oedipus. Strange, that a highwayman should be so daring—
  Unless some faction here bribed him to do it.
Creon. We thought of that. But after Laïos' death
  New troubles arose and we had no avenger.   130
Oedipus. What troubles could prevent your hunting down the killers?
Creon. The riddling Sphinx's song
  Made us deaf to all mysteries but her own.
Oedipus. Then once more I must bring what is dark to light.
  It is most fitting that Apollo shows,
  As you do, this compunction for the dead.
  You shall see how I stand by you, as I should,
  To avenge the city and the city's god,
  And not as though it were for some distant friend,
  But for my own sake, to be rid of evil.   140
  Whoever killed King Laïos might—who knows?—
  Decide at any moment to kill me as well.
  By avenging the murdered king I protect myself.
  Come, then, my children: leave the altar steps,
  Lift up your olive boughs!
                        One of you go
  And summon the people of Kadmos to gather here.
  I will do all that I can; you may tell them that.

[*Exit a page.*]

So, with the help of God,
We shall be saved—or else indeed we are lost.
Priest. Let us rise, children. It was for this we came,   150
And now the King has promised it himself.
Phoibos[6] has sent us an oracle; may he descend
Himself to save us and drive out the plague.

[*Exeunt Oedipus and Creon into the palace by the central door. The Priest and the suppliants disperse R and L. After a short pause the Chorus enters the orchestra.*]

PÁRODOS[7]

Chorus. What is God singing in his profound   [*Strophe 1*]
Delphi of gold and shadow?
What oracle for Thebes, the sunwhipped city?
Fear unjoints me, the roots of my heart tremble.
Now I remember, O Healer, your power, and wonder;
Will you send doom like a sudden cloud, or weave it
Like nightfall of the past?
Speak, speak to us, issue of holy sound:
Dearest to our expectancy: be tender!

Let me pray to Athenê, the immortal daughter of Zeus,   [*Antistrophe 1*]
And to Artemis her sister
Who keeps her famous throne in the market ring,
And to Apollo, bowman at the far butts of heaven —

O gods, descend! Like three streams leap against
The fires of our grief, the fires of darkness;
Be swift to bring us rest!

As in the old time from the brilliant house
Of air you stepped to save us, come again!

Now our afflictions have no end,   [*Strophe 2*]
Now all our stricken host lies down   20
And no man fights off death with his mind;

The noble plowland bears no grain,
And groaning mothers can not bear—

---

[6] Phoebus Apollo, god of the sun.   [7] The *Párodos* is the ode sung by the Chorus as it entered the theater and moved down the aisles to the playing area. The *strophe*, in Greek tragedy, is the unit of verse the Chorus chanted as it moved to the left in a dance rhythm. The Chorus sang the *antistrophe* as it moved to the right, and the *epode* while standing still.

See, how our lives like birds take wing,
Like sparks that fly when a fire soars,
To the shore of the god of evening.

The plague burns on, it is pitiless,   [*Antistrophe 2*]
Though pallid children laden with death
Lie unwept in the stony ways,

And old gray women by every path   30
Flock to the strand about the altars
There to strike their breasts and cry
Worship of Phoibos in wailing prayers:
Be kind, God's golden child!

There are no swords in this attack by fire,   [*Strophe 3*]
No shields, but we are ringed with cries.
Send the besieger plunging from our homes
Into the vast sea-room of the Atlantic
Or into the waves that foam eastward of Thrace—
For the day ravages what the night spares—   40
Destroy our enemy, lord of the thunder!
Let him be riven by lightning from heaven!

Phoibos Apollo, stretch the sun's bowstring,   [*Antistrophe 3*]
That golden cord, until it sing for us,
Flashing arrows in heaven!
                              Artemis, Huntress
Race with flaring lights upon our mountains!
O scarlet god, O golden-banded brow,
O Theban Bacchos in a storm of Maenads,[8]

[*Enter Oedipus, C.*]

Whirl upon Death, that all the Undying hate!
Come with blinding cressets, come in joy!   50

SCENE I

Oedipus. Is this your prayer? It may be answered. Come,
   Listen to me, act as the crisis demands,
   And you shall have relief from all these evils.

---

[8] Bacchos is the god of wine and revelry; hence he is scarlet-faced. The Maenads were Bacchos's
female attendants.

Until now I was a stranger to this tale,
As I had been a stranger to the crime.
Could I track down the murderer without a clue?
But now, friends,
As one who became a citizen after the murder,
I make this proclamation to all Thebans:
If any man knows by whose hand Laïos, son of Labdakos,   10
Met his death, I direct that man to tell me everything,
No matter what he fears for having so long withheld it.
Let it stand as promised that no further trouble
Will come to him, but he may leave the land in safety.

Moreover: If anyone knows the murderer to be foreign,
Let him not keep silent: he shall have his reward from me.
However, if he does conceal it, if any man
Fearing for his friend or for himself disobeys this edict,
Hear what I propose to do:

I solemnly forbid the people of this country,   20
Where power and throne are mine, ever to receive that man
Or speak to him, no matter who he is, or let him
Join in sacrifice, lustration, or in prayer.
I decree that he be driven from every house,
Being, as he is, corruption itself to us: the Delphic
Voice of Zeus has pronounced this revelation.
Thus I associate myself with the oracle
And take the side of the murdered king.

As for the criminal, I pray to God—
Whether it be a lurking thief, or one of a number—   30
I pray that that man's life be consumed in evil and wretchedness.
And as for me, this curse applies no less
If it should turn out that the culprit is my guest here,
Sharing my hearth.
                        You have heard the penalty.
I lay it on you now to attend to this
For my sake, for Apollo's, for the sick
Sterile city that heaven has abandoned.
Suppose the oracle had given you no command:
Should this defilement go uncleansed for ever?
You should have found the murderer: your king,   40
A noble king, had been destroyed!
                        Now I,
Having the power that he held before me,
Having his bed, begetting children there

Upon his wife, as he would have, had he lived—
Their son would have been my children's brother,
If Laïos had had luck in fatherhood!
(But surely ill luck rushed upon his reign)—
I say I take the son's part, just as though
I were his son, to press the fight for him
And see it won! I'll find the hand that brought   50
Death to Labdakos' and Polydoros' child,
Heir of Kadmos' and Agenor's line.
And as for those who fail me,
May the gods deny them the fruit of the earth,
Fruit of the womb, and may they rot utterly!
Let them be wretched as we are wretched, and worse!

For you, for loyal Thebans, and for all
Who find my actions right, I pray the favor
Of justice, and of all the immortal gods.
Choragos.[9] Since I am under oath, my lord, I swear   60
I did not do the murder. I can not name
The murderer. Might not the oracle
That has ordained the search tell where to find him?
Oedipus. An honest question. But no man in the world
Can make the gods do more than the gods will.
Choragos. There is one last expedient—
Oedipus.   Tell me what it is.
Though it seem slight, you must not hold it back.
Choragos. A lord clairvoyant to the lord Apollo,
As we all know, is the skilled Teiresias.
One might learn much about this from him, Oedipus.   70
Oedipus. I am not wasting time:
Creon spoke of this, and I have sent for him—
Twice, in fact; it is strange that he is not here.
Choragos. The other matter—that old report—seems useless.
Oedipus. Tell me. I am interested in all reports.
Choragos. The King was said to have been killed by highwaymen.
Oedipus. I know. But we have no witnesses to that.
Choragos. If the killer can feel a particle of dread,
Your curse will bring him out of hiding!
Oedipus.   No.
The man who dared that act will fear no curse.   80

[*Enter the blind seer Teiresias, led by a page.*]

---

[9] Choragos is the leader of the Chorus.

Choragos. But there is one man who may detect the criminal.
　This is Teiresias, this is the holy prophet
　In whom, alone of all men, truth was born.
Oedipus. Teiresias: seer: student of mysteries,
　Of all that's taught and all that no man tells,
　Secrets of Heaven and secrets of the earth:
　Blind though you are, you know the city lies
　Sick with plague; and from this plague, my lord,
　We find that you alone can guard or save us.

　Possibly you did not hear the messengers?　　　　　　　　　　　90
　Apollo, when we sent to him,
　Sent us back word that this great pestilence
　Would lift, but only if we established clearly
　The identity of those who murdered Laïos.
　They must be killed or exiled.
　　　　　　　　　　　　　　　Can you use
　Birdflight or any art of divination
　To purify yourself, and Thebes, and me
　From this contagion? We are in your hands.
　There is no fairer duty
　Than that of helping others in distress.　　　　　　　　　　　100
Teiresias. How dreadful knowledge of the truth can be
　When there's no help in truth! I knew this well,
　But did not act on it: else I should not have come.
Oedipus. What is troubling you? Why are your eyes so cold?
Teiresias. Let me go home. Bear your own fate, and I'll
　Bear mine. It is better so: trust what I say.
Oedipus. What you say is ungracious and unhelpful
　To your native country. Do not refuse to speak.
Teiresias. When it comes to speech, your own is neither
　temperate
　Nor opportune. I wish to be more prudent.　　　　　　　　　110
Oedipus. In God's name, we all beg you—
Teiresias.　　　　　　　　　　　　　You are all ignorant.
　No; I will never tell you what I know.
　Now it is my misery; then, it would be yours.
Oedipus. What! You do know something, and will not tell us?
　You would betray us all and wreck the State?
Teiresias. I do not intend to torture myself, or you.
　Why persist in asking? You will not persuade me.
Oedipus. What a wicked old man you are! You'd try a stone's
　Patience! Out with it! Have you no feeling at all?
Teiresias. You call me unfeeling. If you could only see　　　　120
　The nature of your own feelings . . .

Oedipus.   Why,
  Who would not feel as I do? Who could endure
  Your arrogance toward the city?
Teiresias.   What does it matter!
  Whether I speak or not, it is bound to come.
Oedipus. Then, if "it" is bound to come, you are bound to tell me.
Teiresias. No, I will not go on. Rage as you please.
Oedipus. Rage? Why not!
                              And I'll tell you what I think:
  You planned it, you had it done, you all but
  Killed him with your own hands: if you had eyes,
  I'd say the crime was yours, and yours alone.   130
Teiresias. So? I charge you, then,
  Abide by the proclamation you have made:
  From this day forth
  Never speak again to these men or to me;
  You yourself are the pollution of this country.
Oedipus. You dare say that! Can you possibly think you have
  Some way of going free, after such insolence?
Teiresias. I have gone free. It is the truth sustains me.
Oedipus. Who taught you shamelessness? It was not your craft.
Teiresias. You did. You made me speak. I did not want to.   140
Oedipus. Speak what? Let me hear it again more clearly.
Teiresias. Was it not clear before? Are you tempting me?
Oedipus. I did not understand it. Say it again.
Teiresias. I say that you are the murderer whom you seek.
Oedipus. Now twice you have spat out infamy! You'll pay for it!
Teiresias. Would you care for more? Do you wish to be really angry?
Oedipus. Say what you will. Whatever you say is worthless.
Teiresias. I say you live in hideous shame with those
  Most dear to you. You can not see the evil.
Oedipus. It seems you can go on mouthing like this for ever.   150
Teiresias. I can, if there is power in truth.
Oedipus.   There is:
  But not for you, not for you,
  You sightless, witless, senseless, mad old man!
Teiresias. You are the madman. There is no one here
  Who will not curse you soon, as you curse me.
Oedipus. You child of endless night! You can not hurt me
  Or any other man who sees the sun.
Teiresias. True: it is not from me your fate will come.
  That lies within Apollo's competence,
  As it is his concern.
Oedipus.   Tell me: 160
  Are you speaking for Creon or for yourself?

Teiresias. Creon is no threat. You weave your own doom.

Oedipus. Wealth, power, craft of statesmanship!
Kingly position, everywhere admired!
What savage envy is stored up against these,
If Creon, whom I trusted, Creon my friend,
For this great office which the city once
Put in my hands unsought—if for this power
Creon desires in secret to destroy me!

He has brought this decrepit fortune-teller, this   170
Collector of dirty pennies, this prophet fraud—
Why, he is no more clairvoyant than I am!
                                                    Tell us:
Has your mystic mummery ever approached the truth?
When that hellcat the Sphinx was performing here,
What help were you to these people?
Her magic was not for the first man who came along:
It demanded a real exorcist. Your birds—
What good were they? or the gods, for the matter of that?
But I came by,
Oedipus, the simple man, who knows nothing—   180
I thought it out for myself, no birds helped me!
And this is the man you think you can destroy,
That you may be close to Creon when he's king!
Well, you and your friend Creon, it seems to me,
Will suffer most. If you were not an old man,
You would have paid already for your plot.

Choragos. We can not see that his words or yours
Have been spoken except in anger, Oedipus,
And of anger we have no need. How can God's will
Be accomplished best? That is what most concerns us.   190

Teiresias. You are a king. But where argument's concerned
I am your man, as much a king as you.
I am not your servant, but Apollo's.
I have no need of Creon to speak for me.

Listen to me. You mock my blindness, do you?
But I say that you, with both your eyes, are blind:
You can not see the wretchedness of your life,
Nor in whose house you live, no, nor with whom.
Who are your father and mother? Can you tell me?
You do not even know the blind wrongs   200
That you have done them, on earth and in the world below.
But the double lash of your parents' curse will whip you
Out of this land some day, with only night

Upon your precious eyes.
Your cries then—where will they not be heard?
What fastness of Kithairon[10] will not echo them?
And that bridal-descant of yours—you'll know it then,
The song they sang when you came here to Thebes
And found your misguided berthing.
All this, and more, that you can not guess at now,   210
Will bring you to yourself among your children.

Be angry, then. Curse Creon. Curse my words.
I tell you, no man that walks upon the earth
Shall be rooted out more horribly than you.
Oedipus. Am I to bear this from him?—Damnation
   Take you! Out of this place! Out of my sight!
Teiresias. I would not have come at all if you had not asked me.
Oedipus. Could I have told that you'd talk nonsense, that
   You'd come here to make a fool of yourself, and of me?
Teiresias. A fool? Your parents thought me sane enough.   220
Oedipus. My parents again!—Wait: who were my parents?
Teiresias. This day will give you a father, and break your heart.
Oedipus. Your infantile riddles! Your damned abracadabra!
Teiresias. You were a great man once at solving riddles.
Oedipus. Mock me with that if you like; you will find it true.
Teiresias. It was true enough. It brought about your ruin.
Oedipus. But if it saved this town?
Teiresias [**to the page**].   Boy, give me your hand.
Oedipus. Yes, boy; lead him away.
                              While you are here
   We can do nothing. Go; leave us in peace.   230
Teiresias. I will go when I have said what I have to say.
   How can you hurt me? And I tell you again:
   The man you have been looking for all this time,
   The damned man, the murderer of Laïos,
   That man is in Thebes. To your mind he is foreignborn,
   But it will soon be shown that he is a Theban,
   A revelation that will fail to please.
                              A blind man,
   Who has his eyes now; a penniless man, who is rich now;
   And he will go tapping the strange earth with his staff;
   To the children with whom he lives now he will be   240
   Brother and father—the very same; to her
   Who bore him, son and husband—the very same

---

[10] A mountain range near Thebes where the infant Oedipus was left to die.

Who came to his father's bed, wet with his father's blood.
Enough. Go think that over.
If later you find error in what I have said,
You may say that I have no skill in prophecy.

[*Exit Teiresias, led by his page. Oedipus goes into the palace.*]

ODE I

Chorus.   The Delphic stone of prophecies   [*Strophe 1*]
    Remembers ancient regicide
    And a still bloody hand.
    That killer's hour of flight has come.
    He must be stronger than riderless
    Coursers of untiring wind,
    For the son of Zeus[11] armed with his father's thunder
    Leaps in lightning after him;
    And the Furies follow him, the sad Furies.[12]

    Holy Parnassos' peak of snow   [*Antistrophe 1*]
    Flashes and blinds that secret man,
    That all shall hunt him down:
    Though he may roam the forest shade
    Like a bull gone wild from pasture
    To rage through glooms of stone.
    Doom comes down on him; flight will not avail him;
    For the world's heart calls him desolate,
    And the immortal Furies follow, for ever follow.

    But now a wilder thing is heard   [*Strophe 2*]
    From the old man skilled at hearing Fate in the wingbeat of a bird.   20
    Bewildered as a blown bird, my soul hovers and can not find
    Foothold in this debate, or any reason or rest of mind.
    But no man ever brought—none can bring
    Proof of strife between Thebes' royal house,
    Labdakos' line, and the son of Polybus;[13]
    And never until now has any man brought word
    Of Laïos' dark death staining Oedipus the King.

    Divine Zeus and Apollo hold   [*Antistrophe 2*]
    Perfect intelligence alone of all tales ever told;

---

[11] I.e., Apollo (see note 4).   [12] The goddesses of divine vengeance.   [13] Labdakos was an early king of Thebes and an ancestor of Oedipus. Oedipus is mistakenly referred to as the son of Polybus.

And well though this diviner works, he works in his own night;   30
No man can judge that rough unknown or trust in second sight,
For wisdom changes hands among the wise.
Shall I believe my great lord criminal
At a raging word that a blind old man let fall?
I saw him, when the carrion woman faced him of old,
Prove his heroic mind! These evil words are lies.

SCENE II

Creon. Men of Thebes:
I am told that heavy accusations
Have been brought against me by King Oedipus.

I am not the kind of man to bear this tamely.

If in these present difficulties
He holds me accountable for any harm to him
Through anything I have said or done—why, then,
I do not value life in this dishonor.
It is not as though this rumor touched upon
Some private indiscretion. The matter is grave.   10
The fact is that I am being called disloyal
To the State, to my fellow citizens, to my friends.
Choragos. He may have spoken in anger, not from his mind.
Creon. But did you not hear him say I was the one
Who seduced the old prophet into lying?
Choragos. The thing was said; I do not know how seriously.
Creon. But you were watching him! Were his eyes steady?
Did he look like a man in his right mind?
Choragos.   I do not know.
I can not judge the behavior of great men.
But here is the King himself.

[*Enter Oedipus.*]

Oedipus.   So you dared come back.   20
Why? How brazen of you to come to my house,
You murderer!
                Do you think I do not know
That you plotted to kill me, plotted to steal my throne?
Tell me, in God's name: am I coward, a fool,
That you should dream you could accomplish this?

A fool who could not see your slippery game?
A coward, not to fight back when I saw it?
You are the fool, Creon, are you not? hoping
Without support or friends to get a throne?
Thrones may be won or bought: you could do neither.   30
Creon. Now listen to me. You have talked; let me talk, too.
    You can not judge unless you know the facts.
Oedipus. You speak well: there is one fact; but I find it hard
    To learn from the deadliest enemy I have.
Creon. That above all I must dispute with you.
Oedipus. That above all I will not hear you deny.
Creon. If you think there is anything good in being stubborn
    Against all reason, then I say you are wrong.
Oedipus. If you think a man can sin against his own kind
    And not be punished for it, I say you are mad.   40
Creon. I agree. But tell me: what have I done to you?
Oedipus. You advised me to send for that wizard, did you not?
Creon. I did. I should do it again.
Oedipus.   Very well. Now tell me:
    How long has it been since Laïos —
Creon.   What of Laïos?
Oedipus. Since he vanished in that onset by the road?
Creon. It was long ago, a long time.
Oedipus.   And this prophet,
    Was he practicing here then?
Creon.   He was; and with honor, as now.
Oedipus. Did he speak of me at that time?
Creon.   He never did;
    At least, not when I was present.
Oedipus.   But . . . the enquiry?
    I suppose you held one?
Creon.   We did, but we learned nothing.   50
Oedipus. Why did the prophet not speak against me then?
Creon. I do not know; and I am the kind of man
    Who holds his tongue when he has no facts to go on.
Oedipus. There's one fact that you know, and you could tell it.
Creon. What fact is that? If I know it, you shall have it.
Oedipus. If he were not involved with you, he could not say
    That it was I who murdered Laïos.
Creon. If he says that, you are the one that knows it!—
    But now it is my turn to question you.
Oedipus. Put your questions. I am no murderer.   60
Creon. First then: You married my sister?
Oedipus.   I married your sister.
Creon. And you rule the kingdom equally with her?

Oedipus. Everything that she wants she has from me.
Creon. And I am the third, equal to both of you?
Oedipus. That is why I call you a bad friend.
Creon. No. Reason it out, as I have done.
Think of this first. Would any sane man prefer
Power, with all a king's anxieties,
To that same power and the grace of sleep?
Certainly not I.   70
I have never longed for the king's power—only his rights.
Would any wise man differ from me in this?
As matters stand, I have my way in everything
With your consent, and no responsibilities.
If I were king, I should be a slave to policy.

How could I desire a scepter more
Than what is now mine—untroubled influence?
No, I have not gone mad; I need no honors,
Except those with the perquisites I have now.
I am welcome everywhere; every man salutes me,   80
And those who want your favor seek my ear,
Since I know how to manage what they ask.
Should I exchange this ease for that anxiety?
Besides, no sober mind is treasonable.
I hate anarchy
And never would deal with any man who likes it.

Test what I have said. Go to the priestess
At Delphi, ask if I quoted her correctly.
And as for this other thing: if I am found
Guilty of treason with Teiresias,   90
Then sentence me to death! You have my word
It is a sentence I should cast my vote for
But not without evidence!
                    You do wrong
When you take good men for bad, bad men for good.
A true friend thrown aside—why, life itself
Is not more precious!
                    In time you will know this well:
For time, and time alone, will show the just man,
Though scoundrels are discovered in a day.
Choragos. This is well said, and a prudent man would ponder it.
Judgments too quickly formed are dangerous.   100
Oedipus. But is he not quick in his duplicity?
And shall I not be quick to parry him?
Would you have me stand still, hold my peace, and let

This man win everything, through my inaction?
Creon. And you want—what is it, then? To banish me?
Oedipus. No, not exile. It is your death I want,
   So that all the world may see what treason means.
Creon. You will persist, then? You will not believe me?
Oedipus. How can I believe you?
Creon.   Then you are a fool.
Oedipus. To save myself?
Creon.   In justice, think of me.   110
Oedipus. You are evil incarnate.
Creon.   But suppose that you are wrong?
Oedipus. Still I must rule.
Creon.   But not if you rule badly.
Oedipus. O city, city!
Creon.   It is my city, too!
Choragos. Now, my lords, be still. I see the Queen,
   Iocastê, coming from her palace chambers;
   And it is time she came, for the sake of you both.
   This dreadful quarrel can be resolved through her.

[*Enter Iocastê.*]

Iocastê.   Poor foolish men, what wicked din is this?
   With Thebes sick to death, is it not shameful
   That you should rake some private quarrel up?   120
   [*To Oedipus.*] Come into the house.
                       —And you, Creon, go now:
   Let us have no more of this tumult over nothing.
Creon. Nothing? No, sister: what your husband plans for me
   Is one of two great evils: exile or death.
Oedipus. He is right.
                Why, woman I have caught him squarely
   Plotting against my life.
Creon.   No! Let me die
   Accurst if ever I have wished you harm!
Iocastê.   Ah, believe it, Oedipus!
   In the name of the gods, respect this oath of his
   For my sake, for the sake of these people here!   130

Choragos. Open your mind to her my lord. Be ruled by her,   [*Strophe 1*]
   I beg you!
Oedipus. What would you have me do?
Choragos. Respect Creon's word. He has never spoken like a fool,
   And now he has sworn an oath.
Oedipus.   You know what you ask?

Choragos.   I do.
Oedipus.   Speak on, then.
Choragos. A friend so sworn should not be baited so,
    In blind malice, and without final proof.
Oedipus. You are aware, I hope, that what you say
    Means death for me, or exile at the least.

Choragos. No, I swear by Helios,[14] first in Heaven!   [*Strophe 2*]
    May I die friendless and accurst,   140
    The worst of deaths, if ever I meant that!
        It is the withering fields
            That hurt my sick heart:
        Must we bear all these ills,
            And now your bad blood as well?
Oedipus. Then let him go. And let me die, if I must,
    Or be driven by him in shame from the land of Thebes.
    It is your unhappiness, and not his talk,
    That touches me.
                    As for him—
    Wherever he is, I will hate him as long as I live.   150
Creon. Ugly in yielding, as you were ugly in rage!
    Natures like yours chiefly torment themselves.
Oedipus. Can you not go? Can you not leave me?
Creon.   I can.
    You do not know me; but the city knows me,
    And in its eyes I am just, if not in yours.

[*Exit Creon.*]

Choragos. Lady Iocastê, did you not ask the King to go   [*Antistrophe 1*]
    to his chambers?
Iocastê.   First tell me what has happened
Choragos. There was suspicion without evidence; yet it rankled
    As even false charges will.
Iocastê.   On both sides?
Choragos.   On both.
Iocastê.   But what was said?
Choragos. Oh let it rest, let it be done with!   160
    Have we not suffered enough?
Oedipus. You see to what your decency has brought you:
    You have made difficulties where my heart saw none.

---

[14] The sun god.

Choragos. Oedipus, it is not once only I have told you— [*Antistrophe 2*]
  You must know I should count myself unwise
  To the point of madness, should I now forsake you—
    You, under whose hand,
      In the storm of another time,
      Our dear land sailed out free.
        But now stand fast at the helm! 170
Iocastê. In God's name, Oedipus, inform your wife as well:
  Why are you so set in this hard anger?
Oedipus. I will tell you, for none of these men deserves
  My confidence as you do. It is Creon's work,
  His treachery, his plotting against me.
Iocastê. Go on, if you can make this clear to me.
Oedipus. He charges me with the murder of Laïos.
Iocastê. Has he some knowledge? Or does he speak from hearsay?
Oedipus. He would not commit himself to such a charge,
  But he has brought in that damnable soothsayer 180
  To tell his story.
Iocastê.   Set your mind at rest.
  If it is a question of soothsayers, I tell you
  That you will find no man whose craft gives knowledge
  Of the unknowable.
                  Here is my proof:

  An oracle was reported to Laïos once
  (I will not say from Phoibos himself, but from
  His appointed ministers, at any rate)
  That his doom would be death at the hands of his own son—
  His son, born of his flesh and of mine!

  Now, you remember the story: Laïos was killed 190
  By marauding strangers where three highways meet;
  But his child had not been three days in this world
  Before the King had pierced the baby's ankles
  And left him to die on a lonely mountainside.

  Thus, Apollo never caused that child
  To kill his father, and it was not Laïos' fate
  To die at the hands of his son, as he had feared.
  This is what prophets and prophecies are worth!
  Have no dread of them.
                  It is God himself
  Who can show us what he wills, in his own way. 200
Oedipus. How strange a shadowy memory crossed my mind,
  Just now while you were speaking; it chilled my heart.

Iocastê. What do you mean? What memory do you speak of?

Oedipus. If I understand you, Laïos was killed
    At a place where three roads meet.

Iocastê.   So it was said;
    We have no later story.

Oedipus.   Where did it happen?

Iocastê. Phokis, it is called: at a place where the Theban Way
    Divides into the roads towards Delphi and Daulia.

Oedipus. When?

Iocastê.   We had the news not long before you came
    And proved the right to your succession here.   210

Oedipus. Ah, what net has God been weaving for me?

Iocastê. Oedipus! Why does this trouble you?

Oedipus.   Do not ask me yet.
    First, tell me how Laïos looked, and tell me
    How old he was.

Iocastê.   He was tall, his hair just touched
    With white; his form was not unlike your own.

Oedipus. I think that I myself may be accurst
    By my own ignorant edict.

Iocastê.   You speak strangely.
    It makes me tremble to look at you, my King.

Oedipus. I am not sure that the blind man can not see.
    But I should know better if you were to tell me—   220

Iocastê. Anything — though I dread to hear you ask it.

Oedipus. Was the King lightly escorted, or did he ride
    With a large company, as a ruler should?

Iocastê. There were five men with him in all. One was a herald;
    And a single chariot, which he was driving.

Oedipus. Alas, that makes it plain enough!
                         But who—
    Who told you how it happened?

Iocastê.   A household servant,
    The only one to escape.

Oedipus.   And is he still
    A servant of ours?

Iocastê.   No; for when he came back at last
    And found you enthroned in the place of the dead king,   230
    He came to me, touched my hand with his, and begged
    That I would send him away to the frontier district
    Where only the shepherds go —
    As far away from the city as I could send him.
    I granted his prayer; for although the man was a slave,
    He had earned more than this favor at my hands.

Oedipus. Can he be called back quickly?

Iocastê.   Easily.
  But why?
Oedipus. I have taken too much upon myself
  Without enquiry; therefore I wish to consult him.
Iocastê. Then he shall come.

                              But am I not one also   240
  To whom you might confide these fears of yours?
Oedipus. That is your right; it will not be denied you,
  Now least of all; for I have reached a pitch
  Of wild foreboding. Is there anyone
  To whom I should sooner speak?
  Polybus of Corinth is my father.
  My mother is a Dorian: Meropê.
  I grew up chief among the men of Corinth
  Until a strange thing happened—
  Not worth my passion, it may be, but strange.   250

At a feast, a drunken man maundering in his cups
Cries out that I am not my father's son!

I contained myself that night, though I felt anger
And a sinking heart. The next day I visited
My father and mother, and questioned them. They stormed,
Calling it all the slanderous rant of a fool;
And this relieved me. Yet the suspicion
Remained always aching in my mind;
I knew there was talk; I could not rest;
And finally, saying nothing to my parents,   270
I went to the shrine at Delphi.
The god dismissed my question without reply;
He spoke of other things.
                    Some were clear,
Full of wretchedness, dreadful, unbearable:
As, that I should lie with my own mother, breed
Children from whom all men would turn their eyes;
And that I should be my father's murderer.

I heard all this, and fled. And from that day
Corinth to me was only in the stars
Descending in that quarter of the sky,   270
As I wandered farther and farther on my way
To a land where I should never see the evil
Sung by the oracle. And I came to this country
Where, so you say, King Laïos was killed.

I will tell you all that happened there, my lady.

There were three highways
Coming together at a place I passed;
And there a herald came towards me, and a chariot
Drawn by horses, with a man such as you describe
Seated in it. The groom leading the horses   280
Forced me off the road at his lord's command;
But as this charioteer lurched over towards me
I struck him in my rage. The old man saw me
And brought his double goad down upon my head
As I came abreast.
                          He was paid back, and more!
Swinging my club in this right hand I knocked him
Out of his car, and he rolled on the ground.
                                                I killed him.

I killed them all.
Now if that stranger and Laïos were—kin,
Where is a man more miserable than I?   290
More hated by the gods? Citizen and alien alike
Must never shelter me or speak to me—
I must be shunned by all.
                          And I myself
Pronounced this malediction upon myself!

Think of it: I have touched you with these hands,
These hands that killed your husband. What defilement!

Am I all evil, then? It must be so,
Since I must flee from Thebes, yet never again
See my own countrymen, my own country,
For fear of joining my mother in marriage   300
And killing Polybus, my father.
                          Ah,
If I was created so, born to this fate,
Who could deny the savagery of God?

O holy majesty of heavenly powers!
May I never see that day! Never!
Rather let me vanish from the race of men
Than know the abomination destined me!
Choragos. We too, my lord, have felt dismay at this.
But there is hope: you have yet to hear the shepherd.
Oedipus. Indeed, I fear no other hope is left me.   310

Iocastê. What do you hope from him when he comes?
Oedipus.   This much:
  If his account of the murder tallies with yours,
  Then I am cleared.
Iocastê.   What was it that I said
  Of such importance?
Oedipus.   Why, "marauders," you said,
  Killed the King, according to this man's story.
  If he maintains that still, if there were several,
  Clearly the guilt is not mine: I was alone.
  But if he says one man, singlehanded, did it,
  Then the evidence all points to me.
Iocastê. You may be sure that he said there were several;   320
  And can he call back that story now? He can not.
  The whole city heard it as plainly as I.
  But suppose he alters some detail of it:
  He can not ever show that Laïos' death
  Fulfilled the oracle: For Apollo said
  My child was doomed to kill him; and my child—
  Poor baby!—it was my child that died first.

  No. From now on, where oracles are concerned,
  I would not waste a second thought on any.
Oedipus. You may be right.
                    But come: let someone go   330
  For the shepherd at once. This matter must be settled.
Iocastê. I will send for him.
  I would not wish to cross you in anything.
  And surely not in this.—Let us go in.

[*Exeunt into the palace.*]

ODE II

Chorus. Let me be reverent in the ways of right,   [*Strophe 1*]
  Lowly the paths I journey on;
  Let all my words and actions keep
  The laws of the pure universe
  From highest Heaven handed down.
  For Heaven is their bright nurse,
  Those generations of the realms of light;
  Ah, never of mortal kind were they begot,

Nor are they slaves of memory, lost in sleep:
Their Father is greater than Time, and ages not.   10

The tyrant is a child of Pride   [*Antistrophe 1*]
Who drinks from his great sickening cup
Recklessness and vanity,
Until from his high crest headlong
He plummets to the dust of hope.
That strong man is not strong.
But let no fair ambition be denied;
May God protect the wrestler for the State
In government, in comely policy,
Who will fear God, and on His ordinance wait.   20

Haughtiness and the high hand of disdain   [*Strophe 2*]
Tempt and outrage God's holy law;
And any mortal who dares hold
No immortal Power in awe
Will be caught up in a net of pain:
The price for which his levity is sold.
Let each man take due earnings, then,
And keep his hands from holy things,
And from blasphemy stand apart—
Else the crackling blast of heaven   30
Blows on his head, and on his desperate heart;
Though fools will honor impious men,
In their cities no tragic poet sings.

Shall we lose faith in Delphi's obscurities,   [*Antistrophe 2*]
We who have heard the world's core
Discredited, and the sacred wood
Of Zeus at Elis praised no more?
The deeds and the strange prophecies
Must make a pattern yet to be understood.
Zeus, if indeed you are lord of all,   40
Throned in light over night and day,
Mirror this in your endless mind:
Our masters call the oracle
Words on the wind, and the Delphic vision blind!
Their hearts no longer know Apollo,
And reverence for the gods has died away.

SCENE III

[*Enter Iocastê.*]

Iocastê. Princes of Thebes, it has occurred to me
    To visit the altars of the gods, bearing
    These branches as a suppliant, and this incense.
    Our King is not himself: his noble soul
    Is overwrought with fantasies of dread,
    Else he would consider
    The new prophecies in the light of the old.
    He will listen to any voice that speaks disaster,
    And my advice goes for nothing.

[*She approaches the altar, R.*]

                      To you, then, Apollo,
    Lycean lord, since you are nearest, I turn in prayer.   10
    Receive these offerings, and grant us deliverance
    From defilement. Our hearts are heavy with fear
    When we see our leader distracted, as helpless sailors
    Are terrified by the confusion of their helmsman.

[*Enter Messenger.*]

Messenger. Friends, no doubt you can direct me:
    Where shall I find the house of Oedipus,
    Or, better still, where is the King himself?
Choragos. It is this very place, stranger; he is inside.
    This is his wife and mother of his children.
Messenger. I wish her happiness in a happy house,   20
    Blest in all the fulfillment of her marriage.
Iocastê. I wish as much for you: your courtesy
    Deserves a like good fortune. But now, tell me:
    Why have you come? What have you to say to us?
Messenger. Good news, my lady, for your house and your husband.
Iocastê. What news? Who sent you here?
Messenger.   I am from Corinth.
    The news I bring ought to mean joy for you,
    Though it may be you will find some grief in it.
Iocastê. What is it? How can it touch us in both ways?
Messenger. The people of Corinth, they say,   30
    Intend to call Oedipus to be their king.
Iocastê. But old Polybus—is he not reigning still?

Messenger. No. Death holds him in his sepulchre.

Iocastê. What are you saying? Polybus is dead?

Messenger. If I am not telling the truth, may I die myself.

Iocastê [*to a maidservant*]. Go in, go quickly; tell this to your master.
O riddlers of God's will, where are you now!
This was the man whom Oedipus, long ago,
Feared so, fled so, in dread of destroying him—
But it was another fate by which he died.   40

[*Enter Oedipus, C.*]

Oedipus. Dearest Iocastê, why have you sent for me?

Iocastê. Listen to what this man says, and then tell me
What has become of the solemn prophecies.

Oedipus. Who is this man? What is his news for me?

Iocastê. He has come from Corinth to announce your father's death!

Oedipus. Is it true, stranger? Tell me in your own words.

Messenger. I can not say it more clearly: the King is dead.

Oedipus. Was it by treason? Or by an attack of illness?

Messenger. A little thing brings old men to their rest.

Oedipus. It was sickness, then?

Messenger.   Yes, and his many years.   50

Oedipus. Ah!
Why should a man respect the Pythian hearth,[15] or
Give heed to the birds that jangle above his head?
They prophesied that I should kill Polybus,
Kill my own father; but he is dead and buried,
And I am here—I never touched him, never,
Unless he died of grief for my departure,
And thus, in a sense, through me. No. Polybus
Has packed the oracles off with him underground.
They are empty words.

Iocastê.   Had I not told you so?   60

Oedipus. You had; it was my faint heart that betrayed me.

Iocastê. From now on never think of those things again.

Oedipus. And yet—must I not fear my mother's bed?

Iocastê. Why should anyone in this world be afraid,
Since Fate rules us and nothing can be foreseen?
A man should live only for the present day.

Have no more fear of sleeping with your mother:
How many men, in dreams, have lain with their mothers!
No reasonable man is troubled by such things.

---

[15] Delphi, where Apollo spoke through an oracle.

Oedipus. That is true; only— 70
 If only my mother were not still alive!
 But she is alive. I can not help my dread.
Iocastê. Yet this news of your father's death is wonderful.
Oedipus. Wonderful. But I fear the living woman.
Messenger. Tell me, who is this woman that you fear?
Oedipus. It is Meropê, man; the wife of King Polybus.
Messenger. Meropê? Why should you be afraid of her?
Oedipus. An oracle of the gods, a dreadful saying.
Messenger. Can you tell me about it or are you sworn to silence?
Oedipus. I can tell you, and I will. 80
 Apollo said through his prophet that I was the man
 Who should marry his own mother, shed his father's blood
 With his own hands. And so, for all these years
 I have kept clear of Corinth, and no harm has come—
 Though it would have been sweet to see my parents again.
Messenger. And is this the fear that drove you out of Corinth?
Oedipus. Would you have me kill my father?
Messenger.   As for that
 You must be reassured by the news I gave you.
Oedipus. If you could reassure me, I would reward you.
Messenger. I had that in mind, I will confess: I thought 90
 I could count on you when you returned to Corinth.
Oedipus. No: I will never go near my parents again.
Messenger. Ah, son, you still do not know what you are doing—
Oedipus. What do you mean? In the name of God tell me!
Messenger. —If these are your reasons for not going home.
Oedipus. I tell you, I fear the oracle may come true.
Messenger. And guilt may come upon you through your parents?
Oedipus. That is the dread that is always in my heart.
Messenger. Can you not see that all your fears are groundless?
Oedipus. How can you say that? They are my parents, surely? 100
Messenger. Polybus was not your father.
Oedipus.   Not my father?
Messenger. No more your father than the man speaking to you.
Oedipus. But you are nothing to me!
Messenger.   Neither was he.
Oedipus. Then why did he call me son?
Messenger.   I will tell you:
 Long ago he had you from my hands, as a gift.
Oedipus. Then how could he love me so, if I was not his?
Messenger. He had no children, and his heart turned to you.
Oedipus. What of you? Did you buy me? Did you find me by chance?
Messenger. I came upon you in the crooked pass of Kithairon.
Oedipus. And what were you doing there?

Messenger.   Tending my flocks.   110

Oedipus. A wandering shepherd?

Messenger.   But your savior, son, that day.

Oedipus. From what did you save me?

Messenger.   Your ankles should tell you that.

Oedipus. Ah, stranger, why do you speak of that childhood pain?

Messenger. I cut the bonds that tied your ankles together.

Oedipus. I have had the mark as long as I can remember.

Messenger. That was why you were given the name you bear.[16]

Oedipus. God! Was it my father or my mother who did it?
    Tell me!

Messenger. I do not know. The man who gave you to me
    Can tell you better than I.   120

Oedipus. It was not you that found me, but another?

Messenger. It was another shepherd gave you to me.

Oedipus. Who was he? Can you tell me who he was?

Messenger. I think he was said to be one of Laïos' people.

Oedipus. You mean the Laïos who was king here years ago?

Messenger. Yes; King Laïos; and the man was one of his herdsmen.

Oedipus. Is he still alive? Can I see him?

Messenger.   These men here
    Know best about such things.

Oedipus.   Does anyone here
    Know this shepherd that he is talking about?
    Have you seen him in the fields, or in the town?   130
    If you have, tell me. It is time things were made plain.

Choragos. I think the man he means is that same shepherd
    You have already asked to see. Iocastê perhaps
    Could tell you something.

Oedipus.   Do you know anything
    About him, Lady? Is he the man we have summoned?
    Is that the man this shepherd means?

Iocastê.   Why think of him?
    Forget this herdsman. Forget it all.
    This talk is a waste of time.

Oedipus.   How can you say that?
    When the clues to my true birth are in my hands?

Iocastê. For God's love, let us have no more questioning!   140
    Is your life nothing to you?
    My own is pain enough for me to bear.

Oedipus. You need not worry. Suppose my mother a slave,
    And born of slaves: no baseness can touch you.

Iocastê. Listen to me, I beg you: do not do this thing!

---

[16] *Oedipus* literally means "swollen-foot."

Oedipus. I will not listen; the truth must be made known.

Iocastê. Everything that I say is for your own good!

Oedipus.   My own good
     Snaps my patience, then; I want none of it.

Iocastê. You are fatally wrong! May you never learn who you are!

Oedipus. Go, one of you, and bring the shepherd here.   150
     Let us leave this woman to brag of her royal name.

Iocastê. Ah, miserable!
     That is the only word I have for you now.
     That is the only word I can ever have.

[Exit into the palace.]

Choragos. Why has she left us, Oedipus? Why has she gone
     In such a passion of sorrow? I fear this silence:
     Something dreadful may come of it.

Oedipus.   Let it come!
     However base my birth, I must know about it.
     The Queen, like a woman, is perhaps ashamed
     To think of my low origin. But I   160
     Am a child of Luck; I can not be dishonored.
     Luck is my mother; the passing months, my brothers,
     Have seen me rich and poor.
                                          If this is so,
     How could I wish that I were someone else?
     How could I not be glad to know my birth?

ODE III

Chorus.   If ever the coming time were known   *[Strophe]*
     To my heart's pondering,
     Kithairon, now by Heaven I see the torches
     At the festival of the next full moon,
     And see the dance, and hear the choir sing
     A grace to your gentle shade:
     Mountain where Oedipus was found,
     O mountain guard of a noble race!
     May the god who heals us lend his aid,
     And let that glory come to pass   10
     For our king's cradling-ground.

     Of the nymphs that flower beyond the years,   *[Antistrophe]*
     Who bore you, royal child,

To Pan of the hills or the timberline Apollo,
Cold in delight where the upland clears,
Or Hermês for whom Kyllenê's heights are piled?[17]
Or flushed as evening cloud,
Great Dionysos, roamer of mountains,
He—was it he who found you there,
And caught you up in his own proud   20
Arms from the sweet god-ravisher
Who laughed by the Muses' fountains?

SCENE IV

Oedipus. Sirs: though I do not know the man,
   I think I see him coming, this shepherd we want:
   He is old, like our friend here, and the men
   Bringing him seem to be servants of my house.
   But you can tell, if you have ever seen him.

[*Enter Shepherd escorted by servants.*]

Choragos. I know him, he was Laïos' man. You can trust him.
Oedipus. Tell me first, you from Corinth: is this the shepherd
   We were discussing?
Messenger.   This is the very man.
Oedipus [*to Shepherd*].   Come here. No, look at me. You must answer
   Everything I ask. You belonged to Laïos?   10
Shepherd. Yes: born his slave, brought up in his house.
Oedipus. Tell me what kind of work did you do for him?
Shepherd. I was a shepherd of his, most of my life.
Oedipus. Where mainly did you go for pasturage?
Shepherd. Sometimes Kithairon, sometimes the hills near by.
Oedipus. Do you remember ever seeing this man out there?
Shepherd. What would he be doing there? This man?
Oedipus. This man standing here. Have you ever seen him before?
Shepherd. No. At least, not to my recollection.
Messenger. And that is not strange, my lord. But I'll refresh   20
   His memory: he must remember when we two
   Spent three whole seasons together, March to September,
   On Kithairon or thereabouts. He had two flocks;

---

[17] Hermês, the herald of the Olympian gods, was born on the mountain of Kyllenê.

I had one. Each autumn I'd drive mine home
And he would go back with his to Laïos' sheepfold.—
Is this not true, just as I have described it?
Shepherd. True, yes; but it was all so long ago.
Messenger. Well, then: do you remember, back in those days
    That you gave me a baby boy to bring up as my own?
Shepherd. What if I did? What are you trying to say?   30
Messenger. King Oedipus was once that little child.
Shepherd. Damn you, hold your tongue!
Oedipus.   No more of that!
    It is your tongue needs watching, not this man's.
Shepherd. My King, my Master, what is it I have done wrong?
Oedipus. You have not answered his question about the boy.
Shepherd. He does not know . . . He is only making trouble . . .
Oedipus. Come, speak plainly, or it will go hard with you.
Shepherd. In God's name, do not torture an old man!
Oedipus. Come here, one of you; bind his arms behind him.
Shepherd. Unhappy king! What more do you wish to learn?   40
Oedipus. Did you give this man the child he speaks of?
Shepherd.   I did.
    And I would to God I had died that very day.
Oedipus. You will die now unless you speak the truth.
Shepherd. Yet if I speak the truth, I am worse than dead.
Oedipus. Very well; since you insist on delaying—
Shepherd. No! I have told you already that I gave him the boy.
Oedipus. Where did you get him? From your house? From somewhere else?
Shepherd. Not from mine, no. A man gave him to me.
Oedipus. Is that man here? Do you know whose slave he was?
Shepherd. For God's love, my King, do not ask me any more!   50
Oedipus. You are a dead man if I have to ask you again.
Shepherd. Then . . . Then the child was from the palace of Laïos.
Oedipus. A slave child? or a child of his own line?
Shepherd. Ah, I am on the brink of dreadful speech!
Oedipus. And I of dreadful hearing. Yet I must hear.
Shepherd. If you must be told, then . . .
                                They said it was Laïos' child,
    But it is your wife who can tell you about that.
Oedipus. My wife!—Did she give it to you?
Shepherd.   My lord, she did.
Oedipus. Do you know why?
Shepherd.   I was told to get rid of it.
Oedipus. An unspeakable mother!
Shepherd.   There had been prophecies . . .   60
Oedipus. Tell me.
Shepherd.   It was said that the boy would kill his own father.

Oedipus. Then why did you give him over to this old man?
Shepherd. I pitied the baby, my King,
 And I thought that this man would take him far away
 To his own country.
      He saved him—but for what a fate!
 For if you are what this man says you are,
 No man living is more wretched than Oedipus.
Oedipus. Ah God!
 It was true!
   All the prophecies!
     —Now,
 O Light, may I look on you for the last time!   70
 I, Oedipus,
 Oedipus, damned in his birth, in his marriage damned,
 Damned in the blood he shed with his own hand!

[*He rushes into the palace.*]

ODE IV

Chorus. Alas for the seed of men.   [*Strophe 1*]

 What measure shall I give these generations
 That breathe on the void and are void
 And exist and do not exist?

 Who bears more weight of joy
 Than mass of sunlight shifting in images,
 Or who shall make his thought stay on
 That down time drifts away?

 Your splendor is all fallen.

 O naked brow of wrath and tears,   10
 O change of Oedipus!
 I who saw your days call no man blest—
 Your great days like ghosts gone.

 That mind was a strong bow.   [*Antistrophe 1*]

 Deep, how deep you drew it then, hard archer,
 At a dim fearful range,
 And brought dear glory down!

You overcame the stranger—
The virgin with her hooking lion claws—
And though death sang, stood like a tower   20
To make pale Thebes take heart.

Fortress against our sorrow!

Divine king, giver of laws,
Majestic Oedipus!
No prince in Thebes had ever such renown,
No prince won such grace of power.

And now of all men ever known   [*Strophe 2*]
Most pitiful is this man's story:
His fortunes are most changed, his state
Fallen to a low slave's   30
Ground under bitter fate.

O Oedipus, most royal one!
The great door that expelled you to the light
Gave at night—ah, gave night to your glory:
As to the father, to the fathering son.

All understood too late.

How could that queen whom Laïos won,
The garden that he harrowed at his height,
Be silent when that act was done?

But all eyes fail before time's eye,   [*Antistrophe 2*]
All actions come to justice there
Though never willed, though far down the deep past,
Your bed, your dread sirings,
Are brought to book at last.

Child by Laïos doomed to die,
Then doomed to lose that fortunate little death,
Would God you never took breath in this air
That with my wailing lips I take to cry:

For I weep the world's outcast.

I was blind, and now I can tell why: 50
Asleep, for you had given ease of breath
To Thebes, while the false years went by.

EXODOS

[*Enter, from the palace, Second Messenger.*]

Second Messenger. Elders of Thebes, most honored in this land,
What horrors are yours to see and hear, what weight
Of sorrow to be endured, if, true to your birth,
You venerate the line of Labdakos!
I think neither Istros nor Phasis, those great rivers,
Could purify this place of the corruption
It shelters now, or soon must bring to light—
Evil not done unconsciously, but willed.

The greatest griefs are those we cause ourselves.
Choragos. Surely, friend, we have grief enough already;   10
What new sorrow do you mean?
Second Messenger. The Queen is dead.
Choragos. Iocastê? Dead? But at whose hand?
Second Messenger.   Her own.
The full horror of what happened you can not know,
For you did not see it; but I, who did, will tell you
As clearly as I can how she met her death.

When she had left us,
In passionate silence, passing through the court,
She ran to her apartment in the house,
Her hair clutched by the fingers of both hands.

She closed the doors behind her; then, by that bed   20
Where long ago the fatal son was conceived—
The son who should bring about his father's death—
We heard her call upon Laïos, dead so many years,
And heard her wail for the double fruit of her marriage,
A husband by her husband, children by her child.

Exactly how she died I do not know:
For Oedipus burst in moaning and would not let us
Keep vigil to the end: it was by him
As he stormed about the room that our eyes were caught.
From one to another of us he went, begging a sword,   30
Cursing the wife who was not his wife, the mother
Whose womb had carried his own children and himself.
I do not know: it was none of us aided him,

But surely one of the gods was in control!
For with a dreadful cry
He hurled his weight, as though wrenched out of himself,
At the twin doors: the bolts gave, and he rushed in.
And there we saw her hanging, her body swaying
From the cruel cord she had noosed about her neck.
A great sob broke from him, heartbreaking to hear,   40
As he loosed the rope and lowered her to the ground.

I would blot out from my mind what happened next!
For the King ripped from her gown the golden brooches
That were her ornament, and raised them, and plunged them down
Straight into his own eyeballs, crying, "No more,
No more shall you look on the misery about me,
The horrors of my own doing! Too long have you known
The faces of those whom I should never have seen,
Too long been blind to those for whom I was searching!
From this hour, go in darkness!" And as he spoke,   50
He struck at his eyes — not once, but many times;
And the blood spattered his beard,
Bursting from his ruined sockets like red hail.

So from the unhappiness of two this evil has sprung,
A curse on the man and woman alike. The old
Happiness of the house of Labdakos
Was happiness enough: where is it today?
It is all wailing and ruin, disgrace, death—all
The misery of mankind that has a name—
And it is wholly and for ever theirs.   60
Choragos. Is he in agony still? Is there no rest for him?
Second Messenger. He is calling for someone to lead him to the gates
So that all the children of Kadmos may look upon
His father's murderer, his mother's—no,
I can not say it!
            And then he will leave Thebes,
Self-exiled, in order that the curse
Which he himself pronounced may depart from the house.
He is weak, and there is none to lead him,
So terrible is his suffering.
                  But you will see:
Look, the doors are opening; in a moment   70
You will see a thing that would crush a heart of stone.

[*The central door is opened; Oedipus, blinded, is led in.*]

Choragos. Dreadful indeed for men to see.
　Never have my own eyes
　Looked on a sight so full of fear.

　Oedipus!
　What madness came upon you, what daemon
　Leaped on your life with heavier
　Punishment than a mortal man can bear?
　No: I can not even
　Look at you, poor ruined one.　　　　　　　　　　　　　　　　80
　And I would speak, question, ponder,
　If I were able. No.
　You make me shudder.
Oedipus. God. God.
　Is there a sorrow greater?
　Where shall I find harbor in this world?
　My voice is hurled far on a dark wind.
　What has God done to me?
Choragos. Too terrible to think of, or to see.

Oedipus. O cloud of night,　　　　　　　　　　　　　　　　*[Strophe 1]*
　Never to be turned away: night coming on,
　I can not tell how: night like a shroud!

　My fair winds brought me here.
　　　　　　　　　　　　Oh God. Again
　The pain of the spikes where I had sight,
　The flooding pain
　Of memory, never to be gouged out.
Choragos. This is not strange.
　You suffer it all twice over, remorse in pain,
　Pain in remorse.

Oedipus. Ah dear friend　　　　　　　　　　　　　　　　*[Antistrophe 1]*
　Are you faithful even yet, you alone?
　Are you still standing near me, will you stay here,
　Patient, to care for the blind?
　　　　　　　　　　　　　The blind man!
　Yet even blind I know who it is attends me,
　By the voice's tone—
　Though my new darkness hide the comforter.
Choragos. Oh fearful act!
　What god was it drove you to rake black
　Night across your eyes?

Oedipus. Apollo. Apollo. Dear   [*Strophe 2*]
    Children, the god was Apollo.
    He brought my sick, sick fate upon me.
    But the blinding hand was my own!
    How could I bear to see
    When all my sight was horror everywhere?
Choragos. Everywhere; that is true.
Oedipus. And now what is left?
    Images? Love? A greeting even,
    Sweet to the senses? Is there anything?
    Ah no, friends: lead me away.   120
    Lead me away from Thebes.
                          Lead the great wreck
    And hell of Oedipus, whom the gods hate.
Choragos. Your fate is clear, you are not blind to that.
    Would God you had never found it out!

Oedipus. Death take the man who unbound   [*Antistrophe 2*]
    My feet on that hillside
    And delivered me from death to life! What life?
    If only I had died,
    This weight of monstrous doom
    Could not have dragged me and my darlings down.   130
Choragos. I would have wished the same.
Oedipus. Oh never to have come here
    With my father's blood upon me! Never
    To have been the man they call his mother's husband!
    Oh accurst! Oh child of evil,
    To have entered that wretched bed—
                      the selfsame one!
    More primal than sin itself, this fell to me.
Choragos. I do not know how I can answer you.
    You were better dead than alive and blind.
Oedipus. Do not counsel me any more. This punishment   140
    That I have laid upon myself is just.
    If I had eyes,
    I do not know how I could bear the sight
    Of my father, when I came to the house of Death,
    Or my mother: for I have sinned against them both
    So vilely that I could not make my peace
    By strangling my own life.
                    Or do you think my children,
    Born as they were born, would be sweet to my eyes?
    Ah never, never! Nor this town with its high walls,
    Nor the holy images of the gods.
                 For I,   150

Thrice miserable!—Oedipus, noblest of all the line
Of Kadmos, have condemned myself to enjoy
These things no more, by my own malediction
Expelling that man whom the gods declared
To be a defilement in the house of Laïos.
After exposing the rankness of my own guilt,
How could I look men frankly in the eyes?
No, I swear it,
If I could have stifled my hearing at its source,
I would have done it and made all this body   160
A tight cell of misery, blank to light and sound:
So I should have been safe in a dark agony
Beyond all recollection.

           Ah Kithairon!
Why did you shelter me? When I was cast upon you,
Why did I not die? Then I should never
Have shown the world my execrable birth.

Ah Polybus! Corinth, city that I believed
The ancient seat of my ancestors: how fair
I seemed, your child! And all the while this evil
Was cancerous within me!

           For I am sick   170
In my daily life, sick in my origin.

O three roads, dark ravine, woodland and way
Where three roads met: you, drinking my father's blood,
My own blood, spilled by my own hand: can you remember
The unspeakable things I did there, and the things
I went on from there to do?

           O marriage, marriage!
The act that engendered me, and again the act
Performed by the son in the same bed—

               Ah, the net
Of incest, mingling fathers, brothers, sons,
With brides, wives, mothers; the last evil   180
That can be known by men: no tongue can say
How evil!

       No. For the love of God, conceal me
Somewhere far from Thebes; or kill me; or hurl me
Into the sea, away from men's eyes for ever.
Come, lead me. You need not fear to touch me.
Of all men, I alone can bear this guilt.

[*Enter Creon.*]

Choragos. We are not the ones to decide; but Creon here
    May fitly judge of what you ask. He only
    Is left to protect the city in your place.
Oedipus. Alas, how can I speak to him? What right have I   190
    To beg his courtesy whom I have deeply wronged?
Creon. I have not come to mock you, Oedipus,
    Or to reproach you, either.
    [*To attendants.*]   —You, standing there:
    If you have lost all respect for man's dignity,
    At least respect the flame of Lord Helios:
    Do not allow this pollution to show itself
    Openly here, an affront to the earth
    And Heaven's rain and the light of day. No, take him
    Into the house as quickly as you can.
    For it is proper   200
    That only the close kindred see his grief.
Oedipus. I pray you in God's name, since your courtesy
    Ignores my dark expectation, visiting
    With mercy this man of all men most execrable:
    Give me what I ask—for your good, not for mine.
Creon. And what is it that you would have me do?
Oedipus. Drive me out of this country as quickly as may be
    To a place where no human voice can ever greet me.
Creon. I should have done that before now—only,
    God's will had not been wholly revealed to me.   210
Oedipus. But his command is plain: the parricide
    Must be destroyed. I am that evil man.
Creon. That is the sense of it, yes; but as things are,
    We had best discover clearly what is to be done.
Oedipus. You would learn more about a man like me?
Creon. You are ready now to listen to the god.
Oedipus. I will listen. But it is to you
    That I must turn for help. I beg you, hear me.

    The woman in there—
    Give her whatever funeral you think proper: 220
    She is your sister.
                    —But let me go, Creon!
    Let me purge my father's Thebes of the pollution
    Of my living here, and go out to the wild hills,
    To Kithairon, that has won such fame with me,
    The tomb my mother and father appointed for me,
    And let me die there, as they willed I should.
    And yet I know
    Death will not ever come to me through sickness

Or in any natural way: I have been preserved
For some unthinkable fate. But let that be.   230
As for my sons, you need not care for them.
They are men, they will find some way to live.
But my poor daughters, who have shared my table,
Who never before have been parted from their father—
Take care of them, Creon; do this for me.
And will you let me touch them with my hands
A last time, and let us weep together?
Be kind, my lord,
Great prince, be kind!

               Could I but touch them,
They would be mine again, as when I had my eyes.   240

[Enter Antigone and Ismene, attended.]

Ah, God!
Is it my dearest children I hear weeping?
Has Creon pitied me and sent my daughters?
Creon. Yes, Oedipus: I knew that they were dear to you
In the old days, and know you must love them still.
Oedipus. May God bless you for this—and be a friendlier
Guardian to you than he has been to me!

Children, where are you?
Come quickly to my hands: they are your brother's—
Hands that have brought your father's once clear eyes   250
To this way of seeing—

              Ah dearest ones,
I had neither sight nor knowledge then, your father
By the woman who was the source of his own life!
And I weep for you—having no strength to see you—,
I weep for you when I think of the bitterness
That men will visit upon you all your lives.
What homes, what festivals can you attend
Without being forced to depart again in tears?

And when you come to marriageable age,
Where is the man, my daughters, who would dare   260
Risk the bane that lies on all my children?
Is there any evil wanting? Your father killed
His father; sowed the womb of her who bore him;
Engendered you at the fount of his own existence!
That is what they will say of you.

               Then whom

Can you ever marry? There are no bridegrooms for you,
And your lives must wither away in sterile dreaming.
O Creon, son of Menoikeus!
You are the only father my daughters have,
Since we, their parents, are both of us gone for ever.   270
They are your own blood: you will not let them
Fall into beggary and loneliness;
You will keep them from the miseries that are mine!
Take pity on them; see, they are only children,
Friendless except for you. Promise me this,
Great Prince, and give me your hand in token of it.

[*Creon clasps his right hand.*]

Children:
I could say much, if you could understand me,
But as it is, I have only this prayer for you:
Live where you can, be as happy as you can—   280
Happier, please God, than God has made your father!
Creon. Enough. You have wept enough. Now go within.
Oedipus. I must; but it is hard.
Creon.   Time eases all things.
Oedipus. But you must promise—
Creon.   Say what you desire.
Oedipus. Send me from Thebes!
Creon.   God grant that I may!
Oedipus. But since God hates me . . .
Creon.   No, he will grant your wish.
Oedipus. You promise?
Creon.   I can not speak beyond my knowledge.
Oedipus. Then lead me in.
Creon.   Come now, and leave your children.
Oedipus. No! Do not take them from me!
Creon.   Think no longer
That you are in command here, but rather think   290
How, when you were, you served your own destruction.

[*Exeunt into the house all but the Chorus; the Choragos chants directly to the audience.*]

Choragos. Men of Thebes: look upon Oedipus.

This is the king who solved the famous riddle
And towered up, most powerful of men.
No mortal eyes but looked on him with envy,

Yet in the end ruin swept over him.
Let every man in mankind's frailty
Consider his last day; and let none
Presume on his good fortune until he find
Life, at his death, a memory without pain.   300

FOR ANALYSIS

1. How does the prologue establish the mood and theme of the play? What aspects of Oedipus's character are revealed there?

2. Sophocles' audience knew the Oedipus story as others, for instance, know the story of the Buddha or of the crucifixion of Jesus. What literary devices does Sophocles use nonetheless to create suspense and interest in the outcome of the action?

3. Describe the conflict in the play. Who or what is the **antagonist** that opposes Oedipus, the **protagonist**?

4. A classic **tragedy** tells the story of a noble and heroic protagonist who is brought down by arrogance and pride. Do you find that Oedipus suffers from these frailties? Explain.

5. Teiresias is one of many figures in legend and literature whose wisdom and spirituality are somehow connected with blindness. What do you think the connection is based on?

6. What function does the exodos serve?

MAKING CONNECTIONS

1. Compare Oedipus and Shakespeare's Othello (p. 958) as classic tragic protagonists.

2. Although Oedipus is a king, a man of great power and high station, and Willy Loman, in Arthur Miller's *Death of a Salesman* (p. 1234), is an ordinary man and a seeming failure, what connection can be made between the two protagonists?

WRITING TOPICS

1. In the Exodos, Oedipus declares that Apollo "brought my sick, sick fate upon me, / But the blinding hand was my own!" (ll. 112–13) and "this punishment / That I have laid upon myself is just" (ll. 140–41); later he declares, "the parricide / Must be destroyed. I am that evil man" (ll. 211–12). How can Oedipus's acceptance of responsibility for his fate be reconciled with the fact that his fate was divinely ordained? Consider a similar paradox in Christian theology, which holds that God is all-knowing and has foreknowledge and yet humans exercise free will and thus are responsible for their acts.

2. Analyze scene IV, the shortest of the four scenes, as the climax of the play, bringing together all the threads of the drama.

3. Find out who Electra was in ancient Greek dramatic literature. What did she do, and why? What is the Electra complex?

ARISTOTLE   (384–322 B.C.)

FROM THE POETICS   CA. 340 B.C.

Let us now discuss tragedy, bringing together the definition of its essence that
has emerged from what we have already said. Tragedy is, then, an imitation of a
noble and complete action, having the proper magnitude;[1] it employs language that has been artistically enhanced by each of the kinds of linguistic
adornment, applied separately in the various parts of the play; it is presented
in dramatic, not narrative form, and achieves, through the representation of
pitiable and fearful incidents, the catharsis of such pitiable and fearful incidents. I mean by "language that has been artistically enhanced," that which is
accompanied by rhythm and harmony and song; and by the phrase "each of
the kinds of linguistic adornment, applied separately in the various parts of
the play," I mean that some parts are accomplished by meter alone and others,
in turn, through song. . . .

Now I mean by the plot the arrangement of the incidents, and by character that element in accordance with which we say that agents are of a certain
type; and by thought I mean that which is found in whatever things men say
when they prove a point or, it may be, express a general truth. It is necessary,
therefore, that tragedy as a whole have six parts in accordance with which,
as a genre, it achieves its particular quality. These parts are plot, character,
diction, thought, spectacle, and melody. . . . Plots are divided into the simple
and the complex, for the actions of which the plots are imitations are naturally of this character. An action that is, as has been defined, continuous and
unified I call simple when its change of fortune arises without reversal and
recognition, and complex when its change of fortune arises through recognition or reversal or both. Now these aspects of the plot must develop
directly from the construction of the plot itself, so that they occur from
prior events either out of necessity or according to the laws of probability.
For it makes quite a difference whether they occur *because* of those events
or merely *after* them.

Reversal is the change of fortune in the action of the play to the opposite
state of affairs, just as has been said; and this change, we argue, should be in
accordance with probability and necessity. Thus, in the *Oedipus* the messenger comes to cheer Oedipus and to remove his fears in regard to his mother;
but by showing him who he actually is he accomplishes the very opposite
effect. . . .

---

[1] There is no word in the Greek text for *proper,* but I have followed the practice of several other
translators who add a modifier to the term *magnitude* where it is logically warranted. The term *representation* has also been added to the final clause of this sentence because of Aristotle's insistence that
the pleasure of tragedy is achieved *through imitation* (Ch. 14, ll. 18–19). See L. Golden, "Catharsis,"
TAPA 93 (1962): 58. [Tr.]

Recognition, as the same indicates, is a change from ignorance to knowledge, bringing about either a state of friendship or one of hostility on the part of those who have been marked out for good fortune or bad. The most effective recognition is one that occurs together with reversal, for example, as in the *Oedipus*. . . . For such a recognition and reversal will evoke pity or fear, and we have defined tragedy as an imitation of actions of this type; and furthermore, happiness and misery will appear in circumstances of this type. . . .

Now then, these are two parts of the plot, reversal and recognition, and there is 5 also a third part, suffering. Of these, reversal and recognition have been discussed; the incident of suffering results from destructive or painful action such as death on the stage, scenes of very great pain, the infliction of wounds, and the like. . . .

Since the plots of the best tragedies must be complex, not simple, and the plot of a tragedy must be an imitation of pitiable and fearful incidents (for this is the specific nature of the imitation under discussion), it is clear, first of all, that unqualifiedly good human beings must not appear to fall from good fortune to bad; for that is neither pitiable nor fearful; it is, rather, repellent. Nor must an extremely evil man appear to move from bad fortune to good fortune for that is the most untragic situation of all because it has none of the necessary requirements of tragedy; it both violates our human sympathy and contains nothing of the pitiable or fearful in it. Furthermore, a villainous man should not appear to fall from good fortune to bad. For, although such a plot would be in accordance with our human sympathy, it would not contain the necessary elements of pity and fear; for pity is aroused by someone who undeservedly falls into misfortune, and fear is evoked by our recognizing that it is someone like ourselves who encounters this misfortune (pity, as I say, arising for the former reason, fear for the latter). Therefore the emotional effect of the situation just mentioned will be neither pitiable nor fearful. What is left, after our considerations, is someone in between these extremes. This would be a person who is neither perfect in virtue and justice, nor one who falls into misfortune through vice and depravity; but rather, one who succumbs through some miscalculation. He must also be a person who enjoys great reputation and good fortune, such as Oedipus, Thyestes, and other illustrious men from similar families. It is necessary, furthermore, for the well-constructed plot to have a single rather than a double construction, as some urge, and to illustrate a change of fortune not from bad fortune to good but, rather, the very opposite, from good fortune to bad, and for this to take place not because of depravity but through some great miscalculation on the part of the type of person we have described (or a better rather than a worse one). . . .

Pity and fear can arise from the spectacle and also from the very structure of the plot, which is the superior way and shows the better poet. The poet should construct the plot so that even if the action is not performed before spectators, one who merely hears the incidents that have occurred both shudders and feels pity from the way they turn out. That is what anyone who hears the plot of the *Oedipus* would experience. The achievement of this effect through the spectacle does not have much to do with poetic art and really belongs to the business of producing the play. Those who use the spectacle to create not the fearful but only the monstrous have no share in the creation of tragedy; for we should not seek every pleasure from tragedy but only the one proper to it.

Since the poet should provide pleasure from pity and fear through imitation, it is apparent that this function must be worked into the incidents. Let us try to understand what type of occurrences appear to be terrifying and pitiable. It is, indeed, necessary that any such action occur either between those who are friends or enemies to each other, or between those who have no relationship, whatsoever, to each other. If an enemy takes such an action against an enemy, there is nothing pitiable in the performance of the act or in the intention to perform it, except the suffering itself. Nor would there be anything pitiable if neither party had any relationship with the other. But whenever the tragic incidents occur in situations involving strong ties of affection—for example, if a brother kills or intends to kill a brother or a son a father or a mother a son or a son a mother or commits some equally terrible act—there will be something pitiable. These situations, then, are the ones to be sought. Now, it is not possible for a poet to alter completely the traditional stories. I mean, for example, the given fact that Clytemnestra dies at the hands of Orestes, and Eriphyle at the hands of Alcmaeon; but it is necessary for the poet to be inventive and skillful in adapting the stories that have been handed down. Let us define more clearly what we mean by the skillful adaptation of a story. It is possible for the action to occur, as our early poets handled it, with the characters knowing and understanding what they are doing, as indeed Euripides makes Medea kill her children. It is also possible to have the deed done with those who accomplish the terrible deed in ignorance of the identity of their victim, only later recognizing the relationship as in Sophocles' *Oedipus*. . . .

In character, as in the construction of the incidents, we must always seek for either the necessary or the probable, so that a given type of person says or does certain kinds of things, and one event follows another according to necessity or probability. Thus, it is apparent that the resolutions of the plots should also occur through the plot itself and not by means of the deus ex machina, as in the *Medea*, and also in regard to the events surrounding the department of the fleet in the *Iliad*. The deus ex machina must be reserved for the events that lie outside the plot, either those that happened before it that are not capable of being known by men, or those that occur after that need to be announced and spoken of beforehand. For we grant to the gods the power of seeing all things. There should, then, be nothing improbable in the action; but if this is impossible, it should be outside the plot as, for example, in Sophocles' *Oedipus*.

Because tragedy is an imitation of the nobler sort of men it is necessary for poets to imitate good portrait painters. For even though they reproduce the specific characteristics of their subjects and represent them faithfully, they also paint them better than they are. Thus, also, the poet imitating men who are prone to anger or who are indifferent or who are disposed in other such ways

10

in regard to character makes them good as well, even though they have such characteristics, just as Agathon[2] and Homer portray Achilles.

FOR ANALYSIS

1. How does Aristotle define the dramatic representations we call *tragedy*?

2. He asserts that a tragedy must have six parts: "plot, character, diction, thought, spectacle, and melody" (para. 2). Plot and character are relatively easy to define; what does he mean by the other four elements?

3. What are *reversal* and *recognition*?

4. *Pity* and *fear* play an important part in this discussion of tragedy. What produces pity and fear? What doesn't?

5. What is *hamartia*?

6. Can you justify Aristotle's assertion that "tragedy is an imitation of the nobler sort of men" (para. 10)? Or do you agree with Arthur Miller's view that "the common man is as apt a subject for tragedy . . . as kings were" (p. 241)? Explain.

---

[2] Tragic poet (ca. 450–ca. 399 B.C.) mentioned by Aristophanes and Plato.

SIGMUND FREUD   (1856–1939)

THE OEDIPUS COMPLEX   1900

In my experience, which is already extensive, the chief part in the mental lives of all children who later become psychoneurotics is played by their parents. Being in love with the one parent and hating the other are among the essential constituents of the stock of psychical impulses which is formed at that time and which is of such importance in determining the symptoms of the later neurosis. It is not my belief, however, that psychoneurotics differ sharply in this respect from other human beings who remain normal—that they are able, that is, to create something absolutely new and peculiar to themselves. It is far more probable—and this is confirmed by occasional observations on normal children—that they are only distinguished by exhibiting on a magnified scale feelings of love and hatred to their parents which occur less obviously and less intensely in the minds of most children.

This discovery is confirmed by a legend that has come down to us from classical antiquity: a legend whose profound and universal power to move can only be understood if the hypothesis I have put forward in regard to the psychology of children has an equally universal validity. What I have in mind is the legend of King Oedipus and Sophocles' drama which bears his name.

Oedipus, son of Laius, King of Thebes, and of Jocasta, was exposed as an infant because an oracle had warned Laius that the still unborn child would be his father's murderer. The child was rescued and grew up as a prince in an alien court, until, in doubts as to his origin, he too questioned the oracle and was warned to avoid his home since he was destined to murder his father and take his mother in marriage. On the road leading away from what he believed was his home, he met King Laius and slew him in a sudden quarrel. He came next to Thebes and solved the riddle set him by the Sphinx who barred his way. Out of gratitude the Thebans made him their king and gave him Jocasta's hand in marriage. He reigned long in peace and honor, and she who, unknown to him, was his mother bore him two sons and two daughters. Then at last a plague broke out and the Thebans made inquiry once more of the oracle. It is at this point that Sophocles' tragedy opens. The messengers bring back the reply that the plague will cease when the murderer of Laius has been driven from the land.

> But he, where is he? Where shall now be read
> The fading record of this ancient guilt?[1]

The action of the play consists in nothing other than the process of revealing, with cunning delays and ever-mounting excitement—a process that can be likened to the work of a psychoanalysis—that Oedipus himself is the murderer of Laius, but further that he is the son of the murdered man and of Jocasta. Appalled at the abomination which he has unwittingly perpetrated, Oedipus blinds himself and forsakes his home. The oracle has been fulfilled.

Oedipus Rex is what is known as a tragedy of destiny. Its tragic effect is said to lie in the contrast between the supreme will of the gods and the vain attempts of mankind to escape the evil that threatens them. The lesson which, it is said, the deeply moved spectator should learn from the tragedy is submission to the divine will and realization of his own impotence. Modern dramatists have accordingly tried to achieve a similar tragic effect by weaving the same contrast into a plot invented by themselves. But the spectators have looked on unmoved while a curse or an oracle was fulfilled in spite of all the efforts of some innocent man: later tragedies of destiny have failed in their effect.

If *Oedipus Rex* moves a modern audience no less than it did the contemporary 5 Greek one, the explanation can only be that its effect does not lie in the contrast between destiny and human will, but is to be looked for in the particular nature of the material on which that contrast is exemplified. There must be something which makes a voice within us ready to recognize the compelling force of destiny in the *Oedipus*, while we can dismiss as merely arbitrary such dispositions as are laid down in [Grillparzer's] *Die Ahnfrau* or other modern tragedies of destiny. And a factor of this kind is in fact involved in the story of King Oedipus. His destiny moves us only because it might have been ours—because the oracle laid the same curse upon us before our birth as upon him. It is the fate of all of us, perhaps, to direct our first sexual impulse toward our mother and our first hatred and our first murderous wish against our father. Our dreams convince us that

---

[1] Lewis Campbell's translation (1883), lines 108ff.

that is so. King Oedipus, who slew his father Laius and married his mother Jocasta, merely shows us the fulfillment of our own childhood wishes. But, more fortunate than he, we have meanwhile succeeded, in so far as we have not become psychoneurotics, in detaching our sexual impulses from our mothers and in forgetting our jealousy of our fathers. Here is one in whom these primeval wishes of our childhood have been fulfilled, and we shrink back from him with the whole force of the repression by which those wishes have since that time been held down within us. While the poet, as he unravels the past, brings to light the guilt of Oedipus, he is at the same time compelling us to recognize our own inner minds, in which those same impulses, though suppressed, are still to be found. The contrast with which the closing Chorus leaves us confronted—

... Fix on Oedipus your eyes,
Who resolved the dark enigma, noblest champion and most wise.
Like a star his envied fortune mounted beaming far and wide:
Now he sinks in seas of anguish, whelmed beneath a raging tide . . .[2]

—strikes as a warning at ourselves and our pride, at us who since our childhood have grown so wise and so mighty in our own eyes. Like Oedipus, we live in ignorance of these wishes, repugnant to morality, which have been forced upon us by Nature, and after their revelation we may all of us well seek to close our eyes to the scenes of our childhood.[3]

There is an unmistakable indication in the text of Sophocles' tragedy itself that the legend of Oedipus sprang from some primeval dream material which had as its content the distressing disturbance of a child's relation to his parents owing to the first stirrings of sexuality. At a point when Oedipus, though he is not yet enlightened, has begun to feel troubled by his recollection of the oracle, Jocasta consoles him by referring to a dream which many people dream, though, as she thinks, it has no meaning:

Many a man ere now in dreams hath lain
With her who bare him. He hath least annoy
Who with such omens troubleth not his mind.[4]

Today, just as then, many men dream of having sexual relations with their mothers, and speak of the fact with indignation and astonishment. It is clearly

---

[2] Lewis Campbell's translation, lines 1524ff.

[3] [*Footnote added by Freud in 1914 edition.*] None of the findings of psychoanalytic research has provoked such embittered denials, such fierce opposition—or such amusing contortions—on the part of critics as this indication of the childhood impulses toward incest which persist in the unconscious. An attempt has even been made recently to make out, in the face of all experience, that the incest should only be taken as "symbolic."—Ferenczi (1912) has proposed an ingenious "overinterpretation" of the Oedipus myth, based on a passage in one of Schopenhauer's letters. [*Added 1919.*] Later studies have shown that the "Oedipus complex," which was touched upon for the first time in the above paragraphs in the *Interpretation of Dreams,* throws a light of undreamt-of importance on the history of the human race and the evolution of religion and morality.

[4] Lewis Campbell's translation, lines 982ff.

the key to the tragedy and the complement to the dream of the dreamer's father being dead. The story of Oedipus is the reaction of the imagination to these two typical dreams. And just as these dreams, when dreamt by adults, are accompanied by feelings of repulsion, so too the legend must include horror and self-punishment. Its further modification originates once again in a misconceived secondary revision of the material, which has sought to exploit it for theological purposes. . . . The attempt to harmonize divine omnipotence with human responsibility must naturally fail in connection with this subject matter just as with any other.

FOR ANALYSIS

1. "The story of Oedipus," Freud writes, "is the reaction of the imagination to these two typical dreams" (para. 6). What are the two dreams? Why, according to Freud, do men have them?

2. Freud claims that the story of Oedipus is "a legend whose profound and universal power to move can only be understood" by reference to his theories of childhood psychology (para. 2). Were you moved emotionally when you read *Oedipus Rex*? Do you think it was because of the reason Freud posits here? Can you offer possible alternate explanations to Freud's?

FRANCIS FERGUSSON   (1904–1986)

OEDIPUS, MYTH AND PLAY   1949

When Sophocles came to write his play he had the myth of Oedipus to start with. Laius and Jocasta, King and Queen of Thebes, are told by the oracle that their son will grow up to kill his father and marry his mother. The infant, his feet pierced, is left on Mount Kitharon to die. But a shepherd finds him and takes care of him; at last gives him to another shepherd, who takes him to Corinth, and there the King and Queen bring him up as their own son. But Oedipus—"Clubfoot"—is plagued in his turn by the oracle; he hears that he is fated to kill his father and marry his mother; and to escape that fate he leaves Corinth never to return. On his journey he meets an old man with his servants; gets into a dispute with him, and kills him and all his followers. He comes to Thebes at the time when the Sphinx is preying upon that City; solves the riddle which the Sphinx propounds, and saves the City. He marries the widowed Queen, Jocasta; has several children by her; rules prosperously for many years. But, when Thebes is suffering under a plague and a drought, the oracle reports that the gods are angry because Laius's slayer is unpunished. Oedipus, as King, undertakes to find him; discovers that he is himself the culprit and that Jocasta is his own mother. He blinds himself and goes into exile. From this time forth he becomes a sort of sacred relic, like the bones of a saint; perilous, but "good medicine" for the community that possesses him.

He dies, at last, at Athens, in a grove sacred to the Eumenides, female spirits of fertility and night.

It is obvious, even from this sketch, that the myth, which covers several generations, has as much narrative material as *Gone with the Wind*. We do not know what versions of the story Sophocles used. It is the way of myths that they generate whole progenies of elaborations and varying versions. They are so suggestive, seem to say so much, yet so mysteriously, that the mind cannot rest content with any single form, but must add, or interpret, or simplify—reduce to terms which the reason can accept. Mr. William Troy suggests that "what is possibly most in order at the moment is a thoroughgoing refurbishment of the medieval fourfold method of interpretation, which was first developed, it will be recalled, for just such a purpose—to make at least partially available to the reason that complex of human problems which are embedded, deep and imponderable, in the Myth."[1] It appears that Sophocles, in his play, succeeded in preserving the suggestive mystery of the Oedipus myth, while presenting it in a wonderfully unified dramatic form; and this drama has all the dimensions which the fourfold method was intended to explore.

Everyone knows that when Sophocles planned the plot of the play itself, he started almost at the end of the story, when the plague descends upon the City of Thebes which Oedipus and Jocasta had been ruling with great success for a number of years. The action of the play takes less than a day, and consists of Oedipus's quest for Laius's slayer—his consulting the Oracle of Apollo, his examination of the Prophet, Tiresias, and of a series of witnesses, ending with the old Shepherd who gave him to the King and Queen of Corinth. The play ends when Oedipus is unmistakably revealed as himself the culprit.

At this literal level, the play is intelligible as a murder mystery. Oedipus takes the role of District Attorney; and when he at last convicts himself, we have a twist, a *coup de théâtre*, of unparalleled excitement. But no one who sees or reads the play can rest content with its literal coherence. Questions as to its meaning arise at once: Is Oedipus really guilty, or simply a victim of the gods, or his famous complex, of fate, of original sin? How much did he know, all along? How much did Jocasta know? The first, and most deeply instinctive effort of the mind, when confronted with this play, is to endeavor to reduce its meanings to some set of rational categories.

The critics of the Age of Reason tried to understand it as a fable of the enlightened moral will, in accordance with the philosophy of that time. Voltaire's version of the play, following Corneille, and his comments upon it, may be taken as typical. He sees it as essentially a struggle between a strong and righteous Oedipus, and the malicious and very human gods, aided and abetted by the corrupt priest Tiresias; he makes it an antireligious tract, with an unmistakable moral to satisfy the needs of the discursive intellect. In order to

[1] William Troy, "Myth, Method and the Future," *Chimera*, Spring 1946.

make Oedipus "sympathetic" to his audience, he elides, as much as possible, the incest motif; and he adds an irrelevant love story. He was aware that his version and interpretation were not those of Sophocles but, with the complacent provinciality of his period, he attributes the difference to the darkness of the age in which *Sophocles* lived.

Other attempts to rationalize *Oedipus Rex* are subtler than Voltaire's, and take us further toward an understanding of the play. Freud's reduction of the play to the concepts of his psychology reveals a great deal, opens up perspectives which we are still exploring. If one reads *Oedipus* in the light of Fustel de Coulanges's *The Ancient City*, one may see it as the expression of the ancient patriarchal religion of the Greeks. And other interpretations of the play, theological, philosophical, historical, are available, none of them wrong, but all partial, all reductions of Sophocles' masterpiece to an alien set of categories. For the peculiar virtue of Sophocles' presentation of the myth is that it preserves the ultimate mystery by focusing upon the tragic human at a level beneath, or prior to any rationalization whatever. The plot is so arranged that we see the action, as it were, illumined from many sides at once.

By starting the play at the end of the story, and showing on stage only the last crucial episode in Oedipus's life, the past and present action of the protagonist are revealed together; and, in each other's light, are at last felt as one. Oedipus's quest for the slayer of Laius becomes a quest for the hidden reality of his own past; and as that slowly comes into focus, like repressed material under psychoanalysis—with sensory and emotional immediacy, yet in the light of acceptance and understanding—his immediate quest also reaches its end: he comes to see himself (the Savior of the City) and the guilty one, the plague of Thebes, at once and at one.

This presentation of the myth of Oedipus constitutes, in one sense, an "interpretation" of it. What Sophocles saw as the essence of Oedipus's nature and destiny is not what Seneca or Dryden or Cocteau saw; and one may grant that even Sophocles did not exhaust the possibilities in the materials of the myth. But Sophocles' version of the myth does not constitute a "reduction" in the same sense as the rest.

I have said that the action which Sophocles shows is a quest, the quest for Laius's slayer; and that as Oedipus's past is unrolled before us his whole life is seen as a kind of quest for his true nature and destiny. But since the object of this quest is not clear until the end, the seeking action takes many forms, as its object appears in different lights. The object, indeed, the final perception, the "truth," looks so different at the end from what it did at the beginning that Oedipus' action itself may seem not a quest, but its opposite, a flight. Thus it would be hard to say, simply, that Oedipus either succeeds or fails. He succeeds; but his success is his undoing. He fails to find what, in one way, he sought; yet from another point of view his search is brilliantly successful. The same ambiguities surround his effort to discover who and what he is. He seems to find that he is nothing; yet thereby finds himself. And what of his relation to the gods? His quest may be regarded as a heroic attempt to escape their decrees, or as an attempt, based upon some deep natural faith, to discover what their wishes are, and what true obedience would be. In one sense Oedipus suffers forces he can neither control nor understand, the puppet of fate; yet at the same time he wills and intelligently intends his every move.

The meaning, or spiritual content of the play, is not to be sought by trying to 10 resolve such ambiguities as these. The spiritual content of the play is the tragic action which Sophocles directly presents; and this action is in its essence *zweideutig*: triumph and destruction, darkness and enlightenment, mourning and rejoicing, at any moment we care to consider it. But this action has also a shape: a beginning, middle, and end, in time. It starts with the reasoned purpose of finding Laius's slayer. But this aim meets unforeseen difficulties, evidences which do not fit, and therefore shake the purpose as it was first understood; and so the characters suffer the piteous and terrible sense of the mystery of the human situation. From this suffering or passion, with its shifting visions, a new perception of the situation emerges; and on that basis the purpose of the action is redefined, and a new movement starts. This movement, or *tragic rhythm of action*, constitutes the shape of the play as a whole; it is also the shape of each episode, each discussion between principals with the chorus following. Mr. Kenneth Burke has studied the tragic rhythm in his *Philosophy of Literary Form*, and also in *A Grammar of Motives*, where he gives the three moments traditional designations which are very suggestive: *Poiema, Pathema, Mathema*. They may also be called, for convenience, Purpose, Passion (or Suffering), and Perception. It is this tragic rhythm of action which is the substance or spiritual content of the play, and the clue to its extraordinarily comprehensive form.

In order to illustrate these points in more detail, it is convenient to examine the scene between Oedipus and Tiresias with the chorus following it. This episode, being early in the play (the first big agon), presents, as it were, a preview of the whole action and constitutes a clear and complete example of action in the tragic rhythm. . . .

The Cambridge School of Classical Anthropologists has shown in great detail that the form of Greek tragedy follows the form of a very ancient ritual, that of the *Enniautos-Daimon*, or seasonal god. This was one of the most influential discoveries of the last few generations, and it gives us new insights into Oedipus which I think are not yet completely explored. The clue to Sophocles' dramatizing of the myth of Oedipus is to be found in this ancient ritual, which had a similar form and meaning—that is, it also moved in the "tragic rhythm."

Experts in classical anthropology, like experts in other fields, dispute innumerable questions of fact and of interpretation which the layman can only pass over in respectful silence. One of the thornier questions seems to be whether myth or ritual came first. Is the ancient ceremony merely an enactment of the Ur-Myth of the year-god—Attis, or Adonis, or Osiris, or the "Fisher-King"—in any case that Hero-King-Father-High-Priest who fights with his rival, is slain and dismembered, then rises anew with the spring season? Or did the innumerable myths of this kind arise to "explain" a ritual which was perhaps mimed or danced or sung to celebrate the annual change of seasons?

For the purpose of understanding the form and meaning of *Oedipus,* it is not necessary to worry about the answer to this question of historic fact. The figure of Oedipus himself fulfills all the requirements of the scapegoat, the dismembered king or god-figure. The situation in which Thebes is presented at the beginning of the play—in peril of its life; its crops, its herds, its women mysteriously infertile, signs of a mortal disease of the City, and the disfavor of the gods—is like the withering which winter brings, and calls, in the same way, for struggle, dismemberment, death, and renewal. And this tragic sequence is the substance of the play. It is enough to know that myth and ritual are close together in their genesis, two direct imitations of the perennial experience of the race.

But when one considers *Oedipus* as a ritual one understands it in ways 15 which one cannot by thinking of it merely as a dramatization of a story, even that story. Harrison has shown that the Festival of Dionysos, based ultimately upon the yearly vegetation ceremonies, included *rites de passage,* like that celebrating the assumption of adulthood—celebrations of the mystery of individual growth and development. At the same time, it was a prayer for the welfare of the whole City; and this welfare was understood not only as material prosperity, but also as the natural order of the family, the ancestors, the present members, and the generations still to come, and, by the same token, obedience to the gods who were jealous, each in his own province, of this natural and divinely sanctioned order and proportion.

We must suppose that Sophocles' audience (the whole population of the City) came early, prepared to spend the day in the bleachers. At their feet was the semicircular dancing-ground for the chorus, and the thrones for the priests, and the altar. Behind that was the raised platform for the principal actors, backed by the all-purpose, emblematic façade, which would presently be taken to represent Oedipus's palace in Thebes. The actors were not professionals in our sense, but citizens selected for a religious office, and Sophocles himself had trained them and the chorus.

This crowd must have had as much appetite for thrills and diversion as the crowds who assemble in our day for football games and musical comedies, and Sophocles certainly holds the attention with an exciting show. At the same time his audience must have been alert for the fine points of poetry and dramaturgy, for *Oedipus* is being offered in competition with other plays on the same bill. But the element which distinguishes this theater, giving it its unique directness and depth, is the *ritual expectancy* which Sophocles assumed in his audience. The nearest thing we have to this ritual sense of theater is, I suppose, to be found at an Easter performance of the *Mattias Passion.* We also can observe something similar in the dances and ritual mummery of the Pueblo Indians. Sophocles' audience must have been prepared, like the Indians standing around their plaza, to consider the playing, the make-believe it was about to see—the choral invocations, with dancing and chanting; the reasoned discourses and the terrible combats of the protagonists; the mourning, the rejoicing, and the contemplation of the final stage-picture of epiphany—as imitating and celebrating the mystery of human nature and destiny. And this mystery was at once that of individual growth and development, and that of the precarious life of the human City.

I have indicated how Sophocles presents the life of the mythic Oedipus in the tragic rhythm, the mysterious quest of life. Oedipus is shown seeking his own true being; but at the same time and by the same token, the welfare of the City. When one considers the ritual form of the whole play, it becomes evident that it presents the tragic but perennial, even normal, quest of the whole City for its well-being. In this larger action, Oedipus is only the protagonist, the first and most important champion. This tragic quest is realized by all the characters in their various ways; but in the development of the action as a whole it is the chorus alone that plays a part as important as that of Oedipus; its counterpart, in fact. The chorus holds the balance between Oedipus and his antagonists, marks the progress of their struggles, and restates the main theme, and its new variation, after each dialogue or agon. The ancient ritual was probably performed by a chorus alone without individual developments and variations, and the chorus, in *Oedipus,* is still the element that throws most light on the ritual form of the play as a whole.

The chorus consists of twelve or fifteen "Elders of Thebes." This group is not intended to represent literally all of the citizens either of Thebes or of Athens. The play opens with a large delegation of Theban citizens before Oedipus's palace, and the chorus proper does not enter until after the prologue. Nor does the chorus speak directly for the Athenian audience; we are asked throughout to make-believe that the theater is the agora at Thebes; and at the same time Sophocles' audience is witnessing a ritual. It would, I think, be more accurate to say that the chorus represents the point of view and the faith of Thebes as a whole, and, by analogy, of the Athenian audience. Their errand before Oedipus's palace is like that of Sophocles' audience in the theater: they are watching a sacred combat, in the issue of which they have an all-important and official stake. Thus they represent the audience and the citizens in a particular way—not as a mob formed in response to some momentary feeling, but rather as an organ of a highly self-conscious community: something closer to the "conscience of the race" than to the overheated affectivity of a mob.

According to Aristotle, a Sophoclean chorus is a character that takes an [20] important role in the action of the play, instead of merely making incidental music between the scenes, as in the plays of Euripides. The chorus may be described as a group personality, like an old Parliament. It has its own traditions, habits of thought and feeling, and mode of being. It exists, in a sense, as a living entity, but not with the sharp actuality of an individual. It perceives; but its perception is at once wider and vaguer than that of a single man. It shares, in its way, the seeking action of the play as a whole; but it cannot act in all the modes; it depends upon the chief agonists to invent and try out the detail of policy, just as a rather helpless but critical Parliament depends upon the Prime Minister to act but, in its less specific form of life, survives his destruction.

When the chorus enters after the prologue, with its questions, its invocation of the various gods, and its focus upon the hidden and jeopardized welfare of the City—Athens or Thebes — the list of essential *dramatis personae,* as well as the elements needed to celebrate the ritual, is complete, and the main action can begin. It is the function of the chorus to mark the stages of this action, and to perform the suffering and perceiving part of the tragic rhythm. The protagonist and his antagonists develop the "purpose" with which the tragic sequence begins; the chorus, with its less than individual being, broods over the agons, marks their stages with a word (like that of the chorus leader in the middle of the Tiresias scene), and (expressing its emotions and visions in song and dance) suffers the results, and the new perception at the end of the fight.

The choral odes are lyrics but they are not to be understood as poetry, the art of words, only, for they are intended also to be danced and sung. And though each chorus has its own shape, like that of a discrete lyric—its beginning, middle, and end—it represents also one passion or pathos in the changing action of the whole. This passion, like the other moments in the tragic rhythm, is felt at so general or, rather, so deep a level that it seems to contain both the mob ferocity that Nietzsche felt in it and, at the other extreme, the patience of prayer. It is informed by faith in the unseen order of nature and the gods, and moves through a sequence of modes of suffering. This may be illustrated from the chorus I have quoted at the end of the Tiresias scene.

It begins (close to the savage emotion of the end of the fight) with images suggesting that cruel "Bacchic frenzy" which is supposed to be the common root of tragedy and of the "old" comedy: "In panoply of fire and lightning/The son of Zeus now springs upon him." In the first antistrophe these images come together more clearly as we relish the chase; and the fleeing culprit, as we imagine him, begins to resemble Oedipus, who is lame, and always associated with the rough wilderness of Kitharon. But in the second strophe, as though appalled by its ambivalent feelings and the imagined possibilities, the chorus sinks back into a more dark and patient posture of suffering, "in awe," "hovering in hope." In the second antistrophe this is developed into something like the orthodox Christian attitude of prayer, based on faith, and assuming the possibility of a hitherto unimaginable truth and answer: "Zeus and Apollo are wise," etc. The whole chorus then ends with a new vision of Oedipus, of the culprit, and of the direction in which the welfare of the City is to be sought. This vision is still colored by the chorus's human love of Oedipus as Hero, for the chorus has still its own purgation to complete, cannot as yet accept completely either the suffering in store for it, or Oedipus as scapegoat. But it marks the end of the first complete "purpose-passion-perception" unit, and lays the basis for the new purpose which will begin the next unit.

It is also to be noted that the chorus changes the scene which we, as audience, are to imagine. During the agon between Oedipus and Tiresias, our attention is fixed upon their clash, and the scene is literal, close, and immediate: before Oedipus's palace. When the fighters depart and the choral music starts, the focus suddenly widens, as though we had been removed to a distance. We become aware of the interested City around the bright arena; and beyond that, still more dimly, of Nature, sacred to the hidden gods. Mr. Burke has expounded the fertile notion that human action may be understood in terms of the scene in which it occurs, and vice versa: the scene is defined by the mode of action. The chorus's action is not limited by the sharp, rationalized purposes of the protagonist; its mode of action, more patient, less sharply realized, is cognate with a wider, if less accurate, awareness of the scene of human life. But the chorus's action, as I have remarked, is not that of passion itself (Nietzsche's cosmic void of night) but suffering informed by the faith of the tribe in a human and a divinely sanctioned natural order: "If such deeds as these are honored," the chorus asks after Jocasta's impiety, "why should I dance and sing?" Thus it is one of the most important functions of the chorus to reveal, in its widest and most mysterious extent, the theater of human life which the play, and indeed the whole Festival of Dionysos, assumed. Even when the chorus does not speak, but only watches, it maintains this theme and this perspective—ready to take the whole stage when the fighters depart.

If one thinks of the movements of the play, it appears that the tragic rhythm 25 analyzes human action temporally into successive modes, as a crystal analyzes a white beam of light spatially into the colored bands of the spectrum. The chorus, always present, represents one of these modes, and at the recurrent moments when reasoned purpose is gone, it takes the stage with its faith-informed passion, moving through an ordered succession of modes of suffering, to a new perception of the immediate situation.

FOR ANALYSIS

1. Do you see Oedipus as a scapegoat? Why or why not?

2. At the heart of Fergusson's analysis is the claim that "when one considers *Oedipus* as a ritual one understands it in ways which one cannot by thinking of it merely as a dramatization of a story" (para. 15). What does it mean to understand the play in this way? If modern audiences are unable to watch the play in the same way the original Greek audiences did, how should they watch it?

D. W. LUCAS (1905–1985)

THE DRAMA OF OEDIPUS 1950

There was once a collision in a fog between a liner and an aircraft carrier in the Mediterranean; one of the carrier's aircraft exercising above the fog, and powerless to intervene, could see the converging mastheads of the two vessels and the disaster in which their courses must end. That is a type of situation to which the term "dramatic" is applied; it is by no means the only kind of drama, but it is a recognizable category, and no plot could be better raw material for such a drama of "the convergence of the twain" than that supplied by the myth of Oedipus.

Oedipus was famous for his cleverness, yet this cleverness serves only to enmesh him in a net of illusion. He starts, through no fault of his own, from a false premise; he does not know who he is, that is his *hamartia*. Tiresias tells him of his guilt, and he jumps, not indeed unreasonably from the evidence in his possession, to the conclusion that Creon and Tiresias are conspiring against him. Jocasta intervenes to stop the quarrel between her husband and her brother, but in attempting to show the absurdity of the charge that he had murdered Laius she gives him a clue to his guilt. The final discovery depends on putting together the evidence of two parties each of whom knows only half the truth. The Theban Herdsman knows that the child he was ordered to expose was Jocasta's and that Laius was killed by Oedipus; he does not know that Oedipus was the child. The Corinthian Herdsman knows that Oedipus is the baby that he received from the Theban Herdsman. When the two are brought together, the pieces of the puzzle fit. Nothing could exceed the brilliance and dexterity with which Sophocles handles his material so as to extract the last ounce of drama from it.

Some readers may find these claims highly irritating, for it is possible to look at the play in another way. The actual story is puerile, the antecedents of the play are full of impossibilities, and the play itself contains not a few things which will not bear looking into; Oedipus's ignorance about his predecessor, his failure to respond to the plainest hints in spite of early doubts about his parentage, and the extreme irritability of Tiresias which leads to such momentous indiscretion, all these can be made the subject of easy wit, which would be justified if Oedipus was intended to be a Sherlock Holmes. The answer is that when the play is acting we do not think of looking into these things, and Sophocles never troubled himself to provide answers to questions which were not going to enter the mind of his audience. The simple and poetic fancy which contrives the folk-tale is puerile when judged from a certain angle; Sophocles, if less simple, is still moving in the world of poetry, and his plays can only be seen or read by those who are prepared to enter that world leaving all irrelevant cleverness behind.

The question of the guilt of Oedipus has been much discussed; here we are troubled by fundamental differences between primitive and sophisticated thought. Though things were moving fast when the *Oedipus* was written, men were finding great difficulty in escaping from the notion that certain acts brought with them a physical contamination as definite as the infection conveyed by contact with a leper. To this sort of guilt intention is irrelevant, though the Greeks at all times distinguished between acts done willingly and under compulsion. The incestuous parricide is a pariah; it is futile to try to analyse the horror felt by Oedipus and the Chorus at the discovery, but it is clear that they did not feel the purity of his intentions to be relevant. In the

Oedipus Coloneus written many years later Oedipus does feel this, but he still thinks that his touch conveys contamination. It is not, however, allowable to infer anything about the ideas implicit in an earlier play from the views expressed later in the poet's life.

FOR ANALYSIS

1. Do you agree with Lucas's assertion that Oedipus "does not know who he is, that is his *hamartia*" (para. 2)? Explain. Would Aristotle agree?

2. Oedipus strove to do the right thing—to avoid the horror that the oracles decreed—and yet Lucas still finds him guilty. Why?

ARTHUR MILLER   (1915-2005)

TRAGEDY AND THE COMMON MAN   1949

In this age few tragedies are written. It has often been held that the lack is due to a paucity of heroes among us, or else that modern man has had the blood drawn out of his organs of belief by the skepticism of science, and the heroic attack on life cannot feed on an attitude of reserve and circumspection. For one reason or another, we are often held to be below tragedy—or tragedy above us. The inevitable conclusion is, of course, that the tragic mode is archaic, fit only for the very highly placed, the kings or the kingly, and where this admission is not made in so many words it is most often implied.

I believe that the common man is as apt a subject for tragedy in its highest sense as kings were. On the face of it this ought to be obvious in the light of modern psychiatry, which bases its analysis upon classic formulations, such as the Oedipus and Orestes complexes, for instance, which were enacted by royal beings, but which apply to everyone in similar emotional situations.

More simply, when the question of tragedy in art is not at issue, we never hesitate to attribute to the well-placed and the exalted the very same mental processes as the lowly. And finally, if the exaltation of tragic action were truly a property of the high-bred character alone, it is inconceivable that the mass of mankind should cherish tragedy above all other forms, let alone be capable of understanding it.

As a general rule, to which there may be exceptions unknown to me, I think the tragic feeling is evoked in us when we are in the presence of a character who is ready to lay down his life, if need be, to secure one thing—his sense of personal dignity. From Orestes to Hamlet, Medea to Macbeth, the underlying struggle is that of the individual attempting to gain his "rightful" position in his society.

Sometimes he is one who has been displaced from it, sometimes one who 5 seeks to attain it for the first time, but the fateful wound from which the inevitable events spiral is the wound of indignity, and its dominant force is indignation. Tragedy, then, is the consequence of a man's total compulsion to evaluate himself justly.

In the sense of having been initiated by the hero himself, the tale always reveals what has been called his "tragic flaw," a failing that is not peculiar to grand or elevated characters. Nor is it necessarily a weakness. The flaw, or crack in the character, is really nothing—and need be nothing—but his inherent unwillingness to remain passive in the face of what he conceives to be a challenge to his dignity, his image of his rightful status. Only the passive, only those who accept their lot without active retaliation, are "flawless." Most of us are in that category.

But there are among us today, as there always have been, those who act against the scheme of things that degrades them, and in the process of action, everything we have accepted out of fear or insensitivity or ignorance is shaken before us and examined and from this total onslaught by an individual against the seemingly stable cosmos surrounding us—from this total examination of the "unchangeable" environment—comes the terror and the fear that is classically associated with tragedy.

More important, from this total questioning of what has been previously unquestioned, we learn. And such a process is not beyond the common man. In revolutions around the world, these past thirty years, he has demonstrated again and again this inner dynamic of all tragedy.

Insistence upon the rank of the tragic hero, or the so-called nobility of his character, is really but a clinging to the outward forms of tragedy. If rank or nobility of character was indispensable, then it would follow that the problems of those with rank were the particular problems of tragedy. But surely the right of one monarch to capture the domain from another no longer raises our passions, nor are our concepts of justice what they were to the mind of an Elizabethan king.

The quality in such plays that does shake us, however, derives from the underlying fear of being displaced, the disaster inherent in being torn away from our chosen image of what and who we are in this world. Among us today this fear is as strong, and perhaps stronger, than it ever was. In fact, it is the common man who knows this fear best. 10

Now, if it is true that tragedy is the consequence of a man's total compulsion to evaluate himself justly, his destruction in the attempt posits a wrong or an evil in his environment. And this is precisely the morality of tragedy and its lesson. The discovery of the moral law, which is what the enlightenment of tragedy consists of, is not the discovery of some abstract or metaphysical quantity.

The tragic right is a condition of life, a condition in which the human personality is able to flower and realize itself. The wrong is the condition which suppresses man, perverts the flowing out of his love and creative instinct. Tragedy enlightens—and it must, in that it points the heroic finger at the enemy of man's freedom. The thrust for freedom is the quality in tragedy which exalts. The revolutionary questioning of the stable environment is what terrifies. In no way is the common man debarred from such thoughts or such actions.

Seen in this light, our lack of tragedy may be partially accounted for by the turn which modern literature has taken toward the purely psychiatric view of life, or the purely sociological. If all our miseries, our indignities, are born and bred within our minds, then all action, let alone heroic action, is obviously impossible.

And if society alone is responsible for the cramping of our lives, then the protagonist must need be so pure and faultless as to force us to deny his validity as a character. From neither of these views can tragedy derive, simply because neither represents a balanced concept of life. Above all else, tragedy requires the finest appreciation by the writer of cause and effect.

No tragedy can therefore come about when its author fears to question 15 absolutely everything, when he regards any institution, habit or custom as being either everlasting, immutable or inevitable. In the tragic view the need of man to wholly realize himself is the only fixed star, and whatever it is that hedges his nature and lowers it is ripe for attack and examination. Which is not to say that tragedy must preach revolution.

The Greeks could probe the very heavenly origin of their ways and return to confirm the rightness of laws. And Job could face God in anger, demanding his right, and end in submission. But for a moment everything is in suspension, nothing is accepted, and in this stretching and tearing apart of the cosmos, in the very action of so doing, the character gains "size," the tragic stature which is spuriously attached to the royal or the high born in our minds. The commonest of men may take on that stature to the extent of his willingness to throw all he has into the contest, the battle to secure his rightful place in his world.

There is a misconception of tragedy with which I have been struck in review after review, and in many conversations with writers and readers alike. It is the idea that tragedy is of necessity allied to pessimism. Even the dictionary says nothing more about the word than that it means a story with a sad or unhappy ending. This impression is so firmly fixed that I almost hesitate to claim that in truth tragedy implies more optimism in its author than does comedy, and that its final result ought to be the reinforcement of the onlooker's brightest opinions of the human animal.

For, if it is true to say that in essence the tragic hero is intent upon claiming his whole due as a personality, and if this struggle must be total and without reservation, then it automatically demonstrates the indestructible will of man to achieve his humanity.

The possibility of victory must be there in tragedy. Where pathos rules, where pathos is finally derived, a character has fought a battle he could not possibly have won. The pathetic is achieved when the protagonist is, by virtue of his witlessness, his insensitivity, or the very air he gives off, incapable of grappling with a much superior force.

Pathos truly is the mode for the pessimist. But tragedy requires a nicer 20 balance between what is possible and what is impossible. And it is curious, although edifying, that the plays we revere, century after century, are the tragedies. In them, and in them alone, lies the belief—optimistic, if you will— in the perfectibility of man.

It is time, I think, that we who are without kings, took up this bright thread of our history and followed it to the only place it can possibly lead our time—the heart and spirit of the average man.

FOR ANALYSIS

1. In what fundamental way does Miller's view of tragedy differ from Aristotle's?

2. Historically, what political changes underlie Miller's view?

3. Ancient comedies depicted ordinary people on the stage. Why were they appropriate subjects for comedies but not for tragedies?

DAVID WILES (B. 1951)

ON OEDIPUS THE KING AS A POLITICAL PLAY 2000

Oedipus becomes a political play when we focus on the interaction of actor and chorus, and see how the chorus form a democratic mass jury. Each sequence of dialogue takes the form of a contest for the chorus' sympathy, with Oedipus sliding from the role of prosecutor to that of defendant, and each choral dance offers a provisional verdict. After Oedipus's set-to with Teiresias the soothsayer, the chorus decide to trust Oedipus on the basis of his past record; after his argument with his brother-in-law Creon, the chorus show their distress and urge compromise. Once Oedipus has confessed to a killing and Jocasta has declared that oracles have no force, the chorus are forced to think about political tyranny, torn between respect for divine law and trust in their rulers. In the next dance they assume that the contradiction is resolved and Oedipus has turned out to be the son of a god. Finally a slave's evidence reveals that the man most honoured by society is in fact the least to be envied. The political implications are clear: there is no space in democratic society for such as Oedipus. Athenians, like the chorus of the play, must reject the temptation to believe one man can calculate the future.

—From *Greek Theatre Performance: An Introduction*

FOR ANALYSIS

1. The title for Sophocles' play in the original Greek is *Oedipus Tyrannus*. *Tyrannus* did not carry the connotation of tyranny that we hear in it, but how does Wiles's analysis echo the original title?

2. People are naturally anxious about the future because anything can happen and nobody really knows what will. In a democracy, does our willingness to grant power to political leaders come from this anxiety about the future? Why would the governed trust politicians to lead them into an uncertain future?

MAKING CONNECTIONS

1. It is possible to read *Oedipus* and be struck by the unlikeliness of the convergence of the two plotlines. Is this a flaw in the play or a source of its power? Which of the commentaries helps you best answer this question?

2. Many of the critical responses to *Oedipus*, from Aristotle on, follow the structure of the plot, that is, the way in which the play orders events. Whose explanation of the order do you find most agreeable?

3. Both Fergusson and Wiles focus on the chorus but read its judgment in different ways, using it as evidence for alternate readings of the play. How do their interpretations of the chorus' role and judgment differ? Whose argument do you find more convincing?

4. Lucas argues that the "incestuous parricide is a pariah; it is futile to try to analyse the horror felt by Oedipus and the Chorus at the discovery" (para. 4). Did Freud agree? Do you?

SUZAN-LORI PARKS   (B. 1963)

FATHER COMES HOME FROM THE WARS[1]   2006

FATHER COMES HOME FROM THE WARS (PART 1)

Father. Hi honey, Im home.
Mother. Yr home.
Father. Yes.
Mother. I wasnt expecting you. Ever.
Father. Should I go back out and come back in again?
Mother. Please.

He goes back out and comes back in again.

Mother. Once more.
Father. Yr kidding.
Mother. Please.

He goes back out and comes back in again.

Mother. Yr home.
Father. Yes.
Mother. Let me get a good look at you.
Father. I'll just turn around.
Mother. Please.

He turns around once. Counterclockwise,

Mother. They should of sent a letter. A letter saying you were coming home. Or at least a telephone call. That is the least they could do. Give a woman and her family and her friends and neighbors a chance to get ready. A chance to spruce things up. Put new ribbons in the hair of the dog. Get the oil changed. Have everything running. Smoothly. And

Father. They sent a letter saying I was coming or at least they telephoned. Maybe you didnt open the letter. I dont blame you. It could have been bad news. I see yr unopened envelopes piled up. I dont blame you. I dont blame you at all. They called several times. Maybe you were out. Maybe you were screwing the yard man. If you had known

[1] The following twelve plays are from *365 Days/365 Plays* by Suzan-Lori Parks.

246

Mother (cont). bake a cake of course. Hang streamers. Tell the yard man to—tidy up his act. Oh God. Long story. Oh God. Long story. Oh God. Long story. I woulda invited the neighbors over. Had everyone on the block jump out from their hiding places from behind the brand-new furniture with the plastic still on it and say— WHAT? Say: "Welcome Home" of course. And then after a few slices of cake and a few drinks theyd all get the nerve to say what theyre really thinking. For now itll stay unthought and unsaid. Well. You came home. All in one piece looks like. We're lucky. I guess. We're lucky, right? Hhhhh.

Father (cont). I was coming you woulda put new ribbons in the hair of the dog, got the oil changed, baked a cake and invited all the neighbors over so they could jump out of their various hiding places behind the brand-new furniture purchased with the blood of some people I used to know—and some blood of some people I used to kill. Oh God. Long story. Oh God. Long story. And theyd shout at me— WHAT? "Welcome Home" of course. And then after a few slices of cake and a few drinks theyd get the nerve to tell me what they really think: "Murderer, baby killer, racist, government pawn, ultimate patsy, stooge, fall guy, camp follower, dumbass, dope fiend, loser." Hhhhh.

Mother
Father

(Rest)

Mother. I cant understand a word yr saying.
Father. I dont speak English anymore.
Mother. I dont blame you. SIT DOWN, I'LL FIX YOU SOMETHING.

He sits. She takes a heavy frying pan and holds it over his head. Almost murder. She lowers the pan.

Mother
Father

(Rest)

He sits. Again she raises the frying pan and holds it over his head. Almost murder.' She lowers the pan.

Father. Where are the children?
Mother. What children?

Sound of the wind and the rain.

FATHER COMES HOME FROM THE WARS (PART 2)

A Family (Mother, Father, Children) sitting. Neatly dressed. Theyre posing for a family portrait. Painter walks in.

Painter. Lets take up where we left off yesterday, shall we?
Mother. Thatll do nicely.

Painter paints. Children fidget. Mother eyes them or slaps them on their hands and they do their best to keep still. Painter paints. Soldier Man arrives, dressed in battle dress. It does not matter from what war; the Trojan war, WWI, American Civil, Iran-Iraq, Napoleonic, Spanish Civil, Crimean, Zulu, ANC against the Powers that Were, whatever, the Chinese-Tibetan conflict, the War of the Worlds, whatever, it does not matter. Soldier Man taps the Father of the Family on the shoulder, relieving him from duty. The Father was only a father figure, and, very graciously bows, clicks his heels and leaves. The Family does not flinch. The Painter continues to paint. After posing for awhile with his Family, Soldier Man wanders away. He puts on a record. Opera. A Puccini aria. He starts moving around.

Soldier Man. Lets have a sing-along, shall we?

He reaches out to the Family. They cringe and shrink from his touch. He can live with it. He dances around. Its clear that he's missing an eye, a leg, an arm—he sings and dances, quite beautifully, though, all the same. The Family watches him, with mounting horror, spoiling the portrait. The Painter turns to the audience:

Painter. Oh, this will never do!

The Family snaps back into polite alignment. The Painter continues painting. The Soldier Man's hearing is now gone too. He turns up the record player and continues singing and dancing as the Family, very bravely, you understand, holds very very still.

FATHER COMES HOME FROM THE WARS (PART 3)

Father, surrounded by his Soldiers, stands at the door. The Family is at dinner.

Father. Hi, honey, Im home.

The Family stares.

1st Soldier. When you hear the word "war" what comes to mind?
Father. Dont start that talk here. Im home.

2nd Soldier. You dont mind if we wait here do you?
Father. Do what you gotta do. Im home.

Father sits in his easy chair. His Soldiers wait.

Father. Come on, Junior. Lets watch some game shows.
Mother. Yr not hungry?
Sister. Mother and me made a welcome home pie for you. See the
    writing: "Welcome home from the wars, Father!"
(Rest)
Yr not even looking.
Father. All I wanna do is watch some goddamn game shows.
Junior. All thats on is war movies.
Father. Fine.
Mother. Who are yr friends, honey?
Father. Turn up the volume, Junior.
Junior. Im gonna be a soldier just like yr a soldier, right, Pop?

Father
Father

Father. You betcha.

*Junior turns up the volume and the Soldiers in the doorway make loud war sounds.
Father leans back and relaxes.*

FATHER COMES HOME FROM THE WARS (PART 4)

A man, the Father, comes in wearing army fatigues.

Father. Hello? Im home. Made it home in one piece! Anybody home?

*He looks for the Family, finds no one. Even goes looking offstage. No one. He spies
a note.*

Father. "Gone to the store. Back soon. Love, Family."
(Rest)
Thats nice.
(Rest)
Gives me plenty of time to change.

*He opens his pack. Changes into an army-issued business suit. Complete with army-
issued shoes and socks, a necktie, and a pipe and tobacco.*

Father. Army issue. Could be worse. Made in a country I cant even pronounce. Could be worse. I got a full suit. Some guys just get the jacket or just the shoes. Some guys dont got a need for the shoes, cause they dont got feet. There was a guy I knew, he used to be 6′4″: Save that story. Dont tell the kids. Dont tell the missus. Not suitable. Tell the soldiers at the VA hospital when you go in for yr shots. Right. Some lost their feet or their arms. Or their minds. Or they house. Or they wife and kids. Put that in yr army-issue pipe and smoke it. Leave yr edge at the door. Think: "Peace." Think: "Lucky You." Think: "Same Old Same Old." Sit in my favorite chair. Watch my army-issue tv. All I need is an army-issue dog. "Gone to the store. Back soon." I'll wait.

(Rest)

Im a lucky man.

FATHER COMES HOME FROM THE WARS (PART 5)

Cocktails before dinner. Very stylish. The den of an early 1960s home. Sophisticated but not over-the-top. Joe and Lovey (husband and wife) are the center of attention.

Joe. Crawling. For miles.
Host. Yr exaggerating.
Hostess. Let him tell his story.
Host. Just as long as you dont exaggerate.
Hostess. He loves tales, he hates tall tales.

Joe gives Lovey's hand a squeeze. Too hard.

Lovey. Its not a tall tale. Its the facts.
Host. Miles?
Joe. Scout's honor.

After a beat. The girls laugh in a stylish upscale manner.

Next Door Neighbor. Crawling for miles in the dirt? Go on—
Joe. In the *sand*.
Host. Tall tale.
Lovey. Not at all. He had so much sand in his boots. There was barely any room for his feet!

More stylish laughter.

Joe. I had sand in my mouth too. And every other uniform I saw—
Next Door Neighbor. Had the enemy in it.
Lovey. Worse.
Joe. Had a dead man in it.

Joe
Joe

(Rest)

A Kitchen Servant appears and whispers to the Host.

Host. The cook is making yr favorite dish, Joe. He wants to know how you like yr meat.
Joe. Raw.
Host. You mean rare.
Joe. 1 mean raw. With the skin of the animal still on it. Right, Lovey?

He hugs Lovey too hard.

Lovey. Joe's such a kidder.

Host
Joe

Host. How about well-done, Joe?
Joe. How about well-done, Sam?
Lovey. Yr home now, Joe.
Hostess. How about well-done, Joe?
Joe. Well-done it is. Im home now. After all.
Host. 3 cheers for Joe.

They toast Joe.

FATHER COMES HOME FROM THE WARS (PART 6)

The same people—minus Joe. All are many years older.

Host. 3 cheers for Joe. Come on.

They toast Joe.

Lovey. They wanted me to testify against him.
Hostess. No!
Lovey. They wanted me to say he beat me.
Next Door Neighbor. And after all he's done for this country.

Lovey
Host

Hostess
Next Door Neighbor

(Rest)

Host. Good old Joe!

(Rest)

Next Door Neighbor. Lovey, how about I sit on the picnic bench and you do for me what you do for Joe? Whaddayathink?
Lovey. I dont think so, K?
Next Door Neighbor. Dont hurt to ask, does it?

(Rest)

Hostess. Does Joe like it better at the Front?
Host. Its where he can be himself with no pretense.
Lovey. He writes to me every day. I have a whole room full of letters and theyre all love letters. And sometimes, when he writes about something—Top Secret— you know something he knows but that he's not supposed to know, something he knows that he's not supposed to say he knows, the censors crop it out. And—

Lovey
Lovey

Hostess. Well at least he doesnt come home with blood on his clothes anymore.
Host. Thats something.
Lovey. He doesnt come home at all.

They raise their glasses and laugh politely.

MOTHER COMES HOME FROM THE WARS

A Man looks up at the sky. A Woman enters.

Man. Yr back.
Woman. I got in last night.
Man. I heard they freed you.
Woman. Ive been doing interviews nonstop. The National Publisher wants to buy rights to my story.
Man. The National Publisher?
Woman. That means big money.
Man. Wow.

Woman. There was a picture of me on the front page of the paper.
Man. I missed it.
Woman. Ive got a copy for you.
Man. Thanks.

Woman
Man

Woman. Hon?
Man. What.
Woman. What are you looking at?
Man. God.
Woman. Youll go blind.

The Man lowers his head—he wears black spectacles.

Woman. Yr blind already.
Man. Yep.

The Man lifts his glasses and smiles.

Man. Just kidding.
Woman. Yr such a joker. I could have you shot. I had a lot of men shot. They were
all just like you. Just like you but—
Man. Foreign.
Woman. Just like you but foreign. Yes.

Man
Woman

Man. Welcome home, hon.

They embrace. We can see that their embrace, while warm and passionate, causes
them both excruciating pain.

PLAYING CHOPSTICKS (FATHER COMES
HOME FROM THE WARS, PART 7)

A Soldier Dad in an army uniform, like he's just come in from jungle combat. He's
still got a camouflage suit on, and dark paint covers his face. Maybe even jungle twigs
and branches stick out of his helmet and clothing. He sits on a campstool, a Kid sits
with him. The Soldier Dad is teaching the Kid to use chopsticks. They are moving a
mountain of rice into another pile, far across the other side of the stage, making

another, hopefully identical mountain. The Soldier Dad is great with chopsticks. The Kid is hopeless. Somewhere offstage someone plays the piano. Theyre playing "Chopsticks" over and over.

Soldier Dad. You wanted yr dad to bring you back something from over there. I brought you something, right?
Kid. Right.
(Rest)
Whats "gonorrhea"?

(Rest)

Soldier Dad. Thats something for adults, Kid. Lets stick to our chopsticks.
Kid. I heard Mom telling Grandmom that you brought her some "gonorrhea" home from the war.

Soldier Dad
Soldier Dad

Soldier Dad. I brought you something nice and yr acting like you dont like it, Kid. Here. Watch Dad do it.

Soldier Dad effortlessly picks up a piece of rice and walks over to the other side of the stage where he arranges it carefully on the pile.

Soldier Dad. The idea is to pick up the rice with the chopsticks, carry it over here and put the rice down. And put it down in such a way as we remake the rice mountain over here.
Kid. Right.
Soldier Dad. Its good practice.
Kid. For what?

Soldier Dad
Kid

Soldier Dad smacks Kid upside the head. The move comes so fast and seemingly out of nowhere. Like a flash flood. The Kid's head snaps horribly back, but then, just as quickly, the Soldier Dad's anger is spent. The Kid doesnt cry or anything.

Soldier Dad. Try it again. Go on. You gotta learn it.

The Kid tries moving the rice with the chopsticks again.

Soldier Dad. Not much better. Ok, a little better, but, watch.

Soldier Dad moves several pieces of rice, all one at a time, very quickly and with great fanfare, talking as he moves them.

Soldier Dad. Soldier Dad can move them quick. Soldier Dad can hold the chopsticks in his right hand and move rice, and he can hold them in his left hand too. Makes no difference. Soldier Dad can hold the sticks behind his back, he doesnt have to look, its just that easy. And every piece of rice gets put in its place!

The Kid watches with mounting awe and mounting anger. Offstage the piano playing gets louder.

Soldier Dad *(Yelling to the offstage piano).* CUT THAT OUT, HUH? HOW AM I SUPPOSED TO FUCKING THINK WITH YOU FUCKING, FUCKING THAT MUSIC UP??!!

The music stops.

Kid
Soldier Dad

Kid. You want me to try it again?
Soldier Dad. Yr mother used to be a concert pianist.
Kid. You want me to try it again?
Soldier Dad. Yeah. Go ahead.

The Kid tries moving the rice again. He's much better this time—like a miracle happened—and now he's actually pretty good.

Soldier Dad. Wow! Great job, Kid.
Kid. Thanks.
Soldier Dad. Chip off the old block after all. I was worried I'd been away for so long and you—you couldnt do the rice thing.
(Rest)
It was the only thing I brought you back and you couldnt do it and I was worried. But you can do it. My Kid's my Kid! Good. So lets get to work, huh?

The music starts up again and the Kid and Soldier Dad get back to work. Each is amazing at moving the rice. And they are enjoying themselves. It is horrible to see them enjoying themselves doing such a pointless task. But they are building a monument together—and this monument will be a fortress against the future pain. And the music, playing all the while, seeps into the walls of the fortress, seeps in and holds it like stone.

FATHER COMES HOME FROM THE WARS (PART 8)

Mother stares out toward the audience into space. Father enters dragging an enormous bloody sword.

Father. Im home.
Mother. At last.
Father. Yes

(Rest)

Mother. Where were you?
Father. The wars.
Mother. And then?
Father. Lost.
Mother. Oh.
Father. Where are the children?
Mother. Grown up and moved away.
Father. Oh.

Sounds of the sea in the near distance

FATHER COMES HOME FROM THE WARS (PART 9)

Several Fathers, men in army suits or uniforms, are sitting in a row: a Soldier, a Sailor, a Janitor with a broom, a Security Guard with a badge and a gun, a Mechanic with an oily rag and a wrench, a Businessman with a suit and a briefcase, maybe an Astronaut even. They are all young-looking: fresh-faced, and firm-limbed; but very, very old-acting in the most typical of ways: forgetful, passive, paranoid, sad, weak, infirm, angry. The Mechanic wipes his head. The Security Guard peers worriedly at the audience. The Janitor sweeps. The Businessman opens his briefcase, realizes its empty, and closes it The Soldier and Sailor are having a conversation:

Soldier. "Father's Home—Comes from the Wars."
Sailor. You got the title wrong.
Soldier. Did not.
Sailor. Did too.
Soldier. You got water in yr ears. You wanna step outside?
Sailor. You got the title wrong. Im just trying to—
Soldier. What the hell is it, then?
Sailor. I dont know. But "Father's Home—Comes from the Wars" it aint.

(Rest)

Janitor. They put me in the doghouse. Thats not a lie. Do you know how hard it was? A man my size, living in a house so small. And in the backyard.

Mechanic. Least they didnt put you on the junk pile. Thats where they put me. Cause I'd cost them an arm and a leg to fix. So they junked me. After that, I turned to junk. Drugs, you know. Thats what I did. Lots of drugs. What else could I do?

Security Guard. Look! The war!

They strain their necks downstage to get a better look.

Businessman. Its something, isnt it?
Soldier. Its bloody.
Businessman. Cant have a war without blood.
Janitor. Why have a war at all?
Businessman. Clean-up. Theres money in the clean-up.
Sailor. Its closer than it was yesterday. I can feel the heat from the fire on my face.

They all lean in their chairs slightly, like heliotropism, when flowers crane and strain and turn beautifully toward the sun. Theres the sound of a high-pitched whine underneath, like the barely audible (but sustained) screeching of fingernails on a blackboard. The lights grow very bright and then pop out.

SWEET (FATHER COMES HOME FROM THE WARS, PART 10)

A Man eats slowly, but like an animal. A Woman watches.

Woman. Yr home.
Man. I know.

His plate is empty. The Woman piles more food onto his plate.

Man. Im home but I still got the taste for killing, you know?
Woman. Lemmie put some sugar on. It tastes like shit without sugar.

She pours a lot of sugar on his food. He continues eating. At last his plate is empty. He puts his knife in its sheath.

Man. Im gonna go out for awhile.
Woman. Where to?
Man. Nowhere special. I'll just, you know—
Woman. Walk around.
Man. Yeah.

(Rest)

Woman. Just smell them before you cut them, ok?
Man. Have I ever killed one of our own?
Woman. No, but—
Man. Yr talking to me like I killed one of our own.
Woman. You never done nothing like that—its just—I worry.
Man. If you kept them in the house you wouldnt have no worries.
Woman. Theyre grown. And the house is small.
Man. So I'll get us a bigger house. WHEN I GET A BIGGER JOB!
(Rest)
In the meantime, I gotta go out.

Woman
Man

(Rest)

Man. Itll wear off in awhile. The taste for it.
Woman. Lets hope.

He goes. She frets, then cleans up the dishes. A Young Man enters.

Junior. Hey Mom. Wheres Pop?—
Woman. Out bowling—with his bowling buddies, Junior.
Junior. Sweet. Im history, K?
Woman. Oh no yr not.
Junior. Come on, I did my homework. And my chores.
Woman. One step out there and yr grounded, mister.
Junior. You cant ground me, Ive served my country.
(Rest)
Later. K, Mom?

He kisses her and goes. As soon as he has cleared the stage, Sister comes on.

Sister. Wheres Junior and Pop?
Woman. Out and about.
Sister. Im—
Woman. Dont—
Sister. Hey—
Woman. Sure. Yr history. I know. Whatever. Sweet.

Sister
Woman

Sister goes. The Woman very meticulously cleans up the dishes and sits. Then she quickly gets up, puts on a coat and hat and hurries out the door. The house is empty. No foul play will happen to any of them, although, of course, they may cause foul play to others, and, of course, none of them will ever ever return.

FATHER COMES HOME FROM THE WARS (PART 11: HIS ETERNAL RETURN—A PLAY FOR MY FATHER)

During this play we hear a war news-in-brief soundtrack, laced with military band music thats played at a slower than normal speed. The action is as follows: A never-ending loop of action—Servicemen walk downstage together. All wear military uniforms from the same side of the same war, but not necessarily the same branch of Service. They stand upstage and walk very vibrantly and heroically downstage. Theyre returning home as heroes. As they reach centerstage, 5 women, their Servicewives, stand up from the audience, and run toward the men. Just as the Servicemen reach the downstage edge, the Servicewives meet them. The Servicemen pick up their Servicewives, twirling them around very joyfully. Before each Wife returns to the ground a Child comes onstage and, racing toward its respective Mother and Father, jumps for joy. This action repeats. New Servicemen walk downstage, new Wives leap up from the audience and rush into their arms, new Children run in to cheer. The action repeats eternally. Long after the audience has emptied of Women; long after the Men have grown out of the desire to be hugged and kissed and welcomed; long after the Children have become less cheerful and more sensible and have taken up trades, like accounting or teaching or real estate or politics; long after the Children's Children have outgrown joy and have all grown-up and moved away. Forever.

FOR ANALYSIS

1. Would you describe these short plays as realistic or unrealistic? How does their realism or irrealism serve their subject?

2. It is typical to think of soldiers who make it back from wars, and the families to whom they return, as lucky. Is that how these short plays present this situation? How else do they portray these soldiers and their families?

MAKING CONNECTIONS

1. Compare Parks's techniques for reflecting on war to those employed by Wilfred Owen in "Dulce et Decorum Est" (p. 435). Do they have similar things to say? How does the way they say them affect their their meaning?

2. Compare the depictions of Father by Parks to one of the fathers in "Connecting Poems: Remembering Fathers" in "Love and Hate" (p. 943). Based on the settings, what are fathers "supposed" to be like? How, in these works, do they really behave?

WRITING TOPICS

1. Characterize the stance these different *Father Comes Home from the Wars* plays have toward war. Are they prowar? Antiwar? Prosoldier? Antisoldier? Explain your characterization with support from specific moments in the plays.

2. In *Father Comes Home from the Wars (Part 4)*, Father says, "Save that story. Dont tell the kids. Dont tell the missus. Not suitable" (p. 250). What kind of story is Father not telling? How does Parks herself do the same thing and to what effect?

NONFICTION

LANGSTON HUGHES   (1902–1967)

SALVATION   1940

I was saved from sin when I was going on thirteen. But not really saved. It happened like this. There was a big revival at my Auntie Reed's church. Every night for weeks there had been much preaching, singing, praying, and shouting, and some very hardened sinners had been brought to Christ, and the membership of the church had grown by leaps and bounds. Then just before the revival ended, they held a special meeting for children, "to bring the young lambs to the fold." My aunt spoke of it for days ahead. That night I was escorted to the front row and placed on the mourners' bench with all the other young sinners, who had not yet been brought to Jesus.

My aunt told me that when you were saved you saw a light, and something happened to you inside! And Jesus came into your life! And God was with you from then on! She said you could see and hear and feel Jesus in your soul. I believed her. I had heard a great many old people say the same thing and it seemed to me they ought to know. So I sat there calmly in the hot, crowded church, waiting for Jesus to come to me.

The preacher preached a wonderful rhythmical sermon, all moans and shouts and lonely cries and dire pictures of hell, and then he sang a song about the ninety and nine safe in the fold, but one little lamb was left out in the cold. Then he said: "Won't you come? Won't you come to Jesus? Young lambs, won't you come?" And he held out his arms to all us young sinners there on the mourners' bench. And the little girls cried. And some of them jumped up and went to Jesus right away. But most of us just sat there.

A great many old people came and knelt around us and prayed, old women with jet-black faces and braided hair, old men with work-gnarled hands. And the church sang a song about the lower lights are burning, some poor sinners to be saved. And the whole building rocked with prayer and song.

Still I kept waiting to *see* Jesus.   5

Finally all the young people had gone to the altar and were saved, but one boy and me. He was a rounder's son named Westley. Westley and I were surrounded by sisters and deacons praying. It was very hot in the church, and getting late now. Finally Westley said to me in a whisper: "God damn! I'm tired o' sitting here. Let's get up and be saved." So he got up and was saved.

Then I was left all alone on the mourners' bench. My aunt came and knelt at my knees and cried, while prayers and song swirled all around me in the little church. The whole congregation prayed for me alone, in a mighty wail of moans and voices. And I kept waiting serenely for Jesus, waiting, waiting—but he didn't come. I wanted to see him, but nothing happened to me. Nothing! I wanted something to happen to me, but nothing happened.

I heard the songs and the minister saying: "Why don't you come? My dear child, why don't you come to Jesus? Jesus is waiting for you. He wants you. Why don't you come? Sister Reed, what is this child's name?"

"Langston," my aunt sobbed.

"Langston, why don't you come? Why don't you come and be saved? Oh, 10 Lamb of God! Why don't you come?"

Now it was really getting late. I began to be ashamed of myself, holding everything up so long. I began to wonder what God thought about Westley, who certainly hadn't seen Jesus either, but who was now sitting proudly on the platform, swinging his knickerbockered legs and grinning down at me, surrounded by deacons and old women on their knees praying. God had not struck Westley dead for taking his name in vain or for lying in the temple. So I decided that maybe to save further trouble, I'd better lie, too, and say that Jesus had come, and get up and be saved.

So I got up.

Suddenly the whole room broke into a sea of shouting, as they saw me rise. Waves of rejoicing swept the place. Women leaped in the air. My aunt threw her arms around me. The minister took me by the hand and led me to the platform.

When things quieted down, in a hushed silence, punctuated by a few ecstatic "Amens," all the new young lambs were blessed in the name of God. Then joyous singing filled the room.

That night, for the last time in my life but one—for I was a big boy twelve 15 years old—I cried. I cried, in bed alone, and couldn't stop. I buried my head under the quilts, but my aunt heard me. She woke up and told my uncle I was crying because the Holy Ghost had come into my life, and because I had seen Jesus. But I was really crying because I couldn't bear to tell her that I had lied, that I had deceived everybody in the church, that I hadn't seen Jesus, and that now I didn't believe there was a Jesus any more, since he didn't come to help me.

FOR ANALYSIS

1. Is the **tone** of this essay comic or serious or both? Explain.
2. What role does Westley (para. 6) play in the narrative?

3. Can the word *salvation* as Hughes uses it be construed in more than one way? Explain.

4. Discuss how the **point of view** of a narrator who looks back on a childhood experience helps define the meaning of the experience.

MAKING CONNECTIONS

1. Compare and contrast Hughes's loss of innocence with that of Sylvia in Bambara's "The Lesson" (p. 110).

2. Compare and contrast the narrator's attitude toward adult authority in this story with Sylvia's in Bambara's "The Lesson" (p. 110).

WRITING TOPIC

Describe an experience in which public pressure forced you either to express an opinion or a belief that you didn't really hold or to act in a way you otherwise would not have.

JOAN DIDION   (B. 1934)

ON MORALITY   1965

As it happens I am in Death Valley, in a room at the Enterprise Motel and Trailer Park, and it is July, and it is hot. In fact it is 119°. I cannot seem to make the air conditioner work, but there is a small refrigerator, and I can wrap ice cubes in a towel and hold them against the small of my back. With the help of the ice cubes I have been trying to think, because *The American Scholar*[1] asked me to, in some abstract way about "morality," a word I distrust more every day, but my mind veers inflexibly toward the particular.

Here are some particulars. At midnight last night, on the road in from Las Vegas to Death Valley Junction, a car hit a shoulder and turned over. The driver, very young and apparently drunk, was killed instantly. His girl was found alive but bleeding internally, deep in shock. I talked this afternoon to the nurse who had driven the girl to the nearest doctor, 185 miles across the floor of the Valley and three ranges of lethal mountain road. The nurse explained that her husband, a talc miner, had stayed on the highway with the boy's body until the coroner could get over the mountains from Bishop, at dawn today. "You can't just leave a body on the highway," she said. "It's immoral."

It was one instance in which I did not distrust the word, because she meant something quite specific. She meant that if a body is left alone for even a few minutes on the desert, the coyotes close in and eat the flesh. Whether or not a corpse is torn apart by coyotes may seem only a sentimental consideration, but of course it is more: one of the promises we make to one another is that we will try to retrieve our casualties, try not to abandon our dead to the coyotes. If we have been taught to keep our promises—if, in the simplest terms, our upbringing is good enough—we stay with the body, or have bad dreams.

I am talking, of course, about the kind of social code that is sometimes called, usually pejoratively, "wagon-train morality." In fact that is precisely what it is. For better or worse, we are what we learned as children: my own childhood was illuminated by graphic litanies of the grief awaiting those who failed in their loyalties to each other. The Donner-Reed Party,[2] starving in the Sierra snows, all the ephemera of civilization gone save that one vestigial taboo, the provision that no one should eat his own blood kin. The Jayhawkers, who quarreled and separated not far from where I am tonight. Some of them

---

[1] A general-interest journal published by the Phi Beta Kappa Society.

[2] A group of eighty-seven people who tried to cross the mountains into California during the stormy winter of 1846. The forty-seven who survived the ordeal ate the flesh of those who died.

died in the Funerals[3] and some of them died down near Badwater and most of the rest of them died in the Panamints. A woman who got through gave the Valley its name. Some might say that the Jayhawkers were killed by the desert summer, and the Donner Party by the mountain winter, by circumstances beyond control; we were taught instead that they had somewhere abdicated their responsibilities, somehow breached their primary loyalties, or they would not have found themselves helpless in the mountain winter or the desert summer, would not have given way to acrimony, would not have deserted one another, would not have *failed*. In brief, we heard such stories as cautionary tales, and they still suggest the only kind of "morality" that seems to me to have any but the most potentially mendacious meaning.

You are quite possibly impatient with me by now; I am talking, you want to   5 say, about a "morality" so primitive that it scarcely deserves the name, a code that has as its point only survival, not the attainment of the ideal good. Exactly. Particularly out here tonight, in this country so ominous and terrible that to live in it is to live with antimatter, it is difficult to believe that "the good" is a knowable quantity. Let me tell you what it is like out here tonight. Stories travel at night on the desert. Someone gets in his pickup and drives a couple of hundred miles for a beer, and he carries news of what is happening, back wherever he came from. Then he drives another hundred miles for another beer, and passes along stories from the last place as well as from the one before; it is a network kept alive by people whose instincts tell them that if they do not keep moving at night on the desert they will lose all reason. Here is a story that is going around the desert tonight: over across the Nevada line, sheriff's deputies are diving in some underground pools, trying to retrieve a couple of bodies known to be in the hole. The widow of one of the drowned boys is over there; she is eighteen, and pregnant, and is said not to leave the hole. The divers go down and come up, and she just stands there and stares into the water. They have been diving for ten days but have found no bottom to the caves, no bodies and no trace of them, only the black 90° water going down and down and down, and a single translucent fish, not classified. The story tonight is that one of the divers has been hauled up incoherent, out of his head, shouting—until they got him out of there so that the widow could not hear—about water that got hotter instead of cooler as he went down, about light flickering through the water, about magma, about underground nuclear testing.

That is the tone stories take out here, and there are quite a few of them tonight. And it is more than the stories alone. Across the road at the Faith Community Church a couple of dozen old people, come here to live in trailers and die in the sun, are holding a prayer sing. I cannot hear them and do not want to. What I can hear are occasional coyotes and a constant chorus of "Baby the Rain Must Fall" from the jukebox in the Snake Room next door, and if I were also to hear those dying voices, those Midwestern voices drawn to this

---

[3] The Funerals and the Panamints are mountain ranges close to Death Valley.

lunar country for some unimaginable atavistic rites, *rock of ages cleft for me,* I think I would lose my own reason. Every now and then I imagine I hear a rattlesnake, but my husband says that it is a faucet, a paper rustling, the wind. Then he stands by a window, and plays a flashlight over the dry wash outside.

What does it mean? It means nothing manageable. There is some sinister hysteria in the air out here tonight, some hint of the monstrous perversion to which any human idea can come. "I followed my own conscience." "I did what I thought was right." How many madmen have said it and meant it? How many murderers? Klaus Fuchs said it, and the men who committed the Mountain Meadows Massacre said it, and Alfred Rosenberg[4] said it. And, as we are rotely and rather presumptuously reminded by those who would say it now, Jesus said it. Maybe we have all said it, and maybe we have been wrong. Except on that most primitive level—our loyalties to those we love—what could be more arrogant than to claim the primacy of personal conscience? ("Tell me," a rabbi asked Daniel Bell when he said, as a child, that he did not believe in God. "Do you think God cares?") At least some of the time, the world appears to me as a painting by Hieronymus Bosch;[5] were I to follow my conscience then, it would lead me out onto the desert with Marion Faye, out to where he stood in *The Deer Park*[6] looking east to Los Alamos and praying, as if for rain, that it would happen: "*. . . let it come and clear the rot and the stench and the stink, let it come for all of everywhere, just so it comes and the world stands clear in the white dead dawn.*"

Of course you will say that I do not have the right, even if I had the power, to inflict that unreasonable conscience upon you; nor do I want you to inflict your conscience, however reasonable, however enlightened, upon me. ("We must be aware of the dangers which lie in our most generous wishes," Lionel Trilling[7] once wrote. "Some paradox of our nature leads us, when once we have made our fellow men the objects of our enlightened interest, to go on to make them the objects of our pity, then of our wisdom, ultimately of our coercion.") That the ethic of conscience is intrinsically insidious seems scarcely a revelatory point, but it is one raised with increasing infrequency; even those who do raise it tend to *segue* with troubling readiness into the quite contradictory position that the ethic of conscience is dangerous when it is "wrong," and admirable when it is "right."

---

[4] Klaus Fuchs fled Germany to the United States, where he worked on the development of the atomic bomb during World War II. He moved to Great Britain to assume an important position at the British atomic energy center. He was convicted and imprisoned for providing atomic energy secrets to the Soviet Union. The Mountain Meadows Massacre occurred in September 1857 in Utah. A group of 130 to 140 emigrants heading for California were attacked by Indians incited and joined by Mormons angry at the treatment they had received during their earlier trek across the continent. All but seventeen children were massacred. Alfred Rosenberg was a Nazi leader often called "The Grand Inquisitor of the Third Reich." He was hanged for war crimes in 1946.

[5] Hieronymus Bosch (ca. 1450–ca. 1516), a Dutch painter of fantastic and hellish images.

[6] A novel by Norman Mailer.

[7] Lionel Trilling (1905–1975), an eminent critic of literature and modern culture.

You see I want to be quite obstinate about insisting that we have no way of knowing—beyond that fundamental loyalty to the social code—what is "right" and what is "wrong," what is "good" and what "evil." I dwell so upon this because the most disturbing aspect of "morality" seems to me to be the frequency with which the word now appears; in the press, on television, in the most perfunctory kinds of conversation. Questions of straightforward power (or survival) politics, questions of quite indifferent public policy, questions of almost anything: they are all assigned these factitious moral burdens. There is something facile going on, some self-indulgence at work. Of course we would all like to "believe" in something, like to assuage our private guilts in public causes, like to lose our tiresome selves; like, perhaps, to transform the white flag of defeat at home into the brave white banner of battle away from home. And of course it is all right to do that; that is how, immemorially, things have gotten done. But I think it is all right only so long as we do not delude ourselves about what we are doing, and why. It is all right only so long as we remember that all the *ad hoc* committees, all the picket lines, all the brave signatures in *The New York Times,* all the tools of agitprop straight across the spectrum, do not confer upon anyone any *ipso facto* virtue. It is all right only so long as we recognize that the end may or may not be expedient, may or may not be a good idea, but in any case has nothing to do with "morality." Because when we start deceiving ourselves into thinking not that we want something or need something, not that it is a pragmatic necessity for us to have it, but that it is a *moral imperative* that we have it, then is when we join the fashionable madmen, and then is when the thin whine of hysteria is heard in the land, and then is when we are in bad trouble. And I suspect we are already there.

FOR ANALYSIS

1. What instances of "wagon-train" or "primitive" morality does Didion cite? How would you characterize that morality? Why is Didion comfortable with that sort of morality?

2. Why is Didion pleased that the music from a jukebox drowns out the singing of the prayer meeting near the motel (para. 6)? How does her identification of the musical pieces contribute to the argument of this essay?

3. What is the point of her including the speech from *The Deer Park* (para. 7)?

4. What names and, by implication, events does Didion use to illustrate some possibilities of abstract morality?

5. What role does the quotation from Lionel Trilling (para. 8) play in the essay?

MAKING CONNECTIONS

1. Didion says that "we are what we learned as children" (para. 4). Do your own moral values reflect what you learned as a child, or did those values change as you grew older? Explain.

2. Compare and contrast Didion's views on morality with King's in "Letter from Birmingham Jail" (p. 529).

WRITING TOPICS

1. Focusing on the next-to-last sentence of this piece, write an essay in which you distinguish between *needs, wants,* and *pragmatic necessities* on the one hand, and *moral imperatives* on the other. Why is it dangerous to convert *needs, wants,* and *pragmatic necessities* into *moral imperatives?* Conclude with your own judgment on the usefulness or necessity of moral imperatives.

2. Write an essay describing a personal experience that required you to choose among alternatives that were not clearly "right" or "wrong." Explain how you resolved the dilemma.

AMERICAN HISTORY   1993

I once read in a *Ripley's Believe It or Not* column that Paterson, New Jersey, is the place where the Straight and Narrow (streets) intersect. The Puerto Rican tenement known as El Building was one block up from Straight. It was, in fact, the corner of Straight and Market; not "at" the corner, but *the* corner. At almost any hour of the day, El Building was like a monstrous jukebox, blasting out *salsas* from open windows as the residents, mostly new immigrants just up from the island, tried to drown out whatever they were currently enduring with loud music. But the day President Kennedy was shot, there was a profound silence in El Building, even the abusive tongues of viragoes, the cursing of the unemployed, and the screeching of small children had been somehow muted. President Kennedy was a saint to these people. In fact, soon his photograph would be hung along-side the Sacred Heart and over the spiritist altars that many women kept in their apartments. He would become part of the hierarchy of martyrs they prayed to for favors that only one who had died for a cause would understand.

On the day that President Kennedy was shot, my ninth grade class had been out in the fenced playground of Public School Number 13. We had been given "free" exercise time and had been ordered by our P.E. teacher, Mr. DePalma, to "keep moving." That meant that the girls should jump rope and the boys toss basketballs through a hoop at the far end of the yard. He in the meantime would "keep an eye" on us from just inside the building.

It was a cold gray day in Paterson. The kind that warns of early snow. I was miserable, since I had forgotten my gloves and my knuckles were turning red and raw from the jump rope. I was also taking a lot of abuse from the black girls for not turning the rope hard and fast enough for them.

"Hey, Skinny Bones, pump it, girl. Ain't you got no energy today?" Gail, the biggest of the black girls who had the other end of the rope yelled, "Didn't you eat your rice and beans and pork chops for breakfast today?"

The other girls picked up the "pork chop" and made it into a refrain: "pork ⁵ chop, pork chop, did you eat your pork chop?" They entered the double ropes in pairs and exited without tripping or missing a beat. I felt a burning on my cheeks, and then my glasses fogged up so that I could not manage to coordinate the jump rope with Gail. The chill was doing to me what it always did, entering my bones, making me cry, humiliating me. I hated the city, especially in winter. I hated Public School Number 13. I hated my skinny flat-chested body, and I envied the black girls who could jump rope so fast that their legs became a blur. They always seemed to be warm while I froze.

There was only one source of beauty and light for me that school year. The only thing I had anticipated at the start of the semester. That was seeing Eugene. In August, Eugene and his family had moved into the only house on the block that had a yard and trees. I could see his place from my window in El Building. In fact, if I sat on the fire escape I was literally suspended above Eugene's backyard. It was my favorite spot to read my library books in the summer. Until that August the house had been occupied by an old Jewish couple. Over the years I had become part of their family, without their knowing it, of course. I had a view of their kitchen and their backyard, and though I could not hear what they said, I knew when they were arguing, when one of them was sick, and many other things. I knew all this by watching them at mealtimes. I could see their kitchen table, the sink and the stove. During good times, he sat at the table and read his newspapers while she fixed the meals. If they argued, he would leave and the old woman would sit and stare at nothing for a long time. When one of them was sick, the other would come and get things from the kitchen and carry them out on a tray. The old man had died in June. The last week of school I had not seen him at the table at all. Then one day I saw that there was a crowd in the kitchen. The old woman had finally emerged from the house on the arm of a stocky middle-aged woman whom I had seen there a few times before, maybe her daughter. Then a man had carried out suitcases. The house had stood empty for weeks. I had had to resist the temptation to climb down into the yard and water the flowers the old lady had taken such good care of.

By the time Eugene's family moved in, the yard was a tangled mass of weeds. The father had spent several days mowing, and when he finished, I didn't see the red, yellow, and purple clusters that meant flowers to me from where I sat. I didn't see this family sit down at the kitchen table together. It was just the mother, a red-headed tall woman who wore a white uniform—a nurse's, I guessed it was; the father was gone before I got up in the morning and was never there at dinner time. I only saw him on weekends when they sometimes sat on lawn chairs under the oak tree, each hidden behind a section of the newspaper; and there was Eugene. He was tall and blond, and he wore glasses. I liked him right away because he sat at the kitchen table and read books for hours. That summer, before we had even spoken one word to each other, I kept him company on my fire escape.

Once school started I looked for him in all my classes, but P.S. 13 was a huge, overpopulated place and it took me days and many discreet questions to discover that Eugene was in honors classes for all his subjects; classes that were not open to me because English was not my first language, though I was a straight A student. After much maneuvering I managed "to run into him" in the hallway where his locker was—on the other side of the building from mine—and in study hall at the library, where he first seemed to notice me but did not speak; and finally, on the way home after school one day when I decided to approach him directly, though my stomach was doing somersaults.

I was ready for rejection, snobbery, the worst. But when I came up to him, practically panting in my nervousness, and blurted out: "You're Eugene. Right?" He smiled, pushed his glasses up on his nose, and nodded. I saw then that he was blushing deeply. Eugene liked me, but he was shy. I did most of the talking that day. He nodded and smiled a lot. In the weeks that followed, we walked home together. He would linger at the corner of El Building for a few minutes then walk down to his two-story house. It was not until Eugene moved into that house that I noticed that El Building blocked most of the sun and that the only spot that got a little sunlight during the day was the tiny square of earth the old woman had planted with flowers.

I did not tell Eugene that I could see inside his kitchen from my bedroom. I felt dishonest, but I liked my secret sharing of his evenings, especially now that I knew what he was reading, since we chose our books together at the school library.

One day my mother came into my room as I was sitting on the windowsill staring out. In her abrupt way she said: "Elena, you are acting 'moony.'" *Enamorada* was what she really said—that is, like a girl stupidly infatuated. Since I had turned fourteen and started menstruating my mother had been more vigilant than ever. She acted as if I was going to go crazy or explode or something if she didn't watch me and nag me all the time about being a señorita now. She kept talking about virtue, morality, and other subjects that did not interest me in the least. My mother was unhappy in Paterson, but my father had a good job at the blue jeans factory in Passaic, and soon, he kept assuring us, we would be moving to our own house there. Every Sunday we drove out to the suburbs of Paterson, Clifton, and Passaic, out to where people mowed grass on Sundays in the summer and where children made snowmen in the winter from pure white snow, not like the gray slush of Paterson, which seemed to fall from the sky in that hue. I had learned to listen to my parents' dreams, which were spoken in Spanish, as fairy tales, like the stories about life in the island paradise of Puerto Rico before I was born. I had been to the island once as a little girl, to grandmother's funeral, and all I remembered was wailing women in black, my mother becoming hysterical and being given a pill that made her sleep two days, and me feeling lost in a crowd of strangers all claiming to be my aunts, uncles, and cousins. I had actually been glad to return to the city. We had not been back there since then, though my parents talked constantly about buying a house on the beach someday, retiring on the island—that was a common topic among the residents of El Building. As for me, I was going to go to college and become a teacher.

But after meeting Eugene I began to think of the present more than of the future. What I wanted now was to enter that house I had watched for so many years. I wanted to see the other rooms where the old people had lived and where the boy I liked spent his time. Most of all, I wanted to sit at the kitchen table with Eugene like two adults, like the old man and his wife had done, maybe drink some coffee and talk about books. I had started reading *Gone with the Wind*. I was enthralled by it, with the daring and the passion of the beautiful girl living in a mansion, and with her devoted parents and the slaves who did everything for them. I didn't believe such a world had ever really existed, and I wanted to ask Eugene some questions, since he and his parents, he had told me, had come up from Georgia, the same place where the novel was set. His father worked for a company that had transferred him to Paterson. His mother was very unhappy, Eugene said, in his beautiful voice that rose and fell over words in a strange, lilting way. The kids at school called him the Hick and made fun of the way he talked. I knew I was his only friend so far, and I liked that, though I felt sad for him sometimes. Skinny Bones and the Hick, was what they called us at school when we were seen together.

The day Mr. DePalma came out into the cold and asked us to line up in front of him was the day that President Kennedy was shot. Mr. DePalma, a short, muscular man with slicked-down black hair, was the science teacher, P.E. coach, and disciplinarian at P.S. 13. He was the teacher to whose homeroom you got assigned if you were a troublemaker, and the man called out to break up playground fights, and to escort violently angry teenagers to the office. And Mr. DePalma was the man who called your parents in for "a conference."

That day, he stood in front of two rows of mostly black and Puerto Rican kids, brittle from their efforts to "keep moving" on a November day that was turning bitter cold. Mr. DePalma, to our complete shock, was crying. Not just silent adult tears, but really sobbing. There were a few titters from the back of the line where I stood, shivering.

"Listen," Mr. DePalma raised his arms over his head as if he were about to 15 conduct an orchestra. His voice broke, and he covered his face with his hands. His barrel chest was heaving. Someone giggled behind me.

"Listen," he repeated, "something awful has happened." A strange gurgling came from his throat, and he turned around and spit on the cement behind him.

"Gross," someone said, and there was a lot of laughter.

"The president is dead, you idiots. I should have known that wouldn't mean anything to a bunch of losers like you kids. Go home." He was shrieking now. No one moved for a minute or two, but then a big girl let out a "yeah!" and ran to get her books piled up with the others against the brick wall of the school building. The others followed in a mad scramble to get to their things before somebody caught on. It was still an hour to the dismissal bell.

A little scared, I headed for El Building. There was an eerie feeling on the streets. I looked into Mario's drugstore, a favorite hangout for the high school crowd, but there were only a couple of old Jewish men at the soda bar, talking with the short order cook in tones that sounded almost angry, but they were keeping their voices low. Even the traffic on one of the busiest intersections in Paterson—Straight Street and Park Avenue—seemed to be moving slower. There were no horns blasting that day. At El Building, the usual little group of unemployed men were not hanging out on the front stoop, making it difficult for women to enter the front door. No music spilled out from open doors in the hallway. When I walked into our apartment, I found my mother sitting in front of the grainy picture of the television set.

She looked up at me with a tear-streaked face and just said: "Dios mío," 20 turning back to the set as if it were pulling at her eyes. I went into my room.

Though I wanted to feel the right thing about President Kennedy's death, I could not fight the feeling of elation that stirred in my chest. Today was the day I was to visit Eugene in his house. He had asked me to come over after school to study for an American history test with him. We had also planned to walk to the public library together. I looked down into his yard. The oak tree was bare of leaves, and the ground looked gray with ice. The light through the large kitchen window of his house told me that El Building blocked the sun to such an extent that they had to turn lights on in the middle of the day. I felt ashamed about it. But the white kitchen table with the lamp hanging just above it looked cozy and inviting. I would soon sit there, across from Eugene, and I would tell him about my perch just above his house. Maybe I would.

In the next thirty minutes I changed clothes, put on a little pink lipstick, and got my books together. Then I went in to tell my mother that I was going to a friend's house to study. I did not expect her reaction.

"You are going out *today?*" The way she said "today" sounded as if a storm warning had been issued. It was said in utter disbelief. Before I could answer, she came toward me and held my elbows as I clutched my books.

"*Hija,* the president has been killed. We must show respect. He was a great man. Come to church with me tonight."

She tried to embrace me, but my books were in the way. My first impulse 25 was to comfort her, she seemed so distraught, but I had to meet Eugene in fifteen minutes.

"I have a test to study for, Mama. I will be home by eight."

"You are forgetting who you are, *Niña.* I have seen you staring down at that boy's house. You are heading for humiliation and pain." My mother said this in Spanish and in a resigned tone that surprised me, as if she had no intention of stopping me from "heading for humiliation and pain." I started for the door. She sat in front of the TV, holding a white handkerchief to her face.

I walked out to the street and around the chain-link fence that separated El Building from Eugene's house. The yard was neatly edged around the little walk that led to the door. It always amazed me how Paterson, the inner core of the city, had no apparent logic to its architecture. Small, neat, single residences like this one could be found right next to huge, dilapidated apartment buildings like El Building. My guess was that the little houses had been there first, then the immigrants had come in droves, and the monstrosities had been raised for them—the Italians, the Irish, the Jews, and now us, the Puerto Ricans, and the blacks. The door was painted a deep green: *verde,* the color of hope. I had heard my mother say it: *Verde-Esperanza.*

I knocked softly. A few suspenseful moments later the door opened just a crack. The red, swollen face of a woman appeared. She had a halo of red hair floating over a delicate ivory face—the face of a doll—with freckles on the nose. Her smudged eye makeup made her look unreal to me, like a mannequin seen through a warped store window.

"What do you want?" Her voice was tiny and sweet-sounding, like a little 30
girl's, but her tone was not friendly.

"I'm Eugene's friend. He asked me over. To study." I thrust out my books, a
silly gesture that embarrassed me almost immediately.

"You live there?" She pointed up to El Building, which looked particularly
ugly, like a gray prison with its many dirty windows and rusty fire escapes. The
woman had stepped halfway out, and I could see that she wore a white nurse's
uniform with "St. Joseph's Hospital" on the name tag.

"Yes. I do."

She looked intently at me for a couple of heartbeats, then said as if to herself,
"I don't know how you people do it." Then directly to me: "Listen. Honey.
Eugene doesn't want to study with you. He is a smart boy. Doesn't need help.
You understand me. I am truly sorry if he told you you could come over. He
cannot study with you. It's nothing personal. You understand? We won't be in
this place much longer, no need for him to get close to people—it'll just make
it harder for him later. Run back home now."

I couldn't move. I just stood there in shock at hearing these things said to me 35
in such a honey-drenched voice. I had never heard an accent like hers except
for Eugene's softer version. It was as if she were singing me a little song.

"What's wrong? Didn't you hear what I said?" She seemed very angry, and I
finally snapped out of my trance. I turned away from the green door and heard
her close it gently.

Our apartment was empty when I got home. My mother was in someone else's
kitchen, seeking the solace she needed. Father would come in from his late shift at
midnight. I would hear them talking softly in the kitchen for hours that night.
They would not discuss their dreams for the future, or life in Puerto Rico, as they
often did; that night they would talk sadly about the young widow and her two
children, as if they were family. For the next few days, we would observe *luto* in
our apartment; that is, we would practice restraint and silence—no loud music or
laughter. Some of the women of El Building would wear black for weeks.

That night, I lay in my bed, trying to feel the right thing for our dead president. But the tears that came up from a deep source inside me were strictly for
me. When my mother came to the door, I pretended to be sleeping. Sometime
during the night, I saw from my bed the streetlight come on. It had a pink halo
around it. I went to my window and pressed my face to the cool glass. Looking
up at the light I could see the white snow falling like a lace veil over its face. I
did not look down to see it turning gray as it touched the ground below.

FOR ANALYSIS

1. Suggest a reason why the narrator spies on the neighbors.

2. Why does Elena's mother warn her that "[y]ou are forgetting who you are" and
that "[y]ou are heading for humiliation and pain" (para. 27)?

3. What does Eugene's mother reveal when she says, "I don't know how you people
do it" (para. 34)? Why does she refuse to let Elena study with Eugene?

4. How would you describe the **tone** of this essay? Is it bitter? Belligerent? Argumentative? Accepting? Explain.

5. Discuss the implications of the essay's title.

Writing Topic

Explain which event—President Kennedy's death or Eugene's mother's remarks—more significantly shapes the narrator's view of American history.

BRIAN DOYLE (B. 1956)

POP ART 2001

In nine years I have been graced with three children and here is what I have learned about them. They are engines of incalculable joy and agonizing despair. They are comedy machines. Their language is their own and the order of their new halting words has never been heard before in the whole history of the world. They are headlong and hilarious. Their hearts are enormous and sensitive beyond calculation by man or machine. Their pride is vast. They are cruel, and move in herds and gaggles and mobs, and woe unto the silent one, the one who looks funny, the one who speaks awkwardly, the fat one, for she will be shouldered aside, he will never get the ball, she will never be asked to jump rope, he will not be invited to the pool party, she will weep with confusion and rage, he will lash out with sharp small fists. Yet they are endlessly kind, kind by nature, and among them there is often an artless democracy, a linking of arms against the vast puzzle of the long people. They search for rules and rank, for what is allowed and what is forbidden, and poke the rules to see which bends and which is steel, for they wish to know their place in the world, where they might walk, what they may wear, which shows are allowed, how far they can go, who they are. They rise early in excitement and return reluctantly to barracks at night for fear of missing a shred of the daily circus. They eat nothing to speak of but grow at stunning rates that produce mostly leg. They are absorbed by dogs and toast. Mud and jelly accrue to them. They are at war with wasps. They eat no green things. Once they learn sarcasm they use it with abandon, slashing here and there without control and wreaking havoc. When they weep they weep utterly from the marrows of their lonely bones. They will not speak of death but when it comes, a dark hooded hawk on the fence, they face it without fear. They are new creatures hourly, and what you think you know of them is already lost in the river. Their hearts are dense books no one can read. They speak many languages of the body. To them you are a stone who has always been and will always be. When they are ill they shrivel. To father them is not a brief noun but an endless verb that exhausts, enrages, edifies, elevates, educates; I am a thinner and grayer man than I was; and closer to joy. They frighten me, for they will make a new world on the bowed back of the one I love; but they delight me, for to have loved them is to have tasted the furious love the Maker has for what He made, and fathers still, and always will.

FOR ANALYSIS

1. Why do you think Doyle chose "Pop Art" as his title?

2. Describe the **tone** of "Pop Art." Does it have only one, or is it varied? Can you chart its changes? What effect do these changes have?

MAKING CONNECTIONS

1. In "Those Winter Sundays," Hayden writes, "What did I know, what did I know / of love's austere and lonely offices?" (p. 944). In what ways could "Pop Art" be seen as a response to Hayden's speaker's innocence of fathering?

2. Both "Pop Art" and Galway Kinnell's "After Making Love We Hear Footsteps" (p. 953) connect two things readers know are related—conceiving and raising children—but are not often written about together. How does bringing the children back to bed, as it were, contribute (perhaps differently) to the meanings of each work?

WRITING TOPICS

1. "Pop Art" first appeared in a creative nonfiction venue called *Brevity*. Write an essay in which you describe the effects "Pop Art" makes with its brevity. Can you imagine it longer? How would it change?

2. Write your own short piece, modeled on Doyle's, in which you list descriptions of something or someone in a way that adds up to more than a roster of characteristics and reveals the nature of the subject.

CONNECTING NONFICTION:
ADVICE TO GRADUATES

The college experience is a significant stage in the passage from adolescence to adulthood, from school to work, from dependence to independence, and from innocence to experience. College is also the place where students learn to think differently about the world in which they live. No matter what students learn, the college experience is part of the process through which they find out who they are and their place in the world. While you read the selections in this unit, pay attention to the ways the movement from teenage innocence to adult experience is connected with the education college offers, not just about the world, but about the students themselves. Also look for the ways the essays reveal that the college experience is sometimes about learning that the world is a bigger, more complicated place than students thought it was.

LOUIS MENAND   (B. 1952)

THE GRADUATES   2007

On your first sleepover, your best friend's mother asks if you would like a tuna-fish-salad sandwich. Your own mother gives you tuna-fish-salad sandwiches all the time, so you say, "Sure." When you bite into the sandwich, though, you realize, too late, that your best friend's mother's tuna-fish salad tastes nothing like the tuna-fish salad your mother makes. You never dreamed that it was possible for there to be more than one way to prepare tuna-fish salad. And what's with the bread? It's brown, and appears to have tiny seeds in it. What is more unnerving is the fact that your best friend obviously considers his mother's tuna-fish salad to be perfectly normal and has been eating it with enjoyment all his life. Later on, you discover that the pillows in your best friend's house are filled with some kind of foam-rubber stuff instead of feathers. The toilet paper is pink. What kind of human beings are these? At two o'clock in the morning, you throw up, and your mother comes and takes you home.

College, from which some 1.5 million people will graduate this year, is, basically, a sleepover with grades. In college, it is not so cool to throw up or for your mother to come and take you home. But plenty of students do throw up, and undergo other forms of mental and bodily distress, and plenty take time off from school or drop out. Almost half the people who go to college never graduate. Except in the case of a few highfliers and a somewhat larger number of inveterate slackers, college is a stressful experience.

American colleges notoriously inflate grades, but they can never inflate them enough, because education in the United States has become hypercompetitive and every little difference matters. In 1960, Harvard College had around five thousand applicants and accepted roughly 30 percent; this year, it had almost twenty-three thousand applicants and accepted 9 percent. And the narrower the funnel, the finer applicants grind themselves in order to squeeze through it. Perversely, though, the competitiveness is a sign that the system is doing what Americans want it to be doing. Americans want education to be two things, universal and meritocratic. They want everyone to have a slot who wants one, and they want the slots to be awarded according to merit. The system is not perfect: children from higher-income families enjoy an advantage in competing for the top slots. But there are lots of slots. There are more than four thousand institutions of higher education in the United States, enrolling more than seventeen million students. Can you name fifty colleges? Even if you could name a thousand, there would be three thousand you hadn't heard of. Most of these schools accept virtually all qualified applicants.

What makes for the stress is meritocracy. Meritocratic systems are democratic (since, in theory, everyone gets a place at the starting line) and efficient (since resources are not wasted on the unqualified), but they are huge engines of anxiety. The more purely meritocratic the system—the more open, the more efficient, the *fairer*—the more anxiety it produces, because there is no haven from competition. Your mother can't come over and help you out—that would be cheating! You're on your own. Everything you do in a meritocratic society is some kind of test, and there is never a final exam. There is only another test. People seem to pick up on this earlier and earlier in their lives, and at some point it starts to get in the way of their becoming educated. You can't learn when you're afraid of being wrong.

The biggest undergraduate major by far in the United States today is busi- 5 ness. Twenty-two percent of bachelor's degrees are awarded in that field. Eight percent are awarded in education, five percent in the health professions. By contrast, fewer than four percent of college graduates major in English, and only two percent major in history. There are more bachelor's degrees awarded every year in Parks, Recreation, Leisure, and Fitness Studies than in all foreign languages and literatures combined. The Carnegie Foundation for the Advancement of Teaching, which classifies institutions of higher education, no longer uses the concept "liberal arts" in making its distinctions. This makes the obsession of some critics of American higher education with things like whether Shakespeare is being required of English majors beside the point. The question isn't what the English majors aren't taking; the question is what everyone else isn't taking.

More than 50 percent of Americans spend some time in college, and American higher education is the most expensive in the world. The average annual tuition at a four-year private college is more than twenty-two thousand dollars.

What do we want from college, though? It is hard to imagine that there could be one answer that was right for each of the 1.5 million or so people graduating this year, one part of the college experience they all must have had. Any prescription that had to spread itself across that many institutions would not be very deep. One thing that might be hoped for, though, is that, somewhere along the way, every student had a moment of vertigo (without unpleasant side effects). In commencement speeches and the like, people say that education is all about opportunity and expanding your horizons. But some part of it is about shrinking people, about teaching them that they are not the measure of everything. College should give them the intellectual equivalent of their childhood sleepover experience. We want to give graduates confidence to face the world, but we also want to protect the world a little from their confidence. Humility is good. There is not enough of it these days.

FOR ANALYSIS

1. How does Menand think the college experience should be, in part, like the first childhood sleepover?

2. What is a *meritocracy*? What other kinds of social arrangements exist? Which fits best with what some have called the American Dream? Are there other arrangements that also might correspond to American reality?

WRITING TOPIC

Write a short response in which you agree or disagree with Menand's statement that college is a stressful experience. Write from your own experience, and try to draw conclusions from that particular evidence.

DAVID FOSTER WALLACE   (1962–2008)

COMMENCEMENT SPEECH, KENYON COLLEGE[1]   2005

There are these two young fish swimming along, and they happen to meet an older fish swimming the other way, who nods at them and says, "Morning, boys, how's the water?" And the two young fish swim on for a bit, and then eventually one of them looks over at the other and goes, "What the hell is water?"

If at this moment, you're worried that I plan to present myself here as the wise old fish explaining what water is to you younger fish, please don't be. I am

---

[1] Adapted from a commencement speech given by David Foster Wallace to the 2005 graduating class at Kenyon College. Mr. Wallace, 46, died on September 12, 2008, after committing suicide.

not the wise old fish. The immediate point of the fish story is that the most obvious, ubiquitous, important realities are often the ones that are the hardest to see and talk about. Stated as an English sentence, of course, this is just a banal platitude—but the fact is that, in the day-to-day trenches of adult existence, banal platitudes can have life-or-death importance. That may sound like hyperbole, or abstract nonsense.

A huge percentage of the stuff that I tend to be automatically certain of is, it turns out, totally wrong and deluded. Here's one example of the utter wrongness of something I tend to be automatically sure of: everything in my own immediate experience supports my deep belief that I am the absolute center of the universe, the realest, most vivid, and important person in existence. We rarely talk about this sort of natural, basic self-centeredness, because it's so socially repulsive, but it's pretty much the same for all of us, deep down. It is our default-setting, hard-wired into our boards at birth. Think about it: there is no experience you've had that you were not at the absolute center of. The world as you experience it is right there in front of you, or behind you, to the left or right of you, on your TV, or your monitor, or whatever. Other people's thoughts and feelings have to be communicated to you somehow, but your own are so immediate, urgent, *real*—you get the idea. But please don't worry that I'm getting ready to preach to you about compassion or other-directedness or the so-called virtues. This is not a matter of virtue—it's a matter of my choosing to do the work of somehow altering or getting free of my natural, hard-wired default-setting, which is to be deeply and literally self-centered, and to see and interpret everything through this lens of self.

People who can adjust their natural default-setting this way are often described as being "well adjusted," which I suggest to you is not an accidental term.

Given the triumphal academic setting here, an obvious question is how   5 much of this work of adjusting our default-setting involves actual knowledge or intellect. This question gets tricky. Probably the most dangerous thing about college education, at least in my own case, is that it enables my tendency to over-intellectualize stuff, to get lost in abstract arguments inside my head instead of simply paying attention to what's going on right in front of me. Paying attention to what's going on inside me. As I'm sure you guys know by now, it is extremely difficult to stay alert and attentive instead of getting hypnotized by the constant monologue inside your own head. Twenty years after my own graduation, I have come gradually to understand that the liberal-arts cliché about "teaching you how to think" is actually shorthand for a much deeper, more serious idea: "learning how to think" really means learning how to exercise some control over how and what you think. It means being conscious and aware enough to choose what you pay attention to and to choose how you construct meaning from experience. Because if you cannot exercise this kind of choice in adult life, you will be totally hosed. Think of the old cliché about "the mind being an excellent servant but a terrible master." This, like many clichés, so lame and unexciting on the surface, actually expresses a great and terrible truth. It is not the least bit coincidental that adults who commit suicide with firearms almost always shoot themselves in the head. And the truth is that most of these suicides are actually dead long before they pull the trigger. And I submit that this is what the real, no-bull-value of your liberal-arts education is supposed to be about: how to keep from going through your comfortable, prosperous, respectable adult life dead, unconscious, a slave to your head and to your natural default-setting of being uniquely, completely, imperially alone, day in and day out.

That may sound like hyperbole, or abstract nonsense. So let's get concrete. The plain fact is that you graduating seniors do not yet have any clue what "day in, day out" really means. There happen to be whole large parts of adult American life that nobody talks about in commencement speeches. One such part involves boredom, routine, and petty frustration. The parents and older folks here will know all too well what I'm talking about.

By way of example, let's say it's an average day, and you get up in the morning, go to your challenging job, and you work hard for nine or ten hours, and at the end of the day you're tired, and you're stressed out, and all you want is to go home and have a good supper and maybe unwind for a couple of hours and then hit the rack early because you have to get up the next day and do it all again. But then you remember there's no food at home—you haven't had time to shop this week, because of your challenging job—and so now after work you have to get in your car and drive to the supermarket. It's the end of the workday, and the traffic's very bad, so getting to the store takes way longer than it should, and when you finally get there the supermarket is very crowded, because of course it's the time of day when all the other people with jobs also try to squeeze in some grocery shopping, and the store's hideously, fluorescently lit, and infused with soul-killing Muzak or corporate pop, and it's pretty much the last place you want to be, but you can't just get in and quickly out: you have to wander all over the huge, overlit store's crowded aisles to find the stuff you want, and you have to maneuver your junky cart through all these other tired, hurried people with carts, and of course there are also the glacially slow old people and the spacey people and the ADHD kids who all block the aisle and you have to grit your teeth and try to be polite as you ask them to let you by, and eventually, finally, you get all your supper supplies, except now it turns out there aren't enough checkout lanes open even though it's the end-of-the-day-rush, so the checkout line is incredibly long, which is stupid and infuriating, but you can't take your fury out on the frantic lady working the register.

Anyway, you finally get to the checkout line's front, and pay for your food, and wait to get your check or card authenticated by a machine, and then get told to "Have a nice day" in a voice that is the absolute voice of *death*, and then you have to take your creepy flimsy plastic bags of groceries in your cart through the crowded, bumpy, littery parking lot, and try to load the bags in your car in such a way that everything doesn't fall out of the bags and roll around in the trunk on the way home, and then you have to drive all the way home through slow, heavy, SUV-intensive rush-hour traffic, etcetera, etcetera.

The point is that petty, frustrating crap like this is exactly where the work of choosing comes in. Because the traffic jams and crowded aisles and long checkout lines give me time to think, and if I don't make a conscious decision about how to think and what to pay attention to, I'm going to be pissed and miserable every time I have to food-shop, because my natural default-setting is the certainty that situations like this are really all about *me*, about my hungriness and my fatigue and my desire to just get home, and it's going to seem, for all the world, like everybody else is just *in my way*, and who are all these people in my way? And look at how repulsive most of them are and how stupid and cow-like and dead-eyed and nonhuman they seem here in the checkout line, or at how annoying and rude it is that people are talking loudly on cell phones in the middle of the line, and look at how deeply unfair this is: I've worked really hard all day and I'm starved and tired and I can't even get home to eat and unwind because of all these stupid g-d- *people*.

Or, of course, if I'm in a more socially conscious form of my default-setting, 10 I can spend time in the end-of-the-day traffic jam being angry and disgusted at all the huge, stupid, lane-blocking SUVs and Hummers and V-12 pickup trucks burning their wasteful, selfish, forty-gallon tanks of gas, and I can dwell on the fact that the patriotic or religious bumper stickers always seem to be on the biggest, most disgustingly selfish vehicles driven by the ugliest, most inconsiderate and aggressive drivers, who are usually talking on cell phones as they cut people off in order to get just twenty stupid feet ahead in a traffic jam, and I can think about how our children's children will despise us for wasting all the future's fuel and probably screwing up the climate, and how spoiled and stupid and disgusting we all are, and how it all just *sucks*, and so on and so forth. . . .

Look, if I choose to think this way, fine, lots of us do—except that thinking this way tends to be so easy and automatic It doesn't *have* to be a choice. Thinking this way is my natural default-setting. It's the automatic, unconscious way that I experience the boring, frustrating, crowded parts of adult life when I'm operating on the automatic, unconscious belief that I am the center of the world and that my immediate needs and feelings are what should determine the world's priorities. The thing is that there are obviously different ways to think about these kinds of situations. In this traffic, all these vehicles stuck and idling in my way: it's not impossible that some of these people in SUVs have been in horrible auto accidents in the past and now find driving so traumatic that their therapist has all but ordered them to get a huge, heavy SUV so they can feel safe enough to drive; or that the Hummer that just cut me off is maybe being driven by a father whose little child is hurt or sick in the seat next to him, and he's trying to rush to the hospital, and he's in a way bigger, more legitimate hurry than I am—it is actually *I* who am in *his* way. Or I can choose to force myself to consider the likelihood that everyone else in the supermarket's checkout line is just as bored and frustrated as I am, and that some of these people probably have much harder, more tedious or painful lives than I do, overall.

Again, please don't think that I'm giving you moral advice, or that I'm say-ing you're "supposed to" think this way, or that anyone expects you to just automatically do it, because it's hard, it takes will and mental effort, and if you're like me, some days you won't be able to do it, or you just flat-out won't want to. But most days, if you're aware enough to give yourself a choice, you can choose to look differently at this fat, dead-eyed, over-made-lady who just screamed at her little child in the checkout line—maybe she's not usually like this; maybe she's been up three straight nights holding the hand of her hus-band who's dying of bone cancer, or maybe this very lady is the low-wage clerk at the Motor Vehicles Department, who just yesterday helped your spouse resolve a nightmarish red-tape problem through some small act of bureau-cratic kindness. Of course, none of this is likely, but it's also not impossible—it just depends on what you want to consider. If you're automatically sure that you know what reality is and who and what is really important—if you want to operate on your default-setting—then you, like me, will not consider possibil-ities that aren't pointless and annoying. But if you've really learned how to think, how to pay attention, then you will know you have other options. It will actually be within your power to experience a crowded, loud, slow, consumer-hell-type situation as not only meaningful but sacred, on fire with the same force that lit the stars—compassion, love, the subsurface unity of all things. Not that that mystical stuff's necessarily true: the only thing that's capital-T True is that you get to *decide* how you're going to try to see it. You get to con-sciously decide what has meaning and what doesn't. You get to decide what to worship. . . .

Because here's something else that's true. In the day-to-day trenches of adult life, there is actually no such thing as atheism. There is no such thing as not wor-shipping. Everybody worships. The only choice we get is *what* to worship. And an outstanding reason for choosing some sort of God or spiritual-type thing to worship—be it J.C. or Allah, be it Yahweh or the Wiccan mother-goddess or the Four Noble Truths or some infrangible set of ethical principles—is that pretty much anything else you worship will eat you alive. If you worship money and things—if they are where you tap real meaning in life—then you will never have enough. Never feel you have enough. It's the truth. Worship your own body and beauty and sexual allure and you will always feel ugly, and when time and age start showing, you will die a million deaths before they finally plant you. On one level, we all know this stuff already—it's been codified as myths, proverbs, clichés, bromides, epigrams, parables: the skeleton of every great story. The trick is keeping the truth up front in daily consciousness. Worship power—you will feel weak and afraid, and you will need ever more power over others to keep the fear at bay. Worship your intellect, being seen as smart—you will end up feeling stupid, a fraud, always on the verge of being found out. And so on.

Look, the insidious thing about these forms of worship is not that they're evil or sinful; it is that they are *unconscious*. They are default-settings. They're the kind of worship you just gradually slip into, day after day, getting more and more selective about what you see and how you measure value without ever being fully aware that that's what you're doing. And the world will not discourage you from operating on your default-settings, because the world of men and money and power hums along quite nicely on the fuel of fear and contempt and frustration and craving and the worship of self. Our own present culture has harnessed these forces in ways that have yielded extraordinary wealth and comfort and personal freedom. The freedom to be lords of our own tiny skull-sized kingdoms, alone at the center of all creation. This kind of freedom has much to recommend it. But of course there are all different kinds of freedom, and the kind that is most precious you will not hear much talked about in the great outside world of winning and achieving and displaying. The really important kind of freedom involves attention, and awareness, and discipline, and effort, and being able truly to care about other people and to sacrifice for them, over and over, in myriad petty little unsexy ways, every day. That is real freedom. The alternative is unconsciousness, the default-setting, the "rat race"—the constant gnawing sense of having had and lost some infinite thing.

I know that this stuff probably doesn't sound fun and breezy or grandly 15 inspirational. What it is, so far as I can see, is the truth with a whole lot of rhetorical bullshit pared away. Obviously, you can think of it whatever you wish. But please don't dismiss it as some finger-wagging Dr. Laura sermon. None of this is about morality, or religion, or dogma, or big fancy questions of life after death. The capital-T Truth is about life *before* death. It is about making it to thirty, or maybe fifty, without wanting to shoot yourself in the head. It is about simple awareness—awareness of what is so real and essential, so hidden in plain sight all around us, that we have to keep reminding ourselves, over and over: "This is water, this is water."

It is unimaginably hard to do this, to stay conscious and alive, day in and day out.

FOR ANALYSIS

1. What does Wallace mean when he says, "This is water" (para. 15)?

2. "That may sound like hyperbole, or abstract nonsense," Wallace comments on something he's said, "So let's get concrete" (para. 6). What are Wallace's abstractions? How does he use the concrete to anchor them?

WRITING TOPIC

Write your own reflection on an everyday event, like Wallace's on the checkout line (or the traffic jam). Try to make a more general statement based on these reflections.

MAKING CONNECTIONS

1. Wallace writes, "A huge percentage of the stuff that I tend to be automatically certain of is, it turns out, totally wrong and deluded" (para. 3). Education, especially higher education, is often thought of as the place people prepare themselves for careers by mastering particular thinking skills and bodies of knowledge. How do Wallace and Menand challenge this idea?

2. Whose vision of higher education's value appeals to you more? Why?

3. Compare Wallace's writing style to Menand's. Both have been praised as stylists, but they write very differently. How do they write? Think about different elements of writing—**diction,** sentence structure, voice—and different adjectives used to describe writing—flowery, spare, hard-edged, sophisticated, showy, smug, generous. Do you like one's style more? Why?

FURTHER QUESTIONS
FOR THINKING AND WRITING

1. How do the works in this section illustrate Thomas Gray's well-known observation that "where ignorance is bliss, / 'Tis folly to be wise"? **Writing Topic:** Use Gray's observation as the basis for an analysis of Toni Cade Bambara's "The Lesson" (p. 110) or Hanan Mikha'il 'Ashrawi's "From the Diary of an Almost-Four-Year-Old" (p. 163).

2. In poems such as William Blake's "The Garden of Love" (p. 139), Robert Frost's "Birches" (p. 150), and Stevie Smith's "To Carry the Child" (p. 153), growing up is seen as a growing away from a kind of truth and reality; in other poems, such as Gerard Manley Hopkins's "Spring and Fall" (p. 145) and Dylan Thomas's "Fern Hill" (p. 155), growing up is seen as growing into truth and reality. Do these two groups of poems embody contradictory and mutually exclusive conceptions of childhood? Explain. **Writing Topic:** Select one poem from each of these two groups, and contrast the conception of childhood embodied in each.

3. An eighteenth-century novelist wrote: "Oh Innocence, how glorious and happy a portion art thou to the breast that possesses thee! Thou fearest neither the eyes nor the tongues of men. Truth, the most powerful of all things, is thy strongest friend; and the brighter the light is in which thou art displayed, the more it discovers thy transcendent beauties." Which works in this section support this assessment of innocence? Which works contradict it? How would you characterize the relationship between "truth" and "innocence" in the fiction, drama, and essays presented here? **Writing Topic:** Use this observation as the basis for an analysis of Nathaniel Hawthorne's "Young Goodman Brown" (p. 81) or Toni Cade Bambara's "The Lesson" (p. 110).

4. James Joyce's "Araby" (p. 92) and John Updike's "A & P" (p. 127) deal with some aspect of sexuality as a force that moves the protagonist from innocence toward experience. How does the recognition of sexuality function in each of the stories? **Writing Topic:** Discuss the relationship between sexuality and innocence in these stories.

5. Which poems in this section depend largely on **irony** for their force? Why do you think irony is a useful device in literature that portrays innocence and experience? **Writing Topic:** Analyze the function of irony in Blake's "The Garden of Love" (p. 139) and Hardy's "The Ruined Maid" (p. 144).

6. Some authors treat the passage from innocence to experience as comedy, while others treat it more seriously, even as tragedy. Do you find one or the other treatment more satisfying? Explain. **Writing Topic:** Select one short story, and show how the author achieves either a comic or a serious tone.

CONFORMITY
AND REBELLION

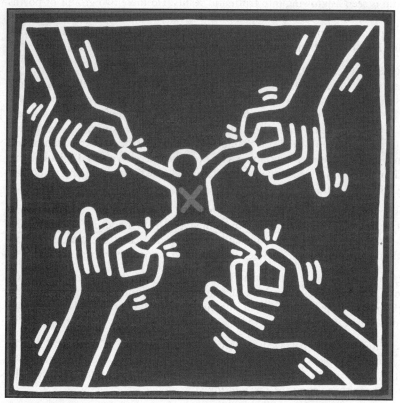

Untitled, 1985, by Keith Haring. © Keith Haring Foundation. Used by permission.

The works in this section, "Conformity and Rebellion," feature a clash between two well-articulated positions in which a rebel, on principle, confronts and struggles with established authority. Central in these works are powerful external forces—the state, the church, tradition—which sometimes can be obeyed only at the expense of conscience and humanity. At the most general level, these works confront a dilemma older than the one Othello encountered in Venice: the very organizations men and women establish to protect and nurture the individual often demand—on pain of economic ruin, social ostracism, even spiritual or physical death—that individuals violate their most deeply cherished beliefs. In these works, some individuals refuse such a demand and translate their awareness of a hostile social order into action against it. In *A Doll's House*, Nora realizes that dehumanization is too high a price to pay for domestic tranquillity. On a different note, in Melville's "Bartleby, the Scrivener" the crisis arises out of the protagonist's passive refusal to conform to the expectations of society.

Many of the works in this section, particularly the poems, do not treat the theme of conformity and rebellion quite so explicitly and dramatically. Some, like Emily Dickinson's "She rose to His Requirement," reveal the painful injustice of certain traditional values; others, like W. H. Auden's "The Unknown Citizen," tell us that the price exacted for total conformity to the industrial superstate is spiritual death. In "Easter 1916," William Butler Yeats meditates on the awesome meaning of the lives and deaths of political revolutionaries, and in "Harlem," Langston Hughes warns that an inflexible and constricting social order will generate explosion.

While in many of the works the individual is caught up in a crisis that forces him or her into rebellion, in other works the focus may be on the individual's failure to move from awareness into action. For example, the portrait of Auden's unknown citizen affirms the necessity for rebellion by rendering so effectively the hollow life of mindless conformity.

Although diverse in treatment and technique, all the works in this section are about individuals struggling with complex sets of external forces that regulate and define their lives. As social beings, these individuals may recognize that they must be controlled for some larger good; yet they are aware that

289

established social power is often abusive. The institution at its best can act as a conserving force, keeping in check the individual's disruptive impulse to abandon and destroy, without cause, old ways and ideas. At its worst, the power of social institutions is self-serving. It is up to the individual to judge whether power is being abused. Because the power of the individual is often negligible beside that of abusive social forces, it is not surprising that many artists find a fundamental human dignity in the resistance of the individual to organized society.

QUESTIONS FOR THINKING AND WRITING

Before you begin reading the selections in "Conformity and Rebellion," consider the following questions. Then write out your thoughts informally in a reading journal, if you are keeping one, as a way of preparing to respond to the selections. Or you may wish to make your response to one of these questions the basis for a formal essay.

1. How do you define *conformity?* What forms of rebellion are possible for a person in your situation? Do you perceive yourself as a conformist? A rebel? Some combination of the two? Explain.

2. How do you define *sanity?* Based on your definition, do you know an insane person? What form does that insanity take? Do you agree or disagree with Emily Dickinson's assertion that "Much Madness is divinest Sense"? Explain.

3. Discuss this proposition: governments routinely engage in behavior for which an individual would be imprisoned or institutionalized.

4. Freewrite an extended response to each of the following questions: Is war sane? Should one obey an "unjust" law? Should one be guided absolutely by religious principles?

FICTION

HERMAN MELVILLE   (1819–1891)

BARTLEBY, THE SCRIVENER   1853

A STORY OF WALL STREET

I am a rather elderly man. The nature of my avocations, for the last thirty years, has brought me into more than ordinary contact with what would seem an interesting and somewhat singular set of men, of whom, as yet, nothing, that I know of, has ever been written—I mean, the law-copyists, or scriveners. I have known very many of them, professionally and privately, and, if I pleased, could relate divers histories, at which good-natured gentlemen might smile, and sentimental souls might weep. But I waive the biographies of all other scriveners, for a few passages in the life of Bartleby, who was a scrivener, the strangest I ever saw, or heard of. While, of other law-copyists, I might write the complete life, of Bartleby nothing of that sort can be done. I believe that no materials exist for a full and satisfactory biography of this man. It is an irreparable loss to literature. Bartleby was one of those beings of whom nothing is ascertainable, except from the original sources, and, in his case, those are very small. What my own astonished eyes saw of Bartleby, *that* is all I know of him, except, indeed, one vague report, which will appear in the sequel.

Ere introducing the scrivener, as he first appeared to me, it is fit I make some mention of myself, my employees, my business, my chambers, and general surroundings; because some such description is indispensable to an adequate understanding of the chief character about to be presented. Imprimis: I am a man who, from his youth upwards, has been filled with a profound conviction that the easiest way of life is the best. Hence, though I belong to a profession proverbially energetic and nervous, even to turbulence, at times, yet nothing of that sort have I ever suffered to invade my peace. I am one of those unambitious lawyers who never addresses a jury, or in any way draws down public applause; but, in the cool tranquillity of a snug retreat, do a snug business among rich men's bonds, and mortgages, and title-deeds. All who know me, consider me an eminently *safe* man. The late John Jacob Astor,[1] a personage little given to poetic enthusiasm, had no hesitation in pronouncing my first grand point to be prudence; my next, method. I do not speak it in vanity, but simply record the fact, that I was not unemployed in my profession by the late John Jacob Astor; a name which, I admit, I love to repeat; for it hath a rounded and orbicular sound to it, and rings like unto bullion. I will freely add, that I was not insensible to the late John Jacob Astor's good opinion.

Some time prior to the period at which this little history begins, my avocations had been largely increased. The good old office, now extinct in the State of New York, of a Master in Chancery,[2] had been conferred upon me. It was not a very arduous office, but very pleasantly remunerative. I seldom lose my temper; much more seldom indulge in dangerous indignation at wrongs and outrages; but, I must be permitted to be rash here, and declare that I consider the sudden and violent abrogation of the office of Master in Chancery, by the new Constitution, as a—premature act; inasmuch as I had counted upon a lifelease of the profits, whereas I only received those of a few short years. But this is by the way.

My chambers were up stairs, at No. —— Wall Street. At one end, they looked upon the white wall of the interior of a spacious sky-light shaft, penetrating the building from top to bottom.

This view might have been considered rather tame than otherwise, deficient 5 in what landscape painters call "life." But, if so, the view from the other end of my chambers offered, at least, a contrast, if nothing more. In that direction, my windows commanded an unobstructed view of a lofty brick wall, black by age and everlasting shade; which wall required no spyglass to bring out its lurking beauties, but, for the benefit of all near-sighted spectators, was pushed up to within ten feet of my window panes. Owing to the great height of the surrounding buildings, and my chambers being on the second floor, the interval between this wall and mine not a little resembled a huge square cistern.

At the period just preceding the advent of Bartleby, I had two persons as copyists in my employment, and a promising lad as an office-boy. First, Turkey; second, Nippers; third, Ginger Nut. These may seem names, the like of which are not usually found in the Directory. In truth, they were nicknames, mutually conferred upon each other by my three clerks, and were deemed expressive of their respective persons or characters. Turkey was a short, pursy Englishman, of about my own age—that is, somewhere not far from sixty. In the morning, one might say, his face was of a fine florid hue, but after twelve o'clock, meridian—his dinner hour—it blazed like a grate full of Christmas coals; and continued blazing—but, as it were, with a gradual wane—till six o'clock P.M., or thereabouts; after which, I saw no more of the proprietor of the face, which, gaining its meridian with the sun, seemed to set with it, to rise, culminate, and decline the following day, with the like regularity and

---

[1] A poor immigrant from Germany who became one of the great business tycoons of the nineteenth century.
[2] Courts of Chancery often adjudicated business disputes.

undiminished glory. There are many singular coincidences I have known in the course of my life, not the least among which was the fact, that, exactly when Turkey displayed his fullest beams from his red and radiant countenance, just then, too, at that critical moment, began the daily period when I considered his business capacities as seriously disturbed for the remainder of the twenty-four hours. Not that he was absolutely idle, or averse to business, then; far from it. The difficulty was, he was apt to be altogether too energetic. There was a strange, inflamed, flurried, flighty recklessness of activity about him. He would be incautious in dipping his pen into his inkstand. All his blots upon my documents were dropped there after twelve o'clock meridian. Indeed, not only would he be reckless, and sadly given to making blots in the afternoon, but, some days, he went further, and was rather noisy. At such times, too, his face flamed with augmented blazonry, as if cannel coal had been heaped on anthracite. He made an unpleasant racket with his chair; spilled his sand-box; in mending his pens, impatiently split them all to pieces, and threw them on the floor in a sudden passion; stood up, and leaned over his table, boxing his papers about in a most indecorous manner, very sad to behold in an elderly man like him. Nevertheless, as he was in many ways a most valuable person to me, and all the time before twelve o'clock meridian, was the quickest, steadiest creature, too, accomplishing a great deal of work in a style not easily to be matched—for these reasons, I was willing to overlook his eccentricities, though, indeed, occasionally, I remonstrated with him. I did this very gently, however, because, though the civilest, nay, the blandest and most reverential of men in the morning, yet, in the afternoon, he was disposed, upon provocation, to be slightly rash with his tongue—in fact, insolent. Now, valuing his morning services as I did, and resolved not to lose them—yet, at the same time, made uncomfortable by his inflamed ways after twelve o'clock—and being a man of peace, unwilling by my admonitions to call forth unseemly retorts from him, I took upon me, one Saturday noon (he was always worse on Saturdays) to hint to him, very kindly, that, perhaps, now that he was growing old, it might be well to abridge his labors; in short, he need not come to my chambers after twelve o'clock, but, dinner over, had best go home to his lodgings, and rest himself till tea-time. But no; he insisted upon his afternoon devotions. His countenance became intolerably fervid, as he oratorically assured me—gesticulating with a long ruler at the other end of the room—that if his services in the morning were useful, how indispensable, then, in the afternoon?

"With submission, sir," said Turkey, on this occasion, "I consider myself your right-hand man. In the morning I but marshal and deploy my columns; but in the afternoon I put myself at their head, and gallantly charge the foe, thus"— and he made a violent thrust with the ruler.

"But the blots, Turkey," intimated I.

"True; but, with submission, sir, behold these hairs! I am getting old. Surely, sir, a blot or two of a warm afternoon is not to be severely urged against gray hairs. Old age—even if it blot the page—is honorable. With submission, sir, we *both* are getting old."

This appeal to my fellow-feeling was hardly to be resisted. At all events, I   10
saw that go he would not. So, I made up my mind to let him stay, resolving,
nevertheless, to see to it that, during the afternoon, he had to do with my less
important papers.

Nippers, the second on my list, was a whiskered, sallow, and, upon the
whole, rather piratical-looking young man, of about five and twenty. I always
deemed him the victim of two evil powers—ambition and indigestion. The
ambition was evinced by a certain impatience of the duties of a mere copyist,
an unwarrantable usurpation of strictly professional affairs, such as the original drawing up of legal documents. The indigestion seemed betokened in an
occasional nervous testiness and grinning irritability, causing the teeth to
audibly grind together over mistakes committed in copying; unnecessary
maledictions, hissed, rather than spoken, in the heat of business; and especially
by a continual discontent with the height of the table where he worked.
Though of a very ingenious, mechanical turn, Nippers could never get this
table to suit him. He put chips under it, blocks of various sorts, bits of paste-
board, and at last went so far as to attempt an exquisite adjustment, by final
pieces of folded blotting-paper. But no invention would answer. If, for the sake
of easing his back, he brought the table-lid at a sharp angle well up towards his
chin, and wrote there like a man using the steep roof of a Dutch house for his
desk, then he declared that it stopped the circulation in his arms. If now he
lowered the table to his waistbands, and stooped over it in writing, then there
was a sore aching in his back. In short, the truth of the matter was, Nippers
knew not what he wanted. Or, if he wanted anything, it was to be rid of a
scrivener's table altogether. Among the manifestations of his diseased ambition was a fondness he had for receiving visits from certain ambiguous-look-
ing fellows in seedy coats, whom he called his clients. Indeed, I was aware that
not only was he, at times, considerable of a ward-politician, but he occasionally did a little business at the Justices' courts, and was not unknown on the
steps of the Tombs.[3] I have good reason to believe, however, that one individual who called upon him at my chambers, and who, with a grand air, he
insisted was his client, was no other than a dun, and the alleged title-deed, a
bill. But, with all his failings, and the annoyances he caused me, Nippers, like
his compatriot Turkey, was a very useful man to me; wrote a neat, swift hand;
and, when he chose, was not deficient in a gentlemanly sort of deportment.
Added to this, he always dressed in a gentlemanly sort of way; and so, inciden-
tally, reflected credit upon my chambers. Whereas, with respect to Turkey, I
had much ado to keep him from being a reproach to me. His clothes were apt
to look oily, and smell of eating houses. He wore his pantaloons very loose and
baggy in summer. His coats were execrable, his hat not to be handled. But
while the hat was a thing of indifference to me, inasmuch as his natural civility
and deference, as a dependent Englishman, always led him to doff it the
moment he entered the room, yet his coat was another matter. Concerning his

[3] A prison in New York City.

coats, I reasoned with him; but with no effect. The truth was, I suppose, that a man with so small an income could not afford to sport such a lustrous face and a lustrous coat at one and the same time. As Nippers once observed, Turkey's money went chiefly for red ink. One winter day, I presented Turkey with a highly respectable-looking coat of my own—a padded gray coat, of a most comfortable warmth, and which buttoned straight up from the knee to the neck. I thought Turkey would appreciate the favor, and abate his rashness and obstreperousness of afternoons. But no; I verily believe that buttoning himself up in so downy and blanket-like a coat had a pernicious effect upon him— upon the same principle that too much oats are bad for horses. In fact, precisely as a rash, restive horse is said to feel his oats, so Turkey felt his coat. It made him insolent. He was a man whom prosperity harmed.

Though, concerning the self-indulgent habits of Turkey, I had my own private surmises, yet, touching Nippers, I was well persuaded that, whatever might be his faults in other respects, he was, at least, a temperate young man. But, indeed, nature herself seemed to have been his vintner, and, at his birth, charged him so thoroughly with an irritable, brandy-like disposition, that all subsequent potations were needless. When I consider how, amid the stillness of my chambers, Nippers would sometimes impatiently rise from his seat, and stooping over his table, spread his arms wide apart, seize the whole desk, and move it, and jerk it, with a grim, grinding motion on the floor, as if the table were a perverse voluntary agent and vexing him, I plainly perceive that, for Nippers, brandy-and-water were altogether superfluous.

It was fortunate for me that, owing to its peculiar cause—indigestion—the irritability and consequent nervousness of Nippers were mainly observable in the morning, while in the afternoon he was comparatively mild. So that, Turkey's paroxysms only coming on about twelve o'clock, I never had to do with their eccentricities at one time. Their fits relieved each other, like guards. When Nippers's was on, Turkey's was off; and *vice versa*. This was a good natural arrangement, under the circumstances.

Ginger Nut, the third on my list, was a lad, some twelve years old. His father was a car-man, ambitious of seeing his son on the bench instead of a cart, before he died. So he sent him to my office, as student at law, errand-boy, cleaner and sweeper, at the rate of one dollar a week. He had a little desk to himself; but he did not use it much. Upon inspection, the drawer exhibited a great array of shells of various sorts of nuts. Indeed, to this quick-witted youth, the whole noble science of the law was contained in a nutshell. Not the least among the employments of Ginger Nut, as well as one which he discharged with the most alacrity, was his duty as cake and apple purveyor for Turkey and Nippers. Copying law-papers being proverbially a dry, husky sort of business, my two scriveners were fain to moisten their mouths very often with Spitzenbergs,[4] to be had at the numerous stalls nigh the Custom House and Post Office. Also, they sent Ginger Nut very frequently for that peculiar

---

[4] A variety of apple.

cake—small, flat, round, and very spicy—after which he had been named by them. Of a cold morning, when business was but dull, Turkey would gobble up scores of these cakes, as if they were mere wafers—indeed, they sell them at the rate of six or eight for a penny—the scrape of his pen blending with the crunching of the crisp particles in his mouth. Rashest of all the fiery afternoon blunders and flurried rashnesses of Turkey, was his once moistening a ginger-cake between his lips, and clapping it on to a mortgage, for a seal. I came within an ace of dismissing him then. But he mollified me by making an oriental bow, and saying—

"With submission, sir, it was generous of me to find you in stationery on my own account." 15

Now my original business—that of a conveyancer and title hunter, and drawer-up of recondite documents of all sorts—was considerably increased by receiving the master's office. There was now great work for scriveners. Not only must I push the clerks already with me, but I must have additional help.

In answer to my advertisement, a motionless young man one morning stood upon my office threshold, the door being open, for it was summer. I can see that figure now—pallidly neat, pitiably respectable, incurably forlorn! It was Bartleby.

After a few words touching his qualifications, I engaged him, glad to have among my corps of copyists a man of so singularly sedate an aspect, which I thought might operate beneficially upon the flighty temper of Turkey, and the fiery one of Nippers.

I should have stated before that ground-glass folding-doors divided my premises into two parts, one of which was occupied by my scriveners, the other by myself. According to my humor, I threw open these doors, or closed them. I resolved to assign Bartleby a corner by the folding-doors, but on my side of them, so as to have this quiet man within easy call, in case any trifling thing was to be done. I placed his desk close up to a small side-window in that part of the room, a window which originally had afforded a lateral view of certain grimy backyards and bricks, but which, owing to subsequent erections, commanded at present no view at all, though it gave some light. Within three feet of the panes was a wall, and the light came down from far above, between two lofty buildings, as from a very small opening in a dome. Still further to a satisfactory arrangement, I procured a high green folding screen, which might entirely isolate Bartleby from my sight, though not remove him from my voice. And thus, in a manner, privacy and society were conjoined.

At first, Bartleby did an extraordinary quantity of writing. As if long famishing for something to copy, he seemed to gorge himself on my documents. There was no pause for digestion. He ran a day and night line, copying by sun-light and by candle-light. I should have been quite delighted with his application, had he been cheerfully industrious. But he wrote on silently, palely, mechanically. 20

It is, of course, an indispensable part of a scrivener's business to verify the accuracy of his copy, word by word. Where there are two or more scriveners in an office, they assist each other in this examination, one reading from the copy, the other holding the original. It is a very dull, wearisome, and lethargic affair. I can readily imagine that, to some sanguine temperaments, it would be altogether intolerable. For example, I cannot credit that the mettlesome poet, Byron, would have contentedly sat down with Bartleby to examine a law document of, say five hundred pages, closely written in a crimpy hand.

Now and then, in the haste of business, it had been my habit to assist in comparing some brief document myself, calling Turkey or Nippers for this purpose. One object I had, in placing Bartleby so handy to me behind the screen, was to avail myself of his services on such trivial occasions. It was on the third day, I think, of his being with me, and before any necessity had arisen for having his own writing examined, that, being much hurried to complete a small affair I had in hand, I abruptly called to Bartleby. In my haste and natural expectancy of instant compliance, I sat with my head bent over the original on my desk, and my right hand sideways, and somewhat nervously extended with the copy, so that, immediately upon emerging from his retreat, Bartleby might snatch it and proceed to business without the least delay.

In this very attitude did I sit when I called to him, rapidly stating what it was I wanted him to do—namely, to examine a small paper with me. Imagine my surprise, nay, my consternation, when, without moving from his privacy, Bartleby, in a singularly mild, firm voice, replied, "I would prefer not to."

I sat awhile in perfect silence, rallying my stunned faculties. Immediately it occurred to me that my ears had deceived me, or Bartleby had entirely misunderstood my meaning. I repeated my request in the clearest tone I could assume; but in quite as clear a one came the previous reply, "I would prefer not to."

"Prefer not to," echoed I, rising in high excitement, and crossing the room 25 with a stride. "What do you mean? Are you moon-struck? I want you to help me compare this sheet here—take it," and I thrust it towards him.

"I would prefer not to," said he.

I looked at him steadfastly. His face was leanly composed; his gray eye dimly calm. Not a wrinkle of agitation rippled him. Had there been the least uneasiness, anger, impatience, or impertinence in his manner; in other words, had there been any thing ordinarily human about him, doubtless I should have violently dismissed him from the premises. But as it was, I should have as soon thought of turning my pale plaster-of-paris bust of Cicero out of doors. I stood gazing at him awhile, as he went on with his own writing, and then reseated myself at my desk. This is very strange, thought I. What had one best do? But my business hurried me. I concluded to forget the matter for the present, reserving it for my future leisure. So calling Nippers from the other room, the paper was speedily examined.

A few days after this, Bartleby concluded four lengthy documents, being quadruplicates of a week's testimony taken before me in my High Court of Chancery. It became necessary to examine them. It was an important suit, and great accuracy was imperative. Having all things arranged, I called Turkey, Nippers, and Ginger Nut from the next room, meaning to place the four copies in the hands of my four clerks, while I should read from the original. Accordingly, Turkey,

Nippers, and Ginger Nut had taken their seats in a row, each with his document in his hand, when I called to Bartleby to join this interesting group.

"Bartleby! quick, I am waiting."

I heard a slow scrape of his chair legs on the uncarpeted floor, and soon he 30
appeared standing at the entrance of his hermitage.

"What is wanted?" said he, mildly.

"The copies, the copies," said I, hurriedly. "We are going to examine them. There—" and I held towards him the fourth quadruplicate.

"I would prefer not to," he said, and gently disappeared behind the screen.

For a few moments I was turned into a pillar of salt, standing at the head of my seated column of clerks. Recovering myself, I advanced towards the screen, and demanded the reason for such extraordinary conduct.

"*Why* do you refuse?"   35

"I would prefer not to."

With any other man I should have flown outright into a dreadful passion, scorned all further words, and thrust him ignominiously from my presence. But there was something about Bartleby that not only strangely disarmed me, but in a wonderful manner, touched and disconcerted me. I began to reason with him.

"These are your own copies we are about to examine. It is labor saving to you, because one examination will answer for your four papers. It is common usage. Every copyist is bound to help examine his copy. Is it not so? Will you not speak? Answer!"

"I prefer not to," he replied in a flutelike tone. It seemed to me that, while I had been addressing him, he carefully revolved every statement that I made; fully comprehended the meaning; could not gainsay the irresistible conclusion; but, at the same time, some paramount consideration prevailed with him to reply as he did.

"You are decided, then, not to comply with my request—a request made 40
according to common usage and common sense?"

He briefly gave me to understand, that on that point my judgment was sound. Yes: his decision was irreversible.

It is not seldom the case that, when a man is browbeaten in some unprecedented and violently unreasonable way, he begins to stagger in his own plainest faith. He begins, as it were, vaguely to surmise that, wonderful as it may be, all the justice and all the reason is on the other side. Accordingly, if any disinterested persons are present, he turns to them for some reinforcement of his own faltering mind.

"Turkey," said I, "what do you think of this? Am I not right?"

"With submission, sir," said Turkey, in his blandest tone, "I think that you are."

"Nippers," said I, "what do *you* think of it?"   45

"I think I should kick him out of the office."

(The reader, of nice perceptions, will here perceive that, it being morning, Turkey's answer is couched in polite and tranquil terms, but Nippers replies in ill-tempered ones. Or, to repeat a previous sentence, Nippers's ugly mood was on duty, and Turkey's off.)

"Ginger Nut," said I, willing to enlist the smallest suffrage in my behalf, "what do *you* think of it?"

"I think, sir, he's a little *luny*," replied Ginger Nut, with a grin.

"You hear what they say," said I, turning towards the screen, "come forth and 50 do your duty."

But he vouchsafed no reply. I pondered a moment in sore perplexity. But once more business hurried me. I determined again to postpone the consideration of this dilemma to my future leisure. With a little trouble we made out to examine the papers without Bartleby, though at every page or two Turkey deferentially dropped his opinion, that this proceeding was quite out of the common; while Nippers, twitching in his chair with a dyspeptic nervousness, ground out, between his set teeth, occasional hissing maledictions against the stubborn oaf behind the screen. And for his (Nippers's) part, this was the first and the last time he would do another man's business without pay.

Meanwhile Bartleby sat in his hermitage, oblivious to everything but his own peculiar business there.

Some days passed, the scrivener being employed upon another lengthy work. His late remarkable conduct led me to regard his ways narrowly. I observed that he never went to dinner; indeed, that he never went anywhere. As yet I had never, of my personal knowledge, known him to be outside of my office. He was a perpetual sentry in the corner. At about eleven o'clock though, in the morning, I noticed that Ginger Nut would advance toward the opening in Bartleby's screen, as if silently beckoned thither by a gesture invisible to me where I sat. The boy would then leave the office, jingling a few pence, and reappear with a handful of ginger-nuts, which he delivered in the hermitage, receiving two of the cakes for his trouble.

He lives, then, on ginger-nuts, thought I; never eats a dinner, properly speaking; he must be a vegetarian, then; but no; he never eats even vegetables; he eats nothing but ginger-nuts. My mind then ran on in reveries concerning the probable effects upon the human constitution of living entirely on ginger-nuts. Ginger-nuts are so called, because they contain ginger as one of their peculiar constituents, and the final flavoring one. Now, what was ginger? A hot, spicy thing. Was Bartleby hot and spicy? Not at all. Ginger, then, had no effect upon Bartleby. Probably he preferred it should have none.

Nothing so aggravates an earnest person as a passive resistance. If the indi- 55 vidual so resisted be of a not inhumane temper, and the resisting one perfectly harmless in his passivity, then, in the better moods of the former, he will endeavor charitably to construe to his imagination what proves impossible to be solved by his judgment. Even so, for the most part, I regarded Bartleby and his ways. Poor fellow! thought I, he means no mischief; it is plain he intends no insolence; his aspect sufficiently evinces that his eccentricities are involuntary. He is useful to me. I can get along with him. If I turn him away, the chances are he will fall in with some less-indulgent employer, and then he will be rudely treated, and perhaps driven forth miserably to starve. Yes. Here I can cheaply purchase a delicious self-approval. To befriend Bartleby; to humor him in his strange willfulness, will cost me little or nothing, while I lay up in my soul what will eventually prove a sweet morsel for my conscience. But this mood was not invariable with me. The passiveness of Bartleby sometimes irritated me. I felt strangely goaded on to encounter him in new opposition—to elicit some angry spark from him answerable to my own. But, indeed, I might as well have essayed to strike fire with my knuckles against a bit of Windsor soap. But one afternoon the evil impulse in me mastered me, and the following little scene ensued:

"Bartleby," said I, "when those papers are all copied, I will compare them with you."

"I would prefer not to."

"How? Surely you do not mean to persist in that mulish vagary?"

No answer.

I threw open the folding-doors near by, and, turning upon Turkey and Nip- 60
pers, exclaimed:

"Bartleby a second time says, he won't examine his papers. What do you think of it, Turkey?"

It was afternoon, be it remembered. Turkey sat glowing like a brass boiler; his bald head steaming; his hands reeling among his blotted papers.

"Think of it?" roared Turkey; "I think I'll just step behind his screen, and black his eyes for him!"

So saying, Turkey rose to his feet and threw his arms into a pugilistic position. He was hurrying away to make good his promise, when I detained him, alarmed at the effect of incautiously rousing Turkey's combativeness after dinner.

"Sit down, Turkey," said I, "and hear what Nippers has to say. What do you 65
think of it, Nippers? Would I not be justified in immediately dismissing Bartleby?"

"Excuse me, that is for you to decide, sir. I think his conduct quite unusual, and, indeed, unjust, as regards Turkey and myself. But it may only be a passing whim."

"Ah," exclaimed I, "you have strangely changed your mind, then—you speak very gently of him now."

"All beer," cried Turkey; "gentleness is effects of beer—Nippers and I dined together to-day. You see how gentle *I* am, sir. Shall I go and black his eyes?"

"You refer to Bartleby, I suppose. No, not to-day, Turkey," I replied; "pray, put up your fists."

I closed the doors, and again advanced towards Bartleby. I felt additional 70
incentives tempting me to my fate. I burned to be rebelled against again. I remembered that Bartleby never left the office.

"Bartleby," said I, "Ginger Nut is away; just step around to the post office, won't you? (it was but a three minutes' walk), and see if there is anything for me."

"I would prefer not to."

"You *will* not?"

"I *prefer* not."

I staggered to my desk, and sat there in a deep study. My blind inveteracy 75
returned. Was there any other thing in which I could procure myself to be
ignominiously repulsed by this lean, penniless wight?—my hired clerk? What
added thing is there, perfectly reasonable, that he will be sure to refuse to do?
"Bartleby!"

No answer.

"Bartleby," in a louder tone.

No answer.

"Bartleby," I roared.

Like a very ghost, agreeably to the laws of magical invocation, at the third 80
summons, he appeared at the entrance of his hermitage.

"Go to the next room, and tell Nippers to come to me."

"I prefer not to," he respectfully and slowly said and mildly disappeared.

"Very good, Bartleby," said I, in a quiet sort of serenely-severe, self-possessed
tone, intimating the unalterable purpose of some terrible retribution very
close at hand. At the moment I half intended something of the kind. But upon
the whole, as it was drawing towards my dinner-hour, I thought it best to put
on my hat and walk home for the day, suffering much from perplexity and distress of mind.

Shall I acknowledge it? The conclusion of this whole business was, that it
soon became a fixed fact of my chambers, that a pale young scrivener, by the
name of Bartleby, had a desk there; that he copied for me at the usual rate of
four cents a folio (one hundred words); but he was permanently exempt from
examining the work done by him, that duty being transferred to Turkey and
Nippers, out of compliment, doubtless, to their superior acuteness; moreover,
said Bartleby was never, on any account, to be dispatched on the most trivial
errand of any sort; and that even if entreated to take upon him such a matter, it
was generally understood that he would "prefer not to"—in other words, he
would refuse point blank.

As days passed on, I became considerably reconciled to Bartleby. His steadi- 85
ness, his freedom from all dissipation, his incessant industry (except when he
chose to throw himself into a standing revery behind his screen), his great stillness, his unalterableness of demeanor under all circumstances, made him a
valuable acquisition. One prime thing was this—*he was always there*—first in
the morning, continually through the day, and the last at night. I had a singular
confidence in his honesty. I felt my most precious papers perfectly safe in his
hands. Sometimes, to be sure, I could not, for the very soul of me, avoid falling
into sudden spasmodic passions with him. For it was exceeding difficult to
bear in mind all the time those strange peculiarities, privileges, and unheard of
exemptions, forming the tacit stipulations on Bartleby's part under which he
remained in my office. Now and then, in the eagerness of dispatching pressing
business, I would inadvertently summon Bartleby, in a short, rapid tone, to put
his finger, say, on the incipient tie of a bit of red tape with which I was about

compressing some papers. Of course, from behind the screen the usual answer, "I prefer not to," was sure to come; and then, how could a human creature, with the common infirmities of our nature, refrain from bitterly exclaiming upon such perverseness—such unreasonableness? However, every added repulse of this sort which I received only tended to lessen the probability of my repeating the inadvertence.

Here it must be said, that according to the custom of most legal gentlemen occupying chambers in densely-populated law buildings, there were several keys to my door. One was kept by a woman residing in the attic, which person weekly scrubbed and daily swept and dusted my apartments. Another was kept by Turkey for convenience sake. The third I sometimes carried in my own pocket. The fourth I knew not who had.

Now, one Sunday morning I happened to go to Trinity Church, to hear a celebrated preacher, and finding myself rather early on the ground I thought I would walk round to my chambers for a while. Luckily I had my key with me; but upon applying it to the lock, I found it resisted by something inserted from the inside. Quite surprised, I called out; when to my consternation a key was turned from within; and thrusting his lean visage at me, and holding the door ajar, the apparition of Bartleby appeared, in his shirt sleeves, and otherwise in a strangely tattered *déshabillé*, saying quietly that he was sorry, but he was deeply engaged just then, and—preferred not admitting me at present. In a brief word or two, he moreover added, that perhaps I had better walk around the block two or three times, and by that time he would probably have concluded his affairs.

Now, the utterly unsurmised appearance of Bartleby, tenanting my law-chambers of a Sunday morning, with his cadaverously gentlemanly *nonchalance*, yet withal firm and self-possessed, had such a strange effect upon me, that incontinently I slunk away from my own door, and did as desired. But not without sundry twinges of impotent rebellion against the mild effrontery of this unaccountable scrivener. Indeed, it was his wonderful mildness chiefly, which not only disarmed me, but unmanned me as it were. For I consider that one, for the time, is somehow unmanned when he tranquilly permits his hired clerk to dictate to him, and order him away from his own premises. Furthermore, I was full of uneasiness as to what Bartleby could possibly be doing in my office in his shirt sleeves, and in an otherwise dismantled condition of a Sunday morning. Was anything amiss going on? Nay, that was out of the question. It was not to be thought of for a moment that Bartleby was an immoral person. But what could he be doing there?—copying? Nay again, whatever might be his eccentricities, Bartleby was an eminently decorous person. He would be the last man to sit down to his desk in any state approaching to nudity. Besides, it was Sunday; and there was something about Bartleby that forbade the supposition that he would by any secular occupation violate the proprieties of the day.

Nevertheless, my mind was not pacified; and full of a restless curiosity, at last I returned to the door. Without hindrance I inserted my key, opened it, and entered. Bartleby was not to be seen. I looked round anxiously, peeped behind his screen; but it was very plain that he was gone. Upon more closely examining the place, I surmised that for an indefinite period Bartleby must have eaten, dressed, and slept in my office, and that, too, without plate, mirror, or bed. The cushioned seat of a rickety old sofa in one corner bore the faint impress of a lean, reclining form. Rolled away under his desk, I found a blanket; under the empty grate, a blacking box and brush; on a chair, a tin basin, with soap and a ragged towel; in a newspaper a few crumbs of ginger-nuts and a morsel of cheese. Yes, thought I, it is evident enough that Bartleby has been making his home here, keeping bachelor's hall all by himself. Immediately then the thought came sweeping across me, what miserable friendlessness and loneliness are here revealed! His poverty is great; but his solitude, how horrible! Think of it. Of a Sunday, Wall Street is deserted as Petra;[5] and every night of every day it is an emptiness. This building, too, which of week-days hums with industry and life, at nightfall echoes with sheer vacancy, and all through Sunday is forlorn. And here Bartleby makes his home; sole spectator of a solitude which he has seen all populous—a sort of innocent and transformed Marius brooding among the ruins of Carthage![6]

For the first time in my life a feeling of over-powering stinging melancholy 90 seized me. Before, I had never experienced aught but a not unpleasing sadness. The bond of a common humanity now drew me irresistibly to gloom. A fraternal melancholy! For both I and Bartleby were sons of Adam. I remembered the bright silks and sparkling faces I had seen that day, in gala trim, swan-like sailing down the Mississippi of Broadway; and I contrasted them with the pallid copyist, and thought to myself, Ah, happiness courts the light, so we deem the world is gay; but misery hides aloof, so we deem that misery there is none. These sad fancyings—chimeras, doubtless, of a sick and silly brain—led on to other and more special thoughts, concerning the eccentricities of Bartleby. Presentiments of strange discoveries hovered round me. The scrivener's pale form appeared to me laid out, among uncaring strangers, in its shivering winding sheet.

Suddenly I was attracted by Bartleby's closed desk, the key in open sight left in the lock.

I mean no mischief, seek the gratification of no heartless curiosity, thought I; besides, the desk is mine, and its contents, too, so I will make bold to look within. Everything was methodically arranged, the papers smoothly placed. The pigeon holes were deep, and removing the files of documents, I groped into their recesses. Presently I felt something there, and dragged it out. It was an old bandanna handkerchief, heavy and knotted. I opened it, and saw it was a saving's bank.

I now recalled all the quiet mysteries which I had noted in the man. I remembered that he never spoke but to answer; that, though at intervals he had considerable time to himself, yet I had never seen him reading—no, not even a

---

[5] A city in Palestine found by explorers in 1812. It had been deserted and lost for centuries.

[6] Gaius Marius (155–86 B.C.), a plebeian general who was forced to flee from Rome. Nineteenth-century democratic literature sometimes pictured him old and alone among the ruins of Carthage.

newspaper; that for long periods he would stand looking out, at his pale window behind the screen, upon the dead brick wall; I was quite sure he never visited any refectory or eating house; while his pale face clearly indicated that he never drank beer like Turkey; or tea and coffee even, like other men; that he never went anywhere in particular that I could learn; never went out for a walk, unless, indeed, that was the case at present; that he had declined telling who he was, or whence he came, or whether he had any relatives in the world; that though so thin and pale, he never complained of ill health. And more than all, I remembered a certain unconscious air of pallid—how shall I call it?—of pallid haughtiness, say, or rather an austere reserve about him, which had positively awed me into my tame compliance with his eccentricities, when I had feared to ask him to do the slightest incidental thing for me, even though I might know, from his long-continued motionlessness, that behind his screen he must be standing in one of those dead-wall reveries of his.

Revolving all these things, and coupling them with the recently discovered fact, that he made my office his constant abiding place and home, and not forgetful of his morbid moodiness; revolving all these things, a prudential feeling began to steal over me. My first emotions had been those of pure melancholy and sincerest pity; but just in proportion as the forlornness of Bartleby grew and grew to my imagination, did that same melancholy merge into fear, that pity into repulsion. So true it is, and so terrible, too, that up to a certain point the thought or sight of misery enlists our best affections; but, in certain special cases, beyond that point it does not. They err who would assert that invariably this is owing to the inherent selfishness of the human heart. It rather proceeds from a certain hopelessness of remedying excessive and organic ill. To a sensitive being, pity is not seldom pain. And when at last it is perceived that such pity cannot lead to effectual succor, common sense bids the soul be rid of it. What I saw that morning persuaded me that the scrivener was the victim of innate and incurable disorder. I might give alms to his body; but his body did not pain him; it was his soul that suffered, and his soul I could not reach.

I did not accomplish the purpose of going to Trinity Church that morning. 95 Somehow, the things I had seen disqualified me for the time from churchgoing. I walked homeward, thinking what I would do with Bartleby. Finally, I resolved upon this—I would put certain calm questions to him the next morning, touching his history, etc., and if he declined to answer them openly and unreservedly (and I supposed he would prefer not), then to give him a twenty dollar bill over and above whatever I might owe him, and tell him his services were no longer required; but that if in any other way I could assist him, I would be happy to do so, especially if he desired to return to his native place, wherever that might be, I would willingly help to defray the expenses. Moreover, if, after reaching home, he found himself at any time in want of aid, a letter from him would be sure of a reply.

The next morning came.

"Bartleby," said I, gently calling to him behind his screen.

No reply.

"Bartleby," said I, in a still gentler tone, "come here; I am not going to ask you to do anything you would prefer not to do—I simply wish to speak to you."

Upon this he noiselessly slid into view. 100

"Will you tell me, Bartleby, where you were born?"

"I would prefer not to."

"Will you tell me *anything* about yourself?"

"I would prefer not to."

"But what reasonable objection can you have to speak to me? I feel friendly 105 towards you."

He did not look at me while I spoke, but kept his glance fixed upon my bust of Cicero, which, as I then sat, was directly behind me, some six inches above my head.

"What is your answer, Bartleby," said I, after waiting a considerable time for a reply, during which his countenance remained immovable, only there was the faintest conceivable tremor of the white attenuated mouth.

"At present I prefer to give no answer," he said, and retired into his hermitage.

It was rather weak in me I confess, but his manner, on this occasion, nettled me. Not only did there seem to lurk in it a certain calm disdain, but his perverseness seemed ungrateful, considering the undeniable good usage and indulgence he had received from me.

Again I sat ruminating what I should do. Mortified as I was at his behavior, 110 and resolved as I had been to dismiss him when I entered my office, nevertheless I strangely felt something superstitious knocking at my heart, and forbidding me to carry out my purpose, and denouncing me for a villain if I dared to breathe one bitter word against this forlornest of mankind. At last, familiarly drawing my chair behind his screen, I sat down and said: "Bartleby, never mind, then, about revealing your history; but let me entreat you, as a friend, to comply as far as may be with the usages of this office. Say now, you will help to examine papers tomorrow or next day: in short, say now, that in a day or two you will begin to be a little reasonable—say so, Bartleby."

"At present I would prefer not to be a little reasonable," was his mildly cadaverous reply.

Just then the folding-doors opened, and Nippers approached. He seemed suffering from an unusually bad night's rest, induced by severer indigestion than common. He overheard those final words of Bartleby.

"*Prefer not*, eh?" gritted Nippers—"I'd *prefer* him, if I were you, sir," addressing me—"I'd *prefer* him; I'd give him preferences, the stubborn mule! What is it, sir, pray, that he *prefers* not to do now?"

Bartleby moved not a limb.

"Mr. Nippers," said I, "I'd prefer that you would withdraw for the present." 115

Somehow, of late, I had got into the way of involuntarily using this word "prefer" upon all sorts of not exactly suitable occasions. And I trembled to think that my contact with the scrivener had already and seriously affected me in a mental way. And what further and deeper aberration might it not yet produce? This apprehension had not been without efficacy in determining me to summary measures.

As Nippers, looking very sour and sulky, was departing, Turkey blandly and deferentially approached.

"With submission, sir," said he, "yesterday I was thinking about Bartleby here, and I think that if he would but prefer to take a quart of good ale every day, it would do much towards mending him, and enabling him to assist in examining his papers."

"So you have got the word, too," said I, slightly excited.

"With submission, what word, sir," asked Turkey, respectfully crowding 120 himself into the contracted space behind the screen, and by so doing, making me jostle the scrivener. "What word, sir?"

"I would prefer to be left alone here," said Bartleby, as if offended at being mobbed in his privacy.

"*That's* the word, Turkey," said I—"*that's* it."

"Oh, *prefer?* oh yes—queer word. I never use it myself. But, sir, as I was saying, if he would but prefer—"

"Turkey," interrupted I, "you will please withdraw."

"Oh certainly, sir, if you prefer that I should." 125

As he opened the folding-door to retire, Nippers at his desk caught a glimpse of me, and asked whether I would prefer to have a certain paper copied on blue paper or white. He did not in the least roguishly accent the word prefer. It was plain that it involuntarily rolled from his tongue. I thought to myself, surely I must get rid of a demented man, who already has in some degree turned the tongues, if not the heads of myself and clerks. But I thought it prudent not to break the dismission at once.

The next day I noticed that Bartleby did nothing but stand at his window in his dead-wall revery. Upon asking him why he did not write, he said that he had decided upon doing no more writing.

"Why, how now? What next?" exclaimed I, "do no more writing?"

"No more."

"And what is the reason?" 130

"Do you not see the reason for yourself?" he indifferently replied.

I looked steadfastly at him, and perceived that his eyes looked dull and glazed. Instantly it occurred to me, that his unexampled diligence in copying by his dim window for the first few weeks of his stay with me might have temporarily impaired his vision.

I was touched. I said something in condolence with him. I hinted that of course he did wisely in abstaining from writing for a while; and urged him to embrace that opportunity of taking wholesome exercise in the open air. This, however, he did not do. A few days after this, my other clerks being absent, and being in a great hurry to dispatch certain letters by the mail, I thought that, having nothing else earthly to do, Bartleby would surely be less inflexible than usual, and carry these letters to the post office. But he blankly declined. So, much to my inconvenience, I went myself.

Still added days went by. Whether Bartleby's eyes improved or not, I could not say. To all appearance, I thought they did. But when I asked him if they did, he vouchsafed no answer. At all events, he would do no copying. At last, in reply to my urgings, he informed me that he had permanently given up copying.

"What!" exclaimed I; "suppose your eyes should get entirely well—better 135 than ever before—would you not copy then?"

"I have given up copying," he answered, and slid aside.

He remained as ever, a fixture in my chamber. Nay—if that were possible— he became still more of a fixture than before. What was to be done? He would do nothing in the office; why should he stay there? In plain fact, he had now become a millstone to me, not only useless as a necklace, but afflictive to bear. Yet I was sorry for him. I speak less than truth when I say that, on his own account, he occasioned me uneasiness. If he would but have named a single relative or friend, I would instantly have written, and urged their taking the poor fellow away to some convenient retreat. But he seemed alone, absolutely alone in the universe. A bit of wreck in the mid-Atlantic. At length, necessities connected with my business tyrannized over all other considerations. Decently as I could, I told Bartleby that in six days time he must unconditionally leave the office. I warned him to take measures, in the interval, for procuring some other abode. I offered to assist him in this endeavor, if he himself would but take the first step towards a removal. "And when you finally quit me, Bartleby," added I, "I shall see that you go not away entirely unprovided. Six days from this hour, remember."

At the expiration of that period, I peeped behind the screen, and lo! Bartleby was there.

I buttoned up my coat, balanced myself; advanced slowly towards him, touched his shoulder, and said, "The time has come; you must quit this place; I am sorry for you; here is money; but you must go."

"I would prefer not," he replied, with his back still towards me. 140

"You *must*."

He remained silent.

Now I had an unbounded confidence in this man's common honesty. He had frequently restored to me sixpences and shillings carelessly dropped upon the floor, for I am apt to be very reckless in such shirt-button affairs. The proceeding, then, which followed will not be deemed extraordinary.

"Bartleby," said I, "I owe you twelve dollars on account; here are thirty-two, the odd twenty are yours—Will you take it?" and I handed the bills towards him.

But he made no motion. 145

"I will leave them here, then," putting them under a weight on the table. Then taking my hat and cane and going to the door, I tranquilly turned and added—"After you have removed your things from these offices, Bartleby, you will of course lock the door—since every one is now gone for the day but you—and if you please, slip your key underneath the mat, so that I may have it in the morning. I shall not see you again; so good-by to you. If, hereafter, in your new place of abode, I can be of any service to you, do not fail to advise me by letter. Good-by, Bartleby, and fare you well."

But he answered not a word; like the last column of some ruined temple, he remained standing mute and solitary in the middle of the otherwise deserted room.

As I walked home in a pensive mood, my vanity got the better of my pity. I could not but highly plume myself on my masterly management in getting rid of Bartleby. Masterly I call it, and such it must appear to any dispassionate thinker. The beauty of my procedure seemed to consist in its perfect quietness. There was no vulgar bullying, no bravado of any sort, no choleric hectoring, and striding to and fro across the apartment, jerking out vehement commands for Bartleby to bundle himself off with his beggarly traps. Nothing of the kind. Without loudly bidding Bartleby depart—as an inferior genius might have done—I *assumed* the ground that depart he must; and upon that assumption built all I had to say. The more I thought over my procedure, the more I was charmed with it. Nevertheless, next morning, upon awakening, I had my doubts—I had somehow slept off the fumes of vanity. One of the coolest and wisest hours a man has, is just after he awakes in the morning. My procedure seemed as sagacious as ever—but only in theory. How it would prove in practice—there was the rub. It was truly a beautiful thought to have assumed Bartleby's departure; but, after all, that assumption was simply my own, and none of Bartleby's. The great point was, not whether I had assumed that he would quit me, but whether he would prefer to do so. He was more a man of preferences than assumptions.

After breakfast, I walked down town, arguing the probabilities *pro* and *con.* One moment I thought it would prove a miserable failure, and Bartleby would be found all alive at my office as usual; the next moment it seemed certain that I should find his chair empty. And so I kept veering about. At the corner of Broadway and Canal Street, I saw quite an excited group of people standing in earnest conversation.

"I'll take odds he doesn't," said a voice as I passed.

150

"Doesn't go?—done!" said I; "put up your money."

I was instinctively putting my hand in my pocket to produce my own, when I remembered that this was an election day. The words I had overheard bore no reference to Bartleby, but to the success or non-success of some candidate for the mayoralty. In my intent frame of mind, I had, as it were, imagined that all Broadway shared in my excitement, and were debating the same question with me. I passed on, very thankful that the uproar of the street screened my momentary absent-mindedness.

As I had intended, I was earlier than usual at my office door. I stood listening for a moment. All was still. He must be gone. I tried the knob. The door was locked. Yes, my procedure had worked to a charm; he indeed must be vanished. Yet a certain melancholy mixed with this: I was almost sorry for my brilliant success. I was fumbling under the door mat for the key, which Bartleby was to have left there for me, when accidentally my knee knocked against a panel, producing a summoning sound, and in response a voice came to me from within—"Not yet; I am occupied."

It was Bartleby.

I was thunderstruck. For an instant I stood like the man who, pipe in mouth, 155 was killed one cloudless afternoon long ago in Virginia, by summer lightning; at his own warm open window he was killed, and remained leaning out there upon the dreamy afternoon, till some one touched him, when he fell.

"Not gone!" I murmured at last. But again obeying that wondrous ascendancy which the inscrutable scrivener had over me, and from which ascendancy, for all my chafing, I could not completely escape, I slowly went down stairs and out into the street, and while walking round the block, considered what I should next do in this unheard-of perplexity. Turn the man out by an actual thrusting I could not; to drive him away by calling him hard names would not do; calling in the police was an unpleasant idea; and yet, permit him to enjoy his cadaverous triumph over me—this, too, I could not think of. What was to be done? or, if nothing could be done, was there anything further that I could *assume* in the matter? Yes, as before I had prospectively assumed that Bartleby would depart, so now I might retrospectively assume that departed he was. In the legitimate carrying out of this assumption, I might enter my office in a great hurry, and pretending not to see Bartleby at all, walk straight against him as if he were air. Such a proceeding would in a singular degree have the appearance of a home-thrust. It was hardly possible that Bartleby could withstand such an application of the doctrine of assumption. But upon second thoughts the success of the plan seemed rather dubious. I resolved to argue the matter over with him again.

"Bartleby," said I, entering the office, with a quietly severe expression, "I am seriously displeased. I am pained, Bartleby. I had thought better of you. I had imagined you of such a gentlemanly organization, that in any delicate dilemma a slight hint would suffice—in short, an assumption. But it appears I am deceived. Why," I added, unaffectedly starting, "you have not even touched that money yet," pointing to it, just where I had left it the evening previous.

He answered nothing.

"Will you, or will you not, quit me?" I now demanded in a sudden passion, advancing close to him.

"I would prefer *not* to quit you," he replied, gently emphasizing the *not*. 160

"What earthly right have you to stay here? Do you pay any rent? Do you pay my taxes? Or is this property yours?"

He answered nothing.

"Are you ready to go on and write now? Are your eyes recovered? Could you copy a small paper for me this morning? or help examine a few lines? or step round to the post office? In a word, will you do anything at all, to give a coloring to your refusal to depart the premises?"

He silently retired into his hermitage.

I was now in such a state of nervous resentment that I thought it but prudent 165 to check myself at present from further demonstrations. Bartleby and I were alone. I remembered the tragedy of the unfortunate Adams and the still more unfortunate Colt in the solitary office of the latter; and how poor Colt, being dreadfully incensed by Adams, and imprudently permitting himself to get wildly excited, was at unawares hurried into his fatal act—an act which certainly no man could possibly deplore more than the actor himself.[7] Often it had occurred to me in my ponderings upon the subject that had that altercation taken place in the public street, or at a private residence, it would not have terminated as it did. It was the circumstance of being alone in a solitary office, up stairs, of a building entirely unhallowed by humanizing domestic associations—an uncarpeted office, doubtless, of a dusty, haggard sort of appearance—this it must have been, which greatly helped to enhance the irritable desperation of the hapless Colt.

But when this old Adam of resentment rose in me and tempted me concerning Bartleby, I grappled him and threw him. How? Why, simply by recalling the divine injunction: "A new commandment give I unto you, that ye love one another." Yes, this it was that saved me. Aside from higher considerations, charity often operates as a vastly wise and prudent principle—a great safeguard to its possessor. Men have committed murder for jealousy's sake, and anger's sake, and hatred's sake, and selfishness' sake, and spiritual pride's sake; but no man, that ever I heard of, ever committed a diabolical murder for sweet charity's sake. Mere self-interest, then, if no better motive can be enlisted, should, especially with high-tempered men, prompt all beings to charity and philanthropy. At any rate, upon the occasion in question, I strove to drown my exasperated feelings towards the scrivener by benevolently construing his conduct. Poor fellow, poor fellow! thought I, he don't mean anything; and besides, he has seen hard times, and ought to be indulged.

I endeavored, also, immediately to occupy myself, and at the same time to comfort my despondency. I tried to fancy, that in the course of the morning, at such time as might prove agreeable to him, Bartleby, of his own free accord, would emerge from his hermitage and take up some decided line of march in the direction of the door. But no. Half-past twelve o'clock came; Turkey began to glow in the face, overturn his inkstand, and become generally obstreperous; Nippers abated down into quietude and courtesy; Ginger Nut munched his noon apple; and Bartleby remained standing at his window in one of his profoundest dead-wall reveries. Will it be credited? Ought I to acknowledge it? That afternoon I left the office without saying one further word to him.

Some days now passed, during which, at leisure intervals I looked a little into "Edwards on the Will," and "Priestley on Necessity."[8] Under the circumstances, those books induced a salutary feeling. Gradually I slid into the persuasion that these troubles of mine, touching the scrivener, had been all predestinated from eternity, and Bartleby was billeted upon me for some mysterious purpose of an all-wise Providence, which it was not for a mere mortal like me to fathom. Yes, Bartleby, stay there behind your screen, thought I; I shall persecute you no more; you are harmless and noiseless as any of these old chairs; in short, I never feel so private as when I know you are here. At last I see it, I feel it; I penetrate to

---

[7] A sensational 1841 homicide case in which John C. Colt murdered printer Samuel Adams in a fit of passion.

[8] Jonathan Edwards (1703–1758), American theologian, and Joseph Priestley (1733–1804), English clergyman and chemist, both held that a person's life was predetermined.

the predestinated purpose of my life. I am content. Others may have loftier parts to enact; but my mission in this world, Bartleby, is to furnish you with office-room for such period as you may see fit to remain.

I believe that this wise and blessed frame of mind would have continued with me, had it not been for the unsolicited and uncharitable remarks obtruded upon me by my professional friends who visited the rooms. But thus it often is, that the constant friction of illiberal minds wears out at last the best resolves of the more generous. Though to be sure, when I reflected upon it, it was not strange that people entering my office should be struck by the peculiar aspect of the unaccountable Bartleby, and so be tempted to throw out some sinister observations concerning him. Sometimes an attorney, having business with me, and calling at my office, and finding no one but the scrivener there, would undertake to obtain some sort of precise information from him touching my whereabouts; but without heeding his idle talk, Bartleby would remain standing immovable in the middle of the room. So after contemplating him in that position for a time, the attorney would depart, no wiser than he came.

Also, when a reference was going on, and the room full of lawyers and wit- 170 nesses, and business driving fast, some deeply-occupied legal gentleman present, seeing Bartleby wholly unemployed, would request him to run round to his (the legal gentleman's) office and fetch some papers for him. Thereupon, Bartleby would tranquilly decline, and yet remain idle as before. Then the lawyer would give a great stare, and turn to me. And what could I say? At last I was made aware that all through the circle of my professional acquaintance, a whisper of wonder was running round, having reference to the strange creature I kept at my office. This worried me very much. And as the idea came upon me of his possibly turning out a long-lived man, and keep occupying my chambers, and denying my authority; and perplexing my visitors; and scandalizing my professional reputation; and casting a general gloom over the premises; keeping soul and body together to the last upon his savings (for doubtless he spent but half a dime a day), and in the end perhaps outlive me, and claim possession of my office by right of his perpetual occupancy: as all these dark anticipations crowded upon me more and more, and my friends continually intruded their relentless remarks upon the apparition in my room; a great change was wrought in me. I resolved to gather all my faculties together, and forever rid me of this intolerable incubus.

Ere revolving any complicated project, however, adapted to this end, I first simply suggested to Bartleby the propriety of his permanent departure. In a calm and serious tone, I commended the idea to his careful and mature consideration. But, having taken three days to meditate upon it, he apprised me, that his original determination remained the same; in short, that he still preferred to abide with me.

What shall I do? I now said to myself, buttoning up my coat to the last button. What shall I do? what ought I to do? what does conscience say I *should* do with this man, or, rather, ghost. Rid myself of him, I must; go, he shall. But how? You will not thrust him, the poor, pale, passive mortal—you will not thrust such a helpless creature out of your door? you will not dishonor yourself by such cruelty? No, I will not, I cannot do that. Rather would I let him live and die here, and then mason up his remains in the wall. What, then, will you do? For all your coaxing, he will not budge. Bribes he leaves under your own paper-weight on your table; in short, it is quite plain that he prefers to cling to you.

Then something severe, something unusual must be done. What! surely you will not have him collared by a constable, and commit his innocent pallor to the common jail? And upon what ground could you procure such a thing to be done?—a vagrant, is he? What! he a vagrant, a wanderer, who refuses to budge? It is because he will *not* be a vagrant, then, that you seek to count him *as* a vagrant. That is too absurd. No visible means of support: there I have him. Wrong again: for indubitably he *does* support himself, and that is the only unanswerable proof that any man can show of his possessing the means so to do. No more, then. Since he will not quit me, I must quit him. I will change my offices; I will move elsewhere, and give him fair notice, that if I find him in my new premises I will then proceed against him as a common trespasser.

Acting accordingly, next day I thus addressed him: "I find these chambers too far from the City Hall; the air is unwholesome. In a word, I propose to remove my offices next week, and shall no longer require your services. I tell you this now, in order that you may seek another place."

He made no reply, and nothing more was said.   175

On the appointed day I engaged carts and men, proceeded to my chambers, and, having but little furniture, everything was removed in a few hours. Throughout, the scrivener remained standing behind the screen, which I directed to be removed the last thing. It was withdrawn; and, being folded up like a huge folio, left him the motionless occupant of a naked room. I stood in the entry watching him a moment, while something from within me upbraided me.

I re-entered, with my hand in my pocket—and—and my heart in my mouth.

"Good-by, Bartleby; I am going—good-by, and God some way bless you; and take that," slipping something in his hand. But it dropped upon the floor, and then—strange to say—I tore myself from him whom I had so longed to be rid of.

Established in my new quarters, for a day or two I kept the door locked, and started at every footfall in the passages. When I returned to my rooms, after any little absence, I would pause at the threshold for an instant, and attentively listen, ere applying my key. But these fears were needless. Bartleby never came nigh me.

I thought all was going well, when a perturbed-looking stranger visited   180
me, inquiring whether I was the person who had recently occupied rooms at No. ——— Wall Street.

Full of forebodings, I replied that I was.

"Then, sir," said the stranger, who proved a lawyer, "you are responsible for the man you left there. He refuses to do any copying; he refuses to do anything; he says he prefers not to; and he refuses to quit the premises."

"I am very sorry, sir," said I, with assumed tranquillity, but an inward tremor, "but, really, the man you allude to is nothing to me—he is no relation or apprentice of mine, that you should hold me responsible for him."

"In mercy's name, who is he?"

"I certainly cannot inform you. I know nothing about him. Formerly I em- 185 ployed him as a copyist; but he has done nothing for me now for some time past."

"I shall settle him, then—good morning, sir."

Several days passed, and I heard nothing more; and, though I often felt a charitable prompting to call at the place and see poor Bartleby, yet a certain squeamishness, of I know not what, withheld me.

All is over with him, by this time, thought I, at last, when, through another week, no further intelligence reached me. But, coming to my room the day after, I found several persons waiting at my door in a high state of nervous excitement.

"That's the man—here he comes," cried the foremost one, whom I recognized as the lawyer who had previously called upon me alone.

"You must take him away, sir, at once," cried a portly person among them, ad- 190 vancing upon me, and whom I knew to be the landlord of No. —— Wall Street. "These gentlemen, my tenants, cannot stand it any longer; Mr. B——," pointing to the lawyer, "has turned him out of his room, and he now persists in haunting the building generally, sitting upon the banisters of the stairs by day, and sleeping in the entry by night. Everybody is concerned; clients are leaving the offices; some fears are entertained of a mob; something you must do, and that without delay."

Aghast at this torrent, I fell back before it, and would fain have locked myself in my new quarters. In vain I persisted that Bartleby was nothing to me—no more than to any one else. In vain—I was the last person known to have anything to do with him, and they held me to the terrible account. Fearful, then, of being exposed in the papers (as one person present obscurely threatened), I considered the matter, and, at length, said, that if the lawyer would give me a confidential interview with the scrivener, in his (the lawyer's) own room, I would, that afternoon, strive my best to rid them of the nuisance they complained of.

Going up stairs to my old haunt, there was Bartleby silently sitting upon the banister at the landing.

"What are you doing here, Bartleby?" said I.

"Sitting upon the banister," he mildly replied.

I motioned him into the lawyer's room, who then left us. 195

"Bartleby," said I, "are you aware that you are the cause of great tribulation to me, by persisting in occupying the entry after being dismissed from the office?"

No answer.

"Now one of two things must take place. Either you must do something, or something must be done to you. Now what sort of business would you like to engage in? Would you like to re-engage in copying for some one?"

"No; I would prefer not to make any change."

"Would you like a clerkship in a dry-goods store?"   200

"There is too much confinement about that. No, I would not like a clerkship; but I am not particular."

"Too much confinement," I cried, "why, you keep yourself confined all the time!"

"I would prefer not to take a clerkship," he rejoined, as if to settle that little item at once.

"How would a bar-tender's business suit you? There is no trying of the eyesight in that."

"I would not like it at all; though, as I said before, I am not particular."   205

His unwonted wordiness inspirited me. I returned to the charge.

"Well, then, would you like to travel through the country collecting bills for the merchants? That would improve your health."

"No, I would prefer to be doing something else."

"How, then, would going as a companion to Europe, to entertain some young gentleman with your conversation—how would that suit you?"

"Not at all. It does not strike me that there is anything definite about that. I   210 like to be stationary. But I am not particular."

"Stationary you shall be, then," I cried, now losing all patience, and, for the first time in all my exasperating connection with him, fairly flying into a passion. "If you do not go away from these premises before night, I shall feel bound— indeed, I *am* bound—to—to—to quit the premises myself!" I rather absurdly concluded, knowing not with what possible threat to try to frighten his immobility into compliance. Despairing of all further efforts, I was precipitately leaving him, when a final thought occurred to me—one which had not been wholly unindulged before.

"Bartleby," said I, in the kindest tone I could assume under such exciting circumstances, "will you go home with me now—not to my office, but my dwelling—and remain there till we can conclude upon some convenient arrangement for you at our leisure? Come, let us start now, right away."

"No: at present I would prefer not to make any change at all."

I answered nothing; but, effectually dodging every one by the suddenness and rapidity of my flight, rushed from the building, ran up Wall Street towards Broadway, and, jumping into the first omnibus, was soon removed from pursuit. As soon as tranquillity returned, I distinctly perceived that I had now done all that I possibly could, both in respect to the demands of the landlord and his tenants, and with regard to my own desire and sense of duty, to benefit Bartleby, and shield him from rude persecution. I now strove to be entirely care-free and quiescent; and my conscience justified me in the attempt; though, indeed, it was not so successful as I could have wished. So fearful was I of being again hunted out by the incensed landlord and his exasperated tenants, that, surrendering my business to Nippers, for a few days, I drove about the upper part of the town and through the suburbs, in my rockaway; crossed over to Jersey City and Hoboken, and paid fugitive visits to Manhattanville and Astoria. In fact, I almost lived in my rockaway for the time.

When again I entered my office, lo, a note from the landlord lay upon the 215 desk. I opened it with trembling hands. It informed me that the writer had sent to the police, and had Bartleby removed to the Tombs as a vagrant. Moreover, since I knew more about him than any one else, he wished me to appear at that place, and make a suitable statement of the facts. These tidings had a conflicting effect upon me. At first I was indignant; but, at last, almost approved. The landlord's energetic, summary disposition, had led him to adopt a procedure which I do not think I would have decided upon myself; and yet, as a last resort, under such peculiar circumstances, it seemed the only plan.

As I afterwards learned, the poor scrivener, when told that he must be conducted to the Tombs, offered not the slightest obstacle, but, in his pale, unmoving way, silently acquiesced.

Some of the compassionate and curious by-standers joined the party; and headed by one of the constables arm in arm with Bartleby, the silent procession filed its way through all the noise, and heat, and joy of the roaring thoroughfares at noon.

The same day I received the note, I went to the Tombs, or, to speak more properly, the Halls of Justice. Seeking the right officer, I stated the purpose of my call, and was informed that the individual I described was, indeed, within. I then assured the functionary that Bartleby was a perfectly honest man, and greatly to be compassionated, however unaccountably eccentric. I narrated all I knew, and closed by suggesting the idea of letting him remain in as indulgent confinement as possible, till something less harsh might be done—though, indeed, I hardly knew what. At all events, if nothing else could be decided upon, the alms-house must receive him. I then begged to have an interview.

Being under no disgraceful charge, and quite serene and harmless in all his ways, they had permitted him freely to wander about the prison, and, especially, in the inclosed grass-platted yards thereof. And so I found him there, standing all alone in the quietest of the yards, his face towards a high wall, while all around, from the narrow slits of the jail windows, I thought I saw peering out upon him the eyes of murderers and thieves.

"Bartleby!" 220

"I know you," he said, without looking round—"and I want nothing to say to you."

"It was not I that brought you here, Bartleby," said I, keenly pained at his implied suspicion. "And to you, this should not be so vile a place. Nothing reproachful attaches to you by being here. And see, it is not so sad a place as one might think. Look, there is the sky, and here is the grass."

"I know where I am," he replied, but would say nothing more, and so I left him.

As I entered the corridor again, a broad meat-like man, in an apron, accosted me, and, jerking his thumb over his shoulder, said—"Is that your friend?"

"Yes." 225

"Does he want to starve? If he does, let him live on the prison fare, that's all."

"Who are you?" asked I, not knowing what to make of such an unofficially speaking person in such a place.

"I am the grub-man. Such gentlemen as have friends here, hire me to provide them with something good to eat."

"Is this so?" said I, turning to the turnkey.

He said it was.   230

"Well, then," said I, slipping some silver into the grub-man's hands (for so they called him), "I want you to give particular attention to my friend there; let him have the best dinner you can get. And you must be as polite to him as possible."

"Introduce me, will you?" said the grub-man, looking at me with an expression which seemed to say he was all impatience for an opportunity to give a specimen of his breeding.

Thinking it would prove of benefit to the scrivener, I acquiesced; and, asking the grub-man his name, went up with him to Bartleby.

"Bartleby, this is a friend; you will find him very useful to you."

"Your sarvant, sir, your sarvant," said the grub-man, making a low salutation   235
behind his apron. "Hope you find it pleasant here, sir; nice grounds—cool apartments—hope you'll stay with us some time—try to make it agreeable. What will you have for dinner to-day?"

"I prefer not to dine to-day," said Bartleby, turning away. "It would disagree with me; I am unused to dinners." So saying, he slowly moved to the other side of the inclosure, and took up a position fronting the deadwall.

"How's this?" said the grub-man, addressing me with a stare of astonishment. "He's odd, ain't he?"

"I think he is a little deranged," said I, sadly.

"Deranged? deranged is it? Well, now, upon my word, I thought that friend of yourn was a gentleman forger; they are always pale and genteel-like, them forgers. I can't help pity 'em—can't help it, sir. Did you know Monroe Edwards?" he added, touchingly, and paused. Then, laying his hand piteously on my shoulder, sighed, "he died of consumption at Sing-Sing.[9] So you weren't acquainted with Monroe?"

"No, I was never socially acquainted with any forgers. But I cannot stop   240
longer. Look to my friend yonder. You will not lose by it. I will see you again."

Some few days after this, I again obtained admission to the Tombs, and went through the corridors in quest of Bartleby; but without finding him.

"I saw him coming from his cell not long ago," said a turnkey, "may be he's gone to loiter in the yards."

So I went in that direction.

"Are you looking for the silent man?" said another turnkey, passing me. "Yonder he lies—sleeping in the yard there. 'Tis not twenty minutes since I saw him lie down."

The yard was entirely quiet. It was not accessible to the common prisoners.   245
The surrounding walls of amazing thickness, kept off all sounds behind them.

[9] The state prison near Ossining, New York.

The Egyptian character of the masonry weighed upon me with its gloom. But a soft imprisoned turf grew under foot. The heart of the eternal pyramids, it seemed, wherein, by some strange magic, through the clefts, grass-seed, dropped by birds, had sprung.

Strangely huddled at the base of the wall, his knees drawn up, and lying on his side, his head touching the cold stones, I saw the wasted Bartleby. But nothing stirred. I paused; then went close up to him; stooped over, and saw that his dim eyes were open; otherwise he seemed profoundly sleeping. Something prompted me to touch him. I felt his hand, when a tingling shiver ran up my arm and down my spine to my feet.

The round face of the grub-man peered upon me now. "His dinner is ready. Won't he dine to-day, either? Or does he live without dining?"

"Lives without dining," said I, and closed the eyes.

"Eh!—He's asleep, ain't he?"

"With kings and counselors," murmured I.

250

There would seem little need for proceeding further in this history. Imagination will readily supply the meagre recital of poor Bartleby's interment. But, ere parting with the reader, let me say, that if this little narrative has sufficiently interested him, to awaken curiosity as to who Bartleby was, and what manner of life he led prior to the present narrator's making his acquaintance, I can only reply, that in such curiosity I fully share, but am wholly unable to gratify it. Yet here I hardly know whether I should divulge one little item of rumor, which came to my ear a few months after the scrivener's decease. Upon what basis it rested, I could never ascertain; and hence, how true it is I cannot now tell. But, inasmuch as this vague report has not been without a certain suggestive interest to me, however said, it may prove the same with some others; and so I will briefly mention it. The report was this: that Bartleby had been a subordinate clerk in the Dead Letter[10] Office at Washington, from which he had been suddenly removed by a change in the administration. When I think over this rumor, hardly can I express the emotions which seize me. Dead letters! does it not sound like dead men? Conceive a man by nature and misfortune prone to a pallid hopelessness, can any business seem more fitted to heighten it than that of continually handling these dead letters, and assorting them for the flames? For by the cart-load they are annually burned. Some times from out the folded paper the pale clerk takes a ring—the finger it was meant for, perhaps, moulders in the grave; a banknote sent in swiftest charity—he whom it would relieve, nor eats nor hungers any more; pardon for those who died despairing; hope for those who died unhoping; good tidings for those who died stifled by unrelieved calamities. On errands of life, these letters speed to death.

Ah, Bartleby! Ah, humanity!

---

[10] A letter that is undeliverable and unreturnable.

FOR ANALYSIS

1. List a half dozen adjectives that describe the narrator. Would the narrator agree that these adjectives are accurate?

2. What is it about Bartleby that so intrigues and fascinates the narrator? Why does the narrator continue to feel a moral obligation to an employee who refuses to work and curtly rejects kind offers of help?

3. What thematic function do Turkey and Nippers serve?

4. As the narrator congratulates himself on the cleverness of his scheme to dismiss Bartleby, he becomes fascinated with his "assumptions" about how Bartleby will behave. Examine the passage (paras. 149–56), and show how it advances the narrator's growing awareness of what Bartleby represents.

5. Readers differ as to whether this is the story of Bartleby or the lawyer-narrator. What is your view?

6. Would it be fair to describe Bartleby as a rebel without a cause, as a young man who refuses to participate in a comfortable and well-ordered business world but fails to offer any alternative way of life? Write a paragraph or two explaining why or why not.

MAKING CONNECTIONS

Compare and contrast Bartleby's form of rebellion with the rebellion of those who leave Omelas in Le Guin's "The Ones Who Walk Away from Omelas" (p. 346)?

WRITING TOPICS

1. About midway through the story (paras. 87–94), the narrator discovers that Bartleby has been living in the law offices, and he is profoundly moved when his eyes fall on the scrivener's worldly possessions. Reread those paragraphs, and write an analysis showing how they describe the narrator's growing awareness of who Bartleby is.

2. With his final utterance, "Ah, Bartleby! Ah, humanity!" the narrator apparently penetrates the mystery of the silent scrivener. The comment suggests that the narrator sees Bartleby as a representative of humanity. In what sense might the narrator have come to see Bartleby in this light?

3. Why does Melville allow the narrator (and the reader) to discover so little about Bartleby and the causes of his behavior? All we learn of Bartleby's past is told in the next-to-last paragraph. What clues does this paragraph give us to the narrator's fascination with Bartleby?

FRANZ KAFKA   (1883–1924)

A HUNGER ARTIST[1]   1924

During these last decades the interest in professional fasting has markedly diminished. It used to pay very well to stage such great performances under one's own management, but today that is quite impossible. We live in a different world now. At one time the whole town took a lively interest in the hunger artist; from day to day of his fast the excitement mounted; everybody wanted to see him at least once a day; there were people who bought season tickets for the last few days and sat from morning till night in front of his small barred cage; even in the nighttime there were visiting hours, when the whole effect was heightened by torch flares; on fine days the cage was set out in the open air, and then it was the children's special treat to see the hunger artist; for their elders he was often just a joke that happened to be in fashion, but the children stood open-mouthed, holding each other's hands for greater security, marveling at him as he sat there pallid in black tights, with his ribs sticking out so prominently, not even on a seat but down among straw on the ground, sometimes giving a courteous nod, answering questions with a constrained smile, or perhaps stretching an arm through the bars so that one might feel how thin it was, and then again withdrawing deep into himself, paying no attention to anyone or anything, not even to the all-important striking of the clock that was the only piece of furniture in his cage, but merely staring into vacancy with half shut eyes, now and then taking a sip from a tiny glass of water to moisten his lips.

Besides casual onlookers there were also relays of permanent watchers selected by the public, usually butchers, strangely enough, and it was their task to watch the hunger artist day and night, three of them at a time, in case he should have some secret recourse to nourishment. This was nothing but a formality, instituted to reassure the masses, for the initiates knew well enough that during his fast the artist would never in any circumstances, not even under forcible compulsion, swallow the smallest morsel of food; the honor of his profession forbade it. Not every watcher, of course, was capable of understanding this; there were often groups of night watchers who were very lax in carrying out their duties and deliberately huddled together in a retired corner to play cards with great absorption, obviously intending to give the hunger artist the chance of a little refreshment, which they supposed he could draw from some private hoard. Nothing annoyed the artist more than such watchers; they made him miserable; they made his fast seem unendurable; sometimes he mastered his

[1] Translated by Edwin and Willa Muir.

319

feebleness sufficiently to sing during their watch for as long as he could keep going, to show them how unjust their suspicions were. But that was of little use; they only wondered at his cleverness in being able to fill his mouth even while singing. Much more to his taste were the watchers who sat close up to the bars, who were not content with the dim night lighting of the hall but focused him in the full glare of the electric pocket torch given them by the impresario. The harsh light did not trouble him at all, in any case he could never sleep properly, and he could always drowse a little, whatever the light, at any hour, even when the hall was thronged with noisy onlookers. He was quite happy at the prospect of spending a sleepless night with such watchers; he was ready to exchange jokes with them, to tell them stories out of his nomadic life, anything at all to keep them awake and demonstrate to them again that he had no eatables in his cage and that he was fasting as not one of them could fast. But his happiest moment was when the morning came and an enormous breakfast was brought them, at his expense, on which they flung themselves with the keen appetite of healthy men after a weary night of wakefulness. Of course there were people who argued that this breakfast was an unfair attempt to bribe the watchers, but that was going rather too far, and when they were invited to take on a night's vigil without a breakfast, merely for the sake of the cause, they made themselves scarce, although they stuck stubbornly to their suspicions.

Such suspicions, anyhow, were a necessary accompaniment to the profession of fasting. No one could possibly watch the hunger artist continuously, day and night, and so no one could produce first-hand evidence that the fast had really been rigorous and continuous; only the artist himself could know that, he was therefore bound to be the sole completely satisfied spectator of his own fast. Yet for other reasons he was never satisfied; it was not perhaps mere fasting that had brought him to such skeleton thinness that many people had regretfully to keep away from his exhibitions, because the sight of him was too much for them, perhaps it was dissatisfaction with himself that had worn him down. For he alone knew, what no other initiate knew, how easy it was to fast. It was the easiest thing in the world. He made no secret of this, yet people did not believe him, at the best they set him down as modest; most of them, however, thought he was out for publicity or else was some kind of cheat who found it easy to fast because he had discovered a way of making it easy, and then had the impudence to admit the fact, more or less. He had to put up with all that, and in the course of time had got used to it, but his inner dissatisfaction always rankled, and never yet, after any term of fasting—this must be granted to his credit—had he left the cage of his own free will. The longest period of fasting was fixed by his impresario at forty days, beyond that term he was not allowed to go, not even in great cities, and there was good reason for it, too. Experience had proved that for about forty days the interest of the public could be stimulated by a steadily increasing pressure of advertisement, but after that the town began to lose interest, sympathetic support began notably to fall off; there were of course local variations as between one town and another or one country and another, but as a general rule forty days marked the limit. So on the fortieth day the flower bedecked cage was opened, enthusiastic spectators filled the hall, a military band played, two doctors entered the cage to measure the results of the fast, which were announced through a megaphone, and finally two young ladies appeared, blissful at having been selected for the honor, to help the hunger artist down the few steps leading to a small table on which was spread a carefully chosen invalid repast. And at this very moment the artist always turned stubborn. True, he would entrust his bony arms to the outstretched helping hands of the ladies bending over him, but stand up he would not. Why stop fasting at this particular moment, after forty days of it? He had held out for a long time, an illimitably long time; why stop now, when he was in his best fasting form, or rather, not yet quite in his best fasting form? Why should he be cheated of the fame he would get for fasting longer, for being not only the record hunger artist of all time, which presumably he was already, but for beating his own record by a performance beyond human imagination, since he felt that there were no limits to his capacity for fasting? His public pretended to admire him so much, why should it have so little patience with him; if he could endure fasting longer, why shouldn't the public endure it? Besides, he was tired, he was comfortable sitting in the straw, and now he was supposed to lift himself to his full height and go down to a meal the very thought of which gave him a nausea that only the presence of the ladies kept him from betraying, and even that with an effort. And he looked up into the eyes of the ladies who were apparently so friendly and in reality so cruel, and shook his head, which felt too heavy on its strengthless neck. But then there happened yet again what always happened. The impresario came forward, without a word— for the band made speech impossible—lifted his arms in the air above the artist, as if inviting Heaven to look down upon its creature here in the straw, this suffering martyr, which indeed he was, although in quite another sense; grasped him round the emaciated waist, with exaggerated caution, so that the frail condition he was in might be appreciated; and committed him to the care of the blenching ladies, not without secretly giving him a shaking so that his legs and body tottered and swayed. The artist now submitted completely; his head lolled on his breast as if it had landed there by chance; his body was hollowed out; his legs in a spasm of self-preservation clung close to each other at the knees, yet scraped on the ground as if it were not really solid ground, as if they were only trying to find solid ground; and the whole weight of his body, a feather-weight after all, relapsed onto one of the ladies, who, looking round for help and panting a little—this post of honor was not at all what she had expected it to be—first stretched her neck as far as she could to keep her face at least free from contact with the artist, when finding this impossible, and her more fortunate companion not coming to her aid but merely holding extended on her own trembling hand the little bunch of knucklebones that was the artist's, to the great delight of the spectators burst into tears and had to be replaced by an attendant who had long been stationed in readiness. Then came the food, a little of which the impresario managed to get between the artist's lips, while he sat in a kind of half-fainting trance, to the accompaniment of cheerful patter designed to distract the public's attention from the artist's condition; after that a toast was drunk to the public, supposedly prompted by a whisper from the artist in the impresario's ear; the band confirmed it with a mighty flourish, the spectators melted away, and no one had any cause to be dissatisfied with the proceedings, no one except the hunger artist himself, he only, as always.

So he lived for many years, with small regular intervals of recuperation, in visible glory, honored by the world, yet in spite of that troubled in spirit, and all the more troubled because no one would take his trouble seriously. What comfort could he possibly need? What more could he possibly wish for? And if some good-natured person, feeling sorry for him, tried to console him by pointing out that his melancholy was probably caused by fasting; it could happen, especially when he had been fasting for some time, that he reacted with an outburst of fury and to the general alarm began to shake the bars of his cage like a wild animal. Yet the impresario had a way of punishing these outbreaks which he rather enjoyed putting into operation. He would apologize publicly for the artist's behavior, which was only to be excused, he admitted, because of the irritability caused by fasting; a condition hardly to be understood by well-fed people; then by natural transition he went on to mention the artist's equally incomprehensible boast that he could fast for much longer than he was doing; he praised the high ambition, the good will, the great self-denial undoubtedly implicit in such a statement; and then quite simply countered it by bringing out photographs, which were also on sale to the public, showing the artist on the fortieth day of a fast lying in bed almost dead from exhaustion. This perversion of the truth, familiar to the artist though it was, always unnerved him afresh and proved too much for him. What was a consequence of the premature ending of his fast was here presented as the cause of it! To fight against this lack of understanding, against a whole world of nonunderstanding, was impossible. Time and again in good faith he stood by the bars listening to the impresario, but as soon as the photographs appeared he always let go and sank with a groan back on to his straw, and the reassured public could once more come close and gaze at him.

A few years later when the witnesses of such scenes called them to mind, they often failed to understand themselves at all. For meanwhile the aforementioned change in public interest had set in; it seemed to happen almost overnight; there may have been profound causes for it, but who was going to bother about that; at any rate the pampered hunger artist suddenly found himself deserted one fine day by the amusement seekers, who were streaming past him to other more favored attractions. For the last time the impresario hurried him over half Europe to discover whether the old interest might still survive here and there; all in vain; everywhere, as if by secret agreement, a positive revulsion from professional fasting was in evidence. Of course it could not really have sprung up so suddenly as all that, and many premonitory symptoms which had not been sufficiently remarked or suppressed during the rush and glitter of success now came retrospectively to mind, but it was now too late to take any countermeasures. Fasting would surely come into fashion again at some future date, yet that was no comfort for those living in the present. What, then, was the hunger artist to do? He had been applauded by thousands in his time and could hardly come down to showing himself in a street booth at village fairs, and as for adopting another profession, he was not only too old for that but too frantically devoted to fasting. So he took leave of the impresario, his partner in an unparalleled career, and hired himself to a large circus; in order to spare his own feelings he avoided reading the conditions of his contract.

A large circus with its enormous traffic in replacing and recruiting men, animals, and apparatus can always find a use for people at any time, even for a hunger artist, provided of course that he does not ask too much, and in this particular case anyhow it was not only the artist who was taken on but his famous and long-known name as well, indeed considering the peculiar nature of his performance, which was not impaired by advancing age, it could not be objected that there was an artist past his prime, no longer at the height of his professional skill, seeking a refuge in some quiet corner of a circus; on the contrary, the hunger artist averred that he could fast as well as ever, which was entirely credible; he even alleged that if he were allowed to fast as he liked, and this was at once promised him without more ado, he could astound the world by establishing a record never yet achieved, a statement which certainly provoked a smile among the other professionals, since it left out of account the change in public opinion, which the hunger artist in his zeal conveniently forgot.

He had not, however, actually lost his sense of the real situation and took it as a matter of course that he and his cage should be stationed, not in the middle of the ring as a main attraction, but outside, near the animal cages, on a site that was after all easily accessible. Large and gaily painted placards made a frame for the cage and announced what was to be seen inside it. When the public came thronging out in the intervals to see the animals, they could hardly avoid passing the hunger artist's cage and stopping there for a moment; perhaps they might even have stayed longer had not those pressing behind them in the narrow gangway, who did not understand why they should be held up on their way toward the excitements of the menagerie, made it impossible for anyone to stand gazing quietly for any length of time. And that was the reason why the hunger artist, who had of course been looking forward to these visiting hours as the main achievement of his life, began instead to shrink from them. At first he could hardly wait for the intervals; it was exhilarating to watch the crowds come streaming his way, until only too soon—not even the most obstinate self-deception, clung to almost consciously, could hold out against the fact—the conviction was borne in upon him that these people, most of them, to judge from their actions, again and again, without exception, were all on their way to the menagerie. And the first sight of them from the distance remained the best. For when they reached his cage he was at once deafened by the storm of shouting and abuse that arose from the two contending factions, which renewed themselves continuously, of those who wanted to stop and stare at him—he soon began to dislike them more than the others—not out of real interest but only out of obstinate self-assertiveness, and those who wanted to go straight on to the animals. When the first great rush was past, the stragglers came along, and these, whom nothing could have prevented from stopping to look at him as long as they had breath, raced past with long strides, hardly even glancing at him, in their haste to get to the menagerie in time. And all too rarely did it happen that he had a stroke of luck, when some father of a family fetched up before him with his children, pointed a finger at the hunger artist, and explained at length what the phenomenon meant, telling stories of earlier years when he himself had watched similar but much more thrilling performances, and the children, still rather uncomprehending, since neither inside nor outside school had they been sufficiently prepared for this lesson—what did they care about fasting?— yet showed by the brightness of their intent eyes that new and better times might be coming. Perhaps, said the hunger artist to himself many a time, things would be a little better if his cage were set not quite so near the menagerie. That made it too easy for people to make their choice, to say nothing of what he suffered from the stench of the menagerie, the animals' restlessness by night, the carrying past of raw lumps of flesh for the beasts of prey, the roaring at feeding times, which depressed him continually. But he did not dare to lodge a complaint with the management; after all, he had the animals to thank for the troops of people who passed his cage, among whom there might always be one here and there to take an interest in him, and who could tell where they might seclude him if he called attention to his existence and thereby to the fact that, strictly speaking, he was only an impediment on the way to the menagerie.

A small impediment, to be sure, one that grew steadily less. People grew familiar with the strange idea that they could be expected, in times like these, to take an interest in a hunger artist, and with this familiarity the verdict went out against him. He might fast as much as he could, and he did so; but nothing could save him now, people passed him by. Just try to explain to anyone the art of fasting! Anyone who has no feeling for it cannot be made to understand it. The fine placards grew dirty and illegible, they were torn down; the little notice board telling the number of fast days achieved, which at first was changed carefully every day, had long stayed at the same figure, for after the first few weeks even this small task seemed pointless to the staff; and so the artist simply fasted on and on, as he had once dreamed of doing, and it was no trouble to him, just as he had always foretold, but no one counted the days, no one, not even the artist himself, knew what records he was already breaking, and his heart grew heavy. And when once in a time some leisurely passerby stopped, made merry over the old figure on the board, and spoke of swindling, that was in its way the stupidest lie ever invented by indifference and inborn malice, since it was not the hunger artist who was cheating; he was working honestly, but the world was cheating him of his reward.

Many more days went by, however, and that too came to an end. An overseer's eye fell on the cage one day and asked the attendants why this perfectly good cage should be left standing there unused with dirty straw inside it; nobody knew, until one man, helped out by the notice board, remembered about the hunger artist. They poked into the straw with sticks and found him in it. "Are you still fasting?" asked the overseer. "When on earth do you mean to stop?" "Forgive me, everybody," whispered the hunger artist; only the overseer, who had his ear to the bars, understood him. "Of course," said the overseer, and tapped his forehead with a finger to let the attendants know what state the man was in, "we forgive you." "I always wanted you to admire my fasting," said the hunger artist. "We do admire it," said the overseer, affably. "But you shouldn't admire it," said the hunger artist. "Well, then we don't admire it," said the overseer, "but why shouldn't we admire it?" "Because I have to fast, I can't help it," said the hunger artist. "What a fellow you are," said the overseer, "and why can't you help it?" "Because," said the hunger artist, lifting his head a little and speaking, with his lips pursed, as if for a kiss, right into the overseer's ear, so that no syllable might be lost, "because I couldn't find the food I liked. If I had found it, believe me, I should have made no fuss and stuffed myself like you or anyone else." These were his last words, but in his dimming eyes remained the firm though no longer proud persuasion that he was still continuing to fast.

"Well, clear this out now!" said the overseer, and they buried the hunger 10 artist, straw and all. Into the cage they put a young panther. Even the most insensitive felt it refreshing to see this wild creature leaping around the cage that had so long been dreary. The panther was all right. The food he liked was brought him without hesitation by the attendants; he seemed not even to miss his freedom; his noble body, furnished almost to the bursting point with all that it needed, seemed to carry freedom around with it too; somewhere in his jaws it seemed to lurk; and the joy of life streamed with such ardent passion from his throat that for the onlookers it was not easy to stand the shock of it. But they braced themselves, crowded round the cage, and did not want ever to move away.

FOR ANALYSIS

1. Many readers interpret this story as a parable of the artist in the modern world, while others see it as a religious parable. What evidence do you find in the story to support either interpretation?

2. Suggest reasons for Kafka's selection of an expert in fasting (rather than a priest or a singer, for example) as the central figure in the story.

3. How does Kafka manage to achieve such a bizarre, dreamlike effect with dry and factual prose?

4. Since his greatest achievements involve inwardness and withdrawal, why does the hunger artist nevertheless seem to need an audience?

MAKING CONNECTIONS

1. Compare this story with Hawthorne's "Young Goodman Brown" (p. 81) and Melville's "Bartleby the Scrivener" (p. 291). What similarities do the central figures in the three stories share? What differences do you find? How does the alienation of each of the central figures contribute to each story's theme?

2. Describe feelings of isolation and alienation that you have experienced. What caused those feelings? How did you cope with them? How, finally, do you differ from the hunger artist?

WRITING TOPICS

1. Should the hunger artist be admired for his passionate and single-minded devotion to his art or condemned for his withdrawal from humanity and his sickness of will? Why? Be sure to discuss the significance of the panther put in the cage after the artist's death.

2. In an essay, compare the hunger artist with Melville's Bartleby. Discuss the origins, rationale, consequences, and significance of their behavior.

RALPH ELLISON (1914–1994)

BATTLE ROYAL 1952

It goes a long way back, some twenty years. All my life I had been looking for something, and everywhere I turned someone tried to tell me what it was. I accepted their answers too, though they were often in contradiction and even self-contradictory. I was naive. I was looking for myself and asking everyone except myself questions which I, and only I, could answer. It took me a long time and much painful boomeranging of my expectations to achieve a realization everyone else appears to have been born with: that I am nobody but myself. But first I had to discover that I am an invisible man!

And yet I am no freak of nature, nor of history. I was in the cards, other things having been equal (or unequal) eighty-five years ago. I am not ashamed of my grandparents for having been slaves. I am only ashamed of myself for having at one time been ashamed. About eighty-five years ago they were told that they were free, united with others of our country in everything pertaining to the common good, and, in everything social, separate like the fingers of the hand. And they believed it. They exulted in it. They stayed in their place, worked hard, and brought up my father to do the same. But my grandfather is the one. He was an odd old guy, my grandfather, and I am told I take after him. It was he who caused the trouble. On his deathbed he called my father to him and said, "Son, after I'm gone I want you to keep up the good fight. I never told you, but our life is a war and I have been a traitor all my born days, a spy in the enemy's country ever since I give up my gun back in the Reconstruction. Live with your head in the lion's mouth. I want you to overcome 'em with yeses, undermine 'em with grins, agree 'em to death and destruction, let 'em swoller you till they vomit or bust wide open." They thought the old man had gone out of his mind. He had been the meekest of men. The younger children were rushed from the room, the shades drawn, and the flame of the lamp turned so low that it sputtered on the wick like the old man's breathing. "Learn it to the younguns," he whispered fiercely; then he died.

But my folks were more alarmed over his last words than over his dying. It was as though he had not died at all, his words caused so much anxiety. I was warned emphatically to forget what he had said and, indeed, this is the first time it has been mentioned outside the family circle. It had a tremendous effect upon me, however. I could never be sure of what he meant. Grandfather had been a quiet old man who never made any trouble, yet on his deathbed he had called himself a traitor and a spy, and he had spoken of his meekness as a dangerous activity. It became a constant puzzle which lay unanswered in the back of my mind. And whenever things went well for me I remembered my grandfather and felt guilty and uncomfortable. It was as though I was carrying out his advice in spite of myself. And to make it worse, everyone loved me for it. I was praised by the most lily-white men of the town. I was considered an example of desirable conduct—just as my grandfather had been. And what puzzled me was that the old man had defined it as *treachery*. When I was praised for my conduct I felt a guilt that in some way I was doing something that was really against the wishes of the white folks, that if they had understood they would have desired me to act just the opposite, that I should have been sulky and mean, and that that really would have been what they wanted, even though they were fooled and thought they wanted me to act as I did. It made me afraid that some day they would look upon me as a traitor and I would be lost. Still I was more afraid to act any other way because they didn't like that at all. The old man's words were like a curse. On my graduation day I delivered an oration in which I showed that humility was the secret, indeed, the very essence of progress. (Not that I believed this—how could I, remembering my grandfather?—I only believed that it worked.) It was a great success. Everyone praised me and I was invited to give the speech at a gathering of the town's leading white citizens. It was a triumph for our whole community.

It was in the main ballroom of the leading hotel. When I got there I discovered that it was on the occasion of a smoker, and I was told that since I was to be there anyway I might as well take part in the battle royal to be fought by some of my schoolmates as part of the entertainment. The battle royal came first.

All of the town's big shots were there in their tuxedoes, wolfing down the buffet foods, drinking beer and whiskey and smoking black cigars. It was a large room with a high ceiling. Chairs were arranged in neat rows around three sides of a portable boxing ring. The fourth side was clear, revealing a gleaming space of polished floor. I had some misgivings over the battle royal, by the way. Not from a distaste for fighting, but because I didn't care too much for the other fellows who were to take part. They were tough guys who seemed to have no grandfather's curse worrying their minds. No one could mistake their toughness. And besides, I suspected that fighting a battle royal might detract from the dignity of my speech. In those pre-invisible days I visualized myself as a potential Booker T. Washington. But the other fellows didn't care too much for me either, and there were nine of them. I felt superior to them in my way, and I didn't like the manner in which we were all crowded together into the servants' elevator. Nor did they like my being there. In fact, as the warmly lighted floors flashed past the elevator we had words over the fact that I, by taking part in the fight, had knocked one of their friends out of a night's work.

We were led out of the elevator through a rococo hall into an anteroom and told to get into our fighting togs. Each of us was issued a pair of boxing gloves and ushered out into the big mirrored hall, which we entered looking cautiously about us and whispering, lest we might accidentally be heard above the noise of the room. It was foggy with cigar smoke. And already the whiskey was taking effect. I was shocked to see some of the most important men of the town quite tipsy. They were all there—bankers, lawyers, judges, doctors, fire chiefs, teachers, merchants. Even one of the more fashionable pastors. Something we could not see was going on up front. A clarinet was vibrating sensuously and the men were standing up and moving eagerly forward. We were a small tight group, clustered together, our bare upper bodies touching and shining with anticipatory sweat; while up front the big shots were becoming increasingly excited over something we still could not see. Suddenly I heard the school superintendent, who had told me to come, yell, "Bring up the shines, gentlemen! Bring up the little shines!"

We were rushed up to the front of the ballroom, where it smelled even more strongly of tobacco and whiskey. Then we were pushed into place. I almost wet my pants. A sea of faces, some hostile, some amused, ringed around us, and in the center, facing us, stood a magnificent blonde—stark naked. There was dead silence. I felt a blast of cold air chill me. I tried to back away, but they were behind me and around me. Some of the boys stood with lowered heads, trembling. I felt a wave of irrational guilt and fear. My teeth chattered, my skin turned to goose flesh, my knees knocked. Yet I was strongly attracted and looked in spite of myself. Had the price of looking been blindness, I would have looked. The hair was yellow like that of a circus kewpie doll, the face heavily powdered and rouged, as though to form an abstract mask, the eyes hollow and smeared a cool blue, the color of a baboon's butt. I felt a desire to spit upon her as my eyes brushed slowly over her body. Her breasts were firm and round as the domes of East Indian temples, and I stood so close as to see the fine skin texture and beads of pearly perspiration glistening like dew around the pink and erected buds of her nipples. I wanted at one and the same time to run from the room, to sink through the floor, or go to her and cover her from my eyes and the eyes of the others with my body; to feel the soft thighs, to caress her and destroy her, to love her and murder her, to hide from her, and yet to stroke where below the small American flag tattooed upon her belly her thighs formed a capital V. I had a notion that of all in the room she saw only me with her impersonal eyes.

And then she began to dance, a slow sensuous movement; the smoke of a hundred cigars clinging to her like the thinnest of veils. She seemed like a fair bird-girl girdled in veils calling to me from the angry surface of some gray and threatening sea. I was transported. Then I became aware of the clarinet playing and the big shots yelling at us. Some threatened us if we looked and others if we did not. On my right I saw one boy faint. And now a man grabbed a silver pitcher from a table and stepped close as he dashed ice water upon him and stood him up and forced two of us to support him as his head hung and moans issued from his thick bluish lips. Another boy began to plead to go home. He was the largest of the group, wearing dark red fighting trunks much too small to conceal the erection which projected from him as though in answer to the insinuating low-registered moaning of the clarinet. He tried to hide himself with his boxing gloves.

And all the while the blonde continued dancing, smiling faintly at the big shots who watched her with fascination, and faintly smiling at our fear. I noticed a certain merchant who followed her hungrily, his lips loose and drooling. He was a large man who wore diamond studs in a shirtfront which swelled with the ample paunch underneath, and each time the blonde swayed her undulating hips he ran his hand through the thin hair of his bald head and, with his arms upheld, his posture clumsy like that of an intoxicated panda, wound his belly in a slow and obscene grind. This creature was completely hypnotized. The music had quickened. As the dancer flung herself about with a detached expression on her face, the men began reaching out to touch her. I could see their beefy fingers sink into her soft flesh. Some of the others tried to stop them and she began to move around the floor in graceful circles, as they gave chase, slipping and sliding over the polished floor. It was mad. Chairs went crashing, drinks were spilt, as they ran laughing and howling after her. They caught her just as she reached a door, raised her from the floor, and tossed her as college boys are tossed at a hazing, and above her red fixed-smiling lips I saw the terror and disgust in her eyes, almost like my own terror and that which I saw in some of the other boys. As I watched, they tossed her twice and her soft breasts seemed to flatten against the air and her legs flung wildly as she spun. Some of the more sober ones helped her to escape. And I started off the floor, heading for the anteroom with the rest of the boys.

Some were still crying and in hysteria. But as we tried to leave we were   10
stopped and ordered to get into the ring. There was nothing to do but what we were told. All ten of us climbed under the ropes and allowed ourselves to be blindfolded with broad bands of white cloth. One of the men seemed to feel a bit sympathetic and tried to cheer us up as we stood with our backs against the ropes. Some of us tried to grin. "See that boy over there?" one of the men said. "I want you to run across at the bell and give it to him right in the belly. If you don't get him, I'm going to get you. I don't like his looks." Each of us was told the same. The blindfolds were put on. Yet even then I had been going over my speech. In my mind each word was as bright as flame. I felt the cloth pressed into place, and frowned so that it would be loosened when I relaxed.

But now I felt a sudden fit of blind terror. I was unused to darkness. It was as though I had suddenly found myself in a dark room filled with poisonous cottonmouths. I could hear the bleary voices yelling insistently for the battle royal to begin.

"Get going in there!"

"Let me at that big nigger!"

I strained to pick up the school superintendent's voice, as though to squeeze some security out of that slightly more familiar sound.

"Let me at those black sonsabitches!" someone yelled.   15

"No, Jackson, no!" another voice yelled. "Here, somebody, help me hold Jack."

"I want to get at that ginger-colored nigger. Tear him limb from limb," the first voice yelled.

I stood against the ropes trembling. For in those days I was what they called ginger-colored, and he sounded as though he might crunch me between his teeth like a crisp ginger cookie.

Quite a struggle was going on. Chairs were being kicked about and I could hear voices grunting as with a terrific effort. I wanted to see, to see more desperately than ever before. But the blindfold was as tight as a thick skin-puckering scab and when I raised my gloved hands to push the layers of white aside a voice yelled, "Oh, no you don't, black bastard! Leave that alone!"

"Ring the bell before Jackson kills him a coon!" someone boomed in the   20 sudden silence. And I heard the bell clang and the sound of the feet scuffling forward.

A glove smacked against my head. I pivoted, striking out stiffly as someone went past, and felt the jar ripple along the length of my arm to my shoulder. Then it seemed as though all nine of the boys had turned upon me at once. Blows pounded me from all sides while I struck out as best I could. So many blows landed upon me that I wondered if I were not the only blindfolded fighter in the ring, or if the man called Jackson hadn't succeeded in getting me after all.

Blindfolded, I could no longer control my motions. I had no dignity. I stumbled about like a baby or a drunken man. The smoke had become thicker and with each new blow it seemed to sear and further restrict my lungs. My saliva became like hot bitter glue. A glove connected with my head, filling my mouth with warm blood. It was everywhere. I could not tell if the moisture I felt upon my body was sweat or blood. A blow landed hard against the nape of my neck. I felt myself going over, my head hitting the floor. Streaks of blue light filled the black world behind the blindfold. I lay prone, pretending that I was knocked out, but felt myself seized by hands and yanked to my feet. "Get going, black boy! Mix it up!" My arms were like lead, my head smarting from blows. I managed to feel my way to the ropes and held on, trying to catch my breath. A glove landed in my mid-section and I went over again, feeling as though the smoke had become a knife jabbed into my guts. Pushed this way and that by the legs milling around me, I finally pulled erect and discovered that I could see the black, sweat-washed forms weaving in the smoky-blue atmosphere like drunken dancers weaving to the rapid drum like thuds of blows.

Everyone fought hysterically. It was complete anarchy. Everybody fought everybody else. No group fought together for long. Two, three, four, fought one, then turned to fight each other, were themselves attacked. Blows landed below the belt and in the kidney, with the gloves open as well as closed, and with my eye partly opened now there was not so much terror. I moved carefully, avoiding blows, although not too many to attract attention, fighting from group to group. The boys groped about like blind, cautious crabs crouching to protect their mid-sections, their heads pulled in short against their shoulders, their arms stretched nervously before them, with their fists testing the smoke-filled air like the knobbed feelers of hypersensitive snails. In one corner I glimpsed a boy violently punching the air and heard him scream in pain as he smashed his hand against a ring post. For a second I saw him bent over holding his hand, then going down as a blow caught his unprotected head. I played one group against the other, slipping in and throwing a punch then stepping out of range while pushing the others into the melee to take the blows blindly aimed at me. The smoke was agonizing and there were no rounds, no bells at three minute intervals to relieve our exhaustion. The room spun round me, a swirl of lights, smoke, sweating bodies surrounded by tense white faces. I bled from both nose and mouth, the blood spattering upon my chest.

The men kept yelling, "Slug him, black boy! Knock his guts out!"

"Uppercut him! Kill him! Kill that big boy!"   25

Taking a fake fall, I saw a boy going down heavily beside me as though we were felled by a single blow, saw a sneaker-clad foot shoot into his groin as the two who had knocked him down stumbled upon him. I rolled out of range, feeling a twinge of nausea.

The harder we fought the more threatening the men became. And yet, I had begun to worry about my speech again. How would it go? Would they recognize my ability? What would they give me?

I was fighting automatically and suddenly I noticed that one after another of the boys was leaving the ring. I was surprised, filled with panic, as though I had been left alone with an unknown danger. Then I understood. The boys had arranged it among themselves. It was the custom for the two men left in the ring to slug it out for the winner's prize. I discovered this too late. When the bell sounded two men in tuxedoes leaped into the ring and removed the blindfold. I found myself facing Tatlock, the biggest of the gang. I felt sick at my stomach. Hardly had the bell stopped ringing in my ears than it clanged again and I saw him moving swiftly toward me. Thinking of nothing else to do I hit him smash on the nose. He kept coming, bringing the rank sharp violence of stale sweat. His face was a black blank of a face, only his eyes alive—with hate of me and aglow with a feverish terror from what had happened to us all. I became anxious. I wanted to deliver my speech and he came at me as though he meant to beat it out of me. I smashed him again and again, taking his blows as they came. Then on a sudden impulse I struck him lightly and as we clinched, I whispered, "Fake like I knocked you out, you can have the prize."

"I'll break your behind," he whispered hoarsely.

"For *them*?"   30

"For *me*, sonofabitch!"

They were yelling for us to break it up and Tatlock spun me half around with a blow, and as a joggled camera sweeps in a reeling scene, I saw the howling red faces crouching tense beneath the cloud of blue-gray smoke. For a moment the world wavered, unraveled, flowed, then my head cleared and Tatlock bounced before me. That fluttering shadow before my eyes was his jabbing left hand. Then falling forward, my head against his damp shoulder, I whispered,

"I'll make it five dollars more."

"Go to hell!"

But his muscles relaxed a trifle beneath my pressure and I breathed, "Seven!"   35

"Give it to your ma," he said, ripping me beneath the heart.

And while I still held him I butted him and moved away. I felt myself bombarded with punches. I fought back with hopeless desperation. I wanted to deliver my speech more than anything else in the world, because I felt that only these men could judge truly my ability, and now this stupid clown was ruining my chances. I began fighting carefully now, moving in to punch him and out again with my greater speed. A lucky blow to his chin and I had him going too—until I heard a loud voice yell, "I got my money on the big boy."

Hearing this, I almost dropped my guard. I was confused: Should I try to win against the voice out there? Would not this go against my speech, and was not this a moment for humility, for nonresistance? A blow to my head as I danced about sent my right eye popping like a jack-in-the-box and settled my dilemma. The room went red as I fell. It was a dream fall, my body languid and fastidious as to where to land, until the floor became impatient and smashed up to meet me. A moment later I came to. An hypnotic voice said FIVE emphatically. And I lay there, hazily watching a dark red spot of my own blood shaping itself into a butterfly, glistening and soaking into the soiled gray world of the canvas.

When the voice drawled TEN I was lifted up and dragged to a chair. I sat dazed. My eye pained and swelled with each throb of my pounding heart and I wondered if now I would be allowed to speak. I was wringing wet, my mouth still bleeding. We were grouped along the wall now. The other boys ignored me as they congratulated Tatlock and speculated as to how much they would be paid. One boy whimpered over his smashed hand. Looking up front, I saw attendants in white jackets rolling the portable ring away and placing a small square rug in the vacant space surrounded by chairs. Perhaps, I thought, I will stand on the rug to deliver my speech.

Then the M.C. called to us, "Come on up here boys and get your money." 40

We ran forward to where the men laughed and talked in their chairs, waiting. Everyone seemed friendly now.

"There it is on the rug," the man said. I saw the rug covered with coins of all dimensions and a few crumpled bills. But what excited me, scattered here and there, were the gold pieces.

"Boys, it's all yours," the man said. "You get all you grab."

"That's right, Sambo," a blond man said, winking at me confidentially.

I trembled with excitement, forgetting my pain. I would get the gold and the 45
bills, I thought. I would use both hands. I would throw my body against the boys nearest me to block them from the gold.

"Get down around the rug now," the man commanded, "and don't anyone touch it until I give the signal."

"This ought to be good," I heard.

As told, we got around the square rug on our knees. Slowly the man raised his freckled hand as we followed it upward with our eyes.

I heard, "These niggers look like they're about to pray!"

Then, "Ready," the man said. "Go!" 50

I lunged for a yellow coin lying on the blue design of the carpet, touching it and sending a surprised shriek to join those rising around me. I tried frantically to remove my hand but could not let go. A hot, violent force tore through my body, shaking me like a wet rat. The rug was electrified. The hair bristled up on my head as I shook myself free. My muscles jumped, my nerves jangled, writhed. But I saw that this was not stopping the other boys. Laughing in fear and embarrassment, some were holding back and scooping up the coins knocked off by the painful contortions of the others. The men roared above us as we struggled.

"Pick it up, goddamnit, pick it up!" someone called like a bass-voiced parrot. "Go on, get it!"

I crawled rapidly around the floor, picking up the coins, trying to avoid the coppers and to get greenbacks and the gold. Ignoring the shock by laughing, as I brushed the coins off quickly, I discovered that I could contain the electricity—a contradiction, but it works. Then the men began to push us onto the rug. Laughing embarrassedly, we struggled out of their hands and kept after the coins. We were all wet and slippery and hard to hold. Suddenly I saw a boy lifted into the air, glistening with sweat like a circus seal, and dropped, his wet back landing flush upon the charged rug, heard him yell and saw him literally dance upon his back, his elbows beating a frenzied tatoo upon the floor, his muscles twitching like the flesh of a horse stung by many flies. When he finally rolled off, his face was gray and no one stopped him when he ran from the floor amid booming laughter.

"Get the money," the M.C. called. "That's good hard American cash!"

And we snatched and grabbed, snatched and grabbed. I was careful not to 55
come too close to the rug now, and when I felt the hot whiskey breath descend upon me like a cloud of foul air I reached out and grabbed the leg of a chair. It was occupied and I held on desperately.

"Leggo, nigger! Leggo!"

The huge face wavered down to mine as he tried to push me free. But my body was slippery and he was too drunk. It was Mr. Colcord, who owned a chain of movie houses and "entertainment palaces." Each time he grabbed me I slipped out of his hands. It became a real struggle. I feared the rug more than I did the drunk, so I held on, surprising myself for a moment by trying to topple *him* upon the rug. It was such an enormous idea that I found myself actually carrying it out. I tried not to be obvious, yet when I grabbed his leg, trying to tumble him out of the chair, he raised up roaring with laughter, and, looking at me with soberness dead in the eye, kicked me viciously in the chest. The chair leg flew out of my hand. I felt myself going and rolled. It was as though I had rolled through a bed of hot coals. It seemed a whole century would pass before I would roll free, a century in which I was seared through the deepest levels of my body to the fearful breath within me and the breath seared and heated to the point of explosion. It'll all be over in a flash, I thought as I rolled clear. It'll all be over in a flash.

But not yet, the men on the other side were waiting, red faces swollen as though from apoplexy as they bent forward in their chairs. Seeing their fingers coming toward me I rolled away as a fumbled football rolls off the receiver's fingertips, back into the coals. That time I luckily sent the rug sliding out of place and heard the coins ringing against the floor and the boys scuffling to pick them up and the M.C. calling, "All right, boys, that's all. Go get dressed and get your money."

I was limp as a dish rag. My back felt as though it had been beaten with wires.

When we had dressed the M.C. came in and gave us each five dollars, except 60 Tatlock, who got ten for being last in the ring. Then he told us to leave. I was not to get a chance to deliver my speech, I thought. I was going out into the dim alley in despair when I was stopped and told to go back. I returned to the ballroom, where the men were pushing back their chairs and gathering in groups to talk.

The M.C. knocked on a table for quiet. "Gentlemen," he said, "we almost forgot an important part of the program. A most serious part, gentlemen. This boy was brought here to deliver a speech which he made at his graduation yesterday. . . ."

"Bravo!"

"I'm told that he is the smartest boy we've got out there in Greenwood. I'm told that he knows more big words than a pocket-sized dictionary."

Much applause and laughter.

"So now, gentlemen, I want you to give him your attention." 65

There was still laughter as I faced them, my mouth dry, my eye throbbing. I began slowly, but evidently my throat was tense, because they began shouting, "Louder! Louder!"

"We of the younger generation extol the wisdom of that great leader and educator," I shouted, "who first spoke these flaming words of wisdom: 'A ship lost at sea for many days suddenly sighted a friendly vessel. From the mast of the unfortunate vessel was seen a signal: "Water, water; we die of thirst!" The answer from the friendly vessel came back: "Cast down your bucket where you are." The captain of the distressed vessel, at last heeding the injunction, cast down his bucket, and it came up full of fresh sparkling water from the mouth of the Amazon River.' And like him I say, and in his words, 'To those of my race who depend upon bettering their condition in a foreign land, or who underestimate the importance of cultivating friendly relations with the Southern white man, who is his next-door neighbor, I would say: "Cast down your bucket where you are"—cast it down in making friends in every manly way of the people of all races by whom we are surrounded. . . .'"

I spoke automatically and with such fervor that I did not realize that the men were still talking and laughing until my dry mouth, filling up with blood from the cut, almost strangled me. I coughed, wanting to stop and go to one of the tall brass, sand-filled spittoons to relieve myself, but a few of the men, especially the superintendent, were listening and I was afraid. So I gulped it down, blood, saliva, and all, and continued. (What powers of endurance I had during those days! What enthusiasm! What a belief in the rightness of things!) I spoke even louder in spite of the pain. But still they talked and still they laughed, as though deaf with cotton in dirty ears. So I spoke with greater emotional emphasis. I closed my ears and swallowed blood until I was nauseated. The speech seemed a hundred times as long as before, but I could not leave out a single word. All had to be said, each memorized nuance considered, rendered. Nor was that all. Whenever I uttered a word of three or more syllables a group of voices would yell for me to repeat it. I used the phrase "social responsibility" and they yelled:

"What's the word you say, boy?"

"Social responsibility," I said.   70

"What?"

"Social . . ."

"Louder."

". . . responsibility."

"More!"   75

"Respon —"

"Repeat!"

"—sibility."

The room filled with the uproar of laughter until, no doubt, distracted by having to gulp down my blood, I made a mistake and yelled a phrase I had often seen denounced in newspaper editorials, heard debated in private.

"Social . . ."   80

"What?" they yelled.

". . . equality —"

The laughter hung smokelike in the sudden stillness. I opened my eyes, puzzled. Sounds of displeasure filled the room. The M.C. rushed forward. They shouted hostile phrases at me. But I did not understand.

A small dry mustached man in the front row blared out, "Say that slowly, son!"

"What sir?"   85

"What you just said!"

"Social responsibility, sir," I said.

"You weren't being smart, were you, boy?" he said, not unkindly.

"No, sir!"

"You sure that about 'equality' was a mistake?"   90

"Oh, yes, sir," I said. "I was swallowing blood."

"Well, you had better speak more slowly so we can understand. We mean to do right by you, but you've got to know your place at all times. All right, now, go on with your speech."

I was afraid. I wanted to leave but I wanted also to speak and I was afraid they'd snatch me down.

"Thank you, sir," I said, beginning where I had left off, and having them ignore me as before.

Yet when I finished there was a thunderous applause. I was surprised to see 95 the superintendent come forth with a package wrapped in white tissue paper, and, gesturing for quiet, address the men.

"Gentlemen, you see that I did not overpraise this boy. He makes a good speech and some day he'll lead his people in the proper paths. And I don't have to tell you that that is important in these days and times. This is a good, smart boy, and so to encourage him in the right direction, in the name of the Board of Education I wish to present him a prize in the form of this . . ."

He paused, removing the tissue paper and revealing a gleaming calfskin brief case.

". . . in the form of this first-class article from Shad Whitmore's shop."

"Boy," he said, addressing me, "take this prize and keep it well. Consider it a badge of office. Prize it. Keep developing as you are and some day it will be filled with important papers that will help shape the destiny of your people."

I was so moved that I could hardly express my thanks. A rope of bloody 100 saliva forming a shape like an undiscovered continent drooled upon the leather and I wiped it quickly away. I felt an importance that I had never dreamed.

"Open it and see what's inside," I was told.

My fingers a-tremble, I complied, smelling the fresh leather and finding an official-looking document inside. It was a scholarship to the state college for Negroes. My eyes filled with tears and I ran awkwardly off the floor.

I was overjoyed; I did not even mind when I discovered that the gold pieces I had scrambled for were brass pocket tokens advertising a certain make of automobile.

When I reached home everyone was excited. Next day the neighbors came to congratulate me. I even felt safe from grandfather, whose deathbed curse usually spoiled my triumphs. I stood beneath his photograph with my brief case in hand and smiled triumphantly into his stolid black peasant's face. It was a face that fascinated me. The eyes seemed to follow everywhere I went.

That night I dreamed I was at a circus with him and that he refused to laugh 105 at the clowns no matter what they did. Then later he told me to open my brief case and read what was inside and I did, finding an official envelope stamped with the state seal; and inside the envelope I found another and another, end-lessly, and I thought I would fall of weariness. "Them's years," he said. "Now open that one." And I did and in it I found an engraved document containing a short message in letters of gold. "Read it," my grandfather said. "Out loud."

"To Whom It May Concern," I intoned. "Keep This Nigger-Boy Running."

I awoke with the old man's laughter ringing in my ears.

(It was a dream I was to remember and dream again for many years after. But at the time I had no insight into its meaning. First I had to attend college.)

FOR ANALYSIS

1. What phrase does the **narrator** inadvertently utter, causing the room to go quiet? Why does it have such an effect?

2. Why is it significant that the naked woman in the story is white?

3. The meaning of the grandfather's last words, recounted at the story's opening, are ambiguous; the narrator even says, "I could never be sure of what he meant" (para. 3). Does the meaning become clearer by the end of the story? What do you think it is, and how is it revealed?

MAKING CONNECTIONS

1. There is much more action in "Battle Royal" than in Bambara's "The Lesson" (p. 110). It is more obvious, then, that Bambara's story is about what its main **character** sees and what she learns from it. How, in spite of Ellison's story's differences, is it like Bambara's? Does the main character learn a lesson? How? What is it?

2. Read "Battle Royal" in the context of the connections unit "Voices of Experience" (p. 176). What voices of experience speak in this story, including but not limited to the grandfather? What advice do they give? How is it taken? To which of the poems in "Voices of Experience" is "Battle Royal" most similar? To which is it most different?

WRITING TOPICS

1. Write about the **symbolism** in "Battle Royal." For what might the different objects and different activities stand? How do they fit together? Why do you think Ellison has his **protagonist** see and experience these symbolic things?

2. Write a reflective personal essay on invisibility. Possible topics for this essay include ways in which you are invisible, ways in which other people you know or see are invisible, ways in which you are guilty of not seeing others.

SHIRLEY JACKSON   (1919–1965)

THE LOTTERY   1948

The morning of June 27th was clear and sunny, with the fresh warmth of a full-summer day; the flowers were blossoming profusely and the grass was richly green. The people of the village began to gather in the square, between the post office and the bank, around ten o'clock; in some towns there were so many people that the lottery took two days and had to be started on June 26th, but in this village, where there were only about three hundred people, the whole lottery took less than two hours, so it could begin at ten o'clock in the morning and still be through in time to allow the villagers to get home for noon dinner.

The children assembled first, of course. School was recently over for the summer, and the feeling of liberty sat uneasily on most of them; they tended to gather together quietly for a while before they broke into boisterous play, and their talk was still of the classroom and the teacher, of books and reprimands. Bobby Martin had already stuffed his pockets full of stones, and the other boys soon followed his example, selecting the smoothest and roundest stones; Bobby and Harry Jones and Dickie Delacroix—the villagers pronounced his name "Dellacroy"—eventually made a great pile of stones in one corner of the square and guarded it against the raids of the other boys. The girls stood aside, talking among themselves, looking over their shoulders at the boys, and the very small children rolled in the dust or clung to the hands of their older brothers or sisters.

Soon the men began to gather, surveying their own children, speaking of planting and rain, tractors and taxes. They stood together, away from the pile of stones in the corner, and their jokes were quiet and they smiled rather than laughed. The women, wearing faded house dresses and sweaters, came shortly after their menfolk. They greeted one another and exchanged bits of gossip as they went to join their husbands. Soon the women, standing by their husbands, began to call to their children, and the children came reluctantly, having to be called four or five times. Bobby Martin ducked under his mother's grasping hand and ran, laughingly, back to the pile of stones. His father spoke up sharply, and Bobby came quickly and took his place, between his father and his oldest brother.

The lottery was conducted—as were the square dances, the teenage club, the Halloween program—by Mr. Summers, who had time and energy to devote to civic activities. He was a round-faced, jovial man and he ran the coal business, and people were sorry for him, because he had no children and his wife was a scold. When he arrived in the square, carrying the black wooden box, there was a murmur of conversation among the villagers, and he waved and called "Little late today, folks." The postmaster, Mr. Graves, followed him, carrying a three-legged stool, and the stool was put in the center of the square and Mr. Summers set the black box down on it. The villagers kept their distance, leaving a space between themselves and the stool, and when Mr. Summers said, "Some of you fellows want to give me a hand?" there was a hesitation before two men, Mr. Martin and his oldest son, Baxter, came forward to hold the box steady on the stool while Mr. Summers stirred up the papers inside it.

The original paraphernalia for the lottery had been lost long ago, and the 5 black box now resting on the stool had been put into use even before Old Man Warner, the oldest man in town, was born. Mr. Summers spoke frequently to the villagers about making a new box, but no one liked to upset even as much tradition as was represented by the black box. There was a story that the present box had been made with some pieces of the box that had preceded it, the one that had been constructed when the first people settled down to make a village here. Every year, after the lottery, Mr. Summers began talking about a new box, but every year the subject was allowed to fade off without anything's being done. The black box grew shabbier each year; by now it was no longer completely black but splintered badly along one side to show the original wood color, and in some places faded and stained.

Mr. Martin and his oldest son, Baxter, held the black box securely on the stool until Mr. Summers had stirred the papers thoroughly with his hand. Because so much of the ritual had been forgotten or discarded, Mr. Summers had been successful in having slips of paper substituted for the chips of wood that had been used for generations. Chips of wood, Mr. Summers had argued, had been all very well when the village was tiny, but now that the population was more than three hundred and likely to keep on growing, it was necessary to use something that would fit more easily into the black box. The night before the lottery, Mr. Summers and Mr. Graves made up the slips of paper and put them in the box, and it was then taken to the safe of Mr. Summers's coal company and locked up until Mr. Summers was ready to take it to the square the next morning. The rest of the year, the box was put away, sometimes one place, sometimes another; it had spent one year in Mr. Graves's barn and another year underfoot in the post office, and sometimes it was set on a shelf in the Martin grocery and left there.

There was a great deal of fussing to be done before Mr. Summers declared the lottery open. There were the lists to make up—of heads of families, heads of households in each family, members of each household in each family. There was the proper swearing-in of Mr. Summers by the postmaster, as the official of the lottery; at one time, some people remembered, there had been a recital of some sort, performed by the official of the lottery, a perfunctory, tuneless chant that had been rattled off duly each year; some people believed that the official of the lottery used to stand just so when he said or sang it, others believed that he was supposed to walk among the people, but years and years ago this part of the ritual had been allowed to lapse. There had been, also, a ritual salute, which the official of the lottery had had to use in addressing each person who came up to draw from the box, but this also had changed with time, until now it was felt necessary only for the official to speak to each person approaching. Mr. Summers was very good at all this; in his clean white shirt and blue jeans, with one hand resting carelessly on the black box, he seemed very proper and important as he talked interminably to Mr. Graves and the Martins.

Just as Mr. Summers finally left off talking and turned to the assembled villagers, Mrs. Hutchinson came hurriedly along the path to the square, her sweater thrown over her shoulders, and slid into place in the back of the crowd. "Clean forgot what day it was," she said to Mrs. Delacroix, who stood next to her, and they both laughed softly. "Thought my old man was out back stacking wood," Mrs. Hutchinson went on, "and then I looked out the window and the kids were gone, and then I remembered it was the twenty-seventh and came a-running." She dried her hands on her apron, and Mrs. Delacroix said, "You're in time, though. They're still talking away up there."

Mrs. Hutchinson craned her neck to see through the crowd and found her husband and children standing near the front. She tapped Mrs. Delacroix on the arm as a farewell and began to make her way through the crowd. The people separated good-humoredly to let her through; two or three people said, in voices just loud enough to be heard across the crowd, "Here comes your Missus, Hutchinson," and "Bill, she made it after all." Mrs. Hutchinson reached her husband, and Mr. Summers, who had been waiting, said cheerfully, "Thought we were going to have to get on without you, Tessie." Mrs. Hutchinson said, grinning, "Wouldn't have me leave m'dishes in the sink, now, would you, Joe?" and soft laughter ran through the crowd as the people stirred back into position after Mrs. Hutchinson's arrival.

"Well, now," Mr. Summers said soberly, "guess we better get started, get this over with, so's we can go back to work. Anybody ain't here?"   10

"Dunbar," several people said. "Dunbar, Dunbar."

Mr. Summers consulted his list. "Clyde Dunbar," he said. "That's right. He's broke his leg, hasn't he? Who's drawing for him?"

"Me, I guess," a woman said, and Mr. Summers turned to look at her. "Wife draws for her husband," Mr. Summers said. "Don't you have a grown boy to do it for you, Janey?" Although Mr. Summers and everyone else in the village knew the answer perfectly well, it was the business of the official of the lottery to ask such questions formally. Mr. Summers waited with an expression of polite interest while Mrs. Dunbar answered.

"Horace's not but sixteen yet," Mrs. Dunbar said regretfully. "Guess I gotta fill in for the old man this year."

"Right," Mr. Summers said. He made a note on the list he was holding. Then   15 he asked, "Watson boy drawing this year?"

A tall boy in the crowd raised his hand. "Here," he said. "I'm drawing for m'mother and me." He blinked his eyes nervously and ducked his head as several voices in the crowd said things like "Good fellow, Jack," and "Glad to see your mother's got a man to do it."

"Well," Mr. Summers said, "guess that's everyone. Old Man Warner make it?"

"Here," a voice said, and Mr. Summers nodded.

A sudden hush fell on the crowd as Mr. Summers cleared his throat and looked at the list. "All ready?" he called. "Now, I'll read the names—heads of families first—and the men come up and take a paper out of the box. Keep the paper folded in your hand without looking at it until everyone has had a turn. Everything clear?"

The people had done it so many times that they only half listened to the 20 directions; most of them were quiet, wetting their lips, not looking around. Then Mr. Summers raised one hand high and said, "Adams." A man disengaged himself from the crowd and came forward. "Hi, Steve," Mr. Summers said, and Mr. Adams said, "Hi, Joe." They grinned at one another humorlessly and nervously. Then Mr. Adams reached into the black box and took out a folded paper. He held it firmly by one corner as he turned and went hastily back to his place in the crowd, where he stood a little apart from his family, not looking down at his hand.

"Allen." Mr. Summers said. "Anderson. . . . Betham."

"Seems like there's no time at all between lotteries any more," Mrs. Delacroix said to Mrs. Graves in the back row. "Seems like we got through the last one only last week."

"Time sure goes fast," Mrs. Graves said.

"Clark. . . . Delacroix."

"There goes my old man," Mrs. Delacroix said. She held her breath while her 25 husband went forward.

"Dunbar," Mr. Summers said, and Mrs. Dunbar went steadily to the box while one of the women said, "Go on, Janey," and another said, "There she goes."

"We're next," Mrs. Graves said. She watched while Mr. Graves came around from the side of the box, greeted Mr. Summers gravely, and selected a slip of paper from the box. By now, all through the crowd there were men holding the small folded papers in their large hands, turning them over and over nervously. Mrs. Dunbar and her two sons stood together, Mrs. Dunbar holding the slip of paper.

"Harburt. . . . Hutchinson."

"Get up there, Bill," Mrs. Hutchinson said, and the people near her laughed.

"Jones."   30

"They do say," Mr. Adams said to Old Man Warner, who stood next to him, "that over in the north village they're talking of giving up the lottery."

Old Man Warner snorted. "Pack of crazy fools," he said. "Listening to the young folks, nothing's good enough for *them*. Next thing you know, they'll be wanting to go back to living in caves, nobody work any more, live *that* way for a while. Used to be a saying about 'Lottery in June, corn be heavy soon.' First thing you know, we'd all be eating stewed chickweed and acorns. There's *always* been a lottery," he added petulantly. "Bad enough to see young Joe Summers up there joking with everybody."

"Some places have already quit lotteries," Mrs. Adams said.

"Nothing but trouble in *that*," Old Man Warner said stoutly. "Pack of young fools."

"Martin." And Bobby Martin watched his father go forward. "Overdyke. . . . 35
Percy."

"I wish they'd hurry," Mrs. Dunbar said to her older son. "I wish they'd hurry."

"They're almost through," her son said.

"You get ready to run tell Dad," Mrs. Dunbar said.

Mr. Summers called his own name and then stepped forward precisely and selected a slip from the box. Then he called, "Warner."

"Seventy-seventh year I been in the lottery," Old Man Warner said as he 40
went through the crowd. "Seventy-seventh time."

"Watson." The tall boy came awkwardly through the crowd. Someone said, "Don't be nervous, Jack," and Mr. Summers said, "Take your time, son."

"Zanini."

After that, there was a long pause, a breathless pause, until Mr. Summers, holding his slip of paper in the air, said, "All right fellows." For a minute, no one moved, and then all the slips of paper were opened. Suddenly, all the women began to speak at once, saying, "Who is it" "Who's got it?" "Is it the Dunbars?" "Is it the Watsons?" Then the voices began to say, "It's Hutchinson. It's Bill," "Bill Hutchinson's got it."

"Go tell your father," Mrs. Dunbar said to her older son.

People began to look around to see the Hutchinsons. Bill Hutchinson was 45
standing quiet, staring down at the paper in his hand. Suddenly, Tessie Hutchinson shouted to Mr. Summers, "You didn't give him time enough to take any paper he wanted. I saw you. It wasn't fair!"

"Be a good sport, Tessie," Mrs. Delacroix called, and Mrs. Graves said, "All of us took the same chance."

"Shut up, Tessie," Bill Hutchinson said.

"Well, everyone," Mr. Summers said, "That was done pretty fast, and now we've got to be hurrying a little more to get it done in time." He consulted his next list. "Bill," he said, "you draw for the Hutchinson family. You got any other households in the Hutchinsons?"

"There's Don and Eva," Mrs. Hutchinson yelled. "Make *them* take their chance!"

"Daughters draw with their husbands' families, Tessie," Mr. Summers said 50
gently. "You know that as well as anyone else."

"It wasn't *fair*," Tessie said.

"I guess not, Joe," Bill Hutchinson said regretfully. "My daughter draws with her husband's family, that's only fair. And I've got no other family except the kids."

"Then, as far as drawing for families is concerned, it's you," Mr. Summers said in explanation, "and as far as drawing for households is concerned, that's you, too. Right?"

"Right," Bill Hutchinson said.

"How many kids, Bill?" Mr. Summers asked formally. 55

"Three," Bill Hutchinson said. "There's Bill, Jr., and Nancy, and little Dave. And Tessie and me."

"All right then," Mr. Summers said. "Harry, you got their tickets back?"

Mr. Graves nodded and held up the slips of paper. "Put them in the box, then," Mr. Summers directed. "Take Bill's and put it in."

"I think we ought to start over," Mrs. Hutchinson said, as quietly as she could. "I tell you it wasn't *fair*. You didn't give him time enough to choose. *Every*body saw that."

Mr. Graves had selected the five slips and put them in the box, and he dropped all the papers but those onto the ground, where the breeze caught them and lifted them off. 60

"Listen, everybody," Mrs. Hutchinson was saying to the people around her.

"Ready, Bill?" Mr. Summers asked, and Bill Hutchinson, with one quick glance around at his wife and children, nodded.

"Remember," Mr. Summers said, "take the slips and keep them folded until each person has taken one. Harry, you help little Dave." Mr. Graves took the hand of the little boy, who came willingly with him up to the box. "Take a paper out of the box, Davy," Mr. Summers said. Davy put his hand into the box and laughed. "Take just *one* paper," Mr. Summers said. "Harry, you hold it for him." Mr. Graves took the child's hand and removed the folded paper from the tight fist and held it while little Dave stood next to him and looked up at him wonderingly.

"Nancy next," Mr. Summers said. Nancy was twelve, and her school friends breathed heavily as she went forward, switching her skirt, and took a slip daintily from the box. "Bill, Jr.," Mr. Summers said, and Billy, his face red and his feet over-large, nearly knocked the box over as he got a paper out. "Tessie," Mr. Summers said. She hesitated for a minute, looking around defiantly, and then set her lips and went up to the box. She snatched a paper out and held it behind her.

"Bill," Mr. Summers said, and Bill Hutchinson reached into the box and felt around, bringing his hand out at last with the slip of paper in it. 65

The crowd was quiet. A girl whispered, "I hope it's not Nancy," and the sound of the whisper reached the edges of the crowd.

"It's not the way it used to be," Old Man Warner said clearly. "People ain't the way they used to be."

"All right," Mr. Summers said. "Open the papers. Harry, you open little Dave's."

Mr. Graves opened the slip of paper and there was a general sigh through the crowd as he held it up and everyone could see that it was blank. Nancy and Bill, Jr., opened theirs at the same time, and both beamed and laughed, turning around to the crowd and holding their slips of paper above their heads.

"Tessie," Mr. Summers said. There was a pause, and then Mr. Summers looked at Bill Hutchinson, and Bill unfolded his paper and showed it. It was blank. 70

"It's Tessie," Mr. Summers said, and his voice was hushed. "Show us her paper, Bill."

Bill Hutchinson went over to his wife and forced the slip of paper out of her hand. It had a black spot on it, the black spot Mr. Summers had made the night before with the heavy pencil in the coal-company office. Bill Hutchinson held it up, and there was a stir in the crowd.

"All right, folks," Mr. Summers said. "Let's finish quickly."

Although the villagers had forgotten the ritual and lost the original black box, they still remembered to use stones. The pile of stones the boys had made earlier was ready; there were stones on the ground with the blowing scraps of paper that had come out of the box. Mrs. Delacroix selected a stone so large she had to pick it up with both hands and turned to Mrs. Dunbar. "Come on," she said. "Hurry up."

Mrs. Dunbar had small stones in both hands, and she said, gasping for 75 breath, "I can't run at all. You'll have to go ahead and I'll catch up with you."

The children had stones already, and someone gave little Davy Hutchinson a few pebbles.

Tessie Hutchinson was in the center of a cleared space by now, and she held her hands out desperately as the villagers moved in on her. "It isn't fair," she said. A stone hit her on the side of the head.

Old Man Warner was saying, "Come on, come on, everyone." Steve Adams was in the front of the crowd of villagers, with Mrs. Graves beside him.

"It isn't fair, it isn't right," Mrs. Hutchinson screamed, and then they were upon her.

FOR ANALYSIS

1. What evidence in the story suggests that the lottery is a ritualistic ceremony?

2. Does the straightforward narrative style describing the holiday atmosphere diminish or intensify the horror of the story's conclusion? Explain.

3. Might the story be a comment on religious orthodoxy? Explain.

MAKING CONNECTIONS

Compare this story with Silko's "The Man to Send Rain Clouds" (p. 1164). What similarities do you find? What differences?

WRITING TOPICS

1. Explain the purpose of the lottery, and identify contemporary rituals that exhibit similar purposes.

2. Magic and religion differ because magicians can compel change whereas priests can only ask for change. Comment on this distinction. Can you identify magical elements in religion?

URSULA K. LE GUIN (B. 1929)

THE ONES WHO WALK
AWAY FROM OMELAS   1974

With a clamor of bells that set the swallows soaring, the Festival of Summer came to the city Omelas, bright-towered by the sea. The rigging of the boats in harbor sparkled with flags. In the streets between houses with red roofs and painted walls, between old moss-grown gardens and under avenues of trees, past great parks and public buildings, processions moved. Some were decorous: old people in long stiff robes of mauve and grey, grave master workmen, quiet, merry women carrying their babies and chatting as they walked. In other streets the music beat faster, a shimmering of gong and tambourine, and the people went dancing, the procession was a dance. Children dodged in and out, their high calls rising like the swallows' crossing flights over the music and the singing. All the processions wound towards the north side of the city, where on the great water-meadow called the Green Fields boys and girls, naked in the bright air, with mud-stained feet and ankles and long, lithe arms, exercised their restive horses before the race. The horses wore no gear at all but a halter without bit. Their manes were braided with streamers of silver, gold, and green. They flared their nostrils and pranced and boasted to one another; they were vastly excited, the horse being the only animal who has adopted our ceremonies as his own. Far off to the north and west the mountains stood up half encircling Omelas on her bay. The air of morning was so clear that the snow still crowning the Eighteen Peaks burned with white-gold fire across the miles of sunlit air, under the dark blue of the sky. There was just enough wind to make the banners that marked the racecourse snap and flutter now and then. In the silence of the broad green meadows one could hear the music winding through the city streets, farther and nearer and ever approaching, a cheerful faint sweetness of the air that from time to time trembled and gathered together and broke out into the great joyous clanging of the bells.

Joyous! How is one to tell about joy? How describe the citizens of Omelas?

They were not simple folk, you see, though they were happy. But we do not say the words of cheer much any more. All smiles have become archaic. Given a description such as this one tends to make certain assumptions. Given a description such as this one tends to look next for the King, mounted on a splendid stallion and surrounded by his noble knights, or perhaps in a golden litter borne by great-muscled slaves. But there was no king. They did not use swords, or keep slaves. They were not barbarians. I do not know the rules and laws of their society, but I suspect that they were singularly few. As they did without monarchy and slavery, so they also got on without the stock exchange, the advertisement, the secret police, and the bomb. Yet I repeat that these were not simple folk, not dulcet shepherds, noble savages, bland utopians. They were not less complex than us. The trouble is that we have a bad habit, encouraged by pedants and sophisticates, of considering happiness as something rather stupid. Only pain is intellectual, only evil interesting. This is the treason of the artist: a refusal to admit the banality of evil and the terrible boredom of pain. If you can't lick 'em, join 'em. If it hurts, repeat it. But to praise despair is to condemn delight, to embrace violence is to lose hold of everything else. We have almost lost hold; we can no longer describe a happy man, nor make any celebration of joy. How can I tell you about the people of Omelas? They were not naïve and happy children—though their children were, in fact, happy. They were mature, intelligent, passionate adults whose lives were not wretched. O miracle! but I wish I could describe it better. I wish I could convince you. Omelas sounds in my words like a city in a fairy tale, long ago and far away, once upon a time. Perhaps it would be best if you imagined it as your own fancy bids, assuming it will rise to the occasion, for certainly I cannot suit you all. For instance, how about technology? I think that there would be no cars or helicopters in and above the streets; this follows from the fact that the people of Omelas are happy people. Happiness is based on a just discrimination of what is necessary, what is neither necessary nor destructive, and what is destructive. In the middle category, however—that of the unnecessary but undestructive, that of comfort, luxury, exuberance, etc.—they could perfectly well have central heating, subway trains, washing machines, and all kinds of marvelous devices not yet invented here, floating light-sources, fuelless power, a cure for the common cold. Or they could have none of that: it doesn't matter. As you like it. I incline to think that people from towns up and down the coast have been coming in to Omelas during the last days before the Festival on very fast little trains and double decker trams, and that the train station of Omelas is actually the handsomest building in town, though plainer than the magnificent Farmers' Market. But even granted trams, I fear that Omelas so far strikes some of you as goody-goody. Smiles, bells, parades, horses, bleh. If so, please add an orgy. If an orgy would help, don't hesitate. Let us not, however, have temples from which issue beautiful nude priests and priestesses already half in ecstasy and ready to copulate with any man or woman, lover or stranger, who desires union with the deep godhead of the blood, although that was my first idea. But really it would be better not to have any temples in Omelas—at least, not manned temples. Religion yes, clergy no. Surely the beautiful nudes can just wander about, offering themselves like divine soufflés to the hunger of the needy and the rapture of the flesh. Let them join the processions. Let tambourines be struck above the copulations, and the glory of desire be proclaimed upon the gongs, and (a not unimportant point) let the offspring of these delightful rituals be beloved and looked after by all. One thing I know there is none of in Omelas is guilt. But what else should there be? I thought at first there were no drugs, but that is puritanical. For those who like it, the faint insistent sweetness of *drooz* may perfume the ways of the city, *drooz* which first brings a great lightness and brilliance to the mind and limbs, and then after some hours a dreamy languor, and wonderful visions at last of the very arcana and inmost secrets of the Universe, as well as exciting the pleasure of sex beyond all belief; and it is not habit-forming. For more modest tastes I think there ought to be beer. What else, what else belongs in the joyous city? The sense of victory, surely, the celebration of courage. But as we did without clergy, let us do without soldiers. The joy built upon successful slaughter is not the right kind of joy; it will not do; it is fearful and it is trivial. A boundless and generous contentment, a magnanimous triumph felt not against some outer enemy but in communion with the finest and fairest in the souls of all men everywhere and the splendor of the world's summer: this is what swells the hearts of the people of Omelas, and the victory they celebrate is that of life. I really don't think many of them need to take *drooz*.

Most of the processions have reached the Green Fields by now. A marvelous smell of cooking goes forth from the red and blue tents of the provisioners. The faces of small children are amiably sticky; in the benign grey beard of a man a couple of crumbs of rich pastry are entangled. The youths and girls have mounted their horses and are beginning to group around the starting line of the course. An old woman, small, fat, and laughing, is passing out flowers from a basket, and tall young men wear her flowers in their shining hair. A child of nine or ten sits at the edge of the crowd, alone, playing on a wooden flute. People pause to listen, and they smile, but they do not speak to him, for he never ceases playing and never sees them, his dark eyes wholly rapt in the sweet, thin magic of the tune.

He finishes, and slowly lowers his hands holding the wooden flute.   5

As if that little private silence were the signal, all at once a trumpet sounds from the pavilion near the starting line: imperious, melancholy, piercing. The horses rear on their slender legs, and some of them neigh in answer. Sober-faced, the young riders stroke the horses' necks and soothe them, whispering, "Quiet, quiet, there my beauty, my hope. . . ." They begin to form in rank along the starting line. The crowds along the racecourse are like a field of grass and flowers in the wind. The Festival of Summer has begun.

Do you believe? Do you accept the festival, the city, the joy? No? Then let me describe one more thing.

In a basement under one of the beautiful public buildings of Omelas, or per-haps in the cellar of one of its spacious private homes, there is a room. It has one locked door, and no window. A little light seeps in dustily between cracks in the boards, secondhand from a cobwebbed window somewhere across the cellar. In one corner of the little room a couple of mops, with stiff, clotted, foul-smelling heads, stand near a rusty bucket. The floor is dirt, a little damp to the touch, as cellar dirt usually is. The room is about three paces long and two wide: a mere broom closet or disused tool room. In the room a child is sitting. It could be a boy or a girl. It looks about six, but actually is nearly ten. It is fee-ble-minded. Perhaps it was born defective, or perhaps it has become imbecile through fear, malnutrition, and neglect. It picks its nose and occasionally fumbles vaguely with its toes or genitals, as it sits hunched in the corner far-thest from the bucket and the two mops. It is afraid of the mops. It finds them horrible. It shuts its eyes, but it knows the mops are still standing there; and the door is locked; and nobody will come. The door is always locked; and nobody ever comes, except that sometimes—the child has no understanding of time or interval—sometimes the door rattles terribly and opens, and a person, or sev-eral people, are there. One of them may come in and kick the child to make it stand up. The others never come close, but peer in at it with frightened, dis-gusted eyes. The food bowl and the water jug are hastily filled, the door is locked, the eyes disappear. The people at the door never say anything, but the child, who has not always lived in the tool room, and can remember sunlight and its mother's voice, sometimes speaks. "I will be good," it says. "Please let me out. I will be good!" They never answer. The child used to scream for help at night, and cry a good deal, but now it only makes a kind of whining, "eh-haa, eh-haa," and it speaks less and less often. It is so thin there are no calves to its legs; its belly protrudes; it lives on a half-bowl of corn meal and grease a day. It is naked. Its buttocks and thighs are a mass of festered sores, as it sits in its own excrement continually.

They all know it is there, all the people of Omelas. Some of them have come to see it, others are content merely to know it is there. They all know that it has to be there. Some of them understand why, and some do not, but all under-stand that their happiness, the beauty of their city, the tenderness of their friendships, the health of their children, the wisdom of their scholars, the skill of their makers, even the abundance of their harvest and the kindly weathers of their skies, depend wholly on this child's abominable misery.

This is usually explained to children when they are between eight and 10 twelve, whenever they seem capable of understanding; and most of those who come to see the child are young people, though often enough an adult comes, or comes back, to see the child. No matter how well the matter has been explained to them, these young spectators are always shocked and sickened at the sight. They feel disgust, which they had thought themselves superior to. They feel anger, outrage, impotence, despite all the explanations. They would like to do something for the child. But there is nothing they can do. If the child were brought up into the sunlight out of that vile place, if it were cleaned and fed and comforted, that would be a good thing, indeed; but if it were done, in that day and hour all the prosperity and beauty and delight of Omelas would wither and be destroyed. Those are the terms. To exchange all the good-ness and grace of every life in Omelas for that single, small improvement: to throw away the happiness of thousands for the chance of the happiness of one: that would be to let guilt within the walls indeed.

The terms are strict and absolute; there may not even be a kind word spoken to the child.

Often the young people go home in tears, or in a tearless rage, when they have seen the child and faced this terrible paradox. They may brood over it for weeks or years. But as time goes on they begin to realize that even if the child could be released, it would not get much good of its freedom: a little vague pleasure of warmth and food, no doubt, but little more. It is too degraded and imbecile to know any real joy. It has been afraid too long ever to be free of fear. Its habits are too uncouth for it to respond to humane treatment. Indeed, after so long it would probably be wretched without walls about it to protect it, and darkness for its eyes, and its own excrement to sit in. Their tears at the bitter injustice dry when they begin to perceive the terrible justice of reality, and to accept it. Yet it is their tears and anger, the trying of their generosity and the acceptance of their helplessness, which are perhaps the true source of the splendor of their lives. Theirs is no vapid, irresponsible happiness. They know that they, like the child, are not free. They know compassion. It is the existence of the child, and their knowledge of its existence, that makes possible the nobility of their architecture, the poignancy of their music, the profundity of their science. It is because of the child that they are so gentle with children. They know that if the wretched one were not there snivelling in the dark, the other one, the flute-player, could make no joyful music as the young riders line up in their beauty for the race in the sunlight of the first morning of summer.

Now do you believe in them? Are they not more credible? But there is one more thing to tell, and this is quite incredible.

At times one of the adolescent girls or boys who go to see the child does not go home to weep or rage, does not, in fact, go home at all. Sometimes also a man or woman much older falls silent for a day or two, and then leaves home. These people go out into the street, and walk down the street alone. They keep walking, and walk straight out of the city of Omelas, through the beautiful gates. They keep walking across the farmlands of Omelas. Each one goes alone, youth or girl, man or woman. Night falls; the traveler must pass down village streets, between the houses with yellow-lit windows, and on out into the darkness of the fields. Each alone, they go west or north, towards the mountains. They go on. They leave Omelas, they walk ahead into the darkness, and they do not come back. The place they go towards is a place even less imaginable to most of us than the city of happiness. I cannot describe it at all. It is possible that it does not exist. But they seem to know where they are going, the ones who walk away from Omelas.

FOR ANALYSIS

1. Who is the **narrator**? What are her feelings about Omelas, particularly about the misery of the child on which the happiness of the city depends?

2. Does the narrator sympathize with those who walk away? Or with those who remain? Or is she ambivalent?

3. Is Omelas described in sufficient detail, or are there other things about the city you wish the author had included?

4. Look up the dictionary definition of *utopia*. Does Omelas fit that definition?

5. How would you describe the **conflict** in this story? Is there a **protagonist** and an **antagonist**? Who are they?

MAKING CONNECTIONS

1. This story, Hawthorne's "Young Goodman Brown" (p. 81), and Ellison's "'Repent, Harlequin!' Said the Ticktockman" (p. 372) all rely on fantasy. What advantages does the use of fantasy give the authors?

2. Compare the statement this story makes about the human spirit with that made by Ellison's "'Repent, Harlequin!' Said the Ticktockman" (p. 372). Do the ones who walk away from Omelas share any of the attributes of the Harlequin?

WRITING TOPICS

1. The narrator comments, "The trouble is that we have a bad habit, encouraged by pedants and sophisticates, of considering happiness as something rather stupid. Only pain is intellectual, only evil interesting. This is the treason of the artist: a refusal to admit the banality of evil and the terrible boredom of pain" (para. 3). Write an essay examining this statement. Are the narrator's claims persuasive?

2. Is Le Guin's story, first published in 1974, still relevant? Why or why not?

TWO KINDS   1989

M y mother believed you could be anything you wanted to be in America. You could open a restaurant. You could work for the government and get good retirement. You could buy a house with almost no money down. You could become rich. You could become instantly famous.

"Of course you can be prodigy, too," my mother told me when I was nine. "You can be best anything. What does Auntie Lindo know? Her daughter, she is only best tricky."

America was where all my mother's hopes lay. She had come here in 1949 after losing everything in China: her mother and father, her family home, her first husband, and two daughters, twin baby girls. But she never looked back with regret. There were so many ways for things to get better.

We didn't immediately pick the right kind of prodigy. At first my mother thought I could be a Chinese Shirley Temple. We'd watch Shirley's old movies on TV as though they were training films. My mother would poke my arm and say, "*Ni kan*"—You watch. And I would see Shirley tapping her feet, or singing a sailor song, or pursing her lips into a very round O while saying, "Oh my goodness."

"*Ni kan*," said my mother as Shirley's eyes flooded with tears. "You already 5 know how. Don't need talent for crying!"

Soon after my mother got this idea about Shirley Temple, she took me to a beauty training school in the Mission district and put me in the hands of a student who could barely hold the scissors without shaking. Instead of getting big fat curls, I emerged with an uneven mass of crinkly black fuzz. My mother dragged me off to the bathroom and tried to wet down my hair.

"You look like Negro Chinese," she lamented, as if I had done this on purpose.

The instructor of the beauty training school had to lop off these soggy clumps to make my hair even again. "Peter Pan is very popular these days," the instructor assured my mother. I now had hair the length of a boy's, with straight-across bangs that hung at a slant two inches above my eyebrows. I liked the haircut and it made me actually look forward to my future fame.

In fact, in the beginning, I was just as excited as my mother, maybe even more so. I pictured this prodigy part of me as many different images, trying each one on for size. I was a dainty ballerina girl standing by the curtains, waiting to hear the right music that would send me floating on my tiptoes. I was like the Christ child lifted out of the straw manger, crying with holy indignity. I was Cinderella stepping from her pumpkin carriage with sparkly cartoon music filling the air.

In all of my imaginings, I was filled with a sense that I would soon become 10
perfect. My mother and father would adore me. I would be beyond reproach. I
would never feel the need to sulk for anything.

But sometimes the prodigy in me became impatient. "If you don't hurry up
and get me out of here, I'm disappearing for good," it warned. "And then you'll
always be nothing."

Every night after dinner, my mother and I would sit at the Formica kitchen
table. She would present new tests, taking her examples from stories of amazing children she had read in *Ripley's Believe It or Not,* or *Good Housekeeping,*
Reader's Digest, and a dozen other magazines she kept in a pile in our bathroom. My mother got these magazines from people whose houses she cleaned.
And since she cleaned many houses each week, we had a great assortment. She
would look through them all, searching for stories about remarkable children.

The first night she brought out a story about a three-year-old boy who knew
the capitals of all the states and even of most of the European countries. A
teacher was quoted as saying the little boy could also pronounce the names of
the foreign cities correctly.

"What's the capital of Finland?" my mother asked me, looking at the magazine story.

All I knew was the capital of California, because Sacramento was the name 15
of the street we lived on in Chinatown. "Nairobi!" I guessed, saying the most
foreign word I could think of. She checked to see if that was possibly one way
to pronounce "Helsinki" before showing me the answer.

The tests got harder—multiplying numbers in my head, finding the queen of
hearts in a deck of cards, trying to stand on my head without using my hands,
predicting the daily temperatures in Los Angeles, New York, and London.

One night I had to look at a page from the Bible for three minutes and then
report everything I could remember. "Now Jehoshaphat had riches and honor
in abundance and . . . that's all I remember, Ma," I said.

And after seeing my mother's disappointed face once again, something
inside of me began to die. I hated the tests, the raised hopes and failed expectations. Before going to bed that night, I looked in the mirror above the bathroom sink and when I saw only my face staring back—and that it would always
be this ordinary face—I began to cry. Such a sad, ugly girl! I made high-pitched noises like a crazed animal, trying to scratch out the face in the mirror.

And then I saw what seemed to be the prodigy side of me—because I had
never seen that face before. I looked at my reflection, blinking so I could see
more clearly. The girl staring back at me was angry, powerful. This girl and I
were the same. I had new thoughts, willful thoughts, or rather thoughts filled
with lots of won'ts. I won't let her change me, I promised myself. I won't be
what I'm not.

So now on nights when my mother presented her tests, I performed listlessly, 20
my head propped on one arm. I pretended to be bored. And I was. I got so
bored I started counting the bellows of the foghorns out on the bay while my

mother drilled me in other areas. The sound was comforting and reminded me of the cow jumping over the moon. And the next day, I played a game with myself, seeing if my mother would give up on me before eight bellows. After a while I usually counted only one, maybe two bellows at most. At last she was beginning to give up hope.

Two or three months had gone by without any mention of my being a prodigy again. And then one day my mother was watching *The Ed Sullivan Show* on TV. The TV was old and the sound kept shorting out. Every time my mother got halfway up from the sofa to adjust the set, the sound would come back on and Ed would be talking. As soon as she sat down, Ed would go silent again. She got up, the TV broke into loud piano music. She sat down. Silence. Up and down, back and forth, quiet and loud. It was like a stiff embraceless dance between her and the TV set. Finally she stood by the set with her hand on the sound dial.

She seemed entranced by the music, a little frenzied piano piece with this mesmerizing quality, sort of quick passages and then teasing lilting ones before it returned to the quick playful parts.

"*Ni kan,*" my mother said, calling me over with hurried hand gestures, "Look here."

I could see why my mother was fascinated by the music. It was being pounded out by a little Chinese girl, about nine years old, with a Peter Pan haircut. The girl had the sauciness of a Shirley Temple. She was proudly modest like a proper Chinese child. And she also did a fancy sweep of a curtsy, so that the fluffy skirt of her white dress cascaded slowly to the floor like the petals of a large carnation.

In spite of these warning signs, I wasn't worried. Our family had no piano 25 and we couldn't afford to buy one, let alone reams of sheet music and piano lessons. So I could be generous in my comments when my mother bad-mouthed the little girl on TV.

"Play note right, but doesn't sound good! No singing sound," complained my mother.

"What are you picking on her for?" I said carelessly. "She's pretty good. Maybe she's not the best, but she's trying hard." I knew almost immediately I would be sorry I said that.

"Just like you," she said. "Not the best. Because you not trying." She gave a little huff as she let go of the sound dial and sat down on the sofa.

The little Chinese girl sat down also to play an encore of "Anitra's Dance" by Grieg.[1] I remember the song, because later on I had to learn how to play it.

Three days after watching *The Ed Sullivan Show,* my mother told me what my 30 schedule would be for piano lessons and piano practice. She had talked to Mr. Chong, who lived on the first floor of our apartment building. Mr. Chong was a retired piano teacher, and my mother had traded housecleaning services for

[1] From Edvard Grieg's (1843–1907) incidental music composed for Henrik Ibsen's play *Peer Gynt.*

weekly lessons and a piano for me to practice on every day, two hours a day, from four until six.

When my mother told me this, I felt as though I had been sent to hell. I whined and then kicked my foot a little when I couldn't stand it anymore.

"Why don't you like me the way I am? I'm *not* a genius! I can't play the piano. And even if I could, I wouldn't go on TV if you paid me a million dollars!" I cried.

My mother slapped me. "Who ask you be genius?" she shouted. "Only ask you be your best. For you sake. You think I want you be genius? Hnnh! What for! Who ask you!"

"So ungrateful," I heard her mutter in Chinese. "If she had as much talent as she has temper, she would be famous now."

Mr. Chong, whom I secretly nicknamed Old Chong, was very strange, 35 always tapping his fingers to the silent music of an invisible orchestra. He looked ancient in my eyes. He had lost most of the hair on top of his head and he wore thick glasses and had eyes that always looked tired and sleepy. But he must have been younger than I thought, since he lived with his mother and was not yet married.

I met Old Lady Chong once and that was enough. She had this peculiar smell like a baby that had done something in its pants. And her fingers felt like a dead person's, like an old peach I once found in the back of the refrigerator; the skin just slid off the meat when I picked it up.

I soon found out why Old Chong had retired from teaching piano. He was deaf. "Like Beethoven!" he shouted to me. "We're both listening only in our head!" And he would start to conduct his frantic silent sonatas.

Our lessons went like this. He would open the book and point to different things, explaining their purpose: "Key! Treble! Bass! No sharps or flats! So this is C major! Listen now and play after me!"

And then he would play the C scale a few times, a simple chord, and then, as if inspired by an old unreachable itch, he would gradually add more notes and running trills and a pounding bass until the music was really something quite grand.

I would play after him, the simple scale, the simple chord, and then I just 40 played some nonsense that sounded like a cat running up and down on top of garbage cans. Old Chong smiled and applauded and then said, "Very good! But now you must learn to keep time!"

So that's how I discovered that Old Chong's eyes were too slow to keep up with the wrong notes I was playing. He went through the motions in half-time. To help me keep rhythm, he stood behind me, pushing down on my right shoulder for every beat. He balanced pennies on top of my wrists so I would keep them still as I slowly played scales and arpeggios. He had me curve my hand around an apple and keep that shape when playing chords. He marched stiffly to show me how to make each finger dance up and down, staccato like an obedient little soldier.

He taught me all these things, and that was how I also learned I could be lazy and get away with mistakes, lots of mistakes. If I hit the wrong notes because I hadn't practiced enough, I never corrected myself. I just kept playing in rhythm. And Old Chong kept conducting his own private reverie.

So maybe I never really gave myself a fair chance. I did pick up the basics pretty quickly, and I might have become a good pianist at that young age. But I was so determined not to try, not to be anybody different that I learned to play only the most ear-splitting preludes, the most discordant hymns.

Over the next year, I practiced like this, dutifully in my own way. And then one day I heard my mother and her friend Lindo Jong both talking in a loud bragging tone of voice so others could hear. It was after church, and I was leaning against the brick wall wearing a dress with stiff white petticoats. Auntie Lindo's daughter, Waverly, who was about my age, was standing farther down the wall about five feet away. We had grown up together and shared all the closeness of two sisters squabbling over crayons and dolls. In other words, for the most part, we hated each other. I thought she was snotty. Waverly Jong had gained a certain amount of fame as "Chinatown's Littlest Chinese Chess Champion."

"She bring home too many trophy," lamented Auntie Lindo that Sunday. "All 45 day she play chess. All day I have no time do nothing but dust off her winnings." She threw a scolding look at Waverly, who pretended not to see her.

"You lucky you don't have this problem," said Auntie Lindo with a sigh to my mother.

And my mother squared her shoulders and bragged: "Our problem worser than yours. If we ask Jing-mei wash dish, she hear nothing but music. It's like you can't stop this natural talent."

And right then I was determined to put a stop to her foolish pride.

A few weeks later, Old Chong and my mother conspired to have me play in a talent show which would be held in the church hall. By then, my parents had saved up enough to buy me a secondhand piano, a black Wurlitzer spinet with a scarred bench. It was the showpiece of our living room.

For the talent show, I was to play a piece called "Pleading Child" from 50 Schumann's *Scenes from Childhood*. It was a simple, moody piece that sounded more difficult than it was. I was supposed to memorize the whole thing, playing the repeat parts twice to make the piece sound longer. But I dawdled over it, playing a few bars and then cheating, looking up to see what notes followed. I never really listened to what I was playing. I daydreamed about being somewhere else, about being someone else.

The part I liked to practice best was the fancy curtsy: right foot out, touch the rose on the carpet with a pointed foot, sweep to the side, left leg bends, look up, and smile.

My parents invited all the couples from the Joy Luck Club to witness my debut. Auntie Lindo and Uncle Tin were there. Waverly and her two older brothers had also come. The first two rows were filled with children both younger and older than I was. The littlest ones got to go first. They recited simple nursery rhymes, squawked out tunes on miniature violins, twirled Hula Hoops, pranced in pink ballet tutus, and when they bowed or curtsied, the audience would sigh in unison, "Awww," and then clap enthusiastically.

When my turn came, I was very confident. I remember my childish excitement. It was as if I knew, without a doubt, that the prodigy side of me really
did exist. I had no fear whatsoever, no nervousness. I remember thinking to
myself, This is it! This is it! I looked out over the audience, at my mother's
blank face, my father's yawn, Auntie Lindo's stiff-lipped smile, Waverly's sulky
expression. I had on a white dress, layered with sheets of lace, and a pink bow
in my Peter Pan haircut. As I sat down, I envisioned people jumping to their
feet and Ed Sullivan rushing up to introduce me to everyone on TV.

And I started to play. It was so beautiful. I was so caught up in how lovely I
looked that at first I didn't worry how I would sound. So it was a surprise to
me when I hit the first wrong note and I realized something didn't sound
quite right. And then I hit another and another followed that. A chill started
at the top of my head and began to trickle down. Yet I couldn't stop playing,
as though my hands were bewitched. I kept thinking my fingers would adjust
themselves back, like a train switching to the right track. I played this strange
jumble through two repeats, the sour notes staying with me all the way to
the end.

When I stood up, I discovered my legs were shaking. Maybe I had just been   55
nervous and the audience, like Old Chong, had seen me go through the right
motions and had not heard anything wrong at all. I swept my right foot out,
went down on my knee, looked up and smiled. The room was quiet, except for
Old Chong, who was beaming and shouting, "Bravo! Bravo! Well done!" But
then I saw my mother's face, her stricken face. The audience clapped weakly,
and as I walked back to my chair, with my whole face quivering as I tried not to
cry, I heard a little boy whisper loudly to his mother, "That was awful," and the
mother whispered, "Well, she certainly tried."

And now I realized how many people were in the audience, the whole world,
it seemed. I was aware of eyes burning into my back. I felt the shame of my
mother and father as they sat stiffly throughout the rest of the show.

We could have escaped during intermission. Pride and some strange sense
of honor must have anchored my parents to their chairs. And so we watched it
all: the eighteen-year-old boy with a fake moustache who did a magic show
and juggled flaming hoops while riding a unicycle. The breasted girl with
white makeup who sang an aria from *Madama Butterfly* and got an honorable
mention. And the eleven-year-old boy who won first prize playing a tricky violin song that sounded like a busy bee.

After the show, the Hsus, the Jongs, and the St. Clairs from the Joy Luck
Club came up to my mother and father.

"Lots of talented kids," Auntie Lindo said vaguely, smiling broadly.

"That was somethin' else," my father said, and I wondered if he was referring   60
to me in a humorous way, or whether he even remembered what I had done.

Waverly looked at me and shrugged her shoulders. "You aren't a genius like
me," she said matter-of-factly. And if I hadn't felt so bad, I would have pulled
her braids and punched her stomach.

But my mother's expression was what devastated me: a quiet, blank look
that said she had lost everything. I felt the same way, and it seemed as if everybody

were now coming up, like gawkers at the scene of an accident, to see what parts were actually missing. When we got on the bus to go home, my father was humming the busy-bee tune and my mother was silent. I kept thinking she wanted to wait until we got home before shouting at me. But when my father unlocked the door to our apartment, my mother walked in and then went to the back, into the bedroom. No accusations. No blame. And in a way, I felt disappointed. I had been waiting for her to start shouting, so I could shout back and cry and blame her for all my misery.

I assumed my talent-show fiasco meant I never had to play the piano again. But two days later, after school, my mother came out of the kitchen and saw me watching TV.

"Four clock," she reminded me as if it were any other day. I was stunned, as though she were asking me to go through the talent-show torture again. I wedged myself more tightly in front of the TV.

"Turn off TV," she called from the kitchen five minutes later.   65

I didn't budge. And then I decided. I didn't have to do what my mother said anymore. I wasn't her slave. This wasn't China. I had listened to her before, and look what happened. She was the stupid one.

She came out of the kitchen and stood in the arched entryway of the living room. "Four clock," she said once again, louder.

"I'm not going to play anymore," I said nonchalantly. "Why should I? I'm not a genius."

She stood in front of the TV. I saw her chest was heaving up and down in an angry way.

"No!" I said, and I now felt stronger, as if my true self had finally emerged.   70
So this was what had been inside me all along.

"No! I won't!" I screamed.

She yanked me by the arm, pulled me off the floor, snapped off the TV. She was frighteningly strong, half pulling, half carrying me toward the piano as I kicked the throw rugs under my feet. She lifted me up and onto the hard bench. I was sobbing by now, looking at her bitterly. Her chest was heaving even more and her mouth was open, smiling crazily as if she were pleased that I was crying.

"You want me to be someone that I'm not!" I sobbed. "I'll never be the kind of daughter you want me to be!"

"Only two kinds of daughters," she shouted in Chinese. "Those who are obedient and those who follow their own mind! Only one kind of daughter can live in this house. Obedient daughter!"

"Then I wish I weren't your daughter. I wish you weren't my mother," I   75
shouted. As I said these things I got scared. It felt like worms and toads and slimy things crawling out of my chest, but it also felt good, as if this awful side of me had surfaced, at last.

"Too late change this," said my mother shrilly.

And I could sense her anger rising to its breaking point. I wanted to see it spill over. And that's when I remembered the babies she had lost in China, the ones we never talked about. "Then I wish I'd never been born!" I shouted. "I wish I were dead! Like them."

It was as if I had said the magic words. Alakazam!—and her face went blank, her mouth closed, her arms went slack, and she backed out of the room, stunned, as if she were blowing away like a small brown leaf, thin, brittle, lifeless.

It was not the only disappointment my mother felt in me. In the years that followed, I failed her so many times, each time asserting my own will, my right to fall short of expectations. I didn't get straight As. I didn't become class president. I didn't get into Stanford. I dropped out of college.

For unlike my mother, I did not believe I could be anything I wanted to be. I 80 could only be me.

And for all those years, we never talked about the disaster at the recital or my terrible accusations afterward at the piano bench. All that remained unchecked, like a betrayal that was now unspeakable. So I never found a way to ask her why she had hoped for something so large that failure was inevitable.

And even worse, I never asked her about what frightened me the most: Why had she given up hope?

For after our struggle at the piano, she never mentioned my playing again. The lessons stopped. The lid to the piano was closed, shutting out the dust, my misery, and her dreams.

So she surprised me. A few years ago, she offered to give me the piano, for my thirtieth birthday. I had not played in all those years. I saw the offer as a sign of forgiveness, a tremendous burden removed.

"Are you sure?" I asked shyly. "I mean, won't you and Dad miss it?"   85

"No, this your piano," she said firmly. "Always your piano. You only one can play."

"Well, I probably can't play anymore," I said. "It's been years."

"You pick up fast," said my mother, as if she knew this was certain. "You have natural talent. You could been genius if you want to."

"No I couldn't."

"You just not trying," said my mother. And she was neither angry nor sad. She 90 said it as if to announce a fact that could never be disproved. "Take it," she said.

But I didn't at first. It was enough that she had offered it to me. And after that, every time I saw it in my parents' living room, standing in front of the bay windows, it made me feel proud, as if it were a shiny trophy that I had won back.

Last week I sent a tuner over to my parents' apartment and had the piano reconditioned, for purely sentimental reasons. My mother had died a few months before and I had been getting things in order for my father, a little bit at a time. I put the jewelry in special silk pouches. The sweaters she had knitted in yellow, pink, bright orange—all the colors I hated—I put those in mothproof boxes. I found some old Chinese silk dresses, the kind with little slits up the sides. I rubbed the old silk against my skin, then wrapped them in tissue and decided to take them home with me.

After I had the piano tuned, I opened the lid and touched the keys. It sounded even richer than I remembered. Really, it was a very good piano. Inside the bench were the same exercise notes with handwritten scales, the same secondhand music books with their covers held together with yellow tape.

I opened up the Schumann book to the dark little piece I had played at the recital. It was on the left-hand page, "Pleading Child." It looked more difficult than I remembered. I played a few bars, surprised at how easily the notes came back to me.

And for the first time, or so it seemed, I noticed the piece on the right-hand side. It was called "Perfectly Contented." I tried to play this one as well. It had a lighter melody but the same flowing rhythm and turned out to be quite easy. "Pleading Child" was shorter but slower; "Perfectly Contented" was longer, but faster. And after I played them both a few times, I realized they were two halves of the same song.

FOR ANALYSIS

1. Do you think the **conflict** between the mother and daughter is unique to this family? To Asian American families? To any group of families? Why or why not?

2. What does the mother want for her daughter? What does the daughter want for herself?

3. What is the significance of the story's last paragraph?

MAKING CONNECTIONS

Several of the stories in "Conformity and Rebellion" are driven by tensions between parents and children. Compare "Two Kinds" with stories from elsewhere in this anthology: Faulkner's "A Rose for Emily" (p. 622), Achebe's "Marriage Is a Private Affair" (p. 585), and Walker's "Everyday Use" (p. 590). Each of these stories deals with a different culture. What similarities do you find among them? What substantive differences?

WRITING TOPICS

1. Describe the similarities or the differences between the mother's attempt to influence her daughter's life and your own family's attempt to influence yours.

2. Defend or attack this proposition: children should be allowed to choose their own paths.

HARI KUNZRU (B. 1969)

RAJ, BOHEMIAN 2008

We liked to do things casually. We called at the last minute. We messaged one another from our hand-held devices. Sometimes our names were on exclusive guest lists (though we were poor, we were beautiful, and people liked to have us around), but often we preferred to do something else—attend a friend's opening, drink in after-hours clubs or the room above a pub, trek off to remote suburbs to see a band play in a warehouse. We went dancing whenever we felt like it (none of us had regular jobs), and when we didn't we stayed in, watching movies and getting high. Someone always had something new or special—illegal prereleases of Hollywood blockbusters, dubs of 8-mm shorts from the nineteen-seventies. We watched next summer's exploding airplanes, Viennese Actionists masturbating onto operating tables. Raw meat and Nick Cage. Whatever we watched was, by definition, good, because we'd watched it, because it had belonged—at least, temporarily—to us. By the time the wider world caught up—which always happened, sooner or later—we'd usually got bored and moved on. We had long since given up mourning the loss of our various enthusiasms. We'd learned to discard them lightly. It was the same with clubs and bars. Wherever we went would be written about in magazines three or four months later. A single mention on a blog, and a place that had been spangled with beautiful, interesting faces would be swamped by young bankers in button-down shirts, nervously analyzing the room to see if they were having fun.

I must make it clear that we didn't plan for our lives to be this way. We despised trendies—fashion kids who tried too hard, perennially hoping to get hosed down by the paps or interviewed about their hair. With us, it wasn't a neurotic thing. We put on public events—salons, gigs, parties, shows. But once in a while, in the midst of our hectic social gyrations, we liked to do something for one another, something that didn't drain our energy, that made us feel private again.

My friend Sunita had a sense of theatre. She loved formality, intrigue. She had a certain archaic style, which would have been pompous or tediously ironic if it hadn't been for her cracked sense of humor, her painful, charming earnestness. For Sunita, the world was a kind of tragic game. When she threw one of her dinner parties, there were handmade invitations, a dress code. Once, she held a surrealist dinner, all diving suits and lobsters, over which she presided in a sheer green dress that was almost completely transparent. Another time, her theme was war. You might think it bad taste to hold a war-themed dinner party—now, of all times—but Sunita pulled it off. We arrived

361

carrying toy guns, wearing helmets daubed with bloodthirsty slogans. Some of us sniggered; others muttered about our hostess's poor taste. Yet somehow the evening, which should have been ludicrous, took on an unexpected aura of profundity. How? Sunita turned it into a wake. We raised our glasses to the millions of dead, to all the people who had had to endure what we merely watched on television. We had escaped, and we felt very guilty about it. Our childish carnival costumes were a sign of our shame. Donkeys' ears, dunces' caps.

When word got around that Sunita was holding another dinner, people immediately started angling for invitations. Everyone knew that she and I were close. Friends called, more or less begging me to get them in. I had to apologize and say that there was nothing I could do. It was a rule, an unofficial rule: no liggers and no hangers-on.

Sunita lived in an old textile warehouse, a big, echoing building that was due 5 to be converted into apartments. It had pools of water in the basement and a goods lift that clanked its way up to the third floor, where she'd set up home, plumbing in a kitchen and partitioning off a bedroom and a bathroom. The main space was a studio where she made her drawings, ramified patterns of abstract nested lines that had grown, in the time I'd known her, from tiny quadrants smaller than a paperback into huge things that rambled over sheets of paper in uncertain arcs. The landlord, a Greek named Constantine who had a dozen other properties in the area, was waiting for the market to improve before he redeveloped. In the meantime, Sunita lived rent free. She and Constantine had some kind of deal; I never knew the details. I would occasionally find him there when I went to visit, a portly man in a cashmere coat, sitting at her huge pine table shelling pistachios. He often brought nuts, sometimes cherries or boxes of gluey sweets. Sunita seemed able to handle him well enough.

The card for Sunita's latest dinner was minimal: a thick piece of cream-colored paper, with the words "Eating Is Honest" printed in an old-fashioned cursive font. Date and time, address, the cryptic instruction "Dress sincerely." I spent a long time debating what to wear. Sunita was typically tight-lipped about how her theme should be interpreted. "No, I won't help you," she said. "You know it would ruin everything." So I phoned around. No one had a clue. Vikram was his usual scatological self. "Toilets," he said. "She's going to do the thing out of the Buñuel film with the toilets. She's going to make all of us take a shit around a dining table and then eat in little locked cubicles."

I ended up adopting a sort of ironic nerd look, with thick, plastic-framed glasses and a clip-on tie. I wasn't very satisfied with it. I considered wearing my "own" clothes, on the ground that it would have been the most sincere response— to dress as if there were no dress code—but I couldn't work out what the most neutral choice would be. How to let everyone know that not only was I myself, I was *expressing* myself? Damn Sunita, I thought. Damn her clever ideas.

When I arrived at the warehouse, I found that she'd transformed the place into a kind of kitsch Christian heaven. White sheets were draped over the walls. A long table was arrayed with flowers and candelabra and lavish silver platters of food. When you got up close, you saw that it was all aluminum foil and spray paint, but by candlelight the scene looked sumptuous, romantic. Next to each place setting was a little hand mirror. Evidently, self-examination was part of the rubric. A number of old–fashioned medical illustrations were tacked incongruously on the wall, demonstrating the digestive system. Sunita was dressed in a white linen shift, and welcomed us with a short speech that, as far as I could tell, was composed of cut-up extracts from diet books. The food was simple and plain—fruit, cheeses, loaves of crusty bread—and while we ate it there was a program of entertainment. Michel read several of his poems. Hengist and Horsa played folk songs. A woman called Kevin did some kind of improvised dance, a flurry of arm-swirling that made me feel embarrassed and slightly uncomfortable. I took that as a good sign. If a piece of art makes me uncomfortable or, better still, angry, that seems to be a reason to pay attention to it.

It was all very pure and calming, an atmosphere that Faye de Way (when we finally managed to steer her away from the perennial topic of her operation) labeled "Baroque detox." If that was the effect our hostess was shooting for, it was slightly spoiled by her guests, who were all smoking like chimneys. "Chew twenty times!" Sunita admonished. "Once for each person at the table." I was seated next to Thanh, who'd cut her hair into a fringe. She looked like a Vietnamese Nico. I told her she was an inscrutable Oriental, and she told me I was a round-eyed pervert who would cry like a little baby when she cut my cock off. How we laughed! I was in a beautiful place, surrounded by talented people. No one was showing off, no one was being pushy, but somehow everyone shone. For one night, we were glorious.

Gradually, we all swapped chairs, clustering in groups to chat. Vikram stood 10 by the record player, putting on seven-inch singles. The table, which had looked so pristine, was strewn with a wreckage of empty bottles and ashtrays and plastic cups. Sunita sat down beside me and asked if I was enjoying myself. I told her I was. She hugged me and I kissed her on the lips. "You should save that for Thanh," she warned. "If you're not careful, Raj will get hold of her."

Raj was one of the few people at the party that I didn't know. He was good-looking, in that conventional way which seems to sabotage any chance of depth or credibility in a person. Are handsome men doomed to become skin-care-obsessed dullards simply because no one talks to them about serious things? Or are looks linked in some genetic way to intelligence? Raj's hair was gelled and teased into spikes. He wore a fussy beard, shaved into a fine line around the contours of his jaw. He was flirting with Thanh, which annoyed me, since I'd weighed things up and decided that I definitely wanted to go home with her. Still, I swallowed my distaste—after all, the guy was a friend of Sunita's—and was gratified to find that when I moved over to sit beside Thanh he ceded possession graciously enough.

As we chatted, I decided that he was actually rather charming. He even ventured an occasional shot at self-deprecation, which I certainly hadn't expected from someone like him. He'd brought along several bottles of vodka, an unfamiliar brand. He poured a shot for each of us, telling us that he'd just discovered it and rhapsodizing about how fragrant it was, how smooth. We talked about a number of other things—I can't remember what—and he took a few pictures with his phone, which I thought was lame. I mean, if you're too busy recording the experience, are you actually having it in the first place? I came away thinking that he was all right. A little suburban, a little bland, but sweet enough.

As I'd hoped, I went home with Thanh, and for a few weeks my memories of Sunita's party were filtered through my new relationship with her. We'd lie for hours on a rug on her studio floor, fucking and listening to music. One evening, while she got dressed to go back to the boyfriend with whom she had a complex but live-in relationship, I was idly typing our names into a search engine—sort of the digital equivalent of scratching initials into the trunk of a tree—when I came across a picture of the two of us, arms around each other, our cheeks mashed together as we blew kisses at the camera. In the foreground was a vodka bottle. For a moment, I couldn't work out where the photograph had been taken. Then, to my surprise, I realized that it was from Sunita's party. The site it was on was a corporate advertorial affair called something like Get-the-Taste, or Feel-the-Refreshment. There was a competition and an unpopulated "community." Across the screen scrolled similar photos of sexy young things in social situations, always with the vodka bottle in the shot. None of the pictures seemed posed.

It took me a minute or two to put it together, and when I did I wasn't happy. The bastard. The two-faced little fucker. Raj had been getting paid to take those pictures. He'd come to our party, and not just any party, to Sunita's party, the most beautiful gathering imaginable, and he'd shamelessly used it to sell us—to sell me—a product. The more I thought about it, the more angry I became. All that trash about the vodka being smooth: his whole conversation had been a sales pitch. It was creepy. More than creepy. It was sinister. Furious, I told Thanh to come over and have a look. She peered at the monitor, doing up her blouse.

"You came out pretty well," she said. "I like your glam-rock pout."   15

"But look at it. That bastard made us into an advert."

"Are we credited?"

"Only our first names."

"Shame. And I look so drunk."

"I suppose you—no, no, no! That's not the point. I mean, don't you feel   20 used?"

"What are you so upset about? You don't look nearly as wasted as me. It's hardly fair. You were downing those shots all night."

"But what about Raj? He never asked us whether we wanted to be on his damn vodka Web site. And all that patter about how smooth it tasted!"

"It *was* smooth."

"But to talk to people and secretly be trying to sell them something—isn't that, I don't know, unethical? Surely you agree that it's completely out of order."

"He didn't ask us to buy anything. He gave us free drinks."   25

"I know, but the point was to get us to buy something later on. That particular brand. We generate buzz. We recommend it to our friends, it becomes hip, blah-blah-blah."

"He should have given me image approval. Look at my chin! I'm going to have words next time I see him."

"For fuck's sake, Thanh! He was just using us. He wanted to make us into— into early adopters."

"But we *are* early adopters. I got a free phone a few months ago. All I had to do was watch a film and say how it made me feel."

"Jesus, you really are a shallow bitch." 30

Thanh and I more or less stopped seeing each other after that. I couldn't understand why she didn't feel more angry. Something precious to me had been violated, something I'd been holding on to. A secret pleasure that I hadn't wanted to throw into the big commercial vat with all the rest of the stuff—all the other moments and memories that get recycled into processed trends, like so many cheese triangles. Sunita's party had been private. That is the only way I can put it. The party had been private and he'd made it public.

I went to tell Sunita. "That's so Raj," she said.

I was confused. What did she mean, "so Raj"? Didn't she think that he'd betrayed her trust? Wasn't his behavior sleazy and underhanded?

"He was just being himself." She laughed. "He's a hustler. That's something you'll learn about Raj when you get to know him better."

One thing I must admit here: I find anger tricky. Anger is a very sincere 35 emotion. We live under the rule of cool, and we are expected to encounter the vicissitudes of the world with a certain degree of irony. Sincerity, as any hipster will tell you, is for awkward teens and people on SSRIs. Think about it—sincerity is gauche, gauche is boring, and boring is rude, so it's only a matter of ordinary politeness not to take things too seriously. But I really couldn't deal with Sunita laughing at me. When you're truly vexed, so vexed that it makes you incoherent and frustrated, there's nothing worse than being laughed at. You cunt, I thought. You fucking cunt. You're not who I thought you were.

Just as I was making up my mind to say something, I was saved by the intercom. Sunita buzzed up fat Constantine, who was hefting a box of mangoes in his meaty hands. He nodded to me, installed himself at the table, and started to peel and slice them. Sunita sat down beside him. I stood by the sink, my fists balled, so consumed with irritation that I couldn't think of anything to say. Constantine fed Sunita slices of mango, spearing them on the tip of his knife. She took them between her teeth, making eyes at him. Eventually, he looked up at me. "Don't let me interrupt," he said.

"He was talking about my friend Raj," Sunita explained, wiping her mouth with a napkin. "He's a bit of a wheeler-dealer."

"My kind of guy," Constantine said.

Sunita smiled at me. "Raj has the greatest car. Have you seen it?"

No, I hadn't. 40

"It's a big metallic purple thing, with under-floor lighting and 'Rude Mercs' written on the back window. It's hilarious."

"How did you and Raj meet?"

"Oh, around."

That was her standard euphemism for sleeping with someone. There had never been anything serious between Sunita and me, but all the same I felt a pang.

"I can't believe it, Sunny. He's an idiot."

"What's the problem?" Constantine asked. "Who is this Raj?"

"No one," Sunita said. "Just a guy who's been treading on someone's little tootsies."

Constantine gestured to his plate. "Try a mango," he said. "They're Alfonsos. Very sweet."

That night, I couldn't get to sleep. Round and round it went in my mind: Raj, vodka. Of course, it wasn't about the vodka. I'd enjoyed the damn vodka. And surely there was nothing intrinsically wrong with accepting a free drink. But there must come a time when you're allowed to stop being a consumer. There has to be some respite from all that choosing, a time, well, just to *be*. Sunita's party had been cool. Add as many quotation marks around the word as you like, but it was true. Most people never get the chance to attend a party like that. And, yes, there had been an element of performance to it. But I'd thought that we were just being cool for one another, to stave off boredom for a few hours, not to make some poor shell-suited kid on a housing estate feel jealous. I mean, jealousy just breeds resentment, right? Violence. People could get mugged because of Raj and his pictures. People could get raped. I started to look at my lifestyle in a new, fearful light. What did I have that people might want to take? Did people get burgled for their cultural capital?

I'd assumed that Raj's betrayal of trust would be obvious to everyone, but, to my shock, none of my friends seemed to see anything wrong. Otto was a long-haired German who shot music promos. "I need information, man," he said, shrugging. We were sitting in a sushi bar, drinking green tea. "I don't care how it gets to me."

"It's not information," I argued, waving my cup around. "The speed of light, the date of the moon landing. That's information."

"Uh, they recently invented this thing called the Internet."

"Piss off, Otto. You know what I mean."

"Get over yourself, man. You're acting so old-fashioned, like some kind of Communist. I have the right to perform acts of rational consumer choice: our ancestors fought wars for it. And I think I'm clever enough to filter a little bit of spin, don't you? Look, why don't you check out this band I'm working with?" He handed me a sleek little music player. I listened for a while, out of politeness.

"They're the final wave of New Wave," he explained. "After this, there will never be another reason to wear a Blondie T-shirt."

I nodded listlessly. I felt too despondent to argue anymore. Otto, smiling at me as he bounced his head to the beat of the music he couldn't hear, seemed not to notice. "I knew you'd like them. Aren't those headphones great, though? Optional noise cancellation. Amazing dynamic range. Particularly the bass— really rich, considering how small they are."

A sudden suspicion crossed my mind. But, no, this wasn't some suburban wide-boy. This was Otto.

And yet . . . Over the next few days, I started to notice something odd. Every time I met a friend, he or she would immediately make a recommendation, urge me to try something new. Lucas had been to a club on the other side of town and insisted that it was the best night out he'd had in ages. Janine almost forced me to take home a bottle of her "new favorite nutritional supplement." At first, I shrugged it off. But, deep down, I knew that it had something to do with Raj and his vodka. Every night, I'd turn the incident over in my mind. I swallowed Ativan and Valium and Paxil (I had a compliant doctor), hoping that my anxiety would pass. It didn't. There was Joe and his new running shoes. Razia's bike. All my friends seemed to be dropping snippets of advertising copy into their conversation, short messages from their sponsors. They were constantly stating preferences for particular brands, dishing out free samples.

Perhaps nothing had changed. We'd always shared new music with one another or recommended places to eat. But now there was something different. A tone? It was hard to say. I found myself wondering if Sasha was telling me that the sushi at Bar Fugu was "to die for" because he meant it or because it was a snappy slogan. Vikram started talking to me at nauseating length about tires. Steel radials, depth of tread. I hadn't even known that Vikram had a car. When Wei Lin began rhapsodizing about the streaming capabilities of his new video projector, I snapped.

"Don't start this shit on me, Wei. I'm sick of it." 60

"What?"

"This sales patter. I can't take it anymore. Frankly, you disgust me."

"I what?"

"It's not even as if you need the money. You're loaded."

"I don't understand why you're being so hostile." 65

"Your daddy in Shanghai owns a fucking construction company. We all know, Wei. It's not a secret. So why do you need to do this? There's no reason! Is it fun? Does it get you laid?"

Afterward, he told everyone that I'd physically threatened him. He said to Thanh that he thought I might be on crack.

I was shaken up. I tried to get on with my life, working on my designs, speaking to people—even going out, just as if things were normal. But they weren't. I felt I was under immense mental pressure, in constant danger of some unforeseen catastrophic event, a psychological bridge collapse. I found parties increasingly traumatic: the bombardment of messages, the pitches coming at me from every side. It was impossible to untangle what was being said because the speaker felt or believed it from what was merely repetition. When were people being themselves and when were they acting? I began, ever so slightly, to doubt the reality of other minds. People seemed to zone in and out of existence. Sometimes they were fully present, animated by something original and real. But mostly they were just zombies, empty vessels operated by corporate remote control.

I tell you, I was afraid. Becoming a hermit was looking like a good option. A cave in the Hebrides. The lonely sea and the sky. I was ready to batten down the hatches and crawl into the submarine of my own paranoia when I met Zoe. She understood me immediately, saw that my life had been stripped of all humor, all scope and playfulness, that it was irising down to the enforced sincerity of the locked ward.

Zoe didn't like being in physical proximity to too many people, because she thought it made her sick, though as far as I could tell she was a perfectly healthy person. She didn't go outside much, and always went to the shops with a tub of antiseptic wipes in her bag. On bad days, she wore a face mask. Despite her eccentricities, she was no introvert, was a lively presence on various online sites and game worlds. We spent a lot of time indoors, smoking and talking. She wasn't physically beautiful, but I didn't want someone beautiful; I wanted someone who made me feel safe, which Zoe did—until the night I mentioned her ring.

It was a large copper band with a number of tiny stones set into it, a trashy-looking thing with a vaguely *Lord of the Rings* aesthetic. I asked her what it was.

"This?" she said absent-mindedly, sticking one hand out as she manipulated a joystick with the other, careering through some virtual maze. "It's an appetite-reduction ring. See the tiny gems? There are nine of them. It helps correct biochemical imbalances in the body by reverse-actuating the ionic flow in my bloodstream. You should get one."

Zombie-speech. She had reeled it off without a pause.

"Oh, no, Zoe."

She paused her game. "What?"

"Not you, too."

"I don't understand. Are you all right?"

"Zoe, I'm going to ask you something, and you'd better tell me the truth."

"What are you talking about? You look pale."

"Is someone paying you to say that stuff?"

She giggled. "Sorry, babe, it just pops out sometimes. I didn't mean to pitch you. I'm supposed only to do it to my girlfriends."

"What?"

"Ignore me. You know how hard it is to keep track of one's placements."

"Placements?"

"Placements. Why are you making that face? You're looking at me like I'm some kind of freak."

"You have a lot of—placements?"

"Oh, don't get on your high horse. You don't work, either. What do you do for cash? If a girl doesn't want a straight job, she has to monetize her social network."

I'm not proud of what I did then. I just couldn't control myself. I slapped her. I told her that she was a fake, a zombie. Before I walked out, I took a last look at her, pathetically scrubbing at her cheek with a cloth.

At my flat, I looked at the presents she'd bought me during our short relationship—a pair of shoes, a scarf. I decided to give them to charity. I found a cardboard box, but it was big and the shoes and scarf didn't take up much space, so I added a few more things. The experience was oddly pleasurable.

Once I'd started, it was hard to stop. Soon I'd filled several boxes, then several more. They were too heavy to carry to the charity shop, so I just left them on the street outside my building. For the rest of the day, I watched from the balcony as people stopped to rummage and carry things away. That night, I put the rest of my stuff out. All of it—clothes, books and records, furniture, even the cans of food from my kitchen cupboards. Everything I owned. By the following afternoon, it was all gone.

I spent the next couple of days squatting on my haunches in a corner of my 90 empty flat. Something in me had snapped, was broken beyond repair. My taste had been central to my identity. I'd cultivated it, kept it fed and watered like an exotic flowering plant. Now I realized that what I thought had been an expression of my innermost humanity was nothing but a cloud of lifestyle signals, available to anyone at the click of a mouse. How had this happened?

I couldn't understand. There had to be something else. What was a personality if it wasn't a drop-down menu, a collection of likes and dislikes? And now that my possessions were gone, what would I put in their place? Who was I without my private pressings, my limited editions, my vintage one-offs? How could I signal to potential allies across the vast black reaches of interpersonal space?

It was then that I realized I'd been robbed. I'd been forcibly expropriated from myself. And who had done this to me? Who was the cause of all my loss and pain? I stormed around to Sunita's to ask for Raj's address. The door was opened by Constantine, wearing a quilted paisley dressing gown.

"She's out," he said, tightening the cord around his paunch. "She says don't come around no more." He burped.

"Sunita doesn't want to see me?"

"That's right. She says you have a bad energy." 95

I didn't know quite how to process that information. "Whatever. For now, I just need a number for Raj."

"Raj is it? He's a nice guy."

"So you know him?"

"Sure. Everyone knows Raj."

"So how do I get hold of him?" 100

"I've got his card somewhere."

He disappeared and came back holding a business card. On it was written, in a cheesy futuristic font, "Raj, Bohemian." I couldn't tell if it was a company name or a job description. The office address was close by.

"Thanks."

Constantine looked at me solicitously. "You know your problem?"

"Tell me my problem." 105

"Stress. You should get a massage. I'll give you another number. It's local. The girls are very attentive."

I turned my back on him and pressed the call button on the lift.

The trip to Raj's office passed in a dream. I was a ghost, floating through a world of moving signage, people carrying shopping bags, immigrants handing out flyers for bars and language schools. I went into a department store, dazzled by chrome and glass and brushed steel. It was a palace of mirrors, zombie heaven. Girls at the makeup counter, dressed like slutty pharmacists. Rich men with ski tans fingering cashmere sweaters. In the housewares department was a display cabinet of knives, gleaming with surgical allure. I bought the largest and headed back up the escalator to the teeming street.

Raj's office wasn't what I'd expected. I was imagining—I don't know what I was imagining. A flashy loft. A lifestyle statement. It turned out to be a shared suite, a dreary place with grubby tube lights and contract carpeting, where freelancers rented desks, huddling together to make themselves feel less alone. One or two people looked up from their work as I walked in. I felt dizzy, disoriented, carrying the knife wrapped in a yellow plastic bag.

"Hey, man! Good to see you!"   110

Raj was standing up behind a desk piled high with paper and promotional knickknacks. Across the top of his computer monitor paraded a little line of toys. He looked tired and drab, his eyes rimmed with dark circles, a reddish stain disfiguring his crisp white polo shirt. Raj, my nemesis. So ordinary. I had gone there to kill him, to make him into nothing for having made me into nothing. But now that he stood in front of me he was just a guy with a greasy forehead and a pimple on his top lip. Now that I saw the reality of his life, the plastic bags full of free samples, the half-eaten sandwich balanced on a teetering stack of magazines, I knew that any confrontation would be absurd. I sank down onto a swivel chair and spun in little half circles, while he hovered over me, this person who'd polluted my whole life without even realizing it. Someone else was there. A woman. I think he was trying to introduce her to me. I shook my head mutely. What was I? A sorting device. A filter. A human bivalve, culture accreting in me like a mercury deposit. I looked around the office at the young workers wearing headphones, typing, talking into phones with their feet on their desks. This was the world, just the same indoors and out, a place of total nullity. How could anything make any difference? Unless you managed to keep your head underwater, to immerse yourself in the endless metonymic shuffling of objects, it would be intolerable.

"You look awful," Raj said. "Are you feeling O.K.?"

I stared up at him. He was holding out a glass of water.

"Is it good?" I asked.

He shook his head, not understanding.   115

"Is it better than other brands of water?"

"It's just water. From the tap."

I took a sip.

"Are you sick?" he asked gently.

"No."   120

"What is it, then?"

I closed my eyes. "I'm not sure. I think I might be bored."

"Ah."

"Is there anything going on tonight?"

He smiled and started to tell me about a party, a guest list, a secret venue. I   125
took out my phone to punch in the contact number.

FOR ANALYSIS

1. Why does the **narrator** get rid of all his possessions? At the end of the story, do you think he will continue to live without things?

2. What is it that makes the narrator want to kill Raj? Why does he not follow through with his plan?

3. Why do you think Kunzru chose to use Raj's name in the title? How do you think the second part of the title is meant to be taken?

MAKING CONNECTIONS

1. Melville's "Bartleby, the Scrivener" (p. 291) and Kafka's "A Hunger Artist" (p. 319) both feature eponymous **protagonists** who, in the words of Bartleby, "prefer not to." Compare the main character in "Raj, Bohemian" to one or both of these **characters**. How are they similar, and how are they different? Compare especially the things they prefer not to do and their reasons for not doing them.

2. Compare "Raj, Bohemian" to any or all of the selections in "Connecting Poems: Revisiting Fairy Tales" (p. 169). How does each of these works take up the issue of conformity?

WRITING TOPICS

1. Write an essay in which you reflect on how your tastes—the things you wear, carry, listen to, watch—define who you are. How did you come to like these things? What do you think they say about you?

2. Write an essay in which you discuss the workings of identification in this story. How do you feel about the **characters**—the **narrator,** and Sunita, and their circle of friends? Do you find them ridiculous or sad or likable? Do you see yourself in them, or do you see yourself as completely different? What do you think the author wants you to feel about them? why?

CONNECTING STORIES:
SUPERANTIHEROES

The hero, a figure as old as mythology, embodies the ideals of cultures: their self-images, their hopes, and their fantasies. Superman, for instance, represented the immigrant American Dream with his arrival from another planet and his bulletproof invincibility. The power of heroes to embody ideals, however, can sometimes be undermined by the questioning of those same ideals in the wake of historical change. A man in patriotic-colored tights was perceived differently during the Vietnam War—or the war in Iraq—than he was at the height of World War II. As you read Harlan Ellison's and Jonathan Lethem's stories, think about the role of the hero—and the superhero—and think about the connections between what makes that role possible and what makes it impossible.

HARLAN ELLISON (B. 1934)

"REPENT, HARLEQUIN!"
SAID THE TICKTOCKMAN 1965

There are always those who ask, what is it all about? For those who need to ask, for those who need points sharply made, who need to know "where it's at," this:

> *The mass of men serve the state thus, not as men mainly, but as machines, with their bodies. They are the standing army, and the militia, jailors, constables, posse comitatus, etc. In most cases there is no free exercise whatever of the judgment or of the moral sense; but they put themselves on a level with wood and earth and stones; and wooden men can perhaps be manufactured that will serve the purpose as well. Such command no more respect than men of straw or a lump of dirt. They have the same sort of worth only as horses and dogs. Yet such as these even are commonly esteemed good citizens. Others—as most legislators, politicians, lawyers, ministers, and officeholders—serve the state chiefly with their heads; and, as they rarely make any moral distinctions, they are as likely to serve the Devil, without intending it, as God. A very few, as heroes, patriots, martyrs, reformers in the great sense, and men, serve the state with their consciences also, and so necessarily resist it for the most part; and they are commonly treated as enemies by it.*

> Henry David Thoreau
> CIVIL DISOBEDIENCE

That is the heart of it. Now begin in the middle, and later learn the beginning; the end will take care of itself.

But because it was the very world it was, the very world they had allowed it to *become*, for months his activities did not come to the alarmed attention of The Ones Who Kept The Machine Functioning Smoothly, the ones who poured the very best butter over the cams and mainsprings of the culture. Not until it had become obvious that somehow, someway, he had become a notoriety, a celebrity, perhaps even a hero for (what Officialdom inescapably tagged) "an emotionally disturbed segment of the populace," did they turn it over to the Ticktockman and his legal machinery. But by then, because it was the very world it was, and they had no way to predict he would happen—possibly a strain of disease long-defunct, now, suddenly, reborn in a system where immunity had been forgotten, had lapsed—he had been allowed to become too real. Now he had form and substance.

He had become a *personality*, something they had filtered out of the system many decades before. But there it was, and there *he* was, a very definitely imposing personality. In certain circles—middle-class circles—it was thought disgusting. Vulgar ostentation. Anarchistic. Shameful. In others, there was only sniggering: those strata where thought is subjugated to form and ritual, niceties, proprieties. But down below, ah, down below, where the people always needed their saints and sinners, their bread and circuses, their heroes and villains, he was considered a Bolivar; a Napoleon; a Robin Hood; a Dick Bong (Ace of Aces); a Jesus; a Jomo Kenyatta.

And at the top—where, like socially-attuned Shipwreck Kellys, every tremor 5 and vibration threatening to dislodge the wealthy, powerful and titled from their flagpoles—he was considered a menace; a heretic; a rebel; a disgrace; a peril. He was known down the line, to the very heartmeat core, but the important reactions were high above and far below. At the very top, at the very bottom.

So his file was turned over, along with his time card and his cardioplate, to the office of the Ticktockman.

The Ticktockman: very much over six feet tall, often silent, a soft purring man when things went timewise. The Ticktockman.

Even in the cubicles of the hierarchy, where fear was generated, seldom suffered, he was called the Ticktockman. But no one called him that to his mask.

You don't call a man a hated name, not when that man, behind his mask, is capable of revoking the minutes, the hours, the days and nights, the years of your life. He was called the Master Timekeeper to his mask. It was safer that way.

"This is *what* he is," said the Ticktockman with genuine softness, "but not 10 *who* he is. This time-card I'm holding in my left hand has a name on it, but it is the name of *what* he is, not *who* he is. The cardioplate here in my right hand is also named, but not *whom* named, merely *what* named. Before I can exercise proper revocation, I have to know *who* this *what* is."

To his staff, all the ferrets, all the loggers, all the finks, all the commex, even the mineez, he said, "Who is this Harlequin?"

He was not purring smoothly. Timewise, it was jangle.

However, it *was* the longest speech they had ever heard him utter at one time, the staff, the ferrets, the loggers, the finks, the commex, but not the mineez, who usually weren't around to know, in any case. But even they scurried to find out.

Who is the Harlequin?

High above the third level of the city, he crouched on the humming 15 aluminum-frame platform of the air-boat (foof! air-boat, indeed! swizzleskid is what it was, with a tow-rack jerry-rigged) and he stared down at the neat Mondrian arrangement of the buildings.

Somewhere nearby, he could hear the metronomic left-right-left of the 2:47 PM shift, entering the Timkin roller-bearing plant in their sneakers. A minute later, precisely, he heard the softer right-left-right of the 5:00 AM formation, going home.

An elfin grin spread across his tanned features, and his dimples appeared for a moment. Then, scratching at his thatch of auburn hair, he shrugged within his motley, as though girding himself for what came next, and threw the joystick forward, and bent into the wind as the air-boat dropped. He skimmed over a slidewalk, purposely dropping a few feet to crease the tassels of the ladies of fashion, and—inserting thumbs in large ears—he stuck out his tongue, rolled his eyes, and went wugga-wugga-wugga. It was a minor diversion. One pedestrian skittered and tumbled, sending parcels every-whichway, another wet herself, a third keeled slantwise and the walk was stopped automatically by the servitors till she could be resuscitated. It was a minor diversion.

Then he swirled away on a vagrant breeze, and was gone. Hi-ho. As he rounded the cornice of the Time-Motion Study Building, he saw the shift, just boarding the slidewalk. With practiced motion and an absolute conservation of movement, they sidestepped up onto the slow-strip and (in a chorus line reminiscent of a Busby Berkeley film of the antediluvian 1930s) advanced across the strips ostrich-walking till they were lined up on the expresstrip.

Once more, in anticipation, the elfin grin spread, and there was a tooth missing back there on the left side. He dipped, skimmed, and swooped over them; and then, scrunching about on the air-boat, he released the holding pins that fastened shut the ends of the home-made pouring troughs that kept his cargo from dumping prematurely. And as he pulled the trough-pins, the air-boat slid over the factory workers and one hundred and fifty thousand dollars' worth of jelly beans cascaded down on the expresstrip.

Jelly beans! Millions and billions of purples and yellows and greens and 20 licorice and grape and raspberry and mint and round and smooth and crunchy outside and soft-mealy inside and sugary and bouncing jouncing tumbling clittering clattering skittering fell on the heads and shoulders and hardhats and carapaces of the Timkin workers, tinkling on the slidewalk and bouncing away and rolling about underfoot and filling the sky on their way down with all the colors of joy and childhood and holidays, coming down in a steady rain, a solid wash, a torrent of color and sweetness out of the sky from above, and entering a universe of sanity and metronomic order with quite-mad coocoo newness. Jelly beans!

The shift workers howled and laughed and were pelted, and broke ranks, and the jelly beans managed to work their way into the mechanism of the slidewalks after which there was a hideous scraping as the sound of a million fingernails rasped down a quarter of a million blackboards, followed by a coughing and a sputtering, and then the slidewalks all stopped and everyone was dumped thisawayandthataway in a jackstraw tumble, still laughing and popping little jelly bean eggs of childish color into their mouths. It was a holiday, and a jollity, an absolute insanity, a giggle. But . . .

The shift was delayed seven minutes.

They did not get home for seven minutes.

The master schedule was thrown off by seven minutes.

Quotas were delayed by inoperative slidewalks for seven minutes.   25

He had tapped the first domino in the line, and one after another, like chik chik chik, the others had fallen.

The System had been seven minutes' worth of disrupted. It was a tiny matter, one hardly worthy of note, but in a society where the single driving force was order and unity and equality and promptness and clocklike precision and attention to the clock, reverence of the gods of the passage of time, it was a disaster of major importance.

So he was ordered to appear before the Ticktockman. It was broadcast across every channel of the communications web. He was ordered to be *there* at 7:00 dammit on time. And they waited, and they waited, but he didn't show up till almost ten-thirty, at which time he merely sang a little song about moonlight in a place no one had ever heard of, called Vermont, and vanished again. But they had all been waiting since seven, and it wrecked *hell* with their schedules. So the question remained: Who is the Harlequin?

But the *unasked* question (more important of the two) was: how did we get *into* this position, where a laughing, irresponsible japer of jabberwocky and jive could disrupt our entire economic and cultural life with a hundred and fifty thousand dollars' worth of jelly beans . . .

Jelly for God's sake *beans!* This is madness! Where did he get the money to 30 buy a hundred and fifty thousand dollars' worth of jelly beans? (They knew it would have cost that much, because they had a team of Situation Analysts pulled off another assignment, and rushed to the slidewalk scene to sweep up and count the candies, and produce findings, which disrupted *their* schedules and threw their entire branch at least a day behind.) Jelly beans! Jelly . . . *beans?* Now wait a second—a second accounted for—no one has manufactured jelly beans for over a hundred years. Where did he get jelly beans?

That's another good question. More than likely it will never be answered to your complete satisfaction. But then, how many questions ever are?

.   .   .

The middle you know. Here is the beginning. How it starts:

A DESK PAD. DAY FOR DAY, AND TURN EACH DAY. 9:00—OPEN THE MAIL. 9:45—APPOINTMENT WITH PLANNING COMMISSION BOARD. 10:30—DISCUSS INSTALLATION PROGRESS CHARTS WITH J.L. 11:45—PRAY FOR RAIN. 12:00—LUNCH. *AND SO IT GOES.*

"I'm sorry, Miss Grant, but the time for interviews was set at 2:30, and it's almost five now. I'm sorry you're late, but those are the rules. You'll have to wait till next year to submit application for this college again." *And so it goes.*

The 10:10 local stops at Cresthaven, Galesville, Tonawanda Junction, Selby, and 35 Farnhurst, but not at Indiana City, Lucasville and Colton, except on Sunday. The 10:35 express stops at Galesville, Selby, and Indiana City, except on Sundays & Holidays, at which time it stops at . . . *and so it goes.*

```
"I couldn't wait, Fred. I had to be at Pierre Car-
tain's by 3:00, and you said you'd meet me under the
clock in the terminal at 2:45, and you weren't there, so
I had to go on. You're always late, Fred. If you'd been
there, we could have sewed it up together, but as it
was, well, I took the order alone . . ." And so it goes.
```

Dear Mr. and Mrs. Atterley: In reference to your son Gerold's constant tardiness, I am afraid we will have to suspend him from school unless some more reliable method can be instituted guaranteeing he will arrive at his classes on time. Granted he is an exemplary student, and his marks are high, his constant flouting of the schedules of this school makes it impractical to maintain him in a system where the other children seem capable of getting where they are supposed to be on time *and so it goes.*

YOU CANNOT VOTE UNLESS YOU APPEAR AT 8:45 AM.

"I don't care if the script is *good*, I need it Thursday!"

CHECK-OUT TIME IS 2:00 PM.   40

"You got here late. The job's taken. Sorry."

YOUR SALARY HAS BEEN DOCKED FOR TWENTY MINUTES TIME LOST.

"God, what time is it, I've gotta run!"

And so it goes. And so it goes. And so it goes. And so it goes goes goes goes goes tick tock tick tock tick tock and one day we no longer let time serve us, we serve time and we are slaves of the schedule, worshippers of the sun's passing, bound into a life predicated on restrictions because the system will not function if we don't keep the schedule tight.

Until it becomes more than a minor inconvenience to be late. It becomes a   45
sin. Then a crime. Then a crime punishable by this:

> EFFECTIVE 15 JULY 2389 12:00:00 midnight, the office of the Master
> Timekeeper will require all citizens to submit their time-cards and car-
> dioplates for processing. In accordance with Statute 555-7-SGH-999
> governing the revocation of time per capita, all cardioplates will be
> keyed to the individual holder and—

What they had done was devise a method of curtailing the amount of life a
person could have. If he was ten minutes late, he lost ten minutes of his life. An
hour was proportionately worth more revocation. If someone was consistently
tardy, he might find himself, on a Sunday night, receiving a communiqué from
the Master Timekeeper that his time had run out, and he would be "turned off"
at high noon on Monday, please straighten your affairs, sir, madame, or bisex.

And so, by this simple scientific expedient (utilizing a scientific process held
dearly secret by the Ticktockman's office) the System was maintained. It was
the only expedient thing to do. It was, after all, patriotic. The schedules had to
be met. After all, there *was* a war on!

But, wasn't there always?

"Now that is really disgusting," the Harlequin said, when Pretty Alice   50
showed him the wanted poster. "Disgusting and *highly* improbable. After all,
this isn't the Day of the Desperado. A *wanted* poster!"

"You know," Pretty Alice noted, "you speak with a great deal of inflection."

"I'm sorry," said the Harlequin, humbly.

"No need to be sorry. You're always saying 'I'm sorry.' You have such massive
guilt, Everett, it's really very sad."

"I'm sorry," he said again, then pursed his lips so the dimples appeared
momentarily. He hadn't wanted to say that at all. "I have to go out again. I have
to *do* something."

Pretty Alice slammed her coffee-bulb down on the counter. "Oh for God's   55
sake, Everett, can't you stay home just *one* night! Must you always be out in that
ghastly clown suit, running around annoying people?"

"I'm—" He stopped, and clapped the jester's hat onto his auburn thatch
with a tiny tinkling of bells. He rose, rinsed out his coffee-bulb at the spray,
and put it into the dryer for a moment. "I have to go."

She didn't answer. The faxbox was purring, and she pulled a sheet out,
read it, threw it toward him on the counter. "It's about you. Of course. You're
ridiculous."

He read it quickly. It said the Ticktockman was trying to locate him. He
didn't care, he was going out to be late again. At the door, dredging for an exit
line, he hurled back petulantly, "Well, *you* speak with inflection, *too!*"

Pretty Alice rolled her pretty eyes heavenward. "You're ridiculous."

The Harlequin stalked out, slamming the door, which sighed shut softly, and   60
locked itself.

There was a gentle knock, and Pretty Alice got up with an exhalation of exasperated breath, and opened the door. He stood there. "I'll be back about ten-thirty, okay?"

She pulled a rueful face. "Why do you tell me that? Why? You *know* you'll be late! You *know* it! You're *always* late, so why do you tell me these dumb things?" She closed the door.

On the other side, the Harlequin nodded to himself. *She's right. She's always right. I'll be late. I'm always late. Why* do *I tell her these dumb things?*

He shrugged again, and went off to be late once more.

He had fired off the firecracker rockets that said: I will attend the 115th annual International Medical Association Invocation at 8:00 PM precisely. I do hope you will all be able to join me. 65

The words had burned in the sky, and of course the authorities were there, lying in wait for him. They assumed, naturally, that he would be late. He arrived twenty minutes early, while they were setting up the spiderwebs to trap and hold him. Blowing a large bullhorn, he frightened and unnerved them so, their own moisturized encirclement webs sucked closed, and they were hauled up, kicking and shrieking, high above the amphitheater's floor. The Harlequin laughed and laughed, and apologized profusely. The physicians, gathered in solemn conclave, roared with laughter, and accepted the Harlequin's apologies with exaggerated bowing and posturing, and a merry time was had by all, who thought the Harlequin was a regular foofaraw in fancy pants; all, that is, but the authorities, who had been sent out by the office of the Ticktockman; they hung there like so much dockside cargo, hauled up above the floor of the amphitheater in a most unseemly fashion.

(In another part of the same city where the Harlequin carried on his "activities," totally unrelated in every way to what concerns us here, save that it illustrates the Ticktockman's power and import, a man named Marshall Delahanty received his turn-off notice from the Ticktockman's office. His wife received the notification from the gray-suited minee who delivered it, with the traditional "look of sorrow" plastered hideously across his face. She knew what it was, even without unsealing it. It was a billet-doux of immediate recognition to everyone these days. She gasped, and held it as though it were a glass slide tinged with botulism, and prayed it was not for her. Let it be for Marsh, she thought, brutally, realistically, or one of the kids, but not for me, please dear God, not for me. And then she opened it, and it *was* for Marsh, and she was at one and the same time horrified and relieved. The next trooper in the line had caught the bullet. "Marshall," she screamed, "Marshall! Termination, Marshall! OhmiGod, Marshall, whattl we do, whattl we do, Marshall omigodmarshall . . ." and in their home that night was the sound of tearing paper and fear, and the stink of madness went up the flue and there was nothing, absolutely nothing they could do about it.

(But Marshall Delahanty tried to run. And early the next day, when turn-off time came, he was deep in the Canadian forest two hundred miles away, and the office of the Ticktockman blanked his cardioplate, and Marshall

Delahanty keeled over, running, and his heart stopped, and the blood dried up on its way to his brain, and he was dead that's all. One light went out on the sector map in the office of the Master Timekeeper, while notification was entered for fax reproduction, and Georgette Delahanty's name was entered on the dole roles till she could remarry. Which is the end of the footnote, and all the point that need be made, except don't laugh, because that is what would happen to the Harlequin if ever the Ticktockman found out his real name. It isn't funny.)

The shopping level of the city was thronged with the Thursday-colors of the buyers. Women in canary yellow chitons and men in pseudo-Tyrolean outfits that were jade and leather and fit very tightly, save for the balloon pants.

When the Harlequin appeared on the still-being-constructed shell of the new Efficiency Shopping Center, his bullhorn to his elfishly-laughing lips, everyone pointed and stared, and he berated them: 70

"Why let them order you about? Why let them tell you to hurry and scurry like ants or maggots? Take your time! Saunter a while! Enjoy the sunshine, enjoy the breeze, let life carry you at your own pace! Don't be slaves of time, it's a helluva way to die, slowly, by degrees . . . down with the Ticktockman!"

Who's the nut? most of the shoppers wanted to know. Who's the nut oh wow I'm gonna be late I gotta run . . .

And the construction gang on the Shopping Center received an urgent order from the office of the Master Timekeeper that the dangerous criminal known as the Harlequin was atop their spire, and their aid was urgently needed in apprehending him. The work crew said no, they would lose time on their construction schedule, but the Ticktockman managed to pull the proper threads of governmental webbing, and they were told to cease work and catch that nitwit up there on the spire; up there with the bullhorn. So a dozen and more burly workers began climbing into their construction platforms, releasing the a-grav plates, and rising toward the Harlequin.

After the debacle (in which, through the Harlequin's attention to personal safety, no one was seriously injured), the workers tried to reassemble, and assault him again, but it was too late. He had vanished. It had attracted quite a crowd, however, and the shopping cycle was thrown off by hours, simply hours. The purchasing needs of the system were therefore falling behind, and so measures were taken to accelerate the cycle for the rest of the day, but it got bogged down and speeded up and they sold too many float-valves and not nearly enough wegglers, which meant that the popli ratio was off, which made it necessary to rush cases and cases of spoiling Smash-O to stores that usually needed a case only every three or four hours. The shipments were bollixed, the transshipments were misrouted, and in the end, even the swizzleskid industries felt it.

"Don't come back till you have him!" the Ticktockman said, very quietly, 75 very sincerely, extremely dangerously.

They used dogs. They used probes. They used cardioplate crossoffs. They used teepers. They used bribery. They used stiktytes. They used intimidation. They used torment. They used torture. They used finks. They used cops. They used search&seizure. They used fallaron. They used betterment incentive. They used fingerprints. They used the Bertillon system. They used cunning. They used guile. They used treachery. They used Raoul Mitgong, but he didn't help much. They used applied physics. They used techniques of criminology.

And what the hell: they caught him.

After all, his name was Everett C. Marm, and he wasn't much to begin with, except a man who had no sense of time.

"Repent, Harlequin!" said the Ticktockman.

"Get stuffed!" the Harlequin replied, sneering.   80

"You've been late a total of sixty-three years, five months, three weeks, two days, twelve hours, forty-one minutes, fifty-nine seconds, point oh three six one one one microseconds. You've used up everything you can, and more. I'm going to turn you off."

"Scare someone else. I'd rather be dead than live in a dumb world with a bogeyman like you."

"It's my job."

"You're full of it. You're a tyrant. You have no right to order people around and kill them if they show up late."

"You can't adjust. You can't fit in."   85

"Unstrap me, and I'll fit my fist into your mouth."

"You're a nonconformist."

"That didn't used to be a felony."

"It is now. Live in the world around you."

"I hate it. It's a terrible world."   90

"Not everyone thinks so. Most people enjoy order."

"I don't, and most of the people I know don't."

"That's not true. How do you think we caught you?"

"I'm not interested."

"A girl named Pretty Alice told us who you were."   95

"That's a lie."

"It's true. You unnerve her. She wants to belong; she wants to conform; I'm going to turn you off."

"Then do it already, and stop arguing with me."

"I'm not going to turn you off."

"You're an idiot!"   100

"Repent, Harlequin!" said the Ticktockman.

"Get stuffed."

So they sent him to Coventry. And in Coventry they worked him over. It was just like what they did to Winston Smith in NINETEEN EIGHTY-FOUR, which was a book none of them knew about, but the techniques are really quite ancient, and so they did it to Everett C. Marm; and one day, quite a long time later, the Harlequin appeared on the communications web, appearing elfin and dimpled and bright-eyed, and not at all brainwashed, and he said he had been wrong, that it was a good, a very good thing indeed, to belong, to be right on time hip-ho and away we go, and everyone stared up at him on the public screens that covered an entire city block, and they said to themselves, well, you see, he was just a nut after all, and if that's the way the system is run, then let's do it that way, because it doesn't pay to fight city hall, or in this case, the Ticktockman. So Everett C. Marm was destroyed, which was a loss, because of what Thoreau said earlier, but you can't make an omelet without breaking a few eggs, and in every revolution a few die who shouldn't, but they have to, because that's the way it happens, and if you make only a little change, then it seems to be worthwhile. Or, to make the point lucidly:

"Uh, excuse me, sir, I, uh, don't know how to uh, to uh, tell you this, but you were three minutes late. The schedule is a little, uh, bit off."

He grinned sheepishly.   105

"That's ridiculous!" murmured the Ticktockman behind his mask. "Check your watch." And then he went into his office, going *mrmee, mrmee, mrmee, mrmee.*

FOR ANALYSIS

1. What are the connotations of the names *Harlequin* and *Everett C. Marm*? Is the contrast between the names similar to that between, say, *Superman* and *Clark Kent*?

2. What is it about his society that drives Everett C. Marm to rebel?

3. What is Pretty Alice's role in the story?

4. Explain the final section of the story (paras. 104–6). Has the Ticktockman triumphed?

MAKING CONNECTIONS

1. Compare the statement this story makes about the human spirit with that made in Le Guin's "The Ones Who Walk Away from Omelas" (p. 346). Does Everett C. Marm share any of the attributes of the ones who walk away from Omelas?

2. Compare Everett C. Marm and the **narrator** in Ellison's "Battle Royal" (p. 327) as rebels. Who is more successful as a rebel? As a conformist? Will the narrator of "Battle Royal" grow up to be like the Harlequin?

WRITING TOPICS

1. Carefully read the passage (para. 1) taken from Thoreau's "Civil Disobedience." Write an essay explaining why you do or do not agree (in whole or in part) with Thoreau's view of "the state" and with his classification of citizens as those who serve the state with their "bodies," those who serve it with their "heads," and those who serve it with their "consciences." Where would you place Everett C. Marm?

2. Characterize Pretty Alice. Why does she turn Everett in?

JONATHAN LETHEM   (B. 1964)

SUPER GOAT MAN   2004

When Super Goat Man moved into the commune on our street, I was ten years old. Though I liked superheroes, I wasn't familiar with Super Goat Man. His presence didn't mean much to me or to the other kids in the neighborhood. For us, as we ran and screamed and played our secret games on the sidewalk, Super Goat Man was only another of the guys who sat on stoops in sleeveless undershirts on hot summer days, watching the slow progress of life on the block. The two little fleshy horns on his forehead didn't make him especially interesting. We weren't struck by his fall from grace, out of the world of comic-book heroes, among which he had been at best a minor star, to land here in Cobble Hill, Brooklyn, in a single room in what was basically a dorm for college dropouts, a hippie group shelter, any more than we were by the tufts of extra hair at his throat and behind his ears. We had eyes only for Spider-Man and Batman in those days, superheroes in two dimensions, with lunchboxes and television shows and theme songs. Super Goat Man had none of those.

It was our dads who cared. They were unmistakably drawn to the strange figure who'd moved to our block, as though for them he represented some lost possibility in their own lives. My father in particular seemed fascinated with Super Goat Man, though he disguised this interest by acting as though it was on my behalf. One day toward the end of that summer, he and I walked to Montague Street to visit the comics shop there. This was a tiny storefront filled with long white boxes packed with carefully archived comics, protected by plastic bags and cardboard backing. The boxes contained ancient runs of back issues of titles I'd heard of, as well as thousands of other comics featuring characters I'd never encountered. The shop was presided over by a nervous young pedant with long hair and a beard, a collector type himself, an old man in spirit who distrusted children in his store, as he ought to have. He helped my father to find what he sought, deep in the alphabetical archive: a five-issue run of *The Remarkable Super Goat Man,* from Electric Comics. These were the only comics in which Super Goat Man had appeared. There were just five issues because after five the title had been forever canceled. My father seemed satisfied with what he'd found. We paid for the five issues and left.

I didn't know how to explain to my father that Electric wasn't one of the major comics publishers. The stories the comics contained, when we inspected them together, were both ludicrous and boring. Super Goat Man's five issues showed him rescuing old ladies from swerving trucks and kittens from lightning-struck trees, and battling dull villains like Vest Man and False Dave. The drawings were amateurish, cut-rate, antiquated. I couldn't have articulated these judgments then, of course. I knew only that I disliked the comics, found them embarrassing, for myself, for Super Goat Man, and for my dad. They languished in my room, unread, and were eventually cleaned up—I mean, thrown out—by my mom.

For the next few years, Super Goat Man was less than a minor curiosity to me. I didn't waste thought on him. The younger men and women who lived in the commune took him for granted, as anyone should have, so far as I knew. We kids would see him in their company, moving furniture up the stoop and into the house—discarded dressers and couches and lamps they'd found on the street—or taping up posters on lampposts announcing demonstrations against nuclear power or in favor of day-care centers, or weeding in the commune's pathetic front yard, which was intended as a vegetable garden but was choked not only with uninvited growth but with ice-cream wrappers and soda bottles—we kids used the commune's yard as a dumping ground. It didn't occur to me that Super Goat Man was much older, really, than the commune's other occupants, that in fact they might be closer to my age than to his. However childish their behavior, the hippies all seemed as dull and remote as grown-ups to me.

It was the summer when I was thirteen that my parents allowed me to 5 accompany them to one of the commune's potluck dinners. The noise and vibrancy of that house's sporadic celebrations were impossible to ignore on our street, and I knew that my parents had attended a few earlier parties— warily, I imagined. The inhabitants of the commune were always trying to sweep their neighbors into dubious causes, and it might be a mistake to be seduced by frivolity into some sticky association. But my parents liked fun, too. And had too little of it. Their best running jokes concerned the dullness of their friends' dinner parties. This midsummer evening, they brought me along to see inside the life of the scandalous, anomalous house.

The house was already full, many of the guests bearded and jeweled and scruffy, reeking of patchouli and musk, others, like my parents, dressed in their hippest collarless shirts and paisley blouses, wearing their fattest beads and bracelets. The offerings, nearly all casseroles brimming with exotic gray proteins—beans and tofu and eggplant and more I couldn't name—were lined up on a long side table, mostly ignored. This was a version of cocktail hour, with beer drunk from the bottle and well-rolled marijuana cigarettes. I didn't see whether my parents indulged in the latter. My mother accepted a glass of orange juice, surely spiked. I meant not to pay them any attention, so I moved for the stairs. There were partyers leaning on the bannister at the first landing, and music was playing in upstairs rooms, so I didn't doubt that the whole house was open to wandering.

There was no music coming from the garden-facing room on the second floor, but the door was open and three figures were visible inside, seated on cushions on a mattress on the floor: a young couple and Super Goat Man. From his bare hairy feet on the mattress, I guessed that it was his room I'd entered. The walls were sparse apart from a low bookcase, on which I spotted, laid crosswise in the row of upright spines, Norman Mailer's *Armies of the Night*, Sergei Eisenstein's *Film Form/The Film Sense*, and Thomas Pynchon's *V*. The three titles stuck in my head; I would later attempt to read all three in college, succeeding only with the Mailer. Next to the bookcase was a desk heaped with papers, and behind it a few black-and-white postcards had been thumbtacked to the wall. One of the postcard images I recognized as Charlie Parker, clutching a saxophone with his meaty hands. The jazzman was an idol of my father's, perhaps a symbol of his vanished youth.

The young man on the mattress was holding a book: *Memories, Dreams, Reflections,* by Carl Jung. Super Goat Man had evidently just pressed it on him, and had likely been extolling its virtues when I walked into the room.

"Hello," the young woman said, her voice warm. I must have been staring from my place in the middle of the room.

"You're Everett, aren't you?" Super Goat Man said, before I could speak.   10

"How'd you know my name?"

"You live on the block," Super Goat Man said. "I've seen you running around."

"I think we'll head down, Super Goat Man," the young man said abruptly, tucking the book under his arm as he got up from the mattress. "Get something to eat before it's too late."

"I want to hit the dance floor," the young woman said.

"See you down there," Super Goat Man said. With that, the young couple   15
were gone.

"You checking out the house?" Super Goat Man said once we were alone. "Casing the joint?"

"I'm looking for my friend," I lied.

"I think some kids are hanging out in the backyard."

"No, she went upstairs." I wanted him to think I had a girlfriend.

"O.K., cool," Super Goat Man said. He smiled. I suppose he was waiting for   20
me to leave, but he didn't give any sign that I was bothering him by staying.

"Why do you live here?" I asked.

"These are my friends," he said. "They helped me out when I lost my job."

"You're not a superhero anymore, are you?"

Super Goat Man shrugged. "Some people felt I was being too outspoken about the war. Anyway, I wanted to accomplish things on a more local level."

"Why don't you have a secret identity?"   25

"I wasn't that kind of superhero."

"But what was your name before?"

"Ralph Gersten."

"What did Ralph Gersten do?"

"He was a college teacher, for a couple of years."   30

"So why aren't you Ralph Gersten now?"

"Sometime around when they shot Kennedy I just realized that Ralph Gersten wasn't who I was. He was a part of an old life I was holding on to. So I became Super Goat Man. I've come to understand that this is who I am, for better or worse."

This was a bit much for me to assimilate, so I changed the subject. "Do you smoke pot?"

"Sometimes."

"Were Mr. and Mrs. Gersten sad when you gave up your secret identity?"   35

"Who?"

"Your parents."

Super Goat Man smiled. "They weren't my real parents. I was adopted."

Suddenly I was done. "I'm going downstairs, Super Goat Man."

"O.K., Everett," he said. "See you down there, probably."   40

I made my way downstairs to the commune's muddy and ill-lit backyard, milling with the other teenagers and children stranded there by the throngs of frolickers—for the party was now overflowing its bounds, and we were free to steal beers from the counter and carry on our own tentative party, our own fumbling flirtations. I had no girlfriend, but I did play spin the bottle that night, crouched on the ground beneath a fig tree.

Then, near midnight, I went back inside. The living room was jammed with bodies—dancers on a parquet floor that had been revealed when the vast braided rug was rolled up against the base of the mantelpiece. Colored Christmas lights were bunched in one corner, and some of them blinked to create a gently eerie strobe. I smelled sweat and smoke. Feeling perverse and thrilled by the kisses I'd exchanged in the mud beneath the tree, I meandered into the web of celebrants.

Super Goat Man was there. He was dancing with my mother. She was as I'd never seen her, braceleted wrists crossed above her head, swaying to the reggae—I think it was the sound track to *The Harder They Come*. Super Goat Man was more dressed up than he'd been in his room upstairs. He wore a felt brocade vest and striped pants. He danced in tiny little steps, as though losing and regaining his balance, his arms loose at his sides, fingers snapping. Mostly he moved his head to the beat, shaking it back and forth as if saying no-no-no, no-no-no. He shook his head at my mother's dancing, as if he couldn't approve of the way she was moving but couldn't quit paying attention, either.

My father? He was seated on the rolled-up rug, his back against the mantelpiece, elbows on his knees, dangling with forefinger and thumb a nearly empty paper cup of red wine. Like me, he was watching my mom and Super Goat Man. It didn't look as if it bothered him at all.

My junior year at Corcoran College, in Corcoran, New Hampshire, Super   45
Goat Man was brought in to fill the Walt Whitman Chair in the Humanities. This was 1981, the dawn of Reagan. The chair was required to teach one course; Super Goat Man's was listed in the catalog as "Dissidence and Desire: Marginal Heroics in American Life, 1955–1975." The reading list included Franz Fanon, Roland Barthes, and Timothy Leary. It was typical of Corcoran that it would choose that particular moment to recuperate a figure associated with sixties protest, to enshrine what had once been at the vigorous center of the culture in the harmless pantheon of academia. It was Super Goat Man's first teaching job since the fifties. The commune on our street had shut down at some point in my high-school years, and I don't know where Super Goat Man had been in the intervening time. I certainly hadn't thought about him since departing for college.

He'd gained a little weight, but was otherwise unchanged. I first spotted him moving across the Commons lawn on a September afternoon, the scent of fallen and fermenting crab apples on the breeze. It was one of those rare, sweet days on either side of the long New Hampshire winter, when the school year was either falsely fresh before its plunge into bleak December or exhausted and ready to give way to summer. Super Goat Man wore a forest-green corduroy suit and a wide salmon tie, but his feet were still bare. A couple of Corcoran girls trailed alongside him. He had a book open as he walked—perhaps he was reading them a poem.

The college had assigned Super Goat Man a dormitory apartment—a suite of rooms built into Sweeney House, one of the student residences. That is to say, he lived on the edge of the vast Commons lawn, and we students felt his watchful presence much as I had on our street in Brooklyn. I didn't take Super Goat Man's class, which was full of freshmen and those renegade history and rhetoric majors who'd been seduced by French strains of philosophy and literary theory. I fancied myself a classics scholar then—though I'd soon divert into a major in history—and wasn't curious about contemporary political theory; nor did I believe Super Goat Man to be a superior teacher. I wasn't certain that he had nothing to offer the Corcoran students, but whatever he did have to offer it wasn't summed up by the title of his class.

I did, however, participate in one of the late-night salons in the living room of Sweeney House. Super Goat Man had begun appearing there casually, showing up after a few students had occupied the couches and lit a fire or opened a bottle of red wine. Increasingly, his presence was relied upon; soon he was the center of an unnamed tradition. Though Corcoran College was then in the midst of a wave of glamorous eighties-style binge parties, and cocaine had begun to infiltrate our sanctum in the New Hampshire woods, the Sweeney House salons were a return to an earlier temperature of college socializing. Bearded art students who disdained dancing in favor of bull sessions, Woolfian-Plathian girls in long vintage dresses, and lonely gay virgins of both genders—these were the types who found their way to Sweeney to sit at Super Goat Man's feet. There were also, from what I observed, a handful of quiet superhero-comic-book fans who revered Super Goat Man in that capacity and were covertly basking in his aura, ashamed to ask the sorts of questions I'd peppered him with in his room in the communal house so long ago.

The evening I sat in, Super Goat Man had dragged his phonograph out from his apartment and set it up in the living room so that he could play Lenny Bruce records for his acolytes. He spoke intermittently, his voice unhurried and reflective, explaining the context of the famous comedian's arrests and courtroom battles before dropping the needle on a given track. After a while, conversation drifted to other subjects. Cross talk arose, though whenever Super Goat Man began to speak, in his undemonstrative way, all fell deferentially silent. Then Super Goat Man went into his apartment and brought out an Ornette Coleman LP.

"You know a bit about jazz, don't you, Everett?" It was the first time he'd 50 addressed me directly. I hadn't known he'd recognized me.

"A thing or two, I guess."

"Everett's father was the one who turned me on to Rahsaan Roland Kirk," Super Goat Man told a teenager I recognized, a bespectacled sophomore who'd impressively talked his way into a classics seminar that was meant for upperclassmen. "I always thought that stuff was too gimmicky, but I'd never really listened."

I tried to imagine when Super Goat Man and my dad had spent so much time together. It was almost impossible to picture, but Super Goat Man didn't have any reason to be lying about it. It was one of the first times I was forced to consider the possibility that my parents had social lives—that they had lives.

"Does your father write about jazz?" the sophomore asked me, wide-eyed. I suppose he'd misunderstood Super Goat Man's remark. There were plenty of famous—or at least interesting—fathers at Corcoran College, but mine wasn't one of them.

"My father works for New York State," I said. "Department of Housing and 55 Urban Development. Well, he just lost his job, in fact."

"He's a good five-card-stud player, too," said Super Goat Man. "Cleaned me out a few times, I don't mind saying."

"Oh, yeah, my dad's a real supervillain," I said with the heaviest sarcasm I could muster. I was embarrassed to think of my father sucking up to Super Goat Man, as he surely had during their long evenings together, whoever had taken the bulk of the chips.

Then the squeaky jazz began playing, and Super Goat Man, though seated in one of the dormitory's ratty armchairs, closed his eyes and began shaking his head as if transported back to the commune's dance floor, or perhaps to some even earlier time. I studied his face. The tufts around his ears and throat were graying. I puzzled over his actual age. Had Super Goat Man once spent decades frozen in a block of ice, like Captain America? If Ralph Gersten had been a college teacher in the fifties, he was probably older than my dad.

Eight months later, the campus was green again. The term was almost finished, all of us nearly freed to summer, when it happened: the incident at the Campanile. A Saturday, late in a balmy night of revels, the Commons lawn full of small groups crossing from dorm to dorm, cruising the parties that flared like bonfires in the landscape of the campus. Many of us still owed papers, others would have to sit in a final class the following Monday, but the mood was one of expulsive release from our labors. It was nearly three in the morning when Rudy Krugerrand and Seth Brummell, two of the wealthiest and most widely reviled frat boys at Corcoran, scaled the Campanile and began bellowing.

I was among those awake and near enough by to be drawn by the commo- 60 tion into the small crowd at the dark base of the Campanile tower. When I first gazed up at Rudy and Seth, I was confused by what I saw: were there four figures spotlit against the clock beneath the bells? And where were the campus authorities? It was as though this night had been officially ceded to some bacchanalian imperative.

That spring, a sculpture student had, as his thesis project, decorated the Commons with oversized office supplies—a stapler in the dimensions of a limousine, a log painted as a No. 2 pencil, and a pile of facsimile paper clips, each the height of a human being, fashioned out of plastic piping and silver paint. I suppose the work was derivative of Claes Oldenburg, but the result made an impressive spectacle. It was two of the paper-clip sculptures that Rudy Krugerrand and Seth Brummell had managed to attach to their belts like mannequin dance partners and drag with them out onto the ledge of the Campanile clock, where they stood now, six stories from the ground. Their faces uplit in the floodlights, Rudy and Seth were almost like players in the climax of some gothic silent-film drama, but they didn't have the poise or imagination to know it. They were only college pranksters, reeling drunk, Seth with a three-quarters-empty bottle of Jack Daniel's still in his hand, and at first it was hard to make out what they were shouting. We on the ground predictably shouted "Jump!" back at them, knowing that they loved themselves too dearly ever to consider it.

Then Rudy Krugerrand's slurred voice rose above the din—or perhaps it was only that I picked it out of the din for the first time. "Calling Super Goat Man! Calling Super Goat Man!" He shouted this until his voice broke hoarse. "This looks like a job for Super Goat Man! Come out, come out, wherever you are!"

"What's going on?" I asked a student beside me.

He shrugged. "I guess they're calling out Super Goat Man. They want to see if he can get them down from the ledge."

"What do you mean?"

65

"They want to see him use his powers."

From the clock tower, Seth Brummell screamed now, in a girlish falsetto, "Oh, Super Goat Man, where are you?"

A stirring had begun in the crowd, which had grown to a hundred or more. A murmuring. Under the guise of concern for Rudy and Seth, but certainly with a shiver of voyeuristic anticipation, some had begun to speak of going to the Sweeney House apartment to see if Super Goat Man could be found. There was a hint of outrage: Why wasn't he here already? What kind of Super Goat Man was he, anyway?

Now a group of fifteen or twenty broke out and streamed down the hill toward Sweeney House. Others trailed after them, myself included. I hid in the crowd, feeling like an observer, though I suppose I was as complicit as anyone. Were we only curious, or part of a mob? It seemed, anyway, that we were under the direction of Rudy and Seth.

"That's right," mocked Rudy. "Only Super Goat Man can save us now!"

70

Those who'd led the charge hammered on Super Goat Man's apartment door for a good few minutes before getting a result. Bold enough to have woken him, they inched backward at the sight of him on his threshold, dressed only in a flowery silk kimono, blinking groggily at the faces arrayed on the hill. Then someone stepped forward, took his arm, and pointed him toward the Campanile. Any conversation was drowned by the sound of sirens, as the campus police belatedly pulled up to the tower. Super Goat Man shook his head sorrowfully, but he began the trek up the hill toward the Campanile. We all fell in around and behind him, emboldened at marching to the beat of a superhero's step, feeling the pulse of the script that it now appeared would be played out, and ignoring the fact that it had been written by Rudy and Seth and Jack Daniel's. Super Goat Man's kimono fluttered slightly, not quite a cape. He tightened the sash, then strode, rubbing at his eyes with balled fists.

This success seemed only to enrage Rudy and Seth, who writhed and scorned from atop their perch. "Baaahh, baaahh, Super Goat Man!" they roared. "What's the matter with your goaty senses? Smoke too much dope tonight? Fuck you, Super Goat Man!" Seth lifted his giant paper clip above his head and shook it like a fake strongman's prop barbell.

The campus police had begun to herd the students away from the base of the tower, but our arriving throng pushed the opposite way. In the confusion, the young policemen seemed utterly helpless, and fell back. Straining on tiptoe to see over the heads of the crowd, I followed the progress of the lime-green kimono as Super Goat Man was thrust to the fore, not necessarily by his own efforts. Above, Seth was strumming air-guitar chords on his paper clip, then waggling it over our heads like an enormous phallus.

"Bite my crank, Super Goat Man!"

The crowd gasped as Super Goat Man shed his garb—for mobility, I suppose— 75 and started shimmying, almost scampering, up the face of the tower. His pelt was glossy in the moonlight, but nobody could have mistaken the wide streak of white above his dusky buttocks for sheen. Super Goat Man was aging. He scurried through the leaf-blobby shade that a tree branch cast against the side of the tower, then back into the light. Whether it was the pressure of expectation on a still sleepy mind or possibly a genuine call to heroics, a hope that he could do some good here, Super Goat Man had taken the bait. His limbs worked miraculously as he ascended the tower, yet one could only dread what would happen if he reached the idiot boys at the top, who were growing more agitated and furious with every inch he achieved. Rudy had lifted his own paper clip, to match Seth, and now he swung it out over us.

The plummet silenced us. It was over before we could swallow our words and form a cry to replace them. Six stories is no distance at all. Rudy's paper clip had overbalanced him. Super Goat Man had braced three limbs, and reached out with a fourth—some of us saw, others only imagined afterward— but he didn't come away with Rudy. Super Goat Man caught the paper clip in mid-flight with the prehensile toes of his left foot, and the sculpture was jerked free from Rudy as he fell. That's how firm was Super Goat Man's hold on the tower's third story: it was left for later to speculate whether he might have been able to halt a human body's fall. Rudy came to earth, shattering at the feet of the policemen there at the tower's base. Now the nude furry figure could only undertake a sober, methodical descent, paper clip tucked beneath one arm. At the clockface, Seth Brummell was mute, clinging to a post, waiting for the security men who would soon unlock the small door in the tower behind him and angrily yank him to safety.

Rudy Krugerrand survived his fall. It cost him the use of his legs, cost him all feeling below some point at his middle. Only a junior, he rather courageously reappeared in a motorized wheelchair the following September, resumed his studies, resumed drinking, too, though his temperament had mellowed. He'd be seen at parties dozing in the corner after the dance floor had filled—it took very little beer to knock his dwindled body out. If Rudy had died, or never returned, the incident likely would have been avidly discussed, etched into campus legend. Instead it was covered in a clumsy hush. The coexistence in the same small community of Rudy and Super Goat Man—who'd been offered a seat in the social sciences, and accepted—created a kind of odd, insoluble puzzle: Had the hero failed the crisis? Caused it, by some innate provocation? Or was the bogus crisis unworthy, and the outcome its own reward? Who'd shamed whom?

I contemplated this koan, or didn't, for just another year. My graduate studies took me to the University of California, Irvine, three thousand grateful miles from Corcoran. I didn't see Super Goat Man or think of him again for more than a decade.

The sweetest student I ever had was an Italian girl named Angela Verucci. Tall, bronze-skinned, with a quizzical, slightly humorless cast, dressed no matter the weather in neat pants suits or skirts with stockings, she wore heavy tortoiseshell eyeglasses and kept her blond hair knit in a tight, almost Japanese bun. She had an aura of seriousness and a Mediterranean lustre that outshone to near invisibility the blandly corn-fed and T-shirted students in whose midst she had materialized. Angela Verucci was not so much a girl, really: twenty-four years old, she'd studied at Oxford before winning the Reeves Fellowship that brought her to America. She spoke immaculate English, and though her accreditation was a mess, she was nearly as accomplished a medievalist as I was the day she appeared in my class. This was at Oregon State University, in Corvallis, where I'd been given a two-year postdoc after my six years at Irvine. Oregon State was the third stop in Angela Verucci's American tour—she'd spent a year at Columbia and, as it happened, a term at Corcoran.

What does a single thirty-year-old history professor do with the sweetest 80 student he's ever had? He waits until the end of the semester, then he asks her out. We were married two years later.

I was at Rutgers by then, on a second postdoc, and hungry for a tenure-track position. My job interviews weren't exactly unsuccessful: I was never summarily dismissed. Instead I was always called back for second and third visits, always asked to teach a sample class. Afterward, polite notes flew back and forth, candidate and committee reassuring each other of how fine the experience had been, how glad we both were to have met. Only I never got a job.

By the time I got the invitation to interview for a position at Corcoran, the New England pastures of my alma mater didn't look like such a poor fate. It was the week of Halloween, the weather glorious, so at the very least the day of the interview would be a nice jaunt. We left early, to roam a few New Hampshire back roads, then ate a picnic lunch beside Corcoran Pond before I checked in for an afternoon of meetings.

Corcoran looked implacable, though I knew it was changed. The school had been through financial shake-ups and tenure scandals that had, in turn, purged most of the administrators and faculty I'd known. But the grounds, the crab-apple trees and white clapboard, were as eternal as a country-store calendar. While Angela took a memory tour, heading for her old dorm, I showed up for my scheduled tribunal. There I was debriefed by peers, a couple of them younger than myself. The room was full of the usual tensions: some of these people had an investment in my candidacy, some had bets on other tables. No one was in the least sentimental about my status as an alumnus—that was reserved, I supposed, for the dinner that night, arranged in my honor at the President's House. After a final round of polite handclasps, I was ferried to the president's office for a private meeting. I figured this was a good sign.

The president asked how I felt about the interview; we made this and other small talk. She asked about my years at Corcoran, which I painted in rosy tones. Then she said, "Did you know Super Goat Man when you were a student here?"

"Sure," I said. "I mean, I never took a class with him."   85

"He surprised me by asking to join us at the dinner tonight—he doesn't usually bother with faculty socializing anymore."

"He's still here?" I was amazed that Super Goat Man, of all people, had threaded his way through so many personnel shake-ups.

"Yes, though he's reduced to a kind of honorary presence. He doesn't actually teach now. I don't know if he'd be capable of it. But he's beloved. The students joke that he can be spotted strolling across Commons lawn twice a semester. And that if you want to get any time with him you can join him on the stroll."

"He recognized my name?"

"He seemed to, yes. You should prepare yourself. He's quite infirm."   90

"How—how old is he?"

"Measured in years, I don't know. But there's been an accelerated aging process. You'll see."

Perhaps superheroism was a sort of toxin, like a steroid, one with a punitive cost to the body. I mused on this as I crossed the Commons and headed through the parking lot and downhill to find the bench beside Corcoran Creek, a favorite spot, where Angela had said she'd wait. I saw my wife before she saw me, her feet tucked up on the slats, abandoned shoes beneath, her body curled around a big hardback biography of Rousseau. In the distance, dying October light drew long saddle-shaped curves on the White Mountains of New Hampshire. Suddenly, I could picture us here for a long time, and picture it happily.

"How did it go?" she asked when she noticed me.

"Par: two friends, two enemies, one sleeper."   95

"And the president?"

"Nice, but she wasn't giving anything away."

She closed the book. "You seem distant," she said. "Memories?"

"Yes." In fact, I was thinking about Super Goat Man. I'd never before considered the sacrifice he'd made by enunciating his political views so long ago. Fruitlessly, it seemed to me. What had he gained in exchange for his iconic, trapped-in-amber status? Had Super Goat Man really accomplished much outside the parameters of his comics? However unglamorous the chores, didn't kittens need rescuing from trees? Didn't Vest Man require periodic defeating? Why jettison Ralph Gersten if in the end all you attained was the life of a campus mascot?

I wanted to convey some of this to Angela, but didn't know where to begin. 100 "When you were here," I said, "did you know Super Goat Man?"

I saw her stiffen. "Of course. Everybody knew him," she said.

"He's still here." I watched her as I spoke. Her gaze dipped to the ground.

"You saw him?"

"No, but we will at dinner tonight."

"How . . . unexpected." Now Angela was the one in fugue.   105

"Did you study with him?"

"He rarely taught. I attended a few talks."

"I thought you didn't like that stuff."

She shrugged. "I was curious."

I waited to understand. Crickets had begun a chorus in the grass. Soon we'd 110 need to visit our off-campus bed-and-breakfast, to change into fresh clothes for the dinner party. Ordinarily such gatherings were clumsy at best, with grudges incompletely smothered under the surface of the talk, among tenured faculty who knew one another far too well. Something in me now curdled at the prospect of this one. In fact, I'd begun to dread it.

"Everett." There was something Angela wanted to tell me.

I made a preemptive guess. "Did you have some sort of thing with Super Goat Man?" This was how she and I blundered through each other's past liaisons—we'd never been systematic.

"Just an—affair. Nothing."

"What's nothing?"

She shrugged, and flipped her fingers as though dispelling a small fog. "We 115 fooled around a few times. It was stupid."

I felt the poison of bitterness leach into my bloodstream. "I don't know why, but I find that totally disgusting."

"Oh, Everett." Angela raised her arms, moved to assuage me, knowing as she did my visceral possessiveness, the bolt of jealousy that shot through me when contemplating her real past, anytime it arose. Of course she couldn't understand my special history with Super Goat Man. How could she if I didn't? I'd never even mentioned him.

"I was a silly girl." She spoke gently. "And I didn't know you yet."

Unsatisfied, I wished her to declare that the encounter had been abusive, an ethical violation. Not that I had any ground to stand on. Anyway, she was Italian in this, as in all things. It was just an affair.

"Do you want to skip the dinner?" 120

She scowled. "That's unnecessary. He wouldn't even remember. And I don't care. It's really nothing, my darling. My love."

At the president's house, Super Goat Man was the last to arrive, so I was allowed briefly to fantasize that I'd been spared. The sight, when he did come in, was startling. He'd not only aged but shrunk—I doubted if he was even five feet tall. He was, as ever, barefoot, and he wore white muslin pajamas with purple piping. The knees of the pajama bottoms were smudged with mud. As he entered the room, creeping in amid us as we stood with our cocktail glasses, I quickly saw the reason for the smudges: as Super Goat Man's rickety steps faltered, he dropped briefly to all fours. There, on the ground, he shook himself, like a wet dog. Then he rose again, on palsied limbs.

No one took notice of this. The guests, the other faculty, were inured, polite. In this halting manner, Super Goat Man made his way past us to the dining room. Apparently he wasn't capable of mingling, or even necessarily of speech. He took a seat at the long table, his bunched face, his squinting eyes and wrinkled horns, nearly at the level of his place setting. We began drifting in behind him, almost guiltily. The president's husband showed us to our places, which had been carefully designated, though an accommodation was evidently being made for Super Goat Man, who'd plopped down where he liked and wasn't to be budged. I was at the right hand of the president, and the left of the chair of the hiring committee. Another good sign. Angela sat across from me, Super Goat Man many places away, at the other end of the table.

I actually managed to forget him for the duration of the meal. He was, so far as I could tell, silent at his feed, and the women on either side of him turned to their other partners or conversed across the width of the table. Toward the end, we were served Cognac and dessert, and the president's husband passed around cigars, which he bragged were Cuban. Some of the women fled their chairs to avoid the smoke; other guests rose and mingled in the corners of the room. It was in this interval of disarrangement that Super Goat Man pushed himself off his chair and made his way to the seat at my left, which the president had vacated. He had to collapse to his knees only once on the way, and he offered no evidence of sacrificed dignity as he rose from the floor.

Angela remained in her seat. Unlike any of the American women, she'd 125 accepted a cigar, and now leaned it into the flame of a lighter proffered by an older professor she'd been entertaining throughout the meal. Her eyes found mine as Super Goat Man approached. Her expression was curious, and not unsympathetic.

Super Goat Man prodded my arm with a finger. I turned and considered him. Black pupils gleamed behind a hedge of eyebrows. His resplendent tufts had thinned and spread—the hair of his face had been redistributed, to form a merciful gauze across his withered features.

"I . . . knew . . . your . . . father." His voice was mossy, sepulchral.

"Yes," I said simply, keeping my voice low. No one was paying any attention to us, yet, apart from Angela.

"You . . . remember . . . ?"

"Of course."   130

"We . . . love . . . jazz . . ."

I wondered whether he meant my father or, somehow, me. I had in fact over the years come around to my father's love of jazz, though my preference was not so much Ornette Coleman and Rahsaan Roland Kirk as Duke Ellington and Fletcher Henderson.

". . . poker . . ."

"He cleaned you out," I reminded him.

"Yezz . . . good times . . . beautiful women . . ." He struggled, swallowed hard,   135 blinked. "All this controversy . . . not worth it . . ."

"My father was never involved in any controversy," I heard myself say, though I knew Super Goat Man was speaking only of himself, his lost career.

"No . . . absolutely true . . . knew how to live . . ."

Angela had leaned back, pursing her lips to savor the cigar. I might have noticed that the room's gabble of conversation had dampened somewhat— might have noticed sooner, I mean.

"So . . . many . . . hangovers . . ."

"But you and I have something in common besides my father," I told Super   140 Goat Man.

"Yezz . . . yezz . . . ?"

"Of course we do," I began, and though I now understood that we had the attention of the entire room, that the novelty of Super Goat Man's reminis-cences had drawn every ear, I found myself unable to quit before I finished the thought. Further, having gained their attention, I allowed my voice to rise to a garrulous, plummy tone, as if I were starring in dinner theater. Before the line was half out of my mouth, I knew that the words, by airing the sort of laundry so desperately repressed in a community as precious as Corcoran, damned my candidacy. But that was a prize I no longer sought. Broader repercussions I could only guess at. My wife's eyes were on me now, her cigar's blunt tip flar-ing. I'd answer to her later, if she gave me the chance.

It was the worst thing I could think to say. The impulse had formed in the grip of sexual jealousy, of course. But before it crossed my lips I knew that my loathing had its origins in an even deeper place, in the mind of a child wonder-ing at his father's own susceptibility to the notion of a hero.

What I said was this: "I once saw you rescue a paper clip."

FOR ANALYSIS

1. Why is the connection between Everett's father and Super Goat Man so important? How does it relate to the former relationship between Super Goat Man and Angela?

2. What does it mean to Everett when Super Goat Man catches only the giant paper clip? Does the author relate the event in a manner that is sympathetic to the **narrator**? Are readers supposed to agree with Everett's feelings about the incident and about Super Goat Man?

WRITING TOPICS

1. Write your own serious parody of a genre story—it can be a superhero story, a Western, a war story, or a sports story. Try to incorporate turns on your chosen genre similar to some Lethem makes on his. Then reflect on your parody: What does it say about the conventions of the genre, such as heroism, morality, or fairness?

2. Super Goat Man is very much the focus of another's gaze in this story—he is seen and described by someone else. Turn one scene of the story around and write it from his point of view. What changes?

MAKING CONNECTIONS

1. Compare Ellison's and Lethem's stories in terms of their realism. How does each use fantasy? Is one story more fantastic than the other and one more realistic? How does each writer use the improbable/impossible to tell his story?

2. Compare Everetts: How does each conform and/or rebel? How does each think about the status quo? What might Lethem's Everett think of Ellison's?

3. What do these stories' treatments of their heroes have to say about the world in which they are set—or written? Are these worlds in which heroism is still possible, no longer possible, or very difficult to achieve or recognize?

POETRY

GEORGE HERBERT   (1593–1633)

THE COLLAR   1633

I struck the board and cried, "No more;
   I will abroad!
What? shall I ever sigh and pine?
My lines and life are free, free as the road,
 Loose as the wind, as large as store.
    Shall I be still in suit?
  Have I no harvest but a thorn
  To let me blood, and not restore
What I have lost with cordial fruit?
    Sure there was wine   10
  Before my sighs did dry it; there was corn
   Before my tears did drown it.
  Is the year only lost to me?
   Have I no bays to crown it,
No flowers, no garlands gay? All blasted?
    All wasted?
  Not so, my heart; but there is fruit,
    And thou hast hands.
  Recover all thy sigh-blown age
On double pleasures: leave thy cold dispute   20
Of what is fit, and not. Forsake thy cage,
   Thy rope of sands,
Which petty thoughts have made, and made to thee
  Good cable, to enforce and draw,
    And be thy law,
  While thou didst wink and wouldst not see.
    Away! take heed;
    I will abroad.
Call in thy death's-head there; tie up thy fears.
    He that forbears   30
   To suit and serve his need,
    Deserves his load."

But as I raved and grew more fierce and wild
      At every word,
Methought I heard one calling, *Child!*
      And I replied, *My Lord.*

FOR ANALYSIS

1. What images of restraint other than the collar does Herbert include in his poem? What do you think is restraining the speaker in the poem?

2. In the end, is the speaker "free, free as the road," as he insists early in the poem? Does he still want to be? Why or why not?

WRITING TOPIC

"The Collar" is largely a complaint, a poetic cry of dissatisfaction. The lines within quotation marks are a kind of **monologue** or speech by the poetic **persona,** arrested by the speaker's statement that he thought he heard another voice talking to him. Write a response, in poetry or prose, from the voice the speaker thinks he hears talking to him. What might that voice say if allowed to speak further?

PHILLIS WHEATLEY   (1753–1784)

ON BEING BROUGHT FROM AFRICA TO AMERICA   1773

'Twas mercy brought me from my pagan land,
Taught my benighted soul to understand
That there's a God, that there's a Savior too:
Once I redemption neither sought nor knew.
Some view our sable race with scornful eye,
"Their color is a diabolic die.°"   dye
Remember, Christians, Negros, black as Cain,
May be refined, and join th' angelic train.

FOR ANALYSIS

1. Wheatley was brought from Senegal or Gambia to the United States and sold as a slave to the Wheatley family in Boston when she was seven or eight years old. What is your response to the poem's first three lines? Why?

2. Paraphrase "Negros, black as Cain, / May be refined, and join th' angelic train."

3. What historical conditions would perhaps account for the fame of the poet and the extraordinary contemporary wonder at her achievements?

4. Can you imagine an African American poet writing a similar poem in the twenty-first century? Explain.

WRITING TOPIC

First write a review of this poem based on your perception of eighteenth-century society in Massachusetts; then write a twenty-first-century review.

WILLIAM WORDSWORTH (1770–1850)

THE WORLD IS
TOO MUCH WITH US 1807

The world is too much with us; late and soon,
Getting and spending, we lay waste our powers;
Little we see in Nature that is ours;
We have given our hearts away, a sordid boon!
This Sea that bares her bosom to the moon,
The winds that will be howling at all hours,
And are up-gathered now like sleeping flowers,
For this, for everything, we are out of tune;
It moves us not.—Great God! I'd rather be
A Pagan suckled in a creed outworn;   10
So might I, standing on this pleasant lea,
Have glimpses that would make me less forlorn;
Have sight of Proteus rising from the sea;
Or hear old Triton blow his wreathèd horn.[1]

FOR ANALYSIS

1. What does "world" mean in line 1?

2. What does Wordsworth complain of in the first four lines?

3. In lines 4–8 Wordsworth tells us what we have lost; in the concluding lines he suggests a remedy. What is that remedy? What do Proteus and Triton symbolize?

WRITING TOPIC

In what ways does Wordsworth's use of images both define what we have lost and suggest a remedy for this loss?

---

[1] Proteus and Triton are both figures from Greek mythology. Proteus had the power to assume different forms; Triton was often represented blowing on a conch shell.

ALFRED, LORD TENNYSON   (1809–1892)

ULYSSES[1]   1833

It little profits that an idle king,
By this still hearth, among these barren crags,
Matched with an agéd wife, I mete and dole
Unequal laws unto a savage race,
That hoard, and sleep, and feed, and know not me.

I cannot rest from travel; I will drink
Life to the lees. All times I have enjoyed
Greatly, have suffered greatly, both with those
That loved me, and alone; on shore, and when
Through scudding drifts the rainy Hyades[2]   10
Vexed the dim sea. I am become a name;
For always roaming with a hungry heart
Much have I seen and known—cities of men
And manners, climates, councils, governments,
Myself not least, but honored of them all—
And drunk delight of battle with my peers,
Far on the ringing plains of windy Troy.
I am a part of all that I have met;
Yet all experience is an arch wherethrough
Gleams that untraveled world whose margin fades   20
Forever and forever when I move.
How dull it is to pause, to make an end,
To rust unburnished, not to shine in use!
As though to breathe were life. Life piled on life
Were all too little, and of one to me
Little remains; but every hour is saved
From that eternal silence, something more,
A bringer of new things; and vile it were
For some three suns to store and hoard myself,
And this gray spirit yearning in desire   30
To follow knowledge like a sinking star,
Beyond the utmost bound of human thought.

This is my son, mine own Telemachus,
To whom I leave the scepter and the isle—

---

[1] Ulysses, according to Greek legend, was the king of Ithaca and a hero of the Trojan War. Tennyson represents him as eager to resume the life of travel and adventure.
[2] A group of stars in the constellation Taurus. According to Greek mythology, the rising of these stars with the sun foretold rain.

Well-loved of me, discerning to fulfill
This labor, by slow prudence to make mild
A rugged people, and through soft degrees
Subdue them to the useful and the good.
Most blameless is he, centered in the sphere
Of common duties, decent not to fail   40
In offices of tenderness, and pay
Meet° adoration to my household gods,   proper
When I am gone. He works his work, I mine.

    There lies the port; the vessel puffs her sail;
There gloom the dark, broad seas. My mariners,
Souls that have toiled, and wrought, and thought with me—
That ever with a frolic welcome took
The thunder and the sunshine, and opposed
Free hearts, free foreheads—you and I are old;
Old age hath yet his honor and his toil.   50
Death closes all; but something ere the end,
Some work of noble note, may yet be done,
Not unbecoming men that strove with Gods.
The lights begin to twinkle from the rocks;
The long day wanes; the slow moon climbs; the deep
Moans round with many voices. Come, my friends,
'Tis not too late to seek a newer world.
Push off, and sitting well in order smite
The sounding furrows; for my purpose holds
To sail beyond the sunset, and the baths   60
Of all the western stars, until I die.
It may be that the gulfs will wash us down;
It may be we shall touch the Happy Isles,[3]
And see the great Achilles, whom we knew.
Though much is taken, much abides; and though
We are not now that strength which in old days
Moved earth and heaven, that which we are, we are—
One equal temper of heroic hearts,
Made weak by time and fate, but strong in will
To strive, to seek, to find, and not to yield.   70

FOR ANALYSIS

1. Is Ulysses' desire to abdicate his duties as king irresponsible?

2. Contrast Ulysses with his son Telemachus (see ll. 33–43). Is Telemachus admirable?

3. At the conclusion of the poem, Ulysses is determined not to yield. Yield to what?

---

[3] The Islands of the Blessed (also Elysium), thought to be in the far western oceans, where those favored by the gods, such as Achilles, enjoyed life after death.

EMILY DICKINSON   (1830–1886)
MUCH MADNESS IS
DIVINEST SENSE—   1862

Much Madness is divinest Sense—
To a discerning Eye—
Much Sense—the starkest Madness—
'Tis the Majority
In this, as All, prevail—
Assent—and you are sane—
Demur—you're straightway dangerous—
And handled with a Chain—

SHE ROSE TO HIS
REQUIREMENT   CA. 1863

She rose to His Requirement—dropt
The Playthings of Her Life
To take the honorable Work
Of Woman, and of Wife—

If ought° She missed in Her new Day,   anything
Of Amplitude, or Awe
Or first Prospective—Or the Gold
In using, wear away,

It lay unmentioned—as the Sea
Develope Pearl, and Weed,   10
But only to Himself—be known
The Fathoms they abide—

FOR ANALYSIS

1. What are the "Playthings" referred to in line 2?

2. Why does the poet refer to both "Woman" and "Wife" in line 4, since a wife is also a woman?

3. Look up the words *amplitude, awe,* and *prospective* in your dictionary, and consider how these words help you to understand the woman's losses.

4. What does "It" in the third stanza refer to?

5. Why is the sea image at the end of the poem appropriate? What does the contrast between "Pearl" and "Weed" suggest?

6. The last word of the poem, *abide*, has several meanings. Which of them are relevant to the meaning of the poem?

MAKING CONNECTIONS

Compare and contrast the attitudes toward marriage in this poem with those in Achebe's "Marriage Is a Private Affair" (p. 585).

WRITING TOPIC

Write an essay describing a woman you know who gave up an important part of herself to be a wife.

WILLIAM BUTLER YEATS   (1865–1939)

EASTER 1916[1]   1916

I have met them at close of day
Coming with vivid faces
From counter or desk among grey
Eighteenth-century houses.
I have passed with a nod of the head
Or polite meaningless words,
Or have lingered awhile and said
Polite meaningless words,
And thought before I had done
Of a mocking tale or a gibe   10
To please a companion
Around the fire at the club,
Being certain that they and I
But lived where motley is worn:
All changed, changed utterly:
A terrible beauty is born.

That woman's days were spent
In ignorant good-will,
Her nights in argument
Until her voice grew shrill.   20
What voice more sweet than hers
When, young and beautiful,

---

[1] On Easter Monday in 1916, a group of Irish nationalists seized key points in Ireland, including the Dublin Post Office, from which they proclaimed an independent Irish Republic. At first, most of the Irish were indifferent to the nationalists' futile yet heroic gesture, but as the rebellion was crushed and the leaders executed, they became heroes in the eyes of their fellow citizens. Some of those leaders are alluded to in the second stanza and are named in lines 75 and 76.

She rode to harriers?[2]
This man had kept a school
And rode our wingéd horse;[3]
This other his helper and friend
Was coming into his force;
He might have won fame in the end,
So sensitive his nature seemed,
So daring and sweet his thought.   30
This other man I had dreamed
A drunken, vainglorious lout.
He had done most bitter wrong
To some who are near my heart,
Yet I number him in the song;
He, too, has resigned his part
In the casual comedy;
He, too, has been changed in his turn,
Transformed utterly:
A terrible beauty is born.   40

Hearts with one purpose alone
Through summer and winter seem
Enchanted to a stone
To trouble the living stream.
The horse that comes from the road,
The rider, the birds that range
From cloud to tumbling cloud,
Minute by minute they change;
A shadow of cloud on the stream
Changes minute by minute;   50
A horse-hoof slides on the brim,
And a horse plashes within it;
The long-legged moor-hens dive,
And hens to moor-cocks call;
Minute by minute they live:
The stone's in the midst of all.

Too long a sacrifice
Can make a stone of the heart.
O when may it suffice?
That is Heaven's part, our part   60
To murmur name upon name,
As a mother names her child

---

[2] In the aristocratic sport of hare hunting, a "pack of harriers" refers to the hounds as well as the persons following the chase.

[3] In Greek mythology, a winged horse is associated with poetic inspiration.

When sleep at last has come
On limbs that had run wild.
What is it but nightfall?
No, no, not night but death;
Was it needless death after all?
For England may keep faith
For all that is done and said.
We know their dream; enough   70
To know they dreamed and are dead;
And what if excess of love
Bewildered them till they died?
I write it out in a verse—
MacDonagh and MacBride
And Connolly and Pearse⁴
Now and in time to be,
Wherever green is worn,
Are changed, changed utterly:
A terrible beauty is born.   80

FOR ANALYSIS

1. What is "changed utterly"? In what sense can beauty be "terrible" (ll. 15–16)?

2. Who or what does "they" in line 55 refer to? What does the "stone" in lines 43 and 56 symbolize? What is Yeats contrasting?

3. How does the poet answer the question he asks in line 67?

WRITING TOPIC

In the first stanza, the attitude of the poet toward the people he is describing is indifferent, even contemptuous. How is that attitude modified in the rest of the poem?

THE SECOND COMING¹   1921

Turning and turning in the widening gyre°   spiral
The falcon cannot hear the falconer;
Things fall apart; the center cannot hold;

Easter 1916
⁴ Thomas MacDonagh, John MacBride, James Connolly, and Patrick Pearse, shot by a firing squad at Kilmainham Jail in Dublin following the Easter Rising.

The Second Coming
¹ The New Testament (Matthew 24:29–44) describes the Second Coming of Christ as following a period of tribulation to judge the living and the dead and to inaugurate the millennium. Yeats, who believed in historical cycles, foresees the end of civil warfare in his native Ireland and the beginning of a new millennium.

Mere anarchy is loosed upon the world,
The blood-dimmed tide is loosed, and everywhere
The ceremony of innocence is drowned;
The best lack all conviction, while the worst
Are full of passionate intensity.

Surely some revelation is at hand;
Surely the Second Coming is at hand; 10
The Second Coming! Hardly are those words out
When a vast image out of *Spiritus Mundi*[2]
Troubles my sight: somewhere in sands of the desert
A shape with lion body and the head of a man,
A gaze blank and pitiless as the sun,
Is moving its slow thighs, while all about it
Reel shadows of the indignant desert birds.
The darkness drops again; but now I know
That twenty centuries of stony sleep
Were vexed to nightmare by a rocking cradle, 20
And what rough beast, its hour come round at last,
Slouches towards Bethlehem to be born?

EDWIN ARLINGTON ROBINSON (1869–1935)

MINIVER CHEEVY 1910

Miniver Cheevy, child of scorn,
    Grew lean while he assailed the seasons;
He wept that he was ever born,
    And he had reasons.

Miniver loved the days of old
    When swords were bright and steeds were prancing;
The vision of a warrior bold
    Would set him dancing.

Miniver sighed for what was not,
    And dreamed, and rested from his labors; 10

The Second Coming
   [2] The Soul or Spirit of the Universe, which Yeats believed constituted a fund of racial images and memories.

He dreamed of Thebes and Camelot,
    And Priam's neighbors.[1]

Miniver mourned the ripe renown
    That made so many a name so fragrant,
He mourned Romance, now on the town,
    And Art, a vagrant.

Miniver loved the Medici,[2]
    Albeit he had never seen one;
He would have sinned incessantly
    Could he have been one.   20

Miniver cursed the commonplace
    And eyed a khaki suit with loathing;
He missed the medieval grace
    Of iron clothing.

Miniver scorned the gold he sought,
    But sore annoyed was he without it;
Miniver thought, and thought, and thought,
    And thought about it.

Miniver Cheevy, born too late,
    Scratched his head and kept on thinking;   30
Miniver coughed, and called it fate,
    And kept on drinking.

WALLACE STEVENS   (1879–1955)

SUNDAY MORNING   1923

I

Complacencies of the peignoir, and late
Coffee and oranges in a sunny chair,
And the green freedom of a cockatoo
Upon a rug mingle to dissipate

Miniver Cheevy
  [1] Thebes was an ancient Greek city, famous in history and legend; Camelot was the site of the legendary King Arthur's court; Priam was king of Troy during the Trojan War.
  [2] A family of bankers and statesmen, notorious for their cruelty, who ruled Florence for nearly two centuries during the Italian Renaissance.

The holy hush of ancient sacrifice.
She dreams a little, and she feels the dark
Encroachment of that old catastrophe,
As a calm darkens among water-lights.
The pungent oranges and bright, green wings
Seem things in some procession of the dead,   10
Winding across wide water, without sound.
The day is like wide water, without sound,
Stilled for the passing of her dreaming feet
Over the seas, to silent Palestine,
Dominion of the blood and sepulchre.

                    II

Why should she give her bounty to the dead?
What is divinity if it can come
Only in silent shadows and in dreams?
Shall she not find in comforts of the sun,
In pungent fruit and bright, green wings, or else   20
In any balm or beauty of the earth,
Things to be cherished like the thought of heaven?
Divinity must live within herself:
Passions of rain, or moods in falling snow;
Grievings in loneliness, or unsubdued
Elations when the forest blooms; gusty
Emotions on wet roads on autumn nights;
All pleasures and all pains, remembering
The bough of summer and the winter branch.
These are the measures destined for her soul.   30

                    III

Jove in the clouds had his inhuman birth.¹
No mother suckled him, no sweet land gave
Large-mannered motions to his mythy mind
He moved among us, as a muttering king,
Magnificent, would move among his hinds,°   farm servants
Until our blood, commingling, virginal,
With heaven, brought such requital to desire
The very hinds discerned it, in a star.
Shall our blood fail? Or shall it come to be
The blood of paradise? And shall the earth   40

---

¹ Jove is Jupiter, the principal god of the Romans, who, unlike Jesus, had an "inhuman birth."

Seem all of paradise that we shall know?
The sky will be much friendlier then than now,
A part of labor and a part of pain,
And next in glory to enduring love,
Not this dividing and indifferent blue.

IV

She says, "I am content when wakened birds,
Before they fly, test the reality
Of misty fields, by their sweet questionings;
But when the birds are gone, and their warm fields
Return no more, where, then, is paradise?"   50
There is not any haunt of prophecy,
Nor any old chimera[2] of the grave,
Neither the golden underground, nor isle
Melodious, where spirits gat them home,
Nor visionary south, nor cloudy palm
Remote on heaven's hill, that has endured
As April's green endures; or will endure
Like her remembrance of awakened birds,
Or her desire for June and evening, tipped
By the consummation of the swallow's wings.   60

V

She says, "But in contentment I still feel
The need of some imperishable bliss."
Death is the mother of beauty; hence from her,
Alone, shall come fulfilment to our dreams
And our desires. Although she strews the leaves
Of sure obliteration on our paths,
The path sick sorrow took, the many paths
Where triumph rang its brassy phrase, or love
Whispered a little out of tenderness,
She makes the willow shiver in the sun   70
For maidens who were wont to sit and gaze
Upon the grass, relinquished to their feet.
She causes boys to pile new plums and pears
On disregarded plate. The maidens taste
And stray impassioned in the littering leaves.

---

[2] A monster with a lion's head, a goat's body, and a serpent's tail. Here an emblem for the belief in other worlds described in the following lines.

VI

Is there no change of death in paradise?
Does ripe fruit never fall? Or do the boughs
Hang always heavy in that perfect sky,
Unchanging, yet so like our perishing earth,
With rivers like our own that seek for seas   80
They never find, the same receding shores
That never touch with inarticulate pang?
Why set the pear upon those river-banks
Or spice the shores with odors of the plum?
Alas, that they should wear our colors there,
The silken weavings of our afternoons,
And pick the strings of our insipid lutes!
Death is the mother of beauty, mystical,
Within whose burning bosom we devise
Our earthly mothers waiting, sleeplessly.   90

VII

Supple and turbulent, a ring of men
Shall chant in orgy on a summer morn
Their boisterous devotion to the sun,
Not as a god, but as a god might be,
Naked among them, like a savage source.
Their chant shall be a chant of paradise,
Out of their blood, returning to the sky;
And in their chant shall enter, voice by voice,
The windy lake wherein their lord delights,
The trees, like serafin,[3] and echoing hills,   100
That choir among themselves long afterward.
They shall know well the heavenly fellowship
Of men that perish and of summer morn.
And whence they came and whither they shall go
The dew upon their feet shall manifest.

VIII

She hears, upon that water without sound,
A voice that cries, "The tomb in Palestine
Is not the porch of spirits lingering.
It is the grave of Jesus, where he lay."

---

[3] The plural form of *seraph*, an angel.

We live in an old chaos of the sun,   110
Or old dependency of day and night,
Or island solitude, unsponsored, free,
Of that wide water, inescapable.
Deer walk upon our mountains, and the quail
Whistle about us their spontaneous cries;
Sweet berries ripen in the wilderness;
And, in the isolation of the sky,
At evening, casual flocks of pigeons make
Ambiguous undulations as they sink,
Downward to darkness, on extended wings.   120

FOR ANALYSIS

1. In the opening stanza, the woman's enjoyment of a late Sunday morning breakfast in a relaxed and sensuous atmosphere is troubled by thoughts of what Sunday morning *should* mean to her. What are the thoughts that disturb her complacency?

2. What does the speaker mean when he says, "Death is the mother of beauty" (ll. 63 and 88)?

3. In stanza VI, what is the speaker's attitude toward the conventional concept of paradise?

4. Stanza VII presents the speaker's vision of an alternative religion. How does it differ from the paradise of stanza VI?

5. In what ways does the cry of the voice in the final stanza (ll. 107–9) state the woman's dilemma? How do the lines about the pigeons at the end of the poem sum up the speaker's belief?

WRITING TOPIC

This poem is, in a sense, a commentary by the speaker on the woman's desire for truth and certainty more enduring than the physical world can provide. Is the speaker sympathetic to her quest?

ANNA AKHMATOVA   (1889–1966)

FROM REQUIEM   1963

Translated by Judith Hemschemeyer

No, not under the vault of alien skies,
And not under the shelter of alien wings—
I was with my people then,
There, where my people, unfortunately, were.

Instead of a Preface

In the terrible years of the Yezhov terror,[1] I spent seventeen months in the prison lines of Leningrad. Once, someone "recognized" me. Then a woman with bluish lips standing behind me, who, of course, had never heard me called by name before, woke up from the stupor to which everyone had succumbed and whispered in my ear (everyone spoke in whispers there):   10

"Can you describe this?"

And I answered: "Yes, I can."

Then something that looked like a smile passed over what had once been her face.

Dedication

Mountains bow down to this grief,
Mighty rivers cease to flow,
But the prison gates hold firm,
And behind them are the "prisoners' burrows"
And mortal woe.
For someone a fresh breeze blows,
For someone the sunset luxuriates—   20
We wouldn't know, we are those who everywhere
Hear only the rasp of the hateful key
And the soldiers' heavy tread.
We rose as if for an early service,
Trudged through the savaged capital
And met there, more lifeless than the dead;
The sun is lower and the Neva[2] mistier,
But hope keeps singing from afar.
The verdict . . . And her tears gush forth,   30
Already she is cut off from the rest,
As if they painfully wrenched life from her heart,
As if they brutally knocked her flat,
But she goes on . . . Staggering . . . Alone . . .
Where now are my chance friends
Of those two diabolical years?
What do they imagine is in Siberia's storms,
What appears to them dimly in the circle of the moon?
I am sending my farewell greeting to them.

---

[1] Nikolai Yezhov was chief of secret police under Josef Stalin during the Soviet Union's Great Purge of 1936–1938.

[2] River that flows through Leningrad.

Prologue

That was when the ones who smiled   40
Were the dead, glad to be at rest.
And like a useless appendage, Leningrad
Swung from its prisons.
And when, senseless from torment,
Regiments of convicts marched,
And the short songs of farewell
Were sung by locomotive whistles.
The stars of death stood above us
And innocent Russia writhed
Under bloody boots   50
And under the tires of the Black Marias.[3]

. . . .

Epilogue I

I learned how faces fall,
How terror darts from under eyelids,
How suffering traces lines
Of stiff cuneiform on cheeks,
How locks of ashen-blonde or black
Turn silver suddenly,
Smiles fade on submissive lips
And fear trembles in a dry laugh.
And I pray not for myself alone,   60
But for all those who stood there with me
In cruel cold, and in July's heat,
At that blind, red wall.

Epilogue II

Once more the day of remembrance[4] draws near.
I see, I hear, I feel you:

The one they almost had to drag at the end,
And the one who tramps her native land no more,

And the one who, tossing her beautiful head,
Said: "Coming here's like coming home."

---

[3] Paddywagons, or cars used to transport prisoners.
[4] Literally, Remembrance Day, the first anniversary of someone's death and the day on which the Russian Orthodox Church holds a memorial service for the deceased.

I'd like to name them all by name, 70
But the list has been confiscated and is nowhere to be found.

I have woven a wide mantle for them
From their meager, overheard words.

I will remember them always and everywhere,
I will never forget them no matter what comes.

And if they gag my exhausted mouth
Through which a hundred million scream,

Then may the people remember me
On the eve of my remembrance day.

And if ever in this country 80
They decide to erect a monument to me,

I consent to that honor
Under these conditions—that it stand

Neither by the sea, where I was born:
My last tie with the sea is broken,

Nor in the tsar's garden near the cherished pine stump,[5]
Where an inconsolable shade looks for me,

But here, where I stood for three hundred hours,
And where they never unbolted the doors for me

This, lest in blissful death 90
I forget the rumbling of the Black Marias,

Forget how that detested door slammed shut
And an old woman howled like a wounded animal.

And may the melting snow stream like tears
From my motionless lids of bronze,

And a prison dove coo in the distance,
And the ships of the Neva sail calmly on.

---

[5] Old imperial estate south of Leningrad.

CLAUDE MCKAY   (1890-1948)

IF WE MUST DIE   1922

If we must die, let it not be like hogs
Hunted and penned in an inglorious spot,
While round us bark the mad and hungry dogs,
Making their mock at our accurséd lot.
If we must die, O let us nobly die,
So that our precious blood may not be shed
In vain; then even the monsters we defy
Shall be constrained to honor us though dead!
O kinsmen! we must meet the common foe!
Though far outnumbered let us show us brave,   10
And for their thousand blows deal one deathblow!
What though before us lies the open grave?
Like men we'll face the murderous, cowardly pack,
Pressed to the wall, dying, but fighting back!

LANGSTON HUGHES   (1902-1967)

HARLEM   1951

What happens to a dream deferred?

　　Does it dry up
　　like a raisin in the sun?
　　Or fester like a sore—
　　And then run?
　　Does it stink like rotten meat?
　　Or crust and sugar over—
　　like a syrupy sweet?

　　Maybe it just sags
　　like a heavy load.   10

　　Or does it explode?

414

W. H. Auden (1907–1973)

THE UNKNOWN CITIZEN 1940

(To JS/07/M/378
THIS MARBLE MONUMENT
IS ERECTED BY THE STATE)

He was found by the Bureau of Statistics to be
One against whom there was no official complaint,
And all the reports on his conduct agree
That, in the modern sense of an old-fashioned word, he was a saint,
For in everything he did he served the Greater Community.
Except for the War till the day he retired
He worked in a factory and never got fired,
But satisfied his employers, Fudge Motors Inc.
Yet he wasn't a scab or odd in his views,
For his Union reports that he paid his dues,   10
(Our report on his Union shows it was sound)
And our Social Psychology workers found
That he was popular with his mates and liked a drink.
The Press are convinced that he bought a paper every day
And that his reactions to advertisements were normal in every way.
Policies taken out in his name prove that he was fully insured,
And his Health card shows he was once in hospital but left it cured.
Both Producers Research and High-Grade Living declare
He was fully sensible to the advantages of the Installment Plan
And had everything necessary to the Modern Man,   20
A phonograph, radio, a car and a frigidaire.
Our researchers into Public Opinion are content
That he held the proper opinions for the time of year;
When there was peace, he was for peace; when there was war, he went.
He was married and added five children to the population,
Which our Eugenist says was the right number for a parent of his generation,
And our teachers report that he never interfered with their education.
Was he free? Was he happy? The question is absurd:
Had anything been wrong, we should certainly have heard.

MURIEL RUKEYSER (1913–1980)

MYTH 1973

Long afterward, Oedipus, old and blinded, walked the
roads.[1]   He smelled a familiar smell.   It was
the Sphinx.   Oedipus said, "I want to ask one question.
Why didn't I recognize my mother?"   "You gave the
wrong answer," said the Sphinx.   "But that was what
made everything possible," said Oedipus.   "No," she said.
"When I asked, What walks on four legs in the morning,
two at noon, and three in the evening, you answered,
Man.   You didn't say anything about woman."
"When you say Man," said Oedipus, "you include women   10
too. Everyone knows that."   She said, "That's what
you think."

DUDLEY RANDALL (1914–2000)

BALLAD OF BIRMINGHAM 1969

(ON THE BOMBING OF A CHURCH IN
BIRMINGHAM, ALABAMA, 1963)[1]

"Mother dear, may I go downtown
Instead of out to play,
And march the streets of Birmingham
In a Freedom March today?"

"No, baby, no, you may not go,
For the dogs are fierce and wild,
And clubs and hoses, guns and jails
Aren't good for a little child."

"But, mother, I won't be alone.
Other children will go with me,   10

Myth
    [1] Oedipus became king of Thebes when he solved the riddle of the Sphinx quoted in the poem. He
blinded himself when he discovered that he had killed his father and married his own mother.
Ballad of Birmingham
    [1] This poem commemorates the murder of four young African American girls when a bomb was
thrown into the Sixteenth Street Baptist Church in 1963, one of the early and most traumatic events in
the modern civil rights movement.

And march the streets of Birmingham
To make our country free."

"No, baby, no, you may not go,
For I fear those guns will fire.
But you may go to church instead
And sing in the children's choir."

She has combed and brushed her night-dark hair,
And bathed rose petal sweet.
And drawn white gloves on her small brown hands,
And white shoes on her feet.   20

The mother smiled to know her child
Was in the sacred place,
But that smile was the last smile
To come upon her face.

For when she heard the explosion,
Her eyes grew wet and wild.
She raced through the streets of Birmingham
Calling for her child.

She clawed through bits of glass and brick,
Then lifted out a shoe.   30
"Oh, here's the shoe my baby wore,
But, baby, where are you?"

HENRY REED   (1914–1986)

NAMING OF PARTS   1946

Today we have naming of parts. Yesterday,
We had daily cleaning. And tomorrow morning
We shall have what to do after firing. But today,
Today we have naming of parts. Japonica
Glistens like coral in all of the neighboring gardens,
    And today we have naming of parts.

This is the lower sling swivel. And this
Is the upper sling swivel, whose use you will see,
When you are given your slings. And this is the piling swivel,
Which in your case you have not got. The branches   10

Hold in the gardens their silent, eloquent gestures,
  Which in our case we have not got.

This is the safety-catch, which is always released
With an easy flick of the thumb. And please do not let me
See anyone using his finger. You can do it quite easy
If you have any strength in your thumb. The blossoms
Are fragile and motionless, never letting anyone see
  Any of them using their finger.

And this you can see is the bolt. The purpose of this
Is to open the breech, as you see. We can slide it   20
Rapidly backwards and forwards: we call this
Easing the spring. And rapidly backwards and forwards
The early bees are assaulting and fumbling the flowers:
  They call it easing the Spring.

They call it easing the Spring: it is perfectly easy
If you have any strength in your thumb: like the bolt,
And the breech, and the cocking-piece, and the point of balance,
Which in our case we have not got; and the almond-blossom
Silent in all of the gardens and the bees going backwards and forwards,
  For today we have naming of parts.   30

FOR ANALYSIS

1. The poem has two speakers. Identify their voices, and describe the speakers.

2. The last line of each stanza repeats a phrase from within the stanza. What is the effect of the repetition?

WRITING TOPIC

This poem incorporates a subtle underlying sexuality. Trace the language that generates it. What function does this sexuality serve in the poem?

GWENDOLYN BROOKS   (1917–2000)

WE REAL COOL   1959

THE POOL PLAYERS
SEVEN AT THE GOLDEN SHOVEL.

We real cool. We
Left school. We

Lurk late. We
Strike straight. We

Sing sin. We
Thin gin. We

Jazz June. We
Die soon.

TAWFIQ ZAYYAD   (1932–1994)

HERE WE SHALL STAY[1]   1966

As though we were twenty impossibilities
In Lydda, Ramla,[2] and Galilee

Here we shall stay
Like a brick wall upon your breast
And in your throat
Like a splinter of glass, like spiky cactus
And in your eyes
A chaos of fire.

Here we shall stay
Like a wall upon your breast   10
Washing dishes in idle, buzzing bars
Pouring drinks for our overlords
Scrubbing floors in blackened kitchens
To snatch a crumb for our children
From between your blue fangs.

Here we shall stay
A hard wall on your breast.
We hunger
Have no clothes
We defy   20
Sing our songs
Sweep the sick streets with our angry dances
Saturate the prisons with dignity and pride
Keep on making children
One revolutionary generation
After another
As though we were twenty impossibilities
In Lydda, Ramla, and Galilee!

Here We Shall Stay
[1] Translated by Sharif Elmusa and Jack Collom, 1992.
[2] Towns between Jaffa and Jerusalem.

Here we shall stay.
Do your worst.   30
We guard the shade
Of olive and fig.
We blend ideas
Like yeast in dough.
Our nerves are packed with ice
And hellfire warms our hearts.

If we get thirsty
We'll squeeze the rocks.
If we get hungry
We'll eat dirt   40
And never leave.
Our blood is pure
But we shall not hoard it.
Our past lies before us
Our present inside us
Our future on our backs.
As though we were twenty impossibilities
In Lydda, Ramla and Galilee
O living roots hold fast
And—still—reach deep in the earth.   50

It is better for the oppressor
To correct his accounts
Before the pages riffle back
"To every deed . . ."—listen
To what the Book says.

FOR ANALYSIS

1. To what geographical region does the poem refer?

2. Throughout the poem, to whom does the word *your* refer?

3. What is the condition of those referred to as "we" in the poem? Will that condition change? How?

4. How do you interpret the lines "Our blood is pure / But we shall not hoard it"?

5. To what "Book" does the last line refer? Why should the oppressor "correct his accounts"?

WRITING TOPICS

1. Analyze this poem as a call designed to encourage political resistance. What elements contribute to its success? What features seem wishful but impotent?

2. Consider such words as "splinter of glass," "spiky cactus," "chaos of fire," "your blue fangs," and "hellfire." Explain how such language conveys the poem's intent.

MARGE PIERCY   (B. 1936)

THE MARKET ECONOMY   1973

Suppose some peddler offered
you can have a color TV
but your baby will be
born with a crooked spine;
you can have polyvinyl cups
and wash and wear
suits but it will cost
you your left lung
rotted with cancer; suppose
somebody offered you   10
a frozen precooked dinner
every night for ten years
but at the end
your colon dies
and then you do,
slowly and with much pain.
You get a house in the suburbs
but you work in a new plastics
factory and die at fifty-one
when your kidneys turn off.   20
But where else will you
work? where else can
you rent but Smog City?
The only houses for sale
are under the yellow sky.
You've been out of work for
a year and they're hiring
at the plastics factory.
Don't read the fine
print, there isn't any.   30

FOR ANALYSIS

1. Characterize the **tone** of this poem.

2. Would this still be a poem if it were printed as a paragraph? Compare this poem
with Forché's "The Colonel" (p. 423), which is written as a paragraph. Which do you
find more "poetic"? Explain.

3. What is meant by the last two lines of the poem?

WRITING TOPIC

One theory of literature says that fiction allows us to vicariously experience moral dilemmas and test our own reactions. Discuss this poem and Le Guin's story "The Ones Who Walk Away from Omelas" (p. 346) from this perspective. How would you answer the poet's questions? Would you walk away from Omelas?

RICHARD GARCIA   (B. 1941)

WHY I LEFT THE CHURCH   1993

Maybe it was
because the only time
I hit a baseball
it smashed the neon cross
on the church across
the street. Even
twenty-five years later
when I saw Father Harris
I would wonder
if he knew it was me.   10
Maybe it was the demon-stoked
rotisseries of purgatory
where we would roast
hundreds of years
for the smallest of sins.
Or was it the day
I wore my space helmet
to catechism? Clear plastic
with a red-and-white
inflatable rim.   20
Sister Mary Bernadette
pointed toward the door
and said, "Out! Come back
when you're ready."
I rose from my chair
and kept rising
toward the ceiling
while the children
screamed and Sister
kept crossing herself.   30
The last she saw of me
was my shoes disappearing

through cracked plaster
I rose into the sky and beyond.
It is a good thing
I am wearing my helmet,
I thought as I floated
and turned in the blackness
and brightness of outer space,
my body cold on one side and hot   40
on the other. It would
have been very quiet
if my blood had not been
rumbling in my ears so loud.
I remember thinking,
Maybe I will come back
when I'm ready.
But I won't tell
the other children
what it was like.   50
I'll have to make something up.

FOR ANALYSIS

1. What are the meanings of the third word in the title? Why does Garcia have the poem's **persona** imagine leaving the church this way? Or does he actually do it—is the "something" he says he'll have to "make up" (l. 51) something other than this exit by ceiling? Is the poem's meaning affected by your answer?

2. What is the answer to the poem's title? Do you think the speaker will be going back?

WRITING TOPIC

Write a short poem, set in a real place you often find yourself, in which something fantastic happens to you. What kind of poetic/intellectual effects can such an occurrence have? How can it make you see that place, yourself, or especially yourself in that place differently?

CAROLYN FORCHÉ   (B. 1950)

THE COLONEL   1981

What you have heard is true. I was in his house. His wife carried a tray of coffee and sugar. His daughter filed her nails, his son went out for the night. There were daily papers, pet dogs, a pistol on the cushion beside him. The moon swung bare on its black cord over the house. On the television was a cop show.

It was in English. Broken bottles were embedded in the walls round the house to scoop the kneecaps from a man's legs or cut his hands to lace. On the windows there were gratings like those in liquor stores. We had dinner, rack of lamb, good wine, a gold bell was on the table for calling the maid. The maid brought green mangoes, salt, a type of bread. I was asked how I enjoyed the country. There was a brief commercial in Spanish. His wife took everything 10 away. There was some talk then of how difficult it had become to govern. The parrot said hello on the terrace. The colonel told it to shut up, and pushed himself from the table. My friend said to me with his eyes: say nothing. The colonel returned with a sack used to bring groceries home. He spilled many human ears on the table. They were like dried peach halves. There is no other way to say this. He took one of them in his hands, shook it in our faces, dropped it into a water glass. It came alive there. I am tired of fooling around he said. As for the rights of anyone, tell your people they can go fuck themselves. He swept the ears to the floor with his arm and held the last of his wine in the air. Something for your poetry, no? he said. Some of the ears on the floor caught this scrap of 20 his voice. Some of the ears on the floor were pressed to the ground.

FOR ANALYSIS

1. What is the occasion of this poem? Where is it set? How would you characterize the colonel's family?

2. In line 11 the speaker recounts, "There was some talk then of how difficult it had become to govern." Can you suggest why it had become difficult to govern? How does the colonel respond to these difficulties?

3. What does the last sentence suggest?

4. This piece is printed as if it were prose. Does it have any of the formal characteristics of a poem?

CONNECTING POEMS: REVOLUTIONARY THINKING

"Hurrah for revolution and more cannon-shot!" So begins William Butler Yeats's "The Great Day." In this beginning line—and the title—we hear both the anger some poets have felt about revolution and the energy it can take to oppose popular support of the idea. Throughout history, there has been a romantic attraction to revolution, as there has been to armed struggle. In Yeats's mock cheer, and ironic "Great," readers encounter a poet challenging that romantic attitude. As you read the poems in this unit, think about the different things revolutions can do, the different ways they can end, and especially the different things they can mean—to revolutionaries, to those in power, and to those who engage in revolutionary thinking.

WILLIAM BUTLER YEATS   (1865–1939)

THE GREAT DAY   1939

Hurrah for revolution and more cannon-shot!
A beggar upon horseback lashes a beggar on foot.
Hurrah for revolution and cannon come again!
The beggars have changed places, but the lash goes on.

ROBERT FROST   (1874–1963)

A SEMI-REVOLUTION   1942

I advocate a semi-revolution.
The trouble with a total revolution
(Ask any reputable Rosicrucian)[1]
Is that it brings the same class up on top.
Executives of skillful execution
Will therefore plan to go half-way and stop.
Yes, revolutions are the only salves,
But they're one thing that should be done by halves.

OSCAR WILLIAMS   (1900–1964)

A TOTAL REVOLUTION   1952

(AN ANSWER FOR ROBERT FROST)

I advocate a total revolution.
The trouble with a semi-revolution,
It's likely to be slow as evolution.
Who wants to spend the ages in collusion
With Compromise, Complacence and Confusion?
As for the same class coming up on top

A Semi-Revolution
[1] Rosicrucians are members of a society professing mystic religious principles and a belief in occult knowledge and powers. William Butler Yeats was a member of this group (see his poem "The Great Day" at the top of this page).

425

That's wholecloth from the propaganda shop;
The old saw says there's loads of room on top,
That's where the poor should really plan to stop.
And speaking of those people called the "haves,"   10
Who own the whole cow and must have the calves
(And plant the wounds so they can sell the salves)
They won't be stopped by doing things by halves.

NIKKI GIOVANNI   (B. 1943)

DREAMS   1968

i used to dream militant
dreams of taking
over america to show
these white folks how it should be
done
i used to dream radical dreams
of blowing everyone away with my perceptive powers
of correct analysis
i even used to think i'd be the one
to stop the riot and negotiate the peace   10
then i awoke and dug
that if i dreamed natural
dreams of being a natural
woman doing what a woman
does when she's natural
i would have a revolution

MAKING CONNECTIONS

1. Ten years after Frost's "A Semi-Revolution" appeared, Williams's "A Total Revolution" answered it with thoughts on the topic. How does Williams answer Frost? Do you find one of the poems more convincing or true? Which one? Why?

2. All of these poems make skillful use of **tone,** often hiding **irony** not too far beneath what seem at first straightforward statements. In what ways do these different poems manipulate tone, and to what effect?

3. When we think of revolutions, we often think of action—of warfare—but, as the unit title suggests, these poems instead focus on thinking *about* revolutions. Why is thinking—or to use Giovanni's phrase "militant dream[ing]" (above)—so important to revolutions? What kind of revolution is Giovanni imagining in her poem?

The poems in this unit attest to the truth of the notion that what we do—the activity we spend most of our waking hours on Earth doing—has a lot to do with who we are, in our own eyes and in the eyes of others. "What work is," in Philip Levine's words, is complicated though, as is the exact nature of its connection to our identities and to our relationships with others. The three poems in this unit focus on this last element: how our work affects the way we connect to others. Read the poems with an open mind, of course, but keep an eye out for the ways these poems, even when they are tightly focused on the details of work, are also concerned with workers.

PHILIP LEVINE (B. 1928)

WHAT WORK IS   1991

We stand in the rain in a long line
waiting at Ford Highland Park. For work.
You know what work is—if you're
old enough to read this you know what
work is, although you may not do it.
Forget you. This is about waiting,
shifting from one foot to another.
Feeling the light rain falling like mist
into your hair, blurring your vision
until you think you see your own brother   10
ahead of you, maybe ten places.
You rub your glasses with your fingers,
and of course it's someone else's brother,
narrower across the shoulders than
yours but with the same sad slouch, the grin
that does not hide the stubbornness,
the sad refusal to give in to
rain, to the hours wasted waiting,
to the knowledge that somewhere ahead
a man is waiting who will say, "No,   20
we're not hiring today," for any
reason he wants. You love your brother,
now suddenly you can hardly stand
the love flooding you for your brother,

who's not beside you or behind or
ahead because he's home trying to
sleep off a miserable night shift
at Cadillac so he can get up
before noon to study his German.
Works eight hours a night so he can sing   30
Wagner, the opera you hate most,
the worst music ever invented.
How long has it been since you told him
you loved him, held his wide shoulders,
opened your eyes wide and said those words,
and maybe kissed his cheek? You've never
done something so simple, so obvious,
not because you're too young or too dumb,
not because you're jealous or even mean
or incapable of crying in   40
the presence of another man, no,
just because you don't know what work is.

FOR ANALYSIS

1. What is the poem's **tone?** Is it simple or complicated? Does it evoke one feeling or many?

2. Does the poem supply the definition it promises in its title?

WRITING TOPICS

1. Who is the "you" addressed in this poem? What is the speaker's attitude toward this "you"? Write an essay in which you analyze Levine's use of the second-person **point of view** in this poem. What are the effects of this choice?

2. Write a poem that at first seems to be about a sibling (or another close family member or a friend) but is really as much about you as it is about them.

MARGE PIERCY   (B. 1936)

THE SECRETARY CHANT   1973

My hips are a desk.
From my ears hang
chains of paper clips.
Rubber bands form my hair.
My breasts are wells of mimeograph ink.
My feet bear casters.
Buzz. Click.

My head is a badly organized file.
My head is a switchboard
where crossed lines crackle.   10
Press my fingers
and in my eyes appear
credit and debit.
Zing. Tinkle.
My navel is a reject button.
From my mouth issue canceled reams.
Swollen, heavy, rectangular
I am about to be delivered
of a baby
Xerox machine.   20
File me under W
because I wonce
was
a woman.

FOR ANALYSIS

1. From its first line, this poem is focused on the physical. How does the poem's litany
of traits reveal more about mental and emotional life, more about identity, more
about things other than bodies?

2. Why is it significant to the poem's meaning that the speaker is a woman?

WRITING TOPICS

1. Analyze the structure of "The Secretary Chant." What words get repeated? How do
these repetitions—and other repeated elements, like kinds of sentences and images—
structure the poem? Where are these repetitions broken, and to what effect? Why do
you think Piercy chose to have the poem end with an imperative sentence?

2. Write your own chant about a job or social position. Make it funny but also serious, like Piercy's.

JIMMY SANTIAGO BACA   (B. 1952)

TIRE SHOP   2001

I went down yesterday
to fix a leak in my tire. Off Bridge street
there's a place 95 cents
flats fixed,
smeary black paint on warped wood plank
between two bald tires.

I go in, an old Black man
with a Jackie Gleason hat greasy soft
        with a mashed cigar stub in mouth
and another old Chicano man   10
working the other
pneumatic hissing tire changer. The walls are black with rubber
soot blown black dust everywhere
and rows of worn tires on gnawed board racks for sale,
air hoses snaking and looped over the floor.
I greet the two old men
        "Yeah, how's it going!"
No response.
They look up at me as if I just gave them a week to live.
        "I got a tire needs a tube."   20
Rudy, a young Chicano emerges from the black part of the room
pony tailed and plump
walks me out to my truck and looks at the tire.
"It'll cost you five bucks to take off and change."
        I nod.
He tells the old Chicano, who pulls the roller jack
        with a long steel handle outside,
and I wait in the middle of the grunting oval tire
changing machines,
while the old guy goes out and returns with my tire.   30
        He looks at me like a disgruntled Carny
        handling the ferriswheel
for the millionth time
and I'm just another ache in the arm,
        a spoiled kid.
I watch the two old men work the tire machines
        step on the foot levers that send the bars around
flipping the tire from the rim
and I wonder what brought these two old men to work here
        on this gray evening in February—   40
        are they ex-cons?
Drunks or addicts?
He whips the tube out, "Rudy" he yells
        and I see a gaping hole in the tube,
"Can't patch that," Rudy says
        Then in Spanish Slang says, "no podemos pachiarlo,"
"we got a pile of old tubes over there, we'll do it for ten
dollars."
At first I think he might be taking me
        but I hedge away from that thought   50
        and I watch the machines work

the spleesh of air
the final begrudging phoof! of rubber popped loose
    then the holy clank of steel bar
against steel
and every gently the old Chicano man, instead of throwing the bar
on me floor,
takes the iron bar and wipes it clean of rubber bits
    and oil
and slides it gently into his waist belt,   60
    in such a way
I've only seen mother wipe their infant's mouth.
And I wonder where they live these two old guys
I turn and watch MASH on a tv suspended from the ceiling
    six '0 clock news comes on
Hunnington beach blackened with oil.
Rudy comes behind me and says,
"Fucking shame they do that to our shores."
I suddenly realize how I love these working men
working in half dark with bald tires   70
like medieval hunchbacks in a dungeon.
They eat soup and scrape along in their lives—
how can they live I wonder on 95 cents a tire change
in today's world?
I am pleased to be with them
and feel how barrio Chicanos love this too—
how some give up nice jobs
in foreign places
to live by friends working in these places
and out of these men revolutions have started.   80
    The old Chicano is mumbling at me
    how cheap I am
when he learns my four tires are bald
    and spare flat,
    shaking his head as he works the tube into the tirewell.
I notice his heels are chewed to the nails
his fingernails black
his face a weary room and board stairwell
    of a downtown motel
given over to drunks and derelicts, his face hand worn   90
    by drunks leaning their full weight on it
wooden steps grooved by hard soled men just out
    of prison, a face condemned by life to live out more days
    in futility.
I bid goodbye to the Black man chomping his ancient cigar
the Chicano man with his head down

and I feel ashamed, somehow, that I cannot live
    their lives a while for them.
Grateful they are here, I respect such men, who have stories
that will never be told, who bring back to me   100
    my simple boyish days, when men
in oily pants and grubby hands talked in rough tones
    and worked at simply work, getting three meals a day
    on the table the hard way.
They live in an imperfect world,
unlike men with money who have places
to put their shame
these men have none,
other put their shame on planes or Las Vegas
these have no place   110
but to put their shame on their endurance
    their mothers
their kids
    themselves
unlike men who put their shame
on new cars
condos
bank accounts
so they never have to face their shame
    these men in the tire shop   120
    have become more human with shame.
And I thought of the time my brother betrayed
    me leaving me at 14
when we vowed we'd always be together
    he left to live with some rich folks
and I was taken to the Detention Center for kids
with no place to live—
    I became a juvenile
    filled with anger at my brother who left me alone.
These tire shop men made choices   130
never to leave their brothers,
in them I saw shame with no place to go
    but in a man's face, hands, work and silence.
    And as I drove away, nearing my farm
I saw a water sprinkler shooting an arc of water
    far over the fence and grass
it was intended to water—
    the fountain of water hitting a weedy stickered spot
that grew the only single flower anywhere around
    in the midst of rubble brush and stones
    the water hit   140

and touched a dormant seed that blossomed all itself
    into what it was
despite the surroundings.
Something made sense to me then
and I'm not quite sure what—
    an unconditional love of being and living,
    and taking what came one's way
    with dignity.
That night in my dream   150
I cried for my brother as he was leaving,
    all the words I used against myself
    rotten, no good, shitty, failure,
    dissolved in my tears,
my tears poured out of me in my dream and I wept
for my brother and wept when I turned after he left
    and I reached for my sister and she was having coffee
with a friend—
    I wept in my dream because she was not available for me
when I needed her,   160
and all my tears flowed, and how I wept, my feeling my pain
    of abandonment,
    all my tears became that arc of water
    and I became the flower, by sheer accident in the middle
    of nowhere, blossoming . . .

FOR ANALYSIS

1. Why is the speaker "pleased to be with" the men who work in the tire shop? What do they make him feel, and why?

2. In what way does the speaker become the flower he sees in the field?

WRITING TOPIC

One great thing about Baca's poem is the way he uses imagery to paint a vivid picture of the tire shop. Compile your own list of physical details, described actions, and other things that would help you write a vivid poem about a place you have lived, worked, or visited.

MAKING CONNECTIONS

1. In some of these poems, the workers are people other than the speakers. In poems about work, why might poets choose to have the voice be that of an observer instead of a worker?

2. The speakers in "What Work Is" and "Tire Shop" both talk about their brothers. How does each poem make a reflection on working become a reflection about family?

War is many things to many people; however, it is rarely described as "quaint and curious," as the speaker in Hardy's "The Man He Killed" (below) says it is. Hardy's speaker arrives at this conclusion as he confronts the realization, after shooting someone, that his victim was probably just a regular guy like he is, someone he'd loan a little money to or buy a drink for. As you read the poems in this unit, think about the different voices in them and the different realizations they have about war and the people who fight and die in them. Think also about the times and places these poets wrote from—England before and after the Great War (what we now call World War I), the Middle East in the late 1980s, the United States during the Iraq War—and about what changes and what stays the same, across place and time, in these war poems.

THOMAS HARDY (1840–1928)

THE MAN HE KILLED   1902

"Had he and I but met
  By some old ancient inn,
We should have sat us down to wet
  Right many a nipperkin!

"But ranged as infantry,
  And staring face to face,
I shot at him as he at me,
  And killed him in his place.

"I shot him dead because—
  Because he was my foe,   10
Just so: my foe of course he was:
  That's clear enough; although

"He thought he'd 'list, perhaps,
  Off-hand-like—just as I—
Was out of work—had sold his traps—
  No other reason why.

"Yes; quaint and curious war is!
  You shoot a fellow down
You'd treat, if met where any bar is,
  Or help to half-a-crown."   20

WILFRED OWEN   (1893–1918)

DULCE ET DECORUM EST   1920

Bent double, like old beggars under sacks,
Knock-kneed, coughing like hags, we cursed through sludge,
Till on the haunting flares we turned our backs,
And towards our distant rest began to trudge.
Men marched asleep. Many had lost their boots,
But limped on, blood-shod. All went lame, all blind;
Drunk with fatigue; deaf even to the hoots
Of gas-shells dropping softly behind.

Gas! GAS! Quick, boys!—An ecstasy of fumbling,
Fitting the clumsy helmets just in time,   10
But someone still was yelling out and stumbling
And flound'ring like a man in fire or lime.—
Dim through the misty panes and thick green light,
As under a green sea, I saw him drowning.
In all my dreams before my helpless sight
He plunges at me, guttering, choking, drowning.

If in some smothering dreams, you too could pace
Behind the wagon that we flung him in,
And watch the white eyes writhing in his face,
His hanging face, like a devil's sick of sin,   20
If you could hear, at every jolt, the blood
Come gargling from the froth-corrupted lungs
Bitter as the cud
Of vile, incurable sores on innocent tongues,—
My friend, you would not tell with such high zest
To children ardent for some desperate glory,
The old lie: *Dulce et decorum est*
Pro patria mori.[1]

---

[1] A quotation from the Latin poet Horace, "It is sweet and fitting to die for one's country."

Hanan Mikha'il 'Ashrawi (b. 1946)

Night Patrol 1988

(An Israeli Soldier on the West Bank)

It's not the sudden hail
of stones, nor the mocking of
their jeers, but this deliberate
quiet in their eyes that
threatens to wipe itself
around my well-armed uniformed
presence and drag me into
depths of confrontation I
never dared to probe.

Their stares bounce off stone,   10
walls and amateur barricades, and
I'm forced to listen
to the echo of my own
gun fire and tear gas
grenades in the midst of
a deafening silence which
I could almost touch, almost
But not quite.
I refuse to be made
into a figment of my   20
own imagination. I catch
myself, at times, glimpsing
glimpsing the child I
was in one of them. That
same old recklessness, a daredevil
stance, a secret wisdom only
youth can impart as it hurtles
towards adulthood. Then I
begin to take substance before
my very eyes, and   30
shrink back in terror—as
an organism on its long
evolutionary trek recoils at the
touch of a human hand.

If I should once, just
once, grasp the elusive
end of the thread which

ties my being here with
their being there, I
could unravel the beginning . . . no,   40
no, it was not an act
of will that brought me
here, and I shall wrap myself in
fabric woven by hands
other than mine, perhaps
lie down and take a nap.

Should I admit then into
my hapless dreams a thousand
eyes, a thousand hands, and allow
unknowingly the night's   50
silence to conceal me, I
would have done no
more or less than what
thousands have done before, turning
over in sleep clutching my
cocoon of army issue blankets,
and hope for a different posting
in the morning.

FOR ANALYSIS

1. Why do the children from the West Bank hurl stones at the soldier?

2. This Palestinian poet speaks with the voice of an Israeli soldier. In the first stanza, how would "this deliberate / quiet in their eyes" drag the soldier into "depths of confrontation I / never dared to probe"? How does this confrontation differ from the "hail of stones"? How would you characterize the "depths of confrontation"? Why had the speaker "never dared to probe" such a confrontation?

3. In the second stanza, what is the consequence for the speaker when he perceives himself "glimpsing the child I / was in one of them"?

4. Why does the speaker "hope for a different posting / in the morning"?

WRITING TOPICS

1. Evaluate the character of the Israeli soldier on night patrol. Is he a good person or an evil one? A true patriot or a troubled one? What human and moral imperatives embody his consciousness?

2. Compare and contrast 'Ashrawi's and Zayyad's (p. 419) poems. Who do you think is the more effective spokesperson for the Palestinian resistance to the Israeli presence? Justify your response.

STEVE EARLE (B. 1955)

RICH MAN'S WAR   2004

Jimmy joined the army 'cause he had no place to go
There ain't nobody hirin'
'round here since all the jobs went
down to Mexico
Reckoned that he'd learn himself a trade maybe see the world
Move to the city someday and marry a black-haired girl
Somebody somewhere had another plan
Now he's got a rifle in his hand
Rollin' into Baghdad wonderin' how he got this far
Just another poor boy off to fight a rich man's war   10

Bobby had an eagle and a flag tattooed on his arm
Red white and blue to the bone when he landed in Kandahar[1]
Left behind a pretty young wife and a baby girl
A stack of overdue bills and went off to save the world
Been a year now and he's still there
Chasin' ghosts in the thin dry air
Meanwhile back at home the finance company took his car
Just another poor boy off to fight a rich man's war

When will we ever learn
When will we ever see   20
We stand up and take our turn
And keep tellin' ourselves we're free

Ali was the second son of a second son
Grew up in Gaza throwing bottles and rocks when the tanks would come
Ain't nothin' else to do around here just a game children play
Somethin' 'bout livin' in fear all your life makes you hard that way

He answered when he got the call
Wrapped himself in death and praised Allah
A fat man in a new Mercedes drove him to the door
Just another poor boy off to fight a rich man's war   30

FOR ANALYSIS

1. Do the words of this song attack war in general, or only the Israeli-Palestinian, Afghanistan, and Iraq conflicts? Explain.

---

[1] A southern Afghanistan city, bombed by U.S. forces in late 2001 to punish the Taliban for harboring Al Qaeda militants responsible for the September 11, 2001, attacks on the United States.

2. What purpose does a protest song such as Earle's serve? Can such songs affect people's behavior? Explain.

3. Explain lines 19–22. What is it that "we" need to learn?

WRITING TOPIC

Describe the differences and the similarities between Bobby and Ali as they relate to the theme of Earle's **lyric**.

MAKING CONNECTIONS

1. Compare the different effects achieved by the choice of **persona** in these poems. Hardy's, for example, is entirely within quotation marks, a speech delivered by someone—the "He" of the title—while Owen's poem ranges from first-person plural to first-person singular to second-person **point of views.** How do these choices help shape the effects of these poems?

2. What do these poems have to say about the reasons for war? Which seem unconcerned with this question or seem to think it doesn't matter? Which seem more concerned with the reasons individuals become soldiers than the reasons nations enter armed conflict? Do you think poetry is possibly more suited to exploring the former concern?

3. None of these poems seems interested in defending the old idea that, to paraphrase Owen quoting Horace, it is sweet and proper to die for one's country. Are there any voices within the poems who say that or might say that? Are there voices who actually believe it or might say it without believing?

DRAMA

HENRIK IBSEN   (1828–1906)

A DOLL'S HOUSE[1]   1879

CHARACTERS

Torvald Helmer, a lawyer
Nora, his wife
Dr. Rank
Mrs. Linde
Krogstad

The Helmers' three small
   children
Anne, the children's nurse
A Maid
A Porter

ACT I

Scene

A room furnished comfortably and tastefully, but not extravagantly. At the back, a door to the right leads to the entrance hall, another to the left leads to Helmer's study. Between the doors stands a piano. In the middle of the left-hand wall is a door, and beyond it a window. Near the window are a round table, armchairs and a small sofa. In the right-hand wall, at the farther end, another door; and on the same side, nearer the footlights, a stove, two easy chairs and a rocking-chair; between the stove and the door, a small table. Engravings on the walls; a cabinet with china and other small objects; a small book-case with well-bound books. The floors are carpeted, and a fire burns in the stove. It is winter.

A bell rings in the hall; shortly afterwards the door is heard to open. Enter Nora, humming a tune and in high spirits. She is in out-door dress and carries a number of parcels; these she lays on the table to the right. She leaves the outer door open after her, and through it is seen a Porter who is carrying a Christmas tree and a basket, which he gives to the Maid who has opened the door.

Nora. Hide the Christmas tree carefully, Helen. Be sure the children do not see it till this evening, when it is dressed. *(To the Porter, taking out her purse.)* How much?
Porter. Sixpence.

---

[1] Translated by R. Farquharson Sharp.

Nora. There is a shilling. No, keep the change. (*The Porter thanks her, and goes out. Nora shuts the door. She is laughing to herself, as she takes off her hat and coat. She takes a packet of macaroons from her pocket and eats one or two; then goes cautiously to her husband's door and listens.*) Yes, he is in.

(*Still humming, she goes to the table on the right.*)

Helmer (*calls out from his room*). Is that my little lark twittering out there?
Nora (*busy opening some of the parcels*). Yes, it is!
Helmer. Is it my little squirrel bustling about?
Nora. Yes!
Helmer. When did my squirrel come home?
Nora. Just now. (*Puts the bag of macaroons into her pocket and wipes her mouth.*) Come in here, Torvald, and see what I have bought.
Helmer. Don't disturb me. (*A little later, he opens the door and looks into the room, pen in hand.*) Bought, did you say? All these things? Has my little spendthrift been wasting money again?
Nora. Yes, but, Torvald, this year we really can let ourselves go a little. This is the first Christmas that we have not needed to economise.
Helmer. Still, you know, we can't spend money recklessly.
Nora. Yes, Torvald, we may be a wee bit more reckless now, mayn't we? Just a tiny wee bit! You are going to have a big salary and earn lots and lots of money.
Helmer. Yes, after the New Year; but then it will be a whole quarter before the salary is due.
Nora. Pooh! we can borrow till then.
Helmer. Nora! (*Goes up to her and takes her playfully by the ear.*) The same little featherhead! Suppose, now, that I borrowed fifty pounds to-day, and you spent it all in the Christmas week, and then on New Year's Eve a slate fell on my head and killed me, and——
Nora (*putting her hands over his mouth*). Oh! don't say such horrid things.
Helmer. Still, suppose that happened,—what then?
Nora. If that were to happen, I don't suppose I should care whether I owed money or not.
Helmer. Yes, but what about the people who had lent it?
Nora. They? Who would bother about them? I should not know who they were.
Helmer. That is like a woman! But seriously, Nora, you know what I think about that. No debt, no borrowing. There can be no freedom or beauty about a home life that depends on borrowing and debt. We two have kept bravely on the straight road so far, and we will go on the same way for the short time longer that there need be any struggle.
Nora (*moving towards the stove*). As you please, Torvald.
Helmer (*following her*). Come, come, my little skylark must not droop her wings. What is this! Is my little squirrel out of temper? (*Taking out his purse.*) Nora, what do you think I have got here?
Nora (*turning round quickly*). Money!

Helmer. There you are. (*Gives her some money.*) Do you think I don't know what a lot is wanted for house-keeping at Christmas-time?

Nora (*counting*). Ten shillings—a pound—two pounds! Thank you, thank you, Torvald; that will keep me going for a long time.

Helmer. Indeed it must.

Nora. Yes, yes, it will. But come here and let me show you what I have bought. And all so cheap! Look, here is a new suit for Ivar, and a sword; and a horse and a trumpet for Bob; and a doll and dolly's bedstead for Emmy,—they are very plain, but anyway she will soon break them in pieces. And here are dress-lengths and handkerchiefs for the maids; old Anne ought really to have something better.

Helmer. And what is in this parcel?

Nora (*crying out*). No, no! you mustn't see that till this evening.

Helmer. Very well. But now tell me something reasonable that you would particularly like to have.

Nora. No, I really can't think of anything—unless, Torvald——

Helmer. Well?

Nora (*playing with his coat buttons, and without raising her eyes to his*). If you really want to give me something, you might—you might——

Helmer. Well, out with it!

Nora (*speaking quickly*). You might give me money, Torvald. Only just as much as you can afford; and then one of these days I will buy something with it.

Helmer. But, Nora——

Nora. Oh, do! dear Torvald; please, please do! Then I will wrap it up in beautiful gilt paper and hang it on the Christmas tree. Wouldn't that be fun?

Helmer. What are little people called that are always wasting money?

Nora. Spendthrifts—I know. Let us do as you suggest, Torvald, and then I shall have time to think what I am most in want of. That is a very sensible plan, isn't it?

Helmer (*smiling*). Indeed it is—that is to say, if you were really to save out of the money I give you, and then really buy something for yourself. But if you spend it all on the housekeeping and any number of unnecessary things, then I merely have to pay up again.

Nora. Oh but, Torvald——

Helmer. You can't deny it, my dear little Nora. (*Puts his arm round her waist.*) It's a sweet little spendthrift, but she uses up a deal of money. One would hardly believe how expensive such little persons are!

Nora. It's a shame to say that. I do really save all I can.

Helmer (*laughing*). That's very true,—all you can. But you can't save anything!

Nora (*smiling quietly and happily*). You haven't any idea how many expenses we skylarks and squirrels have, Torvald.

Helmer. You are an odd little soul. Very like your father. You always find some new way of wheedling money out of me, and, as soon as you have got it, it seems to melt in your hands. You never know where it has gone. Still, one must take you as you are. It is in the blood; for indeed it is true that you can inherit these things, Nora.

Nora. Ah, I wish I had inherited many of papa's qualities.

Helmer. And I would not wish you to be anything but just what you are, my sweet little skylark. But, do you know, it strikes me that you are looking rather—what shall I say—rather uneasy to-day?

Nora. Do I?

Helmer. You do, really. Look straight at me.

Nora (*looks at him*). Well?

Helmer (*wagging his finger at her*). Hasn't Miss Sweet-Tooth been breaking rules in town to-day?

Nora. No; what makes you think that?

Helmer. Hasn't she paid a visit to the confectioner's?

Nora. No, I assure you, Torvald——

Helmer. Not been nibbling sweets?

Nora. No, certainly not.

Helmer. Not even taken a bite at a macaroon or two?

Nora. No, Torvald, I assure you really——

Helmer. There, there, of course I was only joking.

Nora (*going to the table on the right*). I should not think of going against your wishes.

Helmer. No, I am sure of that! Besides, you gave me your word——(*Going up to her.*) Keep your little Christmas secrets to yourself, my darling. They will all be revealed to-night when the Christmas tree is lit, no doubt.

Nora. Did you remember to invite Doctor Rank?

Helmer. No. But there is no need; as a matter of course he will come to dinner with us. However, I will ask him, when he comes in this morning. I have ordered some good wine. Nora, you can't think how I am looking forward to this evening.

Nora. So am I! And how the children will enjoy themselves, Torvald!

Helmer. It is splendid to feel that one has a perfectly safe appointment, and a big enough income. It's delightful to think of, isn't it?

Nora. It's wonderful!

Helmer. Do you remember last Christmas? For a full three weeks beforehand you shut yourself up every evening till long after midnight, making ornaments for the Christmas tree and all the other fine things that were to be a surprise to us. It was the dullest three weeks I ever spent!

Nora. I didn't find it dull.

Helmer (*smiling*). But there was precious little result, Nora.

Nora. Oh, you shouldn't tease me about that again. How could I help the cat's going in and tearing everything to pieces?

Helmer. Of course you couldn't, poor little girl. You had the best of intentions to please us all, and that's the main thing. But it is a good thing that our hard times are over.

Nora. Yes, it is really wonderful.

Helmer. This time I needn't sit here and be dull all alone, and you needn't ruin your dear eyes and your pretty little hands——

Nora (*clapping her hands*). No, Torvald, I needn't any longer, need I! It's wonderfully lovely to hear you say so! (*Taking his arm.*) Now I will tell you how I have been thinking we ought to arrange things, Torvald. As soon as Christmas is over———(*A bell rings in the hall.*) There's the bell. (*She tidies the room a little.*) There's someone at the door. What a nuisance!

Helmer. If it is a caller, remember I am not at home.

Maid (*in the doorway*). A lady to see you, ma'am,—a stranger.

Nora. Ask her to come in.

Maid (*to Helmer*). The doctor came at the same time, sir.

Helmer. Did he go straight into my room?

Maid. Yes, sir.

(*Helmer goes into his room. The Maid ushers in Mrs. Linde, who is in traveling dress, and shuts the door.*)

Mrs. Linde (*in a dejected and timid voice*). How do you do, Nora?

Nora (*doubtfully*). How do you do———

Mrs. Linde. You don't recognise me, I suppose.

Nora. No, I don't know—yes, to be sure, I seem to———(*Suddenly.*) Yes! Christine! Is it really you?

Mrs. Linde. Yes, it is I.

Nora. Christine! To think of my not recognising you! And yet how could I———(*In a gentle voice.*) How you have altered, Christine!

Mrs. Linde. Yes, I have indeed. In nine, ten long years———

Nora. Is it so long since we met? I suppose it is. The last eight years have been a happy time for me, I can tell you. And so now you have come into the town, and have taken this long journey in winter—that was plucky of you.

Mrs. Linde. I arrived by steamer this morning.

Nora. To have some fun at Christmas-time, of course. How delightful! We will have such fun together! But take off your things. You are not cold, I hope. (*Helps her.*) Now we will sit down by the stove, and be cosy. No, take this arm-chair; I will sit here in the rocking-chair. (*Takes her hands.*) Now you look like your old self again; it was only the first moment———You are a little paler, Christine, and perhaps a little thinner.

Mrs. Linde. And much, much older, Nora.

Nora. Perhaps a little older; very, very little; certainly not much. (*Stops suddenly and speaks seriously.*) What a thoughtless creature I am, chattering away like this. My poor, dear Christine, do forgive me.

Mrs. Linde. What do you mean, Nora?

Nora (*gently*). Poor Christine, you are a widow.

Mrs. Linde. Yes; it is three years ago now.

Nora. Yes, I knew; I saw it in the papers. I assure you, Christine, I meant ever so often to write to you at the time, but I always put it off and something always prevented me.

Mrs. Linde. I quite understand, dear.

Nora. It was very bad of me, Christine. Poor thing, how you must have suffered. And he left you nothing?

Mrs. Linde. No.

Nora. And no children?

Mrs. Linde. No.

Nora. Nothing at all, then?

Mrs. Linde. Not even any sorrow or grief to live upon.

Nora *(looking incredulously at her).* But, Christine, is that possible?

Mrs. Linde *(smiles sadly and strokes her hair).* It sometimes happens, Nora.

Nora. So you are quite alone. How dreadfully sad that must be. I have three lovely children. You can't see them just now, for they are out with their nurse. But now you must tell me all about it.

Mrs. Linde. No, no; I want to hear you.

Nora. No, you must begin. I mustn't be selfish to-day, to-day I must only think of your affairs. But there is one thing I must tell you. Do you know we have just had a great piece of good luck?

Mrs. Linde. No, what is it?

Nora. Just fancy, my husband has been made manager of the Bank!

Mrs. Linde. Your husband? What good luck!

Nora. Yes, tremendous! A barrister's profession is such an uncertain thing, especially if he won't undertake unsavoury cases; and naturally Torvald has never been willing to do that, and I quite agree with him. You may imagine how pleased we are! He is to take up his work in the Bank at the New Year, and then he will have a big salary and lots of commissions. For the future we can live quite differently—we can do just as we like. I feel so relieved and so happy, Christine! It will be splendid to have heaps of money and not need to have any anxiety, won't it?

Mrs. Linde. Yes, anyhow I think it would be delightful to have what one needs.

Nora. No, not only what one needs, but heaps and heaps of money.

Mrs. Linde *(smiling).* Nora, Nora, haven't you learnt sense yet? In our schooldays you were a great spendthrift.

Nora *(laughing).* Yes, that is what Torvald says now. *(Wags her finger at her.)* But "Nora, Nora" is not so silly as you think. We have not been in a position for me to waste money. We have both had to work.

Mrs. Linde. You too?

Nora. Yes; odds and ends, needlework, crochet work, embroidery, and that kind of thing. *(Dropping her voice.)* And other things as well. You know Torvald left his office when we were married? There was no prospect of promotion there, and he had to try and earn more than before. But during the first year he overworked himself dreadfully. You see, he had to make money every way he could, and he worked early and late; but he couldn't stand it, and fell dreadfully ill, and the doctors said it was necessary for him to go south.

Mrs. Linde. You spent a whole year in Italy, didn't you?

Nora. Yes. It was no easy matter to get away, I can tell you. It was just after Ivar was born; but naturally we had to go. It was a wonderfully beautiful journey, and it saved Torvald's life. But it cost a tremendous lot of money, Christine.

Mrs. Linde. So I should think.

Nora. It cost about two hundred and fifty pounds. That's a lot, isn't it?

Mrs. Linde. Yes, and in emergencies like that it is lucky to have the money.

Nora. I ought to tell you that we had it from papa.

Mrs. Linde. Oh, I see. It was just about that time that he died, wasn't it?

Nora. Yes; and, just think of it, I couldn't go and nurse him. I was expecting little Ivar's birth every day and I had my poor sick Torvald to look after. My dear, kind father—I never saw him again, Christine. That was the saddest time I have known since our marriage.

Mrs. Linde. And your husband came back quite well?

Nora. As sound as a bell!

Mrs. Linde. But—the doctor?

Nora. What doctor?

Mrs. Linde. I thought your maid said the gentleman who arrived here just as I did was the doctor?

Nora. Yes, that was Doctor Rank, but he doesn't come here professionally. He is our greatest friend, and comes in at least once every day. No, Torvald has not had an hour's illness since then, and our children are strong and healthy and so am I. *(Jumps up and claps her hands.)* Christine! Christine! it's good to be alive and happy!—— But how horrid of me; I am talking of nothing but my own affairs. *(Sits on a stool near her, and rests her arms on her knees.)* You mustn't be angry with me. Tell me, is it really true that you did not love your husband? Why did you marry him?

Mrs. Linde. My mother was alive then, and was bedridden and helpless, and I had to provide for my two younger brothers; so I did not think I was justified in refusing his offer.

Nora. No, perhaps you were quite right. He was rich at that time, then?

Mrs. Linde. I believe he was quite well off. But his business was a precarious one; and, when he died, it all went to pieces and there was nothing left.

Nora. And then?——

Mrs. Linde. Well, I had to turn my hand to anything I could find—first a small shop, then a small school, and so on. The last three years have seemed like one long working-day, with no rest. Now it is at an end, Nora. My poor mother needs me no more, for she is gone; and the boys do not need me either; they have got situations and can shift for themselves.

Nora. What a relief you must feel it——

Mrs. Linde. No, indeed; I only feel my life unspeakably empty. No one to live for any more. *(Gets up restlessly.)* That was why I could not stand the life in my little backwater any longer. I hope it may be easier here to find something which will busy me and occupy my thoughts. If only I could have the good luck to get some regular work—office work of some kind——

Nora. But, Christine, that is so frightfully tiring, and you look tired out now. You had far better go away to some watering-place.

Mrs. Linde *(walking to the window).* I have no father to give me money for a journey, Nora.

Nora *(rising).* Oh, don't be angry with me.

Mrs. Linde *(going up to her).* It is you that must not be angry with me, dear. The worst of a position like mine is that it makes one so bitter. No one to work for, and yet obliged to be always on the look-out for chances. One must live, and so one becomes selfish. When you told me of the happy turn your fortunes have taken—you will hardly believe it—I was delighted not so much on your account as on my own.

Nora. How do you mean?—Oh, I understand. You mean that perhaps Torvald could get you something to do.

Mrs. Linde. Yes, that was what I was thinking of.

Nora. He must, Christine. Just leave it to me; I will broach the subject very cleverly—I will think of something that will please him very much. It will make me so happy to be of some use to you.

Mrs. Linde. How kind you are, Nora, to be so anxious to help me! It is doubly kind in you, for you know so little of the burdens and troubles of life.

Nora. I——? I know so little of them?

Mrs. Linde (smiling). My dear! Small household cares and that sort of thing!— You are a child, Nora.

Nora (tosses her head and crosses the stage). You ought not to be so superior.

Mrs. Linde. No?

Nora. You are just like the others. They all think that I am incapable of anything really serious——

Mrs. Linde. Come, come——

Nora. —that I have gone through nothing in this world of cares.

Mrs. Linde. But, my dear Nora, you have just told me all your troubles.

Nora. Pooh!—those were trifles. (Lowering her voice.) I have not told you the important thing.

Mrs. Linde. The important thing? What do you mean?

Nora. You look down upon me altogether, Christine—but you ought not to. You are proud, aren't you, of having worked so hard and so long for your mother?

Mrs. Linde. Indeed, I don't look down on any one. But it is true that I am both proud and glad to think that I was privileged to make the end of my mother's life almost free from care.

Nora. And you are proud to think of what you have done for your brothers.

Mrs. Linde. I think I have the right to be.

Nora. I think so, too. But now, listen to this; I too have something to be proud and glad of.

Mrs. Linde. I have no doubt you have. But what do you refer to?

Nora. Speak low. Suppose Torvald were to hear! He mustn't on any account—no one in the world must know, Christine, except you.

Mrs. Linde. But what is it?

Nora. Come here. (Pulls her down on the sofa beside her.) Now I will show you that I too have something to be proud and glad of. It was I who saved Torvald's life.

Mrs. Linde. "Saved"? How?

Nora. I told you about our trip to Italy. Torvald would never have recovered if he had not gone there——

Mrs. Linde. Yes, but your father gave you the necessary funds.

Nora (smiling). Yes, that is what Torvald and all the others think, but——

Mrs. Linde. But——

Nora. Papa didn't give us a shilling. It was I who procured the money.

Mrs. Linde. You? All that large sum?

Nora. Two hundred and fifty pounds. What do you think of that?

Mrs. Linde. But, Nora, how could you possibly do it? Did you win a prize in the Lottery?

Nora (*contemptuously*). In the Lottery? There would have been no credit in that.

Mrs. Linde. But where did you get it from, then?

Nora (*humming and smiling with an air of mystery*). Hm, hm! Aha!

Mrs. Linde. Because you couldn't have borrowed it.

Nora. Couldn't I? Why not?

Mrs. Linde. No, a wife cannot borrow without her husband's consent.

Nora (*tossing her head*). Oh, if it is a wife who has any head for business—a wife who has the wit to be a little bit clever——

Mrs. Linde. I don't understand it at all, Nora.

Nora. There is no need you should. I never said I had borrowed the money. I may have got it some other way. (*Lies back on the sofa.*) Perhaps I got it from some other admirer. When anyone is as attractive as I am——

Mrs. Linde. You are a mad creature.

Nora. Now, you know you're full of curiosity, Christine.

Mrs. Linde. Listen to me, Nora dear. Haven't you been a little bit imprudent?

Nora (*sits up straight*). Is it imprudent to save your husband's life?

Mrs. Linde. It seems to me imprudent, without his knowledge, to——

Nora. But it was absolutely necessary that he should not know! My goodness, can't you understand that? It was necessary he should have no idea what a dangerous condition he was in. It was to me that the doctors came and said that his life was in danger, and that the only thing to save him was to live in the south. Do you suppose I didn't try, first of all, to get what I wanted as if it were for myself? I told him how much I should love to travel abroad like other young wives; I tried tears and entreaties with him; I told him that he ought to remember the condition I was in, and that he ought to be kind and indulgent to me; I even hinted that he might raise a loan. That nearly made him angry, Christine. He said I was thoughtless, and that it was his duty as my husband not to indulge me in my whims and caprices—as I believe he called them. Very well I thought, you must be saved—and that was how I came to devise a way out of the difficulty——

Mrs. Linde. And did your husband never get to know from your father that the money had not come from him?

Nora. No, never. Papa died just at that time. I had meant to let him into the secret and beg him never to reveal it. But he was so ill then—alas, there never was any need to tell him.

Mrs. Linde. And since then have you never told your secret to your husband?

Nora. Good Heavens, no! How could you think so? A man who has such strong opinions about these things! And besides, how painful and humiliating it would be for Torvald, with his manly independence, to know that he owed me anything! It would upset our mutual relations altogether; our beautiful happy home would no longer be what it is now.

Mrs. Linde. Do you mean never to tell him about it?

Nora (*meditatively, and with a half smile*). Yes—some day, perhaps, after many years, when I am no longer as nice-looking as I am now. Don't laugh at me! I mean, of course, when Torvald is no longer as devoted to me as he is now; when my dancing and dressing-up and reciting have palled on him; then it may be a good thing to have something in reserve——(*Breaking off.*) What nonsense! That time will never come. Now, what do you think of my great secret, Christine? Do you still think I am of no use? I can tell you, too, that this affair has caused me a lot of worry. It has been by no means easy for me to meet my engagements punctually. I may tell you that there is something that is called, in business, quarterly interest, and another thing called payment in instalments, and it is always so dreadfully difficult to manage them. I have had to save a little here and there, where I could, you understand. I have not been able to put aside much from my housekeeping money, for Torvald must have a good table. I couldn't let my children be shabbily dressed; I have felt obliged to use up all he gave me for them, the sweet little darlings!

Mrs. Linde. So it has all had to come out of your own necessaries of life, poor Nora?

Nora. Of course. Besides, I was the one responsible for it. Whenever Torvald has given me money for new dresses and such things, I have never spent more than half of it; I have always bought the simplest and cheapest things. Thank Heaven, any clothes look well on me, and so Torvald has never noticed it. But it was often very hard on me, Christine—because it is delightful to be really well dressed, isn't it?

Mrs. Linde. Quite so.

Nora. Well, then I have found other ways of earning money. Last winter I was lucky enough to get a lot of copying to do; so I locked myself up and sat writing every evening until quite late at night. Many a time I was desperately tired; but all the same it was a tremendous pleasure to sit there working and earning money. It was like being a man.

Mrs. Linde. How much have you been able to pay off in that way?

Nora. I can't tell you exactly. You see, it is very difficult to keep an account of a business matter of that kind. I only know that I have paid every penny that I could scrape together. Many a time I was at my wits' end. (*Smiles.*) Then I used to sit here and imagine that a rich old gentleman had fallen in love with me——

Mrs. Linde. What! Who was it?

Nora. Be quiet!—that he had died; and that when his will was opened it contained, written in big letters, the instruction: "The lovely Mrs. Nora Helmer is to have all I possess paid over to her at once in cash."

Mrs. Linde. But, my dear Nora—who could the man be?

Nora. Good gracious, can't you understand? There was no old gentleman at all; it was only something that I used to sit here and imagine, when I couldn't think of any way of procuring money. But it's all the same now; the tiresome old person can stay where he is, as far as I am concerned; I don't care about him or his will either, for I am free from care now. (*Jumps up.*) My goodness, it's delightful to think of, Christine! Free from care! To be able to be free from care, quite free from care; to be able to play and romp with the children; to be able to keep the house beautifully and have everything just as Torvald likes it! And, think of it, soon the spring will come and the big blue sky! Perhaps we shall be able to take a little trip—perhaps I shall see the sea again! Oh, it's a wonderful thing to be alive and be happy. *(A bell is heard in the hall.)*

Mrs. Linde *(rising).* There is the bell; perhaps I had better go.

Nora. No, don't go; no one will come in here; it is sure to be for Torvald.

Servant *(at the hall door).* Excuse me, ma'am—there is a gentleman to see the master, and as the doctor is with him——

Nora. Who is it?

Krogstad *(at the door).* It is I, Mrs. Helmer. *(Mrs. Linde starts, trembles, and turns to the window.)*

Nora *(takes a step towards him, and speaks in a strained, low voice).* You? What is it? What do you want to see my husband about?

Krogstad. Bank business—in a way. I have a small post in the Bank, and I hear your husband is to be our chief now——

Nora. Then it is——

Krogstad. Nothing but dry business matters, Mrs. Helmer; absolutely nothing else.

Nora. Be so good as to go into the study, then. *(She bows indifferently to him and shuts the door into the hall; then comes back and makes up the fire in the stove.)*

Mrs. Linde. Nora—who was that man?

Nora. A lawyer, of the name of Krogstad.

Mrs. Linde. Then it really was he.

Nora. Do you know the man?

Mrs. Linde. I used to—many years ago. At one time he was a solicitor's clerk in our town.

Nora. Yes, he was.

Mrs. Linde. He is greatly altered.

Nora. He made a very unhappy marriage.

Mrs. Linde. He is a widower now, isn't he?

Nora. With several children. There now, it is burning up.

(Shuts the door of the stove and moves the rocking-chair aside.)

Mrs. Linde. They say he carries on various kinds of business.

Nora. Really! Perhaps he does; I don't know anything about it. But don't let us think of business; it is so tiresome.

Doctor Rank *(comes out of Helmer's study. Before he shuts the door he calls to him).* No, my dear fellow, I won't disturb you; I would rather go in to your wife for a little while. *(Shuts the door and sees Mrs. Linde.)* I beg your pardon; I am afraid I am disturbing you too.

Nora. No, not at all. *(Introducing him.)* Doctor Rank, Mrs. Linde.

Rank. I have often heard Mrs. Linde's name mentioned here. I think I passed you on the stairs when I arrived, Mrs. Linde?

Mrs. Linde. Yes, I go up very slowly; I can't manage stairs well.

Rank. Ah! some slight internal weakness?

Mrs. Linde. No, the fact is I have been overworking myself.

Rank. Nothing more than that? Then I suppose you have come to town to amuse yourself with our entertainments?

Mrs. Linde. I have come to look for work.

Rank. Is that a good cure for overwork?

Mrs. Linde. One must live, Doctor Rank.

Rank. Yes, the general opinion seems to be that it is necessary.

Nora. Look here, Doctor Rank—you know you want to live.

Rank. Certainly. However wretched I may feel, I want to prolong the agony as long as possible. All my patients are like that. And so are those who are morally diseased; one of them, and a bad case too, is at this very moment with Helmer——

Mrs. Linde (*sadly*). Ah!

Nora. Whom do you mean?

Rank. A lawyer of the name of Krogstad, a fellow you don't know at all. He suffers from a diseased moral character, Mrs. Helmer; but even he began talking of its being highly important that he should live.

Nora. Did he? What did he want to speak to Torvald about?

Rank. I have no idea; I only heard that it was something about the Bank.

Nora. I didn't know this—what's his name—Krogstad had anything to do with the Bank.

Rank. Yes, he has some sort of appointment there. (*To Mrs. Linde.*) I don't know whether you find also in your part of the world that there are certain people who go zealously snuffing about to smell out moral corruption, and, as soon as they have found some, put the person concerned into some lucrative position where they can keep their eye on him. Healthy natures are left out in the cold.

Mrs. Linde. Still I think the sick are those who most need taking care of.

Rank (*shrugging his shoulders*). Yes, there you are. That is the sentiment that is turning Society into a sickhouse.

(*Nora, who has been absorbed in her thoughts, breaks out into smothered laughter and claps her hands.*)

Rank. Why do you laugh at that? Have you any notion what Society really is?

Nora. What do I care about tiresome Society? I am laughing at something quite different, something extremely amusing. Tell me, Doctor Rank, are all the people who are employed in the Bank dependent on Torvald now?

Rank. Is that what you find so extremely amusing?

Nora (*smiling and humming*). That's my affair! (*Walking about the room.*) It's perfectly glorious to think that we have—that Torvald has so much power over so many people. (*Takes the packet from her pocket.*) Doctor Rank, what do you say to a macaroon?

Rank. What, macaroons? I thought they were forbidden here.

Nora. Yes, but these are some Christine gave me.

Mrs. Linde. What! I?——

Nora. Oh, well, don't be alarmed! You couldn't know that Torvald had forbidden them. I must tell you that he is afraid they will spoil my teeth. But, bah!—once in a way——That's so, isn't it, Doctor Rank? By your leave? *(Puts a macaroon into his mouth.)* You must have one too, Christine. And I shall have one, just a little one—or at most two. *(Walking about.)* I am tremendously happy. There is just one thing in the world now that I should dearly love to do.

Rank. Well, what is that?

Nora. It's something I should dearly love to say, if Torvald could hear me.

Rank. Well, why can't you say it?

Nora. No, I daren't; it's so shocking.

Mrs. Linde. Shocking?

Rank. Well, I should not advise you to say it. Still, with us you might. What is it you would so much like to say if Torvald could hear you?

Nora. I should just love to say—Well, I'm damned!

Rank. Are you mad?

Mrs. Linde. Nora, dear——!

Rank. Say it, here he is!

Nora *(hiding the packet).* Hush! Hush! Hush!

(Helmer comes out of his room, with his coat over his arm and his hat in his hand.)

Nora. Well, Torvald dear, have you got rid of him?

Helmer. Yes, he has just gone.

Nora. Let me introduce you—this is Christine, who has come to town.

Helmer. Christine——? Excuse me, but I don't know——

Nora. Mrs. Linde, dear; Christine Linde.

Helmer. Of course. A school friend of my wife's, I presume?

Mrs. Linde. Yes, we have known each other since then.

Nora. And just think, she has taken a long journey in order to see you.

Helmer. What do you mean?

Mrs. Linde. No, really, I——

Nora. Christine is tremendously clever at book-keeping, and she is frightfully anxious to work under some clever man, so as to perfect herself——

Helmer. Very sensible, Mrs. Linde.

Nora. And when she heard you had been appointed manager of the Bank—the news was telegraphed, you know—she travelled here as quick as she could, Torvald, I am sure you will be able to do something for Christine, for my sake, won't you?

Helmer. Well, it is not altogether impossible. I presume you are a widow, Mrs. Linde?

Mrs. Linde. Yes.

Helmer. And have had some experience of book-keeping?

Mrs. Linde. Yes, a fair amount.

Helmer. Ah! well, it's very likely I may be able to find something for you——

Nora (*clapping her hands*). What did I tell you? What did I tell you?

Helmer. You have just come at a fortunate moment, Mrs. Linde.

Mrs. Linde. How am I to thank you?

Helmer. There is no need. (*Puts on his coat.*) But to-day you must excuse me——

Rank. Wait a minute; I will come with you.

(*Brings his fur coat from the hall and warms it at the fire.*)

Nora. Don't be long away, Torvald dear.

Helmer. About an hour, not more.

Nora. Are you going too, Christine?

Mrs. Linde (*putting on her cloak*). Yes, I must go and look for a room.

Helmer. Oh, well then, we can walk down the street together.

Nora (*helping her*). What a pity it is we are so short of space here; I am afraid it is impossible for us——

Mrs. Linde. Please don't think of it! Good-bye, Nora dear, and many thanks.

Nora. Good-bye for the present. Of course you will come back this evening. And you too, Dr. Rank. What do you say? If you are well enough? Oh, you must be! Wrap yourself up well.

(*They go to the door all talking together. Children's voices are heard on the staircase.*)

Nora. There they are. There they are! (*She runs to open the door. The Nurse comes in with the children.*) Come in! Come in! (*Stoops and kisses them.*) Oh, you sweet blessings! Look at them, Christine! Aren't they darlings?

Rank. Don't let us stand here in the draught.

Helmer. Come along, Mrs. Linde; the place will only be bearable for a mother now!

(*Rank, Helmer and Mrs. Linde go downstairs. The Nurse comes forward with the children; Nora shuts the hall door.*)

Nora. How fresh and well you look! Such red cheeks!—like apples and roses. (*The children all talk at once while she speaks to them.*) Have you had great fun? That's splendid! What, you pulled both Emmy and Bob along on the sledge?—both at once?—that *was* good. You are a clever boy, Ivar. Let me take her for a little, Anne. My sweet little baby doll! (*Takes the baby from the Maid and dances it up and down.*) Yes, yes, mother will dance with Bob too. What! Have you been snowballing? I wish I had been there too! No, no, I will take their things off, Anne; please let me do it, it is such fun. Go in now, you look half frozen. There is some hot coffee for you on the stove.

(*The Nurse goes into the room on the left. Nora takes off the children's things and throws them about, while they all talk to her at once.*)

Nora. Really! Did a big dog run after you? But it didn't bite you? No, dogs don't bite nice little dolly children. You mustn't look at the parcels, Ivar. What are they? Ah, I daresay you would like to know. No, no—it's something nasty! Come, let us have a game! What shall we play at? Hide and Seek? Yes, we'll play Hide and Seek. Bob shall hide first. Must I hide? Very well, I'll hide first.

(She and the children laugh and shout, and romp in and out of the room; at last Nora hides under the table, the children rush in and look for her, but do not see her; they hear her smothered laughter, run to the table, lift up the cloth and find her. Shouts of laughter. She crawls forward and pretends to frighten them. Fresh laughter. Meanwhile there has been a knock at the hall door, but none of them has noticed it. The door is half opened, and Krogstad appears. He waits a little; the game goes on.)

Krogstad. Excuse me, Mrs. Helmer.

Nora *(with a stifled cry, turns round and gets up on to her knees).* Ah! what do you want?

Krogstad. Excuse me, the outer door was ajar; I suppose someone forgot to shut it.

Nora *(rising).* My husband is out, Mr. Krogstad.

Krogstad. I know that.

Nora. What do you want here, then?

Krogstad. A word with you.

Nora. With me?—*(to the children, gently.)* Go in to nurse. What? No, the strange man won't do mother any harm. When he has gone we will have another game. *(She takes the children into the room on the left, and shuts the door after them.)* You want to speak to me?

Krogstad. Yes, I do.

Nora. To-day? It is not the first of the month yet.

Krogstad. No, it is Christmas Eve, and it will depend on yourself what sort of a Christmas you will spend.

Nora. What do you want? To-day it is absolutely impossible for me——

Krogstad. We won't talk about that till later on. This is something different. I presume you can give me a moment?

Nora. Yes—yes, I can—although——

Krogstad. Good. I was in Olsen's Restaurant and saw your husband going down the street——

Nora. Yes?

Krogstad. With a lady.

Nora. What then?

Krogstad. May I make so bold as to ask if it was a Mrs. Linde?

Nora. It was.

Krogstad. Just arrived in town?

Nora. Yes, to-day.

Krogstad. She is a great friend of yours, isn't she?

Nora. She is. But I don't see——

Krogstad. I knew her too, once upon a time.

Nora. I am aware of that.

Krogstad. Are you? So you know all about it; I thought as much. Then I can ask you, without beating about the bush—is Mrs. Linde to have an appointment in the Bank?

Nora. What right have you to question me, Mr. Krogstad?—You, one of my husband's subordinates! But since you ask, you shall know. Yes, Mrs. Linde *is* to have an appointment. And it was I who pleaded her cause, Mr. Krogstad, let me tell you that.

Krogstad. I was right in what I thought, then.

Nora *(walking up and down the stage).*   Sometimes one has a tiny little bit of influence, I should hope. Because one is a woman, it does not necessarily follow that——. When anyone is in a subordinate position, Mr. Krogstad, they should really be careful to avoid offending anyone who—who——

Krogstad. Who has influence?

Nora. Exactly.

Krogstad *(changing his tone).* Mrs. Helmer, you will be so good as to use your influence on my behalf.

Nora. What? What do you mean?

Krogstad. You will be so kind as to see that I am allowed to keep my subordinate position in the Bank.

Nora. What do you mean by that? Who proposes to take your post away from you?

Krogstad. Oh, there is no necessity to keep up the pretence of ignorance. I can quite understand that your friend is not very anxious to expose herself to the chance of rubbing shoulders with me; and I quite understand, too, whom I have to thank for being turned off.

Nora. But I assure you——

Krogstad. Very likely; but, to come to the point, the time has come when I should advise you to use your influence to prevent that.

Nora. But, Mr. Krogstad, I *have* no influence.

Krogstad. Haven't you? I thought you said yourself just now——

Nora. Naturally I did not mean you to put that construction on it. I! What should make you think I have any influence of that kind with my husband?

Krogstad. Oh, I have known your husband from our student days. I don't suppose he is any more unassailable than other husbands.

Nora. If you speak slightingly of my husband, I shall turn you out of the house.

Krogstad. You are bold, Mrs. Helmer.

Nora. I am not afraid of you any longer. As soon as the New Year comes, I shall in a very short time be free of the whole thing.

Krogstad *(controlling himself).* Listen to me, Mrs. Helmer. If necessary, I am prepared to fight for my small post in the Bank as if I were fighting for my life.

Nora. So it seems.

Krogstad. It is not only for the sake of the money; indeed, that weighs least with me in the matter. There is another reason—well, I may as well tell you. My position is this. I daresay you know, like everybody else, that once, many years ago, I was guilty of an indiscretion.

Nora. I think I have heard something of the kind.

Krogstad. The matter never came into court; but every way seemed to be closed to me after that. So I took to the business that you know of. I had to do something; and, honestly, I don't think I've been one of the worst. But now I must cut myself free from all that. My sons are growing up; for their sake I must try and win back as much respect as I can in the town. This post in the Bank was like the first step up for me—and now your husband is going to kick me downstairs again into the mud.

Nora. But you must believe me, Mr. Krogstad; it is not in my power to help you at all.

Krogstad. Then it is because you haven't the will; but I have means to compel you.

Nora. You don't mean that you will tell my husband that I owe you money?

Krogstad. Hm!—suppose I were to tell him?

Nora. It would be perfectly infamous of you. *(Sobbing.)* To think of his learning my secret, which has been my joy and pride, in such an ugly, clumsy way—that he should learn it from you! And it would put me in a horribly disagreeable position——

Krogstad. Only disagreeable?

Nora *(impetuously)*. Well, do it, then!—and it will be the worse for you. My husband will see for himself what a blackguard you are, and you certainly won't keep your post then.

Krogstad. I asked you if it was only a disagreeable scene at home that you were afraid of?

Nora. If my husband does get to know of it, of course he will at once pay you what is still owing, and we shall have nothing more to do with you.

Krogstad *(coming a step nearer)*. Listen to me, Mrs. Helmer. Either you have a very bad memory or you know very little of business. I shall be obliged to remind you of a few details.

Nora. What do you mean?

Krogstad. When your husband was ill, you came to me to borrow two hundred and fifty pounds.

Nora. I didn't know anyone else to go to.

Krogstad. I promised to get you that amount——

Nora. Yes, and you did so.

Krogstad. I promised to get you that amount, on certain conditions. Your mind was so taken up with your husband's illness, and you were so anxious to get the money for your journey, that you seem to have paid no attention to the conditions of our bargain. Therefore it will not be amiss if I remind you of them. Now, I promised to get the money on the security of a bond which I signed.

Nora. Yes, and which I signed.

Krogstad. Good. But below your signature there were a few lines constituting your father a surety for the money; those lines your father should have signed.

Nora. Should? He did sign them.

Krogstad. I had left the date blank; that is to say your father should himself have inserted the date on which he signed the paper. Do you remember that?

Nora. Yes, I think I remember——

Krogstad. Then I gave you the bond to send by post to your father. Is that not so?

Nora. Yes.

Krogstad. And you naturally did so at once, because five or six days afterwards you brought me the bond with your father's signature. And then I gave you the money.

Nora. Well, haven't I been paying it off regularly?

Krogstad. Fairly so, yes. But—to come back to the matter in hand—that must have been a very trying time for you, Mrs. Helmer?

Nora. It was, indeed.

Krogstad. Your father was very ill, wasn't he?

Nora. He was very near his end.

Krogstad. And died soon afterwards?

Nora. Yes.

Krogstad. Tell me, Mrs. Helmer, can you by any chance remember what day your father died?—on what day of the month, I mean.

Nora. Papa died on the 29th of September.

Krogstad. That is correct; I have ascertained it for myself. And, as that is so, there is a discrepancy (*taking a paper from his pocket*) which I cannot account for.

Nora. What discrepancy? I don't know ——

Krogstad. The discrepancy consists, Mrs. Helmer, in the fact that your father signed this bond three days after his death.

Nora. What do you mean? I don't understand——

Krogstad. Your father died on the 29th of September. But, look here; your father has dated his signature the 2nd of October. It is a discrepancy, isn't it? (*Nora is silent.*) Can you explain it to me? (*Nora is still silent.*) It is a remarkable thing, too, that the words "2nd of October," as well as the year, are not written in your father's handwriting but in one that I think I know. Well, of course it can be explained; your father may have forgotten to date his signature, and someone else may have dated it haphazard before they knew of his death. There is no harm in that. It all depends on the signature of the name; and *that* is genuine, I suppose, Mrs. Helmer? It was your father himself who signed his name here?

Nora (*after a short pause, throws her head up and looks defiantly at him*). No, it was not. It was I that wrote papa's name.

Krogstad. Are you aware that is a dangerous confession?

Nora. In what way? You shall have your money soon.

Krogstad. Let me ask you a question; why did you not send the paper to your father?

Nora. It was impossible; papa was so ill. If I had asked him for his signature, I should have had to tell him what the money was to be used for; and when he was so ill himself I couldn't tell him that my husband's life was in danger—it was impossible.

Krogstad. It would have been better for you if you had given up your trip abroad.

Nora. No, that was impossible. That trip was to save my husband's life; I couldn't give that up.

Krogstad. But did it never occur to you that you were committing a fraud on me?

Nora. I couldn't take that into account; I didn't trouble myself about you at all. I couldn't bear you, because you put so many heartless difficulties in my way, although you knew what a dangerous condition my husband was in.

Krogstad. Mrs. Helmer, you evidently do not realise clearly what it is that you have been guilty of. But I can assure you that my one false step, which lost me all my reputation, was nothing more or nothing worse than what you have done.

Nora. You? Do you ask me to believe that you were brave enough to run a risk to save your wife's life?

Krogstad. The law cares nothing about motives.

Nora. Then it must be a very foolish law.

Krogstad. Foolish or not, it is the law by which you will be judged, if I produce this paper in court.

Nora. I don't believe it. Is a daughter not to be allowed to spare her dying father anxiety and care? Is a wife not to be allowed to save her husband's life? I don't know much about law; but I am certain that there must be laws permitting such things as that. Have you no knowledge of such laws—you who are a lawyer? You must be a very poor lawyer, Mr. Krogstad.

Krogstad. Maybe. But matters of business—such business as you and I have had together—do you think I don't understand that? Very well. Do as you please. But let me tell you this—if I lose my position a second time, you shall lose yours with me.

(He bows, and goes out through the hall.)

Nora *(appears buried in thought for a short time, then tosses her head).* Nonsense! Trying to frighten me like that—I am not so silly as he thinks. *(Begins to busy herself putting the children's things in order.)* And yet——? No, it's impossible! I did it for love's sake.

The Children *(in the doorway on the left).* Mother, the stranger man has gone out through the gate.

Nora. Yes, dears, I know. But don't tell anyone about the stranger man. Do you hear? Not even papa.

Children. No, mother; but will you come and play again?

Nora. No, no,—not now.

Children. But, mother, you promised us.

Nora. Yes, but I can't now. Run away in; I have such a lot to do. Run away in, my sweet little darlings. *(She gets them into the room by degrees and shuts the door on them; then sits down on the sofa, takes up a piece of needlework and sews a few stitches, but soon stops.)* No! *(Throws down the work, gets up, goes to the hall door and calls out.)* Helen! bring the tree in. *(Goes to the table on the left, opens a drawer, and stops again.)* No, no! it is quite impossible!

Maid *(coming in with the tree).* Where shall I put it, ma'am?

Nora. Here, in the middle of the floor.

Maid. Shall I get you anything else?

Nora. No, thank you. I have all I want.

(Exit Maid.)

Nora *(begins dressing the tree).* A candle here—and flowers here——. The horrible man! It's all nonsense—there's nothing wrong. The tree shall be splendid! I will do everything I can think of to please you, Torvald!—I will sing for you, dance for you—*(Helmer comes in with some papers under his arm.)* Oh! are you back already?

Helmer. Yes. Has anyone been here?

Nora. Here? No.

Helmer. That is strange. I saw Krogstad going out of the gate.

Nora. Did you? Oh yes, I forgot, Krogstad was here for a moment.

Helmer. Nora, I can see from your manner that he has been here begging you to say a good word for him.

Nora. Yes.

Helmer. And you were to appear to do it of your own accord; you were to conceal from me the fact of his having been here; didn't he beg that of you too?

Nora. Yes, Torvald, but——

Helmer. Nora, Nora, and you would be a party to that sort of thing? To have any talk with a man like that, and give him any sort of promise? And to tell me a lie into the bargain?

Nora. A lie——?

Helmer. Didn't you tell me no one had been here? *(Shakes his finger at her.)* My little song-bird must never do that again. A song-bird must have a clean beak to chirp with—no false notes! *(Puts his arm round her waist.)* That is so, isn't it? Yes, I am sure it is. *(Lets her go.)* We will say no more about it. *(Sits down by the stove.)* How warm and snug it is here!

(Turns over his papers.)

Nora *(after a short pause, during which she busies herself with the Christmas tree).* Torvald!

Helmer. Yes.

Nora. I am looking forward tremendously to the fancy dress ball at the Stenborgs' the day after to-morrow.

Helmer. And I am tremendously curious to see what you are going to surprise me with.

Nora. It was very silly of me to want to do that.

Helmer. What do you mean?

Nora. I can't hit upon anything that will do; everything I think of seems so silly and insignificant.

Helmer. Does my little Nora acknowledge that at last?

Nora *(standing behind his chair with her arms on the back of it).* Are you very busy, Torvald?

Helmer. Well——

Nora. What are all those papers?

Helmer. Bank business.

Nora. Already?

Helmer. I have got authority from the retiring manager to undertake the necessary changes in the staff and in the rearrangement of the work; and I must make use of the Christmas week for that, so as to have everything in order for the new year.

Nora. Then that was why this poor Krogstad——

Helmer. Hm!

Nora *(leans against the back of his chair and strokes his hair).*   If you hadn't been so busy I should have asked you a tremendously big favour, Torvald.

Helmer. What is that? Tell me.

Nora. There is no one has such good taste as you. And I do so want to look nice at the fancy-dress ball. Torvald, couldn't you take me in hand and decide what I shall go as, and what sort of a dress I shall wear?

Helmer. Aha! so my obstinate little woman is obliged to get someone to come to her rescue?

Nora. Yes, Torvald, I can't get along a bit without your help.

Helmer. Very well, I will think it over, we shall manage to hit upon something.

Nora. That *is* nice of you. *(Goes to the Christmas tree. A short pause.)* How pretty the red flowers look——. But, tell me, was it really something very bad that this Krogstad was guilty of?

Helmer. He forged someone's name. Have you any idea what that means?

Nora. Isn't it possible that he was driven to do it by necessity?

Helmer. Yes; or, as in so many cases, by imprudence. I am not so heartless as to condemn a man altogether because of a single false step of that kind.

Nora. No you wouldn't, would you, Torvald?

Helmer. Many a man has been able to retrieve his character, if he has openly confessed his fault and taken his punishment.

Nora. Punishment——?

Helmer. But Krogstad did nothing of that sort; he got himself out of it by a cunning trick, and that is why he has gone under altogether.

Nora. But do you think it would——?

Helmer. Just think how a guilty man like that has to lie and play the hypocrite with everyone, how he has to wear a mask in the presence of those near and dear to him, even before his own wife and children. And about the children—that is the most terrible part of it all, Nora.

Nora. How?

Helmer. Because such an atmosphere of lies infects and poisons the whole life of a home. Each breath the children take in such a house is full of the germs of evil.

Nora *(coming nearer him).* Are you sure of that?

Helmer. My dear, I have often seen it in the course of my life as a lawyer. Almost everyone who has gone to the bad early in life has had a deceitful mother.

Nora. Why do you only say—mother?

Helmer. It seems most commonly to be the mother's influence, though naturally a bad father's would have the same result. Every lawyer is familiar with the fact. This Krogstad, now, has been persistently poisoning his own children with lies and dissimulation; that is why I say he has lost all moral character. *(Holds out his hands to her.)* That is why my sweet little Nora must promise me not to plead his cause. Give me your hand on it. Come, come, what is this? Give me your hand. There now, that's settled. I assure you it would be quite impossible for me to work with him; I literally feel physically ill when I am in the company of such people.

Nora *(takes her hand out of his and goes to the opposite side of the Christmas tree).* How hot it is in here; and I have such a lot to do.

Helmer *(getting up and putting his papers in order).* Yes, and I must try and read through some of these before dinner; and I must think about your costume, too. And it is just possible I may have something ready in gold paper to hang up on the tree. *(Puts his hand on her head.)* My precious little singing-bird!

(He goes into his room and shuts the door after him.)

Nora *(after a pause, whispers).* No, no—it isn't true. It's impossible; it must be impossible.

(The Nurse opens the door on the left.)

Nurse. The little ones are begging so hard to be allowed to come in to mamma.

Nora. No, no, no! Don't let them come in to me! You stay with them, Anne.

Nurse. Very well, ma'am.

(Shuts the door.)

Nora *(pale with terror).* Deprave my little children? Poison my home? *(A short pause. Then she tosses her head.)* It's not true. It can't possibly be true.

ACT II

The Same Scene *The Christmas tree is in the corner by the piano, stripped of its ornaments and with burnt-down candle-ends on its dishevelled branches. Nora's cloak and hat are lying on the sofa. She is alone in the room, walking about uneasily. She stops by the sofa and takes up her cloak.*

Nora *(drops the cloak).* Someone is coming now! *(Goes to the door and listens.)* No—it is no one. Of course, no one will come to-day, Christmas Day—nor tomorrow either. But, perhaps—*(Opens the door and looks out).* No, nothing in the letter-box; it is quite empty. *(Comes forward.)* What rubbish! of course he can't be in earnest about it. Such a thing couldn't happen; it is impossible—I have three little children.

(Enter the Nurse from the room on the left, carrying a big cardboard box.)

Nurse. At last I have found the box with the fancy dress.

Nora. Thanks; put it on the table.

Nurse *(doing so).* But it is very much in want of mending.

Nora. I should like to tear it into a hundred thousand pieces.

Nurse. What an idea! It can easily be put in order—just a little patience.

Nora. Yes, I will go and get Mrs. Linde to come and help me with it.

Nurse. What, out again? In this horrible weather? You will catch cold, ma'am, and make yourself ill.

Nora. Well, worse than that might happen. How are the children?

Nurse. The poor little souls are playing with their Christmas presents, but——

Nora. Do they ask much for me?

Nurse. You see, they are so accustomed to have their mamma with them.

Nora. Yes, but, nurse, I shall not be able to be so much with them now as I was before.

Nurse. Oh well, young children easily get accustomed to anything.

Nora. Do you think so? Do you think they would forget their mother if she went away altogether?

Nurse. Good heavens!—went away altogether?

Nora. Nurse, I want you to tell me something I have often wondered about—how could you have the heart to put your own child out among strangers?

Nurse. I was obliged to, if I wanted to be little Nora's nurse.

Nora. Yes, but how could you be willing to do it?

Nurse. What, when I was going to get such a good place by it? A poor girl who has got into trouble should be glad to. Besides, that wicked man didn't do a single thing for me.

Nora. But I suppose your daughter has quite forgotten you.

Nurse. No, indeed she hasn't. She wrote to me when she was confirmed, and when she was married.

Nora *(putting her arms round her neck).* Dear old Anne, you were a good mother to me when I was little.

Nurse. Little Nora, poor dear, had no other mother but me.

Nora. And if my little ones had no other mother, I am sure you would——What nonsense I am talking! *(Opens the box.)* Go in to them. Now I must——. You will see to-morrow how charming I shall look.

Nurse. I am sure there will be no one at the ball so charming as you, ma'am.

(Goes into the room on the left.)

Nora *(begins to unpack the box, but soon pushes it away from her).* If only I dared go out. If only no one would come. If only I could be sure nothing would happen here in the meantime. Stuff and nonsense! No one will come. Only I mustn't think about it. I will brush my muff. What lovely, lovely gloves! Out of my thoughts, out of my thoughts! One, two, three, four, five, six——*(Screams.)* Ah! there is someone coming——

(Makes a movement towards the door, but stands irresolute. Enter Mrs. Linde from the hall, where she has taken off her cloak and hat.)

Nora. Oh, it's you, Christine. There is no one else out there, is there? How good of you to come!

Mrs. Linde. I heard you were up asking for me.

Nora. Yes, I was passing by. As a matter of fact, it is something you could help me with. Let us sit down here on the sofa. Look here. To-morrow evening there is to be a fancy-dress ball at the Stenborgs', who live above us; and Torvald wants me to go as a Neapolitan fisher-girl, and dance the Tarantella that I learnt at Capri.

Mrs. Linde. I see; you are going to keep up the character.

Nora. Yes, Torvald wants me to. Look, here is the dress; Torvald had it made for me there, but now it is all so torn, and I haven't any idea——

Mrs. Linde. We will easily put that right. It is only some of the trimming come unsewn here and there. Needle and thread? Now then, that's all we want.

Nora. It *is* nice of you.

Mrs. Linde *(sewing)*. So you are going to be dressed up to-morrow, Nora. I will tell you what—I shall come in for a moment and see you in your fine feathers. But I have completely forgotten to thank you for a delightful evening yesterday.

Nora *(gets up, and crosses the stage)*. Well I don't think yesterday was as pleasant as usual. You ought to have come to town a little earlier, Christine. Certainly Torvald does understand how to make a house dainty and attractive.

Mrs. Linde. And so do you, it seems to me; you are not your father's daughter for nothing. But tell me, is Doctor Rank always as depressed as he was yesterday?

Nora. No; yesterday it was very noticeable. I must tell you that he suffers from a very dangerous disease. He has consumption of the spine, poor creature. His father was a horrible man who committed all sorts of excesses, and that is why his son was sickly from childhood, do you understand?

Mrs. Linde *(dropping her sewing)*. But, my dearest Nora, how do you know anything about such things?

Nora *(walking about)*. Pooh! When you have three children, you get visits now and then from—from married women, who know something of medical matters, and they talk about one thing and another.

Mrs. Linde *(goes on sewing. A short silence)*. Does Doctor Rank come here every day?

Nora. Every day regularly. He is Torvald's most intimate friend, and a great friend of mine too. He is just like one of the family.

Mrs. Linde. But tell me this—is he perfectly sincere? I mean, isn't he the kind of man that is very anxious to make himself agreeable?

Nora. Not in the least. What makes you think that?

Mrs. Linde. When you introduced him to me yesterday, he declared he had often heard my name mentioned in this house; but afterwards I noticed that your husband hadn't the slightest idea who I was. So how could Doctor Rank——?

Nora. That is quite right, Christine. Torvald is so absurdly fond of me that he wants me absolutely to himself, as he says. At first he used to seem almost jealous if I mentioned any of the dear folk at home, so naturally I gave up doing so. But I often talk about such things with Doctor Rank, because he likes hearing about them.

Mrs. Linde. Listen to me, Nora. You are still very like a child in many things, and I am older than you in many ways and have a little more experience. Let me tell you this—you ought to make an end of it with Doctor Rank.

Nora. What ought I to make an end of?

Mrs. Linde. Of two things, I think. Yesterday you talked some nonsense about a rich admirer who was to leave you money——

Nora. An admirer who doesn't exist, unfortunately! But what then?

Mrs. Linde. Is Doctor Rank a man of means?

Nora. Yes, he is.

Mrs. Linde. And has no one to provide for?

Nora. No, no one; but——

Mrs. Linde. And comes here every day?

Nora. Yes, I told you so.

Mrs. Linde. But how can this well-bred man be so tactless?

Nora. I don't understand you at all.

Mrs. Linde. Don't prevaricate, Nora. Do you suppose I don't guess who lent you the two hundred and fifty pounds?

Nora. Are you out of your senses? How can you think of such a thing! A friend of ours, who comes here every day! Do you realise what a horribly painful position that would be?

Mrs. Linde. Then it really isn't he?

Nora. No, certainly not. It would never have entered into my head for a moment. Besides, he had no money to lend then; he came into his money afterwards.

Mrs. Linde. Well, I think that was lucky for you, my dear Nora.

Nora. No, it would never have come into my head to ask Doctor Rank. Although I am quite sure that if I had asked him——

Mrs. Linde. But of course you won't.

Nora. Of course not. I have no reason to think it could possibly be necessary. But I am quite sure that if I told Doctor Rank——

Mrs. Linde. Behind your husband's back?

Nora. I must make an end of it with the other one, and that will be behind his back too. I *must* make an end of it with him.

Mrs. Linde. Yes, that is what I told you yesterday, but——

Nora (*walking up and down*). A man can put a thing like that straight much easier than a woman——

Mrs. Linde. One's husband, yes.

Nora. Nonsense! (*Standing still.*) When you pay off a debt you get your bond back, don't you?

Mrs. Linde. Yes, as a matter of course.

Nora. And can tear it into a hundred thousand pieces, and burn it up—the nasty dirty paper!

Mrs. Linde *(looks hard at her, lays down her sewing and gets up slowly).*   Nora, you are concealing something from me.

Nora. Do I look as if I were?

Mrs. Linde. Something has happened to you since yesterday morning. Nora, what is it?

Nora *(going nearer to her).* Christine! *(Listens.)* Hush! there's Torvald come home. Do you mind going in to the children for the present? Torvald can't bear to see dressmaking going on. Let Anne help you.

Mrs. Linde *(gathering some of the things together).*   Certainly—but I am not going away from here till we have had it out with one another.

(She goes into the room on the left, as Helmer comes in from the hall.)

Nora *(going up to Helmer).* I have wanted you so much, Torvald dear.

Helmer. Was that the dressmaker?

Nora. No, it was Christine; she is helping me to put my dress in order. You will see I shall look quite smart.

Helmer. Wasn't that a happy thought of mine, now?

Nora. Splendid! But don't you think it is nice of me, too, to do as you wish?

Helmer. Nice?—because you do as your husband wishes? Well, well, you little rogue, I am sure you did not mean it in that way. But I am not going to disturb you; you will want to be trying on your dress, I expect.

Nora. I suppose you are going to work.

Helmer. Yes. *(Shows her a bundle of papers.)* Look at that. I have just been into the bank.

(Turns to go into his room.)

Nora. Torvald.

Helmer. Yes.

Nora. If your little squirrel were to ask you for something very, very prettily——?

Helmer. What then?

Nora. Would you do it?

Helmer. I should like to hear what it is, first.

Nora. Your squirrel would run about and do all her tricks if you would be nice, and do what she wants.

Helmer. Speak plainly.

Nora. Your skylark would chirp about in every room, with her song rising and falling——

Helmer. Well, my skylark does that anyhow.

Nora. I would play the fairy and dance for you in the moonlight, Torvald.

Helmer. Nora—you surely don't mean that request you made of me this morning?

Nora *(going near him).* Yes, Torvald, I beg you so earnestly——

Helmer. Have you really the courage to open up that question again?

Nora. Yes, dear, you *must* do as I ask; you *must* let Krogstad keep his post in the Bank.

Helmer. My dear Nora, it is his post that I have arranged Mrs. Linde shall have.

Nora. Yes, you have been awfully kind about that; but you could just as well dismiss some other clerk instead of Krogstad.

Helmer. This simply incredible obstinacy! Because you chose to give him a thoughtless promise that you would speak for him, I am expected to——

Nora. That isn't the reason, Torvald. It is for your own sake. This fellow writes in the most scurrilous newspapers; you have told me so yourself. He can do you an unspeakable amount of harm. I am frightened to death of him——

Helmer. Ah, I understand; it is recollections of the past that scare you.

Nora. What do you mean?

Helmer. Naturally you are thinking of your father.

Nora. Yes—yes, of course. Just recall to your mind what these malicious creatures wrote in the papers about papa, and how horribly they slandered him. I believe they would have procured his dismissal if the Department had not sent you over to inquire into it, and if you had not been so kindly disposed and helpful to him.

Helmer. My little Nora, there is an important difference between your father and me. Your father's reputation as a public official was not above suspicion. Mine is, and I hope it will continue to be so, as long as I hold my office.

Nora. You never can tell what mischief these men may contrive. We ought to be so well off, so snug and happy here in our peaceful home, and have no cares— you and I and the children, Torvald! That is why I beg of you so earnestly——

Helmer. And it is just by interceding for him that you make it impossible for me to keep him. It is already known at the Bank that I mean to dismiss Krogstad. Is it to get about now that the new manager has changed his mind at his wife's bidding——

Nora. And what if it did?

Helmer. Of course!—if only this obstinate little person can get her way! Do you suppose I am going to make myself ridiculous before my whole staff, to let people think that I am a man to be swayed by all sorts of outside influence? I should very soon feel the consequences of it, I can tell you! And besides, there is one thing that makes it quite impossible for me to have Krogstad in the Bank as long as I am manager.

Nora. Whatever is that?

Helmer. His moral failings I might perhaps have overlooked, if necessary——

Nora. Yes, you could—couldn't you?

Helmer. And I hear he is a good worker, too. But I knew him when we were boys. It was one of those rash friendships that so often prove an incubus in after life. I may as well tell you plainly, we were once on very intimate terms with one another. But this tactless fellow lays no restraint on himself when other people are present. On the contrary, he thinks it gives him the right to adopt a familiar tone with me, and every minute it is "I say, Helmer, old fellow!" and that sort of thing. I assure you it is extremely painful for me. He would make my position in the Bank intolerable.

Nora. Torvald, I don't believe you mean that.

Helmer. Don't you? Why not?

Nora. Because it is such a narrow-minded way of looking at things.

Helmer. What are you saying? Narrow-minded? Do you think I am narrow-minded?

Nora. No, just the opposite, dear—and it is exactly for that reason.

Helmer. It's the same thing. You say my point of view is narrow-minded, so I must be so too. Narrow-minded! Very well—I must put an end to this. *(Goes to the hall-door and calls.)* Helen!

Nora. What are you going to do?

Helmer *(looking among his papers).* Settle it. *(Enter Maid.)* Look here; take this letter and go downstairs with it at once. Find a messenger and tell him to deliver it, and be quick. The address is on it, and here is the money.

Maid. Very well, sir. *(Exit with the letter.)*

Helmer *(putting his papers together).* Now then, little Miss Obstinate.

Nora *(breathlessly).* Torvald—what was that letter?

Helmer. Krogstad's dismissal.

Nora. Call her back, Torvald! There is still time. Oh Torvald, call her back! Do it for my sake—for your own sake—for the children's sake! Do you hear me, Torvald? Call her back! You don't know what that letter can bring upon us.

Helmer. It's too late.

Nora. Yes, it's too late.

Helmer. My dear Nora, I can forgive the anxiety you are in, although really it is an insult to me. It is, indeed. Isn't it an insult to think that I should be afraid of a starving quill-driver's vengeance? But I forgive you nevertheless, because it is such eloquent witness to your great love for me. *(Takes her in his arms.)* And that is as it should be, my darling Nora. Come what will, you may be sure I shall have both courage and strength if they be needed. You will see I am man enough to take everything upon myself.

Nora *(in a horror stricken voice).* What do you mean by that?

Helmer. Everything, I say——

Nora *(recovering herself).* You will never have to do that.

Helmer. That's right. Well, we will share it, Nora, as man and wife should. That is how it shall be. *(Caressing her.)* Are you content now? There! there!—not these frightened dove's eyes! The whole thing is only the wildest fancy!—Now, you must go and play through the Tarantella and practise with your tambourine. I shall go into the inner office and shut the door, and I shall hear nothing; you can make as much noise as you please. *(Turns back at the door.)* And when Rank comes, tell him where he will find me.

(Nods to her, takes his papers and goes into his room, and shuts the door after him.)

Nora *(bewildered with anxiety, stands as if rooted to the spot, and whispers).* He was capable of doing it. He will do it. He will do it in spite of everything.—No, not that! Never, never! Anything rather than that! Oh, for some help, some way out of it! *(The door-bell rings.)* Doctor Rank! Anything rather than that—any-thing, whatever it is!

(She puts her hands over her face, pulls herself together, goes to the door and opens it. Rank is standing without, hanging up his coat. During the following dialogue it begins to grow dark.)

Nora. Good-day, Doctor Rank. I knew your ring. But you mustn't go into Torvald now; I think he is busy with something.

Rank. And you?

Nora *(brings him in and shuts the door after him).* Oh, you know very well I always have time for you.

Rank. Thank you. I shall make use of as much of it as I can.

Nora. What do you mean by that? As much of it as you can?

Rank. Well, does that alarm you?

Nora. It was such a strange way of putting it. Is anything likely to happen?

Rank. Nothing but what I have long been prepared for. But certainly didn't expect it to happen so soon.

Nora *(gripping him by the arm).* What have you found out? Doctor Rank, you must tell me.

Rank *(sitting down by the stove).* It is all up with me. And it can't be helped.

Nora *(with a sigh of relief).* Is it about yourself?

Rank. Who else? It is no use lying to one's self. I am the most wretched of all my patients, Mrs. Helmer. Lately I have been taking stock of my internal economy. Bankrupt! Probably within a month I shall lie rotting in the churchyard.

Nora. What an ugly thing to say!

Rank. The thing itself is cursedly ugly, and the worst of it is that I shall have to face so much more that is ugly before that. I shall only make one more examina-tion of myself; when I have done that, I shall know pretty certainly when it will be that the horrors of dissolution will begin. There is something I want to tell you. Helmer's refined nature gives him an unconquerable disgust at everything that is ugly; I won't have him in my sick-room.

Nora. Oh, but, Doctor Rank——

Rank. I won't have him there. Not on any account. I bar my door to him. As soon as I am quite certain that the worst has come, I shall send you my card with a black cross on it, and then you will know that the loathsome end has begun.

Nora. You are quite absurd to-day. And I wanted you so much to be in a really good humour.

Rank. With death stalking beside me?—To have to pay this penalty for another man's sin! Is there any justice in that? And in every single family, in one way or another, some such inexorable retribution is being exacted——

Nora *(putting her hands over her ears).* Rubbish! Do talk of something cheerful.

Rank. Oh, it's a mere laughing matter, the whole thing. My poor innocent spine has to suffer for my father's youthful amusements.

Nora *(sitting at the table on the left)*. I suppose you mean that he was too partial to asparagus and pâté de foie gras, don't you.

Rank. Yes, and to truffles.

Nora. Truffles, yes. And oysters too, I suppose?

Rank. Oysters, of course, that goes without saying.

Nora. And heaps of port and champagne. It is sad that all these nice things should take their revenge on our bones.

Rank. Especially that they should revenge themselves on the unlucky bones of those who have not had the satisfaction of enjoying them.

Nora. Yes, that's the saddest part of it all.

Rank *(with a searching look at her)*. Hm!——

Nora *(after a short pause)*. Why did you smile?

Rank. No, it was you that laughed.

Nora. No, it was you that smiled, Doctor Rank!

Rank *(rising)*. You are a greater rascal than I thought.

Nora. I am in a silly mood to-day.

Rank. So it seems.

Nora *(putting her hands on his shoulders)*. Dear, dear Doctor Rank, death mustn't take you away from Torvald and me.

Rank. It is a loss you would easily recover from. Those who are gone are soon forgotten.

Nora *(looking at him anxiously)*. Do you believe that?

Rank. People form new ties, and then——

Nora. Who will form new ties?

Rank. Both you and Helmer, when I am gone. You yourself are already on the high road to it, I think. What did that Mrs. Linde want here last night?

Nora. Oho!—you don't mean to say you are jealous of poor Christine?

Rank. Yes, I am. She will be my successor in this house. When I am done for, this woman will——

Nora. Hush! don't speak so loud. She is in that room.

Rank. To-day again. There, you see.

Nora. She has only come to sew my dress for me. Bless my soul, how unreasonable you are! *(Sits down on the sofa.)* Be nice now, Doctor Rank, and to-morrow you will see how beautifully I shall dance, and you can imagine I am doing it all for you—and for Torvald too, of course. *(Takes various things out of the box.)* Doctor Rank, come and sit down here, and I will show you something.

Rank *(sitting down)*. What is it?

Nora. Just look at those!

Rank. Silk stockings.

Nora. Flesh-coloured. Aren't they lovely? It is so dark here now, but tomorrow—. No, no, no! you must only look at the feet. Oh well, you may have leave to look at the legs too.

Rank. Hm!——

Nora. Why are you looking so critical? Don't you think they will fit me?

Rank. I have no means of forming an opinion about that.

Nora *(looks at him for a moment).* For shame! *(Hits him lightly on the ear with the stockings.)* That's to punish you. *(Folds them up again.)*

Rank. And what other nice things am I to be allowed to see?

Nora. Not a single thing more, for being so naughty. *(She looks among the things, humming to herself.)*

Rank *(after a short silence).* When I am sitting here, talking to you as intimately as this, I cannot imagine for a moment what would have become of me if I had never come into this house.

Nora *(smiling).* I believe you do feel thoroughly at home with us.

Rank *(in a lower voice, looking straight in front of him).* And to be obliged to leave it all——

Nora. Nonsense, you are not going to leave it.

Rank *(as before).* And not be able to leave behind one the slightest token of one's gratitude, scarcely even a fleeting regret—nothing but an empty place which the first comer can fill as well as any other.

Nora. And if I asked you now for a—? No!

Rank. For what?

Nora. For a big proof of your friendship——

Rank. Yes, yes!

Nora. I mean a tremendously big favour——

Rank. Would you really make me so happy for once?

Nora. Ah, but you don't know what it is yet.

Rank. No—but tell me.

Nora. I really can't, Doctor Rank. It is something out of all reason; it means advice, and help, and a favour——

Rank. The bigger a thing it is the better. I can't conceive what it is you mean. Do tell me. Haven't I your confidence?

Nora. More than anyone else. I know you are my truest and best friend, and so I will tell you what it is. Well, Doctor Rank, it is something you must help me to prevent. You know how devotedly, how inexpressibly deeply Torvald loves me; he would never for a moment hesitate to give his life for me.

Rank *(leaning towards her).* Nora—do you think he is the only one——?

Nora *(with a slight start).* The only one—?

Rank. The only one who would gladly give his life for your sake.

Nora *(sadly).* Is that it?

Rank. I was determined you should know it before I went away, and there will never be a better opportunity than this. Now you know it, Nora. And now you know, too, that you can trust me as you would trust no one else.

Nora *(rises, deliberately and quietly).* Let me pass.

Rank *(makes room for her to pass him, but sits still).* Nora!

Nora *(at the hall door).* Helen, bring in the lamp. *(Goes over to the stove.)* Dear Doctor Rank, that was really horrid of you.

Rank. To have loved you as much as anyone else does? Was that horrid?

Nora. No, but to go and tell me so. There was really no need——

Rank. What do you mean? Did you know—? *(Maid enters with lamp, puts it down on the table, and goes out.)* Nora—Mrs. Helmer—tell me, had you any idea of this?

Nora. Oh, how do I know whether I had or whether I hadn't? I really can't tell you— To think you could be so clumsy, Doctor Rank! We were getting on so nicely.

Rank. Well, at all events you know now that you can command me, body and soul. So won't you speak out?

Nora *(looking at him).* After what happened?

Rank. I beg you to let me know what it is.

Nora. I can't tell you anything now.

Rank. Yes, yes. You mustn't punish me in that way. Let me have permission to do for you whatever a man may do.

Nora. You can do nothing for me now. Besides, I really don't need any help at all. You will find that the whole thing is merely fancy on my part. It really is so—of course it is! *(Sits down in the rocking-chair, and looks at him with a smile.)* You are a nice sort of man, Doctor Rank!—don't you feel ashamed of yourself, now the lamp has come?

Rank. Not a bit. But perhaps I had better go—forever?

Nora. No, indeed, you shall not. Of course you must come here just as before. You know very well Torvald can't do without you.

Rank. Yes, but you?

Nora. Oh, I am always tremendously pleased when you come.

Rank. It is just that, that put me on the wrong track. You are a riddle to me. I have often thought that you would almost as soon be in my company as in Helmer's.

Nora. Yes—you see there are some people one loves best, and others whom one would almost always rather have as companions.

Rank. Yes, there is something in that.

Nora. When I was at home, of course I loved papa best. But I always thought it tremendous fun if I could steal down into the maids' room, because they never moralised at all, and talked to each other about such entertaining things.

Rank. I see—it is *their* place I have taken.

Nora *(jumping up and going to him).*   Oh, dear, nice Doctor Rank, I never meant that at all. But surely you can understand that being with Torvald is a little like being with papa——

(Enter Maid from the hall.)

Maid. If you please, ma'am. *(Whispers and hands her a card.)*

Nora *(glancing at the card).*   Oh! *(Puts it in her pocket.)*

Rank. Is there anything wrong?

Nora. No, no, not in the least. It is only something—it is my new dress——

Rank. What? Your dress is lying there.

Nora. Oh, yes, that one; but this is another. I ordered it. Torvald mustn't know about it——

Rank. Oho! Then that was the great secret.

Nora. Of course. Just go in to him; he is sitting in the inner room. Keep him as long as——

Rank. Make your mind easy; I won't let him escape. (*Goes into Helmer's room.*)

Nora (*to the Maid*). And he is standing waiting in the kitchen?

Maid. Yes; he came up the back stairs.

Nora. But didn't you tell him no one was in?

Maid. Yes, but it was no good.

Nora. He won't go away?

Maid. No; he says he won't until he has seen you, ma'am.

Nora. Well, let him come in—but quietly. Helen, you mustn't say anything about it to anyone. It is a surprise for my husband.

Maid. Yes ma'am, I quite understand. (*Exit.*)

Nora. This dreadful thing is going to happen! It will happen in spite of me! No, no, no, it can't happen—it shan't happen!

(*She bolts the door of Helmer's room. The Maid opens the hall door for Krogstad and shuts it after him. He is wearing a fur coat, high boots and a fur cap.*)

Nora (*advancing towards him*). Speak low—my husband is at home.

Krogstad. No matter about that.

Nora. What do you want of me?

Krogstad. An explanation of something.

Nora. Make haste then. What is it?

Krogstad. You know, I suppose, that I have got my dismissal.

Nora. I couldn't prevent it, Mr. Krogstad. I fought as hard as I could on your side, but it was no good.

Krogstad. Does your husband love you so little, then? He knows what I can expose you to, and yet he ventures——

Nora. How can you suppose that he has any knowledge of the sort?

Krogstad. I didn't suppose so at all. It would not be the least like our dear Torvald Helmer to show so much courage—

Nora. Mr. Krogstad, a little respect for my husband, please.

Krogstad. Certainly—all the respect he deserves. But since you have kept the matter so carefully to yourself, I make bold to suppose that you have a little clearer idea, than you had yesterday, of what it actually is that you have done?

Nora. More than you could ever teach me.

Krogstad. Yes, such a bad lawyer as I am.

Nora. What is it you want of me?

Krogstad. Only to see how you were, Mrs. Helmer. I have been thinking about you all day long. A mere cashier, a quill-driver, a—well, a man like me—even he has a little of what is called feeling, you know.

Nora. Show it, then; think of my little children.

Krogstad. Have you and your husband thought of mine? But never mind about that. I only wanted to tell you that you need not take this matter too seriously. In the first place there will be no accusation made on my part.

Nora. No, of course not; I was sure of that.

Krogstad. The whole thing can be arranged amicably; there is no reason why any-one should know anything about it. It will remain a secret between us three.

Nora. My husband must never get to know anything about it.

Krogstad. How will you be able to prevent it? Am I to understand that you can pay the balance that is owing?

Nora. No, not just at present.

Krogstad. Or perhaps that you have some expedient for raising the money soon?

Nora. No expedient that I mean to make use of.

Krogstad. Well, in any case, it would have been of no use to you now. If you stood there with ever so much money in your hand, I would never part with your bond.

Nora. Tell me what purpose you mean to put it to.

Krogstad. I shall only preserve it—keep it in my possession. No one who is not concerned in the matter shall have the slightest hint of it. So that if the thought of it has driven you to any desperate resolution——

Nora. It has.

Krogstad. If you had it in your mind to run away from your home——

Nora. I had.

Krogstad. Or even something worse——

Nora. How could you know that?

Krogstad. Give up the idea.

Nora. How did you know I had thought of *that?*

Krogstad. Most of us think of that at first. I did, too—but I hadn't the courage.

Nora *(faintly).* No more had I.

Krogstad *(in a tone of relief).* No, that's it, isn't it—you hadn't the courage either?

Nora. No, I haven't—I haven't.

Krogstad. Besides, it would have been a great piece of folly. Once the first storm at home is over——. I have a letter for your husband in my pocket.

Nora. Telling him everything?

Krogstad. In as lenient a manner as I possibly could.

Nora *(quickly).* He mustn't get the letter. Tear it up. I will find some means of getting money.

Krogstad. Excuse me, Mrs. Helmer, but I think I told you just now——

Nora. I am not speaking of what I owe you. Tell me what sum you are asking my husband for, and I will get the money.

Krogstad. I am not asking your husband for a penny.

Nora. What do you want, then?

Krogstad. I will tell you. I want to rehabilitate myself, Mrs. Helmer; I want to get on; and in that your husband must help me. For the last year and a half I have not had a hand in anything dishonourable, and all that time I have been strug-gling in most restricted circumstances. I was content to work my way up step by step. Now I am turned out, and I am not going to be satisfied with merely being taken into favour again. I want to get on, I tell you. I want to get into the Bank again, in a higher position. Your husband must make a place for me——

Nora. That he will never do!

Krogstad. He will; I know him; he dare not protest. And as soon as I am in there again with him, then you will see! Within a year I shall be the manager's right hand. It will be Nils Krogstad and not Torvald Helmer who manages the Bank.

Nora. That's a thing you will never see!

Krogstad. Do you mean that you will——?

Nora. I have courage enough for it now.

Krogstad. Oh, you can't frighten me. A fine, spoilt lady like you——

Nora. You will see, you will see.

Krogstad. Under the ice, perhaps? Down into the cold, coal-black water? And then, in the spring, to float up to the surface, all horrible and unrecognisable, with your hair fallen out——

Nora. You can't frighten me.

Krogstad. Nor you me. People don't do such things, Mrs. Helmer. Besides, what use would it be? I should have him completely in my power all the same.

Nora. Afterwards? When I am no longer——

Krogstad. Have you forgotten that it is I who have the keeping of your reputation? *(Nora stands speechlessly looking at him.)* Well, now, I have warned you. Do not do anything foolish. When Helmer has had my letter, I shall expect a message from him. And be sure you remember that it is your husband himself who has forced me into such ways as this again. I will never forgive him for that. Good-bye, Mrs. Helmer. *(Exit through the hall.)*

Nora *(goes to the hall door, opens it slightly and listens).* He is going. He is not putting the letter in the box. Oh no, no! that's impossible! *(Opens the door by degrees.)* He is going. He is standing outside. He is not going downstairs. Is he hesitating? Can he——

(A letter drops into the box; then Krogstad's footsteps are heard, till they die away as he goes downstairs. Nora utters a stifled cry and runs across the room to the table by the sofa. A short pause.)

Nora. In the letter-box. *(Steals across to the hall door.)* There it lies—Torvald, Torvald, there is no hope for us now!

(Mrs. Linde comes in from the room on the left carrying the dress.)

Mrs. Linde. There, I can't see anything more to mend now. Would you like to try it on——?

Nora *(in a hoarse whisper).* Christine, come here.

Mrs. Linde *(throwing the dress down on the sofa).* What is the matter with you? You look so agitated!

Nora. Come here. Do you see that letter? There look—you can see it through the glass in the letter-box.

Mrs. Linde. Yes, I see it.

Nora. That letter is from Krogstad.

Mrs. Linde. Nora—it was Krogstad who lent you the money!

Nora. Yes, and now Torvald will know all about it.

Mrs. Linde. Believe me, Nora, that's the best thing for both of you.

Nora. You don't know all. I forged a name.

Mrs. Linde. Good heavens——!

Nora. I only want to say this to you, Christine—you must be my witness.

Mrs. Linde. Your witness? What do you mean? What am I to—?

Nora. If I should go out of my mind—and it might easily happen——

Mrs. Linde. Nora!

Nora. Or if anything else should happen to me—anything, for instance, that might prevent my being here—

Mrs. Linde. Nora! Nora! you are quite out of your mind.

Nora. And if it should happen that there were someone who wanted to take all the responsibility, all the blame, you understand——

Mrs. Linde. Yes, yes—but how can you suppose—?

Nora. Then you must be my witness, that it is not true, Christine. I am not out of my mind at all; I am in my right senses now, and I tell you no one else has known anything about it; I, and I alone, did the whole thing. Remember that.

Mrs. Linde. I will, indeed. But I don't understand all this.

Nora. How should you understand it? A wonderful thing is going to happen.

Mrs. Linde. A wonderful thing?

Nora. Yes, a wonderful thing!—But it is so terrible, Christine; it *mustn't* happen, not for all the world.

Mrs. Linde. I will go at once and see Krogstad.

Nora. Don't go to him; he will do you some harm.

Mrs. Linde. There was a time when he would gladly do anything for my sake.

Nora. He?

Mrs. Linde. Where does he live?

Nora. How should I know? Yes (*feeling in her pocket*) here is his card. But the letter, the letter——!

Helmer (*calls from his room, knocking at the door*). Nora!

Nora (*cries out anxiously*). Oh, what's that? What do you want?

Helmer. Don't be so frightened. We are not coming in; you have locked the door. Are you trying on your dress?

Nora. Yes, that's it. I look so nice, Torvald.

Mrs. Linde (*who has read the card*). I see he lives at the corner here.

Nora. Yes, but it's no use. It is hopeless. The letter is lying there in the box.

Mrs. Linde. And your husband keeps the key?

Nora. Yes, always.

Mrs. Linde. Krogstad must ask for his letter back unread, he must find some pretence——

Nora. But it is just at this time that Torvald generally——

Mrs. Linde. You must delay him. Go in to him in the meantime. I will come back as soon as I can.

(She goes out hurriedly through the hall door.)

Nora *(goes to Helmer's door, opens it and peeps in).* Torvald!

Helmer *(from the inner room).* Well? May I venture at last to come into my own room again? Come along, Rank, now you will see— *(Halting in the doorway.)* But what is this?

Nora. What is what, dear?

Helmer. Rank led me to expect a splendid transformation.

Rank *(in the doorway).* I understood so, but evidently I was mistaken.

Nora. Yes, nobody is to have the chance of admiring me in my dress until tomorrow.

Helmer. But, my dear Nora, you look so worn out. Have you been practising too much?

Nora. No, I have not practised at all.

Helmer. But you will need to—

Nora. Yes, indeed I shall, Torvald. But I can't get on a bit without you to help me; I have absolutely forgotten the whole thing.

Helmer. Oh, we will soon work it up again.

Nora. Yes, help me, Torvald. Promise that you will! I am so nervous about it—all the people—. You must give yourself up to me entirely this evening. Not the tiniest bit of business—you mustn't even take a pen in your hand. Will you promise, Torvald dear?

Helmer. I promise. This evening I will be wholly and absolutely at your service, you helpless little mortal. Ah, by the way, first of all I will just——

(Goes towards the hall door.)

Nora. What are you going to do there?

Helmer. Only see if any letters have come.

Nora. No, no! don't do that, Torvald!

Helmer. Why not?

Nora. Torvald, please don't. There is nothing there.

Helmer. Well, let me look. *(Turns to go to the letter-box. Nora at the piano, plays the first bars of the Tarantella. Helmer stops in the doorway.)* Aha!

Nora. I can't dance to-morrow if I don't practise with you.

Helmer *(going up to her).* Are you really so afraid of it, dear?

Nora. Yes, so dreadfully afraid of it. Let me practise at once; there is time now, before we go to dinner. Sit down and play for me, Torvald dear; criticise me, and correct me as you play.

Helmer. With great pleasure, if you wish me to.

(Sits down at the piano.)

Nora (*takes out of the box a tambourine and a long variegated shawl. She hastily drapes the shawl round her. Then she springs to the front of the stage and calls out*). Now play for me! I am going to dance!

(*Helmer plays and Nora dances. Rank stands by the piano behind Helmer and looks on.*)

Helmer (*as he plays*). Slower, slower!

Nora. I can't do it any other way.

Helmer. Not so violently, Nora!

Nora. This is the way.

Helmer (*stops playing*). No, no—that is not a bit right.

Nora (*laughing and swinging the tambourine*). Didn't I tell you so?

Rank. Let me play for her.

Helmer (*getting up*). Yes, do. I can correct her better then.

(*Rank sits down at the piano and plays. Nora dances more and more wildly. Helmer has taken up a position beside the stove, and during her dance gives her frequent instructions. She does not seem to hear him; her hair comes down and falls over her shoulders; she pays no attention to it, but goes on dancing. Enter Mrs. Linde.*)

Mrs. Linde (*standing as if spell-bound in the doorway*). Oh!——

Nora (*as she dances*). Such fun, Christine!

Helmer. My dear darling Nora, you are dancing as if your life depended on it.

Nora. So it does.

Helmer. Stop, Rank; this is sheer madness. Stop, I tell you! (*Rank stops playing, and Nora suddenly stands still. Helmer goes up to her.*) I could never have believed it. You have forgotten everything I taught you.

Nora (*throwing away the tambourine*). There, you see.

Helmer. You will want a lot of coaching.

Nora. Yes, you see how much I need it. You must coach me up to the last minute. Promise me that, Torvald!

Helmer. You can depend on me.

Nora. You must not think of anything but me, either to-day or to-morrow; you mustn't open a single letter—not even open the letter-box——

Helmer. Ah, you are still afraid of that fellow——

Nora. Yes, indeed I am.

Helmer. Nora, I can tell from your looks that there is a letter from him lying there.

Nora. I don't know; I think there is; but you must not read anything of that kind now. Nothing horrid must come between us till this is all over.

Rank (*whispers to Helmer*). You mustn't contradict her.

Helmer (*taking her in his arms*). The child shall have her way. But to-morrow night, after you have danced——

Nora. Then you will be free.

(*The Maid appears in the doorway to the right.*)

Maid. Dinner is served, ma'am.

Nora. We will have champagne, Helen.

Maid. Very good, ma'am. *(Exit.)*

Helmer. Hullo!—are we going to have a banquet?

Nora. Yes, a champagne banquet till the small hours. *(Calls out.)* And a few maca-roons, Helen—lots, just for once!

Helmer. Come, come, don't be so wild and nervous. Be my own little skylark, as you used.

Nora. Yes, dear, I will. But go in now and you too, Doctor Rank. Christine, you must help me to do up my hair.

Rank *(whispers to Helmer as they go out)*. I suppose there is nothing—she is not expecting anything?

Helmer. Far from it, my dear fellow; it is simply nothing more than this childish nervousness I was telling you of.

(They go into the right-hand room.)

Nora. Well!

Mrs. Linde. Gone out of town.

Nora. I could tell from your face.

Mrs. Linde. He is coming home to-morrow evening. I wrote a note for him.

Nora. You should have let it alone; you must prevent nothing. After all, it is splen-did to be waiting for a wonderful thing to happen.

Mrs. Linde. What is it that you are waiting for?

Nora. Oh, you wouldn't understand. Go in to them, I will come in a moment. *(Mrs. Linde goes into the dining-room. Nora stands still for a little while, as if to compose herself. Then she looks at her watch.)* Five o'clock. Seven hours till midnight. Then the Tarantella will be over. Twenty-four and seven? Thirty-one hours to live.

Helmer *(from the doorway on the right)*. Where's my little skylark?

Nora *(going to him with her arms outstretched)*. Here she is!

ACT III

The Same Scene *The table has been placed in the middle of the stage, with chairs round it. A lamp is burning on the table. The door into the hall stands open. Dance music is heard in the room above. Mrs. Linde is sitting at the table idly turning over the leaves of a book; she tries to read, but does not seem able to collect her thoughts. Every now and then she listens intently for a sound at the outer door.*

Mrs. Linde *(looking at her watch)*. Not yet—and the time is nearly up. If only he does not—. *(Listens again.)* Ah, there he is. *(Goes into the hall and opens the outer door carefully. Light footsteps are heard on the stairs. She whispers.)* Come in. There is no one here.

Krogstad (*in the doorway*). I found a note from you at home. What does this mean?

Mrs. Linde. It is absolutely necessary that I should have a talk with you.

Krogstad. Really? And is it absolutely necessary that it should be here?

Mrs. Linde. It is impossible where I live; there is no private entrance to my rooms. Come in; we are quite alone. The maid is asleep, and the Helmers are at the dance upstairs.

Krogstad (*coming into the room*). Are the Helmers really at a dance to-night?

Mrs. Linde. Yes, why not?

Krogstad. Certainly—why not?

Mrs. Linde. Now, Nils, let us have a talk.

Krogstad. Can we two have anything to talk about?

Mrs. Linde. We have a great deal to talk about.

Krogstad. I shouldn't have thought so.

Mrs. Linde. No, you have never properly understood me.

Krogstad. Was there anything else to understand except what was obvious to all the world—a heartless woman jilts a man when a more lucrative chance turns up?

Mrs. Linde. Do you believe I am as absolutely heartless as all that? And do you believe that I did it with a light heart?

Krogstad. Didn't you?

Mrs. Linde. Nils, did you really think that?

Krogstad. If it were as you say, why did you write to me as you did at the time?

Mrs. Linde. I could do nothing else. As I had to break with you, it was my duty also to put an end to all that you felt for me.

Krogstad (*wringing his hands*). So that was it. And all this—only for the sake of money!

Mrs. Linde. You must not forget that I had a helpless mother and two little brothers. We couldn't wait for you, Nils, your prospects seemed hopeless then.

Krogstad. That may be so, but you had no right to throw me over for anyone else's sake.

Mrs. Linde. Indeed I don't know. Many a time did I ask myself if I had the right to do it.

Krogstad (*more gently*). When I lost you, it was as if all the solid ground went from under my feet. Look at me now—I am a shipwrecked man clinging to a bit of wreckage.

Mrs. Linde. But help may be near.

Krogstad. It *was* near; but then you came and stood in my way.

Mrs. Linde. Unintentionally, Nils. It was only to-day that I learnt it was your place I was going to take in the Bank.

Krogstad. I believe you, if you say so. But now that you know it, are you not going to give it up to me?

Mrs. Linde. No, because that would not benefit you in the least.

Krogstad. Oh, benefit, benefit—I would have done it whether or no.

Mrs. Linde. I have learnt to act prudently. Life, and hard, bitter necessity have taught me that.

Krogstad. And life has taught me not to believe in fine speeches.

Mrs. Linde. Then life has taught you something very reasonable. But deeds you must believe in?

Krogstad. What do you mean by that?

Mrs. Linde. You said you were like a shipwrecked man clinging to some wreckage.

Krogstad. I had good reason to say so.

Mrs. Linde. Well, I am like a shipwrecked woman clinging to some wreckage— no one to mourn for, no one to care for.

Krogstad. It was your own choice.

Mrs. Linde. There was no other choice—then.

Krogstad. Well, what now?

Mrs. Linde. Nils, how would it be if we two shipwrecked people could join forces?

Krogstad. What are you saying?

Mrs. Linde. Two on the same piece of wreckage would stand a better chance than each on their own.

Krogstad. Christine!

Mrs. Linde. What do you suppose brought me to town?

Krogstad. Do you mean that you gave me a thought?

Mrs. Linde. I could not endure life without work. All my life, as long as I can remember, I have worked, and it has been my greatest and only pleasure. But now I am quite alone in the world—my life is so dreadfully empty and I feel so forsaken. There is not the least pleasure in working for one's self. Nils, give me someone and something to work for.

Krogstad. I don't trust that. It is nothing but a woman's overstrained sense of generosity that prompts you to make such an offer of yourself.

Mrs. Linde. Have you ever noticed anything of the sort in me?

Krogstad. Could you really do it? Tell me—do you know all about my past life?

Mrs. Linde. Yes.

Krogstad. And do you know what they think of me here?

Mrs. Linde. You seemed to me to imply that with me you might have been quite another man.

Krogstad. I am certain of it.

Mrs. Linde. Is it too late now?

Krogstad. Christine, are you saying this deliberately? Yes, I am sure you are. I see it in your face. Have you really the courage then—?

Mrs. Linde. I want to be a mother to someone, and your children need a mother. We two need each other. Nils, I have faith in your real character—I can dare anything together with you.

Krogstad *(grasps her hands)*. Thanks, thanks, Christine! Now I shall find a way to clear myself in the eyes of the world. Ah, but I forgot——

Mrs. Linde *(listening)*. Hush! The Tarantella! Go, go!

Krogstad. Why? What is it?

Mrs. Linde. Do you hear them up there? When that is over, we may expect them back.

Krogstad. Yes, yes—I will go. But it is all no use. Of course you are not aware what steps I have taken in the matter of the Helmers.

Mrs. Linde. Yes, I know all about that.

Krogstad. And in spite of that have you the courage to—?

Mrs. Linde. I understand very well to what lengths a man like you might be driven by despair.

Krogstad. If I could only undo what I have done!

Mrs. Linde. You cannot. Your letter is lying in the letter-box now.

Krogstad. Are you sure of that?

Mrs. Linde. Quite sure, but——

Krogstad (with a searching look at her). Is that what it all means?—that you want to save your friend at my cost? Tell me frankly. Is that it?

Mrs. Linde. Nils, a woman who has once sold herself for another's sake, doesn't do it a second time.

Krogstad. I will ask for my letter back.

Mrs. Linde. No, no.

Krogstad. Yes, of course I will. I will wait here till Helmer comes; I will tell him he must give me my letter back—that it only concerns my dismissal—that he is not to read it——

Mrs. Linde. No, Nils, you must not recall your letter.

Krogstad. But, tell me, wasn't it for that very purpose that you asked me to meet you here?

Mrs. Linde. In my first moment of fright, it was. But twenty-four hours have elapsed since then, and in that time I have witnessed incredible things in this house. Helmer must know all about it. This unhappy secret must be disclosed; they must have a complete understanding between them, which is impossible with all this concealment and falsehood going on.

Krogstad. Very well, if you will take the responsibility. But there is one thing I can do in any case, and I shall do it at once.

Mrs. Linde (listening). You must be quick and go! The dance is over; we are not safe a moment longer.

Krogstad. I will wait for you below.

Mrs. Linde. Yes, do. You must see me back to my door.

Krogstad. I have never had such an amazing piece of good fortune in my life.

(Goes out through the outer door. The door between the room and the hall remains open.)

Mrs. Linde (tidying up the room and laying her hat and cloak ready). What a difference! what a difference! Someone to work for and live for—a home to bring comfort into. That I will do, indeed. I wish they would be quick and come— (Listens.) Ah, there they are now. I must put on my things.

(Takes up her hat and cloak. Helmer's and Nora's voices are heard outside; a key is turned, and Helmer brings Nora almost by force into the hall. She is in an Italian *costume with a large black shawl round her; he is in evening dress and a black domino*[2] *which is flying open.)*

Nora *(hanging back in the doorway, and struggling with him).* No, no, no!—don't take me in. I want to go upstairs again; I don't want to leave so early.
Helmer. But, my dearest Nora——
Nora. Please, Torvald dear—please, *please*—only an hour more.
Helmer. Not a single minute, my sweet Nora. You know that was our agreement. Come along into the room; you are catching cold standing there.

(He brings her gently into the room, in spite of her resistance.)

Mrs. Linde. Good evening.
Nora. Christine!
Helmer. You here, so late, Mrs. Linde?
Mrs. Linde. Yes, you must excuse me; I was so anxious to see Nora in her dress.
Nora. Have you been sitting here waiting for me?
Mrs. Linde. Yes, unfortunately I came too late, you had already gone upstairs; and I thought I couldn't go away again without having seen you.
Helmer *(taking off Nora's shawl).* Yes, take a good look at her. I think she is worth looking at. Isn't she charming, Mrs. Linde?
Mrs. Linde. Yes, indeed she is.
Helmer. Doesn't she look remarkably pretty? Everyone thought so at the dance. But she is terribly self-willed, this sweet little person. What are we to do with her? You will hardly believe that I had almost to bring her away by force.
Nora. Torvald, you will repent not having let me stay, even if it were only for half an hour.
Helmer. Listen to her, Mrs. Linde! She had danced her Tarantella, and it had been a tremendous success, as it deserved—although possibly the performance was a trifle too realistic—a little more so, I mean, than was strictly compatible with the limitations of art. But never mind about that! The chief thing is, she had made a success—she had made a tremendous success. Do you think I was going to let her remain there after that, and spoil the effect? No indeed! I took my charming little Capri maiden—my capricious little Capri maiden, I should say—on my arm; took one quick turn round the room; a curtsey on either side, and, as they say in novels, the beautiful apparition disappeared. An exit ought always to be effective, Mrs. Linde; but that is what I cannot make Nora understand. Pooh! this room is hot. *(Throws his domino on a chair and opens the door of his room.)* Hullo! it's dark in here. Oh, of course— excuse me——.

(He goes in and lights some candles.)

---

[2] A long, loose, hooded cloak.

Nora (*in a hurried and breathless whisper*). Well?

Mrs. Linde (*in a low voice*). I have had a talk with him.

Nora. Yes, and——

Mrs. Linde. Nora, you must tell your husband all about it.

Nora (*in an expressionless voice*). I knew it.

Mrs. Linde. You have nothing to be afraid of as far as Krogstad is concerned; but you must tell him.

Nora. I won't tell him.

Mrs. Linde. Then the letter will.

Nora. Thank you, Christine. Now I know what I must do. Hush——!

Helmer (*coming in again*). Well, Mrs. Linde, have you admired her?

Mrs. Linde. Yes, and now I will say good-night.

Helmer. What, already? Is this yours, this knitting?

Mrs. Linde (*taking it*). Yes, thank you, I have very nearly forgotten it.

Helmer. So you knit?

Mrs. Linde. Of course.

Helmer. Do you know, you ought to embroider.

Mrs. Linde. Really? Why?

Helmer. Yes, it's far more becoming. Let me show you. You hold the embroidery thus in your left hand, and use the needle with the right—like this—with a long, easy sweep. Do you see?

Mrs. Linde. Yes, perhaps——

Helmer. But in the case of knitting—that can never be anything but ungraceful; look here—the arms close together, the knitting-needles going up and down—it has a sort of Chinese effect—. That was really excellent champagne they gave us.

Mrs. Linde. Well,—good-night, Nora, and don't be self-willed any more.

Helmer. That's right, Mrs. Linde.

Mrs. Linde. Good-night, Mr. Helmer.

Helmer (*accompanying her to the door*). Good-night, good-night. I hope you will get home all right. I should be very happy to—but you haven't any great distance to go. Good-night, good-night. (*She goes out; he shuts the door after her, and comes in again.*) Ah!—at last we have got rid of her. She is a frightful bore, that woman.

Nora. Aren't you very tired, Torvald?

Helmer. No, not in the least.

Nora. Nor sleepy?

Helmer. Not a bit. On the contrary, I feel extraordinarily lively. And you?—you really look both tired and sleepy.

Nora. Yes, I am very tired. I want to go to sleep at once.

Helmer. There, you see it was quite right of me not to let you stay there any longer.

Nora. Everything you do is quite right, Torvald.

Helmer (*kissing her on the forehead*). Now my little skylark is speaking reasonably. Did you notice what good spirits Rank was in this evening?

Nora. Really? Was he? I didn't speak to him at all.

Helmer. And I very little, but I have not for a long time seen him in such good form. (*Looks for a while at her and then goes nearer to her.*) It is delightful to be at home by ourselves again, to be all alone with you—you fascinating, charming little darling!

Nora. Don't look at me like that, Torvald.

Helmer. Why shouldn't I look at my dearest treasure?—at all the beauty that is mine, all my very own?

Nora (*going to the other side of the table*). You mustn't say things like that to me to-night.

Helmer (*following her*). You have still got the Tarantella in your blood, I see. And it makes you more captivating than ever. Listen—the guests are beginning to go now. (*In a lower voice.*) Nora—soon the whole house will be quiet.

Nora. Yes, I hope so.

Helmer. Yes, my own darling Nora. Do you know, when I am out at a party with you like this, why I speak so little to you, keep away from you, and only send a stolen glance in your direction now and then?—do you know why I do that? It is because I make believe to myself that we are secretly in love, and you are my secretly promised bride, and that no one suspects there is anything between us.

Nora. Yes, yes—I know very well your thoughts are with me all the time.

Helmer. And when we are leaving, and I am putting the shawl over your beautiful young shoulders—on your lovely neck—then I imagine that you are my young bride and that we have just come from the wedding, and I am bringing you for the first time into our home—to be alone with you for the first time—quite alone with my shy little darling! All this evening I have longed for nothing but you. When I watched the seductive figures of the Tarantella, my blood was on fire; I could endure it no longer, and that was why I brought you down so early——

Nora. Go away, Torvald! You must let me go. I won't——

Helmer. What's that? You're joking, my little Nora! You won't—you won't? Am I not your husband—?

(*A knock is heard at the outer door.*)

Nora (*starting*). Did you hear——?

Helmer (*going into the hall*). Who is it?

Rank (*outside*). It is I. May I come in for a moment?

Helmer (*in a fretful whisper*). Oh, what does he want now? (*Aloud.*) Wait a minute? (*Unlocks the door.*) Come, that's kind of you not to pass by our door.

Rank. I thought I heard your voice, and felt as if I should like to look in. (*With a swift glance round.*) Ah, yes!—these dear familiar rooms. You are very happy and cosy in here, you two.

Helmer. It seems to me that you looked after yourself pretty well upstairs too.

Rank. Excellently. Why shouldn't I? Why shouldn't one enjoy everything in this world?—at any rate as much as one can, and as long as one can. The wine was capital——

Helmer. Especially the champagne.

Rank. So you noticed that too? It is almost incredible how much I managed to put away!

Nora. Torvald drank a great deal of champagne tonight, too.

Rank. Did he?

Nora. Yes, and he is always in such good spirits afterwards.

Rank. Well, why should one not enjoy a merry evening after a well-spent day?

Helmer. Well spent? I am afraid I can't take credit for that.

Rank (clapping him on the back). But I can, you know!

Nora. Doctor Rank, you must have been occupied with some scientific investigation to-day.

Rank. Exactly.

Helmer. Just listen—little Nora talking about scientific investigations!

Nora. And may I congratulate you on the result?

Rank. Indeed you may.

Nora. Was it favourable, then?

Rank. The best possible, for both doctor and patient—certainty.

Nora (quickly and searchingly). Certainty?

Rank. Absolute certainty. So wasn't I entitled to make a merry evening of it after that?

Nora. Yes, you certainly were, Doctor Rank.

Helmer. I think so too, so long as you don't have to pay for it in the morning.

Rank. Oh well, one can't have anything in this life without paying for it.

Nora. Doctor Rank—are you fond of fancy-dress balls?

Rank. Yes, if there is a fine lot of pretty costumes.

Nora. Tell me—what shall we two wear at the next?

Helmer. Little featherbrain!—are you thinking of the next already?

Rank. We two? Yes, I can tell you. You shall go as a good fairy——

Helmer. Yes, but what do you suggest as an appropriate costume for that?

Rank. Let your wife go dressed just as she is in everyday life.

Helmer. That was really very prettily turned. But can't you tell us what you will be?

Rank. Yes, my dear friend, I have quite made up my mind about that.

Helmer. Well?

Rank. At the next fancy dress ball I shall be invisible.

Helmer. That's a good joke!

Rank. There is a big black hat—have you never heard of hats that make you invisible? If you put one on, no one can see you.

Helmer (suppressing a smile). Yes, you are quite right.

Rank. But I am clean forgetting what I came for. Helmer, give me a cigar—one of the dark Havanas.

Helmer. With the greatest pleasure.

(Offers him his case.)

Rank (takes a cigar and cuts off the end). Thanks.

Nora (striking a match). Let me give you a light.

Rank. Thank you. (*She holds the match for him to light his cigar.*) And now good-bye!

Helmer. Good-bye, good-bye, dear old man!

Nora. Sleep well, Doctor Rank.

Rank. Thank you for that wish.

Nora. Wish me the same.

Rank. You? Well, if you want me to—sleep well! And thanks for the light.

(*He nods to them both and goes out.*)

Helmer (*in a subdued voice*). He has drunk more than he ought.

Nora (*absently*). Maybe. (*Helmer takes a bunch of keys out of his pocket and goes into the hall.*) Torvald! what are you going to do there?

Helmer. Empty the letter-box; it is quite full; there will be no room to put the newspaper in to-morrow morning.

Nora. Are you going to work to-night?

Helmer. You know quite well I'm not. What is this? Some one has been at the lock.

Nora. At the lock—?

Helmer. Yes, someone has. What can it mean? I should never have thought the maid—. Here is a broken hairpin. Nora, it is one of yours.

Nora (*quickly*). Then it must have been the children—

Helmer. Then you must get them out of those ways. There, at last I have got it open. (*Takes out the contents of the letter-box, and calls to the kitchen.*) Helen!—Helen, put out the light over the front door. (*Goes back into the room and shuts the door into the hall. He holds out his hand full of letters.*) Look at that—look what a heap of them there are. (*Turning them over.*) What on earth is that?

Nora (*at the window*). The letter—No! Torvald, no!

Helmer. Two cards—of Rank's.

Nora. Of Doctor Rank's?

Helmer (*looking at them*). Doctor Rank. They were on the top. He must have put them in when he went out.

Nora. Is there anything written on them?

Helmer. There is a black cross over the name. Look there—what an uncomfortable idea! It looks as if he were announcing his own death.

Nora. It is just what he is doing.

Helmer. What? Do you know anything about it? Has he said anything to you?

Nora. Yes. He told me that when the cards came it would be his leave-taking from us. He means to shut himself up and die.

Helmer. My poor old friend. Certainly I knew we should not have him very long with us. But so soon! And so he hides himself away like a wounded animal.

Nora. If it has to happen, it is best it should be without a word—don't you think so, Torvald?

Helmer (*walking up and down*). He had so grown into our lives. I can't think of him as having gone out of them. He, with his sufferings and his loneliness, was like a cloudy background to our sunlit happiness. Well, perhaps it is best so. For him, anyway. (*Standing still.*) And perhaps for us too, Nora. We two are thrown quite upon each other now. (*Puts his arms round her.*) My darling wife, I don't feel as if I could hold you tight enough. Do you know, Nora, I have often wished that you might be threatened by some great danger, so that I might risk my life's blood, and everything, for your sake.

Nora (*disengages herself, and says firmly and decidedly*). Now you must read your letters, Torvald.

Helmer. No, no; not to-night. I want to be with you, my darling wife.

Nora. With the thought of your friend's death——

Helmer. You are right, it has affected us both. Something ugly has come between us—the thought of the horrors of death. We must try and rid our minds of that. Until then—we will each go to our own room.

Nora (*hanging on his neck*). Good-night, Torvald—Good-night!

Helmer (*kissing her on the forehead*). Good-night, my little singing-bird. Sleep sound, Nora. Now I will read my letters through.

(*He takes his letters and goes into his room, shutting the door after him.*)

Nora (*gropes distractedly about, seizes Helmer's domino, throws it round her, while she says in quick, hoarse, spasmodic whispers*). Never to see him again. Never! Never! (*Puts her shawl over her head.*) Never to see my children again either— never again. Never! Never!—Ah! the icy, black water—the unfathomable depths—If only it were over! He has got it now—now he is reading it. Good- bye, Torvald and my children!

(*She is about to rush out through the hall, when Helmer opens his door hurriedly and stands with an open letter in his hand.*)

Helmer. Nora!

Nora. Ah!——

Helmer. What is this? Do you know what is in this letter?

Nora. Yes, I know. Let me go! Let me get out!

Helmer (*holding her back*). Where are you going?

Nora (*trying to get free*). You shan't save me, Torvald!

Helmer (*reeling*). True? Is this true, what I read here? Horrible! No, no—it is impossible that it can be true.

Nora. It is true. I have loved you above everything else in the world.

Helmer. Oh, don't let us have any silly excuses.

Nora (*taking a step towards him*). Torvald——!

Helmer. Miserable creature—what have you done?

Nora. Let me go. You shall not suffer for my sake. You shall not take it upon yourself.

Helmer. No tragedy airs, please. (*Locks the hall door.*) Here you shall stay and give me an explanation. Do you understand what you have done? Answer me? Do you understand what you have done?

Nora (*looks steadily at him and says with a growing look of coldness in her face*). Yes, now I am beginning to understand thoroughly.

Helmer (*walking about the room*). What a horrible awakening! All these eight years—she who was my joy and pride—a hypocrite, a liar—worse, worse—a criminal! The unutterable ugliness of it all! For shame! For shame! (*Nora is silent and looks steadily at him. He stops in front of her.*) I ought to have suspected that something of the sort would happen. I ought to have foreseen it. All your father's want of principle—be silent!—all your father's want of principle has come out in you. No religion, no morality, no sense of duty—. How I am punished for having winked at what he did! I did it for your sake, and this is how you repay me.

Nora. Yes, that's just it.

Helmer. Now you have destroyed all my happiness. You have ruined all my future. It is horrible to think of! I am in the power of an unscrupulous man; he can do what he likes with me, ask anything he likes of me, give me any orders he pleases—I dare not refuse. And I must sink to such miserable depths because of a thoughtless woman!

Nora. When I am out of the way, you will be free.

Helmer. No fine speeches, please. Your father had always plenty of those ready, too. What good would it be to me if you were out of the way, as you say? Not the slightest. He can make the affair known everywhere; and if he does, I may be falsely suspected of having been a party to your criminal action. Very likely people will think I was behind it all—that it was I who prompted you! And I have to thank you for all this—you whom I have cherished during the whole of our married life. Do you understand now what it is you have done for me?

Nora (*coldly and quietly*). Yes.

Helmer. It is so incredible that I can't take it in. But we must come to some understanding. Take off that shawl. Take it off, I tell you. I must try and appease him some way or another. The matter must be hushed up at any cost. And as for you and me, it must appear as if everything between us were just as before—but naturally only in the eyes of the world. You will still remain in my house, that is a matter of course. But I shall not allow you to bring up the children; I dare not trust them to you. To think that I should be obliged to say so to one whom I have loved so dearly, and whom I still——. No, that is all over. From this moment happiness is not the question; all that concerns us is to save the remains, the fragments, the appearance——

(*A ring is heard at the front-door bell.*)

Helmer (*with a start*). What is that? So late! Can the worst——? Can he——? Hide yourself, Nora. Say you are ill.

(*Nora stands motionless. Helmer goes and unlocks the hall door.*)

Maid (*half-dressed, comes to the door*). A letter for the mistress.

Helmer. Give it to me. (*Takes the letter, and shuts the door.*) Yes, it is from him. You shall not have it; I will read it myself.

Nora. Yes, read it.

Helmer (*standing by the lamp*). I scarcely have the courage to do it. It may mean ruin for both of us. No, I must know. (*Tears open the letter, runs his eye over a few lines, looks at a paper enclosed and gives a shout of joy.*) Nora! (*She looks at him questioningly.*) Nora!—No, I must read it once again——. Yes, it is true! I am saved! Nora, I am saved!

Nora. And I?

Helmer. You too, of course; we are both saved, both you and I. Look, he sends you your bond back. He says he regrets and repents—that a happy change in his life—never mind what he says! We are saved, Nora! No one can do anything to you. Oh, Nora, Nora!—no, first I must destroy these hateful things. Let me see——. (*Takes a look at the bond.*) No, no, I won't look at it. The whole thing shall be nothing but a bad dream to me. (*Tears up the bond and both letters, throws them all into the stove, and watches them burn.*) There—now it doesn't exist any longer. He says that since Christmas Eve you——. These must have been three dreadful days for you, Nora.

Nora. I have fought a hard fight these three days.

Helmer. And suffered agonies, and seen no way out but——. No, we won't call any of the horrors to mind. We will only shout with joy, and keep saying, "It's all over! It's all over!" Listen to me, Nora. You don't seem to realise that it is all over. What is this?—such a cold, set face! My poor little Nora, I quite understand; you don't feel as if you could believe that I have forgiven you. But it is true, Nora, I swear it; I have forgiven you everything. I know that what you did, you did out of love for me.

Nora. That is true.

Helmer. You have loved me as a wife ought to love her husband. Only you had not sufficient knowledge to judge of the means you used. But do you suppose you are any the less dear to me, because you don't understand how to act on your own responsibility? No, no; only lean on me; I will advise you and direct you. I should not be a man if this womanly helplessness did not just give you a double attractiveness in my eyes. You must not think any more about the hard things I said in my first moment of consternation, when I thought everything was going to overwhelm me. I have forgiven you, Nora; I swear to you I have forgiven you.

(*She goes out through the door to the right.*)

Helmer. No, don't go——. (*Looks in.*) What are you doing in there?

Nora (*from within*). Taking off my fancy dress.

Helmer (*standing at the open door*). Yes, do. Try and calm yourself, and make your mind easy again, my frightened little singing-bird. Be at rest, and feel secure; I have broad wings to shelter you under. (*Walks up and down by the door.*) How warm and cosy our home is, Nora. Here is shelter for you; here I will protect you like a hunted dove that I have saved from a hawk's claws. I will bring peace to your poor beating heart. It will come, little by little, Nora, believe me.

Tomorrow morning you will look upon it all quite differently; soon everything will be just as it was before. Very soon you won't need me to assure you that I have forgiven you; you will yourself feel the certainty that I have done so. Can you suppose I should ever think of such a thing as repudiating you, or even reproaching you? You have no idea what a true man's heart is like, Nora. There is something so indescribably sweet and satisfying, to a man, in the knowledge that he has forgiven his wife—forgiven her freely, and with all his heart. It seems as if that had made her, as it were, doubly his own; he has given her a new life, so to speak; and she has in a way become both wife and child to him. So you shall be for me after this, my little scared, helpless darling. Have no anxiety about anything, Nora; only be frank and open with me, and I will serve as will and conscience both to you——. What is this? Not gone to bed? Have you changed your things?

Nora (*in everyday dress*). Yes, Torvald, I have changed my things now.

Helmer. But what for?—so late as this.

Nora. I shall not sleep to-night.

Helmer. But, my dear Nora——

Nora (*looking at her watch*). It is not so very late. Sit down here, Torvald. You and I have much to say to one another.

(*She sits down at one side of the table.*)

Helmer. Nora—what is this?—this cold, set face?

Nora. Sit down. It will take some time; I have a lot to talk over with you.

Helmer (*sits down at the opposite side of the table*). You alarm me, Nora!—and I don't understand you.

Nora. No, that is just it. You don't understand me, and I have never understood you either—before to-night. No, you mustn't interrupt me. You must simply listen to what I say. Torvald, this is a settling of accounts.

Helmer. What do you mean by that?

Nora (*after a short silence*). Isn't there one thing that strikes you as strange in our sitting here like this?

Helmer. What is that?

Nora. We have been married now eight years. Does it not occur to you that this is the first time we two, you and I, husband and wife, have had a serious conversation?

Helmer. What do you mean by serious?

Nora. In all these eight years—longer than that—from the very beginning of our acquaintance, we have never exchanged a word on any serious subject.

Helmer. Was it likely that I would be continually and for ever telling you about worries that you could not help me to bear?

Nora. I am not speaking about business matters. I say that we have never sat down in earnest together to try and get at the bottom of anything.

Helmer. But, dearest Nora, would it have been any good to you?

Nora. That is just it; you have never understood me. I have been greatly wronged, Torvald—first by papa and then by you.

Helmer. What! By us two—by us two, who have loved you better than anyone else in the world?

Nora (*shaking her head*). You have never loved me. You have only thought it pleasant to be in love with me.

Helmer. Nora, what do I hear you saying?

Nora. It is perfectly true, Torvald. When I was at home with papa, he told me his opinion about everything, and so I had the same opinions; and if I differed from him I concealed the fact, because he would not have liked it. He called me his doll-child, and he played with me just as I used to play with my dolls. And when I came to live with you——

Helmer. What sort of an expression is that to use about our marriage?

Nora (*undisturbed*). I mean that I was simply transferred from papa's hands into yours. You arranged everything according to your own taste, and so I got the same tastes as you—or else I pretended to, I am really not quite sure which—I think sometimes the one and sometimes the other. When I look back on it, it seems to me as if I had been living here like a poor woman—just from hand to mouth. I have existed merely to perform tricks for you, Torvald. But you would have it so. You and papa have committed a great sin against me. It is your fault that I have made nothing of my life.

Helmer. How unreasonable and how ungrateful you are, Nora! Have you not been happy here?

Nora. No, I have never been happy. I thought I was, but it has never really been so.

Helmer. Not—not happy!

Nora. No, only merry. And you have always been so kind to me. But our home has been nothing but a playroom. I have been your doll-wife, just as at home I was papa's doll-child; and here the children have been my dolls. I thought it great fun when you played with me, just as they thought it great fun when I played with them. That is what our marriage has been, Torvald.

Helmer. There is some truth in what you say—exaggerated and strained as your view of it is. But for the future it shall be different. Playtime shall be over, and lesson-time shall begin.

Nora. Whose lessons? Mine, or the children's?

Helmer. Both your and the children's, my darling Nora.

Nora. Alas, Torvald, you are not the man to educate me into being a proper wife for you.

Helmer. And you can say that!

Nora. And I—how am I fitted to bring up the children?

Helmer. Nora!

Nora. Didn't you say so yourself a little while ago—that you dare not trust me to bring them up?

Helmer. In a moment of anger! Why do you pay any heed to that?

Nora. Indeed, you were perfectly right. I am not fit for the task. There is another task I must undertake first. I must try and educate myself—you are not the man to help me in that. I must do that for myself. And that is why I am going to leave you now.

Helmer (*springing up*). What do you say?

Nora. I must stand quite alone, if I am to understand myself and everything about me. It is for that reason that I cannot remain with you any longer.

Helmer. Nora! Nora!

Nora. I am going away from here now, at once. I am sure Christine will take me in for the night——

Helmer. You are out of your mind! I won't allow it! I forbid you!

Nora. It is no use forbidding me anything any longer. I will take with me what belongs to myself. I will take nothing from you, either now or later.

Helmer. What sort of madness is this!

Nora. To-morrow I shall go home—I mean, to my old home. It will be easiest for me to find something to do there.

Helmer. You blind, foolish woman!

Nora. I must try and get some sense, Torvald.

Helmer. To desert your home, your husband and your children! And you don't consider what people will say!

Nora. I cannot consider that at all. I only know that it is necessary for me.

Helmer. It's shocking. This is how you would neglect your most sacred duties.

Nora. What do you consider my most sacred duties?

Helmer. Do I need to tell you that? Are they not your duties to your husband and your children?

Nora. I have other duties just as sacred.

Helmer. That you have not. What duties could those be?

Nora. Duties to myself.

Helmer. Before all else, you are a wife and a mother.

Nora. I don't believe that any longer. I believe that before all else I am a reasonable human being, just as you are—or, at all events, that I must try and become one. I know quite well, Torvald, that most people would think you right, and that views of that kind are to be found in books; but I can no longer content myself with what most people say, or with what is found in books. I must think over things for myself and get to understand them.

Helmer. Can you not understand your place in your own home? Have you not a reliable guide in such matters as that?—have you no religion?

Nora. I am afraid, Torvald, I do not exactly know what religion is.

Helmer. What are you saying?

Nora. I know nothing but what the clergyman said, when I went to be confirmed. He told us that religion was this, and that, and the other. When I am away from all this, and am alone, I will look into that matter too. I will see if what the clergyman said is true, or at all events if it is true for me.

Helmer. This is unheard of in a girl of your age! But if religion cannot lead you aright, let me try and awaken your conscience. I suppose you have some moral sense? Or—answer me—am I to think you have none?

Nora. I assure you, Torvald, that is not an easy question to answer. I really don't know. The thing perplexes me altogether. I only know that you and I look at it in quite another light. I am learning, too, that the law is quite another thing from what I supposed; but I find it impossible to convince myself that the law is right. According to it a woman has no right to spare her old dying father, or to save her husband's life. I can't believe that.

Helmer. You talk like a child. You don't understand the conditions of the world in which you live.

Nora. No, I don't. But now I am going to try. I am going to see if I can make out who is right, the world or I.

Helmer. You are ill, Nora; you are delirious; I almost think you are out of your mind.

Nora. I have never felt my mind so clear and certain as to-night.

Helmer. And is it with a clear and certain mind that you forsake your husband and your children?

Nora. Yes, it is.

Helmer. Then there is only one possible explanation.

Nora. What is that?

Helmer. You do not love me any more.

Nora. No, that is just it.

Helmer. Nora!—and you can say that?

Nora. It gives me great pain, Torvald, for you have always been so kind to me, but I cannot help it. I do not love you any more.

Helmer (regaining his composure). Is that a clear and certain conviction too?

Nora. Yes, absolutely clear and certain. That is the reason why I will not stay here any longer.

Helmer. And can you tell me what I have done to forfeit your love?

Nora. Yes, indeed I can. It was to-night, when the wonderful thing did not happen; then I saw you were not the man I had thought you.

Helmer. Explain yourself better—I don't understand you.

Nora. I have waited so patiently for eight years; for, goodness knows, I knew very well that wonderful things don't happen every day. Then this horrible misfortune came upon me; and then I felt quite certain that the wonderful thing was going to happen at last. When Krogstad's letter was lying out there, never for a moment did I imagine that you would consent to accept this man's conditions. I was so absolutely certain that you would say to him: Publish the thing to the whole world. And when that was done——

Helmer. Yes, what then?—when I had exposed my wife to shame and disgrace?

Nora. When that was done, I was so absolutely certain, you would come forward and take everything upon yourself, and say: I am the guilty one.

Helmer. Nora——!

Nora. You mean that I would never have accepted such a sacrifice on your part? No, of course not. But what would my assurances have been worth against yours? That was the wonderful thing which I hoped for and feared; and it was to prevent that, that I wanted to kill myself.

Helmer. I would gladly work night and day for you, Nora—bear sorrow and want for your sake. But no man would sacrifice his honour for the one he loves.

Nora. It is a thing hundreds of thousands of women have done.

Helmer. Oh, you think and talk like a heedless child.

Nora. Maybe. But you neither think nor talk like the man I could bind myself to. As soon as your fear was over—and it was not fear for what threatened me, but for what might happen to you—when the whole thing was past, as far as you were concerned it was exactly as if nothing at all had happened. Exactly as before, I was your little skylark, your doll, which you would in future treat with doubly gentle care, because it was so brittle and fragile. *(Getting up.)* Torvald— it was then it dawned upon me that for eight years I had been living here with a strange man, and had borne him three children——. Oh, I can't bear to think of it! I could tear myself into little bits!

Helmer *(sadly).* I see, I see. An abyss has opened between us—there is no denying it. But, Nora, would it not be possible to fill it up?

Nora. As I am now, I am no wife for you.

Helmer. I have it in me to become a different man.

Nora. Perhaps—if your doll is taken away from you.

Helmer. But to part!—to part from you! No, no, Nora, I can't understand that idea.

Nora *(going out to the right).* That makes it all the more certain that it must be done.

(She comes back with her cloak and hat and a small bag which she puts on a chair by the table.)

Helmer. Nora, Nora, not now! Wait till to-morrow.

Nora *(putting on her cloak).* I cannot spend the night in a strange man's room.

Helmer. But can't we live here like brother and sister——?

Nora *(putting on her hat).* You know very well that would not last long. *(Puts the shawl round her.)* Good-bye, Torvald. I won't see the little ones. I know they are in better hands than mine. As I am now, I can be of no use to them.

Helmer. But some day, Nora—some day?

Nora. How can I tell? I have no idea what is going to become of me.

Helmer. But you are my wife, whatever becomes of you.

Nora. Listen, Torvald. I have heard that when a wife deserts her husband's house, as I am doing now, he is legally freed from all obligations towards her. In any case I set you free from all your obligations. You are not to feel yourself bound in the slightest way, any more than I shall. There must be perfect freedom on both sides. See here is your ring back. Give me mine.

Helmer. That too?

Nora. That too.

Helmer. Here it is.

Nora. That's right. Now it is all over. I have put the keys here. The maids know all about everything in the house—better than I do. To-morrow, after I have left her, Christine will come here and pack up my own things that I brought with me from home. I will have them sent after me.

Helmer. All over! All over!—Nora, shall you never think of me again?

Nora. I know I shall often think of you and the children and this house.

Helmer. May I write to you, Nora?

Nora. No—never. You must not do that.

Helmer. But at least let me send you——

Nora. Nothing—nothing——

Helmer. Let me help you if you are in want.

Nora. No. I can receive nothing from a stranger.

Helmer. Nora—can I never be anything more than a stranger to you?

Nora (*taking her bag*). Ah, Torvald, the most wonderful thing of all would have to happen.

Helmer. Tell me what that would be!

Nora. Both you and I would have to be so changed that——. Oh, Torvald, I don't believe any longer in wonderful things happening.

Helmer. But I will believe in it. Tell me? So changed that——?

Nora. That our life together would be a real wedlock. Good-bye.

(*She goes out through the hall.*)

Helmer (*sinks down on a chair at the door and buries his face in his hands*). Nora! Nora! (*Looks round, and rises.*) Empty. She is gone. (*A hope flashes across his mind.*) The most wonderful thing of all——?

(*The sound of a door shutting is heard from below.*)

FOR ANALYSIS

1. What evidence can you find to support the interpretation that this play is not only about the Helmers' marriage but also about the institution of marriage itself?

2. What does the first meeting between Nora and Mrs. Linde tell us about Nora's character?

3. On a number of occasions, Nora recalls her father. What relevance do these recollections have to the development of the **theme**?

4. Is Krogstad presented as a conventional villain, or are we meant to sympathize with him? Explain.

5. What function does Dr. Rank serve in the play?

6. Examine the stage directions at the beginning of each act. In what ways do they contribute to and reflect the developing action?

7. Acts I and II contain early dialogues between Nora and Torvald. What changes in Nora does a comparison between the two dialogues reveal?

8. At what point in the action does Nora begin to understand the truth of her situation and take responsibility for her life?

9. Summarize the various arguments Torvald uses in his attempt to persuade Nora not to leave.

10. Is the feminist **theme** of the play weakened by Ibsen's failure to suggest how Nora could conceivably make it on her own in such a patriarchal society? Explain.

MAKING CONNECTIONS

Compare the attitudes toward women revealed in this play with those in Susan Glaspell's *Trifles* (p. 1050) and Lorraine Hansberry's *A Raisin in the Sun* (p. 695)?

WRITING TOPICS

1. Does the fact that Nora abandons her children undermine her otherwise heroic decision to walk out on a hollow marriage? For an 1880 German production, Ibsen—in response to public demand—provided an alternate ending in which Nora, after struggling with her conscience, decides that she cannot abandon her children. Do you think this is a better ending than the original one?

2. How does the **subplot** involving the relationship between Mrs. Linde and Krogstad add force to the main **plot** of *A Doll's House*?

3. Have you ever defied social pressure because the cost of conforming was too high? Describe the source of the pressure, the issues at stake, and the consequences of your refusal. Since then, have you had second thoughts about your actions?

4. Write a brief description of a marriage you are familiar with that endured only out of inertia, economic pressure, or fear.

NONFICTION

JONATHAN SWIFT (1667–1745)

A MODEST PROPOSAL 1729

I t is a melancholy object to those who walk through this great town[1] or travel in the country, when they see the streets, the roads, and cabin doors, crowded with beggars of the female sex, followed by three, four, or six children, all in rags and importuning every passenger for an alms. These mothers, instead of being able to work for their honest livelihood, are forced to employ all their time in strolling to beg sustenance for their helpless infants, who, as they grow up, either turn thieves for want of work, or leave their dear native country to fight for the Pretender in Spain, or sell themselves to the Barbados.[2]

I think it is agreed by all parties that this prodigious number of children in the arms, or on the backs, or at the heels of their mothers, and frequently of their fathers, is in the present deplorable state of the kingdom a very great additional grievance; and therefore whoever could find out a fair, cheap, and easy method of making these children sound, useful members of the commonwealth would deserve so well of the public as to have his statue set up for a preserver of the nation.

But my intention is very far from being confined to provide only for the children of professed beggars; it is of a much greater extent, and shall take in the whole number of infants at a certain age who are born of parents in effect as little able to support them as those who demand our charity in the streets.

As to my own part, having turned my thoughts for many years upon this important subject, and maturely weighed the several schemes of other projectors,[3] I have always found them grossly mistaken in their computation. It is true, a child just dropped from its dam may be supported by her milk for a solar year,

[1] Dublin.
[2] Many Irish men joined the army of the exiled James Stuart (1688–1766), who laid claim to the British throne. Others exchanged their labor for passage to the British colony of Barbados, in the Caribbean.
[3] People with projects.

with little other nourishment; at most not above the value of two shillings,[4] which the mother may certainly get, or the value in scraps, by her lawful occupation of begging; and it is exactly at one year that I propose to provide for them in such a manner as instead of being a charge upon their parents or the parish, or wanting food and raiment for the rest of their lives, they shall on the contrary contribute to the feeding, and partly to the clothing, of many thousands.

There is likewise another great advantage in my scheme, that it will prevent 5 those voluntary abortions, and that horrid practice of women murdering their bastard children, alas, too frequent among us, sacrificing the poor innocent babes, I doubt, more to avoid the expense than the shame, which would move tears and pity in the most savage and inhuman breast.

The number of souls in this kingdom being usually reckoned one million and a half, of these I calculate there may be about two hundred thousand couples whose wives are breeders; from which number I subtract thirty thousand couples who are able to maintain their own children, although I apprehend there cannot be so many under the present distress of the kingdom; but this being granted, there will remain an hundred and seventy thousand breeders. I again subtract fifty thousand for those women who miscarry, or whose children die by accident or disease within the year. There only remain an hundred and twenty thousand children of poor parents annually born. The question therefore is, how this number shall be reared and provided for, which, as I have already said, under the present situation of affairs, is utterly impossible by all the methods hitherto proposed. For we can neither employ them in handicraft or agriculture; we neither build houses (I mean in the country) nor cultivate land. They can very seldom pick up a livelihood by stealing till they arrive at six years old except where they are of towardly parts;[5] although I confess they learn the rudiments much earlier, during which time they can however be looked upon only as probationers, as I have been informed by a principal gentleman in the country of Cavan, who protested to me that he never knew above one or two instances under the age of six, even in a part of the kingdom so renowned for the quickest proficiency in that art.

I am assured by our merchants that a boy or a girl before twelve years old is no salable commodity; and even when they come to this age they will not yield above three pounds, or three pounds and half a crown at most on the Exchange;[6] which cannot turn to account either to the parents or the kingdom, the charge of nutriment and rags having been at least four times that value.

I shall now therefore humbly propose my own thoughts, which I hope will not be liable to the least objection.

I have been assured by a very knowing American of my acquaintance in London, that a young healthy child well nursed is at a year old a most delicious,

---

[4] A shilling was worth about twenty-five cents.
[5] Able and eager to learn.
[6] A pound was twenty shillings; a crown, five shillings.

nourishing, and wholesome food, whether stewed, roasted, baked, or boiled; and I make no doubt that it will equally serve in a fricassee or a ragout.

I do therefore humbly offer it to public consideration that of the hundred and twenty thousand children, already computed, twenty thousand may be reserved for breed, whereof only one fourth part to be males, which is more than we allow to sheep, black cattle, or swine; and my reason is that these children are seldom the fruits of marriage, a circumstance not much regarded by our savages, therefore one male will be sufficient to serve four females. That the remaining hundred thousand may at a year old be offered in sale to the persons of quality and fortune through the kingdom, always advising the mother to let them suck plentifully in the last month, so as to render them plump and fat for a good table. A child will make two dishes at an entertainment for friends; and when the family dines alone, the fore or hind quarter will make a reasonable dish, and seasoned with a little pepper or salt will be very good boiled on the fourth day, especially in winter.

I have reckoned upon a medium that a child just born will weigh twelve pounds, and in a solar year if tolerably nursed increaseth to twenty-eight pounds.

I grant this food will be somewhat dear, and therefore very proper for landlords, who, as they have already devoured most of the parents, seem to have the best title to the children.

Infant's flesh will be in season throughout the year, but more plentiful in March, and a little before and after. For we are told by a grave author, an eminent French physician,[7] that fish being a prolific diet, there are more children born in Roman Catholic countries about nine months after Lent than at any other season; therefore, reckoning a year after Lent, the markets will be more glutted than usual, because the number of popish infants is at least three to one in this kingdom; and therefore it will have one other collateral advantage, by lessening the number of Papists among us.

I have already computed the charge of nursing a beggar's child (in which list I reckon all cottagers, laborers, and four-fifths of the farmers) to be about two shillings per annum, rags included; and I believe no gentleman would repine to give ten shillings for the carcass of a good fat child, which, as I have said, will make four dishes of excellent nutritive meat, when he hath only some particular friend or his own family to dine with him. Thus the squire will learn to be a good landlord, and grow popular among the tenants; the mother will have eight shillings net profit, and be fit for work till she produces another child.

Those who are more thrifty (as I must confess the times require) may flay the carcass; the skin of which artificially[8] dressed will make admirable gloves for ladies, and summer boots for fine gentlemen.

As to our city of Dublin, shambles[9] may be appointed for this purpose in the most convenient parts of it, and butchers we may be assured will not be wanting;

[7] François Rabelais, sixteenth-century French comic writer.
[8] Skillfully.
[9] Slaughterhouses.

although I rather recommend buying the children alive, and dressing them hot from the knife as we do roasting pigs.

A very worthy person, a true lover of his country, and whose virtues I highly esteem, was lately pleased in discoursing on this matter to offer a refinement upon my scheme. He said that many gentlemen of his kingdom, having of late destroyed their deer, he conceived that the want of venison might be well supplied by the bodies of young lads and maidens, not exceeding fourteen years of age nor under twelve, so great a number of both sexes in every country being now ready to starve for want of work or service; and these to be disposed of by their parents, if alive, or otherwise by their nearest relations. But with due deference to so excellent a friend and so deserving a patriot, I cannot be altogether in his sentiments; for as to the males, my American acquaintance assured me from frequent experience that their flesh was generally tough and lean, like that of our schoolboys, by continual exercise, and their taste disagreeable; and to fatten them would not answer the charge. Then as to the females; it would, I think with humble submission, be a loss to the public, because they soon would become breeders themselves; and besides, it is not improbable that some scrupulous people might be apt to censure such a practice (although indeed very unjustly) as a little bordering upon cruelty; which, I confess, hath always been with me the strongest objection against any project, how well soever intended.

But in order to justify my friend, he confessed that this expedient was put into his head by the famous Psalmanazar,[10] a native of the island Formosa, who came from thence to London above twenty years ago, and in conversation told my friend that in his country when any young person happened to be put to death, the executioner sold the carcass to persons of quality as a prime dainty; and that in his time the body of a plump girl of fifteen, who was crucified for an attempt to poison the emperor, was sold to his Imperial Majesty's prime minister of state, and other great mandarins of the court, in joints from the gibbet, at four hundred crowns. Neither indeed can I deny that if the same use were made of several plump young girls in this town, who without one single groat[11] to their fortunes cannot stir abroad without a chair,[12] and appear at the playhouse and assemblies in foreign fineries which they never will pay for, the kingdom would not be the worse.

Some persons of a desponding spirit are in great concern about the vast number of poor people who are aged, diseased, or maimed, and I have been desired to employ my thoughts what course may be taken to ease the nation of so grievous an encumberance. But I am not in the least pain upon the matter, because it is very well known that they are every day dying and rotting by cold and famine, and filth and vermin, as fast as can be reasonably expected. And as

---

[10] George Psalmanazar was a Frenchman who passed himself off as a native of Formosa (the former name for Taiwan).

[11] A coin worth about four cents.

[12] A sedan chair, an enclosed chair carried by poles on the front and back.

to the younger laborers, they are now in almost as hopeful a condition. They cannot get work, and consequently pine away for want of nourishment to a degree that if any time they are accidently hired to common labor, they have not the strength to perform it; and thus the country and themselves are happily delivered from the evils to come.

I have too long digressed, and therefore I shall return to my subject. I think the advantages by the proposal which I have made are obvious and many, as well as of the highest importance.

For first, I have already observed, it would greatly lessen the number of Papists, with whom we are yearly overrun, being the principal breeders of the nation as well as our most dangerous enemies; and who stay at home on purpose to deliver the kingdom to the Pretender, hoping to take their advantage by the absence of so many good Protestants, who have chose rather to leave their country than to stay at home and pay tithes against their conscience to an Episcopal curate.

Secondly, the poorer tenants will have something valuable of their own, which by law may be made liable to distress,[13] and help to pay their landlord's rent, their corn and cattle being already seized and money a thing unknown.

Thirdly, whereas the maintenance of a hundred thousand children, from two years old and upwards, cannot be computed at less than ten shillings a piece per annum, the nation's stock will be thereby increased fifty thousand pounds per annum, besides the profit of a new dish introduced to the tables of all gentlemen of fortune in the kingdom who have any refinement in taste. And all the money will circulate among ourselves, the goods being entirely of our own growth and manufacture.

Fourthly, the constant breeders, besides the gain of eight shillings sterling per annum by the sale of their children, will be rid of the charge of maintaining them after the first year.

Fifthly, this food would likewise bring great custom to taverns, where the vintners will certainly be so prudent as to procure the best receipts[14] for dressing it to perfection, and consequently have their houses frequented by all the fine gentlemen, who justly value themselves upon their knowledge in good eating; and a skillful cook, who understands how to oblige his guests, will contrive to make it as expensive as they please.

Sixthly, this would be a great inducement to marriage, which all wise nations have either encouraged by rewards or enforced by laws and penalties. It would increase the care and tenderness of mothers towards their children, when they were sure of a settlement for life to the poor babes, provided in some sort by the public, to their annual profit instead of expense. We should see an honest emulation among the married women, which of them could bring the fattest child to the market. Men would become as fond of their wives during the time of their pregnancy as they are now of their mares in foal, their

---

[13] Seizure for payment of debts.
[14] Recipes.

cows in calf, or sows when they are ready to farrow; nor offer to beat or kick them (as is too frequent a practice) for fear of a miscarriage.

Many other advantages might be enumerated. For instance, the addition of some thousand carcasses in our exportation of barreled beef, the propagation of swine's flesh, and improvements in the art of making good bacon, so much wanted among us by the great destruction of pigs, too frequent at our tables, which are no way comparable in taste or magnificence to a well-grown, fat, yearling child, which roasted whole will make a considerable figure at a lord mayor's feast or any other public entertainment. But this and many others I omit, being studious of brevity.

Supposing that one thousand families in this city would be constant customers for infants' flesh, besides others who might have it at merry meetings, particularly weddings and christenings, I compute that Dublin would take off annually about twenty thousand carcasses, and the rest of the kingdom (where probably they will be sold somewhat cheaper) the remaining eighty thousand.

I can think of no one objection that will possibly be raised against this proposal unless it should be urged that the number of people will be thereby much lessened in the kingdom. This I freely own, and it was indeed one principal design in offering it to the world. I desire the reader will observe, that I calculate my remedy for this one individual kingdom of Ireland and for no other that ever was, is, or I think ever can be upon earth. Therefore let no man talk to me of other expedients: of taxing our absentees at five shillings a pound: of using neither clothes nor household furniture except what is of our own growth and manufacture: of utterly rejecting the materials and instruments that promote foreign luxury: of curing the expensiveness of pride, vanity, idleness, and gaming in our women: of introducing a vein of parsimony, prudence, and temperance: of learning to love our country, in the want of which we differ even from Laplanders and the inhabitants of Topinamboo:[15] of quitting our animosities and factions, nor acting any longer like the Jews, who were murdering one another at the very moment their city was taken:[16] of being a little cautious not to sell our country and conscience for nothing: of teaching landlords to have at least one degree of mercy toward their tenants: lastly, of putting a spirit of honesty, industry, and skill into our shopkeepers; who, if a resolution could now be taken to buy only our native goods, would immediately unite to cheat and exact upon us in the price, the measure, and the goodness, nor could ever yet be brought to make one fair proposal of just dealing, though often and earnestly invited to it.

Therefore, I repeat, let no man talk to me of these and the like expedients, 30 till he hath at least some glimpse of hope that there will be some hearty and sincere attempt to put them in practice.

[15] A district in Brazil, inhabited in Swift's day by primitive tribes.
[16] While the Roman emperor Titus laid siege to Jerusalem in A.D. 70, bloody fighting erupted among factions within the city.

But as to myself, having been wearied out for many years of offering vain, idle, visionary thoughts, and at length utterly despairing of success, I fortunately fell upon this proposal, which, as it is wholly new, so it hath something solid and real, of no expense and little trouble, full in our own power, and whereby we can incur no danger in disobliging England. For this kind of commodity will not bear exportation, the flesh being of too tender a consistence to admit a long continuance in salt, although perhaps I could name a country[17] which would be glad to eat up our whole nation without it.

After all, I am not so violently bent upon my own opinion as to reject any offer proposed by wise men, which shall be found equally innocent, cheap, easy, and effectual. But before something of that kind shall be advanced in contradiction to my scheme, and offering a better, I desire the author or authors will be pleased maturely to consider two points. First, as things now stand, how they will be able to find food and raiment for an hundred thousand useless mouths and backs. And secondly, there being a round million of creatures in human figure throughout this kingdom, whose sole subsistence put into a common stock would leave them in debt two millions of pounds sterling, adding those who are beggars by profession to the bulk of farmers, cottagers, and laborers, with their wives and children who are beggars in effect; I desire those politicians who dislike my overture, and may perhaps be so bold to attempt to answer, that they will first ask the parents of these mortals whether they would not at this day think it a great happiness to have been sold for food at a year old in this manner I prescribe, and thereby have avoided such a perpetual scene of misfortunes as they have since gone through by the oppression of landlords, the impossibility of paying rent without money or trade, the want of common sustenance, with neither house nor clothes to cover them from the inclemencies of the weather, and the most inevitable prospect of entailing the like or greater miseries upon their breed forever.

I profess, in the sincerity of my heart, that I have not the least personal interest in endeavoring to promote this necessary work, having no other motive than the public good of my country, by advancing our trade, providing for infants, relieving the poor, and giving some pleasure to the rich. I have no children by which I can propose to get a single penny; the youngest being nine years old, and my wife past childbearing.

FOR ANALYSIS

1. What kind of person is the speaker? What does his tone of voice reveal about who he is? Is his voice direct and transparent, or does it seem deliberately created to achieve a specific effect?

2. In what sense is the proposal "modest"?

3. Where are the major divisions of the essay? What function does each serve?

---

[17] England.

4. What function does paragraph 29 serve?

5. Explain what Swift means when he says in paragraph 20, "I have too long digressed."

6. Whom is Swift addressing in this essay?

MAKING CONNECTIONS

Some other works in this anthology that use **satire** include e. e. cummings, "the Cambridge ladies who live in furnished souls" (p. 650); W. H. Auden, "The Unknown Citizen" (p. 415) and Harlan Ellison, "'Repent, Harlequin!' Said the Ticktockman" (p. 372). Compare and contrast the use of satire in one of these works with Swift's use of satire.

WRITING TOPICS

1. Some background information on Swift's life, as well as familiarity with his other works, would make it clear that in this essay he is being satiric. Without that background—that is, on the basis of this essay alone—would you conclude that Swift is writing satire? Explain.

2. In one brief paragraph, paraphrase the major arguments Swift uses to support his plan.

ELLEN LEVY

MASTERING THE ART
OF FRENCH COOKING   2005

I have no photograph of my mother cooking, but when I recall my childhood this is how I picture her: standing in the kitchen of our suburban ranch house, a blue-and-white-checked terrycloth apron tied at her waist, her lovely head bent over a recipe, a hiss of frying butter, a smell of onions and broth, and open like a hymnal on the counter beside her, a copy of Julia Child's *Mastering the Art of French Cooking*.

The book's cover is delicately patterned like wallpaper—white with miniature red fleurs-de-lis and tiny teal stars—the title and authors' names modestly scripted in a rectangular frame no larger than a recipe card: a model of feminine self-effacement.

This unassuming book was my mother's most reliable companion throughout my childhood, and from the table laid with a blue cotton cloth, not yet set with flatware and plates and glasses of ice water, not yet laid with bowls of broccoli spears, *boeuf bourguignon*, potatoes sautéed in butter, I observed her as she sought in its pages an elusive balance between the bitter and sweet.

It is a scene less remembered than invoked, an amalgam of the many evenings when I sat and watched my mother cook at the copper gas stove whose handles glowed a soft burnished too human pink. Tall and remote as statuary, dressed stylishly in cashmere and pumps, a chestnut bouffant framing her face and its high cheekbones, her pale-blue eyes cast down, my mother consulted her recipes night after night. It is a scene suffused in memory with a diffuse golden light and a sense of enormous safety and an awareness that beyond that radiant kitchen lay the shadow-draped lawn, the cold, starry night of another midwestern autumn.

My mother had few pleasures when I was growing up. She liked to read. She 5 liked to play the piano. She liked to cook. Of these, she did a good deal of the first, very little of the second, and a great deal of the third. She was of that generation of women caught in the sexual cross fire of women's liberation, who knew enough to probe for their desires, but not enough to practice them.

Born into the permissive '60s, raised in the disillusioned '70s, the third of three children, I came of age in a world where few rules were trusted, few applied. Of those that did, the rules contained in my mother's cookbooks were paramount.

The foods of my childhood were romantic. *Boeuf bourguignon*. *Vichyssoise*. *Salade Niçoise*. *Bouillabaisse*. *Béarnaise*. *Mousseline au Chocolat*. Years before I

505

could spell these foods, I learned their names from my mother's lips, their smells by heart.

At the time I took no notice of the gustatory schizophrenia that governed our meals. The extravagant French cuisine prepared on the nights my father dined with us; the Swanson TV dinners on the nights we ate alone, we three kids and my mother, nights that came more frequently as the sixties ebbed into the seventies. On those nights we ate our dinners in silence and watched the Vietnam War on television, and I took a childish proprietary delight in having a dinner of my own, served in its aluminum tray, with each portion precisely fitted to its geometrical place. These dinners were heated under thin tin foil and served on plates, and we ate directly from the metal trays our meals of soft whipped potatoes, brown gravy, sliced turkey, cubed carrots, and military-green peas.

Had I noticed these culinary cycles, I doubt that I would have recognized them for the strategic maneuvers they seem to me in retrospect. Precisely what my parents were warring over I'm not sure, but it seems clear to me now that in the intricate territorial maneuvers that for years defined their marriage, cooking was my mother's principal weapon. Proof of her superiority. My father might not feel tenderness, but he would have to admire her. My mother cooked with a vengeance in those years, or perhaps I should say she cooked for revenge. In her hands, cuisine became a martial art.

My mother spent herself in cooking. Whipping egg whites by hand with her 10 muscular forearm, rubbing down a turkey with garlic and butter and rosemary and thyme, she sublimated her enormous unfeminine ambition in extravagant hubristic cuisine. Disdainful of the Sisyphean chores of housecleaning, she threw herself into the task of feeding us in style. If we were what we ate, she was hell bent on making her brood singular, Continental, and I knew throughout my childhood that I would disappoint her.

In the kitchen, my mother could invent for herself a coterie of scent and flavor, a retinue of exquisite associates, even though she would later have to eat them. What she craved in those years was a companion, not children, but my father was often gone, and I was ill suited to the role.

I lacked utterly the romance my mother craved. Indifferent to books, unsociable, I could not master French. Though I would study the language for five years in high school I would never get beyond the rudiments of ordering in restaurants and asking directions to the municipal pool (*Je voudrais un bifteck, s'il vous plaît. Où est la piscine?*). In the face of my mother's yearning, I became a spectator of desire, passive, watchful, wary. Well into my twenties I remained innocent of my tastes, caught up in observing my mother's passions and fearful too that I might betray her, call into question her unswerving desires with desires of my own.

Julia Child was the only reliable companion my mother had in those years, other than the woman who came once a week to clean the house. Across the street the Segals had a "live-in girl," a local college student who came in to watch the children in the afternoons, while Mrs. Segal nursed a nervous breakdown.

Each year these live-in girls changed: now blond, now brunette, with names like Stacy and Joanne. They taught us how to shoot hoops, how to ride bikes, how to appreciate soap operas. In our house there was no "live-in girl," there was only Mrs. Williams, the "cleaning lady."

I was quiet on the days when Mrs. Williams came to clean, embarrassed that we needed someone to help us keep our lives in order, embarrassed too by the fact that she was black and we were white. On the afternoons she came to clean I could not help but see my family as White People, part of a pattern of white folks who hired black folks to pick up after them. I felt ashamed when I saw my mother and Mrs. Williams chatting over coffee at our kitchen table. I saw their silhouettes against history and they made an ugly broken line. I read in it patronage, condescension, exploitation, thwarted rage.

I thought at the time that it was misapplied gentility that prompted my mother 15 to sit with Mrs. Williams, while she ate lunch. Their conversations seemed to me a matter of polite routine. They spoke generally. Of the latest space launch, Watergate, the price of oil. The conversation was not intimate. But they shared it. Later, when Mrs. Williams was dying of breast cancer, she told my mother that my mother had been her *best* friend. Her best friend. My mother told me this with wonder, as if she were amazed that anyone had ever considered her a friend. Now I wonder if the declaration moved her too because she understood its corollary: that Mrs. Williams had been her best, perhaps her only, friend.

Cooking was not the only medium in which my mother excelled. She organized birthday parties on an epic scale—fashioning piñatas out of crepe paper and papier-mâché, organizing haunted houses, and games of smell and memory—and she made us prize-winning costumes well beyond the point at which we should rightly have given up masquerading.

I was fifteen when I won the final prize in a series of prizes won for her costumes, for a banana suit she'd made me, a full-length, four-paneled yellow cotton shift worn over a conical cardboard cap to shape the crown, and yellow tights. My mother had ingeniously designed the suit with a triangular front panel that could be secured with Velcro to the crown or "peeled" down to reveal—through a round hole in the cloth—my face.

The prize for this costume, my father reminds me, was a radio designed to look like a box of frozen niblet corn—a square, yellow-plastic radio with an authentic Green Giant label. This was the late seventies and in America you could buy a lot of things that looked like food but weren't. You could buy a scented candle in the shape of a chocolate sundae, sculpted in a tulip glass with piles of frothy false whipped cream and a perfect wax cherry. You could buy a soda glass tipped on its side out of which a carbonated cola-colored liquid spilled into a puddle of clear plastic. There was shampoo that smelled of herbs or lemons; tiny soaps in the shape of peaches and green apples; paperweights shaped like giant aspirin, four inches in diameter, cast in plaster; the plastic simulacrum of a slice of pineapple or a fried egg dangling at the end of a key chain.

It was an era of food impersonation. A cultural critic might dismiss this as conspicuous consumption: possessed of abundance, we could mock necessity. Food, for us, could be a plaything—revenge for all those childhood admonitions not to play with your food. But I think that there was in this as well a sign of political disaffection—an ironic commentary on the unreliability of appearances in the wake of Watergate and Vietnam (in South Africa such objects were also popular at the time, a Fulbright scholar from Zimbabwe will tell me years later)—and a measure of spiritual dislocation. As if, glutted with comfort and suspicious of appearances, we had lost touch with what sustains us and had relinquished faith in even the most elementary source of life. Food.

Mixed marriage. The phrase itself recalls cuisine: mixed greens, mixed vegetables, "mix carefully two cups sifted flour with. . . ." As if marriage were a form of sentimental cookery, a blending of disparate ingredients—man and woman—to produce a new and delectable whole. "She's my honey bun, my sweet pea, my cookie, sugar"; "You can't make an omelet without breaking a few eggs." 20

English is spiced with phrases that attest to our enduring attachment to food as metaphor, and point to our abiding faith in affection's ability to sustain us as vitally as food. But the phrase *mixed marriage* suggests as well the limits of love, its inability to transform difference, and is a warning. In the mythic goulash of American culture, the melting pot is supposed to inspire amity, not love. One should melt, it seems, not mix. Marriage, of the kind my parents ventured to embrace—between gentile and Jew—went, according to the conventions of the time, too far.

It was in part because of their differences that my mother married my father. He must have seemed to her exotic, with his dark skin, jet eyes, his full sensuous mouth; at seventy he will look like Rossano Brazzi, but at age thirty-one, when my parents meet at the University of Minnesota on the stairs of Eddy Hall as my beautiful mother descends from a library in the tower where she has finished her day's research and my father ascends to his office where he is a young professor of psychology, he is more handsome even than a movie star—I can see this in photos from the time—because his face is radiant with expectation for his future.

For my father, son of Russian and Lithuanian immigrants, marrying my mother must have seemed like marrying America itself. Her ancestors had come over in 1620 on that first and famous boat and though my mother's family was of modest means, her speech and gestures bespeak gentility. Her English is precise, peppered with Latinate words and French phrases, her pronunciations are distinctive and slightly anglicized (not cer-EE-bral, she corrects me, CER-eh-bral). She possesses all the Victorian virtues: widely read, she is an accomplished pianist and a gifted painter; she speaks French and Czech, is knowledgeable in art and history, physics, physiology, and philosophy. Although she is a passionate conversationalist, she has a habit of concluding her sentences on a slight descending note as if she has discovered part way through speech that it were too wearying to converse after all, and so has given up. My mother's verbal inflections are the telltale signs of class in classless America and marrying her, my father crossed the tracks. He could not know how he would resent the crossing; she could not know how she would resent the role of wife.

My mother's enormous ambitions were channeled by her marriage into a narrow course—like a great roaring river forced against its nature to straighten and be dammed, resulting in floods, lost canyons—and her desires became more powerful for having been restrained. It seemed to me only a matter of time before she'd reassert her claim to wilder, broader terrain. Throughout my childhood, I waited for my mother to leave.

Given the centrality of culinary concerns in my childhood, it is unsurprising 25 perhaps that my first act on leaving home was to codify my eating. My first term at college, I eschewed the freshman ritual of room decoration—the requisite Manet prints, the tacky O'Keeffe's—in favor of regulations: I tacked a single notice to the bulletin board beside my desk specifying what I could and could not eat. My schema was simple: 1,000 calories each day, plus, if absolutely necessary, a pack of sugarless gum and as much as a pound of carrots (my skin, in certain photos from the period, is tinted orange from excess carotene). I swam my meals off each morning with a two-mile swim at dawn, and a cold shower.

My saporous palette was unimaginative and highly unaesthetic and varied little from an essentially white and brown motif: poached white fish, bran cereal, skim milk, egg whites, with the occasional splash out into carrots. I practiced a sort of secular asceticism, in which repression of desire was for its own sake deemed a virtue.

In time, I grew thin, then I grew fat. My senior year, by an inverse of my earlier illogic, I ate almost without cessation: lacking authentic desire to guide me, I consumed indiscriminately. Unpracticed in the exercise of tastes, I lumbered insensibly from one meal to the next. I often ate dinner twice, followed up by a pound bag of M & Ms or a slice of pizza. The pop psychology of the day informed me that my eating habits were an effort to "stuff rage," but it seemed to me that I was after ballast. Something to weight me to the world, as love was said to do. Despite my heft, I felt insubstantial as steam, airy and faint as an echo.

Therapy was merely insulting. One waiflike counselor, who had herself been anorectic and spoke in a breathy, childlike voice, insisted earnestly and frequently, whenever I confessed to a thought, "*that* it is your bulimia speaking." She said this irrespective of my statements, like a spiritualist warning of demons in the ether. I raged, I wept, I reasoned. But it was not me, she averred, but my bulimia—*speaking*. She made it sound as if I had a troll living inside me. And I knew it was a lie. I told her I thought this whole thing, my eating and all was about desire, about being attracted to women. But she set me straight.

In the space of two years I would pass through half a dozen women's hands (none of them a lover's)—therapists, social workers, Ph.D. candidates, even a stern Irish psychiatrist, who looked unnervingly like the actress Colleen Dewhurst—and all of them in short order would assure me that I was not desirous of women. As if it were unthinkable, a thing scripted on the body at birth, a thing you could read in the face, the hands; as if sexual desire were not after all an acquired taste.

I was twenty-five before I went to bed with a woman and when I did I found 30 that all along I had been right. Though it strains credulity, the following morning I woke and found that I had lost ten pounds in the night and had recovered my sense of taste. I never again had trouble with food, though my tastes surprised me. Things I never knew I liked suddenly glowed on the gustatory horizon like beacons. Plump oily avocados. The dainty lavender-sheathed teeth of garlic. Ginger. Tonic and Tanqueray gin. Green olives. Blood oranges. Pungent Italian cheese.

If education is ultimately the fashioning of a self through the cultivation of discernment and taste, this was my education, and with it came an acute craving for books and music and film. I discovered in that summer the writings of Virginia Woolf and the films of Ingmar Bergman, the paintings of Jasper Johns and Gertrude Stein's prose and John Cage's symphonies, Italian wines and sex. And I began, tentatively, fearfully, to write (though even the effort to keep a journal was an ordeal; I was tortured by doubt: How could I know what was worthy of recording, what I liked enough, what mattered enough to note and keep?).

"Do you love him?" I once asked my mother, when I was thirteen and still young enough to think that was a simple question, a thing one had or didn't have, the thing that mattered; when I did not yet understand all the other painful, difficult things that bind people more surely than love ever will.

"I like your father," she said. "That is more important."

I do not misremember this. It remains with me like a recipe I follow scrupulously, an old family recipe. And when in my first year of graduate school my lover asks me if I love her, I try to form an answer as precise as my mother's before me; I say "I am very fond of you, I like and respect you," and watch as pain rises in her face like a leavening loaf. I have learned from my mother and Julia Child how to master French cooking, but I have no mastery when it comes to love. It will take me a long time to get the hang of this; it will take practice.

In my second year of graduate school, I enroll in an introductory French class. 35 The instructor is a handsome man from Haiti, and the whole class is a little in love with him. In Minneapolis, the home of the sartorially challenged, where a prominent uptown billboard exhorts passersby to "Dress like you're not from around here," he is a fashion oasis. An anomaly in these rooms of unmodulated beige, he is dressed this drear January morning in a black turtleneck, chinos, belt, heavy gold chain, ring, watch. He looks like he might go straight from this 11:15 A.M. class to a nightclub—or as if he has just come from one.

Born thirty miles east of Cap-Haitien, the second largest city in Haiti, he is an unlikely figure in these rooms filled with privileged white kids from the suburbs. His own education, he recalls, was "sketchy," snatched from stints in lycée (the equivalent of an American public school) in Cap-Haitien. His parents did not live together and life under Duvalier was difficult; he did, he says, what was necessary to survive.

All my adult life I have sought out people like this, people who I sense can instruct me in how to live in the world. Who know how to survive, to hustle.

How to make it from one day to the next. The things my mother and father couldn't teach me or never knew. I will spend my twenties and early thirties seeking out people like this, like a junkie; I can't get enough of certitude or attitude.

The questions you ask in an introductory language class are always the important ones, the original ones that the raw fact of language inspires, the ones we ask as children then forget when we grow up. On the first day of class I dutifully copy into my notebook the questions the instructor has written on the board: *Qui suis-je? Qui êtes-vous?* It is only later, while scanning the pages of this notebook, that I am startled to see the questions I have scribbled there, demanding an answer: Who am I? Who are you?

I had been in junior high or high school when I first began to imagine that my parents would separate as soon as their children left home. I had come to expect this, so that when my siblings and I did leave I was genuinely shocked, even disappointed, that my parents stayed together. I didn't understand that they were, after all those years, if not fond of one another, at least established, that they were afraid of loneliness, that approaching sixty, approaching seventy, they were too tired to fight and so perhaps could make room as they hadn't previously for tenderness. I didn't understand that it is not that time heals all, but that in time the simple fact of having survived together can come to outweigh other concerns, that if you're not careful, you can forget that you ever hoped for something more than sustenance.

"Your parents seem so comfortable," a friend of mine commented after we 40 had dined with my parents in New York City a few years back, when my folks were visiting me. "Yes," I said, with something like regret, recognizing in that moment for the first time their surrender in a long-waged battle. "I think they are." These days my mother orders in Thanksgiving dinner from a restaurant in St. Paul. She orders unlikely foods: in place of the traditional turkey with trimmings, there is a large, squat, hat-box-shaped vegetable torte with marinara sauce, green salad, cranberries from the can. At dinner, she presides from the head of the table, opposite my father, smiling. Sedate as a pudding.

In college, I met a young woman who had corresponded throughout her childhood with Julia Child. It was from her that I first heard that Child had been an alcoholic and often was drunk on the set. My mother, if she recognized drunkenness for what it was, nevertheless cast the story differently: she laughed about how Child, having dropped a chicken on the floor during a taping, had had the aplomb to pick it up and cooked it anyhow. This delighted my mother, this imperturbability, the ability in the face of disappointment to carry on.

I have asked my mother if she regrets her marriage, her choices; and she has told me it is pointless to regret. That she did what she could do. What more can we ask of ourselves? I want to tell her, but do not, that we must ask for so much more, for everything, for love and tenderness and decency and courage. That we must be much more than comfortable, that we must be better than we think we can be, so that if in some foreign tongue we are confronted with those childhood questions—*"Qui êtes-vous?" "Qui suis-je?"*—we will not be afraid to answer.

A few weeks ago, I came across a copy of *Mastering the Art of French Cooking* in a second-hand shop, unused, for $7.49. I bought it and took it home. Fingering its rough pulpy pages, consulting its index for names that conjure my long-ago abandoned childhood, I scanned its pages as if they could provide an explanation, as if it were a secret record of my mother's thwarted passion. I held it in my lap, hesitant to read it, as if it were after all a private matter, a diary of those bygone days when it still seemed possible in this country, in our lives, to bring together disparate elements and mix them—artfully, beautifully—and make of them some new and marvelous whole.

FOR ANALYSIS

1. If this essay is not about cooking, why do you think Levy titled it "Mastering the Art of French Cooking"?

2. What are the other things that are mastered in this essay? What are the things that need to be mastered or that the author or her mother try to master? Are there things in the essay, or in life, that cannot be mastered? What does it mean to "master" something?

MAKING CONNECTIONS

1. Compare "Mastering the Art of French Cooking" to Kunzru's "Raj, Bohemian" (p. 361). Do these two pieces talk about taste in the same way? What does taste mean to each speaker? Which way of looking at taste is more congenial to you?

2. Levy writes that her mother tried to find, in the pages of a cookbook, "an elusive balance between the bitter and sweet" (para. 3). Look in Levy's essay and Doyle's "Pop Art" (p. 276) for ways in which they try to find, in the stories they tell about their lives, the same two things.

WRITING TOPICS

1. Toward the end of the essay, Levy repeats the questions from her first day in French class, one of which is "Who am I?" (para. 38). "Mastering the Art of French Cooking"—while it is about cooking, the author's mother, female sexuality in the second half of the twentieth century, and many other things—is very much about the author's discovery of and creation of her identity; we find out who she is as she tells the story of finding herself. Trace the way she does this by drawing a line down the middle of the paper, entering her personal characteristics on the left, and on the right, the way we learn of that characteristic. Finally, write a short account of how the revelation of the characteristics on the left side of the line is made by the elements of the essay on the right.

2. Read this passage from Levy's essay aloud: "Things I never knew I liked suddenly glowed on the gustatory horizon like beacons. Plump oily avocados. The dainty lavender-sheathed teeth of garlic. Ginger. Tonic and Tanqueray gin. Green olives. Blood oranges. Pungent Italian cheese" (para. 30). Describe the imagery, the sounds, the rhythms. What effects does Levy achieve through her use of these things? Why do you think she might have wanted to achieve these particular effects at this moment in the essay?

For much of human history, religious belief has been an inextricable and unexamined part of culture—it was unthinkable for individuals to doubt their culture's singular story of creation and divine involvement in daily life. In the modern world, it is much more possible to weigh belief—to choose to believe or not to believe, to adhere to one or a number of available religions, or to choose to disbelieve in any theological explanation whatsoever of existence.

The world has recently seen an upsurge in fundamentalism, in styles of religious belief that offer a return to the time before doubt. The two essays in this unit deal with this phenomenon in different ways, but both speak from outside fundamentalist religious belief, examining it in itself and in its (to them) unavoidable historical and social contexts. As you read Rushdie's and Doctorow's thoughts, "imagine" discussions of religious belief that avoid these framing issues. Is it possible to critically examine religion, or any system of belief or ostensible knowledge, without taking into account other, ever-changing elements of human experience?

E. L. DOCTOROW (B 1931)

WHY WE ARE INFIDELS 2003

We have lately been called infidels. Yet we are perhaps the most prayerful nation in the world. Both Tocqueville and Dickens[1] when they came over here to have a look at us were astonished at how much God there was in American society. True, the infidel is not necessarily a nonbeliever; he may also be a believer of the wrong stripe. But I think, given the variety of religious practice in our country, including that of Islam, that the term infidel as it has lately been applied to us probably does not refer to any particular religion we may as a nation subscribe to, but to the fact that we subscribe, within our population of three hundred million, to all of them.

Of course most of our religions, including Christianity, Judaism, Islam, Buddhism, landed here at different times from other parts of the world. They have been vulnerable as religions usually are to such denominational fracture as to offer a potential parishioner a virtual supermarket of spiritual choice. Some of our religions, Mormonism, Christian Science, Native American Anthropomorphism, were invented, or revealed, right here. And if we think even casually of the

[1] Alexis de Tocqueville (1805–1859), an eminent French statesman who traveled to the United States in 1831 to study its prison system. His general observations on democratic government were recorded in *Democracy in America* (1835). The popular English novelist Charles Dickens (1812–1870) recorded his views of American life gathered during a trip in 1842.

parade of creative and influential religionists on our shores[2]—from the colonists Anne Hutchinson and Roger Williams, George Fox, Jonathan Edwards, and Cotton Mather to our citizen evangelicals Aimee Semple McPherson, Billy Sunday, Father Divine, and Billy Graham, we notice immediately that we have left out the Adventists, the Millerites, the Shakers, Swedenborgians, and Perfectionists of the nineteenth century, to say nothing of the stadium-filling brides and grooms of the Reverend Moon's Unification Church, or the suicidal cultists of Jim Jones, or the unfortunate Branch Davidians of Waco, Texas, or the Heaven's Gate believers who castrated themselves and took their own lives in order to board the Hale-Bopp comet when it flew past in 1997.

One of the less scintillating debates among theologians is on the distinction between a religion and a cult. But all together, our religions or religious cults testify to the deeply serious American thirst for celestial connection. We want a spiritual release from the society we have made out of secular humanism.

That our God-soaked country is, as political science, secular, may be indicated by the fact that the word for the state of being of an infidel, *infidelity*, brings to our minds not a violation of faith in the true God but a violation of the marriage contract between ordinary mortals. Philandering husbands and adulterous wives may be viewed as immoral and looked upon with contempt or pity, but they are not usually regarded as infidels. The term however may be justly applied to all of us, including the most pious and monogamous among us, because of a major national sin committed over two hundred years ago when religion and the American state were rent asunder and all worship was consigned to private life. It was Jefferson who said, "Our civil rights have no dependence on our religious opinions, any more than our opinions in physics or geometry." And while it is precisely because of this principle of religious freedom that we enjoy such a continuous national uproar of praying and singing and studying and fasting and confessing and atoning and praising and preaching and dancing and dunking and vowing and quaking and shaking and abstaining and ordaining, a paradox arises from this expression of our religious democracy: if you have extracted the basic ethics of religious invention and found the mechanism for installing them in the statutes of the secular civil order, as we have with our Constitution and our Bill of Rights, but have consigned all the doctrine and rite and ritual, all the symbols and traditional practices to the precincts of private life, you are saying there is no one proven path to salvation, there are only traditions. If you relegate the old stories to the personal choices of private worship, you admit the ineffable[3] is ineffable, and in terms of a possible theological triumphalism everything is up for grabs.

Our pluralism has to be a profound offense to the fundamentalist who by def- 5 inition is an absolutist intolerant of all forms of belief but his own, all stories but

---

[2] Doctorow alludes to a number of persons and religious constructs in paragraph 2. Use a search engine to find information on those unfamiliar to you.

[3] Indescribable; too awesome to be spoken.

his own. In our raucous democracy fundamentalist religious belief has organized itself with political acumen to promulgate law that would undermine just those secular humanist principles that encourage it to flourish in freedom. Of course there has rarely been a period in our history when God has not been called upon to march. The abolitionists decried slavery as a sin against God. The South claimed biblical authority for its slaveholding. The civil disobedience of Dr. Martin Luther King Jr.'s civil rights movement drew its strength from prayer and the examples of Christian fortitude, while the Ku Klux Klan and other white supremacy groups invoked Jesus as a sponsor of their racism. But there is a crucial difference of emphasis between these traditional invocations and the politically astute and well-funded actions in recent years of the leaders of the movement known as the Christian Right, who do not call upon their faith to certify their politics as much as they call for a country that certifies their faith.

Fundamentalism really cannot help itself—it is absolutist and can compromise with nothing, not even democracy. It is not surprising that immediately after the Islamic fundamentalist attack on the World Trade Center and the Pentagon two prominent Christian fundamentalists were reported to have accounted it as justifiable punishment by God for our secularism, our civil libertarianism, our feminists, our gay and lesbian citizens, our abortion providers, and everything and everyone else which their fundamentalist belief condemns. In thus honoring the foreign killers of over three thousand Americans as agents of God's justice, they established their own consanguinity with the principle of righteous warfare in the name of all that is holy, and gave their pledge of allegiance to the theocratic ideal of government of whatever sacred text.

Not just on other shores are we considered a nation of infidels.

FOR ANALYSIS

1. In religious terms, what is an infidel?

2. What are religious fundamentalists? How would they respond to the presumptions of a religion different from their own?

3. What is the official relationship between religion and government in the United States? Do you approve or disapprove of that relationship? Explain.

4. Two American religious leaders asserted that the Islamic attackers who killed over 3,000 people on September 11, 2001, were used by God to punish the country for allowing behavior "which their fundamentalist belief condemns." How does Doctorow characterize this argument? How do you?

5. On what issues does the conflict between civil government and religious conviction often center? Describe the positions that animate such disagreements.

WRITING TOPICS

1. If a majority of Americans voted to abolish the separation between church and state embedded in the Constitution, should the United States amend the Constitution to reflect that position and become a Protestant Christian theocratic state? Upon what assumptions does your position rest?

2. America's justification for its presence in the Middle East is that it wishes to bring "freedom and democracy" to Afghanistan, Iraq, and the entire region; what do you believe should be the response of the United States if one or more of these nations, in a fair and open election, chooses to have a theocratic authoritarian government?

3. Discuss Doctorow's view of the relationship between religion and politics in the modern world.

SALMAN RUSHDIE (B. 1947)

"IMAGINE THERE'S NO HEAVEN"[1] 1997

A LETTER TO THE SIX BILLIONTH WORLD CITIZEN

[Written for a UN-backed anthology of such letters]

Dear little Six Billionth Living Person,

As the newest member of a notoriously inquisitive species, you'll probably soon be asking the two sixty-four-thousand-dollar questions with which the other 5,999,999,999 of us have been wrestling for some time: How did we get here? And, now that we are here, how shall we live?

Oddly—as if six billion of us weren't enough to be going on with—it will almost certainly be suggested to you that the answer to the question of origins requires you to believe in the existence of a further, invisible, ineffable Being "somewhere up there," an omnipotent creator whom we poor limited creatures are unable even to perceive, much less to understand. That is, you will be strongly encouraged to imagine a heaven, with at least one god in residence. This sky-god, it's said, made the universe by churning its matter in a giant pot. Or, he danced. Or, he vomited Creation out of himself. Or, he simply called it into being, and lo, it Was. In some of the more interesting creation stories, the single mighty sky-god is subdivided into many lesser forces—junior deities, avatars, gigantic metamorphic "ancestors" whose adventures create the landscape, or the whimsical, wanton, meddling, cruel pantheons of the great polytheisms, whose wild doings will convince you that the real engine of creation was lust: for infinite power, for too easily broken human bodies, for clouds of glory. But it's only fair to add that there are also stories which offer the message that the primary creative impulse was, and is, love.

Many of these stories will strike you as extremely beautiful, and therefore seductive. Unfortunately, however, you will not be required to make a purely

---

[1] Rushdie takes his title from the first line of "Imagine," a song by John Lennon (1940–1980).

literary response to them. Only the stories of "dead" religions can be appreciated for their beauty. Living religions require much more of you. So you will be
told that belief in "your" stories, and adherence to the rituals of worship that
have grown up around them, must become a vital part of your life in the
crowded world. They will be called the heart of your culture, even of your individual identity. It is possible that they may at some point come to feel
inescapable, not in the way that the truth is inescapable but in the way that a
jail is. They may at some point cease to feel like the texts in which human
beings have tried to solve a great mystery and feel, instead, like the pretexts for
other, properly anointed human beings to order you around. And it's time that
human history is full of the public oppression wrought by the charioteers of
the gods. In the opinion of religious people, however, the private comfort that
religion brings more than compensates for the evil done in its name.

As human knowledge has grown, it has also become plain that every religious story ever told about how we got here is quite simply wrong. This, finally,
is what all religions have in common. They didn't get it right. There was no
celestial churning, no maker's dance, no vomiting of galaxies, no snake or kan-
garoo ancestors, no Valhalla, no Olympus, no six-day conjuring trick followed
by a day of rest. Wrong, wrong, wrong. But here's something genuinely odd.
The wrongness of the sacred tales hasn't lessened the zeal of the devout in the
least. If anything, the sheer out-of-step zaniness of religion leads the religious
to insist ever more stridently on the importance of blind faith.

As a result of this faith, by the way, it has proved impossible, in many parts of 5
the world, to prevent the human race's numbers from swelling alarmingly.
Blame the overcrowded planet at least partly on the misguidedness of the
race's spiritual guides. In your own lifetime, you may well witness the arrival of
the nine billionth world citizen. If you're Indian (and there's a one in six
chance that you are) you will be alive when, thanks to the failure of family
planning schemes in that poor, God-ridden land, its population surges past
China's. And if too many people are being born as a result, in part, of religious
strictures against birth control, then too many people are also dying because
religious culture, by refusing to face the facts of human sexuality, also refuses
to fight against the spread of sexually transmitted diseases.

There are those who say that the great wars of the new century will once
again be wars of religion, jihads and crusades, as they were in the Middle Ages.
I don't believe them, or not in the way they mean it. Take a look at the Muslim
world, or rather the *Islamist* world, to use the word coined to describe Islam's
present-day "political arm." The divisions between its great powers (Afghanistan versus Iran versus Iraq versus Saudi Arabia versus Syria versus Egypt) are
what strike you most forcefully. There's very little resembling a common purpose. Even after the non-Islamic NATO fought a war for the Muslim Kosovar
Albanians, the Muslim world was slow in coming forward with much-needed
humanitarian aid.

The real wars of religion are the wars religions unleash against ordinary citizens within their "spheres of influence." They are wars of the godly against the

largely defenseless—American fundamentalists against pro-choice doctors, Iranian mullahs against their country's Jewish minority, the Taliban against the people of Afghanistan, Hindu fundamentalists in Bombay against that city's increasingly fearful Muslims.

The victors in that war must not be the closed-minded, marching into battle with, as ever, God on their side. To choose unbelief is to choose mind over dogma, to trust in our humanity instead of all these dangerous divinities. So, how did we get here? Don't look for the answer in storybooks. Imperfect human knowledge may be a bumpy, potholed street, but it's the only road to wisdom worth taking. Virgil, who believed that the apiarist Aristaeus could spontaneously generate new bees from the rotting carcass of a cow, was closer to a truth about origins than all the revered old books.

The ancient wisdoms are modern nonsenses. Live in your own time, use what we know, and as you grow up, perhaps the human race will finally grow up with you and put aside childish things.

As the song says, "It's easy if you try."   10

As for morality, the second great question—how to live? What is right action, and what wrong?—it comes down to your willingness to think for yourself. Only you can decide if you want to be handed down the law by priests, and accept that good and evil are somehow external to ourselves. To my mind religion, even at its most sophisticated, essentially infantilizes our ethical selves by setting infallible moral Arbiters and irredeemably immoral Tempters above us; the eternal parents, good and bad, light and dark, of the supernatural realm.

How, then, are we to make ethical choices without a divine rulebook or judge? Is unbelief just the first step on the long slide into the brain-death of cultural relativism,[2] according to which many unbearable things—female circumcision, to name just one—can be excused on culturally specific grounds, and the universality of human rights, too, can be ignored? (This last piece of moral unmaking finds supporters in some of the world's most authoritarian regimes and also, unnervingly, on the op-ed pages of *The Daily Telegraph*.)

Well, no, it isn't, but the reasons for saying so aren't clear-cut. Only hard-line ideology is clear-cut. Freedom, which is the word I use for the secular-ethical position, is inevitably fuzzier. Yes, freedom is that space in which contradiction can reign, it is a never-ending debate. It is not in itself the answer to the question of morals but the conversation about that question.

And it is much more than mere relativism, because it is not merely a never-ending talk-shop, but a place in which choices are made, values defined and defended. Intellectual freedom, in European history, has mostly meant freedom from the restraints of the Church, not the State. This is the battle

---

[2] The view that truth is relative and may differ depending on the believer's situation, and that all beliefs are equally valid. Cultural relativism developed in the late nineteenth century as a backlash against the Western tendency to perceive culture as advancing from ignorant savagery to enlightened civilization.

Voltaire[3] was fighting, and it's also what all six billion of us could do for ourselves, the revolution in which each of us could play our small, six-billionth part: once and for all we could refuse to allow priests, and the fictions on whose behalf they claim to speak, to be the policemen of our liberties and behavior. Once and for all we could put the stories back into the books, put the books back on the shelves, and see the world undogmatized and plain.

Imagine there's no heaven, my dear Six Billionth, and at once the sky's the   15
limit.

FOR ANALYSIS

1. Rushdie argues from the point of view of a "secular-ethical" humanist. How do his arguments differ from those a religious leader might put forward?

2. Using a search engine, try to identify the sources of the "creation myths" that Rushdie enumerates in paragraph 2.

3. At the end of paragraph 4, Rushdie speaks of "blind faith." How does blind faith differ from faith?

4. In paragraph 5, Rushdie argues that overpopulation and certain diseases are the direct result of religious strictures. Do you agree or disagree? Explain.

5. Since this essay was written in 1997, much has changed in the "Islamist world." Do you find Rushdie's assertions about the struggle among Islamic nations (paras. 6–7) convincing or misguided? Explain.

6. In Rushdie's world without religion, what will determine "right action"? Do you find Rushdie's position valid or foolish? Explain.

7. In paragraph 12, Rushdie alludes to the "brain-death of cultural relativism." What is cultural relativism? Why would the author characterize it as "brain-death"?

8. Rushdie promotes "freedom" (paras. 13–14) as the appropriate source of ethical choices and behavior. Do you find his argument convincing? Explain.

WRITING TOPICS

1. The essay embodies this seminal assertion: "To choose unbelief is to choose mind over dogma, to trust in our humanity instead of all these dangerous divinities." Defend or rebut this assertion.

2. Distinguish between what Rushdie calls "cultural relativism" and "freedom."

3. Defend or rebut Rushdie's argument by examining the significance of religious principles as the source of rules that make social organization possible.

4. Hinduism, Jainism, Buddhism, Judaism, Christianity, Islam, Taoism, Shintoism, animism, Bahaism—these "great" religions—exist side by side throughout the world. And these religious structures are complicated by internal divisions. There are Reform, Conservative, and Orthodox Jews; Catholic and Protestant Christians; Orthodox Catholics (Russian, Greek, and others) and Roman Catholics. Protestants include Baptists, Methodists, Lutherans, Anglicans, Seventh-Day Adventists, and

---

[3] The pen name of François-Marie Arouet (1694–1778), author of *Candide* and a major antiecclesiastical writer of his time.

many other churches. Buddhism includes many competing congregations. Islam is divided (bitterly in some regions) into Sunni and Shiite congregations, with further prominent divisions within each group. In an essay, suggest (1) the conditions under which these disparate and competing systems might peacefully coexist, or (2) describe the likely outcome of the ultimate collision between such disparate worldviews.

MAKING CONNECTIONS

1. Compare and contrast Rushdie's and Doctorow's essays. Which do you find more stirring? More persuasive? Do they both advocate the same principles?

2. While both of these essays take a negative stance toward their shared subject, they adopt a variety of **tones** over the course of their arguments. Describe the tones adopted in each essay. How do Rushdie and Doctorow each use shifts in tone to help get across their messages?

3. If you do not agree with one or both of these essays, what would you say in defense of the thing they attack? Are Rushdie and Doctorow unreasonably harsh about religious belief? How so? What might you say, if writing your own essay, to counter their arguments?

CASE STUDY

"LETTER FROM BIRMINGHAM JAIL" IN HISTORICAL CONTEXT

During the 1950s and 1960s, black citizens of the American South engaged in a great struggle to win the civil rights accorded to other U.S. citizens as a matter of course. That struggle nurtured many leaders, but none as charismatic and eloquent as Martin Luther King Jr., who wrote, from his Birmingham jail cell, the essay at the center of this investigation of one interaction between litera-ture and history. The documents collected here reveal that the seeds of the conflict were planted at the very founding of the Republic. Article I, Section 2, of the U.S. Constitution defined a slave as three-fifths of a person when it established the rules that governed the congressional House of Representa-tives. The Supreme Court, in 1856, found in the Constitution the grounds for denying Dred Scott, a slave who had been taken by his owner into a free terri-tory, the dignity of his own humanity, as is delineated in the excerpted tran-script from that case. After the Civil War, the Fourteenth Amendment to the Constitution (1868) redefined the idea of citizenship to include "all persons born or naturalized in the United States," but the resistance of the defeated Confederate states led to the formulation of the so-called Jim Crow laws—named after an African American character in minstrel shows—that endured well past the middle of the twentieth century. Examples of these laws are included in this section.

When the freedom riders came into the Deep South in the 1960s to organize black citizens, conduct voter registration drives, and demonstrate against unfair laws as well as unfair treatment under the law, many white communities responded fiercely and violently. On Good Friday, April 12, 1963, Martin Luther King Jr. was arrested for participating in a peaceful protest parade that was held without a permit. On April 13, a group of "liberal" white clergymen published a letter—included here, in an article reprinted from the *Birming-ham News*—urging restraint, cautioning against "outsiders," and advising the local African American community to turn to the courts for redress of their grievances. King's famous reply appeared on April 16. After a week of negotia-tions between protest leaders and representatives of the city of Birmingham, the Birmingham Truce Agreement was drafted (May 10, 1963). As can be seen from reading this agreement, included at the end of this section, the terms were very modest; however, it was several years before the city implemented the conditions of the agreement.

Before examining these documents, read the brief biography of Martin Luther King Jr. (p. 1389). Note that the U.S. Constitution and Supreme Court decisions can be found at several Web sites. We downloaded the sample list of Jim Crow laws from http://www.nps.gov/malu/documents/jim_crow_laws.htm.

FROM THE U.S. CONSTITUTION, ARTICLE I, SECTION 2 1787

Representatives and direct Taxes shall be apportioned among the several States which may be included within this Union, according to their respective Numbers, which shall be determined by adding to the whole Number of free Persons, including those bound to Service for a Term of Years, and excluding Indians not taxed, three-fifths of all other Persons. The actual Enumeration shall be made within three Years after the first Meeting of the Congress of the United States, and within every subsequent Term of ten Years, in such Manner as they shall by Law direct. The Number of Representatives shall not exceed one for every thirty Thousand, but each State shall have at Least one Representative; and until such enumeration shall be made, the State of New-Hampshire shall be entitled to chuse three, Massachusetts eight, Rhode-Island and Providence Plantations one, Connecticut five, New-York six, New-Jersey four, Pennsylvania eight, Delaware one, Maryland six, Virginia ten, North-Carolina five, South-Carolina five, and Georgia three.

MAKING CONNECTIONS

A class of persons called "indentured servants" were counted as part of a state's population to determine the number of representatives the state could send to Congress, but the Constitution excludes Native Americans from such a count. Can you suggest a reason for that exclusion? A slave was counted as three-fifths of a person. Can you suggest a reason?

FROM DRED SCOTT V. SANDFORD 1856

4. A free negro of the African race, whose ancestors were brought to this country and sold as slaves, is not a "citizen" within the meaning of the Constitution of the United States.

5. When the Constitution was adopted, they were not regarded in any of the States as members of the community which constituted the State, and were not numbered among its "people or citizens." Consequently, the special rights and immunities guaranteed to citizens do not apply to them. And not being "citizens" within the meaning of the Constitution, they are not entitled to sue in that character in a court of the United States, and the Circuit Court has not jurisdiction in such a suit.

6. The only two clauses in the Constitution which point to this race, treat them as persons whom it was morally lawful to deal in as articles of property and to hold as slaves.

7. Since the adoption of the Constitution of the United States, no State can by any subsequent law make a foreigner or any other description of persons citizens of the United States, nor entitle them to the rights and privileges secured to citizens by that instrument.

8. A State, by its laws passed since the adoption of the Constitution, may put a foreigner or any other description of persons upon a footing with its own citizens, as to all the rights and privileges enjoyed by them within its dominion and by its laws. But that will not make him a citizen of the United States, nor entitle him to sue in its courts, nor to any of the privileges and immunities of a citizen in another State.

9. The change in public opinion and feeling in relation to the African race, which has taken place since the adoption of the Constitution, cannot change its construction and meaning, and it must be construed and administered now according to its true meaning and intention when it was formed and adopted.

10. The plaintiff having admitted, by his demurrer to the plea in abatement, that his ancestors were imported from Africa and sold as slaves, he is not a citizen of the State of Missouri according to the Constitution of the United States, and was not entitled to sue in that character in the Circuit Court.

11. This being the case, the judgment of the court below, in favor of the plaintiff on the plea in abatement, was erroneous.

MAKING CONNECTIONS

1. In 1857, could a person be a "citizen" of a state but not a "citizen" of the United States? Explain.

2. Is such a distinction possible now?

3. Do you find a contradiction between the statements in number 5 and Article I, Section 2, of the Constitution? Explain.

4. Research the consequences of the Dred Scott decision, either at the library or on the Internet. In an essay, describe the immediate consequences of the decision and its impact on constitutional amendments in the mid–nineteenth century.

JIM CROW LAWS CA 1880S–1960S

From the 1880s into the 1960s, a majority of American states enforced segregation through Jim Crow laws, which often imposed legal punishments on people for consorting with members of another race.
Here is a sampling of laws from various states:

Nurses No person or corporation shall require any white female nurse to nurse in wards or rooms in hospitals, either public or private, in which negro men are placed. *Alabama*

Buses All passenger stations in this state operated by any motor transportation company shall have separate waiting rooms or space and separate ticket windows for the white and colored races. *Alabama*

Railroads The conductor of each passenger train is authorized and required to assign each passenger to the car or the division of the car, when it is divided by a partition,   designated for the race to which such passenger belongs. *Alabama*

Restaurants   It shall be unlawful to conduct a restaurant or other place for the serving of food in the city, at which white and colored people are served in the same room, unless such white and colored persons are effectually separated by a solid partition extending from the floor upward to a distance of seven feet or higher, and unless a separate entrance from the street is provided for each compartment. *Alabama*

Pool and Billiard Rooms   It shall be unlawful for a negro and white person to play together or in company with each other at any game of pool or billiards. *Alabama*

Toilet Facilities, Male   Every employer of white or negro males shall provide for such white or negro males reasonably accessible and separate toilet facilities. *Alabama*

Intermarriage   The marriage of a person of Caucasian blood with a Negro, Mongolian, Malay, or Hindu shall be null and void. *Arizona*

Intermarriage   All marriages between a white person and a negro, or between a white person and a person of negro descent to the fourth generation inclusive, are hereby forever prohibited. *Florida*

Cohabitation   Any negro man and white woman, or any white man and negro woman, who are not married to each other, who shall habitually live in and occupy in the nighttime the same room, shall each be punished by imprisonment not exceeding twelve (12) months, or by fine not exceeding five hundred ($500.00) dollars. *Florida*

Education   The schools for white children and the schools for negro children shall be conducted separately. *Florida*

Juvenile Delinquents   There shall be separate buildings, not nearer than one-fourth mile to each other, one for white boys and one for negro boys. White boys and negro boys shall not, in any manner, be associated together or worked together. *Florida*

Intermarriage   It shall be unlawful for a white person to marry anyone except a white person. Any marriage in violation of this section shall be void. *Georgia*

Burial   The officer in charge shall not bury, or allow to be buried, any colored persons upon ground set apart or used for the burial of white persons. *Georgia*

Amateur Baseball   It shall be unlawful for any amateur white baseball team to play baseball on any vacant lot or baseball diamond within two blocks of a playground devoted to the Negro race, and it shall be unlawful for any amateur colored baseball team to play baseball in any vacant lot or baseball diamond within two blocks of any playground devoted to the white race. *Georgia*

Parks   It shall be unlawful for colored people to frequent any park owned or maintained by the city for the benefit, use, and enjoyment of white persons . . . and unlawful for any white person to frequent any park owned or maintained by the city for the use and benefit of colored persons. *Georgia*

Wine and Beer   All persons licensed to conduct the business of selling beer or wine shall serve either white people exclusively or colored people exclusively and shall not sell to the two races within the same room at any time. *Georgia*

Circus Tickets   All circuses, shows, and tent exhibitions, to which the attendance of more than one race is invited or expected to attend, shall provide for the convenience of its patrons not less than two ticket offices with individual ticket sellers, and not less than two entrances to the said performance, with individual ticket takers and receivers, and in the case of outside or tent performances, the said ticket offices shall not be less than twenty-five (25) feet apart. *Louisiana*

Promotion of Equality   Any person . . . who shall be guilty of printing, publishing, or circulating printed, typewritten, or written matter urging or presenting for public acceptance or general information, arguments or suggestions in favor of social equality or of intermarriage between whites and negroes, shall be guilty of a misdemeanor and subject to fine not exceeding five hundred ($500.00) dollars or imprisonment not exceeding six (6) months or both. *Mississippi*

Prisons   The warden shall see that the white convicts shall have separate apartments for both eating and sleeping from the negro convicts. *Mississippi*

Child Custody   It shall be unlawful for any parent, relative, or other white person in this State, having the control or custody of any white child, by right of guardianship, natural or acquired, or otherwise, to dispose of, give, or surrender such white child permanently into the custody, control, maintenance, or support of a negro. *South Carolina*

Libraries   Any white person of such county may use the county free library under the rules and regulations prescribed by the commissioners court and may be entitled to all the privileges thereof. Said court shall make proper provision for the negroes of said county to be served through a separate branch or branches of the county free library, which shall be administered by

[a] custodian of the negro race under the supervision of the county librarian. *Texas*

Education [The County Board of Education] shall provide schools of two kinds, those for white children and those for colored children. *Texas*

MAKING CONNECTIONS

1. Research the term *Jim Crow*. Where does it come from, and what does it mean?

2. Jim Crow laws began to appear in the 1880s. Why do you suppose they did not appear earlier?

3. Note that the grassroots activities for which Martin Luther King Jr. was imprisoned occurred in 1963. Why did the African American community and its allies believe it was necessary to break local laws?

4. Place yourself in the position of an African American southerner in 1950. How would you react to the limitations imposed on you by the Jim Crow laws?

A CALL FOR UNITY FROM
ALABAMA CLERGYMEN[1]   1963

Leading Protestant, Catholic, and Jewish clerics Friday called on local Negro citizens to withdraw support of racial demonstrations and unite for a peaceful Birmingham.

In a prepared statement, the clergy praised the manner in which the 10 days of demonstrations have been handled by the Birmingham Police Department.

The same clergy were among others who recently issued "An Appeal for Law and Order and Common Sense" in dealing with the racial problems in Alabama.

Saturday's statement was signed by C.C.J. Carpenter, Episcopal Bishop of Alabama; Joseph A. Durick, auxiliary bishop, Catholic Diocese of Mobile–Birmingham; Rabbi Milton Grafman, Temple Emanu-El; Bishop Paul Hardin, Bishop of the Alabama–West Florida Conference of the Methodist Church; Bishop Nolan B. Harmen, Bishop of the North Alabama Conference of the Methodist Church; George M. Murray, Bishop Coadjutor, Episcopal Diocese of Alabama; Edward V. Ramage, moderator, Synod of the Alabama Presbyterian Church in the United States, and the Reverend Earl Stallings, pastor, First Baptist Church of Birmingham.

The text of the statement follows: 5

"We, the undersigned clergymen are among those who in January issued 'An Appeal for Law and Order and Common Sense' in dealing with the racial

---

[1] The article appeared in the *Birmingham News* on Saturday, April 13, 1963, under the headline "White Clergymen Urge Local Negroes to Withdraw from Demonstrations."

problems in Alabama. We expressed understanding that honest convictions in racial matters could properly be pursued in the courts, but urged that decisions of these courts should in the meantime be peacefully obeyed.

"Since that time there had been some evidence of increased forbearance and a willingness to face facts. Responsible citizens have undertaken to work on various problems which cause racial friction and unrest.

"In Birmingham recent public events have given indication that we all have opportunity for a new constructive and realistic approach to racial problems.

"However, we are now confronted by a series of demonstrations by some of our Negro citizens directed and led in part by outsiders. We recognize the natural impatience of people who feel their hopes are slow in being realized. But we are convinced that these demonstrations are unwise and untimely.

"We agree rather with certain local Negro leadership which has called for 10 honest and open negotiation of racial issues in our area.

"And we believe this kind of facing issues can best be accomplished by citizens of our own metropolitan area, white and Negro, meeting with their knowledge and experience of the local situation. All of us need to face that responsibility and find proper channels for its accomplishment.

"Just as we formerly pointed out that 'hatred and violence have no sanction in our religious and political traditions,' we also point out that such actions as incite hatred and violence, however technically peaceful those actions may be, have not contributed to the resolution of our local problems.

"We do not believe that these days of new hope are days when extreme measures are justified in Birmingham.

"We commend the community as a whole, and the local news media and law enforcement officials in particular, on the calm manner in which these demonstrations have been handled.

"We urge the public to continue to show restraint should the demonstra- 15 tions continue, and the law enforcement officials to remain calm and continue to protect our city from violence.

"We further strongly urge our own Negro community to withdraw support from these demonstrations, and to unite locally in working peacefully for a better Birmingham.

"When rights are consistently denied, a cause should be pressed in the courts and negotiations among local leaders, and not in the streets.

"We appeal to both our white and Negro citizenry to observe the principles of law and order and common sense."

MAKING CONNECTIONS

1. Do you agree with the Alabama clergymen that "honest convictions in racial matters could properly be pursued in the courts" (para. 6)? Explain.

2. If the courts do not provide a means to redress grievances, what are the alternatives?

3. What were the "racial matters" the clergymen were speaking of?

4. Do you find their views on "outsiders" persuasive? Explain.

5. The clergymen say that "extreme measures" are not justified (para. 13). What do you suppose they mean by "extreme measures"? Are there any circumstances that would justify extreme measures? Explain.

THE BIRMINGHAM TRUCE AGREEMENT 1963

1. Within 3 days after close of demonstrations, fitting rooms will be desegregated.

2. Within 30 days after the city government is established by court order, signs on wash rooms, rest rooms and drinking fountains will be removed.

3. Within 60 days after the city government is established by court order, a program of lunchroom counter desegregation will be commenced.

4. When the city government is established by court order, a program of upgrading Negro employment will be continued and there will be meetings with responsible local leadership to consider further steps.

Within 60 days from the court order determining Birmingham's city government, the employment program will include at least one sales person or cashier.

Within 15 days from the cessation of demonstrations, a Committee on Racial Problems and Employment composed of members of the Senior Citizens' Committee will be established, with a membership made public and the publicly announced purpose of establishing liaison with members of the Negro community to carry out a program of up-grading and improving employment opportunities with the Negro citizens of the Birmingham community.

MAKING CONNECTIONS

1. Do you feel that the Birmingham Truce Agreement represented total victory for the demonstrators? Explain.

2. Research the behavior of the Birmingham city government after May 10, 1963 (the date this agreement was reached). Did the government meet the terms of the truce agreement? Explain.

MARTIN LUTHER KING JR. (1929–1968)

LETTER FROM BIRMINGHAM JAIL[1] 1963

My Dear Fellow Clergymen:

While confined here in the Birmingham city jail, I came across your recent statement calling my present activities "unwise and untimely." Seldom do I pause to answer criticism of my work and ideas. If I sought to answer all the criticisms that cross my desk, my secretaries would have little time for anything other than such correspondence in the course of the day, and I would have no time for constructive work. But since I feel that you are men of genuine good will and that your criticisms are sincerely set forth, I want to try to answer your statement in what I hope will be patient and reasonable terms.

I think I should indicate why I am here in Birmingham, since you have been influenced by the view which argues against "outsiders coming in." I have the honor of serving as president of the Southern Christian Leadership Conference, an organization operating in every southern state, with headquarters in Atlanta, Georgia. We have some eighty-five affiliated organizations across the South, and one of them is the Alabama Christian Movement for Human Rights. Frequently we share staff, educational, and financial resources with our affiliates. Several months ago the affiliate here in Birmingham asked us to be on call to engage in a nonviolent direct-action program if such were deemed necessary. We readily consented, and when the hour came we lived up to our promise. So I, along with several members of my staff, am here because I was invited here. I am here because I have organizational ties here.

But more basically, I am in Birmingham because injustice is here. Just as the prophets of the eighth century B.C. left their villages and carried their "thus saith the Lord" far beyond the boundaries of their home towns, and just as the Apostle Paul left his village of Tarsus[2] and carried the gospel of Jesus Christ to the far corners of the Greco-Roman world, so am I compelled to carry the gospel of freedom beyond my own home town. Like Paul, I must constantly respond to the Macedonian call for aid.[3]

Moreover, I am cognizant of the interrelatedness of all communities and states. I cannot sit idly by in Atlanta and not be concerned about what happens in Birmingham. Injustice anywhere is a threat to justice everywhere. We are

---

[1] This response to a published statement by eight fellow clergymen from Alabama (Bishop C. C. J. Carpenter, Bishop Joseph A. Durick, Rabbi Hilton L. Grafman, Bishop Paul Hardin, Bishop Nolan B. Harmon, the Reverend George M. Murray, the Reverend Edward V. Ramage, and the Reverend Earl Stallings) was composed under somewhat constricting circumstances. Begun on the margins of the newspaper in which the statement appeared while I was in jail, the letter was continued on scraps of writing paper supplied by a friendly Negro trusty, and concluded on a pad my attorneys were eventually permitted to leave me. Although the text remains in substance unaltered, I have indulged in the author's prerogative of polishing it for publication. [King's note]

[2] Birthplace of St. Paul, in present-day Turkey.

[3] St. Paul was frequently called upon to aid the Christian community in Macedonia.

caught in an inescapable network of mutuality, tied in a single garment of destiny. Whatever affects one directly, affects all indirectly. Never again can we afford to live with the narrow, provincial "outside agitator" idea. Anyone who lives inside the United States can never be considered an outsider anywhere within its bounds.

You deplore the demonstrations taking place in Birmingham. But your state- 5 ment, I am sorry to say, fails to express a similar concern for the conditions that brought about the demonstrations. I am sure that none of you would want to rest content with the superficial kind of social analysis that deals merely with effects and does not grapple with the underlying causes. It is unfortunate that demonstrations are taking place in Birmingham, but it is even more unfortunate that the city's white power structure left the Negro community with no alternative.

In any nonviolent campaign there are four basic steps: collection of the facts to determine whether injustices exist; negotiation; self-purification; and direct action. We have gone through all these steps in Birmingham. There can be no gainsaying the fact that racial injustice engulfs this community. Birmingham is probably the most thoroughly segregated city in the United States. Its ugly record of brutality is widely known. Negroes have experienced grossly unjust treatment in the courts. There have been more unsolved bombings of Negro homes and churches in Birmingham than in any other city in the nation. These are the hard, brutal facts of the case. On the basis of these conditions, Negro leaders sought to negotiate with the city fathers. But the latter consistently refused to engage in good-faith negotiation.

Then, last September, came the opportunity to talk with leaders of Birmingham's economic community. In the course of the negotiations, certain promises were made by the merchants—for example, to remove the stores' humiliating racial signs. On the basis of these promises, the Reverend Fred Shuttlesworth and the leaders of the Alabama Christian Movement for Human Rights agreed to a moratorium on all demonstrations. As the weeks and months went by, we realized that we were the victims of a broken promise. A few signs, briefly removed, returned; the others remained.

As in so many past experiences, our hopes had been blasted, and the shadow of deep disappointment settled upon us. We had no alternative except to prepare for direct action, whereby we would present our very bodies as a means of laying our case before the conscience of the local and the national community. Mindful of the difficulties involved, we decided to undertake a process of self-purification. We began a series of workshops on nonviolence, and we repeatedly asked ourselves: "Are you able to accept blows without retaliating?" "Are you able to endure the ordeal of jail?" We decided to schedule our direct-action program for the Easter season, realizing that except for Christmas, this is the main shopping period of the year. Knowing that a strong economic-withdrawal program would be the by-product of direct action, we felt that this would be the best time to bring pressure to bear on the merchants for the needed change.

Then it occurred to us that Birmingham's mayoral election was coming up in March, and we speedily decided to postpone action until after election-day. When we discovered that the Commissioner of Public Safety, Eugene "Bull" Connor, had piled up enough votes to be in the run-off, we decided again to postpone action until the day after the run-off so that the demonstrations could not be used to cloud the issues. Like many others, we waited to see Mr. Connor defeated, and to this end we endured postponement after postponement. Having aided in this community need, we felt that our direct-action program could be delayed no longer.

You may well ask, "Why direct action? Why sit-ins, marches, and so forth? Isn't negotiation a better path?" You are quite right in calling for negotiation. Indeed, this is the very purpose of direct action. Nonviolent direct action seeks to create such a crisis and foster such a tension that a community which has constantly refused to negotiate is forced to confront the issue. It seeks so to dramatize the issue that it can no longer be ignored. My citing the creation of tension as part of the work of the nonviolent-resister may sound rather shocking. But I must confess that I am not afraid of the word "tension." I have earnestly opposed violent tension, but there is a type of constructive, nonviolent tension which is necessary for growth. Just as Socrates[4] felt that it was necessary to create a tension in the mind so that individuals could rise from the bondage of myths and half-truths to the unfettered realm of creative analysis and objective appraisal, so must we see the need for nonviolent gadflies to create the kind of tension in society that will help men rise from the dark depths of prejudice and racism to the majestic heights of understanding and brotherhood.

The purpose of our direct-action program is to create a situation so crisis-packed that it will inevitably open the door to negotiation. I therefore concur with you in your call for negotiation. Too long has our beloved Southland been bogged down in a tragic effort to live in monologue rather than dialogue.

One of the basic points in your statement is that the action that I and my associates have taken in Birmingham is untimely. Some have asked: "Why didn't you give the new city administration time to act?" The only answer that I can give to this query is that the new Birmingham administration must be prodded about as much as the outgoing one, before it will act. We are sadly mistaken if we feel that the election of Albert Boutwell as mayor will bring the millennium to Birmingham. While Mr. Boutwell is a much more gentle person than Mr. Connor, they are both segregationists, dedicated to maintenance of the status quo. I have hoped that Mr. Boutwell will be reasonable enough to see the futility of massive resistance to desegregation. But he will not see this without pressure from devotees of civil rights. My friends, I must say to you that we have not made a single gain in civil rights without determined legal and nonviolent pressure. Lamentably, it is an historical fact that privileged groups seldom give up their privileges voluntarily. Individuals may see the

---

[4] Socrates (469–399 B.C.), a Greek philosopher who often pretended ignorance in arguments to expose the errors in his opponent's reasoning.

moral light and voluntarily give up their unjust posture; but, as Reinhold Niebuhr [5] has reminded us, groups tend to be more immoral than individuals.

We know through painful experience that freedom is never voluntarily given by the oppressor; it must be demanded by the oppressed. Frankly, I have yet to engage in a direct-action campaign that was "well timed" in the view of those who have not suffered unduly from the disease of segregation. For years now I have heard the word "Wait!" It rings in the ear of every Negro with piercing familiarity. This "Wait" has almost always meant "Never." We must come to see, with one of our distinguished jurists, that "justice too long delayed is justice denied."

We have waited for more than 340 years for our constitutional and God-given rights. The nations of Asia and Africa are moving with jetlike speed toward gaining political independence, but we still creep at horse-and-buggy pace toward gaining a cup of coffee at a lunch counter. Perhaps it is easy for those who have never felt the stinging darts of segregation to say, "Wait." But when you have seen vicious mobs lynch your mothers and fathers at will and drown your sisters and brothers at whim; when you have seen hate-filled policemen curse, kick, and even kill your black brothers and sisters; when you see the vast majority of your twenty million Negro brothers smothering in an airtight cage of poverty in the midst of an affluent society; when you suddenly find your tongue twisted and your speech stammering as you seek to explain to your six-year-old daughter why she can't go to the public amusement park that has just been advertised on television, and see tears welling up in her eyes when she is told that Funtown is closed to colored children, and see ominous clouds of inferiority beginning to form in her little mental sky, and see her beginning to distort her personality by developing an unconscious bitterness toward white people; when you have to concoct an answer for a five-year-old son who is asking, "Daddy, why do white people treat colored people so mean?"; when you take a cross-country drive and find it necessary to sleep night after night in the uncomfortable corners of your automobile because no motel will accept you; when you are humiliated day in and day out by nagging signs reading "white" and "colored"; when your first name becomes "nigger," your middle name becomes "boy" (however old you are) and your last name becomes "John," and your wife and mother are never given the respected title "Mrs."; when you are harried by day and haunted by night by the fact that you are a Negro, living constantly at tiptoe stance, never quite knowing what to expect next, and are plagued with inner fears and outer resentments; when you are forever fighting a degenerating sense of "nobodiness"—then you will understand why we find it difficult to wait. There comes a time when the cup of endurance runs over, and men are no longer willing to be plunged into the abyss of despair. I hope, sirs, you can understand our legitimate and unavoidable impatience.

---

[5] Reinhold Niebuhr (1892–1971), American philosopher and theologian.

You express a great deal of anxiety over our willingness to break laws. This is 15 certainly a legitimate concern. Since we so diligently urge people to obey the Supreme Court's decision of 1954 outlawing segregation in the public schools, at first glance it may seem rather paradoxical for us consciously to break laws. One may well ask: "How can you advocate breaking some laws and obeying others?" The answer lies in the fact that there are two types of laws: just and unjust. I would be the first to advocate obeying just laws. One has not only a legal but a moral responsibility to obey just laws. Conversely, one has a moral responsibility to disobey unjust laws. I would agree with St. Augustine that "an unjust law is no law at all."

Now, what is the difference between the two? How does one determine whether a law is just or unjust? A just law is a man-made code that squares with the moral law or the law of God. An unjust law is a code that is out of harmony with the moral law. To put it in the terms of St. Thomas Aquinas: an unjust law is a human law that is not rooted in eternal law and natural law. Any law that uplifts human personality is just. Any law that degrades human personality is unjust. All segregation statutes are unjust because segregation distorts the soul and damages the personality. It gives the segregator a false sense of superiority and the segregated a false sense of inferiority. Segregation, to use the terminology of the Jewish philosopher Martin Buber, substitutes an "I-it" relationship for an "I-thou" relationship and ends up relegating persons to the status of things. Hence segregation is not only politically, economically, and sociologically unsound, it is morally wrong and sinful. Paul Tillich has said that sin is separation. Is not segregation an existential expression of man's tragic separation, his awful estrangement, his terrible sinfulness? Thus it is that I can urge men to obey the 1954 decision of the Supreme Court, for it is morally right; and I can urge them to disobey segregation ordinances, for they are morally wrong.

Let us consider a more concrete example of just and unjust laws. An unjust law is a code that a numerical or power majority group compels a minority group to obey but does not make binding on itself. This is *difference* made legal. By the same token, a just law is a code that a majority compels a minority to follow and that it is willing to follow itself. This is *sameness* made legal.

Let me give another explanation. A law is unjust if it is inflicted on a minority that, as a result of being denied the right to vote, had no part in enacting or devising the law. Who can say that the legislature of Alabama which set up that state's segregation laws was democratically elected? Throughout Alabama all sorts of devious methods are used to prevent Negroes from becoming registered voters, and there are some counties in which, even though Negroes constitute a majority of the population, not a single Negro is registered. Can any law enacted under such circumstances be considered democratically structured?

Sometimes a law is just on its face and unjust in its application. For instance, I have been arrested on a charge of parading without a permit. Now, there is nothing wrong in having an ordinance which requires a permit for a parade. But such an ordinance becomes unjust when it is used to maintain segregation and to deny citizens the First-Amendment privilege of peaceful assembly and protest.

I hope you are able to see the distinction I am trying to point out. In no sense 20
do I advocate evading or defying the law, as would the rabid segregationist.
That would lead to anarchy. One who breaks an unjust law must do so openly,
lovingly, and with a willingness to accept the penalty. I submit that an individual who breaks a law that conscience tells him is unjust, and who willingly
accepts the penalty of imprisonment in order to arouse the conscience of the
community over its injustice, is in reality expressing the highest respect for law.

Of course, there is nothing new about this kind of civil disobedience. It was
evidenced sublimely in the refusal of Shadrach, Meshach, and Abednego to
obey the laws of Nebuchadnezzar, on the ground that a higher moral law was at
stake.[6] It was practiced superbly by the early Christians, who were willing to
face hungry lions and the excruciating pain of chopping blocks rather than
submit to certain unjust laws of the Roman Empire. To a degree, academic freedom is a reality today because Socrates practiced civil disobedience. In our own
nation, the Boston Tea Party represented a massive act of civil disobedience.

We should never forget that everything Adolf Hitler did in Germany was
"legal" and everything the Hungarian freedom fighters did in Hungary was "illegal." It was "illegal" to aid and comfort a Jew in Hitler's Germany. Even so, I
am sure that, had I lived in Germany at the time, I would have aided and comforted my Jewish brothers. If today I lived in a Communist country where certain principles dear to the Christian faith are suppressed, I would openly
advocate disobeying that country's anti-religious laws.

I must make two honest confessions to you, my Christian and Jewish brothers. First, I must confess that over the past few years I have been gravely disappointed with the white moderate. I have almost reached the regrettable
conclusion that the Negro's great stumbling block in his stride toward freedom
is not the white Citizen's Counciler[7] or the Ku Klux Klanner, but the white
moderate, who is more devoted to "order" than to justice; who prefers a negative peace which is the absence of tension to a positive peace which is the presence of justice; who constantly says, "I agree with you in the goal you seek, but I
cannot agree with your methods of direct action"; who paternalistically
believes he can set the timetable for another man's freedom; who lives by a
mythical concept of time and who constantly advises the Negro to wait for a
"more convenient season." Shallow understanding from people of good will is
more frustrating than absolute misunderstanding from people of ill will. Luke-
warm acceptance is much more bewildering than outright rejection.

I had hoped that the white moderate would understand that law and order
exist for the purpose of establishing justice and that when they fail in this
purpose they become the dangerously structured dams that block the flow of
social progress. I had hoped that the white moderate would understand that
the present tension in the South is a necessary phase of the transition from an

---

[6] See Daniel 1:7–3:30.
[7] White Citizen's Councils sprang up in the South after 1954 (the year the Supreme Court declared
segregated education unconstitutional) to fight against desegregation.

obnoxious negative peace, in which the Negro passively accepted his unjust plight, to a substantive and positive peace, in which all men will respect the dignity and worth of human personality. Actually, we who engage in nonviolent direct action are not the creators of tension. We merely bring to the surface the hidden tension that is already alive. We bring it out in the open, where it can be seen and dealt with. Like a boil that can never be cured so long as it is covered up but must be opened with all its ugliness to the natural medicines of air and light, injustice must be exposed, with all the tension its exposure creates, to the light of human conscience and the air of national opinion, before it can be cured.

In your statement you assert that our actions, even though peaceful, must be 25 condemned because they precipitate violence. But is this a logical assertion? Isn't this like condemning a robbed man because his possession of money precipitated the evil act of robbery? Isn't this like condemning Socrates because his unswerving commitment to truth and his philosophical inquiries precipitated the act by the misguided populace in which they made him drink hemlock? Isn't this like condemning Jesus because his unique God-consciousness and never-ceasing devotion to God's will precipitated the evil act of crucifixion? We must come to see that, as the federal courts have consistently affirmed, it is wrong to urge an individual to cease his efforts to gain his basic constitutional rights because the quest may precipitate violence. Society must protect the robbed and punish the robber.

I had also hoped that the white moderate would reject the myth concerning time in relation to the struggle for freedom. I have just received a letter from a white brother in Texas. He writes: "All Christians know that the colored people will receive greater equal rights eventually, but it is possible that you are in too great a religious hurry. It has taken Christianity almost two thousand years to accomplish what it has. The teachings of Christ take time to come to earth." Such an attitude stems from a tragic misconception of time, from the strangely irrational notion that there is something in the very flow of time that will inevitably cure all ills. Actually, time itself is neutral; it can be used either destructively or constructively. More and more I feel that the people of ill will have used time much more effectively than have the people of good will. We will have to repent in this generation not merely for the hateful words and actions of the bad people, but for the appalling silence of the good people. Human progress never rolls in on wheels of inevitability; it comes through the tireless efforts of men willing to be co-workers with God, and without this hard work, time itself becomes an ally of the forces of social stagnation. We must use time creatively, in the knowledge that the time is always ripe to do right. Now is the time to make real the promise of democracy and transform our pending national elegy into a creative psalm of brotherhood. Now is the time to lift our national policy from the quicksand of racial injustice to the solid rock of human dignity.

You speak of our activity in Birmingham as extreme. At first I was rather disappointed that fellow clergymen would see my nonviolent efforts as those of an extremist. I began thinking about the fact that I stand in the middle of two opposing forces in the Negro community. One is a force of complacency, made up in part of Negroes, who, as a result of long years of oppression, are so drained of self-respect and a sense of "somebodiness" that they have adjusted to segregation; and in part of a few middle-class Negroes who, because of a degree of academic and economic security and because in some ways they profit by segregation, have become insensitive to the problems of the masses. The other force is one of bitterness and hatred, and it comes perilously close to advocating violence. It is expressed in the various black nationalist groups that are springing up across the nation, the largest and best-known being Elijah Muhammad's Muslim movement.[8] Nourished by the Negro's frustration over the continued existence of racial discrimination, this movement is made up of people who have lost faith in America, who have absolutely repudiated Christianity, and who have concluded that the white man is an incorrigible "devil."

I have tried to stand between these two forces, saying that we need emulate neither the "do-nothingism" of the complacent nor the hatred and despair of the black nationalist. For there is the more excellent way of love and nonviolent protest. I am grateful to God that, through the influence of the Negro church, the way of nonviolence became an integral part of our struggle.

If this philosophy had not emerged, by now many streets of the South would, I am convinced, be flowing with blood. And I am further convinced that if our white brothers dismiss as "rabble-rousers" and "outside agitators" those of us who employ nonviolent direct action, and if they refuse to support our nonviolent efforts, millions of Negroes will, out of frustration and despair, seek solace and security in black-nationalist ideologies—a development that would inevitably lead to a frightening racial nightmare.

Oppressed people cannot remain oppressed forever. The yearning for freedom eventually manifests itself, and that is what has happened to the American Negro. Something within has reminded him of his birthright of freedom, and something without has reminded him that it can be gained. Consciously or unconsciously, he has been caught up by the *Zeitgeist*,[9] and with his black brothers of Africa and his brown and yellow brothers of Asia, South America, and the Caribbean, the United States Negro is moving with a sense of great urgency toward the promised land of racial justice. If one recognizes this vital urge that has engulfed the Negro community, one should readily understand why public demonstrations are taking place. The Negro has many pent-up resentments and latent frustrations, and he must release them. So let him march; let him make prayer pilgrimages to the city hall; let him go on freedom rides[10]—and try to

30

---

[8] Elijah Muhammad (1897–1975), leader of the Nation of Islam, a black Muslim religious group that rejected integration and called upon blacks to fight to establish their own nation.

[9] The spirit of the time.

[10] In 1961, hundreds of blacks and whites, under the direction of the Congress of Racial Equality (CORE), deliberately violated laws in southern states that required segregation in buses and bus terminals.

understand why he must do so. If his repressed emotions are not released in nonviolent ways, they will seek expression through violence; this is not a threat but a fact of history. So I have not said to my people, "Get rid of your discontent." Rather, I have tried to say that this normal and healthy discontent can be channeled into the creative outlet of nonviolent direct action. And now this approach is being termed extremist.

But though I was initially disappointed at being categorized as an extremist, as I continued to think about the matter I gradually gained a measure of satisfaction from the label. Was not Jesus an extremist for love: "Love your enemies, bless them that curse you, do good to them that hate you, and pray for them that despitefully use you, and persecute you." Was not Amos an extremist for justice: "Let justice roll down like waters and righteousness like an ever-flowing stream." Was not Paul an extremist for the Christian gospel: "I bear in my body the marks of the Lord Jesus." Was not Martin Luther an extremist: "Here I stand; I cannot do otherwise, so help me God." And John Bunyan: "I will stay in jail to the end of my days before I make a butchery of my conscience." And Abraham Lincoln: "This nation cannot survive half slave and half free." And Thomas Jefferson: "We hold these truths to be self-evident, that all men are created equal. . . . " So the question is not whether we will be extremists, but what kind of extremists we will be. Will we be extremists for the preservation of injustice or for the extension of justice? In that dramatic scene on Calvary's hill three men were crucified. We must never forget that all three were crucified for the same crime—the crime of extremism. Two were extremists for immorality, and thus fell below their environment. The other, Jesus Christ, was an extremist for love, truth, and goodness, and thereby rose above his environment. Perhaps the South, the nation, and the world are in dire need of creative extremists.

I had hoped that the white moderate would see this need. Perhaps I was too optimistic; perhaps I expected too much. I suppose I should have realized that few members of the oppressor race can understand the deep groans and passionate yearnings of the oppressed race, and still fewer have the vision to see that injustice must be rooted out by strong, persistent, and determined action. I am thankful, however, that some of our white brothers in the South have grasped the meaning of this social revolution and committed themselves to it. They are still all too few in quantity, but they are big in quality. Some—such as Ralph McGill, Lillian Smith, Harry Golden, James McBride Dabbs, Ann Braden, and Sarah Patton Boyle—have written about our struggle in eloquent and prophetic terms. Others have marched with us down nameless streets of the South. They have languished in filthy, roach-infested jails, suffering the abuse and brutality of policemen who view them as "dirty nigger-lovers." Unlike so many of their moderate brothers and sisters, they have recognized the urgency of the moment and sensed the need for powerful "action" antidotes to combat the disease of segregation.

Let me take note of my other major disappointment. I have been so greatly disappointed with the white church and its leadership. Of course, there are some notable exceptions. I am not unmindful of the fact that each of you has taken some significant stands on this issue. I commend you, Reverend Stallings, for your Christian stand on this past Sunday, in welcoming Negroes to your worship service on a nonsegregated basis. I commend the Catholic leaders of this state for integrating Spring Hill College several years ago.

But despite these notable exceptions, I must honestly reiterate that I have been disappointed with the church. I do not say this as one of those negative critics who can always find something wrong with the church. I say this as a minister of the gospel, who loves the church; who was nurtured in its bosom; who has been sustained by its spiritual blessings and who will remain true to it as long as the cord of life shall lengthen.

When I was suddenly catapulted into the leadership of the bus protest in 35 Montgomery, Alabama, a few years ago, I felt we would be supported by the white church. I felt that the white ministers, priests, and rabbis of the South would be among our strongest allies. Instead, some have been outright opponents, refusing to understand the freedom movement and misrepresenting its leaders; all too many others have been more cautious than courageous and have remained silent behind the anesthetizing security of stained-glass windows.

In spite of my shattered dreams, I came to Birmingham with the hope that the white religious leadership of this community would see the justice of our cause and, with deep moral concern, would serve as the channel through which our just grievances could reach the power structure. I had hoped that each of you would understand. But again I have been disappointed.

I have heard numerous southern religious leaders admonish their worshipers to comply with a desegregation decision because it is the law, but I have longed to hear white ministers declare: "Follow this decree because integration is morally right and because the Negro is your brother." In the midst of blatant injustices inflicted upon the Negro, I have watched white churchmen stand on the sideline and mouth pious irrelevancies and sanctimonious trivialities. In the midst of a mighty struggle to rid our nation of racial and economic injustice, I have heard many ministers say: "Those are social issues, with which the gospel has no real concern." And I have watched many churches commit themselves to a completely otherworldly religion which makes a strange, unBiblical distinction between body and soul, between the sacred and the secular.

I have traveled the length and breadth of Alabama, Mississippi, and all the other southern states. On sweltering summer days and crisp autumn mornings I have looked at the South's beautiful churches with their lofty spires pointing heavenward. I have beheld the impressive outlines of her massive religious-education buildings. Over and over I have found myself asking: "What kind of people worship here? Who is their God? Where were their voices when the lips of Governor Barnett dripped with words of interposition and nullification? Where were they when Governor Wallace gave a clarion call for defiance and hatred? Where were their voices of support when bruised and weary Negro men and women decided to rise from the dark dungeons of complacency to the bright hills of creative protest?"

Yes, these questions are still in mind. In deep disappointment I have wept over the laxity of the church. But be assured that my tears have been tears of love. There can be no deep disappointment where there is not deep love. Yes, I love the church. How could I do otherwise? I am in the rather unique position of being the son, the grandson, and the great-grandson of preachers. Yes, I see the church as the body of Christ. But, oh! How we have blemished and scarred the body through social neglect and through fear of being nonconformists.

There was a time when the church was very powerful—in the time when the early Christians rejoiced at being deemed worthy to suffer for what they believed. In those days the church was not merely a thermometer that transformed the mores of society. Whenever the early Christians entered a town, the people in power became disturbed and immediately sought to convict the Christians for being "disturbers of the peace" and "outside agitators." But the Christians pressed on, in the conviction that they were "a colony of heaven," called to obey God rather than man. Small in number, they were big in commitment. They were too God-intoxicated to be "astronomically intimidated." By their effort and example they brought an end to such ancient evils as infanticide and gladiatorial contests. 40

Things are different now. So often the contemporary church is a weak, ineffectual voice with an uncertain sound. So often it is an archdefender of the status quo. Far from being disturbed by the presence of the church, the power structure of the average community is consoled by the church's silent—and often even vocal—sanction of things as they are.

But the judgment of God is upon the church as never before. If today's church does not recapture the sacrificial spirit of the early church, it will lose its authenticity, forfeit the loyalty of millions, and be dismissed as an irrelevant social club with no meaning for the twentieth century. Every day I meet young people whose disappointment with the church has turned into outright disgust.

Perhaps I have once again been too optimistic. Is organized religion too inextricably bound to the status quo to save our nation and the world? Perhaps I must turn my faith to the inner spiritual church, the church within the church, as the true *ekklesia*[11] and the hope of the world. But again I am thankful to God that some noble souls from the ranks of organized religion have broken loose from the paralyzing chains of conformity and joined us as active partners in the struggle for freedom. They have left their secure congregations and walked the streets of Albany, Georgia, with us. They have gone down the highways of the South on tortuous rides for freedom. Yes, they have gone to jail with us. Some have been dismissed from their churches, have lost the support of their bishops and fellow ministers. But they have acted in the faith that right defeated is stronger than evil triumphant. Their witness has been the spiritual salt that has preserved the true meaning of the gospel in these troubled times. They have carved a tunnel of hope through the dark mountain of disappointment.

---

[11] The Greek New Testament word for the early Christian church.

I hope that the church as a whole will meet the challenge of this decisive hour. But even if the church does not come to the aid of justice, I have no despair about the future. I have no fear about the outcome of our struggle in Birmingham, even if our motives are at present misunderstood. We will reach the goal of freedom in Birmingham and all over the nation, because the goal of America is freedom. Abused and scorned though we may be, our destiny is tied up with America's destiny. Before the pilgrims landed at Plymouth, we were here. Before the pen of Jefferson etched the majestic words of the Declaration of Independence across the pages of history, we were here. For more than two centuries our forebears labored in this country without wages; they made cotton king; they built the homes of their masters while suffering gross injustice and shameful humiliation—and yet out of a bottomless vitality they continued to thrive and develop. If the inexpressible cruelties of slavery could not stop us, the opposition we now face will surely fail. We will win our freedom because the sacred heritage of our nation and the eternal will of God are embodied in our echoing demands.

Before closing I feel impelled to mention one other point in your statement that has troubled me profoundly. You warmly commended the Birmingham police force for keeping "order" and "preventing violence." I doubt that you would have so warmly commended the police force if you had seen its dogs sinking their teeth into unarmed, nonviolent Negroes. I doubt that you would so quickly commend the policemen if you were to observe their ugly and inhumane treatment of Negroes here in the city jail; if you were to watch them push and curse old Negro women and young Negro girls; if you were to see them slap and kick old Negro men and young boys; if you were to observe them, as they did on two occasions, refuse to give us food because we wanted to sing our grace together. I cannot join you in your praise of the Birmingham police department. 45

It is true that the police have exercised a degree of discipline in handling the demonstrators. In this sense they have conducted themselves rather "nonviolently" in public. But for what purpose? To preserve the evil system of segregation. Over the past few years I have consistently preached that nonviolence demands that the means we use must be as pure as the ends we seek. I have tried to make clear that it is wrong to use immoral means to attain moral ends. But now I must affirm that it is just as wrong, or perhaps even more so, to use moral means to preserve immoral ends. Perhaps Mr. Connor and his policemen have been rather nonviolent in public, as was Chief Pritchett in Albany, Georgia, but they have used the moral means of nonviolence to maintain the immoral end of racial injustice. As T. S. Eliot[12] has said, "The last temptation is the greatest treason: To do the right deed for the wrong reason."

I wish you had commended the Negro sit-inners and demonstrators of Birmingham for their sublime courage, their willingness to suffer, and their amazing discipline in the midst of great provocation. One day the South will

[12] Thomas Stearns Eliot (1888–1965), American-born poet.

recognize its real heroes. They will be the James Merediths,[13] with the noble sense of purpose that enables them to face jeering and hostile mobs, and with the agonizing loneliness that characterizes the life of the pioneer. They will be old, oppressed, battered Negro women, symbolized in a seventy-two-year-old woman in Montgomery, Alabama, who rose up with a sense of dignity and with her people decided not to ride segregated buses, and who responded with ungrammatical profundity to one who inquired about her weariness: "My feets is tired, but my soul is at rest." They will be the young high school and college students, the young ministers of the gospel and a host of their elders, courageously and nonviolently sitting in at lunch counters and willingly going to jail for conscience' sake. One day the South will know that when these disinherited children of God sat down at lunch counters, they were in reality standing up for what is best in the American dream and for the most sacred values in our Judaeo-Christian heritage, thereby bringing our nation back to those great wells of democracy which were dug deep by the founding fathers in their formulation of the Constitution and the Declaration of Independence.

Never before have I written so long a letter. I'm afraid it is much too long to take your precious time. I can assure you that it would have been much shorter if I had been writing from a comfortable desk, but what else can one do when he is alone in a narrow jail cell, other than write long letters, think long thoughts, and pray long prayers?

If I have said anything in this letter that overstates the truth and indicates an unreasonable impatience, I beg you to forgive me. If I have said anything that understates the truth and indicates my having a patience that allows me to settle for anything less than brotherhood, I beg God to forgive me.

I hope this letter finds you strong in the faith. I hope that circumstances will 50 soon make it possible for me to meet each of you, not as an integrationist or a civil-rights leader but as a fellow clergyman and a Christian brother. Let us all hope that the dark clouds of a racial prejudice will soon pass away and the deep fog of misunderstanding will be lifted from our fear-drenched communities, and in some not too distant tomorrow the radiant stars of love and brotherhood will shine over our great nation with all their scintillating beauty.

> Yours for the cause of Peace and Brotherhood,
> Martin Luther King Jr.

FOR ANALYSIS

1. What is King's definition of "civil disobedience"?

2. Summarize and explain the argument King makes in paragraph 46 about "means" and "ends."

3. Those opposed to civil disobedience frequently argue that in a democratic society, change should be pursued through legislation and the courts because if people are

---

[13] James Meredith was the first black to be admitted as a student to the University of Mississippi.

allowed to disobey laws with which they disagree, there will be chaos and violence. How does King seek to allay those fears?

4. How does King deal with the charge that he is an outsider meddling in the affairs of others?

5. What are the "four basic steps" (para. 6) in a nonviolent campaign, according to King?

6. What is King's answer to his critics who urge negotiation instead of direct action?

MAKING CONNECTIONS

Swift uses **satire** in "A Modest Proposal" (p. 497) to protest the injustice of British rule in Ireland. King adopts a direct personal **tone** to convey his position. How are these contrasting approaches appropriate for each author's purpose?

WRITING TOPICS

1. King offers a philosophical justification for civil disobedience (paras. 15–22), at the heart of which is his distinction between a just and an unjust law. Do you agree with that distinction? Explain.

2. In your opinion, has the history of race relations in the United States since King's assassination in 1968 strengthened or weakened his arguments on the necessity and value of civil disobedience?

FURTHER QUESTIONS
FOR THINKING AND WRITING

1. What support do the works in this section offer for Emily Dickinson's assertion that "Much Madness is divinest Sense"? **Writing Topic:** The central characters in Herman Melville's "Bartleby the Scrivener" and Harlan Ellison's "'Repent, Harlequin!' Said the Ticktockman" are viewed by society as mad. How might it be argued that they exhibit "divinest sense"?

2. In a number of these works, a single individual rebels against society and suffers defeat or death. Are these works therefore pessimistic and despairing? If not, what is the purpose of the rebellions, and why do the authors choose to bring their characters to such ends? **Writing Topic:** Compare two works from this section that offer support for the idea that a single individual can have a decisive effect on society.

3. Examine some of the representatives of established order—the lawyer in "Bartleby the Scrivener," the Ticktockman—and discuss what attitudes they share and how effectively they function as spokespeople for law and order. **Writing Topic:** Compare and evaluate the kinds of order that each represents.

4. William Butler Yeats's "Easter 1916," Lawrence Ferlinghetti's "In Goya's Greatest Scenes" (p. 1201), and Carolyn Forché's "The Colonel" are poems about political struggle against oppressive rulers. In what ways are the poems similar? In what ways are they different? **Writing Topic:** Select the poem that makes the most powerful and effective case on behalf of the oppressed, and write an argument defending your choice.

5. Most of us live out our lives in the ordinary and humdrum world that is rejected in poems such as William Wordsworth's "The World Is Too Much with Us" and W. H. Auden's "The Unknown Citizen." Can these poems be said to be calls to social irresponsibility? **Writing Topic:** Consider whether "we" in Wordsworth's poem and the unknown citizen are simply objects of scorn or whether they deserve sympathy and perhaps even respect.

6. Characters in several of the works in this section—the Harlequin in "'Repent, Harlequin!' Said the Ticktockman" and Bartleby in "Bartleby the Scrivener"—are rebels. What similarities do you find among these rebels? **Writing Topic:** Explain how the attitudes and actions of these characters constitute an attack on the status quo.

7. Many works in this section deal explicitly with the relationship between individuals and religion. What similarities do you find among them? What differences? **Writing Topic:** Compare and contrast the way that relationship is perceived in Shirley Jackson's "The Lottery," and Salman Rushdie's "Imagine There's No Heaven."

CULTURE AND
IDENTITY

This Is Harlem (detail), 1943, by Jacob Lawrence.

Historically, a group of people bound together by kinship and geography will form a society that exhibits a *culture*—common language, behavioral rules, traditions, skills, mores, religion, and art that define the civilization of that group. Literary works, including folklore and myth, are inseparable from the particular human society from which they emerge.

Until relatively recently, with the invention of trains, automobiles, and airplanes, travel over long distances was difficult. Instant communication—the telephone, the computer network—is an innovation of our time. Originally, information about other societies could be heard only as far away as a human could shout. Letters helped transmit ideas and cultural values over time and distance, but no more quickly than a horse could gallop or a ship could sail. For thousands of years cultures lived in relative isolation from each other, and hence they tended to develop distinctive traits and values. Within China, for instance, there are numerous well-defined cultures: the Uighurs of the northwest, the coastal Chinese of Shanghai, the Tibetan mountain people, the Szechuanese of the southwest. They eat different foods; they practice different religions; they speak different dialects.

Though technological advances have made the world seem smaller and, generally, have ended the geographical isolation of various cultures, these advances have not diminished the powerful cultural distinctions that mark societies all over the world. In fact, modern communication and transport have sometimes served to bring cultures into conflict. The works in this section, varied as they are, share a preoccupation with the connection between culture and identity. Some, such as George Orwell's "Shooting an Elephant," examine the devastating consequences of cultural imperialism. Others, such as Zora Neale Hurston's "How It Feels to Be Colored Me," focus on the way dominant cultural stereotypes distort and undermine the sense of self of those who are different.

The works in this section demonstrate how powerfully culture shapes identity. They reveal the tension generated by interacting cultures, and offer insight into the conflicts that usually emerge. But these works also provide an opportunity for us to step outside the bounds and bonds of our own culture and to experience just how complex, diverse, and interesting the human condition can be.

QUESTIONS FOR THINKING AND WRITING

As you read the selections in this section, consider the questions that follow. You may want to write out your thoughts informally—in a journal, if you are keeping one—as a way of preparing to respond to the selections. Or you may wish to make one of these questions the basis for a formal essay.

1. What cultural tradition(s) do you come from? Describe this tradition as fully as you can. Do you feel that you live in or out of the cultural mainstream? Explain.

2. Except for Native Americans, the people of the United States descended from or arrived as citizens of foreign cultures. Is there, nonetheless, an American culture? Explain. The United States was once called a *cultural melting pot*. Now it is sometimes called a *cultural salad*. Which metaphor strikes you as more apt? Explain.

3. Do economic considerations affect culture? Aside from their wealth, are the rich different from the poor? Explain. Does education strengthen or weaken traditional culture? Explain.

4. What are some of the positive and negative associations you have with the values of the cultural tradition(s) you come from? Is the preservation of these values a good thing or a bad thing? Explain.

FICTION

CHARLOTTE PERKINS GILMAN   (1860 1935)

THE YELLOW WALLPAPER   1892

It is very seldom that mere ordinary people like John and myself secure ancestral halls for the summer.

A colonial mansion, a hereditary estate, I would say a haunted house and reach the height of romantic felicity—but that would be asking too much of fate!

Still I will proudly declare that there is something queer about it.

Else, why should it be let so cheaply? And why have stood so long untenanted?

John laughs at me, of course, but one expects that.   5

John is practical in the extreme. He has no patience with faith, an intense horror of superstition, and he scoffs openly at any talk of things not to be felt and seen and put down in figures.

John is a physician, and *perhaps*—(I would not say it to a living soul, of course, but this is dead paper and a great relief to my mind)—*perhaps* that is one reason I do not get well faster.

You see, he does not believe I am sick! And what can one do?

If a physician of high standing, and one's own husband, assures friends and relatives that there is really nothing the matter with one but temporary nervous depression—a slight hysterical tendency—what is one to do?

My brother is also a physician, and also of high standing, and he says the   10 same thing.

So I take phosphates or phosphites—whichever it is, and tonics, and air and exercise, and journeys, and am absolutely forbidden to "work" until I am well again.

Personally, I disagree with their ideas.

Personally, I believe that congenial work, with excitement and change, would do me good.

But what is one to do?

I did write for a while in spite of them; but it *does* exhaust me a good deal—   15 having to be so sly about it, or else meet with heavy opposition.

I sometimes fancy that in my condition if I had less opposition and more society and stimulus—but John says the very worst thing I can do is to think about my condition, and I confess it always makes me feel bad.

So I will let it alone and talk about the house.

The most beautiful place! It is quite alone, standing well back from the road, quite three miles from the village. It makes me think of English places that you read about, for there are hedges and walls and gates that lock, and lots of separate little houses for the gardeners and people.

There is a *delicious* garden! I never saw such a garden—large and shady, full of box-bordered paths, and lined with long grape-covered arbors with seats under them.

There were greenhouses, too, but they are all broken now.   20

There was some legal trouble, I believe, something about the heirs and co-heirs; anyhow, the place has been empty for years.

That spoils my ghostliness, I am afraid, but I don't care—there is something strange about the house—I can feel it.

I even said so to John one moonlight evening, but he said what I felt was a draught, and shut the window.

I get unreasonably angry with John sometimes. I'm sure I never used to be so sensitive. I think it is due to this nervous condition.

But John says if I feel so I shall neglect proper self-control; so I take pains to   25 control myself—before him, at least, and that makes me very tired.

I don't like our room a bit. I wanted one downstairs that opened onto the piazza and had roses all over the window, and such pretty old-fashioned chintz hangings! But John would not hear of it.

He said there was only one window and not room for two beds, and no near room for him if he took another.

He is very careful and loving, and hardly lets me stir without special direction.

I have a schedule prescription for each hour in the day; he takes all care from me, and so I feel basely ungrateful not to value it more.

He said we came here solely on my account, that I was to have perfect rest   30 and all the air I could get. "Your exercise depends on your strength, my dear," said he, "and your food somewhat on your appetite; but air you can absorb all the time." So we took the nursery at the top of the house.

It is a big, airy room, the whole floor nearly, with windows that look all ways, and air and sunshine galore. It was a nursery first, and then playroom and gymnasium, I should judge, for the windows are barred for little children, and there are rings and things in the walls.

The paint and paper look as if a boys' school had used it. It is stripped off— the paper—in great patches all around the head of my bed, about as far as I can reach, and in a great place on the other side of the room low down. I never saw a worse paper in my life. One of those sprawling, flamboyant patterns committing every artistic sin.

It is dull enough to confuse the eye in following, pronounced enough constantly to irritate and provoke study, and when you follow the lame uncertain curves for a little distance they suddenly commit suicide—plunge off at outrageous angles, destroy themselves in unheard-of contradictions.

The color is repellent, almost revolting; a smouldering unclean yellow, strangely faded by the slow-turning sunlight. It is a dull yet lurid orange in some places, a sickly sulphur tint in others.

No wonder the children hated it! I should hate it myself if I had to live in this 35 room long.

There comes John, and I must put this away—he hates to have me write a word.

We have been here two weeks, and I haven't felt like writing before, since that first day.

I am sitting by the window now, up in this atrocious nursery, and there is nothing to hinder my writing as much as I please, save lack of strength.

John is away all day, and even some nights when his cases are serious.

I'm glad my case is not serious! 40

But these nervous troubles are dreadfully depressing.

John does not know how much I really suffer. He knows there is no reason to suffer, and that satisfies him.

Of course it is only nervousness. It does weigh on me so not to do my duty in any way!

I meant to be such a help to John, such a real rest and comfort, and here I am a comparative burden already!

Nobody would believe what an effort it is to do what little I am able—to 45 dress and entertain, and order things.

It is fortunate Mary is so good with the baby. Such a dear baby!

And yet I *cannot* be with him, it makes me so nervous.

I suppose John never was nervous in his life. He laughs at me so about this wallpaper!

At first he meant to repaper the room, but afterward he said that I was letting it get the better of me, and that nothing was worse for a nervous patient than to give way to such fancies.

He said that after the wallpaper was changed it would be the heavy bed- 50 stead, and then the barred windows, and then that gate at the head of the stairs, and so on.

"You know the place is doing you good," he said, "and really, dear, I don't care to renovate the house just for a three months' rental."

"Then do let us go downstairs," I said. "There are such pretty rooms there."

Then he took me in his arms and called me a blessed little goose, and said he would go down to the cellar, if I wished, and have it whitewashed into the bargain.

But he is right enough about the beds and windows and things.

It is as airy and comfortable a room as anyone need wish, and, of course, I 55 would not be so silly as to make him uncomfortable just for a whim.

I'm really getting quite fond of the big room, all but that horrid paper.

Out of one window I can see the garden—those mysterious deep-shaded arbors, the riotous old-fashioned flowers, and bushes and gnarly trees.

Out of another I get a lovely view of the bay and a little private wharf belonging to the estate. There is a beautiful shaded lane that runs down there from the house. I always fancy I see people walking in these numerous paths and arbors, but John has cautioned me not to give way to fancy in the least. He says that with my imaginative power and habit of story-making, a nervous weakness like mine is sure to lead to all manner of excited fancies, and that I ought to use my will and good sense to check the tendency. So I try.

I think sometimes that if I were only well enough to write a little it would relieve the press of ideas and rest me.

But I find I get pretty tired when I try. 60

It is so discouraging not to have any advice and companionship about my work. When I get really well, John says we will ask Cousin Henry and Julia down for a long visit; but he says he would as soon put fireworks in my pillow-case as to let me have those stimulating people about now.

I wish I could get well faster.

But I must not think about that. This paper looks to me as if it *knew* what a vicious influence it had!

There is a recurrent spot where the pattern lolls like a broken neck and two bulbous eyes stare at you upside down.

I get positively angry with the impertinence of it and the everlastingness. Up 65 and down and sideways they crawl, and those absurd, unblinking eyes are everywhere. There is one place where two breadths didn't match, and the eyes go all up and down the line, one a little higher than the other.

I never saw so much expression in an inanimate thing before, and we all know how much expression they have! I used to lie awake as a child and get more entertainment and terror out of blank walls and plain furniture than most children could find in a toy-store.

I remember what a kindly wink the knobs of our big old bureau used to have, and there was one chair that always seemed like a strong friend.

I used to feel that if any of the other things looked too fierce I could always hop into that chair and be safe.

The furniture in this room is no worse than inharmonious, however, for we had to bring it all from downstairs. I suppose when this was used as a play-room they had to take the nursery things out, and no wonder! I never saw such ravages as the children have made here.

The wallpaper, as I said before, is torn off in spots, and it sticketh closer than 70 a brother—they must have had perseverance as well as hatred.

Then the floor is scratched and gouged and splintered, the plaster itself is dug out here and there, and this great heavy bed, which is all we found in the room, looks as if it had been through the wars.

But I don't mind it a bit—only the paper.

There comes John's sister. Such a dear girl as she is, and so careful of me! I must not let her find me writing.

She is a perfect and enthusiastic housekeeper, and hopes for no better profession. I verily believe she thinks it is the writing which made me sick!

But I can write when she is out, and see her a long way off from these windows. 75

There is one that commands the road, a lovely shaded winding road, and one that just looks off over the country. A lovely country, too, full of great elms and velvet meadows.

This wallpaper has a kind of sub-pattern in a different shade, a particularly irritating one, for you can only see it in certain lights, and not clearly then.

But in the places where it isn't faded and where the sun is just so—I can see a strange, provoking, formless sort of figure that seems to skulk about behind that silly and conspicuous front design.

There's sister on the stairs!

Well, the Fourth of July is over! The people are all gone and I am tired out. 80 John thought it might do me good to see a little company, so we just had Mother and Nellie and the children down for a week.

Of course I didn't do a thing. Jennie sees to everything now.

But it tired me all the same.

John says if I don't pick up faster he shall send me to Weir Mitchell in the fall.

But I don't want to go there at all. I had a friend who was in his hands once, and she says he is just like John and my brother, only more so!

Besides, it is such an undertaking to go so far. 85

I don't feel as if it was worthwhile to turn my hand over for anything, and I'm getting dreadfully fretful and querulous.

I cry at nothing, and cry most of the time.

Of course I don't when John is here, or anybody else, but when I am alone.

And I am alone a good deal just now. John is kept in town very often by serious cases, and Jennie is good and lets me alone when I want her to.

So I walk a little in the garden or down that lovely lane, sit on the porch 90 under the roses, and lie down up here a good deal.

I'm getting really fond of the room in spite of the wallpaper. Perhaps *because* of the wallpaper.

It dwells in my mind so!

I lie here on this great immovable bed—it is nailed down, I believe—and follow that pattern about by the hour. It is as good as gymnastics, I assure you. I start, we'll say, at the bottom, down in the corner over there where it has not been touched, and I determine for the thousandth time that I *will* follow that pointless pattern to some sort of a conclusion.

I know a little of the principle of design, and I know this thing was not arranged on any laws of radiation, or alternation, or repetition, or symmetry, or anything else that I ever heard of.

It is repeated, of course, by the breadths, but not otherwise. 95

Looked at in one way, each breadth stands alone; the bloated curves and flourishes—a kind of "debased Romanesque" with delirium tremens—go waddling up and down in isolated columns of fatuity.

But, on the other hand, they connect diagonally, and the sprawling outlines run off in great slanting waves of optic horror, like a lot of wallowing seaweeds in full chase.

The whole thing goes horizontally, too, at least it seems so, and I exhaust myself in trying to distinguish the order of its going in that direction.

They have used a horizontal breadth for a frieze, and that adds wonderfully to the confusion.

There is one end of the room where it is almost intact, and there, when the crosslights fade and the low sun shines directly upon it, I can almost fancy radiation after all,—the interminable grotesque seems to form around a common center and rush off in headlong plunges of equal distraction.

It makes me tired to follow it. I will take a nap, I guess.

I don't know why I should write this.

I don't want to.

I don't feel able.

And I know John would think it absurd. But I *must* say what I feel and think in some way—it is such a relief!

But the effort is getting to be greater than the relief.

Half the time now I am awfully lazy, and lie down ever so much. John says I musn't lose my strength, and has me take cod liver oil and lots of tonics and things, to say nothing of ale and wine and rare meat.

Dear John! He loves me very dearly, and hates to have me sick. I tried to have a real earnest reasonable talk with him the other day, and tell him how I wish he would let me go and make a visit to Cousin Henry and Julia.

But he said I wasn't able to go, nor able to stand it after I got there; and I did not make out a very good case for myself, for I was crying before I had finished.

It is getting to be a great effort for me to think straight. Just this nervous weakness, I suppose.

And dear John gathered me up in his arms, and just carried me upstairs and laid me on the bed, and sat by me and read to me till it tired my head.

He said I was his darling and his comfort and all he had, and that I must take care of myself for his sake, and keep well.

He says no one but myself can help me out of it, that I must use my will and self-control and not let any silly fancies run away with me.

There's one comfort—the baby is well and happy, and does not have to occupy this nursery with the horrid wallpaper.

If we had not used it, that blessed child would have! What a fortunate escape! Why, I wouldn't have a child of mine, an impressionable little thing, live in such a room for worlds.

I never thought of it before, but it is lucky that John kept me here after all; I can stand it so much easier than a baby, you see.

Of course I never mention it to them any more—I am too wise—but I keep watch of it all the same.

There are things in that wallpaper that nobody knows but me, or ever will.

Behind that outside pattern the dim shapes get clearer every day.

It is always the same shape, only very numerous. 120

And it is like a woman stooping down and creeping about behind that pattern. I don't like it a bit. I wonder—I begin to think—I wish John would take me away from here!

It is so hard to talk with John about my case, because he is so wise, and because he loves me so.

But I tried it last night.

It was moonlight. The moon shines in all around just as the sun does.

I hate to see it sometimes, it creeps so slowly, and always comes in by one 125 window or another.

John was asleep and I hated to waken him, so I kept still and watched the moonlight on that undulating wallpaper till I felt creepy.

The faint figure behind seemed to shake the pattern, just as if she wanted to get out.

I got up softly and went to feel and see if the paper *did* move, and when I came back John was awake.

"What is it, little girl?" he said. "Don't go walking about like that—you'll get cold."

I thought it was a good time to talk, so I told him that I really was not gain- 130 ing here, and that I wished he would take me away.

"Why, darling!" said he, "Our lease will be up in three weeks, and I can't see how to leave before.

"The repairs are not done at home, and I cannot possibly leave town just now. Of course if you were in any danger, I could and would, but you really are better, dear, whether you can see it or not. I am a doctor, dear, and I know. You are gaining flesh and color, your appetite is better, I feel really much easier about you."

"I don't weigh a bit more," said I, "nor as much; and my appetite may be better in the evening when you are here but it is worse in the morning when you are away!"

"Bless her little heart!" said he with a big hug, "She shall be as sick as she pleases! But now let's improve the shining hours by going to sleep, and talk about it in the morning!"

"And you won't go away?" I asked gloomily. 135

"Why, how can I, dear? It is only three weeks more and then we will take a nice little trip of a few days while Jennie is getting the house ready. Really, dear, you are better!"

"Better in body perhaps—" I began, and stopped short, for he sat up straight and looked at me with such a stern, reproachful look that I could not say another word.

"My darling," said he, "I beg of you, for my sake and for our child's sake, as well as for your own, that you will never for one instant let that idea enter your mind! There is nothing so dangerous, so fascinating, to a temperament like yours. It is a false and foolish fancy. Can you trust me as a physician when I tell you so?"

So of course I said no more on that score, and we went to sleep before long. He thought I was asleep first, but I wasn't, and lay there for hours trying to decide whether that front pattern and the back pattern really did move together or separately.

On a pattern like this, by daylight, there is a lack of sequence, a defiance of 140
law, that is a constant irritant to a normal mind.

The color is hideous enough, and unreliable enough, and infuriating enough, but the pattern is torturing.

You think you have mastered it, but just as you get well under way in follow-ing, it turns a back-somersault and there you are. It slaps you in the face, knocks you down, and tramples upon you. It is like a bad dream.

The outside pattern is a florid arabesque, reminding one of a fungus. If you can imagine a toadstool in joints, an interminable string of toadstools, bud-ding and sprouting in endless convolutions—why, that is something like it.

That is, sometimes!

There is one marked peculiarity about this paper, a thing nobody seems to 145
notice but myself, and that is that it changes as the light changes.

When the sun shoots in through the east window—I always watch for that first long, straight ray—it changes so quickly that I never can quite believe it.

That is why I watch it always.

By moonlight—the moon shines in all night when there is a moon—I wouldn't know it was the same paper.

At night in any kind of light, in twilight, candlelight, lamplight, and worst of all by moonlight, it becomes bars! The outside pattern, I mean, and the woman behind it is as plain as can be.

I didn't realize for a long time what the thing was that showed behind, that 150
dim sub-pattern, but now I am quite sure it is a woman.

By daylight she is subdued, quiet. I fancy it is the pattern that keeps her so still. It is so puzzling. It keeps me quiet by the hour.

I lie down ever so much now. John says it is good for me, and to sleep all I can.

Indeed he started the habit by making me lie down for an hour after each meal.

It is a very bad habit, I am convinced, for you see, I don't sleep.

And that cultivates deceit, for I don't tell them I'm awake—oh, no! 155
The fact is I am getting a little afraid of John.

He seems very queer sometimes, and even Jennie has an inexplicable look.

It strikes me occasionally, just as a scientific hypothesis, that perhaps it is the paper!

I have watched John when he did not know I was looking, and come into the room suddenly on the most innocent excuses, and I've caught him several times *looking at the paper!* And Jennie too. I caught Jennie with her hand on it once.

She didn't know I was in the room, and when I asked her in a quiet, a very 160
quiet voice, with the most restrained manner possible, what she was doing

with the paper—she turned around as if she had been caught stealing, and looked quite angry—asked me why I should frighten her so!

Then she said that the paper stained everything it touched, that she had found yellow smooches on all my clothes and John's and she wished we would be more careful!

Did not that sound innocent? But I know she was studying that pattern, and I am determined that nobody shall find it out but myself!

Life is very much more exciting now than it used to be. You see, I have something more to expect, to look forward to, to watch. I really do eat better, and am more quiet than I was.

John is so pleased to see me improve! He laughed a little the other day, and said I seemed to be flourishing in spite of my wallpaper.

I turned it off with a laugh. I had no intention of telling him it was *because* of the wallpaper—he would make fun of me. He might even want to take me away.

I don't want to leave now until I have found it out. There is a week more, and I think that will be enough.

I'm feeling so much better!

I don't sleep much at night, for it is so interesting to watch developments; but I sleep a good deal in the daytime.

In the daytime it is tiresome and perplexing.

There are always new shoots on the fungus, and new shades of yellow all over it. I cannot keep count of them, though I have tried conscientiously.

It is the strangest yellow, that wallpaper! It makes me think of all the yellow things I ever saw—not beautiful ones like buttercups, but old, foul, bad yellow things.

But there is something else about that paper—the smell! I noticed it the moment we came into the room, but with so much air and sun it was not bad. Now we have had a week of fog and rain, and whether the windows are open or not, the smell is here.

It creeps all over the house.

I find it hovering in the dining-room, skulking in the parlor, hiding in the hall, lying in wait for me on the stairs.

It gets into my hair.

Even when I go to ride, if I turn my head suddenly and surprise it—there is that smell!

Such a peculiar odor, too! I have spent hours in trying to analyze it, to find what it smelled like.

It is not bad—at first—and very gentle, but quite the subtlest, most enduring odor I ever met.

In this damp weather it is awful. I wake up in the night and find it hanging over me.

It used to disturb me at first. I thought seriously of burning the house—to reach the smell.

But now I am used to it. The only thing I can think of that it is like is the *color* of the paper! A yellow smell.

There is a very funny mark on this wall, low down, near the mopboard. A streak that runs round the room. It goes behind every piece of furniture, except the bed, a long, straight, even *smooch*, as if it had been rubbed over and over.

I wonder how it was done and who did it, and what they did it for. Round and round and round—round and round and round—it makes me dizzy!

I really have discovered something at last.

Through watching so much at night, when it changes so, I have finally 185 found out.

The front pattern *does* move—and no wonder! The woman behind shakes it!

Sometimes I think there are a great many women behind, and sometimes only one, and she crawls around fast, and her crawling shakes it all over.

Then in the very bright spots she keeps still, and in the very shady spots she just takes hold of the bars and shakes them hard.

And she is all the time trying to climb through. But nobody could climb through that pattern—it strangles so; I think that is why it has so many heads.

They get through, and then the pattern strangles them off and turns them 190 upside down and makes their eyes white!

If those heads were covered or taken off it would not be half so bad.

I think that woman gets out in the daytime!

And I'll tell you why—privately—I've seen her!

I can see her out of every one of my windows!

It is the same woman, I know, for she is always creeping, and most women 195 do not creep by daylight.

I see her in that long shaded lane, creeping up and down. I see her in those dark grape arbors, creeping all around the garden.

I see her on that long road under the trees, creeping along, and when a carriage comes she hides under the blackberry vines.

I don't blame her a bit. It must be very humiliating to be caught creeping by daylight!

I always lock the door when I creep by daylight. I can't do it at night, for I know John would suspect something at once.

And John is so queer now that I don't want to irritate him. I wish he would 200 take another room! Besides, I don't want anybody to get that woman out at night but myself.

I often wonder if I could see her out of all the windows at once.

But, turn as fast as I can, I can only see out of one at one time.

And though I always see her, she *may* be able to creep faster than I can turn! I have watched her sometimes away off in the open country, creeping as fast as a cloud shadow in a high wind.

If only that top pattern could be gotten off from the under one! I mean to try it, little by little.

I have found out another funny thing, but I shan't tell it this time! It does not do to trust people too much.

There are only two more days to get this paper off, and I believe John is beginning to notice. I don't like the look in his eyes.

And I hear him ask Jennie a lot of professional questions about me. She had a very good report to give.

She said I slept a good deal in the daytime.

John knows I don't sleep very well at night, for all I'm so quiet!

He asked me all sorts of questions, too, and pretended to be very loving and kind.

As if I couldn't see through him!

Still, I don't wonder he acts so, sleeping under this paper for three months.

It only interests me, but I feel sure John and Jennie are secretly affected by it.

Hurrah! This is the last day, but it is enough. John is to stay in town over night, and won't be out until this evening.

Jennie wanted to sleep with me—the sly thing; but I told her I should un-doubtedly rest better for a night all alone.

That was clever, for really I wasn't alone a bit! As soon as it was moonlight and that poor thing began to crawl and shake the pattern, I got up and ran to help her.

I pulled and she shook. I shook and she pulled, and before morning we had peeled off yards of that paper.

A strip about as high as my head and half around the room.

And then when the sun came and that awful pattern began to laugh at me, I declared I would finish it to-day!

We go away to-morrow, and they are moving all my furniture down again to leave things as they were before.

Jennie looked at the wall in amazement, but I told her merrily that I did it out of pure spite at the vicious thing.

She laughed and said she wouldn't mind doing it herself, but I must not get tired.

How she betrayed herself that time!

But I am here, and no person touches this paper but Me—not *alive!*

She tried to get me out of the room—it was too patent! But I said it was so quiet and empty and clean now that I believed I would lie down again and sleep all I could, and not to wake me even for dinner—I would call when I woke.

So now she is gone, and the servants are gone, and the things are gone, and there is nothing left but that great bedstead nailed down, with the canvas mat-tress we found on it.

We shall sleep downstairs to-night, and take the boat home to-morrow.

I quite enjoy the room, now it is bare again.

How those children did tear about here!

This bedstead is fairly gnawed!

But I must get to work.

I have locked the door and thrown the key down into the front path.

I don't want to go out, and I don't want to have anybody come in, till John comes.

I want to astonish him.

I've got a rope up here that even Jennie did not find. If that woman does get 235 out, and tries to get away, I can tie her!

But I forgot I could not reach far without anything to stand on!

This bed will *not* move!

I tried to lift and push it until I was lame, and then I got so angry I bit off a little piece at one corner—but it hurt my teeth.

Then I peeled off all the paper I could reach standing on the floor. It sticks horribly and the pattern just enjoys it! All those strangled heads and bulbous eyes and waddling fungus growths just shriek with derision!

I am getting angry enough to do something desperate. To jump out of the 240 window would be admirable exercise, but the bars are too strong even to try.

Besides I wouldn't do it. Of course not. I know well enough that a step like that is improper and might be misconstrued.

I don't like to *look* out of the windows even—there are so many of those creeping women, and they creep so fast.

I wonder if they all come out of that wallpaper as I did?

But I am securely fastened now by my well-hidden rope—you don't get *me* out in the road there!

I suppose I shall have to get back behind the pattern when it comes night, 245 and that is hard!

It is so pleasant to be out in this great room and creep around as I please!

I don't want to go outside. I won't, even if Jennie asks me to.

For outside you have to creep on the ground, and everything is green instead of yellow.

But here I can creep smoothly on the floor, and my shoulder just fits in that long smooch around the wall, so I cannot lose my way.

Why, there's John at the door! 250

It is no use, young man, you can't open it!

How he does call and pound!

Now he's crying to Jennie for an axe.

It would be a shame to break down that beautiful door!

"John, dear!" said I in the gentlest voice, "The key is down by the front steps, 255 under a plantain leaf!"

That silenced him for a few moments.

Then he said—very quietly indeed, "Open the door, my darling!"

"I can't," said I. "The key is down by the front door under a plantain leaf!" And then I said it again, several times, very gently and slowly, and said it so often that he had to go and see, and he got it of course, and came in. He stopped short by the door.

"What is the matter?" he cried. "For God's sake, what are you doing!"

I kept on creeping just the same, but I looked at him over my shoulder.   260

"I've got out at last," said I, "in spite of you and Jane. And I've pulled off most of the paper, so you can't put me back!"

Now why should that man have fainted? But he did, and right across my path by the wall, so that I had to creep over him every time!

FOR ANALYSIS

1. Why have the **narrator** and her husband John rented the mansion?

2. In the opening paragraphs, what **tone** does the narrator's description of the mansion establish?

3. Describe the character of John. Does the narrator's view of him change in the course of the story? Explain.

4. After telling us that her husband John is a physician, the narrator adds that "*perhaps that is one reason I do not get well faster*" (para. 7). What does she mean by this comment?

5. How does the narrator's description of what she sees in the outside world reflect her inner state?

6. Who is Jennie? What is her function in the story?

7. The narrator both accepts her husband's control over her and disobeys him by secretly continuing to write. What effect does writing have on her? Is her husband correct in his judgment that writing will hinder her recovery?

8. What evidence does the story provide to explain the narrator's present state?

9. Can it be argued that, on some level, the narrator refuses to recover? Explain.

10. In what ways does the wallpaper embody the **theme** of the story?

MAKING CONNECTIONS

1. Compare the marriage relationship in this story with the marriage in Ibsen's play *A Doll's House* (p. 440).

2. Compare and contrast the narrator in this story with Emily Grierson in William Faulkner's story "A Rose for Emily" (p. 622) as examples of women wounded by a patriarchal society.

3. Compare the wallpaper in this story with the birdcage in Susan Glaspell's play *Trifles* (p. 1050) as **symbols**. In what ways are they similar? In what ways different? Which do you find more effective? Explain.

4. Considered as a horror story, in what ways is Gilman's narrative similar to Edgar Allan Poe's "The Cask of Amontillado" (p. 1097)? In what ways is it different?

WRITING TOPICS

1. Analyze the way **irony** is used in this story.

2. Write an essay in which you imaginatively reconstruct the early life of the narrator, including her marriage, to explain her illness.

3. Write an essay describing the aptness of wallpaper as a **symbol** for the life of the narrator.

4. In a paragraph, explain why we never learn the narrator's name.

JAMES BALDWIN (1924–1987)

SONNY'S BLUES 1957

I read about it in the paper, in the subway, on my way to work. I read it, and I
couldn't believe it, and I read it again. Then perhaps I just stared at it, at the
newsprint spelling out his name, spelling out the story. I stared at it in the
swinging lights of the subway car, and in the faces and bodies of the people,
and in my own face, trapped in the darkness which roared outside.

It was not to be believed and I kept telling myself that, as I walked from the
subway station to the high school. And at the same time I couldn't doubt it. I
was scared, scared for Sonny. He became real to me again. A great block of ice
got settled in my belly and kept melting there slowly all day long, while I taught
my classes algebra. It was a special kind of ice. It kept melting, sending trickles
of ice water all up and down my veins, but it never got less. Sometimes it hardened and seemed to expand until I felt my guts were going to come spilling out
or that I was going to choke or scream. This would always be at a moment
when I was remembering some specific thing Sonny had once said or done.

When he was about as old as the boys in my classes his face had been bright
and open, there was a lot of copper in it; and he'd had wonderfully direct
brown eyes, and great gentleness and privacy. I wondered what he looked like
now. He had been picked up, the evening before, in a raid on an apartment
downtown, for peddling and using heroin.

I couldn't believe it: but what I mean by that is that I couldn't find any room
for it anywhere inside me. I had kept it outside me for a long time. I hadn't
wanted to know. I had had suspicions, but I didn't name them, I kept putting
them away. I told myself that Sonny was wild, but he wasn't crazy. And he'd
always been a good boy, he hadn't ever turned hard or evil or disrespectful, the
way kids can, so quick, so quick, especially in Harlem. I didn't want to believe
that I'd ever see my brother going down, coming to nothing, all that light in his
face gone out, in the condition I'd already seen so many others. Yet it had happened and here I was, talking about algebra to a lot of boys who might, every
one of them for all I knew, be popping off needles every time they went to the
head. Maybe it did more for them than algebra could.

I was sure that the first time Sonny had ever had horse,[1] he couldn't have 5
been much older than these boys were now. These boys, now, were living as
we'd been living then, they were growing up with a rush and their heads
bumped abruptly against the low ceiling of their actual possibilities. They were
filled with rage. All they really knew were two darknesses, the darkness of their

---

[1] Heroin.

lives, which was now closing in on them, and the darkness of the movies, which had blinded them to that other darkness, and in which they now, vindictively, dreamed, at once more together than they were at any other time, and more alone.

When the last bell rang, the last class ended, I let out my breath. It seemed I'd been holding it for all that time. My clothes were wet—I may have looked as though I'd been sitting in a steam bath, all dressed up, all afternoon. I sat alone in the classroom a long time. I listened to the boys outside, downstairs, shouting and cursing and laughing. Their laughter struck me for perhaps the first time. It was not the joyous laughter which—God knows why—one associates with children. It was mocking and insular, its intent to denigrate. It was disenchanted, and in this, also, lay the authority of their curses. Perhaps I was listening to them because I was thinking about my brother and in them I heard my brother. And myself.

One boy was whistling a tune, at once very complicated and very simple, it seemed to be pouring out of him as though he were a bird, and it sounded very cool and moving through all that harsh, bright air, only just holding its own through all those other sounds.

I stood up and walked over to the window and looked down into the courtyard. It was the beginning of the spring and the sap was rising in the boys. A teacher passed through them every now and again, quickly, as though he or she couldn't wait to get out of that courtyard, to get those boys out of their sight and off their minds. I started collecting my stuff. I thought I'd better get home and talk to Isabel.

The courtyard was almost deserted by the time I got downstairs. I saw this boy standing in the shadow of a doorway, looking just like Sonny. I almost called his name. Then I saw that it wasn't Sonny, but somebody we used to know, a boy from around our block. He'd been Sonny's friend. He'd never been mine, having been too young for me, and, anyway, I'd never liked him. And now, even though he was a grown up man, he still hung around that block, still spent hours on the street corners, was always high and raggy. I used to run into him from time to time and he'd often work around to asking me for a quarter or fifty cents. He always had some real good excuse, too, and I always gave it to him. I don't know why.

But now, abruptly, I hated him. I couldn't stand the way he looked at me, partly like a dog, partly like a cunning child. I wanted to ask him what the hell he was doing in the school courtyard.

He sort of shuffled over to me, and he said, "I see you got the papers. So you already know about it."

"You mean about Sonny? Yes, I already know about it. How come they didn't get you?"

He grinned. It made him repulsive and it also brought to mind what he'd looked like as a kid. "I wasn't there. I stay away from them people."

"Good for you." I offered him a cigarette and I watched him through the smoke. "You come all the way down here just to tell me about Sonny?"

"That's right." He was sort of shaking his head and his eyes looked strange, 15
as though they were about to cross. The bright sun deadened his damp dark
brown skin and it made his eyes look yellow and showed up the dirt in his
kinked hair. He smelled funky. I moved a little away from him and I said, "Well,
thanks. But I already know about it and I got to get home."

"I'll walk you a little ways," he said. We started walking. There were a couple
of kids still loitering in the courtyard and one of them said goodnight to me
and looked strangely at the boy beside me.

"What're you going to do?" he asked me. "I mean, about Sonny?"

"Look. I haven't seen Sonny for over a year, I'm not sure I'm going to do anything. Anyway, what the hell *can* I do?"

"That's right," he said quickly, "ain't nothing you can do. Can't much help
old Sonny no more, I guess."

It was what I was thinking and so it seemed to me he had no right to say it. 20

"I'm surprised at Sonny, though," he went on—he had a funny way of talking, he looked straight ahead as though he were talking to himself—"I thought
Sonny was a smart boy, I thought he was too smart to get hung."

"I guess he thought so too," I said sharply, "and that's how he got hung. And
how about you? You're pretty goddamn smart, I bet."

Then he looked directly at me, just for a minute. "I ain't smart," he said. "If I
was smart, I'd have reached for a pistol a long time ago."

"Look. Don't tell *me* your sad story, if it was up to me, I'd give you one."
Then I felt guilty—guilty, probably, for never having supposed that the poor
bastard *had* a story of his own, much less a sad one, and I asked, quickly,
"What's going to happen to him now?"

He didn't answer this. He was off by himself some place. 25

"Funny thing," he said, and from his tone we might have been discussing
the quickest way to get to Brooklyn, "when I saw the papers this morning, the
first thing I asked myself was if I had anything to do with it. I felt sort of
responsible."

I began to listen more carefully. The subway station was on the corner, just
before us, and I stopped. He stopped, too. We were in front of a bar and he
ducked slightly, peering in, but whoever he was looking for didn't seem to be
there. The juke box was blasting away with something black and bouncy and I
half watched the barmaid as she danced her way from the juke box to her place
behind the bar. And I watched her face as she laughingly responded to something someone said to her, still keeping time to the music. When she smiled
one saw the little girl, one sensed the doomed, still-struggling woman beneath
the battered face of the semi-whore.

"I never *give* Sonny nothing," the boy said finally, "but a long time ago I come
to school high and Sonny asked me how it felt." He paused, I couldn't bear to
watch him, I watched the barmaid, and I listened to the music which seemed to
be causing the pavement to shake. "I told him it felt great." The music stopped,
the barmaid paused and watched the juke box until the music began again.
"It did."

All this was carrying me some place I didn't want to go. I certainly didn't want to know how it felt. It filled everything, the people, the houses, the music, the dark, quicksilver barmaid, with menace; and this menace was their reality.

"What's going to happen to him now?" I asked again. 30

"They'll send him away some place and they'll try to cure him." He shook his head. "Maybe he'll even think he's kicked the habit. Then they'll let him loose"—he gestured, throwing his cigarette into the gutter. "That's all."

"What do you mean, that's *all*?"

But I knew what he meant.

"I *mean*, that's *all*." He turned his head and looked at me, pulling down the corners of his mouth. "Don't you know what I mean?" he asked, softly.

"How the hell *would* I know what you mean?" I almost whispered it, I don't 35 know why.

"That's right," he said to the air, "how would *he* know what I mean?" He turned toward me again, patient and calm, and yet I somehow felt him shaking, shaking as though he were going to fall apart. I felt that ice in my guts again, the dread I'd felt all afternoon; and again I watched the barmaid, moving about the bar, washing glasses, and singing. "Listen. They'll let him out and then it'll just start all over again. That's what I mean."

"You mean—they'll let him out. And then he'll just start working his way back in again. You mean he'll never kick the habit. Is that what you mean?"

"That's right," he said, cheerfully. "*You* see what I mean."

"Tell me," I said at last, "why does he want to die? He must want to die, he's killing himself, why does he want to die?"

He looked at me in surprise. He licked his lips. "He don't want to die. He 40 wants to live. Don't nobody want to die, ever."

Then I wanted to ask him—too many things. He could not have answered, or if he had, I could not have borne the answers. I started walking. "Well, I guess it's none of my business."

"It's going to be rough on old Sonny," he said. We reached the subway station. "This is your station?" he asked. I nodded. I took one step down. "Damn!" he said, suddenly. I looked up at him. He grinned again. "Damn it if I didn't leave all my money home. You ain't got a dollar on you, have you? Just for a couple of days, is all."

All at once something inside gave and threatened to come pouring out of me. I didn't hate him any more. I felt that in another moment I'd start crying like a child.

"Sure," I said. "Don't sweat." I looked in my wallet and didn't have a dollar, I only had a five. "Here," I said. "That hold you?"

He didn't look at it—he didn't want to look at it. A terrible, closed look came 45 over his face, as though he were keeping the number on the bill a secret from him and me. "Thanks," he said, and now he was dying to see me go. "Don't worry about Sonny. Maybe I'll write him or something."

"Sure," I said. "You do that. So long."

"Be seeing you," he said. I went on down the steps.

And I didn't write Sonny or send him anything for a long time. When I finally did, it was just after my little girl died, and he wrote me back a letter which made me feel like a bastard.

Here's what he said:

> Dear brother,
>
> You don't know how much I needed to hear from you. I wanted to write you many a time but I dug how much I must have hurt you and so I didn't write. But now I feel like a man who's been trying to climb up out of some deep, real deep and funky hole and just saw the sun up there, outside. I got to get outside.
>
> I can't tell you much about how I got here. I mean I don't know how to tell you. I guess I was afraid of something or I was trying to escape from something and you know I have never been very strong in the head (smile). I'm glad Mama and Daddy are dead and can't see what's happened to their son and I swear if I'd known what I was doing I would never have hurt you so, you and a lot of other fine people who were nice to me and who believed in me.
>
> I don't want you to think it had anything to do with me being a musician. It's more than that. Or maybe less than that. I can't get anything straight in my head down here and I try not to think about what's going to happen to me when I get outside again. Sometime I think I'm going to flip and never get outside and sometime I think I'll come straight back. I tell you one thing, though, I'd rather blow my brains out than go through this again. But that's what they all say, so they tell me. If I tell you when I'm coming to New York and if you could meet me, I sure would appreciate it. Give my love to Isabel and the kids and I was sure sorry to hear about little Gracie. I wish I could be like Mama and say the Lord's will be done, but I don't know it seems to me that trouble is the one thing that never does get stopped and I don't know what good it does to blame it on the Lord. But maybe it does some good if you believe it.
>
> Your brother,
> Sonny

Then I kept in constant touch with him and I sent him whatever I could and   50
I went to meet him when he came back to New York. When I saw him many things I thought I had forgotten came flooding back to me. This was because I had begun, finally, to wonder about Sonny, about the life that Sonny lived inside. This life, whatever it was, had made him older and thinner and it had deepened the distant stillness in which he had always moved. He looked very unlike my baby brother. Yet, when he smiled, when we shook hands, the baby brother I'd never known looked out from the depths of his private life, like an animal waiting to be coaxed into the light.

"How you been keeping?" he asked me.

"All right. And you?"

"Just fine." He was smiling all over his face. "It's good to see you again."

"It's good to see you."

The seven years' difference in our ages lay between us like a chasm: I won- 55
dered if these years would ever operate between us as a bridge. I was remembering, and it made it hard to catch my breath, that I had been there when he
was born; and I had heard the first words he had ever spoken. When he started
to walk, he walked from our mother straight to me. I caught him just before he
fell when he took the first steps he ever took in this world.

"How's Isabel?"

"Just fine. She's dying to see you."

"And the boys?"

"They're fine, too. They're anxious to see their uncle."

"Oh, come on. You know they don't remember me." 60

"Are you kidding? Of course they remember you."

He grinned again. We got into a taxi. We had a lot to say to each other, far too
much to know how to begin.

As the taxi began to move, I asked, "You still want to go to India?"

He laughed. "You still remember that. Hell, no. This place is Indian enough
for me."

"It used to belong to them," I said. 65

And he laughed again. "They damn sure knew what they were doing when
they got rid of it."

Years ago, when he was around fourteen, he'd been all hipped on the idea of
going to India. He read books about people sitting on rocks, naked, in all kinds
of weather, but mostly bad, naturally, and walking barefoot through hot coals
and arriving at wisdom. I used to say that it sounded to me as though they
were getting away from wisdom as fast as they could. I think he sort of looked
down on me for that.

"Do you mind," he asked, "if we have the driver drive alongside the park? On
the west side—I haven't seen the city in so long."

"Of course not," I said. I was afraid that I might sound as though I were
humoring him, but I hoped he wouldn't take it that way.

So we drove along, between the green of the park and the stony, lifeless ele- 70
gance of hotels and apartment buildings, toward the vivid, killing streets of
our childhood. These streets hadn't changed, though housing projects jutted
up out of them now like rocks in the middle of a boiling sea. Most of the
houses in which we had grown up had vanished, as had the stores from which
we had stolen, the basements in which we had first tried sex, the rooftops from
which we had hurled tin cans and bricks. But houses exactly like the houses of
our past yet dominated the landscape, boys exactly like the boys we once had
been found themselves smothering in these houses, came down into the streets
for light and air and found themselves encircled by disaster. Some escaped the
trap, most didn't. Those who got out always left something of themselves
behind, as some animals amputate a leg and leave it in the trap. It might be
said, perhaps, that I had escaped, after all, I was a school teacher; or that Sonny
had, he hadn't lived in Harlem for years. Yet, as the cab moved uptown through
streets which seemed, with a rush, to darken with dark people, and as I covertly

studied Sonny's face, it came to me that what we both were seeking through our separate cab windows was that part of ourselves which had been left behind. It's always at the hour of trouble and confrontation that the missing member aches.

We hit 110th Street and started rolling up Lenox Avenue. And I'd known this avenue all my life, but it seemed to me again, as it had seemed on the day I'd first heard about Sonny's trouble, filled with a hidden menace which was its very breath of life.

"We almost there," said Sonny.

"Almost." We were both too nervous to say anything more.

We live in a housing project. It hasn't been up long. A few days after it was up it seemed uninhabitably new, now, of course, it's already rundown. It looks like a parody of the good, clean, faceless life—God knows the people who live in it do their best to make it a parody. The beat-looking grass lying around isn't enough to make their lives green, the hedges will never hold out the streets, and they know it. The big windows fool no one, they aren't big enough to make space out of no space. They don't bother with the windows, they watch the TV screen instead. The playground is most popular with the children who don't play at jacks, or skip rope, or roller skate, or swing, and they can be found in it after dark. We moved in partly because it's not too far from where I teach, and partly for the kids; but it's really just like the houses in which Sonny and I grew up. The same things happen, they'll have the same things to remember. The moment Sonny and I started into the house I had the feeling that I was simply bringing him back into the danger he had almost died trying to escape.

Sonny has never been talkative. So I don't know why I was sure he'd be dying 75 to talk to me when supper was over the first night. Everything went fine, the oldest boy remembered him, and the youngest boy liked him, and Sonny had remembered to bring something for each of them; and Isabel, who is really much nicer than I am, more open and giving, had gone to a lot of trouble about dinner and was genuinely glad to see him. And she's always been able to tease Sonny in a way that I haven't. It was nice to see her face so vivid again and to hear her laugh and watch her make Sonny laugh. She wasn't, or, anyway, she didn't seem to be, at all uneasy or embarrassed. She chatted as though there were no subject which had to be avoided and she got Sonny past his first, faint stiffness. And thank God she was there, for I was filled with that icy dread again. Everything I did seemed awkward to me, and everything I said sounded freighted with hidden meaning. I was trying to remember everything I'd heard about dope addiction and I couldn't help watching Sonny for signs. I wasn't doing it out of malice. I was trying to find out something about my brother. I was dying to hear him tell me he was safe.

"Safe!" my father grunted, whenever Mama suggested trying to move to a neighborhood which might be safer for children. "Safe, hell! Ain't no place safe for kids, nor nobody."

He always went on like this, but he wasn't, ever, really as bad as he sounded, not even on weekends, when he got drunk. As a matter of fact, he was always on the lookout for "something a little better," but he died before he found it. He died suddenly, during a drunken weekend in the middle of the war, when Sonny was fifteen. He and Sonny hadn't ever got on too well. And this was partly because Sonny was the apple of his father's eye. It was because he loved Sonny so much and was frightened for him, that he was always fighting with him. It doesn't do any good to fight with Sonny. Sonny just moves back, inside himself, where he can't be reached. But the principal reason that they never hit it off is that they were so much alike. Daddy was big and rough and loud-talking, just the opposite of Sonny, but they both had—that same privacy.

Mama tried to tell me something about this, just after Daddy died. I was home on leave from the army.

This was the last time I ever saw my mother alive. Just the same, this picture gets all mixed up in my mind with pictures I had of her when she was younger. The way I always see her is the way she used to be on a Sunday afternoon, say, when the old folks were talking after the big Sunday dinner. I always see her wearing pale blue. She'd be sitting on the sofa. And my father would be sitting in the easy chair, not far from her. And the living room would be full of church folks and relatives. There they sit, in chairs all around the living room, and the night is creeping up outside, but nobody knows it yet. You can see the darkness growing against the windowpanes and you hear the street noises every now and again, or maybe the jangling beat of a tambourine from one of the churches close by, but it's real quiet in the room. For a moment nobody's talking, but every face looks darkening, like the sky outside. And my mother rocks a little from the waist, and my father's eyes are closed. Everyone is looking at something a child can't see. For a minute they've forgotten the children. Maybe a kid is lying on the rug, half asleep. Maybe somebody's got a kid in his lap and is absent-mindedly stroking the kid's head. Maybe there's a kid, quiet and big-eyed, curled up in a big chair in the corner. The silence, the darkness coming, and the darkness in the faces frighten the child obscurely. He hopes that the hand which strokes his forehead will never stop—will never die. He hopes that there will never come a time when the old folks won't be sitting around the living room, talking about where they've come from, and what they've seen, and what's happened to them and their kinfolk.

But something deep and watchful in the child knows that this is bound to 80 end, is already ending. In a moment someone will get up and turn on the light. Then the old folks will remember the children and they won't talk any more that day. And when light fills the room, the child is filled with darkness. He knows that every time this happens he's moved just a little closer to that darkness outside. The darkness outside is what the old folks have been talking about. It's what they've come from. It's what they endure. The child knows that they won't talk any more because if he knows too much about what's happened to *them*, he'll know too much too soon, about what's going to happen to *him*.

The last time I talked to my mother, I remember I was restless. I wanted to get out and see Isabel. We weren't married then and we had a lot to straighten out between us.

There Mama sat, in black, by the window. She was humming an old church song, *Lord, you brought me from a long ways off.* Sonny was out somewhere. Mama kept watching the streets.

"I don't know," she said, "if I'll ever see you again, after you go off from here. But I hope you'll remember the things I tried to teach you."

"Don't talk like that," I said, and smiled. "You'll be here a long time yet."

She smiled, too, but she said nothing. She was quiet for a long time. And I said, "Mama, don't you worry about nothing. I'll be writing all the time, and you be getting the checks. . . ." 85

"I want to talk to you about your brother," she said, suddenly. "If anything happens to me he ain't going to have nobody to look out for him."

"Mama," I said, "ain't nothing going to happen to you *or* Sonny. Sonny's all right. He's a good boy and he's got good sense."

"It ain't a question of his being a good boy," Mama said, "nor of his having good sense. It ain't only the bad ones, nor yet the dumb ones that gets sucked under." She stopped, looking at me. "Your Daddy once had a brother," she said, and she smiled in a way that made me feel she was in pain. "You didn't never know that, did you?"

"No," I said, "I never knew that," and I watched her face.

"Oh, yes," she said, "your Daddy had a brother." She looked out of the window again. "I know you never saw your Daddy cry. But *I* did—many a time, through all these years." 90

I asked her, "What happened to his brother? How come nobody's ever talked about him?"

This was the first time I ever saw my mother look old.

"His brother got killed," she said, "when he was just a little younger than you are now. I knew him. He was a fine boy. He was maybe a little full of the devil, but he didn't mean nobody no harm."

Then she stopped and the room was silent, exactly as it had sometimes been on those Sunday afternoons. Mama kept looking out into the streets.

"He used to have a job in the mill," she said, "and, like all young folks, he just liked to perform on Saturday nights. Saturday nights, him and your father would drift around to different places, go to dances and things like that, or just sit around with people they knew, and your father's brother would sing, he had a fine voice, and play along with himself on his guitar. Well, this particular Saturday night, him and your father was coming home from some place, and they were both a little drunk and there was a moon that night, it was bright like day. Your father's brother was feeling kind of good, and he was whistling to himself, and he had his guitar slung over his shoulder. They was coming down a hill and beneath them was a road that turned off from the highway. Well, your father's brother, being always kind of frisky, decided to run down this hill, and he did, with that guitar banging and clanging behind him, and he ran across 95 the road, and he was making water behind a tree. And your father was sort of amused at him and he was still coming down the hill, kind of slow. Then he heard a car motor and that same minute his brother stepped from behind the tree, into the road, in the moonlight. And he started to cross the road. And your father started to run down the hill, he says he don't know why. This car was full of white men. They was all drunk, and when they seen your father's brother they let out a great whoop and holler and they aimed the car straight at him. They was having fun, they just wanted to scare him, the way they do sometimes, you know. But they was drunk. And I guess the boy, being drunk, too, and scared, kind of lost his head. By the time he jumped it was too late. Your father says he heard his brother scream when the car rolled over him, and he heard the wood of that guitar when it give, and he heard them strings go flying, and he heard them white men shouting, and the car kept on a-going and it ain't stopped till this day. And, time your father got down the hill, his brother weren't nothing but blood and pulp."

Tears were gleaming on my mother's face. There wasn't anything I could say.

"He never mentioned it," she said, "because I never let him mention it before you children. Your Daddy was like a crazy man that night and for many a night thereafter. He says he never in his life seen anything as dark as that road after the lights of that car had gone away. Weren't nothing, weren't nobody on that road, just your Daddy and his brother and that busted guitar. Oh, yes. Your Daddy never did really get right again. Till the day he died he weren't sure but that every white man he saw was the man that killed his brother."

She stopped and took out her handkerchief and dried her eyes and looked at me.

"I ain't telling you all this," she said, "to make you scared or bitter or to make you hate nobody. I'm telling you this because you got a brother. And the world ain't changed."

I guess I didn't want to believe this. I guess she saw this in my face. She 100 turned away from me, toward the window again, searching those streets.

"But I praise my Redeemer," she said at last, "that He called your Daddy home before me. I ain't saying it to throw no flowers at myself, but, I declare, it keeps me from feeling too cast down to know I helped your father get safely through this world. Your father always acted like he was the roughest, strongest man on earth. And everybody took him to be like that. But if he hadn't had me there—to see his tears!"

She was crying again. Still, I couldn't move. I said, "Lord, Lord, Mama, I didn't know it was like that."

"Oh, honey," she said, "there's a lot that you don't know. But you are going to find out." She stood up from the window and came over to me. "You got to hold on to your brother," she said, "and don't let him fall, no matter what it looks like is happening to him and no matter how evil you gets with him. You going to be evil with him many a time. But don't you forget what I told you, you hear?"

"I won't forget," I said. "Don't you worry, I won't forget. I won't let nothing happen to Sonny."

My mother smiled as though she was amused at something she saw in my 105 face. Then, "You may not be able to stop nothing from happening. But you got to let him know you's *there*."

Two days later I was married, and then I was gone. And I had a lot of things on my mind and I pretty well forgot my promise to Mama until I got shipped home on a special furlough for her funeral.

And, after the funeral, with just Sonny and me alone in the empty kitchen, I tried to find out something about him.

"What do you want to do?" I asked him.

"I'm going to be a musician," he said.

For he had graduated, in the time I had been away, from dancing to the juke 110 box to finding out who was playing what, and what they were doing with it, and he had bought himself a set of drums.

"You mean, you want to be a drummer?" I somehow had the feeling that being a drummer might be all right for other people but not for my brother Sonny.

"I don't think," he said, looking at me very gravely, "that I'll ever be a good drummer. But I think I can play a piano."

I frowned. I'd never played the role of the oldest brother quite so seriously before, had scarcely ever, in fact, *asked* Sonny a damn thing. I sensed myself in the presence of something I didn't really know how to handle, didn't under-stand. So I made my frown a little deeper as I asked: "What kind of musician do you want to be?"

He grinned. "How many kinds do you think there are?"

"Be *serious*," I said.   115

He laughed, throwing his head back, and then looked at me. "I *am* serious."

"Well, then, for Christ's sake, stop kidding around and answer a serious question. I mean, do you want to be a concert pianist, you want to play classi-cal music and all that, or—or what?" Long before I finished he was laughing again. "For Christ's *sake*, Sonny!"

He sobered, but with difficulty. "I'm sorry. But you sound so—*scared!*" and he was off again.

"Well, you may think it's funny now, baby, but it's not going to be so funny when you have to make your living at it, let me tell you *that*." I was furious because I knew he was laughing at me and I didn't know why.

"No," he said, very sober now, and afraid, perhaps, that he'd hurt me, "I 120 don't want to be a classical pianist. That isn't what interests me. I mean"—he paused, looking hard at me, as though his eyes would help me to understand, and then gestured helplessly, as though perhaps his hand would help—"I mean, I'll have a lot of studying to do, and I'll have to study *everything*, but, I mean, I want to play *with*—jazz musicians." He stopped. "I want to play jazz," he said.

Well, the word had never before sounded as heavy, as real, as it sounded that afternoon in Sonny's mouth. I just looked at him and I was probably frowning a real frown by this time. I simply couldn't see why on earth he'd want to spend his time hanging around nightclubs, clowning around on bandstands, while people pushed each other around a dance floor. It seemed—beneath him, somehow. I had never thought about it before, had never been forced to, but I suppose I had always put jazz musicians in a class with what Daddy called "good-time people."

"Are you *serious?*"

"Hell, *yes*, I'm serious."

He looked more helpless than ever, and annoyed, and deeply hurt.

I suggested, helpfully: "You mean—like Louis Armstrong?"[2]   125

His face closed as though I'd struck him. "No. I'm not talking about none of that old-time, down home crap."

"Well, look, Sonny, I'm sorry, don't get mad. I just don't altogether get it, that's all. Name somebody—you know, a jazz musician you admire."

"Bird."

"Who?"

"Bird! Charlie Parker![3] Don't they teach you nothing in the goddamn army?"   130

I lit a cigarette. I was surprised and then a little amused to discover that I was trembling. "I've been out of touch," I said. "You'll have to be patient with me. Now. Who's this Parker character?"

"He's just one of the greatest jazz musicians alive," said Sonny, sullenly, his hands in his pockets, his back to me. "Maybe *the* greatest," he added, bitterly, "that's probably why *you* never heard of him."

"All right," I said, "I'm ignorant. I'm sorry. I'll go out and buy all the cat's records right away, all right?"

"It don't," said Sonny, with dignity, "make any difference to me. I don't care what you listen to. Don't do me no favors."

I was beginning to realize that I'd never seen him so upset before. With   135 another part of my mind I was thinking that this would probably turn out to be one of those things kids go through and that I shouldn't make it seem important by pushing it too hard. Still, I didn't think it would do any harm to ask: "Doesn't all this take a lot of time? Can you make a living at it?"

He turned back to me and half leaned, half sat, on the kitchen table. "Everything takes time," he said, "and—well, yes, sure, I can make a living at it. But what I don't seem to be able to make you understand is that it's the only thing I want to do."

"Well, Sonny," I said, gently, "you know people can't always do exactly what they *want* to do—"

"*No*, I don't know that," said Sonny, surprising me. "I think people *ought* to do what they want to do, what else are they alive for?"

"You getting to be a big boy," I said desperately, "it's time you started thinking about your future."

[2] Louis "Satchmo" Armstrong (1901–1971) played the trumpet and was one of the most innovative and influential figures in the history of jazz.

[3] Charlie "Bird" Parker (1920–1955), a seminal African American saxophonist, was one of the originators of the bebop style of jazz. Parker was also a heroin addict.

"I'm thinking about my future," said Sonny, grimly. "I think about it all the   140
time."

I gave up. I decided, if he didn't change his mind, that we could always talk
about it later. "In the meantime," I said, "you got to finish school." We had
already decided that he'd have to move in with Isabel and her folks. I knew this
wasn't the ideal arrangement because Isabel's folks are inclined to be dicty[4]
and they hadn't especially wanted Isabel to marry me. But I didn't know what
else to do. "And we have to get you fixed up at Isabel's."

There was a long silence. He moved from the kitchen table to the window.
"That's a terrible idea. You know it yourself."

"Do you have a *better* idea?"

He just walked up and down the kitchen for a minute. He was as tall as I was.
He had started to shave. I suddenly had the feeling that I didn't know him at all.

He stopped at the kitchen table and picked up my cigarettes. Looking at me   145
with a kind of mocking, amused defiance, he put one between his lips. "You
mind?"

"You smoking already?"

He lit the cigarette and nodded, watching me through the smoke. "I just
wanted to see if I'd have the courage to smoke in front of you." He grinned and
blew a great cloud of smoke to the ceiling. "It was easy." He looked at my face.
"Come on, now. I bet you was smoking at my age, tell the truth."

I didn't say anything but the truth was on my face, and he laughed. But now
there was something very strained in his laugh. "Sure. And I bet that ain't all
you was doing."

He was frightening me a little. "Cut the crap," I said. "We already decided
that you was going to go and live at Isabel's. Now what's got into you all of a
sudden?"

"*You* decided it," he pointed out. "*I* didn't decide nothing." He stopped in   150
front of me, leaning against the stove, arms loosely folded. "Look, brother. I
don't want to stay in Harlem no more, I really don't." He was very earnest. He
looked at me, then over toward the kitchen window. There was something in
his eyes I'd never seen before, some thoughtfulness, some worry all his own.
He rubbed the muscle of one arm. "It's time I was getting out of here."

"Where do you want to *go*, Sonny?"

"I want to join the army. Or the navy, I don't care. If I say I'm old enough,
they'll believe me."

Then I got mad. It was because I was so scared. "You must be crazy. You goddamn fool, what the hell do you want to go and join the *army* for?"

"I just told you. To get out of Harlem."

"Sonny, you haven't even finished *school*. And if you really want to be a   155
musician, how do you expect to study if you're in the *army*?"

He looked at me, trapped, and in anguish. "There's ways. I might be able to
work out some kind of deal. Anyway, I'll have the G.I. Bill when I come out."

[4] Snobbish.

"*If* you come out." We stared at each other. "Sonny, please. Be reasonable. I know the setup is far from perfect. But we got to do the best we can."

"I ain't learning nothing in school," he said. "Even when I go." He turned away from me and opened the window and threw his cigarette out into the narrow alley. I watched his back. "At least, I ain't learning nothing you'd want me to learn." He slammed the window so hard I thought the glass would fly out, and turned back to me. "And I'm sick of the stink of these garbage cans!"

"Sonny," I said, "I know how you feel. But if you don't finish school now, you're going to be sorry later that you didn't." I grabbed him by the shoulders. "And you only got another year. It ain't so bad. And I'll come back and I swear I'll help you do *whatever* you want to do. Just try to put up with it till I come back. Will you please do that? For me?"

He didn't answer and he wouldn't look at me.   160

"Sonny. You hear me?"

He pulled away. "I hear you. But you never hear anything *I* say."

I didn't know what to say to that. He looked out of the window and then back at me. "OK," he said, and sighed. "I'll try."

Then I said, trying to cheer him up a little, "They got a piano at Isabel's. You can practice on it."

And as a matter of fact, it did cheer him up for a minute. "That's right," he   165
said to himself. "I forgot that." His face relaxed a little. But the worry, the thoughtfulness, played on it still, the way shadows play on a face which is staring into the fire.

But I thought I'd never hear the end of that piano. At first, Isabel would write me, saying how nice it was that Sonny was so serious about his music and how, as soon as he came in from school, or wherever he had been when he was supposed to be at school, he went straight to that piano and stayed there until suppertime. And, after supper, he went back to that piano and stayed there until everybody went to bed. He was at the piano all day Saturday and all day Sunday. Then he bought a record player and started playing records. He'd play one record over and over again, all day long sometimes, and he'd improvise along with it on the piano. Or he'd play one section of the record, one chord, one change, one progression, then he'd do it on the piano. Then back to the record. Then back to the piano.

Well, I really don't know how they stood it. Isabel finally confessed that it wasn't like living with a person at all, it was like living with sound. And the sound didn't make any sense to her, didn't make any sense to any of them—naturally. They began, in a way, to be afflicted by this presence that was living in their home. It was as though Sonny were some sort of god, or monster. He moved in an atmosphere which wasn't like theirs at all. They fed him and he ate, he washed himself, he walked in and out of their door; he certainly wasn't nasty or unpleasant or rude, Sonny isn't any of those things; but it was as though he were all wrapped up in some cloud, some fire, some vision all his own; and there wasn't any way to reach him.

At the same time, he wasn't really a man yet, he was still a child, and they had to watch out for him in all kinds of ways. They certainly couldn't throw him out. Neither did they dare to make a great scene about that piano because even they dimly sensed, as I sensed, from so many thousands of miles away, that Sonny was at that piano playing for his life.

But he hadn't been going to school. One day a letter came from the school board and Isabel's mother got it—there had, apparently, been other letters but Sonny had torn them up. This day, when Sonny came in, Isabel's mother showed him the letter and asked where he'd been spending his time. And she finally got it out of him that he'd been down in Greenwich Village, with musicians and other characters, in a white girl's apartment. And this scared her and she started to scream at him and what came up, once she began—though she denies it to this day—was what sacrifices they were making to give Sonny a decent home and how little he appreciated it.

Sonny didn't play the piano that day. By evening, Isabel's mother had 170 calmed down but then there was the old man to deal with, and Isabel herself. Isabel says she did her best to be calm but she broke down and started crying. She says she just watched Sonny's face. She could tell, by watching him, what was happening with him. And what was happening was that they penetrated his cloud, they had reached him. Even if their fingers had been a thousand times more gentle than human fingers ever are, he could hardly help feeling that they had stripped him naked and were spitting on that nakedness. For he also had to see that his presence, that music, which was life or death to him, had been torture for them and that they had endured it, not at all for his sake, but only for mine. And Sonny couldn't take that. He can take it a little better today than he could then but he's still not very good at it and, frankly, I don't know anybody who is.

The silence of the next few days must have been louder than the sound of all the music ever played since time began. One morning, before she went to work, Isabel was in his room for something and she suddenly realized that all of his records were gone. And she knew for certain that he was gone. And he was. He went as far as the navy would carry him. He finally sent me a postcard from some place in Greece and that was the first I knew that Sonny was still alive. I didn't see him any more until we were both back in New York and the war had long been over.

He was a man by then, of course, but I wasn't willing to see it. He came by the house from time to time, but we fought almost every time we met. I didn't like the way he carried himself, loose and dreamlike all the time, and I didn't like his friends, and his music seemed to be merely an excuse for the life he led. It sounded just that weird and disordered.

Then we had a fight, a pretty awful fight, and I didn't see him for months. By and by I looked him up, where he was living, in a furnished room in the Village, and I tried to make it up. But there were lots of other people in the room and Sonny just lay on his bed, and he wouldn't come downstairs with me, and he treated these other people as though they were his family and I weren't. So I got mad and then he got mad, and then I told him that he might just as well be dead as live the way he was living. Then he stood up and he told me not to worry about him any more in life, that he *was* dead as far as I was concerned. Then he pushed me to the door and the other people looked on as though nothing were happening, and he slammed the door behind me. I stood in the hallway, staring at the door. I heard somebody laugh in the room and then the tears came to my eyes. I started down the steps, whistling to keep from crying, I kept whistling to myself, *You going to need me, baby, one of these cold, rainy days.*

I read about Sonny's trouble in the spring. Little Grace died in the fall. She was a beautiful little girl. But she only lived a little over two years. She died of polio and she suffered. She had a slight fever for a couple of days, but it didn't seem like anything and we just kept her in bed. And we would certainly have called the doctor, but the fever dropped, she seemed to be all right. So we thought it had just been a cold. Then, one day, she was up, playing, Isabel was in the kitchen fixing lunch for the two boys when they'd come in from school, and she heard Grace fall down in the living room. When you have a lot of children you don't always start running when one of them falls, unless they start screaming or something. And, this time, Gracie was quiet. Yet, Isabel says that when she heard that *thump* and then that silence, something happened to her to make her afraid. And she ran to the living room and there was little Grace on the floor, all twisted up, and the reason she hadn't screamed was that she couldn't get her breath. And when she did scream, it was the worst sound, Isabel says, that she'd ever heard in all her life, and she still hears it sometimes in her dreams. Isabel will sometimes wake me up with a low, moaning, strangling sound and I have to be quick to awaken her and hold her to me and where Isabel is weeping against me seems a mortal wound.

I think I may have written Sonny the very day that little Grace was buried. I was sitting in the living room in the dark, by myself, and I suddenly thought of Sonny. My trouble made his real.

One Saturday afternoon, when Sonny had been living with us, or, anyway, been in our house, for nearly two weeks, I found myself wandering aimlessly about the living room, drinking from a can of beer, and trying to work up courage to search Sonny's room. He was out, he was usually out whenever I was home, and Isabel had taken the children to see their grandparents. Suddenly I was standing still in front of the living room window, watching Seventh Avenue. The idea of searching Sonny's room made me still. I scarcely dared to admit to myself what I'd be searching for. I didn't know what I'd do if I found it. Or if I didn't.

On the sidewalk across from me, near the entrance to a barbecue joint, some people were holding an old-fashioned revival meeting. The barbecue cook, wearing a dirty white apron, his conked[5] hair reddish and metallic in the pale

[5] Straightened and greased.

sun, and a cigarette between his lips, stood in the doorway, watching them. Kids and older people paused in their errands and stood there, along with some older men and a couple of very tough-looking women who watched everything that happened on the avenue, as though they owned it, or were maybe owned by it. Well, they were watching this, too. The revival was being carried on by three sisters in black, and a brother. All they had were their voices and their Bibles and a tambourine. The brother was testifying and while he testified two of the sisters stood together, seeming to say, amen, and the third sister walked around with the tambourine outstretched and a couple of people dropped coins into it. Then the brother's testimony ended and the sister who had been taking up the collection dumped the coins into her palm and transferred them to the pocket of her long black robe. Then she raised both hands, striking the tambourine against the air, and then against one hand, and she started to sing. And the two other sisters and the brother joined in.

It was strange, suddenly, to watch, though I had been seeing these meetings all my life. So, of course, had everybody else down there. Yet, they paused and watched and listened and I stood still at the window. " *'Tis the old ship of Zion*," they sang, and the sister with the tambourine kept a steady, jangling beat, "*it has rescued many a thousand!*" Not a soul under the sound of their voices was hearing this song for the first time, not one of them had been rescued. Nor had they seen much in the way of rescue work being done around them. Neither did they especially believe in the holiness of the three sisters and the brother, they knew too much about them, knew where they lived, and how. The woman with the tambourine, whose voice dominated the air, whose face was bright with joy, was divided by very little from the woman who stood watching her, a cigarette between her heavy, chapped lips, her hair a cuckoo's nest, her face scarred and swollen from many beatings, and her black eyes glittering like coal. Perhaps they both knew this, which was why, when, as rarely, they addressed each other, they addressed each other as Sister. As the singing filled the air the watching, listening faces underwent a change, the eyes focusing on something within; the music seemed to soothe a poison out of them; and time seemed, nearly, to fall away from the sullen, belligerent, battered faces, as though they were fleeing back to their first condition, while dreaming of their last. The barbecue cook half shook his head and smiled, and dropped his cigarette and disappeared into his joint. A man fumbled in his pockets for change and stood holding it in his hand impatiently, as though he had just remembered a pressing appointment further up the avenue. He looked furious. Then I saw Sonny, standing on the edge of the crowd. He was carrying a wide, flat notebook with a green cover, and it made him look, from where I was standing, almost like a schoolboy. The coppery sun brought out the copper in his skin, he was very faintly smiling, standing very still. Then the singing stopped, the tambourine turned into a collection plate again. The furious man dropped in his coins and vanished, so did a couple of the women, and Sonny dropped some change in the plate, looking directly at the woman with a little smile. He started across the avenue, toward the house. He has a slow, loping walk, something like the way Harlem hipsters walk, only he's imposed on this his own half-beat. I had never really noticed it before.

I stayed at the window, both relieved and apprehensive. As Sonny disappeared from my sight, they began singing again. And they were still singing when his key turned in the lock.

"Hey," he said. 180

"Hey, yourself. You want some beer?"

"No. Well, maybe." But he came up to the window and stood beside me, looking out. "What a warm voice," he said.

They were singing *If I could only hear my mother pray again!*

"Yes," I said, "and she can sure beat that tambourine."

"But what a terrible song," he said, and laughed. He dropped his notebook 185 on the sofa and disappeared into the kitchen. "Where's Isabel and the kids?"

"I think they went to see their grandparents. You hungry?"

"No." He came back into the living room with his can of beer. "You want to come some place with me tonight?"

I sensed, I don't know how, that I couldn't possibly say no. "Sure. Where?"

He sat down on the sofa and picked up his notebook and started leafing through it. "I'm going to sit in with some fellows in a joint in the Village."

"You mean, you're going to play, tonight?" 190

"That's right." He took a swallow of his beer and moved back to the window. He gave me a sidelong look. "If you can stand it."

"I'll try," I said.

He smiled to himself and we both watched as the meeting across the way broke up. The three sisters and the brother, heads bowed, were singing *God be with you till we meet again.* The faces around them were very quiet. Then the song ended. The small crowd dispersed. We watched the three women and the lone man walk slowly up the avenue.

"When she was singing before," said Sonny, abruptly, "her voice reminded me for a minute of what heroin feels like sometimes—when it's in your veins. It makes you feel sort of warm and cool at the same time. And distant. And—and sure." He sipped his beer, very deliberately not looking at me. I watched his face. "It makes you feel—in control. Sometimes you've got to have that feeling."

"Do you?" I sat down slowly in the easy chair. 195

"Sometimes." He went to the sofa and picked up his notebook again. "Some people do."

"In order," I asked, "to play?" And my voice was very ugly, full of contempt and anger.

"Well"—he looked at me with great, troubled eyes, as though, in fact, he hoped his eyes would tell me things he could never otherwise say—"they *think* so. And *if* they think so—!"

"And what do *you* think?" I asked.

He sat on the sofa and put his can of beer on the floor. "I don't know," he 200 said, and I couldn't be sure if he were answering my question or pursuing his thoughts. His face didn't tell me. "It's not so much to *play*. It's to *stand* it, to be able to make it at all. On any level." He frowned and smiled: "In order to keep from shaking to pieces."

"But these friends of yours," I said, "they seem to shake themselves to pieces pretty goddamn fast."

"Maybe." He played with the notebook. And something told me that I should curb my tongue, that Sonny was doing his best to talk, that I should listen. "But of course you only know the ones that've gone to pieces. Some don't—or at least they haven't *yet* and that's just about all *any* of us can say." He paused. "And then there are some who just live, really, in hell, and they know it and they see what's happening and they go right on. I don't know." He sighed, dropped the notebook, folded his arms. "Some guys, you can tell from the way they play, they on something *all* the time. And you can see that, well, it makes something real for them. But of course," he picked up his beer from the floor and sipped it and put the can down again, "they *want* to, too, you've got to see that. Even some of them that say they don't—*some*, not all."

"And what about you?" I asked—I couldn't help it. "What about you? Do *you* want to?"

He stood up and walked to the window and remained silent for a long time. Then he sighed. "Me," he said. Then: "While I was downstairs before, on my way here, listening to that woman sing, it struck me all of a sudden how much suffering she must have had to go through—to sing like that. It's *repulsive* to think you have to suffer that much."

I said: "But there's no way not to suffer—is there, Sonny?"   205

"I believe not," he said and smiled, "but that's never stopped anyone from trying." He looked at me. "Has it?" I realized, with this mocking look, that there stood between us, forever, beyond the power of time or forgiveness, the fact that I had held silence—so long!—when he had needed human speech to help him. He turned back to the window. "No, there's no way not to suffer. But you try all kinds of ways to keep from drowning in it, to keep on top of it, and to make it seem—well, like *you*. Like you did something, all right, and now you're suffering for it. You know?" I said nothing. "Well you know," he said, impatiently, "why *do* people suffer? Maybe it's better to do something to give it a reason, *any* reason."

"But we just agreed," I said, "that there's no way not to suffer. Isn't it better, then, just to—take it?"

"But nobody just takes it," Sonny cried, "that's what I'm telling you! *Everybody* tries not to. You're just hung up on the *way* some people try—it's not *your* way!"

The hair on my face began to itch, my face felt wet. "That's not true," I said, "that's not true. I don't give a damn what other people do, I don't even care how they suffer. I just care how *you* suffer." And he looked at me. "Please believe me," I said, "I don't want to see you—die—trying not to suffer."

"I won't," he said, flatly, "die trying not to suffer. At least, not any faster than   210 anybody else."

"But there's no need," I said, trying to laugh, "is there? in killing yourself."

I wanted to say more, but I couldn't. I wanted to talk about will power and how life could be—well, beautiful. I wanted to say that it was all within; but was it? or, rather, wasn't that exactly the trouble? And I wanted to promise that I would never fail him again. But it would all have sounded—empty words and lies.

So I made the promise to myself and prayed that I would keep it.

"It's terrible sometimes, inside," he said, "that's what's the trouble. You walk these streets, black and funky and cold, and there's not really a living ass to talk to, and there's nothing shaking, and there's no way of getting it out—that storm inside. You can't talk it and you can't make love with it, and when you finally try to get with it and play it, you realize *nobody's* listening. So *you've* got to listen. You got to find a way to listen."

And then he walked away from the window and sat on the sofa again, as 215 though all the wind had suddenly been knocked out of him. "Sometimes you'll do *anything* to play, even cut your mother's throat." He laughed and looked at me. "Or your brother's." Then he sobered. "Or your own." Then: "Don't worry. I'm all right now and I think I'll *be* all right. But I can't forget—where I've been. I don't mean just the physical place I've been, I mean where I've *been*. And *what* I've been."

"What have you been, Sonny?" I asked.

He smiled—but sat sideways on the sofa, his elbow resting on the back, his fingers playing with his mouth and chin, not looking at me. "I've been something I didn't recognize, didn't know I could be. Didn't know anybody could be." He stopped, looking inward, looking helplessly young, looking old. "I'm not talking about it now because I feel *guilty* or anything like that—maybe it would be better if I did, I don't know. Anyway, I can't really talk about it. Not to you, not to anybody," and now he turned and faced me. "Sometimes, you know, and it was actually when I was most *out* of the world, I felt that I was in it, that I was *with* it, really, and I could play or I didn't really have to *play*, it just came out of me, it was there. And I don't know how I played, thinking about it now, but I know I did awful things, those times, sometimes, to people. Or it wasn't that I *did* anything to them—it was that they weren't real." He picked up the beer can; it was empty; he rolled it between his palms: "And other times—well, I needed a fix, I needed to find a place to lean, I needed to clear a space to *listen*—and I couldn't find it, and I—went crazy, I did terrible things to *me*, I was terrible *for* me." He began pressing the beer can between his hands, I watched the metal begin to give. It glittered, as he played with it like a knife, and I was afraid he would cut himself, but I said nothing. "Oh well. I can never tell you. I was all by myself at the bottom of something, stinking and sweating and crying and shaking, and I smelled it, you know? *my* stink, and I thought I'd die if I couldn't get away from it and yet, all the same, I knew that everything I was doing was just locking me in with it. And I didn't know," he paused, still flattening the beer can, "I didn't know, I still *don't* know, something kept telling me that maybe it was good to smell your own stink, but I didn't think that *that* was what I'd been trying to do—and—who can stand it?" and he abruptly dropped the ruined beer can, looking at me with a small, still smile, and then rose, walking to the window as though it were the lodestone rock. I watched his face, he watched the avenue. "I couldn't tell you when Mama died—but the reason I wanted to leave Harlem so bad was to get away from drugs. And then, when I ran away, that's what I was running from—really. When I came back, nothing had changed, *I* hadn't changed, I was just—older." And he stopped, drumming with his fingers on the windowpane. The sun had vanished, soon darkness would fall. I watched his face. "It can come again," he said, almost as though speaking to himself. Then he turned to me. "It can come again," he repeated. "I just want you to know that."

"All right," I said, at last. "So it can come again. All right."

He smiled, but the smile was sorrowful. "I had to try to tell you," he said.

"Yes," I said. "I understand that."   220

"You're my brother," he said, looking straight at me, and not smiling at all.

"Yes," I repeated, "yes. I understand that."

He turned back to the window, looking out. "All that hatred down there," he said, "all that hatred and misery and love. It's a wonder it doesn't blow the avenue apart."

We went to the only nightclub on a short, dark street, downtown. We squeezed through the narrow, chattering, jampacked bar to the entrance of the big room, where the bandstand was. And we stood there for a moment, for the lights were very dim in this room and we couldn't see. Then, "Hello, boy," said the voice and an enormous black man, much older than Sonny or myself, erupted out of all that atmospheric lighting and put an arm around Sonny's shoulder. "I been sitting right here," he said, "waiting for you."

He had a big voice, too, and heads in the darkness turned toward us.   225

Sonny grinned and pulled a little away, and said, "Creole, this is my brother. I told you about him."

Creole shook my hand. "I'm glad to meet you, son," he said, and it was clear that he was glad to meet me *there,* for Sonny's sake. And he smiled, "You got a real musician in *your* family," and he took his arm from Sonny's shoulder and slapped him, lightly, affectionately, with the back of his hand.

"Well. Now I've heard it all," said a voice behind us. This was another musician, and a friend of Sonny's, a coal-black, cheerful-looking man, built close to the ground. He immediately began confiding to me, at the top of his lungs, the most terrible things about Sonny, his teeth gleaming like a lighthouse and his laugh coming up out of him like the beginning of an earthquake. And it turned out that everyone at the bar knew Sonny, or almost everyone; some were musicians, working there, or nearby, or not working, some were simply hangers-on, and some were there to hear Sonny play. I was introduced to all of them and they were all very polite to me. Yet, it was clear that, for them, I was only Sonny's brother. Here, I was in Sonny's world. Or, rather: his kingdom. Here, it was not even a question that his veins bore royal blood.

They were going to play soon and Creole installed me, by myself, at a table in a dark corner. Then I watched them, Creole, and the little black man, and Sonny, and the others, while they horsed around, standing just below the bandstand. The light from the bandstand spilled just a little short of them and, watching them laughing and gesturing and moving about, I had the feeling that they, nevertheless, were being most careful not to step into that circle of light too suddenly; that if they moved into the light too suddenly, without thinking, they would perish in flame. Then, while I watched, one of them, the small, black man, moved into the light and crossed the bandstand and started fooling around with his drums. Then—being funny and being, also, extremely ceremonious—Creole took Sonny by the arm and led him to the piano. A woman's voice called Sonny's name and a few hands started clapping. And Sonny, also being funny and being ceremonious, and so touched, I think, that he could have cried, but neither hiding it nor showing it, riding it like a man, grinned, and put both hands to his heart and bowed from the waist.

Creole then went to the bass fiddle and a lean, very bright-skinned brown   230 man jumped up on the bandstand and picked up his horn. So there they were, and the atmosphere on the bandstand and in the room began to change and tighten. Someone stepped up to the microphone and announced them. Then there were all kinds of murmurs. Some people at the bar shushed others. The waitress ran around, frantically getting in the last orders, guys and chicks got closer to each other, and the lights on the bandstand, on the quartet, turned to a kind of indigo. Then they all looked different there. Creole looked about him for the last time, as though he were making certain that all his chickens were in the coop, and then he—jumped and struck the fiddle. And there they were.

All I know about music is that not many people ever really hear it. And even then, on the rare occasions when something opens within, and the music enters, what we mainly hear, or hear corroborated, are personal, private, vanishing evocations. But the man who creates the music is hearing something else, is dealing with the roar rising from the void and imposing order on it as it hits the air. What is evoked in him, then, is of another order, more terrible because it has no words, and triumphant, too, for that same reason. And his triumph, when he triumphs, is ours. I just watched Sonny's face. His face was troubled, he was working hard, but he wasn't with it. And I had the feeling that, in a way, everyone on the bandstand was waiting for him, both waiting for him and pushing him along. But as I began to watch Creole, I realized that it was Creole who held them all back. He had them on a short rein. Up there, keeping the beat with his whole body, wailing on the fiddle, with his eyes half closed, he was listening to everything, but he was listening to Sonny. He was having a dialogue with Sonny. He wanted Sonny to leave the shoreline and strike out for the deep water. He was Sonny's witness that deep water and drowning were not the same thing—he had been there, and he knew. And he wanted Sonny to know. He was waiting for Sonny to do the things on the keys which would let Creole know that Sonny was in the water.

And, while Creole listened, Sonny moved, deep within, exactly like someone in torment. I had never before thought of how awful the relationship must be between the musician and his instrument. He has to fill it, this instrument, with the breath of life, his own. He has to make it do what he wants it to do. And a piano is just a piano. It's made out of so much wood and wires and little hammers and big ones, and ivory. While there's only so much you can do with it, the only way to find this out is to try; to try and make it do everything.

And Sonny hadn't been near a piano for over a year. And he wasn't on much better terms with his life, not the life that stretched before him now. He and the piano stammered, started one way, got scared, stopped; started another way, panicked, marked time, started again; then seemed to have found a direction, panicked again, got stuck. And the face I saw on Sonny I'd never seen before. Everything had been burned out of it, and, at the same time, things usually hidden were being burned in, by the fire and fury of the battle which was occurring in him up there.

Yet, watching Creole's face as they neared the end of the first set, I had the feeling that something had happened, something I hadn't heard. Then they finished, there was scattered applause, and then, without an instant's warning, Creole started into something else, it was almost sardonic, it was *Am I Blue.*[6] And, as though he commanded, Sonny began to play. Something began to happen. And Creole let out the reins. The dry, low, black man said something awful on the drums, Creole answered, and the drums talked back. Then the horn insisted, sweet and high, slightly detached perhaps, and Creole listened, commenting now and then, dry, and driving, beautiful and calm and old. Then they all came together again, and Sonny was part of the family again. I could tell this from his face. He seemed to have found, right there beneath his fingers, a damn brand-new piano. It seemed that he couldn't get over it. Then, for a while, just being happy with Sonny, they seemed to be agreeing with him that brand-new pianos certainly were a gas.

Then Creole stepped forward to remind them that what they were playing was the blues. He hit something in all of them, he hit something in me, myself, and the music tightened and deepened, apprehension began to beat the air. Creole began to tell us what the blues were all about. They were not about anything very new. He and his boys up there were keeping it new, at the risk of ruin, destruction, madness, and death, in order to find new ways to make us listen. For, while the tale of how we suffer, and how we are delighted, and how we may triumph is never new, it always must be heard. There isn't any other tale to tell, it's the only light we've got in all this darkness.

And this tale, according to that face, that body, those strong hands on those strings, has another aspect in every country, and a new depth in every generation. Listen, Creole seemed to be saying, listen. Now these are Sonny's blues. He made the little black man on the drums know it, and the bright, brown

235

---

[6] One of the standard tunes in the jazz/blues repertoire.

man on the horn. Creole wasn't trying any longer to get Sonny in the water. He was wishing him Godspeed. Then he stepped back, very slowly, filling the air with the immense suggestion that Sonny speak for himself.

Then they all gathered around Sonny and Sonny played. Every now and again one of them seemed to say, amen. Sonny's fingers filled the air with life, his life. But that life contained so many others. And Sonny went all the way back, he really began with the spare, flat statement of the opening phrase of the song. Then he began to make it his. It was very beautiful because it wasn't hurried and it was no longer a lament. I seemed to hear with what burning he had made it his, and what burning we had yet to make it ours, how we could cease lamenting. Freedom lurked around us and I understood, at last, that he could help us to be free if we would listen, that he would never be free until we did. Yet, there was no battle in his face now, I heard what he had gone through, and would continue to go through until he came to rest in earth. He had made it his: that long line, of which we knew only Mama and Daddy. And he was giving it back, as everything must be given back, so that, passing through death, it can live forever. I saw my mother's face again, and felt, for the first time, how the stones of the road she had walked on must have bruised her feet. I saw the moonlit road where my father's brother died. And it brought something else back to me, and carried me past it, I saw my little girl again and felt Isabel's tears again, and I felt my own tears begin to rise. And I was yet aware that this was only a moment, that the world waited outside, as hungry as a tiger, and that trouble stretched above us, longer than the sky.

Then it was over. Creole and Sonny let out their breath, both soaking wet, and grinning. There was a lot of applause and some of it was real. In the dark, the girl came by and I asked her to take drinks to the bandstand. There was a long pause, while they talked up there in the indigo light and after awhile I saw the girl put a Scotch and milk on top of the piano for Sonny. He didn't seem to notice it, but just before they started playing again, he sipped from it and looked toward me, and nodded. Then he put it back on top of the piano. For me, then, as they began to play again, it glowed and shook above my brother's head like the very cup of trembling.[7]

FOR ANALYSIS

1. Explain the title.

2. What is the relation between the opening events and the end of the story?

3. What function does the narrator's encounter with Sonny's friend at the beginning of the story (paras. 9–47) serve?

---

[7] See the Old Testament, Isaiah 51:17, 22–23: "Awake, awake, stand up, O Jerusalem, which hast drunk at the hand of the Lord the cup of his fury; thou hast drunken the dregs of the cup of trembling, and wrung them out. . . . Behold, I have taken out of thine hand the cup of trembling, even the dregs of the cup of my fury; thou shalt no more drink it again: But I will put it into the hand of them that afflict thee."

4. Does the story offer any explanation for Sonny's addiction? Explain.

5. What adjectives would you use to describe the **narrator?** Does he change in the course of the story? Explain.

6. What effects does Baldwin achieve by rearranging the order of events?

7. What does the final sentence mean?

MAKING CONNECTIONS

1. Compare and contrast the way racism is portrayed in this story with its portrayal in Bambara's "The Lesson" (p. 110).

2. Kafka's "A Hunger Artist" (p. 319) is also about an artist and the process of artistic creation. What similarities or differences do you find between Kafka's story and Baldwin's?

WRITING TOPICS

1. What does this story have to say about the sources of creativity?

2. Discuss the significance of the narrator's observations on the revival meeting (paras. 176–178) to the **theme** of the story.

CHINUA ACHEBE (B. 1930)

MARRIAGE IS A PRIVATE AFFAIR 1972

"Have you written to your dad yet?" asked Nene one afternoon as she sat with Nnaemeka in her room at 16 Kasanga Street, Lagos.[1]

"No. I've been thinking about it. I think it's better to tell him when I get home on leave!"

"But why? Your leave is such a long way off yet—six whole weeks. He should be let into our happiness now."

Nnaemeka was silent for a while, and then began very slowly as if he groped for his words: "I wish I were sure it would be happiness to him."

"Of course it must," replied Nene, a little surprised. "Why shouldn't it?" 5

"You have lived in Lagos all your life, and you know very little about people in remote parts of the country."

"That's what you always say. But I don't believe anybody will be so unlike other people that they will be unhappy when their sons are engaged to marry."

"Yes. They are most unhappy if the engagement is not arranged by them. In our case it's worse—you are not even an Ibo."

This was said so seriously and so bluntly that Nene could not find speech immediately. In the cosmopolitan atmosphere of the city it had always seemed to her something of a joke that a person's tribe could determine whom he married.

At last she said, "You don't really mean that he will object to your marrying 10 me simply on that account? I had always thought you Ibos were kindly disposed to other people."

"So we are. But when it comes to marriage, well, it's not quite so simple. And this," he added, "is not peculiar to the Ibos. If your father were alive and lived in the heart of Ibibio-land he would be exactly like my father."

"I don't know. But anyway, as your father is so fond of you, I'm sure he will forgive you soon enough. Come on then, be a good boy and send him a nice lovely letter . . ."

"It would not be wise to break the news to him by writing. A letter will bring it upon him with a shock. I'm quite sure about that."

"All right, honey, suit yourself. You know your father."

As Nnaemeka walked home that evening he turned over in his mind the dif- 15 ferent ways of overcoming his father's opposition, especially now that he had gone and found a girl for him. He had thought of showing his letter to Nene but decided on second thoughts not to, at least for the moment. He read it again when he got home and couldn't help smiling to himself. He remembered

---

[1] The former capital of Nigeria, Lagos is the largest city in sub-Saharan Africa.

Ugoye quite well, an Amazon of a girl who used to beat up all the boys, himself included, on the way to the stream, a complete dunce at school.

I have found a girl who will suit you admirably—Ugoye Nweke, the eldest daughter of our neighbour, Jacob Nweke. She has a proper Christian upbringing. When she stopped schooling some years ago her father (a man of sound judgment) sent her to live in the house of a pastor where she has received all the training a wife could need. Her Sunday School teacher has told me that she reads her Bible very fluently. I hope we shall begin negotiations when you come home in December.

On the second evening of his return from Lagos Nnaemeka sat with his father under a cassia tree. This was the old man's retreat where he went to read his Bible when the parching December sun had set and a fresh, reviving wind blew on the leaves.[2]

"Father," began Nnaemeka suddenly, "I have come to ask forgiveness."

"Forgiveness? For what, my son?" he asked in amazement.

"It's about this marriage question."

"Which marriage question?" 20

"I can't—we must—I mean it is impossible for me to marry Nweke's daughter."

"Impossible? Why?" asked his father.

"I don't love her."

"Nobody said you did. Why should you?" he asked.

"Marriage today is different . . ." 25

"Look here, my son," interrupted his father, "nothing is different. What one looks for in a wife are a good character and a Christian background."

Nnaemeka saw there was no hope along the present line of argument.

"Moreover," he said, "I am engaged to marry another girl who has all of Ugoye's good qualities, and who . . ."

His father did not believe his ears. "What did you say?" he asked slowly and disconcertingly.

"She is a good Christian," his son went on, "and a teacher in a Girls' School 30 in Lagos."

"Teacher, did you say? If you consider that a qualification for a good wife I should like to point out to you, Emeka, that no Christian woman should teach. St. Paul in his letter to the Corinthians says that women should keep silence." He rose slowly from his seat and paced forwards and backwards. This was his pet subject, and he condemned vehemently those church leaders who encouraged women to teach in their schools. After he had spent his emotion on a long homily he at last came back to his son's engagement, in a seemingly milder tone.

"Whose daughter is she, anyway?"

"She is Nene Atang."

---

[2] Although traditional Ibo religion centers on ancestor and nature worship, many Ibos became Christians under British colonial and missionary influence.

"What!" All the mildness was gone again. "Did you say Neneataga, what does that mean?"

"Nene Atang from Calabar. She is the only girl I can marry." This was a very 35 rash reply and Nnaemeka expected the storm to burst. But it did not. His father merely walked away into his room. This was most unexpected and perplexed Nnaemeka. His father's silence was infinitely more menacing than a flood of threatening speech. That night the old man did not eat.

When he sent for Nnaemeka a day later he applied all possible ways of dissuasion. But the young man's heart was hardened, and his father eventually gave him up as lost.

"I owe it to you, my son, as a duty to show you what is right and what is wrong. Whoever put this idea into your head might as well have cut your throat. It is Satan's work." He waved his son away.

"You will change your mind, Father, when you know Nene."

"I shall never see her," was the reply. From that night the father scarcely spoke to his son. He did not, however, cease hoping that he would realize how serious was the danger he was heading for. Day and night he put him in his prayers.

Nnaemeka, for his own part, was very deeply affected by his father's grief. 40 But he kept hoping that it would pass away. If it had occurred to him that never in the history of his people had a man married a woman who spoke a different tongue, he might have been less optimistic. "It has never been heard," was the verdict of an old man speaking a few weeks later. In that short sentence he spoke for all of his people. This man had come with others to commiserate with Okeke when news went round about his son's behaviour. By that time the son had gone back to Lagos.

"It has never been heard," said the old man again with a sad shake of his head.

"What did Our Lord say?" asked another gentleman. "Sons shall rise against their Fathers; it is there in the Holy Book."

"It is the beginning of the end," said another.

The discussion thus tending to become theological, Madubogwu, a highly practical man, brought it down once more to the ordinary level.

"Have you thought of consulting a native doctor about your son?" he asked 45 Nnaemeka's father.

"He isn't sick," was the reply.

"What is he then? The boy's mind is diseased and only a good herbalist can bring him back to his right senses. The medicine he requires is *Amalile*, the same that women apply with success to recapture their husbands' straying affection."

"Madubogwu is right," said another gentleman. "This thing calls for medicine."

"I shall not call in a native doctor." Nnaemeka's father was known to be obstinately ahead of his more superstitious neighbours in these matters. "I will not be another Mrs. Ochuba. If my son wants to kill himself let him do it with his own hands. It is not for me to help him."

"But it was her fault," said Madubogwu. "She ought to have gone to an hon- 50 est herbalist. She was a clever woman, nevertheless."

"She was a wicked murderess," said Jonathan who rarely argued with his neighbours because, he often said, they were incapable of reasoning. "The medicine was prepared for her husband, it was his name they called in its preparation and I am sure it would have been perfectly beneficial to him. It was wicked to put it into the herbalist's food, and say you were only trying it out."

Six months later, Nnaemeka was showing his young wife a short letter from his father:

It amazes me that you could be so unfeeling as to send me your wedding picture. I would have sent it back. But on further thought I decided just to cut off your wife and send it back to you because I have nothing to do with her. How I wish that I had nothing to do with you either.

When Nene read through this letter and looked at the mutilated picture her eyes filled with tears, and she began to sob.

"Don't cry, my darling," said her husband. "He is essentially good-natured and will one day look more kindly on our marriage." But years passed and that one day did not come.

For eight years, Okeke would have nothing to do with his son, Nnaemeka.   55 Only three times (when Nnaemeka asked to come home and spend his leave) did he write to him.

"I can't have you in my house," he replied on one occasion. "It can be of no interest to me where or how you spend your leave—or your life, for that matter."

The prejudice against Nnaemeka's marriage was not confined to his little village. In Lagos, especially among his people who worked there, it showed itself in a different way. Their women, when they met at their village meeting, were not hostile to Nene. Rather, they paid her such excessive deference as to make her feel she was not one of them. But as time went on, Nene gradually broke through some of this prejudice and even began to make friends among them. Slowly and grudgingly they began to admit that she kept her home much better than most of them.

The story eventually got to the little village in the heart of the Ibo country that Nnaemeka and his young wife were a most happy couple. But his father was one of the few people who knew nothing about this. He always displayed so much temper whenever his son's name was mentioned that everyone avoided it in his presence. By a tremendous effort of will he had succeeded in pushing his son to the back of his mind. The strain had nearly killed him but he had persevered, and won.

Then one day he received a letter from Nene, and in spite of himself he began to glance through it perfunctorily until all of a sudden the expression on his face changed and he began to read more carefully.

. . . Our two sons, from the day they learnt that they have a grandfather, have insisted on being taken to him. I find it impossible to tell them that you will not see them. I implore you to allow Nnaemeka to bring them home for a short time during his leave next month. I shall remain here in Lagos . . .

The old man at once felt the resolution he had built up over so many years 60 falling in. He was telling himself that he must not give in. He tried to steel his heart against all emotional appeals. It was a reenactment of that other struggle. He leaned against a window and looked out. The sky was overcast with heavy black clouds and a high wind began to blow filling the air with dust and dry leaves. It was one of those rare occasions when even Nature takes a hand in a human fight. Very soon it began to rain, the first rain in the year. It came down in large sharp drops and was accompanied by the lightning and thunder which mark a change of season. Okeke was trying hard not to think of his two grandsons. But he knew he was now fighting a losing battle. He tried to hum a favourite hymn but the pattering of large rain drops on the roof broke up the tune. His mind immediately returned to the children. How could he shut his door against them? By a curious mental process he imagined them standing, sad and forsaken, under the harsh angry weather—shut out from his house.

That night he hardly slept, from remorse—and a vague fear that he might die without making it up to them.

For Analysis

1. Who in this story sees marriage as a private affair? Who does not? Why?

2. What role does religion play in this story? What different kinds of religious belief are presented? How does history—in particular, the history of the colonization of Nigeria by the British—play a role in different characters' attitudes about marriage and other things?

3. In some ways, both the taboo against marrying outside the tribe and the desire to know one's grandchildren are about blood—about kinship, relatedness. What does it mean that one trumps the other here?

Making Connections

1. At first, this story seems to be Nnaemeka's, and secondarily Nene's. At some point, it becomes as much about Nnaemeka's father. How does Achebe make this shift? Compare "Marriage Is a Private Affair" to Lethem's "Super Goat Man" (p. 382), which splits its attention to two characters in very different ways.

2. Okeke reacts to his son's news according to Ibo tradition. Compare his relation to tradition to those represented in "Connecting Poems: Voices of Experience" (p. 176).

Writing Topics

1. Compare the seemingly old-fashioned attitudes about marriage portrayed in Achebe's story to your parents' attitudes. Is there someone—a person who could be said to be different from you in some way—whom one or both of your parents would have difficulty accepting as your spouse?

2. Imagine this story told entirely from Nene's point of view. How would the emphasis shift? What would the most dramatic moments be?

ALICE WALKER   (B. 1944)

EVERYDAY USE   1973

FOR YOUR GRANDMAMA

I will wait for her in the yard that Maggie and I made so clean and wavy yesterday afternoon. A yard like this is more comfortable than most people know. It is not just a yard. It is like an extended living room. When the hard clay is swept clean as a floor and the fine sand around the edges lined with tiny, irregular grooves anyone can come and sit and look up into the elm tree and wait for the breezes that never come inside the house.

Maggie will be nervous until after her sister goes: she will stand hopelessly in corners homely and ashamed of the burn scars down her arms and legs, eyeing her sister with a mixture of envy and awe. She thinks her sister has held life always in the palm of one hand, that "no" is a word the world never learned to say to her.

You've no doubt seen those TV shows where the child who has "made it" is confronted, as a surprise, by her own mother and father, tottering in weakly from backstage. (A pleasant surprise, of course: What would they do if parent and child came on the show only to curse out and insult each other?) On TV mother and child embrace and smile into each other's faces. Sometimes the mother and father weep, the child wraps them in her arms and leans across the table to tell how she would not have made it without their help. I have seen these programs.

Sometimes I dream a dream in which Dee and I are suddenly brought together on a TV program of this sort. Out of a dark and soft-seated limousine I am ushered into a bright room filled with many people. There I meet a smiling, gray, sporty man like Johnny Carson who shakes my hand and tells me what a fine girl I have. Then we are on the stage and Dee is embracing me with tears in her eyes. She pins on my dress a large orchid, even though she has told me once that she thinks orchids are tacky flowers.

In real life I am a large, big-boned woman with rough, man-working hands. 5 In the winter I wear flannel nightgowns to bed and overalls during the day. I can kill and clean a hog as mercilessly as a man. My fat keeps me hot in zero weather. I can work outside all day, breaking ice to get water for washing. I can eat pork liver cooked over the open fire minutes after it comes steaming from the hog. One winter I knocked a bull calf straight in the brain between the eyes with a sledge hammer and had the meat hung up to chill before nightfall. But of course all this does not show on television. I am the way my daughter would want me to be: a hundred pounds lighter, my skin like an uncooked barley pancake. My hair glistens in the hot bright lights. Johnny Carson has much to do to keep up with my quick and witty tongue.

But that is a mistake. I know even before I wake up. Who ever knew a Johnson with a quick tongue? Who can even imagine me looking a strange white man in the eye? It seems to me I have talked to them always with one foot raised in flight, with my head turned in whichever way is farthest from them. Dee, though. She would always look anyone in the eye. Hesitation was no part of her nature.

"How do I look, Mama?" Maggie says, showing just enough of her thin body enveloped in pink skirt and red blouse for me to know she's there, almost hidden by the door.

"Come out into the yard," I say.

Have you ever seen a lame animal, perhaps a dog run over by some careless person rich enough to own a car, sidle up to someone who is ignorant enough to be kind to him? That is the way my Maggie walks. She has been like this, chin on chest, eyes on ground, feet in shuffle, ever since the fire that burned the other house to the ground.

Dee is lighter than Maggie, with nicer hair and a fuller figure. She's a woman now, though sometimes I forget. How long ago was it that the other house burned? Ten, twelve years? Sometimes I can still hear the flames and feel Maggie's arms sticking to me, her hair smoking and her dress falling off her in little black papery flakes. Her eyes seemed stretched open, blazed open by the flames reflected in them. And Dee. I see her standing off under the sweet gum tree she used to dig gum out of; a look of concentration on her face as she watched the last dingy gray board of the house fall in toward the red-hot brick chimney. Why don't you do a dance around the ashes? I'd wanted to ask her. She had hated the house that much. 10

I used to think she hated Maggie, too. But that was before we raised the money, the church and me, to send her to Augusta to school. She used to read to us without pity; forcing words, lies, other folks' habits, whole lives upon us two, sitting trapped and ignorant underneath her voice. She washed us in a river of make-believe, burned us with a lot of knowledge we didn't necessarily need to know. Pressed us to her with the serious way she read, to shove us away at just the moment, like dimwits, we seemed about to understand.

Dee wanted nice things. A yellow organdy dress to wear to her graduation from high school; black pumps to match a green suit she'd made from an old suit somebody gave me. She was determined to stare down any disaster in her efforts. Her eyelids would not flicker for minutes at a time. Often I fought off the temptation to shake her. At sixteen she had a style of her own: and knew what style was.

I never had an education myself. After second grade the school was closed down. Don't ask me why: in 1927 colored asked fewer questions than they do now. Sometimes Maggie reads to me. She stumbles along good-naturedly but can't see well. She knows she is not bright. Like good looks and money, quickness passed her by. She will marry John Thomas (who has mossy teeth in an earnest face) and then I'll be free to sit here and I guess just sing church songs to myself. Although I never was a good singer. Never could carry a tune. I was always better at a man's job. I used to love to milk till I was hoofed in the side in '49. Cows are soothing and slow and don't bother you, unless you try to milk them the wrong way.

I have deliberately turned my back on the house. It is three rooms, just like the one that burned, except the roof is tin; they don't make shingle roofs any more. There are no real windows, just some holes cut in the sides, like the port-holes in a ship, but not round and not square, with rawhide holding the shutters up on the outside. This house is in a pasture, too, like the other one. No doubt when Dee sees it she will want to tear it down. She wrote me once that no matter where we "choose" to live, she will manage to come see us. But she will never bring her friends. Maggie and I thought about this and Maggie asked me, "Mama, when did Dee ever *have* any friends?"

She had a few. Furtive boys in pink shirts hanging about on washday after 15 school. Nervous girls who never laughed. Impressed with her they worshiped the well-turned phrase, the cute shape, the scalding humor that erupted like bubbles in lye. She read to them.

When she was courting Jimmy T she didn't have much time to pay to us, but turned all her faultfinding power on him. He *flew* to marry a cheap gal from a family of ignorant flashy people. She hardly had time to recompose herself.

When she comes I will meet—but there they are!

Maggie attempts to make a dash for the house, in her shuffling way, but I stay her with my hand. "Come back here," I say. And she stops and tries to dig a well in the sand with her toe.

It is hard to see them clearly through the strong sun. But even the first glimpse of leg out of the car tells me it is Dee. Her feet were always neat-looking, as if God himself had shaped them with a certain style. From the other side of the car comes a short, stocky man. Hair is all over his head a foot long and hanging from his chin like a kinky mule tail. I hear Maggie suck in her breath. "Uhnnnh," is what it sounds like. Like when you see the wriggling end of a snake just in front of your foot on the road. "Uhnnnh."

Dee next. A dress down to the ground, in this hot weather. A dress so loud it 20 hurts my eyes. There are yellows and oranges enough to throw back the light of the sun. I feel my whole face warming from the heat waves it throws out. Earrings, too, gold and hanging down to her shoulders. Bracelets dangling and making noises when she moves her arm up to shake the folds of the dress out of her armpits. The dress is loose and flows, and as she walks closer, I like it. I hear Maggie go "Uhnnnh" again. It is her sister's hair. It stands straight up like the wool on a sheep. It is black as night and around the edges are two long pigtails that rope about like small lizards disappearing behind her ears.

"Wa-su-zo-Tean-o!" she says, coming on in that gliding way the dress makes her move. The short stocky fellow with the hair to his navel is all grinning and he follows up with "Asalamalakim, my mother and sister!" He moves to hug

Maggie but she falls back, right up against the back of my chair. I feel her trembling there and when I look up I see the perspiration falling off her chin.

"Don't get up," says Dee. Since I am stout it takes something of a push. You can see me trying to move a second or two before I make it. She turns, showing white heels through her sandals, and goes back to the car. Out she peeks next with a Polaroid. She stoops down quickly and lines up picture after picture of me sitting there in front of the house with Maggie cowering behind me. She never takes a shot without making sure the house is included. When a cow comes nibbling around the edge of the yard she snaps it and me and Maggie *and* the house. Then she puts the Polaroid in the back seat of the car, and comes up and kisses me on the forehead.

Meanwhile Asalamalakim is going through motions with Maggie's hand. Maggie's hand is as limp as a fish, and probably as cold, despite the sweat, and she keeps trying to pull it back. It looks like Asalamalakim wants to shake hands but wants to do it fancy. Or maybe he don't know how people shake hands. Anyhow, he soon gives up on Maggie.

"Well," I say. "Dee."

"No, Mama," she says. "Not 'Dee,' Wangero Leewanika Kemanjo!"   25

"What happened to 'Dee'?" I wanted to know.

"She's dead," Wangero said. "I couldn't bear it any longer being named after the people who oppress me."

"You know as well as me you was named after your aunt Dicie," I said. Dicie is my sister. She named Dee. We called her "Big Dee" after Dee was born.

"But who was *she* named after?" asked Wangero.

"I guess after Grandma Dee," I said.   30

"And who was she named after?" asked Wangero.

"Her mother," I said, and saw Wangero was getting tired. "That's about as far back as I can trace it," I said. Though, in fact, I probably could have carried it back beyond the Civil War through the branches.

"Well," said Asalamalakim, "there you are."

"Uhnnnh," I heard Maggie say.

"There I was not," I said, "before 'Dicie' cropped up in our family, so why   35 should I try to trace it that far back?"

He just stood there grinning, looking down on me like somebody inspecting a Model A car. Every once in a while he and Wangero sent eye signals over my head.

"How do you pronounce this name?" I asked.

"You don't have to call me by it if you don't want to," said Wangero.

"Why shouldn't I?" I asked. "If that's what you want us to call you, we'll call you."

"I know it might sound awkward at first," said Wangero.   40

"I'll get used to it," I said. "Ream it out again."

Well, soon we got the name out of the way. Asalamalakim had a name twice as long and three times as hard. After I tripped over it two or three times he told me to just call him Hakim-a-barber. I wanted to ask him was he a barber, but I didn't really think he was, so I didn't ask.

"You must belong to those beef-cattle peoples down the road," I said. They said "Asalamalakim" when they met you, too, but they didn't shake hands. Always too busy: feeding the cattle, fixing the fences, putting up salt-lick shelters, throwing down hay. When the white folks poisoned some of the herd the men stayed up all night with rifles in their hands. I walked a mile and a half just to see the sight.

Hakim-a-barber said, "I accept some of their doctrines, but farming and raising cattle is not my style." (They didn't tell me, and I didn't ask, whether Wangero [Dee] had really gone and married him.)

We sat down to eat and right away he said he didn't eat collards and pork   45 was unclean. Wangero, though, went on through the chitlins and corn bread, the greens and everything else. She talked a blue streak over the sweet potatoes. Everything delighted her. Even the fact that we still used the benches her daddy made for the table when we couldn't afford to buy chairs.

"Oh, Mama!" she cried. Then turned to Hakim-a-barber. "I never knew how lovely these benches are. You can feel the rump prints," she said, running her hands underneath her and along the bench. Then she gave a sigh and her hand closed over Grandma Dee's butter dish. "That's it!" she said. "I knew there was something I wanted to ask you if I could have." She jumped up from the table and went over in the corner where the churn stood, the milk in its clabber by now. She looked at the churn and looked at it.

"This churn top is what I need," she said. "Didn't Uncle Buddy whittle it out of a tree you all used to have?"

"Yes," I said.

"Uh huh," she said happily. "And I want the dasher, too."

"Uncle Buddy whittle that, too?" asked the barber.   50

Dee (Wangero) looked up at me.

"Aunt Dee's first husband whittled the dash," said Maggie so low you almost couldn't hear her. "His name was Henry, but they called him Stash."

"Maggie's brain is like an elephant's," Wangero said, laughing. "I can use the churn top as a centerpiece for the alcove table," she said, sliding a plate over the churn, "and I'll think of something artistic to do with the dasher."

When she finished wrapping the dasher the handle stuck out. I took it for a moment in my hands. You didn't even have to look close to see where hands pushing the dasher up and down to make butter had left a kind of sink in the wood. In fact, there were a lot of small sinks; you could see where thumbs and fingers had sunk into the wood. It was beautiful light yellow wood, from a tree that grew in the yard where Big Dee and Stash had lived.

After dinner Dee (Wangero) went to the trunk at the foot of my bed and   55 started rifling through it. Maggie hung back in the kitchen over the dishpan. Out came Wangero with two quilts. They had been pieced by Grandma Dee and then Big Dee and me had hung them on the quilt frames on the front porch and quilted them. One was in the Lone Star pattern. The other was Walk Around the Mountain. In both of them were scraps of dresses Grandma Dee had worn fifty and more years ago. Bits and pieces of Grandpa Jarrell's Paisley shirts. And one teeny faded blue piece, about the size of a penny matchbox, that was from Great Grandpa Ezra's uniform that he wore in the Civil War.

"Mama," Wangero said sweet as a bird. "Can I have these old quilts?"

I heard something fall in the kitchen, and a minute later the kitchen door slammed.

"Why don't you take one or two of the others?" I asked. "These old things was just done by me and Big Dee from some tops your grandma pieced before she died."

"No," said Wangero. "I don't want those. They are stitched around the borders by machine."

"That'll make them last better," I said.   60

"That's not the point," said Wangero. "These are all pieces of dresses Grandma used to wear. She did all this stitching by hand. Imagine!" She held the quilts securely in her arms, stroking them.

"Some of the pieces, like those lavender ones, come from old clothes her mother handed down to her," I said, moving up to touch the quilts. Dee (Wangero) moved back just enough so that I couldn't reach the quilts. They already belonged to her.

"Imagine!" she breathed again, clutching them closely to her bosom.

"The truth is," I said, "I promised to give them quilts to Maggie, for when she marries John Thomas."

She gasped like a bee had stung her.   65

"Maggie can't appreciate these quilts!" she said. "She'd probably be backward enough to put them to everyday use."

"I reckon she would," I said. "God knows I been saving 'em for long enough with nobody using 'em. I hope she will!" I didn't want to bring up how I had offered Dee (Wangero) a quilt when she went away to college. Then she had told me they were old fashioned, out of style.

"But they're *priceless*!" she was saying now, furiously; for she has a temper. "Maggie would put them on the bed and in five years they'd be in rags. Less than that!"

"She can always make some more," I said. "Maggie knows how to quilt."

Dee (Wangero) looked at me with hatred. "You just will not understand.   70 The point is these quilts, *these* quilts!"

"Well," I said, stumped. "What would *you* do with them?"

"Hang them," she said. As if that was the only thing you *could* do with quilts.

Maggie by now was standing in the door. I could almost hear the sound her feet made as they scraped over each other.

"She can have them, Mama," she said, like somebody used to never winning anything, or having anything reserved for her. "I can 'member Grandma Dee without the quilts."

I looked at her hard. She had filled her bottom lip with checkerberry snuff   75 and it gave her face a kind of dopey, hangdog look. It was Grandma Dee and Big Dee who taught her how to quilt herself. She stood there with her scarred hands hidden in the folds of her skirt. She looked at her sister with something like fear but she wasn't mad at her. This was Maggie's portion. This was the way she knew God to work.

When I looked at her like that something hit me in the top of my head and ran down to the soles of my feet. Just like when I'm in church and the spirit of God touches me and I get happy and shout. I did something I never had done before: hugged Maggie to me, then dragged her on into the room, snatched the quilts out of Miss Wangero's hands and dumped them into Maggie's lap. Maggie just sat there on my bed with her mouth open.

"Take one or two of the others," I said to Dee.

But she turned without a word and went out to Hakim-a-barber.

"You just don't understand," she said, as Maggie and I came out to the car.

"What don't I understand?" I wanted to know.   80

"Your heritage," she said. And then she turned to Maggie, kissed her, and said, "You ought to try to make something of yourself, too, Maggie. It's really a new day for us. But from the way you and Mama still live you'd never know it."

She put on some sunglasses that hid everything above the tip of her nose and her chin.

Maggie smiled; maybe at the sunglasses. But a real smile, not scared. After we watched the car dust settle I asked Maggie to bring me a dip of snuff. And then the two of us sat there just enjoying, until it was time to go in the house and go to bed.

FOR ANALYSIS

1. What are the **narrator's** outstanding traits, her weaknesses, and her strengths?

2. How would you describe the narrator's feelings about her daughter Dee? About her daughter Maggie?

3. How would you describe the narrator's descriptions of herself? Are her actions consistent with the kind of person she says she is? Explain.

4. Why does the narrator recall the burning of the house? How does this event from the past help the reader understand the present action?

5. What are the sources of the story's humor?

6. What does Dee's boyfriend, Asalamalakim, represent?

7. Why does the narrator give the quilts to Maggie?

8. Explain the title. What is the meaning of the subtitle, "For Your Grandmama"?

MAKING CONNECTIONS

Compare Dee in this story and Miss Moore in Bambara's "The Lesson" (p. 110) as characters whose intellectual and educational superiority enables them to unsettle the tranquillity of those around them.

WRITING TOPICS

1. Analyze the opening two paragraphs of the story, showing how they set the **tone** and establish the tension of the story.

2. Write an essay analyzing the **conflict** in the story and the way it is resolved. Is the resolution satisfying? Explain.

SHERMAN ALEXIE (B. 1966)

THIS IS WHAT IT MEANS
TO SAY PHOENIX, ARIZONA 1993

Just after Victor lost his job at the BIA,[1] he also found out that his father had died of a heart attack in Phoenix, Arizona. Victor hadn't seen his father in a few years, only talked to him on the telephone once or twice, but there still was a genetic pain, which was soon to be pain as real and immediate as a broken bone.

Victor didn't have any money. Who does have money on a reservation, except the cigarette and fireworks salespeople? His father had a savings account waiting to be claimed, but Victor needed to find a way to get to Phoenix. Victor's mother was just as poor as he was, and the rest of his family didn't have any use at all for him. So Victor called the Tribal Council.

"Listen," Victor said. "My father just died. I need some money to get to Phoenix to make arrangements."

"Now, Victor," the council said. "You know we're having a difficult time financially."

"But I thought the council had special funds set aside for stuff like this." 5

"Now, Victor, we do have some money available for the proper return of tribal members' bodies. But I don't think we have enough to bring your father all the way back from Phoenix."

"Well," Victor said. "It ain't going to cost all that much. He had to be cremated. Things were kind of ugly. He died of a heart attack in his trailer and nobody found him for a week. It was really hot, too. You get the picture."

"Now, Victor, we're sorry for your loss and the circumstances. But we can really only afford to give you one hundred dollars."

"That's not even enough for a plane ticket."

"Well, you might consider driving down to Phoenix." 10

"I don't have a car. Besides, I was going to drive my father's pickup back up here."

"Now, Victor," the council said. "We're sure there is somebody who could drive you to Phoenix. Or is there somebody who could lend you the rest of the money?"

"You know there ain't nobody around with that kind of money."

"Well, we're sorry, Victor, but that's the best we can do."

Victor accepted the Tribal Council's offer. What else could he do? So he 15
signed the proper papers, picked up his check, and walked over to the Trading Post to cash it.

---

[1] The Bureau of Indian Affairs, a division of the U.S. Department of the Interior, oversees the administration of federal programs for American Indians, Indian tribes, and Alaskan natives.

While Victor stood in line, he watched Thomas Builds-the-Fire standing near the magazine rack, talking to himself. Like he always did. Thomas was a storyteller that nobody wanted to listen to. That's like being a dentist in a town where everybody has false teeth.

Victor and Thomas Builds-the-Fire were the same age, had grown up and played in the dirt together. Ever since Victor could remember, it was Thomas who always had something to say.

Once, when they were seven years old, when Victor's father still lived with the family, Thomas closed his eyes and told Victor this story: "Your father's heart is weak. He is afraid of his own family. He is afraid of you. Late at night he sits in the dark. Watches the television until there's nothing but that white noise. Sometimes he feels like he wants to buy a motorcycle and ride away. He wants to run and hide. He doesn't want to be found."

Thomas Builds-the-Fire had known that Victor's father was going to leave, knew it before anyone. Now Victor stood in the Trading Post with a one-hundred-dollar check in his hand, wondering if Thomas knew that Victor's father was dead, if he knew what was going to happen next.

Just then Thomas looked at Victor, smiled, and walked over to him.   20

"Victor, I'm sorry about your father," Thomas said.

"How did you know about it?" Victor asked.

"I heard it on the wind. I heard it from the birds. I felt it in the sunlight. Also, your mother was just in here crying."

"Oh," Victor said and looked around the Trading Post. All the other Indians stared, surprised that Victor was even talking to Thomas. Nobody talked to Thomas anymore because he told the same damn stories over and over again. Victor was embarrassed, but he thought that Thomas might be able to help him. Victor felt a sudden need for tradition.

"I can lend you the money you need," Thomas said suddenly. "But you have   25
to take me with you."

"I can't take your money," Victor said. "I mean, I haven't hardly talked to you in years. We're not really friends anymore."

"I didn't say we were friends. I said you had to take me with you."

"Let me think about it."

Victor went home with his one hundred dollars and sat at the kitchen table. He held his head in his hands and thought about Thomas Builds-the-Fire, remembered little details, tears and scars, the bicycle they shared for a summer, so many stories.

Thomas Builds-the-Fire sat on the bicycle, waited in Victor's yard. He   30
was ten years old and skinny. His hair was dirty because it was the Fourth of July.

"Victor," Thomas yelled. "Hurry up. We're going to miss the fireworks."

After a few minutes, Victor ran out of his house, jumped the porch railing, and landed gracefully on the sidewalk.

"And the judges award him a 9.95, the highest score of the summer," Thomas said, clapped, laughed.

"That was perfect, cousin," Victor said. "And it's my turn to ride the bike."

Thomas gave up the bike and they headed for the fairgrounds. It was nearly 35 dark and the fireworks were about to start.

"You know," Thomas said. "It's strange how us Indians celebrate the Fourth of July. It ain't like it was *our* independence everybody was fighting for."

"You think about things too much," Victor said. "It's just supposed to be fun. Maybe Junior will be there."

"Which Junior? Everybody on this reservation is named Junior."

And they both laughed.

The fireworks were small, hardly more than a few bottle rockets and a 40 fountain. But it was enough for two Indian boys. Years later, they would need much more.

Afterwards, sitting in the dark, fighting off mosquitoes, Victor turned to Thomas Builds-the-Fire.

"Hey," Victor said. "Tell me a story."

Thomas closed his eyes and told this story: "There were these two Indian boys who wanted to be warriors. But it was too late to be warriors in the old way. All the horses were gone. So the two Indian boys stole a car and drove to the city. They parked the stolen car in front of the police station and then hitchhiked back home to the reservation. When they got back, all their friends cheered and their parents' eyes shone with pride. *You were very brave*, everybody said to the two Indian boys. *Very brave*."

"Ya-hey," Victor said. "That's a good one. I wish I could be a warrior."

"Me, too," Thomas said.   45

They went home together in the dark, Thomas on the bike now, Victor on foot. They walked through shadows and light from streetlamps.

"We've come a long ways," Thomas said. "We have outdoor lighting."

"All I need is the stars," Victor said. "And besides, you still think about things too much."

They separated then, each headed for home, both laughing all the way.

Victor sat at his kitchen table. He counted his one hundred dollars again and 50 again. He knew he needed more to make it to Phoenix and back. He knew he needed Thomas Builds-the-Fire. So he put his money in his wallet and opened the front door to find Thomas on the porch.

"Ya-hey, Victor," Thomas said. "I knew you'd call me."

Thomas walked into the living room and sat down on Victor's favorite chair.

"I've got some money saved up," Thomas said. "It's enough to get us down there, but you have to get us back."

"I've got this hundred dollars," Victor said. "And my dad had a savings account I'm going to claim."

"How much in your dad's account?"   55

"Enough. A few hundred."

"Sounds good. When we leaving?"

When they were fifteen and had long since stopped being friends, Victor and Thomas got into a fistfight. That is, Victor was really drunk and beat Thomas up for no reason at all. All the other Indian boys stood around and watched it happen. Junior was there and so were Lester, Seymour, and a lot of others. The beating might have gone on until Thomas was dead if Norma Many Horses hadn't come along and stopped it.

"Hey, you boys," Norma yelled and jumped out of her car. "Leave him alone."

If it had been someone else, even another man, the Indian boys would've just ignored the warnings. But Norma was a warrior. She was powerful. She could have picked up any two of the boys and smashed their skulls together. But worse than that, she would have dragged them all over to some tipi and made them listen to some elder tell a dusty old story.

The Indian boys scattered, and Norma walked over to Thomas and picked him up.

"Hey, little man, are you okay?" she asked.

Thomas gave her a thumbs up.

"Why they always picking on you?"

Thomas shook his head, closed his eyes, but no stories came to him, no words or music. He just wanted to go home, to lie in his bed and let his dreams tell his stories for him.

Thomas Builds-the-Fire and Victor sat next to each other in the airplane, coach section. A tiny white woman had the window seat. She was busy twisting her body into pretzels. She was flexible.

"I have to ask," Thomas said, and Victor closed his eyes in embarrassment.

"Don't," Victor said.

"Excuse me, miss," Thomas asked. "Are you a gymnast or something?"

"There's no something about it," she said. "I was first alternate on the 1980 Olympic team."

"Really?" Thomas asked.

"Really."

"I mean, you used to be a world-class athlete?" Thomas asked.

"My husband still thinks I am."

Thomas Builds-the-Fire smiled. She was a mental gymnast, too. She pulled her leg straight up against her body so that she could've kissed her kneecap.

"I wish I could do that," Thomas said.

Victor was ready to jump out of the plane. Thomas, that crazy Indian storyteller with ratty old braids and broken teeth, was flirting with a beautiful Olympic gymnast. Nobody back home on the reservation would ever believe it.

"Well," the gymnast said. "It's easy. Try it."

Thomas grabbed at his leg and tried to pull it up into the same position as the gymnast. He couldn't even come close, which made Victor and the gymnast laugh.

"Hey," she asked. "You two are Indian, right?" 80

"Full-blood," Victor said.

"Not me," Thomas said. "I'm half magician on my mother's side and half clown on my father's."

They all laughed.

"What are your names?" she asked.

"Victor and Thomas." 85

"Mine is Cathy. Pleased to meet you all."

The three of them talked for the duration of the flight. Cathy the gymnast complained about the government, how they screwed the 1980 Olympic team by boycotting.[2]

"Sounds like you all got a lot in common with Indians," Thomas said.

Nobody laughed.

After the plane landed in Phoenix and they had all found their way to the 90 terminal, Cathy the gymnast smiled and waved good-bye.

"She was really nice," Thomas said.

"Yeah, but everybody talks to everybody on airplanes," Victor said. "It's too bad we can't always be that way."

"You always used to tell me I think too much," Thomas said. "Now it sounds like you do."

"Maybe I caught it from you."

"Yeah." 95

Thomas and Victor rode in a taxi to the trailer where Victor's father died.

"Listen," Victor said as they stopped in front of the trailer. "I never told you I was sorry for beating you up that time."

"Oh, it was nothing. We were just kids and you were drunk."

"Yeah, but I'm still sorry."

"That's all right." 100

Victor paid for the taxi and the two of them stood in the hot Phoenix summer. They could smell the trailer.

"This ain't going to be nice," Victor said. "You don't have to go in."

"You're going to need help."

Victor walked to the front door and opened it. The stink rolled out and made them both gag. Victor's father had lain in that trailer for a week in hundred-degree temperatures before anyone found him. And the only reason anyone found him was because of the smell. They needed dental records to identify him. That's exactly what the coroner said. They needed dental records.

"Oh, man," Victor said. "I don't know if I can do this." 105

"Well, then don't."

---

[2] The United States withdrew from the 1980 Olympics in Moscow to protest the Soviet Union's invasion of Afghanistan in 1979.

"But there might be something valuable in there."

"I thought his money was in the bank."

"It is. I was talking about pictures and letters and stuff like that."

"Oh," Thomas said as he held his breath and followed Victor into the trailer. 110

When Victor was twelve, he stepped into an underground wasp nest. His foot was caught in the hole, and no matter how hard he struggled, Victor couldn't pull free. He might have died there, stung a thousand times, if Thomas Builds-the-Fire had not come by.

"Run," Thomas yelled and pulled Victor's foot from the hole. They ran then, hard as they ever had, faster than Billy Mills, faster than Jim Thorpe, faster than the wasps could fly.

Victor and Thomas ran until they couldn't breathe, ran until it was cold and dark outside, ran until they were lost and it took hours to find their way home. All the way back, Victor counted his stings.

"Seven," Victor said. "My lucky number."

Victor didn't find much to keep in the trailer. Only a photo album and a 115 stereo. Everything else had that smell stuck in it or was useless anyway.

"I guess this is all," Victor said. "It ain't much."

"Better than nothing," Thomas said.

"Yeah, and I do have the pickup."

"Yeah," Thomas said. "It's in good shape."

"Dad was good about that stuff." 120

"Yeah, I remember your dad."

"Really?" Victor asked. "What do you remember?"

Thomas Builds-the-Fire closed his eyes and told this story: "I remember when I had this dream that told me to go to Spokane, to stand by the Falls in the middle of the city and wait for a sign. I knew I had to go there but I didn't have a car. Didn't have a license. I was only thirteen. So I walked all the way, took me all day, and I finally made it to the Falls. I stood there for an hour waiting. Then your dad came walking up. *What the hell are you doing here?* he asked me. I said, *Waiting for a vision.* Then your father said, *All you're going to get here is mugged.* So he drove me over to Denny's, bought me dinner, and then drove me home to the reservation. For a long time I was mad because I thought my dreams had lied to me. But they didn't. Your dad was my vision. *Take care of each other* is what my dreams were saying. *Take care of each other.*"

Victor was quiet for a long time. He searched his mind for memories of his father, found the good ones, found a few bad ones, added it all up, and smiled.

"My father never told me about finding you in Spokane," Victor said. 125

"He said he wouldn't tell anybody. Didn't want me to get in trouble. But he said I had to watch out for you as part of the deal."

"Really?"

"Really. Your father said you would need the help. He was right."

"That's why you came down here with me, isn't it?" Victor asked.

"I came because of your father."   130

Victor and Thomas climbed into the pickup, drove over to the bank, and claimed the three hundred dollars in the savings account.

Thomas Builds-the-Fire could fly.

Once, he jumped off the roof of the tribal school and flapped his arms like a crazy eagle. And he flew. For a second, he hovered, suspended above all the other Indian boys who were too smart or too scared to jump.

"He's flying," Junior yelled, and Seymour was busy looking for the trick wires or mirrors. But it was real. As real as the dirt when Thomas lost altitude and crashed to the ground.

He broke his arm in two places.   135

"He broke his wing," Victor chanted, and the other Indian boys joined in, made it a tribal song.

"He broke his wing, he broke his wing, he broke his wing," all the Indian boys chanted as they ran off, flapping their wings, wishing they could fly, too. They hated Thomas for his courage, his brief moment as a bird. Everybody has dreams about flying. Thomas flew.

One of his dreams came true for just a second, just enough to make it real.

Victor's father, his ashes, fit in one wooden box with enough left over to fill a cardboard box.

"He always was a big man," Thomas said.   140

Victor carried part of his father and Thomas carried the rest out to the pickup. They set him down carefully behind the seats, put a cowboy hat on the wooden box and a Dodgers cap on the cardboard box. That's the way it was supposed to be.

"Ready to head back home?" Victor asked.

"It's going to be a long drive."

"Yeah, take a couple days, maybe."

"We can take turns," Thomas said.   145

"Okay," Victor said, but they didn't take turns. Victor drove for sixteen hours straight north, made it halfway up Nevada toward home before he finally pulled over.

"Hey, Thomas," Victor said. "You got to drive for a while."

"Okay."

Thomas Builds-the-Fire slid behind the wheel and started off down the road. All through Nevada, Thomas and Victor had been amazed at the lack of animal life, at the absence of water, of movement.

"Where is everything?" Victor had asked more than once.   150

Now when Thomas was finally driving they saw the first animal, maybe the only animal in Nevada. It was a long-eared jackrabbit.

"Look," Victor yelled. "It's alive."

Thomas and Victor were busy congratulating themselves on their discovery when the jackrabbit darted out into the road and under the wheels of the pickup.

"Stop the goddamn car," Victor yelled, and Thomas did stop, backed the pickup to the dead jackrabbit.

"Oh, man, he's dead," Victor said as he looked at the squashed animal. 155
"Really dead."

"The only thing alive in this whole state and we just killed it."

"I don't know," Thomas said. "I think it was suicide."

Victor looked around the desert, sniffed the air, felt the emptiness and loneliness, and nodded his head.

"Yeah," Victor said. "It had to be suicide." 160

"I can't believe this," Thomas said. "You drive for a thousand miles and there ain't even any bugs smashed on the windshield. I drive for ten seconds and kill the only living thing in Nevada."

"Yeah," Victor said. "Maybe I should drive."

"Maybe you should."

Thomas Builds-the-Fire walked through the corridors of the tribal school by himself. Nobody wanted to be anywhere near him because of all those stories. Story after story.

Thomas closed his eyes and this story came to him: "We are all given one 165 thing by which our lives are measured, one determination. Mine are the stories which can change or not change the world. It doesn't matter which as long as I continue to tell the stories. My father, he died on Okinawa in World War II, died fighting for this country, which had tried to kill him for years. My mother, she died giving birth to me, died while I was still inside her. She pushed me out into the world with her last breath. I have no brothers or sisters. I have only my stories which came to me before I even had the words to speak. I learned a thousand stories before I took my first thousand steps. They are all I have. It's all I can do."

Thomas Builds-the-Fire told his stories to all those who would stop and listen. He kept telling them long after people had stopped listening.

Victor and Thomas made it back to the reservation just as the sun was rising. It was the beginning of a new day on earth, but the same old shit on the reservation.

"Good morning," Thomas said.

"Good morning."

The tribe was waking up, ready for work, eating breakfast, reading the news- 170 paper, just like everybody else does. Willene LeBret was out in her garden wearing a bathrobe. She waved when Thomas and Victor drove by.

"Crazy Indians made it," she said to herself and went back to her roses.

Victor stopped the pickup in front of Thomas Builds-the-Fire's HUD house.[3] They both yawned, stretched a little, shook dust from their bodies.

---

[3] The Department of Housing and Urban Development, an agency of the U.S. government, provides subsidized housing for low-income persons.

"I'm tired," Victor said.

"Of everything," Thomas added.

They both searched for words to end the journey. Victor needed to thank 175
Thomas for his help, for the money, and make the promise to pay it all back.

"Don't worry about the money," Thomas said. "It don't make any difference
anyhow."

"Probably not, enit?"

"Nope."

Victor knew that Thomas would remain the crazy storyteller who talked to
dogs and cars, who listened to the wind and pine trees. Victor knew that he
couldn't really be friends with Thomas, even after all that had happened. It was
cruel but it was real. As real as the ashes, as Victor's father, sitting behind the seats.

"I know how it is," Thomas said. "I know you ain't going to treat me any bet- 180
ter than you did before. I know your friends would give you too much shit
about it."

Victor was ashamed of himself. Whatever happened to the tribal ties, the
sense of community? The only real thing he shared with anybody was a bottle
and broken dreams. He owed Thomas something, anything.

"Listen," Victor said and handed Thomas the cardboard box which contained half of his father. "I want you to have this."

Thomas took the ashes and smiled, closed his eyes, and told this story: "I'm
going to travel to Spokane Falls one last time and toss these ashes into the
water. And your father will rise like a salmon, leap over the bridge, over me,
and find his way home. It will be beautiful. His teeth will shine like silver, like a
rainbow. He will rise, Victor, he will rise."

Victor smiled.

"I was planning on doing the same thing with my half," Victor said. "But I 185
didn't imagine my father looking anything like a salmon. I thought it'd be like
cleaning the attic or something. Like letting things go after they've stopped
having any use."

"Nothing stops, cousin," Thomas said. "Nothing stops."

Thomas Builds-the-Fire got out of the pickup and walked up his driveway.
Victor started the pickup and began the drive home.

"Wait," Thomas yelled suddenly from his porch. "I just got to ask one favor."

Victor stopped the pickup, leaned out the window, and shouted back. "What
do you want?"

"Just one time when I'm telling a story somewhere, why don't you stop and 190
listen?" Thomas asked.

"Just once?"

"Just once."

Victor waved his arms to let Thomas know that the deal was good. It was a
fair trade, and that was all Victor had ever wanted from his whole life. So Victor drove his father's pickup toward home while Thomas went into his house,
closed the door behind him, and heard a new story come to him in the silence
afterwards.

FOR ANALYSIS

1. Explain the title. What does "This" refer to?

2. When they were boys, Victor would chide Thomas for thinking too much. Why did he do so? What does Thomas think about?

3. What is the significance of Thomas's conversation with Cathy, the Olympic gymnast, during the plane ride to Phoenix?

4. Why has Thomas evoked such dislike and hostility in Victor and others of the tribe?

5. Why is Victor drawn to Thomas despite the embarrassment he feels at being seen with the reservation pariah?

6. The **narrator** interrupts the flashback describing the Fourth of July celebration to remark, "Years later, they would need much more" (para. 40). Does the narrative, which takes place years after this event, throw light on the meaning of this comment? Explain.

7. How does Victor change in the course of the story?

8. Explain the final sentence.

MAKING CONNECTIONS

Compare this story's orientation in time to that of Lethem's "Super Goat Man" (p. 382). Alexie's story uses flashbacks, while Lethem's, also told from the present, uses a different strategy. How does each work? Do they seem the right choices for the stories they tell?

WRITING TOPICS

1. This story, taken from Alexie's book *The Lone Ranger and Tonto Fistfight in Heaven*, is the basis for the 1998 movie *Smoke Signals* (available on video). After viewing the movie, write a paper about how the story was expanded and changed for the film version.

2. Analyze the ways in which Alexie creates a comic **tone** in this story.

JHUMPA LAHIRI (B. 1967)

HELL-HEAVEN 2004

P ranab Chakraborty wasn't technically my father's younger brother. He was a fellow-Bengali from Calcutta who had washed up on the barren shores of my parents' social life in the early seventies, when they lived in a rented apartment in Central Square and could number their acquaintances on one hand. But I had no real uncles in America, and so I was taught to call him Pranab Kaku. Accordingly, he called my father Shyamal Da, always addressing him in the polite form, and he called my mother Boudi, which is how Bengalis are supposed to address an older brother's wife, instead of using her first name, Aparna. After Pranab Kaku was befriended by my parents, he confessed that on the day we first met him he had followed my mother and me for the better part of an afternoon around the streets of Cambridge, where she and I tended to roam after I got out of school. He had trailed behind us along Massachusetts Avenue, and in and out of the Harvard Coop, where my mother liked to look at discounted housewares. He wandered with us into Harvard Yard, where my mother often sat on the grass on pleasant days and watched the stream of students and professors filing busily along the paths, until, finally, as we were climbing the steps to Widener Library so that I could use the bathroom, he tapped my mother on the shoulder and inquired, in English, if she might be a Bengali. The answer to his question was clear, given that my mother was wearing the red and white bangles unique to Bengali married women, and a common Tangail sari, and had a thick stem of vermillion powder in the center parting of her hair, and the full round face and large dark eyes that are so typical of Bengali women. He noticed the two or three safety pins she wore fastened to the thin gold bangles that were behind the red and white ones, which she would use to replace a missing hook on a blouse or to draw a string through a petticoat at a moment's notice, a practice he associated strictly with his mother and sisters and aunts in Calcutta. Moreover, Pranab Kaku had overheard my mother speaking to me in Bengali, telling me that I couldn't buy an issue of *Archie* at the Coop. But back then, he also confessed, he was so new to America that he took nothing for granted, and doubted even the obvious.

My parents and I had lived in Central Square for three years prior to that day; before that, we had lived in Berlin, where I was born and where my father had finished his training in microbiology before accepting a position as a researcher at Mass General, and before Berlin my mother and father had lived in India, where they had been strangers to each other, and where their marriage had been arranged. Central Square is the first place I can recall living, and in my memories of our apartment, in a dark-brown shingled house on

607

Ashburton Place, Pranab Kaku is always there. According to the story he liked to recall often, my mother invited him to accompany us back to our apartment that very afternoon, and prepared tea for the two of them; then, after learning that he had not had a proper Bengali meal in more than three months, she served him the leftover curried mackerel and rice that we had eaten for dinner the night before. He remained into the evening, for a second dinner, after my father got home, and after that he showed up for dinner almost every night, occupying the fourth chair at our square Formica kitchen table, and becoming a part of our family in practice as well as in name.

He was from a wealthy family in Calcutta and had never had to do so much as pour himself a glass of water before moving to America, to study engineering at M.I.T. Life as a graduate student in Boston was a cruel shock, and in his first month he lost nearly twenty pounds. He had arrived in January, in the middle of a snowstorm, and at the end of a week he had packed his bags and gone to Logan, prepared to abandon the opportunity he'd worked toward all his life, only to change his mind at the last minute. He was living on Trowbridge Street in the home of a divorced woman with two young children who were always screaming and crying. He rented a room in the attic and was permitted to use the kitchen only at specified times of the day, and instructed always to wipe down the stove with Windex and a sponge. My parents agreed that it was a terrible situation, and if they'd had a bedroom to spare they would have offered it to him. Instead, they welcomed him to our meals, and opened up our apartment to him at any time, and soon it was there he went between classes and on his days off, always leaving behind some vestige of himself: a nearly finished pack of cigarettes, a newspaper, a piece of mail he had not bothered to open, a sweater he had taken off and forgotten in the course of his stay.

I remember vividly the sound of his exuberant laughter and the sight of his lanky body slouched or sprawled on the dull, mismatched furniture that had come with our apartment. He had a striking face, with a high forehead and a thick mustache, and overgrown, untamed hair that my mother said made him look like the American hippies who were everywhere in those days. His long legs jiggled rapidly up and down wherever he sat, and his elegant hands trembled when he held a cigarette between his fingers, tapping the ashes into a teacup that my mother began to set aside for this exclusive purpose. Though he was a scientist by training, there was nothing rigid or predictable or orderly about him. He always seemed to be starving, walking through the door and announcing that he hadn't had lunch, and then he would eat ravenously, reaching behind my mother to steal cutlets as she was frying them, before she had a chance to set them properly on a plate with red-onion salad. In private, my parents remarked that he was a brilliant student, a star at Jadavpur who had come to M.I.T. with an impressive assistantship, but Pranab Kaku was cavalier about his classes, skipping them with frequency. "These Americans are learning equations I knew at Usha's age," he would complain. He was stunned that my second-grade teacher didn't assign any homework, and that at the age of seven I hadn't yet been taught square roots or the concept of pi.

He appeared without warning, never phoning beforehand but simply 5
knocking on the door the way people did in Calcutta and calling out "Boudi!"
as he waited for my mother to let him in. Before we met him, I would return
from school and find my mother with her purse in her lap and her trenchcoat
on, desperate to escape the apartment where she had spent the day alone. But
now I would find her in the kitchen, rolling out dough for *luchis,* which she
normally made only on Sundays for my father and me, or putting up new curtains she'd bought at Woolworth's. I did not know, back then, that Pranab
Kaku's visits were what my mother looked forward to all day, that she changed
into a new sari and combed her hair in anticipation of his arrival, and that she
planned, days in advance, the snacks she would serve him with such nonchalance. That she lived for the moment she heard him call out "Boudi!" from the
porch, and that she was in a foul humor on the days he didn't materialize.

It must have pleased her that I looked forward to his visits as well. He
showed me card tricks and an optical illusion in which he appeared to be sev-
ering his own thumb with enormous struggle and strength, and taught me
to memorize multiplication tables well before I had to learn them in school.
His hobby was photography. He owned an expensive camera that required
thought before you pressed the shutter, and I quickly became his favorite subject, round-faced, missing teeth, my thick bangs in need of a trim. They are still
the pictures of myself I like best, for they convey that confidence of youth I no
longer possess, especially in front of a camera. I remember having to run back
and forth in Harvard Yard as he stood with the camera, trying to capture me in
motion, or posing on the steps of university buildings and on the street and
against the trunks of trees. There is only one photograph in which my mother
appears; she is holding me as I sit straddling her lap, her head tilted toward me,
her hands pressed to my ears as if to prevent me from hearing something. In
that picture, Pranab Kaku's shadow, his two arms raised at angles to hold the
camera to his face, hovers in the corner of the frame, his darkened, featureless
shape superimposed on one side of my mother's body. It was always the three
of us. I was always there when he visited. It would have been inappropriate for
my mother to receive him in the apartment alone; this was something that
went without saying.

They had in common all the things she and my father did not: a love of
music, film, leftist politics, poetry. They were from the same neighborhood in
North Calcutta, their family homes within walking distance, the façades familiar to them once the exact locations were described. They knew the same
shops, the same bus and tram routes, the same holes-in-the-wall for the best
jelabis and *moghlai parathas.* My father, on the other hand, came from a suburb twenty miles outside Calcutta, an area that my mother considered the
wilderness, and even in her bleakest hours of homesickness she was grateful
that my father had at least spared her a life in the stern house of her in-laws,
where she would have had to keep her head covered with the end of her sari at
all times and use an outhouse that was nothing but a raised platform with a

hole, and where, in the rooms, there was not a single painting hanging on the walls. Within a few weeks, Pranab Kaku had brought his reel-to-reel over to our apartment, and he played for my mother medley after medley of songs from the Hindi films of their youth. They were cheerful songs of courtship, which transformed the quiet life in our apartment and transported my mother back to the world she'd left behind in order to marry my father. She and Pranab Kaku would try to recall which scene in which movie the songs were from, who the actors were and what they were wearing. My mother would describe Raj Kapoor and Nargis singing under umbrellas in the rain, or Dev Anand strumming a guitar on the beach in Goa. She and Pranab Kaku would argue passionately about these matters, raising their voices in playful combat, confronting each other in a way she and my father never did.

Because he played the part of a younger brother, she felt free to call him Pranab, whereas she never called my father by his first name. My father was thirty-seven then, nine years older than my mother. Pranab Kaku was twenty-five. My father was monkish by nature, a lover of silence and solitude. He had married my mother to placate his parents; they were willing to accept his desertion as long as he had a wife. He was wedded to his work, his research, and he existed in a shell that neither my mother nor I could penetrate. Conversation was a chore for him; it required an effort he preferred to expend at the lab. He disliked excess in anything, voiced no cravings or needs apart from the frugal elements of his daily routine: cereal and tea in the mornings, a cup of tea after he got home, and two different vegetable dishes every night with dinner. He did not eat with the reckless appetite of Pranab Kaku. My father had a survivor's mentality. From time to time, he liked to remark, in mixed company and often with no relevant provocation, that starving Russians under Stalin had resorted to eating the glue off the back of their wallpaper. One might think that he would have felt slightly jealous, or at the very least suspicious, about the regularity of Pranab Kaku's visits and the effect they had on my mother's behavior and mood. But my guess is that my father was grateful to Pranab Kaku for the companionship he provided, freed from the sense of responsibility he must have felt for forcing her to leave India, and relieved, perhaps, to see her happy for a change.

In the summer, Pranab Kaku bought a navy-blue Volkswagen Beetle, and began to take my mother and me for drives through Boston and Cambridge, and soon outside the city, flying down the highway. He would take us to India Tea and Spices in Watertown, and one time he drove us all the way to New Hampshire to look at the mountains. As the weather grew hotter, we started going, once or twice a week, to Walden Pond. My mother always prepared a picnic of hard-boiled eggs and cucumber sandwiches, and talked fondly about the winter picnics of her youth, grand expeditions with fifty of her relatives, all taking the train into the West Bengal countryside. Pranab Kaku listened to these stories with interest, absorbing the vanishing details of her past. He did not turn a deaf ear to her nostalgia, like my father, or listen uncomprehending, like me. At Walden Pond, Pranab Kaku would coax my mother through the woods, and lead her down the steep slope to the water's edge. She would unpack the picnic things and sit and watch us as we swam. His chest was matted with thick dark hair, all the way to his waist. He was an odd sight, with his pole-thin legs and a small, flaccid belly, like an otherwise svelte woman who has had a baby and not bothered to tone her abdomen. "You're making me fat, Boudi," he would complain after gorging himself on my mother's cooking. He swam noisily, clumsily, his head always above the water; he didn't know how to blow bubbles or hold his breath, as I had learned in swimming class. Wherever we went, any stranger would have naturally assumed that Pranab Kaku was my father, that my mother was his wife.

It is clear to me now that my mother was in love with him. He wooed her as 10 no other man had, with the innocent affection of a brother-in-law. In my mind, he was just a family member, a cross between an uncle and a much older brother, for in certain respects my parents sheltered and cared for him in much the same way they cared for me. He was respectful of my father, always seeking his advice about making a life in the West, about setting up a bank account and getting a job, and deferring to his opinions about Kissinger and Watergate. Occasionally, my mother would tease him about women, asking about female Indian students at M.I.T., or showing him pictures of her younger cousins in India. "What do you think of her?" she would ask. "Isn't she pretty?" She knew that she could never have Pranab Kaku for herself, and I suppose it was her attempt to keep him in the family. But, most important, in the beginning he was totally dependent on her, needing her for those months in a way my father never did in the whole history of their marriage. He brought to my mother the first and, I suspect, the only pure happiness she ever felt. I don't think even my birth made her as happy. I was evidence of her marriage to my father, an assumed consequence of the life she had been raised to lead. But Pranab Kaku was different. He was the one totally unanticipated pleasure in her life.

In the fall of 1974, Pranab Kaku met a student at Radcliffe named Deborah, an American, and she began to accompany him to our house. I called Deborah by her first name, as my parents did, but Pranab Kaku taught her to call my father Shyamal Da and my mother Boudi, something with which Deborah gladly complied. Before they came to dinner for the first time, I asked my mother, as she was straightening up the living room, if I ought to address her as Deborah Kakima, turning her into an aunt as I had turned Pranab into an uncle. "What's the point?" my mother said, looking back at me sharply. "In a few weeks, the fun will be over and she'll leave him." And yet Deborah remained by his side, attending the weekend parties that Pranab Kaku and my parents were becoming more involved with, gatherings that were exclusively Bengali with the exception of her. Deborah was very tall, taller than both my parents and nearly as tall as Pranab Kaku. She wore her long brass-colored hair center-parted, as my mother did, but it was gathered into a low ponytail instead of a braid, or it spilled messily over her shoulders and down her back in a way that my mother considered indecent. She wore small silver spectacles and not a trace of makeup, and she studied philosophy. I found her utterly beautiful, but according to my mother she had spots on her face, and her hips were too small.

For a while, Pranab Kaku still showed up once a week for dinner on his own, mostly asking my mother what she thought of Deborah. He sought her approval, telling her that Deborah was the daughter of professors at Boston College, that her father published poetry, and that both her parents had Ph.D.s. When he wasn't around, my mother complained about Deborah's visits, about having to make the food less spicy even though Deborah said she liked spicy food, and feeling embarrassed to put a fried fish head in the dal. Pranab Kaku taught Deborah to say *khub bhalo* and *aacha* and to pick up certain foods with her fingers instead of with a fork. Sometimes they ended up feeding each other, allowing their fingers to linger in each other's mouth, causing my parents to look down at their plates and wait for the moment to pass. At larger gatherings, they kissed and held hands in front of everyone, and when they were out of earshot my mother would talk to the other Bengali women. "He used to be so different. I don't understand how a person can change so suddenly. It's just hell-heaven, the difference," she would say, always using the English words for her self-concocted, backward metaphor.

The more my mother began to resent Deborah's visits, the more I began to anticipate them. I fell in love with Deborah, the way young girls often fall in love with women who are not their mothers. I loved her serene gray eyes, the ponchos and denim wrap skirts and sandals she wore, her straight hair that she let me manipulate into all sorts of silly styles. I longed for her casual appearance; my mother insisted whenever there was a gathering that I wear one of my ankle-length, faintly Victorian dresses, which she referred to as maxis, and have party hair, which meant taking a strand from either side of my head and joining them with a barrette at the back. At parties, Deborah would, eventually, politely slip away, much to the relief of the Bengali women with whom she was expected to carry on a conversation, and she would play with me. I was older than all my parents' friends' children, but with Deborah I had a companion. She knew all about the books I read, about Pippi Longstocking and Anne of Green Gables. She gave me the sorts of gifts my parents had neither the money nor the inspiration to buy: a large book of Grimms' fairy tales with watercolor illustrations on thick, silken pages, wooden puppets with hair fashioned from yarn. She told me about her family, three older sisters and two brothers, the youngest of whom was closer to my age than to hers. Once, after visiting her parents, she brought back three Nancy Drews, her name written in a girlish hand at the top of the first page, and an old toy she'd had, a small paper theatre set with interchangeable backdrops, the exterior of a castle and a ballroom and an open field. Deborah and I spoke freely in English, a language in which, by that age, I expressed myself more easily than Bengali, which I was required to speak at home. Sometimes she asked me how to say this or that in Bengali; once, she asked me what *asobbho* meant. I hesitated, then told her it was what my mother called me if I had done something extremely naughty, and Deborah's face clouded. I felt protective of her, aware that she was unwanted, that she was resented, aware of the nasty things people said.

Outings in the Volkswagen now involved the four of us, Deborah in the front, her hand over Pranab Kaku's while it rested on the gearshift, my mother and I in the back. Soon, my mother began coming up with reasons to excuse herself, headaches and incipient colds, and so I became part of a new triangle. To my surprise, my mother allowed me to go with them, to the Museum of Fine Arts and the Public Garden and the aquarium. She was waiting for the affair to end, for Deborah to break Pranab Kaku's heart and for him to return to us, scarred and penitent. I saw no sign of their relationship foundering. Their open affection for each other, their easily expressed happiness, was a new and romantic thing to me. Having me in the back seat allowed Pranab Kaku and Deborah to practice for the future, to try on the idea of a family of their own. Countless photographs were taken of me and Deborah, of me sitting on Deborah's lap, holding her hand, kissing her on the cheek. We exchanged what I believed were secret smiles, and in those moments I felt that she understood me better than anyone else in the world. Anyone would have said that Deborah would make an excellent mother one day. But my mother refused to acknowledge such a thing. I did not know at the time that my mother allowed me to go off with Pranab Kaku and Deborah because she was pregnant for the fifth time since my birth, and was so sick and exhausted and fearful of losing another baby that she slept most of the day. After ten weeks, she miscarried once again, and was advised by her doctor to stop trying.

By summer, there was a diamond on Deborah's left hand, something my 15 mother had never been given. Because his own family lived so far away, Pranab Kaku came to the house alone one day, to ask for my parents' blessing before giving her the ring. He showed us the box, opening it and taking out the diamond nestled inside. "I want to see how it looks on someone," he said, urging my mother to try it on, but she refused. I was the one who stuck out my hand, feeling the weight of the ring suspended at the base of my finger. Then he asked for a second thing: he wanted my parents to write to his parents, saying that they had met Deborah and that they thought highly of her. He was nervous, naturally, about telling his family that he intended to marry an American girl. He had told his parents all about us, and at one point my parents had received a letter from them, expressing appreciation for taking such good care of their son and for giving him a proper home in America. "It needn't be long," Pranab Kaku said. "Just a few lines. They'll accept it more easily if it comes from you." My father thought neither ill nor well of Deborah, never commenting or criticizing as my mother did, but he assured Pranab Kaku that a letter of endorsement would be on its way to Calcutta by the end of the week. My mother nodded her assent, but the following day I saw the teacup Pranab Kaku had used all this time as an ashtray in the kitchen garbage can, in pieces, and three Band-Aids taped to my mother's hand.

Pranab Kaku's parents were horrified by the thought of their only son marrying an American woman, and a few weeks later our telephone rang in the middle of the night: it was Mr. Chakraborty telling my father that they could not possibly bless such a marriage, that it was out of the question, that if Pranab Kaku dared to marry Deborah he would no longer acknowledge him as a son. Then his wife got on the phone, asking to speak to my mother, and attacked her as if they were intimate, blaming my mother for allowing the affair to develop. She said that they had already chosen a wife for him in Calcutta, that he'd left for America with the understanding that he'd go back after he had finished his studies, and marry this girl. They had bought the neighboring flat in their building for Pranab and his betrothed, and it was sitting empty, waiting for his return. "We thought we could trust you, and yet you have betrayed us so deeply," his mother said, taking out her anger on a stranger in a way she could not with her son. "Is this what happens to people in America?" For Pranab Kaku's sake, my mother defended the engagement, telling his mother that Deborah was a polite girl from a decent family. Pranab Kaku's parents pleaded with mine to talk him out of the engagement, but my father refused, deciding that it was not their place to get embroiled in a situation that had nothing to do with them. "We are not his parents," he told my mother. "We can tell him they don't approve but nothing more." And so my parents told Pranab Kaku nothing about how his parents had berated them, and blamed them, and threatened to disown Pranab Kaku, only that they had refused to give him their blessing. In the face of this refusal, Pranab Kaku shrugged. "I don't care. Not everyone can be as open-minded as you," he told my parents. "Your blessing is blessing enough."

After the engagement, Pranab Kaku and Deborah began drifting out of our lives. They moved in together, to an apartment in Boston, in the South End, a part of the city my parents considered unsafe. We moved as well, to a house in Natick. Though my parents had bought the house, they occupied it as if they were still tenants, touching up scuff marks with leftover paint and reluctant to put holes in the walls, and every afternoon when the sun shone through the living-room window my mother closed the blinds so that our new furniture would not fade. A few weeks before the wedding, my parents invited Pranab Kaku to the house alone, and my mother prepared a special meal to mark the end of his bachelorhood. It would be the only Bengali aspect of the wedding; the rest of it would be strictly American, with a cake and a minister and Deborah in a long white dress and veil. There is a photograph of the dinner, taken by my father, the only picture, to my knowledge, in which my mother and Pranab Kaku appear together. The picture is slightly blurry; I remember Pranab Kaku explaining to my father how to work the camera, and so he is captured looking up from the kitchen table and the elaborate array of food my mother had prepared in his honor, his mouth open, his long arm outstretched and his finger pointing, instructing my father how to read the light meter or some such thing. My mother stands beside him, one hand placed on top of his head in a gesture of blessing, the first and last time she was to touch him in her life. "She will leave him," my mother told her friends afterward. "He is throwing his life away."

The wedding was at a church in Ipswich, with a reception at a country club. It was going to be a small ceremony, which my parents took to mean one or two hundred people as opposed to three or four hundred. My mother was shocked that fewer than thirty people had been invited, and she was more perplexed than honored that, of all the Bengalis Pranab Kaku knew by then, we were the only ones on the list. At the wedding, we sat, like the other guests, first on the hard wooden pews of the church and then at a long table that had been set up for lunch. Though we were the closest thing Pranab Kaku had to a family that day, we were not included in the group photographs that were taken on the grounds of the country club, with Deborah's parents and grandparents and her many siblings, and neither my mother nor my father got up to make a toast. My mother did not appreciate the fact that Deborah had made sure that my parents, who did not eat beef, were given fish instead of filet mignon like everyone else. She kept speaking in Bengali, complaining about the formality of the proceedings, and the fact that Pranab Kaku, wearing a tuxedo, barely said a word to us because he was too busy leaning over the shoulders of his new American in-laws as he circled the table. As usual, my father said nothing in response to my mother's commentary, quietly and methodically working though his meal, his fork and knife occasionally squeaking against the surface of the china, because he was accustomed to eating with his hands. He cleared his plate and then my mother's, for she had pronounced the food inedible, and then he announced that he had overeaten and had a stomach ache. The only time my mother forced a smile was when Deborah appeared behind her chair, kissing her on the cheek and asking if we were enjoying ourselves. When the dancing started, my parents remained at the table, drinking tea, and after two or three songs they decided that it was time for us to go home, my mother shooting me looks to that effect across the room, where I was dancing in a circle with Pranab Kaku and Deborah and the other children at the wedding. I wanted to stay, and when, reluctantly, I walked over to where my parents sat Deborah followed me. "Boudi, let Usha stay. She's having such a good time," she said to my mother "Lots of people will be heading back your way, someone can drop her off in a little while." But my mother said no, I had had plenty of fun already, and forced me to put on my coat over my long puff-sleeved dress. As we drove home from the wedding I told my mother, for the first but not the last time in my life, that I hated her.

The following year, we received a birth announcement from the Chakrabortys, a picture of twin girls, which my mother did not paste into an album or display on the refrigerator door. The girls were named Srabani and Sabitri, but were called Bonny and Sara. Apart from a thank-you card for our wedding gift, it was their only communication; we were not invited to the new house in Marblehead, bought after Pranab Kaku got a high-paying job at Stone & Webster. For a while, my parents and their friends continued to invite the Chakrabortys to gatherings, but because they never came, or left after staying only an hour, the invitations stopped. Their absences were attributed, by my parents and their circle, to

Deborah, and it was universally agreed that she had stripped Pranab Kaku not only of his origins but of his independence. She was the enemy, he was her prey, and their example was invoked as a warning, and as vindication, that mixed marriages were a doomed enterprise. Occasionally, they surprised everyone, appearing at a *pujo* for a few hours with their two identical little girls who barely looked Bengali and spoke only English and were being raised so differently from me and most of the other children. They were not taken to Calcutta every summer, they did not have parents who were clinging to another way of life and exhorting their children to do the same. Because of Deborah, they were exempt from all that, and for this reason I envied them. "Usha, look at you, all grown up and so pretty," Deborah would say whenever she saw me, rekindling, if only for a minute, our bond of years before. She had cut off her beautiful long hair by then, and had a bob. "I bet you'll be old enough to babysit soon," she would say. "I'll call you—the girls would love that." But she never did.

I began to grow out of my girlhood, entering middle school and developing 20 crushes on the American boys in my class. The crushes amounted to nothing; in spite of Deborah's compliments, I was always overlooked at that age. But my mother must have picked up on something, for she forbade me to attend the dances that were held the last Friday of every month in the school cafeteria, and it was an unspoken law that I was not allowed to date. "Don't think you'll get away with marrying an American, the way Pranab Kaku did," she would say from time to time. I was thirteen, the thought of marriage irrelevant to my life. Still, her words upset me, and I felt her grip on me tighten. She would fly into a rage when I told her I wanted to start wearing a bra, or if I wanted to go to Harvard Square with a friend. In the middle of our arguments, she often conjured Deborah as her antithesis, the sort of woman she refused to be. "If *she* were your mother, she would let you do whatever you wanted, because she wouldn't care. Is that what you want, Usha, a mother who doesn't care?" When I began menstruating, the summer before I started ninth grade, my mother gave me a speech, telling me that I was to let no boy touch me, and then she asked if I knew how a woman became pregnant. I told her what I had been taught in science, about the sperm fertilizing the egg, and then she asked if I knew how, exactly, that happened. I saw the terror in her eyes and so, though I knew that aspect of procreation as well, I lied, and told her it hadn't been explained to us.

I began keeping other secrets from her, evading her with the aid of my friends. I told her I was sleeping over at a friend's when really I went to parties, drinking beer and allowing boys to kiss me and fondle my breasts and press their erections against my hip as we lay groping on a sofa or the back seat of a car. I began to pity my mother; the older I got, the more I saw what a desolate life she led. She had never worked, and during the day she watched soap operas to pass the time. Her only job, every day, was to clean and cook for my father and me. We rarely went to restaurants, my father always pointing out, even in cheap ones, how expensive they were compared with eating at home. When my mother complained to him about how much she hated life in the suburbs and how lonely she felt, he said nothing to placate her. "If you are so unhappy, go back to Calcutta," he would offer, making it clear that their separation would not affect him one way or the other. I began to take my cues from my father in dealing with her, isolating her doubly. When she screamed at me for talking too long on the telephone, or for staying too long in my room, I learned to scream back, telling her that she was pathetic, that she knew nothing about me, and it was clear to us both that I had stopped needing her, definitively and abruptly, just as Pranab Kaku had.

Then, the year before I went off to college, my parents and I were invited to the Chakrabortys' home for Thanksgiving. We were not the only guests from my parents' old Cambridge crowd; it turned out that Pranab Kaku and Deborah wanted to have a sort of reunion of all the people they had been friendly with back then. Normally, my parents did not celebrate Thanksgiving; the ritual of a large sit-down dinner and the foods that one was supposed to eat was lost on them. They treated it as if it were Memorial Day or Veterans Day—just another holiday in the American year. But we drove out to Marblehead, to an impressive stone-faced house with a semicircular gravel driveway clogged with cars. The house was a short walk from the ocean; on our way, we had driven by the harbor overlooking the cold, glittering Atlantic, and when we stepped out of the car we were greeted by the sound of gulls and waves. Most of the living-room furniture had been moved to the basement, and extra tables joined to the main one to form a giant U. They were covered with tablecloths, set with white plates and silverware, and had centerpieces of gourds. I was struck by the toys and dolls that were everywhere, dogs that shed long yellow hairs on everything, all the photographs of Bonny and Sara and Deborah decorating the walls, still more plastering the refrigerator door. Food was being prepared when we arrived, something my mother always frowned upon, the kitchen a chaos of people and smells and enormous dirtied bowls.

Deborah's family, whom we remembered dimly from the wedding, was there, her parents and her brothers and sisters and their husbands and wives and boyfriends and babies. Her sisters were in their thirties, but, like Deborah, they could have been mistaken for college students, wearing jeans and clogs and fisherman sweaters, and her brother Matty, with whom I had danced in a circle at the wedding, was now a freshman at Amherst, with wide-set green eyes and wispy brown hair and a complexion that reddened easily. As soon as I saw Deborah's siblings, joking with one another as they chopped and stirred things in the kitchen, I was furious with my mother for making a scene before we left the house and forcing me to wear a shalwar kameez. I knew they assumed, from my clothing, that I had more in common with the other Bengalis than with them. But Deborah insisted on including me, setting me to work peeling apples with Matty, and out of my parents' sight I was given beer to drink. When the meal was ready, we were told where to sit, in an alternating boy-girl formation that made the Bengalis uncomfortable. Bottles of wine were lined up on the table. Two turkeys were brought out, one stuffed with sausage and one without. My mouth watered at the food, but I knew that afterward, on our way home, my mother would complain that it was all tasteless and bland. "Impossible," my mother said, shaking her hand over the top of her glass when someone tried to pour her a little wine.

Deborah's father, Gene, got up to say grace, and asked everyone at the table to join hands. He bowed his head and closed his eyes. "Dear Lord, we thank you today for the food we are about to receive," he began. My parents were seated next to each other, and I was stunned to see that they complied, that my father's brown fingers lightly clasped my mother's pale ones. I noticed Matty seated on the other side of the room, and saw him glancing at me as his father spoke. After the chorus of amens, Gene raised his glass and said, "Forgive me, but I never thought I'd have the opportunity to say this: Here's to Thanksgiving with the Indians." Only a few people laughed at the joke.

Then Pranab Kaku stood up and thanked everyone for coming. He was relaxed 25 from alcohol, his once wiry body beginning to thicken. He started to talk sentimentally about his early days in Cambridge, and then suddenly he recounted the story of meeting me and my mother for the first time, telling the guests about how he had followed us that afternoon. The people who did not know us laughed, amused by the description of the encounter, and by Pranab Kaku's desperation. He walked around the room to where my mother was sitting and draped a lanky arm around her shoulder, forcing her, for a brief moment, to stand up. "This woman," he declared, pulling her close to his side, "this woman hosted my first real Thanksgiving in America. It might have been an afternoon in May, but that first meal at Boudi's table was Thanksgiving to me. If it weren't for that meal, I would have gone back to Calcutta." My mother looked away, embarrassed. She was thirty-eight, already going gray, and she looked closer to my father's age than to Pranab Kaku's; regardless of his waistline, he retained his handsome, carefree looks. Pranab Kaku went back to his place at the head of the table, next to Deborah, and concluded, "And if that had been the case I'd have never met you, my darling," and he kissed her on the mouth in front of everyone, to much applause, as if it were their wedding day all over again.

After the turkey, smaller forks were distributed and orders were taken for three different kinds of pie, written on small pads by Deborah's sisters, as if they were waitresses. After dessert, the dogs needed to go out, and Pranab Kaku volunteered to take them. "How about a walk on the beach?" he suggested, and Deborah's side of the family agreed that that was an excellent idea. None of the Bengalis wanted to go, preferring to sit with their tea and cluster together, at last, at one end of the room, speaking freely after the forced chitchat with the Americans during the meal. Matty came over and sat in the chair beside me that was now empty, encouraging me to join the walk. When I hesitated, pointing to my inappropriate clothes and shoes but also aware of my mother's silent fury at the sight of us together, he said, "I'm sure Deb can lend you something." So I went upstairs, where Deborah gave me a pair of her jeans and a thick sweater and some sneakers, so that I looked like her and her sisters.

She sat on the edge of her bed, watching me change, as if we were girlfriends, and she asked if I had a boyfriend. When I told her no, she said, "Matty thinks you're cute."

"He told you?"

"No, but I can tell."

As I walked back downstairs, emboldened by this information, in the jeans 30 I'd had to roll up and in which I felt finally like myself, I noticed my mother lift her eyes from her teacup and stare at me, but she said nothing, and off I went, with Pranab Kaku and his dogs and his in-laws, along a road and then down some steep wooden steps to the water. Deborah and one of her sisters stayed behind, to begin the cleanup and see to the needs of those who remained. Initially, we all walked together, in a single row across the sand, but then I noticed Matty hanging back, and so the two of us trailed behind, the distance between us and the others increasing. We began flirting, talking of things I no longer remember, and eventually we wandered into a rocky inlet and Matty fished a joint out of his pocket. We turned our backs to the wind and smoked it, our cold fingers touching in the process, our lips pressed to the same damp section of the rolling paper. At first I didn't feel any effect, but then, listening to him talk about the band he was in, I was aware that his voice sounded miles away, and that I had the urge to laugh, even though what he was saying was not terribly funny. It felt as if we were apart from the group for hours, but when we wandered back to the sand we could still see them, walking out onto a rocky promontory to watch the sun set. It was dark by the time we all headed back to the house, and I dreaded seeing my parents while I was still high. But when we got there Deborah told me that my parents, feeling tired, had left, agreeing to let someone drive me home later. A fire had been lit and I was told to relax and have more pie as the leftovers were put away and the living room slowly put back in order. Of course, it was Matty who drove me home, and sitting in my parents' driveway I kissed him, at once thrilled and terrified that my mother might walk onto the lawn in her nightgown and discover us. I gave Matty my phone number, and for a few weeks I thought of him constantly, and hoped foolishly that he would call.

In the end, my mother was right, and fourteen years after that Thanksgiving, after twenty-three years of marriage, Pranab Kaku and Deborah got divorced. It was he who had strayed, falling in love with a married Bengali woman, destroying two families in the process. The other woman was someone my parents knew, though not very well. Deborah was in her forties by then, Bonny and Sara away at college. In her shock and grief, it was my mother whom Deborah turned to, calling and weeping into the phone. Somehow, through all the years, she had continued to regard us as quasi in-laws, sending flowers when my grandparents died, and giving me a compact edition of the O.E.D. as a college-graduation present. "You knew him so well. How could he do something like this?" Deborah asked my mother. And then, "Did you know anything about it?" My mother answered truthfully that she did not. Their hearts had been broken by the same man, only my mother's had long ago mended, and in an odd way, as my parents approached their old age, she and my father had grown fond of each other, out of habit if nothing else. I believe my absence from the house, once I left for college, had something to do with this, because over the years, when I visited, I noticed a warmth between my parents that had not been there before, a quiet teasing, a solidarity, a concern when one of them fell ill. My mother and I had also made peace; she had accepted the fact that I was not only her daughter but a child of America as well. Slowly, she accepted that I dated one American man, and then another, and then yet another, that I slept with them, and even that I lived with one though we were not married. She welcomed my boyfriends into our home and when things didn't work out she told me I would find someone better. After years of being idle, she decided, when she turned fifty, to get a degree in library science at a nearby university.

On the phone, Deborah admitted something that surprised my mother: that all these years she had felt hopelessly shut out of a part of Pranab Kaku's life. "I was so horribly jealous of you back then, for knowing him, understanding him in a way I never could. He turned his back on his family, on all of you, really, but I still felt threatened. I could never get over that." She told my mother that she had tried, for years, to get Pranab Kaku to reconcile with his parents, and that she had also encouraged him to maintain ties with other Bengalis, but he had resisted. It had been Deborah's idea to invite us to their Thanksgiving; ironically, the other woman had been there, too. "I hope you don't blame me for taking him away from your lives, Boudi. I always worried that you did."

My mother assured Deborah that she blamed her for nothing. She confessed nothing to Deborah about her own jealousy of decades before, only that she was sorry for what had happened, that it was a sad and terrible thing for their family. She did not tell Deborah that a few weeks after Pranab Kaku's wedding, while I was at a Girl Scout meeting and my father was at work, she had gone through the house, gathering up all the safety pins that lurked in drawers and tins, and adding them to the few fastened to her bracelets. When she'd found enough, she pinned them to her sari one by one, attaching the front piece to the layer of material underneath, so that no one would be able to pull the garment off her body. Then she took a can of lighter fluid and a box of kitchen matches and stepped outside, into our chilly back yard, which was full of leaves needing to be raked. Over her sari she was wearing a knee-length lilac trench-coat, and to any neighbor she must have looked as though she'd simply stepped out for some fresh air. She opened up the coat and removed the tip from the can of lighter fluid and doused herself, then buttoned and belted the coat. She walked over to the garbage barrel behind our house and disposed of the fluid, then returned to the middle of the yard with the box of matches in her coat pocket. For nearly an hour she stood there, looking at our house, trying to work up the courage to strike a match. It was not I who saved her, or my father, but our next-door neighbor, Mrs. Holcomb, with whom my mother had never been particularly friendly. She came out to rake the leaves in her yard, calling out to my mother and remarking how beautiful the sunset was. "I see you've been admiring it for a while now," she said. My mother agreed, and then she went back into the house. By the time my father and I came home in the early evening, she was in the kitchen boiling rice for our dinner, as if it were any other day.

My mother told Deborah none of this. It was to me that she confessed, after my own heart was broken by a man I'd hoped to marry.

FOR ANALYSIS

1. Who is this story about? The **narrator**? Her mother? Both of them?

2. When the narrator changes out of traditional Indian dress and into some American-style clothing for a walk on the beach, she says that "I felt finally like myself" (para. 30). In this story, who determines who the narrator's self is?

3. At the end of "Hell-Heaven," Lahiri makes two unusual choices: she tells of the most shocking event of the story—the mother's near suicide, years after it happens—almost as an afterthought, and she only mentions (rather than presents as a scene) the important moment when the mother tells the daughter about it. What effect do these choices have? Why do you think Lahiri made them?

MAKING CONNECTIONS

Toward the end of the story, the narrator describes how her parents have grown closer later in life: "I noticed a warmth between my parents that had not been there before, a quiet teasing, a solidarity, a concern when one of them fell ill" (para. 31). Compare this moment in the story to a similar moment in Levy's "Mastering the Art of French Cooking" (p. 505). What purpose does the moment serve in each story?

WRITING TOPICS

1. Clothes and food are two ways immigrants are distinguished, or distinguish themselves, from natives. Make a list of all the moments in the story when these details are included, and see if you can discern any patterns. Are they distributed evenly or randomly or do they cluster around significant moments?

2. Imagine this story with the mother as narrator. How would it be different? Why do you think Lahiri chose to tell the story the way she did?

CONNECTING STORIES:
INSIDERS AND OUTCASTS

William Faulkner's "A Rose for Emily" is a classic example of a story depicting the tension between the community and the individual—a conflict that animates so much fiction. Ha Jin's "The Bridegroom" is a contemporary example, one that equals Faulkner's in addressing the more universal question of the fate of the individual by a world organized by groups. As you read these two stories, think about how the manner of their telling implicates not just the characters on whom the stories focus but also the tellers themselves. Think also about the endings of these stories, which reveal much about the character of the people, the complex social issues of the settings, and the larger difficulties of the human experience.

WILLIAM FAULKNER   (1897–1962)

A ROSE FOR EMILY   1931

I

When Miss Emily Grierson died, our whole town went to her funeral: the men through a sort of respectful affection for a fallen monument, the women mostly out of curiosity to see the inside of her house, which no one save an old manservant—a combined gardener and cook—had seen in at least ten years.

It was a big, squarish frame house that had once been white, decorated with cupolas and spires and scrolled balconies in the heavily lightsome style of the seventies, set on what had once been our most select street. But garages and cotton gins had encroached and obliterated even the august names of that neighborhood; only Miss Emily's house was left, lifting its stubborn and coquettish decay above the cotton wagons and the gasoline pumps—an eyesore among eyesores. And now Miss Emily had gone to join the representatives of those august names where they lay in the cedar-bemused cemetery among the ranked and anonymous graves of Union and Confederate soldiers who fell at the battle of Jefferson.

Alive, Miss Emily had been a tradition, a duty, and a care; a sort of hereditary obligation upon the town, dating from that day in 1894 when Colonel Sartoris, the mayor—he who fathered the edict that no Negro woman should appear on the streets without an apron—remitted her taxes, the dispensation dating from the death of her father on into perpetuity. Not that Miss Emily would have accepted charity. Colonel Sartoris invented an involved tale to the effect that Miss Emily's father had loaned money to the town, which the town, as a matter of business, preferred this way of repaying. Only a man of Colonel

Sartoris's generation and thought could have invented it, and only a woman could have believed it.

When the next generation, with its more modern ideas, became mayors and aldermen, this arrangement created some little dissatisfaction. On the first of the year they mailed her a tax notice. February came, and there was no reply. They wrote her a formal letter, asking her to call at the sheriff's office at her convenience. A week later the mayor wrote her himself, offering to call or to send his car for her, and received in reply a note on paper of an archaic shape, in a thin, flowing calligraphy in faded ink, to the effect that she no longer went out at all. The tax notice was also enclosed, without comment.

They called a special meeting of the Board of Aldermen. A deputation 5 waited upon her, knocked at the door through which no visitor had passed since she ceased giving china-painting lessons eight or ten years earlier. They were admitted by the old Negro into a dim hall from which a stairway mounted into still more shadow. It smelled of dust and disuse—a close, dank smell. The Negro led them into the parlor. It was furnished in heavy, leather-covered furniture. When the Negro opened the blinds of one window, they could see that the leather was cracked; and when they sat down, a faint dust rose sluggishly about their thighs, spinning with slow motions in the single sun-ray. On a tarnished gilt easel before the fireplace stood a crayon portrait of Miss Emily's father.

They rose when she entered—a small, fat woman in black, with a thin gold chain descending to her waist and vanishing into her belt, leaning on an ebony cane with a tarnished gold head. Her skeleton was small and spare; perhaps that was why what would have been merely plumpness in another was obesity in her. She looked bloated, like a body long submerged in motionless water, and of that pallid hue. Her eyes, lost in the fatty ridges of her face, looked like two small pieces of coal pressed into a lump of dough as they moved from one face to another while the visitors stated their errand.

She did not ask them to sit. She just stood in the door and listened quietly until the spokesman came to a stumbling halt. Then they could hear the invisible watch ticking at the end of the gold chain.

Her voice was dry and cold. "I have no taxes in Jefferson. Colonel Sartoris explained it to me. Perhaps one of you can gain access to the city records and satisfy yourselves."

"But we have. We are the city authorities, Miss Emily. Didn't you get a notice from the sheriff, signed by him?"

"I received a paper, yes," Miss Emily said. "Perhaps he considers himself the 10 sheriff . . . I have no taxes in Jefferson."

"But there is nothing on the books to show that, you see. We must go by the—"

"See Colonel Sartoris." (Colonel Sartoris had been dead almost ten years.) "I have no taxes in Jefferson. Tobe!" The Negro appeared. "Show these gentlemen out."

II

So she vanquished them, horse and foot, just as she had vanquished their fathers thirty years before about the smell. That was two years after her father's death and a short time after her sweetheart—the one we believed would marry her—had deserted her. After her father's death she went out very little; after her sweetheart went away, people hardly saw her at all. A few of the ladies had the temerity to call, but were not received, and the only sign of life about the place was the Negro man—a young man then—going in and out with a market basket.

"Just as if a man—any man—could keep a kitchen properly," the ladies said; so they were not surprised when the smell developed. It was another link between the gross, teeming world and the high and mighty Griersons.

A neighbor, a woman, complained to the mayor, Judge Stevens, eighty years old. 15

"But what will you have me do about it, madam?" he said.

"Why, send her word to stop it," the woman said. "Isn't there a law?"

"I'm sure that won't be necessary," Judge Stevens said. "It's probably just a snake or a rat that nigger of hers killed in the yard. I'll speak to him about it."

The next day he received two more complaints, one from a man who came in diffident deprecation. "We really must do something about it, Judge. I'd be the last one in the world to bother Miss Emily, but we've got to do something." That night the Board of Aldermen met—three graybeards and one younger man, a member of the rising generation.

"It's simple enough," he said. "Send her word to have her place cleaned up. 20 Give her a certain time to do it in, and if she don't . . ."

"Dammit, sir," Judge Stevens said, "will you accuse a lady to her face of smelling bad?"

So the next night, after midnight, four men crossed Miss Emily's lawn and slunk about the house like burglars, sniffing along the base of the brickwork and at the cellar openings while one of them performed a regular sowing motion with his hand out of a sack slung from his shoulder. They broke open the cellar door and sprinkled lime there, and in all the outbuildings. As they recrossed the lawn, a window that had been dark was lighted and Miss Emily sat in it, the light behind her, and her upright torso motionless as that of an idol. They crept quietly across the lawn and into the shadow of the locusts that lined the street. After a week or two the smell went away.

That was when people had begun to feel really sorry for her. People in our town, remembering how old lady Wyatt, her great-aunt, had gone completely crazy at last, believed that the Griersons held themselves a little too high for what they really were. None of the young men were quite good enough for Miss Emily and such. We had long thought of them as a tableau, Miss Emily a slender figure in white in the background, her father a spraddled silhouette in the foreground, his back to her and clutching a horsewhip, the two of them framed by the back-flung front door. So when she got to be thirty and was still single, we were not pleased exactly, but vindicated; even with insanity in the family she wouldn't have turned down all of her chances if they had really materialized.

When her father died, it got about that the house was all that was left to her; and in a way, people were glad. At last they could pity Miss Emily. Being left alone, and a pauper, she had become humanized. Now she too would know the old thrill and the old despair of a penny more or less.

The day after his death all the ladies prepared to call at the house and offer 25 condolence and aid, as is our custom. Miss Emily met them at the door, dressed as usual and with no trace of grief on her face. She told them that her father was not dead. She did that for three days, with the ministers calling on her, and the doctors, trying to persuade her to let them dispose of the body. Just as they were about to resort to law and force, she broke down, and they buried her father quickly.

We did not say she was crazy then. We believed she had to do that. We remembered all the young men her father had driven away, and we knew that with nothing left, she would have to cling to that which had robbed her, as people will.

III

She was sick for a long time. When we saw her again, her hair was cut short, making her look like a girl, with a vague resemblance to those angels in colored church windows—sort of tragic and serene.

The town had just let the contracts for paving the sidewalks, and in the summer after her father's death they began the work. The construction company came with niggers and mules and machinery, and a foreman named Homer Barron, a Yankee—a big, dark, ready man, with a big voice and eyes lighter than his face. The little boys would follow in groups to hear him cuss the niggers, and the niggers singing in time to the rise and fall of picks. Pretty soon he knew everybody in town. Whenever you heard a lot of laughing anywhere about the square, Homer Barron would be in the center of the group. Presently we began to see him and Miss Emily on Sunday afternoons driving in the yellow-wheeled buggy and the matched team of bays from the livery stable.

At first we were glad that Miss Emily would have an interest, because the ladies all said, "Of course a Grierson would not think seriously of a Northerner, a day laborer." But there were still others, older people, who said that even grief could not cause a real lady to forget *noblesse oblige*—without calling it *noblesse oblige*. They just said, "Poor Emily. Her kinsfolk should come to her." She had some kin in Alabama; but years ago her father had fallen out with them over the estate of old lady Wyatt, the crazy woman, and there was no communication between the two families. They had not even been represented at the funeral.

And as soon as the old people said, "Poor Emily," the whispering began. "Do 30 you suppose it's really so?" they said to one another. "Of course it is. What else could . . ." This behind their hands; rustling of craned silk and satin behind jalousies closed upon the sun of Sunday afternoon as the thin, swift clop-clop-clop of the matched team passed: "Poor Emily."

She carried her head high enough—even when we believed that she was fallen. It was as if she demanded more than ever the recognition of her dignity as the last Grierson; as if it had wanted that touch of earthiness to reaffirm her imperviousness. Like when she bought the rat poison, the arsenic. That was over a year after they had begun to say "Poor Emily," and while the two female cousins were visiting her.

"I want some poison," she said to the druggist. She was over thirty then, still a slight woman, though thinner than usual, with cold, haughty black eyes in a face the flesh of which was strained across the temples and about the eye-sockets as you imagine a lighthouse-keeper's face ought to look. "I want some poison," she said.

"Yes, Miss Emily. What kind? For rats and such? I'd recom—"

"I want the best you have. I don't care what kind."

The druggist named several. "They'll kill anything up to an elephant. But 35 what you want is—"

"Arsenic," Miss Emily said. "Is that a good one?"

"Is . . . arsenic? Yes, ma'am. But what you want—"

"I want arsenic."

The druggist looked down at her. She looked back at him, erect, her face like a strained flag. "Why, of course," the druggist said. "If that's what you want. But the law requires you to tell what you are going to use it for."

Miss Emily just stared at him, her head tilted back in order to look him eye 40 for eye, until he looked away and went and got the arsenic and wrapped it up. The Negro delivery boy brought her package; the druggist didn't come back. When she opened the package at home there was written on the box, under the skull and bones: "For rats."

IV

So the next day we all said, "She will kill herself"; and we said it would be the best thing. When she had first begun to be seen with Homer Barron, we had said, "She will marry him." Then we said, "She will persuade him yet," because Homer himself had remarked—he liked men, and it was known that he drank with the younger men in the Elks' Club—that he was not a marrying man. Later we said, "Poor Emily" behind the jalousies as they passed on Sunday afternoon in the glittering buggy, Miss Emily with her head high and Homer Barron with his hat cocked and a cigar in his teeth, reins and whip in a yellow glove.

Then some of the ladies began to say that it was a disgrace to the town and a bad example to the young people. The men did not want to interfere, but at last the ladies forced the Baptist minister—Miss Emily's people were Episcopal—to call upon her. He would never divulge what happened during that interview, but he refused to go back again. The next Sunday they again drove about the streets, and the following day the minister's wife wrote to Miss Emily's relations in Alabama.

So she had blood-kin under her roof again and we sat back to watch developments. At first nothing happened. Then we were sure that they were to be married. We learned that Miss Emily had been to the jeweler's and ordered a man's toilet set in silver, with the letters H.B. on each piece. Two days later we learned that she had bought a complete outfit of men's clothing, including a nightshirt, and we said, "They are married." We were really glad. We were glad because the two female cousins were even more Grierson than Miss Emily had ever been.

So we were not surprised when Homer Barron—the streets had been finished some time since—was gone. We were a little disappointed that there was not a public blowing-off, but we believed that he had gone on to prepare for Miss Emily's coming, or to give her a chance to get rid of the cousins. (By that time it was a cabal, and we were all Miss Emily's allies to help circumvent the cousins.) Sure enough, after another week they departed. And, as we had expected all along, within three days Homer Barron was back in town. A neighbor saw the Negro man admit him at the kitchen door at dusk one evening.

And that was the last we saw of Homer Barron. And of Miss Emily for some 45 time. The Negro man went in and out with the market basket, but the front door remained closed. Now and then we would see her at the window for a moment, as the men did that night when they sprinkled the lime, but for almost six months she did not appear on the streets. Then we knew that this was to be expected too; as if that quality of her father which had thwarted her woman's life so many times had been too virulent and too furious to die.

When we next saw Miss Emily, she had grown fat and her hair was turning gray. During the next few years it grew grayer and grayer until it attained an even pepper-and-salt iron-gray, when it ceased turning. Up to the day of her death at seventy-four it was still that vigorous iron gray, like the hair of an active man.

From that time on her front door remained closed, save during a period of six or seven years, when she was about forty, during which she gave lessons in china-painting. She fitted up a studio in one of the downstairs rooms, where the daughters and granddaughters of Colonel Sartoris' contemporaries were sent to her with the same regularity and in the same spirit that they were sent to church on Sundays with a twenty-five-cent piece for the collection plate. Meanwhile her taxes had been remitted.

Then the newer generation became the backbone and the spirit of the town, and the painting pupils grew up and fell away and did not send their children to her with boxes of color and tedious brushes and pictures cut from the ladies' magazines. The front door closed upon the last one and remained closed for good. When the town got free postal delivery, Miss Emily alone refused to let them fasten the metal numbers above her door and attach a mailbox to it. She would not listen to them.

Daily, monthly, yearly we watched the Negro grow grayer and more stooped, going in and out with the market basket. Each December we sent her a tax notice, which would be returned by the post office a week later, unclaimed. Now and then we would see her in one of the downstairs windows—she had evidently shut up the top floor of the house—like the carven torso of an idol in a niche, looking or not looking at us, we could never tell which. Thus she passed from generation to generation—dear, inescapable, impervious, tranquil, and perverse.

And so she died. Fell ill in the house filled with dust and shadows, with only   50 a doddering Negro man to wait on her. We did not even know she was sick; we had long since given up trying to get any information from the Negro. He talked to no one, probably not even to her, for his voice had grown harsh and rusty, as if from disuse.

She died in one of the downstairs rooms, in a heavy walnut bed with a curtain, her gray head propped on a pillow yellow and moldy with age and lack of sunlight.

V

The Negro met the first of the ladies at the front door and let them in, with their hushed, sibilant voices and their quick, curious glances, and then he disappeared. He walked right through the house and out the back and was not seen again.

The two female cousins came at once. They held the funeral on the second day, with the town coming to look at Miss Emily beneath a mass of bought flowers, with the crayon face of her father musing profoundly above the bier and the ladies sibilant and macabre; and the very old men—some in their brushed Confederate uniforms—on the porch and the lawn, talking of Miss Emily as if she had been a contemporary of theirs, believing they had danced with her and courted her perhaps, confusing time with its mathematical progression, as the old do, to whom all the past is not a diminishing road but, instead, a huge meadow which no winter ever quite touches, divided from them now by the narrow bottle-neck of the most recent decade of years.

Already we knew that there was one room in that region above stairs which no one had seen in forty years, and which would have to be forced. They waited until Miss Emily was decently in the ground before they opened it.

The violence of breaking down the door seemed to fill this room with per-   55 vading dust. A thin, acrid pall as of the tomb seemed to lie everywhere upon this room decked and furnished as for a bridal: upon the valance curtains of faded rose color, upon the rose-shaded lights, upon the dressing table, upon the delicate array of crystal and the man's toilet things backed with tarnished silver, silver so tarnished that the monogram was obscured. Among them lay a collar and tie, as if they had just been removed, which, lifted, left upon the surface a pale crescent in the dust. Upon a chair hung the suit, carefully folded; beneath it the two mute shoes and the discarded socks.

The man himself lay in the bed.

For a long while we just stood there, looking down at the profound and fleshless grin. The body had apparently once lain in the attitude of an embrace, but now the long sleep that outlasts love, that conquers even the grimace of love, had cuckolded him. What was left of him, rotted beneath what was left of the nightshirt, had become inextricable from the bed in which he lay; and upon him and upon the pillow beside him lay that even coating of the patient and biding dust.

Then we noticed that in the second pillow was the indentation of a head. One of us lifted something from it, and leaning forward, that faint and invisible dust dry and acrid in the nostrils, we saw a long strand of iron-gray hair.

FOR ANALYSIS

1. Why does Faulkner title the narrative "A Rose for Emily"?

2. At the end of section II, the narrator says, "We remembered all the young men her father had driven away." What is the significance of this statement? How would you characterize Emily's relationship with her father? Her father's relationship with the town?

3. In section III, we learn that "the ladies all said, 'Of course a Grierson would not think seriously of a Northerner, a day laborer.' " Why not? What are Emily's alternatives?

4. What is the effect of the final paragraph?

5. Why does the narrator use the pronoun *we?* The narrator often speaks of "the town." What does "the town" signify?

6. Reread the description of Emily's house in paragraph 2. What does this description suggest?

7. What does the author accomplish by not presenting the story in chronological order?

WRITING TOPICS

1. Write a brief essay discussing the role of time in this story. How does the town's response to the Griersons in general, and Emily in particular, change as time passes?

2. Write an essay arguing for or against the assertion that Emily's father determined the course of her life.

HA JIN (B. 1956)

THE BRIDEGROOM 1999

Before Beina's father died, I promised him that I'd take care of his daughter. He and I had been close friends for twenty years. He left his only child with me because my wife and I had no children of our own. It was easy to keep my word when Beina was still a teenager. As she grew older, it became more difficult, not because she was willful or troublesome but because no man was interested in her, a short, homely girl. When she turned twenty-three and still had no boyfriend,

I began to worry. Where could I find her a husband? Timid and quiet, she didn't know how to get close to a man. I was afraid she'd become an old maid.

Then out of the blue Baowen Huang proposed to her. I found myself at a loss, because they'd hardly known each other. How could he be serious about his offer? I feared he might make a fool of Beina, so I insisted they get engaged if he meant business. He came to my home with two trussed-up capons, four cartons of Ginseng cigarettes, two bottles of Five Grains' Sap, and one tall tin of oolong tea. I was pleased, though not very impressed by his gifts.

Two months later they got married. My colleagues congratulated me, saying, "That was fast, Old Cheng."

What a relief to me. But to many young women in our sewing-machine factory, Beina's marriage was a slap in the face. They'd say, "A hen cooped up a peacock." Or, "A fool always lands in the arms of fortune." True, Baowen had been one of the most handsome unmarried men in the factory, and nobody had expected that Beina, stocky and stout, would win him. What's more, Baowen was good-natured and well educated—a middle-school graduate— and he didn't smoke or drink or gamble. He had fine manners and often smiled politely, showing his bright, straight teeth. In a way he resembled a woman, delicate, clear-skinned, and soft-spoken; he even could knit things out of wool. But no men dared bully him because he was skilled at martial arts. Three times in a row he had won the first prize for kung fu at our factory's annual sports meet. He was very good at the long sword and freestyle boxing. When he was in middle school, bigger boys had often picked on him, so his stepfather had sent him to the martial arts school in their hometown. A year later nobody would ever bug him again.

Sometimes I couldn't help wondering why Baowen had chosen Beina. What 5 in her had caught his heart? Did he really like her fleshy face, which often reminded me of a globefish? Although we had our doubts, my wife and I couldn't say anything negative about the marriage. Our only concern was that Baowen might be too good for our nominal daughter. Whenever I heard that somebody had divorced, I'd feel a sudden flutter of panic.

As the head of the Security Section in the factory, I had some pull and did what I could to help the young couple. Soon after their wedding I secured them a brand-new two-bedroom apartment, which angered some people waiting in line for housing. I wasn't daunted by their criticism. I'd do almost anything to make Beina's marriage stable, because I believed that if it survived the first two years, it might last decades—once Baowen became a father, it would be difficult for him to break loose.

But after they'd been married for eight months, Beina still wasn't pregnant. I was afraid that Baowen would soon grow tired of her and run after another woman, since many young women in the factory were still attracted to him. A brazen one even declared that she'd leave her door open for him all night long. Some of them frequently offered him movie tickets and meat coupons. It seemed that they were determined to wreck Beina's marriage. I hated them, and just the thought of them would give me an earache or a sour stomach.

Fortunately, Baowen hadn't yet done anything outside the bounds of a decent husband.

One morning in early November, Beina stepped into my office. "Uncle," she said in a tearful voice, "Baowen didn't come home last night."

I tried to remain calm, though my head began to swim. "Do you know where he's been?" I asked.

"I don't know. I looked for him everywhere." She licked her cracked lips and 10 took off her green work cap, her hair in a huge bun.

"When did you see him last?"

"At dinner yesterday evening. He said he was going to see somebody. He has lots of buddies in town."

"Is that so?" I didn't know he had many friends. "Don't worry. Go back to your workshop and don't tell anybody about this. I'll call around and find him."

She dragged herself out of my office. She must have gained at least a dozen pounds since the wedding. Her blue dungarees had become so tight that they seemed about to burst. Viewed from behind, she looked like a giant turnip.

I called the Rainbow Movie Theater, Victory Park, and a few restaurants in 15 town. They all said they had not seen anyone matching Baowen's description. Before I could phone the city library, where Baowen sometimes spent his weekends, a call came in. It was from the city's Public Security Bureau. The man on the phone said they'd detained a worker of ours named Baowen Huang. He wouldn't tell me what had happened. He just said, "Indecent activity. Come as soon as you can."

It was a cold day. As I cycled toward downtown, the shrill north wind kept flipping up the front ends of my overcoat. My knees were sore, and I couldn't help shivering. Soon my asthma tightened my throat and I began moaning. I couldn't stop cursing Baowen. "I knew it. I just knew it," I said to myself. I had sensed that sooner or later he'd seek pleasure with another woman. Now he was in the police's hands, and the whole factory would talk about him. How could Beina take this blow?

At the Public Security Bureau I was surprised to see that about a dozen officials from other factories, schools, and companies were already there. I knew most of them, who were in charge of security affairs at their workplaces. A policewoman conducted us into a conference room upstairs, where green silk curtains hung in the windows. We sat down around a long mahogany table and waited to be briefed about the case. The glass tabletop was brand new, its edge still sharp. I saw worry and confusion on the other men's faces. I figured Baowen must have been involved in an organized crime—either an orgy or a gang rape. On second thought I felt he couldn't have been a rapist; by nature he was kindhearted, very gentle. I hoped this was not a political case, which would be absolutely unpardonable. Six or seven years ago a half-wit and a high school graduate had started an association in our city, named the China Liberation Party, which had later recruited nine members. Although the sparrow is small it has a complete set of organs—their party elected a chairman, a secretary, and even a prime minister. But before they could print their manifesto, which expressed their intention to overthrow the government, the police rounded them up. Two of the top leaders were executed, and the rest of the members were jailed.

As I was wondering about the nature of Baowen's crime, a middle-aged man came in. He had a solemn face, and his eyes were half closed. He took off his dark blue tunic, hung it on the back of a chair, and sat down at the end of the table. I recognized him; he was Chief Miao of the Investigation Department. Wearing a sheepskin jerkin, he somehow reminded me of Genghis Khan, thick-boned and round-faced. His hooded eyes were shrewd, though they looked sleepy. Without any opening remarks he declared that we had a case of homosexuality on our hands. At that, the room turned noisy. We'd heard of the term but didn't know what it meant exactly. Seeing many of us puzzled, Chief Miao explained, "It's a social disease, like gambling, or prostitution, or syphilis." He kept on squirming as if itchy with hemorrhoids.

A young man from the city's Fifth Middle School raised his hand. He asked, "What do homosexuals do?"

Miao smiled and his eyes almost disappeared. He said, "People of the same sex have a sexual relationship." 20

"Sodomy!" cried someone.

The room turned quiet for at least ten seconds. Then somebody asked what kind of crime this was.

Chief Miao explained, "Homosexuality originated from Western capitalism and bourgeois lifestyle. According to our law it's dealt with as a kind of hooliganism. Therefore, every one of the men we arrested will serve a sentence, from six months to five years, depending on the severity of his crime and his attitude toward it."

A truck blew its horn on the street and made my heart twinge. If Baowen went to prison, Beina would live like a widow, unless she divorced him. Why had he married her to begin with? Why did he ruin her this way?

What had happened was that a group of men, mostly clerks, artists, and 25 schoolteachers, had formed a club called Men's World, a salon of sorts. Every Thursday evening they'd met in a large room on the third floor of the office building of the Forestry Institute. Since the club admitted only men, the police suspected that it might be a secret association with a leaning toward violence, so they assigned two detectives to mix with the group. True, some of the men appeared to be intimate with each other in the club, but most of the time they talked about movies, books, and current events. Occasionally music was played, and they danced together. According to the detectives' account, it was a bizarre, emotional scene. A few men appeared in pairs, unashamed of necking and cuddling in the presence of others, and some would say with tears, "At last we men have a place for ourselves." A middle-aged painter wearing earrings exclaimed, "Now I feel alive! Only in here can I stop living in hypocrisy." Every week two or three new faces would show up. When the club grew close to the size of thirty men, the police took action and arrested them all.

After Chief Miao's briefing, we were allowed to meet with the criminals for fifteen minutes. A policeman led me into a small room in the basement and let me read Baowen's confession while he went to fetch him. I glanced through the four pages of interrogation notes, which stated that Baowen had been new to the club and that he'd joined them only twice, mainly because he was interested in their talks. Yet he didn't deny that he was a homosexual.

The room smelled of urine, since it was next to a bathroom. The policeman took Baowen in and ordered him to sit opposite me at the table. Baowen, in handcuffs, avoided looking at me. His face was bloated, covered with bruises. A broad welt left by a baton, about four inches long, slanted across his forehead. The collar of his jacket was torn open. Yet he didn't appear frightened. His calm manner angered me, though I felt sorry for him.

I kept a hard face, and said, "Baowen, do you know you committed a crime?"

"I didn't do anything. I just went there to listen to them talk."

"You mean you didn't do that thing with any man?" I wanted to make sure 30 so that I could help him.

He looked at me, then lowered his eyes, saying, "I might've done something, to be honest, but I didn't."

"What's that supposed to mean?"

"I— liked a man in the club, a lot. If he'd asked me, I might've agreed." His lips curled upward as if he prided himself on what he had said.

"You're sick!" I struck the table with my knuckles.

To my surprise, he said, "So? I'm a sick man. You think I don't know that?" 35

I was bewildered. He went on, "Years ago I tried everything to cure myself. I took a lot of herbs and boluses, and even ate baked scorpions, lizards, and toads. Nothing helped me. Still I'm fond of men. I don't know why I'm not interested in women. Whenever I'm with a woman my heart is as calm as a stone."

Outraged by his confession, I asked, "Then why did you marry my Beina? To make fun of her, eh? To throw mud in my face?"

"How could I be that mean? Before we got married, I told her I didn't like women and might not give her a baby."

"She believed you?"

"Yes. She said she wouldn't mind. She just wanted a husband." 40

"She's an idiot!" I unfolded my hanky and blew my clogged nose into it, then asked, "Why did you choose her if you had no feelings for her at all?"

"What was the difference? For me she was similar to other women."

"You're a scoundrel!"

"If I didn't marry her, who would? The marriage helped us both, covering me and saving face for her. Besides, we could have a good apartment—a home. You see, I tried living like a normal man. I've never been mean to Beina."

"But the marriage is a fake! You lied to your mother too, didn't you?" 45

"She wanted me to marry."

The policeman signaled that our meeting was over. In spite of my anger, I told Baowen that I'd see what I could do, and that he'd better cooperate with the police and show a sincere attitude.

What should I do? I was sick of him, but he belonged to my family, at least in name, and I was obligated to help him.

On the way home I pedaled slowly, my mind heavy with thoughts. Gradually I realized that I might be able to do something to prevent him from going to jail. There were two steps I could take: first, I would maintain that he had done nothing in the club, so as to isolate him from those real criminals; second, I would present him as a sick man, so that he might receive medical treatment instead of a prison term. Once he became a criminal, he'd be marked forever as an enemy of society, no longer redeemable. Even his children might suffer. I ought to save him.

Fortunately both the party secretary and the director of our factory were willing to accept Baowen as a sick man, particularly Secretary Zhu, who liked Baowen's kung-fu style and had once let him teach his youngest son how to use a three-section cudgel. Zhu suggested we make an effort to rescue Baowen from the police. He said to me in the men's room inside our office building, "Old Cheng, we must not let Baowen end up in prison." I was grateful for his words.

All of a sudden homosexuality became a popular topic in the factory. A few old workers said that some actors of the Beijing opera had slept together as lovers in the old days, because no women were allowed to perform in any troupe and the actors could spend time with men only. Secretary Zhu, who was well read, said that some emperors in the Han Dynasty had owned male lovers in addition to their large harems. Director Liu had heard that the last emperor, Puyi, had often ordered his eunuchs to suck his penis and caress his testicles. Someone even claimed that homosexuality was an upper-class thing, not something for ordinary people. All the talk sickened me. I felt ashamed of my nominal son-in-law. I wouldn't join them in talking and just listened, pretending I wasn't bothered.

As I expected, rumors went wild in the factory, especially in the foundry shop. Some people said Baowen was impotent. Some believed he was a hermaphrodite, otherwise his wife would've been pregnant long ago.

To console Beina, I went to see her one evening. She had a pleasant home, in which everything was in order. Two bookcases, filled with industrial manuals, biographies, novels, and medical books, stood against the whitewashed wall, on either side of the window. In one corner of the living room was a coat tree on which hung the red feather parka Baowen had bought her before their wedding, and in another corner sat a floor lamp. At the opposite end of the room two pots of blooming flowers, one of cyclamens and the other of Bengal roses, were placed on a pair of low stools kept at an equal distance from each other and from the walls on both sides. Near the inner wall, beside a yellow enamel spittoon, was a large sofa upholstered in orange imitation leather. A black-and-white TV perched on an oak chest against the outer wall.

I was impressed, especially by the floor inlaid with bricks and coated with bright red paint. Even my wife couldn't keep a home so neat. No doubt it was Baowen's work, because Beina couldn't be so tidy. Already the room showed the trace of her sloppy habits—in a corner were scattered an empty flour sack and a pile of soiled laundry. Sipping the tea she had poured me, I said, "Beina, I'm sorry about Baowen. I didn't know he was so bad."

"No, he's a good man." Her round eyes looked at me with a steady light.   55

"Why do you say that?"

"He's been good to me."

"But he can't be a good husband, can he?"

"What do you mean?"

I said bluntly, "He didn't go to bed with you very often, did he?"   60

"Oh, he can't do that because he practices kung fu. He said if he slept with a woman, all his many years' work would be gone. From the very beginning his master told him to avoid women."

"So you don't mind?" I was puzzled, saying to myself, What a stupid girl.

"Not really."

"But you two must've shared the bed a couple of times, haven't you?"

"No, we haven't."   65

"Really? Not even once?"

"No." She blushed a little and looked away, twisting her earlobe with her fingertips.

My head was reeling. After eight months' marriage she was still a virgin! And she didn't mind! I lifted the cup and took a large gulp of the jasmine tea.

A lull settled in. We both turned to watch the evening news; my numb mind couldn't take in what the anchorwoman said about a border skirmish between Vietnamese and Chinese troops.

A moment later I told Beina, "I'm sorry he has such a problem. If only we   70
had known."

"Don't feel so bad, Uncle. In fact he's better than a normal man."

"How so?"

"Most men can't stay away from pretty women, but Baowen just likes to have a few buddies. What's wrong with that? It's better this way, 'cause I don't have to worry about those shameless bitches in our factory. He won't bother to give them a look. He'll never have a lifestyle problem."

I almost laughed, wondering how I should explain to her that he could have a sexual relationship with a man and that he'd been detained precisely because of a lifestyle problem. On second thought I realized it might be better for her to continue to think that way. She didn't need more stress at the moment.

Then we talked about how to help Baowen. I told her to write a report,   75
emphasizing what a good, considerate husband he'd been. Of course she must not mention his celibacy in their marriage. Also, from now on, however vicious her fellow workers' remarks were, she should ignore them and never talk back, as if she'd heard nothing.

That night when I told my wife about Beina's silly notions, she smiled, saying, "Compared with most men, Baowen isn't too bad. Beina's not a fool."

I begged Chief Miao and a high-ranking officer to treat Baowen leniently and even gave each of them two bottles of brandy and a coupon for a Butterfly sewing machine. They seemed willing to help but wouldn't promise me anything. For days I was so anxious that my wife was afraid my ulcer might recur.

One morning the Public Security Bureau called, saying they had accepted our factory's proposal and would have Baowen transferred to the mental hospital in a western suburb, provided our factory agreed to pay for his hospitalization. I accepted the offer readily, feeling relieved. Later, I learned that there wasn't enough space in the city's prison for twenty-seven gay men, who couldn't be mixed with other inmates and had to be put in solitary cells. So only four of them were jailed; the rest were either hospitalized (if their work units agreed to pay for the medical expenses) or sent to some labor farms to be reformed. The two party members among them didn't go to jail, though they were expelled from the party, a very severe punishment that ended their political lives.

The moment I put down the phone, I hurried to the assembly shop and found Beina. She broke into tears at the good news. She ran back home and filled a duffel bag with Baowen's clothes. We met at my office, then together set out for the Public Security Bureau. I rode my bicycle while she sat behind me, embracing the duffel as if it were a baby. With a strong tailwind, the cycling was easy and fast, so we arrived before Baowen left for the hospital. He was waiting for a van in front of the police station, accompanied by two policemen.

The bruises on his face had healed, so he looked handsome again. He smiled   80
at us, and said rather secretively, "I want to ask you a favor." He rolled his eyes as the dark green van rounded the street corner, coming toward us.

"What?" I said.

"Don't let my mother know the truth. She's too old to take it. Don't tell her, please!"

"What should we say to her, then?" I asked.

"Just say I have a temporary mental disorder."

Beina couldn't hold back her tears anymore, saying loudly, "Don't worry. We   85
won't let her know. Take care of yourself and come back soon." She handed him the duffel, which he took without a word.

I nodded to assure him that I wouldn't reveal the truth. He smiled at her, then at me. For some reason his face turned rather sweet—charming and enticing, as though it were a mysterious female face. I blinked my eyes and wondered if he was really a man. It flashed through my mind that if he were a woman he could've been a beauty—tall, slim, muscular, and slightly languid.

My thoughts were cut short by a metallic screech as the van stopped in front of us. Baowen climbed into it; so did the policemen. I walked around the van, and shook his hand, saying that I'd visit him the next week and that meanwhile, if he needed anything, just to give me a ring.

We waved good-bye as the van drew away, its tire chains clattering and flinging up bits of snow. After a blasting toot, it turned left and disappeared from the icy street. I got on my bicycle as a gust of wind blew up and almost threw me down. Beina followed me for about twenty yards, then leaped on the carrier, and together we headed home. She was so heavy. Thank heaven, I was riding a Great Golden Deer, one of the sturdiest makes.

During the following week I heard from Baowen once. He said on the phone that he felt better now and less agitated. Indeed his voice sounded calm and smooth. He asked me to bring him a few books when I came, specifically his *Dictionary of Universal Knowledge,* which was a hefty, rare book translated from the Russian in the late fifties. I had no idea how he had come by it.

I went to see him on Thursday morning. The hospital was on a mountain, 90 six miles southwest of Muji City. As I was cycling on the asphalt road, a few tall smokestacks fumed lazily beyond the larch woods in the west. To my right the power lines along the roadside curved, heavy with fluffy snow, which would drop in little chunks whenever the wind blew across them. Now and then I overtook a horse cart loaded with earless sheaves of wheat, followed by one or two foals. After I pedaled across a stone bridge and turned into the mouth of a valley, a group of brick buildings emerged on a gentle slope, connected with one another by straight cement paths. Farther up the hill, past the buildings, there was a cow pen, in which about two dozen milk cows were grazing on dry grass while a few others huddled together to keep warm.

It was so peaceful here that if you hadn't known this was a mental hospital, you might have imagined it was a sanatorium for ranking officials. Entering Building 9, I was stopped by a guard, who then took me to Baowen's room on the ground floor. It happened that the doctor on duty, a tall fortyish man with tapering fingers, was making the morning rounds and examining Baowen. He shook hands with me and said that my son-in-law was doing fine. His surname was Mai; his whiskered face looked very intelligent. When he turned to give a male nurse instructions about Baowen's treatment, I noticed an enormous wart in his ear almost blocking the ear hole like a hearing aid. In a way he looked like a foreigner. I wondered if he had some Mongolian or Tibetan blood.

"We give him the electric bath," Doctor Mai said to me a moment later.

"What?" I asked, wincing.

"We treat him with the electric bath."

I turned to Baowen. "How is it?" 95

"It's good, really soothing." He smiled, but there was a churlish look in his eyes, and his mouth tightened.

The nurse was ready to take him for the treatment. Never having heard of such a bath, I asked Doctor Mai, "Can I see how it works?"

"All right, you may go with them."

Together we climbed the stairs to the second floor. There was another reason for me to join them. I wanted to find out whether Baowen was a normal man. The rumors in our factory had gotten on my nerves, particularly the one that said he had no penis—that was why he had always avoided bathing in the workers' bathhouse.

After taking off our shoes and putting on plastic slippers, we entered a 100 small room that had pea green walls and a parquet floor. At its center lay a porcelain bathtub, as ghastly as an apparatus of torture. Affixed along the interior wall of the tub were rectangles of black perforated metal. Three thick rubber cords connected them to a tall machine standing by the wall. A control board full of buttons, gauges, and switches slanted atop the machine. The young nurse, burly and square-faced, turned on the faucet; steaming water began to tumble into the tub. Then he went over to operate the machine. He seemed good-natured; his name was Fuhai Dong. He said he came from the countryside, apparently of peasant stock, and had graduated from Jilin Nursing School.

Baowen smiled at me while unbuttoning his zebra-striped hospital robe. He looked fine now—all the bruises had disappeared from his face, which had become pinkish and smooth. I was scared by the tub. It seemed suitable for electrocuting a criminal. However sick I was, I wouldn't lie in it with my back resting against that metal groove. What if there was an electricity leak?

"Does it hurt?" I asked Baowen.

"No."

He went behind a khaki screen in a corner and began taking off his clothes. When the water half filled the tub, the nurse took a small bag of white powder out of a drawer, cut it open with scissors, and poured the stuff into the water. It must have been salt. He tucked up his shirtsleeves and bent double to agitate the solution with both hands, which were large and sinewy.

To my dismay, Baowen came out in a clean pair of shorts. Without hesita- 105
tion he got into the tub and lay down, just as one would enter a lukewarm bathing pool. I was amazed. "Have you given him electricity yet?" I asked Nurse Dong.

"Yes, a little. I'll increase it by and by." He turned to the machine and adjusted a few buttons.

"You know," he said to me, "your son-in-law is a very good patient, always cooperative."

"He should be."

"That's why we give him the bath. Other patients get electric cuffs around their limbs or electric rods on their bodies. Some of them scream like animals every time. We have to tie them up."

"When will he be cured?" 110

"I'm not sure."

Baowen was noiseless in the electrified water, with his eyes shut and his head resting on a black rubber pad at the end of the tub. He looked fine, rather relaxed.

I drew up a chair and sat down. Baowen seemed reluctant to talk, concentrating on the treatment, so I remained silent, observing him. His body was wiry, his legs hairless, and the front of his shorts bulged quite a bit. He looked all right physically. Once in a while he breathed a feeble sigh.

As the nurse increased the electric current, Baowen began to squirm in the tub as if smarting from something. "Are you all right?" I asked, and dared not touch him.

"Yeah." 115

He kept his eyes shut. Glistening beads of sweat gathered on his forehead. He looked pale, his lips curling now and again as though he were thirsty.

Then the nurse gave him more electricity. Baowen began writhing and moaning a little. Obviously he was suffering. This bath couldn't be as soothing as he'd claimed. With a white towel Nurse Dong wiped the sweat off Baowen's face, and whispered, "I'll turn it down in a few minutes."

"No, give me more!" Baowen said resolutely without opening his eyes, his face twisted.

I felt as though he was ashamed of himself. Perhaps my presence made this section of the treatment more uncomfortable to him. His hands gripped the rim of the tub, the arched wrists trembling. For a good three minutes nobody said a word; the room was so quiet that its walls seemed to be ringing.

As the nurse gradually reduced the electricity, Baowen calmed down. His 120 toes stopped wiggling.

Not wanting to bother him further with my presence, I went out to look for Doctor Mai, to thank him and find out when Baowen could be cured. The doctor was not in his office, so I walked out of the building for a breath of air. The sun was high and the snow blazingly white. Once outside, I had to close my eyes for a minute to adjust them. I then sat down on a bench and lit a cigarette. A young woman in an ermine hat and army mittens passed by, holding an empty milk pail and humming the song "Comrade, Please Have a Cup of Tea." She looked handsome, and her crisp voice pleased me. I gazed at the pair of thick braids behind her, which swayed a little in the wind.

My heart was full of pity for Baowen. He was such a fine young man that he ought to be able to love a woman, have a family, and enjoy a normal life.

Twenty minutes later I rejoined him in his room. He looked tired, still shivering a little. He told me that as the electric currents increased, his skin had begun prickling as though stung by hundreds of mosquitoes. That was why he couldn't stay in the tub for longer than half an hour.

I felt for him, and said, "I'll tell our leaders how sincere your attitude is and how cooperative you are."

"Oh sure." He tilted his damp head. "Thanks for bringing the books." 125

"Do you need something else?"

"No." He sounded sad.

"Baowen, I hope you can come home before the New Year. Beina needs you."

"I know. I don't want to be locked up here forever."

I told him that Beina had written to his mother, saying he'd been away on a 130 business trip. Then the bell for lunch rang in the building, and outside the loudspeaker began broadcasting the fiery music of "March of the Volunteers." Nurse Dong walked in with a pair of chopsticks and a plate containing two corn buns. He said cheerily to Baowen, "I'll bring you the dish in a minute. We have tofu stewed with sauerkraut today, also bean sprout soup."

I stood up and took my leave.

When I reported Baowen's condition to the factory leaders, they seemed impressed. The term "electric bath" must have given their imagination free rein. Secretary Zhu kept shaking his head, and said, "I'm sorry Baowen has to go through such a thing."

I didn't explain that the electric bath was a treatment less severe than the other kinds, nor did I describe what the bath was like. I just said, "They steep him in electrified water every day." Let the terror seize their brains, I thought, so that they might be more sympathetic to Baowen when he is discharged from the hospital.

It was mid-December, and Baowen had been in the hospital for a month already. For days Beina went on saying that she wanted to see how her husband was doing; she was eager to take him home before the New Year. Among her fellow workers rumors persisted. One said the electric bath had blistered Baowen; another claimed that his genitals had been shriveled up by the treatment; another added that he had become a vegetarian, nauseated at the mere sight of meat. The young woman who had once declared she'd leave her door open for him had just married and proudly told everybody she was pregnant. People began to be kind and considerate to Beina, treating her like an abused wife. The leaders of the assembly shop assigned her only the daytime shift. I was pleased that Finance still paid Baowen his wages as though he were on sick leave. Perhaps they did this because they didn't want to upset me.

On Saturday Beina and I went to the mental hospital. She couldn't pedal,   135
and it was too far for me to carry her on my bicycle, so we took the bus. She had been there by herself two weeks ago to deliver some socks and a pair of woolen pajamas she'd knitted for Baowen.

We arrived at the hospital early in the afternoon. Baowen looked healthy, in good spirits. It seemed that the bath had helped him. He was happy to see Beina and even cuddled her in my presence. He gave her two toffees; knowing I disliked candies, he didn't give me one. He poured a large mug of malted milk for both of us, since there was only one mug in the room. I didn't touch the milk, unsure whether homosexuality was communicable. I was glad to see that he treated his wife well. He took a genuine interest in what she said about their comrades in our factory, and now and then laughed heartily. What a wonderful husband he could have been if he were not sick.

Having sat with the couple for a few minutes, I left so that they could be alone. I went to the nurses' office upstairs and found Fuhai Dong writing at a desk. The door was open, and I knocked on its frame. Startled, he closed his brown notebook and stood up.

"I didn't mean to scare you," I said.

"No, Uncle, I just didn't expect anyone to come up here."

I took a carton of Peony cigarettes out of my bag and put it on the desk, say-   140
ing, "I won't take too much of your time, young man. Please keep this as a token of my regards." I didn't mean to bribe him. I was sincerely grateful to him for treating Baowen well.

"Oh, don't give me this, please."

"You don't smoke?"

"I do. Tell you what, give it to Doctor Mai. He'll help Baowen more."

I was puzzled. Why didn't he want the top-quality cigarettes if he smoked? Seeing that I was confused, he went on, "I'll be nice to Baowen without any gift from you. He's a good man. It's the doctor's wheels that you should grease."

"I have another carton for him."

145

"One carton's nothing here. You should give him at least two."

I was moved by his words, thanked him, and said good-bye.

Doctor Mai happened to be in his office. When I walked in, he was reading the current issue of *Women's Life,* whose back cover carried a large photo of Madame Mao on trial—she wore black and stood, handcuffed, between two young policewomen. Doctor Mai put the magazine aside and asked me to sit down. In the room, tall shelves, loaded with books and files, lined the walls. A smell of rotten fruit hung in there. He seemed pleased to see me.

After we exchanged a few words, I took out both cartons of cigarettes and handed them to him. "This is just a small token of my gratitude, for the New Year," I said.

He took the cigarettes and put them away under his desk. "Thanks a lot," he whispered.

150

"Doctor Mai, do you think Baowen will be cured before the holiday?" I asked.

"What did you say? Cured?" He looked surprised.

"Yes."

He shook his head slowly, then turned to check that the door was shut. He motioned me to move closer. I pulled the chair forward a little and rested my forearms on the edge of his Bakelite desktop.

"To be honest, there's no cure," he said.

155

"What?"

"Homosexuality isn't an illness, so it has no cure. Don't tell anyone I said this."

"Then why torture Baowen like that?"

"The police sent him here and we couldn't refuse. Besides, we ought to make him feel better and hopeful."

"So it isn't a disease?"

160

"Unfortunately no. Let me say this again: there's no cure for your son-in-law, Old Cheng. It's not a disease. It's just a sexual preference; it may be congenital, like being left-handed. Got it?"

"Then why give him the electric bath?" Still I wasn't convinced.

"Electrotherapy is prescribed by the book—a standard treatment required by the Department of Public Health. I have no choice but to follow the regulations. That's why I didn't give him any of those harsher treatments. The bath is very mild by comparison. You see, I've done everything in my power to help him. Let me tell you another fact: according to the statistics, so far electrotherapy has cured only one out of a thousand homosexuals. I bet cod liver oil, or chocolate, or fried pork, anything, could produce a better result. All right, enough of this. I've talked too much."

At last his words sank in. For a good while I sat there motionless with a numb mind. A flock of sparrows were flitting about in the naked branches outside the window, chasing the one that held a tiny ear of millet in its bill. Another of them dragged a yellow string tied around its leg, unable to fly as nimbly as the others. I rose to my feet and thanked the doctor for his candid words. He stubbed out his cigarette in the ashtray on the windowsill, and said, "I'll take special care of your son-in-law. Don't worry."

I rejoined Beina downstairs. Baowen looked quite cheerful, and it seemed   165 they'd had a good time. He said to me, "If I can't come home soon, don't try too hard to get me out. They won't keep me here forever."

"I'll see what I can do."

In my heart I was exasperated, because if Doctor Mai's words were true, there'd be little I could do for Baowen. If homosexuality wasn't a disease, why had he felt sick and tried to have himself cured? Had he been shamming? It was unlikely.

Beina had been busy cleaning their home since her last visit to the hospital. She bought two young drakes and planned to make drunk duck, a dish she said Baowen liked best. My heart was heavy. On the one hand, I'd have loved to have him back for the holiday; on the other hand, I was unsure what would happen if his condition hadn't improved. I dared not reveal my thoughts to anybody, not even to my wife, who had a big mouth. Because of her, the whole factory knew that Beina was still a virgin, and some people called her the Virgin Bride.

For days I pondered what to do. I was confused. Everybody thought homosexuality was a disease except for Doctor Mai, whose opinion I dared not mention to others. The factory leaders would be mad at me if they knew there was no cure for homosexuality. We had already spent over three thousand yuan on Baowen. I kept questioning in my mind, If homosexuality is a natural thing, then why are there men and women? Why can't two men get married and make a baby? Why didn't nature give men another hole? I was beset by doubts. If only I could have seen a trustworthy doctor for a second opinion. If only there were a knowledgeable, honest friend I could have talked with.

I hadn't yet made up my mind about what to do when Chief Miao called   170 from the Public Security Bureau five days before the holiday. He informed me that Baowen had repeated his crime, so the police had taken him out of the hospital and sent him to the prison in Tangyuan County. "This time he did it," said the chief.

"Impossible!" I cried.

"We have evidence and witnesses. He doesn't deny it himself."

"Oh." I didn't know how to continue.

"He has to be incarcerated now."

"Are you sure he's not a hermaphrodite?" I mentioned that as a last resort.   175

Miao chuckled dryly. "No, he's not. We had him checked. Physically he's a man, healthy and normal. Obviously it's a mental, moral disease, like an addiction to opium."

Putting down the phone, I felt dizzy, cursing Baowen for having totally ruined himself. What had happened was that he and Fuhai Dong had developed a relationship secretly. The nurse often gave him a double amount of meat or fish at dinner. Baowen, in return, unraveled his woolen pajamas and knitted Dong a pullover with the wool. One evening when they were lying in each other's arms in the nurses' office, an old cleaner passed by in the corridor and coughed. Fuhai Dong was terrified and convinced that the man had seen what they had been doing. For days, however hard Baowen tried to talk him out of his conviction, Dong wouldn't change his mind, blaming Baowen for having misled him. He said that the old cleaner often smiled at him meaningfully and would definitely turn them in. Finally Fuhai Dong went to the hospital leaders and confessed everything. So, unlike Baowen, who got three and a half years in jail, Nurse Dong was merely put on probation; if he worked harder and criticized himself well, he might keep his current job.

That evening I went to tell Beina about the new development. As I was talking, she sobbed continually. Although she'd been cleaning the apartment for several days, her home was in shambles, most of the flowers half-dead, and dishes and pots piled in the sink. Mopping her face with a pink towel, she asked me, "What should I tell my mother-in-law?"

"Tell her the truth."

She made no response. I said again, "You should consider a divorce."   180

"No!" Her sobbing turned into wailing. "He—he's my husband and I'm his wife. If I die my soul belongs to him. We've sworn never to leave each other. Let others say whatever they want, I know he's a good man."

"Then why did he go to bed with a guy?"

"He just wanted to have a good time. That was all. It's nothing like adultery or bigamy, is it?"

"But it's a crime that got him into jail," I said. Although in my heart I admitted that Baowen in every way was a good fellow except for his fondness for men, I had to be adamant about my position. I was in charge of security for our factory; if I had a criminal son-in-law, who would listen to me? Wouldn't I be removed from my office soon? If I lost my job, who could protect Beina? Sooner or later she would be laid off, since a criminal's wife was not supposed to have the same opportunities for employment as others. Beina remained silent; I asked again, "What are you going to do?"

"Wait for him."   185

I took a few spiced pumpkin seeds from a bowl, stood up, and went over to the window. Under the sill the radiator was hissing softly with a tiny steam leak. Outside, in the distance, firecrackers one after another scattered clusters of sparks into the indigo dusk. I turned around, and said, "He's not worth waiting for. You must divorce him."

"No, I won't," she moaned.

"Well, it's impossible for me to have a criminal as my son-in-law. I've been humiliated enough. If you want to wait for him, don't come to see me again."

I put the pumpkin seeds back into the bowl, picked up my fur hat, and dragged myself out the door.

FOR ANALYSIS

1. Toward the end of the story, the **narrator** asks himself of Baowen, "If homosexuality wasn't a disease, why had he felt sick and tried to have himself cured?" (para. 167). What do you think is the story's answer to this question?

2. Why does the doctor continue Baowen's treatment if he knows homosexuality is not a disease that can be cured?

3. While this story is about a small number of **characters,** it is also about an entire society. What do the events in this story imply about contemporary China? Consider both the actions taken by and against Baowen and the actions taken by his wife and father-in-law. Consider also the attitudes and behaviors of "the people" generally, such as those of the factory workers and the bureaucrats.

WRITING TOPICS

1. While the story is called "The Bridegroom," it is really as much about the narrator as it is about Baowen. What kind of man is the narrator? How do you feel about him? Do your feelings about him change over the course of the story? How about at the end?

2. How would this story be different if it were narrated by Baowen? What would be gained, in terms of understanding the situation and the events? What would be lost?

MAKING CONNECTIONS

1. In spite of the very different settings and situations in these two stories, what makes Miss Emily and Baowen similar?

2. At the center of both stories is the relation of the main characters to their societies. This is true beyond the title characters, Baowen and Miss Emily; for example, the relationship of the narrator of "The Bridegroom" to his society is very important to the story. Is there an analogous figure in "A Rose for Emily"?

3. Both "A Rose for Emily" and "The Bridegroom" feature judgmental narrating figures. Do the stories (or the authors) seem to agree entirely with these narrators' opinions? Do the stories present these judgments straight, or is there some **ironic** distance between what the narrators say and what you think the stories themselves say?

POETRY

EMILY DICKINSON   (1830–1886)

I'M NOBODY! WHO ARE YOU?   c.1861, 1891

I'm Nobody! Who are you?
Are you—Nobody—Too?
Then there's a pair of us!
Don't tell! they'd advertise—you know!

How dreary—to be—Somebody!
How public—like a Frog—
To tell one's name —the livelong June—
To an admiring Bog!

PAUL LAURENCE DUNBAR   (1872–1906)

WE WEAR THE MASK   1896

We wear the mask that grins and lies,
It hides our cheeks and shades our eyes—
This debt we pay to human guile;
With torn and bleeding hearts we smile,
And mouth with myriad subtleties.

Why should the world be over-wise,
In counting all our tears and sighs?
Nay, let them only see us, while
    We wear the mask.

We smile, but, O great Christ, our cries   10
To thee from tortured souls arise.
We sing, but oh the clay is vile
Beneath our feet, and long the mile;
But let the world dream otherwise,
    We wear the mask!

T. S. Eliot   (1888–1965)

The Love Song of
J. Alfred Prufrock   1917

*S'io credessi che mia risposta fosse
a persona che mai tornasse al mondo,
questa fiamma staria senza più scosse.
Ma per ciò che giammai di questo fondo
non tornò vivo alcun, s'i'odo il vero,
senza tema d'infamia ti rispondo.*[1]

Let us go then, you and I,
When the evening is spread out against the sky
Like a patient etherized upon a table;
Let us go, through certain half-deserted streets,
The muttering retreats
Of restless nights in one-night cheap hotels
And sawdust restaurants with oyster shells:
Streets that follow like a tedious argument
Of insidious intent
To lead you to an overwhelming question . . .   10
Oh, do not ask, "What is it?"
Let us go and make our visit.

In the room the women come and go
Talking of Michelangelo.

The yellow fog that rubs its back upon the windowpanes,
The yellow smoke that rubs its muzzle on the windowpanes
Licked its tongue into the corners of the evening,
Lingered upon the pools that stand in drains,
Let fall upon its back the soot that falls from chimneys,
Slipped by the terrace, made a sudden leap,   20
And seeing that it was a soft October night,
Curled once about the house, and fell asleep.

And indeed there will be time
For the yellow smoke that slides along the street,
Rubbing its back upon the windowpanes;

---

[1] From Dante, *Inferno*, XXVII, 61–66. The speaker is Guido da Montefeltro, who is imprisoned in a flame in the level of hell reserved for false counselors. He tells Dante and Virgil, "If I thought my answer were given to one who might return to the world, this flame would stay without further movement. But since from this depth none has ever returned alive, if what I hear is true, I answer you without fear of infamy."

There will be time, there will be time
To prepare a face to meet the faces that you meet;
There will be time to murder and create,
And time for all the works and days of hands
That lift and drop a question on your plate;   30
Time for you and time for me,
And time yet for a hundred indecisions,
And for a hundred visions and revisions,
Before the taking of a toast and tea.

In the room the women come and go
Talking of Michelangelo.

And indeed there will be time
To wonder, "Do I dare?" and, "Do I dare?"
Time to turn back and descend the stair,
With a bald spot in the middle of my hair—   40
(They will say: "How his hair is growing thin!")
My morning coat, my collar mounting firmly to the chin,
My necktie rich and modest, but asserted by a simple pin—
(They will say: "But how his arms and legs are thin!")
Do I dare
Disturb the universe?
In a minute there is time
For decisions and revisions which a minute will reverse.

For I have known them all already, known them all—
Have known the evenings, mornings, afternoons,   50
I have measured out my life with coffee spoons;
I know the voices dying with a dying fall
Beneath the music from a farther room.
    So how should I presume?

And I have known the eyes already, known them all—
The eyes that fix you in a formulated phrase,
And when I am formulated, sprawling on a pin,
When I am pinned and wriggling on the wall,
Then how should I begin
To spit out all the butt-ends of my days and ways?   60
    And how should I presume?

And I have known the arms already, known them all—
Arms that are braceleted and white and bare
(But in the lamplight, downed with light brown hair!)
Is it perfume from a dress

That makes me so digress?
Arms that lie along a table, or wrap about a shawl.
   And should I then presume?
   And how should I begin?

       . . . . .

Shall I say, I have gone at dusk through narrow streets   70
And watched the smoke that rises from the pipes
Of lonely men in shirt-sleeves, leaning out of windows? . . .

I should have been a pair of ragged claws
Scuttling across the floors of silent seas.

       . . . .

And the afternoon, the evening, sleeps so peacefully!
Smoothed by long fingers,
Asleep . . . tired . . . or it malingers,
Stretched on the floor, here beside you and me.
Should I, after tea and cakes and ices,
Have the strength to force the moment to its crisis?   80
But though I have wept and fasted, wept and prayed,
Though I have seen my head (grown slightly bald) brought in upon a platter,[2]
I am no prophet—and here's no great matter;
I have seen the moment of my greatness flicker,
And I have seen the eternal Footman hold my coat, and snicker,
And in short, I was afraid.

And would it have been worth it, after all,
After the cups, the marmalade, the tea,
Among the porcelain, among some talk of you and me,
Would it have been worth while,   90
To have bitten off the matter with a smile,
To have squeezed the universe into a ball
To roll it toward some overwhelming question,
To say: "I am Lazarus,[3] come from the dead,
Come back to tell you all, I shall tell you all"—
If one, settling a pillow by her head,
   Should say: "That is not what I meant at all.
   That is not it, at all."

And would it have been worth it, after all,
Would it have been worth while,   100

[2] Like the head of John the Baptist. See Matthew 14:3–12.
[3] See John 11:1–14 and Luke 16:19–26.

After the sunsets and the dooryards and the sprinkled streets,
After the novels, after the teacups, after the skirts that trail along the floor—
And this, and so much more?—
It is impossible to say just what I mean!
But as if a magic lantern threw the nerves in patterns on a screen:
Would it have been worth while
If one, settling a pillow or throwing off a shawl,
And turning toward the window, should say:
    "That is not it at all,
      That is not what I meant, at all."   110

. . . . .

No! I am not Prince Hamlet, nor was meant to be;
Am an attendant lord, one that will do
To swell a progress,° start a scene or two,   *state journey*
Advise the prince; no doubt, an easy tool,
Deferential, glad to be of use,
Politic, cautious, and meticulous;
Full of high sentence,° but a bit obtuse;   *sententiousness*
At times, indeed, almost ridiculous—
Almost, at times, the Fool.

I grow old . . . I grow old . . .   120
I shall wear the bottoms of my trousers rolled.°   *cuffed*

Shall I part my hair behind? Do I dare to eat a peach?
I shall wear white flannel trousers, and walk upon the beach.
I have heard the mermaids singing, each to each.

I do not think that they will sing to me.

I have seen them riding seaward on the waves
Combing the white hair of the waves blown back
When the wind blows the water white and black.

We have lingered in the chambers of the sea
By sea-girls wreathed with seaweed red and brown   130
Till human voices wake us, and we drown.

FOR ANALYSIS

1. This poem may be understood as a stream of consciousness passing through the mind of Prufrock. The "you and I" of line 1 may be different aspects of his personality. Or perhaps the "you and I" is parallel to Guido da Montefeltro, who speaks the epigraph, and Dante, to whom he tells the story that resulted in his damnation—hence, "you" is the reader and "I" is Prufrock. The poem is disjointed because it proceeds by psychological rather than logical stages. To what social class does Prufrock belong? How does Prufrock respond to the attitudes and values of his class? Does he change in the course of the poem?

2. Line 92 provides a good example of literary **allusion** (see the last stanza of Marvell's "To His Coy Mistress," p. 950). How does an awareness of the allusion contribute to your response?

3. What might the song of the mermaids (l. 124) signify, and why does Prufrock think they will not sing to him (l. 125)?

4. T. S. Eliot once said that some poetry "can communicate without being understood." Is this such a poem?

WRITING TOPIC

What sort of man is J. Alfred Prufrock? How does the poet establish his characteristics?

E. E. CUMMINGS (1894–1962)

THE CAMBRIDGE LADIES WHO LIVE IN FURNISHED SOULS 1923

the Cambridge ladies who live in furnished souls
are unbeautiful and have comfortable minds
(also, with the church's protestant blessings
daughters, unscented shapeless spirited)
they believe in Christ and Longfellow, both dead,
are invariably interested in so many things—
at the present writing one still finds
delighted fingers knitting for the is it Poles?
perhaps. While permanent faces coyly bandy
scandal of Mrs. N. and Professor D.   10
. . . the Cambridge ladies do not care, above
Cambridge if sometimes in its box of
sky lavender and cornerless, the
moon rattles like a fragment of angry candy

FOR ANALYSIS

1. What **images** does the poet use to describe "the Cambridge ladies"? What do the images suggest?

2. What is the effect of the interruption "is it" in line 8?

3. In the final lines, the moon seems to protest against the superficiality of these women. What is the effect of comparing the moon to a fragment of candy?

WRITING TOPICS

1. Compare this poem with Dickinson's "What Soft—Cherubic Creatures—" (p. 685).

2. This poem satirizes the behavior of the Cambridge ladies. Does it imply how they *should* behave?

M. CARL HOLMAN   (1919–1988)

MR. Z   1967

Taught early that his mother's skin was the sign of error,
He dressed and spoke the perfect part of honor;
Won scholarships, attended the best schools,
Disclaimed kinship with jazz and spirituals;
Chose prudent, raceless views for each situation,
Or when he could not cleanly skirt dissension,
Faced up to the dilemma, firmly seized
Whatever ground was Anglo-Saxonized.

In diet, too, his practice was exemplary:
Of pork in its profane forms he was wary;   10
Expert in vintage wines, sauces and salads,
His palate shrank from cornbread, yams and collards.

He was as careful whom he chose to kiss:
His bride had somewhere lost her Jewishness,
But kept her blue eyes; an Episcopalian
Prelate proclaimed them matched chameleon.
Choosing the right addresses, here, abroad,
They shunned those places where they might be barred;
Even less anxious to be asked to dine
Where hosts catered to kosher accent or exotic skin.   20

And so he climbed, unclogged by ethnic weights,
An airborne plant, flourishing without roots.
Not one false note was struck—until he died:
His subtly grieving widow could have flayed
The obit writers, ringing crude changes on a clumsy phrase:
"One of the most distinguished members of his race."

FOR ANALYSIS

1. Explain the title of this poem. What might "Z" stand for?

2. What is the significance of the description of Mr. Z's wife?

3. In what sense is the comment of the final line the only "false note" in an otherwise successful and exemplary life?

4. Describe the use of **irony** in this poem.

WRITING TOPICS

1. Describe an experience in which you successfully conformed to a set of expectations in order to achieve a goal, only to discover that you were denied that goal.

2. If you have lived as a minority (ethnic, religious, racial, or other) in a community, describe the pressures you felt to conform, and the costs (social, economic, or emotional) of your attempts—or your refusal—to conform.

ETHERIDGE KNIGHT (1931–1991)

HARD ROCK RETURNS TO PRISON FROM THE HOSPITAL FOR THE CRIMINAL INSANE 1968

Hard Rock was "known not to take no shit
From nobody," and he had the scars to prove it:
Split purple lips, lumped ears, welts above
His yellow eyes, and one long scar that cut
Across his temple and plowed through a thick
Canopy of kinky hair.

The WORD was that Hard Rock wasn't a mean nigger
Anymore, that the doctors had bored a hole in his head,
Cut out part of his brain, and shot electricity
Through the rest. When they brought Hard Rock back,   10
Handcuffed and chained, he was turned loose,
Like a freshly gelded stallion, to try his new status.
And we all waited and watched, like Indians at a corral,
To see if the WORD was true.

As we waited we wrapped ourselves in the cloak
Of his exploits: "Man, the last time, it took eight
Screws to put him in the Hole." "Yeah, remember when he
Smacked the captain with his dinner tray?" "He set
The record for time in the Hole—67 straight days!"
"Ol Hard Rock! man, that's one crazy nigger."   20
And then the jewel of a myth that Hard Rock had once bit
A screw on the thumb and poisoned him with syphilitic spit.

The testing came, to see if Hard Rock was really tame.
A hillbilly called him a black son of a bitch

And didn't lose his teeth, a screw who knew Hard Rock
From before shook him down and barked in his face.
And Hard Rock did *nothing*. Just grinned and looked silly,
His eyes empty like knot holes in a fence.

And even after we discovered that it took Hard Rock
Exactly 3 minutes to tell you his first name,   30
We told ourselves that he had just wised up,
Was being cool; but we could not fool ourselves for long,
And we turned away, our eyes on the ground. Crushed.

He had been our Destroyer, the doer of things
We dreamed of doing but could not bring ourselves to do,
The fears of years, like a biting whip,
Had cut grooves too deeply across our backs.

WOLE SOYINKA (B. 1934)

TELEPHONE CONVERSATION 1960

The price seemed reasonable, location
Indifferent. The landlady swore she lived
Off premises. Nothing remained
But self-confession. "Madam," I warned,
"I hate a wasted journey—I am African."
Silence. Silenced transmission of
Pressurized good-breeding. Voice, when it came,
Lipstick coated, long gold-rolled
Cigarette-holder pipped. Caught I was, foully.
"HOW DARK?" ... I had not misheard.... "ARE YOU LIGHT   10
OR VERY DARK?" Button B. Button A. Stench
Of rancid breath of public hide-and-speak.
Red booth.[1] Red pillar-box.[2] Red double-tiered
Omnibus squelching tar. It *was* real! Shamed
By ill-mannered silence, surrender
Pushed dumbfoundment to beg simplification.
Considerate she was, varying the emphasis—
"ARE YOU DARK? OR VERY LIGHT?" Revelation came.
"You mean—like plain or milk chocolate?"
Her assent was clinical, crushing in its light   20

Telephone Conversation
[1] Older British public phones, whose booths were painted red, had one button that had to be depressed when a connection was made, and a second one that allowed the caller to disconnect.
[2] A public mailbox.

Impersonality. Rapidly, wave-length adjusted.
I chose. "West African sepia"—and as afterthought,
"Down in my passport." Silence for spectroscopic
Flight of fancy, till truthfulness clanged her accent
Hard on the mouthpiece. "WHAT'S THAT?" conceding
"DON'T KNOW WHAT THAT IS." "Like brunette."
"THAT'S DARK, ISN'T IT?" "Not altogether.
Facially, I am brunette, but madam, you should see
The rest of me. Palm of my hand, soles of my feet
Are a peroxide blonde. Friction, caused—   30
Foolishly madam—by sitting down, has turned
My bottom raven black—One moment madam!"—sensing
Her receiver rearing on the thunderclap
About my ears—"Madam," I pleaded, "wouldn't you rather
See for yourself?"

FOR ANALYSIS

1. Aware of the racism of the culture in which he lives, the speaker volunteers to the landlady that he is African in order to avoid "a wasted journey" (l. 5). Why, then, is he so taken aback when she asks him how dark he is?

2. Describe the meaning and tone of the speaker's comment, "Caught I was, foully" (l. 9).

3. Explain the pun in line 12.

4. What does "It" in line 14 refer to?

WRITING TOPIC

How would the landlady have answered the speaker's question at the end of the poem, and how might she have justified her response?

KAY RYAN   (B. 1945)

ALL SHALL BE RESTORED   1996

The grains shall be collected
from the thousand shores
to which they found their way,
and the boulder restored,
and the boulder itself replaced
in the cliff, and likewise
the cliff shall rise
or subside until the plate of earth
is without fissure. Restoration
knows no half measure. It will   10
not stop when the treasured and lost

bronze horse remounts the steps.
Even this horse will founder backward
to coin, cannon, and domestic pots,
which themselves shall bubble and
drain back to green veins in stone.
And every word written shall lift off
letter by letter, the backward text
read ever briefer, ever more antic
in its effort to insist that nothing   20
shall be lost.

FOR ANALYSIS

1. What process is being reversed in lines 1–9? In lines 10–16? What kind of processes
are these? Are they actually reversible?

2. What does the last sentence of the poem add to its meaning? How is the last
clause—"nothing shall be lost"—related to the poem's title?

3. Describe the **style** of the poem. What kind of voice does Ryan create? How does she
do it?

WRITING TOPICS

One of the most important facts of human experience is that it ends—at least in the
case of individual life. Many different aspects of culture can be seen, in part, to be
dealing with this eventuality: either accepting this natural process or working against
it. What does "All Shall Be Restored" say about the way culture deals with death?

JUAN FELIPE HERRERA   (B. 1948)

187 REASONS MEXICANOS CAN'T CROSS THE BORDER (REMIX) 1994

—Abutebaris modo subjunctivo denuo.[1]

Because Lou Dobbs has been misusing the subjunctive again
Because our suitcases are made with biodegradable maguey fibers
Because we still resemble La Malinche
Because multiplication is our favorite sport
Because we'll dig a tunnel to Seattle
Because Mexico needs us to keep the peso from sinking
Because the Berlin Wall is on the way through Veracruz
Because we just learned we are Huichol
Because someone made our IDs out of corn

---

[1] You've been misusing the subjunctive again.

Because our border thirst is insatiable   10
Because we're on peyote & Coca-Cola & Banamex
Because it's Indian land stolen from our mothers
Because we're too emotional when it comes to our mothers
Because we've been doing it for over five hundred years already
Because it's too easy to say "I am from here"
Because Latin American petrochemical juice flows first
Because what would we do in El Norte
Because Nahuatl, Mayan & Chicano will spread to Canada
Because Zedillo & Salinas & Fox are still on vacation
Because the World Bank needs our abuelita's account   20
Because the CIA trains better with brown targets
Because our accent is unable to hide U.S. colonialism
Because what will the Hispanik MBAs do
Because our voice resembles La Llorona's
Because we are still voting
Because the North is really South
Because we can read about it in an ethnic prison
Because Frida beat us to it
Because U.S. & European Corporations would rather visit us first
Because environmental U.S. industrial pollution suits our color   30
Because of a new form of Overnight Mayan Anarchy
Because there are enough farmworkers in California already
Because we're meant to usher a postmodern gloom into Mexico
Because Nabisco, Exxon, & Union Carbide gave us Mal de Ojo
Because every nacho chip can morph into a Mexican Wrestler
Because it's better to be rootless, unconscious, & rapeable
Because we're destined to have the "Go Back to Mexico" Blues
Because of Pancho Villa's hidden treasure in Chihuahua
Because of Bogart's hidden treasure in the Sierra Madre
Because we need more murals honoring our Indian Past   40
Because we are really dark French Creoles in a Cantínflas costume
Because of this Aztec reflex to sacrifice ourselves
Because we couldn't clean up hurricane Katrina
Because of this Spanish penchant to be polite and aggressive
Because we had a vision of Sor Juana in drag
Because we smell of tamales soaked in Tequila
Because we got hooked listening to Indian Jazz in Chiapas
Because we're still waiting to be cosmic
Because our passport says we're out of date
Because our organ donor got lost in a Bingo game   50
Because we got to learn English first & get in line & pay a little fee
Because we're understanding & appreciative of our Capitalist neighbors
Because our 500-year penance was not severe enough
Because we're still running from La Migra

Because we're still kissing the Pope's hand
Because we're still practicing to be Franciscan priests
Because they told us to sit & meditate & chant "Nosotros los Pobres"
Because of the word "Revolución" & the words "Viva Zapata"
Because we rely more on brujas than lawyers
Because we never finished our Ph.D. in Total United Service   60
Because our identity got mixed up with passion
Because we have visions instead of televisions
Because our huaraches are made with Goodyear & Uniroyal
Because the pesticides on our skin are still glowing
Because it's too easy to say "American Citizen" in cholo
Because you can't shrink-wrap enchiladas
Because a Spy in Spanish sounds too much like "Es Pie" in English
Because our comadres are an International Political Party
Because we believe in The Big Chingazo Theory of the Universe
Because we're still holding our breath in the Presidential Palace in   70
     Mexico City
Because every Mexican is a Living Theatre of Rebellion
Because Hollywood needs its subject matter in proper folkloric costume
Because the Grammys & iTunes are finally out in Spanish
Because the Right is writing an epic poem of apology for our proper edification
Because the Alamo really is pronounced "Alamadre"
Because the Mayan concept of zero means "U.S. Out of Mexico"
Because the oldest ceiba in Yucatán is prophetic
Because England is making plans
Because we can have Nicaragua, Honduras, & Panama anyway
Because 125 million Mexicans can be wrong   80
Because we'll smuggle an earthquake into New York
Because we'll organize like the Vietnamese in San José
Because we'll organize like the Mixtecos in Fresno
Because East L.A. is sinking
Because the Christian Coalition doesn't cater at César Chávez Parque
Because you can't make mace out of beans
Because the computers can't pronounce our names
Because the National Border Police are addicted to us
Because Africa will follow
Because we're still dressed in black rebozos   90
Because we might sing a corrido at any moment
Because our land grants are still up for grabs
Because our tattoos are indecipherable
Because people are hanging milagros on the 2,000 miles of border wire
Because we're locked into Magical Realism
Because Mexican dependence is a form of higher learning
Because making chilaquiles leads to plastic explosives
Because a simple Spanish Fly can mutate into a raging Bird Flu

Because we eat too many carbohydrates
Because we gave enough blood at the Smithfield, Inc., slaughterhouse in   100
    Tar Heel, North Carolina
Because a quinceañera will ruin the concept of American virginity
Because huevos rancheros are now being served at Taco Bell as Wavoritos
Because every Mexican grito undermines English intonation
Because the President has a Mexican maid
Because the Vice President has a Mexican maid
Because it's Rosa López's fault O.J. Simpson was guilty
Because Banda music will take over the White House
Because Aztec sexual aberrations are still in practice
Because our starvation & squalor isn't as glamorous as Somalia's
Because agribusiness will whack us anyway   110
Because the information superhighway is not for Chevys & Impalas
Because white men are paranoid of Frida's mustache
Because the term "mariachi" comes from the word "cucarachi"
Because picking grapes is not a British tradition
Because they are still showing *Zoot Suit* in prisons
Because Richie Valens is alive in West Liberty, Iowa
Because ? & the Mysterians cried 97 tears not 96
Because Hoosgow, Riata and Rodeo are Juzgado, Riata and Rodeo
Because Jackson Hole, Wyoming, will blow as soon as we hit Oceanside
Because U.S. narco-business needs us in Nogales   120
Because the term "Mexican" comes from "Mexicanto"
Because Mexican queers crossed already
Because Mexican lesbians wear Ben Davis pants & sombreros de palma to work
Because VFW halls aren't built to serve cabeza con tripas
Because the National Guard are going international
Because we still bury our feria in the backyard
Because we don't have international broncas for profit
Because we are in love with our sister Rigoberta Menchú
Because California is on the verge of becoming California
Because the PRI is a family affair   130
Because we may start a television series called *No Chingues Conmigo*
Because we are too sweet & obedient & confused & (still) full of rage
Because the CIA needs us in a Third World State of mind
Because brown is the color of the future
Because we turned Welfare into El Huero Fèlix
Because we know what the Jews have been through
Because we know what the Blacks have been through
Because the Irish became the San Patricio Corps at the Battle of Churubusco
Because of our taste for Yiddish gospel raps & tardeadas & salsa limericks
Because El Sistema Nos La Pela   140
Because you can take the boy outta Mexico but not outta the Boycott
Because the Truckers, Arkies and Okies enjoy our telenovelas

Because we'd rather shop at the flea market than Macy's
Because pan dulce feels sexual, especially conchas & the elotes
Because we'll Xerox tamales in order to survive
Because we'll export salsa to Russia & call it "Pikushki"
Because cilantro aromas follow us wherever we go
Because we'll unionize & sing *De Colores*
Because A Day Without a Mexican is a day away
Because we're in touch with our Boricua camaradas   150
Because we are the continental majority
Because we'll build a sweat lodge in front of Bank of America
Because we should wait for further instructions from Televisa
Because 125 million Mexicanos are potential Chicanos
Because we'll take over the Organic Foods business with a
          molcajete
Because 2,000 miles of maquiladoras want to promote us
Because the next Olympics will commemorate the Mexico City
          massacre of 1968
Because there is an Aztec temple beneath our Nopales
Because we know how to pronounce all the Japanese corporations
Because the Comadre network is more accurate than CNN   160
Because the Death Squads are having a hard time with Caló
Because the mayor of San Diego likes salsa medium-picante
Because the Navy, Army, Marines like us topless in Tijuana
Because when we see red, white & blue we just see red
Because when we see the numbers 187 we still see red
Because we need to pay a little extra fee to the Border
Because Mexican Human Rights sounds too Mexican
Because Chrysler is putting out a lowrider
Because they found a lost Chicano tribe in Utah
Because harina white flour bag suits don't cut it at graduation   170
Because we'll switch from AT&T & MCI to Y-que, y-que
Because our hand signs aren't registered
Because Freddy Fender wasn't Baldomar Huerta's real name
Because "lotto" is another Chicano word for "pronto"
Because we won't nationalize a State of Immigrant Paranoia
Because the depression of the '30s was our fault
Because "xenophobia" is a politically correct term
Because we shoulda learned from the Chinese Exclusion Act of 1882
Because we shoulda listened to the Federal Immigration Laws of
          1917, '21, '24 & '30
Because we lack a Nordic/Teutonic approach   180
Because Executive Order 9066 of 1942 shudda had us too
Because Operation Wetback took care of us in the '50s
Because Operation Clean Sweep picked up the loose ends in the '70s
Because one more operation will finish us off anyway

Because you can't deport 12 million migrantes in a Greyhound bus
Because we got this thing about walking out of everything
Because we have a heart that sings rancheras and feet that polka

FOR ANALYSIS

1. In 1994, California voters passed a ballot initiative called Proposition 187 that sought to deny "illegal aliens" a variety of social services guaranteed to legal residents, claiming that such services placed an undue financial burden on the state. The measure was later overturned by federal courts. Why do you think Herrera chose 187 for his title? How many lines are in the poem?

2. Repetition of a word or phrase at the beginning of a sentence, clause, or line of poetry is called *anaphora*. How does Herrera use anaphora, and to what effect?

MAKING CONNECTIONS

Compare the ways in which Erdrich's "Dear John Wayne" (p. 665) and "187 Reasons Mexicanos Can't Cross the Border" are concerned not just with how minorities are seen by the majority culture but also how minorities see themselves.

WRITING TOPICS

1. Write a "because" list poem about some issue of interest to you and in which you dispute reasons or motivations.

2. Describe the complicated use of **irony** in "187 Reasons Mexicanos Can't Cross the Border."

MARK HALLIDAY   (B. 1949)

SEVENTH AVENUE   1992

Late Tuesday afternoon the romantic self weaves
up Seventh Avenue amid too many lookers, too many
feelers: romance hates democracy;

how can *you* be so great and golden inside
if your trunk is shouldered among other trunks
block after block, block after block—

you can't help glimpsing an otherness in others
that is not just surface: they ache,
their aches ache away north and south all Tuesday

in murmurous torsos like yours. . . .   10
What apprehension blossoms even now in Manuel
shifting steaks at the ten-foot grill of Charley O's

beneath the towering chef's hat they make him wear?
When I was twenty I'd have written
that he was only thinking of Cadillacs and sex;

now I'm afraid he's just as worried as I am
about love vs. lesser things and the point of it all.
Manuel, stay there at the sizzling grill till midnight

and then just drink or sleep, man,
don't write poems—   20
do me that favor. It's loud enough already

out here on Seventh Avenue with that cat's boom box
and these three giggle girls being Madonna together
and that guy hawking wind-up titans wielding laser lances.

Who's Wordsworth for any extended period on Seventh Ave?
In this pre-dusk traffic you catch the hint
that Manuel and thou if seers at all are seers only

for seconds—now the steak, taxi, buttocks, headline
and wallet resume their charismatic claim to be what counts.
Soul on Seventh is a sometime on-off quick-flip thing . . .   30

What I want is a poem long as Seventh Avenue
to sprinkle gold on every oppressed minority,
every young woman's subtly female hips,
every sad and suspicious American face
and the quiddity of every mud-tracked pizza shop;
proving, block after block, stanza by stanza
that I'm not just one skinny nervous pedestrian
but the one who matters because he sees and says.
I want that. The Avenue grins and says
"You want, that? How does it feel to want?"   40

FOR ANALYSIS

1. *Quiddity* (l. 35) is the real or essential nature of something. Why is that an important idea in the poem?

2. Is this poem more about Seventh Avenue itself or about the "romantic self" who walks down it? If the latter, who is that self, and what about that self is of concern in the poem?

3. What was your reaction to the last sentence in the poem? What is unusual about it? Why do you think Halliday chose to end the poem this way?

WRITING TOPICS

1. Describe Halliday's use of language. Does he stick to one register—that is, does he use only long, complicated, formal words or everyday words—or switch registers? What effects does he achieve?

2. Write an essay in which you answer the following: Does the poem answer the question of whether the speaker is "just one skinny nervous pedestrian" or "the one who matters because he sees and says" (ll. 37–38)?

RITA DOVE   (B. 1952)

DAYSTAR   1986

She wanted a little room for thinking:
but she saw diapers streaming on the line,
a doll slumped behind the door.

So she lugged a chair behind the garage
to sit out the children's naps.

Sometimes there were things to watch—
the pinched armor of a vanished cricket,
a floating maple leaf. Other days
she stared until she was assured
when she closed her eyes   10
she'd see only her own vivid blood.

She had an hour, at best, before Liza appeared
pouting from the top of the stairs.
and just *what* was mother doing
out back with the field mice? Why,

building a palace. Later
that night when Thomas rolled over and
lurched into her, she would open her eyes
and think of the place that was hers
for an hour—where   20
she was nothing,
pure nothing, in the middle of the day.

FOR ANALYSIS

1. Answer Liza's question: "[A]nd just *what* was mother doing / out back with the field mice?" (ll. 14–15).

2. What *is* the speaker when she is not "pure nothing" (l. 22)?

WRITING TOPIC

Is this poem appropriately placed in the thematic section called "Culture and Identity,"
or does it belong in a different section? Explain.

JUDITH ORTIZ COFER   (B. 1952)

LATIN WOMEN PRAY   1987

Latin women pray
In incense sweet churches
They pray in Spanish to an Anglo God
With a Jewish heritage.

And this Great White Father
Imperturbable in his marble pedestal
Looks down upon his brown daughters
Votive candles shining like lust
In his all seeing eyes
Unmoved by their persistent prayers.   10

Yet year after year
Before his image they kneel
Margarita Josefina Maria and Isabel
All fervently hoping
That if not omnipotent
At least he be bilingual.

MARK DOTY   (B 1953)

ESTA NOCHE   1993

In a dress with a black tulip's sheen
   la fabulosa Lola enters, late, mounts the stairs
to the plywood platform, and begs whoever runs
   the wobbling spot to turn the lights down

to something flattering. When they halo her
   with a petal-toned gel, she sets to haranguing,
shifting in and out of two languages like gowns
   or genders to *please* have a little respect

for the girls, flashing the one entrancing
   and unavoidable gap in the center of her upper teeth.   10
And when the cellophane drop goes black,
   a new spot coronas her in a wig

fit for the end of a century,
   and she tosses back her hair—risky gesture—
and raises her arms like a widow in a blood tragedy,
   all will and black lace, and lipsyncs "You and Me

against the World." She's a man
   you wouldn't look twice at in street clothes,
two hundred pounds of hard living, the gap in her smile
   sadly narrative—but she's a monument,   20

in the mysterious permission of the dress.
   This is Esta Noche, a Latin drag bar in the Mission,
its black door a gap in the face
   of a battered wall. All over the neighborhood

storefront windows show all night
   shrined hats and gloves, wedding dresses,
First Communion's frothing lace:
   gowns of perfection and commencement,

fixed promises glowing. In the dress
   the color of the spaces between streetlamps   30
Lola stands unassailable, the dress
   in which she is in the largest sense

fabulous: a lesson, a criticism and colossus
   of gender, all fire and irony. Her spine's
perfectly erect, only her fluid hands moving
   and her head turned slightly to one side.

She hosts the pageant, Wednesdays and Saturdays,
   and men come in from the streets, the trains,
and the repair shops, lean together to rank
   the artifice of the awkward or lovely   40

Lola welcomes onto the stage: Victoria, Elena,
   Francie, lamé pumps and stockings and always
the rippling night pulled down over broad shoulders
   and flounced around the hips, liquid,

the black silk of esta noche
   proving that perfection and beauty are so alien
they almost never touch. Tonight, she says,
   put it on. The costume is license

and calling. She says you could wear the whole damn
   black sky and all its spangles. It's the only night   50
we have to stand on. Put it on,
   it's the only thing we have to wear.

LOUISE ERDRICH   (B. 1954)

DEAR JOHN WAYNE   1984

August and the drive-in picture is packed.
We lounge on the hood of the Pontiac
surrounded by the slow-burning spirals they sell
at the window, to vanquish the hordes of mosquitoes.
Nothing works. They break through the smoke screen for blood.

Always the lookout spots the Indians first,
spread north to south, barring progress.
The Sioux or some other Plains bunch
in spectacular columns, ICBM missiles,
feathers bristling in the meaningful sunset.   10

The drum breaks. There will be no parlance.
Only the arrows whining, a death-cloud of nerves
swarming down on the settlers
who die beautifully, tumbling like dust weeds
into the history that brought us all here
together: this wide screen beneath the sign of the bear.

The sky fills, acres of blue squint and eye
that the crowd cheers. His face moves over us,
a thick cloud of vengeance, pitted
like the land that was once flesh. Each rut,   20
each scar makes a promise: *It is
not over, this fight, not as long as you resist.*

Everything we see belongs to us.

A few laughing Indians fall over the hood
slipping in the hot spilled butter.
The eye sees a lot, John, but the heart is so blind.
Death makes us owners of nothing.
He smiles, a horizon of teeth
the credits reel over, and then the white fields
again blowing in the true-to-life dark.   30
The dark films over everything.
We get into the car
scratching our mosquito bites, speechless and small
as people are when the movie is done.
We are back in our skins.

How can we help but keep hearing his voice,
the flip side of the sound track, still playing:
Come on, boys, we got them
where we want them, drunk, running.
They'll give us what we want, what we need.   40
Even his disease was the idea of taking everything.
Those cells, burning, doubling, splitting out of their skins.

FOR ANALYSIS

1. Part of the power of "Dear John Wayne" lies in the difference between its two **settings,** or places. What are they? What are their differences, and why are they significant?

2. Describing the "Indians" in the movie, Erdrich calls them "The Sioux, or some other Plains bunch" (l. 8). What **ironic** effect is intended by this last phrase? Note other places where Erdrich is being ironic. What are the effects there?

3. From its very title onward, Erdrich's poem is concerned with the question of audience. Who are the different audiences implied in this poem, intended and actual? Who are the different speakers? As a reader, which audience are you?

WRITING TOPICS

1. Address the issue of this poem's complicated **tone**. What are its various **moods** and attitudes toward its subjects? When and how do they shift, and to what effect?

2. Draw a line down the middle of a piece of paper. In the left column, write down everything the white men in the poem see. In the right column, write down everything the Native Americans in the poem see. Compare the two columns in an essay that discusses the issue of power in seeing and being seen.

CATHY SONG (B. 1955)

STAMP COLLECTING 1988

The poorest countries
have the prettiest stamps
as if impracticality were a major export
shipped with the bananas, t-shirts, and coconuts.
Take Tonga,[1] where the tourists,
expecting a dramatic waterfall replete with birdcalls,
are taken to see the island's peculiar mystery:
hanging bats with collapsible wings
like black umbrellas swing upside down from fruit trees.
The Tongan stamp is a fruit.   10
The banana stamp is scalloped like a butter-varnished seashell.
The pineapple resembles a volcano, a spout of green on top,
and the papaya, a tarnished goat skull.

They look impressive,
these stamps of countries without a thing to sell
except for what is scraped, uprooted and hulled
from their mule-scratched hills.
They believe in postcards,
in portraits of progress: the new dam;
a team of young native doctors   20
wearing stethoscopes like exotic ornaments;
the recently constructed "Facultad de Medicina,"
a building as lack lustre as an American motel.

The stamps of others are predictable.
Lucky is the country that possesses indigenous beauty.
Say a tiger or a queen.
The Japanese can display to the world
their blossoms: a spray of pink on green.
Like pollen, they drift, airborne.
But pity the country that is bleak and stark.   30

Beauty and whimsey are discouraged as indiscreet.
Unbreakable as their climate, a monument of ice,
they issue serious statements, commemorating
factories, tramways and aeroplanes;

---

[1] A group of islands in the southwest Pacific Ocean with a population of around 100,000.

athletes marbled into statues.
They turn their noses upon the world, these countries,
and offer this: an unrelenting procession
of a grim, historic profile.

FOR ANALYSIS

1. What do stamps reveal about the country that creates them? Do you think the poet favors certain kinds of stamps and countries over others? Explain.

2. Contrast the presentation of the Tongan fruit stamps with those of the "countries without a thing to sell" (l. 15). How do they differ in both subject matter and poetic rendering?

3. Describe the countries whose stamps offer "a grim, historic profile" (l. 38).

WRITING TOPIC

Choose a stamp (either domestic or foreign), describe what it depicts, and characterize the mind-set that designed it.

JOSHUA CLOVER   (B. 1962)

THE NEVADA GLASSWORKS   1997

Ka-Boom! They're making glass in Nevada!
Figure August, 1953,
mom's 13, it's hot as a simile.
Ker-Pow! Transmutation in Nevada!
Imagine mom: pre-postModern new teen,
innocent for Elvis, ditto "Korean
conflict," John Paul George Ringo Viet Nam.
Mom's 1 state west of the glassworks, she's
in a tree/K*I*S*S*I*N*G,
lurid cartoon-colored kisses. Ka-Blam!   10
They're blowing peacock-tinted New World glass
in southern Nevada, the alchemists
& architects of mom's duck-&-cover
adolescence, they're making Las Vegas
turn to gold—real neon gold—in the blast
furnace heat that reaches clear to Clover
Ranch in dry Central Valley: O the dust—
It is the Golden State! O the landscape—
dreaming of James Dean! O mom in a tree
close-range kissing as in Nevada just   20

now they're making crazy ground-zero shapes
of radiant see-through geography.
What timing! What kisses! What a fever
this day's become, humming hundred-degree
California afternoon that she's
sure she could never duplicate, *never,*
she feels transparent, gone—isn't this heat
suffocating—no, she forgot to breathe
for a flash while in the Nevada flats
factory glassblowers exhale . . . exhale . . .   30
a philosopher's stone, a crystal ball,
a spectacular machine. Hooray! Hats
off—they're making a window in the sand!
Mom's in the tree—picture this—all alone!
Unforgettable kisses, comic-book
mnemonic kisses. O something's coming
out of the ranch road heat mirage: That drone—
an engine? Mom quits practice & looks
east, cups an ear to the beloved humming,
the hazy gold dust kicked wildly west   40
ahead of something almost . . . in . . . sight. Vroom!
It's the Future, hot like nothing else, dressed
as sonic-boom Cadillac. O mom!
This land *is* your land/This land Amnesia—
they're dropping some new science out there,
a picture-perfect hole blown clear to Asia:
everything in the desert—Shazam!—turns
to glass, gold glass, a picture-window where
the bomb-dead kids are burned & burn & burn

FOR ANALYSIS

1. What exactly is happening in Nevada to make glass? What is the "new science" (l. 45)?

2. When Clover writes, "What timing!" (l. 23), to what is he referring? Why does the poem cut back and forth between Nevada and "1 state west" (l. 8)?

3. Identify Clover's **tone**. What is his attitude toward his subject? Is it directly stated? If not, how do you know what it is?

WRITING TOPIC

1. Clover mixes various kinds of language and **imagery**. Catalog examples of one element—kinds of words, kind of images (remembering that images aren't necessarily only visual)—and group them into different types (for example, long complicated words and simple words). In an essay, consider how and why Clover uses the kinds of elements he does.

KEVIN YOUNG (B. 1970)

NEGATIVE 2005

Wake to find everything black
what was white, all the vice
versa—white maids on TV, black

sitcoms that star white dwarfs
cute as pearl buttons, Black Presidents,
Black Houses, White Horse

candidates. All bleach burns
clothes black. Drive roads
white as you are, white songs

on the radio stolen by black bands   10
like secret pancake recipes, white back-up
singers, ball-players & boxers all

white as tar. Feathers on chickens
dark as everything, boiling in the pot
that called the kettle honky. Even

whites of the eye turn dark, pupils
clear & changing as a cat's.
Is this what we've wanted

& waited for? to see snow
covering everything black   20
as Christmas, dark pages written

white upon? All our eclipses bright,
dark stars shooting across pale
sky, glowing like ash in fire, shower

every skin. Only money keeps
green, still grows & burns like grass
under dark daylight.

CONNECTING POEMS: SELF-DECLARATIONS

The poems in this unit feature speakers declaring who they are; beyond that, the selections diverge wildly. They differ in how their speakers understand their identities; in how they trace the connections between who they are, the world they live in, and the past that produced them; and in how they declare themselves. Many of these poems are formally and stylistically inventive, too. As you read the selections in this unit, take note of the ways in which the poets shape their declarations of what makes a "self," of how we know that "self," of whether a "self" is fixed and discrete or changeable and connected, multiple, even shared.

WALT WHITMAN   (1819–1892)

FROM SONG OF MYSELF   1855

1

I celebrate myself, and sing myself,
And what I assume you shall assume,
For every atom belonging to me as good belongs to you.

I loafe and invite my soul,
I lean and loafe at my ease observing a spear of summer grass.

My tongue, every atom of my blood, form'd from this soil, this air,
Born here of parents born here from parents the same, and their parents
    the same,
I, now thirty-seven years old in perfect health begin,
Hoping to cease not till death.

Creeds and schools in abeyance,   10
Retiring back a while sufficed at what they are, but never forgotten,
I harbor for good or bad, I permit to speak at every hazard,
Nature without check with original energy.

6

A child said *What is the grass?* fetching it to me with full hands;
How could I answer the child? I do not know what it is any more than he.

I guess it must be the flag of my disposition, out of hopeful green stuff woven.

Or I guess it is the handkerchief of the Lord,
A scented gift and remembrancer designedly dropt,

Bearing the owner's name someway in the corners, that we may see and
    remark, and say *Whose?*

Or I guess the grass is itself a child, the produced babe of the vegetation.   20

Or I guess it is a uniform hieroglyphic,
And it means, Sprouting alike in broad zones and narrow zones,
Growing among black folks as among white,
Kanuck, Tuckahoe, Congressman, Cuff, I give them the same, I receive them the same.

And now it seems to me the beautiful uncut hair of graves.

Tenderly will I use you curling grass,
It may be you transpire from the breasts of young men,
It may be if I had known them I would have loved them,
It may be you are from old people, or from offspring taken soon out of
    their mothers' laps,
And here you are the mothers' laps.   30

This grass is very dark to be from the white heads of old mothers,
Darker than the colorless beards of old men,
Dark to come from under the faint red roofs of mouths.

O I perceive after all so many uttering tongues,
And I perceive they do not come from the roofs of mouths for nothing.

I wish I could translate the hints about the dead young men and women,
And the hints about old men and mothers, and the offspring taken soon out
    of their laps.

What do you think has become of the young and old men?
And what do you think has become of the women and children?

They are alive and well somewhere,   40
The smallest sprout shows there is really no death,
And if ever there was it led forward life, and does not wait at the end to arrest it,
And ceas'd the moment life appear'd.

All goes onward and outward, nothing collapses,
And to die is different from what anyone supposed, and luckier.

50

There is that in me—I do not know what it is—but I know it is in me.

Wrench'd and sweaty—calm and cool then my body becomes,
I sleep—I sleep long.

I do not know it—it is without name—it is a word unsaid,
It is not in any dictionary, utterance, symbol.   50

Sometimes it swings on more than the earth I swing on,
To it the creation is the friend whose embracing awakes me.

Perhaps I might tell more. Outlines! I plead for my brothers and sisters.

Do you see O my brothers and sisters?
It is not chaos or death—it is form, union, plan—it is eternal life—it is Happiness.

51

The past and present wilt—I have fill'd them, emptied them.
And proceed to fill my next fold of the future.

Listener up there! what have you to confide to me?
Look in my face while I snuff the sidle of evening,
(Talk honestly, no one else hears you, and I stay only a minute longer.)   60

Do I contradict myself?
Very well then I contradict myself.
(I am large, I contain multitudes.)

I concentrate toward them that are nigh, I wait on the door-slab.

Who has done his day's work? who will soonest be through with his supper?
Who wishes to walk with me?

Will you speak before I am gone? will you prove already too late?

52

The spotted hawk swoops by and accuses me, he complains of my gab
        and my loitering.

I too am not a bit tamed, I too am untranslatable,
I sound my barbaric yawp over the roofs of the world.   70

The last scud of day holds back for me,
It flings my likeness after the rest and true as any on the shadowed wilds,
It coaxes me to the vapor and the dusk.

I depart as air, I shake my white locks at the runaway sun,
I effuse my flesh in eddies, and drift it in lacy jags.

I bequeath myself to the dirt to grow from the grass I love,
If you want me again look for me under your boot-soles.

You will hardly know who I am or what I mean,
But I shall be good health to you nevertheless,
And filter and fibre your blood.

80

Failing to fetch me at first keep encouraged,
Missing me one place search another,
I stop somewhere waiting for you.

FOR ANALYSIS

1. Who or what is the speaker of this poem? List the lines in which he seems to be an individual speaker. Then make a list of the lines in which he seems to be something more.

2. The poem from which these excerpts are drawn is part of a book, *Leaves of Grass*. Why does this poem pay so much attention to grass? What does it mean?

3. How does this poem "contain multitudes" (l. 63)?

WRITING TOPICS

1. Whitman writes, "You will hardly know who I am or what I mean, / But I shall be good health to you nevertheless" (ll. 78–79). How might this poem be intended to be "good" for its readers?

2. "Song of Myself" achieves strong and varied effects. Reread the poem, and keep a log of your reactions—your emotional, intellectual, and hard-to-categorize responses— as you encounter the different parts of the poem. Then write a reflection on this log. Do you see any patterns? As you moved again through "Song of Myself," what did you notice about how it works as a poem and on you as a reader?

LANGSTON HUGHES   (1902–1967)

I, TOO   1926

I, too, sing America.

I am the darker brother.
They send me to eat in the kitchen
When company comes,
But I laugh,
And eat well,
And grow strong.

Tomorrow,
I'll be at the table
When company comes.
Nobody'll dare
Say to me,

10

"Eat in the kitchen,"
Then.

Besides,
They'll see how beautiful I am
And be ashamed—

I, too, am America.

YEVGENY YEVTUSHENKO (B. 1933)

I WOULD LIKE   TRANS. 1962

I would like
          to be born
                    in every country,
have a passport
          for them all,
to throw
          all foreign offices
                    into panic,
be every fish
          in every ocean   10
and every dog
          along the path.
I don't want to bow down
                    before any idols
or play at being
                    an Orthodox church hippy,
but I would like to plunge
                    deep into Lake Baikal[1]
and surface snorting
                    somewhere,   20
                    why not in the Mississippi?
In my beloved universe
                    I would like
to be a lonely weed,
                    but not a delicate Narcissus[2]

[1] A large lake in Siberia, just north of Mongolia.
[2] In Greek myth, a beautiful youth who pines away for love of his own reflection and is changed into a flower.

kissing his own mug
in the mirror.
I would like to be
any of God's creatures
right down to the last mangy hyena—
but never a tyrant
or even the cat of a tyrant.
I would like to be
reincarnated as a man
in any circumstance:
a victim of Paraguayan prison tortures,
a homeless child in the slums of Hong Kong,
a living skeleton in Bangladesh,
a holy beggar in Tibet,
a black in Cape Town, 40
but never
in the image of Rambo
The only people whom I hate
are the hypocrites—
pickled hyenas
in heavy syrup.
I would like to lie
under the knives of all the surgeons in the world,
be hunchbacked, blind,
suffer all kinds of diseases, 50
wounds and scars,
be a victim of war,
or a sweeper of cigarette butts,
just so a filthy microbe of superiority
doesn't creep inside.
I would not like to be in the elite,
nor of course,
in the cowardly herd,
nor be a guard-dog of that herd,
nor a shepherd, 60
sheltered by that herd.
And I would like happiness,
but not at the expense of the unhappy,
and I would like freedom,
but not at the expense of the unfree.
I would like to love
all the women in the world,
and I would like to be a woman, too—
just once. . . .

30

Men have been diminished   70
                 by Mother Nature.
Suppose she'd given motherhood
                    to men?
If an innocent child
               stirred
                  below his heart,
man would probably
                not be so cruel.
I would like to be man's daily bread—
say,   80
    a cup of rice
                 for a Vietnamese woman in mourning,
cheap wine
            in a Neapolitan workers' trattoria,[3]
or a tiny tube of cheese
                   in orbit round the moon:
let them eat me,
                let them drink me,
only let my death
                be of some use.   90
I would like to belong to all times,
                         shock all history so much
that it would be amazed
                  what a smart aleck I was.
I would like to bring Nefertiti
                  to Pushkin in a troika.[4]
I would like to increase
                the space of a moment
                       a hundredfold,
so that in the same moment   100
                  I could drink vodka with fishermen in Siberia
and sit together with Homer,
                 Dante,
                    Shakespeare,
                       and Tolstoy,
drinking anything,
               except of course,
                  Coca-Cola,
—dance to the tom-toms in the Congo,

[3] A small, inexpensive restaurant in Italy.
[4] Nefertiti was a famously beautiful fourteenth-century B.C. queen of Egypt. Aleksandr Sergeyevich Pushkin (1799–1837) was perhaps the greatest Russian writer and poet of his time. A troika is a Russian vehicle drawn by a team of three horses.

—strike at Renault,   110
—chase a ball with Brazilian boys
                              at Copacabana Beach.
I would like
            to know every language,
                              the secret waters under the earth,
and do all kinds of work at once.
                        I would make sure
that one Yevtushenko was merely a poet,
                  the second—an underground fighter,
                                          somewhere,   120
I couldn't say where
                  for security reasons,
the third—a student at Berkeley,
                        the fourth—a jolly Georgian[5] drinker,
and the fifth—
                  maybe a teacher of Eskimo children in Alaska,
the sixth—
            a young president,
                        somewhere, say even in Sierra Leone,
the seventh—   130
            would still be shaking a rattle in his stroller,
and the tenth . . .
                  the hundredth . . .
                              the millionth . . .
For me it's not enough to be myself,
                        let me be everyone!
Every creature
            usually has a double,
but God was stingy
                  with the carbon paper,   140
and in his Paradise Publishing Company
                              made a unique copy of me.
But I shall muddle up
                  all God's cards—
                        I shall confound God!
I shall be in a thousand copies
                        to the end of my days,
so that the earth buzzes with me,
                        and computers go berserk
in the world census of me.   150
I would like to fight on all your barricades,

---

[5] Georgia is one of the republics that made up the former Soviet Union. It lies along the east coast of the Black Sea.

humanity,
dying each night
an exhausted moon,
and being resurrected each morning
like a newborn sun,
with an immortal soft spot
on my skull.
And when I die,
a smart-aleck Siberian François Villon,[6]   160
do not lay me in the earth
of France
or Italy,
but in our Russian, Siberian earth,
on a still green hill,
where I first felt
that I was
everyone.

FOR ANALYSIS

1. The poet declares that he would like to be a certain kind of person. What kind of person? What specific **images** lead you to your judgment?

2. What kind of person does he *not* wish to be? What images support your conclusion?

3. Discuss the images that address chronological time. Discuss those that address geographical distance. Discuss those that address a sort of chain of being among creatures, moving from "low" to "high." How does Yevtushenko use these images to define his social and political views?

WRITING TOPIC

In an essay, describe the poet's notion of an ideal person, and speculate on how that person would get along in the real world. Do you accept, or would you modify, Yevtushenko's ideal? Explain.

TOMAŽ ŠALAMUN   (B. 1941)

HISTORY   2004

Tomaž Šalamun is a monster.
Tomaž Šalamun is a sphere rushing through the air.
He lies down in twilight, he swims in twilight.
People and I, we both look at him amazed,
we wish him well, maybe he is a comet.

I Would Like
  [6] A French balladeer, born in 1431, who was often in trouble with the law.

Maybe he is punishment from the gods,
the boundary stone of the world.
Maybe he is such a speck in the universe
that he will give energy to the planet
when oil, steel, and food run short.   10
He might only be a hump, his head
should be taken off like a spider's.
But something would then suck up
Tomaž Šalamun, possibly the head.
Possibly he should be pressed between
glass, his photo should be taken.
He should be put in formaldehyde, so children
would look at him as they do foetuses,
protei, and mermaids.
Next year, he'll probably be in Hawaii   20
or in Ljubljana. Doorkeepers will scalp
tickets. People walk barefoot
to the university there. The waves can be
a hundred feet high. The city is fantastic,
shot through with people on the make,
the wind is mild.
But in Ljubljana people say: look!
This is Tomaž Šalamun, he went to the store
with his wife Marushka to buy some milk.
He will drink it and this is history.   30

For Analysis

1. How many times does *maybe* appear in this poem? How about *possibly*? Why do you think these words are used so many times?

2. Who is the speaker? What is his relationship to the man named in the first two lines? What is his relationship to the poet?

3. What does the poem directly say "is history" (l. 30)? What does the poem as a whole say about history?

LINDA HOGAN   (B. 1947)

HERITAGE   1978

From my mother, the antique mirror
where I watch my face take on her lines.
She left me the smell of baking bread
to warm fine hairs in my nostrils,

she left the large white breasts that weigh down
my body.

From my father I take his brown eyes,
the plague of locusts that leveled our crops,
they flew in formation like buzzards.

From my uncle the whittled wood   10
that rattles like bones
and is white
and smells like all our old houses
that are no longer there. He was the man
who sang old chants to me, the words
my father was told not to remember.

From my grandfather who never spoke
I learned to fear silence.
I learned to kill a snake
when you're begging for rain.   20

And Grandmother, blue-eyed woman
whose skin was brown,
she used snuff.
When her coffee can full of black saliva
spilled on me
it was like the brown cloud of grasshoppers
that leveled her fields.
It was the brown stain
that covered my white shirt,
my whiteness a shame.   30
That sweet black liquid like the food
she chewed up and spit into my father's mouth
when he was an infant.
It was the brown earth of Oklahoma
stained with oil.
She said tobacco would purge your body of poisons.
It has more medicine than stones and knives
against your enemies.
That tobacco is the dark night that covers me.

She said it is wise to eat the flesh of deer   40
so you will be swift and travel over many miles.
She told me how our tribe has always followed a stick
that pointed west
that pointed east.

From my family I have learned the secrets
of never having a home.

FOR ANALYSIS

1. What kinds of things does the speaker get from her family? Are they all concrete? If not, what abstract things does she get?

2. In what way does the speaker not have a home?

3. Who are the speaker's enemies?

WRITING TOPIC

What have you learned from your family? In an essay, reflect on the ways your parents and grandparents passed on elements of your heritage(s).

MARILYN CHIN   (B. 1955)

HOW I GOT THAT NAME   1994

AN ESSAY ON ASSIMILATION

I am Marilyn Mei Ling Chin.
Oh, how I love the resoluteness
of that first person singular
followed by that stalwart indicative
of "be," without the uncertain i-n-g
of "becoming." Of course,
the name had been changed
somewhere between Angel Island and the sea,
when my father the paperson
in the late 1950s   10
obsessed with a bombshell blonde
transliterated "Mei Ling" to "Marilyn."
And nobody dared question
his initial impulse—for we all know
lust drove men to greatness,
not goodness, not decency.
And there I was, a wayward pink baby,
named after some tragic white woman
swollen with gin and Nembutal.
My mother couldn't pronounce the "r."   20
She dubbed me "Numba one female offshoot"
for brevity: henceforth, she will live and die
in sublime ignorance, flanked
by loving children and the "kitchen deity."

While my father dithers,
a tomcat in Hong Kong trash—
a gambler, a petty thug,
who bought a chain of chopsuey joints
in Piss River, Oregon,
with bootlegged Gucci cash.   30
Nobody dared question his integrity given
his nice, devout daughters
and his bright, industrious sons
as if filial picty were the standard
by which all earthly men were measured.

Oh, how trustworthy our daughters,
how thrifty our sons!
How we've managed to fool the experts
in education, statistics and demography—
We're not very creative but not adverse to rote-learning.   40
Indeed, they can *use* us.
But the "Model Minority" is a tease.
We know you are watching now,
so we refuse to give you any!
Oh, bamboo shoots, bamboo shoots!
The further west we go, we'll hit east;
the deeper down we dig, we'll find China.
History has turned its stomach
on a black polluted beach—
where life doesn't hinge   50
on that red, red wheelbarrow,
but whether or not our new lover
in the final episode of "Santa Barbara"
will lean over a scented candle
and call us a "bitch."
Oh God, where have we gone wrong?
We have no inner resources!

Then, one redolent spring morning
the Great Patriarch Chin
peered down from his kiosk in heaven   60
and saw that his descendants were ugly.
One had a squarish head and a nose without a bridge.
Another's profile—long and knobbed as a gourd.
A third, the sad, brutish one
may never, never marry.
And I, his least favorite—
"not quite boiled, not quite cooked,"

a plump pomfret simmering in my juices—
too listless to fight for my people's destiny.
"To kill without resistance is not slaughter"   70
says the proverb. So, I wait for imminent death.
The fact that this death is also metaphorical
is testament to my lethargy.

So here lies Marilyn Mei Ling Chin,
married once, twice to so-and-so, a Lee and a Wong,
granddaughter of Jack "the patriarch"
and the brooding Suilin Fong,
daughter of the virtuous Yuet Kuen Wong
and G. G. Chin the infamous,
sister of a dozen, cousin of a million,   80
survived by everybody and forgotten by all.
She was neither black nor white,
neither cherished nor vanquished,
just another squatter in her own bamboo grove
minding her poetry—
when one day heaven was unmerciful,
and a chasm opened where she stood.
Like the jowls of a mighty white whale,
or the jaws of a metaphysical Godzilla,
it swallowed her whole.   90
She did not flinch nor writhe,
nor fret about the afterlife,
but stayed! Solid as wood, happily
a little gnawed, tattered, mesmerized
by all that was lavished upon her
and all that was taken away!

FOR ANALYSIS

1. Why does the speaker "love the resoluteness / of that first person singular / followed by that stalwart indicative / of 'be'" (ll. 2–5)?

2. Why is how the poet/**persona** got her name so important?

3. What is wrong, in the speaker's eyes, with being a "Model Minority" (l. 42)?

WRITING TOPICS

1. How is this poem, as its subtitle claims, "An essay on assimilation"? What was "lavished upon her" (l. 95) and what was "taken away" (l. 96)?

2. *Assimilation* is usually meant to indicate what happens to immigrants in a new land. Write about a situation in your life when you had to assimilate in a different sense—not as an international immigrant or a child of immigrants but as a person in a new place. What impact did the experience have on your sense of self?

MAKING CONNECTIONS

1. All of these poems feature *Is*. What do these *Is* have in common? How do they differ? How do they declare themselves?

2. These poems all address identity; many do so in part with reference to the past. What roles does the past play in these poems? How do the poets connect the past to present identities?

3. A number of these poems cast their nets wide, finding images and subjects from around the world and from a variety of human experiences. To what end, or ends, do they do this?

**CONNECTING POEMS:
FASHIONABLE IDENTITIES**

Each of the poems in this unit addresses the pressures women feel to conform to social expectations. From Emily Dickinson's nineteenth-century New England to Taslima Nasrin's contemporary India, women have received, subtly and not so subtly, instructions about what they are supposed to be, what they are supposed to want, and how they are supposed to feel. As you read, note how these poems choose to not simply observe from the outside but instead get inside the heads of women feeling and acting on these pressures—perhaps unknown to themselves—and how they use irony to critique a world in which Barbie holds such power.

EMILY DICKINSON   (1830–1886)

WHAT SOFT—
CHERUBIC CREATURES—   CA. 1862

What Soft—Cherubic Creatures—
These Gentlewomen are—
One would as soon assault a Plush—
Or violate a Star—

Such Dimity Convictions—
A Horror so refined
Of freckled Human Nature—
Of Deity—ashamed—

It's such a common-Glory—
A Fisherman's—Degree—
Redemption—Brittle Lady—
Be so—ashamed of Thee—

10

FOR ANALYSIS

1. How can human nature be seen as "freckled" (l. 7)?

2. What is the poem's **tone**? Does the speaker really think the women are "cherubic"?

3. What is the effect of the use of violence in the third and fourth lines?

JUNE JORDAN (1936–2002)

MEMO: 1980

When I hear some woman say she
has finally decided you can spend time with
other women, I wonder what she means: Her
mother? My mother?
I've always despised my woman friends. Even
if they introduced me to a man I found
attractive I have never let them become
what you could call my intimates. Why
should I? Men are the ones with the money and
the big way with waiters and the passkey   10
to excitement in strange places of real
danger and the power to make things happen
like babies or war and all these great ideas
about mass magazines for members of the weaker sex
who need permission
to eat potatoes or a doctor's opinion on orgasm after death
or the latest word on what the female
executive should do, after hours, wearing
what. They must be morons: women!
Don't you think?   20
I guess you could say
I'm stuck in my ways
as
That Cosmopolitan Girl.

FOR ANALYSIS

1. Explain the title.

2. What do the first three lines mean? Why would a woman feel she *can't* spend time with other women?

3. Does this poem accurately describe the power relations in our society? Explain.

4. Describe the **tone** of this poem.

WRITING TOPIC

Examine a few issues of *Cosmopolitan* magazine, and write an essay imagining how it inspired this poem.

MARGE PIERCY (B. 1936)

BARBIE DOLL 1973

This girlchild was born as usual
and presented dolls that did pee-pee
and miniature GE stoves and irons
and wee lipsticks the color of cherry candy.
Then in the magic of puberty, a classmate said:
You have a great big nose and fat legs.

She was healthy, tested intelligent,
possessed strong arms and back,
abundant sexual drive and manual dexterity.
She went to and fro apologizing.   10
Everyone saw a fat nose on thick legs.

She was advised to play coy,
exhorted to come on hearty,
exercise, diet, smile and wheedle.
Her good nature wore out
like a fan belt.
So she cut off her nose and her legs
and offered them up.

In the casket displayed on satin she lay
with the undertaker's cosmetics painted on,   20
a turned-up putty nose,
dressed in a pink and white nightie.
Doesn't she look pretty? everyone said.
Consummation at last.
To every woman a happy ending.

FOR ANALYSIS

1. In what way does this poem have a "happy ending" (l. 25)? Is it really happy?

2. List the characteristics attributed to the girl in the poem. Which are judged by others to be important? Which are judged unimportant? Why?

3. Why does the girl apologize? Should she?

WRITING TOPICS

1. People have long argued over what makes boys and girls conform to society's expectations. Some argue that the differences are genetic: that boys and girls are intrinsically different. Others argue that gendered behavior is socialized: that differences come not from nature but from nurture. Where does Piercy's poem fall on the nature-nurture question? Where do you fall? Why?

2. Reflect on the turn in line 17. Why is this an unusual moment? What are its effects? Why do you think Piercy chooses to have something like this happen?

TASLIMA NASRIN (B. 1962)

THINGS CHEAPLY HAD[1] 1991

In the market nothing can be had as cheap as women.
If they get a small bottle of *alta*[2] for their feet
       they spend three nights sleepless for sheer joy.
If they get a few bars of soap to scrub their skin
       and some scented oil for their hair
they become so submissive that they scoop out
       chunks of their flesh
to be sold in the flea market twice a week.
If they get a jewel for their nose
       they lick feet for seventy days or so,   10
a full three and a half months
       if it's a single striped sari.[3]

Even the mangy cur of the house barks now and then,
and over the mouths of women cheaply had
       there's a lock
a golden lock.

FOR ANALYSIS

1. Why is the lock in the final line of the poem "golden"?

2. What are the "things" of the title? Do they include more than the items the women "get"?

Things Cheaply Had
  [1] Translated from the Bengali by Carolyne Wright with Mohammad Nurul Huda and the author.
  [2] *Alta*, or lac-dye, is a red liquid with which South Asian women decorate the borders of their feet on ceremonial occasions, such as weddings and dance performances. *Alta* is more in vogue among Hindus, but Bangladeshi women also use it, and it can be seen on the feet of Muslim heroines and harem women in Moghul miniature paintings. [Translator's note.]
  [3] An outer garment worn chiefly by women of India and Pakistan, consisting of a length of cloth wrapped around the waist at one end and draped over the shoulder or head at the other.

MAKING CONNECTIONS

1. How does each of these poems use **irony**? Why is irony an effective tool for poems about this shared subject?

2. Though men are not mentioned in all of these poems, they play a role in each of them. What are those roles, and how are they implicitly or explicitly brought into the poems?

3. Only one of these poems features an explicitly female **persona**, yet all could be said to explore female consciousness. How does each do so, and to what effect?

CONNECTING POEMS: WORKING MOTHERS

The kind of work people do is often partly determined by their gender. Particular jobs are often restricted to or almost always filled by either men or women, and particular kinds of uncompensated tasks, like housework, are too. The poems in this unit address work from the viewpoint of the women who do it or the daughters who watch them do it. As you read, notice the shared point of view but also the different situations in which these women find themselves. How does lifestyle—social class, typical experiences—help shape what these women see when they look at work?

TESS GALLAGHER (B. 1943)

I STOP WRITING THE POEM 1992

to fold the clothes. No matter who lives
or who dies, I'm still a woman.
I'll always have plenty to do.
I bring the arms of his shirt
together. Nothing can stop
our tenderness. I'll get back
to the poem. I'll get back to being
a woman. But for now
there's a shirt, a giant shirt
in my hands, and somewhere a small girl   10
standing next to her mother
watching to see how it's done.

FOR ANALYSIS

1. Does the speaker stop writing the poem? Does the continuation of the title into the first line help answer this question?

2. How does the **enjambment**, or continuation, of the first and second lines help signal an important context for the poem's situation?

3. If the speaker is not being a poet or a woman at the end of the poem, what is she being?

WRITING TOPICS

1. Especially for a self-conscious poem, "I Stop Writing the Poem" is simple, relatively devoid of poetic devices. Reflect on why Gallagher chose to write the poem in this spare style.

2. The "it" in the last line refers to more than shirt-folding; the poem is about more than poetry or laundry, and, though it alludes to a context, it does not explore it. Write a poem about the same situation from the point of view of the speaker's daughter. Is it more or less explicit about the event that precedes the events of the poem? Why?

JULIA ALVAREZ (B. 1950)

WOMAN'S WORK   1996

Who says a woman's work isn't high art?
She'd challenge as she scrubbed the bathroom tiles.
Keep house as if the address were your heart.

We'd clean the whole upstairs before we'd start
downstairs, I'd sigh, hearing my friends outside.
Doing her woman's work was a hard art

to practice when the summer sun would bar
the floor I swept till she was satisfied.
She kept me prisoner in her housebound heart.

She'd shine the tines of forks, the wheels of carts,   10
cut lacy lattices for all her pies.
Her woman's work was nothing less than art.

And I, her masterpiece since I was smart,
was primed, praised, polished, scolded and advised
to keep a house much better than my heart.

I did not want to be her counterpart!
I struck out . . . but became my mother's child:
a woman working at home on her art,
housekeeping paper as if it were her heart.

FOR ANALYSIS

1. How is the speaker her mother's "masterpiece" (l. 13)?

2. To what does "housekeeping paper" (l. 19) refer?

3. Answer the first line's question as if it weren't rhetorical.

WRITING TOPICS

1. Write an account of Alvarez's use of repetition and **rhyme** in "Woman's Work." What effects does Alvarez achieve?

2. **Tone** in this poem is complicated and nuanced. Make a list of words that seem to have positive **connotations**. Then make a list of words that seem to have negative connotations. How do these words express how the speaker feels about the various subjects?

RITA DOVE (B. 1952)

MY MOTHER ENTERS THE WORK FORCE 2000

The path to ABC Business School
was paid for by a lucky sign:
Alterations, Qualified Seamstress Inquire Within.
Tested on Sleeves, hers
never puckered—puffed or sleek,
Leg o' or Raglan—
they barely needed the damp cloth
to steam them perfect.

Those were the afternoons. Evenings
she took in piecework, the treadle machine   10
with its locomotive whir
traveling the lit path of the needle
through quicksand taffeta
or velvet deep as a forest.
And now and now sang the treadle,
I know, I know . . . .

And then it was day again, all morning
at the office machines, their clack and chatter
another journey—rougher,
that would go on forever   20
until she could break a hundred words
with no errors—ah, and then

no more postponed groceries,
and that blue pair of shoes!

FOR ANALYSIS

1. Dove's poem describes the mother's sewing work in great detail. What does the specific nature of this detail express about the daughter-speaker's attitude toward her mother's work?

2. How would you characterize the poem's **tone** overall? What about it informs the tone?

3. What is the treadle saying, and to whom?

WRITING TOPICS

1. Although the poem speaks very little about it, this mother and daughter are not as comfortable economically as they might be. How do we know this? What is the poem's attitude toward this situation?

2. Write a poem about work you have done, or work a parent or another relative or a friend has done. Describe that work in a way that reveals, without being explicit, your (or his or her) feelings about it.

DEBORAH GARRISON   (B. 1965)

SESTINA FOR THE WORKING MOTHER   2007

No time for a sestina for the working mother.
Who has so much to do, from first thing in the morning
When she has to get herself dressed and the children
Too, when they tumble in the pillow pile rather than listening
To her exhortations about brushing teeth, making ready for the day;
They clamor with "up" hugs when she struggles out the door.

Every time, as if shot from a cannon when she shuts the door.
She stomps down the street in her city boots, slipping from mother
Mode into commuter trance, trees swaying at the corner of a new day
Nearly turned, her familiar bus stop cool and welcoming in the morning.   10
She hears her own heart here, though no one else is listening,
And if the bus is late she hears down the block the voices of her children

Bobbing under their oversized backpacks to greet other children
At their own bus stop. They too have come flying from the door,
Brave for the journey, and everyone is talking and no one is listening
As they head off to school. The noisy children of the working mother,
Waiting with their sitter for the bus, are healthy and happy this morning.
And that's the best way, the mother knows, for a day

To begin. The apprehension of what kind of day
It will be in the world of work, blissful without children,   20

Trembles in the anxious and pleasurable pulse of the morning;
It has tamped her down tight and lit her out the door
And away from what she might have been as a mother
At home, perhaps drinking coffee and listening

To NPR, what rapt and intelligent listening
She'd do at home. And volunteering, she thinks, for part of the day
At their school—she'd be a playground monitor, a PTA mother!
She'd see them straggle into the sunshine, her children
Bright in the slipstream, and she a gracious shadow at the school door;
She would not be separated from them for long by the morning.   30

But she has chosen her flight from them, on this and every morning.
She's now so far away she trusts someone else is listening
To their raised voices, applying a Band-Aid, opening the door
For them when the sunshine calls them out into the day.
At certain moments, head bent at her desk, she can see her children,
And feels the quick stab. She hasn't forgotten that she is their mother.

Every weekday morning, every working day,
She listens to her heart and the voices of her children.
Goodbye! they shout, and the door closes behind the working mother.

FOR ANALYSIS

1. *Sestina* is a highly structured traditional form of poetry. Can you guess what the "rules" are for a sestina by figuring out the structure of this one?

2. What is the effect of reading a sestina, or at least this sestina? Considering these effects, why do you think Garrison chose the sestina form for this poem? What about her poem's themes might be expressed by its form?

3. Is the speaker happy to be a working mother? Sad? Both?

WRITING TOPICS

1. What function do lines 23–30 serve? How do they fit into the larger poem? What about the opening of the sixth stanza helps you understand its function and its fit?

2. The final stanza in a sestina, the *envoi*, is often used to comment on the rest of the poem. How does the envoi in "Sestina for the Working Mother" comment on the rest of it?

MAKING CONNECTIONS

1. Three of the four poems in this unit feature a speaker who might be understood to be a poet. How does each of these poems relate poetry to the other things—work, motherhood, and so on—that these poems are about? Is poetry work? Is it more or less than work?

2. All of these poems reflect on issues surrounding women working, sometimes explicitly. Though the first concern is often about social expectations—what work is "appropriate" for women and what isn't—in the background is the question of economics. Which of these poems makes economics a central concern? Which of these does not? Can you read the economics behind one or more that don't foreground it?

3. Address the role housework plays in these poems. Is it drudgery or an art? A necessity or a way to teach work habits?

DRAMA

LORRAINE HANSBERRY   (1930–1965)

A RAISIN IN THE SUN   1959

CHARACTERS (in order of appearance)

Ruth Younger	Travis Younger
Walter Lee Younger, brother	Beneatha Younger
Lena Younger, Mama	Joseph Asagai
George Murchison	Mrs. Johnson
Karl Lindner	Bobo
Moving Men	

The action of the play is set in Chicago's Southside, sometime between World War II and the present.

ACT I

Scene 1.   *(Friday morning.)*

The Younger living room would be a comfortable and well-ordered room if it were not for a number of indestructible contradictions to this state of being. Its furnishings are typical and undistinguished and their primary feature now is that they have clearly had to accommodate the living of too many people for too many years   and they are tired. Still, we can see that at some time, a time probably no longer remembered by the family (except perhaps for Mama), the furnishings of this room were actually selected with care and love and even hope—and brought to this apartment and arranged with taste and pride.

That was a long time ago. Now the once loved pattern of the couch upholstery has to fight to show itself from under acres of crocheted doilies and couch covers which have themselves finally come to be more important than the upholstery. And here a table or a chair has been moved to disguise the worn places in the carpet; but the carpet has fought back by showing its weariness, with depressing uniformity, elsewhere on its surface.

Weariness has, in fact, won in this room. Everything has been polished, washed, sat on, used, scrubbed too often. All pretenses but living itself have long since vanished from the very atmosphere of this room.

Moreover, a section of this room, for it is not really a room unto itself, though the landlord's lease would make it seem so, slopes backward to provide a small kitchen area, where the family prepares the meals that are eaten in the living room proper, which must also serve as dining room. The single window that has been provided for these "two" rooms is located in this kitchen area. The sole natural light the family may enjoy in the course of a day is only that which fights its way through this little window.

At left, a door leads to a bedroom which is shared by Mama and her daughter, Beneatha. At right, opposite, is a second room (which in the beginning of the life of this apartment was probably a breakfast room) which serves as a bedroom for Walter and his wife, Ruth.

Time: Sometime between World War II and the present.

Place: Chicago's Southside.

At Rise: It is morning dark in the living room. Travis is asleep on the make-down bed at center. An alarm clock sounds from within the bedroom at right, and presently Ruth enters from that room and closes the door behind her. She crosses sleepily toward the window. As she passes her sleeping son she reaches down and shakes him a little. At the window she raises the shade and a dusky Southside morning light comes in feebly. She fills a pot with water and puts it on to boil. She calls to the boy, between yawns, in a slightly muffled voice.

Ruth is about thirty. We can see that she was a pretty girl, even exceptionally so, but now it is apparent that life has been little that she expected, and disappointment has already begun to hang in her face. In a few years, before thirty-five even, she will be known among her people as a "settled woman."

She crosses to her son and gives him a good, final, rousing shake.

Ruth. Come on now, boy, it's seven thirty! *(Her son sits up at last, in a stupor of sleepiness.)* I say hurry up, Travis! You ain't the only person in the world got to use a bathroom! *(The child, a sturdy, handsome little boy of ten or eleven, drags himself out of the bed and almost blindly takes his towels and "today's clothes" from drawers and a closet and goes out to the bathroom, which is in an outside hall and which is shared by another family or families on the same floor. Ruth crosses to the bedroom door at right and opens it and calls in to her husband.)* Walter Lee! . . . It's after seven thirty! Lemme see you do some waking up in there now! *(She waits.)* You better get up from there, man! It's after seven thirty I tell you. *(She waits again.)* All right, you just go ahead and lay there and next thing you know Travis be finished and Mr. Johnson'll be in there and you'll be fussing and cussing round here like a madman! And be late too! *(She waits, at the end of patience.)* Walter Lee—it's time for you to GET UP!

She waits another second and then starts to go into the bedroom, but is apparently satisfied that her husband has begun to get up. She stops, pulls the door to, and returns to the kitchen area. She wipes her face with a moist cloth and runs her fingers through her sleep-disheveled hair in a vain effort and ties an apron around her housecoat. The bedroom door at right opens and her husband stands in the doorway in his pajamas, which are rumpled and mismated. He is a lean, intense young man in his middle thirties, inclined to quick nervous movements and erratic speech habits—and always in his voice there is a quality of indictment.

Walter. Is he out yet?

Ruth. What you mean *out?* He ain't hardly got in there good yet.

Walter *(wandering in, still more oriented to sleep than to a new day).* Well, what was you doing all that yelling for if I can't even get in there yet? *(Stopping and thinking.)* Check coming today?

Ruth. They *said* Saturday and this is just Friday and I hopes to God you ain't going to get up here first thing this morning and start talking to me 'bout no money—'cause I 'bout don't want to hear it.

Walter. Something the matter with you this morning?

Ruth. No—I'm just sleepy as the devil. What kind of eggs you want?

Walter. Not scrambled. *(Ruth starts to scramble eggs.)* Paper come? *(Ruth points impatiently to the rolled up Tribune on the table, and he gets it and spreads it out and vaguely reads the front page.)* Set off another bomb yesterday.

Ruth *(maximum indifference).* Did they?

Walter *(looking up).* What's the matter with you?

Ruth. Ain't nothing the matter with me. And don't keep asking me that this morning.

Walter. Ain't nobody bothering you. *(Reading the news of the day absently again.)* Say Colonel McCormick is sick.

Ruth *(affecting tea-party interest).* Is he now? Poor thing.

Walter *(sighing and looking at his watch).* Oh, me. *(He waits.)* Now what is that boy doing in that bathroom all this time? He just going to have to start getting up earlier. I can't be being late to work on account of him fooling around in there.

Ruth *(turning on him)* Oh, no he ain't going to be getting up no earlier no such thing! It ain't his fault that he can't get to bed no earlier nights 'cause he got a bunch of crazy good-for-nothing clowns sitting up running their mouths in what is supposed to be his bedroom after ten o'clock at night . . .

Walter. That's what you mad about, ain't it? The things I want to talk about with my friends just couldn't be important in your mind, could they?

He rises and finds a cigarette in her handbag on the table and crosses to the little window and looks out, smoking and deeply enjoying this first one.

Ruth *(almost matter of factly, a complaint too automatic to deserve emphasis).* Why you always got to smoke before you eat in the morning?

Walter *(at the window).* Just look at 'em down there . . . Running and racing to work . . . *(He turns and faces his wife and watches her a moment at the stove, and then, suddenly.)* You look young this morning, baby.

Ruth *(indifferently).* Yeah?

Walter. Just for a second—stirring them eggs. Just for a second it was—you looked real young again. *(He reaches for her; she crosses away. Then, drily.)* It's gone now—you look like yourself again!

Ruth. Man, if you don't shut up and leave me alone.

Walter *(looking out to the street again).* First thing a man ought to learn in life is not to make love to no colored woman first thing in the morning. You all some eeeevil people at eight o'clock in the morning.

Travis appears in the hall doorway, almost fully dressed and quite wide awake now, his towels and pajamas across his shoulders. He opens the door and signals for his father to make the bathroom in a hurry.

Travis *(watching the bathroom).* Daddy, come on!

Walter gets his bathroom utensils and flies out to the bathroom.

Ruth. Sit down and have your breakfast, Travis.

Travis. Mama, this is Friday. *(Gleefully.)* Check coming tomorrow, huh?

Ruth. You get your mind off money and eat your breakfast.

Travis *(eating).* This is the morning we supposed to bring the fifty cents to school.

Ruth. Well, I ain't got no fifty cents this morning.

Travis. Teacher say we have to.

Ruth. I don't care what teacher say. I ain't got it. Eat your breakfast, Travis.

Travis. I *am* eating.

Ruth. Hush up now and just eat!

The boy gives her an exasperated look for her lack of understanding, and eats grudgingly.

Travis. You think Grandmama would have it?

Ruth. No! And I want you to stop asking your grandmother for money, you hear me?

Travis *(outraged).* Gaaaleee! I don't ask her, she just gimme it sometimes!

Ruth. Travis Willard Younger—I got too much on me this morning to be—

Travis. Maybe Daddy—

Ruth. *Travis!*

The boy hushes abruptly. They are both quiet and tense for several seconds.

Travis *(presently).* Could I maybe go carry some groceries in front of the super-market for a little while after school then?

Ruth. Just hush, I said. *(Travis jabs his spoon into his cereal bowl viciously, and rests his head in anger upon his fists.)* If you through eating, you can get over there and make up your bed.

The boy obeys stiffly and crosses the room, almost mechanically, to the bed and more or less folds the bedding into a heap, then angrily gets his books and cap.

Travis (*sulking and standing apart from her unnaturally*). I'm gone.

Ruth (*looking up from the stove to inspect him automatically*). Come here. (*He crosses to her and she studies his head.*) If you don't take this comb and fix this here head, you better! (*Travis puts down his books with a great sigh of oppression, and crosses to the mirror. His mother mutters under her breath about his "slub-bornness."*) 'Bout to march out of here with that head looking just like chickens slept in it! I just don't know where you get your slubborn ways . . . And get your jacket, too. Looks chilly out this morning.

Travis (*with conspicuously brushed hair and jacket*). I'm gone.

Ruth. Get carfare and milk money—(*Waving one finger.*)—and not a single penny for no caps, you hear me?

Travis (*with sullen politeness*). Yes'm.

He turns in outrage to leave. His mother watches after him as in his frustration he approaches the door almost comically. When she speaks to him, her voice has become a very gentle tease.

Ruth (*mocking; as she thinks he would say it*). Oh, Mama makes me so mad some-times, I don't know what to do! (*She waits and continues to his back as he stands stock-still in front of the door.*) I wouldn't kiss that woman good-bye for nothing in this world this morning! (*The boy finally turns around and rolls his eyes at her, knowing the mood has changed and he is vindicated; he does not, however, move toward her yet.*) Not for nothing in this world! (*She finally laughs aloud at him and holds out her arms to him and we see that it is a way between them, very old and practiced. He crosses to her and allows her to embrace him warmly but keeps his face fixed with masculine rigidity. She holds him back from her presently and looks at him and runs her fingers over the features of his face. With utter gentle-ness—.*) Now—whose little old angry man are you?

Travis (*the masculinity and gruffness start to fade at last*). Aw gaalee Mama . . .

Ruth (*mimicking*). Aw—gaaaaalleeeee, Mama! (*She pushes him, with rough playful-ness and finality, toward the door.*) Get on out of here or you going to be late.

Travis (*in the face of love, new aggressiveness*). Mama, could I please go carry groceries?

Ruth. Honey, it's starting to get so cold evenings.

Walter (*coming in from the bathroom and drawing a make-believe gun from a make-believe holster and shooting at his son*). What is it he wants to do?

Ruth. Go carry groceries after school at the supermarket.

Walter. Well, let him go . . .

Travis (*quickly, to the ally*). I have to—she won't gimme the fifty cents . . .

Walter (*to his wife only*). Why not?

Ruth (*simply, and with flavor*). 'Cause we don't have it.

Walter (*to Ruth only*). What you tell the boy things like that for? (*Reaching down into his pants with a rather important gesture.*) Here, son—

He hands the boy the coin, but his eyes are directed to his wife's. Travis takes the money happily.

Travis. Thanks, Daddy.

He starts out. Ruth watches both of them with murder in her eyes. Walter stands and stares back at her with defiance, and suddenly reaches into his pocket again on an afterthought.

Walter *(without even looking at his son, still staring hard at his wife).* In fact, here's another fifty cents . . . Buy yourself some fruit today—or take a taxicab to school or something!

Travis. Whoopee—

He leaps up and clasps his father around the middle with his legs, and they face each other in mutual appreciation; slowly Walter Lee peeks around the boy to catch the violent rays from his wife's eyes and draws his head back as if shot.

Walter. You better get down now—and get to school, man.

Travis *(at the door).* O.K. Good-bye.

He exits.

Walter *(after him, pointing with pride).* That's *my* boy. *(She looks at him in disgust and turns back to her work.)* You know what I was thinking 'bout in the bathroom this morning?

Ruth. No.

Walter. How come you always try to be so pleasant!

Ruth. What is there to be pleasant 'bout!

Walter. You want to know what I was thinking 'bout in the bathroom or not!

Ruth. I know what you thinking 'bout.

Walter *(ignoring her).* 'Bout what me and Willy Harris was talking about last night.

Ruth *(immediately—a refrain).* Willy Harris is a good-for-nothing loudmouth.

Walter. Anybody who talks to me has got to be a good-for-nothing loudmouth, ain't he? And what you know about who is just a good-for-nothing loudmouth? Charlie Atkins was just a "good-for-nothing loudmouth" too, wasn't he! When he wanted me to go in the dry-cleaning business with him. And now—he's grossing a hundred thousand a year. A hundred thousand dollars a year! You still call *him* a loudmouth!

Ruth *(bitterly).* Oh, Walter Lee . . .

She folds her head on her arms over the table.

Walter *(rising and coming to her and standing over her).* You tired, ain't you? Tired of everything. Me, the boy, the way we live—this beat-up hole—everything. Ain't you? *(She doesn't look up, doesn't answer.)* So tired—moaning and groaning all the time, but you wouldn't do nothing to help, would you? You couldn't be on my side that long for nothing, could you?

Ruth. Walter, please leave me alone.

Walter. A man needs for a woman to back him up . . .

Ruth. Walter—

Walter. Mama would listen to you. You know she listen to you more than she do me and Bennie. She think more of you. All you have to do is just sit down with her when you drinking your coffee one morning and talking 'bout things like you do and—(*He sits down beside her and demonstrates graphically what he thinks her methods and tone should be.*)—you just sip your coffee, see, and say easy like that you been thinking 'bout that deal Walter Lee is so interested in, 'bout the store and all, and sip some more coffee, like what you saying ain't really that important to you—And the next thing you know, she be listening good and asking you questions and when I come home—I can tell her the details. This ain't no fly-by-night proposition, baby. I mean we figured it out, me and Willy and Bobo.

Ruth (*with a frown*). Bobo?

Walter. Yeah. You see, this little liquor store we got in mind cost seventy-five thousand and we figured the initial investment on the place be 'bout thirty thousand, see. That be ten thousand each. Course, there's a couple of hundred you got to pay so's you don't spend your life just waiting for them clowns to let your license get approved—

Ruth. You mean graft?

Walter (*frowning impatiently*). Don't call it that. See there, that just goes to show you what women understand about the world. Baby, don't *nothing* happen for you in the world 'less you pay *somebody* off!

Ruth. Walter, leave me alone! (*She raises her head and stares at him vigorously— then says, more quietly.*) Eat your eggs, they gonna be cold.

Walter (*straightening up from her and looking off*). That's it. There you are. Man say to his woman: I got me a dream. His woman say: Eat your eggs. (*Sadly, but gaining in power.*) Man say: I got to take hold of this here world, baby! And a woman will say: Eat your eggs and go to work. (*Passionately now.*) Man say: I got to change my life, I'm choking to death, baby! And his woman say—(*In utter anguish as he brings his fists down on his thighs.*)—Your eggs is getting cold!

Ruth (*softly*). Walter, that ain't none of our money.

Walter (*not listening at all or even looking at her*). This morning, I was lookin' in the mirror and thinking about it . . . I'm thirty-five years old; I been married eleven years and I got a boy who sleeps in the living room—(*Very, very quietly.*)—and all I got to give him is stories about how rich white people live . . .

Ruth. Eat your eggs, Walter.

Walter (*slams the table and jumps up*). —DAMN MY EGGS—DAMN ALL THE EGGS THAT EVER WAS!

Ruth. Then go to work.

Walter (*looking up at her*). See—I'm trying to talk to you 'bout myself— (*Shaking his head with the repetition.*)—and all you can say is eat them eggs and go to work.

Ruth (*wearily*). Honey, you never say nothing new. I listen to you every day, every night and every morning, and you never say nothing new. (*Shrugging.*) So you would rather *be* Mr. Arnold than be his chauffeur. So—I would *rather* be living in Buckingham Palace.

Walter. That is just what is wrong with the colored woman in this world . . . Don't understand about building their men up and making 'em feel like they somebody. Like they can do something.

Ruth (*drily, but to hurt*). There *are* colored men who do things.

Walter. No thanks to the colored woman.

Ruth. Well, being a colored woman, I guess I can't help myself none.

She rises and gets the ironing board and sets it up and attacks a huge pile of rough-dried clothes, sprinkling them in preparation for the ironing and then rolling them into tight fat balls.

Walter (*mumbling*). We one group of men tied to a race of women with small minds!

His sister Beneatha enters. She is about twenty, as slim and intense as her brother. She is not as pretty as her sister-in-law, but her lean, almost intellectual face has a handsomeness of its own. She wears a bright-red flannel nightie, and her thick hair stands wildly about her head. Her speech is a mixture of many things; it is different from the rest of the family's insofar as education has permeated her sense of English— and perhaps the Midwest rather than the South has finally—at last—won out in her inflection; but not altogether, because over all of it is a soft slurring and transformed use of vowels which is the decided influence of the Southside. She passes through the room without looking at either Ruth or Walter and goes to the outside door and looks, a little blindly, out to the bathroom. She sees that it has been lost to the Johnsons. She closes the door with a sleepy vengeance and crosses to the table and sits down a little defeated.

Beneatha. I am going to start timing those people.

Walter. You should get up earlier.

Beneatha (*her face in her hands. She is still fighting the urge to go back to bed*). Really—would you suggest dawn? Where's the paper?

Walter (*pushing the paper across the table to her as he studies her almost clinically, as though he has never seen her before*). You a horrible-looking chick at this hour.

Beneatha (*drily*). Good morning, everybody.

Walter (*senselessly*). How is school coming?

Beneatha (*in the same spirit*). Lovely. Lovely. And you know, biology is the greatest. (*Looking up at him.*) I dissected something that looked just like you yesterday.

Walter. I just wondered if you've made up your mind and everything.

Beneatha (*gaining in sharpness and impatience*). And what did I answer yesterday morning—and the day before that?

Ruth (*from the ironing board, like someone disinterested and old*). Don't be so nasty, Bennie.

Beneatha *(still to her brother)*. And the day before that and the day before that!

Walter *(defensively)*. I'm interested in you. Something wrong with that? Ain't many girls who decide—

Walter and Beneatha *(in unison)*. —"to be a doctor."

Silence.

Walter. Have we figured out yet just exactly how much medical school is going to cost?

Ruth. Walter Lee, why don't you leave that girl alone and get out of here to work?

Beneatha *(exits to the bathroom and bangs on the door)*. Come on out of there, please!

She comes back into the room.

Walter *(looking at his sister intently)*. You know the check is coming tomorrow.

Beneatha *(turning on him with a sharpness all her own)*. That money belongs to Mama, Walter, and it's for her to decide how she wants to use it. I don't care if she wants to buy a house or a rocket ship or just nail it up somewhere and look at it. It's hers. Not ours—hers.

Walter *(bitterly)*. Now ain't that fine! You just got your mother's interest at heart, ain't you, girl? You such a nice girl—but if Mama got that money she can always take a few thousand and help you through school too—can't she?

Beneatha. I have never asked anyone around here to do anything for me!

Walter. No! And the line between asking and just accepting when the time comes is big and wide—ain't it!

Beneatha *(with fury)*. What do you want from me, Brother—that I quit school or just drop dead, which!

Walter. I don't want nothing but for you to stop acting holy 'round here. Me and Ruth done made some sacrifices for you—why can't you do something for the family?

Ruth. Walter, don't be dragging me in it.

Walter. You are in it—Don't you get up and go work in somebody's kitchen for the last three years to help put clothes on her back?

Ruth. Oh, Walter—that's not fair . . .

Walter. It ain't that nobody expects you to get on your knees and say thank you, Brother; thank you, Ruth; thank you, Mama—and thank you, Travis, for wearing the same pair of shoes for two semesters—

Beneatha *(dropping to her knees)*. Well—I *do*—all right?—thank everybody! And forgive me for ever wanting to be anything at all! *(Pursuing him on her knees across the floor.)* FORGIVE ME, FORGIVE ME, FORGIVE ME!

Ruth. Please stop it! Your mama'll hear you.

Walter. Who the hell told you you had to be a doctor? If you so crazy 'bout messing 'round with sick people—then go be a nurse like other women—or just get married and be quiet . . .

Beneatha. Well—you finally got it said . . . It took you three years but you finally got it said. Walter, give up; leave me alone—it's Mama's money.

Walter. *He was my father, too!*

Beneatha. So what? He was mine, too—and Travis's grandfather—but the insurance money belongs to Mama. Picking on me is not going to make her give it to you to invest in any liquor stores—*(Under breath, dropping into a chair.)*—and I for one say, God bless Mama for that!

Walter *(to Ruth).* See—did you hear? Did you hear!

Ruth. Honey, please go to work.

Walter. Nobody in this house is ever going to understand me.

Beneatha. Because you're a nut.

Walter. Who's a nut?

Beneatha. You—you are a nut. Thee is mad, boy.

Walter *(looking at his wife and his sister from the door, very sadly).* The world's most backward race of people, and that's a fact.

Beneatha *(turning slowly in her chair).* And then there are all those prophets who would lead us out of the wilderness—*(Walter slams out of the house.)*—into the swamps!

Ruth. Bennie, why you always gotta be pickin' on your brother? Can't you be a little sweeter sometimes? *(Door opens. Walter walks in. He fumbles with his cap, starts to speak, clears throat, looks everywhere but at Ruth. Finally:)*

Walter *(to Ruth).* I need some money for carfare.

Ruth *(looks at him, then warms; teasing, but tenderly).* Fifty cents? *(She goes to her bag and gets money.)* Here—take a taxi!

Walter exits. Mama enters. She is a woman in her early sixties, full-bodied and strong. She is one of those women of a certain grace and beauty who wear it so unobtrusively that it takes a while to notice. Her dark-brown face is surrounded by the total whiteness of her hair, and, being a woman who has adjusted to many things in life and overcome many more, her face is full of strength. She has, we can see, wit and faith of a kind that keep her eyes lit and full of interest and expectancy. She is, in a word, a beautiful woman. Her bearing is perhaps most like the noble bearing of the women of the Hereros of Southwest Africa—rather as if she imagines that as she walks she still bears a basket or a vessel upon her head. Her speech, on the other hand, is as careless as her carriage is precise—she is inclined to slur everything—but her voice is perhaps not so much quiet as simply soft.

Mama. Who that 'round here slamming doors at this hour?

She crosses through the room, goes to the window, opens it, and brings in a feeble little plant growing doggedly in a small pot on the window sill. She feels the dirt and puts it back out.

Ruth. That was Walter Lee. He and Bennie was at it again.

Mama. My children and they tempers. Lord, if this little old plant don't get more sun than it's been getting it ain't never going to see spring again. *(She turns from* *the window.)* What's the matter with you this morning, Ruth? You looks right peaked. You aiming to iron all them things? Leave some for me. I'll get to 'em this afternoon. Bennie honey, it's too drafty for you to be sitting 'round half dressed. Where's your robe?

Beneatha. In the cleaners.

Mama. Well, go get mine and put it on.

Beneatha. I'm not cold, Mama, honest.

Mama. I know—but you so thin . . .

Beneatha *(irritably).* Mama, I'm not cold.

Mama *(seeing the make-down bed as Travis has left it).* Lord have mercy, look at that poor bed. Bless his heart—he tries, don't he?

She moves to the bed Travis has sloppily made up.

Ruth. No—he don't half try at all 'cause he knows you going to come along behind him and fix everything. That's just how come he don't know how to do nothing right now—you done spoiled that boy so.

Mama *(folding bedding).* Well—he's a little boy. Ain't supposed to know 'bout housekeeping. My baby, that's what he is. What you fix for his breakfast this morning?

Ruth *(angrily).* I feed my son, Lena!

Mama. I ain't meddling—*(Under breath; busy-bodyish.)* I just noticed all last week he had cold cereal, and when it starts getting this chilly in the fall a child ought to have some hot grits or something when he goes out in the cold—

Ruth *(furious).* I gave him hot oats—is that all right!

Mama. I ain't meddling. *(Pause.)* Put a lot of nice butter on it? *(Ruth shoots her an angry look and does not reply.)* He likes lots of butter.

Ruth *(exasperated).* Lena—

Mama *(to Beneatha. Mama is inclined to wander conversationally sometimes).* What was you and your brother fussing 'bout this morning?

Beneatha. It's not important, Mama.

She gets up and goes to look out at the bathroom, which is apparently free, and she picks up her towels and rushes out.

Mama. What was they fighting about?

Ruth. Now you know as well as I do.

Mama *(shaking her head).* Brother still worrying hisself sick about that money?

Ruth. You know he is.

Mama. You had breakfast?

Ruth. Some coffee.

Mama. Girl, you better start eating and looking after yourself better. You almost thin as Travis.

Ruth. Lena—

Mama. Un-hunh?

Ruth. What are you going to do with it?

Mama. Now don't you start, child. It's too early in the morning to be talking about money. It ain't Christian.

Ruth. It's just that he got his heart set on that store—

Mama. You mean that liquor store that Willy Harris want him to invest in?

Ruth. Yes—

Mama. We ain't no business people, Ruth. We just plain working folks.

Ruth. Ain't nobody business people till they go into business. Walter Lee say colored people ain't never going to start getting ahead till they start gambling on some different kinds of things in the world—investments and things.

Mama. What done got into you, girl? Walter Lee done finally sold you on investing.

Ruth. No. Mama, something is happening between Walter and me. I don't know what it is—but he needs something—something I can't give him any more. He needs this chance, Lena.

Mama (*frowning deeply*). But liquor, honey—

Ruth. Well—like Walter say—I spec people going to always be drinking themselves some liquor.

Mama. Well—whether they drinks it or not ain't none of my business. But whether I go into business selling it to 'em *is,* and I don't want that on my ledger this late in life. (*Stopping suddenly and studying her daughter-in-law.*) Ruth Younger, what's the matter with you today? You look like you could fall over right there.

Ruth. I'm tired.

Mama. Then you better stay home from work today.

Ruth. I can't stay home. She'd be calling up the agency and screaming at them, "My girl didn't come in today—send me somebody! My girl didn't come in!" Oh, she just have a fit . . .

Mama. Well, let her have it. I'll just call her up and say you got the flu—

Ruth (*laughing*). Why the flu?

Mama. 'Cause it sounds respectable to 'em. Something white people get, too. They know 'bout the flu. Otherwise they think you been cut up or something when you tell 'em you sick.

Ruth. I got to go in. We need the money.

Mama. Somebody would of thought my children done all but starved to death the way they talk about money here late. Child, we got a great big old check coming tomorrow.

Ruth (*sincerely, but also self-righteously*). Now that's your money. It ain't got nothing to do with me. We all feel like that—Walter and Bennie and me—even Travis.

Mama (*thoughtfully, and suddenly very far away*). Ten thousand dollars—

Ruth. Sure is wonderful.

Mama. Ten thousand dollars.

Ruth. You know what you should do, Miss Lena? You should take yourself a trip somewhere. To Europe or South America or someplace—

Mama (*throwing up her hands at the thought*). Oh, child!

Ruth. I'm serious. Just pack up and leave! Go on away and enjoy yourself some. Forget about the family and have yourself a ball for once in your life—

Mama *(drily)*. You sound like I'm just about ready to die. Who'd go with me? What I look like wandering 'round Europe by myself?

Ruth. Shoot—these here rich white women do it all the time. They don't think nothing of packing up they suitcases and piling on one of them big steamships and—swoosh!—they gone, child.

Mama. Something always told me I wasn't no rich white woman.

Ruth. Well—what are you going to do with it then?

Mama. I ain't rightly decided. *(Thinking. She speaks now with emphasis.)* Some of it got to be put away for Beneatha and her schoolin'—and ain't nothing going to touch that part of it. Nothing. *(She waits several seconds, trying to make up her mind about something, and looks at Ruth a little tentatively before going on.)* Been thinking that we maybe could meet the notes on a little old two-story somewhere, with a yard where Travis could play in the summertime, if we use part of the insurance for a down payment and everybody kind of pitch in. I could maybe take on a little day work again, few days a week—

Ruth *(studying her mother-in-law furtively and concentrating on her ironing, anxious to encourage without seeming to)*. Well, Lord knows, we've put enough rent into this here rat trap to pay for four houses by now . . .

Mama *(looking up at the words "rat trap" and then looking around and leaning back and sighing—in a suddenly reflective mood—)*. "Rat trap"—yes, that's all it is. *(Smiling.)* I remember just as well the day me and Big Walter moved in here. Hadn't been married but two weeks and wasn't planning on living here no more than a year. *(She shakes her head at the dissolved dream.)* We was going to set away, little by little, don't you know, and buy a little place out in Morgan Park. We had even picked out the house. *(Chuckling a little.)* Looks right dumpy today. But Lord, child, you should know all the dreams I had 'bout buying that house and fixing it up and making me a little garden in the back—*(She waits and stops smiling.)* And didn't none of it happen.

Dropping her hands in a futile gesture.

Ruth *(keeps her head down, ironing)*. Yes, life can be a barrel of disappointments, sometimes.

Mama. Honey, Big Walter would come in here some nights back then and slump down on that couch there and just look at the rug, and look at me and look at the rug and then back at me—and I'd know he was down then . . . really down. *(After a second very long and thoughtful pause; she is seeing back to times that only she can see.)* And then, Lord, when I lost that baby—little Claude—I almost thought I was going to lose Big Walter too. Oh, that man grieved hisself! He was one man to love his children.

Ruth. Ain't nothin' can tear at you like losin' your baby.

Mama. I guess that's how come that man finally worked hisself to death like he done. Like he was fighting his own war with this here world that took his baby from him.

Ruth. He sure was a fine man, all right. I always liked Mr. Younger.

Mama. Crazy 'bout his children! God knows there was plenty wrong with Walter Younger—hard-headed, mean, kind of wild with women—plenty wrong with him. But he sure loved his children. Always wanted them to have something— be something. That's where Brother gets all these notions, I reckon. Big Walter used to say, he'd get right wet in the eyes sometimes, lean his head back with the water standing in his eyes and say, "Seem like God didn't see fit to give the black man nothing but dreams—but He did give us children to make them dreams seem worthwhile." (*She smiles.*) He could talk like that, don't you know.

Ruth. Yes, he sure could. He was a good man, Mr. Younger.

Mama. Yes, a fine man—just couldn't never catch up with his dreams, that's all.

Beneatha comes in, brushing her hair and looking up to the ceiling, where the sound of a vacuum cleaner has started up.

Beneatha. What could be so dirty on that woman's rugs that she has to vacuum them every single day?

Ruth. I wish certain young women 'round here who I could name would take inspiration about certain rugs in a certain apartment I could also mention.

Beneatha (*shrugging*). How much cleaning can a house need, for Christ's sakes.

Mama (*not liking the Lord's name used thus*). Bennie!

Ruth. Just listen to her—just listen!

Beneatha. Oh, God!

Mama. If you use the Lord's name just one more time—

Beneatha (*a bit of a whine*). Oh, Mama—

Ruth. Fresh—just fresh as salt, this girl!

Beneatha (*drily*). Well—if the salt loses its savor—

Mama. Now that will do. I just ain't going to have you 'round here reciting the scriptures in vain—you hear me?

Beneatha. How did I manage to get on everybody's wrong side by just walking into a room?

Ruth. If you weren't so fresh—

Beneatha. Ruth, I'm twenty years old.

Mama. What time you be home from school today?

Beneatha. Kind of late. (*With enthusiasm.*) Madeline is going to start my guitar lessons today.

Mama and Ruth look up with the same expression.

Mama. Your *what* kind of lessons?

Beneatha. Guitar.

Ruth. Oh, Father!

Mama. How come you done taken it in your mind to learn to play the guitar?

Beneatha. I just want to, that's all.

Mama *(smiling).* Lord, child, don't you know what to do with yourself? How long it going to be before you get tired of this now—like you got tired of that little play-acting group you joined last year? *(Looking at Ruth.)* And what was it the year before that?

Ruth. The horseback-riding club for which she bought that fifty-five-dollar riding habit that's been hanging in the closet ever since!

Mama *(to Beneatha).* Why you got to flit so from one thing to another, baby?

Beneatha *(sharply).* I just want to learn to play the guitar. Is there anything wrong with that?

Mama. Ain't nobody trying to stop you. I just wonders sometimes why you has to flit so from one thing to another all the time. You ain't never done nothing with all that camera equipment you brought home—

Beneatha. I don't flit! I—I experiment with different forms of expression—

Ruth. Like riding a horse?

Beneatha. —People have to express themselves one way or another.

Mama. What is it you want to express?

Beneatha *(angrily).* Me! *(Mama and Ruth look at each other and burst into raucous laughter.)* Don't worry—I don't expect you to understand.

Mama *(to change the subject).* Who you going out with tomorrow night?

Beneatha *(with displeasure).* George Murchison again.

Mama *(pleased).* Oh—you getting a little sweet on him?

Ruth. You ask me, this child ain't sweet on nobody but herself—*(Under breath.)* Express herself!

They laugh.

Beneatha. Oh—I like George all right, Mama. I mean I like him enough to go out with him and stuff, but—

Ruth *(for devilment).* What does *and stuff* mean?

Beneatha. Mind your own business.

Mama. Stop picking at her now, Ruth. *(She chuckles—then a suspicious sudden look at her daughter as she turns in her chair for emphasis.)* What DOES it mean?

Beneatha *(wearily).* Oh, I just mean I couldn't ever really be serious about George. He's—he's so shallow.

Ruth. Shallow—what do you mean he's shallow? He's *rich!*

Mama. Hush, Ruth.

Beneatha. I know he's rich. He knows he's rich, too.

Ruth. Well—what other qualities a man got to have to satisfy you, little girl?

Beneatha. You wouldn't even begin to understand. Anybody who married Walter could not possibly understand.

Mama *(outraged).* What kind of way is that to talk about your brother?

Beneatha. Brother is a flip—let's face it.

Mama *(to Ruth, helplessly).* What's a flip?

Ruth *(glad to add kindling).* She's saying he's crazy.

Beneatha. Not crazy. Brother isn't really crazy yet—he—he's an elaborate neurotic.

Mama. Hush your mouth!

Beneatha. As for George. Well. George looks good—he's got a beautiful car and he takes me to nice places and, as my sister-in-law says, he is probably the richest boy I will ever get to know and I even like him sometimes—but if the Youngers are sitting around waiting to see if their little Bennie is going to tie up the family with the Murchisons, they are wasting their time.

Ruth. You mean you wouldn't marry George Murchison if he asked you someday? That pretty, rich thing? Honey, I knew you was odd—

Beneatha. No I would not marry him if all I felt for him was what I feel now. Besides, George's family wouldn't really like it.

Mama. Why not?

Beneatha. Oh, Mama—The Murchisons are honest-to-God-real-*live*-rich colored people, and the only people in the world who are more snobbish than rich white people are rich colored people. I thought everybody knew that. I've met Mrs. Murchison. She's a scene!

Mama. You must not dislike people 'cause they well off, honey.

Beneatha. Why not? It makes just as much sense as disliking people 'cause they are poor, and lots of people do that.

Ruth (*a wisdom-of-the-ages manner. To Mama*). Well, she'll get over some of this—

Beneatha. Get over it? What are you talking about, Ruth? Listen, I'm going to be a doctor. I'm not worried about who I'm going to marry yet—if I ever get married.

Mama and Ruth. *If!*

Mama. Now, Bennie—

Beneatha. Oh, I probably will . . . but first I'm going to be a doctor, and George, for one, still thinks that's pretty funny. I couldn't be bothered with that. I am going to be a doctor and everybody around here better understand that!

Mama (*kindly*). 'Course you going to be a doctor, honey, God willing.

Beneatha (*drily*). God hasn't got a thing to do with it.

Mama. Beneatha—that just wasn't necessary.

Beneatha. Well—neither is God. I get sick of hearing about God.

Mama. Beneatha!

Beneatha. I mean it! I'm just tired of hearing about God all the time. What has He got to do with anything? Does He pay tuition?

Mama. You 'bout to get your fresh little jaw slapped!

Ruth. That's just what she needs, all right!

Beneatha. Why? Why can't I say what I want to around here, like everybody else?

Mama. It don't sound nice for a young girl to say things like that—you wasn't brought up that way. Me and your father went to trouble to get you and Brother to church every Sunday.

Beneatha. Mama, you don't understand. It's all a matter of ideas, and God is just one idea I don't accept. It's not important. I am not going out and be immoral or commit crimes because I don't believe in God. I don't even think about it. It's just that I get tired of Him getting credit for all the things the human race achieves through its own stubborn effort. There simply is no blasted God— there is only man and it is *He* who makes miracles!

Mama absorbs this speech, studies her daughter, and rises slowly and crosses to Beneatha and slaps her powerfully across the face. After, there is only silence and the daughter drops her eyes from her mother's face, and Mama is very tall before her.

Mama. Now—you say after me, in my mother's house there is still God. (*There is a long pause and Beneatha stares at the floor wordlessly. Mama repeats the phrase with precision and cool emotion.*) In my mother's house there is still God.
Beneatha. In my mother's house there is still God.

A long pause.

Mama (*walking away from Beneatha, too disturbed for triumphant posture. Stopping and turning back to her daughter*). There are some ideas we ain't going to have in this house. Not long as I am at the head of this family.
Beneatha. Yes, ma'am.

Mama walks out of the room.

Ruth (*almost gently, with profound understanding*). You think you a woman, Bennie—but you still a little girl. What you did was childish—so you got treated like a child.
Beneatha. I see. (*Quietly.*) I also see that everybody thinks it's all right for Mama to be a tyrant. But all the tyranny in the world will never put a God in the heavens!

She picks up her books and goes out. Pause.

Ruth (*goes to Mama's door*). She said she was sorry.
Mama (*coming out, going to her plant*). They frightens me, Ruth. My children.
Ruth. You got good children, Lena. They just a little off sometimes—but they're good.
Mama. No—there's something come down between me and them that don't let us understand each other and I don't know what it is. One done almost lost his mind thinking 'bout money all the time and the other done commence to talk about things I can't seem to understand in no form or fashion. What is it that's changing, Ruth?
Ruth (*soothingly, older than her years*). Now . . . you taking it all too seriously. You just got strong-willed children and it takes a strong woman like you to keep 'em in hand.
Mama (*looking at her plant and sprinkling a little water on it*). They spirited all right, my children. Got to admit they got spirit—Bennie and Walter. Like this

little old plant that ain't never had enough sunshine or nothing—and look at it . . .

She has her back to Ruth, who has had to stop ironing and lean against something and put the back of her hand to her forehead.

Ruth *(trying to keep Mama from noticing).* You . . . sure . . . loves that little old thing, don't you? . . .

Mama. Well, I always wanted me a garden like I used to see sometimes at the back of the houses down home. This plant is close as I ever got to having one. *(She looks out of the window as she replaces the plant.)* Lord, ain't nothing as dreary as the view from this window on a dreary day, is there? Why ain't you singing this morning, Ruth? Sing that "No Ways Tired." That song always lifts me up so— *(She turns at last to see that Ruth has slipped quietly to the floor, in a state of semi-consciousness.)* Ruth! Ruth honey— what's the matter with you . . . Ruth!

Curtain.

Scene 2. *(The following morning.)*

It is the following morning; a Saturday morning, and house cleaning is in progress at the Youngers'. Furniture has been shoved hither and yon and Mama is giving the kitchen-area walls a washing down. Beneatha, in dungarees, with a handkerchief tied around her face, is spraying insecticide into the cracks in the walls. As they work, the radio is on and a Southside disk-jockey program is inappropriately filling the house with a rather exotic saxophone blues. Travis, the sole idle one, is leaning on his arms, looking out of the window.

Travis. Grandmama, that stuff Bennie is using smells awful. Can I go downstairs, please?

Mama. Did you get all them chores done already? I ain't seen you doing much.

Travis. Yes'm—finished early. Where did Mama go this morning?

Mama *(looking at Beneatha).* She had to go on a little errand.

The phone rings. Beneatha runs to answer it and reaches it before Walter, who has entered from bedroom.

Travis. Where?

Mama. To tend to her business.

Beneatha. Haylo . . . *(Disappointed.)* Yes, he is. *(She tosses the phone to Walter, who barely catches it.)* It's Willie Harris again.

Walter *(as privately as possible under Mama's gaze).* Hello, Willie. Did you get the papers from the lawyer? . . . No, not yet. I told you the mailman doesn't get here till ten-thirty . . . No, I'll come there . . . Yeah! Right away. *(He hangs up and goes for his coat.)*

Beneatha. Brother, where did Ruth go?

Walter *(as he exits).* How should I know!

Travis. Aw come on, Grandma. Can I go outside?

Mama. Oh, I guess so. You stay right in front of the house, though, and keep a good lookout for the postman.

Travis. Yes'm. *(He darts into bedroom for stickball and bat, reenters, and sees Beneatha on her knees spraying under sofa with behind upraised. He edges closer to the target, takes aim, and lets her have it. She screams.)* Leave them poor little cockroaches alone, they ain't bothering you none! *(He runs as she swings the spraygun at him viciously and playfully.)* Grandma! Grandma!

Mama. Look out there, girl, before you be spilling some of that stuff on that child!

Travis *(safely behind the bastion of Mama).* That's right—look out, now! *(He exits.)*

Beneatha *(drily).* I can't imagine that it would hurt him—it has never hurt the roaches.

Mama. Well, little boys' hides ain't as tough as Southside roaches. You better get over there behind the bureau. I seen one marching out of there like Napoleon yesterday.

Beneatha. There's really only one way to get rid of them, Mama—

Mama. How?

Beneatha. Set fire to this building! Mama, where did Ruth go?

Mama *(looking at her with meaning).* To the doctor, I think.

Beneatha. The doctor? What's the matter? *(They exchange glances.)* You don't think—

Mama *(with her sense of drama).* Now I ain't saying what I think. But I ain't never been wrong 'bout a woman neither.

The phone rings.

Beneatha *(at the phone).* Hay-lo . . . *(Pause, and a moment of recognition.)* Well— when did you get back! . . . And how was it? . . . Of course I've missed you—in my way . . . This morning? No . . . house cleaning and all that and Mama hates it if I let people come over when the house is like this . . . You *have?* Well, that's different . . . What is it—Oh, what the hell, come on over . . . Right, see you then. *Arrivederci.*

She hangs up.

Mama *(who has listened vigorously, as is her habit).* Who is that you inviting over here with this house looking like this? You ain't got the pride you was born with!

Beneatha. Asagai doesn't care how houses look, Mama—he's an intellectual.

Mama. *Who?*

Beneatha. Asagai—Joseph Asagai. He's an African boy I met on campus. He's been studying in Canada all summer.

Mama. What's his name?

Beneatha. Asagai, Joseph. Ah-sah-guy . . . He's from Nigeria.

Mama. Oh, that's the little country that was founded by slaves way back . . .

Beneatha. No, Mama—that's Liberia.

Mama. I don't think I never met no African before.

Beneatha. Well, do me a favor and don't ask him a whole lot of ignorant questions about Africans. I mean, do they wear clothes and all that—

Mama. Well, now, I guess if you think we so ignorant 'round here maybe you shouldn't bring your friends here—

Beneatha. It's just that people ask such crazy things. All anyone seems to know about when it comes to Africa is Tarzan—

Mama (*indignantly*). Why should I know anything about Africa?

Beneatha. Why do you give money at church for the missionary work?

Mama. Well, that's to help save people.

Beneatha. You mean save them from *heathenism*—

Mama (*innocently*). Yes.

Beneatha. I'm afraid they need more salvation from the British and the French.

Ruth comes in forlornly and pulls off her coat with dejection. They both turn to look at her.

Ruth (*dispiritedly*). Well, I guess from all the happy faces—everybody knows.

Beneatha. You pregnant?

Mama. Lord have mercy, I sure hope it's a little old girl. Travis ought to have a sister.

Beneatha and Ruth give her a hopeless look for this grandmotherly enthusiasm.

Beneatha. How far along are you?

Ruth. Two months.

Beneatha. Did you mean to? I mean did you plan it or was it an accident?

Mama. What do you know about planning or not planning?

Beneatha. Oh, Mama.

Ruth (*wearily*). She's twenty years old, Lena.

Beneatha. Did you plan it, Ruth?

Ruth. Mind your own business.

Beneatha. It is my business—where is he going to live, on the *roof*? (*There is silence following the remark as the three women react to the sense of it.*) Gee—I didn't mean that, Ruth, honest. Gee, I don't feel like that at all. I—I think it is wonderful.

Ruth (*dully*). Wonderful.

Beneatha. Yes—really.

Mama (*looking at Ruth, worried*). Doctor say everything going to be all right?

Ruth (*far away*). Yes—she says everything is going to be fine . . .

Mama (*immediately suspicious*). "She"—What doctor you went to?

Ruth folds over, near hysteria.

Mama *(worriedly hovering over Ruth).* Ruth honey—what's the matter with you—you sick?

Ruth has her fists clenched on her thighs and is fighting hard to suppress a scream that seems to be rising in her.

Beneatha. What's the matter with her, Mama?

Mama *(working her fingers in Ruth's shoulders to relax her).* She be all right. Women gets right depressed sometimes when they get her way. *(Speaking softly, expertly, rapidly.)* Now you just relax. That's right . . . just lean back, don't think 'bout nothing at all . . . nothing at all—

Ruth. I'm all right . . .

The glassy-eyed look melts and then she collapses into a fit of heavy sobbing. The bell rings.

Beneatha. Oh, my God—that must be Asagai.

Mama *(to Ruth).* Come on now, honey. You need to lie down and rest awhile . . . then have some nice hot food.

They exit, Ruth's weight on her mother-in-law. Beneatha, herself profoundly disturbed, opens the door to admit a rather dramatic-looking young man with a large package.

Asagai. Hello, Alaiyo—

Beneatha *(holding the door open and regarding him with pleasure).* Hello . . . *(Long pause.)* Well—come in. And please excuse everything. My mother was very upset about my letting anyone come here with the place like this.

Asagai *(coming into the room).* You look disturbed too . . . Is something wrong?

Beneatha *(still at the door, absently).* Yes . . . we've all got acute ghetto itus. *(She smiles and comes toward him, finding a cigarette and sitting.)* So—sit down! No! Wait! *(She whips the spraygun off sofa where she had left it and puts the cushions back. At last perches on arm of sofa. He sits.)* So, how was Canada?

Asagai *(a sophisticate).* Canadian.

Beneatha *(looking at him).* Asagai, I'm very glad you are back.

Asagai *(looking back at her in turn).* Are you really?

Beneatha. Yes—very.

Asagai. Why?—you were quite glad when I went away. What happened?

Beneatha. You went away.

Asagai. Ahhhhhhhh.

Beneatha. Before—you wanted to be so serious before there was time.

Asagai. How much time must there be before one knows what one feels?

Beneatha *(stalling this particular conversation. Her hands pressed together, in a deliberately childish gesture).* What did you bring me?

Asagai *(handing her the package).* Open it and see.

Beneatha *(eagerly opening the package and drawing out some records and the colorful robes of a Nigerian woman).* Oh Asagai! . . . You got them for me! . . . How beautiful . . . and the records too! *(She lifts out the robes and runs to the mirror with them and holds the drapery up in front of herself.)*

Asagai *(coming to her at the mirror).* I shall have to teach you how to drape it properly. *(He flings the material about her for the moment and stands back to look at her.)* Ah—Oh-pay-gay-day, oh-gbah-mu-shay. *(A Yoruba exclamation for admiration.)* You wear it well . . . very well . . . mutilated hair and all.

Beneatha *(turning suddenly).* My hair—what's wrong with my hair?

Asagai *(shrugging).* Were you born with it like that?

Beneatha *(reaching up to touch it).* No . . . of course not.

She looks back to the mirror, disturbed.

Asagai *(smiling).* How then?

Beneatha. You know perfectly well how . . . as crinkly as yours . . . that's how.

Asagai. And it is ugly to you that way?

Beneatha *(quickly).* Oh, no—not ugly . . . *(More slowly, apologetically.)* But it's so hard to manage when it's, well—raw.

Asagai. And so to accommodate that—you mutilate it every week?

Beneatha. It's not mutilation!

Asagai *(laughing aloud at her seriousness).* Oh . . . please! I am only teasing you because you are so very serious about these things. *(He stands back from her and folds his arms across his chest as he watches her pulling at her hair and frowning in the mirror.)* Do you remember the first time you met me at school? . . . *(He laughs.)* You came up to me and you said—and I thought you were the most serious little thing I had ever seen—you said: *(He imitates her.)* "Mr. Asagai—I want very much to talk with you. About Africa. You see, Mr. Asagai, I am looking for my *identity!*"

He laughs.

Beneatha *(turning to him, not laughing).* Yes—

Her face is quizzical, profoundly disturbed.

Asagai *(still teasing and reaching out and taking her face in his hands and turning her profile to him).* Well . . . it is true that this is not so much a profile of a Hollywood queen as perhaps a queen of the Nile—*(A mock dismissal of the importance of the question.)* But what does it matter? Assimilationism is so popular in your country.

Beneatha *(wheeling, passionately, sharply).* I am not an assimilationist!

Asagai *(the protest hangs in the room for a moment and Asagai studies her, his laughter fading).* Such a serious one. *(There is a pause.)* So—you like the robes? You must take excellent care of them—they are from my sister's personal wardrobe.

Beneatha *(with incredulity).* You—you sent all the way home—for me?

Asagai *(with charm).* For you—I would do much more . . . Well, that is what I came for. I must go.

Beneatha. Will you call me Monday?

Asagai. Yes . . . We have a great deal to talk about. I mean about identity and time and all that.

Beneatha. Time?

Asagai. Yes. About how much time one needs to know what one feels.

Beneatha. You see! You never understood that there is more than one kind of feeling which can exist between a man and a woman—or, at least, there should be.

Asagai *(shaking his head negatively but gently).* No. Between a man and a woman there need be only one kind of feeling. I have that for you . . . Now even . . . right this moment . . .

Beneatha. I know—and by itself—it won't do. I can find that anywhere.

Asagai. For a woman it should be enough.

Beneatha. I know—because that's what it says in all the novels that men write. But it isn't. Go ahead and laugh—but I'm not interested in being someone's little episode in America or—*(With feminine vengeance.)*—one of them! *(Asagai has burst into laughter again.)* That's funny as hell, huh!

Asagai. It's just that every American girl I have known has said that to me. White—black—in this you are all the same. And the same speech, too!

Beneatha *(angrily).* Yuk, yuk, yuk!

Asagai. It's how you can be sure that the world's most liberated women are not liberated at all. You all talk about it too much!

Mama enters and is immediately all social charm because of the presence of a guest.

Beneatha. Oh—Mama—this is Mr. Asagai.

Mama. How do you do?

Asagai *(total politeness to an elder).* How do you do, Mrs. Younger. Please forgive me for coming at such an outrageous hour on a Saturday.

Mama. Well, you are quite welcome. I just hope you understand that our house don't always look like this. *(Chatterish.)* You must come again. I would love to hear all about—*(Not sure of the name.)*—your country. I think it's so sad the way our American Negroes don't know nothing about Africa 'cept Tarzan and all that. And all that money they pour into these churches when they ought to be helping you people over there drive out them French and Englishmen done taken away your land.

The mother flashes a slightly superior look at her daughter upon completion of the recitation.

Asagai *(taken aback by this sudden and acutely unrelated expression of sympathy).* Yes . . . yes . . .

Mama *(smiling at him suddenly and relaxing and looking him over).* How many miles is it from here to where you come from?

Asagai. Many thousands.

Mama *(looking at him as she would Walter).* I bet you don't half look after yourself, being away from your mama either. I spec you better come 'round here from time to time to get yourself some decent homecooked meals . . .

Asagai *(moved).* Thank you. Thank you very much. *(They are all quiet, then—)* Well . . . I must go. I will call you Monday, Alaiyo.

Mama. What's that he call you?

Asagai. Oh—"Alaiyo." I hope you don't mind. It is what you would call a nickname, I think. It is a Yoruba word. I am a Yoruba.

Mama *(looking at Beneatha).* I—I thought he was from—*(Uncertain.)*

Asagai *(understanding).* Nigeria is my country. Yoruba is my tribal origin—

Beneatha. You didn't tell us what Alaiyo means . . . for all I know, you might be calling me Little Idiot or something . . .

Asagai. Well . . . let me see . . . I do not know how just to explain it . . . The sense of a thing can be so different when it changes languages.

Beneatha. You're evading.

Asagai. No—really it is difficult . . . *(Thinking.)* It means . . . it means One for Whom Bread—Food—Is Not Enough. *(He looks at her.)* Is that all right?

Beneatha *(understanding, softly).* Thank you.

Mama *(looking from one to the other and not understanding any of it).* Well . . . that's nice . . . You must come see us again—Mr.—

Asagai. Ah-sah-guy . . .

Mama. Yes . . . Do come again.

Asagai. Good-bye.

He exits.

Mama *(after him).* Lord, that's a pretty thing just went out here! *(Insinuatingly, to her daughter.)* Yes, I guess I see why we done commence to get so interested in Africa 'round here. Missionaries my aunt Jenny!

She exits.

Beneatha. Oh, Mama! . . .

She picks up the Nigerian dress and holds it up to her in front of the mirror again. She sets the headdress on haphazardly and then notices her hair again and clutches at it and then replaces the headdress and frowns at herself. Then she starts to wriggle in front of the mirror as she thinks a Nigerian woman might. Travis enters and stands regarding her.

Travis. What's the matter, girl, you cracking up?
Beneatha. Shut up.

She pulls the headdress off and looks at herself in the mirror and clutches at her hair again and squinches her eyes as if trying to imagine something. Then, suddenly, she gets her raincoat and kerchief and hurriedly prepares for going out.

Mama *(coming back into the room).* She's resting now. Travis, baby, run next door and ask Miss Johnson to please let me have a little kitchen cleanser. This here can is empty as Jacob's kettle.
Travis. I just came in.
Mama. Do as you told. *(He exits and she looks at her daughter.)* Where you going?
Beneatha *(halting at the door).* To become a queen of the Nile!

She exits in a breathless blaze of glory. Ruth appears in the bedroom doorway.

Mama. Who told you to get up?
Ruth. Ain't nothing wrong with me to be lying in no bed for. Where did Bennie go?
Mama *(drumming her fingers).* Far as I could make out—to Egypt. *(Ruth just looks at her.)* What time is it getting to?
Ruth. Ten twenty. And the mailman going to ring that bell this morning just like he done every morning for the last umpteen years.

Travis comes in with the cleanser can.

Travis. She say to tell you that she don't have much.
Mama *(angrily).* Lord, some people I could name sure is tight-fisted! *(Directing her grandson.)* Mark two cans of cleanser on the list there. If she that hard up for kitchen cleanser, I sure don't want to forget to get her none!
Ruth. Lena—maybe the woman is just short on cleanser—
Mama *(not listening).* —Much baking powder as she done borrowed from me all these years, she could of done gone into the baking business!

The bell sounds suddenly and sharply and all three are stunned—serious and silent—midspeech. In spite of all the other conversations and distractions of the morning, this is what they have been waiting for, even Travis, who looks helplessly from his mother to his grandmother. Ruth is the first to come to life again.

Ruth *(to Travis).* Get down them steps, boy!

Travis snaps to life and flies out to get the mail.

Mama *(her eyes wide, her hand to her breast)*. You mean it done really come?

Ruth *(excited)*. Oh, Miss Lena!

Mama *(collecting herself)*. Well . . . I don't know what we all so excited about 'round here for. We known it was coming for months.

Ruth. That's a whole lot different from having it come and being able to hold it in your hands . . . a piece of paper worth ten thousand dollars . . . *(Travis bursts back into the room. He holds the envelope high above his head, like a little dancer, his face is radiant and he is breathless. He moves to his grandmother with sudden slow ceremony and puts the envelope into her hands. She accepts it, and then merely holds it and looks at it.)* Come on! Open it . . . Lord have mercy, I wish Walter Lee was here!

Travis. Open it, Grandmama!

Mama *(staring at it)*. Now you all be quiet. It's just a check.

Ruth. Open it . . .

Mama *(still staring at it)*. Now don't act silly . . . We ain't never been no people to act silly 'bout no money—

Ruth *(swiftly)*. We ain't never had none before—OPEN IT!

Mama finally makes a good strong tear and pulls out the thin blue slice of paper and inspects it closely. The boy and his mother study it raptly over Mama's shoulders.

Mama. Travis! *(She is counting off with doubt.)* Is that the right number of zeros?

Travis. Yes'm . . . ten thousand dollars. Gaalee, Grandmama, you rich.

Mama *(She holds the check away from her, still looking at it. Slowly her face sobers into a mask of unhappiness)*. Ten thousand dollars. *(She hands it to Ruth.)* Put it away somewhere, Ruth. *(She does not look at Ruth; her eyes seem to be seeing something somewhere very far off.)* Ten thousand dollars they give you. Ten thousand dollars.

Travis *(to his mother, sincerely)*. What's the matter with Grandmama—don't she want to be rich?

Ruth *(distractedly)*. You go on out and play now, baby. *(Travis exits. Mama starts wiping dishes absently, humming intently to herself. Ruth turns to her, with kind exasperation.)* You've gone and got yourself upset.

Mama *(not looking at her)*. I spec if it wasn't for you all . . . I would just put that money away or give it to the church or something.

Ruth. Now what kind of talk is that. Mr. Younger would just be plain mad if he could hear you talking foolish like that.

Mama *(stopping and staring off)*. Yes . . . he sure would. *(Sighing.)* We got enough to do with that money, all right. *(She halts then, and turns and looks at her daughter-in-law hard; Ruth avoids her eyes and Mama wipes her hands with finality and starts to speak firmly to Ruth.)* Where did you go today, girl?

Ruth. To the doctor.

Mama *(impatiently)*. Now, Ruth . . . you know better than that. Old Doctor Jones is strange enough in his way but there ain't nothing 'bout him make somebody slip and call him "she"—like you done this morning.

Ruth. Well, that's what happened—my tongue slipped.

Mama. You went to see that woman, didn't you?

Ruth *(defensively, giving herself away).* What woman you talking about?

Mama *(angrily).* That woman who—

Walter enters in great excitement.

Walter. Did it come?

Mama *(quietly).* Can't you give people a Christian greeting before you start asking about money?

Walter *(to Ruth).* Did it come? *(Ruth unfolds the check and lays it quietly before him, watching him intently with thoughts of her own. Walter sits down and grasps it close and counts off the zeros.)* Ten thousand dollars—*(He turns suddenly, frantically to his mother and draws some papers out of his breast pocket.)* Mama—look. Old Willy Harris put everything on paper—

Mama. Son—I think you ought to talk to your wife . . . I'll go on out and leave you alone if you want—

Walter. I can talk to her later—Mama, look—

Mama. Son—

Walter. WILL SOMEBODY PLEASE LISTEN TO ME TODAY!

Mama *(quietly).* I don't 'low no yellin' in this house, Walter Lee, and you know it—*(Walter stares at them in frustration and starts to speak several times.)* And there ain't going to be no investing in no liquor stores.

Walter. But, Mama, you ain't even looked at it.

Mama. I don't aim to have to speak on that again.

A long pause.

Walter. You ain't looked at it and you don't aim to have to speak on that again? You ain't even looked at it and *you* have decided—*(Crumpling his papers.)* Well, *you* tell that to my boy tonight when you put him to sleep on the living-room couch . . . *(Turning to Mama and speaking directly to her.)* Yeah—and tell it to my wife, Mama, tomorrow when she has to go out of here to look after somebody else's kids. And tell it to *me*, Mama, every time we need a new pair of curtains and I have to watch *you* go out and work in somebody's kitchen. Yeah, you tell me then!

Walter starts out.

Ruth. Where you going?

Walter. I'm going out!

Ruth. Where?

Walter. Just out of this house somewhere—

Ruth *(getting her coat).* I'll come too.

Walter. I don't want you to come!

Ruth. I got something to talk to you about, Walter.

Walter. That's too bad.

Mama *(still quietly).* Walter Lee—*(She waits and he finally turns and looks at her.)* Sit down.

Walter. I'm a grown man, Mama.

Mama. Ain't nobody said you wasn't grown. But you still in my house and my presence. And as long as you are—you'll talk to your wife civil. Now sit down.

Ruth *(suddenly).* Oh, let him go on out and drink himself to death! He makes me sick to my stomach! *(She flings her coat against him and exits to bedroom.)*

Walter *(violently flinging the coat after her).* And you turn mine too, baby! *(The door slams behind her.)* That was my biggest mistake—

Mama *(still quietly).* Walter, what is the matter with you?

Walter. Matter with me? Ain't nothing the matter with *me!*

Mama. Yes there is. Something eating you up like a crazy man. Something more than me not giving you this money. The past few years I been watching it happen to you. You get all nervous acting and kind of wild in the eyes—*(Walter jumps up impatiently at her words.)* I said sit there now, I'm talking to you!

Walter. Mama—I don't need no nagging at me today.

Mama. Seem like you getting to a place where you always tied up in some kind of knot about something. But if anybody ask you 'bout it you just yell at 'em and bust out the house and go out and drink somewheres. Walter Lee, people can't live with that. Ruth's a good, patient girl in her way—but you getting to be too much. Boy, don't make the mistake of driving that girl away from you.

Walter. Why—what she do for me?

Mama. She loves you.

Walter. Mama—I'm going out. I want to go off somewhere and be by myself for a while.

Mama. I'm sorry 'bout your liquor store, son. It just wasn't the thing for us to do. That's what I want to tell you about—

Walter. I got to go out, Mama—

He rises.

Mama. It's dangerous, son.

Walter. What's dangerous?

Mama. When a man goes outside his home to look for peace.

Walter *(beseechingly).* Then why can't there never be no peace in this house then?

Mama. You done found it in some other house?

Walter. No—there ain't no woman! Why do women always think there's a woman somewhere when a man gets restless. *(Picks up the check.)* Do you know what this money means to me? Do you know what this money can do for us? *(Puts it back.)* Mama—Mama—I want so many things . . .

Mama. Yes, son—

Walter. I want so many things that they are driving me kind of crazy . . . Mama— look at me.

Mama. I'm looking at you. You a good-looking boy. You got a job, a nice wife, a fine boy, and—

Walter. A job. *(Looks at her.)* Mama, a job? I open and close car doors all day long. I drive a man around in his limousine and I say, "Yes, sir; no, sir; very good, sir; shall I take the Drive, sir?" Mama, that ain't no kind of job . . . that ain't nothing at all. *(Very quietly.)* Mama, I don't know if I can make you understand.

Mama. Understand what, baby?

Walter *(quietly).* Sometimes it's like I can see the future stretched out in front of me—just plain as day. The future, Mama. Hanging over there at the edge of my days. Just waiting for me—a big, looming blank space—full of *nothing.* Just waiting for *me.* But it don't have to be. *(Pause. Kneeling beside her chair.)* Mama—sometimes when I'm downtown and I pass them cool, quiet-looking restaurants where them white boys are sitting back and talking 'bout things . . . sitting there turning deals worth millions of dollars . . . sometimes I see guys don't look much older than me—

Mama. Son—how come you talk so much 'bout money?

Walter *(with immense passion).* Because it is life, Mama!

Mama *(quietly).* Oh—*(Very quietly.)* So now it's life. Money is life. Once upon a time freedom used to be life—now it's money. I guess the world really do change . . .

Walter. No—it was always money, Mama. We just didn't know about it.

Mama. No . . . something has changed. *(She looks at him.)* You something new, boy. In my time we was worried about not being lynched and getting to the North if we could and how to stay alive and still have a pinch of dignity too . . . Now here come you and Beneatha—talking 'bout things we ain't never even thought about hardly, me and your daddy. You ain't satisfied or proud of nothing we done. I mean that you had a home; that we kept you out of trouble till you was grown; that you don't have to ride to work on the back of nobody's streetcar— You my children—but how different we done become.

Walter *(a long beat. He pats her hand and gets up).* You just don't understand, Mama, you just don't understand.

Mama. Son—do you know your wife is expecting another baby? *(Walter stands, stunned, and absorbs what his mother has said.)* That's what she wanted to talk to you about. *(Walter sinks down into a chair.)* This ain't for me to be telling—but you ought to know. *(She waits.)* I think Ruth is thinking 'bout getting rid of that child.

Walter *(slowly understanding).* —No—no—Ruth wouldn't do that.

Mama. When the world gets ugly enough—a woman will do anything for her family. *The part that's already living.*

Walter. You don't know Ruth, Mama, if you think she would do that.

Ruth opens the bedroom door and stands there a little limp.

Ruth *(beaten).* Yes I would too, Walter. *(Pause.)* I gave her a five-dollar down payment.

There is total silence as the man stares at his wife and the mother stares at her son.

Mama *(presently).* Well—*(Tightly.)* Well—son, I'm waiting to hear you say something . . . *(She waits.)* I'm waiting to hear how you be your father's son. Be the man he was . . . *(Pause. The silence shouts.)* Your wife say she going to destroy your child. And I'm waiting to hear you talk like him and say we a people who give children life, not who destroys them—*(She rises.)* I'm waiting to see you stand up and look like your daddy and say we done give up one baby to poverty and that we ain't going to give up nary another one . . . I'm waiting.

Walter. Ruth—*(He can say nothing.)*

Mama. If you a son of mine, tell her! *(Walter picks up his keys and his coat and walks out. She continues, bitterly.)* You . . . you are a disgrace to your father's memory. Somebody get me my hat!

Curtain.

ACT II

Scene 1.

Time: Later the same day.
   At rise: Ruth is ironing again. She has the radio going. Presently Beneatha's bedroom door opens and Ruth's mouth falls and she puts down the iron in fascination.

Ruth. What have we got on tonight!

Beneatha *(emerging grandly from the doorway so that we can see her thoroughly robed in the costume Asagai brought).* You are looking at what a well-dressed Nigerian woman wears—*(She parades for Ruth, her hair completely hidden by the headdress; she is coquettishly fanning herself with an ornate oriental fan, mistakenly more like Butterfly than any Nigerian that ever was.)* Isn't it beautiful? *(She promenades to the radio and, with an arrogant flourish, turns off the good loud blues that is playing.)* Enough of this assimilationist junk! *(Ruth follows her with her eyes as she goes to the phonograph and puts on a record and turns and waits ceremoniously for the music to come up. Then, with a shout—)* OCOMOGOSIAY!

Ruth jumps. The music comes up, a lovely Nigerian melody. Beneatha listens, enraptured, her eyes far way—"back to the past." She begins to dance. Ruth is dumbfounded.

Ruth. What kind of dance is that?

Beneatha. A folk dance.

Ruth *(Pearl Bailey).* What kind of folks do that, honey?

Beneatha. It's from Nigeria. It's a dance of welcome.

Ruth. Who you welcoming?

Beneatha. The men back to the village.

Ruth. Where they been?

Beneatha. How should I know—out hunting or something. Anyway, they are coming back now . . .

Ruth. Well, that's good.

Beneatha (with the record).

Alundi, alundi
Alundi alunya
Jop pu a jeepua
Ang gu soooooooooo
Ai yai yae . . .
Ayehaye—alundi . . .

Walter comes in during this performance; he has obviously been drinking. He leans against the door heavily and watches his sister, at first with distaste. Then his eyes look off—"back to the past"—as he lifts both his fists to the roof, screaming.

Walter. YEAH . . . AND ETHIOPIA STRETCH FORTH HER HANDS AGAIN! . . .

Ruth (drily, looking at him). Yes—and Africa sure is claiming her own tonight. (She gives them both up and starts ironing again.)

Walter (all in a drunken, dramatic shout). Shut up! . . . I'm diggin them drums . . . them drums move me! . . . (He makes his weaving way to his wife's face and leans in close to her.) In my heart of hearts—(He thumps his chest.)—I am much warrior!

Ruth (without even looking up). In your heart of hearts you are much drunkard.

Walter (coming away from her and starting to wander around the room, shouting). Me and Jomo . . . (Intently, in his sister's face. She has stopped dancing to watch him in this unknown mood.) That's my man, Kenyatta. (Shouting and thumping his chest.) FLAMING SPEAR! HOT DAMN! (He is suddenly in possession of an imaginary spear and actively spearing enemies all over the room.) OCOMO-GOSIAY . . .

Beneatha (to encourage Walter, thoroughly caught up with this side of him). OCOMOGOSIAY, FLAMING SPEAR!

Walter. THE LION IS WAKING . . . OWIMOWEH!

He pulls his shirt open and leaps up on the table and gestures with his spear.

Beneatha. OWIMOWEH!

Walter (on the table, very far gone, his eyes pure glass sheets. He sees what we cannot, that he is a leader of his people, a great chief, a descendant of Chaka, and that the hour to march has come). Listen, my black brothers—

Beneatha. OCOMOGOSIAY!

Walter. —Do you hear the waters rushing against the shores of the coastlands—
Beneatha. OCOMOGOSIAY!
Walter. —Do you hear the screeching of the cocks in yonder hills beyond where
the chiefs meet in council for the coming of the mighty war—
Beneatha. OCOMOGOSIAY!

And now the lighting shifts subtly to suggest the world of Walter's imagination, and the mood shifts from pure comedy. It is the inner Walter speaking: the Southside chauffeur has assumed an unexpected majesty.

Walter. —Do you hear the beating of the wings of the birds flying low over the
mountains and the low places of our land—
Beneatha. OCOMOGOSIAY!
Walter. —Do you hear the singing of the women, singing the war songs of our
fathers to the babies in the great houses? Singing the sweet war songs! *(The
doorbell rings.)* OH, DO YOU HEAR, MY *BLACK* BROTHERS!
Beneatha *(completely gone).* We hear you, Flaming Spear—

Ruth shuts off the phonograph and opens the door. George Murchison enters.

Walter. Telling us to prepare for the GREATNESS OF THE TIME! *(Lights back to
normal. He turns and sees George.)* Black Brother!

He extends his hand for the fraternal clasp.

George. Black Brother, hell!
Ruth *(having had enough, and embarrassed for the family).* Beneatha, you got
company—what's the matter with you? Walter Lee Younger, get down off that
table and stop acting like a fool . . .

Walter comes down off the table suddenly and makes a quick exit to the bathroom.

Ruth. He's had a little to drink . . . I don't know what her excuse is.
George *(to Beneatha).* Look honey, we're going to the theater—we're not going to
be *in* it . . . so go change, huh?

*Beneatha looks at him and slowly, ceremoniously, lifts her hands and pulls off the
headdress. Her hair is close-cropped and unstraightened. George freezes mid-sentence
and Ruth's eyes all but fall out of her head.*

George. What in the name of—
Ruth *(touching Beneatha's hair).* Girl, you done lost your natural mind? Look at
your head!
George. What have you done to your head—I mean your hair!

Beneatha. Nothing—except cut it off.

Ruth. Now that's the truth—it's what ain't been done to it! You expect this boy to go out with you with your head all nappy like that?

Beneatha *(looking at George).* That's up to George. If he's ashamed of his heritage—

George. Oh, don't be so proud of yourself, Bennie—just because you look eccentric.

Beneatha. How can something that's natural be eccentric?

George. That's what being eccentric means—being natural. Get dressed.

Beneatha. I don't like that, George.

Ruth. Why must you and your brother make an argument out of everything people say?

Beneatha. Because I hate assimilationist Negroes!

Ruth. Will somebody please tell me what assimila-whoever means!

George. Oh, it's just a college girl's way of calling people Uncle Toms—but that isn't what it means at all.

Ruth. Well, what does it mean?

Beneatha *(cutting George off and staring at him as she replies to Ruth).* It means someone who is willing to give up his own culture and submerge himself completely in the dominant, and in this case *oppressive* culture!

George. Oh, dear, dear, dear! Here we go! A lecture on the African past! On our Great West African Heritage! In one second we will hear all about the great Ashanti empires; the great Songhay civilizations; and the great sculpture of Bénin—and then some poetry in the Bantu—and the whole monologue will end with the word *heritage!* *(Nastily.)* Let's face it, baby, your heritage is nothing but a bunch of raggedy-assed spirituals and some grass huts!

Beneatha. GRASS HUTS! *(Ruth crosses to her and forcibly pushes her toward the bedroom.)* See there . . . you are standing there in your splendid ignorance talking about people who were the first to smelt iron on the face of the earth! *(Ruth is pushing her through the door.)* The Ashanti were performing surgical operations when the English—*(Ruth pulls the door to, with Beneatha on the other side, and smiles graciously at George. Beneatha opens the door and shouts the end of the sentence defiantly at George.)*—were still tattooing themselves with blue dragons! *(She goes back inside.)*

Ruth. Have a seat, George. *(They both sit. Ruth folds her hands rather primly on her lap, determined to demonstrate the civilization of the family.)* Warm, ain't it? I mean for September. *(Pause.)* Just like they always say about Chicago weather: if it's too hot or cold for you, just wait a minute and it'll change. *(She smiles happily at this cliché of clichés.)* Everybody say it's got to do with them bombs and things they keep setting off. *(Pause.)* Would you like a nice cold beer?

George. No, thank you. I don't care for beer. *(He looks at his watch.)* I hope she hurries up.

Ruth. What time is the show?

George. It's an eight-thirty curtain. That's just Chicago, though. In New York standard curtain time is eight forty.

He is rather proud of this knowledge.

Ruth *(properly appreciating it).* You get to New York a lot?
George *(offhand).* Few times a year.
Ruth. Oh—that's nice. I've never been to New York.

Walter enters. We feel he has relieved himself, but the edge of unreality is still with him.

Walter. New York ain't got nothing Chicago ain't. Just a bunch of hustling people all squeezed up together—being "Eastern."

He turns his face into a screw of displeasure.

George. Oh—you've been?
Walter. *Plenty* of times.
Ruth *(shocked at the lie).* Walter Lee Younger!
Walter *(staring her down).* Plenty! *(Pause.)* What we got to drink in this house? Why don't you offer this man some refreshment. *(To George.)* They don't know how to entertain people in this house, man.
George. Thank you—I don't really care for anything.
Walter *(feeling his head; sobriety coming).* Where's Mama?
Ruth. She ain't come back yet.
Walter *(looking Murchison over from head to toe, scrutinizing his carefully casual tweed sports jacket over cashmere V-neck sweater over soft eyelet shirt and tie, and soft slacks, finished off with white buckskin shoes).* Why all you college boys wear them faggoty-looking white shoes?
Ruth. Walter Lee!

George Murchison ignores the remark.

Walter *(to Ruth).* Well, they look crazy as hell—white shoes, cold as it is.
Ruth *(crushed).* You have to excuse him—
Walter. No he don't! Excuse me for what? What you always excusing me for! I'll excuse myself when I needs to be excused! *(A pause.)* They look as funny as them black knee socks Beneatha wears out of here all the time.
Ruth. It's the college *style*, Walter.
Walter. Style, hell. She looks like she got burnt legs or something!
Ruth. Oh, Walter—
Walter *(an irritable mimic).* Oh, Walter! Oh, Walter! *(To Murchison.)* How's your old man making out? I understand you all going to buy that big hotel on the Drive? *(He finds a beer in the refrigerator, wanders over to Murchison, sipping and wiping his lips with the back of his hand, and straddling a chair backwards to talk to the other man.)* Shrewd move. Your old man is all right, man. *(Tapping his head and half winking for emphasis.)* I mean he knows how

to operate. I mean he thinks *big*, you know what I mean, I mean for a *home*, you know? But I think he's kind of running out of ideas now. I'd like to talk to him. Listen, man, I got some plans that could turn this city upside down. I mean think like he does. *Big*. Invest big, gamble big, hell, lose *big* if you have to, you know what I mean. It's hard to find a man on this whole Southside who understands my kind of thinking—you dig? *(He scrutinizes Murchison again, drinks his beer, squints his eyes and leans in close, confidential, man to man.)* Me and you ought to sit down and talk sometimes, man. Man, I got me some ideas . . .

Murchison *(with boredom)*. Yeah—sometimes we'll have to do that, Walter.

Walter *(understanding the indifference, and offended)*. Yeah—well, when you get the time, man. I know you a busy little boy.

Ruth. Walter, please—

Walter *(bitterly, hurt)*. I know ain't nothing in this world as busy as you colored college boys with your fraternity pins and white shoes . . .

Ruth *(covering her face with humiliation)*. Oh, Walter Lee—

Walter. I see you all all the time—with the books tucked under your arms—going to your *(British A—a mimic.)* "clahsses." And for what! What the hell you learning over there? Filling up your heads—*(Counting off on his fingers.)*—with the sociology and the psychology—but they teaching you how to be a man? How to take over and run the world? They teaching you how to run a rubber plantation or a steel mill? Naw—just to talk proper and read books and wear them faggoty-looking white shoes . . .

George *(looking at him with distaste, a little above it all)*. You're all wacked up with bitterness, man.

Walter *(intently, almost quietly, between the teeth, glaring at the boy)*. And you— ain't you bitter, man? Ain't you just about had it yet? Don't you see no stars gleaming that you can't reach out and grab? You happy?—You contented son-of-a-bitch—you happy? You got it made? Bitter? Man, I'm a volcano. Bitter? Here I am a giant—surrounded by ants! Ants who can't even understand what it is the giant is talking about.

Ruth *(passionately and suddenly)*. Oh, Walter—ain't you with nobody!

Walter *(violently)*. No! 'Cause ain't nobody with me! Not even my own mother!

Ruth. Walter, that's a terrible thing to say!

Beneatha enters, dressed for the evening in a cocktail dress and earrings, hair natural.

George. Well—hey—*(Crosses to Beneatha; thoughtful, with emphasis, since this is a reversal.)* You look great!

Walter *(seeing his sister's hair for the first time)*. What's the matter with your head?

Beneatha *(tired of the jokes now)*. I cut it off, Brother.

Walter *(coming close to inspect it and walking around her)*. Well, I'll be damned. So that's what they mean by the African bush . . .

Beneatha. Ha ha. Let's go, George.

George *(looking at her).* You know something? I like it. It's sharp. I mean it really is. *(Helps her into her wrap.)*

Ruth. Yes—I think so, too. *(She goes to the mirror and starts to clutch at her hair.)*

Walter. Oh no! You leave yours alone, baby. You might turn out to have a pin-shaped head or something!

Beneatha. See you all later.

Ruth. Have a nice time.

George. Thanks. Good night. *(Half out the door, he reopens it. To Walter.)* Good night, Prometheus!

Beneatha and George exit.

Walter *(to Ruth).* Who is Prometheus?

Ruth. I don't know. Don't worry about it.

Walter *(in fury, pointing after George).* See there—they get to a point where they can't insult you man to man—they got to go talk about something ain't nobody never heard of!

Ruth. How do you know it was an insult? *(To humor him.)* Maybe Prometheus is a nice fellow.

Walter. Prometheus! I bet there ain't even no such thing! I bet that simpleminded clown—

Ruth. Walter—

She stops what she is doing and looks at him.

Walter *(yelling).* Don't start!

Ruth. Start what?

Walter. Your nagging! Where was I? Who was I with? How much money did I spend?

Ruth *(plaintively).* Walter Lee—why don't we just try to talk about it . . .

Walter *(not listening).* I been out talking with people who understand me. People who care about the things I got on my mind.

Ruth *(wearily).* I guess that means people like Willy Harris.

Walter. Yes, people like Willy Harris.

Ruth *(with a sudden flash of impatience).* Why don't you all just hurry up and go into the banking business and stop talking about it!

Walter. Why? You want to know why? 'Cause we all tied up in a race of people that don't know how to do nothing but moan, pray, and have babies!

The line is too bitter even for him and he looks at her and sits down.

Ruth. Oh, Walter . . . *(Softly.)* Honey, why can't you stop fighting me?

Walter *(without thinking).* Who's fighting you? Who even cares about you?

This line begins the retardation of his mood.

Ruth. Well—*(She waits a long time, and then with resignation starts to put away her things.)* I guess I might as well go on to bed . . . *(More or less to herself.)* I don't know where we lost it . . . but we have . . . *(Then, to him.)* I—I'm sorry about this new baby, Walter. I guess maybe I better go on and do what I started . . . I guess I just didn't realize how bad things was with us . . . I guess I just didn't really realize—*(She starts out to the bedroom and stops.)* You want some hot milk?

Walter. Hot milk?

Ruth. Yes—hot milk.

Walter. Why hot milk?

Ruth. 'Cause after all that liquor you come home with you ought to have something hot in your stomach.

Walter. I don't want no milk.

Ruth. You want some coffee then?

Walter. No, I don't want no coffee. I don't want nothing hot to drink. *(Almost plaintively.)* Why you always trying to give me something to eat?

Ruth *(standing and looking at him helplessly).* What *else* can I give you, Walter Lee Younger?

She stands and looks at him and presently turns to go out again. He lifts his head and watches her going away from him in a new mood which began to emerge when he asked her "Who cares about you?"

Walter. It's been rough, ain't it, baby? *(She hears and stops but does not turn around and he continues to her back.)* I guess between two people there ain't never as much understood as folks generally thinks there is. I mean like between me and you —*(She turns to face him.)* How we gets to the place where we scared to talk softness to each other. *(He waits, thinking hard himself.)* Why you think it got to be like that? *(He is thoughtful, almost as a child would be.)* Ruth, what is it gets into people ought to be close?

Ruth. I don't know, honey. I think about it a lot.

Walter. On account of you and me, you mean? The way things are with us. The way something done come down between us.

Ruth. There ain't so much between us, Walter . . . Not when you come to me and try to talk to me. Try to be with me . . . a little even.

Walter *(total honesty).* Sometimes . . . sometimes . . . I don't even know how to try.

Ruth. Walter—

Walter. Yes?

Ruth *(coming to him, gently and with misgiving, but coming to him).* Honey . . . life don't have to be like this. I mean sometimes people can do things so that things are better . . . You remember how we used to talk when Travis was born . . .

about the way we were going to live . . . the kind of house . . . *(She is stroking his head.)* Well, it's all starting to slip away from us . . .

He turns her to him and they look at each other and kiss, tenderly and hungrily. The door opens and Mama enters—Walter breaks away and jumps up. A beat.

Walter. Mama, where have you been?

Mama. My—them steps is longer than they used to be. Whew! *(She sits down and ignores him.)* How you feeling this evening, Ruth?

Ruth shrugs, disturbed at having been interrupted and watching her husband knowingly.

Walter. Mama, where have you been all day?

Mama *(still ignoring him and leaning on the table and changing to more comfortable shoes).* Where's Travis?

Ruth. I let him go out earlier and he ain't come back yet. Boy, is he going to get it!

Walter. Mama!

Mama *(as if she has heard him for the first time).* Yes, son?

Walter. Where did you go this afternoon?

Mama. I went downtown to tend to some business that I had to tend to.

Walter. What kind of business?

Mama. You know better than to question me like a child, Brother.

Walter *(rising and bending over the table).* Where were you, Mama? *(Bringing his fists down and shouting.)* Mama, you didn't go do something with that insurance money, something crazy?

The front door opens slowly, interrupting him, and Travis peeks his head in, less than hopefully.

Travis *(to his mother).* Mama, I—

Ruth. "Mama I" nothing! You're going to get it, boy! Get on in that bedroom and get yourself ready!

Travis. But I—

Mama. Why don't you all never let the child explain hisself.

Ruth. Keep out of it now, Lena.

Mama clamps her lips together, and Ruth advances toward her son menacingly.

Ruth. A thousand times I have told you not to go off like that—

Mama *(holding out her arms to her grandson).* Well—at least let me tell him something. I want him to be the first one to hear . . . Come here, Travis. *(The boy obeys, gladly.)* Travis—*(She takes him by the shoulder and looks into his face.)*— you know that money we got in the mail this morning?

Travis. Yes'm—

Mama. Well—what you think your grandmama gone and done with that money?

Travis. I don't know, Grandmama.

Mama (*putting her finger on his nose for emphasis*). She went out and she bought you a house! (*The explosion comes from Walter at the end of the revelation and he jumps up and turns away from all of them in a fury. Mama continues, to Travis.*) You glad about the house? It's going to be yours when you get to be a man.

Travis. Yeah—I always wanted to live in a house.

Mama. All right, gimme some sugar then—(*Travis puts his arms around her neck as she watches her son over the boy's shoulder. Then, to Travis, after the embrace.*) Now when you say your prayers tonight, you thank God and your grandfather—'cause it was him who give you the house—in his way.

Ruth (*taking the boy from Mama and pushing him toward the bedroom*). Now you get out of here and get ready for your beating.

Travis. Aw, Mama—

Ruth. Get on in there—(*Closing the door behind him and turning radiantly to her mother-in-law.*) So you went and did it!

Mama (*quietly, looking at her son with pain*). Yes, I did.

Ruth (*raising both arms classically*). PRAISE GOD! (*Looks at Walter a moment, who says nothing. She crosses rapidly to her husband.*) Please, honey—let me be glad . . . you be glad too. (*She has laid her hands on his shoulders, but he shakes himself free of her roughly, without turning to face her.*) Oh, Walter . . . a home . . . a home. (*She comes back to Mama.*) Well—where is it? How big is it? How much it going to cost?

Mama. Well—

Ruth. When we moving?

Mama (*smiling at her*). First of the month.

Ruth (*throwing back her head with jubilance*). *Praise God!*

Mama (*tentatively, still looking at her son's back turned against her and Ruth*). It's—it's a nice house too . . . (*She cannot help speaking directly to him. An imploring quality in her voice, her manner, makes her almost like a girl now.*) Three bedrooms—nice big one for you and Ruth . . . Me and Beneatha still have to share our room, but Travis have one of his own—and (*With difficulty.*) I figure if the—new baby—is a boy, we could get one of them double-decker outfits . . . And there's a yard with a little patch of dirt where I could maybe get to grow me a few flowers . . . And a nice big basement . . .

Ruth. Walter honey, be glad —

Mama (*still to his back, fingering things on the table*). 'Course I don't want to make it sound fancier than it is . . . It's just a plain little old house—but it's made good and solid—and it will be *ours*. Walter Lee—it makes a difference in a man when he can walk on floors that belong to *him* . . .

Ruth. Where is it?

Mama (*frightened at this telling*). Well—well—it's out there in Clybourne Park—

Ruth's radiance fades abruptly, and Walter finally turns slowly to face his mother with incredulity and hostility.

Ruth. Where?

Mama *(matter-of-factly).* Four o six Clybourne Street, Clybourne Park.

Ruth. Clybourne Park? Mama, there ain't no colored people living in Clybourne Park.

Mama *(almost idiotically).* Well, I guess there's going to be some now.

Walter *(bitterly).* So that's the peace and comfort you went out and bought for us today!

Mama *(raising her eyes to meet his finally).* Son—I just tried to find the nicest place for the least amount of money for my family.

Ruth *(trying to recover from the shock).* Well—well—'course I ain't one never been 'fraid of no crackers, mind you—but—well, wasn't there no other houses nowhere?

Mama. Them houses they put up for colored in them areas way out all seem to cost twice as much as other houses. I did the best I could.

Ruth *(struck senseless with the news, in its various degrees of goodness and trouble, she sits a moment, her fists propping her chin in thought, and then she starts to rise, bringing her fists down with vigor, the radiance spreading from cheek to cheek again).* Well—well—All I can say is—if this is my time in life—MY TIME—to say good-bye—*(And she builds with momentum as she starts to circle the room with an exuberant, almost tearfully happy release.)*—to these Goddamned cracking walls!—*(She pounds the walls.)*—and these marching roaches!—*(She wipes at an imaginary army of marching roaches.)*—and this cramped little closet which ain't now or never was no kitchen! . . . then I say it loud and good, HAL-LELUJAH! AND GOOD-BYE MISERY . . . I DON'T NEVER WANT TO SEE YOUR UGLY FACE AGAIN! *(She laughs joyously, having practically destroyed the apartment, and flings her arms up and lets them come down happily, slowly, reflectively, over her abdomen, aware for the first time perhaps that the life therein pulses with happiness and not despair.)* Lena?

Mama *(moved, watching her happiness).* Yes, honey?

Ruth *(looking off).* Is there—is there a whole lot of sunlight?

Mama *(understanding).* Yes, child, there's a whole lot of sunlight.

Long pause.

Ruth *(collecting herself and going to the door of the room Travis is in).* Well—I guess I better see 'bout Travis. *(To Mama.)* Lord, I sure don't feel like whipping nobody today!

She exits.

Mama *(the mother and son are left alone now and the mother waits a long time, considering deeply, before she speaks).* Son—you—you understand what I done, don't you? (*Walter is silent and sullen.*) I—I just seen my family falling apart today . . . just falling to pieces in front of my eyes . . . We couldn't of gone on like we was today. We was going backwards 'stead of forwards—talking 'bout killing babies and wishing each other was dead . . . When it gets like that in life—you just got to do something different, push on out and do something bigger . . . (*She waits.*) I wish you say something, son . . . I wish you'd say how deep inside you you think I done the right thing—

Walter (*crossing slowly to his bedroom door and finally turning there and speaking measuredly*). What you need me to say you done right for? *You* the head of this family. You run our lives like you want to. It was your money and you did what you wanted with it. So what you need for me to say it was all right for? (*Bitterly, to hurt her as deeply as he knows is possible.*) So you butchered up a dream of mine—you—who always talking 'bout your children's dreams . . .

Mama. Walter Lee—

He just closes the door behind him. Mama sits alone, thinking heavily.

Curtain.

Scene 2.

Time: Friday night, a few weeks later.
   At rise: Packing crates mark the intention of the family to move. Beneatha and George come in, presumably from an evening out again.

George. O.K. . . . O.K., whatever you say . . . (*They both sit on the couch. He tries to kiss her. She moves away.*) Look, we've had a nice evening; let's not spoil it, huh? . . .

He again turns her head and tries to nuzzle in and she turns away from him, not with distaste but with momentary lack of interest; in a mood to pursue what they were talking about.

Beneatha. I'm *trying* to talk to you.
George. We always talk.
Beneatha. Yes—and I love to talk.
George (*exasperated; rising*). I know it and I don't mind it sometimes . . . I want you to cut it out, see—The moody stuff, I mean. I don't like it. You're a nice-looking girl . . . all over. That's all you need, honey, forget the atmosphere. Guys aren't going to go for the atmosphere—they're going to go for what they see. Be glad for that. Drop the Garbo routine. It doesn't go with you. As for myself, I want a nice— (*Groping.*)—simple (*Thoughtfully.*)—sophisticated girl . . . not a poet—O.K.?

He starts to kiss her, she rebuffs him again and he jumps up.

Beneatha. Why are you angry, George?

George. Because this is stupid! I don't go out with you to discuss the nature of "quiet desperation" or to hear all about your thoughts—because the world will go on thinking what it thinks regardless—

Beneatha. Then why read books? Why go to school?

George *(with artificial patience, counting on his fingers).* It's simple. You read books—to learn facts—to get grades—to pass the course—to get a degree. That's all—it has nothing to do with thoughts.

A long pause.

Beneatha. I see. *(He starts to sit.)* Good night, George.

George looks at her a little oddly, and starts to exit. He meets Mama coming in.

George. Oh—hello, Mrs. Younger.

Mama. Hello, George, how you feeling?

George. Fine—fine, how are you?

Mama. Oh, a little tired. You know them steps can get you after a day's work. You all have a nice time tonight?

George. Yes—a fine time. A fine time.

Mama. Well, good night.

George. Good night. *(He exits. Mama closes the door behind her.)*

Mama. Hello, honey. What you sitting like that for?

Beneatha. I'm just sitting.

Mama. Didn't you have a nice time?

Beneatha. No.

Mama. No? What's the matter?

Beneatha. Mama, George is a fool—honest. *(She rises.)*

Mama *(hustling around unloading the packages she has entered with. She stops).* Is he, baby?

Beneatha. Yes.

Beneatha makes up Travis's bed as she talks.

Mama. You sure?

Beneatha. Yes.

Mama. Well—I guess you better not waste your time with no fools.

Beneatha looks up at her mother, watching her put groceries in the refrigerator. Finally she gathers up her things and starts into the bedroom. At the door she stops and looks back at her mother.

Beneatha. Mama—

Mama. Yes, baby—

Beneatha. Thank you.

Mama. For what?

Beneatha. For understanding me this time.

She exits quickly and the mother stands, smiling a little, looking at the place where Beneatha just stood. Ruth enters.

Ruth. Now don't you fool with any of this stuff, Lena—

Mama. Oh, I just thought I'd sort a few things out. Is Brother here?

Ruth. Yes.

Mama *(with concern)*. Is he—

Ruth *(reading her eyes)*. Yes.

Mama is silent and someone knocks on the door. Mama and Ruth exchange weary and knowing glances and Ruth opens it to admit the neighbor, Mrs. Johnson,[1] who is a rather squeaky wide-eyed lady of no particular age, with a newspaper under her arm.

Mama *(changing her expression to acute delight and a ringing cheerful greeting)*. Oh—hello there, Johnson.

Johnson *(this is a woman who decided long ago to be enthusiastic about EVERYTHING in life and she is inclined to wave her wrist vigorously at the height of her exclamatory comments)*. Hello there, yourself! H'you this evening, Ruth?

Ruth *(not much of a deceptive type)*. Fine, Mis' Johnson, h'you?

Johnson. Fine. *(Reaching out quickly, playfully, and patting Ruth's stomach.)* Ain't you starting to poke out none yet! *(She mugs with delight at the over familiar remark and her eyes dart around looking at the crates and packing preparation; Mama's face is a cold sheet of endurance.)* Oh, ain't we getting ready round here, though! Yessir! Lookathere! I'm telling you the Youngers is really getting ready to "move on up a little higher!"—Bless God!

Mama *(a little drily, doubting the total sincerity of the Blesser)*. Bless God.

Johnson. He's good, ain't He?

Mama. Oh yes, He's good.

Johnson. I mean sometimes He works in mysterious ways . . . but He works, don't He!

Mama *(the same)*. Yes, He does.

Johnson. I'm just soooooo happy for y'all. And this here child—*(About Ruth.)* looks like she could just pop open with happiness, don't she. Where's all the rest of the family?

Mama. Bennie's gone to bed—

[1] This character and the scene of her visit were cut from the original production and early editions of the play.

Johnson. Ain't no . . . (*The implication is pregnancy.*) sickness done hit you—I hope . . . ?

Mama. No—she just tired. She was out this evening.

Johnson (*all is a coo, an emphatic coo*). Aw—ain't that lovely. She still going out with the little Murchison boy?

Mama (*drily*). Ummmm huh.

Johnson. That's lovely. You sure got lovely children, Younger. Me and Isaiah talks all the time 'bout what fine children you was blessed with. We sure do.

Mama. Ruth, give Mis' Johnson a piece of sweet potato pie and some milk.

Johnson. Oh honey, I can't stay hardly a minute—I just dropped in to see if there was anything I could do. (*Accepting the food easily.*) I guess y'all seen the news what's all over the colored paper this week . . .

Mama. No—didn't get mine yet this week.

Johnson (*lifting her head and blinking with the spirit of catastrophe*). You mean you ain't read 'bout them colored people that was bombed out their place out there?

Ruth straightens with concern and takes the paper and reads it. Johnson notices her and feeds commentary.

Johnson. Ain't it something how bad these here white folks is getting here in Chicago! Lord, getting so you think you right down in Mississippi! (*With a tremendous and rather insincere sense of melodrama.*) 'Course I thinks it's wonderful how our folk keeps on pushing out. You hear some of these Negroes round here talking 'bout how they don't go where they ain't wanted and all that—but not me, honey! (*This is a lie.*) Wilhemenia Othella Johnson goes anywhere, any time she feels like it! (*With head movement for emphasis.*) Yes I do! Why if we left it up to these here crackers, the poor niggers wouldn't have nothing—(*She clasps her hand over her mouth.*) Oh, I always forgets you don't 'low that word in your house.

Mama (*quietly, looking at her*). No—I don't 'low it.

Johnson (*vigorously again*). Me neither! I was just telling Isaiah yesterday when he come using it in front of me—I said, "Isaiah, it's just like Mis' Younger says all the time—"

Mama. Don't you want some more pie?

Johnson. No—no thank you; this was lovely. I got to get on over home and have my midnight coffee. I hear some people say it don't let them sleep but I finds I can't close my eyes right lessen I done had that laaaast cup of coffee . . . (*She waits. A beat. Undaunted.*) My Goodnight coffee, I calls it!

Mama (*with much eye-rolling and communication between herself and Ruth*). Ruth, why don't you give Mis' Johnson some coffee.

Ruth gives Mama an unpleasant look for her kindness.

Johnson (*accepting the coffee*). Where's Brother tonight?

Mama. He's lying down.

Johnson. Mmmmmmm, he sure gets his beauty rest, don't he? Good-looking man. Sure is a good-looking man! *(Reaching out to pat Ruth's stomach again.)* I guess that's how come we keep on having babies around here. *(She winks at Mama.)* One thing 'bout Brother, he always know how to have a *good* time. And soooooo ambitious! I bet it was his idea y'all moving out to Clybourne Park. Lord—I bet this time next month y'all's names will have been in the papers plenty—*(Holding up her hands to mark off each word of the headline she can see in front of her.)* "NEGROES INVADE CLYBOURNE PARK—BOMBED!"

Mama *(she and Ruth look at the woman in amazement).* We ain't exactly moving out there to get bombed.

Johnson. Oh honey—you know I'm praying to God every day that don't nothing like that happen! But you have to think of life like it is—and these here Chicago peckerwoods is some baaaad peckerwoods.

Mama *(wearily).* We done thought about all that Mis' Johnson.

Beneatha comes out of the bedroom in her robe and passes through to the bathroom. Mrs. Johnson turns.

Johnson. Hello there, Bennie!

Beneatha *(crisply).* Hello, Mrs. Johnson.

Johnson. How is school?

Beneatha *(crisply).* Fine, thank you. *(She goes out.)*

Johnson *(insulted).* Getting so she don't have much to say to nobody.

Mama. The child was on her way to the bathroom.

Johnson. I know—but sometimes she act like ain't got time to pass the time of day with nobody ain't been to college. Oh—I ain't criticizing her none. It's just—you know how some of our young people gets when they get a little education *(Mama and Ruth say nothing, just look at her.)* Yes—well. Well, I guess I better get on home. *(Unmoving.)* 'Course I can understand how she must be proud and everything—being the only one in the family to make something of herself. I know just being a chauffeur ain't never satisfied Brother none. He shouldn't feel like that, though. Ain't nothing wrong with being a chauffeur.

Mama. There's plenty wrong with it.

Johnson. What?

Mama. Plenty. My husband always said being any kind of a servant wasn't a fit thing for a man to have to be. He always said a man's hands was made to make things, or to turn the earth with—not to drive nobody's car for 'em—or—*(She looks at her own hands.)* carry they slop jars. And my boy is just like him—he wasn't meant to wait on nobody.

Johnson *(rising, somewhat offended).* Mmmmmmmmmm. The Youngers is too much for me! *(She looks around.)* You sure one proud-acting bunch of colored folks. Well—I always thinks like Booker T. Washington said that time—"Education has spoiled many a good plow hand"—

Mama. Is that what old Booker T. said?

Johnson. He sure did.

Mama. Well, it sounds just like him. The fool.

Johnson (*indignantly*). Well—he was one of our great men.

Mama. Who said so?

Johnson (*nonplussed*). You know, me and you ain't never agreed about some things, Lena Younger. I guess I better be going—

Ruth (*quickly*). Good night.

Johnson. Good night. Oh—(*Thrusting it at her.*) You can keep the paper! (*With a trill.*) 'Night.

Mama. Good night, Mis' Johnson.

Mrs. Johnson exits.

Ruth. If ignorance was gold . . .

Mama. Shush. Don't talk about folks behind their backs.

Ruth. You do.

Mama. I'm old and corrupted. (*Beneatha enters.*) You was rude to Mis' Johnson, Beneatha, and I don't like it at all.

Beneatha (*at her door*). Mama, if there are two things we, as a people, have got to overcome, one is the Ku Klux Klan—and the other is Mrs. Johnson. (*She exits.*)

Mama. Smart aleck.

The phone rings.

Ruth. I'll get it.

Mama. Lord, ain't this a popular place tonight.

Ruth (*at the phone*). Hello—Just a minute. (*Goes to door.*) Walter, it's Mrs. Arnold. (*Waits. Goes back to the phone. Tense.*) Hello. Yes, this is his wife speaking . . . He's lying down now. Yes . . . well, he'll be in tomorrow. He's been very sick. Yes—I know we should have called, but we were so sure he'd be able to come in today. Yes—yes, I'm very sorry. Yes . . . Thank you very much. (*She hangs up. Walter is standing in the doorway of the bedroom behind her.*) That was Mrs. Arnold.

Walter (*indifferently*). Was it?

Ruth. She said if you don't come in tomorrow that they are getting a new man . . .

Walter. Ain't that sad—ain't that crying sad.

Ruth. She said Mr. Arnold has had to take a cab for three days . . . Walter, you ain't been to work for three days! (*This is a revelation to her.*) Where you been, Walter Lee Younger? (*Walter looks at her and starts to laugh.*) You're going to lose your job.

Walter. That's right . . . (*He turns on the radio.*)

Ruth. Oh, Walter, and with your mother working like a dog every day—

A steamy, deep blues pours into the room.

Walter. That's sad too—Everything is sad.

Mama. What you been doing for these three days, son?

Walter. Mama—you don't know all the things a man what got leisure can find to do in this city . . . What's this—Friday night? Well—Wednesday I borrowed Willy Harris's car and I went for a drive . . . just me and myself and I drove and drove . . . Way out . . . way past South Chicago, and I parked the car and I sat and looked at the steel mills all day long. I just sat in the car and looked at them big black chimneys for hours. Then I drove back and I went to the Green Hat. *(Pause.)* And Thursday—Thursday I borrowed the car again and I got in it and I pointed it the other way and I drove the other way—for hours—way, way up to Wisconsin, and I looked at the farms. I just drove and looked at the farms. Then I drove back and I went to the Green Hat. *(Pause.)* And today—today I didn't get the car. Today I just walked. All over the Southside. And I looked at the Negroes and they looked at me and finally I just sat down on the curb at Thirty-ninth and South Parkway and I just sat there and watched the Negroes go by. And then I went to the Green Hat. You all sad? You all depressed? And you know where I am going right now—

Ruth goes out quietly.

Mama. Oh, Big Walter, is this the harvest of our days?

Walter. You know what I like about the Green Hat? I like this little cat they got there who blows a sax . . . He blows. He talks to me. He ain't but 'bout five feet tall and he's got a conked head and his eyes is always closed and he's all music—

Mama *(rising and getting some papers out of her handbag).* Walter—

Walter. And there's this other guy who plays the piano . . . and they got a sound. I mean they can work on some music . . . They got the best little combo in the world in the Green Hat . . . You can just sit there and drink and listen to them three men play and you realize that don't nothing matter worth a damn, but just being there—

Mama. I've helped do it to you, haven't I, son? Walter I been wrong.

Walter. Naw—you ain't never been wrong about nothing, Mama.

Mama. Listen to me, now. I say I been wrong, son. That I been doing to you what the rest of the world been doing to you. *(She turns off the radio.)* Walter—*(She stops and he looks up slowly at her and she meets his eyes pleadingly.)* What you ain't never understood is that I ain't got nothing, don't own nothing, ain't never really wanted nothing that wasn't for you. There ain't nothing as precious to me . . . There ain't nothing worth holding on to, money, dreams, nothing else— if it means—if it means it's going to destroy my boy. *(She takes an envelope out of her handbag and puts it in front of him and he watches her without speaking or moving.)* I paid the man thirty-five hundred dollars down on the house. That leaves sixty-five hundred dollars. Monday morning I want you to take this money and take three thousand dollars and put it in a savings account for Beneatha's medical schooling. The rest you put in a checking account—with your name on it. And from now on any penny that come out of it or that go in it is for you to look after. For you to decide. *(She drops her hands a little help-lessly.)* It ain't much, but it's all I got in the world and I'm putting it in your hands. I'm telling you to be the head of this family from now on like you sup-posed to be.

Walter *(stares at the money).* You trust me like that, Mama?

Mama. I ain't never stop trusting you. Like I ain't never stop loving you.

She goes out, and Walter sits looking at the money on the table. Finally, in a decisive gesture, he gets up, and, in mingled joy and desperation, picks up the money. At the same moment, Travis enters for bed.

Travis. What's the matter, Daddy? You drunk?

Walter *(sweetly, more sweetly than we have ever known him).* No, Daddy ain't drunk. Daddy ain't going to never be drunk again . . .

Travis. Well, good night, Daddy.

The father has come from behind the couch and leans over, embracing his son.

Walter. Son, I feel like talking to you tonight.

Travis. About what?

Walter. Oh, about a lot of things. About you and what kind of man you going to be when you grow up . . . Son—son, what do you want to be when you grow up?

Travis. A bus driver.

Walter *(laughing a little).* A what? Man, that ain't nothing to want to be!

Travis. Why not?

Walter. 'Cause, man—it ain't big enough—you know what I mean.

Travis. I don't know then. I can't make up my mind. Sometimes Mama asks me that too. And sometimes when I tell her I just want to be like you—she says she don't want me to be like that and sometimes she says she does. . . .

Walter *(gathering him up in his arms).* You know what, Travis? In seven years you going to be seventeen years old. And things is going to be very different with us in seven years, Travis. . . . One day when you are seventeen I'll come home—home from my office downtown somewhere—

Travis. You don't work in no office, Daddy.

Walter. No—but after tonight. After what your daddy gonna do tonight, there's going to be offices—a whole lot of offices. . . .

Travis. What you gonna do tonight, Daddy?

Walter. You wouldn't understand yet, son, but your daddy's gonna make a trans-action . . . a business transaction that's going to change our lives. . . . That's how come one day when you 'bout seventeen years old I'll come home and I'll be pretty tired, you know what I mean, after a day of conferences and secretaries getting things wrong the way they do . . . 'cause an executive's life is hell, man— *(The more he talks the farther away he gets.)* And I'll pull the car up on the drive-way . . . just a plain black Chrysler, I think, with white walls—no—black tires.

More elegant. Rich people don't have to be flashy . . . though I'll have to get something a little sportier for Ruth—maybe a Cadillac convertible to do her shopping in. . . . And I'll come up the steps to the house and the gardener will be clipping away at the hedges and he'll say, "Good evening, Mr. Younger." And I'll say, "Hello, Jefferson, how are you this evening?" And I'll go inside and Ruth will come downstairs and meet me at the door and we'll kiss each other and she'll take my arm and we'll go up to your room to see you sitting on the floor with the catalogues of all the great schools in America around you. . . . All the great schools in the world! And—and I'll say, all right son—it's your seventeenth birthday, what is it you've decided? . . . Just tell me where you want to go to school and you'll go. Just tell me, what it is you want to be—and you'll *be* it. . . . Whatever you want to be—Yessir! (*He holds his arms open for Travis.*) You just name it, son . . . (*Travis leaps into them.*) and I hand you the world!

Walter's voice has risen in pitch and hysterical promise and on the last line he lifts Travis high.

    Blackout.

Scene 3.

Time. Saturday, moving day, one week later.
    Before the curtain rises, Ruth's voice, a strident, dramatic church alto, cuts through the silence.
    It is, in the darkness, a triumphant surge, a penetrating statement of expectation: "Oh, Lord, I don't feel no ways tired! Children, oh, glory hallelujah!"
    As the curtain rises we see that Ruth is alone in the living room, finishing up the family's packing. It is moving day. She is nailing crates and tying cartons. Beneatha enters, carrying a guitar case, and watches her exuberant sister-in-law.

Ruth. Hey!
Beneatha (*putting away the case*). Hi.
Ruth (*pointing at a package*). Honey— look in that package there and see what I found on sale this morning at the South Center. (*Ruth gets up and moves to the package and draws out some curtains.*) Lookahere—hand-turned hems!
Beneatha. How do you know the window size out there?
Ruth (*who hadn't thought of that*). Oh—Well, they bound to fit something in the whole house. Anyhow, they was too good a bargain to pass up. (*Ruth slaps her head, suddenly remembering something.*) Oh, Bennie—I meant to put a special note on that carton over there. That's your mama's good china and she wants 'em to be very careful with it.
Beneatha. I'll do it.

Beneatha finds a piece of paper and starts to draw large letters on it.

Ruth. You know what I'm going to do soon as I get in that new house?

Beneatha. What?

Ruth. Honey—I'm going to run me a tub of water up to here . . . *(With her fingers practically up to her nostrils.)* And I'm going to get in it—and I am going to sit . . . and sit . . . and sit in that hot water and the first person who knocks to tell *me* to hurry up and come out—

Beneatha. Gets shot at sunrise.

Ruth *(laughing happily).* You said it, sister! *(Noticing how large Beneatha is absent-mindedly making the note)*: Honey, they ain't going to read that from no airplane.

Beneatha *(laughing herself).* I guess I always think things have more emphasis if they are big, somehow.

Ruth *(looking up at her and smiling).* You and your brother seem to have that as a philosophy of life. Lord, that man—done changed so 'round here. You know— you know what we did last night? Me and Walter Lee?

Beneatha. What?

Ruth *(smiling to herself).* We went to the movies. *(Looking at Beneatha to see if she understands.)* We went to the movies. You know the last time me and Walter went to the movies together?

Beneatha. No.

Ruth. Me neither. That's how long it been. *(Smiling again.)* But we went last night. The picture wasn't much good, but that didn't seem to matter. We went—and we held hands.

Beneatha. Oh, Lord!

Ruth. We held hands—and you know what?

Beneatha. What?

Ruth. When we come out of the show it was late and dark and all the stores and things was closed up . . . and it was kind of chilly and there wasn't many people on the streets . . . and we was still holding hands, me and Walter.

Beneatha. You're killing me.

Walter enters with a large package. His happiness is deep in him; he cannot keep still with his newfound exuberance. He is singing and wiggling and snapping his fingers. He puts his package in a corner and puts a phonograph record, which he has brought in with him, on the record player. As the music, soulful and sensuous, comes up he dances over to Ruth and tries to get her to dance with him. She gives in at last to his raunchiness and in a fit of giggling allows herself to be drawn into his mood. They dip and she melts into his arms in a classic, body-melting "slow drag."

Beneatha *(regarding them a long time as they dance, then drawing in her breath for a deeply exaggerated comment which she does not particularly mean).* Talk about— olddddddddddd-fashionedddddddd—Negroes!

Walter *(stopping momentarily).* What kind of Negroes?

He says this in fun. He is not angry with her today, nor with anyone. He starts to dance with his wife again.

Beneatha. Old-fashioned.

Walter (*as he dances with Ruth*). You know, when these *New Negroes* have their convention—(*Pointing at his sister.*)—that is going to be the chairman of the Committee on Unending Agitation. (*He goes on dancing, then stops.*) Race, race, race! . . . Girl, I do believe you are the first person in the history of the entire human race to successfully brainwash yourself. (*Beneatha breaks up and he goes on dancing. He stops again, enjoying his tease.*) Damn, even the N double A C P takes a holiday sometimes! (*Beneatha and Ruth laugh. He dances with Ruth some more and starts to laugh and stops and pantomimes someone over an operating table.*) I can just see that chick someday looking down at some poor cat on an operating table and before she starts to slice him, she says . . . (*Pulling his sleeves back maliciously.*) "By the way, what are your views on civil rights down there? . . ."

He laughs at her again and starts to dance happily. The bell sounds.

Beneatha. Sticks and stones may break my bones but . . . words will never hurt me!

Beneatha goes to the door and opens it as Walter and Ruth go on with the clowning. Beneatha is somewhat surprised to see a quiet-looking middle-aged white man in a business suit holding his hat and a briefcase in his hand and consulting a small piece of paper.

Man. Uh—how do you do, miss. I am looking for a Mrs.—(*He looks at the slip of paper.*) Mrs. Lena Younger? (*He stops short, struck dumb at the sight of the oblivious Walter and Ruth.*)

Beneatha (*smoothing her hair with slight embarrassment*). Oh—yes, that's my mother. Excuse me. (*She closes the door and turns to quiet the other two.*) Ruth! Brother! (*Enunciating precisely but soundlessly: "There's a white man at the door!" They stop dancing, Ruth cuts off the phonograph, Beneatha opens the door. The man casts a curious quick glance at all of them.*) Uh—come in please.

Man (*coming in*). Thank you.

Beneatha. My mother isn't here just now. Is it business?

Man. Yes . . . well, of a sort.

Walter (*freely, the Man of the House*). Have a seat. I'm Mrs. Younger's son. I look after most of her business matters.

Ruth and Beneatha exchange amused glances.

Man (*regarding Walter, and sitting*). Well—My name is Karl Lindner . . .

Walter (*stretching out his hand*). Walter Younger. This is my wife—(*Ruth nods politely.*)—and my sister.

Lindner. How do you do.

Walter (*amiably, as he sits himself easily on a chair, leaning forward on his knees with interest and looking expectantly into the newcomer's face*). What can we do for you, Mr. Lindner!

Lindner (*some minor shuffling of the hat and briefcase on his knees*). Well—I am a representative of the Clybourne Park Improvement Association—

Walter (*pointing*). Why don't you sit your things on the floor?

Lindner. Oh—yes. Thank you. (*He slides the briefcase and hat under the chair.*) And as I was saying—I am from the Clybourne Park Improvement Association and we have had it brought to our attention at the last meeting that you people—or at least your mother—has bought a piece of residential property at—(*He digs for the slip of paper again.*)—four o six Clybourne Street . . .

Walter. That's right. Care for something to drink? Ruth, get Mr. Lindner a beer.

Lindner (*upset for some reason*). Oh—no, really. I mean thank you very much, but no thank you.

Ruth (*innocently*). Some coffee?

Lindner. Thank you, nothing at all.

Beneatha is watching the man carefully.

Lindner. Well, I don't know how much you folks know about our organization. (*He is a gentle man; thoughtful and somewhat labored in his manner.*) It is one of these community organizations set up to look after—oh, you know, things like block upkeep and special projects and we also have what we call our New Neighbors Orientation Committee . . .

Beneatha (*drily*). Yes—and what do they do?

Lindner (*turning a little to her and then returning the main force to Walter*). Well— it's what you might call a sort of welcoming committee, I guess. I mean they, we—I'm the chairman of the committee—go around and see the new people who move into the neighborhood and sort of give them the lowdown on the way we do things out in Clybourne Park.

Beneatha (*with appreciation of the two meanings, which escape Ruth and Walter*). Un-huh.

Lindner. And we also have the category of what the association calls—(*He looks elsewhere.*)—uh—special community problems . . .

Beneatha. Yes—and what are some of those?

Walter. Girl, let the man talk.

Lindner (*with understated relief*). Thank you. I would sort of like to explain this thing in my own way. I mean I want to explain to you in a certain way.

Walter. Go ahead.

Lindner. Yes. Well. I'm going to try to get right to the point. I'm sure we'll all appreciate that in the long run.

Beneatha. Yes.

Walter. Be still now!

Lindner. Well—

Ruth (*still innocently*). Would you like another chair—you don't look comfortable.

Lindner (*more frustrated than annoyed*). No, thank you very much. Please. Well— to get right to the point, I—(*A great breath, and he is off at last.*) I am sure you people must be aware of some of the incidents which have happened in various parts of the city when colored people have moved into certain areas—*(Beneatha exhales heavily and starts tossing a piece of fruit up and down in the air.)* Well—because we have what I think is going to be a unique type of organization in American community life—not only do we deplore that kind of thing—but we are trying to do something about it. *(Beneatha stops tossing and turns with a new and quizzical interest to the man.)* We feel—*(gaining confidence in his mission because of the interest in the faces of the people he is talking to.)*—we feel that most of the trouble in this world, when you come right down to it—*(He hits his knee for emphasis.)*—most of the trouble exists because people just don't sit down and talk to each other.

Ruth *(nodding as she might in church, pleased with the remark).* You can say that again, mister.

Lindner *(more encouraged by such affirmation).* That we don't try hard enough in this world to understand the other fellow's problem. The other guy's point of view.

Ruth. Now that's right.

Beneatha and Walter merely watch and listen with genuine interest.

Lindner. Yes—that's the way we feel out in Clybourne Park. And that's why I was elected to come here this afternoon and talk to you people. Friendly like, you know, the way people should talk to each other and see if we couldn't find some way to work this thing out. As I say, the whole business is a matter of *caring* about the other fellow. Anybody can see that you are a nice family of folks, hard working and honest I'm sure. *(Beneatha frowns slightly, quizzically, her head tilted regarding him.)* Today everybody knows what it means to be on the outside of *something*. And of course, there is always somebody who is out to take advantage of people who don't always understand.

Walter. What do you mean?

Lindner. Well—you see our community is made up of people who've worked hard as the dickens for years to build up that little community. They're not rich and fancy people; just hard-working, honest people who don't really have much but those little homes and a dream of the kind of community they want to raise their children in. Now, I don't say we are perfect and there is a lot wrong in some of the things they want. But you've got to admit that a man, right or wrong, has the right to want to have the neighborhood he lives in a certain kind of way. And at the moment the overwhelming majority of our people out there feel that people get along better, take more of a common interest in the life of the community, when they share a common background. I want you to believe me when I tell you that race prejudice simply doesn't enter into it. It is a matter of the people of Clybourne Park believing, rightly or wrongly, as I say, that for the happiness of all concerned that our Negro families are happier when they live in their *own* communities.

Beneatha *(with a grand and bitter gesture).* This, friends, is the Welcoming Committee!

Walter *(dumfounded, looking at Lindner)*. Is this what you came marching all the way over here to tell us?

Lindner. Well, now we've been having a fine conversation. I hope you'll hear me all the way through.

Walter *(tightly)*. Go ahead, man.

Lindner. You see—in the face of all the things I have said, we are prepared to make your family a very generous offer . . .

Beneatha. Thirty pieces and not a coin less!

Walter. Yeah?

Lindner *(putting on his glasses drawing a form out of the briefcase)*. Our association is prepared, through the collective effort of our people, to buy the house from you at a financial gain to your family.

Ruth. Lord have mercy, ain't this the living gall!

Walter. All right, you through?

Lindner. Well, I want to give you the exact terms of the financial arrangement—

Walter. We don't want to hear no exact terms of no arrangements. I want to know if you got any more to tell us 'bout getting together?

Lindner *(taking off his glasses)*. Well—I don't suppose that you feel . . .

Walter. Never mind how I feel—you got any more to say 'bout how people ought to sit down and talk to each other? . . . Get out of my house, man.

He turns his back and walks to the door.

Lindner *(looking around at the hostile faces and reaching and assembling his hat and briefcase)*. Well—I don't understand why you people are reacting this way. What do you think you are going to gain by moving into a neighborhood where you just aren't wanted and where some elements—well—people can get awful worked up when they feel that their whole way of life and everything they've ever worked for is threatened.

Walter. Get out.

Lindner *(at the door, holding a small card)*. Well—I'm sorry it went like this.

Walter. Get out.

Lindner *(almost sadly regarding Walter)*. You just can't force people to change their hearts, son.

He turns and puts his card on a table and exits. Walter pushes the door to with stinging hatred, and stands looking at it. Ruth just sits and Beneatha just stands. They say nothing. Mama and Travis enter.

Mama. Well—this all the packing got done since I left out of here this morning. I testify before God that my children got all the energy of the *dead!* What time the moving men due?

Beneatha. Four o'clock. You had a caller, Mama.

She is smiling, teasingly.

Mama. Sure enough—who?

Beneatha *(her arms folded saucily).* The Welcoming Committee.

Walter and Ruth giggle.

Mama *(innocently).* Who?

Beneatha. The Welcoming Committee. They said they're sure going to be glad to see you when you get there.

Walter *(devilishly).* Yeah, they said they can't hardly wait to see your face.

Laughter.

Mama *(sensing their facetiousness).* What's the matter with you all?

Walter. Ain't nothing the matter with us. We just telling you 'bout the gentleman who came to see you this afternoon. From the Clybourne Park Improvement Association.

Mama. What he want?

Ruth *(in the same mood as Beneatha and Walter).* To welcome you, honey.

Walter. He said they can't hardly wait. He said the one thing they don't have, that they just *dying* to have out there is a fine family of fine colored people! *(To Ruth and Beneatha.)* Ain't that right!

Ruth *(mockingly).* Yeah! He left his card—

Beneatha *(handing card to Mama).* In case.

Mama reads and throws it on the floor—understanding and looking off as she draws her chair up to the table on which she has put her plant and some sticks and some cord.

Mama. Father, give us strength *(Knowingly—and without fun.)* Did he threaten us?

Beneatha. Oh—Mama—they don't do it like that any more. He talked Brotherhood. He said everybody ought to learn how to sit down and hate each other with good Christian fellowship.

She and Walter shake hands to ridicule the remark.

Mama *(sadly).* Lord, protect us . . .

Ruth. You should hear the money those folks raised to buy the house from us. All we paid and then some.

Beneatha. What they think we going to do—eat 'em?

Ruth. No, honey, marry 'em.

Mama *(shaking her head).* Lord, Lord, Lord . . .

Ruth. Well—that's the way the crackers crumble. *(A beat.)* Joke.

Beneatha *(laughingly noticing what her mother is doing).* Mama, what are you doing?

Mama. Fixing my plant so it won't get hurt none on the way . . .
Beneatha. Mama, you going to take *that* to the new house?
Mama. Un-huh—
Beneatha. That raggedy-looking old thing?
Mama *(stopping and looking at her).* It expresses ME!
Ruth *(with delight, to Beneatha).* So there, Miss Thing!

Walter comes to Mama suddenly and bends down behind her and squeezes her in his arms with all his strength. She is overwhelmed by the suddenness of it and, though delighted, her manner is like that of Ruth and Travis.

Mama. Look out now, boy! You make me mess up my thing here!
Walter *(his face lit, he slips down on his knees beside her, his arms still about her).*
     Mama . . . you know what it means to climb up in the chariot?
Mama *(gruffly, very happy).* Get on away from me now . . .
Ruth *(near the gift-wrapped package, trying to catch Walter's eye).* Psst—
Walter. What the old song say, Mama . . .
Ruth. Walter—Now?

She is pointing at the package.

Walter *(speaking the lines, sweetly, playfully, in his mother's face).*

     I got wings . . . you got wings . . .
     All God's Children got wings . . .

Mama. Boy—get out of my face and do some work . . .
Walter.

     When I get to heaven gonna put on my wings,
     Gonna fly all over God's heaven . . .

Beneatha *(teasingly, from across the room).* Everybody talking 'bout heaven ain't going there!
Walter *(to Ruth, who is carrying the box across to them).* I don't know, you think we ought to give her that . . . Seems to me she ain't been very appreciative around here.
Mama *(eying the box, which is obviously a gift).* What is that?
Walter *(taking it from Ruth and putting it on the table in front of Mama).* Well— what you all think? Should we give it to her?
Ruth. Oh—she was pretty good today.
Mama. I'll good you—

She turns her eyes to the box again.

Beneatha. Open it, Mama.

She stands up, looks at it, turns and looks at all of them, and then presses her hands together and does not open the package.

Walter *(sweetly).* Open it, Mama. It's for you. *(Mama looks in his eyes. It is the first present in her life without its being Christmas. Slowly she opens her package and lifts out, one by one, a brand-new sparkling set of gardening tools. Walter continues, prodding.)* Ruth made up the note—read it . . .

Mama *(picking up the card and adjusting her glasses).* "To our own Mrs. Miniver— Love from Brother, Ruth, and Beneatha." Ain't that lovely . . .

Travis *(tugging at his father's sleeve).* Daddy, can I give her mine now?

Walter. All right, son. *(Travis flies to get his gift.)*

Mama. Now I don't have to use my knives and forks no more . . .

Walter. Travis didn't want to go in with the rest of us, Mama. He got his own. *(Somewhat amused.)* We don't know what it is . . .

Travis *(racing back in the room with a large hatbox and putting it in front of his grandmother).* Here!

Mama. Lord have mercy, baby. You done gone and bought your grandmother a hat?

Travis *(very proud).* Open it!

She does and lifts out an elaborate, but very elaborate, wide gardening hat, and all the adults break up at the sight of it.

Ruth. Travis, honey, what is that?

Travis *(who thinks it is beautiful and appropriate).* It's a gardening hat! Like the ladies always have on in the magazines when they work in their gardens.

Beneatha *(giggling fiercely).* Travis—we were trying to make Mama Mrs. Miniver—not Scarlett O'Hara!

Mama *(indignantly).* What's the matter with you all! This here is a beautiful hat! *(Absurdly.)* I always wanted me one just like it!

She pops it on her head to prove it to her grandson, and the hat is ludicrous and considerably oversized.

Ruth. Hot dog! Go, Mama!

Walter *(doubled over with laughter).* I'm sorry, Mama—but you look like you ready to go out and chop you some cotton sure enough!

They all laugh except Mama, out of deference to Travis's feelings.

Mama *(gathering the boy up to her).* Bless your heart—this is the prettiest hat I ever owned—*(Walter, Ruth, and Beneatha chime in—noisily, festively, and insincerely congratulating Travis on his gift.)* What are we all standing around here for? We ain't finished packin' yet. Bennie, you ain't packed one book.

The bell rings.

Beneatha. That couldn't be the movers . . . it's not hardly two good yet—

Beneatha goes into her room. Mama starts for door.

Walter *(turning, stiffening).* Wait—wait—I'll get it.

He stands and looks at the door.

Mama. You expecting company, son?
Walter *(just looking at the door).* Yeah—yeah . . .

Mama looks at Ruth, and they exchange innocent and unfrightened glances.

Mama *(not understanding).* Well, let them in, son.
Beneatha *(from her room).* We need some more string.
Mama. Travis—you run to the hardware and get me some string cord.

Mama goes out and Walter turns and looks at Ruth. Travis goes to a dish for money.

Ruth. Why don't you answer the door, man?
Walter *(suddenly bounding across the floor to embrace her).* 'Cause sometimes it
  hard to let the future begin! *(Stooping down in her face.)*

  I got wings! You got wings!
  All God's children got wings!

*He crosses to the door and throws it open. Standing there is a very slight little man in a
not-too-prosperous business suit and with haunted frightened eyes and a hat pulled
down tightly, brim up, around his forehead. Travis passes between the men and exits.
Walter leans deep in the man's face, still in his jubilance.*

  When I get to heaven gonna put on my wings,
  Gonna fly all over God's heaven . . .

The little man just stares at him.

  Heaven—

Suddenly he stops and looks past the little man into the empty hallway.

  Where's Willy, man?
Bobo. He ain't with me.
Walter *(not disturbed).* Oh—come on in. You know my wife.
Bobo *(dumbly, taking off his hat).* Yes—h'you, Miss Ruth.

Ruth (*quietly, a mood apart from her husband already, seeing Bobo*). Hello, Bobo.
Walter. You right on time today . . . Right on time. That's the way! (*He slaps Bobo on his back.*) Sit down . . . lemme hear.

Ruth stands stiffly and quietly in back of them, as though somehow she senses death, her eyes fixed on her husband.

Bobo (*his frightened eyes on the floor, his hat in his hands*). Could I please get a drink of water, before I tell you about it, Walter Lee?

Walter does not take his eyes off the man. Ruth goes blindly to the tap and gets a glass of water and brings it to Bobo.

Walter. There ain't nothing wrong, is there?
Bobo. Lemme tell you—
Walter. Man—didn't nothing go wrong?
Bobo. Lemme tell you—Walter Lee. (*Looking at Ruth and talking to her more than to Walter.*) You know how it was. I got to tell you how it was. I mean first I got to tell you how it was all the way . . . I mean about the money I put in, Walter Lee . . .
Walter (*with taut agitation now*). What about the money you put in?
Bobo. Well—it wasn't much as we told you—me and Willy—(*He stops.*) I'm sorry, Walter. I got a bad feeling about it. I got a real bad feeling about it . . .
Walter. Man, what you telling me about all this for? . . . Tell me what happened in Springfield . . .
Bobo. Springfield.
Ruth (*like a dead woman*). What was supposed to happen in Springfield?
Bobo (*to her*). This deal that me and Walter went into with Willy—Me and Willy was going to go down to Springfield and spread some money 'round so's we wouldn't have to wait so long for the liquor license . . . That's what we were going to do. Everybody said that was the way you had to do, you understand, Miss Ruth?
Walter. Man—what happened down there?
Bobo (*a pitiful man, near tears*). I'm trying to tell you, Walter.
Walter (*screaming at him suddenly*). THEN TELL ME, GODDAMMIT . . . WHAT'S THE MATTER WITH YOU?
Bobo. Man . . . I didn't go to no Springfield, yesterday.
Walter (*halted, life hanging in the moment*). Why not?
Bobo (*the long way, the hard way to tell*). 'Cause I didn't have no reasons to . . .
Walter. Man, what are you talking about!
Bobo. I'm talking about the fact that when I got to the train station yesterday morning—eight o'clock like we planned . . . Man—*Willy didn't never show up.*
Walter. Why . . . where was he . . . where is he?
Bobo. That's what I'm trying to tell you . . . I don't know . . . I waited six hours . . . I called his house . . . and I waited . . . six hours . . . I waited in that

train station six hours . . . *(Breaking into tears.)* That was all the extra money I had in the world . . . *(Looking up at Walter with the tears running down his face.)* Man, *Willy is gone.*

Walter. Gone, what you mean Willy is gone? Gone where? You mean he went by himself. You mean he went off to Springfield by himself—to take care of getting the license—*(Turns and looks anxiously at Ruth.)* You mean maybe he didn't want too many people in on the business down there? *(Looks to Ruth again, as before.)* You know Willy got his own ways. *(Looks back to Bobo.)* Maybe you was late yesterday and he just went on down there without you. Maybe—maybe—he's been callin' you at home tryin' to tell you what happened or something. Maybe—maybe—he just got sick. He's somewhere— he's got to be somewhere. We just got to find him—me and you got to find him. *(Grabs Bobo senselessly by the collar and starts to shake him.)* We got to!

Bobo *(in sudden angry, frightened agony).* What's the matter with you, Walter! When a cat take off with your money he don't leave you no road maps!

Walter *(turning madly, as though he is looking for Willy in the very room).* Willy! . . . Willy . . . don't do it . . . Please don't do it . . . Man, not with that money . . . Man, please, not with that money . . . Oh, God . . . Don't let it be true . . . *(He is wandering around, crying out for Willy and looking for him or perhaps for help from God.)* Man . . . I trusted you . . . Man, I put my life in your hands . . . *(He starts to crumple down on the floor as Ruth just covers her face in horror. Mama opens the door and comes into the room, with Beneatha behind her.)* Man . . . *(He starts to pound the floor with his fists, sobbing wildly.)* THAT MONEY IS MADE OUT OF MY FATHER'S FLESH—

Bobo *(standing over him helplessly).* I'm sorry, Walter . . . *(only Walter's sobs reply. Bobo puts on his hat.)* I had my life staked on this deal, too . . .

He exits.

Mama *(to Walter).* Son—*(She goes to him, bends down to him, talks to his bent head.)* Son . . . Is it gone? Son, I gave you sixty-five hundred dollars. Is it gone? All of it? Beneatha's money too?

Walter *(lifting his head slowly).* Mama . . . I never . . . went to the bank at all . . .

Mama *(not wanting to believe him).* You mean . . . your sister's school money . . . you used that too . . . Walter? . . .

Walter. Yessss! All of it . . . It's all gone . . .

There is total silence. Ruth stands with her face covered with her hands; Beneatha leans forlornly against a wall, fingering a piece of red ribbon from the mother's gift. Mama stops and looks at her son without recognition and then, quite without thinking about it, starts to beat him senselessly in the face. Beneatha goes to them and stops it.

Beneatha. Mama!

Mama stops and looks at both of her children and rises slowly and wanders vaguely, aimlessly away from them.

Mama. I seen . . . him . . . night after night . . . come in . . . and look at that rug . . . and then look at me . . . the red showing in his eyes . . . the veins moving in his head . . . I seen him grow thin and old before he was forty . . . working and working and working like somebody's old horse . . . killing himself . . . and you—you give it all away in a day—(*She raises her arms to strike him again.*)

Beneatha. Mama—

Mama. Oh, God . . . (*She looks up to Him.*) Look down here—and show me the strength.

Beneatha. Mama—

Mama (*folding over*). Strength . . .

Beneatha (*plaintively*). Mama . . .

Mama. Strength!

Curtain.

ACT III

Time: An hour later.

At curtain, there is a sullen light of gloom in the living room, gray light not unlike that which began the first scene of Act I. At left we can see Walter within his room, alone with himself. He is stretched out on the bed, his shirt out and open, his arms under his head. He does not smoke, he does not cry out, he merely lies there, looking up at the ceiling, much as if he were alone in the world.

In the living room Beneatha sits at the table, still surrounded by the now almost ominous packing crates. She sits looking off. We feel that this is a mood struck perhaps an hour before, and it lingers now, full of the empty sound of profound disappointment. We see on a line from her brother's bedroom the sameness of their attitudes. Presently the bell rings and Beneatha rises without ambition or interest in answering. It is Asagai, smiling broadly, striding into the room with energy and happy expectation and conversation.

Asagai. I came over . . . I had some free time. I thought I might help with the packing. Ah, I like the look of packing crates! A household in preparation for a journey! It depresses some people . . . but for me . . . it is another feeling. Something full of the flow of life, do you understand? Movement, progress . . . It makes me think of Africa.

Beneatha. Africa!

Asagai. What kind of a mood is this? Have I told you how deeply you move me?

Beneatha. He gave away the money, Asagai . . .

Asagai. Who gave away what money?

Beneatha. The insurance money. My brother gave it away.

Asagai. Gave it away?

Beneatha. He made an investment! With a man even Travis wouldn't have trusted with his most worn-out marbles.

Asagai. And it's gone?

Beneatha. Gone!

Asagai. I'm very sorry . . . And you, now?

Beneatha. Me? . . . Me? . . . Me, I'm nothing . . . Me. When I was very small . . . we used to take our sleds out in the wintertime and the only hills we had were the ice-covered stone steps of some houses down the street. And we used to fill them in with snow and make them smooth and slide down them all day . . . and it was very dangerous, you know . . . far too steep . . . and sure enough one day a kid named Rufus came down too fast and hit the sidewalk and we saw his face just split open right there in front of us . . . And I remember standing there looking at his bloody open face thinking that was the end of Rufus. But the ambulance came and they took him to the hospital and they fixed the broken bones and they sewed it all up . . . and the next time I saw Rufus he just had a little line down the middle of his face . . . I never got over that . . .

Asagai. What?

Beneatha. That that was what one person could do for another, fix him up—sew up the problem, make him all right again. That was the most marvelous thing in the world . . . I wanted to do that. I always thought it was the one concrete thing in the world that a human being could do. Fix up the sick, you know—and make them whole again. This was truly being God . . .

Asagai. You wanted to be God?

Beneatha. No—I wanted to cure. It used to be so important to me. I wanted to cure. It used to matter. I used to care. I mean about people and how their bodies hurt . . .

Asagai. And you've stopped caring?

Beneatha. Yes—I think so.

Asagai. Why?

Beneatha (bitterly). Because it doesn't seem deep enough, close enough to what ails mankind! It was a child's way of seeing things—or an idealist's.

Asagai. Children see things very well sometimes—and idealists even better.

Beneatha. I know that's what you think. Because you are still where I left off. You with all your talk and dreams about Africa! You still think you can patch up the world. Cure the Great Sore of Colonialism—(Loftily, mocking it.) with the Penicillin of Independence—!

Asagai. Yes!

Beneatha. Independence and then what? What about all the crooks and thieves and just plain idiots who will come into power and steal and plunder the same as before—only now they will be black and do it in the name of the new Independence—WHAT ABOUT THEM?!

Asagai. That will be the problem for another time. First we must get there.

Beneatha. And where does it end?

Asagai. End? Who even spoke of an end? To life? To living?

Beneatha. An end to misery! To stupidity! Don't you see there isn't any real progress, Asagai, there is only one large circle that we march in, around and around, each of us with our own little picture in front of us—our own little mirage that we think is the future.

Asagai. That is the mistake.

Beneatha. What?

Asagai. What you just said—about the circle. It isn't a circle—it is simply a long line—as in geometry, you know, one that reaches into infinity. And because we cannot see the end—we also cannot see how it changes. And it is very odd but those who see the changes—who dream, who will not give up—are called idealists . . . and those who see only the circle—we call *them* the "realists"!

Beneatha. Asagai, while I was sleeping in that bed in there, people went out and took the future right out of my hands! And nobody asked me, nobody consulted me—they just went out and changed my life!

Asagai. Was it your money?

Beneatha. What?

Asagai. Was it your money he gave away?

Beneatha. It belonged to all of us.

Asagai. But did you earn it? Would you have had it at all if your father had not died?

Beneatha. No.

Asagai. Then isn't there something wrong in a house—in a world—where all dreams, good or bad, must depend on the death of a man? I never thought to see *you* like this, Alaiyo. You! Your brother made a mistake and you are grateful to him so that now you can give up the ailing human race on account of it! You talk about what good is struggle, what good is anything! Where are we all going and why are we bothering!

Beneatha. AND YOU CANNOT ANSWER IT!

Asagai (*shouting over her*). *I LIVE THE ANSWER!* (*Pause.*) In my village at home it is the exceptional man who can even read a newspaper . . . or who ever sees a book at all. I will go home and much of what I will have to say will seem strange to the people of my village. But I will teach and work and things will happen, slowly and swiftly. At times it will seem that nothing changes at all . . . and then again the sudden dramatic events which make history leap into the future. And then quiet again. Retrogression even. Guns, murder, revolution. And I even will have moments when I wonder if the quiet was not better than all that death and hatred. But I will look about my village at the illiteracy and disease and ignorance and I will not wonder long. And perhaps . . . perhaps I will be a great man . . . I mean perhaps I will hold on to the substance of truth and find my way always with the right course . . . and perhaps for it I will be butchered in my bed some night by the servants of empire . . .

Beneatha. *The martyr!*

Asagai (*he smiles*). . . . or perhaps I shall live to be a very old man, respected and esteemed in my new nation . . . And perhaps I shall hold office and this is what I'm trying to tell you, Alaiyo: perhaps the things I believe now for my country will be wrong and outmoded, and I will not understand and do terrible things to have things my way or merely to keep my power. Don't you see that there will be young men and women—not British soldiers then, but my own black countrymen—to step out of the shadows some evening and slit my then useless throat? Don't you see they have always been there . . . that they always will be. And that such a thing as my own death will be an advance? They who might kill me even . . . actually replenish all that I was.

Beneatha. Oh, Asagai, I know all that.

Asagai. Good! Then stop moaning and groaning and tell me what you plan to do.

Beneatha. Do?

Asagai. I have a bit of a suggestion.

Beneatha. What?

Asagai *(rather quietly for him).* That when it is all over—that you come home with me—

Beneatha *(staring at him and crossing away with exasperation).* Oh—Asagai—at this moment you decide to be romantic!

Asagai *(quickly understanding the misunderstanding).* My dear, young creature of the New World—I do not mean across the city—I mean across the ocean: home—to Africa.

Beneatha *(slowly understanding and turning to him with murmured amazement).* To Africa?

Asagai. Yes! . . . *(smiling and lifting his arms playfully.)* Three hundred years later the African Prince rose up out of the seas and swept the maiden back across the middle passage over which her ancestors had come—

Beneatha *(unable to play).* To—to Nigeria?

Asagai. Nigeria. Home. *(Coming to her with genuine romantic flippancy.)* I will show you our mountains and our stars; and give you cool drinks from gourds and teach you the old songs and the ways of our people—and, in time, we will pretend that—*(Very softly.)*—you have only been away for a day. Say that you'll come—*(He swings her around and takes her full in his arms in a kiss which proceeds to passion.)*

Beneatha *(pulling away suddenly).* You're getting me all mixed up—

Asagai. Why?

Beneatha. Too many things—too many things have happened today. I must sit down and think. I don't know what I feel about anything right this minute.

She promptly sits down and props her chin on her fist.

Asagai *(charmed).* All right, I shall leave you. No—don't get up. *(Touching her, gently, sweetly.)* Just sit awhile and think . . . Never be afraid to sit awhile and think. *(He goes to door and looks at her.)* How often I have looked at you and said, "Ah—so this is what the New World hath finally wrought . . ."

He exits. Beneatha sits on alone. Presently Walter enters from his room and starts to rummage through things, feverishly looking for something. She looks up and turns in her seat.

Beneatha (*hissingly*). Yes—just look at what the New World hath wrought! . . . Just look! (*She gestures with bitter disgust.*) There he is! *Monsieur le petit bourgeois noir*[2]—himself! There he is—Symbol of a Rising Class! Entrepreneur! Titan of the system! (*Walter ignores her completely and continues frantically and destructively looking for something and hurling things to floor and tearing things out of their place in his search. Beneatha ignores the eccentricity of his actions and goes on with the monologue of insult.*) Did you dream of yachts on Lake Michigan, Brother? Did you see yourself on that Great Day sitting down at the Conference Table, surrounded by all the mighty bald-headed men in America? All halted, waiting, breathless, waiting for your pronouncements on industry? Waiting for you—Chairman of the Board! (*Walter finds what he is looking for— a small piece of white paper—and pushes it in his pocket and puts on his coat and rushes out without ever having looked at her. She shouts after him.*) I look at you and I see the final triumph of stupidity in the world!

The door slams and she returns to just sitting again. Ruth comes quickly out of Mama's room.

Ruth. Who was that?
Beneatha. Your husband.
Ruth. Where did he go?
Beneatha. Who knows—maybe he has an appointment at U.S. Steel.
Ruth (*anxiously, with frightened eyes*). You didn't say nothing bad to him, did you?
Beneatha. Bad? Say anything bad to him? No —I told him he was a sweet boy and full of dreams and everything is strictly peachy keen, as the ofay kids say!

Mama enters from her bedroom. She is lost, vague, trying to catch hold, to make some sense of her former command of the world, but it still eludes her. A sense of waste overwhelms her gait; a measure of apology rides on her shoulders. She goes to her plant, which has remained on the table, looks at it, picks it up and takes it to the window sill and sits it outside, and she stands and looks at it a long moment. Then she closes the window, straightens her body with effort and turns around to her children.

Mama. Well— ain't it a mess in here, though? (*A false cheerfulness, a beginning of something.*) I guess we all better stop moping around and get some work done. All this unpacking and everything we got to do. (*Ruth raises her head slowly in response to the sense of the line; and Beneatha in similar manner turns very slowly to look at her mother.*) One of you all better call the moving people and tell 'em not to come.
Ruth. Tell 'em not to come?
Mama. Of course, baby. Ain't no need in 'em coming all the way here and having to go back. They charges for that too. (*She sits down, fingers to her brow, thinking.*) Lord, ever since I was a little girl, I always remembers people saying, "Lena—Lena Eggleston, you aims too high all the time. You needs to slow down

---

[2] Mr. Black Bourgeoisie.

and see life a little more like it is. Just slow down some." That's what they always used to say down home—"Lord, that Lena Eggleston is a high-minded thing. She'll get her due one day!"

Ruth. No, Lena . . .

Mama. Me and Big Walter just didn't never learn right.

Ruth. Lena, no! We gotta go. Bennie—tell her . . .

She rises and crosses to Beneatha with her arms outstretched. Beneatha doesn't respond.

Tell her we can still move . . . the notes ain't but a hundred and twenty-five a month. We got four grown people in this house—we can work . . .

Mama *(to herself).* Just aimed too high all the time—

Ruth *(turning and going to Mama fast—the words pouring out with urgency and desperation).* Lena—I'll work . . . I'll work twenty hours a day in all the kitchens in Chicago . . . I'll strap my baby on my back if I have to and scrub all the floors in America and wash all the sheets in America if I have to—but we got to MOVE! We got to get OUT OF HERE!!

Mama reaches out absently and pats Ruth's hand.

Mama. No—I sees things differently now. Been thinking 'bout some of the things we could do to fix this place up some. I seen a second-hand bureau over on Maxwell Street just the other day that could fit right there. *(She points to where the new furniture might go. Ruth wanders away from her.)* Would need some new handles on it and then a little varnish and it look like something brand-new. And—we can put up them new curtains in the kitchen . . . Why this place be looking fine. Cheer us all up so that we forget trouble ever come . . . *(To Ruth.)* And you could get some nice screens to put up in your room round the baby's bassinet . . . *(She looks at both of them pleadingly.)* Sometimes you just got to know when to give up some things . . . and hold on to what you got . . .

Walter enters from the outside, looking spent and leaning against the door, his coat hanging from him.

Mama. Where you been, son?

Walter *(breathing hard).* Made a call.

Mama. To who, son?

Walter. To The Man. *(He heads for his room.)*

Mama. What man, baby?

Walter *(stops in the door).* The Man, Mama. Don't you know who The Man is?

Ruth. Walter Lee?

Walter. *The Man.* Like the guys in the streets say—The Man. Captain Boss—Mistuh Charley . . . Old Cap'n Please Mr. Bossman . . .

Beneatha *(suddenly).* Lindner!

Walter. That's right! That's good. I told him to come right over.

Beneatha (*fiercely, understanding*). For what? What do you want to see him for!

Walter (*looking at his sister*). We going to do business with him.

Mama. What you talking 'bout, son?

Walter. Talking 'bout life, Mama. You all always telling me to see life like it is. Well—I laid in there on my back today . . . and I figured it out. Life just like it is. Who gets and who don't get. (*He sits down with his coat on and laughs.*) Mama, you know it's all divided up. Life is. Sure enough. Between the takers and the "tooken." (*He laughs.*) I've figured it out finally. (*He looks around at them.*) Yeah. Some of us always getting "tooken." (*He laughs.*) People like Willy Harris, they don't never get "tooken." And you know why the rest of us do? 'Cause we all mixed up. Mixed up bad. We get to looking 'round for the right and the wrong; and we worry about it and cry about it and stay up nights trying to figure out 'bout the wrong and the right of things all the time . . . And all the time, man, them takers is out there operating, just taking and taking. Willy Harris? Shoot—Willy Harris don't even count. He don't even count in the big scheme of things. But I'll say one thing for old Willy Harris . . . he's taught me something. He's taught me to keep my eye on what counts in this world. Yeah—(*Shouting out a little.*) Thanks, Willy!

Ruth. What did you call that man for, Walter Lee?

Walter. Called him to tell him to come on over to the show. Gonna put on a show for the man. Just what he wants to see. You see, Mama, the man came here today and he told us that them people out there where you want us to move—well they so upset they willing to pay us *not* to move! (*He laughs again.*) And—and oh, Mama—you would of been proud of the way me and Ruth and Bennie acted. We told him to get out . . . Lord have mercy! We told the man to get out! Oh, we was some proud folks this afternoon, yeah. (*He lights a cigarette.*) We were still full of that old-time stuff . . .

Ruth (*coming toward him slowly*). You talking 'bout taking them people's money to keep us from moving in that house?

Walter. I ain't just talking 'bout it, baby—I'm telling you that's what's going to happen!

Beneatha. Oh, God! Where is the bottom! Where is the real honest-to-God bottom so he can't go any farther!

Walter. See—that's the old stuff. You and that boy that was here today. You all want everybody to carry a flag and a spear and sing some marching songs, huh? You wanna spend your life looking into things and trying to find the right and the wrong part, huh? Yeah. You know what's going to happen to that boy someday—he'll find himself sitting in a dungeon, locked in forever—and the takers will have the key! Forget it, baby! There ain't no causes—there ain't nothing but taking in this world, and he who takes most is smartest—and it don't make a damn bit of difference *how.*

Mama. You making something inside me cry, son. Some awful pain inside me.

Walter. Don't cry, Mama. Understand. That white man is going to walk in that door able to write checks for more money than we ever had. It's important to him and I'm going to help him . . . I'm going to put on the show, Mama.

Mama. Son—I come from five generations of people who was slaves and share-croppers—but ain't nobody in my family never let nobody pay 'em no money that was a way of telling us we wasn't fit to walk the earth. We ain't never been that poor. *(Raising her eyes and looking at him.)* We ain't never been that—dead inside.

Beneatha. Well—we are dead now. All the talk about dreams and sunlight that goes on in this house. It's all dead now.

Walter. What's the matter with you all! I didn't make this world! It was give to me this way! Hell, yes, I want me some yachts someday! Yes, I want to hang some real pearls 'round my wife's neck. Ain't she supposed to wear no pearls? Some-body tell me—tell me, who decides which women is suppose to wear pearls in this world. I tell you I am a *man*—and I think my wife should wear some pearls in this world!

This last line hangs a good while and Walter begins to move about the room. The word "Man" has penetrated his consciousness; he mumbles it to himself repeatedly between strange agitated pauses as he moves about.

Mama. Baby, how you going to feel on the inside?

Walter. Fine! . . . Going to feel fine . . . a man . . .

Mama. You won't have nothing left then, Walter Lee.

Walter *(coming to her).* I'm going to feel fine, Mama. I'm going to look that son-of-a-bitch in the eyes and say—*(He falters.)*—and say, "All right, Mr. Lindner—*(He falters even more.)*—that's *your* neighborhood out there! You got the right to keep it like you want! You got the right to have it like you want! Just write the check and—the house is yours." And—and I am going to say—*(His voice almost breaks.)* "And you—you people just put the money in my hand and you won't have to live next to this bunch of stinking niggers! . . ." *(He straightens up and moves away from his mother, walking around the room.)* And maybe—maybe I'll just get down on my black knees . . . *(He does so; Ruth and Bennie and Mama watch him in frozen horror.)* "Captain, Mistuh, Bossman—*(Groveling and grin-ning and wringing his hands in profoundly anguished imitation of the slow-witted movie stereotype.)* A-hee-hee-hee! Oh, yassuh boss! Yasssssuh! Great white—*(Voice breaking, he forces himself to go on.)*—Father, just gi' ussen de money, fo' God's sake, and we's—we's ain't gwine come out deh and dirty up yo' white folks neighborhood . . ." *(He breaks down completely.)* And I'll feel fine! Fine! FINE! *(He gets up and goes into the bedroom.)*

Beneatha. That is not a man. That is nothing but a toothless rat.

Mama. Yes—death done come in this here house. *(She is nodding, slowly, reflec-tively.)* Done come walking in my house on the lips of my children. You what supposed to be my beginning again. You—what supposed to be my harvest. *(To Beneatha.)* You—you mourning your brother?

Beneatha. He's no brother of mine.

Mama. What you say?

Beneatha. I said that that individual in that room is no brother of mine.

Mama. That's what I thought you said. You feeling like you better than he is today? *(Beneatha does not answer.)* Yes? What you tell him a minute ago? That he wasn't a man? Yes? You give him up for me? You done wrote his epitaph too—like the rest of the world? Well, who give you the privilege?

Beneatha. Be on my side for once! You saw what he just did, Mama! You saw him—down on his knees. Wasn't it you who taught me to despise any man who would do that? Do what he's going to do?

Mama. Yes—I taught you that. Me and your daddy. But I thought I taught you something else too . . . I thought I taught you to love him.

Beneatha. Love him? There is nothing left to love.

Mama. There is *always* something left to love. And if you ain't learned that, you ain't learned nothing. *(Looking at her.)* Have you cried for that boy today? I don't mean for yourself and for the family 'cause we lost the money. I mean for him: what he been through and what it done to him. Child, when do you think is the time to love somebody the most? When they done good and made things easy for everybody? Well then, you ain't through learning—because that ain't the time at all. It's when he's at his lowest and can't believe in hisself 'cause the world done whipped him so! When you starts measuring somebody, measure him right, child, measure him right. Make sure you done taken into account what hills and valleys he come through before he got to wherever he is.

Travis bursts into the room at the end of the speech, leaving the door open.

Travis. Grandmama—the moving men are downstairs! The truck just pulled up.

Mama *(turning and looking at him).* Are they, baby? They downstairs?

She sighs and sits. Lindner appears in the doorway. He peers in and knocks lightly, to gain attention, and comes in. All turn to look at him.

Lindner *(hat and briefcase in hand).* Uh—hello . . .

Ruth crosses mechanically to the bedroom door and opens it and lets it swing open freely and slowly as the lights come up on Walter within, still in his coat, sitting at the far corner of the room. He looks up and out through the room to Lindner.

Ruth. He's here.

A long minute passes and Walter slowly gets up.

Lindner *(coming to the table with efficiency, putting his briefcase on the table and starting to unfold papers and unscrew fountain pens).* Well, I certainly was glad to hear from you people. (*Walter has begun the trek out of the room, slowly and awkwardly, rather like a small boy, passing the back of his sleeve across his mouth* *from time to time.)* Life can really be so much simpler than people let it be most of the time. Well—with whom do I negotiate? You, Mrs. Younger, or your son here? *(Mama sits with her hands folded on her lap and her eyes closed as Walter advances. Travis goes closer to Lindner and looks at the papers curiously.)* Just some official papers, sonny.

Ruth. Travis, you go downstairs—

Mama *(opening her eyes and looking into Walter's).* No. Travis, you stay right here. And you make him understand what you doing, Walter Lee. You teach him good. Like Willy Harris taught you. You show where our five generations done come to. *(Walter looks from her to the boy, who grins at him innocently.)* Go ahead, son—*(She folds her hands and closes her eyes.)* Go ahead.

Walter *(at last crosses to Lindner, who is reviewing the contract).* Well, Mr. Lindner. *(Beneatha turns away.)* We called you—*(There is a profound, simple groping quality in his speech.)*—because, well, me and my family *(He looks around and shifts from one foot to the other.)* Well—we are very plain people . . .

Lindner. Yes—

Walter. I mean—I have worked as a chauffeur most of my life—and my wife here, she does domestic work in people's kitchens. So does my mother. I mean—we are plain people . . .

Lindner. Yes, Mr. Younger—

Walter *(really like a small boy, looking down at his shoes and then up at the man).* And—uh—well, my father, well, he was a laborer most of his life. . . .

Lindner *(absolutely confused).* Uh, yes—yes, I understand. *(He turns back to the contract.)*

Walter *(a beat; staring at him).* And my father—*(With sudden intensity.)* My father almost *beat a man to death* once because this man called him a bad name or something, you know what I mean?

Lindner *(looking up, frozen).* No, no, I'm afraid I don't—

Walter *(a beat. The tension hangs; then Walter steps back from it).* Yeah. Well—what I mean is that we come from people who had a lot of *pride.* I mean—we are very proud people. And that's my sister over there and she's going to be a doctor—and we are very proud—

Lindner. Well—I am sure that is very nice, but—

Walter. What I am telling you is that we called you over here to tell you that we are very proud and that this—*(Signaling to Travis.)* Travis, come here. *(Travis crosses and Walter draws him before him facing the man.)* This is my son, and he makes the sixth generation our family in this country. And we have all thought about your offer—

Lindner. Well, good . . . good—

Walter. And we have decided to move into our house because my father—my father—he earned it for us brick by brick. *(Mama has her eyes closed and is rocking back and forth as though she were in church, with her head nodding the Amen yes.)* We don't want to make no trouble for nobody or fight no causes, and we will try to be good neighbors. And that's *all* we got to say about that. *(He looks* *the man absolutely in the eyes.)* We don't want your money. *(He turns and walks away.)*

Lindner *(looking around at all of them).* I take it then—that you have decided to occupy . . .

Beneatha. That's what the man said.

Lindner *(to Mama in her reverie).* Then I would like to appeal to you, Mrs. Younger. You are older and wiser and understand things better I am sure . . .

Mama. I am afraid you don't understand. My son said we was going to move and there ain't nothing left for me to say. *(Briskly.)* You know how these young folks is nowadays, mister. Can't do a thing with 'em! *(As he opens his mouth, she rises.)* Good-bye.

Lindner *(folding up his materials).* Well—if you are that final about it . . . there is nothing left for me to say. *(He finishes, almost ignored by the family, who are concentrating on Walter Lee. At the door Lindner halts and looks around.)* I sure hope you people know what you're getting into.

He shakes his head and exits.

Ruth *(looking around and coming to life).* Well, for God's sake—if the moving men are here—LET'S GET THE HELL OUT OF HERE!

Mama *(into action).* Ain't it the truth! Look at all this here mess. Ruth, put Travis's good jacket on him . . . Walter Lee, fix your tie and tuck your shirt in, you look like somebody's hoodlum! Lord have mercy, where is my plant? *(She flies to get it amid the general bustling of the family, who are deliberately trying to ignore the nobility of the past moment.)* You all start on down . . . Travis child, don't go empty-handed . . . Ruth, where did I put that box with my skillets in it? I want to be in charge of it myself . . . I'm going to make us the biggest dinner we ever ate tonight . . . Beneatha, what's the matter with them stockings? Pull them things up, girl . . .

The family starts to file out as two moving men appear and begin to carry out the heavier pieces of furniture, bumping into the family as they move about.

Beneatha. Mama, Asagai asked me to marry him today and go to Africa—

Mama *(in the middle of her getting-ready activity).* He did? You ain't old enough to marry nobody—*(Seeing the moving men lifting one of her chairs precariously.)* Darling, that ain't no bale of cotton, please handle it so we can sit in it again! I had that chair twenty-five years . . .

The movers sigh with exasperation and go on with their work.

Beneatha *(girlishly and unreasonably trying to pursue the conversation).* To go to Africa, Mama—be a doctor in Africa . . .

Mama *(distracted).* Yes, baby—

Walter. *Africa!* What he want you to go to Africa for?

Beneatha. To practice there . . .

Walter. Girl, if you don't get all them silly ideas out your head! You better marry yourself a man with some loot . . .

Beneatha (*angrily, precisely as in the first scene of the play*). What have you got to do with who I marry!

Walter. Plenty. Now I think George Murchison—

Beneatha. *George Murchison!* I wouldn't marry him if he was Adam and I was Eve!

Walter and Beneatha go out yelling at each other vigorously and the anger is loud and real till their voices diminish. Ruth stands at the door and turns to Mama and smiles knowingly.

Mama (*fixing her hat at last*). Yeah—they something all right, my children . . .

Ruth. Yeah—they're something. Let's go, Lena.

Mama (*stalling, starting to look around at the house*). Yes—I'm coming. Ruth—

Ruth. Yes?

Mama (*quietly, woman to woman*). He finally come into his manhood today, didn't he? Kind of like a rainbow after the rain . . .

Ruth (*biting her lip lest her own pride explode in front of Mama*). Yes, Lena.

Walter's voice calls for them raucously.

Walter (*off stage*). Y'all come on! These people charges by the hour, you know!

Mama (*waving Ruth out vaguely*). All right, honey—go on down. I be down directly.

Ruth hesitates, then exits. Mama stands, at last alone in the living room, her plant on the table before her as the lights start to come down. She looks around at all the walls and ceilings and suddenly, despite herself, while the children call below, a great heaving thing rises in her and she puts her fist to her mouth to stifle it, takes a final desperate look, pulls her coat about her, pats her hat, and goes out. The lights dim down. The door opens and she comes back in, grabs her plant, and goes out for the last time.

Curtain.

FOR ANALYSIS

1. In what ways does the opening dialogue between Ruth and Walter establish the major themes of the play?

2. Describe the shared values and dreams that give the family its cohesiveness.

3. Describe Walter's view of women. Is his view validated by the actions of the women? Explain.

4. Describe the contrast between Beneatha's two suitors, George Murchison and Joseph Asagai, and explain how it contributes to the theme of the play.

5. What is the significance of Mama's plant?

6. In what ways does the dialogue between Beneatha and Asagai that opens act III advance the theme of the play and prepare us for the ending?

7. Karl Lindner asserts that "the overwhelming majority of our people out there feel that people get along better, take more of a common interest in the life of the community, when they share a common background" (act II, scene 3). Is this a reasonable argument? Or is Lindner a racist? Explain.

8. In what sense is this play a celebration of African American life and culture?

9. Describe the speech patterns of the main characters. What function do the differences in **diction** serve? Is there any relationship between a character's diction and his or her moral standing in the play? Explain.

10. Even though he is dead, Big Walter is an important presence in the play. Examine the ways in which his presence is created, and explain what he represents.

MAKING CONNECTIONS

Compare and contrast the dynamics of family life in this play with those of the family in Walker's "Everyday Use" (p. 590). Which family do you think is more successful in coping with its problems? Explain.

WRITING TOPICS

1. Argue for or against the proposition that this play, written in 1959, is dated in its portrayal of black life and race relations.

2. Read Hughes's poem "Harlem" (p. 414), from which the title of the play is taken, and write an essay describing why you think Hansberry found the line appropriate as the title for her play.

3. Describe the significance of money in the play.

4. Write an essay in which you speculate on what happens to the members of the Younger family once they have moved into their new home.

DAVID HENRY HWANG (B. 1957)

TRYING TO FIND CHINATOWN 1996

CHARACTERS

Benjamin, Caucasian male, early twenties.
Ronnie, Asian American male, mid-twenties.

Time and Place

A street corner on the Lower East Side, New York City. The present.

Note on Music

Obviously, it would be foolish to require that the actor portraying Ronnie perform the specified violin music live. The score of this play can be played on tape over the house speakers, and the actor can feign playing the violin using a bow treated with soap. However, in order to effect a convincing illusion, it is desirable that the actor possess some familiarity with the violin or another stringed instrument.

> *Darkness. Over the house speakers, sound fades in: Hendrix-like virtuoso rock 'n' roll riffs—heavy feedback, distortion, phase shifting, wah-wah—amplified over a tiny Fender pug-nose.*
>
> *Lights fade up to reveal that the music's being played over a solid-body electric violin by Ronnie, a Chinese American male in his mid-twenties; he is dressed in retro-'60s clothing and has a few requisite '90s body mutilations. He's playing on a sidewalk for money, his violin case open before him; change and a few stray bills have been left by previous passersby.*
> *Benjamin enters; he's in his early twenties, blond, blue-eyed, a midwestern tourist in the big city. He holds a scrap of paper in his hands, scanning street signs for an address. He pauses before Ronnie, listens for a while. With a truly bravura run, Ronnie concludes the number and falls to his knees, gasping. Benjamin applauds.*

Benjamin. Good. That was really great. *(Pause)* I didn't . . . I mean, a fiddle . . . I mean, I'd heard them at square dances, on country stations and all, but I never . . . wow, this must really be New York City!

(Benjamin applauds, starts to walk on. Still on his knees, Ronnie clears his throat loudly.)

Oh, I . . . you're not just doing this for your health, right?

(Benjamin reaches in his pocket, pulls out a couple of coins. Ronnie clears his throat again.)

Look, I'm not a millionaire, I'm just . . .

(Benjamin pulls out his wallet, removes a dollar bill. Ronnie nods his head and gestures toward the violin case as he takes out a pack of cigarettes, lights one.)

Ronnie. And don't call it a "fiddle," OK?

Benjamin. Oh. Well, I didn't mean to—

Ronnie. You sound like a wuss. A hick. A dipshit.

Benjamin. It just slipped out. I didn't really—

Ronnie. If this was a fiddle, I'd be sitting here with a cob pipe, stomping my cowboy boots and kicking up hay. Then I'd go home and fuck my cousin.

Benjamin. Oh! Well, I don't really think—

Ronnie. Do you see a cob pipe? Am I fucking my cousin?

Benjamin. Well, no, not at the moment, but—

Ronnie. All right. Then this is a violin, now you give me your money, and I ignore the insult. Herein endeth the lesson.

(Pause.)

Benjamin. Look, a dollar's more than I've ever given to a . . . to someone asking for money.

Ronnie. Yeah, well, this is New York. Welcome to the cost of living.

Benjamin. What I mean is, maybe in exchange, you could help me—?

Ronnie. Jesus Christ! Do you see a sign around my neck reading "Big Apple Fucking Tourist Bureau"?

Benjamin. I'm just looking for an address, I don't think it's far from here, maybe you could . . . ?

(Benjamin holds out his scrap of paper, Ronnie snatches it away.)

Ronnie. You're lucky I'm such a goddamn softy. *(He looks at the paper)* Oh, fuck you. Just suck my dick, you and the cousin you rode in on.

Benjamin. I don't get it! What are you—?

Ronnie. Eat me. You know exactly what I—

Benjamin. I'm just asking for a little—

Ronnie. "13 Doyers Street"? Like you don't know where that is?

Benjamin. Of course I don't know! That's why I'm asking—

Ronnie. C'mon, you trailer-park refugee. You don't know that's Chinatown?

Benjamin. Sure I know that's Chinatown.

Ronnie. I know you know that's Chinatown.

Benjamin. So? That doesn't mean I know where Chinatown—

Ronnie. So why is it that you picked *me*, of all the street musicians in the city—to point you in the direction of Chinatown? Lemme guess—is it the earring? No, I don't think so. The Hendrix riffs? Guess again, you fucking moron.

Benjamin. Now, wait a minute. I see what you're—

Ronnie. What are you gonna ask me next? Where you can find the best dim sum in the city? Whether I can direct you to a genuine opium den? Or do I happen to know how you can meet Miss Saigon for a night of nookie-nookie followed by a good old-fashioned ritual suicide? Now, get your white ass off my sidewalk. One dollar doesn't even begin to make up for all this aggravation. Why don't you go back home and race bullfrogs, or whatever it is you do for—?

Benjamin. Brother, I can absolutely relate to your anger. Righteous rage, I suppose, would be a more appropriate term. To be marginalized, as we are, by a white racist patriarchy, to the point where the accomplishments of our people are obliterated from the history books, this is cultural genocide of the first order, leading to the fact that you must do battle with all of Euro-America's emasculating and brutal stereotypes of Asians—the opium den, the sexual objectification of the Asian female, the exoticized image of a tourist's China-town which ignores the exploitation of workers, the failure to unionize, the high rate of mental illness and tuberculosis—against these, each day, you rage, no, not as a victim, but as a survivor, yes, brother, a glorious warrior survivor!

(Silence.)

Ronnie. Say what?
Benjamin. So, I hope you can see that my request is not—
Ronnie. Wait, wait.
Benjamin. —motivated by the sorts of racist assumptions—
Ronnie. But, but where . . . how did you learn all that?
Benjamin. All what?
Ronnie. All that—you know—oppression stuff—tuberculosis . . .
Benjamin. It's statistically irrefutable. TB occurs in the community at a rate—
Ronnie. Where did *you* learn it?
Benjamin. I took Asian American studies. In college.
Ronnie. Where did you go to college?
Benjamin. University of Wisconsin. Madison.
Ronnie. Madison, Wisconsin?
Benjamin. That's not where the bridges are, by the way.
Ronnie. Huh? Oh, right . . .
Benjamin. You wouldn't believe the number of people who—
Ronnie. They have Asian American studies in Madison, Wisconsin? Since when?
Benjamin. Since the last Third World Unity hunger strike. *(Pause)* Why do you look so surprised? We're down.
Ronnie. I dunno. It just never occurred to me, the idea of Asian students in the Midwest going on a hunger strike.
Benjamin. Well, a lot of them had midterms that week, so they fasted in shifts. *(Pause)* The administration never figured it out. The Asian students put that "They all look alike" stereotype to good use.
Ronnie. OK, so they got Asian American studies. That still doesn't explain—
Benjamin. What?
Ronnie. Well . . . what *you* were doing taking it?
Benjamin. Just like everyone else. I wanted to explore my roots. And, you know, the history of oppression which is my legacy. After a lifetime of assimilation, I wanted to find out who I really am.

(Pause.)

Ronnie. And did you?

Benjamin. Sure. I learned to take pride in my ancestors who built the railroads, my Popo who would make me a hot bowl of jok with thousand-day-old eggs when the white kids chased me home yelling, "Gook! Chink! Slant-eyes!"

Ronnie. OK, OK, that's enough!

Benjamin. Painful to listen to, isn't it?

Ronnie. I don't know what kind of bullshit ethnic studies program they're running over in Wuss-consin, but did they bother to teach you that in order to find your Asian "roots," it's a good idea to first be Asian?

(Pause.)

Benjamin. Are you speaking metaphorically?

Ronnie. No! Literally! Look at your skin!

Benjamin. You know, it's very stereotypical to think that all Asian skin tones conform to a single hue.

Ronnie. You're white! Is this some kind of redneck joke or something? Am I the first person in the world to tell you this?

Benjamin. Oh! Oh! Oh!

Ronnie. I know real Asians are scarce in the Midwest, but . . . Jesus!

Benjamin. No, of course, I . . . I see where your misunderstanding arises.

Ronnie. Yeah. It's called, "You white."

Benjamin. It's just that—in my hometown of Tribune, Kansas, and then at school—see, everyone knows me—so this sort of thing never comes up. *(He offers his hand)* Benjamin Wong. I forget that a society wedded to racial constructs constantly forces me to explain my very existence.

Ronnie. Ronnie Chang. Otherwise known as "The Bow Man."

Benjamin. You see, I was adopted by Chinese American parents at birth. So, clearly, I'm an Asian American—

Ronnie. Even though you're blond and blue-eyed.

Benjamin. Well, you can't judge my race by my genetic heritage alone.

Ronnie. If genes don't determine race, what does?

Benjamin. Perhaps you'd prefer that I continue in denial, masquerading as a white man?

Ronnie. You can't just wake up and say, "Gee, I *feel* black today."

Benjamin. Brother, I'm just trying to find what you've already got.

Ronnie. What do I got?

Benjamin. A home. With your people. Picketing with the laundry workers. Taking refuge from the daily slights against your masculinity in the noble image of Gwan Gung.

Ronnie. Gwan who?

Benjamin. C'mon—the Chinese god of warriors and—what do you take me for? There're altars to him up all over the community.

Ronnie. I dunno what community you're talking about, but it's sure as hell not mine.

(Pause.)

Benjamin. What do you mean?

Ronnie. I mean, if you wanna call Chinatown *your* community, OK, knock your-self out, learn to use chopsticks, big deal. Go ahead, try and find your "roots" in some dim sum parlor with headless ducks hanging in the window. Those places don't tell you a thing about who *I* am.

Benjamin. Oh, I get it.

Ronnie. You get what?

Benjamin. You're one of those self-hating, *assimilated* Chinese Americans, aren't you?

Ronnie. Oh, Jesus.

Benjamin. You probably call yourself "Oriental," huh? Look, maybe I can help you. I have some books I can—

Ronnie. Hey, I read all those Asian identity books when you were still slathering on industrial-strength sunblock. *(Pause)* Sure, I'm Chinese. But folks like you act like that means something. Like, all of a sudden, you know who I am. You think identity's that simple? That you can wrap it all up in a neat package and say, "I have ethnicity, therefore I am"? All you fucking ethnic fundamentalists. Always settling for easy answers. You say you're looking for identity, but you can't begin to face the real mysteries of the search. So instead, you go skin-deep, and call it a day. *(Pause. He turns away from Benjamin and starts to play his violin—slow and bluesy.)*

Benjamin. So what are you? "Just a human being"? That's like saying you *have* no identity. If you asked me to describe my dog, I'd say more than, "He's just a dog."

Ronnie. What—you think if I deny the importance of my race, I'm nobody? There're worlds out there, worlds you haven't even begun to understand. Open your eyes. Hear with your ears.

(Ronnie holds his violin at chest level, but does not attempt to play during the following monologue. As he speaks, rock and jazz violin tracks fade in and out over the house speakers, bringing to life the styles of music he describes.)

I concede—it was called a fiddle long ago—but that was even before the birth of jazz. When the hollering in the fields, the rank injustice of human bondage, the struggle of God's children against the plagues of the devil's white man, when all these boiled up into that bittersweet brew, called by later generations, the blues. That's when fiddlers like Son Sims held their chin rests at their chests, and sawed away like the hillbillies still do today. And with the coming of ragtime appeared the pioneer Stuff Smith, who sang as he stroked the catgut, with his raspy, Louis Armstrong–voice—gruff and sweet like the timber of horsehair riding south below the fingerboard—and who finally sailed for Europe to find ears that would hear. Europe—where Stephane Grappelli initiated a magical French vio-lin, to be passed from generation to generation—first he, to Jean-Luc Ponty, then Ponty to Didier Lockwood. Listening to Grappelli play "A Nightingale Sang in Berkeley Square" is to understand not only the song of birds, but also how they learn to fly, fall in love on the wing, and finally falter one day, to wait for darkness beneath a London street lamp. And Ponty—he showed how the mod-ern violin man can accompany the shadow of his own lead lines, which cascade, one over another, into some nether world beyond the range of human hearing. Joe Venuti. Noel Pointer. Sven Asmussen. Even the Kronos Quartet, with their arrangement of "Purple Haze." Now, tell me, could any legacy be more rich, more crowded with mythology and heroes to inspire pride? What can I say if the banging of a gong or the clinking of a pickax on the Transcontinental Railroad fails to move me even as much as one note, played through a violin MIDI controller by Michael Urbaniak? *(He puts his violin to his chin, begins to play a jazz composition of his own invention)* Does it have to sound like Chinese opera before people like you decide I know who I am?

(Benjamin stands for a long moment, listening to Ronnie play. Then, he drops his dollar into the case, turns and exits right. Ronnie continues to play a long moment. Then Benjamin enters downstage left, illuminated in his own spotlight. He sits on the floor of the stage, his feet dangling off the lip. As he speaks, Ronnie continues playing his tune, which becomes underscoring for Benjamin's monologue. As the music continues, does it slowly begin to reflect the influence of Chinese music?)

Benjamin. When I finally found Doyers Street, I scanned the buildings for Number 13. Walking down an alley where the scent of freshly steamed char siu bao lingered in the air, I felt immediately that I had entered a world where all things were finally familiar. *(Pause)* An old woman bumped me with her shopping bag—screaming to her friend in Cantonese, though they walked no more than a few inches apart. Another man—shouting to a vendor in Sze-Yup. A youth, in white undershirt, perhaps a recent newcomer, bargaining with a grocer in Hokkien. I walked through this ocean of dialects, breathing in the richness with deep gulps, exhilarated by the energy this symphony brought to my step. And when I finally saw the number 13, I nearly wept at my good fortune. An old tenement, paint peeling, inside walls no doubt thick with a century of grease and broken dreams—and yet, to me, a temple—the house where my father was born. I suddenly saw it all: Gung Gung, coming home from his sixteen-hour days pressing shirts he could never afford to own, bringing with him candies for my father, each sweet wrapped in the hope of a better life. When my father left the ghetto, he swore he would never return. But he had, this day, in the thoughts and memories of his son, just six months after his death. And as I sat on the stoop, I pulled a hua-moi from my pocket, sucked on it, and felt his spirit returning. To this place where his ghost, and the dutiful hearts of all his descendants, would always call home. *(He listens for a long moment)* And I felt an ache in my heart for all those lost souls, denied this most important of revelations: to know who they truly are.

(Benjamin sucks his salted plum and listens to the sounds around him. Ronnie continues to play. The two remain oblivious of one another. Lights fade slowly to black.)

End of play

FOR ANALYSIS

1. Two things about Benjamin are revealed in his first big speech (p. 770). What are they? What two different sets of stereotypes make them surprising?

2. Why does Benjamin consider himself Chinese? Why does Ronnie disagree?

3. The second-to-last stage direction (not counting "End of play") ends: "As the music continues, does it slowly begin to reflect the influence of Chinese music?" (p. 773). Why might Hwang have written this stage direction? What comment might it be making about the discussion the two **characters** have been having?

MAKING CONNECTIONS

1. Compare this play to Chin's poem "How I Got That Name" (p. 682). How does each work relate Chinese identity to mainstream "white" American identity?

2. Compare Ronnie's attitudes about Asian stereotypes to the responses about gender stereotypes by the speakers in "Connecting Poems: Working Mothers." How are these responses—and the issues they concern—similar? How are they different?

WRITING TOPICS

1. Hwang writes dialogue in a very particular way for each character. Describe the **style** of each character's lines, and compare them. What does the way each talks say about him as a person? What do the similarities and differences between the ways they talk say about the similarities and differences between them as people?

2. Ronnie and Benjamin disagree about the importance of ethnic heritage to identity. Do you agree more with one than the other? In a brief essay, explain why.

NONFICTION

VIRGINIA WOOLF   (1882–1941)

WHAT IF SHAKESPEARE HAD HAD A SISTER?[1]   1928

It was disappointing not to have brought back in the evening some important statement, some authentic fact. Women are poorer than men because—this or that. Perhaps now it would be better to give up seeking for the truth, and receiving on one's head an avalanche of opinion hot as lava, discoloured as dish-water. It would be better to draw the curtains; to shut out distractions; to light the lamp; to narrow the enquiry and to ask the historian, who records not opinions but facts, to describe under what conditions women lived, not throughout the ages, but in England, say in the time of Elizabeth.

For it is a perennial puzzle why no woman wrote a word of that extraordinary literature when every other man, it seemed, was capable of song or sonnet. What were the conditions in which women lived, I asked myself; for fiction, imaginative work that is, is not dropped like a pebble upon the ground, as science may be; fiction is like a spider's web, attached ever so lightly perhaps, but still attached to life at all four corners. Often the attachment is scarcely perceptible; Shakespeare's plays, for instance, seem to hang there complete by themselves. But when the web is pulled askew, hooked up at the edge, torn in the middle, one remembers that these webs are not spun in midair by incorporeal creatures, but are the work of suffering human beings, and are attached to grossly material things, like health and money and the houses we live in.

I went, therefore, to the shelf where the histories stand and took down one of the latest, Professor Trevelyan's *History of England.* Once more I looked up

---

[1] *A Room of One's Own,* from which this essay is taken, is based on two lectures Woolf delivered on women and literature at Newnham College and Girton College, Cambridge University. In the opening chapter, Woolf declares that without "money and a room of her own," a woman cannot write fiction. In the following chapter, she recounts her unsuccessful attempt to turn up information at the British Library on the lives of women. This essay is from Chapter 3, from which a few passages are omitted. The essay ends with the concluding paragraph of the book.

Women, found "position of," and turned to the pages indicated. "Wife-beating," I read, "was a recognized right of man, and was practiced without shame by high as well as low. . . . Similarly," the historian goes on, "the daughter who refused to marry the gentleman of her parents' choice was liable to be locked up, beaten and flung about the room, without any shock being inflicted on public opinion. Marriage was not an affair of personal affection, but of family avarice, particularly in the 'chivalrous' upper classes. . . . Betrothal often took place while one or both of the parties was in the cradle, and marriage when they were scarcely out of the nurses' charge." That was about 1470, soon after Chaucer's time. The next reference to the position of women is some two hundred years later, in the time of the Stuarts. "It was still the exception for women of the upper and middle class to choose their own husbands, and when the husband had been assigned, he was lord and master, so far at least as law and custom could make him. Yet even so," Professor Trevelyan concludes, "neither Shakespeare's women nor those of authentic seventeenth-century memoirs, like the Verneys and the Hutchinsons, seem wanting in personality and character." Certainly, if we consider it, Cleopatra must have had a way with her; Lady Macbeth, one would suppose, had a will of her own; Rosalind, one might conclude, was an attractive girl. Professor Trevelyan is speaking no more than the truth when he remarks that Shakespeare's women do not seem wanting in personality and character. Not being a historian, one might go even further and say that women have burnt like beacons in all the works of all the poets from the beginning of time—Clytemnestra, Antigone, Cleopatra, Lady Macbeth, Phèdre, Cressida, Rosalind, Desdemona, the Duchess of Malfi, among the dramatists; then among the prose writers: Millamant, Clarissa, Becky Sharp, Anna Karenina, Emma Bovary, Madame de Guermantes[2]—the names flock to mind, nor do they recall women "lacking in personality and character." Indeed, if woman had no existence save in the fiction written by men, one would imagine her a person of the utmost importance; very various; heroic and mean; splendid and sordid; infinitely beautiful and hideous in the extreme; as great as a man, some think even greater. But this is woman in fiction. In fact, as Professor Trevelyan points out, she was locked up, beaten and flung about the room.

A very queer, composite being thus emerges. Imaginatively she is of the highest importance; practically she is completely insignificant. She pervades poetry from cover to cover; she is all but absent from history. She dominates the lives of kings and conquerors in fiction; in fact she was the slave of any boy whose parents forced a ring upon her finger. Some of the most inspired words, some of the most profound thoughts in literature fell from her lips; in real life she could hardly read, could scarcely spell, and was the property of her husband.

It was certainly an odd monster that one made up by reading the historians 5 first and the poets afterwards—a worm winged like an eagle; the spirit of life and beauty in a kitchen chopping up suet. But these monsters, however amusing

[2] Female characters from great works of literature.

to the imagination, have no existence in fact. What one must do to bring her to life was to think poetically and prosaically at one and the same moment, thus keeping in touch with fact—that she is Mrs. Martin, aged thirty-six, dressed in blue, wearing a black hat and brown shoes; but not losing sight of fiction either—that she is a vessel in which all sorts of spirits and forces are coursing and flashing perpetually. The moment, however, that one tries this method with the Elizabethan woman, one branch of illumination fails; one is held up by the scarcity of facts. One knows nothing detailed, nothing perfectly true and substantial about her. History scarcely mentions her. And I turned to Professor Trevelyan again to see what history meant to him. I found by looking at his chapter headings that it meant—

"The Manor Court and the Methods of Open-field Agriculture . . . The Cistercians and Sheep-farming . . . The Crusades . . . The University . . . The House of Commons . . . The Hundred Years' War . . . The Wars of the Roses . . . The Renaissance Scholars . . . The Dissolution of the Monasteries . . . Agrarian and Religious Strife . . . The Origin of English Seapower . . . The Armada . . ." and so on. Occasionally an individual woman is mentioned, an Elizabeth, or a Mary; a queen or a great lady. But by no possible means could middle-class women with nothing but brains and character at their command have taken part in any one of the great movements which, brought together, constitute the historian's view of the past. Nor shall we find her in any collection of anecdotes. Aubrey hardly mentions her.[3] She never writes her own life and scarcely keeps a diary; there are only a handful of her letters in existence. She left no plays or poems by which we can judge her . . . Here am I asking why women did not write poetry in the Elizabethan age, and I am not sure how they were educated; whether they were taught to write; whether they had sitting-rooms to themselves; how many women had children before they were twenty-one; what, in short, they did from eight in the morning till eight at night. They had no money evidently, according to Professor Trevelyan they were married whether they liked it or not before they were out of the nursery, at fifteen or sixteen very likely. It would have been extremely odd, even upon this showing, had one of them suddenly written the plays of Shakespeare, I concluded, and I thought of that old gentleman, who is dead now, but was a bishop, I think, who declared that it was impossible for any woman, past, present, or to come, to have the genius of Shakespeare. He wrote to the papers about it. He also told a lady who applied to him for information that cats do not as a matter of fact go to heaven, though they have, he added, souls of a sort. How much thinking those old gentlemen used to save one! How the borders of ignorance shrank back at their approach! Cats do not go to heaven. Women cannot write the plays of Shakespeare.

Be that as it may, I could not help thinking, as I looked at the works of Shakespeare on the shelf, that the bishop was right at least in this; it would

[3] John Aubrey (1626–1697), author of *Brief Lives,* a biographical work.

have been impossible, completely and entirely, for any woman to have written the plays of Shakespeare in the age of Shakespeare. Let me imagine, since facts are so hard to come by, what would have happened had Shakespeare had a wonderfully gifted sister, called Judith, let us say. Shakespeare himself went, very probably—his mother was an heiress—to the grammar school, where he may have learnt Latin—Ovid, Virgil and Horace—and the elements of grammar and logic. He was, it is well known, a wild boy who poached rabbits, perhaps shot a deer, and had, rather sooner than he should have done, to marry a woman in the neighbourhood, who bore him a child rather quicker than was right. That escapade sent him to seek his fortune in London. He had, it seemed, a taste for the theatre; he began by holding horses at the stage door. Very soon he got work in the theatre, became a successful actor, and lived in the hub of the universe, meeting everybody, knowing everybody, practising his art on the boards, exercising his wits in the streets, and even getting access to the palace of the queen. Meanwhile his extraordinarily gifted sister, let us suppose, remained at home. She was as adventurous, as imaginative, as agog to see the world as he was. But she was not sent to school. She had no chance of learning grammar and logic, let alone of reading Horace and Virgil. She picked up a book now and then, one of her brother's perhaps, and read a few pages. But then her parents came in and told her to mend the stockings or mind the stew and not moon about with books and papers. They would have spoken sharply but kindly, for they were substantial people who knew the conditions of life for a woman and loved their daughter—indeed, more likely than not she was the apple of her father's eye. Perhaps she scribbled some pages up in an apple loft on the sly, but was careful to hide them or set fire to them. Soon, however, before she was out of her teens, she was to be betrothed to the son of a neighbouring wool-stapler. She cried out that marriage was hateful to her, and for that she was severely beaten by her father. Then he ceased to scold her. He begged her instead not to hurt him, not to shame him in this matter of her marriage. He would give her a chain of beads or a fine petticoat, he said; and there were tears in his eyes. How could she disobey him? How could she break his heart? The force of her own gift alone drove her to it. She made up a small parcel of her belongings, let herself down by a rope one summer's night and took the road to London. She was not seventeen. The birds that sang in the hedge were not more musical than she was. She had the quickest fancy, a gift like her brother's, for the tune of words. Like him, she had a taste for the theatre. She stood at the stage door; she wanted to act, she said. Men laughed in her face. The manager—a fat, loose-lipped man—guffawed. He bellowed something about poodles dancing and women acting—no woman, he said, could possibly be an actress.[4] He hinted—you can imagine what. She could get no training in her craft. Could she even seek her dinner in a tavern or roam the streets at midnight? Yet her genius was for

---

[4] In Shakespeare's day, women's roles were played by males.

fiction and lusted to feed abundantly upon the lives of men and women and the study of their ways. At last—for she was very young, oddly like Shakespeare the poet in her face, with the same grey eyes and rounded brows—at last Nick Greene the actor-manager took pity on her; she found herself with child by that gentleman and so—who shall measure the heat and violence of the poet's heart when caught and tangled in a woman's body?—killed herself one winter's night and lies buried at some cross-roads where the omnibuses now stop outside the Elephant and Castle.[5]

That, more or less, is how the story would run, I think, if a woman in Shakespeare's day had had Shakespeare's genius. But for my part, I agree with the deceased bishop, if such he was—it is unthinkable that any woman in Shakespeare's day should have had Shakespeare's genius. For genius like Shakespeare's is not born among labouring, uneducated, servile people. It was not born in England among the Saxons and the Britons. It is not born today among the working classes. How, then, could it have been born among women whose work began, according to Professor Trevelyan, almost before they were out of the nursery, who were forced to it by their parents and held to it by all the power of law and custom? Yet genius of a sort must have existed among women as it must have existed among the working classes. Now and again an Emily Brontë or a Robert Burns blazes out and proves its presence.[6] But certainly it never got itself on to paper. When, however, one reads of a witch being ducked, of a woman possessed by devils, of a wise woman selling herbs, or even of a very remarkable man who had a mother, then I think we are on the track of a lost novelist, a suppressed poet, of some mute and inglorious[7] Jane Austen, some Emily Brontë who dashed her brains out on the moor or moped and mowed about the highways crazed with the torture that her gift had put her to. Indeed, I would venture to guess that Anon, who wrote so many poems without signing them, was often a woman. It was a woman Edward Fitzgerald,[8] I think, suggested who made the ballads and the folk-songs, crooning them to her children, beguiling her spinning with them, or the length of the winter's night.

This may be true or it may be false—who can say?—but what is true in it, so it seemed to me, reviewing the story of Shakespeare's sister as I had made it, is that any woman born with a great gift in the sixteenth century would certainly have gone crazed, shot herself, or ended her days in some lonely cottage outside the village, half witch, half wizard, feared and mocked at. For it needs little skill in psychology to be sure that a highly gifted girl who had tried to use her gift for poetry would have been so thwarted and hindered by other people, so tortured and pulled asunder by her own contrary instincts, that she must have lost her health and sanity to a certainty. No girl could have walked to London

[5] A tavern.

[6] Emily Brontë (1818–1848), English novelist, and Robert Burns (1759–1796), Scottish poet.

[7] Thomas Gray's description in "Elegy Written in a Country Churchyard" of a peasant whose underdeveloped poetic genius might be as powerful as the great John Milton's.

[8] Edward FitzGerald (1809–1883), translator and poet.

and stood at a stage door and forced her way into the presence of actor-managers without doing herself a violence and suffering an anguish which may have been irrational—for chastity may be a fetish invented by certain societies for unknown reasons—but were none the less inevitable. Chastity had then, it has even now, a religious importance in a woman's life, and has so wrapped itself round with nerves and instincts that to cut it free and bring it to the light of day demands courage of the rarest. To have lived a free life in London in the sixteenth century would have meant for a woman who was poet and playwright a nervous stress and dilemma which might well have killed her. Had she survived, whatever she had written would have been twisted and deformed, issuing from a strained and morbid imagination. And undoubtedly, I thought, looking at the shelf where there are no plays by women, her work would have gone unsigned. That refuge she would have sought certainly. It was the relic of the sense of chastity that dictated anonymity to women even so late as the nineteenth century. Currer Bell, George Eliot, George Sand,[9] all the victims of inner strife as their writings prove, sought ineffectively to veil themselves by using the name of a man. Thus they did homage to the convention, which if not implanted by the other sex was liberally encouraged by them (the chief glory of a woman is not to be talked of, said Pericles,[10] himself a much-talked-of man), that publicity in women is detestable. . . .

That woman, then, who was born with a gift of poetry in the sixteenth cen-   10
tury, was an unhappy woman, a woman at strife against herself. All the conditions of her life, all her own instincts, were hostile to the state of mind which is needed to set free whatever is in the brain. But what is the state of mind that is most propitious to the act of creation, I asked? Can one come by any notion of the state that furthers and makes possible that strange activity? Here I opened the volume containing the Tragedies of Shakespeare. What was Shakespeare's state of mind, for instance, when he wrote *Lear* and *Antony and Cleopatra*? It was certainly the state of mind most favourable to poetry that there has ever existed. But Shakespeare himself said nothing about it. We only know casually and by chance that he "never blotted a line."[11] Nothing indeed was ever said by the artist himself about his state of mind until the eighteenth century perhaps. Rousseau[12] perhaps began it. At any rate, by the nineteenth century self-consciousness had developed so far that it was the habit for men of letters to describe their minds in confessions and autobiographies. Their lives also were written, and their letters were printed after their deaths. Thus, though we do not know what Shakespeare went through when he wrote *Lear,* we do know what Carlyle went through when he wrote the *French Revolution;* what

---

[9] The pseudonyms of Charlotte Brontë (1816–1855) and Mary Ann Evans (1819–1880), English novelists, and Amandine-Aurore-Lucie Dupin (1804–1876), French novelist.

[10] Pericles (ca. 495–429 B.C.), Athenian statesman and general.

[11] According to Ben Jonson, Shakespeare's contemporary.

[12] Jean-Jacques Rousseau (1712–1778), French philosopher, author of *The Confessions of Jean-Jacques Rousseau.*

Flaubert went through when he wrote *Madame Bovary;* what Keats was going through when he tried to write poetry against the coming of death and the indifference of the world.

And one gathers from this enormous modern literature of confession and self-analysis that to write a work of genius is almost always a feat of prodigious difficulty. Everything is against the likelihood that it will come from the writer's mind whole and entire. Generally material circumstances are against it. Dogs will bark; people will interrupt; money must be made; health will break down. Further, accentuating all these difficulties and making them harder to bear is the world's notorious indifference. It does not ask people to write poems and novels and histories; it does not need them. It does not care whether Flaubert finds the right word or whether Carlyle scrupulously verifies this or that fact. Naturally, it will not pay for what it does not want. And so the writer, Keats, Flaubert, Carlyle, suffers, especially in the creative years of youth, every form of distraction and discouragement. A curse, a cry of agony, rises from those books of analysis and confession. "Mighty poets in their misery dead"[13]—that is the burden of their song. If anything comes through in spite of this, it is a miracle, and probably no book is born entire and uncrippled as it was conceived.

But for women, I thought, looking at the empty shelves, these difficulties were infinitely more formidable. In the first place, to have a room of her own, let alone a quiet room or a sound-proof room, was out of the question, unless her parents were exceptionally rich or very noble, even up to the beginning of the nineteenth century. Since her pin money, which depended on the good will of her father, was only enough to keep her clothed, she was debarred from such alleviations as came even to Keats or Tennyson or Carlyle, all poor men, from a walking tour, a little journey to France, from the separate lodging which, even if it were miserable enough, sheltered them from the claims and tyrannies of their families. Such material difficulties were formidable; but much worse were the immaterial. The indifference of the world which Keats and Flaubert and other men of genius have found so hard to bear was in her case not indifference but hostility. The world did not say to her as it said to them, Write if you choose; it makes no difference to me. The world said with a guffaw, Write? What's the good of your writing? . . .

I told you in the course of this paper that Shakespeare had a sister; but do not look for her in Sir Sidney Lee's life of the poet. She died young—alas, she never wrote a word. She lies buried where the omnibuses now stop, opposite the Elephant and Castle. Now my belief is that this poet who never wrote a word and was buried at the cross-roads still lives. She lives in you and me, and in many other women who are not here tonight, for they are washing up the dishes and putting the children to bed. But she lives; for great poets do not die;

---

[13] From William Wordsworth's poem "Resolution and Independence."

they are continuing presences; they need only the opportunity to walk among us in the flesh. This opportunity, as I think, it is now coming within your power to give her. For my belief is that if we live another century or so—I am talking of the common life which is the real life and not of the little separate lives which we live as individuals—and have five hundred a year each of us and rooms of our own; if we have the habit of freedom and the courage to write exactly what we think; if we escape a little from the common sitting-room and see human beings not always in their relation to each other but in relation to reality; and the sky, too, and the trees or whatever it may be in themselves; if we look past Milton's bogey, for no human being should shut out the view; if we face the fact, for it is a fact, that there is no arm to cling to, but that we go alone and that our relation is to the world of reality and not only to the world of men and women, then the opportunity will come and the dead poet who was Shakespeare's sister will put on the body which she has so often laid down. Drawing her life from the lives of the unknown who were her forerunners, as her brother did before her, she will be born. As for her coming without that preparation, without that effort on our part, without that determination that when she is born again she shall find it possible to live and write her poetry, that we cannot expect, for that would be impossible. But I maintain that she would come if we worked for her, and that so to work, even in poverty and obscurity, is worth while.

FOR ANALYSIS

1. How does Woolf explain the contrast between the women of fact and women as they have been portrayed in fiction?

2. What answers do historians provide to the "perennial puzzle" Woolf mentions in the first sentence of paragraph 2? What generalizations might we make about the meaning of "history" on the basis of Woolf's research into the status of women?

3. Analyze the effect of Woolf's concluding remarks about the bishop (para. 6): "Cats do not go to heaven. Women cannot write the plays of Shakespeare." Then consider her later comment (para. 8), "I agree with the deceased bishop, if such he was—it is unthinkable that any woman in Shakespeare's day should have had Shakespeare's genius." Does this contradict what she has been saying?

4. Explain the link Woolf makes between chastity and the problem of the gifted woman writer (para. 9).

5. In what ways does the first part of Woolf's essay prepare the reader to accept her imagined life of Shakespeare's sister?

MAKING CONNECTIONS

1. Among the women who "have burnt like beacons" (para. 3) in the works of great male writers, Woolf cites Desdemona in Shakespeare's *Othello* (p. 958). Do you agree with her assessment? Might Woolf have included Nora in Ibsen's *A Doll's House* (p. 440) and Mama in Hansberry's *A Raisin in the Sun* (p. 695)? Explain.

2. What do you think Woolf would think of Mrs. Peters and Mrs. Hale in Glaspell's *Trifles* (p. 1050) and Calixta in Kate Chopin's "The Storm" (p. 805)?

WRITING TOPICS

1. Do you believe that our culture has changed so significantly in its attitudes toward women that Woolf's arguments have lost their relevance? Write an essay explaining why or why not.

2. Speculate on why, while being as economically dependent on men as servants were throughout much of Western history, women were sometimes portrayed in fiction as being "as great as a man, some think even greater" (para. 3).

ZORA NEALE HURSTON (1891–1960)

HOW IT FEELS TO BE
COLORED ME 1928

I am colored but I offer nothing in the way of extenuating circumstances
except the fact that I am the only Negro in the United States whose grandfather on the mother's side was *not* an Indian chief.

I remember the very day that I became colored. Up to my thirteenth year I
lived in the little Negro town of Eatonville, Florida. It is exclusively a colored
town. The only white people I knew passed through the town going to or coming from Orlando. The native whites rode dusty horses, the Northern tourists
chugged down the sandy village road in automobiles. The town knew the
Southerners and never stopped cane chewing when they passed. But the
Northerners were something else again. They were peered at cautiously from
behind the curtains by the timid. The more venturesome would come out on
the porch to watch them go past and got just as much pleasure out of the
tourists as the tourists got out of the village.

The front porch might seem a daring place for the rest of the town, but it
was a gallery seat for me. My favorite place was atop the gate-post. Proscenium
box[1] for a born first-nighter. Not only did I enjoy the show, but I didn't mind
the actors knowing that I liked it. I usually spoke to them in passing. I'd wave at
them and when they returned my salute, I would say something like this:
"Howdy-do-well-I-thank-you-where-you-goin'?" Usually automobile or the
horse paused at this, and after a queer exchange of compliments, I would
probably "go a piece of the way" with them, as we say in farthest Florida. If one
of my family happened to come to the front in time to see me, of course negotiations would be rudely broken off. But even so, it is clear that I was the first
"welcome-to-our-state" Floridian, and I hope the Miami Chamber of Com-
merce will please take notice.

During this period, white people differed from colored to me only in that
they rode through town and never lived there. They liked to hear me "speak
pieces" and sing and wanted to see me dance the parse-me-la, and gave me
generously of their small silver for doing these things, which seemed strange to
me for I wanted to do them so much that I needed bribing to stop. Only they
didn't know it. The colored people gave no dimes. They deplored any joyful
tendencies in me, but I was their Zora nevertheless. I belonged to them, to the
nearby hotels, to the county—everybody's Zora.

---

[1] A box seat close to the stage.

But changes came in the family when I was thirteen, and I was sent to school 5 in Jacksonville. I left Eatonville, the town of the oleanders, as Zora. When I disembarked from the river-boat at Jacksonville, she was no more. It seemed that I had suffered a sea change. I was not Zora of Orange County any more, I was now a little colored girl. I found it out in certain ways. In my heart as well as in the mirror, I became a fast brown—warranted not to rub nor run.

But I am not tragically colored. There is no great sorrow dammed up in my soul, nor lurking behind my eyes. I do not mind at all. I do not belong to the sobbing school of Negrohood who hold that nature somehow has given them a lowdown dirty deal and whose feelings are all hurt about it. Even in the helter-skelter skirmish that is my life, I have seen that the world is to the strong regardless of a little pigmentation more or less. No, I do not weep at the world—I am too busy sharpening my oyster knife.

Someone is always at my elbow reminding me that I am the granddaughter of slaves. It fails to register depression with me. Slavery is sixty years in the past. The operation was successful and the patient is doing well, thank you. The terrible struggle that made me an American out of a potential slave said "On the line!" The Reconstruction said "Get set!"; and the generation before said "Go!" I am off to a flying start and I must not halt in the stretch to look behind and weep. Slavery is the price I paid for civilization, and the choice was not with me. It is a bully adventure and worth all that I have paid through my ancestors for it. No one on earth ever had a greater chance for glory. The world to be won and nothing to be lost. It is thrilling to think—to know that for any act of mine, I shall get twice as much praise or twice as much blame. It is quite exciting to hold the center of the national stage, with the spectators not knowing whether to laugh or to weep.

The position of my white neighbor is much more difficult. No brown specter pulls up a chair beside me when I sit down to eat. No dark ghost thrusts its leg against mine in bed. The game of keeping what one has is never so exciting as the game of getting.

I do not always feel colored. Even now I often achieve the unconscious Zora of Eatonville before the Hegira.[2] I feel most colored when I am thrown against a sharp white background.

For instance at Barnard. "Beside the waters of the Hudson" I feel my race. 10 Among the thousand white persons, I am a dark rock surged upon, and overswept, but through it all, I remain myself. When covered by the waters, I am; and the ebb but reveals me again.

Sometimes it is the other way around. A white person is set down in our midst, but the contrast is just as sharp for me. For instance, when I sit in the drafty basement that is The New World Cabaret[3] with a white person, my color

[2] A flight or journey to a better place.
[3] A Harlem nightclub popular in the 1920s.

comes. We enter chatting about any little nothing that we have in common and are seated by the jazz waiters. In the abrupt way that jazz orchestras have, this one plunges into a number. It loses no time in circumlocutions, but gets right down to business. It constricts the thorax and splits the heart with its tempo and narcotic harmonies. This orchestra grows rambunctious, rears on its hind legs and attacks the tonal veil with primitive fury, rending it, clawing it until it breaks through to the jungle beyond. I follow those heathen—follow them exultingly. I dance wildly inside myself; I yell within, I whoop; I shake my assegai[4] above my head, I hurl it true to the mark *yeeeeooww!* I am in the jungle and living in the jungle way. My face is painted red and yellow and my body is painted blue. My pulse is throbbing like a war drum. I want to slaughter some-thing—give pain, give death to what, I do not know. But the piece ends. The men of the orchestra wipe their lips and rest their fingers. I creep back slowly to the veneer we call civilization with the last tone and find the white friend sit-ting motionless in his seat—smoking calmly.

"Good music they have here," he remarks, drumming the table with his fingertips.

Music. The great blobs of purple and red emotion have not touched him. He has only heard what I felt. He is far away and I see him but dimly across the ocean and the continent that have fallen between us. He is so pale with his whiteness then and I am *so* colored.

At certain times I have no race, I am *me*. When I set my hat at a certain angle and saunter down Seventh Avenue, Harlem City, feeling as snooty as the lions in front of the Forty-Second Street Library, for instance. So far as my feelings are concerned, Peggy Hopkins Joyce on the Boule Mich[5] with her gorgeous rai-ment, stately carriage, knees knocking together in a most aristocratic manner, has nothing on me. The cosmic Zora emerges. I belong to no race nor time. I am the eternal feminine with its string of beads.

I have no separate feeling about being an American citizen and colored. I am   15
merely a fragment of the Great Soul that surges within the boundaries. My country, right or wrong.

Sometimes, I feel discriminated against, but it does not make me angry. It merely astonishes me. How *can* any deny themselves the pleasure of my com-pany? It's beyond me.

But in the main, I feel like a brown bag of miscellany propped against a wall. Against a wall in company with other bags, white, red, and yellow. Pour out the contents, and there is discovered a jumble of small things priceless and worth-less. A first-water diamond, an empty spool, bits of broken glass, lengths of string, a key to a door long since crumbled away, a rusty knife-blade, old shoes saved for a road that never was and never will be, a nail bent under the weight

---

[4] An iron-tipped spear used by the Bantu peoples of Africa.
[5] Peggy Hopkins Joyce (1893–1957) was a media icon of her day, celebrated for her beauty and suc-cession of rich husbands. Boule Mich, short for Boulevard St-Michel, is a famous street on the Left Bank in Paris.

of things too heavy for any nail, a dried flower or two still a little fragrant. In your hand is the brown bag. On the ground before you is the jumble it held— so much like the jumble in the bags, could they be emptied, that all might be dumped in a single heap and the bags refilled without altering the content of any greatly. A bit of colored glass more or less would not matter. Perhaps that is how the Great Stuffer of Bags filled them in the first place—who knows?

FOR ANALYSIS

1. Describe the **tone** established in the opening paragraph. Is that tone maintained throughout? Explain.

2. What does Hurston mean by the first sentence of paragraph 6?

3. Describe Hurston's feelings about her African ancestry.

4. What does Hurston mean in paragraph 7 when she says, "Slavery is the price I paid for civilization"?

5. Is Hurston's argument in paragraph 7 convincing? Explain.

6. How do the four sections of the essay relate to one another?

MAKING CONNECTIONS

1. Compare Hurston's feelings about the connection between her racial/cultural identity and who she is with those of Kincaid in "Girl" (p. 117).

2. Compare the meaning of jazz music in this essay with its meaning in Baldwin's "Sonny's Blues" (p. 560).

WRITING TOPICS

1. Describe Hurston's sense of what it means to be black.

2. Write an essay either supporting or taking issue with the validity of Hurston's declaration that "At certain times I have no race, I am *me*" (para. 14).

3. Use the following passage from W. E. B. Du Bois's book *The Souls of Black Folk* (1903) as the basis for an analysis of Hurston's essay.

> It is a peculiar sensation, this double-consciousness, this sense of always looking at one's self through the eyes of others, of measuring one's soul by the tape of a world that looks on in amused contempt and pity. One ever feels his two-ness—an American, a Negro; two souls, two thoughts, two unreconciled strivings; two warring ideals in one dark body, whose dogged strength alone keeps it from being torn asunder.

GEORGE ORWELL   (1903–1950)

SHOOTING AN ELEPHANT   1936

In Moulmein, in lower Burma, I was hated by large numbers of people—the only time in my life that I have been important enough for this to happen to me. I was sub-divisional police officer of the town, and in an aimless, petty kind of way anti-European feeling was very bitter. No one had the guts to raise a riot, but if a European woman went through the bazaars alone somebody would probably spit betel juice over her dress. As a police officer I was an obvious target and was baited whenever it seemed safe to do so. When a nimble Burman tripped me up on the football field and the referee (another Burman) looked the other way, the crowd yelled with hideous laughter. This happened more than once. In the end the sneering yellow faces of young men that met me everywhere, the insults hooted after me when I was at a safe distance, got badly on my nerves. The young Buddhist priests were the worst of all. There were several thousands of them in the town and none of them seemed to have anything to do except stand on street corners and jeer at Europeans.

All this was perplexing and upsetting. For at that time I had already made up my mind that imperialism was an evil thing and the sooner I chucked up my job and got out of it the better. Theoretically—and secretly, of course—I was all for the Burmese and all against their oppressors, the British. As for the job I was doing, I hated it more bitterly than I can perhaps make clear. In a job like that you see the dirty work of Empire at close quarters. The wretched prisoners huddling in the stinking cages of the lock-ups, the grey, cowed faces of the long-term convicts, the scarred buttocks of the men who had been flogged with bamboos—all these oppressed me with an intolerable sense of guilt. But I could get nothing into perspective. I was young and ill-educated and I had had to think out my problems in the utter silence that is imposed on every Englishman in the East. I did not even know that the British Empire is dying, still less did I know that it is a great deal better than the younger empires that are going to supplant it. All I knew was that I was stuck between my hatred of the empire I served and my rage against the evil-spirited little beasts who tried to make my job impossible. With one part of my mind I thought of the British[1] as an unbreakable tyranny, as something clamped down, *in saecula saeculorum*,[2] upon the will of prostrate peoples; with another part I thought that the greatest joy in the world would be to drive a bayonet into a Buddhist priest's guts. Feelings like these are the normal by-products of imperialism; ask any Anglo-Indian official, if you can catch him off duty.

[1] The imperial British government of India and Burma.
[2] For eternity.

788

One day something happened which in a roundabout way was enlightening. It was a tiny incident in itself, but it gave me a better glimpse than I had had before of the real nature of imperialism—the real motive for which despotic governments act. Early one morning the sub-inspector at a police station the other end of the town rang me up on the 'phone and said that an elephant was ravaging the bazaar. Would I please come and do something about it? I did not know what I could do, but I wanted to see what was happening and I got on to a pony and started out. I took my rifle, an old .44 Winchester and much too small to kill an elephant, but I thought the noise might be useful *in terrorem.* Various Burmans stopped me on the way and told me about the elephant's doings. It was not, of course, a wild elephant, but a tame one which had gone "must." It had been chained up, as tame elephants always are when their attack of "must" is due, but on the previous night it had broken its chain and escaped. Its mahout,[3] the only person who could manage it when it was in that state, had set out in pursuit, but had taken the wrong direction and was now twelve hours' journey away, and in the morning the elephant had suddenly reappeared in the town. The Burmese population had no weapons and were quite helpless against it. It had already destroyed somebody's bamboo hut, killed a cow and raided some fruit-stalls and devoured the stock; also it had met the municipal rubbish van and, when the driver jumped out and took to his heels, had turned the van over and inflicted violences upon it.

The Burmese sub-inspector and some Indian constables were waiting for me in the quarter where the elephant had been seen. It was a very poor quarter, a labyrinth of squalid bamboo huts, thatched with palm-leaf, winding all over a steep hillside. I remember that it was a cloudy, stuffy morning at the beginning of the rains. We began questioning the people as to where the elephant had gone and, as usual, failed to get any definite information. That is invariably the case in the East; a story always sounds clear enough at a distance, but the nearer you get to the scene of events the vaguer it becomes. Some of the people said that the elephant had gone in one direction, some said that he had gone in another, some professed not even to have heard of any elephant. I had almost made up my mind that the whole story was a pack of lies, when we heard yells a little distance away. There was a loud, scandalized cry of "Go away, child! Go away this instant!" and an old woman with a switch in her hand came round the corner of a hut, violently shooing away a crowd of naked children. Some more women followed, clicking their tongues and exclaiming; evidently there was something that the children ought not to have seen. I rounded the hut and saw a man's dead body sprawling in the mud. He was an Indian, a black Dravidian coolie, almost naked, and he could not have been dead many minutes. The people said that the elephant had come suddenly upon him round the corner of the hut, caught him with its trunk, put its foot on his back and ground him into the earth. This was the rainy season and the

---

[3] The keeper and driver of an elephant.

ground was soft, and his face had scored a trench a foot deep and a couple of yards long. He was lying on his belly with arms crucified and head sharply twisted to one side. His face was coated with mud, the eyes wide open, the teeth bared and grinning with an expression of unendurable agony. (Never tell me, by the way, that the dead look peaceful. Most of the corpses I have seen look devilish.) The friction of the great beast's foot had stripped the skin from his back as neatly as one skins a rabbit. As soon as I saw the dead man I sent an orderly to a friend's house nearby to borrow an elephant rifle. I had already sent back the pony, not wanting it to go mad with fright and throw me if it smelt the elephant.

The orderly came back in a few minutes with a rifle and five cartridges, and 5 meanwhile some Burmans had arrived and told us that the elephant was in the paddy fields below, only a few hundred yards away. As I started forward practically the whole population of the quarter flocked out of the houses and followed me. They had seen the rifle and were all shouting excitedly that I was going to shoot the elephant. They had not shown much interest in the elephant when he was merely ravaging their homes, but it was different now that he was going to be shot. It was a bit of fun to them, as it would be to an English crowd; besides they wanted the meat. It made me vaguely uneasy. I had no intention of shooting the elephant—I had merely sent for the rifle to defend myself if necessary—and it is always unnerving to have a crowd following you. I marched down the hill, looking and feeling a fool, with the rifle over my shoulders and an ever-growing army of people jostling at my heels. At the bottom, when you got away from the huts, there was a metalled road and beyond that a miry waste of paddy fields a thousand yards across, not yet ploughed but soggy from the first rains and dotted with coarse grass. The elephant was standing eight yards from the road, his left side towards us. He took not the slightest notice of the crowd's approach. He was tearing up branches of grass, beating them against his knees to clean them and stuffing them into his mouth.

I had halted on the road. As soon as I saw the elephant I knew with perfect certainty that I ought not to shoot him. It is a serious matter to shoot a working elephant—it is comparable to destroying a huge and costly piece of machinery—and obviously one ought not to do it if it can possibly be avoided. And at that distance, peacefully eating, the elephant looked no more dangerous than a cow. I thought then and I think now that his attack of "must" was already passing off; in which case he would merely wander harmlessly about until the mahout came back and caught him. Moreover, I did not in the least want to shoot him. I decided that I would watch him for a little while to make sure that he did not turn savage again, and then go home.

But at that moment I glanced round at the crowd that had followed me. It was an immense crowd, two thousand at the least and growing every minute. It blocked the road for a long distance on either side. I looked at the sea of yellow faces above the garish clothes—faces all happy and excited over this bit of fun, all certain that the elephant was going to be shot. They were watching me as they would watch a conjurer about to perform a trick. They did not like me, but with the magical rifle in my hands I was momentarily worth watching. And suddenly I realized that I should have to shoot the elephant after all. The people expected it of me and I had got to do it; I could feel their two thousand wills pressing me forward, irresistibly. And it was at this moment, as I stood there with the rifle in my hands, that I first grasped the hollowness, the futility of the white man's dominion in the East. Here was I, the white man with his gun, standing in front of the unarmed native crowd—seemingly the leading actor of the piece; but in reality I was only an absurd puppet pushed to and fro by the will of those yellow faces behind. I perceived in this moment that when the white man turns tyrant it is his own freedoms that he destroys. He becomes a sort of hollow, posing dummy, the conventionalized figure of a sahib. For it is the condition of his rule that he shall spend his life in trying to impress the "natives," and so in every crisis he has got to do what the "natives" expect of him. He wears a mask, and his face grows to fit it. I had got to shoot the elephant. I had committed myself to doing it when I sent for the rifle. A sahib has got to act like a sahib; he has got to appear resolute, to know his own mind and do definite things. To come all that way, rifle in hand, with two thousand people marching at my heels, and then to trail feebly away, having done nothing—no, that was impossible. The crowd would laugh at me. And my whole life, every white man's life in the East, was one long struggle not to be laughed at.

But I did not want to shoot the elephant. I watched him beating his bunch of grass against his knees, with that preoccupied grandmotherly air that elephants have. It seemed to me that it would be murder to shoot him. At that age I was not squeamish about killing animals, but I had never shot an elephant and never wanted to. (Somehow it always seems worse to kill a *large* animal.) Besides, there was the beast's owner to be considered. Alive, the elephant was worth at least a hundred pounds; dead, he would only be worth the value of his tusks, five pounds, possibly. But I had to act quickly. I turned to some experienced-looking Burmans who had been there when we arrived, and asked them how the elephant had been behaving. They all said the same thing: he took no notice of you if you left him alone, but he might charge if you went too close to him.

It was perfectly clear to me what I ought to do. I ought to walk up to within, say, twenty-five yards of the elephant and test his behavior. If he charged, I could shoot; if he took no notice of me, it would be safe to leave him until the mahout came back. But also I knew that I was going to do no such thing. I was a poor shot with a rifle and the ground was soft mud into which one would sink at every step. If the elephant charged and I missed him, I should have about as much chance as a toad under a steam-roller. But even then I was not thinking particularly of my own skin, only of the watchful yellow faces behind. For at that moment, with the crowd watching me, I was not afraid in the ordinary sense, as I would have been if I had been alone. A white man mustn't be frightened in front of "natives"; and so, in general, he isn't frightened. The sole thought in my mind was that if anything went wrong those two thousand Burmans would see me pursued, caught, trampled on and reduced to a grinning corpse like that Indian up the hill. And if that happened it was quite probable that some of them would laugh. That would never do. There was only one alternative. I shoved the cartridges into the magazine and lay down on the road to get a better aim.

The crowd grew very still, and a deep, low, happy sigh, as of people who see 10 the theatre curtain go up at last, breathed from innumerable throats. They were going to have their bit of fun after all. The rifle was a beautiful German thing with cross-hair sights. I did not then know that in shooting an elephant one would shoot to cut an imaginary bar running from ear-hole to ear-hole. I ought, therefore, as the elephant was sideways on, to have aimed straight at his ear-hole; actually I aimed several inches in front of this, thinking the brain would be further forward.

When I pulled the trigger I did not hear the bang or feel the kick—one never does when a shot goes home—but I heard the devilish roar of glee that went up from the crowd. In that instant, in too short a time, one would have thought, even for the bullet to get there, a mysterious, terrible change had come over the elephant. He neither stirred nor fell, but every line of his body had altered. He looked suddenly stricken, shrunken, immensely old, as though the frightful impact of the bullet had paralysed him without knocking him down. At last, after what seemed a long time—it might have been five seconds, I dare say—he sagged flabbily to his knees. His mouth slobbered. An enormous senility seemed to have settled upon him. One could have imagined him thousands of years old. I fired again into the same spot. At the second shot he did not collapse but climbed with desperate slowness to his feet and stood weakly upright, with legs sagging and head drooping. I fired a third time. That was the shot that did for him. You could see the agony of it jolt his whole body and knock the last remnant of strength from his legs. But in falling he seemed for a moment to rise, for as his hind legs collapsed beneath him he seemed to tower upward like a huge rock toppling, his trunk reaching skywards like a tree. He trumpeted, for the first and only time. And then down he came, his belly towards me, with a crash that seemed to shake the ground even where I lay.

I got up. The Burmans were already racing past me across the mud. It was obvious that the elephant would never rise again, but he was not dead. He was breathing very rhythmically with long rattling gasps, his great mound of a side painfully rising and falling. His mouth was wide open—I could see far down into caverns of pale pink throat. I waited a long time for him to die, but his breathing did not weaken. Finally I fired my two remaining shots into the spot where I thought his heart must be. The thick blood welled out of him like red velvet, but still he did not die. His body did not even jerk when the shots hit him, the tortured breathing continued without a pause. He was dying, very slowly and in great agony, but in some world remote from me where not even a bullet could damage him further. I felt that I had got to put an end to that dreadful noise. It seemed dreadful to see the great beast lying there, powerless to move and yet powerless to die, and not even to be able to finish him. I sent back for my small rifle and poured shot after shot into his heart and down his throat. They seemed to make no impression. The tortured gasps continued as steadily as the ticking of a clock.

In the end I could not stand it any longer and went away. I heard later that it took him half an hour to die. Burmans were bringing dahs[4] and baskets even before I left, and I was told they had stripped his body almost to the bones by the afternoon.

Afterwards, of course, there were endless discussions about the shooting of the elephant. The owner was furious, but he was only an Indian and could do nothing. Besides, legally I had done the right thing, for a mad elephant has to be killed, like a mad dog, if its owner fails to control it. Among the Europeans opinion was divided. The older men said I was right, the younger men said it was a damn shame to shoot an elephant for killing a coolie, because an elephant was worth more than any damn Coringhee coolie. And afterwards I was very glad that the coolie had been killed; it put me legally in the right and it gave me a sufficient pretext for shooting the elephant. I often wondered whether any of the others grasped that I had done it solely to avoid looking a fool.

FOR ANALYSIS

1. Examine carefully paragraphs 11 and 12, in which Orwell describes the death of the elephant. Is the reader meant to take the passage only literally, or can a case be made that the elephant's death is imbued with symbolic meaning? Explain.

2. Orwell tells us repeatedly that his sympathies are with the Burmese. Yet he describes them as "evil-spirited little beasts" (para. 2). Explain this ambivalence.

3. What does the experience described in paragraph 7 teach Orwell?

4. Do you agree with Orwell's rationalization that under the circumstances he had no choice but "to shoot the elephant" (para. 7)?

5. What is your reaction to Orwell's final comment: "I was very glad that the coolie had been killed; it put me legally in the right and it gave me a sufficient pretext for shooting the elephant. I often wondered whether any of the others grasped that I had done it solely to avoid looking a fool"?

6. Midway through the essay (para. 7), Orwell discloses the significance the event had for him. Why does he disclose it then rather than save it for the conclusion?

MAKING CONNECTIONS

1. Compare the techniques and arguments used in this essay to attack imperialism with those used in Swift's "A Modest Proposal" (p. 497).

2. While they are dissimilar in subject matter, this story and Bambara's "The Lesson" (p. 110) culminate in climactic events that change the **protagonists**. Compare those events and their effect on the two protagonists.

---

[4] Knives.

WRITING TOPICS

1. In a brief paragraph, summarize the lesson Orwell learned from his experience.

2. What does Orwell conclude about the position of foreign authorities in a hostile country?

3. Describe a situation in which you were required to behave in an official capacity in a way that contradicted your personal beliefs.

Immigrants often experience a dislocation that is more than geographical, as their cultural environment changes while individual identity lags behind. This position can give immigrant writers a unique vantage point on their new homes. As you read these essays, think about what the experiences of these authors allow them to see. Do they see things in America that native-born Americans may not? Do they see things about the homes they have left that those who stayed behind may not? Do they see themselves differently too?

BHARATI MUKHERJEE   (B. 1940)

TWO WAYS TO BELONG IN AMERICA   1996

This is a tale of two sisters from Calcutta, Mira and Bharati, who have lived in the United States for some thirty-five years, but who find themselves on different sides in the current debate over the status of immigrants.

I am an American citizen and she is not. I am moved that thousands of long-term residents are finally taking the oath of citizenship. She is not.

Mira arrived in Detroit in 1960 to study child psychology and preschool education. I followed her a year later to study creative writing at the University of Iowa. When we left India, we were almost identical in appearance and attitude. We dressed alike, in saris; we expressed identical views on politics, social issues, love, and marriage in the same Calcutta convent-school accent. We would endure our two years in America, secure our degrees, then return to India to marry the grooms of our father's choosing.

Instead, Mira married an Indian student in 1962 who was getting his business administration degree at Wayne State University. They soon acquired the labor certifications necessary for the green card of hassle-free residence and employment.

Mira still lives in Detroit, works in the Southfield, Michigan, school system, and has become nationally recognized for her contributions in the fields of preschool education and parent-teacher relationships. After thirty-six years as a legal immigrant in this country, she clings passionately to her Indian citizenship and hopes to go home to India when she retires.

In Iowa City in 1963, I married a fellow student, an American of Canadian parentage. Because of the accident of his North Dakota birth, I bypassed labor-certification requirements and the race-related "quota" system that favored the applicant's country of origin over his or her merit. I was prepared for (and even welcomed) the emotional strain that came with marrying outside my ethnic community. In thirty-three years of marriage, we have lived in every part of North America. By choosing a husband who was not my father's selection, I was opting for fluidity, self-invention, blue jeans and T-shirts, and renouncing three thousand years (at least) of caste-observant, "pure culture" marriage in the Mukherjee family. My books have often been read as unapologetic (and in some quarters overenthusiastic) texts for cultural and psychological "mongrelization." It's a word I celebrate.

Mira and I have stayed sisterly close by phone. In our regular Sunday morning conversations, we are unguardedly affectionate. I am her only blood relative on this continent. We expect to see each other through the looming crises of aging and ill health without being asked. Long before Vice President Gore's "Citizenship U.S.A." drive, we'd had our polite arguments over the ethics of retaining an overseas citizenship while expecting the permanent protection and economic benefits that come with living and working in America.

Like well-raised sisters, we never said what was really on our minds, but we probably pitied one another. She, for the lack of structure in my life, the erasure of Indianness, the absence of an unvarying daily core. I, for the narrowness of her perspective, her uninvolvement with the mythic depths or the superficial pop culture of this society. But, now, with the scapegoating of "aliens" (documented or illegal) on the increase, and the targeting of long-term legal immigrants like Mira for new scrutiny and new self-consciousness, she and I find ourselves unable to maintain the same polite discretion. We were always unacknowledged adversaries, and we are now, more than ever, sisters.

"I feel used," Mira raged on the phone the other night. "I feel manipulated and discarded. This is such an unfair way to treat a person who was invited to stay and work here because of her talent. My employer went to the I.N.S. and petitioned for the labor certification. For over thirty years, I've invested my creativity and professional skills into the improvement of this country's preschool system. I've obeyed all the rules, I've paid my taxes, I love my work, I love my students, I love the friends I've made. How dare America now change its rules in midstream? If America wants to make new rules curtailing benefits of legal immigrants, they should apply only to immigrants who arrive after those rules are already in place." To my ears, it sounded like the description of a long-enduring, comfortable yet loveless marriage, without risk or recklessness. Have we the right to demand, and to expect, that we be loved? (That, to me, is the subtext of the arguments by immigration advocates.) My sister is an expatriate, professionally generous and creative, socially courteous and gracious, and that's as far as her Americanization can go. She is here to maintain an identity, not to transform it.

I asked her if she would follow the example of others who have decided to 10 become citizens because of the anti-immigration bills in Congress. And here, she surprised me. "If America wants to play the manipulative game, I'll play it too," she snapped. "I'll become a U.S. citizen for now, then change back to Indian when I'm ready to go home. I feel some kind of irrational attachment to India that I don't to America. Until all this hysteria against legal immigrants, I was totally happy. Having my green card meant I could visit any place in the world I wanted to and then come back to a job that's satisfying and that I do very well."

In one family, from two sisters alike as peas in a pod, there could not be a wider divergence of immigrant experience. America spoke to me—I married it—I embraced the demotion from expatriate aristocrat to immigrant nobody, surrendering those thousands of years of "pure culture," the saris, the delightfully accented English. She retained them all. Which of us is the freak?

Mira's voice, I realize, is the voice not just of the immigrant South Asian community but of an immigrant community of the millions who have stayed rooted in one job, one city, one house, one ancestral culture, one cuisine, for the entirety of their productive years. She speaks for greater numbers than I possibly can. Only the fluency of her English and the anger, rather than fear, born of confidence from her education, differentiate her from the seamstresses, the domestics, the technicians, the shop owners, the millions of hardworking but effectively silenced documented immigrants as well as their less fortunate "illegal" brothers and sisters.

Nearly twenty years ago, when I was living in my husband's ancestral homeland of Canada, I was always well employed but never allowed to feel part of the local Quebec or larger Canadian society. Then, through a Green Paper that invited a national referendum on the unwanted side effects of "nontraditional" immigration, the government officially turned against its immigrant communities, particularly those from South Asia.

I felt then the same sense of betrayal that Mira feels now.

I will never forget the pain of that sudden turning, and the casual racist outbursts the Green Paper elicited. That sense of betrayal had its desired effect and drove me, and thousands like me, from the country.   15

Mira and I differ, however, in the ways in which we hope to interact with the country that we have chosen to live in. She is happier to live in America as expatriate Indian than as an immigrant American. I need to feel like a part of the community I have adopted (as I tried to feel in Canada as well). I need to put roots down, to vote and make the difference that I can. The price that the immigrant willingly pays, and that the exile avoids, is the trauma of self-transformation.

FOR ANALYSIS

1. What does Mukherjee mean by "mongrelization" (para. 6)?

2. What is the "trauma of self-transformation" (para. 16)? Are there traumas felt by those who choose to remain faithful to their original identity?

3. What are Mukherjee's feelings about the culture she left behind? What does she value? To what does she object?

WRITING TOPICS

1. Mukherjee's sister describes her attachment to India as "irrational" (para. 10), yet she maintains it. Does Mukherjee agree with her sister? Is she similarly attached to her nation, only her new one rather than her old one? Do you think feeling a deep connection to a nation and culture is irrational?

2. Immigration is a controversial political issue. Where do you stand on it? Should the United States make it easier or harder for immigrants to enter the country, to gain access to social services, to stay without becoming citizens, or to become citizens?

GARY SHTEYNGART   (B. 1972)

SIXTY-NINE CENTS   2007

When I was fourteen years old, I lost my Russian accent. I could, in theory, walk up to a girl and the words "Oh, hi there" would not sound like *Okht Hyzer*, possibly the name of a Turkish politician. There were three things I wanted to do in my new incarnation: go to Florida, where I understood that our nation's best and brightest had built themselves a sandy, vice-filled paradise; have a girl, preferably native-born, tell me that she liked me in some way; and eat all my meals at McDonald's. I did not have the pleasure of eating at McDonald's often. My parents believed that going to restaurants and buying clothes not sold by weight on Orchard Street were things done only by the very wealthy or the very profligate, maybe those extravagant "welfare queens" we kept hearing about on television. Even my parents, however, as uncritically in love with America as only immigrants can be, could not resist the iconic pull of Florida, the call of the beach and the Mouse.

And so, in the midst of my Hebrew-school winter vacation, two Russian families crammed into a large used sedan and took I-95 down to the Sunshine State. The other family—three members in all—mirrored our own, except that their single offspring was a girl and they were, on the whole, more ample; by contrast, my entire family weighed three hundred pounds. There's a picture of us beneath the monorail at EPCOT Center, each of us trying out a different smile to express the déjà-vu feeling of standing squarely in our new country's greatest attraction, my own megawatt grin that of a turn-of-the-century Jewish peddler scampering after a potential sidewalk sale. The Disney tickets were a freebie, for which we had had to sit through a sales pitch for an Orlando time-share. "You're from Moscow?" the time-share salesman asked, appraising the polyester cut of my father's jib.

"Leningrad."

"Let me guess: mechanical engineer?"

"Yes, mechanical engineer. . . . Eh, please Disney tickets now."   5

The ride over the MacArthur Causeway to Miami Beach was my real naturalization ceremony. I wanted all of it—the palm trees, the yachts bobbing beside the hard-currency mansions, the concrete-and-glass condominiums preening at their own reflections in the azure pool water below, the implicit availability of relations with amoral women. I could see myself on a balcony eating a Big Mac, casually throwing fries over my shoulder into the sea-salted air. But I would have to wait. The hotel reserved by my parents' friends featured army cots instead of beds and a half-foot-long cockroach evolved enough to wave what looked like a fist at us. Scared out of Miami Beach, we decamped for Fort Lauderdale, where a Yugoslav woman sheltered us in a faded motel, beach adjacent and featuring free UHF reception. We always seemed to be at the margins of places: the driveway of the Fontainebleau Hilton, or the glassed-in elevator leading to a rooftop restaurant where we could momentarily peek over the "Please Wait to Be Seated" sign at the endless ocean below, the Old World we had left behind so far and yet deceptively near.

To my parents and their friends, the Yugoslav motel was an unquestioned paradise, a lucky coda to a set of difficult lives. My father lay magnificently beneath the sun in his red-and-black striped imitation Speedo while I stalked down the beach, past baking midwestern girls. "Oh, hi there." The words, perfectly American, not a birthright but an acquisition, perched between my lips, but to walk up to one of those girls and say something so casual required a deep rootedness to the hot sand beneath me, a historical presence thicker than the green card embossed with my thumbprint and freckled face. Back at the motel, the *Star Trek* reruns looped endlessly on Channel 73 or 31 or some other prime number, the washed-out Technicolor planets more familiar to me than our own.

On the drive back to New York, I plugged myself firmly into my Walkman, hoping to forget our vacation. Sometime after the palm trees ran out, somewhere in southern Georgia, we stopped at a McDonald's. I could already taste it: the sixty-nine-cent hamburger. The ketchup, red and decadent, embedded with little flecks of grated onion. The uplift of the pickle slices; the obliterating rush of fresh Coca-Cola; the soda tingle at the back of the throat signifying that the act was complete. I ran into the meat-fumigated coldness of the magical place, the larger Russians following behind me, lugging something big and red. It was a cooler, packed, before we left the motel, by the other mother, the kindly, round-faced equivalent of my own mother. She had prepared a full Russian lunch for us. Soft-boiled eggs wrapped in tinfoil; *vinigret*, the Russian beet salad, overflowing a reused container of sour cream; cold chicken served between crisp white furrows of a *hulka*. "But it's not allowed," I pleaded. "We have to buy the food here."

I felt coldness, not the air-conditioned chill of southern Georgia but the coldness of a body understanding the ramifications of its own demise, the pointlessness of it all. I sat down at a table as far away from my parents and their friends as possible. I watched the spectacle of the newly tanned resident aliens eating their ethnic meal—jowls working, jowls working—the soft-boiled eggs that quivered lightly as they were brought to the mouth; the girl, my coeval, sullen like me but with a hint of pliant equanimity; her parents, dishing out the chunks of beet with plastic spoons; my parents, getting up to use free McDonald's napkins and straws while American motorists with their noisy towheaded children bought themselves the happiest of meals.

My parents laughed at my haughtiness. Sitting there hungry and all alone—what a strange man I was becoming! So unlike them. My pockets were filled with several quarters and dimes, enough for a hamburger and a small Coke. I considered the possibility of redeeming my own dignity, of leaving behind our beet-salad heritage. My parents didn't spend money, because they lived with the idea that disaster was close at hand, that a liver-function test would come back marked with a doctor's urgent scrawl, that they would be fired from their jobs because their English did not suffice. We were all representatives of a shadow society, cowering under a cloud of bad tidings that would never come. The silver coins stayed in my pocket, the anger burrowed and expanded into some future ulcer. I was my parents' son. 10

FOR ANALYSIS

1. To what does the title refer? Why do you think Shteyngart chose this title?

2. What are the two main symbols of "Americanness" in this essay? Why does the author, at fourteen, feel they are unattainable?

3. Which do you think embarrasses the author more: his family's bringing food into a restaurant or the kind of food they bring?

WRITING TOPICS

1. Shteyngart remembers watching *Star Trek* while on vacation and finding the alien worlds more familiar than his own. Write about a time when the world you found yourself in—a new home, school, or other unfamiliar setting—felt like a foreign planet.

2. How are you, as Shteyngart says of himself at the end of his essay, your "parents' son [or daughter]"? In what ways have you been formed by the people who raised you?

MAKING CONNECTIONS

1. Both of these essays are about what Mukherjee calls "the trauma of self-transformation." Does Shteyngart have the same feelings about this process? What are the traumas in "Sixty-Nine Cents"? Is self-transformation possible?

2. Immigration is not just about ways of eating and talking and dressing—about culture—but also about economics. How do class and money figure in each of these essays?

3. Mukherjee laments her sister's "uninvolvement with the mythic depths or the superficial pop culture" of the United States. How do these two essays involve them-selves in these things? On what elements of popular culture do they comment? On what myths?

FURTHER QUESTIONS
FOR THINKING AND WRITING

1. Explain how Woolf's observations in "What If Shakespeare Had Had a Sister?" illuminate Emily's situation in Faulkner's "A Rose for Emily." **Writing Topic:** In an essay, argue for or against the proposition that women have achieved absolute equality in the United States.

2. Cummings's "the Cambridge ladies who live in furnished souls" and Dickinson's "What Soft—Cherubic Creatures—" both address certain culturally determined behavior patterns among women. Describe the behavior depicted in these poems. How do the authors feel about the behavior? What devices reveal the authors' attitudes? **Writing Topic:** Define the social tradition that produced the women in these poems. Either defend that tradition as crucial to the social order, or offer a cultural variation that would give women a different social role.

3. The speakers in Yevtushenko's "I Would Like" and Eliot's "The Love Song of J. Alfred Prufrock" exhibit quite different attitudes about their identities. Describe each speaker's attitude toward his identity, and identify which aspects of the poems define those attitudes. In what sense are the speakers' identities culturally determined? **Writing Topic:** In an imaginative essay, describe each speaker's early life, and suggest what cultural forces shaped him.

4. Some of the works in this section focus on intergenerational tensions within a culture. Compare such tensions among parents and offspring in Walker's "Everyday Use" and Achebe's "Marriage Is a Private Affair."

5. The struggle of women to achieve equality is the subject of many works in this section. **Writing Topic:** Examine some of the feminist works in this section. What, if any, common threads do you find running through them, either in content or in the use of literary devices?

6. Homer in Faulkner's "A Rose for Emily" and Prufrock in Eliot's "The Love Song of J. Alfred Prufrock," are both in some sense, cultural outsiders. **Writing Topic:** Compare their positions in the dominant culture, the resulting conflicts or tensions, and the strategies they employ in dealing with their status.

LOVE AND HATE

Two Lovers, 1630, by Riza 'Abbasi.

Love and death, it is often noted, are the two great themes of literature. Many of the literary works we have placed in the sections "Innocence and Experience," "Conformity and Rebellion," and "Culture and Identity" speak of love and death as well. But in those works, other thematic interests dominate. In this section, we gather a number of works in which love and hate are thematically central.

The rosy conception of love presented in many popular and sentimental stories does not prepare us for the complicated reality we face. We know that the course of true love never runs smoothly, but in those popular stories the obstacles that hinder the lovers are simple and external. If the young lover can land the high-paying job or convince the beloved's parents that he or she is worthy despite social differences, all will be well. But love in life is rarely that simple. The external obstacles may be insuperable, or the obstacles may lie deep within the personality. The major obstacle may well be an individual's difficult and painful effort to understand that he or she has been deceived by an immature or sentimental conception of love.

In this age of psychological awareness, the claims of the flesh are well recognized. But psychology teaches us, as well, to recognize the aggressive aspect of the human condition. The omnipresent selfishness that civilization attempts to check may be aggressively violent as well as lustful. Thus, on one hand, we have the simple eroticism of Kate Chopin's "The Storm" and, on the other, the more complicated, dangerous attraction of Kate Braverman's "Tall Tales from the Mekong Delta." And Matthew Arnold in "Dover Beach" finds love the only refuge from a chaotic world in which "ignorant armies clash by night."

The cliché has it that love and hate are closely related, and much evidence supports this proposition. But why should love and hate, seeming opposites, lie so close together in the emotional lives of men and women? We are all egos, separate from each other. And as separate individuals, we develop elaborate behavior mechanisms that defend us from each other. But the erotic love relationship differs from other relationships in that it may be defined as a rejection of separateness. The common metaphor speaks of two lovers as joining, as merging into one. That surrender of the "me" to join in an "us" leaves lovers uniquely vulnerable to psychic injury. In short, the defenses are down, and the self-esteem of each of the lovers depends importantly on the behavior of the other. If the lover is betrayed by the beloved, the emotional consequences are uniquely disastrous—hence the peculiarly close relationship between passionate hatred and erotic love.

Words like *love* and *hate* are so general that poets rarely use them except as one term in a metaphor designed to project sharply some aspect of emotional life. The simple sexuality in poems such as Andrew Marvell's "To His Coy Mistress" and Christopher Marlowe's "The Passionate Shepherd to His Love" may be juxtaposed with the hatred and violence generated in *Othello* by sexual jealousy or with the quick reprisal of the slighted Barbara Allan. And Sharon Olds's description of lust in "Sex without Love" notes an aspect of love quite overlooked by Robert Burns in "A Red, Red Rose."

Perhaps more than anything, the works in this section celebrate the elemental impulses of men and women that run counter to those rational formulations by which we govern our lives. We pursue Othello's love for Desdemona and Iago's hate for Othello and arrive at an irreducible mystery, for neither Othello's love nor Iago's hate yields satisfactorily to rational explanation. Reason does not tell us why Othello and Desdemona love one another or why Iago hates rather than honors Othello.

Love is an act of faith springing from our deep-seated need to join with another human being not only in physical nakedness but in emotional and spiritual nakedness as well. While hate is a denial of that faith and therefore a retreat into spiritual isolation, love is an attempt to break out of the isolation.

QUESTIONS FOR THINKING AND WRITING

As you read the selections in this section, consider the following questions. You may want to write out your thoughts informally in a journal or notebook as a way of preparing to respond to the selections, or you may wish to make one of these questions the basis for a formal essay.

1. What is love? What is the source of your definition (literature, personal observation, discussions with those you trust)? Have you ever been in love? How did you know? Do you know someone who is in love? How has it changed that person?

2. Have you ever truly hated someone or something? Describe the circumstances, and characterize your hatred.

3. Do you believe that love and hate are closely related? Have you experienced a change from love to hatred, or do you know someone who has? Explain.

4. There are different kinds of love—love of family, of humankind, of a cause. Describe several different kinds of love, and examine your own motives and behavior in different love relationships. Is it possible that certain kinds of love necessarily generate certain hatreds? Explain.

FICTION

KATE CHOPIN   (1851–1904)

THE STORM   1898

I

The leaves were so still that even Bibi thought it was going to rain. Bobinôt, who was accustomed to converse on terms of perfect equality with his little son, called the child's attention to certain sombre clouds that were rolling with sinister intention from the west, accompanied by a sullen, threatening roar. They were at Friedheimer's store and decided to remain there till the storm had passed. They sat within the door on two empty kegs. Bibi was four years old and looked very wise.

"Mama'll be 'fraid, yes," he suggested with blinking eyes.

"She'll shut the house. Maybe she got Sylvie helpin' her this evenin'," Bobinôt responded reassuringly.

"No; she ent got Sylvie. Sylvie was helpin' her yiotiday," piped Bibi.

Bobinôt arose and going across to the counter purchased a can of shrimps, 5 of which Calixta was very fond. Then he returned to his perch on the keg and sat stolidly holding the can of shrimps while the storm burst. It shook the wooden store and seemed to be ripping great furrows in the distant field. Bibi laid his little hand on his father's knee and was not afraid.

II

Calixta, at home, felt no uneasiness for their safety. She sat at a side window sewing furiously on a sewing machine. She was greatly occupied and did not notice the approaching storm. But she felt very warm and often stopped to mop her face on which the perspiration gathered in beads. She unfastened her white sacque at the throat. It began to grow dark, and suddenly realizing the situation she got up hurriedly and went about closing windows and doors.

Out on the small front gallery she had hung Bobinôt's Sunday clothes to air and she hastened out to gather them before the rain fell. As she stepped outside,

Alcée Laballière rode in at the gate. She had not seen him very often since her marriage, and never alone. She stood there with Bobinôt's coat in her hands, and the big rain drops began to fall. Alcée rode his horse under the shelter of a side projection where the chickens had huddled and there were plows and a harrow piled up in the corner.

"May I come and wait on your gallery till the storm is over, Calixta?" he asked.

"Come 'long in, M'sieur Alcée."

His voice and her own startled her as if from a trance, and she seized Bo- 10 binôt's vest. Alcée, mounting to the porch, grabbed the trousers and snatched Bibi's braided jacket that was about to be carried away by a sudden gust of wind. He expressed an intention to remain outside, but it was soon apparent that he might as well have been out in the open: the water beat in upon the boards in driving sheets, and he went inside, closing the door after him. It was even necessary to put something beneath the door to keep the water out.

"My! what a rain! It's good two years since it rain' like that," exclaimed Calixta as she rolled up a piece of bagging and Alcée helped her to thrust it beneath the crack.

She was a little fuller of figure than five years before when she married; but she had lost nothing of her vivacity. Her blue eyes still retained their melting quality; and her yellow hair, dishevelled by the wind and rain, kinked more stubbornly than ever about her ears and temples.

The rain beat upon the low, shingled roof with a force and clatter that threatened to break an entrance and deluge them there. They were in the dining room—the sitting room—the general utility room. Adjoining was her bed room, with Bibi's couch along side her own. The door stood open, and the room with its white, monumental bed, its closed shutters, looked dim and mysterious.

Alcée flung himself into a rocker and Calixta nervously began to gather up from the floor the lengths of a cotton sheet which she had been sewing.

"If this keeps up, *Dieu sait*[1] if the levees goin' to stan' it!" she exclaimed. 15

"What have you got to do with the levees?"

"I got enough to do! An' there's Bobinôt with Bibi out in that storm—if he only didn' left Friedheimer's!"

"Let us hope, Calixta, that Bobinôt's got sense enough to come in out of a cyclone."

She went and stood at the window with a greatly disturbed look on her face. She wiped the frame that was clouded with moisture. It was stiflingly hot. Alcée got up and joined her at the window, looking over her shoulder. The rain was coming down in sheets obscuring the view of far-off cabins and enveloping the distant wood in a gray mist. The playing of the lightning was incessant. A bolt struck a tall chinaberry tree at the edge of the field. It filled all visible space with a blinding glare and the crash seemed to invade the very boards they stood upon.

---

[1] God knows.

Calixta put her hands to her eyes, and with a cry, staggered backward. Alcée's 20 arm encircled her, and for an instant he drew her close and spasmodically to him.

"*Bonté!*"[2] she cried, releasing herself from his encircling arm and retreating from the window, "the house'll go next! If I only knew w'ere Bibi was!" She would not compose herself; she would not be seated. Alcée clasped her shoulders and looked into her face. The contact of her warm, palpitating body when he had unthinkingly drawn her into his arms, had aroused all the old-time infatuation and desire for her flesh.

"Calixta," he said, "don't be frightened. Nothing can happen. The house is too low to be struck, with so many tall trees standing about. There! aren't you going to be quiet? say, aren't you?" He pushed her hair back from her face that was warm and steaming. Her lips were as red and moist as pomegranate seed. Her white neck and a glimpse of her full, firm bosom disturbed him powerfully. As she glanced up at him the fear in her liquid blue eyes had given place to a drowsy gleam that unconsciously betrayed a sensuous desire. He looked down into her eyes and there was nothing for him to do but to gather her lips in a kiss. It reminded him of Assumption.[3]

"Do you remember—in Assumption, Calixta?" he asked in a low voice broken by passion. Oh! she remembered; for in Assumption he had kissed her and kissed and kissed her; until his senses would well nigh fail, and to save her he would resort to a desperate flight. If she was not an immaculate dove in those days, she was still inviolate; a passionate creature whose very defenselessness had made her defense, against which his honor forbade him to prevail. Now—well, now—her lips seemed in a manner free to be tasted, as well as her round, white throat and her whiter breasts.

They did not heed the crashing torrents, and the roar of the elements made her laugh as she lay in his arms. She was a revelation in that dim, mysterious chamber; as white as the couch she lay upon. Her firm, elastic flesh that was knowing for the first time its birthright, was like a creamy lily that the sun invites to contribute its breath and perfume to the undying life of the world.

The generous abundance of her passion, without guile or trickery, was like a 25 white flame which penetrated and found response in depths of his own sensuous nature that had never yet been reached.

When he touched her breasts they gave themselves up in quivering ecstasy, inviting his lips. Her mouth was a fountain of delight. And when he possessed her, they seemed to swoon together at the very borderland of life's mystery.

He stayed cushioned upon her, breathless, dazed, enervated, with his heart beating like a hammer upon her. With one hand she clasped his head, her lips lightly touching his forehead. The other hand stroked with a soothing rhythm his muscular shoulders.

---

[2] An exclamation: Goodness!

[3] A holiday commemorating the ascent of the Virgin Mary to heaven. Assumption is also the name of a Louisiana parish (county) where Calixta and Alcée had a rendezvous in an earlier story.

The growl of the thunder was distant and passing away. The rain beat softly upon the shingles, inviting them to drowsiness and sleep. But they dared not yield.

The rain was over; and the sun was turning the glistening green world into a palace of gems. Calixta, on the gallery, watched Alcée ride away. He turned and smiled at her with a beaming face; and she lifted her pretty chin in the air and laughed aloud.

III

Bobinôt and Bibi, trudging home, stopped without at the cistern to make themselves presentable. 30

"My! Bibi, w'at will yo' mama say! You ought to be ashame'. You oughtn' put on those good pants. Look at 'em! An' that mud on yo' collar! How you got that mud on yo' collar, Bibi? I never saw such a boy!" Bibi was the picture of pathetic resignation. Bobinôt was the embodiment of serious solicitude as he strove to remove from his own person and his son's the signs of their tramp over heavy roads and through wet fields. He scraped the mud off Bibi's bare legs and feet with a stick and carefully removed all traces from his heavy brogans. Then, prepared for the worst—the meeting with an over-scrupulous housewife, they entered cautiously at the back door.

Calixta was preparing supper. She had set the table and was dripping coffee at the hearth. She sprang up as they came in.

"Oh, Bobinôt! You back! My! but I was uneasy. W'ere you been during the rain? An' Bibi? he ain't wet? he ain't hurt?" She had clasped Bibi and was kissing him effusively. Bobinôt's explanations and apologies which he had been composing all along the way, died on his lips as Calixta felt him to see if he were dry, and seemed to express nothing but satisfaction at their safe return.

"I brought you some shrimps, Calixta," offered Bobinôt, hauling the can from his ample side pocket and laying it on the table.

"Shrimps! Oh, Bobinôt! you too good fo' anything!" and she gave him a smacking kiss on the cheek that resounded. "*J'vous réponds*,[4] we'll have a feas' to night! umph-umph!" 35

Bobinôt and Bibi began to relax and enjoy themselves, and when the three seated themselves at table they laughed much and so loud that anyone might have heard them as far away as Laballière's.

IV

Alcée Laballière wrote to his wife, Clarisse, that night. It was a loving letter, full of tender solicitude. He told her not to hurry back, but if she and the babies liked it at Biloxi, to stay a month longer. He was getting on nicely; and though

---

[4] I'm telling you.

he missed them, he was willing to bear the separation a while longer—realizing that their health and pleasure were the first things to be considered.

V

As for Clarisse, she was charmed upon receiving her husband's letter. She and the babies were doing well. The society was agreeable; many of her old friends and acquaintances were at the bay. And the first free breath since her marriage seemed to restore the pleasant liberty of her maiden days. Devoted as she was to her husband, their intimate conjugal life was something which she was more than willing to forego for a while.

So the storm passed and everyone was happy.

FOR ANALYSIS

1. Aside from the child Bibi, there are four characters in this story—two married couples. How did you respond to each of these characters? What are the sources for your reactions?

2. How do the characters in the story feel about themselves? About each other? On what evidence in the story do you base your response?

3. Discuss the title of the story.

4. During the second half of the nineteenth century, certain American writers, including Kate Chopin, evoked a sense of region in their work. What region of the United States provides the **setting** for this story? How do you know?

5. What aspects of this story's **style** contribute to its realism?

MAKING CONNECTIONS

Read this story against Kinnell's "After Making Love We Hear Footsteps" (p. 933). How do the children function in relation to the sex in each work? What does the boy's presence after the act mean in each selection?

WRITING TOPICS

1. Write an essay on modern marriage, using this story to support your analysis.

2. Comment on the story's final line. Is "the storm" literal or symbolic? If everyone is "happy," do you believe they have the right to be? Or is such a question irrelevant? Explain.

ERNEST HEMINGWAY (1899–1961)

HILLS LIKE WHITE ELEPHANTS 1927

The hills across the valley of the Ebro were long and white. On this side there was no shade and no trees and the station was between two lines of rails in the sun. Close against the side of the station there was the warm shadow of the building and a curtain, made of strings of bamboo beads, hung across the open door into the bar, to keep out flies. The American and the girl with him sat at a table in the shade, outside the building. It was very hot and the express from Barcelona would come in forty minutes. It stopped at this junction for two minutes and went on to Madrid.

"What should we drink?" the girl asked. She had taken off her hat and put it on the table.

"It's pretty hot," the man said.

"Let's drink beer."

"*Dos cervezas*," the man said into the curtain.

"Big ones?" a woman asked from the doorway.

"Yes. Two big ones."

The woman brought two glasses of beer and two felt pads. She put the felt pads and the beer glasses on the table and looked at the man and the girl. The girl was looking off at the line of hills. They were white in the sun and the country was brown and dry.

"They look like white elephants," she said.

"I've never seen one," the man drank his beer.

"No, you wouldn't have."

"I might have," the man said. "Just because you say I wouldn't have doesn't prove anything."

The girl looked at the bead curtain. "They've painted something on it," she said. "What does it say?"

"Anis del Toro. It's a drink."

"Could we try it?"

The man called "Listen" through the curtain. The woman came out from the bar.

"Four reales."

"We want two Anis del Toro."

"With water?"

"Do you want it with water?"

"I don't know," the girl said. "Is it good with water?"

"It's all right."

"You want them with water?" asked the woman.

"Yes, with water."

"It tastes like licorice," the girl said and put the glass down.   25

"That's the way with everything."

"Yes," said the girl. "Everything tastes of licorice. Especially all the things you've waited so long for, like absinthe."

"Oh, cut it out."

"You started it," the girl said. "I was being amused. I was having a fine time."

"Well, let's try and have a fine time."   30

"All right. I was trying. I said the mountains looked like white elephants. Wasn't that bright?"

"That was bright."

"I wanted to try this new drink: that's all we do, isn't it—look at things and try new drinks?"

"I guess so."

The girl looked across at the hills.   35

"They're lovely hills," she said. "They don't really look like white elephants. I just meant the coloring of their skin through the trees."

"Should we have another drink?"

"All right."

The warm wind blew the bead curtain against the table.

"The beer's nice and cool," the man said.   40

"It's lovely," the girl said.

"It's really an awfully simple operation, Jig," the man said. "It's not really an operation at all."

The girl looked at the ground the table legs rested on.

"I know you wouldn't mind it, Jig. It's really not anything. It's just to let the air in."

The girl did not say anything.   45

"I'll go with you and I'll stay with you all the time. They just let the air in and then it's all perfectly natural."

"Then what will we do afterward?"

"We'll be fine afterward. Just like we were before."

"What makes you think so?"

"That's the only thing that bothers us. It's the only thing that's made us   50
unhappy."

The girl looked at the bead curtain, put her hand out, and took hold of two of the strings of beads.

"And you think then we'll be all right and be happy."

"I know we will. You don't have to be afraid. I've known lots of people that have done it."

"So have I," said the girl. "And afterward they were all so happy."

"Well," the man said, "if you don't want to you don't have to. I wouldn't have   55
you do it if you didn't want to. But I know it's perfectly simple."

"And you really want to?"

"I think it's the best thing to do. But I don't want you to do it if you don't really want to."

"And if I do it you'll be happy and things will be like they were and you'll love me?"

"I love you now. You know I love you."

"I know. But if I do it, then it will be nice again if I say things are like white 60 elephants, and you'll like it?"

"I'll love it. I love it now but I just can't think about it. You know how I get when I worry."

"If I do it you won't ever worry?"

"I won't worry about that because it's perfectly simple."

"Then I'll do it. Because I don't care about me."

"What do you mean?"   65

"I don't care about me."

"Well, I care about you."

"Oh, yes. But I don't care about me. And I'll do it and then everything will be fine."

"I don't want you to do it if you feel that way."

The girl stood up and walked to the end of the station. Across, on the other 70 side, were fields of grain and trees along the banks of the Ebro. Far away, beyond the river, were mountains. The shadow of a cloud moved across the field of grain and she saw the river through the trees.

"And we could have all this," she said. "And we could have everything and every day we make it more impossible."

"What did you say?"

"I said we could have everything."

"We can have everything."

"No, we can't."

"We can have the whole world."   75

"No, we can't."

"We can go everywhere."

"No, we can't. It isn't ours any more."

"It's ours."

"No, it isn't. And once they take it away, you never get it back."   80

"But they haven't taken it away."

"We'll wait and see."

"Come on back in the shade," he said. "You mustn't feel that way."

"I don't feel any way," the girl said. "I just know things."   85

"I don't want you to do anything that you don't want to do——"

"Nor that isn't good for me," she said. "I know. Could we have another beer?"

"All right. But you've got to realize——"

"I realize," the girl said. "Can't we maybe stop talking?"

They sat down at the table and the girl looked across at the hills on the dry 90 side of the valley and the man looked at her and at the table.

"You've got to realize," he said, "that I don't want you to do it if you don't want to. I'm perfectly willing to go through with it if it means anything to you."

"Doesn't it mean anything to you? We could get along."

"Of course it does. But I don't want anybody but you. I don't want any one else. And I know it's perfectly simple."

"Yes, you know it's perfectly simple."

"It's all right for you to say that, but I do know it."   95

"Would you do something for me now?"

"I'd do anything for you."

"Would you please please please please please please please stop talking?"

He did not say anything but looked at the bags against the wall of the station. There were labels on them from all the hotels where they had spent nights.

"But I don't want you to," he said, "I don't care anything about it."   100

"I'll scream," the girl said.

The woman came out through the curtains with two glasses of beer and put them down on the damp felt pads. "The train comes in five minutes," she said.

"What did she say?" asked the girl.

"That the train is coming in five minutes."

The girl smiled brightly at the woman, to thank her.   105

"I'd better take the bags over to the other side of the station," the man said. She smiled at him.

"All right. Then come back and we'll finish the beer."

He picked up the two heavy bags and carried them around the station to the other tracks. He looked up the tracks but could not see the train. Coming back, he walked through the barroom, where people waiting for the train were drinking. He drank an Anis at the bar and looked at the people. They were all waiting reasonably for the train. He went out through the bead curtain. She was sitting at the table and smiled at him.

"Do you feel better?" he asked.

"I feel fine," she said. "There's nothing wrong with me. I feel fine."   110

FOR ANALYSIS

1. What is a "white elephant"?

2. What do you think the couple is arguing about? Is it more than one thing?

3. How do you think their story will turn out? Is there a happy ending in store for this couple?

MAKING CONNECTIONS

1. Early in the story, the woman says, "that's all we do, isn't it—look at things and try new drinks?" (p. 811). Compare Hemingway's story to one of the poems from "Connecting Poems: Working Mothers" (p. 689) in "Culture and Identity." On the spare evidence Hemingway provides, what about this woman's life—the way she spends her time—shapes who she is and how she deals with the situation at the center of this story? How might one or more of the women in the poems deal with it differently?

2. In Hemingway's story, much of the "business"—what the characters do while they talk—concerns buying drinks. Think about this in light of where they are and why, and compare it to similar food-and-drink related business in Shteyngart's "Sixty-Nine Cents" (p. 798). How does being tourists compare to being immigrants in this regard?

WRITING TOPICS

1. How would you characterize Hemingway's **style**? Focus on what he includes and what he leaves out. What are the effects of his stylistic choices?

2. Much attention is paid in the story to **setting**—to where the main characters are sitting in relation to the things around them. Write an analysis of setting in this story. What might the relations of the characters to their surroundings mean? How might it reinforce certain ideas about their situation?

KATHERINE MIN (B.1959)

COURTING A MONK 1996

When I first saw my husband he was sitting cross-legged under a tree on the quad, his hair as short as peach fuzz, large blue eyes staring upward, the smile on his face so wide and undirected as to seem moronic. I went flying by him every minute or two, guarding man-to-man, or chasing down a pass, and out of the corner of my eye I would see him watching and smiling. What I noticed about him most was his tremendous capacity for stillness. His hands were like still-life objects resting on his knees; his posture was impeccable. He looked so rooted there, like some cheerful, exotic mushroom, that I began to feel awkward in my exertion. Sweat funneled into the valley of my back, cooling and sticking when I stopped, hands on knees, to regain my breath. I tried to stop my gape-mouthed panting, refashioned my ponytail, and wiped my hands on the soft front of my sweatpants.

He was still there two plays later when my team was down by one. Sully stole a pass and flipped to Graham. Graham threw me a long bomb that sailed wide and I leapt for it, sailing with the Frisbee for a moment in a parallel line— floating, flying, reaching—before coming down whap! against the ground. I groaned. I'd taken a tree root in the solar plexus. The wind was knocked out of me. I lay there, the taste of dry leaves in my mouth.

"Sorry, Gina. Lousy pass," Graham said, coming over. "You O.K.?"

"Fine," I gasped, fingering my ribs. "Just let me sit out for a while."

I sat down in the leaves, breathing carefully as I watched them play. The day was growing dark and the Frisbee was hard to see. Everyone was tired and played in a sloppy rhythm of errant throws and dropped passes.

Beside me on the grass crept the guy from under the tree. I had forgotten about him. He crouched shyly next to me, leaves cracking under his feet, and, when I looked up, he whispered, "You were magnificent," and walked away smiling.

I spotted him the next day in the vegetarian dining hall. I was passing through with my plate of veal cordon bleu when I saw him sitting by himself next to the window. He took a pair of wooden chopsticks out of the breast pocket of his shirt and poked halfheartedly at his tofu and wilted mung beans. I sat down across from him and demanded his life story.

It turned out he wanted to be a monk. Not the Chaucerian kind, bald-pated and stout, with a hooded robe, ribald humor, and penchant for wine. Something even more baffling—a Buddhist. He had just returned from a semester in Nepal, studying in a monastery in the Himalayas. His hair was coming back in in soft spikes across his head and he had a watchful manner—not cautious but receptive, waiting.

815

He was from King of Prussia, off the Philadelphia Main Line, and this made me mistrust the depth of his beliefs. I have discovered that a fascination for the East is often a prelude to a pass, a romantic overture set in motion by an "I think Oriental girls are so beautiful," and a viselike grip on the upper thigh. But Micah was different. He understood I was not impressed by his belief, and he did not aim to impress.

"My father was raised Buddhist," I told him. "But he's a scientist now." 10
"Oh," said Micah. "So, he's not spiritual."
"Spirit's insubstantial," I said. "He doesn't hold with intangibility."
"Well, you can't hold atoms in your hand," Micah pointed out.
"Ah," I said, smiling, "but you can count them."

I told Micah my father was a man of science, and this was true. He was a 15 man, also, of silence. Unlike Micah, whose reticence seemed calming, so undisturbed, like a pool of light on still water, my father's silence was like the lid on a pot, sealing off some steaming, inner pressure.

Words were not my father's medium. "Language," my father liked to say, "is an imprecise instrument." (For though he said little, when he hit upon a phrase he liked, he said it many times.) He was fond of Greek letters and numerals set together in intricate equations, symbolizing a certain physical law or experimental hypothesis. He filled yellow legal pads in a strong, vertical hand, writing these beauties down in black, indelible felt-tip pen. I think it was a source of tremendous irritation to him that he could not communicate with other people in so ordered a fashion, that he could not simply draw an equals sign after something he'd said, have them solve for x or y.

That my father's English was not fluent was only part of it. He was not a garrulous man, even in Korean, among visiting relatives, or alone with my mother. And with me, his only child—who could speak neither of his preferred languages, Korean or science—my father had conspicuously little to say. "Pick up this mess," he would tell me, returning from work in the evening. "Homework finished?" he would inquire, raising an eyebrow over his rice bowl as I excused myself to go watch television.

He limited himself to the imperative mood, the realm of injunction and command; the kinds of statement that required no answer, that left no opening for discussion or rejoinder. These communications were my father's verbal equivalent to his neat numerical equations. They were hermetically sealed.

When I went away to college, my father's parting words constituted one of the longest speeches I'd heard him make. Surrounded by station wagons packed with suitcases, crates of books, and study lamps, amid the excited chattering and calling out of students, among the adults with their nervous, parental surveillance of the scene, my father leaned awkwardly forward with his hands in his pockets, looking at me intently. He said, "Study hard. Go to bed early. Do not goof off. And do not let the American boys take advantages."

This was the same campus my father had set foot on twenty years before, 20 when he was a young veteran of the Korean War, with fifty dollars in his pocket and about that many words of English. Stories of his college years constituted family legend and, growing up, I had heard them so often they were as vivid and dreamlike as my own memories. My father in the dorm bathroom over Christmas, vainly trying to hard-boil an egg in a sock by running it under hot water; his triumph in the physics lab where his ability with the new language did not impede him, and where his maturity and keen scientific mind garnered him highest marks and the top physics prize in his senior year—these were events I felt I'd witnessed, like some obscure, envious ghost.

In the shadow of my father's achievements then, on the same campus where he had first bowed his head to a microscope, lost in a chalk-dust mathematical dream, I pursued words, English words. I committed myself to expertise. I studied Shakespeare and Eliot, Hardy and Conrad, Joyce and Lawrence, and Hemingway and Fitzgerald. It was important to get it right, every word, every nuance, to fill in my father's immigrant silences, the gaps he had left for me.

Other gaps he'd left. Staying up late and studying little, I did things my father would have been too shocked to merely disapprove. As for American boys, I heeded my father's advice and did not let them take advantage. Instead I took advantage of them, of their proximity, their good looks, and the amiable way they would fall into bed with you if you gave them the slightest encouragement. I liked the way they moved in proud possession of their bodies, the rough feel of their unshaven cheeks, their shoulders and smooth, hairless chests, the curve of their backs like burnished wood. I liked the way I could look up at them, or down, feeling their shuddering climax like a distant earthquake; I could make it happen, moving in undulant circles from above or below, watching them, holding them, making them happy. I collected boys like baubles, like objects not particularly valued, which you stash away in the back of some drawer. It was the pleasant interchangeability of their bodies I liked. They were all white boys.

Micah refused to have sex with me. It became a matter of intellectual disagreement between us. "Sex saps the will," he said.

"Not necessarily," I argued. "Just reroutes it."

"There are higher forms of union," he said.   25

"Not with your clothes off," I replied.

"Gina," he said, looking at me with kindness, a concern that made me flush with anger. "What need do you have that sex must fill?"

"Fuck you, Micah," I said. "Be a monk, not a psychologist."

He laughed. His laughter was always a surprise to me, like a small disturbance to the universe. I wanted to seduce him, this was true. I considered Micah the only real challenge among an easy field. But more than seduction, I wanted to rattle him, to get under that sense of peace, that inward contentment. No one my age, I reasoned, had the right to such self-possession.

We went for walks in the bird sanctuary, rustling along the paths slowly, dis-   30
cussing Emily Dickinson or maple-syrup-making, but always I brought the subject around.

"What a waste of a life," I said once. "Such indulgence. All that monkly devotion and quest for inner peace. Big deal. It's selfish. Not only is it selfish, it's a cop-out. An escape from this world and its messes."

Micah listened, a narrow smile on his lips, shaking his head regretfully. "You're so wonderfully passionate, Gina, so alive and in the world. I can't make you see. Maybe it is a cop-out, as you say, but Buddhism makes no distinction between the world outside or the world within the monastery. And historically, monks have been in the middle of political protest and persecution. Look at Tibet."

"I was thinking about, ahem, something more basic," I said.

Micah laughed. "Of course," he said. "You don't seem to understand, Gina, Buddhism is all about the renunciation of desire."

I sniffed. "What's wrong with desire? Without desire, you might as well not 35 be alive."

The truth was that I was fascinated by this idea, the renunciation of desire. My life was fueled by longing, by vast and clamorous desires; a striving toward things I did not have and, perhaps, had no hope of having. I could vaguely imagine an end, some point past desiring, of satiety, but I could not fathom the laying down of desire, walking away in full appetite.

"The desire to renounce desire," I said now, "is still desire, isn't it?"

Micah sunk his hands into his pockets and smiled. "It's not," he said, walking ahead of me. "It's a conscious choice."

We came to a pond, sun-dappled in a clearing, bordered by white birch and maples with the bright leaves of mid-autumn. A fluttering of leaves blew from the trees, landing on the water as gently as if they'd been placed. The color of the pond was a deep canvas green; glints of light snapped like sparks above the surface. There was the lyric coo of a mourning dove, the chitter-chitter of late-season insects. Micah's capacity for appreciation was vast. Whether this had anything to do with Buddhism, I didn't know, but watching him stand on the edge of the pond, his head thrown back, his eyes eagerly taking in the light, I felt his peace and also his sense of wonder. He stood motionless for a long time.

I pulled at ferns, weaved their narrow leaves in irregular samplers, braided 40 tendrils together, while Micah sat on a large rock and, taking his chopsticks from his breast pocket, began to tap them lightly against one another in a solemn rhythm.

"Every morning in the monastery," he said, "we woke to the prayer drum. Four o'clock and the sky would be dark and you'd hear the hollow wooden sound—plock, plock, plock—summoning you to meditation." He smiled dreamily. The chopsticks made a somewhat less effectual sound, a sort of ta ta ta. I imagined sunrise across a Himalayan valley—the wisps of pink-tinged cloud on a cold spring morning, the austerity of a monk's chamber.

Micah had his eyes closed, face to the sun. He continued to tap the chopsticks together slowly. He looked singular and new, sitting on that rock, like an advance scout for some new tribe, with his crest of hair and calm, and the attentiveness of his body to his surroundings.

I think it was then I fell in love with him, or, it was in that moment that my longing for him became so great that it was no longer a matter of simple gratification. I needed his response. I understood what desire was then, the disturbance of a perfect moment in anticipation of another.

"Wake-up call," I said. I peeled off my turtleneck and sweater in one clever motion and tossed them at Micah's feet. Micah opened his eyes. I pulled my pants off and my underwear and stood naked. "Plock, plock, who's there?"

Micah did not turn away. He looked at me, his chopsticks poised in the air. 45 He raised one toward me and held it, as though he were an artist with a paintbrush raised for a proportion, or a conductor ready to lead an orchestra. He held the chopstick suspended in the space between us, and it was as though I couldn't move for as long as he held it. His eyes were fathomless blue. My nipples constricted with the cold. Around us leaves fell in shimmering lights to the water, making a soft rustling sound like the rub of stiff fabric. He brought his hand down and I was released. I turned and leapt into the water.

A few nights later I bought a bottle of cheap wine and goaded Micah into drinking it with me. We started out on the steps of the library after it had closed for the night, taking sloppy swigs from a brown paper bag. The lights of the Holyoke range blinked in the distance, across the velvet black of the freshman quad. From there we wandered the campus, sprawling on the tennis courts, bracing a stiff wind from the terrace of the science center, sedately rolling down Memorial Hill like a pair of tumbleweeds.

"J'a know what a koan is?" he asked me, when we were perched at the top of the bleachers behind home plate. We unsteadily contemplated the steep drop off the back side.

"You mean like ice cream?" I said.

"No, a ko-an. In Buddhism."

"Nope." 50

"It's a question that has no answer, sort of like a riddle. You know, like 'What is the sound of one hand clapping?' Or 'What was your face before you were born?'"

"'What was my face before it was born?' That makes no sense."

"Exactly. You're supposed to contemplate the koan until you achieve a greater awareness."

"Of what?"

"Of life, of meaning." 55

"Oh, O.K.," I said. "I've got it." I was facing backwards, the bag with the bottle in both my hands. "How 'bout, 'What's the sound of one cheek farting?'"

He laughed for a long time, then retched off the side of the bleachers. I got him home and put him to bed; his forehead was feverish, his eyes glassy with sickness.

"Sorry," I said. "I'm a bad influence." I kissed him. His lips were hot and slack.

"Don't mind," he murmured, half-asleep.

The next night we slept in the same bed together for the first time. He kept 60
his underwear on and his hands pressed firmly to his sides, like Gandhi among
his young virgins. I was determined to make it difficult for him. I kept brushing my naked body against him, draping a leg across his waist, stroking his narrow chest with my fingertips. He wiggled and pushed away, feigning sleep.
When I woke in the morning, he was gone and the *Ode to Joy* was blasting from
my stereo.

Graham said he missed me. We'd slept together a few times before I met
Micah, enjoying the warm, healthful feeling we got from running or playing
Ultimate, taking a quick sauna, and falling into bed. He was good-looking,
dark and broad, with sinewy arms and a tight chest. He made love to a woman
like he was lifting Nautilus, all grim purpose and timing. It was hard to believe
that had ever been appealing. I told him I was seeing someone else.

"Not the guy with the crew cut?" he said. "The one who looks like a baby seal?"
I shrugged.

Graham looked at me skeptically. "He doesn't seem like your type," he said.

"No," I agreed. "But at least he's not yours." 65

Meanwhile I stepped up my attack. I asked endless questions about Buddhist teaching. Micah talked about *dukkha;* the four noble truths; the five
aggregates of attachment; the noble eightfold path to enlightenment. I listened
dutifully, willing to acknowledge that it all sounded nice, that the goal of perfect awareness and peace seemed worth attaining. While he talked, I stretched
my feet out until my toes touched his thigh; I slid my hand along his back; or
leaned way over so he could see down my loose, barely-buttoned blouse.

"Too bad you aren't Tantric," I said. I'd been doing research.

Micah scoffed. "Hollywood Buddhism," he said, "Heavy breathing and
theatrics."

"They believe in physical desire," I said. "They have sex."

"Buddha believes in physical desire," Micah said. "It's impermanent, that's 70
all. Something to get beyond."

"To get beyond it," I said petulantly, "you have to do it."

Micah sighed. "Gina," he said, "you are beautiful, but I can't. There are a lot
of guys who will."

"A lot of them do."

He smiled a bit sadly. "Well, then . . ."

I leaned down to undo his shoelaces. I tied them together in double knots. 75
"But I want you," I said.

My parents lived thirty miles from campus and my mother frequently asked
me to come home for dinner. I went only once that year, and that was with
Micah. My parents were not the kind of people who enjoyed the company of
strangers. They were insular people who did not like to socialize much or go
out—or anyway, my father was that way, and my mother accommodated herself to his preferences.

My mother had set the table in the dining room with blue linen. There were crystal wine glasses and silver utensils in floral patterns. She had made some dry baked chicken with overcooked peas and carrots—the meal she reserved for when Americans came to dinner. When it came to Korean cooking, my mother was a master. She made fabulous marinated short ribs and sautéed transparent bean noodles with vegetables and beef, pork dumplings and batter-fried shrimp, and cucumber and turnip kimchis which she made herself and fermented in brown earthenware jars. But American cuisine eluded her; it bored her. I think she thought it was meant to be tasteless.

"Just make Korean," I had urged her on the phone. "He'll like that."

My mother was skeptical. "Too spicy," she said. "I know what Americans like."

"Not the chicken dish," I pleaded. "He's a vegetarian." 80

"We'll see," said my mother, conceding nothing.

Micah stared down at his plate. My mother smiled serenely. Micah nodded. He ate a forkful of vegetables, took a bite of bread. His Adam's apple seemed to be doing a lot of work. My father, too, was busy chewing, his Adam's apple moving up and down his throat like the ratchets of a tire jack. No one had said a thing since my father had uncorked the Chardonnay and read to us the description from his well-creased paperback edition of *The New York Times Guide to Wine*.

The sound of silverware scraping on ceramic plates seemed amplified. I was aware of my own prolonged chewing. My father cleared his throat. My mother looked at him expectantly. He coughed.

"Micah studied Buddhism in Nepal," I offered into the silence.

"Oh!" my mother exclaimed. She giggled. 85

My father kept eating. He swallowed exaggeratedly and looked up. "That so?" he said, sounding almost interested.

Micah nodded. "I was only there four months," he said. "Gina tells me you were brought up Buddhist."

My father grunted. "Well, of course," he said, "in Korea in those days, our families were all Buddhist. I do not consider myself a Buddhist now."

Micah and I exchanged a look.

"It's become quite fashionable, I understand," my father went on. "With you 90 American college kids. Buddhism has become fad."

I saw Micah wince.

"I think it is wonderful, Hi Joon," my mother interceded, "for Americans to learn about Asian religion and philosophy. I was a philosophy major in college, Micah. I studied Whitehead, American pragmatism."

My father leaned back in his chair and watched, frowning, while my mother and Micah talked. It was like he was trying to analyze Micah, not as a psychiatrist analyzes—my father held a dim view of psychology—but as a chemist would, breaking him down to his basic elements, the simple chemical formula that would define his makeup.

Micah was talking about the aggregates of matter, sensation, perception, mental formations, and consciousness that comprise being in Buddhist teaching. "It's a different sense of self than in Christian religions," he explained, looking at my mother.

"Nonsense," my father interrupted. "There is no self in Buddhist doctrine..." 95

My mother and I watched helplessly as they launched into discussion. I was surprised that my father seemed to know so much about it, and by how much he was carrying forth. I was surprised also by Micah's deference. He seemed to have lost all his sureness, the walls of his conviction. He kept nodding and conceding to my father certain points that he had rigorously defended to me before. "I guess I don't know as much about it," he said more than once, and "Yes, I see what you mean" several times, with a sickening air of humility.

I turned from my father's glinting, pitiless intelligence, to Micah's respectfulness, his timid manner, and felt a rising irritation I could not place, anger at my father's belligerence, at Micah's backing down, at my own strange motives for having brought them together. Had I really expected them to get along? And yet, my father was concentrating on Micah with such an intensity—almost as though he were a rival—in a way in which he never focused on me.

When the dialogue lapsed, and after we had consumed as much of the food as we deemed polite, my mother took the dishes away and brought in a bowl of rice with kimchi for my father. Micah's eyes lit up. "May I have some of that, too, Mrs, Kim?"

My mother looked doubtful. "Too spicy," she said.

"Oh, I love spicy food," Micah assured her. My mother went to get him a 100 bowl.

"You can use chopsticks?" my mother said, as Micah began eating with them.

"Mom, it's no big deal," I said.

My father looked up from his bowl. Together, my parents watched while Micah ate a large piece of cabbage kimchi.

"Hah!" my father said, suddenly smiling. "Gina doesn't like kimchi," he said. He looked at me. "Gina," he said. "This boy more Korean than you."

"Doesn't take much," I said. 105

My father ignored me. "Gina always want to be American," he told Micah. "Since she was little girl, she want blue eyes, yellow hair." He stabbed a chopstick toward Micah's face. "Like yours."

"If I had hair," said Micah, grinning, rubbing a hand across his head.

My father stared into his bowl. "She doesn't want to be Korean girl. She thinks she can be 100 percent American, but she cannot. She has Korean blood—100 percent. Doesn't matter where you grow up—blood is most important. What is in the blood." He gave Micah a severe look. "You think you can become Buddhist. Same way. But it is not in your blood. You cannot know real Buddha's teaching. You should study Bible."

"God, Dad!" I said. "You sound like a Nazi!"

"Gina!" my mother warned. 110

"You're embarrassing me," I said. "Being rude to my guest. Discussing me as if I wasn't here. You can say what you want, Dad, I'm American whether you like it or not. Blood's got nothing to do with it. It's what's up here." I tapped my finger to my temple.

"It's not Nazi," my father said. "Is fact! What you have here," he pointed to his forehead, "is all from blood, from genetics. You got from me!"

"Heaven help me," I said.

"Gina!" my mother implored.

"Mr. Kim—" Micah began.

"You just like American girl in one thing," my father shouted. "You have no respect for father. In Korea, daughters do not talk back to their parents, is big shame!"

"In Korea, girls are supposed to be submissive doormats for fathers to wipe their feet on!" I shouted back.

"What do you know about Korea? You went there only once when you were six years old."

"It's in my blood," I said. I stood up. "I'm not going to stay here for this. Come on, Micah."

Micah looked at me uncertainly, then turned to my father.

My father was eating again, slowly levering rice to his mouth with his chopsticks. He paused. "She was always this way," he said, seeming to address the table. "So angry. Even as a little girl."

"Mr. Kim," Micah said, "Um, thank you very much. We're . . . I think we're heading out now."

My father chewed ruminatively. "I should never have left Korea," he said quietly, with utter conviction.

"Gina," my mother said. "Sit down. Hi Joon, please!"

"Micah," I said. "You coming?"

We left my father alone at the dining-room table.

"I should have sent you to live with Auntie Soo!" he called after me.

My mother followed us out to the driveway with a Tupperware container of chicken Micah hadn't eaten.

On the way home we stopped for ice cream. Koans, I told Micah. "What is the sound of Swiss chocolate almond melting?" I asked him. "What was the vanilla before it was born?"

Inside the ice-cream parlor the light was too strong, a ticking fluorescence bleaching everything bone-white. Micah leaned down to survey the cardboard barrels of ice cream in their plastic cases. He looked shrunken, subdued. He ordered a scoop of mint chocolate chip and one of black cherry on a sugar cone and ate it with the long, regretful licks of a child who'd spent the last nickel of his allowance. There was a ruefulness to his movements, a sense of apology. He had lost his monklike stillness and seemed suddenly adrift.

The cold of the ice cream gave me a headache, all the blood vessels in my temples seemed strung out and tight. I shivered and the cold was like fury, spreading through me with the chill.

Micah rubbed my back.

"You're hard on your father," he said. "He's not a bad guy."

"Forget it," I said. "Let's go."

We walked from the dorm parking lot in silence. There were lights going on 135
across the quad and music spilling from the windows out into the cool air.
What few stars there were seemed too distant to wage a constant light.

Back in my room, I put on the Rolling Stones at full blast. Mick Jagger's
voice was taunting and cruel. I turned out the lights and lit a red candle.

"O.K., this is going to stop," I said. I felt myself trembling. I pushed Micah
back on the bed. I was furious. He had ruined it for me, the lightness, the skim-
ming quality of my life. It had seemed easy, with the boys, the glib words and
feelings, the simple heat and surface pleasures. It was like the sensation of flying, leaping for the Frisbee and sailing through the air. For a moment you lose
a feeling for gravity, for the consciousness of your own skin or species. For a
moment you are free.

I started to dance, fast, swinging and swaying in front of the bed. I closed my
eyes and twirled wildly, bouncing off the walls like a pinball, stumbling on my
own stockings. I danced so hard the stereo skipped, Jagger forced to stutter in
throaty monosyllables, gulping repetitions. I whirled and circled, threw my
head from side to side until I could feel the baffled blood, brought my hair up
off my neck and held it with both hands.

Micah watched me dance. His body made an inverted-S upon my bed, his
head propped by the pillar of his own arm. The expression on his face was the
same as he'd had talking with my father, that look of deference, of fawn-eyed
yielding. But I could see there was something hidden.

With white-knuckled fingers, I undid the buttons of my sweater and ripped 140
my shirt lifting it off my head. I danced out of my skirt and underthings, kicking them into the corner, danced until the song was over, until I was soaked
with sweat and burning—and then I jumped him.

It was like the taste of food after a day's starvation—unexpectedly strong
and substantial. Micah responded to my fury, met it with his own mysterious
passion; it was like a brawl, a fight, with something at stake that neither of us
wanted to lose. Afterward we sat up in bed and listened to *Ode to Joy* while
Micah, who had a surplus supply of chopsticks lying around the room, did his
Leonard Bernstein impersonation. Later, we went out for a late-night snack to
All-Star Dairy and Micah admitted to me that he was in love.

My father refused to attend the wedding. He liked Micah, but he did not
want me to marry a Caucasian. It became a joke I would tell people. Korean
custom, I said, to give the bride away four months before the ceremony.

Micah became a high-school biology teacher. I am an associate dean of students at the local college. We have two children. When Micah tells the story of
our courtship, he tells it with great self-deprecation and humor. He makes it
sound as though he were crazy to ever consider becoming a monk. "Think of
it," he tells our kids. "Your dad."

Lately I've taken to reading books about Buddhism. Siddhartha Gotama was
thirty-five years old when he sat under the Bodhi-tree on the bank of the river
Neranjara and gained Enlightenment. Sometimes, when I see my husband

looking at me across the breakfast table, or walking toward me from the other side of a room, I catch a look of distress on his face, a blinking confusion, as though he cannot remember who I am. I have happened on him a few times, on a Sunday when he has disappeared from the house, sitting on a bench with the newspaper in his lap staring across the town common, so immersed in his thoughts that he is not roused by my calling of his name.

I remember the first time I saw him, that tremendous stillness he carried, the 145 contentment in his face. I remember how he looked on the rocks by that pond, like a pioneer in a new land, and I wonder if he regrets, as I do, the loss of his implausible faith. Does he miss the sound of the prayer drum, the call to an inner life without the configuration of desire? I think of my father, running a sock under heated water thousands of miles from home, as yet unaware of the daughter he will raise with the same hopeful, determined, and ultimately futile, effort. I remember the way I used to play around with koans, and I wonder, "What is the sound of a life not lived?"

FOR ANALYSIS

1. When Gina first sees Micah, how does she describe him? When does her sense of him change? How does her seeing him in a similar position at the end of the story connect to this earlier sighting?

2. How is sex described in this story? Do the descriptions conform to romantic stereotypes of sex?

3. What might the last line of the story mean? Which life or lives are not lived?

MAKING CONNECTIONS

1. Gina's father believes that genetics, "[w]hat is in the blood" (para. 108), is the only important thing in determining identity. Compare the story's reflections on this proposition and on the immigrant experience, as embodied in Gina's father, to those in Mukherjee's "Two Ways to Belong in America" (p. 795).

2. The setting of "Courting a Monk" is crucial to the story. How does the college experience of Gina and Micah relate to Menand's and Wallace's reflections on college in "Connecting Essays: Advice to Graduates" (p. 278)?

WRITING TOPICS

1. At the end of the story, the narrator seems to reconsider her rejection of her father's spirituality and her steering of her future husband away from his. What do you think of her actions in this story?

2. Graham tells Gina that Micah doesn't seem like her "type" (para. 64). Do you believe that people have "types"? Why or why not? If so, where do types come from—what makes one man like tall blondes and one woman like men with scruffy beards? If not, why do other people believe in types?

DAVID MEANS (B. 1961)

THE SECRET GOLDFISH 2004

He had a weird growth along his dorsal fin, and that gape-mouth grimace you see in older fish. Way too big for his tank, too, having outgrown the standard goldfish age limit. Which is what? About one month? He was six years old—outlandishly old for a fish. One afternoon, Teddy, as he was called then, now just Ted, took notice of the condition of Fish's tank: a wedge of sunlight plunged through the window of his bedroom and struck the water's surface, disappearing. The water was so clotted it had become a solid mass, a putty within which Fish was presumably swimming, or dead. Most likely dead. Where's Fish? Where's Fish? Teddy yelled to his mom. She came into his room, caught sight of the tank, and gave a small yelp. Once again, a fish had been neglected.

Everyone knows the story. The kids beg and plead: Please, please get us a fish (or a dog), we'll feed it, we will, honest, we'll take care of it and you won't have to do a single thing. We'll clean the tank walls with the brush and make sure the filter charcoal is replaced regularly and refill the water when it evaporates. Please, please, we can handle it, we're old enough now, we are, it'll be so much fun, it will, so much fun. But in the end they don't. They dump too much food in no matter how often they're told to be careful, to use just a pinch, and even after they've read biblical-sounding fables about the fish who ate too much and grew too large for its bowl, shattering the sides, they watch gleefully while he consumes like mad, unable to stop. It's fun to watch him eat, to witness the physical manifestation of a fact: the level of Fish's hunger is permanently set too high. In the metaphysics of the fish universe, gluttony is not a sin. The delicate wafers of food fall lightly onto the water, linger on the surface tension, and are broken apart on infinitely eager lips. She overfeeds, too (on the days when she's pretty sure the kids haven't fed him). Her shaking mechanics are sloppy. The light flakes become moist, collude, collect their inertia, and all too often fall out of the can in a large clump. Really, she hasn't neglected the poor fish. *Neglect* seems a word too heavy with submerged intent. Something was bound to slip to the side amid the chaos of the domestic arena. But Fish has sustained himself in terrible conditions. He is the king of all goldfish survivors.

Her own childhood goldfish—named Fred—ended his days in Grayling Pond, a hole near her house in northern Michigan, dug out by the state D.N.R. on a pond-production grant. (Why the Great Lakes state needed more ponds is anyone's guess.) Garnished with a wide band of lily pads, the water a pale yellow, speckled with skeeter-bug ripples, the pond was close to becoming a marsh. Hope you survive, Fred, her father had said as he slopped the fish out of the pail and into the pond. She did not forget the sight of her beloved fish as he slipped from the lip of the bucket and rode the glassine tube of water into the pond. The rest of the summer she imagined his orange form—brilliantly bright and fluorescent against the glimmer of water—in a kind of slow-motion replay. Dumbest animals on earth, she remembered her father adding. Nothing dumber than a carp. Except maybe a catfish, or your goddamn mother.

Not long after that afternoon at Grayling Pond, her father left the house in a fit of rage. Gone for good, her mother said. Thank Christ. Then, a few months later, he was killed in a freak accident, crushed between hunks of ice and the hull of a container ship in Duluth. Superior's slush ice was temperamental that winter, chewing up the coastline, damaging bulkheads. Her father had signed on as one of the men who went down with poles and gave furtive pokes and prods, in the tradition of those Michigan rivermen who had once dislodged logjams with their peaveys and pike poles, standing atop the timber in their spiked boots, sparring with magnificent forces. Accounts varied, but the basic story was that the ice shifted, some kind of crevasse formed, and he slipped in. Then the lake gave a heave and his legs were crushed, clamped in the jaw of God's stupid justice. As she liked to imagine it, he had just enough time to piece together a little prayer asking for forgiveness for being a failure of a father ("Dear Heavenly Father, forgive me for my huge failings as a father to my dear daughter and even more for my gaping failure as a husband to my wife") and for dumping Fred ("and for getting rid of that fish my daughter loved more than me"), and then to watch as the pale winter sun slipped quickly away while the other men urged him to remain calm and told him that he'd be fine and they'd have him out in a minute or so, while knowing for certain that they wouldn't.

Long after her father was gone, she imagined Fred lurking in the lower reaches of Grayling Pond, in the coolest pockets, trying to conserve his energy. Sometimes, when she was cleaning upstairs and dusting Teddy's room, she would pause in the deep, warm, silent heart of a suburban afternoon and watch Fish as he dangled asleep, wide-eyed, unmoving, just fluffing his fins softly on occasion. One time she even tried it herself, standing still, suspended in the dense fluid of an unending array of demanding tasks—cleaning, cooking, washing, grocery shopping, snack getting—while outside the birds chirped and the traffic hissed past on the parkway.

The marriage had fallen apart abruptly. Her husband—who worked in the city as a corporate banker and left the house each morning at dawn with the *Times*, still wrapped in its bright-blue delivery bag, tucked beneath his arm— had betrayed his vows. One evening, he'd arrived home from work with what seemed to be a new face: his teeth were abnormally white. He'd had them bleached in the city. (In retrospect, she saw that his bright teeth were the first hint of his infidelity.) He had found a dentist on Park Avenue. Soon he was coming home late on some nights and not at all on others, under the vague pretense of work obligations. In Japan, he explained, people sleep overnight in town as a sign of their dedication to business; they rent cubicles just wide enough for a body, like coffins, he said, and for days when he did not return she thought of those small compartments and she chose to believe him. (Of course I know about the Japanese, she had said, emphatically.) Then one night she found him in the bathroom with a bar of soap, rubbing it gently against his wedding ring. It's too tight, he said. I'm just trying to loosen it. When others were perplexed by the fact that she had not deduced his infidelity, picked up on the clues, during those fall months, she felt compelled (though she never did) to describe the marriage in all of its long complexity—fifteen years—starting with the honeymoon in Spain: the parador in Chinchón, outside Madrid, that had once been a monastery, standing naked with him at the balcony door in the dusky night air listening to the sounds of the village and the splash of the pool. She had given up her career for the relationship, for the family. She had given up plenty in order to stay home for Teddy's and Annie's formative years, to make sure those brain synapses formed correctly, to be assured that the right connections were fused. (Because studies had made it clear that a kid's success depends on the first few years. It was important to develop the fine motor skills, to have the appropriate hand play, not to mention critical reasoning skills, before the age of four!) So, yes, she guessed the whole decision to give herself over to the domestic job had been an act of free will, but now it felt as though the act itself had been carried out in the conditions of betrayal that would eventually unfold before her.

Fish had come into the family fold in a plastic Baggie of water, bulging dangerously, knotted at the top, with a mate, Sammy, who would end up a floater two days later. Pet Universe had given free goldfish to all the kids on a preschool field trip. In less than a year, Fish had grown too big for his starter bowl and begun to tighten his spiraled laps, restricted in his movements by his gathering bulk and the glass walls of the bowl. Then he graduated to a classic five-gallon bowl, where, in the course of the next few years, he grew, until one afternoon, still deep in what seemed to be a stable domestic situation, with the kids off at school, she went out to Pet Universe and found a large tank and some water-prep drops and a filter unit, one that sat on the rim and produced a sleek, fountainlike curl of water, and some turquoise gravel and a small figurine to keep the fish company: a cartoonish pirate galleon—a combination of Mark Twain riverboat and man-of-war—with an exaggerated bow and an orange plastic paddle wheel that spun around in the tank's currents until it gobbed up and stuck. The figurine, which was meant to please the eyes of children, had that confused mix of design that put commercial viability ahead of the truth. Teddy and Annie hated it. Ultimately, the figure served one purpose. It rearranged the conceptual space of the tank and gave the illusion that Fish now had something to do, something to work around, during his languorous afternoon laps, and she found herself going in to watch him, giving deep philosophical consideration to his actions: Did Fish remember that he had passed that way before? Was he aware of his eternal hell, caught in the tank's glass grip? Or did he feel wondrously free, swimming—for all he knew—in Lake Superior, an abundant, wide field of water, with some glass obstructions here and there? Was he basically free of wants, needs, and everything else? Did he wonder at the food miraculously appearing atop the surface tension, food to be approached with parted lips?

One evening, after observing Fish, when she was at the sink looking out the window at the yard, she saw her husband there, along the south side, holding his phone to his ear and lifting his free hand up and down from his waist in a slight flapping gesture that she knew indicated that he was emotionally agitated.

Shortly after that, the tank began to murk up. Through the dim months of January and February, the filter clotted, the flow stopped, and stringy green silk grew on the lip of the waterfall. The murk thickened. In the center of the darkness, Fish swam in random patterns and became a sad, hopeless entity curled into his plight. He was no longer fooled by his short-term memory into thinking that he was eternally free. Nor was he bored by the repetitive nature of his laps, going around the stupid ship figurine, sinking down into the gravel, picking—typical bottom-feeder—for scraps. Instead, he was lost in the eternal roar of an isotropic universe, flinging himself wildly within the expanding big bang of tank murk. On occasion, he found his way to the light and rubbed his eye against the glass, peering out in a judgmental way. But no one was there to see him. No one seemed available to witness these outward glances. Until the day when Teddy, now just Ted, noticed and said, Mom, Mom, the tank, and she went and cleaned it, but only after she had knocked her knuckle a few times on the glass and seen that he was alive, consumed in the dark but moving and seemingly healthy. Then she felt awe at the fact that life was sustainable even under the most abhorrent conditions. She felt a fleeting connection between this awe and the possibility that God exists. But then she reminded herself that it was only Fish. Just frickin' Fish, she thought. Here I am so weepy and sad, trying to make sense of my horrible situation, that something like this will give me hope. Of course, she was probably also thinking back to that afternoon, watching her father sluice Fred down into the warm waters of the shallow pond in Michigan. Her memory of it was profoundly clear. The vision of the fish itself—pristine and orange—travelling through the water as it spilled from the bucket was exact and perfect.

She set to work scooping out the water with an old Tupperware bowl, replacing it in increments so the chlorine would evaporate, driving to Pet Universe to get another cotton filter, some water-clarifying drops, and a pound sack of activated charcoal nuggets. She disassembled the pump mechanism—a small magnet attached to a ring of plastic that hovered, embraced by a larger magnet. Somehow the larger magnet cooperated with the magnet on the plastic device and used physical laws of some sort to suck the water up and through the filter, where it cascaded over the wide lip and twisted as it approached the surface. It seemed to her as her fingers cleaned the device that it was not only a thing of great simplicity and beauty but also something much deeper, a tool meant to sustain Fish's life and, in turn, his place in the family.

The afternoon was clear, blue-skied, wintry bright—and out the kitchen window she saw the uncut lawn, dark straw brown, matted down in van Gogh swirls, frosted with cold. Past the lawn, the woods, through which she could see the cars moving on the parkway, stood stark and brittle in the direct implications of the winter light. It was a fine scene, embarrassingly suburban, but certainly fine. Back upstairs, she saw Fish swimming jauntily in his new conditions and she was pretty sure that he was delighted, moving with swift strokes from one end of the tank to the other, skirting the figurine professionally, wagging his back fin—what was that called? was it the caudal fin?—fashionably, like a cabaret dancer working her fan. A beautiful tail, unfurling in a windswept motion in the clearing water. When she leaned down for a closer look, it became apparent that the fin was much, much larger than it seemed when it was in action and twining in on itself. When Fish paused, it swayed open beautifully—a fine, healthy, wide carp tail. Along his sides, he had the usual scars of an abused fish, a wound or two, a missing scale, a new, smaller growth of some kind down near his anal fin. But otherwise he seemed big, brutally healthy, still blinking off the shock of the sudden glare.

Then the tank fell back into its murk, got worse, stank up, and became, well, completely, utterly, fantastically murky. Here one might note tangentially: if, as Aristotle claims, poetry is something of graver import than history—partly because of the naturalness of its statements—then Fish was more important than any domestic history, because Fish was poetic, in that he had succumbed to the darkness that had formed around him, and yet he was unwilling to die—or, rather, he *did not* die. He kept himself alive. He kept at it. Somehow he gathered enough oxygen from the water—perhaps by staying directly under the trickle that made its way over the lip of the filter. Of course, by nature he was a bottom-feeder, a mudfish, accustomed to slime and algae and to an environment that, for other fish, would be insufferable. No trout could sustain itself in these conditions. Not even close. A good brookie would've gone belly up long ago. A brookie would want cool pockets of a fast-moving stream, sweet riffles, bubbling swirls, to live a good life. But Fish stood in his cave of slime, graver than the history of the household into which his glass enclave had been placed: Dad packing his suitcases, folding and refolding his trousers and taking his ties off the electric tie rack and carefully folding them inside sheets of tissue, and then taking his shoes and putting each pair, highly glossed oxfords (he was one of the few to make regular use of the shoeshine stand at Grand Central), into cotton drawstring sacks, and then emptying his top dresser drawer, taking his cuff links, his old wallets, and a few other items. All of this stuff, the history of the house, the legal papers signed and sealed and the attendant separation agreement and, of course, the divorce that left her the house—all this historical material was transpiring outside the gist of Fish. He could chart his course and touch each corner of the tank and still not know shit. But he understood something. That much was clear. The world is a mucky mess. It gets clotted up, submerged in its own gunk. End of story.

He brushed softly against the beard of algae that hung from the filter device, worked his way over to the figurine, leaned his flank against her side, and felt the shift of temperature as night fell—Teddy liked to sleep with the window cracked a bit—and the oxygen content increased slightly as the water cooled. During the day, the sun cranked through the window, the tank grew warm, and he didn't move at all, unless someone came into the room and knocked on the tank or the floor, and then he jerked forward slightly before quickly settling down. A few times the downstairs door slammed hard enough to jolt him awake. Or there was a smashing sound from the kitchen. Or voices. "What in the world should we do?" "I would most certainly like this to be amicable, for the sake of the kids." Or a shoe striking the wall in the adjacent master bedroom. At times he felt a kinship with the figurine, as if another carp were there alongside him, waiting, hovering. Other times he felt a slight kinship with the sides of the tank, which touched his gill flaps when he went in search of light. God, if only he knew that he, Fish, was at the very center of the domestic arena, holding court with his own desire to live. He might have died happily right there! But he was not a symbolic fish. He seemed to have no desire to stand as the tragic hero in this drama.

Sent out, told to stay out, the kids were playing together down in the yard so that, inside, the two central figures, Dad and Mom, might have one final talk. The kids were standing by the playhouse—which itself was falling to decrepitude, dark-gray smears of mildew growing on its fake logs—pretending to be a mom and a dad themselves, although they were a bit too old and self-conscious for play-acting. Perhaps they were old enough to know that they were faking it on two levels, regressing to a secondary level of play-acting they'd pretty much rejected but playing Mom and Dad anyway, Teddy saying, I'm gonna call my lawyer if you don't settle with me, and Annie responding, in her high sweet voice, I knew you'd lawyer up on me, I just knew it, and then both kids giggling in that secretive, all-knowing way they have. Overhead, the tree branches were fuzzed with the first buds of spring, but it was still a bit cold, and words hovered in vapor from their mouths and darkness was falling fast over the trees, and beyond the trees the commuter traffic hissed unnoticed.

If you were heading south on the Merritt Parkway on the afternoon of April 3rd, and you happened to look to your right through the trees after Exit 35, you might've seen them, back beyond the old stone piles, the farm fences that no longer held significance except maybe as a reminder of the Robert Frost poem about good fences and good neighbors and all of that: two kids leaning against an old playhouse while the house behind them appeared cozy, warm, and, clearly, expensive. A fleeting tableau without much meaning to the commuting folk aside from the formulaic economics of the matter: near the parkway = reduced value, but an expensive area + buffer of stone walls + old trees + trendiness of area = more value.

There is something romantic and heartening about seeing those homes 15 through the trees from the vantage of the parkway—those safe, confided

Connecticut lives. Inside the house, the secret goldfish is going about his deeply moving predicament, holding his life close to the gills, subdued by the dark but unwilling to relinquish his cellular activities, the Krebs cycle still spinning its carbohydrate breakdown. The secret goldfish draws close to the center of the cosmos. In the black hole of familial carelessness, he awaits the graceful moment when the mother, spurred on by Teddy, will give yet another soft shriek. She'll lean close to the glass and put her eye there to search for Fish. Fish will be there, of course, hiding in the core of the murk near the figurine, playing possum, so that she will, when she sees him, feel the pitiful sinking in her gut—remembering the preschool field trip to Pet Universe—and a sorrow so deep it will send her to her knees to weep. She'll think of the sad little pet funeral she hoped to perform when Fish died (when Fish's sidekick died, Dad flushed him away): a small but deeply meaningful moment in the backyard, with the trowel, digging a shoebox-size hole, putting the fish in, performing a small rite ("Dear Lord, dear Heavenly Father, dear Fish God, God of Fish, in Fish's name we gather here to put our dear fish to rest"), and then placing atop the burial mound a big rock painted with the word FISH. It would be a moment designed to teach the children the ways of loss, and the soft intricacies of seeing something that was once alive now dead, and to clarify that sharp defining difference, to smooth it over a bit, so that they will remember the moment and know, later, recalling it, that she was a good mother, the kind who would hold pet funerals.

But Fish is alive. His big old carp gills clutch and lick every tiny trace of oxygen from the froth of depravity in the inexplicably determinate manner that only animals have. He will have nothing to do with this household. And later that evening, once Dad is gone, they'll hold a small party to celebrate his resurrection, because they had assumed—as was natural in these circumstances—that he was dead, or near enough death to be called dead, having near-death visions, as the dead are wont: that small pinpoint of light at the end of the tunnel and visions of an existence as a fish in some other ethery world, a better world for a fish, with fresh clear water bursting with oxygen and other carp large and small in communal bliss and just enough muck and mud for good pickings. After the celebration, before bedtime, they'll cover the top of the clean tank in plastic wrap and, working together, moving slowly with the unison of pallbearers, being careful not to slosh the water, carry it down the stairs to the family room, where with a soft patter of congratulatory applause they'll present Fish with a new home, right next to the television set.

FOR ANALYSIS

1. What kinds of events or situations are repeated over the years in this story? What connects them?

2. From Fish's survival in a dirty, uncared-for tank, we learn that "life was sustainable even under the most abhorrent conditions" (para. 9). In spite of the **narrator**'s insistence that Fish "was not a symbolic fish" (para. 12), how does this lesson apply more broadly in the story?

3. "The Secret Goldfish" ends with Fish, presumed dead, again being found alive. What does this near-resurrection mean for the story? How does it point to the future?

MAKING CONNECTIONS

1. When the woman in this story leaves behind her career to stay home and raise her children, she describes it as doing "the domestic job" (para. 6). Compare the story in this regard to one or more of the poems in "Connecting Poems: Working Mothers" (p. 689) in "Culture and Identity." How do these works explore the tension many women feel between working outside the home and working inside it?

2. The death of the wife's father early in the story describes him as being "clamped in the jaw of God's stupid justice" (para. 4). What does this choice of wording convey? Compare this description to those of the deaths in O'Connor's "A Good Man Is Hard to Find" (p. 97). What kind of justice is presented in these two stories?

WRITING TOPICS

1. Write a short story or scene from the **point of view** of an animal. What does the use of such a point of view offer a writer? What do animals see that people don't? What might they "think" that people might not?

2. "Fish was more important than any domestic history, because Fish was poetic" (para. 11). How does Means turn the story of a fish—and a woman and her family going through the crumbling of a marriage—into poetry? Reflect on the devices Means uses, the strategies, the use of **point of view** and **imagery** and language, to turn these stories into poetry. As you do this, consider what "poetry"—which you can understand for these purposes as "literature"—is, and what it does.

Z.Z. PACKER (B. 1973)

DRINKING COFFEE ELSEWHERE 2000

Orientation games began the day I arrived at Yale from Baltimore. In my group we played heady, frustrating games for smart people. One game appeared to be charades reinterpreted by existentialists; another involved listening to rocks. Then a freshman counselor made everyone play Trust. The idea was that if you had the faith to fall backward and wait for four scrawny former high-school geniuses to catch you, just before your head cracked on the slate sidewalk, then you might learn to trust your fellow students. Russian roulette sounded like a better game.

"No way," I said. The white boys were waiting for me to fall, holding their arms out for me, sincerely, gallantly. "No fucking way."

"It's all cool, it's all cool," the counselor said. Her hair was a shade of blond I'd seen only on *Playboy* covers, and she raised her hands as though backing away from a growling dog. "Sister," she said, in an I'm-down-with-the-struggle voice, "you don't have to play this game. As a person of color, you shouldn't have to fit into any white, patriarchal system."

I said, "It's a bit too late for that."

In the next game, all I had to do was wait in a circle until it was my turn to 5 say what inanimate object I wanted to be. One guy said he'd like to be a gadfly, like Socrates. "Stop me if I wax Platonic," he said. The girl next to him was eating a rice cake. She wanted to be the Earth, she said. Earth with a capital *E*.

There was one other black person in the circle. He wore an Exeter T-shirt and his overly elastic expressions resembled a series of facial exercises. At the end of each person's turn, he smiled and bobbed his head with unfettered enthusiasm. "Oh, that was good," he said, as if the game were an experiment he'd set up and the results were turning out better than he'd expected. "Good, good, good!"

When it was my turn I said, "My name is Dina, and if I had to be any object, I guess I'd be a revolver." The sunlight dulled as if on cue. Clouds passed rapidly overhead, presaging rain. I don't know why I said it. Until that moment I'd been good in all the ways that were meant to matter. I was an honor-roll student—though I'd learned long ago not to mention it in the part of Baltimore where I lived. Suddenly I was hard-bitten and recalcitrant, the kind of kid who took pleasure in sticking pins into cats; the kind who chased down smart kids to spray them with mace.

"A revolver," a counselor said, stroking his chin, as if it had grown a rabbinical beard. "Could you please elaborate?"

The black guy cocked his head and frowned, as if the beakers and Erlenmeyer flasks of his experiment had grown legs and scurried off.

"You were just kidding," the dean said, "about wiping out all of mankind. 10 That, I suppose, was a joke." She squinted at me. One of her hands curved atop the other to form a pink, freckled molehill on her desk.

"Well," I said, "maybe I meant it at the time." I quickly saw that that was not the answer she wanted. "I don't know. I think it's the architecture."

Through the dimming light of the dean's-office window, I could see the fortress of the old campus. On my ride from the bus station to the campus, I'd barely glimpsed New Haven—a flash of crumpled building here, a trio of straggly kids there. A lot like Baltimore. But everything had changed when we reached those streets hooded by the gothic buildings. I imagined how the college must have looked when it was founded, when most of the students owned slaves. I pictured men wearing tights and knickers, smoking pipes.

"The architecture," the dean repeated. She bit her lip and seemed to be making a calculation of some sort. I noticed that she blinked less often than most people. I sat there, waiting to see how long it would be before she blinked again.

My revolver comment won me a year's worth of psychiatric counseling, weekly meetings with Dean Guest, and—since the parents of the roommate I'd never met weren't too hip on the idea of their Amy sharing a bunk bed with a budding homicidal loony—my very own room.

Shortly after getting my first D, I also received the first knock on my door. 15 The female counselors never knocked. The dean had spoken to them; I was a priority. Every other day, right before dinnertime, they'd look in on me, unannounced. "Just checking up," a counselor would say. It was the voice of a suburban mother in training. By the second week, I had made a point of sitting in a chair in front of the door, just when I expected a counselor to pop her head around. This was intended to startle them. I also made a point of being naked. The unannounced visits ended.

The knocking persisted. Through the peephole I saw a white face, distorted and balloonish.

"Let me in." The person looked like a boy but sounded like a girl. "Let me in," the voice repeated.

"Not a chance," I said.

Then the person began to sob, and I heard a back slump against the door. If I hadn't known the person was white from the peephole, I'd have known it from a display like this. Black people didn't knock on strangers' doors, crying. Not that I understood the black people at Yale. There was something pitiful in how cool they were. Occasionally one would reach out to me with missionary zeal, but I'd rebuff that person with haughty silence.

"I don't have anyone to talk to!" the person on the other side of the door cried. 20

"That is correct."

"When I was a child," the person said, "I played by myself in a corner of the school yard all alone. I hated dolls and I hated games, animals were not friendly and birds flew away. If anyone was looking for me I hid behind a tree and cried out 'I am an orphan—'"

I opened the door. It was a she.

"Plagiarist!" I yelled. She had just recited a Frank O'Hara poem as though she'd thought it up herself. I knew the poem because it was one of the few things I'd been forced to read that I wished I'd written myself.

The girl turned to face me, smiling weakly, as though her triumph were not 25 in getting me to open the door but in the fact that she was able to smile at all when she was so accustomed to crying. She was large but not obese, and crying had turned her face the color of raw chicken. She blew her nose into the waist end of her T-shirt, revealing a pale belly.

"How do you know that poem?"

She sniffed. "I'm in your Contemporary Poetry class."

She was Canadian and her name was Heidi, although she said she wanted people to call her *Henrik*. "That's a guy's name," I said. "What do you want? A sex change?"

She looked at me with so little surprise that I suspected she hadn't discounted this as an option. Then her story came out in teary, hiccup-like bursts. She had sucked some "cute guy's dick" and he'd told everybody and now people thought she was "a slut."

"Why'd you suck his dick? Aren't you a lesbian?" 30

She fit the bill. Short hair, hard, roach-stomping shoes. Dressed like an aspiring plumber. The lesbians I'd seen on TV were wiry, thin strips of muscle, but Heidi was round and soft and had a moonlike face. Drab mud-colored hair. And lesbians had cats. "Do you have a cat?" I asked.

Her eyes turned glossy with new tears. "No," she said, her voice wavering, "and I'm not a lesbian. Are you?"

"Do I look like one?" I said.

She didn't answer.

"O.K." I said. "I could suck a guy's dick, too, if I wanted. But I don't. The 35 human penis is one of the most germ-ridden objects there is." Heidi looked at me, unconvinced. "What I meant to say," I began again, "is that I don't like anybody. Period. Guys or girls. I'm a misanthrope."

"I am, too."

"No," I said, guiding her back through my door and out into the hallway. "You're not."

"Have you had dinner?" she asked. "Let's go to Commons."

I pointed to a pyramid of ramen-noodle packages on my windowsill. "See that? That means I never have to go to Commons. Aside from class, I have contact with no one."

"I hate it here, too," she said. "I should have gone to McGill, eh." 40

"The way to feel better," I said, "is to get some ramen and lock yourself in your room. Everyone will forget about you and that guy's dick and you won't have to see anyone ever again. If anyone looks for you—"

"I'll hide behind a tree."

"A revolver?" Dr. Raeburn said, flipping through a manila folder. He looked up at me as if to ask another question, but he didn't.

Dr. Raeburn was the psychiatrist. He had the gray hair and whiskers of a Civil War general. He was also a chain smoker with beige teeth and a navy wool jacket smeared with ash. He asked about the revolver at the beginning of my first visit. When I was unable to explain myself he smiled, as if this were perfectly respectable.

"Tell me about your parents."   45

I wondered what he already had on file. The folder was thick, though I hadn't said a thing of significance since Day One.

"My father was a dick and my mother seemed to like him."

He patted his pockets for his cigarettes. "That's some heavy stuff," he said. "How do you feel about Dad?" The man couldn't say the word *father*. "Is Dad someone you see often?"

"I hate my father almost as much as I hate the word *Dad*."

He started tapping his cigarette.   50

"You can't smoke in here."

"That's right," he said, and slipped the cigarette back into the packet. He smiled, widening his eyes brightly. "Don't ever start."

I thought that that first encounter would be the last of Heidi, but then her head appeared in a window of Linsly-Chit during my Chaucer class. Next, she swooped down a flight of stairs in Harkness. She hailed me from across Elm Street and found me in the Sterling Library stacks. After one of my meetings with Dr. Raeburn, she was waiting for me outside Health Services, legs crossed, cleaning her fingernails.

"You know," she said, as we walked through Old Campus, "you've got to stop eating ramen. Not only does it lack a single nutrient but it's full of MSG."

"I like eating chemicals," I said. "It keeps the skin radiant."   55

"There's also hepatitis." She already knew how to get my attention—mention a disease.

"You get hepatitis from unwashed lettuce," I said. "If there's anything safe from the perils of the food chain, it's ramen."

"But you refrigerate what you don't eat. Each time you reheat it, you're killing good bacteria, which then can't keep the bad bacteria in check. A guy got sick from reheating Chinese noodles, and his son died from it. I read it in the *Times*." With this, she put a jovial arm around my neck. I continued walking, a little stunned. Then, just as quickly, she dropped her arm and stopped walking. I stopped, too.

"Did you notice that I put my arm around you?"

"Yes," I said. "Next time, I'll have to chop it off."   60

"I don't want you to get sick," she said. "Let's eat at Commons."

In the cold air, her arm had felt good.

The problem with Commons was that it was too big; its ceiling was as high as a cathedral's, but below it there were no awestruck worshippers, only eighteen-year-olds at heavy wooden tables, chatting over veal patties and Jell-O.

We got our food, tacos stuffed with meat substitute, and made our way through the maze of tables. The Koreans had a table. Each singing group had a table. The crew team sat at a long table of its own. We passed the black table. The sheer quantity of Heidi's flesh accentuated just how white she was.

"How you doing, sista?" a guy asked, his voice full of accusation, eyeballing 65 me as though I were clad in a Klansman's sheet and hood. "I guess we won't see you till graduation."

"If," I said, "you graduate."

The remark was not well received. As I walked past, I heard protests, angry and loud, as if they'd discovered a cheat at their poker game. Heidi and I found an unoccupied table along the periphery, which was isolated and dark. We sat down. Heidi prayed over her tacos.

"I thought you didn't believe in God," I said.

"Not in the God depicted in the Judeo-Christian Bible, but I do believe that nature's essence is a spirit that—"

"All right," I said. I had begun to eat, and cubes of diced tomato fell from my 70 mouth when I spoke. "Stop right there. Tacos and spirits don't mix."

"You've always got to be so flip," she said. "I'm going to apply for another friend."

"There's always Mr. Dick," I said. "Slurp, slurp."

"You are so lame. So unbelievably lame. I'm going out with Mr. Dick. Thursday night at Atticus. His name is Keith."

Heidi hadn't mentioned Mr. Dick since the day I'd met her. That was more than a month ago and we'd spent a lot of that time together. I checked for signs that she was lying; her habit of smiling too much, her eyes bright and cheeks full, so that she looked like a chipmunk. But she looked normal. Pleased, even, to see me so flustered.

"You're insane! What are you going to do this time?" I asked. "Sleep with 75 him? Then when he makes fun of you, what? Come pound your head on my door reciting the *Collected Poems of Sylvia Plath*?"

"He's going to apologize for before. And don't call me insane. You're the one going to the psychiatrist."

"Well, I'm not going to suck his dick, that's for sure."

She put her arm around me in mock comfort, but I pushed it off, and ignored her. She touched my shoulder again, and I turned, annoyed, but it wasn't Heidi after all; a sepia-toned boy dressed in khakis and a crisp plaid shirt was standing behind me. He handed me a hot-pink square of paper without a word, then briskly made his way toward the other end of Commons, where the crowds blossomed. Heidi leaned over and read it: "Wear Black Leather—the Less, the Better."

"It's a gay party," I said, crumpling the card. "He thinks we're fucking gay."

Heidi and I signed on to work at the Saybrook Dining Hall as dishwashers. 80 The job consisted of dumping food from plates and trays into a vat of rushing water. It seemed straightforward, but then I learned better. You wouldn't believe what people could do with food until you worked in a dish room. Let-tuce and crackers and soup would be bullied into a pulp in the bowl of some bored anorexic; ziti would be mixed with honey and granola; trays would appear heaped with mashed-potato snow women with melted chocolate ice cream for hair. Frat boys arrived at the dish-room window, en masse. They liked to fill glasses with food, then seal them, airtight, onto their trays. If you tried to prize them off, milk, Worcestershire sauce, peas, chunks of bread vom-ited onto your dish-room uniform.

When this happened one day in the middle of the lunch rush, for what seemed like the hundredth time, I tipped the tray toward one of the frat boys, popping the glasses off so that the mess spurted onto his Shetland sweater.

He looked down at his sweater. "Lesbo bitch!"

"No," I said, "that would be your mother."

Heidi, next to me, clenched my arm in support, but I remained motionless, waiting to see what the frat boy would do. He glared at me for a minute, then walked away.

"Let's take a smoke break," Heidi said.

I didn't smoke, but Heidi had begun to, because she thought it would help her lose weight. As I hefted a stack of glasses through the steamer, she lit up. "Soft packs remind me of you," she said. "Just when you've smoked them all and you think there's none left, there's always one more, hiding in that little crushed corner." Before I could respond she said, "Oh, God. Not another mouse. You know whose job that is."

By the end of the rush, the floor mats got full and slippery with food. This was when mice tended to appear, scurrying over our shoes; more often than not, a mouse got caught in the grating that covered the drains in the floor. Sometimes the mouse was already dead by the time we noticed it. This one was alive.

"No way," I said. "This time you're going to help. Get some gloves and a trash bag."

"That's all I'm getting. I'm not getting that mouse out of there."

"Put on the gloves," I ordered. She winced, but put them on. "Reach down," I said. "At an angle, so you get at its middle. Otherwise, if you try to get it by its tail, the tail will break off."

"This is filthy, eh."

"That's why we're here," I said. "To clean up filth. Eh."

She reached down, but would not touch the mouse. I put my hand around her arm and pushed it till her hand made contact. The cries from the mouse were soft, songlike. "Oh, my God," she said. "Oh, my God, ohmigod." She wres-tled it out of the grating and turned her head away.

"Don't you let it go," I said.

"Where's the food bag? It'll smother itself if I drop it in the food bag. Quick," she said, her head still turned away, her eyes closed. "lead me to it."

"No. We are not going to smother this mouse. We've got to break its neck."

"You're one heartless bitch."

I wondered how to explain that if death is unavoidable it should be quick and painless. My mother had died slowly. At the hospital, they'd said it was kidney failure, but I knew that, in the end, it was my father. He made her scared to live in her own home, until she was finally driven away from it in an ambulance.

"Breaking its neck will save it the pain of smothering," I said. "Breaking its 100 neck is more humane. Take the trash bag and cover it so you won't get any blood on you, then crush."

The loud jets of the steamer had shut off automatically and the dish room grew quiet. Heidi breathed in deeply, then crushed the mouse. She shuddered, disgusted. "Now what?"

"What do you mean, 'now what?' Throw the little bastard in the trash."

At our third session, I told Dr. Raeburn I didn't mind if he smoked. He sat on the sill of his open window, smoking behind a jungle screen of office plants.

We spent the first ten minutes discussing the *Iliad*, and whether or not the text actually states that Achilles had been dipped in the River Styx. He said it did, and I said it didn't. After we'd finished with the *Iliad*, and with my new job in what he called "the scullery," he asked more questions about my parents. I told him nothing. It was none of his business. Instead, I talked about Heidi. I told him about that day in Commons, Heidi's plan to go on a date with Mr. Dick, and the invitation we'd been given to the gay party.

"You seem preoccupied by this soirée." He arched his eyebrows at the word 105 *soirée*.

"Wouldn't you be?"

"Dina," he said slowly, in a way that made my name seem like a song title, "have you ever had a romantic interest?"

"You want to know if I've ever had a boyfriend?" I said. "Just go ahead and ask if I've ever fucked anybody."

This appeared to surprise him. "I think that you are having a crisis of identity," he said.

"Oh, is that what this is?" 110

His profession had taught him not to roll his eyes. Instead, his exasperation revealed itself with a tiny pursing of his lips, as though he'd just tasted something awful and were trying very hard not to offend the cook.

"It doesn't have to be, as you say, someone you've fucked, it doesn't have to be a boyfriend," he said.

"Well, what are you trying to say? If it's not a boy, then you're saying it's a girl—"

"Calm down. It could be a crush, Dina." He lit one cigarette off another. "A crush on a male teacher, a crush on a dog, for heaven's sake. An interest. Not necessarily a relationship."

It was sacrifice time. If I could spend the next half hour talking about some 115 boy, then I'd have given him what he wanted.

So I told him about the boy with the nice shoes.

I was sixteen and had spent the last few coins in my pocket on bus fare to buy groceries. I didn't like going to the Super Fresh two blocks away from my house, plunking government food stamps into the hands of the cashiers.

"There she go reading," one of them once said, even though I was only carrying a book. "Don't your eyes get tired?"

On Greenmount Avenue you could read schoolbooks—that was understandable. The government and your teachers forced you to read them. But anything else was antisocial. It meant you'd rather submit to the words of some white dude than shoot the breeze with your neighbors.

I hated those cashiers, and I hated them seeing me with food stamps, so I took the bus and shopped elsewhere. That day, I got off the bus at Govans, and though the neighborhood was black like my own—hair salon after hair salon of airbrushed signs promising arabesque hair styles and inch-long fingernails—the houses were neat and orderly, nothing at all like Greenmount, where every other house had at least one shattered window. The store was well swept, and people quietly checked long grocery lists—no screaming kids, no loud cashier-customer altercations. I got the groceries and left the store. 120

I decided to walk back. It was a fall day, and I walked for blocks. Then I sensed someone following me. I walked more quickly, my arms around the sack, the leafy lettuce tickling my nose. I didn't want to hold the sack so close that it would break the eggs or squash the hamburger buns, but it was slipping, and as I looked behind a boy my age, maybe older, rushed toward me.

"Let me help you," he said.

"That's all right." I set the bag on the sidewalk. Maybe I saw his face, maybe it was handsome enough, but what I noticed first, splayed on either side of the bag, were his shoes. They were nice shoes, real leather, a stitched design like a widow's peak on each one, or like birds' wings, and for the first time in my life I understood what people meant when they said "wing tip shoes."

"I watched you carry them groceries out that store, then you look around, like you're lost, but like you liked being lost, then you walk down the sidewalk for blocks and blocks. Rearranging that bag, it almost gone to slip, then hefting it back up again."

"Huh, huh," I said. 125

"And then I passed my own house and was still following you. And then your bag really look like it was gone crash and everything. So I just thought I'd help." He sucked in his bottom lip, as if to keep it from making a smile. "What's your name?" When I told him, he said, "Dina, my name is Cecil." Then he said, "D comes right after C."

"Yes," I said, "it does, doesn't it."

Then, half question, half statement, he said, "I could carry your groceries for you? And walk you home?"

I stopped the story there. Dr. Raeburn kept looking at me. "Then what happened?"

I couldn't tell him the rest: that I had not wanted the boy to walk me home, that I didn't want someone with such nice shoes to see where I lived. 130

Dr. Raeburn would only have pitied me if I'd told him that I ran down the sidewalk after I told the boy no, that I fell, the bag slipped, and the eggs cracked, their yolks running all over the lettuce. Clear amniotic fluid coated the can of cinnamon rolls. I left the bag there on the sidewalk, the groceries spilled out randomly like cards loosed from a deck. When I returned home, I told my mother that I'd lost the food stamps.

"Lost?" she said. I'd expected her to get angry, I'd wanted her to get angry, but she hadn't. "Lost?" she repeated. Why had I been so clumsy and nervous around a harmless boy? I could have brought the groceries home and washed off the egg yolk, but, instead, I'd just left them there. "Come on," mama said, snuffing her tears, pulling my arm, trying to get me to join her and start yanking cushions off the couch. "We'll find enough change here. We got to get something for dinner before your father gets back."

We'd already searched the couch for money the previous week, and I knew there'd be nothing now, but I began to push my fingers into the couch's boniest corners, pretending that it was only a matter of time before I'd find some change or a lost watch or an earring. Something pawnable, perhaps.

"What happened next?" Dr. Raeburn asked again. "Did you let the boy walk you home?"

"My house was far, so we went to his house instead." Though I was sure Dr. Raeburn knew that I was making this part up, I continued. "We made out on his sofa. He kissed me."

Dr. Raeburn lit his next cigarette like a detective. Cool, suspicious. "How did it feel?"

"You know," I said. "Like a kiss feels. It felt nice. The kiss felt very, very nice."

Raeburn smiled gently, though he seemed unconvinced. When he called time on our session his cigarette had become one long pole of ash. I left his office, walking quickly down the corridor, afraid to look back. It would be like him to trot after me, his navy blazer flapping, just to eke the truth out of me. *You never kissed anyone.* The words slid from my brain, and knotted in my stomach.

When I reached my dorm, I found an old record player blocking my door and a Charles Mingus LP propped beside it. I carried them inside and then, lying on the floor, I played the Mingus over and over again until I fell asleep. I slept feeling as though Dr. Raeburn had attached electrodes to my head, willing into my mind a dream about my mother. I saw the lemon meringue of her skin, the long bone of her arm as she reached down to clip her toenails. I'd come home from a school trip to an aquarium, and I was explaining the differences between baleen and sperm whales according to the size of their heads, the range of their habitats, their feeding patterns.

I awoke remembering the expression on her face after I'd finished my dizzying whale lecture. She looked like a tourist who'd asked for directions to a place she thought was simple enough to get to only to hear a series of hypothetical turns, alleys, one-way streets. Her response was to nod politely at the perilous elaborateness of it all; to nod in the knowledge that she would never be able to get where she wanted to go.

The dishwashers always closed down the dining hall. One night, after every-one else had punched out, Heidi and I took a break, and though I wasn't a smoker, we set two milk crates upside down on the floor and smoked ciga-rettes.

The dishwashing machines were off, but steam still rose from them like a jungle mist. Outside in the winter air, students were singing carols in their groomed and tailored singing-group voices. The Whiffenpoofs were back in New Haven after a tour around the world, and I guess their return was a huge deal. Heidi and I craned our necks to watch the year's first snow through an open window.

"What are you going to do when you're finished?" Heidi asked. Sexy ques-tion marks of smoke drifted up to the windows before vanishing.

"Take a bath."

She swatted me with her free hand. "No, silly. Three years from now. When 145 you leave Yale."

"I don't know. Open up a library. Somewhere where no one comes in for books. A library in a desert."

She looked at me as though she'd expected this sort of answer and didn't know why she'd asked in the first place.

"What are you going to do?" I asked her.

"Open up a psych clinic. In a desert. And my only patient will be some wacko who runs a library."

"Ha," I said. "Whatever you do, don't work in a dish room ever again. You're 150 no good." I got up from the crate. "C'mon. Let's hose the place down."

We put out our cigarettes on the floor, since it was our job to clean it, any-way. We held squirt guns in one hand and used the other to douse the floors with the standard-issue, eye-burning cleaning solution. We hosed the dish room, the kitchen, the serving line, sending the water and crud and suds into the drains. Then we hosed them again so the solution wouldn't eat holes in our shoes as we left. Then I had an idea. I unbuckled my belt.

"What the hell are you doing?" Heidi said.

"Listen, it's too cold to go outside with our uniforms all wet. We could just take a shower right here. There's nobody but us."

"What the fuck, eh?"

I let my pants drop, then took off my shirt and panties. I didn't wear a bra, 155 since I didn't have much to fill one. I took off my shoes and hung my clothes on the stepladder.

"You've flipped," Heidi said. "I mean, really, psych-ward flipped."

I soaped up with the liquid hand soap until I felt as glazed as a ham. "Stand back and spray me."

"Oh, my God," she said. I didn't know whether she was confused or delighted, but she picked up the squirt gun and sprayed me. She was laughing. Then she got too close and the water started to sting.

"God damn it!" I said. "That hurt!"

"I was wondering what it would take to make you say that." 160

When all the soap had been rinsed off, I put on my regular clothes and said, "O.K. You're up next."

"No way," she said.

"Yes way."

She started to take off her uniform shirt, then stopped.

"What?" 165

"I'm too fat."

"You goddam right." She always said she was fat. One time, I'd told her that she should shut up about it, that large black women wore their fat like mink coats. "You're big as a house," I said now. "Frozen yogurt may be low in calories but not if you eat five tubs of it. Take your clothes off. I want to get out of here."

She began taking off her uniform, then stood there, hands cupped over her breasts, crouching at the pubic bone.

"Open up," I said, "or we'll never get done."

Her hands remained where they were. I threw the bottle of liquid soap at 170 her, and she had to catch it, revealing herself as she did.

I turned on the squirt gun, and she stood there, stiff, arms at her sides, eyes closed, as though awaiting mummification. I began with the water on low, and she turned around in a full circle, hesitantly, letting the droplets from the spray fall on her as if she were submitting to a death by stoning.

When I increased the water pressure, she slipped and fell on the sudsy floor. She stood up and then slipped again. This time she laughed and remained on the floor, rolling around on it as I sprayed.

I think I began to love Heidi that night in the dish room, but who is to say that I hadn't begun to love her the first time I met her? I sprayed her and sprayed her, and she turned over and over like a large beautiful dolphin, lolling about in the sun.

Heidi started sleeping at my place. Sometimes she slept on the floor; sometimes we slept sardinelike, my feet at her head, until she complained that my feet were "taunting" her. When we finally slept head to head, she said, "Much better." She was so close I could smell her toothpaste. "I like your hair," she told me, touching it through the darkness. "You should wear it out more often."

"White people always say that about black people's hair. The worse it looks, 175 the more they say they like it."

I'd expected her to disagree, but she kept touching my hair, her hands passing through it till my scalp tingled. When she began to touch the hair around the edge of my face, I felt myself quake. Her fingertips stopped for a moment, as if checking my pulse, then resumed.

"I like how it feels right here. See, mine just starts with the same old texture as the rest of my hair." She found my hand under the blanket and brought it to her hairline. "See," she said.

It was dark. As I touched her hair, it seemed as though I could smell it, too. Not a shampoo smell. Something richer, murkier. A bit dead, but sweet, like the decaying wood of a ship. She guided my hand.

"I see," I said. The record she'd given me was playing in my mind, and I kept trying to shut it off. I could also hear my mother saying that this is what happens when you've been around white people: things get weird. So weird I could hear the stylus etching its way into the flat vinyl of the record. "Listen," I said finally, when the bass and saxes started up. I heard Heidi breathe deeply, but she said nothing.

We spent the winter and some of the spring in my room—never hers— 180 missing tests, listening to music, looking out my window to comment on people who wouldn't have given us a second thought. We read books related to none of our classes. I got riled up by *The Autobiography of Malcolm X* and *The Chomsky Reader*; Heidi read aloud passages from *The Anxiety of Influence*. We guiltily read mysteries and *Clan of the Cave Bear*, then immediately threw them away. Once, we looked up from our books at exactly the same moment, as though trapped at a dinner table with nothing to say. A pleasant trap of silence.

Then one weekend I went back to Baltimore. When I returned, to a sleepy, tree-scented spring, a group of students were holding what was called "Coming Out Day." I watched it from my room.

The MC was the sepia boy who'd invited us to that party months back. His speech was strident but still smooth, and peppered with jokes. There was a speech about AIDS, with lots of statistics: nothing that seemed to make "coming out" worth it. Then the women spoke. One girl pronounced herself "out" as casually as if she'd announced the time. Another said nothing at all: she appeared at the microphone accompanied by a woman who began cutting off her waist-length, bleached-blond hair. The woman doing the cutting tossed the shorn hair in every direction as she cut. People were clapping and cheering and catching the locks of hair.

And then there was Heidi. She was proud that she liked girls, she said when she reached the microphone. She loved them, wanted to sleep with them. She was a dyke, she said repeatedly, stabbing her finger to her chest in case anyone was unsure to whom she was referring. She could not have seen me. I was across the street, three stories up. And yet, when everyone clapped for her, she seemed to be looking straight at me.

Heidi knocked. "Let me in." It was like the first time I met her. The tears, the raw pink of her face.

We hadn't spoken in weeks. Outside, pink-and-white blossoms hung from 185 the Old Campus trees. Students played hackeysack in T-shirts and shorts. Though I was the one who'd broken away after she went up to that podium, I still half expected her to poke her head out a window in Linsly-Chit, or tap on my back in Harkness, or even join me in the Commons dining hall, where I'd asked for my dish-room shift to be transferred. She did none of these.

"Well," I said, "what is it?"

She looked at me. "My mother," she said.

She continued to cry, but it seemed to have grown so silent in my room I wondered if I could hear the numbers change on my digital clock.

"When my parents were getting divorced," she said, "my mother bought a car. A used one. An El Dorado. It was filthy. It looked like a huge crushed can coming up the street. She kept trying to clean it out. I mean—"

I nodded and tried to think what to say in the pause she left behind. Finally I 190 said, "We had one of those," though I was sure ours was an Impala.

She looked at me, eyes steely from trying not to cry. "Anyway, she'd drive me around in it and although she didn't like me to eat in it, I always did. One day, I was eating cantaloupe slices, spitting the seeds on the floor. Maybe a month later, I saw this little sprout, growing right up from the car floor. I just started laughing and she kept saying what, what? I was laughing and then I saw she was so—"

She didn't finish. So what? So sad? So awful? Heidi looked at me with what seemed to be a renewed vigor. "We could have gotten a better car, eh?"

"It's all right. It's not a big deal," I said.

Of course, that was the wrong thing to say. And I really didn't mean it to sound the way it had come out.

I told Dr. Raeburn about Heidi's mother having cancer and how I'd said it 195 wasn't a big deal, though I'd wanted to say exactly the opposite. I meant that I knew what it was like to have a parent die. My mother had died. I knew how eventually one accustoms oneself to the physical world's lack of sympathy: the buses that still run on time, the kids who still play in the street, the clocks that won't stop ticking for the person who's gone.

"You're pretending," Dr. Raeburn said, not sage or professional but a little shocked by the discovery, as if I'd been trying to hide a pack of his cigarettes behind my back.

"I'm pretending?" I shook my head. "All those years of psych grad," I said. "And to tell me *that*?"

"You construct stories about yourself and dish them out—one for you, one for you—" here he reenacted the process, showing me handing out lies as if they were apples.

"Pretending. I believe the professional name for it might be denial," I said. "Are you calling me gay?"

He pursed his lips noncommittally. "No, Dina. I don't think you're gay." 200

I checked his eyes. I couldn't read them.

"No. Not at all," he said, sounding as if he were telling a subtle joke. "But maybe you'll finally understand."

"Understand what?"

"That constantly saying what one doesn't mean accustoms the mouth to meaningless phrases." His eyes narrowed. "Maybe you'll understand that when you need to express something truly significant, your mouth will revert to the insignificant nonsense it knows so well." He looked at me, his hands sputtering in the air in a gesture of defeat. "Who knows?" he asked, with a glib, psychiatric smile I'd never seen before. "Maybe it's your survival mechanism. Black living in a white world."

I heard him, but only vaguely. I'd hooked on to that one word, *pretending*. What Dr. Raeburn would never understand was that pretending was what had got me this far. I remembered the morning of my mother's funeral. I'd been given milk to settle my stomach; I'd pretended it was coffee. I imagined I was drinking coffee elsewhere. Some Arabic-speaking country where the thick coffee served in little cups was so strong it could keep you awake for days. Some Arabic country where I'd sit in a tented café and be more than happy to don a veil.

Heidi wanted me to go with her to the funeral. She'd sent this message through the dean. "We'll pay for your ticket to Vancouver," the dean said.

"What about my ticket back?" I asked. "Maybe the shrink will pay for that."

The dean looked at me as though I were an insect she'd like to squash. "We'll pay for the whole thing. We might even pay for some lessons in manners."

So I packed my suitcase and walked from my suicide-single dorm to Heidi's room. A thin wispy girl in ragged cutoffs and a shirt that read "LSBN!" answered the door. A group of short-haired girls in thick black leather jackets, bundled up despite the summer heat, encircled Heidi in a protective fairy ring. They looked at me critically, clearly wondering if Heidi was too fragile for my company.

"You've got our numbers," one said, holding onto Heidi's shoulder. "And Vancouver's got a great gay community."

"Oh God," I said. "She's going to a funeral, not a 'Save the Dykes' rally."

One of the girls stepped in front of me.

"It's O.K., Cynthia," Heidi said. Then she ushered me into her bedroom and closed the door. A suitcase was on her bed, half packed. She folded a polka-dotted T-shirt that was wrong for any occasion. "Why haven't you talked to me?" she said. "Why haven't you talked to me in two months?"

"I don't know," I said.

"You don't know," she said, each syllable seeped in sarcasm. "You don't know. Well, I know. You thought I was going to try to sleep with you."

"Try to? We slept together all winter!"

"Smelling your feet is not 'sleeping together.' You've got a lot to learn." She seemed thinner and meaner.

"So tell me," I said. "What can you show me that I need to learn?" But as soon as I said it I somehow knew that she still hadn't slept with anyone.

"Am I supposed to come over there and sweep your enraged self into my arms?" I said. "Like in the movies? Is this the part where we're both so mad we kiss each other?"

She shook her head and smiled weakly. "You don't get it," she said. "My mother is dead." She closed her suitcase, clicking shut the old-fashioned locks. "My mother is dead," she said again, this time reminding herself. She set the suitcase upright on the floor and sat on it. She looked like someone waiting for a train.

"Fine," I said. "And she's going to be dead for a long time." Though it sounded stupid, I felt good saying it. As though I had my own locks to click shut.

Heidi went to Vancouver for her mother's funeral. I didn't go. Instead, I went back to Baltimore and moved in with an aunt I barely knew. Every day was the same: I read and smoked outside my aunt's apartment, studying the row of hair salons across the street, where girls in denim cutoffs and tank tops would troop in and come out hours later, a flash of neon nails, coifs the color and sheen of patent leather. And every day I imagined visiting Heidi in Vancouver. Her house would not be large, but it would be clean. Flowery shrubs would line the walks. The Canadian wind would whip us about like pennants. I'd be visiting her at some vague time in the future, deliberately vague, for people like me, who realign past events to suit themselves. In that future time, you always have a chance to catch the groceries before they fall, your words can always be rewound and erased, rewritten and revised.

But once I imagined Heidi visiting me. There would be no psychiatrists or deans. No boys with nice shoes or flip cashiers. Just me in my single room. She would knock on the door and say, "Open up."

FOR ANALYSIS

1. Dina's psychiatrist tells her he thinks she's having a "crisis of identity" (para. 109). Is she? What is the crisis? Is there more than one—that is, more than one identity or aspect of herself with which she is struggling?

2. Why are "orientation games" (para. 1) a fitting beginning for this story?

3. Why do you think Packer ends the story with the **narrator** imagining Heidi knocking on her door and saying, "Open up" (para. 223)?

MAKING CONNECTIONS

1. The relationship between love and sex is an endlessly fraught subject. Compare "Drinking Coffee Elsewhere" to Min's "Courting a Monk" (p. 815) in this regard. Does love equal sex? Is it possible to have one without the other? Are both necessary?

2. In this story, the **narrator** reflects on past actions and wishes her words could be "rewound and erased, rewritten and revised" (para. 222). Compare Packer's story to Lethem's "Super Goat Man" (p. 382). How do Packer's and Lethem's narrators think about the past? How do their stories connect individual past to identity—that is, where they come from and what they do to who they become?

WRITING TOPICS

1. The **narrator** says her mother "would never be able to get where she wanted to go" (para. 140). While college can be a place to discover who you are, even to experiment with different possible selves, it can also be a place that enables you to improve your economic condition. Reflect on the ways in which this story is about social class.

2. Dina and Heidi struggle to come to grips with their sexual orientations. The results of their struggles—whether they accept who they are and are comfortable in a world that does not always concur—are not known at story's end. Write a short sequel to "Drinking Coffee Elsewhere" in which Heidi and Dina meet up later in life. How have they turned out? How have their struggles turned out?

PERCEPTUAL THINKING CO

CONNECTING STORIES:
DANGEROUS SEDUCERS

Both stories in this unit are about dangerous men and the women (or girls) who love them. The reasons for their attraction—the deep-rooted or hidden motivations for risking so much to be with men so obviously dangerous—come out in a variety of ways. As you read, watch for the revelation of these reasons, but also pay attention to the way the writers use point of view to let readers in on the way the protagonists see these men. How they make what seem to be obviously bad choices plausible is part of their magic.

JOYCE CAROL OATES   (B. 1938)

WHERE ARE YOU GOING,
WHERE HAVE YOU BEEN?   1970

FOR BOB DYLAN[1]

Her name was Connie. She was fifteen and she had a quick nervous giggling habit of craning her neck to glance into mirrors, or checking other people's faces to make sure her own was all right. Her mother, who noticed everything and knew everything and who hadn't much reason any longer to look at her own face, always scolded Connie about it. "Stop gawking at yourself, who are you? You think you're so pretty?" she would say. Connie would raise her eyebrows at these familiar complaints and look right through her mother, into a shadowy vision of herself as she was right at that moment: she knew she was pretty and that was everything. Her mother had been pretty once too, if you could believe those old snapshots in the album, but now her looks were gone and that was why she was always after Connie.

"Why don't you keep your room clean like your sister? How've you got your hair fixed—what the hell stinks? Hair spray? You don't see your sister using that junk."

Her sister June was twenty-four and still lived at home. She was a secretary in the high school Connie attended, and if that wasn't bad enough—with her in the same building—she was so plain and chunky and steady that Connie had to hear her praised all the time by her mother and her mother's sisters. June did this, June did that, she saved money and helped clean the house and cooked and Connie couldn't do a thing, her mind was all filled with trashy daydreams. Their father was away at work most of the time and when he came

---

[1] Bob Dylan (b. 1941) is an influential folk-rock musician and songwriter. Oates has commented that she had in mind Dylan's song "It's All Over Now, Baby Blue" when she wrote this story.

home he wanted supper and he read the newspaper at supper and after supper he went to bed. He didn't bother talking much to them, but around his bent head Connie's mother kept picking at her until Connie wished her mother was dead and she herself was dead and it was all over. "She makes me want to throw up sometimes," she complained to her friends. She had a high, breathless, amused voice which made everything she said sound a little forced, whether it was sincere or not.

There was one good thing: June went places with girl friends of hers, girls who were just as plain and steady as she, and so when Connie wanted to do that her mother had no objections. The father of Connie's best girl friend drove the girls the three miles to town and left them off at a shopping plaza, so that they could walk through the stores or go to a movie, and when he came to pick them up again at eleven he never bothered to ask what they had done.

They must have been familiar sights, walking around that shopping plaza in their shorts and flat ballerina slippers that always scuffed the sidewalk, with charm bracelets jingling on their thin wrists; they would lean together to whisper and laugh secretly if someone passed by who amused or interested them. Connie had long dark blond hair that drew anyone's eye to it, and she wore part of it pulled up on her head and puffed out and the rest of it she let fall down her back. She wore a pull-over jersey blouse that looked one way when she was at home and another way when she was away from home. Everything about her had two sides to it, one for home and one for anywhere that was not home: her walk that could be childlike and bobbing, or languid enough to make anyone think she was hearing music in her head, her mouth which was pale and smirking most of the time, but bright and pink on these evenings out, her laugh which was cynical and drawling at home—"Ha, ha, very funny"— but high-pitched and nervous anywhere else, like the jingling of the charms on her bracelet.

Sometimes they did go shopping or to a movie, but sometimes they went across the highway, ducking fast across the busy road, to a drive-in restaurant where older kids hung out. The restaurant was shaped like a big bottle, though squatter than a real bottle, and on its cap was a revolving figure of a grinning boy who held a hamburger aloft. One night in mid-summer they ran across, breathless with daring, and right away someone leaned out a car window and invited them over, but it was just a boy from high school they didn't like. It made them feel good to be able to ignore him. They went up through the maze of parked and cruising cars to the bright-lit, fly-infested restaurant, their faces pleased and expectant as if they were entering a sacred building that loomed out of the night to give them what haven and what blessing they yearned for. They sat at the counter and crossed their legs at the ankles, their thin shoulders rigid with excitement, and listened to the music that made everything so good: the music was always in the background like music at a church service, it was something to depend upon.

A boy named Eddie came in to talk with them. He sat backwards on his stool, turning himself jerkily around in semi-circles and then stopping and turning again, and after a while he asked Connie if she would like something to eat. She said she did and so she tapped her friend's arm on her way out—her friend pulled her face up into a brave droll look—and Connie said she would meet her at eleven, across the way. "I just hate to leave her like that," Connie said earnestly, but the boy said that she wouldn't be alone for long. So they went out to his car and on the way Connie couldn't help but let her eyes wander over the windshields and faces all around her, her face gleaming with a joy that had nothing to do with Eddie or even this place; it might have been the music. She drew her shoulders up and sucked in her breath with the pure pleasure of being alive, and just at that moment she happened to glance at a face just a few feet from hers. It was a boy with shaggy black hair, in a convertible jalopy painted gold. He stared at her and then his lips widened into a grin. Connie slit her eyes at him and turned away, but she couldn't help glancing back and there he was still watching her. He wagged a finger and laughed and said, "Gonna get you, baby," and Connie turned away without Eddie noticing anything.

She spent three hours with him, at the restaurant where they ate hamburgers and drank Cokes in wax cups that were always sweating, and then down an alley a mile or so away, and when he left her off at five to eleven only the movie house was still open at the plaza. Her girl friend was there, talking with a boy. When Connie came up the two girls smiled at each other and Connie said, "How was the movie?" and the girl said, "*You* should know." They rode off with the girl's father, sleepy and pleased, and Connie couldn't help but look at the darkened shopping plaza with its big empty parking lot and its signs that were faded and ghostly now, and over at the drive-in restaurant where cars were still circling tirelessly. She couldn't hear the music at this distance.

Next morning June asked her how the movie was and Connie said, "So-so."

She and that girl and occasionally another girl went several times a week 10 that way, and the rest of the time Connie spent around the house—it was summer vacation—getting in her mother's way and thinking, dreaming, about the boys she met. But all the boys fell back and dissolved into a single face that was not even a face, but an idea, a feeling, mixed up with the urgent insistent pounding of the music and the humid night air of July. Connie's mother kept dragging her back to the daylight by finding things for her to do or saying, suddenly, "What's this about the Pettinger girl?"

And Connie would say nervously, "Oh, her. That dope." She always drew thick clear lines between herself and such girls, and her mother was simple and kindly enough to believe her. Her mother was so simple, Connie thought, that it was maybe cruel to fool her so much. Her mother went scuffling around the house in old bedroom slippers and complained over the telephone to one sister about the other, then the other called up and the two of them complained about the third one. If June's name was mentioned her mother's tone was approving, and if Connie's name was mentioned it was disapproving. This did not really mean she disliked Connie and actually Connie thought that her mother preferred her to June because she was prettier, but the two of them kept up a pretense of exasperation, a sense that they were tugging and struggling over something of little value to either of them. Sometimes, over coffee, they were almost friends, but something would come up—some vexation that was like a fly buzzing suddenly around their heads—and their faces went hard with contempt.

One Sunday Connie got up at eleven—none of them bothered with church—and washed her hair so that it could dry all day long, in the sun. Her parents and sister were going to a barbecue at an aunt's house and Connie said no, she wasn't interested, rolling her eyes to let her mother know just what she thought of it. "Stay home alone then," her mother said sharply. Connie sat out back in a lawn chair and watched them drive away, her father quiet and bald, hunched around so that he could back the car out, her mother with a look that was still angry and not at all softened through the windshield, and in the back seat poor old June all dressed up as if she didn't know what a barbecue was, with all the running yelling kids and the flies. Connie sat with her eyes closed in the sun, dreaming and dazed with the warmth about her as if this were a kind of love, the caresses of love, and her mind slipped over onto thoughts of the boy she had been with the night before and how nice he had been, how sweet it always was, not the way someone like June would suppose but sweet, gentle, the way it was in movies and promised in songs; and when she opened her eyes she hardly knew where she was, the back yard ran off into weeds and a fence-line of trees and behind it the sky was perfectly blue and still. The asbestos "ranch house" that was now three years old still startled her—it looked small. She shook her head as if to get awake.

It was too hot. She went inside the house and turned on the radio to drown out the quiet. She sat on the edge of her bed, barefoot, and listened for an hour and a half to a program called XYZ Sunday Jamboree, record after record of hard, fast, shrieking songs she sang along with, interspersed by exclamations from "Bobby King": "An' look here you girls at Napoleon's—Son and Charley want you to pay real close attention to this song coming up!"

And Connie paid close attention herself, bathed in a glow of slow-pulsed joy that seemed to rise mysteriously out of the music itself and lay languidly about the airless little room, breathed in and breathed out with each gentle rise and fall of her chest.

After a while she heard a car coming up the drive. She sat up at once, startled, because it couldn't be her father so soon. The gravel kept crunching all the way in from the road—the driveway was long—and Connie ran to the window. It was a car she didn't know. It was an open jalopy, painted a bright gold that caught the sunlight opaquely. Her heart began to pound and her fingers snatched at her hair, checking it, and she whispered "Christ. Christ," wondering how bad she looked. The car came to a stop at the side door and the horn sounded four short taps as if this were a signal Connie knew.

She went into the kitchen and approached the door slowly, then hung out the screen door, her bare toes curling down off the step. There were two boys in the car and now she recognized the driver: he had shaggy, shabby black hair that looked crazy as a wig and he was grinning at her.

"I ain't late, am I?" he said.

"Who the hell do you think you are?" Connie said.

"Toldja I'd be out, didn't I?"

"I don't even know who you are." 20

She spoke sullenly, careful to show no interest or pleasure, and he spoke in a fast bright monotone. Connie looked past him to the other boy, taking her time. He had fair brown hair, with a lock that fell onto his forehead. His sideburns gave him a fierce, embarrassed look, but so far he hadn't even bothered to glance at her. Both boys wore sunglasses. The driver's glasses were metallic and mirrored everything in miniature.

"You wanta come for a ride?" he said.

Connie smirked and let her hair fall loose over one shoulder.

"Don'tcha like my car? New paint job," he said. "Hey."

"What?" 25

"You're cute."

She pretended to fidget, chasing flies away from the door.

"Don'tcha believe me, or what?" he said.

"Look, I don't even know who you are," Connie said in disgust.

"Hey, Ellie's got a radio, see. Mine's broke down." He lifted his friend's arm 30 and showed her the little transistor the boy was holding, and now Connie began to hear the music. It was the same program that was playing inside the house.

"Bobby King?" she said.

"I listen to him all the time. I think he's great."

"He's kind of great," Connie said reluctantly.

"Listen, that guy's *great*. He knows where the action is."

Connie blushed a little, because the glasses made it impossible for her to see 35 just what this boy was looking at. She couldn't decide if she liked him or if he was just a jerk, and so she dawdled in the doorway and wouldn't come down or go back inside. She said, "What's all that stuff painted on your car?"

"Can'tcha read it?" He opened the door very carefully, as if he was afraid it might fall off. He slid out just as carefully, planting his feet firmly on the ground, the tiny metallic world in his glasses slowing down like gelatine hardening and in the midst of it Connie's bright green blouse. "This here is my name, to begin with," he said. ARNOLD FRIEND was written in tarlike black letters on the side, with a drawing of a round grinning face that reminded Connie of a pumpkin, except it wore sunglasses. "I wanta introduce myself, I'm Arnold Friend and that's my real name and I'm gonna be your friend, honey, and inside the car's Ellie Oscar, he's kinda shy." Ellie brought his transistor radio up to his shoulder and balanced it there. "Now these numbers are a secret code, honey," Arnold Friend explained. He read off the numbers 33, 19, 17 and raised his eyebrows at her to see what she thought of that, but she didn't think much of it. The left rear fender had been smashed and around it was written on the gleaming gold background: DONE BY CRAZY WOMAN DRIVER. Connie had to laugh at that. Arnold Friend was pleased at her laughter and looked up at her. "Around the other side's a lot more—you wanta come and see them?"

"No."

"Why not?"

"Why should I?"

"Don'tcha wanta see what's on the car? Don'tcha wanta go for a ride?"   40

"I don't know."

"Why not?"

"I got things to do."

"Like what?"

"Things."   45

He laughed as if she had said something funny. He slapped his thighs. He was standing in a strange way, leaning back against the car as if he were balancing himself. He wasn't tall, only an inch or so taller than she would be if she came down to him. Connie liked the way he was dressed, which was the way all of them dressed: tight faded jeans stuffed into black, scuffed boots, a belt that pulled his waist in and showed how lean he was, and a white pull-over shirt that was a little soiled and showed the hard small muscles of his arms and shoulders. He looked as if he possibly did hard work, lifting and carrying things. Even his neck looked muscular. And his face was a familiar face, somehow: the jaw and chin and cheeks slightly darkened, because he hadn't shaved for a day or two, and the nose long and hawk-like, sniffing as if she were a treat he was going to gobble up and it was all a joke.

"Connie, you ain't telling the truth. This is your day set aside for a ride with me and you know it," he said, still laughing. The way he straightened and recovered from his fit of laughing showed that it had been all fake.

"How do you know what my name is?" she said suspiciously.

"It's Connie."

"Maybe and maybe not."   50

"I know my Connie," he said, wagging his finger. Now she remembered him even better, back at the restaurant, and her cheeks warmed at the thought of how she sucked in her breath just at the moment she passed him—how she must have looked to him. And he had remembered her. "Ellie and I came out here especially for you," he said. "Ellie can sit in back. How about it?"

"Where?"

"Where what?"

"Where're we going?"

He looked at her. He took off the sunglasses and she saw how pale the skin   55 around his eyes was, like holes that were not in shadow but instead in light. His eyes were chips of broken glass that catch the light in an amiable way. He smiled. It was as if the idea of going for a ride somewhere, to some place, was a new idea to him.

"Just for a ride, Connie sweetheart."

"I never said my name was Connie," she said.

"But I know what it is. I know your name and all about you, lots of things," Arnold Friend said. He had not moved yet but stood still leaning back against the side of his jalopy. "I took a special interest in you, such a pretty girl, and found out all about you like I know your parents and sister are gone somewheres and I know where and how long they're going to be gone, and I know who you were with last night, and your best girl friend's name is Betty. Right?"

He spoke in a simple lilting voice, exactly as if he were reciting the words to a song. His smile assured her that everything was fine. In the car, Ellie turned up the volume on his radio and did not bother to look around at them.

"Ellie can sit in the back seat," Arnold Friend said. He indicated his friend with a casual jerk of his chin, as if Ellie did not count and she should not bother with him. 60

"How'd you find out all that stuff?" Connie said.

"Listen: Betty Schultz and Tony Fitch and Jimmy Pettinger and Nancy Pettinger," he said, in a chant. "Raymond Stanley and Bob Hutter—"

"Do you know all those kids?"

"I know everybody."

"Look, you're kidding. You're not from around here." 65

"Sure."

"But—how come we never saw you before?"

"Sure you saw me before," he said. He looked down at his boots, as if he were a little offended. "You just don't remember."

"I guess I'd remember you," Connie said.

"Yeah?" He looked up at this, beaming. He was pleased. He began to mark time with the music from Ellie's radio, tapping his fists lightly together. Connie looked away from his smile to the car, which was painted so bright it almost hurt her eyes to look at it. She looked at that name, ARNOLD FRIEND. And up at the front fender was an expression that was familiar—MAN THE FLYING SAUCERS. It was an expression kids had used the year before, but didn't use this year. She looked at it for a while as if the words meant something to her that she did not yet know. 70

"What're you thinking about? Huh?" Arnold Friend demanded. "Not worried about your hair blowing around in the car, are you?"

"No."

"Think I maybe can't drive good?"

"How do I know?"

"You're a hard girl to handle. How come?" he said. "Don't you know I'm your friend? Didn't you see me put my sign in the air when you walked by?" 75

"What sign?"

"My sign." And he drew an X in the air, leaning out toward her. They were maybe ten feet apart. After his hand fell back to his side, the X was still in the air, almost visible. Connie let the screen door close and stood perfectly still inside it, listening to the music from her radio and the boy's blend together. She stared at Arnold Friend. He stood there so stiffly relaxed, pretending to be relaxed, with one hand idly on the door handle as if he were keeping himself up that way and had no intention of ever moving again. She recognized most things about him, the tight jeans that showed his thighs and buttocks and the greasy leather boots and the tight shirt, and even that slippery friendly smile of his, that sleepy dreamy smile that all the boys used to get across ideas they didn't want to put into words. She recognized all this and also the singsong way he talked, slightly mocking, kidding, but serious and a little melancholy, and she recognized the way he tapped one fist against the other in homage to the perpetual music behind him. But all these things did not come together.

She said suddenly, "Hey, how old are you?"

His smile faded. She could see then that he wasn't a kid, he was much older—thirty, maybe more. At this knowledge her heart began to pound faster.

"That's a crazy thing to ask. Can'tcha see I'm your own age?" 80

"Like hell you are."

"Or maybe a couple years older, I'm eighteen."

"Eighteen?" she said doubtfully.

He grinned to reassure her and lines appeared at the corners of his mouth. His teeth were big and white. He grinned so broadly his eyes became slits and she saw how thick the lashes were, thick and black as if painted with a black tarlike material. Then he seemed to become embarrassed, abruptly, and looked over his shoulder at Ellie. "*Him,* he's crazy," he said. "Ain't he a riot, he's a nut, a real character." Ellie was still listening to the music. His sunglasses told nothing about what he was thinking. He wore a bright orange shirt unbuttoned halfway to show his chest, which was a pale, bluish chest and not muscular like Arnold Friend's. His shirt collar was turned up all around and the very tips of the collar pointed out past his chin as if they were protecting him. He was pressing the transistor radio up against his ear and sat there in a kind of daze, right in the sun.

"He's kinda strange," Connie said. 85

"Hey, she says you're kinda strange! Kinda strange!" Arnold Friend cried. He pounded on the car to get Ellie's attention. Ellie turned for the first time and Connie saw with shock that he wasn't a kid either—he had a fair, hairless face, cheeks reddened slightly as if the veins grew too close to the surface of his skin, the face of a forty-year-old baby. Connie felt a wave of dizziness rise in her at this sight and she stared at him as if waiting for something to change the shock of the moment, make it all right again. Ellie's lips kept shaping words, mumbling along, with the words blasting in his ear.

"Maybe you two better go away," Connie said faintly.

"What? How come?" Arnold Friend cried. "We come out here to take you for a ride. It's Sunday." He had the voice of the man on the radio now. It was the same voice, Connie thought. "Don'tcha know it's Sunday all day and honey, no matter who you were with last night today you're with Arnold Friend and don't you forget it!—Maybe you better step out here," he said, and this last was in a different voice. It was a little flatter, as if the heat was finally getting to him.

"No. I got things to do."

"Hey." 90

"You two better leave."

"We ain't leaving until you come with us."

"Like hell I am—"

"Connie, don't fool around with me. I mean, I mean, don't fool *around,*" he said, shaking his head. He laughed incredulously. He placed his sunglasses on top of his head, carefully, as if he were indeed wearing a wig, and brought the stems down behind his ears. Connie stared at him, another wave of dizziness and fear rising in her so that for a moment he wasn't even in focus but was just a blur, standing there against his gold car, and she had the idea that he had driven up the driveway all right but had come from nowhere before that and belonged nowhere and that everything about him and even about the music that was so familiar to her was only half real.

"If my father comes and sees you—"   95

"He ain't coming. He's at the barbecue."

"How do you know that?"

"Aunt Tillie's. Right now they're—uh—they're drinking. Sitting around," he said vaguely, squinting as if he were staring all the way to town and over to Aunt Tillie's backyard. Then the vision seemed to get clear and he nodded energetically. "Yeah. Sitting around. There's your sister in a blue dress, huh? And high heels, the poor sad bitch—nothing like you, sweetheart! And your mother's helping some fat woman with the corn, they're cleaning the corn—husking the corn—"

"What fat woman?" Connie cried.

"How do I know what fat woman. I don't know every goddam fat woman in   100 the world!" Arnold Friend laughed.

"Oh, that's Mrs. Hornby. . . . Who invited her?" Connie said. She felt a little light-headed. Her breath was coming quickly.

"She's too fat. I don't like them fat. I like them the way you are, honey," he said, smiling sleepily at her. They stared at each other for awhile, through the screen door. He said softly, "Now what you're going to do is this: you're going to come out that door. You're going to sit up front with me and Ellie's going to sit in the back, the hell with Ellie, right? This isn't Ellie's date. You're my date. I'm your lover, honey."

"What? You're crazy—"

"Yes, I'm your lover. You don't know what that is but you will," he said. "I know that too. I know all about you. But look: it's real nice and you couldn't ask for nobody better than me, or more polite. I always keep my word. I'll tell you how it is, I'm always nice at first, the first time. I'll hold you so tight you won't think you have to try to get away or pretend anything because you'll know you can't. And I'll come inside you where it's all secret and you'll give in to me and you'll love me—"

"Shut up! You're crazy!" Connie said. She backed away from the door. She   105 put her hands against her ears as if she'd heard something terrible, something not meant for her. "People don't talk like that, you're crazy," she muttered. Her heart was almost too big now for her chest and its pumping made sweat break out all over her. She looked out to see Arnold Friend pause and then take a step toward the porch lurching. He almost fell. But, like a clever drunken man, he managed to catch his balance. He wobbled in high boots and grabbed hold of one of the porch posts.

"Honey?" he said. "You still listening?"

"Get the hell out of here!"

"Be nice, honey. Listen."

"I'm going to call the police—"

He wobbled again and out of the side of his mouth came a fast spat curse, an 110
aside not meant for her to hear. But even this "Christ!" sounded forced. Then
he began to smile again. She watched this smile come, awkward as if he were
smiling from inside a mask. His whole face was a mask, she thought wildly,
tanned down onto his throat but then running out as if he had plastered makeup on his face but had forgotten about his throat.

"Honey—? Listen, here's how it is. I always tell the truth and I promise you
this: I ain't coming in the house after you."

"You better not! I'm going to call the police if you—if you don't—"

"Honey," he said, talking right through her voice, "honey, I'm not coming in
there but you are coming out here. You know why?"

She was panting. The kitchen looked like a place she had never seen before,
some room she had run inside but which wasn't good enough, wasn't going to
help her. The kitchen window had never had a curtain, after three years, and
there were dishes in the sink for her to do—probably—and if you ran your
hand across the table you'd probably feel something sticky there.

"You listening, honey? Hey?"   115

"— going to call the police—"

"Soon as you touch the phone I don't need to keep my promise and can
come inside. You won't want that."

She rushed forward and tried to lock the door. Her fingers were shaking.
"But why lock it," Arnold Friend said gently, talking right into her face. "It's
just a screen door. It's just nothing." One of his boots was at a strange angle, as
if his foot wasn't in it. It pointed out to the left, bent at the ankle. "I mean, anybody can break through a screen door and glass and wood and iron or anything else he needs to, anybody at all and specially Arnold Friend. If the place
got lit up with a fire honey you'd come running out into my arms, right into
my arms and safe at home—like you knew I was your lover and'd stopped
fooling around. I don't mind a nice shy girl but I don't like no fooling around."
Part of those words were spoken with a slight rhythmic lilt, and Connie somehow recognized them—the echo of a song from last year, about a girl rushing
into her boy friend's arms and coming home again—

Connie stood barefoot on the linoleum floor, staring at him. "What do you
want?" she whispered.

"I want you," he said.   120

"What?"

"Seen you that night and thought, that's the one, yes sir. I never needed to
look any more."

"But my father's coming back. He's coming to get me. I had to wash my hair
first—" She spoke in a dry, rapid voice, hardly raising it for him to hear.

"No, your daddy is not coming and yes, you had to wash your hair and you
washed it for me. It's nice and shining and all for me, I thank you, sweetheart,"

he said, with a mock bow, but again he almost lost his balance. He had to bend and adjust his boots. Evidently his feet did not go all the way down; the boots must have been stuffed with something so that he would seem taller. Connie stared out at him and behind him Ellie in the car, who seemed to be looking off toward Connie's right, into nothing. This Ellie said, pulling the words out of the air one after another as if he were just discovering them, "You want me to pull out the phone?"

"Shut your mouth and keep it shut," Arnold Friend said, his face red from 125 bending over or maybe from embarrassment because Connie had seen his boots. "This ain't none of your business."

"What—what are you doing? What do you want?" Connie said. "If I call the police they'll get you, they'll arrest you—"

"Promise was not to come in unless you touch that phone, and I'll keep that promise," he said. He resumed his erect position and tried to force his shoulders back. He sounded like a hero in a movie, declaring something important. He spoke too loudly and it was as if he were speaking to someone behind Connie. "I ain't made plans for coming in that house where I don't belong but just for you to come out to me, the way you should. Don't you know who I am?"

"You're crazy," she whispered. She backed away from the door but did not want to go into another part of the house, as if this would give him permission to come through the door. "What do you . . . You're crazy, you . . ."

"Huh? What're you saying, honey?"

Her eyes darted everywhere in the kitchen. She could not remember what it 130 was, this room.

"This is how it is, honey: you come out and we'll drive away, have a nice ride. But if you don't come out we're gonna wait till your people come home and then they're all going to get it."

"You want that telephone pulled out?" Ellie said. He held the radio away from his ear and grimaced, as if without the radio the air was too much for him.

"I toldja shut up, Ellie," Arnold Friend said, "you're deaf, get a hearing aid, right? Fix yourself up. This little girl's no trouble and's gonna be nice to me, so Ellie keep to yourself, this ain't your date—right? Don't hem in on me. Don't hog. Don't crush. Don't bird dog. Don't trail me," he said in a rapid meaningless voice, as if he were running through all the expressions he'd learned but was no longer sure which one of them was in style, then rushing on to new ones, making them up with his eyes closed, "Don't crawl under my fence, don't squeeze in my chipmunk hole, don't sniff my glue, suck my popsicle, keep your own greasy fingers on yourself!" He shaded his eyes and peered in at Connie, who was backed against the kitchen table. "Don't mind him honey he's just a creep. He's a dope. Right? I'm the boy for you and like I said you come out here nice like a lady and give me your hand, and nobody else gets hurt, I mean, your nice old bald-headed daddy and your mummy and your sister in her high heels. Because listen: why bring them in this?"

"Leave me alone," Connie whispered.

"Hey, you know that old woman down the road, the one with the chickens   135
and stuff—you know her?"

"She's dead!"

"Dead? What? You know her?" Arnold Friend said.

"She's dead—"

"Don't you like her?"

"She's dead—she's—she isn't here any more—"   140

"But don't you like her, I mean, you got something against her? Some
grudge or something?" Then his voice dipped as if he were conscious of a
rudeness. He touched the sunglasses perched on top of his head as if to make
sure they were still there. "Now you be a good girl."

"What are you going to do?"

"Just two things, or maybe three," Arnold Friend said. "But I promise it
won't last long and you'll like me that way you get to like people you're close to.
You will. It's all over for you here, so come on out. You don't want your people
in any trouble, do you?"

She turned and bumped against a chair or something, hurting her leg, but
she ran into the back room and picked up the telephone. Something roared in
her ear, a tiny roaring, and she was so sick with fear that she could do nothing
but listen to it—the telephone was clammy and very heavy and her fingers
groped down to the dial but were too weak to touch it. She began to scream
into the phone, into the roaring. She cried out, she cried for her mother, she
felt her breath start jerking back and forth in her lungs as if it were something
Arnold Friend were stabbing her with again and again with no tenderness. A
noisy sorrowful wailing rose all about her and she was locked inside it the way
she was locked inside that house.

After a while she could hear again. She was sitting on the floor with her wet   145
back against the wall.

Arnold Friend was saying from the door, "That's a good girl. Put the phone
back."

She kicked the phone away from her.

"No, honey. Pick it up. Put it back right."

She picked it up and put it back. The dial tone stopped.

"That's a good girl. Now come outside."   150

She was hollow with what had been fear, but what was now just an emptiness. All that screaming had blasted it out of her. She sat, one leg cramped
under her, and deep inside her brain was something like a pinpoint of light
that kept going and would not let her relax. She thought, I'm not going to see
my mother again. She thought, I'm not going to sleep in my bed again. Her
bright green blouse was all wet.

Arnold Friend said, in a gentle-loud voice that was like a stage voice, "The
place where you came from ain't there any more, and where you had in mind
to go is cancelled out. This place you are now—inside your daddy's house—is
nothing but a cardboard box I can knock down any time. You know that and
always did know it. You hear me?"

She thought, I have got to think. I have to know what to do.

"We'll go out to a nice field, out in the country here where it smells so nice and it's sunny," Arnold Friend said. "I'll have my arms around you so you won't need to try to get away and I'll show you what love is like, what it does. The hell with this house! It looks solid all right," he said. He ran a fingernail down the screen and the noise did not make Connie shiver, as it would have the day before. "Now put your hand on your heart, honey. Feel that? That feels solid too but we know better, be nice to me, be sweet like you can because what else is there for a girl like you but to be sweet and pretty and give in?—and get away before her people come back?"

She felt her pounding heart. Her hand seemed to enclose it. She thought for   155 the first time in her life that it was nothing that was hers, that belonged to her, but just a pounding, living thing inside this body that wasn't really hers either.

"You don't want them to get hurt," Arnold Friend went on. "Now get up, honey. Get up all by yourself."

She stood up.

"Now turn this way. That's right. Come over here to me—Ellie, put that away, didn't I tell you? You dope. You miserable creepy dope," Arnold said. His words were not angry but only part of an incantation. The incantation was kindly. "Now come out through the kitchen to me honey and let's see a smile, try it, you're a brave sweet little girl and now they're eating corn and hotdogs cooked to bursting over an outdoor fire, and they don't know one thing about you and never did and honey, you're better than them because not a one of them would have done this for you."

Connie felt the linoleum under her feet; it was cool. She brushed her hair back out of her eyes. Arnold Friend let go of the post tentatively and opened his arms for her, his elbows pointing in toward each other and his wrists limp, to show that this was an embarrassed embrace and a little mocking, he didn't want to make her self-conscious.

She put out her hand against the screen. She watched herself push the door   160 slowly open as if she were safe back somewhere in the other doorway, watching this body and this head of long hair moving out into the sunlight where Arnold Friend waited.

"My sweet little blue-eyed girl," he said, in a half-sung sigh that had nothing to do with her brown eyes but was taken up just the same by the vast sunlit reaches of the land behind him and on all sides of him, so much land that Connie had never seen before and did not recognize except to know that she was going to it.

FOR ANALYSIS

1. Describe Connie in your own words. What are the sources of her values? What sort of love experience does she imagine?

2. When she agrees to go with Eddie, what do you suppose they did in the "alley a mile or so away" (para. 8)?

3. How does Arnold Friend differ from Eddie?

4. Why is attention paid in the story to Arnold's boots?

5. How does Ellie's repeated proposal that Arnold pull out the phone affect your understanding of Arnold and Ellie's motives?

6. Does Connie go to Arnold simply to protect her family from his threats? Explain.

7. What is going to happen to Connie? Why?

8. The story is told by a **third-person narrator**—yet it is limited, essentially, to Connie's viewpoint. Would multiple viewpoints—her mother's, June's, Eddie's, her friend's, Arnold's—enhance or impair the story's impact?

WRITING TOPICS

1. In your experience, do some women find dangerous and unstable men more attractive than gentle and kind men? Support your arguments with **allusions** to Oates's story and other stories you have read.

2. Using evidence from the story, argue that Arnold Friend is an incarnation of the devil or some fairy-tale villain.

KATE BRAVERMAN   (B. 1950)

TALL TALES FROM THE MEKONG DELTA   1990

It was in the fifth month of her sobriety. It was after the hospital. It was after her divorce. It was autumn. She had even stopped smoking. She was wearing pink aerobic pants, a pink T-shirt with KAUAI written in lilac across the chest, and tennis shoes. She had just come from the gym. She was walking across a parking lot bordering a city park in West Hollywood. She was carrying cookies for the AA meeting. She was in charge of bringing the food for the meeting. He fell into step with her. He was short, fat, pale. He had bad teeth. His hair was dirty. Later, she would freeze this frame in her mind and study it. She would say he seemed frightened and defeated and trapped, cagey was the word she used to describe his eyes, how he measured and evaluated something in the air between them. The way he squinted through hazel eyes, it had nothing to do with the sunlight.

"I'm Lenny," he said, extending his hand. "What's your name?"

She told him. She was holding a bag with packages of cookies in it. After the meeting, she had an appointment with her psychiatrist, then a manicure. She kept walking.

"You a teacher? You look like a teacher," he said.

"I'm a writer," she told him. "I teach creative writing."   5

"You look like a teacher," Lenny said.

"I'm not just a teacher," she told him. She was annoyed.

"Okay. You're a writer. And you're bad. You're one of those bad girls from Beverly Hills. I've had my eye on you," Lenny said.

She didn't say anything. He was wearing blue jeans, a black leather jacket zipped to his throat, a long red wool scarf around his neck, and a Dodgers baseball cap. It was too hot a day for the leather jacket and scarf. She didn't find that detail significant. It caught her attention, she touched it briefly and then let it go. She looked but did not see. They were standing on a curb. The meeting was in a community room across the boulevard. She wasn't afraid yet.

"You do drugs? What do you do? Drink too much?" he asked.   10

"I'm a cocaine addict," she told him.

"Me too. Let's see your tracks. Show me your tracks." Lenny reached out for her arm.

"I don't have any now." She glanced at her arm. She extended her arm into the yellow air between them. The air was already becoming charged and disturbed. "They're gone."

"I see them," Lenny told her, inspecting her arm, turning it over, holding it in the sunlight. He touched the part of her arm behind her elbow where the vein rose. "They're beautiful."

"But there's nothing there," she said.   15

"Yeah, there is. There always is if you know how to look," Lenny told her. "How many people by the door? How many steps?"

He was talking about the door across the boulevard. His back was turned. She didn't know.

"Four steps," Lenny said. "Nine people. Four women. One old man. I look. I see."

She was counting the people on the steps in front of the meeting. She didn't say anything.

"Let's get a coffee later. That's what you do, right? You can't get a drink? You 20 go out for coffee?" Lenny was studying her face.

"I don't think so," she said.

"You don't think so? Come on. I'll buy you coffee. You can explain AA to me. You like that Italian shit? That French shit? The little cups?" Lenny was staring at her.

"No, thank you. I'm sorry," she said. He was short and fat and sweating. He looked like he was laughing at her with his eyes.

"You're sorry. I'll show you sorry. Listen. I know what you want. You're one of those smart-ass teachers from Beverly Hills," Lenny said.

"Right," she said. She didn't know why she bothered talking to him.   25

"You want to get in over your head. You want to see what's on the other side. I'll show you. I'll take you there. It'll be the ride of your life," Lenny said.

"Goodbye," she answered.

Lenny was at her noon meeting the next day. She saw him immediately as she walked through the door. She wondered how he knew that she would be there. As she approached her usual chair, she saw a bouquet of long-stemmed pink roses.

"You look beautiful," Lenny said. "You knew I'd be here. That's why you put that crap on your face. You didn't have that paint on yesterday. Don't do that. You don't need that. Those whores from Beverly Hills need it. Not you. You're a teacher. I like that. Sit down." He picked the roses up. "Sit next to me. You glad to see me?"

"I don't think so." She sat down. Lenny handed the roses to her. She put 30 them on the floor.

"Yeah. You're glad to see me. You were hoping I'd be here. And here I am. You want me to chase you? I'll chase you. Then I'll catch you. Then I'll show you what being in over your head means." Lenny was smiling.

She turned away. When the meeting was over, she stood up quickly and began moving, even before the prayer was finished. "I have to go," she said, softly, over her shoulder. She felt she had to apologize. She felt she had to be careful.

"You don't have to go," Lenny said. He caught up with her on the steps. "Yeah. Don't look surprised. Lenny's fast, real fast. And you're lying. Don't ever lie to me. You think I'm stupid? Yeah, you think Lenny's stupid. You think you can get away from me? You can't get away. You got an hour. You don't pick that kid up for the dance school until four. Come on. I'll buy you coffee."

"What are you talking about?" She stopped. Her breath felt sharp and fierce. It was a warm November. The air felt like glass.

"I know all about you. I know your routine. I been watching you for two 35 weeks. Ever since I got to town. I saw you my first day. You think I'd ask you out on a date and not know your routine?" Lenny stared at her.

She felt her eyes widen. She started to say something but she changed her mind.

"You live at the top of the hill, off of Doheny. You pick up that kid, what's her name, Annie something? You pick her up and take her to dance school. You get coffee next door. Table by the window. You read the paper. Then you go home. Just the two of you. And that Mex cleaning lady. Maria. That her name? Maria? They're all called *Maria*. And the gardener Friday afternoons. That's it." Lenny lit a cigarette.

"You've been following me?" She was stunned. Her mouth opened.

"Recon," Lenny said.

"I beg you pardon?" 40

"In Nam. We called it recon. Fly over, get a lay of the land. Or stand behind some trees. Count the personnel. People look but they don't see. I'll tell you about it. Get coffee. You got an hour. Want to hear about Vietnam? I got stories. Choppers? I like choppers. You can take your time, aim. You can hit anything, even dogs. Some days we'd go out just aiming at dogs. Or the black market? Want to hear about that? Profiteering in smack? You're a writer, right? You like stories. I got some tall tales from the Mekong Delta for you, sweetheart. Knock your socks off. Come on." He reached out and touched her arm.

"Later you can have your own war stories. I can be one of your tall tales. I can be the tallest."

The sun was strong. The world was washed with white. The day seemed somehow clarified. He was wearing a leather jacket and shaking. It occurred to her that he was sick.

"Excuse me. I must go," she said. "If you follow me, I shall have someone call the police."

"Okay. Okay. Calm down," Lenny was saying behind her. "I'll save you a seat tomorrow, okay?"

She didn't reply. She sat in her car. It was strange how blue the sky seemed, 45 etched with the blue of radium or narcotics. Or China blue, perhaps. Was that a color? The blue of the China Sea? The blue of Vietnam. When he talked about Asia, she could imagine that blue, luminescent with ancient fever, with promises and bridges broken, with the harvest lost in blue flame. Always there were barbarians, shooting the children and dogs.

She locked her car and began driving. It occurred to her, suddenly, that the Chinese took poets as concubines. Their poets slept with warlords. They wrote with gold ink. They ate orchids and smoked opium. They were consecrated by nuance, by birds and silk and the ritual birthdays of gods and nothing changed for a thousand years. And afternoon was absinthe yellow and almond, burnt orange and chrysanthemum. And in the abstract sky, a litany of kites.

She felt herself look for him as she walked into the meeting the next day at noon. The meeting was in the basement of a church. Lenny was standing near the coffeepot with his back to the wall. He was holding two cups of coffee as if he was expecting her. He handed one to her.

"I got seats," he said. He motioned for her to follow. She followed. He pointed to a chair. She sat in it. An older woman was standing at the podium, telling the story of her life. Lenny was wearing a white warm-up suit with a green neon stripe down the sides of the pants and the arms of the jacket. He was wearing a baseball cap. His face seemed younger and tanner than she had remembered.

"Like how I look? I look like a lawyer on his way to tennis, right? I even got a tan. Fit right in. Chameleon Lenny. The best, too." He lit a cigarette. He held the pack out to her.

She shook her head, no. She was staring at the cigarette in his mouth, in his 50 fingers. She could lean her head closer, part her lips, take just one puff.

"I got something to show you," Lenny said.

The meeting was over. They were walking up the stairs from the basement of the church. The sun was strong. She blinked in the light. It was the yellow of a hot autumn, a yellow that seemed amplified and redeemed. She glanced at her watch.

"Don't do that," Lenny said. He was touching the small of her back with his hand. He was helping her walk.

"What?"

"Looking at that fucking watch all the time. Take it off," Lenny said. 55

"My watch?" She was looking at her wrist as if she had never seen it before.

"Give it here, come on." Lenny put his hand out. He motioned with his fingers. She placed her watch in the palm of his hand.

"That's a good girl," Lenny was saying. "You don't need it. You don't have to know what time it is. You're with me. Don't you get it? You're hungry, I feed you. You're tired, I find a hotel. You're in a structured environment now. You're protected. I protect you. It doesn't matter what time it is." He put her watch in his pocket. "Forget it. I'll buy you a new one. A better one. That was junk. I was embarrassed for you to wear junk like that. Want a Rolex?"

"You can't afford a Rolex," she said. She felt intelligent. She looked into his face.

"I got a drawerful," Lenny told her. "I got all the colors. Red. Black. Gold." 60

"Where?" She studied his face. They were walking on a side street in Hollywood. The air was a pale blue, bleeding into the horizon, taking the sky.

"In the bank," Lenny said. "In the safety deposit with everything else. All the cash that isn't buried." Lenny smiled.

"What else?" She put her hands on her hips.

"Let's go for a ride," Lenny said.

They were standing at the curb. They were two blocks from the church. A 65 motorcycle was parked there. Lenny took out a key.

"Get on," he said.

"I don't want to get on a motorcycle." She was afraid.

"Yes, you do," Lenny told her. "Sit down on it. Wrap your arms around me. Just lean into me. Nothing else. You'll like it. You'll be surprised. It's a beautiful day. It looks like Hong Kong today. Want to go to the beach? Want lunch? I know a place in Malibu. You like seafood? Crab? Scampi? Watch the waves?" Lenny was doing something to the motorcycle. He looked at her face.

"No," she said.

"How about Italian? I got a place near the Marina. Owner owes for ten kilos. 70 We'll get a good table. You like linguini?" Lenny sat down on the motorcycle.

She shook her head, no.

"Okay. You're not hungry. You're skinny. You should eat. Come on. We'll go around the block. Get on. Once around the block and I'll bring you back to the church." Lenny reached out his hand through the warm white air.

She looked at his hand and how the air seemed blue near his fingers. It's simply a blue glaze, she was thinking. In Malibu, in Hilo, in the China Sea, forms of blue, confusion and remorse, a dancing dress, a daughter with a mouth precisely your own and it's done, all of it.

Somewhere it was carnival night in the blue wash of a village on the China Sea. On the river, boats passed with low-slung antique masts sliding silently to the blue of the ocean, to the inverted delta where the horizon concluded itself in a rapture of orchid and pewter. That's what she was thinking when she took his hand.

She did not see him for a week. She changed her meeting schedule. She 75
went to women's meetings in the Pacific Palisades and the Valley. She went to
meetings she had never been to before. She trembled when she thought
about him.

She stopped her car at a red light. It occurred to her that it was an early afternoon in autumn in her thirty-eighth year. Then she found herself driving to
the community center. The meeting was over. There was no one left on the
street. Just one man, sitting alone on the front steps, smoking. Lenny looked
up at her and smiled.

"I was expecting you," Lenny said. "I told you. You can't get away from me."

She could feel his eyes on her face, the way when she lived with a painter, she
had learned to feel lamplight on her skin. When she had learned to perceive
light as an entity. She began to cry.

"Don't cry," Lenny said, his voice soft. "I can't stand you crying. Let's make
up. I'll buy you dinner."

"I can't." She didn't look at him.   80

"Yeah. You can. I'll take you someplace good. Spago? You like those little piz-
zas with the duck and shit? Lobster? You want the Palm? The Rangoon Racket
Club? Yeah. Don't look surprised. I know the places. I made deals in all those
places. What did you think?" He was lighting a cigarette and she could feel his
eyes on her skin.

She didn't say anything. They were walking across a parking lot. The
autumn made everything ache. Later, it would be worse. At dusk, with the
subtle irritation of lamps.

"Yeah. I know what you think. You think Lenny looks like he just crawled
out from a rock. This is a disguise. Blue jeans, sneakers. I fit right in. I got a
gang of angry Colombians on my ass. Forget it." Lenny stared at her. "You got a
boyfriend?"

"What's it to you?"

"What's it to me? That's sharp. I want to date you. I probably want to marry 85
you. You got a boyfriend, I got to hurt him." Lenny smiled.

"I can't believe you said that." She put her hands on her hips.

"You got a boyfriend? I'm going to cut off his arm and beat him with it.
Here. Look at this." He was bending over and removing something from his
sock. He held it in the palm of his hand.

"Know what this is?" Lenny asked.

She shook her head, no.

"It's a knife, sweetheart," Lenny said.   90

She could see that now, even before he opened it. A push-button knife.
Lenny was reaching behind to his back. He was pulling out something from
behind his belt, under his shirt. It was another knife.

"Want to see the guns?"

She felt dizzy. They were standing near her car. It was early in December.
The Santa Anas had been blowing. She felt that it had been exceptionally
warm for months.

"Don't get in the car," Lenny said. "I can't take it when you leave. Stay near me. Just let me breathe the same air as you. I love you."

"You don't even know me," she said.   95

"But you know me. You been dreaming me. I'm your ticket to the other side, remember?" Lenny had put his knives away. "Want to hear some more Nam stories? How we ran smack into Honolulu? You'll like this. You like the dope stories. You want to get loaded?"

She shook her head, no.

"You kidding me? You don't want to get high?" Lenny smiled.

"I like being sober," she said.

"Sure," Lenny said. "Let me know when that changes. One phone call. I got   100
the best dope in the world."

They were standing in front of her car. The street beyond the parking lot seemed estranged, the air was tarnished. She hadn't thought about drugs in months. Lenny was handing her something, thin circles of metal. She looked down at her hand. Two dimes seemed to glare in her palm.

"For when you change your mind," Lenny said. He was still smiling.

They were sitting on the grass of a public park after a meeting. Lenny was wearing Bermuda shorts and a green T-shirt that said CANCUN. They were sitting in a corner of the park with a stucco wall behind them.

"It's our anniversary," Lenny told her. "We been in love four weeks."

"I've lost track of time," she said. She didn't have a watch anymore. The air   105
felt humid, green, stalled. It was December in West Hollywood. She was think-ing that the palms were livid with green death. They could be the palms of Vietnam.

"I want to fuck you," Lenny said. "Let's go to your house."

She shook her head, no. She turned away from him. She began to stand up.

"Okay. Okay. You got the kid. I understand that. Let's go to a hotel. You want the Beverly Wilshire? I can't go to the Beverly Hills Hotel. I got a problem there. What about the Four Seasons? You want to fuck in the Four Seasons?"

"You need to get an AIDS test," she said.

"Why?" Lenny looked amused.   110

"Because you're a heroin addict. Because you've been in jail," she began.

"Who told you that?" Lenny sat up.

"You told me," she said. "Terminal Island. Chino. Folsom? Is it true?"

"Uh-huh," Lenny said. He lit a cigarette. "Five years in Folsom. Consecutive. Sixty months. I topped out."

She stared at him. She thought how easy it would be, to reach and take a cig- 115
arette. Just one, once.

"Means I finished my whole sentence. No time off for good behavior. Lenny did the whole sixty." He smiled. "I don't need an AIDS test."

"You're a heroin addict. You shoot cocaine. You're crazy. Who knows what you do or who you do it with?" She was beginning to be afraid.

"You think I'd give you a disease?" Lenny looked hurt.

Silence. She was looking at Lenny's legs, how white the exposed skin was. She was thinking that he brought his sick body to her, that he was bloated enormous with pathology and bad history, with jails and demented resentments.

"Listen. You got nothing to worry about. I don't need a fucking AIDS test. 120 Listen to me. Are you hearing me? You get that disease, I take care of you. I take you to Bangkok. I keep a place there, on the river. Best smack in the world. Fifty cents. I keep you loaded. You'll never suffer. You start hurting, I'll take you out. I'll kill you myself. With my own hands. I promise," Lenny said.

Silence. She was thinking that he must be drawn to her vast emptiness, could he sense that she was aching and hot and always listening? There is always a garish carnival across the boulevard. We are born, we eat and sleep, conspire and mourn, a birth, a betrayal, an excursion to the harbor, and it's done. All of it, done.

"Come here." Lenny extended his arm. "Come here. You're like a child. Don't be afraid. I want to give you something."

She moved her body closer to his. There are blue enormities, she was thinking, horizons and boulevards. Somewhere, there are blue rocks and they burn.

"Close your eyes," Lenny said. "Open your mouth."

She closed her eyes. She opened her mouth. There was something pressing 125 against her lip. Perhaps it was a flower.

"Close your mouth and breathe," Lenny said.

It was a cigarette. She felt the smoke in her lungs. It had been six months since she smoked. Her hand began to tremble.

"There," Lenny was saying. "You need to smoke. I can tell. It's okay. You can't give up everything at once. Here. Share it. Give me a hit."

They smoked quietly. They passed the cigarette back and forth. She was thinking that she was like a sacked capital. Nothing worked in her plazas. The palm trees were on fire. The air was smoky and blue. No one seemed to notice.

"Sit on my lap. Come on. Sit down. Closer. On my lap," Lenny was saying. 130 "Good. Yeah. Good. I'm not going to bite you. I love you. Want to get married? Want to have a baby? Closer. Let me kiss you. You don't do anything. Let me do it. Now your arms. Yeah. Around my neck. Tighter. Tighter. You worried? You got nothing to worry about. You get sick, I keep you whacked on smack. Then I kill you. So what are you worried? Closer. Yeah. Want to hear about R and R in Bangkok? Want to hear about what you get for a hundred bucks on the river? You'll like this. Lean right up against me. Yeah. Close your eyes."

"Look. It's hot. You want to swim. You like that? Swimming? You know how to swim?" Lenny looked at her. "Yeah? Let's go. I got a place in Bel Air."

"You have a place in Bel Air?" she asked. It was after the meeting. It was the week before Christmas. It was early afternoon.

"Guy I used to know. I did a little work for him. I introduced him to his wife. He owes me some money. He gave me the keys." Lenny reached in his pocket. He was wearing a white-and-yellow warm-up suit. He produced a key ring. It hung in the hot air between them. "It's got everything there. Food. Booze. Dope. Pool. Tennis court. Computer games. You like that? Pac Man?"

She didn't say anything. She felt she couldn't move. She lit a cigarette. She was buying two packages at a time again. She would be buying cartons soon.

"Look. We'll go for a drive. I'll tell you some more war stories. Come on. I got a nice car today. I got a brand-new red Ferrari. Want to see it? Just take a look. One look. It's at the curb. Give me your hand." Lenny reached out for her hand. 135

She could remember being a child. It was a child's game in a child's afternoon, before time or distance were factors. When you were told you couldn't move or couldn't see. And for those moments you are paralyzed or blind. You freeze in place. You don't move. You feel that you have been there for years. It does not occur to you that you can move. It does not occur to you that you can break the rules. The world is a collection of absolutes and spells. You know words have a power. You are entranced. The world is a soft blue.

"There. See. I'm not crazy. A red Ferrari. A hundred forty grand. Get in. We'll go around the block. Sit down. Nice interior, huh? Nice stereo. But I got no fucking tapes. Go to the record store with me? You pick out the tapes, okay? Then we'll go to Bel Air. Swim a little. Watch the sunset. Listen to some music. Want to dance? I love to dance. You can't get a disease doing that, right?" Lenny was holding the car door open for her.

She sat down. The ground seemed enormous. It seemed to leap up at her face.

"Yeah. I'm a good driver. Lean back. Relax. I used to drive for a living," Lenny told her.

"What did you drive? A bus?" She smiled. 140

"A bus? That's sharp. You're sharp. You're one of those sharp little Jewish girls from Beverly Hills with a cocaine problem. Yeah. I know what you're about. All of you. I drove some cars on a few jobs. Couple of jewelry stores, a few banks. Now I fly," Lenny said.

Lenny turned the car onto Sunset Boulevard. In the gardens of the houses behind the gates, everything was in bloom. Patches of color slid past so fast she thought they might be hallucinations. Azaleas and camellias and hibiscus. The green seemed sullen and half asleep. Or perhaps it was opiated, dazed, exhausted from pleasure.

"You fly?" she repeated.

"Planes. You like planes? I'll take you up. I got a plane. Company plane," Lenny told her. "It's in Arizona."

"You're a pilot?" She put out her cigarette and immediately lit another. 145

"I fly planes for money. Want to fly? I'm going next week. Every second Tuesday. Want to come?" Lenny looked at her.

"Maybe," she said. They had turned on a street north of Sunset. They were winding up a hill. The street was narrow. The bougainvillea was a kind of net near her face. The air smelled of petals and heat.

"Yeah. You'll come with me. I'll show you what I do. I fly over a stretch of desert looks like the moon. There's a small manufacturing business down there.

Camouflaged. You'd never see it. I drop some boxes off. I pick some boxes up. Three hours' work. Fifteen grand," Lenny said. "Know what I'm talking about?"

"No."

"Yeah. You don't want to know anything about this. Distribution," Lenny said. "That's federal." 150

"You do that twice a month?" she asked. They were above Sunset Boulevard. The bougainvillea was a magenta web. There were sounds of birds and insects. They were winding through pine trees. "That's thirty thousand dollars a month."

"That's nothing. The real money's the Bogota run," Lenny said. "Mountains leap up out of the ground, out of nowhere. The Bogota run drove me crazy. Took me a month to come down. Then the Colombians got mad. You know what I'm talking about?"

"No."

"That's good. You don't want to know anything about the Colombians," Lenny said again.

She was thinking about the Colombians and Bogota and the town where 155 Lenny said he had a house, Medellin. She was thinking they would have called her gitana, with her long black hair and bare feet. She could have fanned herself with handfuls of hundred-dollar bills like a green river. She could have borne sons for men crossing borders, searching for the definitive run, the one you don't return from. She would dance in bars in the permanently hot nights. They would say she was intoxicated with grief and dead husbands. Sadness made her dance. When she thought about this, she laughed.

The driveway seemed sudden and steep. They were approaching a walled villa. Lenny pushed numbers on a console. The gate opened.

He parked the red Ferrari. He opened the car door for her. She followed him up a flight of stone steps. The house looked like a Spanish fortress.

A large Christmas wreath with pine cones and a red ribbon hung on the door. The door was unlocked. The floor was tile. They were walking on an Oriental silk carpet, past a piano, a fireplace, a bar. There were ceiling-high glass cabinets in which Chinese artifacts were displayed, vases and bowls and carvings. They were walking through a library, then a room with a huge television, stereo equipment, a billiard table. She followed him out a side door.

The pool was built on the edge of the hill. The city below seemed like a sketch for a village, something not quite formed beneath the greenery. Pink and yellow roses had been planted around two sides of the pool. There were beds of azaleas with ferns between them and red camellias, yellow lilies, white daisies, and birds-of-paradise.

"Time to swim," Lenny said. 160

She was standing near the pool, motionless. "We don't have suits," she said.

"Don't tell nobody, okay?" Lenny was pulling his shirt over his head. He stared at her, a cigarette in his mouth. "It's private. It's walled. Just a cliff out here. And Bernie and Phyllis aren't coming back. Come on. Take off your clothes. What are you? Scared? You're like a child. Come here. I'll help you. Daddy'll help you. Just stand near me. Here. See? Over your head. Over baby's head. Did that hurt? What's that? One of those goddamn French jobs with the hooks in front? You do it. What are you looking at? I put on a few pounds. Okay? I'm a little out of shape. I need some weights. I got to buy some weights. What are you? Skinny? You're so skinny. You one of those vomiters? I'm not going to bite. Come here. Reach down. Take off my necklace. Unlock the chain. Yeah. Good. Now we swim."

The water felt strange and icy. It was nothing like she expected. There were shadows on the far side of the pool. The shadows were hideous. There was nothing ambiguous about them. The water beneath the shadows looked remote and troubled and green. It looked contaminated. The more she swam, the more the infected blue particles clustered on her skin. There would be no way to remove them.

"I have to leave," she said.

The sun was going down. It was an unusual sunset for Los Angeles, red and protracted. Clouds formed islands in the red sky. The sprinklers came on. The air smelled damp and green like a forest. There were pine trees beyond the rose garden. She thought of the smell of camp at nightfall, when she was a child.

"What are you? Crazy? You kidding me? I want to take you out," Lenny said. He wrapped a towel around his waist. Then he wrapped a towel around her shoulders. "Don't just stand there. Dry off. Come on. You'll get sick. Dry yourself."

He lit a cigarette for her. "You want to get dressed up, right? I know you skinny broads from Beverly Hills. You want to get dressed up. Look. Let me show you something. You'll like it. I know. Come on." He put out his hand for her. She took it.

They were walking up a marble stairway to the bedroom. The bedroom windows opened onto a tile balcony. There were sunken tubs in the bathroom. Everything was black marble. The faucets were gold. There were gold chandeliers hanging above them. Every wall had mirrors bordered by bulbs and gold. Lenny was standing in front of a closet.

"Pick something out. Go on. Walk in. Pink. You like pink? No. You like it darker. Yeah. Keep walking. Closet big as a tennis court. They got no taste, right? Looks like Vegas, right? You like red? No. Black. That's you. Here. Black silk." Lenny came out of the closet. He was holding an evening gown. "This your size? All you skinny broads wear the same size."

Lenny handed the dress to her. He stretched out on the bed. "Yeah. Let go of the towel. That's right. Only slower."

He was watching her. He lit a cigarette. His towel had come apart. He was holding something near his lap. It was a jewelry box.

"After you put that crap on your face, the paint, the lipstick, we'll pick out a little something nice for you. Phyllis won't need it. She's not coming back.

Yeah." Lenny laughed. "Bernie and Phyllis are entertaining the Colombians by now. Give those boys from the jungle something to chew on. Don't look like that. You like diamonds? I know you like diamonds."

Lenny was stretched out on the bed. The bed belonged to Bernie and Phyllis but they weren't coming back. Lenny was holding a diamond necklace out to her. She wanted it more than she could remember wanting anything.

"I'll put it on you. Come here. Sit down. I won't touch you. Not unless you ask me. I can see you're all dressed up. Just sit near me. I'll do the clasp for you," Lenny offered.

She sat down. She could feel the stones around her throat, cool, individual, 175 like the essence of something that lives in the night. Or something more ancient, part of the fabric of the night itself.

"Now you kiss me. Come on. You want to. I can tell. Kiss me. Know what this costs?" Lenny touched the necklace at her throat with his fingertips. He studied the stones. He left his fingers on her throat. "Sixty, seventy grand maybe. You can kiss me now."

She turned her face toward him. She opened her lips. Outside, the Santa Ana winds were startling, howling as if from a mouth. The air smelled of scorched lemons and oranges, of something delirious and intoxicated. When she closed her eyes, everything was blue.

She didn't see him at her noon meeting the next day or the day after. She thought, Well, that's it. She wasn't sorry. She got a manicure. She went to her psychiatrist. She began taking a steam bath after her aerobics class at the gym. She went Christmas shopping. She bought her daughter a white rabbit coat trimmed with blue fox. She was spending too much money. She didn't care.

It was Christmas Eve when the doorbell rang. There were carols on the radio. She was wearing a silk robe and smoking. She told Maria that she would answer the door.

"You promised never to come here." She was angry. "You promised to 180 respect my life. To recognize my discrete borders."

"Discrete borders?" Lenny repeated. "I'm in serious trouble. Look at me. Can't you see there's something wrong? You look but you don't see."

There was nothing unusual about him. He was wearing blue jeans and a black leather jacket. He was carrying an overnight bag. She could see the motorcycle near the curb. Maybe the Colombians had the red Ferrari. Maybe they were chewing on that now. She didn't ask him in.

"This is it," Lenny was saying. He brushed past her and walked into the living room. He was talking quickly. He was telling her what had happened in the desert, what the Colombians had done. She felt like she was being electrocuted, that her hair was standing on end. It occurred to her that it was a sensation so singular that she might come to enjoy it. There were small blue wounded sounds in the room now. She wondered if they were coming from her.

"I disappear in about five minutes." Lenny looked at her. "You coming?"

She thought about it. "I can't come, no," she said finally. "I have a child." 185

"We take her," Lenny offered.

She shook her head, no. The room was going dark at the edges, she noticed. Like a field of blue asters, perhaps. Or ice when the sun strikes it. And how curious the blue becomes when clouds cross the sun, when the blue becomes broken, tawdry.

"I had plans for you. I was going to introduce you to some people. I should of met you fifteen years ago. I could have retired. Get me some ice," Lenny said. "Lets have a drink."

"We're in AA. Are you crazy?" She was annoyed.

"I need a drink. I need a fix. I need an automatic weapon. I need a plane," he 190 said. He looked past her to the den. Maria was watching television and wrapping Christmas presents.

"You need a drink, too," Lenny said. "Don't even think about it. The phone. You're an accessory after the fact. You can go to jail. What about your kid then?"

They were standing in her living room. There was a noble pine tree near the fireplace. There were wrapped boxes beneath the branches. Maria asked in Spanish if she needed anything. She said not at the moment. Two glasses with ice, that was all.

"Have a drink," Lenny said. "You can always go back to the meetings. They take you back. They don't mind. I do it all the time. All over the world. I been doing it for ten years."

"I didn't know that," she said. It was almost impossible to talk. It occurred to her that her sanity was becoming intermittent, like a sudden stretch of intact road in an abandoned region. Or radio music, blatant after months of static.

"Give me the bottle. I'll pour you one. Don't look like that. You look like 195 you're going down for the count. Here." Lenny handed the glass to her. She could smell the vodka. "Open your mouth, goddamn it."

She opened her mouth. She took a sip. Then she lit a cigarette.

"Wash the glass when I leave," Lenny said. "They can't prove shit. You don't know me. You were never anywhere. Nothing happened. You listening? You don't look like you're listening. You look like you're on tilt. Come on, baby. Listen to Daddy. That's good. Take another sip."

She took another sip. Lenny was standing near the door. "You're getting off easy, you know that? I ran out of time. I had plans for you," he was saying.

He was opening the door. "Some ride, huh? Did Daddy do like he said? Get you to the other side? You catch a glimpse? See what's there? I think you're starting to see. Can't say Lenny lied to you, right?"

She took another sip. "Right," she agreed. When this glass was finished she 200 would pour another. When the bottle was empty, she would buy another.

Lenny closed the door. The night stayed outside. She was surprised. She opened her mouth but no sound came out. Instead, blue things flew in, pieces of glass or tin, or necklaces of blue diamonds, perhaps. The air was the blue of a pool when there are shadows, when clouds cross the turquoise surface, when you suspect something contagious is leaking, something camouflaged and disrupted. There is only this infected blue enormity elongating defiantly. The blue that knows you and where you live and it's never going to forget.

FOR ANALYSIS

1. When they first meet, the **protagonist** thinks that she doesn't "know why she bothered talking to him" (para. 25). Why *does* she talk to Lenny?

2. What function does the color blue serve in this story? Where in the story does it appear? What kinds of moments is it connected to?

3. Do you think the main character will return to sobriety after the story's end? Why or why not?

WRITING TOPICS

1. When Lenny first starts trying to convince the protagonist to be with him, he says, "I can be one of your tall tales" (para. 41). What does this moment do to the reader's "willing suspension of disbelief"? In what ways is Braverman's story a tall tale?

2. Much of the story is dialogue, and much of that is Lenny's voice. How does Braverman write Lenny's dialogue? What makes it so distinctive? How does it draw you in as a reader—just as it draws the **protagonist** in—in spite of his saying things like, "You start hurting, I'll take you out. I'll kill you myself. With my own hands. I promise" (para. 120).

MAKING CONNECTIONS

1. Are Arnold Friend and Lenny physically attractive? What is the source of their attraction for these women?

2. Both Connie and Braverman's **protagonist** are drawn to danger. Are their reasons the same? Similar? Different?

3. Can you imagine these stories told from different **points of view**? From Arnold's and Lenny's? From characters outside these "relationships"? How would the stories be different? Would they work?

CASE STUDY

RAYMOND CARVER: A WRITER REVISING

When we read a story or a poem, we encounter it as a finished product, set down in black and white on bound pages. As a result, we don't often think of the process of literature's composition, of the changes a work might have gone through as the writer set down his initial thoughts, changed direction, or got feedback from editors. In this casebook, however, we have the chance to read different versions of the same stories, and so to engage with works of literature not as fixed objects but as things produced by a craftsman, sometimes collaboratively. As a result, we are better able to think about the choices a writer makes.

Raymond Carver's career offers us the rare opportunity to do this kind of thinking. Carver, who died in 1988, was edited early in his career by magazine and book editor Gordon Lish. On the evidence of Lish's claims since Carver's death, correspondence between the two, and copies of drafts of the stories, it is clear that Lish edited with a heavy hand, cutting whole pages of Carver's work and radically altering the style and structure of his stories. It is also clear that Carver came to chafe at the restrictions Lish's editing imposed on his writing, as well perhaps at the debt his work owed to an unsigned collaborator. Breaking from Lish in the early 1980s, Carver's stories became more expansive, fuller, more like the uncovered drafts of his earlier work before Lish made his edits. While critical opinion varies over which is better, the fact that we have two Carvers—although complicating his legacy—makes reading Carver in some ways a richer experience.

While you read these stories, think about them as created works, but also think about how changes made in different versions alter the way these stories say things about their subject: love.

RAYMOND CARVER   (1938–1988)

MINE   1977

During the day the sun had come out and the snow melted into dirty water. Streaks of water ran down from the little, shoulder-high window that faced the backyard. Cars slushed by on the street outside. It was getting dark, outside and inside.

He was in the bedroom pushing clothes into a suitcase when she came to the door.

I'm glad you're leaving, I'm glad you're leaving! she said. Do you hear?

He kept on putting his things into the suitcase and didn't look up.

Sonofabitch! I'm so glad you're leaving! She began to cry. You can't even 5 look me in the face, can you? Then she noticed the baby's picture on the bed and picked it up.

He looked at her and she wiped her eyes and stared at him before turning and going back to the living room.

Bring that back.

Just get your things and get out, she said.

He did not answer. He fastened the suitcase, put on his coat, and looked at the bedroom before turning off the light. Then he went out to the living room. She stood in the doorway of the little kitchen, holding the baby.

I want the baby, he said.   10

Are you crazy?

No, but I want the baby. I'll get someone to come by for his things.

You can go to hell! You're not touching this baby.

The baby had begun to cry and she uncovered the blanket from around its head.

Oh, oh, she said, looking at the baby.   15

He moved towards her.

For God's sake! she said. She took a step back into the kitchen.

I want the baby.

Get out of here!

She turned and tried to hold the baby over in a corner behind the stove as he   20
came up.

He reached across the stove and tightened his hands on the baby.

Let go of him, he said.

Get away, get away! she cried.

The baby was red-faced and screaming. In the scuffle they knocked down a little flower pot that hung behind the stove.

He crowded her into the wall then, trying to break her grip, holding onto the   25
baby and pushing his weight against her arm.

Let go of him, he said.

Don't, she said, you're hurting him!

He didn't talk again. The kitchen window gave no light. In the near dark he worked on her fisted fingers with one hand and with the other hand he gripped the screaming baby up under an arm near the shoulder.

She felt her fingers being forced open and the baby going from her. No, she said, just as her hands came loose. She would have it, this baby whose chubby face gazed up at them from the picture on the table. She grabbed for the baby's other arm. She caught the baby around the wrist and leaned back.

He would not give. He felt the baby going out of his hands and he pulled   30
back hard. He pulled back very hard.

In this manner they decided the issue.

For Analysis

1. What might be the significance of the first paragraph's noting the weather outside the house?

2. Why might the story be titled as it is? How does the title prepare the reader for the story?

1. Would the man in the story have demanded the baby if the woman had not picked up the baby's photograph?

2. How would you describe Carver's style? What kinds of words does he use? How would you characterize his sentences—in terms of length, complexity, **tone**? How does the style affect the telling of the story?

POPULAR MECHANICS 1981

Early that day the weather turned and the snow was melting into dirty water. Streaks of it ran down from the little shoulder-high window that faced the backyard. Cars slushed by on the street outside, where it was getting dark. But it was getting dark on the inside too.

He was in the bedroom pushing clothes into a suitcase when she came to the door.

I'm glad you're leaving! I'm glad you're leaving! she said. Do you hear?

He kept on putting his things into the suitcase.

Son of a bitch! I'm so glad you're leaving! She began to cry. You can't even 5
look me in the face, can you?

Then she noticed the baby's picture on the bed and picked it up.

He looked at her and she wiped her eyes and stared at him before turning and going back to the living room.

Bring that back, he said.

Just get your things and get out, she said.

He did not answer. He fastened the suitcase, put on his coat, looked around 10
the bedroom before turning off the light. Then he went out to the living room.

She stood in the doorway of the little kitchen, holding the baby.

I want the baby, he said.

Are you crazy?

No, but I want the baby. I'll get someone to come by for his things.

You're not touching this baby, she said. 15

The baby had begun to cry and she uncovered the blanket from around his head.

Oh, oh, she said, looking at the baby.

He moved toward her.

For God's sake! she said. She took a step back into the kitchen.

I want the baby. 20

Get out of here!

She turned and tried to hold the baby over in a corner behind the stove.

But he came up. He reached across the stove and tightened his hands on the baby.

Let go of him, he said.

Get away, get away! she cried. 25

The baby was red-faced and screaming. In the scuffle they knocked down a flowerpot that hung behind the stove.

He crowded her into the wall then, trying to break her grip. He held on to the baby and pushed with all his weight.

Let go of him, he said.

Don't, she said. You're hurting the baby, she said.

I'm not hurting the baby, he said.

The kitchen window gave no light. In the near-dark he worked on her fisted fingers with one hand and with the other hand he gripped the screaming baby up under an arm near the shoulder.

She felt her fingers being forced open. She felt the baby going from her.

No! she screamed just as her hands came loose.

She would have it, this baby. She grabbed for the baby's other arm. She caught the baby around the wrist and leaned back.

But he would not let go. He felt the baby slipping out of his hands and he pulled back very hard.

In this manner, the issue was decided.

FOR ANALYSIS

1. "Popular Mechanics" is also the name of a magazine. What might that association have to do with the story?

2. We are not told the names of the **characters** in this story. Why might Carver have chosen not to give them names?

WRITING TOPICS

1. This version of Carver's story appeared under two different titles—"Little Things" and "Popular Mechanics"—in different collections. What does each title mean in the context of the story? Which title do you like more? Why?

2. Does it matter that we don't know what has happened to the characters' relationship? How would knowing change the story? Why might Carver have chosen not to supply that information?

BEGINNERS   2007

My friend Herb McGinnis, a cardiologist, was talking. The four of us were sitting around his kitchen table drinking gin. It was Saturday afternoon. Sunlight filled the kitchen from the big window behind the sink. There were Herb and I and his second wife, Teresa—Terri, we called her—and my wife, Laura. We lived in Albuquerque, but we were all from somewhere else. There was an ice bucket on the table. The gin and the tonic water kept going around, and we somehow got on the subject of love. Herb thought real love was nothing less than spiritual love. When he was young he'd spent five years in a seminary before quitting to go to medical school. He'd left the Church at the same time, but he said he still looked back to those years in the seminary as the most important in his life.

Terri said the man she lived with before she lived with Herb loved her so much he tried to kill her. Herb laughed after she said this. He made a face. Terri looked at him. Then she said, "He beat me up one night, the last night we lived together. He dragged me around the living room by my ankles, all the while saying, 'I love you, don't you see? I love you, you bitch.' He went on dragging me around the living room, my head knocking on things." She looked around the table at us and then looked at her hands on her glass. "What do you do with love like that?" she said. She was a bone-thin woman with a pretty face, dark eyes, and brown hair that hung down her back. She liked necklaces made of turquoise, and long pendant earrings. She was fifteen years younger than Herb, had suffered periods of anorexia, and during the late sixties, before she'd gone to nursing school, had been a dropout, a "street person," as she put it. Herb sometimes called her, affectionately, his hippie.

"My God, don't be silly. That's not love, and you know it," Herb said. "I don't know what you'd call it—madness is what I'd call it—but it's sure as hell not love."

"Say what you want to, but I know he loved me," Terri said. "I know he did. It may sound crazy to you, but it's true just the same. People are different, Herb. Sure, sometimes he may have acted crazy. O.K. But he loved me. In his own way, maybe, but he loved me. There was love there, Herb. Don't deny me that."

Herb let out breath. He held his glass and turned to Laura and me. "He 5 threatened to kill *me*, too." He finished his drink and reached for the gin bottle. "Terri's a romantic. Terri's of the 'Kick-me-so-I'll-know-you-love-me' school. Terri, hon, don't look that way." He reached across the table and touched her cheek with his fingers. He grinned at her.

"Now he wants to make up," Terri said. "After he tries to dump on me." She wasn't smiling.

"Make up what?" Herb said. "What is there to make up? I know what I know, and that's all."

"What would you call it then?" Terri said. "How'd we get started on this subject anyway?" She raised her glass and drank. "Herb always has love on his mind," she said. "Don't you, honey?" She smiled now, and I thought that was the last of it.

"I just wouldn't call Carl's behavior love, that's all I'm saying, honey," Herb said. "What about you guys?" he said to Laura and me. "Does that sound like love to you?"

I shrugged. "I'm the wrong person to ask. I didn't even know the man. I've 10 only heard his name mentioned in passing. Carl. I wouldn't know. You'd have to know all the particulars. Not in my book it isn't, but who's to say? There're lots of different ways of behaving and showing affection. That way doesn't happen to be mine. But what you're saying, Herb, is that love is an absolute?"

"The kind of love I'm talking about is," Herb said. "The kind of love I'm talking about, you don't try to kill people."

Laura, my sweet, big Laura, said evenly, "I don't know anything about Carl, or anything about the situation. Who can judge anyone else's situation? But, Terri, I didn't know about the violence."

I touched the back of Laura's hand. She gave me a quick smile, then turned her gaze back to Terri. I picked up Laura's hand. The hand was warm to the touch, the nails polished, perfectly manicured. I encircled the broad wrist with my fingers, like a bracelet, and held her.

"When I left he drank rat poison," Terri said. She clasped her arms with her hands. "They took him to the hospital in Santa Fe where we lived then and they saved his life, and his gums separated. I mean they pulled away from his teeth. After that his teeth stood out like fangs. My God," she said. She waited a minute, then let go of her arms and picked up her glass.

"What people won't do!" Laura said. "I'm sorry for him and I don't even   15
think I like him. Where is he now?"

"He's out of the action," Herb said. "He's dead." He handed me the saucer of limes. I took a section of lime, squeezed it over my drink, and stirred the ice cubes with my finger.

"It gets worse," Terri said. "He shot himself in the mouth, but he bungled that, too. Poor Carl," she said. She shook her head.

"Poor Carl nothing," Herb said. "He was dangerous." Herb was forty-five years old. He was tall and rangy with wavy, graying hair. His face and arms were brown from the tennis he played. When he was sober, his gestures, all his movements, were precise and careful.

"He did love me, though, Herb, grant me that," Terri said. "That's all I'm ask-ing. He didn't love me the way you love me, I'm not saying that. But he loved me. You can grant me that, can't you? That's not much to ask."

"What do you mean, 'He bungled it'?" I asked. Laura leaned forward with   20
her glass. She put her elbows on the table and held her glass in both hands. She glanced from Herb to Terri and waited with a look of bewilderment on her open face, as if amazed that such things happened to people you knew. Herb finished his drink. "How'd he bungle it when he killed himself?" I said again.

"I'll tell you what happened," Herb said. "He took this .22 pistol he'd bought to threaten Terri and me with—oh, I'm serious, he wanted to use it. You should have seen the way we lived in those days. Like fugitives. I even bought a gun myself, and I thought I was a nonviolent sort. But I bought a gun for self-defense and carried it in the glove compartment. Sometimes I'd have to leave the apartment in the middle of the night, you know, to go to the hospital. Terri and I weren't married then and my first wife had the house and kids, the dog, everything, and Terri and I were living in this apartment. Sometimes, as I say, I'd get a call in the middle of the night and have to go in to the hospital at two or three in the morning. It'd be dark out there in the parking lot and I'd break into a sweat before I could even get to my car. I never knew if he was going to come up out of the shrubbery or from behind a car and start shooting. I mean, he was crazy. He was capable of wiring a bomb to my car, anything. He used to call my answering service at all hours and say he needed to talk to the doctor, and when I'd return the call he'd say, 'Son of a bitch, your days are numbered.' Little things like that. It was scary, I'm telling you."

"I still feel sorry for him," Terri said. She sipped her drink and gazed at Herb. Herb stared back.

"It sounds like a nightmare," Laura said. "But what exactly happened after he shot himself?" Laura is a legal secretary. We'd met in a professional capacity, lots of other people around, but we'd talked and I'd asked her to have dinner with me. Before we knew it, it was a courtship. She's thirty-five, three years younger than I am. In addition to being in love, we like each other and enjoy one another's company. She's easy to be with. "What happened?" Laura asked again.

Herb waited a minute and turned the glass in his hand. Then he said, "He shot himself in the mouth in his room. Someone heard the shot and told the manager. They came in with a passkey, saw what had happened, and called an ambulance. I happened to be there when they brought him in to the emergency room. I was there on another case. He was still alive, but beyond anything anyone could do for him. Still, he lived for three days. I'm serious, though, his head swelled up to twice the size of a normal head. I'd never seen anything like it, and I hope I never do again. Terri wanted to go in and sit with him when she found out about it. We had a fight over it. I didn't think she'd want to see him like that. I didn't think she should see him, and I still don't."

"Who won the fight?" Laura said.   25

"I was in the room with him when he died," Terri said. "He never regained consciousness, and there was no hope for him, but I sat with him. He didn't have anyone else."

"He was dangerous," Herb said. "If you call that love, you can have it."

"It was love," Terri said. "Sure it was abnormal in most people's eyes, but he was willing to die for it. He did die for it."

"I sure as hell wouldn't call it love," Herb said. "You don't know what he died for. I've seen a lot of suicides, and I couldn't say anyone close to them ever knew for sure. And when they claimed to be the cause, well I don't know." He put his hands behind his neck and leaned on the back legs of his chair. "I'm not interested in that kind of love. If that's love, you can have it."

After a minute, Terri said, "We were afraid. Herb even made a will out and   30
wrote to his brother in California who used to be a Green Beret. He told him who to look for if something happened to him mysteriously. Or not so mysteriously!" She shook her head and laughed at it now. She drank from her glass. She went on. "But we did live a little like fugitives. We *were* afraid of him, no question. I even called the police at one point, but they were no help. They said they couldn't do anything to him, they couldn't arrest him or do anything unless he actually *did* something to Herb. Isn't that a laugh?" Terri said. She poured the last of the gin into her glass and wagged the bottle. Herb got up from the table and went to the cupboard. He took down another bottle of gin.

"Well, Nick and I are in love," Laura said. "Aren't we, Nick?" She bumped my knee with her knee. "You're supposed to say something now," she said, and turned a large smile on me. "We get along really well, I think. We like doing things together, and neither of us has beaten up on the other yet, thank God. Knock on wood. I'd say we're pretty happy. I guess we should count our blessings."

For answer, I took her hand and raised it to my lips with a flourish. I made a production out of kissing her hand. Everyone was amused. "We're lucky," I said.

"You guys," Terri said. "Stop that now. You're making me sick! You're still on a honeymoon, that's why you can act like this. You're still gaga over each other yet. Just wait. How long have you been together now? How long has it been? A year? Longer than a year."

"Going on a year and a half," Laura said, still flushed and smiling.

"You're still on the honeymoon," Terri said again. "Wait a while." She held   35
her drink and gazed at Laura. "I'm only kidding," she said.

Herb had opened the gin and gone around the table with the bottle. "Terri, Jesus, you shouldn't talk like that, even if you're not serious, even if you are kidding. It's bad luck. Here, you guys. Let's have a toast. I want to propose a toast. A toast to love. True love," Herb said. We touched glasses.

"To love," we said.

Outside, in the backyard, one of the dogs began to bark. The leaves of the aspen tree that leaned past the window flickered in the breeze. The afternoon sunlight was like a presence in the room. There was suddenly a feeling of ease and generosity around the table, of friendship and comfort. We could have been anywhere. We raised our glasses again and grinned at each other like children who had agreed on something for once.

"I'll tell you what real love is," Herb said finally, breaking the spell. "I mean I'll give you a good example of it, and then you can draw your own conclusions." He poured a little more gin into his glass. He added an ice cube and a piece of lime. We waited and sipped our drinks. Laura and I touched knees again. I put a hand on her warm thigh and left it there.

"What do any of us really know about love?" Herb said. "I kind of mean   40
what I'm saying, too, if you'll pardon me for saying it. But it seems to me we're just rank beginners at love. We say we love each other and we do, I don't doubt it. We love each other and we love hard, all of us. I love Terri and Terri loves me, and you guys love each other. You know the kind of love I'm talking about now. Sexual love, that attraction to the other person, the partner, as well as just the plain everyday kind of love, love of the other person's being, the loving to be with the other, the little things that make up everyday love. Carnal love, then and, well, call it sentimental love, the day-to-day caring about the other. But sometimes I have a hard time accounting for the fact that I must have loved my first wife, too. But I did, I know I did. So I guess before you can say anything, I *am* like Terri in that regard. Terri and Carl." He thought about it a minute and then went on, "But at one time I thought I loved my first wife more

than life itself, and we had the kids together. But now I hate her guts. I do. How do you figure that? What happened to that love? Did that love just get erased from the big board, as if it was never up there, as if it never happened? What happened to it is what I'd like to know. I wish someone could tell me. Then there's Carl. O.K., we're back to Carl. He loved Terri so much he tries to kill her and winds up killing himself." He stopped talking and shook his head. "You guys have been together eighteen months and you love each other, it shows all over you, you simply glow with it, but you've loved other people, too, before you met each other. You've both been married before, just like us. And you probably loved other people before that. Terri and I have been together five years, been married for four. And the terrible thing, the terrible thing is, but the good thing, too, the saving grace, you might say, is that if something happened to one of us—excuse me for saying this—but if something happened to one of us tomorrow, I think the other one, the other partner, would mourn for a while, you know, but then the surviving party would go out and love again, have someone else soon enough and all this, all of this love—Jesus, how can you figure it?—it would just be memory. Maybe not even memory. Maybe that's the way it's supposed to be. But am I wrong? Am I way off base? I know that's what would happen with us, with Terri and me, as much as we may love each other. With any one of us for that matter. I'll stick my neck out that much. We've all proved it anyhow. I just don't understand. Set me straight if you think I'm wrong. I want to know. I don't know anything, and I'm the first to admit it."

"Herb, for God's sake," Terri said. "This is depressing stuff. This could get very depressing. Even if you think it's true," she said, "it's still depressing." She reached out to him and took hold of his forearm near the wrist. "Are you getting drunk, Herb? Honey, are you drunk?"

"Honey, I'm just talking, all right," Herb said. "I don't have to be drunk to say what's on my mind, do I? I'm not drunk. We're just talking, right?" Herb said. Then his voice changed. "But if I want to get drunk I will, God damn it. I can do anything I want today." He fixed his eyes on her.

"Honey, I'm not criticizing," she said. She picked up her glass.

"I'm not on call today," Herb said. "I can do anything I want today. I'm just tired, that's all."

"Herb, we love you," Laura said.   45

Herb looked at Laura. It was as if he couldn't place her for a minute. She kept looking at him, holding her smile. Her cheeks were flushed and the sun was hitting her in the eyes, so she squinted to see him. His features relaxed. "Love you, too, Laura. And you, Nick. I'll tell you, you're our pals," Herb said. He picked up his glass. "Well, what was I saying? Yeah. I wanted to tell you about something that happened a while back. I think I wanted to prove a point, and I will if I can just tell this thing the way it happened. This happened a few months ago, but it's still going on right now. You might say that, yeah. But it ought to make us all feel ashamed when we talk like we know what we were talking about, when we talk about love."

"Herb, come on now," Terri said. "You are too drunk. Don't talk like this. Don't talk like you're drunk if you're not drunk."

"Just shut up for a minute, will you?" Herb said. "Let me tell this. It's been on my mind. Just shut up for a minute. I told you a little about it when it first happened. That old couple who got into an accident out on the interstate? A kid hit them, and they were all battered up and not given much chance to pull through. Let me tell this, Terri. Now just shut up for a minute. O.K.?"

Terri looked at us and then looked back at Herb. She seemed anxious, that's the only word for it. Herb handed the bottle around the table.

"Surprise me, Herb," Terri said. "Surprise me beyond all thought and reason." 50

"Maybe I will," Herb said. "Maybe so. I'm constantly surprised with things myself. Everything in my life surprises me." He stared at her for a minute. Then he began talking.

"I was on call that night. It was in May or June. Terri and I had just sat down to dinner, when the hospital called. There'd been an accident out on the interstate. A drunk kid, a teen-ager, had plowed his dad's pickup into a camper with this old couple in it. They were up in their mid-seventies. The kid, he was eighteen or nineteen, he was D.O.A. when they brought him in. He'd taken the steering wheel through his sternum and must have died instantly. But the old couple, they were still alive, but just barely. They had multiple fractures and contusions, lacerations, the works, and they each had themselves a concussion. They were in a bad way, believe me. And, of course, their age was against them. She was even a little worse off than he was. She had a ruptured spleen and along with everything else, both kneecaps were broken. But they'd been wearing their seat belts and, God knows, that's the only thing that saved them."

"Folks, this is an advertisement for the National Safety Council," Terri said. "This is your spokesman, Dr. Herb McGinnis, talking. Listen up now," Terri said and laughed, then lowered her voice. "Herb, you're just too much sometimes. I love you, honey."

We all laughed. Herb laughed, too. "Honey, I love you. But you know that, don't you?" He leaned across the table, Terri met him halfway, and they kissed. "Terri's right, everybody," Herb said as he settled himself again. "Buckle up for safety. Listen to what Dr. Herb is telling you. But, seriously, they were in bum shape, those old people. By the time I got down there, the intern and nurses were already at work on them. The kid was dead, as I said. He was off in a corner, laid out on a gurney. Someone had already notified the next of kin, and the funeral-home people were on the way. I took one look at the old couple and told the E.R. nurse to get me a neurologist and an orthopedic man down there right away. I'll try and make a long story short. The other fellows showed up, and we took the old couple up to the operating room and worked on them most of the night. They must have had incredible reserves, those old people, you see that once in a while. We did everything that could be done, and toward morning we were giving them a fifty-fifty chance, maybe less than that, maybe thirty-seventy for the wife. Anna Gates was her name, and she was quite a woman. But they were still alive the next morning, and we moved them into the I.C.U. where we could monitor every breath and keep a twenty-four-hour watch on them. They were in intensive care for nearly two weeks, she a little longer, before their condition improved enough so we could transfer them out and down the hall to their own rooms."

Herb stopped talking. "Here," he said, "let's drink this gin. Let's drink it up. 55 Then we're going to dinner, right? Terri and I know a place. It's a new place. That's where we'll go, this new place we know about. We'll go when we finish this gin."

"It's called the Library," Terri said. "You haven't eaten there yet, have you?" she said, and Laura and I shook our heads. "It's some place. They say it's part of a new chain, but it's not like a chain, if you know what I mean. They actually have bookshelves in there with real books on them. You can browse around after dinner and take a book out and bring it back the next time you come to eat. You won't believe the food. And Herb's reading *Ivanhoe*! He took it out when we were there last week. He just signed a card. Like in a real library."

"I like *Ivanhoe*," Herb said. "*Ivanhoe*'s great. If I had it to do over again, I'd study literature. Right now I'm having an identity crisis. Right, Terri?" Herb said. He laughed. He twirled the ice in his glass. "I've been having an identity crisis for years. Terri knows. Terri can tell you. But let me say this. If I could come back again in a different life, a different time and all, you know what? I'd like to come back as a knight. You were pretty safe wearing all that armor. It was all right being a knight until gunpowder and muskets and .22 pistols came along."

"Herb would like to ride a white horse and carry a lance," Terri said, and laughed.

"Carry a woman's garter with you everywhere," Laura said.

"Or just a woman," I said.   60

"That's right," Herb said. "There you go. You know what's what, don't you, Nick?" he said. "Also, you'd carry around their perfumed hankies with you wherever you rode. Did they have perfumed hankies in those days? It doesn't matter. Some little forget-me-not. A token, that's what I'm trying to say. You needed some token to carry around with you in those days. Anyway, whatever, it was better in those days being a knight than a serf," Herb said.

"It's always better," Laura said.

"The serfs didn't have it so good in those days," Terri said.

"The serfs have never had it good," Herb said. "But I guess even the knights were vessels to someone. Isn't that the way it worked in those days? But, then, everyone is always a vessel to someone else. Isn't that right? Terri? But what I liked about knights, besides their ladies, was that they had that suit of armor, you know, and they couldn't get hurt very easy. No cars in those days, man. No drunk teen-agers to run over you."

"Vassals," I said.   65

"What?" Herb said.

"Vassals," I said. "They were called *vassals*, Doc, not *vessels*."

"Vassals," Herb said. "Vassals, vessels, ventricles, vas deferens. Well, you knew what I meant anyway. You're all better educated in these matters than I am,"

Herb said. "I'm not educated. I learned my stuff. I'm a heart surgeon, sure, but really I'm just a mechanic. I just go in and fix things that go wrong with the body. I'm just a mechanic."

"Modesty somehow doesn't become you, Herb," Laura said, and Herb grinned at her.

"He's just a humble doctor, folks," I said. "But sometimes they suffocated in all that armor, Herb. They'd even have heart attacks if it got too hot and they were too tired and worn out. I read somewhere that they'd fall off their horses and not be able to get up because they were too tired to stand with all that armor on them. They got trampled by their own horses sometimes." 70

"That's terrible," Herb said. "That's a terrible image, Nicky. I guess they'd just lay there then and wait until someone, the enemy, came along and made a shish kebab out of them."

"Some other vassal," Terri said.

"That's right, some other vassal," Herb said. "There you have it. Some other vassal would come along and spear his fellow-knight in the name of love. Or whatever it was they fought over in those days. Same things we fight over these days, I guess," Herb said.

"Politics," Laura said. "Nothing's changed." The color was still in Laura's cheeks. Her eyes were bright. She brought her glass to her lips.

Herb poured himself another drink. He looked at the label closely, as if studying the little figures of the Beefeater guards. Then he slowly put the bottle down on the table and reached for the tonic water. 75

"What about this old couple, Herb?" Laura said. "You didn't finish that story you started." Laura was having a hard time lighting her cigarette. Her matches kept going out. The light inside the room was different now, changing, getting weaker. The leaves outside the window were still shimmering, and I stared at the fuzzy pattern they made on the pane and the Formica counter under it. There was no sound except for Laura striking her matches.

"What about that old couple?" I said after a minute. "The last we heard they were just getting out of intensive care."

"Older but wiser," Terri said.

Herb stared at her.

"Herb, don't give me that kind of look," Terri said. "Go on with your story. I was only kidding. Then what happened? We all want to know." 80

"Terri, sometimes," Herb said.

"Please, Herb," she said. "Honey, don't always be so serious. Please go on with the story. I was joking, for God's sake. Can't you take a joke?"

"This is nothing to joke about," Herb said. He held his glass and gazed steadily at her.

"What happened then, Herb?" Laura said. "We really want to know."

Herb fixed his eyes on Laura. Then he broke off and grinned. "Laura, if I didn't have Terri and love her so much, and Nick wasn't my friend, I'd fall in love with you. I'd carry you off." 85

"Herb, you shit," Terri said. "Tell your story. If I weren't in love with you, I damn sure well wouldn't be here in the first place, you can bet on it. Honey, what do you say? Finish your story. Then we'll go to the Library. O.K.?"

"O.K.," Herb said. "Where was I? Where am I? That's a better question. Maybe I should ask that." He waited a minute, and then began to talk.

"When they were finally out of the woods, we were able to move them out of intensive care, after we could see they were going to make it. I dropped in to see each of them every day, sometimes twice a day if I was up doing other calls anyway. They were both in casts and bandages, head to foot. You know, you've seen it in the movies even if you haven't seen the real thing. But they were bandaged head to foot, man, and I mean head to foot. That's just the way they looked, just like those phony actors in the movies after some big disaster. But this was the real thing. Their heads were bandaged—they just had eye holes and a place for their mouths and noses. Anna Gates had to have her legs elevated, too. She was worse off than he was, I told you that. Both of them were on intravenous and glucose for a time. Well, Henry Gates was very depressed for the longest while. Even after he found out that his wife was going to pull through and recover, he was still very depressed. Not just about the accident itself, though of course that had gotten to him, as those things will. There you are one minute, you know, everything just dandy, then *blam,* you're staring into the abyss. You come back. It's like a miracle. But it's left its mark on you. It does that. One day, I was sitting in a chair beside his bed and he described to me, talking slowly, talking through his mouth hole so sometimes I had to get up to his face to hear him, telling me what it looked like to him, what it felt like, when that kid's car crossed the center line onto his side of the road and kept coming. He said he knew it was all up for them, that was the last look of anything he'd have on this earth. This was it. But he said nothing flew into his mind, his life didn't pass before his eyes, nothing like that. He said he just felt sorry to not be able to see any more of his Anna, because they'd had this fine life together. That was his only regret. He looked straight ahead, just gripped the wheel and watched the kid's car coming at them. And there was nothing he could do except say, 'Anna! Hold on, Anna!'"

"It gives me the shivers," Laura said. "Brrr," she said, shaking her head.

Herb nodded. He went on talking, caught up in it now. "I'd sit awhile every day beside the bed. He'd lay there in his bandages staring out the window at the foot of his bed. The window was too high for him to see anything except the tops of trees. That's all he saw for hours at a stretch. He couldn't turn his head without assistance, and he was only allowed to do that twice a day. Each morning for a few minutes and every evening, he was allowed to turn his head. But during our visits he had to look at the window when he talked. I'd talk a little, ask a few questions, but mostly I'd listen. He was very depressed. What was most depressing to him, after he was assured his wife was going to be all right, that she was recovering to everyone's satisfaction, what was most depressing was the fact they couldn't be physically together. That he couldn't see her and be with her every day. He told me they'd married in 1927, and since that time they'd only been apart from each other for any time on two occasions. Even when their children were born, they were born there on the ranch and Henry and the missus still saw each other every day and talked and were together around the place. But he said they'd only been away from each other for any real time on two occasions—once when her mother died, in 1940, and Anna had to take a train to St. Louis to settle matters there. And again in 1952, when her sister died in Los Angeles, and she had to go down there to claim the body. I should tell you they had a little ranch seventy-five miles or so outside of Bend, Oregon, and that's where they'd lived most of their lives. They'd sold the ranch and moved into the city of Bend just a few years ago. When this accident happened, they were on their way down from Denver, where they'd gone to see his sister. They were going on to visit a son and some of their grandchildren in El Paso. But in all of their married life they'd only been apart from each other for any length of time on just those two occasions. Imagine that. But, Jesus, he was lonely for her. I'm telling you he *pined* for her. I never knew what that word meant before, *pined*, until I saw it happening to this man. He missed her something fierce. He just longed for her company, that old man did. Of course, he felt better, he'd brighten, when I'd give him my daily report on Anna's progress—that she was mending, that she was going to be fine, just a question of a little more time. He was out of his casts and bandages now, but he was still extremely lonely. I told him that just as soon as he was able, maybe in a week, I'd put him into a wheelchair and take him visiting, take him down the corridor to see his wife. Meanwhile, I called on him and we'd talk. He told me a little about their lives out there on the ranch in the late nineteen-twenties and during the early thirties." He looked around the table at us and shook his head at what he was going to say, or just maybe at the impossibility of all this. "He told me that in the winter it would do nothing but snow, and for maybe months at a time they couldn't leave the ranch, the road would be closed. Besides, he had to feed cattle every day through those winter months. They would just be there together, the two of them, him and his wife. The kids hadn't come along yet. They'd come along later. But, month in, month out, they'd be there together, the two of them, the same routine, the same everything, never anyone else to talk to or to visit with during those winter months. But they had each other. That's all and every-thing they had, each other. 'What would you do for entertainment?' I asked him. I was serious. I wanted to know. I didn't see how people could live like that. I don't think anyone can live like that these days. You think so? It seems impossible to me. You know what he said? Do you want to know what he answered? He lay there and considered the question. He took some time. Then he said, 'We'd go to the dances every night.' 'What?' I said. 'Pardon me, Henry,' I said, and leaned closer, thinking I hadn't heard right. 'We'd go to the dances every night,' he said again. I wondered what he meant. I didn't know what he was talking about, but I waited for him to go on. He thought back to that time again, and in a little while he said, 'We had a Victrola and some records, Doctor. We'd play the Victrola every night and listen to the records and dance there in the living room. We'd do that every night. Sometimes it'd be snowing outside and the temperature down below zero. The temperature really drops on you up there in January or February. But we'd listen to the records and dance in our stocking feet in the living room until we'd gone through all the records. And then I'd build up the fire and turn out the lights, all but one, and we'd go to bed. Some nights it'd be snowing, and it'd be so still outside you could hear the snow falling. It's true, Doc,' he said, 'you can do that. Sometimes you can hear the snow falling. If you're quiet and your mind is clear and you're at peace with yourself and all things, you can lay in the dark and hear it snow. You try it sometimes,' he said. 'You get snow down here once in a while, don't you? You try it sometimes. Anyway, we'd go to the dances every night. And then we'd go to bed under a lot of quilts and sleep warm until morning. When you woke up you could see your breath,' he said.

"When he'd recovered enough to be moved in a wheelchair, his bandages were long gone by then, a nurse and I wheeled him down the corridor to where his wife was. He'd shaved that morning and put on some lotion. He was in his bathrobe and hospital gown, he was still recovering, you know, but he held himself erect in the wheelchair. Still, he was nervous as a cat, you could see that. As we came closer to her room, his color rose and he got this look of anticipation to his face, a look I can't begin to describe. I pushed his chair, and the nurse walked along beside me. She knew something about the situation, she'd picked up things. Nurses, you know, they've seen everything, and not much gets to them after a while, but this one was strung a little tight herself that morning. The door was open and I wheeled Henry right into the room. Mrs. Gates, Anna, she was still immobilized, but she could move her head and her left arm. She had her eyes closed, but they snapped open when we entered the room. She was still in bandages, but only from the pelvic area down. I pushed Henry up to the left side of her bed and said, 'You have some company, Anna. Company, dear.' But I couldn't say any more than that. She gave a little smile and her face lit up. Out came her hand from under the sheet. It was bluish and bruised-looking. Henry took the hand in his hands. He held it and kissed it. Then he said, 'Hello, Anna. How's my babe? Remember me?' Tears started down her cheeks. She nodded. 'I've missed you,' he said. She kept nodding. The nurse and I got the hell out of there. She began blubbering once we were outside the room, and she's a tough lot, that nurse. It was an experience, I'm telling you. But after that he was wheeled down there every morning and every afternoon. We arranged it so they could have lunch and dinner together in her room. In between times, they'd just sit and hold hands and talk. They had no end of things to talk about."

"You didn't tell me this before, Herb," Terri said. "You just said a little about it when it first happened. You didn't tell me any of this, damn you. Now you're telling me this to make me cry. Herb, this story better not have an unhappy ending. It doesn't, does it? You're not setting us up, are you? If you are, I don't want to hear another word. You don't have to go any farther with it, you can stop right there. Herb?"

"What happened to them, Herb?" Laura said. "Finish the story, for God's sake. Is there more? But I'm like Terri, I don't want anything to happen to them. That's really something."

"Are they all right now?" I asked. I was involved in the story, too, but I was getting drunk. It was hard to keep things in focus. The light seemed to be draining out of the room, going back through the window where it had come from in the first place. Yet nobody made a move to get up from the table or to turn on an electric light.

"Sure, they're all right," Herb said. "They were discharged a while later. Just a   95
few weeks ago, in fact. After a time, Henry was able to get around on crutches and then he went to a cane and then he was just all over the place. But his spirits were up now, his spirits were fine, he just improved every day once he got to see his missus again. When she was able to be moved, their son from El Paso and his wife drove up in a station wagon and took them back down there with them. She still had some convalescing to do, but she was coming along real fine. I just had a card from Henry a few days ago. I guess that's one of the reasons they're on my mind right now. That, and what we were saying about love earlier.

"Listen," Herb went on. "Let's finish this gin. There's about enough left here for one drink all around. Then let's go eat. Let's go to the Library. What do you say? I don't know, the whole thing was really something to see. It just unfolded day after day. Some of those talks I had with him . . . I won't forget those times. But talking about it now has got me depressed. Jesus, but I feel depressed all of a sudden."

"Don't feel depressed, Herb," Terri said. "Herb, why don't you take a pill, honey?" She turned to Laura and me and said, "Herb takes these mood-elevator pills sometimes. It's no secret, is it, Herb?"

Herb shook his head. "I've taken everything there is to take, at one time or another. No secret."

"My first wife took them, too," I said.

"Did they help her?" Laura said.   100

"No, she still went around depressed. She cried a lot."

"Some people are born depressed, I think," Terri said. "Some people are born unhappy. And unlucky, too. I've known people who were just plain unlucky in everything. Other people—not you, honey, I'm not talking about you, of course—other people just set out to make themselves unhappy and they stay unhappy." She was rubbing at something on the table with her finger. Then she stopped rubbing.

"I think I want to call my kids before we go eat," Herb said. "Is that all right with everybody? I won't be long. I'll take a quick shower to freshen up, then I'll call my kids. Then let's go eat."

"You might have to talk to Marjorie, Herb, if she answers the phone. That's Herb's ex-wife. You guys, you've heard us on the subject of Marjorie. You don't want to talk to her this afternoon, Herb. It'll make you feel even worse."

"No, I don't want to talk to Marjorie," Herb said. "But I want to talk to my kids.   105
I miss them real bad, honey. I miss Steve. I was awake last night remembering

things from when he was little. I want to talk to him. I want to talk to Kathy, too. I miss them, so I'll have to take the chance their mother will answer the phone. That bitch of a woman."

"There isn't a day goes by that Herb doesn't say he wishes she'd get married again, or else die. For one thing," Terri said, "she's bankrupting us. Another is that she has custody of both kids. We get to have the kids down here just for a month during the summer. Herb says it's just to spite him that she won't get married again. She has a boyfriend who lives with them, too, and Herb is supporting him as well."

"She's allergic to bees," Herb said. "If I'm not praying she'll get married again, I'm praying she'll go out in the country and get herself stung to death by a swarm of bees."

"Herb, that's awful," Laura said, and laughed until her eyes welled.

"Awful funny," Terri said. We all laughed. We laughed and laughed.

"*Bzzzzzz*," Herb said, turning his fingers into bees and buzzing them at 110 Terri's throat and necklace. Then he let his hands drop and leaned back, suddenly serious again.

"She's a rotten bitch. It's true," Herb said. "She's vicious. Sometimes when I get drunk, like I am now, I think I'd like to go up there dressed like a beekeeper—you know, that hat that's like a helmet with the plate that comes down over your face, the big thick gloves, and the padded coat. I'd like to just knock on the door and release a hive of bees in the house. First I'd make sure the kids were out of the house, of course." With some difficulty, he crossed one leg over the other. Then he put both feet on the floor and leaned forward, elbows on the table, chin cupped in his hands. "Maybe I won't call the kids right now after all. Maybe you're right, Terri. Maybe it isn't such a hot idea. Maybe I'll just take a quick shower and change my shirt, and then we'll go eat. How does that sound, everybody?"

"Sounds fine to me," I said "Eat or not eat. Or keep drinking. I could head right on into the sunset."

"What does that mean, honey?" Laura said, turning a look on me.

"It just means what I said, honey, nothing else. I mean I could just keep going and going. That's all I meant. It's that sunset maybe." The window had a reddish tint to it now as the sun went down.

"I could eat something myself," Laura said. "I just realized I'm hungry. What 115 is there to snack on?"

"I'll put out some cheese and crackers," Terri said, but she just sat there.

Herb finished his drink. Then he got slowly up from the table and said, "Excuse me. I'll go shower." He left the kitchen and walked slowly down the hall to the bathroom. He shut the door behind him.

"I'm worried about Herb," Terri said. She shook her head. "Sometimes I worry more than other times, but lately I'm really worried." She stared at her glass. She didn't make any move for cheese and crackers. I decided to get up and look in the refrigerator. When Laura says she's hungry, I know she needs to eat. "Help yourself to whatever you can find, Nick. Bring out anything that looks good. Cheese in there, and a salami stick, I think. Crackers in that cupboard over the stove. I forgot. We'll have a snack. I'm not hungry myself, but you guys must be starving. I don't have an appetite anymore. What was I saying?" She closed her eyes and opened them. "I don't think we've told you this, maybe we have, I can't remember, but Herb was very suicidal after his first marriage broke up and his wife moved to Denver with the kids. He went to a psychiatrist for a long while, for months. Sometimes he says he thinks he should still be going." She picked up the empty bottle and turned it upside down over her glass. I was cutting some salami on the counter as carefully as I could. "Dead soldier," Terri said. Then she said, "Lately, he's been talking about suicide again. Especially when he's been drinking. Sometimes I think he's too vulnerable. He doesn't have any defenses. He doesn't have defenses against anything. Well," she said, "gin's gone. Time to cut and run. Time to cut our losses, as my daddy used to say. Time to eat, I guess, though I don't have any appetite. But you guys must be starving. I'm glad to see you eating something. That'll keep you until we get to the restaurant. We can get drinks at the restaurant if we want them. Wait'll you see this place, it's something else. You can take books out of there along with your doggie bag. I guess I should get ready, too. I'll just wash my face and put on some lipstick. I'm going just like I am. If they don't like it, tough. I just want to say this, and that's all. But I don't want it to sound negative. I hope and pray that you guys still love each other five, even three years from now the way you do today. Even four years from now, say. That's the moment of truth, four years. That's all I have to say on the subject." She hugged her thin arms and began running her hands up and down them. She closed her eyes.

I stood up from the table and went behind Laura's chair. I leaned over her and crossed my arms under her breasts and held her. I brought my face down beside hers. Laura pressed my arms. She pressed harder and wouldn't let go.

Terri opened her eyes. She watched us. Then she picked up her glass. "Here's to you guys," she said. "Here's to all of us." She drained the glass, and the ice clicked against her teeth. "Carl, too," she said, and put her glass back on the table. "Poor Carl. Herb thought he was a schmuck, but Herb was genuinely afraid of him. Carl wasn't a schmuck. He loved me, and I loved him. That's all. I still think of him sometimes. It's the truth, and I'm not ashamed to say it. Sometimes I think of him, he'll just pop into my head at any old moment. I'll tell you something, and I hate how soap opera a life can get, so it's not even yours anymore, but this is how it was. I was pregnant by him. It was that first time he tried to kill himself, when he took the rat poison. He didn't know I was pregnant. It gets worse. I decided on an abortion. I didn't tell him about it, either, naturally. I'm not saying anything Herb doesn't know. Herb knows all about it. Final installment. Herb gave me the abortion. Small world, isn't it? But I thought Carl was crazy at the time. I didn't want his baby. Then he goes and kills himself. But after that, after he'd been gone for a while and there was no Carl anymore to talk to and listen to his side of things and

120

help him when he was afraid, I felt real bad about things. I was sorry about his baby, that I hadn't had it. I love Carl, and there's no question of that in my mind. I still love him. But God, I love Herb, too. You can see that, can't you? I don't have to tell you that. Oh, isn't it all too much, all of it?" She put her face in her hands and began to cry. Slowly, she leaned forward and put her head on the table.

Laura put her food down at once. She got up and said, "Terri. Terri, dear," and began rubbing Terri's neck and shoulders. "Terri," she murmured.

I was eating a piece of salami. The room had gotten very dark. I finished chewing what I had in my mouth, swallowed the stuff, and moved over to the window. I looked out into the backyard. I looked past the aspen tree and the two black dogs sleeping in amongst the lawn chairs. I looked past the swimming pool to the little corral with its gate open and the old empty horse barn and beyond. There was a field of wild grass, and then a fence and then another field, and then the interstate connecting Albuquerque with El Paso. Cars moved back and forth on the highway. The sun was going down behind the mountains, and the mountains had gotten dark, shadows everywhere. Yet there was light, too, and it seemed to be softening those things I looked at. The sky was gray near the tops of the mountains, as gray as a dark day in winter. But there was a band of blue sky just above the gray, the blue you see in tropical postcards, the blue of the Mediterranean. The water on the surface of the pool rippled and the same breeze caused the aspen leaves to tremble. One of the dogs raised its head as if on signal, listened a minute with its ears up, and then put its head back down between its paws.

I had the feeling something was going to happen, it was in the slowness of the shadows and the light, and that whatever it was might take me with it. I didn't want that to happen. I watched the wind move in waves across the grass, I could see the grass in the fields bend in the wind and then straighten again. The second field slanted up to the highway, and the wind moved uphill across it, wave after wave. I stood there and waited and watched the grass bend in the wind. I could feel my heart beating. Somewhere toward the back of the house the shower was running. Terri was still crying. Slowly and with an effort, I turned to look at her. She lay with her head on the table, her face turned toward the stove. Her eyes were open, but now and then she would blink away tears. Laura had pulled her chair over, and sat with an arm around Terri's shoulders. She murmured still, her lips against Terri's hair.

"Sure, sure," Terri said. "Tell me about it."

"Terri, sweetheart," Laura said to her tenderly. "It'll be O.K., you'll see. It'll 125
be O.K."

Laura raised her eyes to mine then. Her look was penetrating, and my heart slowed. She gazed into my eyes for what seemed a long time, and then she nodded. That's all she did, the only sign she gave, but it was enough. It was as if she were telling me, Don't worry, we'll get past this, everything is going to be all right with us, you'll see. Easy does it. That's the way I chose to interpret the look anyway, though I could be wrong.

The shower stopped running. In a minute, I heard whistling as Herb opened the bathroom door. I kept looking at the women at the table. Terri was still crying and Laura was stroking her hair. I turned back to the window. The blue layer of sky had given way now and was turning dark like the rest. But stars had appeared. I recognized Venus and, farther off and to the side, not as bright but unmistakably there on the horizon, Mars. The wind had picked up. I looked at what it was doing to the empty fields. I thought unreasonably that it was too bad the McGinnises no longer kept horses. I wanted to imagine horses rushing through those fields in the near-dark, or even just standing quietly with their heads in opposite directions near the fence. I stood at the window and waited. I knew I had to keep still a while longer, keep my eyes out there, outside the house, as long as there was something left to see.

FOR ANALYSIS

1. How would you describe the relationship between Herb and Terri? Between Nick and Laura?

2. The story begins in the sunlight of midday and ends in darkness. How does this transition affect our understanding of what the story says about love and marriage?

WRITING TOPICS

1. Herb and Terri disagree about Carl. With whom do you agree? Why?

2. Have you, or someone you know, ever hated a person once loved or wanted to injure a person once cherished? Why did this happen? How do you, or the subject of your reflection, feel about this emotional turn now?

WHAT WE TALK ABOUT
WHEN WE TALK ABOUT LOVE   1981

My friend Mel McGinnis was talking. Mel McGinnis is a cardiologist, and sometimes that gives him the right.

The four of us were sitting around his kitchen table drinking gin. Sunlight filled the kitchen from the big window behind the sink. There were Mel and me and his second wife, Teresa—Terri, we called her—and my wife, Laura. We lived in Albuquerque then. But we were all from somewhere else.

There was an ice bucket on the table. The gin and the tonic water kept going around, and we somehow got on the subject of love. Mel thought real love was nothing less than spiritual love. He said he'd spent five years in a seminary before quitting to go to medical school. He said he still looked back on those years in the seminary as the most important years in his life.

Terri said the man she lived with before she lived with Mel loved her so much he tried to kill her. Then Terri said, "He beat me up one night. He dragged me around the living room by my ankles. He kept saying, 'I love you, I love you, you bitch.' He went on dragging me around the living room. My head kept knocking on things." Terri looked around the table. "What do you do with love like that?"

She was a bone-thin woman with a pretty face, dark eyes, and brown hair 5 that hung down her back. She liked necklaces made of turquoise, and long pendant earrings.

"My God, don't be silly. That's not love, and you know it," Mel said. "I don't know what you'd call it, but I sure know you wouldn't call it love."

"Say what you want to, but I know it was," Terri said. "It may sound crazy to you, but it's true just the same. People are different, Mel. Sure, sometimes he may have acted crazy. Okay. But he loved me. In his own way maybe, but he loved me. There was love there, Mel. Don't say there wasn't."

Mel let out his breath. He held his glass and turned to Laura and me. "The man threatened to kill me," Mel said. He finished his drink and reached for the gin bottle. "Terri's a romantic. Terri's of the kick-me-so-I'll-know-you-love-me school. Terri, hon, don't look that way." Mel reached across the table and touched Terri's cheek with his fingers. He grinned at her.

"Now he wants to make up," Terri said.

"Make up what?" Mel said. "What is there to make up? I know what I know. 10 That's all."

"How'd we get started on this subject, anyway?" Terri said. She raised her glass and drank from it. "Mel always has love on his mind," she said. "Don't you, honey?" She smiled, and I thought that was the last of it.

"I just wouldn't call Ed's behavior love. That's all I'm saying, honey," Mel said. "What about you guys?" Mel said to Laura and me. "Does that sound like love to you?"

"I'm the wrong person to ask," I said. "I didn't even know the man. I've only heard his name mentioned in passing. I wouldn't know. You'd have to know the particulars. But I think what you're saying is that love is an absolute."

Mel said, "The kind of love I'm talking about is. The kind of love I'm talking about, you don't try to kill people."

Laura said, "I don't know anything about Ed, or anything about the situa- 15 tion. But who can judge anyone else's situation?"

I touched the back of Laura's hand. She gave me a quick smile. I picked up Laura's hand. It was warm, the nails polished, perfectly manicured. I encircled the broad wrist with my fingers, and I held her.

"When I left, he drank rat poison," Terri said. She clasped her arms with her hands. "They took him to the hospital in Sante Fe. That's where we lived then, about ten miles out. They saved his life. But his gums went crazy from it. I mean they pulled away from his teeth. After that, his teeth stood out like fangs. My God," Terri said. She waited a minute, then let go of her arms and picked up her glass.

"What people won't do!" Laura said.

"He's out of the action now," Mel said. "He's dead."

Mel handed me the saucer of limes. I took a section, squeezed it over my 20
drink, and stirred the ice cubes with my finger.

"It gets worse," Terri said. "He shot himself in the mouth. But he bungled
that too. Poor Ed," she said. Terri shook her head.

"Poor Ed nothing," Mel said. "He was dangerous."

Mel was forty-five years old. He was tall and rangy with curly soft hair. His
face and arms were brown from the tennis he played. When he was sober, his
gestures, all his movements, were precise, very careful.

"He did love me though, Mel. Grant me that," Terri said. "That's all I'm asking. He didn't love me the way you love me. I'm not saying that. But he loved
me. You can grant me that, can't you?"

"What do you mean, he bungled it?" I said.   25

Laura leaned forward with her glass. She put her elbows on the table and
held her glass in both hands. She glanced from Mel to Terri and waited with a
look of bewilderment on her open face, as if amazed that such things happened to people you were friendly with.

"How'd he bungle it when he killed himself?" I said.

"I'll tell you what happened," Mel said. "He took this twenty-two pistol he'd
bought to threaten Terri and me with. Oh, I'm serious, the man was always
threatening. You should have seen the way we lived in those days. Like fugitives. I even bought a gun myself. Can you believe it? A guy like me? But I did.
I bought one for self-defense and carried it in the glove compartment. Sometimes I'd have to leave the apartment in the middle of the night. To go to the
hospital, you know? Terri and I weren't married then, and my first wife had the
house and kids, the dog, everything, and Terri and I were living in this apartment here. Sometimes, as I say, I'd get a call in the middle of the night and have
to go in to the hospital at two or three in the morning. It'd be dark out there in
the parking lot, and I'd break into a sweat before I could even get to my car. I
never knew if he was going to come up out of the shrubbery or from behind a
car and start shooting. I mean, the man was crazy. He was capable of wiring a
bomb, anything. He used to call my service at all hours and say he needed to
talk to the doctor, and when I'd return the call, he'd say, 'Son of a bitch, your
days are numbered.' Little things like that. It was scary, I'm telling you."

"I still feel sorry for him," Terri said.

"It sounds like a nightmare," Laura said. "But what exactly happened after 30
he shot himself?"

Laura is a legal secretary. We'd met in a professional capacity. Before we
knew it, it was a courtship. She's thirty-five, three years younger than I am. In
addition to being in love, we like each other and enjoy one another's company.
She's easy to be with.

"What happened?" Laura said.

Mel said, "He shot himself in the mouth in his room. Someone heard the
shot and told the manager. They came in with a passkey, saw what had happened, and called an ambulance. I happened to be there when they brought

him in, alive but past recall. The man lived for three days. His head swelled up to twice the size of a normal head. I'd never seen anything like it, and I hope I never do again. Terri wanted to go in and sit with him when she found out about it. We had a fight over it. I didn't think she should see him like that. I didn't think she should see him, and I still don't."

"Who won the fight?" Laura said.

"I was in the room with him when he died," Terri said. "He never came up 35 out of it. But I sat with him. He didn't have anyone else."

"He was dangerous," Mel said. "If you call that love, you can have it."

"It was love," Terri said. "Sure, it's abnormal in most people's eyes. But he was willing to die for it. He did die for it."

"I sure as hell wouldn't call it love," Mel said. "I mean, no one knows what he did it for. I've seen a lot of suicides, and I couldn't say anyone ever knew what they did it for."

Mel put his hands behind his neck and tilted his chair back. "I'm not interested in that kind of love," he said. "If that's love, you can have it."

Terri said, "We were afraid. Mel even made a will out and wrote to his brother 40 in California who used to be a Green Beret. Mel told him who to look for if something happened to him."

Terri drank from her glass. She said, "But Mel's right—we lived like fugitives. We were afraid. Mel was, weren't you, honey? I even called the police at one point, but they were no help. They said they couldn't do anything until Ed actually did something. Isn't that a laugh?" Terri said.

She poured the last of the gin into her glass and waggled the bottle. Mel got up from the table and went to the cupboard. He took down another bottle.

"Well, Nick and I know what love is," Laura said. "For us, I mean," Laura said. She bumped my knee with her knee. "You're supposed to say something now," Laura said, and turned her smile on me.

For an answer, I took Laura's hand and raised it to my lips. I made a big production out of kissing her hand. Everyone was amused.

"We're lucky," I said. 45

"You guys," Terri said. "Stop that now. You're making me sick. You're still on the honeymoon, for God's sake. You're still gaga, for crying out loud. Just wait. How long have you been together now? How long has it been? A year? Longer than a year?"

"Going on a year and a half," Laura said, flushed and smiling.

"Oh, now," Terri said. "Wait a while."

She held her drink and gazed at Laura.

"I'm only kidding," Terri said. 50

Mel opened the gin and went around the table with the bottle.

"Here, you guys," he said. "Let's have a toast. I want to propose a toast. A toast to love. To true love," Mel said.

We touched glasses.

"To love," we said.

Outside in the backyard, one of the dogs began to bark. The leaves of the 55
aspen that leaned past the window ticked against the glass. The afternoon sun
was like a presence in this room, the spacious light of ease and generosity. We
could have been anywhere, somewhere enchanted. We raised our glasses
again and grinned at each other like children who had agreed on something
forbidden.

"I'll tell you what real love is," Mel said. "I mean, I'll give you a good example. And then you can draw your own conclusions." He poured more gin
into his glass. He added an ice cube and a sliver of lime. We waited and sipped
our drinks. Laura and I touched knees again. I put a hand on her warm thigh
and left it there.

"What do any of us really know about love?" Mel said. "It seems to me we're
just beginners at love. We say we love each other and we do, I don't doubt it. I
love Terri and Terri loves me, and you guys love each other too. You know the
kind of love I'm talking about now. Physical love, that impulse that drives you
to someone special, as well as love of the other person's being, his or her
essence, as it were. Carnal love and, well, call it sentimental love, the day-to-day
caring about the other person. But sometimes I have a hard time accounting
for the fact that I must have loved my first wife too. But I did, I know I did. So I
suppose I am like Terri in that regard. Terri and Ed." He thought about it and
then he went on. "There was a time when I thought I loved my first wife more
than life itself. But now I hate her guts. I do. How do you explain that? What
happened to that love? What happened to it, is what I'd like to know. I wish
someone could tell me. Then there's Ed. Okay, we're back to Ed. He loves Terri
so much he tries to kill her and he winds up killing himself." Mel stopped talking and swallowed from his glass. "You guys have been together eighteen
months and you love each other. It shows all over you. You glow with it. But
you both loved other people before you met each other. You've both been married before, just like us. And you probably loved other people before that too,
even. Terri and I have been together five years, been married for four. And the
terrible thing, the terrible thing is, but the good thing too, the saving grace, you
might say, is that if something happened to one of us—excuse me for saying
this—but if something happened to one of us tomorrow I think the other one,
the other person, would grieve for a while, you know, but then the surviving
party would go out and love again, have someone else soon enough. All this, all
of this love we're talking about, it would just be a memory. Maybe not even a
memory. Am I wrong? Am I way off base? Because I want you to set me
straight if you think I'm wrong. I want to know. I mean, I don't know anything, and I'm the first one to admit it."

"Mel, for God's sake," Terri said. She reached out and took hold of his wrist.
"Are you getting drunk? Honey? Are you drunk?"

"Honey, I'm just talking," Mel said. "All right? I don't have to be drunk to say
what I think. I mean, we're all just talking, right?" Mel said. He fixed his eyes
on her.

"Sweetie, I'm not criticizing," Terri said. 60

She picked up her glass.

"I'm not on call today," Mel said. "Let me remind you of that. I am not on call," he said.

"Mel, we love you," Laura said.

Mel looked at Laura. He looked at her as if he could not place her, as if she was not the woman she was.

"Love you too, Laura," Mel said. "And you, Nick, love you too. You know something?" Mel said. "You guys are our pals," Mel said. 65

He picked up his glass.

Mel said, "I was going to tell you about something. I mean, I was going to prove a point. You see, this happened a few months ago, but it's still going on right now, and it ought to make us feel ashamed when we talk like we know what we're talking about when we talk above love."

"Come on now," Terri said. "Don't talk like you're drunk if you're not drunk."

"Just shut up for once in your life," Mel said very quietly. "Will you do me a favor and do that for a minute? So as I was saying, there's this old couple who had this car wreck out on the interstate. A kid hit them and they were all torn to shit and nobody was giving them much chance to pull through."

Terri looked at us and then back at Mel. She seemed anxious, or maybe that's 70 too strong a word.

Mel was handing the bottle around the table.

"I was on call that night," Mel said. "It was May or maybe it was June. Terri and I had just sat down to dinner when the hospital called. There'd been this thing out on the interstate. Drunk kid, teenager, plowed his dad's pickup into this camper with this old couple in it. They were up in their mid-seventies, that couple. The kid—eighteen, nineteen, something—he was DOA. Taken the steering wheel through his sternum. The old couple, they were alive, you understand. I mean, just barely. But they had everything. Multiple fractures, internal injuries, hemorrhaging, contusions, lacerations, the works, and they each of them had themselves concussions. They were in a bad way, believe me. And, of course, their age was two strikes against them. I'd say she was worse off than he was. Ruptured spleen along with everything else. Both kneecaps broken. But they'd been wearing their seatbelts and, God knows, that's what saved them for the time being."

"Folks, this is an advertisement for the National Safety Council," Terri said. "This is your spokesman, Dr. Melvin R. McGinnis, talking." Terri laughed. "Mel," she said, "sometimes you're just too much. But I love you, hon," she said.

"Honey, I love you," Mel said.

He leaned across the table. Terri met him halfway. They kissed. 75

"Terri's right," Mel said as he settled himself again. "Get those seatbelts on. But seriously, they were in some shape, those oldsters. By the time I got down there, the kid was dead, as I said. He was off in a corner, laid out on a gurney. I took one look at the old couple and told the ER nurse to get me a neurologist and an orthopedic man and a couple of surgeons down there right away."

He drank from his glass. "I'll try to keep this short," he said. "So we took the two of them up to the OR and worked like fuck on them most of the night. They had these incredible reserves, those two. You see that once in a while. So we did everything that could be done, and toward morning we're giving them a fifty-fifty chance, maybe less than that for her. So here they are, still alive the next morning. So, okay, we move them into the ICU, which is where they both kept plugging away at it for two weeks, hitting it better and better on all the scopes. So we transfer them out to their own room."

Mel stopped talking. "Here," he said, "let's drink this cheapo gin the hell up. Then we're going to dinner, right? Terri and I know a new place. That's where we'll go, to this new place we know about. But we're not going until we finish up this cut-rate, lousy gin."

Terri said, "We haven't actually eaten there yet. But it looks good. From the outside, you know."

"I like food," Mel said. "If I had it to do all over again, I'd be a chef, you know? Right, Terri?" Mel said. 80

He laughed. He fingered the ice in his glass.

"Terri knows," he said. "Terri can tell you. But let me say this. If I could come back again in a different life, a different time and all, you know what? I'd like to come back as a knight. You were pretty safe wearing all that armor. It was all right being a knight until gunpowder and muskets and pistols came along."

"Mel would like to ride a horse and carry a lance," Terri said.

"Carry a woman's scarf with you everywhere," Laura said.

"Or just a woman," Mel said. 85

"Shame on you," Laura said.

Terri said, "Suppose you came back as a serf. The serfs didn't have it so good in those days," Terri said.

"The serfs never had it good," Mel said. "But I guess even the knights were vessels to someone. Isn't that the way it worked? But then everyone is always a vessel to someone. Isn't that right? Terri? But what I liked about knights, besides their ladies, was that they had that suit of armor, you know, and they couldn't get hurt very easy. No cars in those days, you know? No drunk teenagers to tear into your ass."

"Vassals," Terri said.

"What?" Mel said. 90

"Vassals," Terri said. "They were called vassals, not vessels."

"Vassals, vessels," Mel said, "what the fuck's the difference? You knew what I meant anyway. All right," Mel said. "So I'm not educated. I learned my stuff. I'm a heart surgeon, sure, but I'm just a mechanic. I go in and I fuck around and I fix things. Shit," Mel said.

"Modesty doesn't become you," Terri said.

"He's just a humble sawbones," I said. "But sometimes they suffocated in all that armor, Mel. They'd even have heart attacks if it got too hot and they were too tired and worn out. I read somewhere that they'd fall off their horses and not be able to get up because they were too tired to stand with all that armor on them. They got trampled by their own horses sometimes."

"That's terrible," Mel said. "That's a terrible thing, Nicky. I guess they'd just 95 lay there and wait until somebody came along and made a shish kebab out of them."

"Some other vessel," Terri said.

"That's right," Mel said. "Some vassal would come along and spear the bastard in the name of love. Or whatever the fuck it was they fought over in those days."

"Same things we fight over these days," Terri said.

Laura said, "Nothing's changed."

The color was still high in Laura's cheeks. Her eyes were bright. She brought 100 her glass to her lips.

Mel poured himself another drink. He looked at the label closely as if studying a long row of numbers. Then he slowly put the bottle down on the table and slowly reached for the tonic water.

"What about the old couple?" Laura said. "You didn't finish that story you started."

Laura was having a hard time lighting her cigarette. Her matches kept going out.

The sunshine inside the room was different now, changing, getting thinner. But the leaves outside the window were still shimmering, and I stared at the pattern they made on the panes and on the Formica counter. They weren't the same patterns, of course.

"What about the old couple?" I said. 105

"Older but wiser," Terri said.

Mel stared at her.

Terri said, "Go on with your story, hon. I was only kidding. Then what happened?"

"Terri, sometimes," Mel said.

"Please, Mel," Terri said. "Don't always be so serious, sweetie. Can't you take 110 a joke?"

"Where's the joke?" Mel said.

He held his glass and gazed steadily at his wife.

"What happened?" Laura said.

Mel fastened his eyes on Laura. He said, "Laura, if I didn't have Terri and if I didn't love her so much, and if Nick wasn't my best friend, I'd fall in love with you, I'd carry you off, honey," he said.

"Tell your story," Terri said. "Then we'll go to that new place, okay?" 115

"Okay," Mel said. "Where was I?" he said. He stared at the table and then he began again.

"I dropped in to see each of them every day, sometimes twice a day if I was up doing other calls anyway. Casts and bandages, head to foot, the both of them. You know, you've seen it in the movies. That's just the way they looked, just like in the movies. Little eye-holes and nose-holes and mouth-holes. And she had to have her legs slung up on top of it. Well, the husband was very depressed for the longest while. Even after he found out that his wife was going to pull through, he was still very depressed. Not about the accident, though. I mean, the accident was one thing, but it wasn't everything. I'd get up to his mouth-hole, you know, and he'd say no, it wasn't the accident exactly but it was because he couldn't see her through his eye-holes. He said that was what was making him feel so bad. Can you imagine? I'm telling you, the man's heart was breaking because he couldn't turn his goddamn head and *see* his goddamn wife."

Mel looked around the table and shook his head at what he was going to say.

"I mean, it was killing the old fart just because he couldn't *look* at the fucking woman."

We all looked at Mel.

"Do you see what I'm saying?" he said.

Maybe we were a little drunk by then. I know it was hard keeping things in focus. The light was draining out of the room, going back through the window where it had come from. Yet nobody made a move to get up from the table to turn on the overhead light.

"Listen," Mel said. "Let's finish this fucking gin. There's about enough left here for one shooter all around. Then let's go eat. Let's go to the new place."

"He's depressed," Terri said. "Mel, why don't you take a pill?"

Mel shook his head. "I've taken everything there is."

"We all need a pill now and then," I said.

"Some people are born needing them," Terri said.

She was using her finger to rub at something on the table. Then she stopped rubbing.

"I think I want to call my kids," Mel said. "Is that all right with everybody? I'll call my kids," he said.

Terri said, "What if Marjorie answers the phone? You guys, you've heard us on the subject of Marjorie? Honey, you know you don't want to talk to Marjorie. It'll make you feel even worse."

"I don't want to talk to Marjorie," Mel said. "But I want to talk to my kids."

"There isn't a day goes by that Mel doesn't say he wishes she'd get married again. Or else die," Terri said. "For one thing," Terri said, "she's bankrupting us. Mel says it's just to spite him that she won't get married again. She has a boyfriend who lives with her and the kids, so Mel is supporting the boyfriend too."

"She's allergic to bees," Mel said. "If I'm not praying she'll get married again, I'm praying she'll get herself stung to death by a swarm of fucking bees."

"Shame on you," Laura said.

"Bzzzzzzz," Mel said, turning his fingers into bees and buzzing them at Terri's throat. Then he let his hands drop all the way to his sides.

120

125

130

135

"She's vicious," Mel said. "Sometimes I think I'll go up there dressed like a beekeeper. You know, that hat that's like a helmet with the plate that comes down over your face, the big gloves, and the padded coat? I'll knock on the door and let loose a hive of bees in the house. But first I'd make sure the kids were out, of course."

He crossed one leg over the other. It seemed to take him a lot of time to do it. Then he put both feet on the floor and leaned forward, elbows on the table, his chin cupped in his hands.

"Maybe I won't call the kids, after all. Maybe it isn't such a hot idea. Maybe we'll just go eat. How does that sound?"

"Sounds fine to me," I said. "Eat or not eat. Or keep drinking. I could head right on out into the sunset."

"What does that mean, honey?" Laura said. 140

"It just means what I said," I said. "It means I could just keep going. That's all it means."

"I could eat something myself," Laura said. "I don't think I've ever been so hungry in my life. Is there something to nibble on?"

"I'll put out some cheese and crackers," Terri said.

But Terri just sat there. She did not get up to get anything.

Mel turned his glass over. He spilled it out on the table. 145

"Gin's gone," Mel said.

Terri said, "Now what?"

I could hear my heart beating. I could hear everyone's heart. I could hear the human noise we sat there making, not one of us moving, not even when the room went dark.

FOR ANALYSIS

1. What is your reaction to Mel? Is he likable? What does his profession—a scientist and a cardiologist—represent?

2. What is the significance of Mel's account of the old couple injured in the car accident?

3. Do Mel's feelings about his ex-wife parallel Ed's feelings about Terri? Explain.

WRITING TOPIC

In an essay, examine the various relationships in the story: Nick and Laura, Mel and Terri, Terri and Ed, Mel and his ex-wife Marjorie, and the injured old couple. Conclude with a comment on "what we talk about when we talk about love."

MAKING CONNECTIONS

1. Compare the first paragraph of "Mine" to the first paragraph of "Popular Mechanics." While they are similar, there are some key changes. What are they? Why might Carver have made them? Are there ways in which they connect to the story's themes?

2. Compare the last paragraph of "Mine" to the last paragraph of "Popular Mechanics." What is changed? Why do you think Carver chose to make the most significant deletion? How might the story be better without it? What about the shape and size of the sentences: How are they different in the revised version of the story, and why might they be better? What might the apparently minor change in voice in the last sentence in the newer version express?

3. "Beginners" is Carver's original version of what became, under the editorial hand of Gordon Lish, "What We Talk About When We Talk About Love." What kind of changes occurred between Carver's original and the Lish-edited version?

4. Many readers like the earlier Carver better than the stories that appeared later in his career. After his death, it became clear that his earlier style was in fact largely the product of Gordon Lish's editing. On the evidence of "Beginners" (unedited Carver) and "What We Talk About When We Talk About Love" (Lish-edited Carver), which Carver do you like more? Why?

POETRY

SAPPHO   (CA. 610-CA. 580 B.C.)

WITH HIS VENOM[1]

With his venom

Irresistible
and bittersweet

that loosener
of limbs, Love

reptile-like
strikes me down

PO CHU-I   (772-846)

GOLDEN BELLS[1]   CA. 010

When I was almost forty
I had a daughter whose name was Golden Bells.
Now it is just a year since she was born;
She is learning to sit and cannot yet talk.
Ashamed—to find that I have not a sage's heart:
I cannot resist vulgar thoughts and feelings.
Henceforward I am tied to things outside myself:
My only reward—the pleasure I am getting now.
If I am spared the grief of her dying young,

With His Venom
   [1] Translated by Mary Barnard.

Golden Bells
   [1] Translated by Arthur Waley.

Then I shall have the trouble of getting her married.   10
My plan for retiring and going back to the hills
Must now be postponed for fifteen years!

REMEMBERING GOLDEN BELLS[1]   CA. 810

Ruined and ill—a man of two score;
Pretty and guileless—a girl of three.
Not a boy—but still better than nothing:
To soothe one's feeling—from time to time a kiss!
There came a day—they suddenly took her from me;
Her soul's shadow wandered I know not where.
And when I remember how just at the time she died
She lisped strange sounds, beginning to learn to talk,
Then I know that the ties of flesh and blood
Only bind us to a load of grief and sorrow.   10

At last, by thinking of the time before she was born,
By thought and reason I drove the pain away.
Since my heart forgot her, many days have passed
And three times winter has changed to spring.
This morning, for a little, the old grief came back,
Because, in the road, I met her foster-nurse.

ANONYMOUS

BONNY BARBARA ALLAN

It was in and about the Martinmas[1] time,
    When the green leaves were a falling,
That Sir John Graeme, in the West Country,
    Fell in love with Barbara Allan.

He sent his man down through the town,
    To the place where she was dwelling:
"O haste and come to my master dear,
    Gin° ye be Barbara Allan."   if

Remembering Golden Bells
    [1] Translated by Arthur Waley.
Bonny Barbara Allan
    [1] November 11.

O hooly,° hooly rose she up,   slowly
    To the place where he was lying,   10
And when she drew the curtain by:
    "Young man, I think you're dying."

"O it's I'm sick, and very, very sick,
    And 'tis a' for Barbara Allan."
"O the better for me ye s'° never be,   ye shall
    Tho your heart's blood were a-spilling."

"O dinna° ye mind,° young man," said she,   don't/remember
    "When ye was in the tavern a drinking,
That ye made the healths gae° round and round,   go
    And slighted Barbara Allan?"   20

He turned his face unto the wall,
    And death was with him dealing:
"Adieu, adieu, my dear friends all,
    And be kind to Barbara Allan."

And slowly, slowly raise she up,
    And slowly, slowly left him,
And sighing said she could not stay,
    Since death of life had reft him.

She had not gane a mile but twa,
    When she heard the dead-bell ringing,   30
And every jow° that the dead-bell geid,°   stroke/gave
    It cried, "Woe to Barbara Allan!"

"O mother, mother, make my bed!
    O make it saft and narrow!
Since my love died for me to-day,
    I'll die for him to-morrow."

WILLIAM SHAKESPEARE   (1564–1616)

SONNETS   1609

18

Shall I compare thee to a summer's day?
Thou art more lovely and more temperate:
Rough winds do shake the darling buds of May,

And summer's lease hath all too short a date:
Sometime too hot the eye of heaven shines,
And often is his gold complexion dimmed;
And every fair from fair sometimes declines,
By chance or nature's changing course untrimmed;
But thy eternal summer shall not fade,
Nor lose possession of that fair thou ow'st,°   owns   10
Nor shall death brag thou wander'st in his shade,
When in eternal lines to time thou grow'st:
    So long as men can breathe, or eyes can see,
    So long lives this, and this gives life to thee.

For Analysis

1. Why does the speaker in the poem argue that "a summer's day" is an inappropriate **metaphor** for his beloved?

2. What is "this" in line 14?

29

When, in disgrace with fortune and men's eyes,
I all alone beweep my outcast state
And trouble deaf heaven with my bootless cries
And look upon myself and curse my fate,
Wishing me like to one more rich in hope,
Featured like him, like him with friends possessed,
Desiring this man's art and that man's scope,
With what I most enjoy contented least;
Yet in these thoughts myself almost despising,
Haply I think on thee, and then my state,   10
Like to the lark at break of day arising
From sullen earth, sings hymns at heaven's gate;
    For thy sweet love remembered such wealth brings
    That then I scorn to change my state with kings.

116

Let me not to the marriage of true minds
Admit impediments. Love is not love
Which alters when it alteration finds,
Or bends with the remover to remove:
Oh, no! it is an ever-fixèd mark,
That looks on tempests and is never shaken;
It is the star to every wandering bark,
Whose worth's unknown, although his height be taken.

Love's not Time's fool, though rosy lips and cheeks
Within his bending sickle's compass come;   10
Love alters not with his brief hours and weeks,
But bears it out even to the edge of doom.
If this be error and upon me proved,
I never writ, nor no man ever loved.

130

My mistress' eyes are nothing like the sun;
Coral is far more red than her lips' red;
If snow be white, why then her breasts are dun;
If hairs be wires, black wires grow on her head.
I have seen roses damasked,° red and white,   variegated
But no such roses see I in her cheeks;
And in some perfumes is there more delight
Than in the breath that from my mistress reeks.
I love to hear her speak, yet well I know
That music hath a far more pleasing sound;   10
I grant I never saw a goddess go;
My mistress, when she walks, treads on the ground.
    And yet, by heaven, I think my love as rare
    As any she belied with false compare.[1]

FOR ANALYSIS

1. It seems at first like the speaker might be insulting his "mistress." Is he? What evidence supports your answer?

2. Annotate the poem so that the sonnet's **rhyme** scheme is clear. Where does the scheme change—that is, where does the pattern of alternating pairs of lines whose last words rhyme (for example, in lines 1–4 "sun," "red," "dun," "head", or ABAB) shift to a different pattern? How does the poem take advantage of this shift to make meaning?

3. How do the last two lines echo the first line?

WRITING TOPIC

This poem plays off the tradition of Petrarchan love poetry, whose conventions include the worshipful idealization of the woman who is the subject of the poem. How does Shakespeare's poem **satirize** this kind of love poetry?

Sonnets
[1] I.e., as any woman misrepresented with false comparisons.

John Donne   (1572–1631)

The Flea   1633

Mark but this flea, and mark in this,
How little that which thou deniest me is;
It sucked me first, and now sucks thee,
And in this flea our two bloods mingled be;
Thou know'st that this cannot be said
A sin, nor shame, nor loss of maidenhead,
 Yet this enjoys before it woo,
 And pampered swells with one blood made of two,
 And this, alas, is more than we would do.

Oh stay, three lives in one flea spare,   10
Where we almost, yea more than married, are.
This flea is you and I, and this
Our marriage bed and marriage temple is;
Though parents grudge, and you, we are met,
And cloistered in these living walls of jet,
 Though use° make you apt to kill me   custom
 Let not to that, self-murder added be,
 And sacrilege, three sins in killing three.

Cruel and sudden, hast thou since
Purpled thy nail, in blood of innocence?   20
Wherein could this flea guilty be,
Except in that drop which it sucked from thee?
Yet thou triumph'st, and say'st that thou
Find'st not thy self nor me the weaker now;
 'Tis true, then learn how false fears be;
 Just so much honor, when thou yield'st to me,
 Will waste, as this flea's death took life from thee.

For Analysis

1. What does the woman addressed in this poem deny the poet (l. 2)?

2. What is the woman about to do at the beginning of the second stanza? What argument does the poet use to save the flea?

3. How does the poet turn the flea's life and death to his own purposes?

Writing Topic

In a paragraph, discuss your response to Donne's use of a flea to animate a seduction poem.

SONG 1633

Go and catch a falling star
　Get with child a mandrake root,[1]
Tell me where all past years are,
　Or who cleft the Devil's foot,
Teach me to hear mermaids singing,
Or to keep off envy's stinging,
　　And find
　　What wind
Serves to advance an honest mind.

If thou be'st born to strange sights,　　　　　　　　　　　　　　　10
　Things invisible to see,
Ride ten thousand days and nights,
　Till age snow white hairs on thee,
Thou, when thou return'st, wilt tell me
　All strange wonders that befell thee,
　　And swear
　　Nowhere
Lives a woman true, and fair.

If thou findst one, let me know,
　Such a pilgrimage were sweet—　　　　　　　　　　　　　　　20
　Yet do not, I would not go,
　Though at next door we might meet;
Though she were true, when you met her,
　And last, till you write your letter,
　　Yet she
　　Will be
False, ere I come, to two or three.

FOR ANALYSIS

1. The first five lines set tasks for the reader. How would you describe those tasks?

2. The tasks set in the remaining lines of the stanza seem different. Discuss the difference.

3. In the second stanza, how does the poet emphasize the difficulty of finding a woman both "true, and fair"?

WRITING TOPICS

1. Describe Donne's attitude toward women in this poem.

2. Describe the poetic devices Donne employs to make his point.

---

[1] A forked root associated with fertility and thought to have magical powers.

A VALEDICTION:
FORBIDDING MOURNING   1633

As virtuous men pass mildly away,
   And whisper to their souls to go,
Whilst some of their sad friends do say
   The breath goes now, and some say, No;

So let us melt, and make no noise,
   No tear-floods, nor sigh-tempests move,
'Twere profanation of our joys
   To tell the laity our love.

Moving of th' earth° brings harms and fears,   *earthquake*
   Men reckon what it did and meant;   10
But trepidation of the spheres,
   Though greater far, is innocent.[1]

Dull sublunary° lovers' love   *under the moon*
   (Whose soul is sense) cannot admit
Absence, because it doth remove
   Those things which elemented it.

But we by a love so much refined
   That our selves know not what it is,
Inter-assuréd of the mind,
   Care less, eyes, lips, and hands to miss.   20

Our two souls therefore, which are one,
   Though I must go, endure not yet
A breach, but an expansion,
   Like gold to airy thinness beat.

If they be two, they are two so
   As stiff twin compasses are two;
Thy soul, the fixed foot, makes no show
   To move, but doth, if th' other do.

And though it in the center sit,
   Yet when the other far doth roam,   30

---

[1] The movement of the heavenly spheres is harmless.

It leans and harkens after it,
    And grows erect, as that comes home.

Such wilt thou be to me, who must
    Like th' other foot, obliquely run;
Thy firmness makes my circle just,
    And makes me end where I begun.

FOR ANALYSIS

1. Two kinds of love are described in this poem: spiritual and physical. How does the **simile** drawn in the first two stanzas help define the differences between them?

2. How does the contrast between earthquakes and the movement of the spheres in stanza 3 further develop the contrast between the two types of love?

3. Explain the comparison between a drawing compass and the lovers in the last three stanzas.

BEN JONSON   (1572–1637)

SONG, TO CELIA[1]   1616

Drink to me only with thine eyes,
    And I will pledge with mine;
Or leave a kiss but in the cup,
    And I'll not look for wine.
The thirst that from the soul doth rise
    Doth ask a drink divine;
But might I of Jove's nectar sup,
    I would not change for thine.
I sent thee late a rosy wreath,
    Not so much honoring thee   10
As giving it a hope, that there
    It could not withered be.
But thou thereon didst only breathe,
    And sent'st it back to me;
Since when it grows, and smells, I swear,
    Not of itself but thee.

[1] A widely recorded song.

LADY MARY WROTH   (CA. 1587–CA. 1651)

AM I THUS CONQUERED?   1621

Am I thus conquered? Have I lost the powers,
   That° to withstand, which joyes° to ruin me?   (love)/delights
   Must I be still while it my strength devours,
   And captive leads me prisoner bound, unfree?
Love first shall leave men's fant'sies to them free,
   Desire shall quench love's flames, spring hate sweet showers,
   Love shall loose all his darts, have sight, and see
   His shame, and wishings hinder happy hours.
Why should we not love's purblind° charms resist?   completely blind
   Must we be servile, doing what he list?°   pleases   10
   No, seek some host to harbor thee: I fly
Thy babish° tricks, and freedom do profess   childish
   But O my hurt makes my lost heart confess
   I love, and must: so farewell liberty.

ROBERT HERRICK   (1591–1674)

TO THE VIRGINS, TO MAKE MUCH OF TIME[1]   1648

Gather ye rosebuds while ye may,
   Old Time is still a-flying;
And this same flower that smiles today,
   Tomorrow will be dying.

The glorious lamp of heaven, the sun,
   The higher he's a-getting,
The sooner will his race be run,
   And nearer he's to setting.

That age is best which is the first,
   When youth and blood are warmer;
But being spent, the worse, and worst   10
   Times still succeed the former.

To the Virgins, to Make Much of Time
[1] Available on CD, *In Praise of Woman* (Hyperion, 1994), composed by Madeleine Dring with Graham Johnson and Anthony Rolfe-Johnson.

916

Then be not coy, but use your time;
And while ye may, go marry:
For having lost but once your prime,
You may for ever tarry.

ANNE BRADSTREET   (CA. 1612–1672)

TO MY DEAR AND LOVING HUSBAND   1678

If ever two were one, then surely we.
If ever man were loved by wife, then thee;
If ever wife was happy in a man,
Compare with me ye women if you can.
I prize thy love more than whole mines of gold
Or all the riches that the East doth hold.
My love is such that rivers cannot quench,
Nor ought but love from thee give recompense.
Thy love is such I can no way repay;
The heavens reward thee manifold, I pray.   10
Then while we live, in love let's so persever,
That when we live no more we may live ever.

APHRA BEHN   (1640–1689)

ON HER LOVING TWO EQUALLY   1684

I

How strongly does my passion flow,
Divided equally twixt two?
Damon had ne'er subdued my heart,
Had not Alexis took his part;
Nor could Alexis powerful prove,
Without my Damon's aid, to gain my love.

II

When my Alexis present is,
Then I for Damon sigh and mourn;
But when Alexis I do miss,

Damon gains nothing but my scorn. 10
But if it chance they both are by,
For both alike I languish, sigh, and die.

III

Cure then, thou mighty wingèd god,
This restless fever in my blood;
One golden-pointed dart take back:
But which, O Cupid, wilt thou take?
If Damon's, all my hopes are crossed;
Or that of my Alexis, I am lost.

FOR ANALYSIS

1. What is the speaker's attitude toward her predicament?

2. What is the poem's attitude toward the speaker's predicament? Is there any difference
between what she feels about loving two men and what the author might feel?

3. Can someone really be "in love" with two people? Can someone feel "true love" for
two people simultaneously? What ideas about romantic love conflict with this possibility?

WRITING TOPICS

1. Write a poem or short prose dialogue from Cupid's **point of view.** What might he
say about this situation? Feel free to be serious or comic.

2. *Damon* and *Alexis* are ancient Greek names connected to the pastoral tradition in
poetry. What does Behn's **allusion** to that tradition, in which idealized romantic figures play in idealized meadows with idealized sheep, mean for her poem? Does her
poem seem to fit within that tradition or work against it?

LADY MARY WORTLEY MONTAGU   (1689–1762)

SONG   (1739?)

Why should you think I live unpleas'd,
   Because I am not pleas'd with you?
My mind is not so far diseas'd,
   To yield when powder'd fops pursue.

My vanity can find no charm
   In common prostituted vows;
Nor can you raise a wish that's warm
   In one that your true value knows.

While cold and careless thus I shun
   The buzz and flutter that you make, 10

Perhaps some giddy girl may run
   To catch the prize that I forsake.

So brightly shines the glittering glare,
   In unexperienc'd children's eyes,
When they with little arts ensnare
   The gaudy painted butterflies.

While they with pride the conquest boast,
   And think the chase deserving care,
Those scorn the useless toil they cost
   Who're us'd to more substantial fare.   20

WILLIAM BLAKE   (1757–1827)

A POISON TREE 1794

I was angry with my friend:
I told my wrath, my wrath did end.
I was angry with my foe:
I told it not, my wrath did grow.

And I watered it in fears,
Night & morning with my tears;
And I sunnéd it with smiles,
And with soft deceitful wiles.

And it grew both day and night,
Till it bore an apple bright.   10
And my foe beheld its shine,
And he knew that it was mine,

And into my garden stole,
When the night had veil'd the pole;
In the morning glad I see
My foe outstretched beneath the tree.

FOR ANALYSIS

1. Is anything gained from the parallel readers might draw between this tree and the tree in the Garden of Eden? Explain.

2. Explain what the "poison" is.

3. Does your own experience verify the first stanza of the poem?

ROBERT BURNS   (1759–1796)

A RED, RED ROSE   1796

O My Luve's like a red, red rose,
   That's newly sprung in June;
O My Luve's like a melodie
   That's sweetly played in tune.

As fair art thou, my bonnie lass,
   So deep in luve am I;
And I will luve thee still, my dear,
   Til a' the seas gang dry.

Till a' the seas gang dry, my dear,
   And the rocks melt wi' the sun:
O I will love thee still, my dear,
   While the sands o' life shall run.

And fare thee weel, my only luve,
   And fare thee weel awhile!
And I will come again, my luve,
   Though it were ten thousand mile.

MATTHEW ARNOLD   (1822–1888)

DOVER BEACH   1867

The sea is calm tonight.
The tide is full, the moon lies fair
Upon the straits; on the French coast the light
Gleams and is gone; the cliffs of England stand,
Glimmering and vast, out in the tranquil bay.
Come to the window, sweet is the night-air!
Only, from the long line of spray
Where the sea meets the moon-blanched land,
Listen! you hear the grating roar
Of pebbles which the waves draw back, and fling,
At their return, up the high strand,
Begin, and cease, and then again begin,
With tremulous cadence slow, and bring
The eternal note of sadness in.

Sophocles long ago
Heard it on the Aegean, and it brought
Into his mind the turbid ebb and flow
Of human misery; we
Find also in the sound a thought,
Hearing it by this distant northern sea.   20

The Sea of Faith
Was once, too, at the full, and round earth's shore
Lay like the folds of a bright girdle furled.
But now I only hear
Its melancholy, long, withdrawing roar,
Retreating, to the breath
Of the night-wind, down the vast edges drear
And naked shingles° of the world.   pebble beaches

Ah, love, let us be true
To one another! for the world, which seems   30
To lie before us like a land of dreams,
So various, so beautiful, so new,
Hath really neither joy, nor love, nor light,
Nor certitude, nor peace, nor help for pain;
And we are here as on a darkling plain
Swept with confused alarms of struggle and flight,
Where ignorant armies clash by night.

GERARD MANLEY HOPKINS   (1844–1889)

PIED BEAUTY   1877

Glory be to God for dappled things—
    For skies of couple-colour as a brinded° cow;   brindled
        For rose-moles all in stipple upon trout that swim;
Fresh-firecoal chestnut-falls;[1] finches' wings;
    Landscape plotted and pieced[2]—fold, fallow, and plough;
        And all trades, their gear and tackle, and trim.°   equipment

Pied Beauty
   [1] Fallen chestnuts, with the outer husks removed, colored like fresh fire coal.
   [2] The variegated pattern of land put to different uses.

All things counter,° original, spare, strange;   °contrasted
    Whatever is fickle, freckled (who knows how?)
      With swift, slow; sweet, sour; adazzle, dim;
He fathers-forth whose beauty is past change: 10
            Praise him.

ROBERT FROST   (1874–1963)

FIRE AND ICE   1923

Some say the world will end in fire,
Some say in ice,
From what I've tasted of desire
I hold with those who favor fire.
But if it had to perish twice,
I think I know enough of hate
To say that for destruction ice
Is also great
And would suffice.

DOROTHY PARKER   (1893–1967)

ONE PERFECT ROSE   1926

A single flow'r he sent me, since we met.
    All tenderly his messenger he chose;
Deep-hearted, pure, with scented dew still wet—
    One perfect rose.

I knew the language of the floweret;
    "My fragile leaves," it said, "his heart enclose."
Love long has taken for his amulet
    One perfect rose.

Why is it no one ever sent me yet
    One perfect limousine, do you suppose?   10
Ah no, it's always just my luck to get
    One perfect rose.

E. E. CUMMINGS   (1894–1962)

SHE BEING BRAND   1926

she being Brand

-new;and you
know consequently a
little stiff i was
careful of her and(having

thoroughly oiled the universal
joint tested my gas felt of
her radiator made sure her springs were O.

K.)i went right to it flooded-the-carburetor cranked her

up, slipped the   10
clutch(and then somehow got into reverse she
kicked what
the hell)next
minute i was back in neutral tried and

again slo-wly;bare,ly nudg. ing (my

lev-er Right-
oh and her gears being in
A 1 shape passed
from low through
second-in-to-high like   20
greasedlightning)just as we turned the corner of Divinity

avenue i touched the accelerator and give

her the juice, good

                    (it

was the first ride and believe i we was
happy to see how nice she acted right up to
the last minute coming back down by the Public
Gardens i slammed on

the
internalexpanding   30

923

&
externalcontracting
brakes Bothatonce and

brought allofher tremB
-ling
to a:dead.

stand-
;Still)

FOR ANALYSIS

1. People often use female gendered language when referring to cars and boats. How does Cummings take advantage of this convention? What conceit in the poem depends on it?

2. What is unusual about the way Cummings places words on the page? What effects does it achieve?

3. Describe the poem's tempo. Where does it speed up? Where does it slow down? If you were to draw a line or an arc depicting its speed, what would it look like? What other phenomenon or phenomena might such a drawing describe?

WRITING TOPICS

1. Automobiles began to be mass-produced at the beginning of the 1920s. How might "she being Brand" be a response to the new widespread availability of cars?

2. Write a poem in which you describe one experience or activity in language suggestive of another. Try to make the connection clear but not explicit.

THEODORE ROETHKE   (1908–1963)

I KNEW A WOMAN   1958

I knew a woman, lovely in her bones,
When small birds sighed, she would sigh back at them;
Ah, when she moved, she moved more ways than one:
The shapes a bright container can contain!
Of her choice virtues only gods should speak,
Or English poets who grew up on Greek
(I'd have them sing in chorus, cheek to cheek).

How well her wishes went! She stroked my chin,
She taught me Turn, and Counter-turn, and Stand;
She taught me Touch, that undulant white skin;   10

I nibbled meekly from her proffered hand;
She was the sickle; I, poor I, the rake,
Coming behind her for her pretty sake
(But what prodigious mowing we did make).

Love likes a gander, and adores a goose:
Her full lips pursed, the errant note to seize;
She played it quick, she played it light and loose;
My eyes, they dazzled at her flowing knees;
Her several parts could keep a pure repose,
Or one hip quiver with a mobile nose   20
(She moved in circles, and those circles moved).

Let seed be grass, and grass turn into hay:
I'm martyr to a motion not my own;
What's freedom for? To know eternity.
I swear she cast a shadow white as stone.
But who would count eternity in days?
These old bones live to learn her wanton ways:
(I measure time by how a body sways).

FOR ANALYSIS

1. What is the **rhyme** scheme of this poem?
2. What does line 3 mean?
3. Describe the two principal images in the second stanza.

WRITING TOPIC

In an essay, describe the role of motion in this celebration of a woman's beauty.

ELIZABETH BISHOP   (1911–1979)

ONE ART   1976

The art of losing isn't hard to master;
so many things seem filled with the intent
to be lost that their loss is no disaster.

Lose something every day. Accept the fluster
of lost door keys, the hour badly spent.
The art of losing isn't hard to master.

Then practice losing farther, losing faster:
places, and names, and where it was you meant
to travel. None of these will bring disaster.

I lost my mother's watch. And look! my last, or   10
next-to-last, of three loved houses went.
The art of losing isn't hard to master.

I lost two cities, lovely ones. And, vaster,
some realms I owned, two rivers, a continent.
I miss them, but it wasn't a disaster.

—Even losing you (the joking voice, a gesture
I love) I shan't have lied. It's evident
the art of losing's not too hard to master
though it may look like (*Write* it!) like disaster.

JOHN FREDERICK NIMS   (1913-1999)

LOVE POEM   1947

My clumbsiest dear, whose hands shipwreck vases,
At whose quick touch all glasses chip and ring,
Whose palms are bulls in china, burrs in linen,
And have no cunning with any soft thing

Except all ill at ease fidgeting people:
The refugee uncertain at the door
You make at home; deftly you steady
The drunk clambering on his undulant floor.

Unpredictable dear, the taxi drivers' terror,
Shrinking from far headlights pale as a dime   10
Yet leaping before red apoplectic streetcars—
Misfit in any space. And never on time.

A wrench in clocks and the solar system. Only
With words and people and love you move at ease.
In traffic of wit expertly maneuver
And keep us, all devotion, at your knees.

Forgetting your coffee spreading on our flannel,
Your lipstick grinning on our coat,

So gayly in love's unbreakable heaven
Our souls on glory of split bourbon float.   20

Be with me darling early and late. Smash glasses—
I will study wry music for your sake.
For should your hands drop white and empty
All the toys of the world would break.

DENISE LEVERTOV   (1923–1997)

THE ACHE OF MARRIAGE   1966

The ache of marriage:

thigh and tongue, beloved,
are heavy with it,
it throbs in the teeth

We look for communion
and are turned away, beloved,
each and each

It is leviathan and we
in its belly
looking for joy, some joy   10
not to be known outside it

two by two in the ark of
the ache of it.

WISLAWA SZYMBORSKA   (B. 1923)

A HAPPY LOVE   1981

A happy love. Is it normal,
is it serious, is it profitable—
what use to the world are two people
who have no eyes for the world?

Elevated each for each, for no apparent merit,
by sheer chance singled out of a million, yet convinced

it had to be so—as reward for what? for nothing,
the light shines from nowhere—
why just on them, and not on others?
Is this an offense to justice? Yes.   10
Does it violate time-honored principles, does it cast
any moral down from the heights? It violates and casts down.

Look at the happy couple:
if they'd at least dissemble a bit,
feign depression and thereby cheer their friends!
Hear how they laugh—offensively.
And the language they speak—it only seems to make sense.
And all those ceremonials, ceremonies,
those elaborate obligations toward each other—
it all looks like a plot behind mankind's back!   20

It's even hard to foresee how far things might go,
if their example could be followed.
What could religions and poetries rely on,
what would be remembered, what abandoned,
who would want to keep within the bounds.

A happy love. Is it necessary?
Tact and common sense advise us to say no more of it
than of a scandal in Life's upper ranks.
Little cherubs get born without its help.
Never, ever could it populate the earth,   30
for it happens so seldom.

Let people who know naught of happy love
assert that nowhere is there a happy love.

With such faith, they would find it easier to live and to die.

LISEL MUELLER (B. 1924)

HAPPY AND UNHAPPY FAMILIES I 1996

If all happy families are alike,[1]
then so are the unhappy families,
whose lives we celebrate

Happy and Unhappy Families I
[1]An allusion to the celebrated opening line of Leo Tolstoy's novel *Anna Karenina* (1873–76).

because they are motion and heat,
because they are what we think of as *life*.
Someone is lying and someone else
is being lied to. Someone is beaten
and someone else is doing the beating.
Someone is praying, or weeps
because she does not know how to pray.   10
Someone drinks all night;
someone cowers in corners;
someone threatens and someone pleads.
Bitter words at the table,
bitter sobs in the bedroom;
reprisal breathed on the bathroom mirror.
The house crackles with secrets;
everyone draws up a plan of escape.
Somebody shatters without a sound.
Sometimes one of them leaves the house   20
on a stretcher, in terrible silence.
How much energy suffering takes!
It is like a fire that burns and burns
but cannot burn down to extinction.
Unhappy families are never idle;
they are where the action is,
unlike the others, the happy ones,
who never raise their voices
and spit no blood, who do nothing
to deserve their happiness   30

FOR ANALYSIS

1. How does the speaker describe unhappy families? What do you think are the characteristics of happy families?

2. Describe the images used to identify the sources of unhappiness.

3. Describe the conditions that generate happy families (ll. 27–30). Do you agree with the speaker? Explain.

4. In line 22, the speaker laments, "How much energy suffering takes!" Do you agree? How much energy does happiness take?

WRITING TOPIC

Argue for or against the proposition that all happy (or unhappy) families are alike. On what assumptions do you base your argument?

CAROLYN KIZER (B. 1925)

BITCH 1984

Now, when he and I meet, after all these years,
I say to the bitch inside me, don't start growling.
He isn't a trespasser anymore,
Just an old acquaintance tipping his hat.
My voice says, "Nice to see you,"
As the bitch starts to bark hysterically.
He isn't an enemy now,
Where are your manners, I say, as I say,
"How are the children? They must be growing up."
At a kind word from him, a look like the old days,   10
The bitch changes her tone: she begins to whimper.
She wants to snuggle up to him, to cringe.
Down, girl! Keep your distance
Or I'll give you a taste of the choke-chain.
"Fine, I'm just fine," I tell him.
She slobbers and grovels.
After all, I am her mistress. She is basically loyal.
It's just that she remembers how she came running
Each evening, when she heard his step;
How she lay at his feet and looked up adoringly   20
Though he was absorbed in his paper;
Or, bored with her devotion, ordered her to the kitchen
Until he was ready to play.
But the small careless kindnesses
When he'd had a good day, or a couple of drinks,
Come back to her now, seem more important
Than the casual cruelties, the ultimate dismissal.
"It's nice to know you are doing so well," I say.
He couldn't have taken you with him;
You were too demonstrative, too clumsy,   30
Not like the well-groomed pets of his new friends.
"Give my regards to your wife," I say. You gag
As I drag you off by the scruff,
Saying, "Goodbye! Goodbye! Nice to have seen you again."

FOR ANALYSIS

1. Who is being addressed in lines 13 and 14?

2. In what ways does the title suit the poem? In answering this question, consider the
tone of "Bitch," as well as the many **connotations** of the word.

3. What is "the ultimate dismissal" referred to in line 27?

4. How would you describe the speaker's present feelings about her former relationship?

ADRIENNE RICH   (B. 1929)

LIVING IN SIN   1955

She had thought the studio would keep itself;
no dust upon the furniture of love.
Half heresy, to wish the taps less vocal,
the panes relieved of grime. A plate of pears,
a piano with a Persian shawl, a cat
stalking the picturesque amusing mouse
had risen at his urging.
Not that at five each separate stair would writhe
under the milkman's tramp; that morning light
so coldly would delineate the scraps   10
of last night's cheese and three sepulchral bottles;
that on the kitchen shelf among the saucers
a pair of beetle-eyes would fix her own—
Envoy from some village in the moldings . . .
Meanwhile, he, with a yawn,
sounded a dozen notes upon the keyboard,
declared it out of tune, shrugged at the mirror,
rubbed at his beard, went out for cigarettes;
while she, jeered by the minor demons,
pulled back the sheets and made the bed and found   20
a towel to dust the table-top,
and let the coffee-pot boil over on the stove.
By evening she was back in love again,
though not so wholly but throughout the night
she woke sometimes to feel the daylight coming
like a relentless milkman up the stairs.

SYLVIA PLATH   (1932–1963)

DADDY   1965

You do not do, you do not do
Any more, black shoe
In which I have lived like a foot

For thirty years, poor and white,
Barely daring to breathe or Achoo.

Daddy, I have had to kill you,
You died before I had time—
Marble-heavy, a bag full of God,
Ghastly statue with one gray toe
Big as a Frisco seal   10

And a head in the freakish Atlantic
Where it pours bean green over blue
In the waters off beautiful Nauset.
I used to pray to recover you.
Ach, du.[1]

In the German tongue, in the Polish town
Scraped flat by the roller
Of wars, wars, wars.
But the name of the town is common.
My Polack friend   20

Says there are a dozen or two.
So I never could tell where you
Put your foot, your root,
I never could talk to you.
The tongue stuck in my jaw.

It stuck in a barb wire snare.
Ich, ich, ich, ich,[2]
I could hardly speak.
I thought every German was you.
And the language obscene   30

An engine, an engine
Chuffing me off like a Jew.
A Jew to Dachau, Auschwitz, Belsen.
I began to talk like a Jew.
I think I may well be a Jew.

The snows of the Tyrol, the clear beer of Vienna
Are not very pure or true.
With my gypsy ancestress and my weird luck

[1] German for "Oh, you."
[2] German for "I, I, I, I."

And my Taroc pack and my Taroc pack
I may be a bit of a Jew.

I have always been scared of *you*,
With your Luftwaffe,[3] your gobbledygoo.
And your neat mustache
And your Aryan eye, bright blue.
Panzer-man,[4] panzer-man, O You—

Not God but a swastika
So black no sky could squeak through.
Every woman adores a Fascist,
The boot in the face, the brute
Brute heart of a brute like you.

You stand at the blackboard, daddy,
In the picture I have of you,
A cleft in your chin instead of your foot
But no less a devil for that, no not
Any less the black man who

Bit my pretty red heart in two.
I was ten when they buried you.
At twenty I tried to die
And get back, back, back to you.
I thought even the bones would do

But they pulled me out of the sack,
And they stuck me together with glue.
And then I knew what to do.
I made a model of you,
A man in black with a Meinkampf[5] look

And a love of the rack and the screw.
And I said I do, I do.
So daddy, I'm finally through.
The black telephone's off at the root,
The voices just can't worm through.

If I've killed one man, I've killed two—
The vampire who said he was you
And drank my blood for a year,

---

[3] Name of the German air force during World War II.
[4] *Panzer* refers to German armored divisions during World War II.
[5] *My Struggle*, the title of Adolf Hitler's autobiography.

Seven years, if you want to know.
Daddy, you can lie back now.

There's a stake in your fat black heart
And the villagers never liked you.
They are dancing and stamping on you.
They always *knew* it was you.
Daddy, daddy, you bastard, I'm through.   80

FOR ANALYSIS

1. How do the **allusions** to Nazism function in the poem?

2. Does the poem exhibit the speaker's love for her father or her hatred of him? Explain.

3. What type of man does the speaker marry (see ll. 61–70)?

4. How does the speaker characterize her husband and her father in the last two stanzas? Might the "Daddy" of the last line of the poem refer to something more than the speaker's father? Explain.

WRITING TOPICS

1. What is the effect of the peculiar structure, idiosyncratic **rhyme**, unusual words (such as *achoo, gobbledygoo*), and repetitions in the poem?

2. What emotional associations does the title "Daddy" possess? Are those associations reinforced or contradicted by the poem?

AUDRE LORDE   (1934–1992)

POWER[1]   1978

The difference between poetry and rhetoric
is being
ready to kill
yourself
instead of your children.

I am trapped on a desert of raw gunshot wounds
and a dead child dragging his shattered black

Power
[1] "'Power'... is a poem written about Clifford Glover, the ten-year-old Black child shot by a cop who was acquitted by a jury on which a Black woman sat. In fact, the day I heard on the radio that O'Shea had been acquitted, I was going across town on Eighty-eighth Street and I had to pull over. A kind of fury rose up in me; the sky turned red. I felt so sick. I felt as if I would drive this car into a wall, into the next person I saw. So I pulled over. I took out my journal just to air some of my fury, to get it out of my fingertips. Those expressed feelings are that poem" (Audre Lorde, "My Words Will Be There," in *Black Women Writers* (1950–1980), ed. Mari Evans, New York, 1983, p. 266).

face off the edge of my sleep
blood from his punctured cheeks and shoulders
is the only liquid for miles and my stomach   10
churns at the imagined taste while
my mouth splits into dry lips
without loyalty or reason
thirsting for the wetness of his blood
as it sinks into the whiteness
of the desert where I am lost
without imagery or magic
trying to make power out of hatred and destruction
trying to heal my dying son with kisses
only the sun will bleach his bones quicker.   20

The policeman who shot down a 10-year-old in Queens[2]
stood over the boy with his cop shoes in childish blood
and a voice said "Die you little motherfucker" and
there are tapes to prove that. At his trial
this policeman said in his own defense
"I didn't notice the size or nothing else
only the color." and
there are tapes to prove that, too.

Today that 37-year-old white man with 13 years of police forcing
has been set free   30
by 11 white men who said they were satisfied
justice had been done
and one black woman who said
"They convinced me" meaning
they had dragged her 4' 10" black woman's frame
over the hot coals of four centuries of white male approval
until she let go the first real power she ever had
and lined her own womb with cement
to make a graveyard for our children.

I have not been able to touch the destruction within me.   40
But unless I learn to use
the difference between poetry and rhetoric
my power too will run corrupt as poisonous mold
or lie limp and useless as an unconnected wire
and one day I will take my teenaged plug
and connect it to the nearest socket
raping an 85-year-old white woman

---

[2] A borough of New York City.

who is somebody's mother
and as I beat her senseless and set a torch to her bed
a greek chorus will be singing in ¾ time[3]   50
"Poor thing. She never hurt a soul. What beasts they are."

LUCILLE CLIFTON   (B. 1936)

THERE IS A GIRL INSIDE   1977

there is a girl inside.
she is randy as a wolf.
she will not walk away
and leave these bones
to an old woman.

she is a green tree
in a forest of kindling.
she is a green girl
in a used poet.

she has waited   10
patient as a nun
for the second coming,
when she can break through gray hairs
into blossom

and her lovers will harvest
honey and thyme
and the woods will be wild
with the damn wonder of it.

FOR ANALYSIS

1. Who is the "girl" of this poem? What is she "inside" of?

2. What are the "bones" of the first stanza? What does the speaker's statement that she will not defer to an old woman tell us about her?

3. Describe the prevailing **metaphor** of the poem.

WRITING TOPIC

In an essay, discuss the appropriateness of the **images** Clifton uses to make her point.

Power
   [3] In classical Greek tragedy, a chorus chanted in response to the action in the play. Three-quarter time is waltz rhythm.

SEAMUS HEANEY (B. 1939)

VALEDICTION 1966

Lady with the frilled blouse
And simple tartan skirt,
Since you have left the house
Its emptiness has hurt
All thought. In your presence
Time rode easy, anchored
On a smile; but absence
Rocked love's balance, unmoored
The days. They buck and bound
Across the calendar   10
Pitched from the quiet sound
Of your flower-tender
Voice. Need breaks on my strand;
You've gone, I am at sea.
Until you resume command
Self is in mutiny.

FOR ANALYSIS

1. What is the central figure of speech (beginning in the middle of line 5) that animates this poem?

2. How are *time, love's balance,* and *the days* affected by the "lady's" behavior?

3. What sort of voice would a "flower-tender / Voice" (ll. 12–13) be?

WRITING TOPIC

Write an essay or a poem, serious or humorous, in which you use an extended **metaphor** to describe a fundamental emotion or experience — for example, how falling in love is like racing a car, or how the anguish of separation is like a visit to a dentist, or how attending classes is like a long hike through a desert.

BILLY COLLINS (B. 1941)

SONNET 1999

All we need is fourteen lines, well, thirteen now,
and after this one just a dozen
to launch a little ship on love's storm-tossed seas,
then only ten more left like rows of beans.

How easily it goes unless you get Elizabethan[1]
and insist the iambic bongos must be played
and rhymes positioned at the ends of lines,
one for every station of the cross.
But hang on here while we make the turn
into the final six where all will be resolved,
where longing and heartache will find an end,   10
where Laura will tell Petrarch[2] to put down his pen,
take off those crazy medieval tights,
blow out the lights, and come at last to bed.

SHARON OLDS   (B. 1942)

SEX WITHOUT LOVE   1984

How do they do it, the ones who make love
without love? Beautiful as dancers,
gliding over each other like ice skaters
over the ice, fingers hooked
inside each other's bodies, faces
red as steak, wine, wet as the
children at birth whose mothers are going to
give them away. How do they come to the
come to the   come to the   God   come to the
still waters, and not love   10
the one who came there with them, light
rising slowly as steam off their joined
skin? These are the true religious,
the purists, the pros, the ones who will not
accept a false Messiah, love the
priest instead of the God. They do not
mistake the lover for their own pleasure,
they are like great runners: they know they are alone
with the road surface, the cold, the wind,
the fit of their shoes, their over-all cardio-   20
vascular health—just factors, like the partner

Sonnet
  [1] The entry for **sonnet** in the "Glossary of Literary Terms" (p. 1431) distinguishes between the Elizabethan and the Italian, or Petrarchan, sonnet.
  [2] Francesco Petrarca (1304–1374), who employed the sonnet form named for him. Laura was the idealized woman he celebrated in his sonnets.

in the bed, and not the truth, which is the
single body alone in the universe
against its own best time.

FOR ANALYSIS

1. Describe the speaker's attitude toward "the ones who make love / without love" (ll. 1–2).

2. Who are the "These" of line 13?

3. What is the effect of the repetitions in lines 8 and 9?

4. What does "factors" of line 21 refer to?

5. Put into your own words the "truth" referred to in the final three lines. Does the speaker use the word straightforwardly or ironically? Explain.

DEBORAH POPE (B. ?)

GETTING THROUGH 1995

Like a car stuck in gear,
a chicken too stupid to tell
its head is gone,
or sound ratcheting on
long after the film
has jumped the reel,
or a phone
ringing and ringing
in the house they have all
moved away from,   10
through rooms where dust
is a deepening skin,
and the locks unneeded,
so I go on loving you,
my heart blundering on,
a muscle spilling out
what is no longer wanted,
and my words hurtling past,
like a train off its track,
toward a boarded-up station,   20
closed for years,
like some last speaker
of a beautiful language
no one else can hear.

WYATT PRUNTY (B. 1947)

LEARNING THE BICYCLE 2000

FOR HEATHER

The older children pedal past
Stable as little gyros, spinning hard
To supper, bath, and bed, until at last
We also quit, silent and tired
Beside the darkening yard where trees
Now shadow up instead of down.
Their predictable lengths can only tease
Her as, head lowered, she walks her bike alone
Somewhere between her wanting to ride
And her certainty she will always fall.   10

Tomorrow, though I will run behind,
Arms out to catch her, she'll tilt then balance wide
Of my reach, till distance makes her small,
Smaller, beyond the place I stop and know
That to teach her I had to follow
And when she learned to let her go.

FOR ANALYSIS

1. Describe the form and rhyme scheme of this poem. How does it differ from a **sonnet**?

2. What does the speaker learn from the experience of teaching his daughter to ride a bicycle?

WRITING TOPIC

Write an analysis of the poem's formal structure, noting how the poem shifts somewhat at lines 5, 9, and 11. How does the poem's organization and rhyme scheme
mimic a typical sonnet?

TONY HOAGLAND (B. 1953)

THE DOG YEARS 1998

when it seemed every girl I dated
had a friend—
a Sheena or a Scoop, Jerome or Mr. Bones—
a four-legged, longtime furry pal

whose single-minded, tail-shaking
devotion to his mistress
caused me a certain pang,
knowing his relationship with her

would outlast mine;
that he would still be here,   10
jumping on the furniture
long after I was just a memory

beside the toothbrush rack, another
anecdotal mugshot
in the history book of non-commitment.
Still, that animal and I would often,

on a sunny afternoon, promenade together,
sniffing at the pants of strangers,
one of us pausing
while the other peed,   20

having in common both
a short attention span
and an insatiable appetite
for the love of womankind.

How perplexing for that dog
it must have been
when at the midnight hour
it was me, not him,

admitted to the fresh
bower of her bed—   30
and more than once,
in the warm, aromatic dark

full of animal mysteries
and spiritual facts,
I myself felt baffled by my luck,
like a sinner who has woken up

inexplicably in heaven,
while far off in the background
some poor wretch
who had lived by all the rules   40

howled and scratched at the shut door.

SCOTT CAIRNS   (B. 1954)

POSSIBLE ANSWERS TO PRAYER   2002

Your petitions—though they continue to bear
just the one signature—have been duly recorded.
Your anxieties—despite their constant,

relatively narrow scope and inadvertent
entertainment value—nonetheless serve
to bring your person vividly to mind.

Your repentance—all but obscured beneath
a burgeoning, yellow fog of frankly more
conspicuous resentment—is sufficient.

Your intermittent concern for the sick,   10
the suffering, the needy poor is sometimes
recognizable to me, if not to them.

Your angers, your zeal, your lipsmackingly
righteous indignation toward the many
whose habits and sympathies offend you—

these must burn away before you'll apprehend
how near I am, with what fervor I adore
precisely these, the several who rouse your passions.

FOR ANALYSIS

1. Who is the speaker in this poem? How would you describe the speaker's **tone**? Is it
what you might expect?

2. What does the speaker have to say about the "petitions" (l. 1) and other offerings
and thoughts of the addressee? Does he accept them in the spirit in which they were
made or intended?

3. How would you characterize the speaker's point, finally? What is the speaker trying
to tell the addressee?

WRITING TOPICS

1. Describe the characteristics of the world the poem assumes. What kind of people
live in it? How do they act toward each other? What do these different kinds of people
expect of the universe? What might they get?

2. Write your own response to some kind of message or petition that is often delivered
without expectation of explicit written reply. Try to play off both the comedy of the
unexpected reply and the serious expectations of the writers/speakers of the messages.

CONNECTING POEMS: REMEMBERING FATHERS

No relationship is more primary to the human experience than that between parent and child. The relationship of mother or father to baby is one of complete responsibility and complete dependence, but this changes as both grow older and the emotional terrain becomes more tricky and harder to read. The poems in this unit express just a few of the very different kinds of emotions fathers and their children feel for each other, in the context of some of the many difficulties people encounter in life. As you read, take note of how the poems address the ways in which parents' and children's expectations of each other are or are not met and the ways in which feelings are or are not expressed.

THEODORE ROETHKE   (1908–1963)

MY PAPA'S WALTZ   1948

The whiskey on your breath
Could make a small boy dizzy;
But I hung on like death:
Such waltzing was not easy.

We romped until the pans
Slid from the kitchen shelf;
My mother's countenance
Could not unfrown itself.

The hand that held my wrist
Was battered on one knuckle;   10
At every step you missed
My right ear scraped a buckle.

You beat time on my head
With a palm caked hard by dirt,
Then waltzed me off to bed
Still clinging to your shirt.

FOR ANALYSIS

1. Why is iambic trimeter an appropriate **meter** for this poem?
2. What details reveal the kind of person the father is?
3. How would you describe the boy's feelings about his father? The father's about the boy?

WRITING TOPIC

Describe this poem's **tone.** What in the way it describes the events, from the title to the conceit, expresses this tone?

ROBERT HAYDEN   (1913–1980)

THOSE WINTER SUNDAYS   1975

Sundays too my father got up early
and put his clothes on in the blueblack cold,
then with cracked hands that ached
from labor in the weekday weather made
banked fires blaze. No one ever thanked him.

I'd wake and hear the cold splintering, breaking.
When the rooms were warm, he'd call,
and slowly I would rise and dress,
fearing the chronic angers of that house,

Speaking indifferently to him,   10
who had driven out the cold
and polished my good shoes as well.
What did I know, what did I know
of love's austere and lonely offices?

FOR ANALYSIS

1. Why Sundays "too" (l. 1)?

2. What does *offices* mean (l. 14) in this poem? Why do you think Hayden chooses this word?

3. From when in his life does the speaker describe those winter Sundays? How does his relation to the event color his description?

WRITING TOPICS

1. In the last line of the second stanza, the speaker refers to "the chronic angers of that house." How does the anger the speaker fears relate to the "love" of the poem's last line?

2. Has there been a time in your life when you neglected to thank someone you should have or to appreciate something you should have? How does the recollection make you feel?

SAY YOU LOVE ME   1989

What happened earlier I'm not sure of.
Of course he was drunk, but often he was.
His face looked like a ham on a hook above

me—I was pinned to the chair because
he'd hunkered over me with arms like jaws
pried open by the chair arms. "Do you love

me?" he began to sob. "Say you love me!"
I held out. I was probably fifteen.
What had happened? Had my mother—had she

said or done something? Or had he just been   10
drinking too long after work? "He'll get *mean*,"
my sister hissed, "just *tell* him." I brought my knee

up to kick him, but was too scared. Nothing
could have got the words out of me then. Rage
shut me up, yet "DO YOU?" was beginning

to peel, as of live layers of skin, age
from age from age from him until he gazed
through hysteria as a wet baby thing

repeating, "Do you love me? Say you do,"
in baby chokes, only loud, for they came   20
from a man. There wouldn't be a rescue

from my mother, still at work. The same
choking sobs said, "Love me, love me," and my game
was breaking down because I couldn't do

anything, not escape into my own
refusal, *I won't, I won't,* not fantasize
a kind, rich father, not fill the narrowed zone,

empty except for confusion until the size
of my fear ballooned as I saw his eyes,
blurred, taurean°—my sister screamed—unknown,   bull-like   30

unknown to me, a voice rose and leveled
off, "I love you," I said. *"Say 'I love you,
Dad.'* " "I love you, Dad," I whispered, leveled

by defeat into a cardboard image, untrue,
unbending. I was surprised I could move
as I did to get up, but he stayed, burled

onto the chair—my monstrous fear—she screamed,
my sister, "Dad, the phone! Go answer it!"
The phone wasn't ringing, yet he seemed

to move toward it, and I ran. He had a fit—   40
"It's not ringing!"—but I was at the edge of it
as he collapsed into the chair and blamed

both of us at a distance. No, the phone
was not ringing. There was no world out there,
so there we remained, completely alone.

FOR ANALYSIS

1. Is the speaker a child or an adult? Explain.

2. How do the **images** of lines 16–18 capture the speaker's feelings?

3. When the speaker finally capitulates to her father's demand, she describes herself
in lines 33–35 as "leveled / by defeat into a cardboard image, untrue, / unbending."
What does she mean?

4. Explain what the speaker means by "my game" (l. 23).

WRITING TOPIC

What would motivate a parent, even a drunken one, to make the kind of demand the
father makes on his daughter?

LI-YOUNG LEE   (B. 1957)

EATING ALONE   1986

I've pulled the last of the year's young onions.
The garden is bare now. The ground is cold,
brown and old. What is left of the day flames
in the maples at the corner of my

eye. I turn, a cardinal vanishes.
By the cellar door, I wash the onions,
then drink from the icy metal spigot.

Once, years back, I walked beside my father
among the windfall pears. I can't recall
our words. We may have strolled in silence. But   10
I still see him bend that way—left hand braced
on knee, creaky—to lift and hold to my
eye a rotten pear. In it, a hornet
spun crazily, glazed in slow, glistening juice.

It was my father I saw this morning
waving to me from the trees. I almost
called to him, until I came close enough
to see the shovel, leaning where I had
left it, in the flickering, deep green shade.

White rice steaming, almost done. Sweet green peas   20
fried in onions. Shrimp braised in sesame
oil and garlic. And my own loneliness.
What more could I, a young man, want.

FOR ANALYSIS

1. Why is the speaker eating alone?

2. How do the repeated references to youth and age, things being finished or almost done, function in the poem?

3. Why do you think the poet might have chosen to include the image of the hornet?

WRITING TOPICS

1. Read the last stanza closely. What is the effect of the **imagery**? What kind of question is asked in the last line? What do you think Lee was trying to do at the end of his poem?

2. Why do you think the poet chooses to write about a son remembering his father through the preparation of a meal? What is the significance of eating?

MAKING CONNECTIONS

1. Violence—actual or possible—is a presence in many of these poems. How do these poems express violence, explicitly and implicitly? Why is it such a presence?

2. In these poems, love is expressed in funny ways or goes unexpressed even when it is felt. What are some of the different ways in which these poems represent or hint at love?

3. With the modern advent of the nuclear family—consisting of only one set of parents and their unmarried children living together—families could be said to have become more isolated than they were previously. How does what Molly Peacock calls the "world out there" in "Say You Love Me" (p. 945) enter into these poems?

CONNECTING POEMS: PROPOSALS AND REPLIES

The four poems in this unit concern romantic proposals. Paired—the two original proposal poems, by Christopher Marlowe and Andrew Marvell, grouped with the responses they inspire, by Sir Walter Raleigh and Annie Finch—they can be read as statements on the assumptions and expectations encoded in romance, on their gendered nature, and on the use of poetry to talk about love. As you read these poetic conversations, try to take them in not just as individual works but as part of a long tradition of love poetry and a nearly as long tradition of sometimes angry, sometimes funny responses.

SIR WALTER RALEIGH   (1554–1618)

THE NYMPH'S REPLY TO THE SHEPHERD [1]   1600

If all the world and love were young,
And truth in every shepherd's tongue,
These pretty pleasures might me move
To live with thee and be thy love.

Time drives the flocks from field to fold,
When rivers rage and rocks grow cold,
And Philomel° becometh dumb;   the nightingale
The rest complains of cares to come.

The flowers do fade, and wanton fields
To wayward winter reckoning yields;   10
A honey tongue, a heart of gall,
Is fancy's spring, but sorrow's fall.

---

[1] Available on CD, *Voices from the Lost Realms* (Albany Records, 1994), composed by William Mayer, performed by New Calliope Singers, conducted by Peter Schubert.

Thy gowns, thy shoes, thy beds of roses,
Thy cap, thy kirtle, and thy posies
Soon break, soon wither, soon forgotten—
In folly ripe, in reason rotten.

Thy belt of straw and ivy buds,
Thy coral clasps and amber studs,
All these in me no means can move
To come to thee and be thy love.   20

But could youth last and love still breed,
Had joys no date° nor age no need,   end
Then these delights my mind might move
To live with thee and be thy love.

FOR ANALYSIS

1. How does the poet use the natural **setting** to create the poem's **tone**?

2. What seasons are featured in the poem?

3. To what natural/physical phenomena does the speaker connect love's frailty?

WRITING TOPIC

Raleigh's poem was written as a response to Marlowe's "The Passionate Shepherd to
His Love" (below). Write a response in return from the Shepherd to the Nymph.

CHRISTOPHER MARLOWE   (1564–1593)

THE PASSIONATE SHEPHERD
TO HIS LOVE[1] 1600

Come live with me and be my love,
And we will all the pleasures prove
That valleys, groves, hills, and fields,
Woods, or steepy mountain yields.

And we will sit upon the rocks,
Seeing the shepherds feed their flocks,

The Passionate Shepherd to His Love
   [1] The melody for Marlowe's song was published as early as 1603.

By shallow rivers to whose falls
Melodious birds sing madrigals.

And I will make thee beds of roses
And a thousand fragrant posies,
A cap of flowers, and a kirtle°   10
Embroidered all with leaves of myrtle;   skirt

A gown made of the finest wool
Which from our pretty lambs we pull;
Fair lined slippers for the cold,
With buckles of the purest gold;

A belt of straw and ivy buds,
With coral clasps and amber studs:
And if these pleasures may thee move,
Come live with me, and be my love.   20

The shepherds' swains shall dance and sing
For thy delight each May morning:
If these delights thy mind may move,
Then live with me and be my love.

FOR ANALYSIS

1. How would you characterize the poem's **setting**? How does the poem use it to create its mood?

2. Which season or seasons are the setting for the speaker's pleas? Which are not? Why?

3. What aspects of the natural world are absent from this poem?

WRITING TOPIC

What kind of relationship does the shepherd envision? Does the poem go into much depth describing this hypothetical future? Why or why not?

ANDREW MARVELL (1621–1678)

TO HIS COY MISTRESS 1681

Had we but world enough, and time,
This coyness, lady, were no crime.
We would sit down, and think which way

To walk, and pass our long love's day.
Thou by the Indian Ganges' side
Shouldst rubies find; I by the tide
Of Humber would complain. I would
Love you ten years before the flood,
And you should, if you please, refuse
Til the conversion of the Jews.   10
My vegetable love should grow
Vaster than empires and more slow;
An hundred years should go to praise
Thine eyes, and on thy forehead gaze;
Two hundred to adore each breast,
But thirty thousand to the rest;
An age at least to every part,
And the last age should show your heart.
For, lady, you deserve this state,
Nor would I love at lower rate.   20
     But at my back I always hear
Time's wingéd chariot hurrying near;
And yonder all before us lie
Deserts of vast eternity.
Thy beauty shall no more be found,
Nor, in thy marble vault, shall sound
My echoing song; then worms shall try
That long-preserved virginity,
And your quaint honor turn to dust,
And into ashes all my lust: 30
The grave's a fine and private place,
But none, I think, do there embrace.
     Now therefore, while the youthful hue
Sits on thy skin like morning dew,
And while thy willing soul transpires
At every pore with instant fires,
Now let us sport us while we may,
And now, like amorous birds of prey,
Rather at once our time devour
Than languish in his slow chapped° power.   slow-jawed   40
Let us roll our strength and all
Our sweetness up into one ball,
And tear our pleasures with rough strife
Thorough° the iron gates of life: through
Thus, though we cannot make our sun
Stand still, yet we will make him run.

FOR ANALYSIS

1. State the argument of the poem (see ll. 1–2, 21–22, 33–34).

2. Compare the figures of speech in lines 1–20 with those in lines 33–46. How do they differ?

3. Describe the attitude toward life recommended by the poet.

ANNIE FINCH   (B. 1956)

COY MISTRESS   1997

(IN ANSWER TO THE POEM BY ANDREW MARVELL)

Sir, I am not a bird of prey:
a Lady does not seize the day.
I trust that brief Time will unfold
our youth, before he makes us old.
How could we two write lines of rhyme
were we not fond of numbered Time
and grateful to the vast and sweet
trials his days will make us meet:
The Grave's not just the body's curse;
no skeleton can pen a verse!   10
So while this numbered World we see,
let's sweeten Time with poetry,
and Time, in turn, may sweeten Love
and give us time our love to prove.
You've praised my eyes, forehead, breast:
you've all our lives to praise the rest.

FOR ANALYSIS

1. What word appears more than any other in this poem? Why?

2. What is the poem's **tone?** How is it created?

3. What is the thing most valued in this poem?

WRITING TOPIC

Finch's poem is a response to Marvell's "To His Coy Mistress" (p. 950). Imagine a different response to Marvell's poem. What else could be said in reply? Who else could say it?

MAKING CONNECTIONS

1. How does Marlowe use the **pastoral** to press his case? How does Marvell use time? Compare and contrast these authors' dependence on natural phenomena in their arguments.

2. Compare Raleigh's and Finch's responses. How do they counter Marlowe and Marvell?

3. The Marlowe and Marvell poems make great use of **style**. How do the Raleigh and Finch poems respond in their own use of style? That is, how do they write back to the earlier poems, not in terms of argument, but in terms of style?

CONNECTING POEMS: LOVER'S DISCOVERIES

The poems in this unit are all about the things people in romantic relationships learn about themselves, each other, and the experience itself. From the act of love to the things lovers do for and to one another, these poems explore the surprises that lay around the corner and sometimes right in front of people in love. As you read, keep an eye out for the interplay between stability and fragility, between the solid bonds between people and the chaos of daily experience that lays outside—and sometimes creeps in.

GALWAY KINNELL   (B. 1927)

AFTER MAKING LOVE WE HEAR FOOTSTEPS   1980

For I can snore like a bullhorn
or play loud music
or sit up talking with any reasonably sober Irishman
and Fergus will only sink deeper
into his dreamless sleep, which goes by all in one flash,
but let there be that heavy breathing
or a stifled come-cry anywhere in the house
and he will wrench himself awake
and make for it on the run—as now, we lie together,
after making love, quiet, touching along the length of our bodies,   10
familiar touch of the long-married,
and he appears   in his baseball pajamas, it happens,
the neck opening so small
he has to screw them on, which one day may make him wonder
about the mental capacity of baseball players—

and says, "Are you loving and snuggling? May I join?"
He flops down between us and hugs us and snuggles himself to sleep,
his face gleaming with satisfaction at being this very child.

In the half darkness we look at each other
and smile
and touch arms across his little, startlingly muscled body—   20
this one whom habit of memory propels to the ground of his making,
sleeper only the mortal sounds can sing awake,
this blessing love gives again into our arms.

FOR ANALYSIS

1. What two things appear in this poem that rarely appear together in poems? What is it like to read about them together? Why?

2. What expectation is set up by the event related in lines 6–9? Is it met? Does the speaker have the reaction to this event that we expect?

3. What function might lines 12–15 serve? How do they stand apart from the rest of the poem, and how do they fit in?

WRITING TOPICS

1. Do you believe the explanation in line 22? Do you have to for the poem to work?

2. Though it is not explicitly expressed, what might the speaker be said to be discovering in this poem?

JANE KENYON   (1947–1995)

SURPRISE   1996

He suggests pancakes at the local diner,
followed by a walk in search of mayflowers,
while friends convene at the house
bearing casseroles and a cake, their cars
pulled close along the sandy shoulders
of the road, where tender ferns unfurl
in the ditches, and this year's budding leaves
push last year's spectral leaves from the tips
of the twigs of the ash trees. The gathering
itself is not what astounds her, but the casual   10
accomplishment with which he has lied.

FOR ANALYSIS

1. What is the **tone** through the beginning and middle of the poem? Does it change? Where, and how?

2. What is the surprise in this poem? Is there more than one?

3. What function might the seemingly insignificant details concerning the side of the road play?

WRITING TOPICS

1. Reflect on lying in everyday life. Are there different kinds of lies? Which are acceptable and which are thought more serious? Where do these distinctions come from?

2. Do you lie? When? Why?

MICHAEL S. HARPER   (B. 1951)

DISCOVERY   1970

We lay together, darkness all around,
I listen to her constant breath,
and when I thought she slept,
I too fell asleep.
But something stirred me, why I . . .
she was staring at me with her eyes,
her breasts still sturdy,
her thigh warming mine.
And I, a little shaken as she stroked
my skin and kissed my brow,   10
reached for the light turned on,
feeling for the heat which would
reveal how long she had looked
and cared.
The bulb was hot.   It burned my hand.

FOR ANALYSIS

1. What is "the light turned on" (l. 11)? What does it mean that the "bulb" (l. 15) is not just hot but burns the speaker's hand?

2. What does the speaker discover? Does he discover more than one thing?

3. Why do you think the speaker is "shaken"?

WRITING TOPIC

What sense does the poem give of the relationship between the speaker and the woman? Describe it in your own words, explaining what textual evidence supports your description.

SUSAN MINOT (B. 1956)

MY HUSBAND'S BACK 2005

Sunday evening.
Breakdown hour. Weeping into
a pot of burnt rice. Sun dimmed
like a light bulb gone out
behind a gray lawn of snow.
The baby flushed with the flu
asleep on a pillow.
The fire won't catch.
The wet wood's caked
with ice. Sitting   10
on the couch my spine
collides with all its bones
and I watch my husband
peer past the glass grate
and blow.
His back in a snug plaid shirt
gray and white
leaning into the woodstove
is firm and compact
like a young man's back.   20

And the giant world which swirls
in my head
stopping most thought
suddenly ceases
to spin. It sits
right there, the back I love,
animal and gamine, leaning
on one arm.
I could crawl on it forever
the one point in the world   30
turns out
I have travelled everywhere
to get to.

FOR ANALYSIS

1. How is the speaker feeling in the first twenty-five lines? How does she feel in the last nine lines? What changes?

2. What does *gamine* mean? What is the effect of its use on the description of the husband's back?

3. Minot's poem moves from very specific to, in the last five lines, less concrete **imagery.** What is the effect of this movement?

WRITING TOPIC

Why do you think Minot chose the husband's back to focus on? How might it have changed the poem to choose another body part? Make a list of five alternate body parts and list characteristics associated with each that might inform five different poems focused on them.

MAKING CONNECTIONS

1. Sex plays a role in some of these poems. In which poems does it appear? How is it represented? What does it mean in the context of the described relationships?

2. A sense of danger is just beneath the surface of some of these poems. In which poems do love and/or sex appear dangerous? What are the dangers? How do the poems present them?

3. How does the issue of trust appear in these poems? In which is it featured? What is the relationship between trust and love? Between trust and sex?

DRAMA

WILLIAM SHAKESPEARE   (1564–1616)

OTHELLO   CA. 1604

CHARACTERS

Duke of Venice
Brabantio, a Senator
Senators
Gratiano, Brother to Brabantio
Lodovico, Kinsman to Brabantio
Othello, a noble Moor; in the service of the Venetian State
Cassio, his Lieutenant
Iago, his Ancient
Roderigo, a Venetian Gentleman

Montano, Othello's predecessor in the Government of Cyprus
Clown, Servant to Othello
Desdemona, Daughter to Brabantio, and Wife to Othello
Emilia, Wife to Iago
Bianca, Mistress to Cassio
Sailor, Officers, Gentlemen, Messengers, Musicians, Heralds, Attendants

Scene

For the first Act, in Venice; during the rest of the Play, at a Sea-port in Cyprus

---

ACT I

Scene 1.   Venice. A Street.

(Enter Roderigo and Iago.)

Roderigo. Tush! Never tell me; I take it much unkindly
   That thou, Iago, who has had my purse
   As if the strings were thine, shouldst know of this.[1]

---

[1] I.e., Othello's successful courtship of Desdemona.

Iago. 'Sblood,[2] but you will not hear me:
If ever I did dream of such a matter,
Abhor me.

Roderigo. Thou told'st me thou didst hold him[3] in thy hate.

Iago. Despise me if I do not. Three great ones of the city,
In personal suit to make me his lieutenant,
Off-capp'd[4] to him; and, by the faith of man,
I know my price, I am worth no worse a place;   10
But he, as loving his own pride and purposes,
Evades them, with a bombast circumstance[5]
Horribly stuff'd with epithets of war;
And, in conclusion,
Nonsuits[6] my mediators;[7] for, 'Certes,'[8] says he,
'I have already chosen my officer.'
And what was he?
Forsooth, a great arithmetician,
One Michael Cassio, a Florentine,
A fellow almost damn'd in a fair wife;[9]   20
That never set a squadron in the field,
Nor the division of a battle knows
More than a spinster; unless[10] the bookish theoric,[11]
Wherein the togèd consuls can propose
As masterly as he: mere prattle, without practice,
Is all his soldiership. But he, sir, had the election;
And I—of whom his eyes had seen the proof
At Rhodes, at Cyprus, and on other grounds
Christian and heathen—must be be-lee'd[12] and calm'd
By debitor and creditor; this counter-caster,[13]   30
He, in good time, must his lieutenant be,
And I—God bless the mark!—his Moorship's ancient.[14]

Roderigo. By heaven, I rather would have been his hangman.

Iago. Why, there's no remedy: 'tis the curse of service,
Preferment goes by letter and affection,
Not by the old gradation,[15] where each second
Stood heir to the first. Now, sir, be judge yourself,
Whe'r[16] I in any just term am affin'd[17]
To love the Moor.

---

[2] By God's blood.   [3] I.e., Othello.   [4] Took off their caps.   [5] Pompous wordiness, circumlocu-
tion.   [6] Turns down.   [7] Spokesmen.   [8] In truth.   [9] A much debated phrase. In the Italian source
the Captain (i.e., Cassio) was married, and it may be that Shakespeare originally intended Bianca to be
Cassio's wife but later changed his mind and failed to alter the phrase here accordingly. Or perhaps Iago
simply sneers at Cassio as a notorious ladies' man.   [10] Except.   [11] Theory.   [12] Left without wind
for my sails.   [13] Bookkeeper (*cf.* "arithmetician" above).   [14] Ensign (but Iago's position in the play
seems to be that of Othello's aide-de-camp).   [15] Seniority.   [16] Whether.   [17] Obliged.

Roderigo.   I would not follow him then.
Iago. O! sir, content you;   40
  I follow him to serve my turn upon him;
  We cannot all be masters, nor all masters
  Cannot be truly follow'd. You shall mark
  Many a duteous and knee-crooking knave,
  That, doting on his own obsequious bondage,
  Wears out his time, much like his master's ass,
  For nought but provender, and when he's old, cashier'd;
  Whip me such honest knaves. Others there are
  Who, trimm'd in forms and visages of duty,
  Keep yet their hearts attending on themselves,   50
  And, throwing but shows of service on their lords,
  Do well thrive by them, and when they have lin'd their coats
  Do themselves homage: these fellows have some soul;
  And such a one do I profess myself. For, sir,
  It is as sure as you are Roderigo,
  Were I the Moor, I would not be Iago:
  In following him, I follow but myself;
  Heaven is my judge, not I for love and duty,
  But seeming so, for my peculiar end:
  For when my outward action doth demonstrate   60
  The native act and figure of my heart
  In compliment extern,[18] 'tis not long after
  But I will wear my heart upon my sleeve
  For daws to peck at: I am not what I am.
Roderigo. What a full fortune does the thick-lips owe,[19]
  If he can carry 't thus!
Iago.   Call up her father;
  Rouse him, make after him, poison his delight,
  Proclaim him in the streets, incense her kinsmen,
  And, though he in a fertile climate dwell,[20]
  Plague him with flies; though that his joy be joy,   70
  Yet throw such changes of vexation on 't
  As it may lose some colour.
Roderigo. Here is her father's house; I'll call aloud.
Iago. Do; with like timorous[21] accent and dire yell
  As when, by night and negligence, the fire
  Is spied in populous cities.
Roderigo. What, ho! Brabantio: Signior Brabantio, ho!
Iago. Awake! what, ho! Brabantio! thieves! thieves! thieves!
  Look to your house, your daughter, and your bags!
  Thieves! thieves!   80

---

[18] External show.   [19] Own.   [20] I.e., is fortunate.   [21] Frightening.

(Enter Brabantio, above, at a window.)

Brabantio.   What is the reason of this terrible summons?
    What is the matter there?
Roderigo.   Signior, is all your family within?
Iago.   Are your doors lock'd?
Brabantio.   Why? wherefore ask you this?
Iago.   'Zounds!²² sir, you're robb'd; for shame, put on your gown;
    Your heart is burst, you have lost half your soul;
    Even now, now, very now, an old black ram
    Is tupping²³ your white ewe. Arise, arise!
    Awake the snorting²⁴ citizens with the bell,
    Or else the devil will make a grandsire of you.   90
    Arise, I say.
Brabantio.   What! have you lost your wits?
Roderigo.   Most reverend signior, do you know my voice?
Brabantio.   Not I, what are you?
Roderigo.   My name is Roderigo.
Brabantio.   The worser welcome:
    I have charg'd thee not to haunt about my doors:
    In honest plainness thou hast heard me say
    My daughter is not for thee; and now, in madness,
    Being full of supper and distempering draughts,
    Upon malicious knavery dost thou come
    To start my quiet.   100
Roderigo.   Sir, sir, sir!
Brabantio.   But thou must needs be sure
    My spirit and my place²⁵ have in them power
    To make this bitter to thee.
Roderigo.   Patience, good sir.
Brabantio.   What tell'st thou me of robbing? this is Venice;
    My house is not a grange.²⁶
Roderigo.   Most grave Brabantio,
    In simple and pure soul I come to you.
Iago.   'Zounds! sir, you are one of those that will not serve God if the devil bid
    you. Because we come to do you service and you think we are ruffians, you'll
    have your daughter covered with a Barbary horse; you'll have your nephews
    neigh to you; you'll have coursers for cousins and gennets²⁷ for germans.²⁸   110
Brabantio.   What profane wretch art thou?
Iago.   I am one, sir, that comes to tell you, your daughter and the Moor are now
    making the beast with two backs.
Brabantio.   Thou art a villain.

---

²² By God's wounds.   ²³ Copulating.   ²⁴ Snoring.   ²⁵ Position.   ²⁶ Isolated farmhouse.
²⁷ Spanish horses.   ²⁸ Blood relations.

Iago.   You are—a senator.

Brabantio. This thou shalt answer; I know thee, Roderigo.

Roderigo. Sir, I will answer any thing. But, I beseech you,
If 't be your pleasure and most wise consent,—
As partly, I find, it is,—that your fair daughter,
At this odd-even[29] and dull watch o' the night,
Transported with no worse nor better guard   120
But with a knave of common hire, a gondolier,
To the gross clasps of a lascivious Moor,—
If this be known to you, and your allowance,[30]
We then have done you bold and saucy wrongs;
But if you know not this, my manners tell me
We have your wrong rebuke. Do not believe
That, from[31] the sense of all civility,
I thus would play and trifle with your reverence:
Your daughter, if you have not given her leave,
I say again, hath made a gross revolt;   130
Tying her duty, beauty, wit and fortunes
In[32] an extravagant[33] and wheeling stranger
Of here and every where. Straight satisfy yourself:
If she be in her chamber or your house,
Let loose on me the justice of the state
For thus deluding you.

Brabantio.   Strike on the tinder, ho!
Give me a taper! call up all my people!
This accident[34] is not unlike my dream;
Belief of it oppresses me already.
Light, I say! light!   *(Exit, from above.)*   140

Iago.   Farewell, for I must leave you:
It seems not meet nor wholesome to my place
To be produc'd,[35] as, if I stay, I shall,
Against the Moor; for I do know the state,
However this may gall him with some check,[36]
Cannot with safety cast him; for he's embark'd
With such loud reason to the Cyprus wars,—
Which even now stand in act,—that, for their souls,
Another of his fathom[37] they have none,
To lead their business; in which regard,
Though I do hate him as I do hell-pains,   150
Yet, for necessity of present life,
I must show out a flag and sign of love,

---

[29] Between night and morning.   [30] By your approval.   [31] Away from.   [32] To.   [33] Expatriate.
[34] Happening.   [35] I.e., as a witness.   [36] Restraining adversity.   [37] Caliber, ability.

Which is indeed but sign. That you shall surely find him,
Lead to the Sagittary[38] the raised search;
And there will I be with him. So, farewell.   *(Exit.)*

(Enter below, Brabantio, and servants with torches.)

Brabantio. It is too true an evil: gone she is,
   And what's to come of my despised time
   Is nought but bitterness. Now, Roderigo,
   Where didst thou see her? O, unhappy girl!
   With the Moor, sayst thou? Who would be a father!   160
   How didst thou know 'twas she? O, she deceives me
   Past thought. What said she to you? Get more tapers!
   Raise all my kindred! Are they married, think you?
Roderigo. Truly, I think they are.
Brabantio. O heaven! How got she out? O treason of the blood:
   Fathers, from hence trust not your daughters' minds
   By what you see them act. Are there not charms
   By which the property of youth and maidhood
   May be abus'd? Have you not read, Roderigo,
   Of some such thing?
Roderigo.   Yes, sir, I have indeed.   170
Brabantio. Call up my brother. O! that you had had her.
   Some one way, some another! Do you know
   Where we may apprehend her and the Moor?
Roderigo. I think I can discover him, if you please
   To get good guard and go along with me.
Brabantio. Pray you, lead on. At every house I'll call;
   I may command at most. Get weapons, ho!
   And raise some special officers of night.
   On, good Roderigo; I'll deserve[39] your pains.   *(Exeunt.)*

Scene 2.   Another Street.

(Enter Othello, Iago, and Attendants, with torches.)

Iago. Though in the trade of war I have slain men,
   Yet do I hold it very stuff o' the conscience
   To do no contriv'd murder: I lack iniquity
   Sometimes to do me service. Nine or ten times
   I had thought to have yerk'd[40] him here under the ribs.
Othello. 'Tis better as it is.

---

[38] The name of an inn (?).   [39] I.e., reward.   [40] Stabbed.

Iago.   Nay, but he prated,
And spoke such scurvy and provoking terms
Against your honour
That, with the little godliness I have,
I did full hard forbear him. But, I pray, sir,   10
Are you fast married? Be assur'd of this,
That the magnifico[41] is much belov'd,
And hath in his effect a voice potential
As double[42] as the duke's; he will divorce you,
Or put upon you what restraint and grievance
The law—with all his might to enforce it on—
Will give him cable.[43]
Othello.   Let him do his spite:
My services which I have done the signiory[44]
Shall out-tongue his complaints. 'Tis yet to know,[45]
Which when I know that boasting is an honour   20
I shall promulgate, I fetch my life and being
From men of royal siege, and my demerits[46]
May speak unbonneted[47] to as proud a fortune
As this[48] that I have reach'd; for know, Iago,
But that I love the gentle Desdemona,
I would not my unhoused[49] free condition
Put into circumscription and confine
For the sea's worth. But, look! what lights come yond?
Iago. Those are the raised[50] father and his friends:
You were best[51] go in.
Othello.   Not I; I must be found: 30
My parts, my title, and my perfect[52] soul
Shall manifest me rightly. Is it they?
Iago. By Janus,[53] I think no.

(Enter Cassio and certain Officers, with torches.)

Othello. The servants of the duke, and my lieutenant.
The goodness of the night upon you, friends!
What is the news?
Cassio.   The duke does greet you, general,
And he requires your haste-post-haste appearance,
Even on the instant.

---

[41] One of the grandees, or rulers, of Venice; here, Brabantio.   [42] Iago means that Brabantio's influence equals that of the Doge's with his double vote.   [43] I.e., scope.   [44] The Venetian government.   [45] I.e., the signiory does not as yet know.   [46] Merits.   [47] I.e., as equals.   [48] I.e., that of Desdemona's family.   [49] Unconfined.   [50] Aroused.   [51] Had better.   [52] Untroubled by a bad conscience.   [53] The two-faced Roman god of portals and doors and (hence) of beginnings and ends.

Othello.   What is the matter, think you?

Cassio. Something from Cyprus, as I may divine.

It is a business of some heat;[54] the galleys   40

Have sent a dozen sequent[55] messengers

This very night at one another's heels,

And many of the consuls,[56] rais'd and met,

Are at the duke's already. You have been hotly call'd for;

When, being not at your lodging to be found,

The senate hath sent about three several[57] quests

To search you out.

Othello.   'Tis well I am found by you.

I will but spend a word here in the house,

And go with you.   (*Exit.*)

Cassio.   Ancient, what makes he here?

Iago. Faith, he to-night hath boarded a land carrack;[58]   50

If it prove lawful prize, he's made for ever.

Cassio. I do not understand.

Iago.   He's married.

Cassio.   To who?

(*Re-enter Othello.*)

Iago. Marry,[59] to—Come, captain, will you go?

Othello.   Have with you.

Cassio. Here comes another troop to seek for you.

Iago. It is Brabantio. General, be advis'd;

He comes to bad intent.

(*Enter Brabantio, Roderigo, and Officers, with torches and weapons.*)

Othello.   Holla! stand there!

Roderigo. Signior, it is the Moor.

Brabantio.   Down with him, thief!

(*They draw on both sides.*)

Iago. You, Roderigo! Come, sir, I am for you.[60]

Othello. Keep up your bright swords, for the dew will rust them.

Good signior, you shall more command with years   60

Than with your weapons.

Brabantio. O thou foul thief! where hast thou stow'd my daughter?

Damn'd as thou art, thou hast enchanted her;

---

[54] Urgency.   [55] Following one another.   [56] I.e., senators.   [57] Separate.   [58] Treasure ship.
[59] By the Virgin Mary.   [60] Let you and me fight.

For I'll refer me to all things of sense,
If she in chains of magic were not bound,
Whether a maid so tender, fair, and happy,
So opposite to marriage that she shunn'd
The wealthy curled darlings of our nation,
Would ever have, to incur a general mock,
Run from her guardage to the sooty bosom   70
Of such a thing as thou; to fear, not to delight.
Judge me the world, if 'tis not gross in sense[61]
That thou hast practis'd on her with foul charms,
Abus'd her delicate youth with drugs or minerals
That weaken motion:[62] I'll have 't disputed on;
'Tis probable, and palpable to thinking.
I therefore apprehend and do attach[63] thee
For an abuser of the world, a practiser
Of arts inhibited and out of warrant.[64]
Lay hold upon him: if he do resist,   80
Subdue him at his peril.

Othello.   Hold your hands,
Both you of my inclining,[65] and the rest:
Were it my cue to fight, I should have known it
Without a prompter. Where will you that I go
To answer this your charge?

Brabantio.   To prison; till fit time
Of law and course of direct session[66]
Call thee to answer.

Othello.   What if I do obey?
How may the duke be therewith satisfied,
Whose messengers are here about my side,
Upon some present[67] business of the state   90
To bring me to him?

Officer.   'Tis true, most worthy signior;
The duke's in council, and your noble self,
I am sure, is sent for.

Brabantio.   How! the duke in council!
In this time of the night! Bring him away.
Mine's not an idle cause: the duke himself,
Or any of my brothers of the state,[68]
Cannot but feel this wrong as 'twere their own;
For if such actions may have passage free,
Bond-slaves and pagans shall our statesmen be.   (*Exeunt.*)

---

[61] Obvious.   [62] Normal reactions.   [63] Arrest.   [64] Prohibited and illegal.   [65] Party.
[66] Normal process of law.   [67] Immediate, pressing.   [68] Fellow senators.

Scene 3. A Council Chamber.

(The Duke and Senators sitting at a table. Officers attending.)

Duke. There is no composition[69] in these news
   That gives them credit.
First Senator.   Indeed, they are disproportion'd;
   My letters say a hundred and seven galleys.
Duke. And mine, a hundred and forty.
Second Senator.   And mine, two hundred:
   But though they jump[70] not on a just[71] account,—
   As in these cases, where the aim[72] reports,
   'Tis oft with difference,—yet do they all confirm
   A Turkish fleet, and bearing up to Cyprus.
Duke. Nay, it is possible enough to judgment:
   I do not so secure me in[73] the error,
   But the main article[74] I do approve[75]
   In fearful sense.
Sailor *(within).*   What, ho! what, ho! what, ho!
Officer.   A messenger from the galleys.

(Enter a Sailor.)

Duke.   Now, what's the business?
Sailor.   The Turkish preparation makes for Rhodes;
   So was I bid report here to the state
   By Signior Angelo.
Duke. How say you by this change?
First Senator.   This cannot be
   By no[76] assay[77] of reason; 'tis a pageant[78]
   To keep us in false gaze.[79] When we consider
   The importancy of Cyprus to the Turk,
   And let ourselves again but understand,
   That as it more concerns the Turk than Rhodes,
   So may he with more facile question bear[80] it,
   For that it stands not in such warlike brace,[81]
   But altogether lacks the abilities
   That Rhodes is dress'd in: if we make thought of this,
   We must not think the Turk is so unskilful
   To leave that latest which concerns him first,
   Neglecting an attempt of ease and gain,
   To wake and wage a danger profitless.

---

[69] Consistency, agreement.   [70] Coincide.   [71] Exact.   [72] Conjecture.   [73] Draw comfort from.
[74] Substance.   [75] Believe.   [76] Any.   [77] Test.   [78] (Deceptive) show.   [79] Looking in the wrong
direction.   [80] More easily capture.   [81] State of defense.

Duke. Nay, in all confidence, he's not for Rhodes.
Officer. Here is more news.

(Enter a Messenger.)

Messenger. The Ottomites,[82] reverend and gracious,
Steering with due course toward the isle of Rhodes,
Have there injointed[83] them with an after fleet.[84]
First Senator. Ay, so I thought. How many, as you guess?
Messenger. Of thirty sail; and now they do re-stem[85]
Their backward course, bearing with frank appearance
Their purposes toward Cyprus. Signior Montano,
Your trusty and most valiant servitor,   40
With his free duty[86] recommends[87] you thus,
And prays you to believe him.
Duke. 'Tis certain then, for Cyprus.
Marcus Luccicos, is not he in town?
First Senator. He's now in Florence.
Duke. Write from us to him; post-post-haste dispatch.
First Senator. Here comes Brabantio and the valiant Moor.

(Enter Brabantio, Othello, Iago, Roderigo, and Officers.)

Duke. Valiant Othello, we must straight employ you
Against the general enemy Ottoman.
(To Brabantio.) I did not see you; welcome, gentle signior;   50
We lack'd your counsel and your help to-night.
Brabantio. So did I yours. Good your Grace, pardon me;
Neither my place nor aught I heard of business
Hath rais'd me from my bed, nor doth the general care
Take hold of me, for my particular grief
Is of so flood-gate[88] and o'erbearing nature
That it engluts and swallows other sorrows
And it is still itself.
Duke.   Why, what's the matter?
Brabantio. My daughter! O! my daughter.
Duke. }
Senators. }   Dead?
Brabantio.   Ay, to me;
She is abus'd, stol'n from me, and corrupted   60
By spells and medicines bought of mountebanks;
For nature so preposterously to err,

---

[82] Turks.   [83] Joined.   [84] Fleet that followed after.   [85] Steer again.   [86] Unqualified expressions
of respect.   [87] Informs.   [88] Torrential.

Being not deficient, blind, or lame of sense,
Sans[89] witchcraft could not.

Duke. Whoe'er he be that in this foul proceeding
Hath thus beguil'd your daughter of herself
And you of her, the bloody book of law
You shall yourself read in the bitter letter
After your own sense; yea, though our proper[90] son
Stood[91] in your action.[92]

Brabantio.   Humbly I thank your Grace.   70
Here is the man, this Moor; whom now, it seems,
Your special mandate for the state affairs
Hath hither brought.

Duke.   }
                          We are very sorry for it.
Senators. }

Duke *(to Othello).* What, in your own part, can you say to this?

Brabantio. Nothing, but this is so.

Othello. Most potent, grave, and reverend signiors,
My very noble and approv'd[93] good masters,
That I have ta'en away this old man's daughter,
It is most true; true, I have married her:
The very head and front of my offending   80
Hath this extent, no more. Rude am I in my speech,
And little bless'd with the soft phrase of peace;
For since these arms of mine had seven years' pith,[94]
Till now some nine moons wasted,[95] they have us'd
Their dearest action in the tented field;
And little of this great world can I speak,
More than pertains to feats of broil and battle;
And therefore little shall I grace my cause
In speaking for myself. Yet, by your gracious patience,
I will a round[96] unvarnish'd tale deliver   90
Of my whole course of love; what drugs, what charms,
What conjuration, and what mighty magic,
For such proceeding I am charg'd withal,
I won his daughter.

Brabantio.   A maiden never bold;
Of spirit so still and quiet, that her motion
Blush'd at herself;[97] and she, in spite of nature,
Of years, of country, credit, every thing,
To fall in love with what she fear'd to look on!
It is a judgment maim'd and most imperfect

---

[89] Without.   [90] Own.   [91] Were accused.   [92] Suit.   [93] Tested (by past experience).   [94] Strength.
[95] Past.   [96] Blunt.   [97] I.e. (her modesty was such that) she blushed at her own emotions; or: she could not move without blushing.

That will confess[98] perfection so could err   100
Against all rules of nature, and must be driven
To find out practices of cunning hell,
Why this should be. I therefore vouch again
That with some mixtures powerful o'er the blood,
Or with some dram conjur'd to this effect,
He wrought upon her.
Duke.   To vouch this, is no proof,
Without more certain and more overt test
Than these thin habits[99] and poor likelihoods
Of modern[100] seeming do prefer against him.
First Senator. But, Othello, speak: 110
Did you by indirect and forced courses
Subdue and poison this young maid's affections;
Or came it by request and such fair question[101]
As soul to soul affordeth?
Othello.   I do beseech you;
Send for the lady to the Sagittary,
And let her speak of me before her father:
If you do find me foul in her report,
The trust, the office I do hold of you,
Not only take away, but let your sentence
Even fall upon my life.
Duke.   Fetch Desdemona hither.   120
Othello. Ancient, conduct them; you best know the place.

                                        (*Exeunt Iago and Attendants.*)

And, till she come, as truly as to heaven
I do confess the vices of my blood,
So justly to your grave ears I'll present
How I did thrive in this fair lady's love,
And she in mine.
Duke. Say it, Othello.
Othello. Her father lov'd me; oft invited me;
Still[102] question'd me the story of my life
From year to year, the battles, sieges, fortunes   130
That I have pass'd.
I ran it through, even from my boyish days
To the very moment that he bade me tell it;
Wherein I spake of most disastrous chances,
Of moving accidents by flood and field,

---

[98] Assert.   [99] Weak appearances.   [100] Commonplace.   [101] Conversation.   [102] Always, regularly.

Of hair-breadth 'scapes i' the imminent deadly breach,
Of being taken by the insolent foe
And sold to slavery, of my redemption thence
And portance[103] in my travel's history;
Wherein of antres[104] vast and deserts idle,[105]   140
Rough quarries, rocks, and hills whose heads touch heaven,
It was my hint[106] to speak, such was the process;
And of the Cannibals that each other eat,
The Anthropophagi,[107] and men whose heads
Do grow beneath their shoulders. This to hear
Would Desdemona seriously incline;
But still the house-affairs would draw her thence;
Which ever as she could with haste dispatch,
She'd come again, and with a greedy ear
Devour up my discourse. Which I observing,   150
Took once a pliant[108] hour, and found good means
To draw from her a prayer of earnest heart
That I would all my pilgrimage dilate,[109]
Whereof by parcels[110] she had something heard,
But not intentively:[111] I did consent;
And often did beguile her of her tears,
When I did speak of some distressful stroke
That my youth suffer'd. My story being done,
She gave me for my pains a world of sighs:
She swore, in faith, 'twas strange, 'twas passing[112] strange;   160
'Twas pitiful, 'twas wondrous pitiful:
She wish'd she had not heard it, yet she wish'd
That heaven had made her[113] such a man; she thank'd me,
And bade me, if I had a friend that lov'd her,
I should but teach him how to tell my story,
And that would woo her. Upon this hint I spake.
She lov'd me for the dangers I had pass'd,
And I lov'd her that she did pity them.
This only is the witchcraft I have us'd:
Here comes the lady; let her witness it.   170

(Enter Desdemona, Iago, and Attendants.)

Duke. I think this tale would win my daughter too.
  Good Brabantio,
  Take up this mangled matter at the best;

---

[103] Behavior.   [104] Caves.   [105] Empty, sterile.   [106] Opportunity.   [107] Man-eaters.   [108] Suitable.
[109] Relate in full.   [110] Piecemeal.   [111] In sequence.   [112] Surpassing.   [113] Direct object; not
"for her."

Men do their broken weapons rather use
Than their bare hands.

Brabantio.   I pray you, hear her speak:
  If she confess that she was half the wooer,
  Destruction on my head, if my bad blame
  Light on the man! Come hither, gentle mistress:
  Do you perceive in all this noble company
  Where most you owe obedience?

Desdemona.   My noble father,   180
  I do perceive here a divided duty:
  To you I am bound for life and education;
  My life and education both do learn[114] me
  How to respect you; you are the lord of duty,
  I am hitherto your daughter: but here's my husband;
  And so much duty as my mother show'd
  To you, preferring you before her father,
  So much I challenge[115] that I may profess
  Due to the Moor my lord.

Brabantio.   God be with you! I have done.
  Please it your Grace, on to the state affairs;   190
  I had rather to adopt a child than get it.
  Come hither, Moor:
  I here do give thee that with all my heart
  Which, but thou hast[116] already, with all my heart
  I would keep from thee. For your sake,[117] jewel,
  I am glad at soul I have no other child;
  For thy escape would teach me tyranny,
  To hang clogs on them. I have done, my lord.

Duke. Let me speak like yourself and lay a sentence,[118]
  Which as a grize[119] or step, may help these lovers   200
  Into your favour.
  When remedies are past, the griefs are ended
  By seeing the worst, which[120] late on hopes depended.
  To mourn a mischief that is past and gone
  Is the next way to draw new mischief on.
  What cannot be preserv'd when Fortune takes,
  Patience her injury a mockery makes.[121]
  The robb'd that smiles steals something from the thief;
  He robs himself that spends a bootless grief.

Brabantio. So let the Turk of Cyprus us beguile;   210
  We lose it not so long as we can smile.

---

[114] Teach.   [115] Claim as right.   [116] Didn't you have it.   [117] Because of you.   [118] Provide a maxim.   [119] Step.   [120] The antecedent is "griefs."   [121] To suffer an irreparable loss patiently is to make light of injury (i.e., to triumph over adversity).

He bears the sentence[122] well that nothing bears
But the free comfort which from thence he hears;
But he bears both the sentence and the sorrow
That, to pay grief, must of poor patience borrow.
These sentences, to sugar, or to gall,
Being strong on both sides, are equivocal:[123]
But words are words: I never yet did hear
That the bruis'd heart was pierced[124] through the ear.
I humbly beseech you, proceed to the affairs of state.   220

Duke. The Turk with a most mighty preparation makes for Cyprus. Othello, the fortitude[125] of the place is best known to you; and though we have there a substitute of most allowed sufficiency,[126] yet opinion, a sovereign mistress of effects, throws a more safer voice on you:[127] you must therefore be content to slubber[128] the gloss of your new fortunes with this more stubborn[129] and boisterous expedition.

Othello. The tyrant custom, most grave senators,
Hath made the flinty and steel couch of war
My thrice-driven[130] bed of down: I do agnize[131]
A natural and prompt alacrity   230
I find in hardness, and do undertake
These present wars against the Ottomites.
Most humbly therefore bending to your state,[132]
I crave fit disposition[133] for my wife,
Due reference of place and exhibition,[134]
With such accommodation and besort[135]
As levels with[136] her breeding.

Duke.   If you please,
Be 't at her father's.

Brabantio.   I'll not have it so.

Othello. Nor I.

Desdemona. Nor I; I would not there reside,   240
To put my father in impatient thoughts
By being in his eye. Most gracious duke,
To my unfolding[137] lend your gracious ear;
And let me find a charter[138] in your voice
To assist my simpleness.

Duke. What would you, Desdemona?

Desdemona. That I did love the Moor to live with him,
My downright violence and storm of fortunes

---

[122] (1) Verdict, (2) Maxim.   [123] Sententious comfort (like the Duke's trite maxims) can hurt as well as soothe.   [124] (1) Lanced (i.e., cured), (2) Wounded.   [125] Strength.   [126] Admitted competence.   [127] General opinion, which mainly determines action, thinks Cyprus safer with you in command.   [128] Besmear.   [129] Rough.   [130] Made as soft as possible.   [131] Recognize.   [132] Submitting to your authority.   [133] Disposal.   [134] Provision.   [135] Fitness.   [136] Is proper to.   [137] Explanation.   [138] Permission.

May trumpet to the world; my heart's subdu'd
Even to the very quality of my lord;[139]   250
I saw Othello's visage in his mind,
And to his honours and his valiant parts
Did I my soul and fortunes consecrate.
So that, dear lords, if I be left behind,
A moth of peace, and he go to the war,
The rites[140] for which I love him are bereft me,
And I a heavy interim shall support[141]
By his dear[142] absence. Let me go with him.

Othello. Let her have your voices.
Vouch with me, heaven, I therefore beg it not   260
To please the palate of my appetite,
Nor to comply with heat,—the young affects[143]
In me defunct,—and proper satisfaction,
But to be free and bounteous to her mind;
And heaven defend[144] your good souls that you think
I will your serious and great business scant
For[145] she is with me. No, when light-wing'd toys
Of feather'd Cupid seel[146] with wanton dulness
My speculative and offic'd instruments,[147]
That[148] my disports corrupt and taint my business,   270
Let housewives make a skillet of my helm,
And all indign[149] and base adversities
Make head against my estimation![150]

Duke. Be it as you shall privately determine,
Either for her stay or going. The affair cries haste,
And speed must answer it.

First Senator. You must away to-night.

Othello.   With all my heart.

Duke. At nine i' the morning here we'll meet again.
Othello, leave some officer behind,
And he shall our commission bring to you;   280
With such things else of quality and respect
As doth import you.[151]

Othello.   So please your Grace, my ancient;
A man he is of honesty and trust:
To his conveyance I assign my wife,
With what else needful your good grace shall think
To be sent after me.

---

[139] I.e., I have become a soldier, like Othello.   [140] I.e., of marriage, or of war, or of both.
[141] Endure.   [142] Closely concerning (i.e., Desdemona).   [143] The passions of youth (hence, here, *immoderate* sexual passion).   [144] Forbid.   [145] Because.   [146] Blind (v.) by sewing up the eyelids (a term from falconry).   [147] Reflective and executive faculties and organs.   [148] So that.   [149] Shameful.   [150] Reputation.   [151] Concern.

Duke.   Let it be so.
Good-night to every one. *(To Brabantio.)* And, noble signior,
If virtue no delighted[152] beauty lack,
Your son-in-law is far more fair than black.
First Senator. Adieu, brave Moor! use Desdemona well.   290
Brabantio. Look to her, Moor, if thou hast eyes to see:
She has deceiv'd her father, and may thee.

(Exeunt Duke, Senators, Officers, &c.)

Othello. My life upon her faith! Honest Iago,
My Desdemona must I leave to thee:
I prithee, let thy wife attend on her;
And bring them after in the best advantage.[153]
Come, Desdemona; I have but an hour
Of love, of worldly matters and direction,
To spend with thee: we must obey the time.

(Exeunt Othello and Desdemona.)

Roderigo. Iago!   300
Iago. What sayst thou, noble heart?
Roderigo. What will I do, think'st thou?
Iago. Why, go to bed, and sleep.
Roderigo. I will incontinently[154] drown myself.
Iago. Well, if thou dost, I shall never love thee after.
Why, thou silly gentleman!
Roderigo. It is silliness to live when to live is torment; and then have we a pre
scription to die when death is our physician.
Iago. O! villainous; I have looked upon the world for four times seven years, and
since I could distinguish betwixt a benefit and an injury, I never found man that
knew how to love himself. Ere I would say, I would drown myself for the love of
a guinea-hen, I would change my humanity with a baboon.   312
Roderigo. What should I do? I confess it is my shame to be so fond;[155] but it is not
in my virtue[156] to amend it.
Iago. Virtue! a fig! 'tis in ourselves that we are thus, or thus. Our bodies are our
gardens, to the which our wills are gardeners; so that if we will plant nettles or
sow lettuce, set hyssop and weed up thyme, supply it with one gender[157] of herbs
or distract it with many, either to have it sterile with idleness or manured with
industry, why, the power and corrigible[158] authority of this lies in our wills.
If the balance of our lives had not one scale of reason to poise another of
sensuality, the blood and baseness of our natures would conduct us to most

---

[152] Delightful.   [153] Opportunity.   [154] Forthwith.   [155] Infatuated.   [156] Strength.   [157] Kind.
[158] Corrective.

preposterous conclusions; but we have reason to cool our raging motions, our carnal stings, our unbitted[159] lusts, whereof I take this that you call love to be a sect or scion.[160]

Roderigo. It cannot be.

Iago. It is merely a lust of the blood and a permission of the will. Come, be a man. Drown thyself! drown cats and blind puppies. I have professed me thy friend, and I confess me knit to thy deserving with cables of perdurable toughness; I could never better stead thee than now. Put money in thy purse; follow these wars; defeat thy favour[161] with a usurped[162] beard; I say, put money in thy purse. It cannot be that Desdemona should long continue her love to the Moor,—put money in thy purse,—nor he his to her. It was a violent commencement in her, and thou shalt see an answerable sequestration;[163] put but money in thy purse. These Moors are changeable in their wills;—fill thy purse with money:—the food that to him now is as luscious as locusts,[164] shall be to him shortly as bitter as coloquintida.[165] She must change for youth: when she is sated with his body, she will find the error of her choice. She must have change, she must: therefore put money in thy purse. If thou wilt needs damn thyself, do it a more delicate way than drowning. Make all the money thou canst. If sanctimony and a frail vow betwixt an erring[166] barbarian and a supersubtle[167] Venetian be not too hard for my wits and all the tribe of hell, thou shalt enjoy her; therefore make money. A pox of drowning thyself! it is clean out of the way: seek thou rather to be hanged in compassing thy joy than to be drowned and go without her. 344

Roderigo. Wilt thou be fast to my hopes, if I depend on the issue?[168]

Iago. Thou art sure of me: go, make money. I have told thee often, and I retell thee again and again, I hate the Moor; my cause is hearted; thine hath no less reason. Let us be conjunctive[169] in our revenge against him; if thou canst cuckold him, thou dost thyself a pleasure, me a sport. There are many events in the womb of time which will be delivered. Traverse;[170] go: provide thy money. We will have more of this to-morrow. Adieu. 351

Roderigo. Where shall we meet i' the morning?

Iago. At my lodging.

Roderigo. I'll be with thee betimes.

Iago. Go to: farewell. Do you hear, Roderigo?

Roderigo. What say you?

Iago. No more of drowning, do you hear?

Roderigo. I am changed. I'll sell all my land.

Iago. Go to; farewell! put money enough in your purse. *(Exit Roderigo.)*

Thus do I ever make my fool my purse; 360

For I mine own gain'd knowledge should profane,

---

[159] I.e., uncontrolled.   [160] Offshoot.   [161] Change thy appearance (for the worse?).   [162] Assumed.
[163] Estrangement.   [164] Sweet-tasting fruits (perhaps the carob, the edible seedpod of an evergreen tree in the Mediterranean area).   [165] Purgative derived from a bitter apple.   [166] Vagabond.
[167] Exceedingly refined.   [168] Rely on the outcome.   [169] Allied.   [170] March.

If I would time expend with such a snipe[171]
But for my sport and profit. I hate the Moor,
And it is thought abroad[172] that 'twixt my sheets
He has done my office: I know not if 't be true,
But I, for mere suspicion in that kind,
Will do as if for surety.[173] He holds me well;[174]
The better shall my purpose work on him.
Cassio's a proper[175] man; let me see now:
To get his place; and to plume up[176] my will   370
In double knavery; how, how? Let's see:
After some time to abuse Othello's ear
That he[177] is too familiar with his wife:
He hath a person and a smooth dispose[178]
To be suspected; framed[179] to make women false,
The Moor is of a free and open nature,
That thinks men honest that but seem to be so,
And will as tenderly be led by the nose
As asses are.
I have 't; it is engender'd: hell and night   380
Must bring this monstrous birth to the world's light.   (*Exit.*)

ACT II

Scene 1.   A Sea-port Town in Cyprus. An open place near the Quay.

(*Enter Montano and two Gentlemen.*)

Montano. What from the cape can you discern at sea?
First Gentleman   Nothing at all, it is a high-wrought flood;
   I cannot 'twixt the heaven and the main[180]
   Descry a sail.
Montano. Methinks the wind hath spoke aloud at land;
   A fuller blast ne'er shook our battlements;
   If it hath ruffian'd so upon the sea,
   What ribs of oak, when mountains melt on them,
   Can hold the mortise?[181] What shall we hear of this?
Second Gentleman.   A segregation[182] of the Turkish fleet;   10
   For do but stand upon the foaming shore,
   The chidden billow seems to pelt the clouds;

---

[171] Dupe.   [172] People think.   [173] As if it were certain.   [174] In high regard.   [175] Handsome.
[176] Make ready.   [177] I.e., Cassio.   [178] Bearing.   [179] Designed, apt.   [180] Ocean.   [181] Hold the joints
together.   [182] Scattering.

The wind-shak'd surge, with high and monstrous mane,
Seems to cast water on the burning bear[183]
And quench the guards of the ever-fixed pole:[184]
I never did like[185] molestation view
On the enchafed[186] flood.

Montano.   If that[187] the Turkish fleet
Be not enshelter'd and embay'd, they are drown'd;
It is impossible they bear it out.

(Enter a Third Gentleman.)

Third Gentleman.   News, lad! our wars are done.   20
The desperate tempest hath so bang'd the Turks
That their designment halts;[188] a noble ship of Venice
Hath seen a grievous wrack and suffrance[189]
On most part of their fleet.

Montano. How! is this true?

Third Gentleman.   The ship is here put in,
A Veronesa;[190] Michael Cassio,
Lieutenant to the warlike Moor Othello,
Is come on shore: the Moor himself's at sea,
And is in full commission here for Cyprus.

Montano. I am glad on 't; 'tis a worthy governor.   30

Third Gentleman.   But this same Cassio, though he speak of comfort
Touching the Turkish loss, yet he looks sadly
And prays the Moor be safe; for they were parted
With foul and violent tempest.

Montano.   Pray heaven he be;
For I have serv'd him, and the man commands
Like a full soldier. Let's to the sea-side, ho!
As well to see the vessel that's come in
As to throw out our eyes for brave Othello,
Even till we make the main and the aerial blue
An indistinct regard.[191]   40

Third Gentleman. Come, let's do so;
For every minute is expectancy
Of more arrivance.

(Enter Cassio.)

---

[183] Ursa Minor (the Little Dipper).   [184] Polaris, the North Star, almost directly above the Earth's axis, is part of the constellation of the Little Bear, or Dipper.   [185] Similar.   [186] Agitated.   [187] If.   [188] Plan is stopped.   [189] Damage.   [190] Probably a *type* of ship, rather than a ship from Verona—not only because Verona is an inland city but also because of "a noble ship of Venice" above.   [191] Till our (straining) eyes can no longer distinguish sea and sky.

Cassio. Thanks, you the valiant of this warlike isle,
That so approve the Moor. O! let the heavens
Give him defence against the elements,
For I have lost him on a dangerous sea.
Montano. Is he well shipp'd?
Cassio. His bark is stoutly timber'd, and his pilot
Of very expert and approv'd allowance;[192]   50
Therefore my hopes, not surfeited to death,[193]
Stand in bold cure.[194]

(Within, 'A sail!—a sail!—a sail!' Enter a Messenger.)

Cassio. What noise?
Messenger. The town is empty; on the brow o' the sea
Stand ranks of people, and they cry 'A sail!'
Cassio. My hopes do shape him for the governor.

(Guns heard.)

Second Gentleman. They do discharge their shot of courtesy;
Our friends at least.
Cassio.   I pray you, sir, go forth.
And give us truth who 'tis that is arriv'd.
Second Gentleman. I shall.   *(Exit.)*   60
Montano. But, good lieutenant, is your general wiv'd?
Cassio. Most fortunately: he hath achiev'd a maid
That paragons[195] description and wild fame;
One that excels the quirks[196] of blazoning pens,
And in th' essential vesture of creation[197]
Does tire the ingener.[198]

(Re-enter Second Gentleman.)

                    How now! who has put in?
Second Gentleman. 'Tis one Iago, ancient to the general.
Cassio. He has had most favourable and happy speed:
Tempests themselves, high seas, and howling winds,
The gutter'd[199] rocks, and congregated sands,   70
Traitors ensteep'd[200] to clog the guiltless keel,
As having sense of beauty, do omit

---

[192] Admitted and proven to be expert.   [193] Overindulged.   [194] With good chance of being fulfilled.   [195] Exceeds, surpasses.   [196] Ingenuities.   [197] I.e., just as God made her; or: (even in) the (mere) essence of human nature.   [198] Inventor (i.e., of her praises?).   [199] Jagged; or: submerged.   [200] Submerged.

Their mortal[201] natures, letting go safely by
The divine Desdemona.
Montano.   What is she?
Cassio. She that I spake of, our great captain's captain,
Left in the conduct of the bold Iago,
Whose footing[202] here anticipates our thoughts
A se'nnight's[203] speed. Great Jove, Othello guard,
And swell his sail with thine own powerful breath,
That he may bless this bay with his tall[204] ship,   80
Make love's quick pants in Desdemona's arms,
Give renew'd fire to our extinct spirits,
And bring all Cyprus comfort!

(Enter Desdemona, Emilia, Iago, Roderigo, and Attendants.)

                                    O! behold,
The riches of the ship is come on shore.
Ye men of Cyprus, let her have your knees.
Hail to thee, lady! and the grace of heaven,
Before, behind thee, and on every hand,
Enwheel thee round!
Desdemona.   I thank you, valiant Cassio.
What tidings can you tell me of my lord?
Cassio. He is not yet arriv'd; nor know I aught   90
But that he's well, and will be shortly here.
Desdemona. O! but I fear—How lost you company?
Cassio. The great contention of the sea and skies
Parted our fellowship. But hark! a sail.

(Cry within, 'A sail—a sail!' Guns heard.)

Second Gentleman. They give their greeting to the citadel:
This likewise is a friend.
Cassio.   See for the news!   *(Exit Gentleman.)*
Good ancient, you are welcome:—*(To Emilia.)* welcome, mistress.
Let it not gall your patience, good Iago,
That I extend my manners; 'tis my breeding
That gives me this bold show of courtesy.   *(Kissing her.)*   100
Iago. Sir, would she give you so much of her lips
As of her tongue she oft bestows on me,
You'd have enough.
Desdemona.   Alas! she has no speech.

---

[201] Deadly.   [202] Landing.   [203] Week's.   [204] Brave.

Iago. In faith, too much;
  I find it still when I have list[205] to sleep:
  Marry, before your ladyship, I grant,
  She puts her tongue a little in her heart,
  And chides with thinking.[206]

Emilia. You have little cause to say so.

Iago. Come on, come on; you are pictures[207] out of doors,   110
  Bells[208] in your parlours, wild cats in your kitchens,
  Saints in your injuries, devils being offended,
  Players[209] in your housewifery,[210] and housewives[211] in your beds.

Desdemona. O! fie upon thee, slanderer.

Iago. Nay, it is true, or else I am a Turk:
  You rise to play and go to bed to work.

Emilia. You shall not write my praise.

Iago.   No, let me not.

Desdemona. What wouldst thou write of me, if thou shouldst praise me?

Iago. O gentle lady, do not put me to 't,
  For I am nothing if not critical.   120

Desdemona. Come on; assay. There's one gone to the harbour?

Iago. Ay, madam.

Desdemona *(aside)*. I am not merry, but I do beguile
  The thing I am by seeming otherwise.
  (To Iago.) Come, how wouldst thou praise me?

Iago. I am about it; but indeed my invention
  Comes from my pate[212] as birdlime does from frize;[213]
  It plucks out brains and all: but my muse labours
  And thus she is deliver'd.
  If she be fair and wise, fairness and wit,   130
  The one's for use, the other useth it.

Desdemona. Well prais'd! How if she be black and witty?

Iago. If she be black,[214] and thereto have a wit,
  She'll find a white that shall her blackness fit.

Desdemona. Worse and worse.

Emilia. How if fair and foolish?

Iago. She never yet was foolish that was fair,
  For even her folly[215] help'd to an heir.

Desdemona. These are old fond[216] paradoxes to make fools laugh i' the alehouse.
  What miserable praise has thou for her that's foul and foolish?   140

Iago. There's none so foul and foolish thereunto,
  But does foul pranks which fair and wise ones do.

---

[205] Wish.   [206] I.e., without words.   [207] I.e., made up, "painted."   [208] I.e., jangly.   [209] Triflers, wastrels.   [210] Housekeeping.   [211] (1) Hussies, (2) (unduly) frugal with their sexual favors, (3) businesslike, serious.   [212] Head.   [213] Coarse cloth.   [214] Brunette, dark haired.   [215] Here also, wantonness.   [216] Foolish.

Desdemona. O heavy ignorance! thou praisest the worst best. But what praise
couldst thou bestow on a deserving woman indeed, one that, in the authority of
her merit, did justly put on the vouch[217] of very malice itself?

Iago. She that was ever fair and never proud,
Had tongue at will and yet was never loud,
Never lack'd gold and yet went never gay,
Fled from her wish and yet said 'Now I may,'
She that being anger'd, her revenge being nigh,   150
Bade her wrong stay and her displeasure fly,
She that in wisdom never was so frail
To change the cod's head for the salmon's tail,[218]
She that could think and ne'er disclose her mind,
See suitors following and not look behind,
She was a wight, if ever such wight were,—

Desdemona. To do what?

Iago. To suckle fools and chronicle small beer.[219]

Desdemona. O most lame and impotent conclusion! Do not learn of him,
Emilia, though he be thy husband. How say you, Cassio? Is he not a most profane and liberal[220] counsellor?   161

Cassio. He speaks home,[221] madam; you may relish him more in the soldier than
in[222] the scholar.

Iago *(aside).* He takes her by the palm: ay, well said, whisper; with as little a web
as this will I ensnare as great a fly as Cassio. Ay, smile upon her, do; I will gyve[223]
thee in thine own courtship. You say true, 'tis so, indeed. If such tricks as these
strip you out of your lieutenantry, it had been better you had not kissed your
three fingers so oft, which now again you are most apt to play the sir [224] in. Very
good; well kissed! an excellent courtesy! 'tis so, indeed. Yet again your fingers to
your lips? would they were clyster-pipes[225] for your sake! *(A trumpet heard.)* The
Moor! I know his trumpet.[226]   171

Cassio. 'Tis truly so.

Desdemona. Let's meet him and receive him.

Cassio. Lo! where he comes.

(Enter Othello and Attendants.)

Othello. O my fair warrior!

Desdemona.   My dear Othello!

Othello. It gives me wonder great as my content
To see you here before me. O my soul's joy!
If after every tempest come such calms,

---

[217] Compel the approval.   [218] To make a foolish exchange (a bawdy secondary meaning is probable).   [219] I.e., keep petty household accounts.   [220] Free-spoken, licentious.   [221] To the mark, aptly.
[222] As . . . as.   [223] Entangle.   [224] Gentleman.   [225] Syringes, enema pipes.   [226] I.e., Othello's distinctive trumpet call.

May the winds blow till they have waken'd death!
And let the labouring bark climb hills of seas 180
Olympus-high, and duck again as low
As hell's from heaven! If it were now to die,
'Twere now to be most happy, for I fear
My soul hath her content so absolute
That not another comfort like to this
Succeeds in unknown fate.

Desdemona. The heavens forbid
But that our loves and comforts should increase
Even as our days do grow!

Othello. Amen to that, sweet powers!
I cannot speak enough of this content; 190
It stops me here; it is too much of joy:
And this, and this, the greatest discords be *(Kissing her.)*
That e'er our hearts shall make!

Iago *(aside).* O! you are well tun'd now,
But I'll set down[227] the pegs that make this music,
As honest as I am.

Othello. Come, let us to the castle.
News, friends; our wars are done, the Turks are drown'd.
How does my old acquaintance of this isle?
Honey, you shall be well desir'd[228] in Cyprus;
I have found great love amongst them. O my sweet,
I prattle out of fashion, and I dote 200
In mine own comforts. I prithee, good Iago,
Go to the bay and disembark my coffers.
Bring thou the master to the citadel;
He is a good one, and his worthiness
Does challenge much respect. Come, Desdemona,
Once more well met at Cyprus.

(Exeunt all except Iago and Roderigo.)

Iago. Do thou meet me presently at the harbour. Come hither. If thou be'st valiant, as they say base men being in love have then a nobility in their natures more than is native to them, list[229] me. The lieutenant to-night watches on the court of guard:[230] first, I must tell thee this, Desdemona is directly in love with him. 211

Roderigo. With him! Why, 'tis not possible.

Iago. Lay thy finger thus, and let thy soul be instructed. Mark me with what violence she first loved the Moor but for bragging and telling her fantastical lies; and will she love him still for prating? let not thy discreet heart think it.

---

[227] Loosen.   [228] Welcomed.   [229] Listen to.   [230] Guardhouse.

Her eye must be fed; and what delight shall she have to look on the devil? When the blood is made dull with the act of sport, there should be, again to inflame it, and to give satiety a fresh appetite, loveliness in favour, sympathy in years, manners, and beauties; all which the Moor is defective in. Now, for want of these required conveniences, her delicate tenderness will find itself abused, begin to heave the gorge,[231] disrelish and abhor the Moor; very nature will instruct her in it, and compel her to some second choice. Now, sir, this granted, as it is a most pregnant[232] and unforced position, who stands so eminently in the degree of this fortune as Cassio does? a knave very voluble, no further conscionable[233] than in putting on the mere form of civil and humane seeming, for the better compassing of his salt[234] and most hidden loose affection? why, none; why, none: a slipper[235] and subtle knave, a finder-out of occasions, that has an eye can stamp and counterfeit advantages, though true advantage never present itself; a devilish knave! Besides, the knave is handsome, young, and hath all those requisites in him that folly and green minds look after; a pestilent complete knave! and the woman hath found him already.   232

Roderigo. I cannot believe that in her; she is full of most blessed condition.

Iago. Blessed fig's end! the wine she drinks is made of grapes;[236] if she had been blessed she would never have loved the Moor; blessed pudding! Didst thou not see her paddle with the palm of his hand? didst not mark that?

Roderigo. Yes, that I did; but that was but courtesy.

Iago. Lechery, by this hand! an index[237] and obscure prologue to the history of lust and foul thoughts. They met so near with their lips, that their breaths embraced together. Villainous thoughts, Roderigo! when these mutualities so marshal the way, hard at hand comes the master and main exercise, the incorporate[238] conclusion. Pish![239] But, sir, be you ruled by me: I have brought you from Venice. Watch you to-night; for the command, I'll lay 't upon you: Cassio knows you not. I'll not be far from you: do you find some occasion to anger Cassio, either by speaking too loud, or tainting[240] his discipline; or from what other course you please, which the time shall more favourably minister.   246

Roderigo. Well.

Iago. Sir, he is rash and very sudden in choler, and haply may strike at you: provoke him, that he may; for even out of that will I cause these of Cyprus to mutiny, whose qualification[241] shall come into no true taste again but by the displanting of Cassio. So shall you have a shorter journey to your desires by the means I shall then have to prefer[242] them; and the impediment most profitably removed, without the which there were no expectation of our prosperity.

Roderigo. I will do this, if I can bring it to any opportunity.

Iago. I warrant thee. Meet me by and by at the citadel: I must fetch his necessaries ashore. Farewell.

---

[231] Vomit.   [232] Obvious.   [233] Conscientious.   [234] Lecherous.   [235] Slippery.   [236] I.e., she is only flesh and blood.   [237] Pointer.   [238] Carnal.   [239] Exclamation of disgust.   [240] Disparaging.   [241] Appeasement.   [242] Advance.

Roderigo. Adieu. *(Exit.)*

Iago. That Cassio loves her, I do well believe it;

That she loves him, 'tis apt,[243] and of great credit:[244]   260

The Moor, howbeit that I endure him not,

Is of a constant, loving, noble nature;

And I dare think he'll prove to Desdemona

A most dear[245] husband. Now, I do love her too;

Not out of absolute lust,—though peradventure[246]

I stand accountant[247] for as great a sin,—

But partly led to diet my revenge,

For that I do suspect the lusty Moor

Hath leap'd into my seat; the thought whereof

Doth like a poisonous mineral gnaw my inwards;   270

And nothing can or shall content my soul

Till I am even'd with him, wife for wife;

Or failing so, yet that I put the Moor

At least into a jealousy so strong

That judgment cannot cure. Which thing to do,

If this poor trash[248] of Venice, whom I trash[249]

For his quick hunting, stand the putting-on,[250]

I'll have our Michael Cassio on the hip;

Abuse him to the Moor in the rank garb,[251]

For I fear Cassio with my night-cap too,   280

Make the Moor thank me, love me, and reward me

For making him egregiously an ass

And practising upon his peace and quiet

Even to madness. 'Tis here, but yet confus'd:

Knavery's plain face is never seen till us'd.   *(Exit.)*

Scene 2. A Street.

(Enter a Herald with a proclamation; people following.)

Herald.   It is Othello's pleasure, our noble and valiant general, that, upon certain tidings now arrived, importing the mere[252] perdition of the Turkish fleet, every man put himself into triumph; some to dance, some to make bonfires, each man to what sport and revels his addiction leads him; for, besides these beneficial news, it is the celebration of his nuptial. So much was his pleasure should be proclaimed. All offices[253] are open, and there is full liberty of feasting from this present hour of five till the bell have told eleven. Heaven bless the isle of Cyprus and our noble general Othello!   *(Exeunt.)*

---

[243] Natural, probable.   [244] Easily believable.   [245] A pun on the word in the sense of expensive.
[246] Perchance, perhaps.   [247] Accountable.   [248] I.e., Roderigo.   [249] Check, control.   [250] Inciting.
[251] Gross manner.   [252] Utter.   [253] Kitchens and storehouses.

Scene 3.   A Hall in the Castle.

(Enter Othello, Desdemona, Cassio, and Attendants.)

Othello. Good Michael, look you to the guard to-night:
 Let's teach ourselves that honourable stop,[254]
 Not to outsport discretion.
Cassio. Iago hath direction what to do:
 But, notwithstanding, with my personal[255] eye
 Will I look to 't.
Othello.   Iago is most honest.
 Michael, good-night; to-morrow with your earliest
 Let me have speech with you. *(To Desdemona.)* Come, my dear love,
 The purchase made, the fruits are to ensue;
 That profit's yet to come 'twixt me and you.   10
 Good-night.

        (Exeunt Othello, Desdemona, and Attendants.)

(Enter Iago.)

Cassio. Welcome, Iago; we must to the watch.
Iago. Not this hour, lieutenant; 'tis not yet ten o' the clock. Our general casts us
 thus early for the love of his Desdemona, who let us not therefore blame; he
 hath not yet made wanton the night with her, and she is sport for Jove.
Cassio. She's a most exquisite lady.
Iago. And, I'll warrant her, full of game.
Cassio. Indeed, she is a most fresh and delicate creature.
Iago. What an eye she has! methinks it sounds a parley[256] of provocation.
Cassio. An inviting eye: and yet methinks right modest.   20
Iago. And when she speaks, is it not an alarum[257] to love?
Cassio. She is indeed perfection.
Iago. Well, happiness to their sheets! Come, lieutenant, I have a stoup of wine,
 and here without are a brace[258] of Cyprus gallants that would fain have a meas-
 ure to the health of black Othello.
Cassio. Not to-night, good Iago: I have very poor and unhappy brains for
 drinking: I could well wish courtesy would invent some other custom of
 entertainment.
Iago. O! they are our friends; but one cup: I'll drink for you.   29
Cassio. I have drunk but one cup to-night, and that was craftily qualified[259] too,
 and, behold, what innovation[260] it makes here: I am unfortunate in the infirmity, and dare not task my weakness with any more.

---

[254]Discipline. [255]Own. [256]Conference. [257]Call-to-arms. [258]Pair. [259]Diluted. [260]Change, revolution.

Iago. What, man! 'tis a night of revels; the gallants desire it.

Cassio. Where are they?

Iago. Here at the door; I pray you, call them in.

Cassio. I'll do 't; but it dislikes me.   (*Exit.*)

Iago. If I can fasten but one cup upon him,
    With that which he hath drunk to-night already,
    He'll be as full of quarrel and offence
    As my young mistress' dog. Now, my sick fool Roderigo,   40
    Whom love has turn'd almost the wrong side out,
    To Desdemona hath to-night carous'd
    Potations pottle-deep;[261] and he's to watch.
    Three lads of Cyprus, noble swelling spirits,
    That hold their honours in a wary distance,[262]
    The very elements[263] of this warlike isle,
    Have I to-night fluster'd with flowing cups,
    And they watch too. Now, 'mongst this flock of drunkards,
    Am I to put our Cassio in some action
    That may offend the isle. But here they come.   50
    If consequence[264] do but approve my dream,
    My boat sails freely, both with wind and stream.

(*Re-enter Cassio, with him Montano, and Gentlemen. Servant following with wine.*)

Cassio. 'Fore God, they have given me a rouse[265] already.

Montano. Good faith, a little one; not past a pint, as I am a soldier.

Iago. Some wine, ho!
    (*Sings.*) And let me the canakin[266] clink, clink;
            And let me the canakin clink:
            A soldier's a man;
            A life's but a span;
            Why then let a soldier drink.   60
    Some wine, boys!

Cassio. 'Fore God, an excellent song.

Iago. I learned it in England, where indeed they are most potent in potting; your Dane, your German, and your swag-bellied[267] Hollander,—drink ho!—are nothing to your English.

Cassio. Is your Englishman so expert in his drinking?

Iago. Why, he drinks you[268] with facility your Dane dead drunk; he sweats not to overthrow your Almain;[269] he gives your Hollander a vomit ere the next pottle can be filled.

---

[261] Bottoms-up.   [262] Take offense easily.   [263] Types.   [264] Succeeding events.   [265] Drink.   [266] Small cup.   [267] With a pendulous belly.   [268] The "ethical" dative, i.e., you'll see that he drinks.   [269] German.

Cassio. To the health of our general! 70

Montano. I am for it, lieutenant; and I'll do you justice.

Iago. O sweet England!

> (*Sings.*) King Stephen was a worthy peer,
>> His breeches cost him but a crown;
> He held them sixpence all too dear,
>> With that he call'd the tailor lown.[270]
> He was a wight of high renown,
>> And thou art but of low degree:
> 'Tis pride that pulls the country down,
>> Then take thine auld cloak about thee. 80

Some wine, ho!

Cassio. Why, this is a more exquisite song than the other.

Iago. Will you hear 't again?

Cassio. No; for I hold him to be unworthy of his place that does those things. Well, God's above all; and there be souls must be saved, and there be souls must not be saved.

Iago. It's true, good lieutenant.

Cassio. For mine own part,—no offence to the general, nor any man of quality,— I hope to be saved.

Iago. And so do I too, lieutenant. 90

Cassio. Ay; but, by your leave, not before me; the lieutenant is to be saved before the ancient. Let's have no more of this; let's to our affairs. God forgive us our sins! Gentlemen, let's look to our business. Do not think, gentlemen, I am drunk: this is my ancient; this is my right hand, and this is my left hand. I am not drunk now; I can stand well enough, and speak well enough.

All. Excellent well.

Cassio. Why, very well, then; you must not think then that I am drunk.

(*Exit.*)

Montano. To the platform, masters; come, let's set the watch.

Iago. You see this fellow that is gone before;
> He is a soldier fit to stand by Caesar 100
> And give direction; and do but see his vice;
> 'Tis to his virtue a just equinox,[271]
> The one as long as the other; 'tis pity of him.
> I fear the trust Othello puts him in,
> On some odd time of his infirmity,
> Will shake this island.

Montano. But is he often thus?

Iago. 'Tis evermore the prologue to his sleep;
> He'll watch the horologe a double set,[272]
> If drink rock not his cradle.

---

[270] Lout, rascal. [271] Equivalent. [272] Stand watch twice twelve hours.

Montano.   It were well
  The general were put in mind of it.   110
  Perhaps he sees it not; or his good nature
  Prizes the virtue that appears in Cassio,
  And looks not on his evils. Is not this true?

(Enter Roderigo.)

Iago *(aside to him).*   How now, Roderigo!
  I pray you, after the lieutenant; go.   *(Exit Roderigo.)*
Montano. And 'tis great pity that the noble Moor
  Should hazard such a place as his own second
  With one of an ingraft[273] infirmity;
  It were an honest action to say
  So to the Moor.
Iago.   Not I, for this fair island: 120
  I do love Cassio well, and would do much
  To cure him of this evil. But hark! what noise?

(Cry within, 'Help! Help!' Re-enter Cassio, driving in Roderigo.)

Cassio. You rogue! you rascal!
Montano.   What's the matter, lieutenant?
Cassio. A knave teach me my duty!
  I'll beat the knave into a twiggen[274] bottle.
Roderigo. Beat me!
Cassio.   Dost thou prate, rogue?

(Striking Roderigo.)

Montano *(staying him).*   Nay, good lieutenant;
  I pray you, sir, hold your hand.
Cassio.   Let me go, sir,
  Or I'll knock you o'er the mazzard.[275]
Montano.   Come, come; you're drunk.
Cassio. Drunk!   130

(They fight.)

Iago *(aside to Roderigo).*   Away, I say! go out, and cry a mutiny.

                                                              (Exit Roderigo.)

---

[273] Ingrained.   [274] Wicker.   [275] Head.

Nay, good lieutenant! God's will, gentlemen!
Help, ho! Lieutenant! sir! Montano! sir!
Help, masters! Here's a goodly watch indeed!

(Bell rings.)

Who's that that rings the bell? Diablo, ho!
The town will rise: God's will! lieutenant, hold!
You will be sham'd for ever.

(Re-enter Othello and Attendants.)

Othello.   What is the matter here?
Montano. 'Zounds! I bleed still; I am hurt to the death.

(He faints.)

Othello. Hold, for your lives!   140
Iago. Hold, ho, lieutenant! Sir! Montano! gentlemen!
   Have you forgot all sense of place and duty?
   Hold! the general speaks to you; hold for shame!
Othello. Why, how now, ho! from whence ariseth this?
   Are we turn'd Turks, and to ourselves do that
   Which heaven hath forbid the Ottomites?
   For Christian shame put by this barbarous brawl;
   He that stirs next to carve for his own rage
   Holds his soul light; he dies upon his motion.
   Silence that dreadful bell! it frights the isle   150
   From her propriety. What is the matter, masters?
   Honest Iago, that look'st dead with grieving,
   Speak, who began this? On thy love, I charge thee.
Iago. I do not know; friends all but now, even now,
   In quarter[276] and in terms like bride and groom
   Devesting[277] them for bed; and then, but now,—
   As if some planet had unwitted men,—
   Swords out, and tilting one at other's breast,
   In opposition bloody. I cannot speak
   Any beginning to this peevish odds,[278]   160
   And would in action glorious I had lost
   Those legs that brought me to a part of it!
Othello. How comes it, Michael, you are thus forgot?
Cassio. I pray you, pardon me; I cannot speak.

[276] On duty.   [277] Undressing.   [278] Silly quarrel.

Othello. Worthy Montano, you were wont be civil;
  The gravity and stillness of your youth
  The world hath noted, and your name is great
  In mouths of wisest censure:[279] what's the matter,
  That you unlace[280] your reputation thus
  And spend your rich opinion[281] for the name   170
  Of a night-brawler? give me answer to it.
Montano. Worthy Othello, I am hurt to danger;
  Your officer, Iago, can inform you,
  While I spare speech, which something now offends[282] me,
  Of all that I do know; nor know I aught
  By me that 's said or done amiss this night,
  Unless self-charity be sometimes a vice,
  And to defend ourselves it be a sin
  When violence assails us.
Othello.   Now, by heaven,
  My blood begins my safer guides to rule,   180
  And passion, having my best judgment collied,[283]
  Assays to lead the way. If I once stir,
  Or do but lift this arm, the best of you
  Shall sink in my rebuke. Give me to know
  How this foul rout began, who set it on;
  And he that is approv'd[284] in this offence,
  Though he had twinn'd with me—both at a birth—
  Shall lose me. What! in a town of war,
  Yet wild, the people's hearts brimful of fear,
  To manage private and domestic quarrel,   190
  In night, and on the court and guard of safety!
  'Tis monstrous. Iago, who began 't?
Montano. If partially affin'd,[285] or leagu'd in office,
  Thou dost deliver more or less than truth,
  Thou art not soldier.
Iago.   Touch me not so near;
  I had rather[286] have this tongue cut from my mouth
  Than it should do offence to Michael Cassio;
  Yet, I persuade myself, to speak the truth
  Shall nothing wrong him. Thus it is, general.
  Montano and myself being in speech,   200
  There comes a fellow crying out for help,
  And Cassio following with determin'd sword
  To execute upon him. Sir, this gentleman

---

[279] Judgment.   [280] Undo.   [281] High reputation.   [282] Pains, harms.   [283] Clouded.   [284] Proved (i.e., guilty).   [285] Favorably biased (by ties of friendship, or as Cassio's fellow officer).   [286] More quickly.

Steps in to Cassio, and entreats his pause;
Myself the crying fellow did pursue,
Lest by his clamour, as it so fell out,
The town might fall in fright; he, swift of foot,
Outran my purpose, and I return'd the rather
For that I heard the clink and fall of swords,
And Cassio high in oath, which till to-night   210
I ne'er might say before. When I came back,—
For this was brief,—I found them close together,
At blow and thrust, even as again they were
When you yourself did part them.
More of this matter can I not report:
But men are men; the best sometimes forget:
Though Cassio did some little wrong to him,
As men in rage strike those that wish them best,
Yet, surely Cassio, I believe, receiv'd
From him that fled some strange indignity,   220
Which patience could not pass.

Othello.   I know, Iago.
Thy honesty and love doth mince[287] this matter,
Making it light to Cassio. Cassio, I love thee;
But never more be officer of mine.

(Enter Desdemona, attended.)

Look! if my gentle love be not rais'd up;
(To Cassio.) I'll make thee an example.
Desdemona.   What's the matter?
Othello. All's well now, sweeting; come away to bed.
Sir, for your hurts, myself will be your surgeon.
Lead him off.   *(Montano is led off.)*
Iago, look with care about the town,   230
And silence those whom this vile brawl distracted.
Come, Desdemona; 'tis the soldier's life,
To have their balmy slumbers wak'd with strife.

(Exeunt all but Iago and Cassio.)

Iago. What! are you hurt, lieutenant?
Cassio. Ay; past all surgery.
Iago. Marry, heaven forbid!

---

[287] Tone down.

Cassio. Reputation, reputation, reputation! O! I have lost my reputation. I have lost the immortal part of myself, and what remains is bestial. My reputation, Iago, my reputation!

Iago. As I am an honest man, I thought you had received some bodily wound; there is more offence in that than in reputation. Reputation is an idle and most false imposition;[288] oft got without merit, and lost without deserving: you have lost no reputation at all, unless you repute yourself such a loser. What! man; there are ways to recover the general again; you are but now cast in his mood,[289] a punishment more in policy[290] than in malice; even so as one would beat his offenceless dog to affright an imperious lion. Sue to him again, and he is yours.

Cassio. I will rather sue to be despised than to deceive so good a commander with so slight, so drunken and so indiscreet an officer. Drunk! and speak parrot![291] and squabble, swagger, swear, and discourse fustian[292] with one's own shadow! O thou invisible spirit of wine! if thou hast no name to be known by, let us call thee devil!

Iago. What was he that you followed with your sword? What hath he done to you?

Cassio. I know not.

Iago. Is 't possible?

Cassio. I remember a mass of things, but nothing distinctly; a quarrel, but nothing wherefore. O God! that men should put an enemy in their mouths to steal away their brains; that we should, with joy, pleasance,[293] revel, and applause, transform ourselves into beasts.   260

Iago. Why, but you are now well enough; how came you thus recovered?

Cassio. It hath pleased the devil drunkenness to give place to the devil wrath; one unperfectness shows me another, to make me frankly despise myself.

Iago. Come, you are too severe a moraler. As the time, the place, and the condition of this country stands, I could heartily wish this had not befallen, but since it is as it is, mend it for your own good.

Cassio. I will ask him for my place again; he shall tell me I am a drunkard! Had I as many mouths as Hydra,[294] such an answer would stop them all. To be now a sensible man, by and by a fool, and presently a beast! O strange! Every inordinate cup is unblessed and the ingredient[295] is a devil.   270

Iago. Come, come; good wine is a good familiar creature if it be well used; exclaim no more against it. And, good lieutenant, I think you think I love you.

Cassio. I have well approved it, sir. I drunk!

Iago. You or any man living may be drunk at some time, man. I'll tell you what you shall do. Our general's wife is now the general; I may say so in this respect, for that he hath devoted and given up himself to the contemplation, mark, and denotement of her parts and graces: confess yourself freely to her; importune

---

[288] Something external.   [289] Dismissed because he is angry.   [290] I.e., more for the sake of the example or to show his fairness.   [291] I.e., without thinking.   [292] I.e., nonsense.   [293] Pleasure.
[294] Many-headed snake in Greek mythology.   [295] Contents.

her; she'll help to put you in your place again. She is of so free, so kind, so apt, so blessed a disposition, that she holds it a vice in her goodness not to do more than she is requested. This broken joint between you and her husband entreat her to splinter;[296] and, my fortunes against any lay[297] worth naming, this crack of your love shall grow stronger than it was before.

Cassio. You advise me well.

Iago. I protest, in the sincerity of love and honest kindness.

Cassio. I think it freely; and betimes in the morning I will beseech the virtuous Desdemona to undertake for me. I am desperate of my fortunes if they check me here.

Iago. You are in the right. Good-night, lieutenant; I must to the watch.

Cassio. Good-night, honest Iago!   *(Exit.)*

Iago. And what's he then that says I play the villain?   290
When this advice is free I give and honest,
Probal[298] to thinking and indeed the course
To win the Moor again? For 'tis most easy
The inclining Desdemona to subdue
In any honest suit; she's fram'd as fruitful[299]
As the free elements. And then for her
To win the Moor, were 't to renounce his baptism,
All seals and symbols of redeemed sin,
His soul is so enfetter'd to her love,
That she may make, unmake, do what she list,   300
Even as her appetite shall play the god
With his weak function.[300] How am I then a villain
To counsel Cassio to this parallel[301] course,
Directly to his good? Divinity of hell!
When devils will the blackest sins put on,
They do suggest at first with heavenly shows,
As I do now; for while this honest fool
Plies Desdemona to repair his fortunes,
And she for him pleads strongly to the Moor,
I'll pour this pestilence into his ear   310
That she repeals[302] him for her body's lust;
And, by how much she strives to do him good,
She shall undo her credit with the Moor.
So will I turn her virtue into pitch,
And out of her own goodness make the net
That shall enmesh them all.

(Re-enter Roderigo.)

---

[296] Bind up with splints.   [297] Wager.   [298] Provable.   [299] Generous.   [300] Faculties.   [301] Purposeful.   [302] I.e., seeks to recall.

Iago.   How now, Roderigo!

Roderigo. I do follow here in the chase, not like a hound that hunts, but one that fills up the cry.[303] My money is almost spent; I have been to-night exceedingly well cudgelled; and I think the issue will be, I shall have so much experience for my pains; and so, with no money at all and a little more wit, return again to Venice.

Iago. How poor are they that have not patience!
What wound did ever heal but by degrees?
Thou know'st we work by wit and not by witchcraft,
And wit depends on dilatory time.
Does 't not go well? Cassio hath beaten thee,
And thou by that small hurt hast cashiered Cassio.
Though other things grow fair against the sun,
Yet fruits that blossom first will first be ripe:
Content thyself awhile. By the mass, 'tis morning;   330
Pleasure and action make the hours seem short.
Retire thee; go where thou art billeted:
Away, I say; thou shalt know more hereafter:
Nay, get thee gone. *(Exit Roderigo.)* Two things are to be done,
My wife must move for Cassio to her mistress;
I'll set her on;
Myself the while to draw the Moor apart,
And bring him jump[304] when he may Cassio find
Soliciting his wife: ay, that's the way:
Dull not device by coldness and delay.   *(Exit.)*

Act III

Scene 1. Cyprus. Before the Castle.

(Enter Cassio, and some Musicians.)

Cassio. Masters, play here, I will content your pains;[305]
Something that's brief; and bid 'Good-morrow, general.'   *(Music.)*

(Enter Clown.)

Clown. Why, masters, have your instruments been in Naples, that they speak i' the nose[306] thus?

---

[303] Pack (hunting term).   [304] At the exact moment.   [305] Reward your efforts.   [306] Naples was notorious for venereal disease, and syphilis was believed to affect the nose.

First Musician. How, sir, how?

Clown. Are these, I pray you, wind-instruments?

First Musician. Ay, marry, are they, sir.

Clown. O! thereby hangs a tale.

First Musician. Whereby hangs a tale, sir?

Clown. Marry, sir, by many a wind-instrument that I know. But, masters, here's money for you; and the general so likes your music, that he desires you, for love's sake, to make no more noise with it.

First Musician. Well, sir, we will not.

Clown. If you have any music that may not be heard, to 't again; but, as they say, to hear music the general does not greatly care.

First Musician. We have none such, sir.

Clown. Then put up your pipes in your bag, for I'll away.
Go; vanish into air; away! *(Exeunt Musicians.)*

Cassio. Dost thou hear, mine honest friend?

Clown. No, I hear not your honest friend; I hear you.   20

Cassio. Prithee, keep up thy quillets.[307] There's a poor piece of gold for thee. If the gentlewoman that attends the general's wife be stirring, tell her there's one Cassio entreats her a little favour of speech: wilt thou do this?

Clown. She is stirring, sir: if she will stir hither, I shall seem to notify unto her.

Cassio. Do, good my friend.   *(Exit Clown.)*

(Enter Iago.)

In happy time, Iago.

Iago. You have not been a-bed, then?

Cassio. Why, no; the day had broke
Before we parted. I have made bold, Iago,
To send in to your wife; my suit to her
Is, that she will to virtuous Desdemona   30
Procure me some access.

Iago.   I'll send her to you presently;
And I'll devise a mean to draw the Moor
Out of the way, that your converse and business
May be more free.

Cassio. I humbly thank you for 't.   *(Exit Iago.)*
                         I never knew
A Florentine more kind and honest.[308]

(Enter Emilia.)

Emilia. Good-morrow, good lieutenant: I am sorry

---

[307] Quibbles.   [308] Cassio means that not even a fellow Florentine could behave to him in a friendlier fashion than does Iago.

For your displeasure,[309] but all will soon be well.
The general and his wife are talking of it,
And she speaks for you stoutly: the Moor replies   40
That he you hurt is of great fame in Cyprus
And great affinity,[310] and that in wholesome wisdom
He might not but refuse you; but he protests he loves you,
And needs no other suitor but his likings
To take the safest occasion by the front[311]
To bring you in again.[312]

Cassio.   Yet, I beseech you,
If you think fit, or that it may be done,
Give me advantage of some brief discourse
With Desdemona alone.

Emilia.   Pray you, come in:
I will bestow you where you shall have time   50
To speak your bosom[313] freely.

Cassio.   I am much bound to you.   *(Exeunt.)*

Scene 2.   A Room in the Castle.

(Enter Othello, Iago, and Gentlemen.)

Othello.   These letters give, Iago, to the pilot,
And by him do my duties to the senate;
That done, I will be walking on the works;
Repair there to me.

Iago.   Well, my good lord, I'll do 't.

Othello.   This fortification, gentlemen, shall we see 't?

Gentlemen.   We'll wait upon your lordship.   *(Exeunt.)*

Scene 3.   Before the Castle.

(Enter Desdemona, Cassio, and Emilia.)

Desdemona.   Be thou assur'd, good Cassio, I will do
All my abilities in thy behalf.

Emilia.   Good madam, do: I warrant it grieves my husband,
As if the case were his.

Desdemona.   O! that's an honest fellow. Do not doubt, Cassio,
But I will have my lord and you again
As friendly as you were.

---

[309] Disgrace.   [310] Family connection.   [311] Forelock.   [312] Restore you (to Othello's favor).
[313] Heart, inmost thoughts.

Cassio.   Bounteous madam,
  Whatever shall become of Michael Cassio,
  He's never any thing but your true servant.
Desdemona. I know 't; I thank you. You do love my lord;   10
  You have known him long; and be you well assur'd
  He shall in strangeness[314] stand no further off
  Than in a politic[315] distance.
Cassio.   Ay, but, lady,
  That policy may either last so long,
  Or feed upon such nice[316] and waterish diet,
  Or breed itself so out of circumstance,
  That, I being absent and my place supplied,
  My general will forget my love and service.
Desdemona. Do not doubt[317] that; before Emilia here
  I give thee warrant of thy place. Assure thee,   20
  If I do vow a friendship, I'll perform it
  To the last article; my lord shall never rest;
  I'll watch him tame,[318] and talk him out of patience;
  His bed shall seem a school, his board a shrift;[319]
  I'll intermingle every thing he does
  With Cassio's suit. Therefore be merry, Cassio;
  For thy solicitor shall rather die
  Than give thy cause away.[320]

(Enter Othello and Iago, at a distance.)

Emilia. Madam, here comes my lord.
Cassio. Madam, I'll take my leave.   30
Desdemona. Why, stay, and hear me speak.
Cassio. Madam, not now; I am very ill at ease,
  Unfit for mine own purposes.
Desdemona. Well, do your discretion.   *(Exit Cassio.)*
Iago. Ha! I like not that.
Othello.   What dost thou say?
Iago. Nothing, my lord: or if—I know not what.
Othello. Was not that Cassio parted from my wife?
Iago. Cassio, my lord? No, sure, I cannot think it,
  That he would steal away so guilty-like,
  Seeing you coming.
Othello.   I do believe 'twas he.   40
Desdemona. How now, my lord!

---

[314] Aloofness.   [315] I.e., dictated by policy.   [316] Slight, trivial.   [317] Fear.   [318] Outwatch him (i.e., keep him awake) till he submits.   [319] Confessional.   [320] Abandon your cause.

I have been talking with a suitor here,
A man that languishes in your displeasure.

Othello. Who is 't you mean?

Desdemona. Why, your lieutenant, Cassio. Good my lord,
If I have any grace or power to move you,
His present[321] reconciliation take;
For if he be not one that truly loves you,
That errs in ignorance and not in cunning,
I have no judgment in an honest face.   50
I prithee[322] call him back.

Othello.   Went he hence now?

Desdemona. Ay, sooth; so humbled,
That he hath left part of his grief with me,
To suffer with him. Good love, call him back.

Othello. Not now, sweet Desdemona; some other time.

Desdemona. But shall 't be shortly?

Othello.   The sooner, sweet, for you.

Desdemona. Shall 't be to-night at supper?

Othello.   No, not to-night.

Desdemona. To-morrow dinner, then?

Othello.   I shall not dine at home;
I meet the captains at the citadel.

Desdemona. Why, then, to-morrow night; or Tuesday morn;   60
Or Tuesday noon, or night; or Wednesday morn:
I prithee name the time, but let it not
Exceed three days: in faith, he's penitent;
And yet his trespass, in our common reason,—
Save that they say, the wars must make examples
Out of their best,—is not almost[323] a fault
To incur a private check.[324] When shall he come?
Tell me, Othello: I wonder in my soul,
What you could ask me, that I should deny,
Or stand so mammering[325] on. What! Michael Cassio,   70
That came a wooing with you, and so many a time,
When I have spoke of you dispraisingly,
Hath ta'en your part; to have so much to do
To bring him in! Trust me, I could do much,—

Othello. Prithee, no more; let him come when he will;
I deny thee nothing.

Desdemona.   Why, this is not a boon;
'Tis as I should entreat you wear your gloves,
Or feed on nourishing dishes, or keep you warm,

---

[321] Immediate. [322] Pray thee. [323] Hardly. [324] (Even) a private reprimand. [325] Shilly-shallying.

Or sue to you to do a peculiar profit
To your own person: nay, when I have a suit   80
Wherein I mean to touch your love indeed,
It shall be full of poise[326] and difficult weight,
And fearful to be granted.

Othello.   I will deny thee nothing:
Whereon, I do beseech thee, grant me this,
To leave me but a little to myself.

Desdemona. Shall I deny you? no: farewell, my lord.

Othello. Farewell, my Desdemona: I'll come to thee straight.

Desdemona. Emilia, come. Be as your fancies teach you;
Whate'er you be, I am obedient.   *(Exit, with Emilia.)*

Othello. Excellent wretch![327] Perdition catch my soul,   90
But I do love thee! and when I love thee not,
Chaos is[328] come again.

Iago. My noble lord,—

Othello.   What dost thou say, Iago?

Iago. Did Michael Cassio, when you woo'd my lady,
Know of your love?

Othello. He did, from first to last: why dost thou ask?

Iago. But for a satisfaction of my thought;
No further harm.

Othello.   Why of thy thought, Iago?

Iago. I did not think he had been acquainted with her.

Othello. O! yes; and went between us very oft.   100

Iago. Indeed!

Othello. Indeed! ay, indeed; discern'st thou aught in that?
Is he not honest?

Iago.   Honest, my lord?

Othello.   Honest! ay, honest.

Iago. My lord, for aught I know.

Othello. What dost thou think?

Iago.   Think, my lord!

Othello.   Think, my lord!
By heaven, he echoes me,
As if there were some monster in his thought
Too hideous to be shown. Thou dost mean something:
I heard thee say but now, thou lik'dst not that,
When Cassio left my wife; what didst not like?   110
And when I told thee he was of my counsel
In my whole course of wooing, thou criedst, 'Indeed!'
And didst contract and purse thy brow together,
As if thou then hadst shut up in thy brain

---

[326] Weight.   [327] Here, a term of endearment.   [328] Will have.

Some horrible conceit.[329] If thou dost love me,
Show me thy thought.

Iago. My lord, you know I love you.

Othello.   I think thou dost;
And, for[330] I know thou art full of love and honesty,
And weigh'st thy words before thou givest them breath,
Therefore these stops[331] of thine fright me the more;   120
For such things in a false disloyal knave
Are tricks of custom, but in a man that's just
They are close dilations,[332] working from the heart
That passion cannot rule.

Iago.   For Michael Cassio,
I dare be sworn I think that he is honest.

Othello. I think so too.

Iago.   Men should be what they seem;
Or those that be not, would they might seem none!

Othello. Certain men should be what they seem.

Iago. Why then, I think Cassio's an honest man.

Othello. Nay, yet there's more in this.   130
I pray thee, speak to me as to thy thinkings,
As thou dost ruminate, and give thy worst of thoughts
The worst of words.

Iago.   Good my lord, pardon me;
Though I am bound to every act of duty,
I am not bound to[333] that all slaves are free to.
Utter my thoughts? Why, say they are vile and false;
As where's that palace whereinto foul things
Sometimes intrude not? who has a breast so pure
But some uncleanly apprehensions[334]
Keep leets and law-days,[335] and in session sit   140
With meditations lawful?

Othello. Thou dost conspire against thy friend, Iago,
If thou but think'st him wrong'd, and mak'st his ear
A stranger to thy thoughts.

Iago.   I do beseech you,
Though I perchance am vicious in my guess,—
As, I confess, it is my nature's plague
To spy into abuses, and oft my jealousy[336]
Shapes faults that are not,—that your wisdom yet,
From one that so imperfectly conceits,
Would take no notice, nor build yourself a trouble   150

---

[329] Fancy.   [330] Because.   [331] Interruptions, hesitations.   [332] Secret (i.e., involuntary, unconscious)
revelations.   [333] Bound with regard to.   [334] Conceptions.   [335] Sittings of the local courts.
[336] Suspicion.

Out of his scattering and unsure observance.
It were not for your quiet nor your good,
Nor for my manhood, honesty, or wisdom,
To let you know my thoughts.

Othello.   What dost thou mean?

Iago. Good name in man and woman, dear my lord,
Is the immediate jewel of [337] their souls:
Who steals my purse steals trash; 'tis something, nothing;
'Twas mine, 'tis his, and has been slave to thousands;
But he that filches from me my good name
Robs me of that which not enriches him,
And makes me poor indeed.   160

Othello. By heaven, I'll know thy thoughts.

Iago. You cannot, if my heart were in your hand;
Nor shall not, whilst 'tis in my custody.

Othello. Ha!

Iago.   O! beware, my lord, of jealousy;
It is the green-ey'd monster which doth mock
The meat it feeds on: that cuckold [338] lives in bliss
Who, certain of his fate, loves not his wronger;
But, O! what damned minutes tells [339] he o'er
Who dotes, yet doubts; suspects, yet soundly loves!   170

Othello. O misery!

Iago. Poor and content is rich, and rich enough,
But riches fineless [340] is as poor as winter
To him that ever fears he shall be poor.
Good heaven, the souls of all my tribe defend
From jealousy!

Othello.   Why, why is this?
Think'st thou I'd make a life of jealousy,
To follow still the changes of the moon
With fresh suspicions? No; to be once in doubt
Is once to be resolved. Exchange me for a goat   180
When I shall turn the business of my soul
To such exsufflicate [341] and blown [342] surmises,
Matching thy inference. 'Tis not to make me jealous
To say my wife is fair, feeds well, loves company,
Is free of speech, sings, plays, and dances well;
Where virtue is, these are more virtuous:
Nor from mine own weak merits will I draw
The smallest fear, or doubt of her revolt;
For she had eyes, and chose me. No, Iago;

---

[337] Jewel closest to.   [338] Husband of an adulterous woman.   [339] Counts.   [340] Boundless.
[341] Spat out (?).   [342] Fly-blown.

I'll see before I doubt; when I doubt, prove;   190
And, on the proof, there is no more but this,
Away at once with love or jealousy!

Iago. I am glad of it; for now I shall have reason
To show the love and duty that I bear you
With franker spirit; therefore, as I am bound,
Receive it from me; I speak not yet of proof.
Look to your wife; observe her well with Cassio;
Wear your eye thus, not jealous nor secure:
I would not have your free and noble nature
Out of self-bounty[343] be abus'd; look to 't: 200
I know our country disposition[344] well;
In Venice they do let heaven see the pranks
They dare not show their husbands; their best conscience
Is not to leave 't undone, but keep 't unknown.

Othello. Dost thou say so?

Iago. She did deceive her father, marrying you;
And when she seem'd to shake and fear your looks,
She lov'd them most.

Othello.   And so she did.

Iago.   Why, go to,[345] then;
She that so young could give out such a seeming,
To seel her father's eyes up close as oak,   210
He thought 'twas witchcraft; but I am much to blame;
I humbly do beseech you of your pardon
For too much loving you.

Othello.   I am bound to thee for ever.

Iago. I see, this hath a little dash'd your spirits.

Othello. Not a jot, not a jot.

Iago.   I' faith, I fear it has.
I hope you will consider what is spoke
Comes from my love. But I do see you're mov'd;
I am to pray you not to strain my speech
To grosser issues nor to larger reach
Than to suspicion.   220

Othello. I will not.

Iago.   Should you do so, my lord,
My speech should fall into such vile success
As my thoughts aim not at. Cassio's my worthy friend—
My lord, I see you're mov'd.

Othello.   No, not much mov'd:
I do not think but Desdemona's honest.[346]

---

[343] Innate generosity.   [344] I.e., that of Venice.   [345] Colloquialism; here, something like "all right."
[346] Chaste.

Iago. Long live she so! and long live you to think so!
Othello. And yet, how nature erring from itself,—
Iago. Ay, there's the point: as, to be bold with you,
    Not to affect many proposed matches
    Of her own clime,[347] complexion, and degree,[348]   230
    Whereto, we see, in all things nature tends;
    Foh! one may smell in such, a will most rank,
    Foul disproportion, thoughts unnatural.
    But pardon me; I do not in position[349]
    Distinctly[350] speak of her, though I may fear
    Her will, recoiling[351] to her better judgment,
    May fall to match you with her country forms
    And happily[352] repent.
Othello.   Farewell, farewell:
    If more thou dost perceive, let me know more;
    Set on thy wife to observe. Leave me, Iago.   240
Iago. My lord, I take my leave.   *(Going.)*
Othello. Why did I marry? This honest creature, doubtless,
    Sees and knows more, much more, than he unfolds.
Iago *(returning).* My lord, I would I might entreat your honour
    To scan this thing no further; leave it to time.
    Although 'tis fit that Cassio have his place,
    For, sure he fills it up with great ability,
    Yet, if you please to hold him off awhile,
    You shall by that perceive him and his means:
    Note if your lady strain his entertainment[353]   250
    With any strong or vehement importunity;
    Much will be seen in that. In the mean time,
    Let me be thought too busy[354] in my fears,
    As worthy cause I have to fear I am,
    And hold her free, I do beseech your honour.
Othello. Fear not my government.
Iago. I once more take my leave.   *(Exit.)*
Othello. This fellow's of exceeding honesty,
    And knows all qualities, with a learned spirit,
    Of human dealings; if I do prove her haggard,[355]   260
    Though that her jesses[356] were my dear heart-strings,
    I'd whistle her off and let her down the wind,[357]
    To prey at fortune. Haply, for I am black,
    And have not those soft parts of conversation

---

[347] Country.   [348] Social rank.   [349] In definite assertion.   [350] Specifically.   [351] Reverting.   [352] Perhaps.   [353] Urge his re-welcome (i.e., to Othello's trust and favor).   [354] Meddlesome.   [355] Wild hawk.   [356] Leather thongs by which the hawk's legs were strapped to the trainer's wrist.   [357] I'd let her go and take care of herself.

That chamberers[358] have, or, for I am declin'd
Into the vale of years—yet that's not much—
She's gone, I am abus'd;[359] and my relief
Must be to loathe her. O curse of marriage!
That we can call these delicate creatures ours,
And not their appetites. I had rather be a toad,   270
And live upon the vapour of a dungeon,
Than keep a corner in the thing I love
For others' uses. Yet, 'tis the plague of great ones;
Prerogativ'd[360] are they less than the base;
'Tis destiny unshunnable, like death:
Even then this forked plague[361] is fated to us
When we do quicken.[362]

                   Look! where she comes.
If she be false, O! then heaven mocks itself.
I'll not believe it.

(Re-enter Desdemona and Emilia.)

Desdemona.   How now, my dear Othello!
  Your dinner and the generous[363] islanders   280
  By you invited, do attend your presence.
Othello. I am to blame.
Desdemona.   Why do you speak so faintly?
  Are you not well?
Othello. I have a pain upon my forehead here.[364]
Desdemona. Faith, that's with watching; 'twill away again:
  Let me but bind it hard, within this hour
  It will be well.
Othello.   Your napkin[365] is too little:

(She drops her handkerchief.)

  Let it alone. Come, I'll go in with you.
Desdemona. I am very sorry that you are not well.

                        (Exeunt Othello and Desdemona.)

Emilia. I am glad I have found this napkin;   290
  This was her first remembrance from the Moor;
  My wayward husband hath a hundred times

---

[358] Courtiers; or (more specifically) gallants, frequenters of bed chambers.   [359] Deceived.
[360] Privileged.   [361] I.e., the cuckold's proverbial horns.   [362] Are conceived, come alive.   [363] Noble.
[364] Othello again refers to his cuckoldom.   [365] Handkerchief.

Woo'd me to steal it, but she so loves the token,
For he conjur'd her she should ever keep it,
That she reserves it evermore about her
To kiss and talk to. I'll have the work ta'en out,[366]
And giv 't Iago:
What he will do with it heaven knows, not I;
I nothing but[367] to please his fantasy.[368]

(Enter Iago.)

Iago. How now! what do you here alone?   300
Emilia. Do not you chide; I have a thing for you.
Iago. A thing for me? It is a common thing—
Emilia. Ha!
Iago. To have a foolish wife.
Emilia. O! is that all? What will you give me now
  For that same handkerchief?
Iago.   What handkerchief?
Emilia. What handkerchief!
  Why, that the Moor first gave to Desdemona:
  That which so often did bid me steal.
Iago. Hath stol'n it from her?   310
Emilia. No, faith; she let it drop by negligence,
  And, to the advantage, I, being there, took 't up.
  Look, here it is.
Iago.   A good wench; give it me.
Emilia. What will you do with 't, that you have been so earnest
  To have me filch it?
Iago.   Why, what's that to you?   *(Snatches it.)*
Emilia. If it be not for some purpose of import
  Give 't me again; poor lady! she'll run mad
  When she shall lack it.
Iago. Be not acknown on 't;[369] I have use for it.
  Go, leave me.   *(Exit Emilia.)*
  I will in Cassio's lodging lose this napkin,
  And let him find it; trifles light as air
  Are to the jealous confirmations strong
  As proofs of holy writ; this may do something.
  The Moor already changes with my poison:
  Dangerous conceits are in their natures poisons,
  Which at the first are scarce found to distaste,[370]

---

[366] Pattern copied.   [367] I.e., only want.   [368] Whim.   [369] You know nothing about it.   [370] Scarce can be tasted.

But with a little act upon the blood,
Burn like the mines of sulphur. I did say so:
Look! where he comes!

(Enter Othello.)

Not poppy,[371] nor mandragora,[372]   330
Nor all the drowsy syrups[373] of the world,
Shall ever medicine thee to that sweet sleep
Which thou ow'dst yesterday.

Othello.   Ha! ha! false to me?

Iago. Why, how now, general! no more of that.

Othello. Avaunt! be gone! thou hast set me on the rack;
I swear 'tis better to be much abus'd
Than but to know 't a little.

Iago.   How now, my lord!

Othello. What sense had I of her stol'n hours of lust?
I saw 't not, thought it not, it harm'd not me;
I slept the next night well, was free and merry;   340
I found not Cassio's kisses on her lips;
He that is robb'd, not wanting what is stol'n,
Let him not know 't, and he's not robb'd at all.

Iago. I am sorry to hear this.

Othello. I had been happy, if the general camp,[374]
Pioners[375] and all, had tasted her sweet body,
So[376] I had nothing known. O! now, for ever
Farewell the tranquil mind; farewell content!
Farewell the plumed troop and the big wars
That make ambition virtue! O, farewell!   350
Farewell the neighing steed, and the shrill trump,
The spirit-stirring drum, the ear-piercing fife,
The royal banner, and all quality,
Pride, pomp, and circumstance[377] of glorious war!
And, O you mortal engines,[378] whose rude throats
The immortal Jove's dread clamours counterfeit,
Farewell! Othello's occupation's gone!

Iago. Is it possible, my lord?

Othello. Villain, be sure thou prove my love a whore,
Be sure of it; give me the ocular proof;   360
Or, by the worth of mine eternal soul,
Thou hadst been better have been born a dog
Than answer my wak'd wrath.

---

[371] Opium.   [372] A soporific.   [373] I.e., soporifics.   [374] Whole army.   [375] Lowest rank of manual laborers in the army.   [376] As long as.   [377] Pageantry.   [378] Deadly artillery.

Iago.   Is 't come to this?

Othello. Make me to see 't; or, at the least, so prove it,
That the probation[379] bear no hinge nor loop
To hang a doubt on; or woe upon thy life!

Iago. My noble lord—

Othello. If thou dost slander her and torture me,
Never pray more; abandon all remorse;
On horror's head horrors accumulate;   370
Do deeds to make heaven weep, all earth amaz'd;
For nothing canst thou to damnation add
Greater than that.

Iago.   O grace! O heaven forgive me!
Are you a man! have you a soul or sense?
God be wi' you; take mine office. O wretched fool!
That liv'st to make thine honesty a vice.
O monstrous world! Take note, take note, O world!
To be direct and honest is not safe.
I thank you for this profit,[380] and, from hence
I'll love no friend, sith[381] love breeds such offence.   380

Othello. Nay, stay; thou shouldst be honest.

Iago. I should be wise; for honesty's a fool,
And loses that it works for.

Othello.   By the world,
I think my wife be honest and think she is not;
I think that thou art just and think thou art not.
I'll have some proof. Her name, that was as fresh
As Dian's[382] visage, is now begrim'd and black
As mine own face. If there be cords or knives,
Poison or fire or suffocating streams,
I'll not endure it. Would I were satisfied!   390

Iago. I see, sir, you are eaten up with passion.
I do repent me that I put it to you.
You would be satisfied?

Othello.   Would! nay, I will.

Iago. And may; but how? how satisfied, my lord?
Would you, the supervisor,[383] grossly gape on;
Behold her tupp'd?

Othello.   Death and damnation! O!

Iago. It were a tedious[384] difficulty, I think,
To bring them to that prospect; damn them then,
If ever mortal eyes do see them bolster[385]

---

[379] Proof.   [380] Lesson.   [381] Since.   [382] Diana's, the goddess of the moon.   [383] Observer.   [384] Laborious.   [385] Lie together.

More[386] than their own! What then? how then?   400
  What shall I say? Where's satisfaction?
  It is impossible you should see this,
  Were they as prime[387] as goats, as hot as monkeys,
  As salt as wolves in pride,[388] and fools as gross
  As ignorance made drunk; but yet, I say,
  If imputation, and strong circumstances,
  Which lead directly to the door of truth,
  Will give you satisfaction, you may have it.

Othello. Give me a living reason she's disloyal.

Iago. I do not like the office;   410
  But, sith I am enter'd in this cause so far,
  Prick'd to 't by foolish honesty and love,
  I will go on. I lay with Cassio lately;
  And, being troubled with a raging tooth,
  I could not sleep.
  There are a kind of men so loose of soul
  That in their sleeps will mutter their affairs;
  One of this kind is Cassio.
  In sleep I heard him say, 'Sweet Desdemona,
  Let us be wary, let us hide our loves!'   420
  And then, sir, would he gripe[389] and wring my hand,
  Cry, 'O, sweet creature!' and then kiss me hard,
  As if he pluck'd up kisses by the roots,
  That grew upon my lips; then laid his leg
  Over my thigh, and sigh'd, and kiss'd; and then
  Cried, 'Cursed fate, that gave thee to the Moor!'

Othello. O monstrous! monstrous!

Iago.   Nay, this was but his dream.

Othello. But this denoted a foregone conclusion:[390]
  'Tis a shrewd doubt,[391] though it be but a dream.

Iago. And this may help to thicken other proofs   430
  That do demonstrate thinly.

Othello.   I'll tear her all to pieces.

Iago. Nay, but be wise; yet we see nothing done;
  She may be honest yet. Tell me but this:
  Have you not sometimes seen a handkerchief
  Spotted with strawberries in your wife's hand?

Othello. I gave her such a one; 'twas my first gift.

Iago. I know not that; but such a handkerchief—
  I am sure it was your wife's—did I to-day
  See Cassio wipe his beard with.

---

[386] Other.   [387] Lustful.   [388] Heat.   [389] Seize.   [390] Previous consummation.   [391] (1) Cursed, (2) Acute, suspicion.

Othello.   If it be that,—

Iago. If it be that, or any that was hers,   440
It speaks against her with the other proofs.

Othello. O! that the slave had forty thousand lives;
One is too poor, too weak for my revenge.
Now do I see 'tis true. Look here, Iago;
All my fond love thus do I blow to heaven:
'Tis gone.
Arise, black vengeance, from the hollow hell!
Yield up, O love! thy crown and hearted throne
To tyrannous hate. Swell, bosom, with thy fraught,[392]
For 'tis of aspics'[393] tongues!

Iago.   Yet be content.[394]   450

Othello. O! blood, blood, blood!

Iago. Patience, I say; your mind, perhaps, may change.

Othello. Never, Iago. Like to the Pontic sea,[395]
Whose icy current and compulsive course
Ne'er feels retiring ebb, but keeps due on
To the Propontic and the Hellespont,[396]
Even so my bloody thoughts, with violent pace,
Shall ne'er look back, ne'er ebb to humble love,
Till that a capable[397] and wide revenge
Swallow them up.   (*Kneels.*)
                    Now, by yond marble heaven,   460
In the due reverence of a sacred vow
I here engage my words.

Iago.   Do not rise yet.   (*Kneels.*)
Witness, you ever-burning lights above!
You elements that clip[398] us round about!
Witness, that here Iago doth give up
The execution of his wit, hands, heart,
To wrong'd Othello's service! Let him command,
And to obey shall be in me remorse,[399]
What bloody business ever.[400]   (*They rise.*)

Othello.   I greet thy love,
Not with vain thanks, but with acceptance bounteous,   470
And will upon the instant put thee to 't:
Within these three days let me hear thee say
That Cassio 's not alive.

Iago. My friend is dead; 'tis done at your request:
But let her live.

---

[392] Burden.   [393] Poisonous snakes.   [394] Patient.   [395] The Black Sea.   [396] The Sea of Marmara,
the Dardanelles.   [397] Comprehensive.   [398] Encompass.   [399] Probably a corrupt line; the meaning
appears to be: "to obey shall be my solemn obligation."   [400] Soever.

Othello.   Damn her, lewd minx! O, damn her!
   Come, go with me apart; I will withdraw.
   To furnish me with some swift means of death
   For the fair devil. Now art thou my lieutenant.
Iago. I am your own for ever.   *(Exeunt.)*

Scene 4. Before the Castle.

(Enter Desdemona, Emilia, and Clown.)

Desdemona. Do you know, sirrah,[401] where Lieutenant Cassio lies?[402]
Clown. I dare not say he lies any where.
Desdemona. Why, man?
Clown. He is a soldier; and for one to say a soldier lies, is stabbing.[403]
Desdemona. Go to;[404] where lodges he?
Clown. To tell you where he lodges is to tell you where I lie.
Desdemona. Can anything be made of this?
Clown. I know not where he lodges, and for me to devise[405] a lodging, and say he
   lies here or he lies there, were to lie in mine own throat.
Desdemona. Can you inquire him out, and be edified by report?   10
Clown. I will catechize the world for him; that is, make questions, and by them
   answer.
Desdemona. Seek him, bid him come hither; tell him I have moved my lord in
   his behalf, and hope all will be well.
Clown. To do this is within the compass of man's wit, and therefore I will attempt
   the doing it.   *(Exit.)*
Desdemona. Where should I lose that handkerchief, Emilia?
Emilia. I know not, madam.
Desdemona. Believe me, I had rather have lost my purse
   Full of cruzadoes;[406] and, but my noble Moor   20
   Is true of mind, and made of no such baseness
   As jealous creatures are, it were enough
   To put him to ill thinking.
Emilia.   Is he not jealous?
Desdemona. Who! he? I think the sun where he was born
   Drew all such humours from him.
Emilia.   Look! where he comes.
Desdemona. I will not leave him now till Cassio
   Be call'd to him.

(Enter Othello.)

---

[401] Common form of address to inferiors. [402] Lives. [403] I.e., is cause for stabbing. [404] Here
apparently: "Come on!" [405] Invent. [406] Portuguese gold coins.

Desdemona.   How is 't with you, my lord?

Othello. Well, my good lady. *(Aside.)* O! hardness to dissemble.
    How do you, Desdemona?

Desdemona.   Well, my good lord.

Othello. Give me your hand. This hand is moist,[407] my lady.   30

Desdemona. It yet has felt no age nor known no sorrow.

Othello. This argues fruitfulness and liberal[408] heart;
    Hot, hot, and moist; this hand of yours requires
    A sequester[409] from liberty, fasting and prayer,
    Much castigation, exercise devout;
    For here 's a young and sweating devil here,
    That commonly rebels. 'Tis a good hand,
    A frank one.

Desdemona. You may, indeed, say so;
    For 'twas that hand that gave away my heart.   40

Othello. A liberal hand; the hearts of old gave hands,
    But our new heraldry[410] is hands not hearts.

Desdemona. I cannot speak of this. Come now, your promise.

Othello. What promise, chuck?[411]

Desdemona. I have sent to bid Cassio come speak with you.

Othello. I have a salt and sorry rheum offends me.
    Lend me thy handkerchief.

Desdemona.   Here, my lord.

Othello. That which I gave you.

Desdemona.   I have it not about me.

Othello. Not?

Desdemona. No, indeed, my lord.

Othello.   That is a fault.
    That handkerchief   50
    Did an Egyptian[412] to my mother give;
    She was a charmer,[413] and could almost read
    The thoughts of people; she told her, while she kept it,
    'Twould make her amiable[414] and subdue my father
    Entirely to her love, but if she lost it
    Or made a gift of it, my father's eye
    Should hold her loathed, and his spirits should hunt
    After new fancies.[415] She dying gave it me;
    And bid me, when my fate would have me wive,
    To give it her. I did so; and take heed on 't;   60
    Make it a darling like your precious eye;

---

[407] A supposed symptom of a lustful nature.   [408] With overtones of: too free, loose.   [409] Separation.   [410] I.e., new heraldic symbolism (Othello means that the new way is not to give the heart together with the hand).   [411] Common term of endearment.   [412] Gypsy.   [413] Sorceress.
[414] Lovable, desirable.   [415] Loves.

To lose 't or give 't away, were such perdition
As nothing else could match.
Desdemona.   Is 't possible?
Othello. 'Tis true; there's magic in the web of it;
A sibyl,[416] that had number'd in the world
The sun to course two hundred compasses,
In her prophetic fury sew'd the work;
The worms were hallow'd that did breed the silk,
And it was dy'd in mummy[417] which the skilful
Conserv'd of maidens' hearts.
Desdemona.   Indeed! is 't true?   70
Othello. Most veritable; therefore look to 't well.
Desdemona. Then would to heaven that I had never seen it!
Othello. Ha! wherefore?
Desdemona. Why do you speak so startingly and rash?
Othello. Is 't lost? is 't gone? speak, is it out o' the way?
Desdemona. Heaven bless us!
Othello. Say you?
Desdemona. It is not lost; but what an if[418] it were?
Othello. How!
Desdemona. I say, it is not lost.
Othello.   Fetch 't, let me see 't!   80
Desdemona. Why, so I can, sir, but I will not now.
This is a trick to put me from my suit:
Pray you let Cassio be receiv'd again.
Othello. Fetch me the handkerchief; my mind misgives.
Desdemona. Come, come;
You'll never meet a more sufficient[419] man.
Othello. The handkerchief!
Desdemona.   I pray, talk[420] me of Cassio.
Othello. The handkerchief!
Desdemona.   A man that all his time
Hath founded his good fortunes on your love,
Shar'd dangers with you,—   90
Othello. The handkerchief!
Desdemona. In sooth, you are to blame.
Othello. Away!   *(Exit.)*
Emilia. Is not this man jealous?
Desdemona. I ne'er saw this before.
Sure, there's some wonder in this handkerchief;
I am most unhappy in the loss of it.

---

[416] Prophetess.   [417] Drug (medicinal or magic) derived from embalmed bodies.   [418] If.   [419] Adequate.   [420] Talk to.

Emilia. 'Tis not a year or two shows us a man;
  They are all but stomachs, and we all but[421] food;
  They eat us hungerly, and when they are full   100
  They belch us. Look you! Cassio and my husband.

(Enter Iago and Cassio.)

Iago. There is no other way; 'tis she must do 't:
  And, lo! the happiness;[422] go and importune her.
Desdemona. How now, good Cassio! what 's the news with you?
Cassio. Madam, my former suit: I do beseech you
  That by your virtuous means I may again
  Exist, and be a member of his love
  Whom I with all the office[423] of my heart
  Entirely honour; I would not be delay'd.
  If my offence be of such mortal kind   110
  That nor my service past, nor present sorrows,
  Nor purpos'd merit in futurity,
  Can ransom me into his love again,
  But to know so must be my benefit;
  So shall I clothe me in a forc'd content,
  And shut myself up in some other course
  To fortune's alms.
Desdemona.   Alas! thrice-gentle Cassio!
  My advocation is not now in tune;
  My lord is not my lord, nor should I know him,
  Were he in favour[424] as in humour alter'd.   120
  So help me every spirit sanctified,
  As I have spoken for you all my best
  And stood within the blank of[425] his displeasure
  For my free speech. You must awhile be patient;
  What I can do I will, and more I will
  Than for myself I dare: let that suffice you.
Iago. Is my lord angry?
Emilia.   He went hence but now,
  And certainly in strange unquietness.
Iago. Can he be angry? I have seen the cannon,
  When it hath blown his ranks[426] into the air,   130
  And, like the devil, from his very arm
  Puff'd his own brother; and can he be angry?

---

[421] Only ... only.   [422] "What luck!"   [423] Duty.   [424] Appearance.   [425] As the target for.   [426] I.e., his soldiers.

Something of moment[427] then; I will go meet him;
There's matter in 't indeed, if he be angry.

Desdemona. I prithee, do so. (*Exit Iago.*) Something, sure, of state,[428]
Either from Venice, or some unhatch'd[429] practice
Made demonstrable here in Cyprus to him,
Hath puddled[430] his clear spirit; and, in such cases
Men's natures wrangle with inferior things,
Though great ones are their object. 'Tis even so;   140
For let our finger ache, and it indues[431]
Our other healthful members even to that sense
Of pain. Nay, we must think men are not gods,
Nor of them look for such observancy[432]
As fits the bridal.[433] Beshrew me much, Emilia,
I was—unhandsome warrior as I am—
Arraigning his unkindness with[434] my soul;
But now I find I had suborn'd the witness,[435]
And he 's indicted falsely.

Emilia. Pray heaven it be state matters, as you think,   150
And no conception,[436] nor no jealous toy[437]
Concerning you.

Desdemona. Alas the day! I never gave him cause.

Emilia. But jealous souls will not be answer'd so;
They are not ever jealous for the cause,
But jealous for they are jealous; 'tis a monster
Begot upon itself, born on itself.

Desdemona. Heaven keep that monster from Othello's mind!

Emilia. Lady, amen.

Desdemona. I will go seek him. Cassio, walk hereabout;   160
If I do find him fit, I'll move your suit
And seek to effect it to my uttermost.

Cassio. I humbly thank your ladyship.

(*Exeunt Desdemona and Emilia.*)

(*Enter Bianca.*)

Bianca. Save you, friend Cassio!

Cassio.   What make you from home?
How is it with you, my most fair Bianca?
I' faith, sweet love, I was coming to your house.

---

[427] Important.   [428] Public affairs.   [429] Abortive or budding plot.   [430] Muddied.   [431] Brings, leads.
[432] Attention.   [433] Wedding.   [434] To.   [435] I.e., caused my soul to bring in wrong charges.   [436] Fancy,
supposition.   [437] Fancy.

Bianca. And I was going to your lodging, Cassio.
What! keep a week away? seven days and nights?
Eight score eight hours? and lovers' absent hours,
More tedious than the dial eight score times?   170
O weary reckoning!
Cassio.   Pardon me, Bianca,
I have this while with leaden thoughts been press'd;
But I shall, in a more continuate[438] time,
Strike off[439] this score of absence. Sweet Bianca,

(Giving her Desdemona's handkerchief.)

Take me this work out.
Bianca.   O Cassio! whence came this?
This is some token from a newer friend;
To the felt absence now I feel a cause;
Is 't come to this? Well, well.
Cassio.   Go to, woman!
Throw your vile guesses in the devil's teeth,
From whence you have them. You are jealous now   180
That this is from some mistress, some remembrance:
No, in good troth, Bianca.
Bianca.   Why, whose is it?
Cassio. I know not, sweet; I found it in my chamber.
I like the work well; ere it be demanded,—[440]
As like enough it will,—I'd have it copied;
Take it and do 't; and leave me for this time.
Bianca. Leave you! wherefore?
Cassio. I do attend here on[441] the general,
And think it no addition,[442] nor my wish,
To have him see me woman'd.
Bianca.   Why, I pray you?   190
Cassio. Not that I love you not.
Bianca.   But that you do not love me.
I pray you, bring me on the way a little
And say if I shall see you soon at night.
Cassio. 'Tis but a little way that I can bring you,
For I attend here; but I'll see you soon.
Bianca. 'Tis very good; I must be circumstanc'd.[443]   *(Exeunt.)*

---

[438] Uninterrupted.   [439] Cancel (i.e., make up for).   [440] Asked for.   [441] Wait for.   [442] Advantage, credit.   [443] Governed by circumstances.

ACT IV

Scene 1. Cyprus. Before the Castle.

(Enter Othello and Iago.)

Iago. Will you think so?
Othello.   Think so, Iago!
Iago.   What!
  To kiss in private?
Othello.   An unauthoriz'd kiss.
Iago. Or to be naked with her friend a-bed
  An hour or more, not meaning any harm?
Othello. Naked a-bed, Iago, and not mean harm?
  It is hypocrisy against the devil:[444]
  They that mean virtuously, and yet do so,
  The devil their virtue tempts, and they tempt heaven.
Iago. If they do nothing, 'tis a venial slip;
  But if I give my wife a handkerchief,—   10
Othello. What then?
Iago. Why, then, 'tis hers, my lord; and, being hers,
  She may, I think, bestow 't on any man.
Othello. She is protectress of her honour too;
  May she give that?
Iago. Her honour is an essence that 's not seen;
  They have it very oft that have it not:[445]
  But for the handkerchief,—
Othello. By heaven, I would most gladly have forgot it:—
  Thou said'st,—O! it comes o'er my memory,   20
  As doth the raven[446] o'er the infected house,
  Boding to all,—he had my handkerchief.
Iago. Ay, what of that?
Othello.   That's not so good now.
Iago.   What,
  If I had said I had seen him do you wrong?
  Or heard him say, as knaves be such abroad,[447]
  Who having, by their own importunate suit,
  Or voluntary dotage[448] of some mistress,
  Convinced or supplied them,[449] cannot choose
  But they must blab.

---

[444] I.e., by not committing the sin which the situation invites. [445] I.e., some unchaste women are thought chaste. [446] (1) A bad omen, (2) A carrier of the plague. [447] As there are some such in the world. [448] Foolish affection. [449] Overcome (their reluctance) or satisfied (their desires).

Othello.   Hath he said any thing?

Iago. He hath, my lord; but be you well assur'd,   30
No more than he'll unswear.

Othello.   What hath he said?

Iago. Faith, that he did— I know not what he did.

Othello. What? what?

Iago. Lie—

Othello. With her?

Iago.   With her, on her; what you will.

Othello. Lie with her; lie on her! We say, lie on her, when they belie her. Lie with
her! that's fulsome. Handkerchief,—confessions,—handkerchief! To confess,
and be hanged for his labour. First, to be hanged, and then to confess: I tremble
at it. Nature would not invest herself in such shadowing passion without some
instruction.[450] It is not words that shake me thus. Pish! Noses, ears, and lips. Is it
possible?—Confess!—Handkerchief!—O devil!

(Falls in a trance.)

Iago. Work on,
My medicine, work! Thus credulous fools are caught;
And many worthy and chaste dames even thus,
All guiltless, meet reproach. What, ho! my lord!
My lord, I say! Othello!

(Enter Cassio.)

                        How now, Cassio!

Cassio. What's the matter?

Iago. My lord is fallen into an epilepsy;[451]
This is his second fit; he had one yesterday.

Cassio. Rub him about the temples.

Iago.   No, forbear;
The lethargy[452] must have his quiet course,   50
If not, he foams at mouth, and by and by
Breaks out to savage madness. Look! he stirs;
Do you withdraw yourself a little while,
He will recover straight; when he is gone,
I would on great occasion[453] speak with you.   *(Exit Cassio.)*
How is it, general? have you not hurt your head?

Othello. Dost thou mock me?[454]

Iago.   I mock you! no, by heaven.
Would you would bear your fortune like a man!

---

[450] I would not fall into such passion unless there were some real grounds for it.   [451] Seizure, fit.
[452] Coma.   [453] Important matter.   [454] Another allusion to the cuckold's horns.

Othello. A horned man's a monster and a beast. 60

Iago. There's many a beast then, in a populous city,
And many a civil[455] monster.

Othello. Did he confess it?

Iago.   Good sir, be a man;
Think every bearded fellow that's but yok'd
May draw[456] with you; there's millions now alive
That nightly lie in those unproper[457] beds
Which they dare swear peculiar;[458] your case is better.
O! 'tis the spite of hell, the fiend's arch-mock,
To lip[459] a wanton in a secure[460] couch,
And to suppose her chaste. No, let me know; 70
And knowing what I am, I know what she shall be.

Othello. O! thou art wise; 'tis certain.

Iago.   Stand you awhile apart;
Confine yourself but in a patient list.[461]
Whilst you were here o'erwhelmed with your grief,—
A passion most unsuiting such a man,—
Cassio came hither; I shifted him away,
And laid good 'scuse upon your ecstasy;[462]
Bade him anon return and here speak with me;
The which he promis'd. Do but encave yourself,
And mark the fleers, the gibes, and notable scorns, 80
That dwell in every region of his face;
For I will make him tell the tale anew,
Where, how, how oft, how long ago, and when
He hath, and is again to cope[463] your wife:
I say, but mark his gesture. Marry, patience;
Or I shall say you are all in all in spleen,[464]
And nothing of a man.

Othello.   Dost thou hear, Iago?
I will be found most cunning in my patience;
But—dost thou hear?—most bloody.

Iago.   That's not amiss:
But yet keep time[465] in all. Will you withdraw?   *(Othello goes apart.)*
Now will I question Cassio of Bianca,
A housewife[466] that by selling her desires
Buys herself bread and clothes; it is a creature
That dotes on Cassio; as 'tis the strumpet's plague
To beguile many and be beguil'd by one.

---

[455] Citizen.   [456] I.e., pull the burden of cuckoldom.   [457] Not exclusively their own.   [458] Exclusively their own.   [459] Kiss.   [460] I.e., without suspicion of having a rival.   [461] Bounds of patience.
[462] Derangement, trance.   [463] Close with.   [464] Completely overcome by passion.   [465] Maintain control.   [466] Hussy.

He, when he hears of her, cannot refrain
From the excess of laughter. Here he comes:

(Re-enter Cassio.)

As he shall smile, Othello shall go mad;
And his unbookish[467] jealousy must construe
Poor Cassio's smiles, gestures, and light behaviour   100
Quite in the wrong. How do you now, lieutenant?

Cassio. The worser that you give me the addition[468]
Whose want[469] even kills me.

Iago. Ply Desdemona well, and you are sure on 't.
(Speaking lower.) Now, if this suit lay in Bianca's power,
How quickly should you speed!

Cassio.   Alas! poor caitiff![470]

Othello. Look! how he laughs already!

Iago. I never knew woman love man so.

Cassio. Alas! poor rogue, I think i' faith, she loves me.

Othello. Now he denies it faintly, and laughs it out.   110

Iago. Do you hear, Cassio?

Othello.   Now he importunes him
To tell it o'er: go to; well said, well said.

Iago. She gives it out that you shall marry her;
Do you intend it?

Cassio. Ha, ha, ha!

Othello. Do you triumph, Roman?[471] do you triumph?

Cassio. I marry her! what? a customer?[472] I prithee, bear some charity to my
wit;[473] do not think it so unwholesome. Ha, ha, ha!

Othello. So, so, so, so. They laugh that win.[474]

Iago. Faith, the cry goes that you shall marry her.   120

Cassio. Prithee, say true.

Iago. I am a very villain else.

Othello. Have you scored me?[475] Well.

Cassio. This is the monkey's own giving out: she is persuaded I will marry her,
out of her own love and flattery, not out of my promise.

Othello. Iago beckons me;[476] now he begins the story.

Cassio. She was here even now; she haunts me in every place. I was the other day
talking on the sea-bank with certain Venetians, and thither comes this bauble,[477]
and, by this hand, she falls me thus about my neck;—

Othello. Crying, 'O dear Cassio!' as it were; his gesture imports it.   130

---

[467] Unpracticed, naive.   [468] Title.   [469] The want of which.   [470] Wretch.   [471] I.e., one who
triumphs (?).   [472] Courtesan, prostitute.   [473] Give me credit for some sense.   [474] "He who laughs
last laughs longest" (?).   [475] Wounded, defaced (?); or: settled my account (?).   [476] Signals.
[477] Plaything.

Cassio. So hangs and lolls and weeps upon me; so hales[478] and pulls me; ha, ha, ha!

Othello. Now he tells how she plucked him to my chamber. O! I see that nose of yours, but not the dog I shall throw it to.

Cassio. Well, I must leave her company.

Iago. Before me![479] look, where she comes.

Cassio. 'Tis such another fitchew![480] marry, a perfumed one.

(Enter Bianca.)

What do you mean by this haunting of me?

Bianca. Let the devil and his dam haunt you! What did you mean by that same handkerchief you gave me even now? I was a fine fool to take it. I must take out the work! A likely piece of work, that you should find it in your chamber, and not know who left it there! This is some minx's token, and I must take out the work! There, give it your hobby-horse;[481] wheresoever you had it I'll take out no work on 't.

Cassio. How now, my sweet Bianca! how now, how now!

Othello. By heaven, that should be[482] my handkerchief!

Bianca. An you'll come to supper to-night, you may; an you will not, come when you are next prepared[483] for.   *(Exit.)*

Iago. After her, after her.

Cassio. Faith, I must; she'll rail in the street else.   150

Iago. Will you sup there?

Cassio. Faith, I intend so.

Iago. Well, I may chance to see you, for I would very fain[484] speak with you.

Cassio. Prithee come; will you?

Iago. Go to; say no more.   *(Exit Cassio.)*

Othello *(advancing).* How shall I murder him, Iago?

Iago. Did you perceive how he laughed at his vice?

Othello. O! Iago!

Iago. And did you see the handkerchief?

Othello. Was that mine?   160

Iago. Yours, by this hand; and to see how he prizes the foolish woman your wife! she gave it him, and he hath given it his whore.

Othello. I would have him nine years a-killing. A fine woman! a fair woman! a sweet woman!

Iago. Nay, you must forget that.

Othello. Ay, let her rot, and perish, and be damned to-night; for she shall not live. No, my heart is turned to stone; I strike it, and it hurts my hand. O! the world

---

[478] Hauls.   [479] An exclamation of surprise.   [480] Polecat, noted both for its strong smell and for its lechery.   [481] Harlot.   [482] I.e., I think that is.   [483] Expected (Bianca means that if he does not come that night, she will never want to see him again).   [484] Gladly.

hath not a sweeter creature; she might lie by an emperor's side and command him tasks.

Iago. Nay, that's not your way.[485]   170

Othello. Hang her! I do but say what she is. So delicate with her needle! An admirable musician! O, she will sing the savageness out of a bear. Of so high and plenteous wit and invention!

Iago. She's the worse for all this.

Othello. O! a thousand, a thousand times. And then, of so gentle a condition![486]

Iago. Ay, too gentle.[487]

Othello. Nay, that's certain;—but yet the pity of it, Iago! O! Iago, the pity of it, Iago!

Iago. If you are so fond over her iniquity, give her patent to offend; for, if it touch not you, it comes near nobody.

Othello. I will chop her into messes.[488] Cuckold me!

Iago. O! 'tis foul in her.

Othello. With mine officer!

Iago. That's fouler.

Othello. Get me some poison, Iago; this night: I'll not expostulate with her, lest her body and beauty unprovide my mind again.[489] This night, Iago.

Iago. Do it not with poison, strangle her in her bed, even the bed she hath contaminated.

Othello. Good, good; the justice of it pleases; very good.   190

Iago. And for Cassio, let me be his undertaker;[490] you shall hear more by midnight.

Othello. Excellent good. *(A trumpet within.)* What trumpet is that same?

Iago. Something from Venice, sure. 'Tis Lodovico, Come from the duke; and see, your wife is with him.

(Enter Lodovico, Desdemona, and Attendants.)

Lodovico. God save you, worthy general!

Othello.   With all my heart, sir.

Lodovico. The duke and senators of Venice greet you.

(Gives him a packet.)

Othello. I kiss the instrument of their pleasures.

(Opens the packet, and reads.)

---

[485] Proper course.   [486] So much the high-born lady.   [487] I.e., yielding.   [488] Bits.   [489] Unsettle my intention.   [490] Dispatcher.

Desdemona. And what's the news, good cousin Lodovico?

Iago. I am very glad to see you, signior;   200
　　Welcome to Cyprus.

Lodovico. I thank you. How does Lieutenant Cassio?

Iago. Lives, sir.

Desdemona. Cousin, there's fall'n between him and my lord
　　An unkind[491] breach; but you shall make all well.

Othello. Are you sure of that?

Desdemona. My lord?

Othello (reads).　'This fail you not to do, as you will'—

Lodovico. He did not call; he's busy in the paper.
　　Is there division[492] twixt my lord and Cassio?   210

Desdemona. A most unhappy one; I would do much
　　To atone[493] them, for the love I bear to Cassio.

Othello. Fire and brimstone!

Desdemona.　　　　　　　My lord?

Othello.　　　　　　　　　　　Are you wise?

Desdemona. What! is he angry?

Lodovico.　　　　　　May be the letter mov'd him;
　　For, as I think, they do command him home,
　　Deputing Cassio in his government.

Desdemona. Trust me, I am glad on 't.

Othello.　　　　　　　　Indeed!

Desdemona.　　　　　　　　　　My lord?

Othello. I am glad to see you mad.

Desdemona.　　　　　　Why, sweet Othello?

Othello. Devil!   (Strikes her.)

Desdemona. I have not deserved this.   220

Lodovico. My lord, this would not be believ'd in Venice,
　　Though I should swear I saw 't; 'tis very much;
　　Make her amends, she weeps.

Othello.　　　　　　　　() devil, devil!
　　If that the earth could teem with woman's tears,
　　Each drop she falls[494] would prove a crocodile.[495]
　　Out of my sight!

Desdemona. I will not stay to offend you.   (Going.)

Lodovico. Truly, an obedient lady;
　　I do beseech your lordship, call her back.

Othello. Mistress!

Desdemona.　　My lord?

Othello.　　　　　　What would you with her, sir?   230

Lodovico. Why, I, my lord?

---

[491] Unnatural.　　[492] Estrangement.　　[493] Reconcile.　　[494] Lets fall.　　[495] The crocodile's tears were supposed to be hypocritical.

Othello. Ay; you did wish that I would make her turn:
    Sir, she can turn, and turn, and yet go on,
    And turn again; and she can weep, sir, weep;
    And she's obedient, as you say, obedient,
    Very obedient. Proceed you in your tears.
    Concerning this, sir—O well-painted passion!—
    I am commanded home. Get you away;
    I'll send for you anon. Sir, I obey the mandate,
    And will return to Venice. Hence! avaunt![496]   *(Exit Desdemona.)*
    Cassio shall have my place. And, sir, to-night,
    I do entreat that we may sup together;
    You are welcome, sir, to Cyprus. Goats and monkeys!   *(Exit.)*
Lodovico. Is this the noble Moor whom our full senate
    Call all-in-all sufficient? is this the noble nature
    Whom passion could not shake? whose solid virtue
    The shot of accident nor dart of chance
    Could neither graze nor pierce?
Iago.   He is much chang'd.
Lodovico. Are his wits safe? is he not light of brain?
Iago. He's that he is; I may not breathe my censure.   250
    What he might be, if, what he might, he is not,
    I would to heaven he were![497]
Lodovico.   What! strike his wife!
Iago. Faith, that was not so well; yet would I knew
    That stroke would prove the worst!
Lodovico.   Is it his use?
    Or did the letters work upon his blood,
    And new-create this fault?
Iago.   Alas, alas!
    It is not honesty in me to speak
    What I have seen and known. You shall observe him,
    And his own courses[498] will denote him so
    That I may save my speech. Do but go after   260
    And mark how he continues.
Lodovico. I am sorry that I am deceiv'd in him.   *(Exeunt.)*

Scene 2. A Room in the Castle.

(Enter Othello and Emilia.)

Othello. You have seen nothing, then?
Emilia. Nor ever heard, nor ever did suspect.

---

[496] Begone!   [497] Another of Iago's gnomic speeches; perhaps approximately: "If now he is not himself, I wish he would be what he could be!"   [498] Actions.

Othello. Yes, you have seen Cassio and her together.

Emilia. But then I saw no harm, and then I heard
Each syllable that breath made up between them.

Othello. What! did they never whisper?

Emilia.   Never, my lord.

Othello. Nor send you out o' the way?

Emilia. Never.

Othello. To fetch her fan, her gloves, her mask, nor nothing?[499]

Emilia. Never, my lord.   10

Othello. That's strange.

Emilia. I durst, my lord, to wager she is honest,
Lay down my soul at stake: if you think other,
Remove your thought; it doth abuse your bosom.
If any wretch have put this in your head,
Let heaven requite it with the serpent's curse!
For, if she be not honest, chaste, and true,
There's no man happy; the purest of their wives
Is foul as slander.

Othello.   Bid her come hither; go.   *(Exit Emilia.)*
She says enough; yet she 's a simple[500] bawd   20
That cannot say as much. This is a subtle whore,
A closet lock and key of villainous secrets;
And yet she 'll kneel and pray; I have seen her do 't.

(Re-enter Emilia with Desdemona.)

Desdemona. My lord, what is your will?

Othello.   Pray, chuck, come hither.

Desdemona. What is your pleasure?

Othello.   Let me see your eyes;
Look in my face.

Desdemona.   What horrible fancy 's this?

Othello *(to Emilia).*   Some of your function,[501] mistress;
Leave procreants alone and shut the door;
Cough or cry 'hem' if any body come;
Your mystery,[502] your mystery; nay, dispatch.   *(Exit Emilia.)*

Desdemona. Upon my knees, what doth your speech import?
I understand a fury in your words.
But not the words.

Othello. Why, what art thou?

Desdemona.   Your wife, my lord; your true
And loyal wife.

---

[499] Anything.   [500] Simpleminded.   [501] To your duty, business.   [502] Trade.

Othello.   Come, swear it, damn thyself;
Lest, being like one of heaven, the devils themselves
Should fear to seize thee; therefore be double-damn'd;
Swear thou art honest.

Desdemona.   Heaven doth truly know it.

Othello. Heaven truly knows that thou art false as hell.

Desdemona. To whom, my lord? with whom? how am I false?   40

Othello. Ah! Desdemona; away, away, away!

Desdemona. Alas, the heavy day!—Why do you weep?
Am I the motive of these tears, my lord?
If haply you my father do suspect
An instrument of this your calling back,
Lay not your blame on me; if you have lost him,
Why, I have lost him too.

Othello.   Had it pleas'd heaven
To try me with affliction, had he rain'd
All kinds of sores and shames on my bare head,
Steep'd me in poverty to the very lips,   50
Given to captivity me and my utmost hopes,
I should have found in some part of my soul
A drop of patience; but, alas! to make me
The fixed figure for the time of scorn[503]
To point his slow and moving finger at;
Yet could I bear that too; well, very well:
But there, where I have garner'd[504] up my heart,
Where either I must live or bear no life,
The fountain from the which my current runs
Or else dries up; to be discarded thence!   60
Or keep it as a cistern for foul toads
To knot and gender in![505] Turn thy complexion there,[506]
Patience, thou young and rose-lipp'd cherubin;
Ay, there, look grim as hell!

Desdemona. I hope my noble lord esteems me honest.

Othello. O! ay; as summer flies are in the shambles,[507]
That quicken even with blowing. O thou weed!
Who art so lovely fair and smell'st so sweet
That the sense aches at thee, would thou hadst ne'er been born.

Desdemona. Alas! what ignorant sin have I committed?   70

Othello. Was this fair paper, this most goodly book,
Made to write 'whore' upon? What committed!
Committed! O thou public commoner![508]
I should make very forges of my cheeks,

---

[503] I.e., the scornful world.   [504] Stored.   [505] Bunch up and procreate.   [506] I.e., change your color to suit the "cistern for foul toads."   [507] Slaughterhouse.   [508] Harlot.

That would to cinders burn up modesty,
Did I but speak thy deeds. What committed!
Heaven stops the nose at it and the moon winks,[509]
The bawdy wind that kisses all it meets
Is hush'd within the hollow mine of earth,
And will not hear it. What committed!   80
Impudent strumpet!

Desdemona.   By heaven, you do me wrong.
Othello. Are not you a strumpet?
Desdemona.   No, as I am a Christian.
If to preserve this vessel for my lord
From any other foul unlawful touch
Be not to be a strumpet, I am none.
Othello. What! not a whore?
Desdemona.   No, as I shall be sav'd.
Othello. Is it possible?
Desdemona. O! heaven forgive us.
Othello.   I cry you mercy,[510] then;
I took you for that cunning whore of Venice
That married with Othello. You, mistress,   90
That have the office opposite to Saint Peter,
And keep the gate of hell!

(Re-enter Emilia.)

                         You, you, ay, you!
We have done our course; there's money for your pains.
I pray you, turn the key and keep our counsel.   *(Exit.)*
Emilia. Alas! what does this gentleman conceive?[511]
How do you, madam? how do you, my good lady?
Desdemona. Faith, half asleep.
Emilia. Good madam, what 's the matter with my lord?
Desdemona. With who?
Emilia. Why, with my lord, madam.   100
Desdemona. Who is thy lord?
Emilia.   He that is yours, sweet lady.
Desdemona. I have none; do not talk to me, Emilia;
I cannot weep, nor answer have I none,
But what should go by water.[512] Prithee, to-night
Lay on my bed my wedding sheets: remember:
And call thy husband hither.
Emilia.   Here is a change indeed!   *(Exit.)*

---

[509] Closes her eyes.   [510] Beg your pardon.   [511] Imagine.   [512] Be conveyed by means of tears.

Desdemona. 'Tis meet I should be us'd so, very meet.
　　How have I been behav'd, that he might stick
　　The small'st opinion on my least misuse? [513]

(Re-enter Emilia, with Iago.)

Iago. What is your pleasure, madam? How is it with you? 　　110
Desdemona. I cannot tell. Those that do teach young babes
　　Do it with gentle means and easy tasks;
　　He might have chid me so; for, in good faith,
　　I am a child to chiding.
Iago. 　　　　　　　　　What 's the matter, lady?
Emilia. Alas, Iago, my lord hath so bewhor'd her,
　　Thrown such despite [514] and heavy terms upon her,
　　As true hearts cannot bear.
Desdemona. Am I that name, Iago?
Iago. 　　　　　　　　　　　What name, fair lady?
Desdemona. Such as she says my lord did say I was.
Emilia. He call'd her whore; a beggar in his drink 　　120
　　Could not have laid such terms upon his callat. [515]
Iago. Why did he so?
Desdemona. I do not know; I am sure I am none such.
Iago. Do not weep, do not weep. Alas the day!
Emilia. Has she forsook so many noble matches,
　　Her father and her country and her friends,
　　To be call'd whore? would it not make one weep?
Desdemona. It is my wretched fortune.
Iago. 　　　　　　　　　　Beshrew [516] him for it!
　　How comes this trick upon him?
Desdemona. 　　　　　　　　Nay, heaven doth know.
Emilia. I will be hang'd, if some eternal villain, 　　130
　　Some busy and insinuating rogue,
　　Some cogging [517] cozening slave, to get some office,
　　Have not devis'd this slander; I'll be hang'd else.
Iago. Fie! there is no such man; it is impossible.
Desdemona. If any such there be, heaven pardon him!
Emilia. A halter pardon him, and hell gnaw his bones!
　　Why should he call her whore? who keeps her company?
　　What place? what time? what form? what likelihood?
　　The Moor 's abus'd by some most villainous knave,
　　Some base notorious knave, some scurvy fellow. 　　140
　　O heaven! that such companions [518] thou'dst unfold,

---

[513] The least suspicion on my slightest misconduct. 　[514] Abuse. 　[515] Slut. 　[516] Curse. 　[517] Cheating.
[518] Fellows (derogatory).

And put in every honest hand a whip
To lash the rascals naked through the world,
Even from the east to west!

Iago.   Speak within door.

Emilia. O! fie upon them. Some such squire he was
That turn'd your wit the seamy side without,[519]
And made you to suspect me with the Moor.

Iago. You are a fool; go to.

Desdemona.   O good Iago,
What shall I do to win my lord again?
Good friend, go to him; for, by this light of heaven,   150
I know not how I lost him. Here I kneel:
If e'er my will did trespass 'gainst his love,
Either in discourse of thought or actual deed,
Or that mine eyes, mine ears, or any sense,
Delighted them[520] in any other form;
Or that I do not yet,[521] and ever did,
And ever will, though he do shake me off
To beggarly divorcement, love him dearly,
Comfort forswear me! Unkindness may do much;
And his unkindness may defeat[522] my life,   160
But never taint my love. I cannot say 'whore':
It does abhor me now I speak the word;
To do the act that might the addition earn
Not the world's mass of vanity could make me.

Iago. I pray you be content, 'tis but his humour;
The business of the state does him offence,
And he does chide with you.

Desdemona.   If 'twere no other,—

Iago. 'Tis but so, I warrant.   (*Trumpets.*)
Hark! how these instruments summon to supper;
The messengers of Venice stay the meat: 170
Go in, and weep not; all things shall be well.

                           (*Exeunt Desdemona and Emilia.*)

(*Enter Roderigo.*)

    How now, Roderigo!

Roderigo. I do not find that thou dealest justly with me.

Iago. What in the contrary?[523]

Roderigo. Every day thou daffest me[524] with some device, Iago; and rather, as
it seems to me now, keepest from me all conveniency,[525] than suppliest me

---

[519] Outward.   [520] Found delight.   [521] Still.   [522] Destroy.   [523] I.e., what reason do you have for
saying that?   [524] You put me off.   [525] Favorable circumstances.

with the least advantage of hope. I will indeed no longer endure it, nor am I yet persuaded to put up[526] in peace what already I have foolishly suffered.

Iago. Will you hear me, Roderigo?

Roderigo. Faith, I have heard too much, for your words and performances are no kin together.

Iago. You charge me most unjustly.

Roderigo. With nought but truth. I have wasted myself out of my means. The jewels you have had from me to deliver to Desdemona would half have corrupted a votarist;[527] you have told me she has received them, and returned me expectations and comforts of sudden respect[528] and acquaintance, but I find none.

Iago. Well; go to; very well.

Roderigo. Very well! go to! I cannot go to, man; nor 'tis not very well: by this hand, I say, it is very scurvy, and begin to find myself fobbed[529] in it.   190

Iago. Very well.

Roderigo. I tell you 'tis not very well. I will make myself known to Desdemona; if she will return me my jewels, I will give over my suit and repent my unlawful solicitation; if not, assure yourself I will seek satisfaction of you.

Iago. You have said now.[530]

Roderigo. Ay, and said nothing, but what I protest intendment of doing.

Iago. Why, now I see there's mettle in thee, and even from this instant do build on thee a better opinion than ever before. Give me thy hand, Roderigo; thou hast taken against me a most just exception; but yet, I protest, I have dealt most directly in thy affair.   200

Roderigo. It hath not appeared.

Iago. I grant indeed it hath not appeared, and your suspicion is not without wit and judgment. But, Roderigo, if thou hast that in thee indeed, which I have greater reason to believe now than ever, I mean purpose, courage, and valour, this night show it: if thou the next night following enjoy not Desdemona, take me from this world with treachery and devise engines for[531] my life.

Roderigo. Well, what is it? is it within reason and compass?

Iago. Sir, there is especial commission come from Venice to depute Cassio in Othello's place.   210

Roderigo. Is that true? why, then Othello and Desdemona return again to Venice.

Iago. O, no! he goes into Mauritania, and takes away with him the fair Desdemona, unless his abode be lingered here by some accident; wherein none can be so determinate[532] as the removing of Cassio.

Roderigo. How do you mean, removing of him?

Iago. Why, by making him uncapable of Othello's place; knocking out his brains.

---

[526] Put up with.   [527] Nun.   [528] Immediate consideration.   [529] Cheated.   [530] I.e., "I suppose you're through?" (?); or: "Now you're talking" (?).   [531] Devices against.   [532] Effective.

Roderigo. And that you would have me do?

Iago. Ay; if you dare do yourself a profit and a right. He sups to-night with a har-lotry,[533] and thither will I go to him; he knows not yet of his honourable for-tune. If you will watch his going thence,—which I will fashion to fall out between twelve and one,—you may take him at your pleasure; I will be near to second your attempt, and he shall fall between us. Come, stand not amazed at it, but go along with me; I will show you such a necessity in his death that you shall think yourself bound to put it on him. It is now high supper-time, and the night grows to waste; about it.

Roderigo. I will hear further reason for this.

Iago. And you shall be satisfied. *(Exeunt.)*

Scene 3. Another Room in the Castle.

(Enter Othello, Lodovico, Desdemona, Emilia, and Attendants.)

Lodovico. I do beseech you, sir, trouble yourself no further.

Othello. O! pardon me; 'twill do me good to walk.

Lodovico. Madam, good-night; I humbly thank your ladyship.

Desdemona. Your honour is most welcome.

Othello.   Will you walk, sir?

O! Desdemona,—

Desdemona. My lord?

Othello. Get you to bed on the instant; I will be returned forthwith; dismiss your attendant there; look it be done.

Desdemona. I will, my lord.   *(Exeunt Othello, Lodovico, and Attendants.)*

Emilia. How goes it now? He looks gentler than he did.   10

Desdemona. He says he will return incontinent;[534]

He hath commanded me to go to bed,

And bade me to dismiss you.

Emilia.   Dismiss me!

Desdemona. It was his bidding; therefore, good Emilia,

Give me my nightly wearing, and adieu:

We must not now displease him.

Emilia. I would you had never seen him.

Desdemona. So would not I; my love doth so approve him,

That even his stubbornness,[535] his checks[536] and frowns,—

Prithee, unpin me,—have grace and favour in them.   20

Emilia. I have laid those sheets you bade me on the bed.

Desdemona. All's one.[537] Good faith! how foolish are our minds!

If I do die before thee, prithee, shroud me

In one of those same sheets.

---

[533] Harlot.   [534] At once.   [535] Roughness.   [536] Rebukes.   [537] I.e., it doesn't matter.

Emilia.   Come, come, you talk.

Desdemona. My mother had a maid call'd Barbara;
She was in love, and he she lov'd prov'd mad[538]
And did forsake her; she had a song of 'willow';
An old thing 'twas, but it express'd her fortune,
And she died singing it; that song to-night
Will not go from my mind; I have much to do   30
But to go hang my head all at one side,
And sing it like poor Barbara. Prithee, dispatch.

Emilia. Shall I go fetch your night-gown?

Desdemona.   No, unpin me here.
This Lodovico is a proper man.

Emilia. A very handsome man.

Desdemona. He speaks well.

Emilia. I know a lady in Venice would have walked barefoot to Palestine for a
touch of his nether lip.

Desdemona (sings).
The poor soul sat sighing by a sycamore tree,
  Sing all a green willow;   40
Her hand on her bosom, her head on her knee,
  Sing willow, willow, willow:
The fresh streams ran by her, and murmur'd her moans;
  Sing willow, willow, willow:
Her salt tears fell from her and soften'd the stones;—

Lay by these:—
  Sing willow, willow, willow:

Prithee, hie thee;[539] he 'll come anon.—

  Sing all a green willow must be my garland.
    Let nobody blame him, his scorn I approve,—   50
Nay, that's not next. Hark! who is it that knocks?

Emilia. It is the wind.

Desdemona.
I call'd my love false love; but what said he then?
  Sing willow, willow, willow:
If I court moe[540] women, you 'll couch with moe men.

So, get thee gone; good-night. Mine eyes do itch;
Doth that bode weeping?

Emilia.   'Tis neither here nor there.

Desdemona. I have heard it said so. O! these men, these men!

---

[538] Wild.   [539] Hurry.   [540] More.

Dost thou in conscience think, tell me, Emilia,
That there be women do abuse their husbands   60
In such gross kind?

Emilia.   There be some such, no question.

Desdemona. Wouldst thou do such a deed for all the world?

Emilia. Why, would not you?

Desdemona.   No, by this heavenly light!

Emilia. Nor I neither by this heavenly light;
I might do 't as well i' the dark.

Desdemona. Wouldst thou do such a deed for all the world?

Emilia. The world is a huge thing; 'tis a great price
For a small vice.

Desdemona.   In troth, I think thou wouldst not.

Emilia. In troth, I think I should, and undo 't when I had done. Marry, I would
not do such a thing for a joint-ring,[541] nor measures of lawn,[542] nor for gowns,
petticoats, nor caps, nor any petty exhibition;[543] but for the whole world, who
would not make her husband a cuckold to make him a monarch? I should venture purgatory for 't.

Desdemona. Beshrew me, if I would do such a wrong
For the whole world.

Emilia. Why, the wrong is but a wrong i' the world; and having the world for
your labour, 'tis a wrong in your own world, and you might quickly make it
right.

Desdemona. I do not think there is any such woman.

Emilia. Yes, a dozen; and as many to the vantage,[544] as   80
Would store[545] the world they played for.
But I do think it is their husbands' faults
If wives do fall. Say that they slack their duties,
And pour our treasures into foreign laps,
Or else break out in peevish jealousies,
Throwing restraint upon us; or say they strike us,
Or scant[546] our former having[547] in despite;
Why, we have galls;[548] and though we have some grace,
Yet have we some revenge. Let husbands know
Their wives have sense like them; they see and smell,   90
And have their palates both for sweet and sour,
As husbands have. What is it that they do
When they change us for others? Is it sport?[549]
I think it is; and doth affection breed it?
I think it doth; is 't frailty that thus errs?
It is so too; and have not we affections,
Desires for sport, and frailty, as men have?

---

[541] Ring made in separable halves.   [542] Fine linen.   [543] Offer, gift.   [544] Over and above.
[545] Populate.   [546] Reduce.   [547] Allowance.   [548] Spirits, temper.   [549] Lust, sexual enjoyment.

Then, let them use us well; else let them know,
The ills we do, their ills instruct us so.
Desdemona. Good-night, good night; heaven me such usage[550] send,   100
Not to pick bad from bad, but by bad mend!   *(Exeunt.)*

ACT V

Scene 1.   Cyprus. A Street.

(Enter Iago and Roderigo.)

Iago. Here, stand behind this bulk,[551] straight will he come:
Wear thy good rapier bare, and put it home.
Quick, quick; fear nothing; I 'll be at thy elbow.
It makes us, or it mars us; think on that,
And fix most firm thy resolution.
Roderigo. Be near at hand; I may miscarry in 't.
Iago. Here, at thy hand: be bold, and take thy stand.   *(Retires.)*
Roderigo. I have no great devotion to the deed;
And yet he has given me satisfying reasons:
'Tis but a man gone: forth, my sword; he dies.   10
Iago. I have rubb'd this young quat[552] almost to the sense,[553]
And he grows angry. Now, whether he kill Cassio,
Or Cassio him, or each do kill the other,
Every way makes my gain: live Roderigo,
He calls me to a restitution large
Of gold and jewels that I bobb'd[554] from him,
As gifts to Desdemona;
It must not be: if Cassio do remain,
He hath a daily beauty in his life
That makes me ugly: and, besides, the Moor   20
May unfold me to him; there stand I in much peril.
No, he must die. But so;[555] I hear him coming.

(Enter Cassio.)

Roderigo. I know his gait; 'tis he. Villain, thou diest!

(Makes a pass at Cassio.)

---

[550] Habits (?), treatment (?).   [551] Jutting part of a wall.   [552] Pimple.   [553] To the quick.
[554] Swindled.   [555] I.e., that's the only way.

Cassio. That thrust had been mine enemy indeed
But that my coat is better than thou know'st;
I will make proof of thine.

(Draws, and wounds Roderigo.)

Roderigo.   O! I am slain.

(Iago from behind wounds Cassio in the leg, and exit.)

Cassio. I am maim'd for ever. Help, ho! murder! murder!   *(Falls.)*

(Enter Othello, at a distance.)

Othello. The voice of Cassio: Iago keeps his word.
Roderigo. O! villain that I am!
Othello.   It is e'en so.
Cassio. O, help, ho! light! a surgeon!   30
Othello. 'Tis he: O brave Iago, honest and just!
That hast such noble sense of thy friend's wrong;
Thou teachest me. Minion,[556] your dear lies dead,
And your unblest fate hies; strumpet, I come!
Forth of my heart those charms, thine eyes, are blotted;
Thy bed lust-stain'd shall with lust's blood be spotted.   *(Exit.)*

(Enter Lodovico and Gratiano, at a distance.)

Cassio. What ho! no watch? no passage?[557] murder! murder!
Gratiano. 'Tis some mischance; the cry is very direful.
Cassio. O, help!
Lodovico. Hark!   40
Roderigo. O wretched villain!
Lodovico. Two or three groans: it is a heavy[558] night;
These may be counterfeits; let 's think 't unsafe
To come in to the cry[559] without more help.
Roderigo. Nobody come? then shall I bleed to death.
Lodovico. Hark!

(Re-enter Iago, with a light.)

Gratiano. Here 's one comes in his shirt, with light and weapons.
Iago. Who 's there? whose noise is this that cries on murder?

---

[556] (Cassio's) darling, i.e., Desdemona.   [557] Passer-by.   [558] Dark.   [559] Where the cry comes from.

Lodovico. We do not know.

Iago.   Did not you hear a cry?

Cassio. Here, here! for heaven's sake, help me.

Iago.   What's the matter?   50

Gratiano. This is Othello's ancient, as I take it.

Lodovico. The same indeed; a very valiant fellow.

Iago. What are you here that cry so grievously?

Cassio. Iago? O! I am spoil'd, undone by villains!
    Give me some help.

Iago. O me, lieutenant! what villains have done this?

Cassio. I think that one of them is hereabout,
    And cannot make away.

Iago.   O treacherous villains!
    (*To Lodovico and Gratiano.*) What are you there? come in, and
    give some help.   60

Roderigo. O! help me here.

Cassio. That's one of them.

Iago.   O murderous slave! O villain!

(Stabs Roderigo.)

Roderigo. O damn'd Iago! O inhuman dog!

Iago. Kill men i' the dark! Where be these bloody thieves?
    How silent is this town! Ho! murder! murder!
    What may you be? are you of good or evil?

Lodovico. As you shall prove us, praise us.

Iago. Signior Lodovico?

Lodovico. He, sir.

Iago. I cry you mercy. Here 's Cassio hurt by villains.   70

Gratiano. Cassio!

Iago. How is it, brother?

Cassio. My leg is cut in two.

Iago.   Marry, heaven forbid.
    Light, gentlemen; I 'll bind it with my shirt.

(Enter Bianca.)

Bianca. What is the matter, ho? who is 't that cried?

Iago. Who is 't that cried!

Bianca. O my dear Cassio! my sweet Cassio!
    O Cassio, Cassio, Cassio!

Iago. O notable strumpet! Cassio, may you suspect
    Who they should be that have thus mangled you?   80

Cassio. No.

Gratiano. I am sorry to find you thus; I have been to seek you.

Iago. Lend me a garter. So. O! for a chair,
　　To bear him easily hence!
Bianca. Alas; he faints! O Cassio, Cassio, Cassio!
Iago. Gentlemen all, I do suspect this trash[560]
　　To be a party in this injury.
　　Patience awhile, good Cassio. Come, come.
　　Lend me a light. Know we this face, or no?
　　Alas! my friend and my dear countryman,　　　　　　　　90
　　Roderigo? no: yes, sure, O heaven! Roderigo.
Gratiano. What! of Venice?
Iago. Even he, sir, did you know him?
Gratiano.　　　　　　　　　　Know him! ay.
Iago. Signior Gratiano? I cry you gentle pardon;
　　These bloody accidents must excuse my manners,
　　That so neglected you.
Gratiano.　　　　　　　I am glad to see you.
Iago. How do you, Cassio? O! a chair, a chair!
Gratiano. Roderigo!

(A chair brought in.)

Iago. He, he, 'tis he,—O! that 's well said; the chair:
　　Some good men bear him carefully from hence;　　　　100
　　I 'll fetch the general's surgeon. *(To Bianca.)* For you, mistress,
　　Save you your labour. He that lies slain here, Cassio,
　　Was my dear friend. What malice was between you?
Cassio. None in the world; nor do I know that man.
Iago *(to Bianca).*　　What! look you pale? O! bear him out o' the air

(Cassio and Roderigo are borne off.)

　　Stay you, good gentlemen. Look you pale, mistress?—
　　Do you perceive the gastness[561] of her eye?
　　Nay, if you stare, we shall hear more anon.
　　Behold her well; I pray you, look upon her.
　　Do you see, gentlemen? nay, guiltiness will speak　　　　110
　　Though tongues were out of use.

(Enter Emilia.)

Emilia. 'Las! what 's the matter? what 's the matter, husband?
Iago. Cassio hath here been set on in the dark

---

[560] I.e., Bianca.　　[561] Terror.

By Roderigo and fellows that are 'scaped:
He 's almost slain, and Roderigo dead.
Emilia. Alas! good gentleman; alas! good Cassio!
Iago. This is the fruit of whoring. Prithee, Emilia,
Go know of Cassio where he supp'd to-night.
(To Bianca.) What! do you shake at that?
Bianca. He supp'd at my house; but I therefore shake not.   120
Iago. O! did he so? I charge you, go with me.
Emilia. Fie, fie, upon thee, strumpet!
Bianca. I am no strumpet, but of life as honest
As you that thus abuse me.
Emilia.   As I! foh! fie upon thee!
Iago. Kind gentlemen, let 's go see poor Cassio dress'd.[562]
Come, mistress, you must tell 's another tale.
Emilia, run you to the citadel,
And tell my lord and lady what hath happ'd.
Will you go on afore? *(Aside.)* This is the night
That either makes me or fordoes[563] me quite.   *(Exeunt.)*

Scene 2.   A Bedchamber in the Castle. Desdemona in bed asleep. A light burning.

(Enter Othello.)

Othello. It is the cause,[564] it is the cause, my soul;
Let me not name it to you, you chaste stars!
It is the cause. Yet I 'll not shed her blood,
Nor scar that whiter skin of hers than snow,
And smooth as monumental alabaster.
Yet she must die, else she 'll betray more men.
Put out the light, and then put out the light:
If I quench thee, thou flaming minister,[565]
I can again thy former light restore,
Should I repent me; but once put out thy light,   10
Thou cunning'st[566] pattern of excelling nature,
I know not where is that Promethean[567] heat
That can thy light relume.[568] When I have pluck'd the rose,
I cannot give it vital growth again,
It needs must wither: I 'll smell it on the tree. *(Kisses her.)*
O balmy breath, that dost almost persuade

---

[562] Bandaged.   [563] Ruins.   [564] I.e., Desdemona's unchastity (Othello means that the severity of the punishment is required by the nature of her sin).   [565] I.e., the candle.   [566] Most intricately wrought.   [567] In Greek mythology the demigod Prometheus stole fire from the gods and gave it to man.   [568] Relight.

Justice to break her sword! One more, one more.
Be thus when thou art dead, and I will kill thee,
And love thee after. One more, and this the last:
So sweet was ne'er so fatal. I must weep,   20
But they are cruel tears; this sorrow 's heavenly,
It strikes where it doth love. She wakes.
Desdemona. Who 's there? Othello?
Othello.   Ay, Desdemona.
Desdemona. Will you come to bed, my lord?
Othello. Have you pray'd to-night, Desdemona?
Desdemona.   Ay, my lord.
Othello. If you bethink yourself of any crime
    Unreconcil'd as yet to heaven and grace,
    Solicit for it straight.
Desdemona. Alas! my lord, what may you mean by that?
Othello. Well, do it, and be brief; I will walk by:[569]   30
    I would not kill thy unprepared spirit;
    No; heaven forfend![570] I would not kill thy soul.
Desdemona. Talk you of killing?
Othello.   Ay, I do.
Desdemona.   Then heaven
    Have mercy on me!
Othello.   Amen! with all my heart.
Desdemona. If you say so, I hope you will not kill me.
Othello. Hum!
Desdemona. And yet I fear you; for you are fatal then
    When your eyes roll so. Why I should fear I know not,
    Since guiltiness I know not; but yet I feel I fear.
Othello. Think on thy sins.
Desdemona.   They are loves I bear to you.   40
Othello. Ay, and for that thou diest.
Desdemona. That death's unnatural that kills for loving.
    Alas! why gnaw you so your nether lip?
    Some bloody passion shakes your very frame;
    These are portents,[571] but yet, I hope, I hope
    They do not point on me.
Othello.   Peace, and be still!
Desdemona. I will so. What 's the matter?
Othello. That handkerchief which I so lov'd and gave thee
    Thou gav'st to Cassio.
Desdemona.   No, by my life and soul!
    Send for the man and ask him.

[569] Nearby.   [570] Forbid.   [571] Omens.

Othello.   Sweet soul, take heed,   50
  Take heed of perjury; thou 'rt on thy death-bed.
Desdemona. Ay, but not yet to die.
Othello.   Yes, presently;[572]
  Therefore confess thee freely of thy sin;
  For to deny each article with oath
  Cannot remove nor choke the strong conception[573]
  That I do groan withal. Thou art to die.
Desdemona. Then Lord have mercy on me!
Othello.   I say, amen.
Desdemona. And have you mercy too! I never did
  Offend you in my life; never lov'd Cassio
  But with such general warranty[574] of heaven   60
  As I might love; I never gave him token.
Othello. By heaven, I saw my handkerchief in 's hand.
  O perjur'd woman! thou dost stone[575] my heart,
  And mak'st me call what I intend to do
  A murder, which I thought a sacrifice:
  I saw the handkerchief.
Desdemona.   He found it then;
  I never gave it him. Send for him hither;
  Let him confess a truth.
Othello.   He had confessed.
Desdemona. What, my lord?
Othello. That he hath us'd thee.
Desdemona.   How? Unlawfully?
Othello.   Ay.   70
Desdemona. He will not say so.
Othello.   No; his mouth is stopp'd:
  Honest Iago hath ta'en order for 't.[576]
Desdemona. O! my fear interprets. What! is he dead?
Othello. Had all his hairs been lives, my great revenge
  Had stomach[577] for them all.
Desdemona. Alas! he is betray'd and I undone.
Othello. Out, strumpet! Weep'st thou for him to my face?
Desdemona. O! banish me, my lord, but kill me not!
Othello. Down, strumpet!
Desdemona. Kill me to-morrow; let me live to-night!   80
Othello. Nay, if you strive,—
Desdemona. But half an hour!
Othello.   Being done, there is no pause.
Desdemona. But while I say one prayer!

---

[572] At once.   [573] Belief.   [574] Permission.   [575] Turn to stone.   [576] Taken steps.   [577] Appetite.

Othello. It is too late. *(He smothers her.)*

Emilia *(within).* My lord, my lord! what, ho! my lord, my lord!

Othello. What noise is this? Not dead? Not yet quite dead?
 I that am cruel am yet merciful;
 I would not have thee linger in thy pain.
 So, so.

Emilia *(within).* What, ho! my lord, my lord!

Othello. Who's there?

Emilia *(within).* O! good my lord, I would speak a word with you!   90

Othello. Yes; 'tis Emilia: by and by.[578] She's dead.
 'Tis like[579] she comes to speak of Cassio's death;
 The noise was high. Ha! no more moving?
 Still as the grave. Shall she come in? were 't good?[580]
 I think she stirs again: no. What 's best to do?
 If she come in she'll sure speak to my wife:
 My wife! my wife! what wife? I have no wife;
 O, insupportable! O heavy hour!
 Methinks it should be now a huge eclipse
 Of sun and moon, and that the affrighted globe   100
 Should yawn[581] at alteration.

Emilia *(within).*   I do beseech you
 That I may speak with you, O! good my lord.

Othello. I had forgot thee: O! come in, Emilia:
 Soft, by and by: let me the curtains draw.
 Where art thou?   *(Unlocks the door.)*

(Enter Emilia.)

  What 's the matter with thee now?

Emilia. O! my good lord, yonder 's foul murder done.

Othello. What! now?

Emilia. But now, my lord.

Othello. It is the very error[582] of the moon;
 She comes more near the earth than she was wont,   110
 And makes men mad.

Emilia. Cassio, my lord, has kill'd a young Venetian
 Call'd Roderigo.

Othello.   Roderigo kill'd!
 And Cassio kill'd?

Emilia.   No, Cassio is not kill'd.

Othello. Not Cassio kill'd! then murder 's out of tune,
 And sweet revenge grows harsh.

---

[578] I.e., "just a moment."   [579] Likely.   [580] Would that be wise.   [581] Open up (as in an earthquake).
[582] Straying.

Desdemona. O! falsely, falsely murder'd.

Emilia. Alas! what cry is that?

Othello. That! what?

Emilia. Out, and alas! that was my lady's voice:
Help! Help, ho! help! O lady, speak again!   120
Sweet Desdemona! O! sweet mistress, speak.

Desdemona. A guiltless death I die.

Emilia. O! who hath done this deed?

Desdemona. Nobody; I myself; farewell:
Commend me to my kind lord. O! farewell!   *(Dies.)*

Othello. Why, how should she be murder'd?

Emilia. Alas! who knows?

Othello. You heard her say herself it was not I.

Emilia. She said so; I must needs report the truth.

Othello. She 's like a liar gone to burning hell;
'Twas I that kill'd her.

Emilia. O! the more angel she,   130
And you the blacker devil.

Othello. She turn'd to folly, and she was a whore.

Emilia. Thou dost belie her, and thou art a devil.

Othello. She was false as water.

Emilia. Thou art rash as fire to say
That she was false! O! she was heavenly true.

Othello. Cassio did tup her; ask thy husband else.
O! I were damn'd beneath all depth in hell
But that I did proceed[583] upon just grounds
To this extremity. Thy husband knew it all.

Emilia. My husband!   140

Othello. Thy husband.

Emilia. That she was false to wedlock?

Othello. Ay, with Cassio. Nay, had she been true,
If heaven would make me such another world
Of one entire and perfect chrysolite,[584]
I'd not have sold her for it.

Emilia. My husband!

Othello. Ay, 'twas he that told me first:
An honest man he is, and hates the slime
That sticks on filthy deeds.

Emilia. My husband!

Othello. What needs this iterance,[585] woman? I say thy husband.   150

Emilia. O mistress! villany hath made mocks with love.
My husband say that she was false!

---

[583] Had I not proceeded.   [584] Topaz.   [585] Repetition.

Othello. He, woman;
  I say, thy husband: dost understand the word?
  My friend, thy husband, honest, honest Iago.
Emilia. If he say so, may his pernicious soul
  Rot half a grain a day! he lies to the heart:
  She was too fond of her most filthy bargain.[586]
Othello. Ha!
Emilia. Do thy worst:
  This deed of thine is no more worthy heaven   160
  Than thou wast worthy her.
Othello. Peace! you were best.[587]
Emilia. Thou hast not half the power to do me harm
  As I have to be hurt. O gull! O dolt!
  As ignorant as dirt! thou hast done a deed,—
  I care not for thy sword; I'll make thee known,
  Though I lost twenty lives. Help! help, ho! help!
  The Moor has kill'd my mistress! murder! murder!

(Enter Montano, Gratiano, Iago, and others.)

Montano. What is the matter? How now, general!
Emilia. O! are you come, Iago? you have done well,
  That men must lay their murders on your neck.   170
Gratiano. What is the matter?
Emilia. Disprove this villain if thou be'st a man:
  He says thou told'st him that his wife was false.
  I know thou didst not, thou 'rt not such a villain.
  Speak, for my heart is full.
Iago. I told him what I thought, and told no more
  Than what he found himself was apt and true.
Emilia. But did you ever tell him she was false?
Iago. I did.
Emilia. You told a lie, an odious damned lie;   180
  Upon my soul, a lie, a wicked lie;
  She false with Cassio! Did you say with Cassio?
Iago. With Cassio, mistress. Go to, charm[588] your tongue.
Emilia. I will not charm my tongue; I am bound to speak.
  My mistress here lies murder'd in her bed.
All. O heavens forfend!
Emilia. And your reports have set the murder on.
Othello. Nay, stare not, masters; it is true, indeed.
Gratiano. 'Tis a strange truth.
Montano. O monstrous act!

---

[586] I.e., Othello.   [587] You'd better be quiet.   [588] I.e., into silence.

Emilia.   Villany! villany! villany!   190
    I think upon 't, I think, I smell 't; O villany!
    I thought so then;[589] I'll kill myself for grief.
    O! villany, villany!
Iago. What! are you mad? I charge you, get you home.
Emilia. Good gentlemen, let me have leave to speak:
    'Tis proper I obey him, but not now.
    Perchance, Iago, I will ne'er go home.
Othello. O! O! O!   (Falls on the bed.)
Emilia.   Nay, lay thee down and roar,
    For thou hast kill'd the sweetest innocent
    That e'er did lift up eye.
Othello.   O! she was foul.   (Rises.)
    I scarce did know you, uncle. There lies your niece,
    Whose breath, indeed, these hands have newly stopp'd:
    I know this act shows terrible and grim.
Gratiano. Poor Desdemona! I am glad thy father 's dead.
    Thy match was mortal to him, and pure grief
    Shore[590] his old thread in twain: did he live now,
    This sight would make him do a desperate turn,
    Yea, curse his better angel from his side,
    And fall to reprobation.[591]
Othello. 'Tis pitiful; but yet Iago knows   210
    That she with Cassio hath the act of shame
    A thousand times committed; Cassio confess'd it:
    And she did gratify[592] his amorous works
    With that recognizance and pledge of love
    Which I first gave her. I saw it in his hand:
    It was a handkerchief, an antique token
    My father gave my mother.
Emilia. O heaven! O heavenly powers!
Iago.   Come, hold your peace.
Emilia. 'Twill out, 'twill out; I hold my peace, sir? no;
    No, I will speak as liberal as the north;[593]   220
    Let heaven and men and devils, let them all,
    All, all, cry shame against me, yet I'll speak.
Iago. Be wise, and get you home.
Emilia.   I will not.

(Iago threatens to stab Emilia.)

---

[589] *Cf.* "I will be hang'd, if some eternal villain, / Some busy and insinuating rogue, / Some cogging cozening slave, to get some office, / Have not devis'd this slander; . . ." (IV, 2, 130 ff.). Emilia means not that she guessed Iago's guilt but that she rightly guessed the slanderer's motive. [590] Cut. [591] Damnation. [592] Reward. [593] I.e., the north wind (?), the supposedly free-spoken people of north England (?).

Gratiano.   Fie!
 Your sword upon a woman!
Emilia. O thou dull Moor! that handkerchief thou speak'st of
 I found by fortune and did give my husband;
 For often, with a solemn earnestness,
 More than, indeed, belong'd to such a trifle,
 He begg'd of me to steal it.
Iago.   Villainous whore!
Emilia. She give it Cassio! no, alas! I found it,   230
 And I did give 't my husband.
Iago.   Filth, thou liest!
Emilia. By heaven, I do not, I do not, gentlemen.
 O murderous coxcomb![594] what should such a fool
 Do with so good a wife?
Othello.   Are there no stones[595] in heaven
 But what serve for the thunder? Precious villain!

(He runs at Iago. Iago stabs Emilia.)

Gratiano. The woman falls; sure, he has kill'd his wife. *(Exit Iago.)*
Emilia. Ay, ay; O! lay me by my mistress' side.
Gratiano. He 's gone; but his wife 's kill'd.
Montano. 'Tis a notorious[596] villain. Take you this weapon,
 Which I have here recover'd from the Moor.   240
 Come, guard the door without; let him not pass,
 But kill him rather. I'll after that same villain,
 For 'tis a damned slave. *(Exeunt Montano and Gratiano.)*
Othello.   I am not valiant neither,
 But every puny whipster[597] gets my sword.
 But why should honour outlive honesty?
 Let it go all.
Emilia. What did thy song bode, lady?
 Hark, canst thou hear me? I will play the swan,
 And die in music:—
 (Sings.)   Willow, willow, willow.
 Moor, she was chaste; she lov'd thee, cruel Moor;
 So come my soul to bliss as I speak true;   250
 So speaking as I think, I die, I die.   *(Dies.)*
Othello. I have another weapon in this chamber;
 It is a sword of Spain, the ice-brook's temper.[598]
 O! here it is. Uncle, I must come forth.

---

[594] Idiot. [595] I.e., thunderbolts (to strike Iago down). [596] Notable. [597] I.e., a small boy whipping a top. [598] Tempered in icy water (or the reference may be to Innsbruck, famed for the quality of its steel, but this hardly fits "a sword of Spain").

Gratiano *(within)*. If thou attempt it, it will cost thee dear:
  Thou hast no weapon, and perforce must suffer.
Othello. Look in upon me then, and speak with me,
  Or, naked[599] as I am, I will assault thee.

(Re-enter Gratiano.)

Gratiano. What is the matter?
Othello.   Behold! I have a weapon;
  A better never did itself sustain   260
  Upon a soldier's thigh: I have seen the day,
  That with this little arm, and this good sword,
  I have made my way through more impediments
  Than twenty times your stop: but, O vain boast!
  Who can control his fate? 'tis not so now.
  Be not afraid, though you do see me weapon'd;
  Here is my journey's end, here is my butt,[600]
  And very sea-mark of my utmost sail.[601]
  Do you go back dismay'd? 'tis a lost fear;
  Man but a rush[602] against Othello's breast,   270
  And he retires. Where should Othello go?
  Now how dost thou look now? O ill-starr'd wench!
  Pale as thy smock! when we shall meet at compt,[603]
  This look of thine will hurl my soul from heaven,
  And fiends will snatch at it. Cold, cold, my girl!
  Even like thy chastity.
  O! cursed, cursed slave. Whip me, ye devils,
  From the possession of this heavenly sight!
  Blow me about in winds! roast me in sulphur!
  Wash me in steep-down gulfs of liquid fire!   280
  O Desdemona! Desdemona! dead!
  Oh! Oh! Oh!

(Enter Lodovico, Montano, Cassio carried in a chair, and Officers with Iago, prisoner.)

Lodovico. Where is this rash and most unfortunate man?
Othello. That's he that was Othello; here I am.
Lodovico. Where is that viper? bring the villain forth.
Othello. I look down towards his feet;[604] but that 's a fable.
  If that thou be'st a devil, I cannot kill thee.   *(Wounds Iago.)*
Lodovico. Wrench his sword from him.   *(Othello is disarmed.)*

---

[599] Unarmed.   [600] Goal, end, limit.   [601] Destination of my farthest journey.   [602] Wield but a reed.   [603] On the day of judgment.   [604] I.e., for the Devil's cloven hoof.

Iago.   I bleed, sir; but not kill'd.

Othello. I am not sorry neither; I'd have thee live;
For, in my sense,[605] 'tis happiness to die.   290

Lodovico. O thou Othello! that wert once so good,
Fall'n in the practice[606] of a damned slave,[607]
What shall be said to thee?

Othello.   Why, any thing:
An honourable murderer, if you will;
For nought did I in hate, but all in honour.

Lodovico. This wretch hath part confess'd his villany:
Did you and he consent in Cassio's death?

Othello. Ay.

Cassio. Dear general, I never gave you cause.

Othello. I do believe it, and I ask your pardon.   300
Will you, I pray, demand that demi-devil
Why he hath thus ensnar'd my soul and body?

Iago. Demand me nothing: what you know, you know:
From this time forth I never will speak word.

Lodovico. What! not to pray?

Gratiano.   Torments will ope[608] your lips.

Othello. Well, thou dost best.

Lodovico. Sir, you shall understand what hath befall'n,
Which, as I think, you know not. Here is a letter
Found in the pocket of the slain Roderigo,
And here another; the one of them imports   310
The death of Cassio to be undertook
By Roderigo.

Othello. O villain!

Cassio.   Most heathenish and most gross!

Lodovico. Now here's another discontented paper,
Found in his pocket too; and this, it seems,
Roderigo meant to have sent this damned villain,
But that, belike,[609] Iago in the interim[610]
Came in and satisfied him.

Othello.   O the pernicious caitiff!
How came you, Cassio, by that handkerchief
That was my wife's?

Cassio.   I found it in my chamber;   320
And he himself confess'd but even now
That there he dropp'd it for a special purpose
Which wrought to his desire.

Othello.   O fool! fool! fool!

---

[605] The way I feel.   [606] Plot, machination.   [607] I.e., Iago.   [608] Open.   [609] Most likely.   [610] In the meantime.

Cassio. There is besides in Roderigo's letter
    How he upbraids Iago that he made him
    Brave me upon the watch; whereon it came
    That I was cast:[611] and even but now he spake,
    After long seeming dead, Iago hurt him,
    Iago set him on.
Lodovico. You must forsake this room and go with us;   330
    Your power and your command is taken off,
    And Cassio rules in Cyprus. For this slave,
    If there be any cunning cruelty
    That can torment him much and hold him long,
    It shall be his. You shall close prisoner rest,
    Till that the nature of your fault be known
    To the Venetian state. Come, bring him away.
Othello. Soft you; a word or two before you go.
    I have done the state some service, and they know 't;
    No more of that. I pray you, in your letters,   340
    When you shall these unlucky deeds relate,
    Speak of me as I am; nothing extenuate,
    Nor set down aught[612] in malice: then, must you speak
    Of one that lov'd not wisely but too well;
    Of one not easily jealous, but, being wrought,
    Perplex'd[613] in the extreme; of one whose hand
    Like the base Indian,[614] threw a pearl away
    Richer than all his tribe; of one whose subdu'd[615] eyes
    Albeit unused to the melting mood,
    Drop tears as fast as the Arabian trees   350
    Their med'cinable gum. Set you down this;
    And say besides, that in Aleppo once,
    Where a malignant and a turban'd Turk
    Beat a Venetian and traduc'd the state,
    I took by the throat the circumcised dog,
    And smote him, thus.   *(Stabs himself.)*
Lodovico. O bloody period![616]
Gratiano.   All that's spoke is marr'd.
Othello. I kiss'd thee ere I killed thee; no way but this.
        (Falling upon Desdemona.)
    Killing myself to die upon a kiss.   *(Dies.)*
Cassio. This did I fear, but thought he had no weapon;   360
    For he was great of heart.
Lodovico *(to Iago).*   O Spartan dog!
    More fell[617] than anguish, hunger, or the sea.

---

[611] Dismissed.   [612] Anything.   [613] Distracted.   [614] The Folio reads "ludean." Both readings denote the foolish infidel who fails to appreciate the treasure he possesses.   [615] Overcome (by grief).
[616] Ending.   [617] Grim, cruel.

Look on the tragic loading of this bed;
This is thy work; the object poisons sight;
Let it be hid. Gratiano, keep the house,
And seize upon the fortunes of the Moor,
For they succeed on you. To you, lord governor,
Remains the censure of this hellish villain,
The time, the place, the torture; O! enforce it.
Myself will straight aboard, and to the state   370
This heavy act with heavy heart relate.   *(Exeunt.)*

FOR ANALYSIS

1. In what sense might it be said that Othello is responsible for his own downfall?

2. Do you find the reasons that Iago gives for his actions consistent and convincing?

3. Discuss the functions of the minor characters, such as Roderigo, Bianca, and Emilia.

4. Is the rapidity of Othello's emotional collapse (act III, scene 3) plausible? Does his race contribute to his emotional turmoil? Explain.

5. The first part of act IV, scene 2 (until Othello exits), is sometimes called the "brothel" scene. What features of Othello's language and behavior justify this designation?

6. Why does Iago kill Roderigo?

7. What are the benefits of moving the main characters to Cyprus rather than setting the drama in Venice?

8. Compare the speeches of Cassio and Iago in act II, scene 1. What do the differences in language and **style** reveal about their characters?

9. Carefully review the play to determine how much time elapses between the arrival in Cyprus and the end of the action. Can you find narrated events that could not possibly have occurred within that time frame? What effect do the chronological inconsistencies have on you? Explain.

MAKING CONNECTIONS

1. Place yourself in Othello's position. How would you respond to Iago's machinations? If you were in Desdemona's position, how would you deal with Othello's apparently bizarre behavior?

2. Compare Desdemona's hope that her virtue will win out to the hope (or cynicism) of the wife in Raymond Carver's "What We Talk About When We Talk About Love" (p. 896). Why do you think Desdemona remains submissive?

WRITING TOPICS

1. Write an analysis of the **figurative language** in Iago's soliloquies at the end of act I and at the end of act II, scene 1.

2. Choose a minor character, such as Roderigo, Emilia, or Bianca, and in a carefully reasoned essay, explain how the character contributes to the design of the play.

3. Discuss the relationship between love and hate in this tragedy.

SUSAN GLASPELL   (1882–1948)

TRIFLES   1916

CHARACTERS

George Henderson, county attorney

Henry Peters, sheriff

Lewis Hale, a neighboring farmer

Mrs. Peters

Mrs. Hale

Scene

The kitchen in the now abandoned farmhouse of John Wright, a gloomy kitchen, and left without having been put in order—the walls covered with a faded wall paper. Down right is a door leading to the parlor. On the right wall above this door is a built-in kitchen cupboard with shelves in the upper portion and drawers below. In the rear wall at right, up two steps is a door opening onto stairs leading to the second floor. In the rear wall at left is a door to the shed and from there to the outside. Between these two doors is an old-fashioned black iron stove. Running along the left wall from the shed door is an old iron sink and sink shelf, in which is set a hand pump. Downstage of the sink is an uncurtained window. Near the window is an old wooden rocker. Center stage is an unpainted wooden kitchen table with straight chairs on either side. There is a small chair down right. Unwashed pans under the sink, a loaf of bread outside the breadbox, a dish towel on the table—other signs of incompleted work. At the rear the shed door opens and the Sheriff comes in followed by the County Attorney and Hale. The Sheriff and Hale are men in middle life, the County Attorney is a young man; all are much bundled up and go at once to the stove. They are followed by the two women—the Sheriff's wife, Mrs. Peters, first; she is a slightly wiry woman, with a thin nervous face. Mrs. Hale is larger and would ordinarily be called more comfortable looking, but she is disturbed now and looks fearfully about as she enters. The women have come in slowly, and stand close together near the door.

County Attorney (*at stove rubbing his hands*). This feels good. Come up to the fire, ladies.

Mrs. Peters (*after taking a step forward*). I'm not—cold.

Sheriff (*unbuttoning his overcoat and stepping away from the stove to right of table as if to mark the beginning of official business*). Now, Mr. Hale, before we move things about, you explain to Mr. Henderson just what you saw when you came here yesterday morning.

County Attorney (*crossing down to left of the table*). By the way, has anything been moved? Are things just as you left them yesterday?

Sheriff (*looking about*). It's just about the same. When it dropped below zero last night I thought I'd better send Frank out this morning to make a fire for us—(*sits right of center table*) no use getting pneumonia with a big case on, but I told him not to touch anything except the stove—and you know Frank.

County Attorney. Somebody should have been left here yesterday.

Sheriff. Oh—yesterday. When I had to send Frank to Morris Center for that man who went crazy—I want you to know I had my hands full yesterday. I knew you could get back from Omaha by today and as long as I went over everything here myself—

County Attorney. Well, Mr. Hale, tell just what happened when you came here yesterday morning.

Hale (*crossing down to above table*). Harry and I started to town with a load of potatoes. We came along the road from my place and as I got here I said, "I'm going to see if I can't get John Wright to go in with me on a party telephone." I spoke to Wright about it once before and he put me off, saying folks talked too much anyway, and all he asked was peace and quiet—I guess you know about how much he talked himself; but I thought maybe if I went to the house and talked about it before his wife, though I said to Harry that I didn't know as what his wife wanted made much difference to John———

County Attorney. Let's talk about that later, Mr. Hale. I do want to talk about that, but tell now just what happened when you got to the house.

Hale. I didn't hear or see anything; I knocked at the door, and still it was all quiet inside. I knew they must be up, it was past eight o'clock. So I knocked again, and I thought I heard somebody say, "Come in." I wasn't sure. I'm not sure yet, but I opened the door—this door (*indicating the door by which the two women are still standing*) and there in that rocker—(*pointing at it*) sat Mrs. Wright. (*They all look at the rocker down left.*)

County Attorney. What—was she doing?

Hale. She was rockin' back and forth. She had her apron in her hand and was kind of—pleating it.

County Attorney. And how did she—look?

Hale. Well, she looked queer.

County Attorney. How do you mean—queer?

Hale. Well, as if she didn't know what she was going to do next. And kind of done up.

County Attorney (*takes out notebook and pencil and sits left of center table*). How did she seem to feel about your coming?

Hale. Why, I don't think she minded—one way or another. She didn't pay much attention. I said, "How do, Mrs. Wright, it's cold, ain't it?" And she said, "Is it?"—and went on kind of pleating at her apron. Well, I was surprised; she didn't ask me to come up to the stove, or to set down, but just sat there, not even looking at me, so I said, "I want to see John." And then she—laughed. I guess you would call it a laugh. I thought of Harry and the team outside, so I said a little sharp: "Can't I see John?" "No," she says, kind o' dull like. "Ain't he home?" says I. "Yes," says she, "he's home." "Then why can't I see him?" I asked her, out of patience. " 'Cause he's dead," says she. "*Dead?*" says I. She just nodded her head, not getting a bit excited, but rockin' back and forth. "Why—where is he?" says I, not knowing what to say. She just pointed upstairs—like that. *(Himself pointing to the room above.)* I started for the stairs, with the idea of going up there. I walked from there to here—then I says, "Why, what did he die of?" "He died of a rope round his neck," says she, and just went on, pleatin' at her apron. Well, I went out and called Harry. I thought I might—need help. We went upstairs and there he was lyin'————

County Attorney. I think I'd rather have you go into that upstairs, where you can point it all out. Just go on now with the rest of the story.

Hale. Well, my first thought was to get that rope off. It looked . . . *(stops; his face twitches)* . . . but Harry, he went up to him, and he said, "No, he's dead all right, and we'd better not touch anything." So we went back downstairs. She was still sitting that same way. "Has anybody been notified?" I asked. "No," says she, unconcerned. "Who did this, Mrs. Wright?" said Harry. He said it businesslike— and she stopped pleatin' of her apron. "I don't know," she says. "You don't *know?*" says Harry. "No," says she. "Weren't you sleepin' in the bed with him?" says Harry. "Yes," says she, "but I was on the inside." "Somebody slipped a rope round his neck and strangled him and you didn't wake up?" says Harry. "I didn't wake up," she said after him. We must 'a' looked as if we didn't see how that could be, for after a minute she said, "I sleep sound." Harry was going to ask her more questions but I said maybe we ought to let her tell her story first to the coroner, or the sheriff, so Harry went fast as he could to Rivers' place, where there's a telephone.

County Attorney. And what did Mrs. Wright do when she knew that you had gone for the coroner?

Hale. She moved from the rocker to that chair over there *(pointing to a small chair in the down right corner)* and just sat there with her hands held together and looking down. I got a feeling that I ought to make some conversation, so I said I had come in to see if John wanted to put in a telephone, and at that she started to laugh, and then she stopped and looked at me—scared. *(The County Attorney, who has had his notebook out, makes a note.)* I dunno, maybe it wasn't scared. I wouldn't like to say it was. Soon Harry got back, and then Dr. Lloyd came and you, Mr. Peters, and so I guess that's all I know that you don't.

County Attorney *(rising and looking around).* I guess we'll go upstairs first— and then out to the barn and around there. *(To the Sheriff.)* You're convinced that there was nothing important here—nothing that would point to any motive?

Sheriff. Nothing here but kitchen things.

(The County Attorney, after again looking around the kitchen, opens the door of a cupboard closet in right wall. He brings a small chair from right—gets on it and looks on a shelf. Pulls his hand away, sticky.)

County Attorney. Here's a nice mess. *(The women draw nearer up center.)*

Mrs. Peters *(to the other woman)*. Oh, her fruit; it did freeze. *(To the Lawyer.)* She worried about that when it turned so cold. She said the fire'd go out and her jars would break.

Sheriff *(rises)*. Well, can you beat the women! Held for murder and worryin' about her preserves.

County Attorney *(getting down from chair)*. I guess before we're through she may have something more serious than preserves to worry about. *(Crosses down right center.)*

Hale. Well, women are used to worrying over trifles. *(The two women move a little closer together.)*

County Attorney *(with the gallantry of a young politician)*. And yet, for all their worries, what would we do without the ladies? *(The women do not unbend. He goes below the center table to the sink, takes a dipperful of water from the pail, and pouring it into a basin, washes his hands. While he is doing this the Sheriff and Hale cross to cupboard, which they inspect. The County Attorney starts to wipe his hands on the roller towel, turns it for a cleaner place.)* Dirty towels! *(Kicks his foot against the pans under the sink.)* Not much of a housekeeper, would you say, ladies?

Mrs. Hale *(stiffly)*. There's a great deal of work to be done on a farm.

County Attorney. To be sure. And yet *(with a little bow to her)* I know there are some Dickson County farmhouses which do not have such roller towels.

(He gives it a pull to expose its full length again.)

Mrs. Hale. Those towels get dirty awful quick. Men's hands aren't always as clean as they might be.

County Attorney. Ah, loyal to your sex, I see. But you and Mrs. Wright were neighbors. I suppose you were friends, too.

Mrs. Hale *(shaking her head)*. I've not seen much of her of late years. I've not been in this house—it's more than a year.

County Attorney *(crossing to women up center)*. And why was that? You didn't like her?

Mrs. Hale. I liked her all well enough. Farmers' wives have their hands full, Mr. Henderson. And then——

County Attorney. Yes—— ?

Mrs. Hale *(looking about)*. It never seemed a very cheerful place.

County Attorney. No—it's not cheerful. I shouldn't say she had the homemaking instinct.

Mrs. Hale. Well, I don't know as Wright had, either.

County Attorney. You mean that they didn't get on very well?

Mrs. Hale. No, I don't mean anything. But I don't think a place'd be any cheerfuller for John Wright's being in it.

County Attorney. I'd like to talk more of that a little later. I want to get the lay of things upstairs now.

(He goes past the women to up right where steps lead to a stair door.)

Sheriff. I suppose anything Mrs. Peters does'll be all right. She was to take in some clothes for her, you know, and a few little things. We left in such a hurry, yesterday.

County Attorney. Yes, but I would like to see what you take, Mrs. Peters, and keep an eye out for anything that might be of use to us.

Mrs. Peters. Yes, Mr. Henderson.

(The men leave by up right door to stairs. The women listen to the men's steps on the stairs, then look about the kitchen.)

Mrs. Hale *(crossing left to sink)*. I'd hate to have men coming into my kitchen, snooping around and criticizing.

(She arranges the pans under sink which the Lawyer had shoved out of place.)

Mrs. Peters. Of course it's no more than their duty.

(Crosses to cupboard up right.)

Mrs. Hale. Duty's all right, but I guess that deputy sheriff that came out to make the fire might have got a little of this on. *(Gives the roller towel a pull.)* Wish I'd thought of that sooner. Seems mean to talk about her for not having things slicked up when she had to come away in such a hurry.

(Crosses right to Mrs. Peters at cupboard.)

Mrs. Peters *(who has been looking through cupboard, lifts one end of towel that covers a pan)*. She had bread set.

(Stands still.)

Mrs. Hale *(eyes fixed on a loaf of bread beside the breadbox, which is on a low shelf of the cupboard)*. She was going to put this in there. *(Picks up a loaf, abruptly drops it. In a manner of returning to familiar things.)* It's a shame about her fruit. I wonder if it's all gone. *(Gets up on the chair and looks.)* I think there's some here that's all right, Mrs. Peters. Yes—here; *(holding it toward the window)* this is cherries, too. *(Looking again.)* I declare I believe that's the only one. *(Gets down, jar in her hand. Goes to the sink and wipes it off on the outside.)* She'll feel awful bad after all her hard work in the hot weather. I remember the afternoon I put up my cherries last summer.

(She puts the jar on the big kitchen table, center of the room. With a sigh, is about to sit down in the rocking chair. Before she is seated realizes what chair it is; with a

slow look at it, steps back. The chair which she has touched rocks back and forth. Mrs. Peters moves to center table and they both watch the chair rock for a moment or two.)

Mrs. Peters *(shaking off the mood which the empty rocking chair has evoked. Now in a businesslike manner she speaks).* Well I must get those things from the front room closet. *(She goes to the door at the right but, after looking into the other room, steps back.)* You coming with me, Mrs. Hale? You could help me carry them. *(They go in the other room; reappear, Mrs. Peters carrying a dress, petticoat, and skirt, Mrs. Hale following with a pair of shoes.)* My, it's cold in there.

(She puts the clothes on the big table and hurries to the stove.)

Mrs. Hale *(right of center table examining the skirt).* Wright was close. I think maybe that's why she kept so much to herself. She didn't even belong to the Ladies' Aid. I suppose she felt she couldn't do her part, and then you don't enjoy things when you feel shabby. I heard she used to wear pretty clothes and be lively, when she was Minnie Foster, one of the town girls singing in the choir. But that—oh, that was thirty years ago. This all you want to take in?

Mrs. Peters. She said she wanted an apron. Funny thing to want, for there isn't much to get you dirty in jail, goodness knows. But I suppose just to make her feel more natural. *(Crosses to cupboard.)* She said they was in the top drawer in this cupboard. Yes, here. And then her little shawl that always hung behind the door. *(Opens stair door and looks.)* Yes, here it is.

(Quickly shuts door leading upstairs.)

Mrs. Hale *(abruptly moving toward her).* Mrs. Peters?
Mrs. Peters. Yes, Mrs. Hale?

(At up right door.)

Mrs. Hale. Do you think she did it?
Mrs. Peters *(in a frightened voice).* Oh, I don't know.
Mrs. Hale. Well, I don't think she did. Asking for an apron and her little shawl. Worrying about her fruit.
Mrs. Peters *(starts to speak, glances up, where footsteps are heard in the room above. In a low voice).* Mr. Peters says it looks bad for her. Mr. Henderson is awful sarcastic in a speech and he'll make fun of her sayin' she didn't wake up.
Mrs. Hale. Well, I guess John Wright didn't wake when they was slipping that rope under his neck.
Mrs. Peters *(crossing slowly to table and placing shawl and apron on table with other clothing).* No, it's strange. It must have been done awful crafty and still. They say it was such a—funny way to kill a man, rigging it all up like that.

Mrs. Hale (*crossing to left of Mrs. Peters at table*). That's just what Mr. Hale said. There was a gun in the house. He says that's what he can't understand.

Mrs. Peters. Mr. Henderson said coming out that what was needed for the case was a motive; something to show anger, or—sudden feeling.

Mrs. Hale (*who is standing by the table*). Well, I don't see any signs of anger around here. (*She puts her hand on the dish towel, which lies on the table, stands looking down at table, one-half of which is clean, the other half messy.*) It's wiped to here. (*Makes a move as if to finish work, then turns and looks at loaf of bread outside the breadbox. Drops towel. In that voice of coming back to familiar things.*) Wonder how they are finding things upstairs. (*Crossing below table to down right.*) I hope she had it a little more red-up[1] up there. You know, it seems kind of *sneaking*. Locking her up in town and then coming out here and trying to get her own house to turn against her!

Mrs. Peters. But, Mrs. Hale, the law is the law.

Mrs. Hale. I s'pose 'tis. (*Unbuttoning her coat.*) Better loosen up your things, Mrs. Peters. You won't feel them when you go out.

(*Mrs. Peters takes off her fur tippet, goes to hang it on chair back left of table, stands looking at the work basket on floor near down left window.*)

Mrs. Peters. She was piecing a quilt.

(*She brings the large sewing basket to the center table and they look at the bright pieces, Mrs. Hale above the table and Mrs. Peters left of it.*)

Mrs. Hale. It's a log cabin pattern. Pretty, isn't it? I wonder if she was goin' to quilt it or just knot it?

(*Footsteps have been heard coming down the stairs. The Sheriff enters followed by Hale and the County Attorney.*)

Sheriff. They wonder if she was going to quilt it or just knot it!

(*The men laugh, the women look abashed.*)

County Attorney (*rubbing his hands over the stove*). Frank's fire didn't do much up there, did it? Well, let's go out to the barn and get that cleared up.

(*The men go outside by up left door.*)

Mrs. Hale (*resentfully*). I don't know as there's anything so strange, our takin' up our time with little things while we're waiting for them to get the evidence.

---

[1] A slang expression for "make attractive."

(She sits in chair right of table smoothing out a block with decision.) I don't see as it's anything to laugh about.

Mrs. Peters *(apologetically).* Of course they've got awful important things on their minds.

(Pulls up a chair and joins Mrs. Hale at the left of the table.)

Mrs. Hale *(examining another block).* Mrs. Peters, look at this one. Here, this is the one she was working on, and look at the sewing! All the rest of it has been so nice and even. And look at this! It's all over the place! Why, it looks as if she didn't know what she was about!

(After she has said this they look at each other, then start to glance back at the door. After an instant Mrs. Hale has pulled at a knot and ripped the sewing.)

Mrs. Peters. Oh, what are you doing, Mrs. Hale?

Mrs. Hale *(mildly).* Just pulling out a stitch or two that's not sewed very good. *(Threading a needle.)* Bad sewing always made me fidgety.

Mrs. Peters *(with a glance at door, nervously).* I don't think we ought to touch things.

Mrs. Hale. I'll just finish up this end. *(Suddenly stopping and leaning forward.)* Mrs. Peters?

Mrs. Peters. Yes, Mrs. Hale?

Mrs. Hale. What do you suppose she was so nervous about?

Mrs. Peters. Oh—I don't know. I don't know as she was nervous. I sometimes sew awful queer when I'm just tired. *(Mrs. Hale starts to say something, looks at Mrs. Peters, then goes on sewing.)* Well, I must get these things wrapped up. They may be through sooner than we think. *(Putting apron and other things together.)* I wonder where I can find a piece of paper, and string.

(Rises.)

Mrs. Hale. In that cupboard, maybe.

Mrs. Peters *(crosses right looking in cupboard).* Why, here's a bird-cage. *(Holds it up.)* Did she have a bird, Mrs. Hale?

Mrs. Hale. Why, I don't know whether she did or not—I've not been here for so long. There was a man around last year selling canaries cheap, but I don't know as she took one; maybe she did. She used to sing real pretty herself.

Mrs. Peters *(glancing around).* Seems funny to think of a bird here. But she must have had one, or why would she have a cage? I wonder what happened to it?

Mrs. Hale. I s'pose maybe the cat got it.

Mrs. Peters. No, she didn't have a cat. She's got that feeling some people have about cats—being afraid of them. My cat got in her room and she was real upset and asked me to take it out.

Mrs. Hale. My sister Bessie was like that. Queer, ain't it?

Mrs. Peters *(examining the cage).* Why, look at this door. It's broke. One hinge is
pulled apart.

(Takes a step down to Mrs. Hale's right.)

Mrs. Hale *(looking too).* Looks as if someone must have been rough with it.

Mrs. Peters. Why, yes.

(She brings the cage forward and puts it on the table.)

Mrs. Hale *(glancing toward up left door).* I wish if they're going to find any evidence they'd be about it. I don't like this place.

Mrs. Peters. But I'm awful glad you came with me, Mrs. Hale. It would be lonesome for me sitting here alone.

Mrs. Hale. It would, wouldn't it? *(Dropping her sewing.)* But I tell you what I do
wish, Mrs. Peters. I wish I had come over sometimes when *she* was here. I—
(looking around the room)—wish I had.

Mrs. Peters. But of course you were awful busy, Mrs. Hale—your house and your
children.

Mrs. Hale *(rises and crosses left).* I could've come. I stayed away because it weren't
cheerful—and that's why I ought to have come. I—*(looking out left window)*—
I've never liked this place. Maybe because it's down in a hollow and you don't
see the road. I dunno what it is, but it's a lonesome place and always was. I wish I
had come over to see Minnie Foster sometimes. I can see now—

(Shakes her head.)

Mrs. Peters *(left of table and above it).* Well, you mustn't reproach yourself, Mrs.
Hale. Somehow we just don't see how it is with other folks until—something
turns up.

Mrs. Hale. Not having children makes less work—but it makes a quiet house, and
Wright out to work all day, and no company when he did come in. *(Turning
from window.)* Did you know John Wright, Mrs. Peters?

Mrs. Peters. Not to know him; I've seen him in town. They say he was a good man.

Mrs. Hale. Yes—good; he didn't drink, and kept his word as well as most, I guess,
and paid his debts. But he was a hard man, Mrs. Peters. Just to pass the time of
day with him—*(Shivers.)* Like a raw wind that gets to the bone. *(Pauses, her eye
falling on the cage.)* I should think she would 'a' wanted a bird. But what do you
suppose went with it?

Mrs. Peters. I don't know, unless it got sick and died.

(She reaches over and swings the broken door, swings it again, both women watch it.)

Mrs. Hale. You weren't raised round here, were you? *(Mrs. Peters shakes her head.)*
You didn't know—her?

Mrs. Peters. Not till they brought her yesterday.

Mrs. Hale. She—come to think of it, she was kind of like a bird herself—real sweet and pretty, but kind of timid and—fluttery. How—she—did—change. (*Silence: then as if struck by a happy thought and relieved to get back to everyday things. Crosses right above Mrs. Peters to cupboard, replaces small chair used to stand on to its original place down right.*) Tell you what, Mrs. Peters, why don't you take the quilt in with you? It might take up her mind.

Mrs. Peters. Why, I think that's a real nice idea, Mrs. Hale. There couldn't possibly be any objection to it could there? Now, just what would I take? I wonder if her patches are in here—and her things.

(*They look in the sewing basket.*)

Mrs. Hale (*crosses to right of table*). Here's some red. I expect this has got sewing things in it. (*Brings out a fancy box.*) What a pretty box. Looks like something somebody would give you. Maybe her scissors are in here. (*Opens box. Suddenly puts her hand to her nose.*) Why————(*Mrs. Peters bends nearer, then turns her face away.*) There's something wrapped up in this piece of silk.

Mrs. Peters. Why, this isn't her scissors.

Mrs. Hale (*lifting the silk*). Oh, Mrs. Peters— it's————

(*Mrs. Peters bends closer.*)

Mrs. Peters. It's the bird.

Mrs. Hale. But, Mrs. Peters—look at it! Its neck! Look at its neck! It's all—other side *to*.

Mrs. Peters. Somebody—wrung—its—neck.

(*Their eyes meet. A look of growing comprehension, of horror. Steps are heard outside. Mrs. Hale slips box under quilt pieces, and sinks into her chair. Enter Sheriff and County Attorney. Mrs. Peters steps down left and stands looking out of window.*)

County Attorney (*as one turning from serious things to little pleasantries*). Well, ladies, have you decided whether she was going to quilt it or knot it?

(*Crosses to center above table.*)

Mrs. Peters. We think she was going to—knot it.

(*Sheriff crosses to right of stove, lifts stove lid, and glances at fire, then stands warming hands at stove.*)

County Attorney. Well, that's interesting, I'm sure. (*Seeing the bird-cage.*) Has the bird flown?

Mrs. Hale (*putting more quilt pieces over the box*). We think the—cat got it.

County Attorney (*preoccupied*). Is there a cat?

(*Mrs. Hale glances in a quick covert way at Mrs. Peters.*)

Mrs. Peters (*turning from window takes a step in*). Well, not *now*. They're superstitious, you know. They leave.

County Attorney (*to Sheriff Peters, continuing an interrupted conversation*). No sign at all of anyone having come from the outside. Their own rope. Now let's go up again and go over it piece by piece. (*They start upstairs.*) It would have to have been someone who knew just the———

(*Mrs. Peters sits down left of table. The two women sit there not looking at one another, but as if peering into something and at the same time holding back. When they talk now it is in the manner of feeling their way over strange ground, as if afraid of what they are saying, but as if they cannot help saying it.*)

Mrs. Hale (*hesitatively and in hushed voice*). She liked the bird. She was going to bury it in that pretty box.

Mrs. Peters (*in a whisper*). When I was a girl—my kitten—there was a boy took a hatchet, and before my eyes—and before I could get there——— (*Covers her face an instant.*) If they hadn't held me back I would have—(*catches herself, looks upstairs where steps are heard, falters weakly*)—hurt him.

Mrs. Hale (*with a slow look around her*). I wonder how it would seem never to have had any children around. (*Pause.*) No, Wright wouldn't like the bird—a thing that sang. She used to sing. He killed that, too.

Mrs. Peters (*moving uneasily*). We don't know who killed the bird.

Mrs. Hale. I knew John Wright.

Mrs. Peters. It was an awful thing was done in this house that night, Mrs. Hale. Killing a man while he slept, slipping a rope around his neck that choked the life out of him.

Mrs. Hale. His neck. Choked the life out of him.

(*Her hand goes out and rests on the bird-cage.*)

Mrs. Peters (*with rising voice*). We don't know who killed him. We don't *know*.

Mrs. Hale (*her own feeling not interrupted*). If there'd been years and years of nothing, then a bird to sing to you, it would be awful—still, after the bird was still.

Mrs. Peters (*something within her speaking*). I know what stillness is. When we homesteaded in Dakota, and my first baby died—after he was two years old, and me with no other then———

Mrs. Hale (*moving*). How soon do you suppose they'll be through looking for the evidence?

Mrs. Peters. I know what stillness is. (*Pulling herself back.*) The law has got to punish crime, Mrs. Hale.

Mrs. Hale (*not as if answering that*). I wish you'd seen Minnie Foster when she wore a white dress with blue ribbons and stood up there in the choir and sang. (*A look around the room.*) Oh, I wish I'd come over here once in a while! That was a crime! That was a crime! Who's going to punish that?

Mrs. Peters (*looking upstairs*). We mustn't—take on.

Mrs. Hale. I might have known she needed help! I know how things can be—for women. I tell you, it's queer, Mrs. Peters. We live close together and we live far apart. We all go through the same things—it's all just a different kind of the same thing. (*Brushes her eyes, noticing the jar of fruit, reaches out for it.*) If I was you I wouldn't tell her her fruit was gone. Tell her it *ain't*. Tell her it's all right. Take this in to prove it to her. She—she may never know whether it was broke or not.

Mrs. Peters (*takes the jar, looks about for something to wrap it in; takes petticoat from the clothes brought from the other room, very nervously begins winding this around the jar. In a false voice*). My, it's a good thing the men couldn't hear us. Wouldn't they just laugh! Getting all stirred up over a little thing like a— dead canary. As if that could have anything to do with—with—wouldn't they laugh!

(*The men are heard coming downstairs.*)

Mrs. Hale (*under her breath*). Maybe they would—maybe they wouldn't.

County Attorney. No, Peters, it's all perfectly clear except a reason for doing it. But you know juries when it comes to women. If there was some definite thing. (*Crosses slowly to above table. Sheriff crosses down right. Mrs. Hale and Mrs. Peters remain seated at either side of table.*) Something to show—something to make a story about—a thing that would connect up with this strange way of doing it———

(*The women's eyes meet for an instant. Enter Hale from outer door.*)

Hale (*remaining by door*). Well, I've got the team around. Pretty cold out there.

County Attorney. I'm going to stay awhile by myself. (*To the Sheriff.*) You can send Frank out for me, can't you? I want to go over everything. I'm not satisfied that we can't do better.

Sheriff. Do you want to see what Mrs. Peters is going to take in?

(*The Lawyer picks up the apron, laughs.*)

County Attorney. Oh, I guess they're not very dangerous things the ladies have picked out. (*Moves a few things about, disturbing the quilt pieces which cover the box. Steps back.*) No, Mrs. Peters doesn't need supervising. For that matter a sheriff's wife is married to the law. Ever think of it that way, Mrs. Peters?

Mrs. Peters. Not—just that way.

Sheriff (*chuckling*). Married to the law. (*Moves to down right door to the other room.*) I just want you to come in here a minute, George. We ought to take a look at these windows.

County Attorney (*scoffingly*). Oh, windows!

Sheriff. We'll be right out, Mr. Hale.

(*Hale goes outside. The Sheriff follows the County Attorney into the room. Then Mrs. Hale rises, hands tight together, looking intensely at Mrs. Peters, whose eyes make a slow turn, finally meeting Mrs. Hale's. A moment Mrs. Hale holds her, then her own eyes point the way to where the box is concealed. Suddenly Mrs. Peters throws back quilt pieces and tries to put the box in the bag she is carrying. It is too big. She opens box, starts to take bird out, cannot touch it, goes to pieces, stands there helpless. Sound of a knob turning in the other room. Mrs. Hale snatches the box and puts it in the pocket of her big coat. Enter County Attorney and Sheriff, who remain down right.*)

County Attorney (*crosses to up left door facetiously*). Well, Henry, at least we found out that she was not going to quilt it. She was going to—what is it you call it, ladies?

Mrs. Hale (*standing center below table facing front, her hand against her pocket*). We call it—knot it, Mr. Henderson.

Curtain.

FOR ANALYSIS

1. What is the meaning of the title? Glaspell titled a short-story version of the play "A Jury of Her Peers." Is that a better title than *Trifles*? Explain.

2. What are the major differences between Mrs. Hale and Mrs. Peters?

3. At one point, Mrs. Peters tells Mrs. Hale a childhood story about a boy who killed her kitten. Why is she reminded of this event? What does it tell us about her reaction to the Wrights' marriage?

4. Which of the two women undergoes the most noticeable character development? Explain.

5. In what ways do the relationships between the two couples—Mrs. Hale and Mrs. Peters, and Henry Peters and Lewis Hale—change by the end of the play?

6. Do Henry Peters and Lewis Hale change in the course of the play?

7. Why are the men unable to see the clues that become obvious to the women?

8. Can you suggest why Mrs. Wright is the only one identified by her birth name?

MAKING CONNECTIONS

1. What similarities in attitudes toward women do you find in this play and in Ibsen's *A Doll's House* (p. 440)?

2. Do you think it is fair to say that Mrs. Wright in this play and the narrator in Gilman's "The Yellow Wallpaper" (p. 547) are people whose lives have been blighted by a patriarchal society that confines women to narrow, stereotypical roles? Explain.

WRITING TOPICS

1. Show how the discussion of Mrs. Wright's quilt embodies the major themes of *Trifles*.

2. Argue for or against the proposition that Mrs. Hale and Mrs. Peters are morally obligated to tell the county attorney what they know about the murder.

NONFICTION

PAUL (D. CA. C.E. 64)

1 CORINTHIANS 13 CA. 56

If I speak in the tongues of men° and of angels, but have not love, I am a noisy gong or a clanging cymbal. [2] And if I have prophetic powers, and understand all mysteries and all knowledge, and if I have all faith, so as to remove mountains, but have not love, I am nothing. [3] If I give away all I have, and if I deliver my body to be burned, but have not love, I gain nothing.

[4] Love is patient and kind; love is not jealous or boastful; [5] it is not arrogant or rude. Love does not insist on its own way; it is not irritable or resentful; [6] it does not rejoice at wrong, but rejoices in the right. [7] Love bears all things, believes all things, hopes all things, endures all things.

[8] Love never ends; as for prophesies, they will pass away; as for tongues, they will cease; as for knowledge, it will pass away. [9] For our knowledge is imperfect and our prophecy is imperfect; [10] but when the perfect comes, the imperfect will pass away. [11] When I was a child, I spoke like a child, I thought like a child, I reasoned like a child; when I became a man, I gave up childish ways. [12] For now we see in a mirror dimly, but then face to face. Now I know in part; then I shall understand fully, even as I have been fully understood. [13] So faith, hope, love abide, these three; but the greatest of these is love.

FOR ANALYSIS

1. How does Paul emphasize the significance of love in verses 1–3?

2. What does Paul mean by "now" and "then" in verse 12?

3. In verse 13, Paul mentions "faith, hope, love" as abiding values. What do you understand by "faith" and "hope"? What do you think "love" means to Paul? Why does he rank it above the others?

°Glossolalia, the ecstatic uttering of unintelligible sounds that some interpret as a deeply religious experience.

MAKING CONNECTIONS

How do you think the characters in Carver's "What We Talk About When We Talk About Love" (p. 896) would respond to Paul's definition of *love* or the absence of love?

WRITING TOPICS

1. Read Paul's First Epistle to the Corinthians (preferably in a well-annotated study Bible), and analyze the relationship of chapter 13 to the rest of the epistle.

2. This text, translated from the original Greek, is taken from the Revised Standard Version of the Bible. Read the same passage in two or three other versions (for example, the King James Version, the Douay Version, the New American Bible), and compare the translations in terms of **style** and effectiveness.

NO NAME WOMAN   1970

Y ou must not tell anyone," my mother said, "what I am about to tell you. In China your father had a sister who killed herself. She jumped into the family well. We say that your father has all brothers because it is as if she had never been born.

"In 1924 just a few days after our village celebrated seventeen hurry-up weddings—to make sure that every young man who went 'out on the road' would responsibly come home—your father and his brothers and your grandfather and his brothers and your aunt's new husband sailed for America, the Gold Mountain. It was your grandfather's last trip. Those lucky enough to get contracts waved good-bye from the decks. They fed and guarded the stowaways and helped them off in Cuba, New York, Bali, Hawaii. 'We'll meet in California next year,' they said. All of them sent money home.

"I remember looking at your aunt one day when she and I were dressing; I had not noticed before that she had such a protruding melon of a stomach. But I did not think, 'She's pregnant,' until she began to look like other pregnant women, her shirt pulling and the white tops of her black pants showing. She could not have been pregnant, you see, because her husband had been gone for years. No one said anything. We did not discuss it. In early summer she was ready to have the child, long after the time when it could have been possible.

"The village had also been counting. On the night the baby was to be born the villagers raided our house. Some were crying. Like a great saw, teeth strung with lights, files of people walked zigzag across our land, tearing the rice. Their lanterns doubled in the disturbed black water, which drained away through the broken bunds. As the villagers closed in, we could see that some of them, probably men and women we knew well, wore white masks. The people with long hair hung it over their faces. Women with short hair made it stand up on end. Some had tied white bands around their foreheads, arms, and legs.

"At first they threw mud and rocks at the house. Then they threw eggs and 5 began slaughtering our stock. We could hear the animals scream their deaths— the roosters, the pigs, a last great roar from the ox. Familiar wild heads flared in our night windows; the villagers encircled us. Some of the faces stopped to peer at us, their eyes rushing like searchlights. The hands flattened against the panes, framed heads, and left red prints.

"The villagers broke in the front and the back doors at the same time, even though we had not locked the doors against them. Their knives dripped with the blood of our animals. They smeared blood on the doors and walls. One woman swung a chicken, whose throat she had slit, splattering blood in red arcs about her. We stood together in the middle of our house, in the family hall with the pictures and tables of the ancestors around us, and looked straight ahead.

"At that time the house had only two wings. When the men came back, we would build two more to enclose our courtyard and a third one to begin a second courtyard. The villagers pushed through both wings, even your grandparents' rooms, to find your aunt's, which was also mine until the men returned. From this room a new wing for one of the younger families would grow. They ripped up her clothes and shoes and broke her combs, grinding them underfoot. They tore her work from the loom. They scattered the cooking fire and rolled the new weaving in it. We could hear them in the kitchen breaking our bowls and banging the pots. They overturned the great waist-high earthenware jugs; duck eggs, pickled fruits, vegetables burst out and mixed in acrid torrents. The old woman from the next field swept a broom through the air and loosed the spirits-of-the-broom over our heads. 'Pig.' 'Ghost.' 'Pig,' they sobbed and scolded while they ruined our house.

"When they left, they took sugar and oranges to bless themselves. They cut pieces from the dead animals. Some of them took bowls that were not broken and clothes that were not torn. Afterward we swept up the rice and sewed it back up into sacks. But the smells from the spilled preserves lasted. Your aunt gave birth in the pigsty that night. The next morning when I went for the water, I found her and the baby plugging up the family well.

"Don't let your father know that I told you. He denies her. Now that you have started to menstruate, what happened to her could happen to you. Don't humiliate us. You wouldn't like to be forgotten as if you had never been born. The villagers are watchful."

Whenever she had to warn us about life, my mother told stories that ran like this one, a story to grow up on. She tested our strength to establish realities. Those in the emigrant generations who could not reassert brute survival died young and far from home. Those of us in the first American generations have had to figure out how the invisible world the emigrants built around our childhoods fit in solid America. [10]

The emigrants confused the gods by diverting their curses, misleading them with crooked streets and false names. They must try to confuse their offspring as well, who, I suppose, threaten them in similar ways—always trying to get things straight, always trying to name the unspeakable. The Chinese I know hide their names; sojourners take new names when their lives change and guard their real names with silence.

Chinese Americans, when you try to understand what things in you are Chinese, how do you separate what is peculiar to childhood, to poverty, insanities, one family, your mother who marked your growing with stories, from what is Chinese? What is Chinese tradition and what is the movies?

If I want to learn what clothes my aunt wore, whether flashy or ordinary, I would have to begin, "Remember Father's drowned-in-the-well sister?" I cannot ask that. My mother has told me once and for all the useful parts. She will add nothing unless powered by Necessity, a riverbank that guides her life. She plants vegetable gardens rather than lawns; she carries the odd-shaped toma-toes home from the fields and eats food left for the gods.

Whenever we did frivolous things, we used up energy; we flew high kites. We children came up off the ground over the melting cones our parents brought home from work and the American movie on New Year's Day—*Oh, You Beautiful Doll* with Betty Grable one year, and *She Wore a Yellow Ribbon* with John Wayne another year. After the one carnival ride each, we paid in guilt; our tired father counted his change on the dark walk home.

Adultery is extravagance. Could people who hatch their own chicks and eat 15 the embryos and the heads for delicacies and boil the feet in vinegar for party food, leaving only the gravel, eating even the gizzard lining—could such people engender a prodigal aunt? To be a woman, to have a daughter in starvation time was a waste enough. My aunt could not have been the lone romantic who gave up everything for sex. Women in the old China did not choose. Some man had commanded her to lie with him and be his secret evil. I wonder whether he masked himself when he joined the raid on her family.

Perhaps she had encountered him in the fields or on the mountain where the daughters-in-law collected fuel. Or perhaps he first noticed her in the market-place. He was not a stranger because the village housed no strangers. She had to have dealings with him other than sex. Perhaps he worked an adjoining field, or he sold her the cloth for the dress she sewed and wore. His demand must have surprised, then terrified her. She obeyed him; she always did as she was told.

When the family found a young man in the next village to be her husband, she had stood tractably beside the best rooster, his proxy, and promised before they met that she would be his forever. She was lucky that he was her age and she would be the first wife, an advantage secure now. The night she first saw him, he had sex with her. Then he left for America. She had almost forgotten what he looked like. When she tried to envision him, she only saw the black and white face in the group photograph the men had had taken before leaving.

The other man was not, after all, much different from her husband. They both gave orders: she followed. "If you tell your family, I'll beat you, I'll kill you. Be here again next week." No one talked sex, ever. And she might have separated the rapes from the rest of living if only she did not have to buy her oil from him or gather wood in the same forest. I want her fear to have lasted just as long as rape lasted so that the fear could have been contained. No drawn-out fear. But women at sex hazarded birth and hence lifetimes. The fear did not stop but permeated everywhere. She told the man, "I think I'm pregnant." He organized the raid against her.

On nights when my mother and father talked about their life back home, sometimes they mentioned an "outcast table" whose business they still seemed to be settling, their voices tight. In a commensal tradition, where food is precious, the powerful older people made wrongdoers eat alone. Instead of letting them start separate new lives like the Japanese, who could become samurais and geishas, the Chinese family, faces averted but eyes glowering sideways, hung on to the offenders and fed them leftovers. My aunt must have lived in the same house as my parents and eaten at an outcast table. My mother spoke about the raid as if she had seen it, when she and my aunt, a daughter-in-law to a different household, should not have been living together at all. Daughters-in-law lived with their husbands' parents, not their own; a synonym for marriage in Chinese is "taking a daughter-in-law." Her husband's parents could have sold her, mortgaged her, stoned her. But they had sent her back to her own mother and father, a mysterious act hinting at disgraces not told me. Perhaps they had thrown her out to deflect the avengers.

She was the only daughter; her four brothers went with her father, husband, 20 and uncles "out on the road" and for some years became Western men. When the goods were divided among the family, three of the brothers took land, and the youngest, my father, chose an education. After my grandparents gave their daughter away to her husband's family, they had dispensed all the adventure and all the property. They expected her alone to keep the traditional ways, which her brothers, now among the barbarians, could fumble without detection. The heavy, deep-rooted women were to maintain the past against the flood, safe for returning. But the rare urge west had fixed upon our family, and so my aunt crossed boundaries not delineated in space.

The work of preservation demands that the feelings playing about in one's guts not be turned into action. Just watch their passing like cherry blossoms. But perhaps my aunt, my forerunner, caught in a slow life, let dreams grow and fade and after some months or years went toward what persisted. Fear at the enormities of the forbidden kept her desires delicate, wire and bone. She looked at a man because she liked the way the hair was tucked behind his ears, or she liked the question-mark line of a long torso curving at the shoulder and straight at the hip. For warm eyes or a soft voice or a slow walk—that's all—a few hairs, a line, a brightness, a sound, a pace, she gave up family. She offered us up for a charm that vanished with tiredness, a pigtail that didn't toss when the wind died. Why, the wrong lighting could erase the dearest thing about him.

It could very well have been, however, that my aunt did not take subtle enjoyment of her friend, but, a wild woman, kept rollicking company. Imagining her free with sex doesn't fit, though. I don't know any women like that, or men either. Unless I see her life branching into mine, she gives me no ancestral help.

To sustain her being in love, she often worked at herself in the mirror, guessing at the colors and shapes that would interest him, changing them frequently in order to hit on the right combination. She wanted him to look back.

On a farm near the sea, a woman who tended her appearance reaped a reputation for eccentricity. All the married women blunt-cut their hair in flaps about their ears or pulled it back in tight buns. No nonsense. Neither style blew easily into heart-catching tangles. And at their weddings they displayed themselves in their long hair for the last time. "It brushed the backs of my knees," my mother tells me. "It was braided, and even so, it brushed the backs of my knees."

At the mirror my aunt combined individuality into her bob. A bun could 25 have been contrived to escape into black streamers blowing in the wind or in quiet wisps about her face, but only the older women in our picture album wear buns. She brushed her hair back from her forehead, tucking the flaps behind her ears. She looped a piece of thread, knotted into a circle between her index fingers and thumbs, and ran the double strand across her forehead. When she closed her fingers as if she were making a pair of shadow geese bite, the string twisted together catching the little hairs. Then she pulled the thread away from her skin, ripping the hairs out neatly, her eyes watering from the needles of pain. Opening her fingers, she cleaned the thread, then rolled it along her hairline and the tops of her eyebrows. My mother did the same to me and my sisters and herself. I used to believe that the expression "caught by the short hairs" meant a captive held with a depilatory string. It especially hurt at the temples, but my mother said we were lucky we didn't have to have our feet bound when we were seven. Sisters used to sit on their beds and cry together, she said, as their mothers or their slave removed the bandages for a few minutes each night and let the blood gush back into their veins. I hope that the man my aunt loved appreciated a smooth brow, that he wasn't just a tits-and-ass man.

Once my aunt found a freckle on her chin, at a spot that the almanac said predestined her for unhappiness. She dug it out with a hot needle and washed the wound with peroxide.

More attention to her looks than these pullings of hairs and pickings at spots would have caused gossip among the villagers. They owned work clothes and good clothes, and they wore good clothes for feasting the new seasons. But since a woman combing her hair hexes beginnings, my aunt rarely found an occasion to look her best. Women looked like great sea snails—the corded wood, babies, and laundry they carried were the whorls on their backs. The Chinese did not admire a bent back; goddesses and warriors stood straight. Still there must have been a marvelous freeing of beauty when a worker laid down her burden and stretched and arched.

Such commonplace loveliness, however, was not enough for my aunt. She dreamed of a lover for the fifteen days of New Year's, the time for families to exchange visits, money, and food. She plied her secret comb. And sure enough she cursed the year, the family, the village, and herself.

Even as her hair lured her imminent lover, many other men looked at her. Uncles, cousins, nephews, brothers would have looked, too, had they been home between journeys. Perhaps they had already been restraining their curiosity, and they left, fearful that their glances, like a field of nesting birds, might be startled and caught. Poverty hurt, and that was their first reason for leaving. But another, final reason for leaving the crowded house was the never-said.

She may have been unusually beloved, the precious only daughter, spoiled 30 and mirror-gazing because of the affection the family lavished on her. When her husband left, they welcomed the chance to take her back from the in-laws;

she could live like the little daughter for just a while longer. There are stories that my grandfather was different from other people, "crazy ever since the little Jap bayoneted him in the head." He used to put his naked penis on the dinner table, laughing. And one day he brought home a baby girl, wrapped up inside his brown Western-style greatcoat. He had traded one of his sons, probably my father, the youngest, for her. My grandmother made him trade back. When he finally got a daughter of his own, he doted on her. They must have all loved her, except perhaps my father, the only brother who never went back to China, having once been traded for a girl.

Brothers and sisters, newly men and women, had to efface their sexual color and present plain miens. Disturbing hair and eyes, a smile like no other, threatened the ideal of five generations living under one roof. To focus blurs, people shouted face to face and yelled from room to room. The immigrants I know have loud voices, unmodulated to American tones even after years away from the village where they called their friendships out across the fields. I have not been able to stop my mother's screams in public libraries or over telephones. Walking erect (knees straight, toes pointed forward, not pigeon-toed, which is Chinese-feminine) and speaking in an inaudible voice, I have tried to turn myself American-feminine. Chinese communication was loud, public. Only sick people had to whisper. But at the dinner table, where the family members came nearest one another, no one could talk, not the outcasts nor any eaters. Every word that falls from the mouth is a coin lost. Silently they gave and accepted food with both hands. A preoccupied child who took his bowl with one hand got a sideways glare. A complete moment of total attention is due everyone alike. Children and lovers have no singularity here, but my aunt used a secret voice, a separate attentiveness.

She kept the man's name to herself throughout her labor and dying; she did not accuse him that he be punished with her. To save her inseminator's name she gave silent birth.

He may have been somebody in her own household, but intercourse with a man outside the family would have been no less abhorrent. All the village were kinsmen, and the titles shouted in loud country voices never let kinship be forgotten. Any man within visiting distance would have been neutralized as a lover—"brother," "younger brother," "older brother"—115 relationship titles. Parents researched birth charts probably not so much to assure good fortune as to circumvent incest in a population that has but one hundred surnames. Everybody has eight million relatives. How useless then sexual mannerisms, how dangerous.

As if it came from an atavism deeper than fear, I used to add "brother" silently to boys' names. It hexed the boys, who would or would not ask me to dance, and made them less scary and as familiar and deserving of benevolence as girls.

But, of course, I hexed myself also—no dates. I should have stood up, both 35 arms waving, and shouted out across libraries, "Hey, you! Love me back." I had no idea, though, how to make attraction selective, how to control its direction and magnitude. If I made myself American-pretty so that the five or six

Chinese boys in the class fell in love with me, everyone else—the Caucasian, Negro, and Japanese boys—would too. Sisterliness, dignified and honorable, made much more sense.

Attraction eludes control so stubbornly that whole societies designed to organize relationships among people cannot keep order, not even when they bind people to one another from childhood and raise them together. Among the very poor and the wealthy, brothers married their adopted sisters, like doves. Our family allowed some romance, paying adult brides' prices and providing dowries so that their sons and daughters could marry strangers. Marriage promises to turn strangers into friendly relatives—a nation of siblings.

In the village structure, spirits shimmered among the live creatures, balanced and held in equilibrium by time and land. But one human being flaring up into violence could open up a black hole, a maelstrom that pulled in the sky. The frightened villagers, who depended on one another to maintain the real, went to my aunt to show her a personal, physical representation of the break she had made in the "roundness." Misallying couples snapped off the future, which was to be embodied in true offspring. The villagers punished her for acting as if she could have a private life, secret and apart from them.

If my aunt had betrayed the family at a time of large grain yields and peace, when many boys were born, and wings were being built on many houses, perhaps she might have escaped such severe punishment. But the men—hungry, greedy, tired of planting in dry soil, cuckolded—had been forced to leave the village in order to send food-money home. There were ghost plagues, bandit plagues, wars with the Japanese, floods. My Chinese brother and sister had died of an unknown sickness. Adultery, perhaps only a mistake during good times, became a crime when the village needed food.

The round moon cakes and round doorways, the round tables of graduated size that fit one roundness inside another, round windows and rice bowls—these talismans had lost their power to warn this family of the law: a family must be whole, faithfully keeping the descent line by having sons to feed the old and the dead, who in turn look after the family. The villagers came to show my aunt and her lover-in-hiding a broken house. The villagers were speeding up the circling of events because she was too shortsighted to see that her infidelity had already harmed the village, that waves of consequences would return unpredictably, sometimes in disguise, as now, to hurt her. This roundness had to be made coin-sized so that she would see its circumference: punish her at the birth of her baby. Awaken her to the inexorable. People who refused fatalism because they could invent small resources insisted on culpability. Deny accidents and wrest fault from the stars.

After the villagers left, their lanterns now scattering in various directions 40 toward home, the family broke their silence and cursed her. "Aiaa, we're going to die. Death is coming. Death is coming. Look what you've done. You've killed us. Ghost! Dead ghost! Ghost! You've never been born." She ran out into the fields, far enough from the house so that she could no longer hear their voices, and pressed herself against the earth, her own land no more. When she felt the birth coming, she thought that she had been hurt. Her body seized together. "They've hurt me too much," she thought. "This is gall, and it will kill me." With forehead and knees against the earth, her body convulsed and then relaxed. She turned on her back, lay on the ground. The black well of sky and stars went out and out and out forever; her body and her complexity seemed to disappear. She was one of the stars, a bright dot in blackness, without home, without a companion, in eternal cold and silence. An agoraphobia rose in her, speeding higher and higher, bigger and bigger; she would not be able to contain it; there would be no end to fear.

Flayed, unprotected against space, she felt pain return, focusing her body. This pain chilled her—a cold, steady kind of surface pain. Inside, spasmodically, the other pain, the pain of the child, heated her. For hours she lay on the ground, alternately body and space. Sometimes a vision of normal comfort obliterated reality: she saw the family in the evening gambling at the dinner table, the young people massaging their elders' backs. She saw them congratulating one another, high joy on the mornings the rice shoots came up. When these pictures burst, the stars drew yet further apart. Black space opened.

She got to her feet to fight better and remembered that old-fashioned women gave birth in their pigsties to fool the jealous, pain-dealing gods, who do not snatch piglets. Before the next spasms could stop her, she ran to the pigsty, each step a rushing out into emptiness. She climbed over the fence and knelt in the dirt. It was good to have a fence enclosing her, a tribal person alone.

Laboring, this woman who had carried her child as a foreign growth that sickened her every day, expelled it at last. She reached down to touch the hot, wet, moving mass, surely smaller than anything human, and could feel that it was human after all—fingers, toes, nails, nose. She pulled it up on to her belly, and it lay curled there, butt in the air, feet precisely tucked one under the other. She opened her loose shirt and buttoned the child inside. After resting, it squirmed and thrashed and she pushed it up to her breast. It turned its head this way and that until it found her nipple. There, it made little snuffling noises. She clenched her teeth at its preciousness, lovely as a young calf, a piglet, a little dog.

She may have gone to the pigsty as a last act of responsibility: she would protect this child as she had protected its father. It would look after her soul, leaving supplies on her grave. But how would this tiny child without family find her grave when there would be no marker for her anywhere, neither in the earth nor the family hall? No one would give her a family hall name. She had taken the child with her into the wastes. At its birth the two of them had felt the same raw pain of separation, a wound that only the family pressing tight could close. A child with no descent line would not soften her life but only trail after her, ghostlike, begging her to give it purpose. At dawn the villagers on their way to the fields would stand around the fence and look.

Full of milk, the little ghost slept. When it awoke, she hardened her breasts 45 against the milk that crying loosens. Toward morning she picked up the baby and walked to the well.

Carrying the baby to the well shows loving. Otherwise abandon it. Turn its face into the mud. Mothers who love their children take them along. It was probably a girl; there is some hope of forgiveness for boys.

"Don't tell anyone you had an aunt. Your father does not want to hear her name. She has never been born." I have believed that sex was unspeakable and words so strong and fathers so frail that "aunt" would do my father mysterious harm. I have thought that my family, having settled among immigrants who had also been their neighbors in the ancestral land, needed to clean their name, and a wrong word would incite the kinspeople even here. But there is more to this silence: they want me to participate in her punishment. And I have.

In the twenty years since I heard this story I have not asked for details nor said my aunt's name; I do not know it. People who can comfort the dead can also chase after them to hurt them further—a reverse ancestor worship. The real punishment was not the raid swiftly inflicted by the villagers, but the family's deliberately forgetting her. Her betrayal so maddened them, they saw to it that she would suffer forever, even after death. Always hungry, always needing, she would have to beg food from other ghosts, snatch and steal it from those whose living descendants give them gifts. She would have to fight the ghosts massed at crossroads for the buns a few thoughtful citizens leave to decoy her away from village and home so that the ancestral spirits could feast unharassed. At peace, they could act like gods, not ghosts, their descent lines providing them with paper suits and dresses, spirit money, paper houses, paper automobiles, chicken, meat, and rice into eternity—essences delivered up in smoke and flames, steam and incense rising from each rice bowl. In an attempt to make the Chinese care for people outside the family, Chairman Mao encourages us now to give our paper replicas to the spirits of outstanding soldiers and workers, no matter whose ancestors they may be. My aunt remains forever hungry. Goods are not distributed evenly among the dead.

My aunt haunts me—her ghost drawn to me because now, after fifty years of neglect, I alone devote pages of paper to her, though not origamied into houses and clothes. I do not think she always means me well. I am telling on her, and she was a spite suicide, drowning herself in the drinking water. The Chinese are always very frightened of the drowned one, whose weeping ghost, wet hair hanging and skin bloated, waits silently by the water to pull down a substitute.

FOR ANALYSIS

1. In what sense did the narrator participate in her aunt's punishment?

2. Given the Chinese belief system, what is the No Name Woman's most significant punishment?

3. What evidence in the essay supports the view that the Chinese villagers favored males over females?

4. Why does the woman enter the pigsty to give birth?

5. What factors intensify the ferocity of the villagers' attack on the house?

6. Discuss the significance of the assertion in paragraph 49: "I alone devote pages of paper to her, though not origamied into houses and clothes."

7. Reread the essay, noting scenes the speaker seems to invent. What reasons might Kingston have for imagining the events that she could not have known?

MAKING CONNECTIONS

Some authors, such as Chopin in "The Storm" (p. 805), seem to treat sexual infidelity casually; others, such as Shakespeare in *Othello* (p. 958), treat it murderously. Give reasons to support each view.

WRITING TOPIC

Describe the No Name Woman's sin. Was it a sin against the absent husband of her hastily arranged marriage, against her extended family, against the village, against the gods?

STUART LISHAN   (B. 1955)

WINTER COUNT, 1964   2005

When Sherri Luna rammed Jerry Kruger's crew-cut head into the hand-ball court wall at Kester Avenue Elementary School on February 15, 1964, I knew she loved him, a swirling, butch, embarrassed sort of love that denied itself even as it was expressed. She loved him the way a nine-year-old, beefy-ankled, white-socked, scuffed-up saddle-shoed, Valley girl chicana loves a drawly, red-necked, red-haired, red-freckled, cracker son of a Pentecostal preacher from Oklahoma who wouldn't let his kid slow dance in Miss Arlington's A4 class, not because Miss Arlington was a wafer-thin woman with a two-foot-high beehive hairdo that made her look like an alien from some planet of white-porcelain doll people with blood-red lips and fingernails long and sharp as steak knives, but because Jerry's preacher pa didn't believe nine-year-olds, much less anybody, should be cradling one another's bodies in their arms and breathing softly on their necks as they swayed to music. Nosiree, Sherri Luna didn't love Jerry that way, the slow dance, fandango way, where holding some-one close is as sweet and natural as lying on your back in the backyard watch-ing the clouds and letting the sunlight kiss your cheek, but she loved him just the same. I knew it when I first saw her rub her body up against Jerry's blue jeans as she slugged him in the arm by the water fountain the first day he came to class that winter. Plus, she didn't want to slow dance, not because she didn't believe in it, but because she was constitutionally against any request that curled out of Miss Arlington's pouty lips.

"Just do it, honey."

"No."

"Please?"

"No, I said!"

So, "Ka-Chunk," went Jerry's head, cradled in Sherri's gentle headlock when Miss Arlington was putting a scratchy waltz on the mono record player that Ricky LaConte had lugged out onto the playground after lunch. Ricky, a fat kid who liked to have us punch his stomach in the boys' room until his bubbly flesh was filled with blotches like lesions, liked to do such favors, his arm shooting up like a rocket ship out of its socket every time Miss Arlington asked with those pouty lips just who would like to do this or that for her. And that's a sort of love, too, don't get me wrong, only it wasn't Sherri Luna's sort of love. She needed to touch the someone she loved, even if she didn't understand what the yearning in her heart was asking her nine-year-old body to do.

So, "Ka-Chunk."

I was breathing my face into Melinda Coates's blond ringlets, getting hairs twisted in my glasses' hinges and imagining myself in heaven and then feeling embarrassed for even thinking such a slack-brained thing as that when I heard it.

"Ka-Chunk," echoing into the mauve plastic handball court wall that rose out of the blacktop playground surrounded by bungalows, chain-link fence, and honeysuckle rustling in the winter breeze like our breaths on one another's necks as we danced.

"Ka-Chunk."

"That was fun," Jerry laughed. "Do it again," with again drawled out so long, so slow, that it slobbered and dribbled out of his mouth into a dopey-grinned, three-syllabled, shrieky a-gaaa-in. 10

"Do it a-gaaa-in."

Poor Ricky. He was right next to me, swaying sort of sad-like, out of time and out of step with Louise Dolan. He wanted to be in that headlock, too, I guess. Maybe he thought that the bumps on his forehead would go with the blotches on his stomach. I don't know, but I know this. Sherri would have none of him. Ricky wasn't Jerry in any way, shape, or form, and Sherri Luna loved Jerry. That was that, end of the story. We were dancing that Strauss waltz you hear in *2001* when the ship docks with the space station, and I swear I saw her gently bend over as pretty as you please and nibble out a tongue-licked hickey on that sunburnt, freckly red neck of his when she thought no one was looking. We stared and stared. Not even the creamy touch of Melinda Coates could keep me from it. No one in Miss Arlington's A4 class in 1964 had ever seen such a thing.

And then she counted to three. And then she did it again.

And then she did it again. And I swear she didn't miss a beat, not a one, not a single one. 15

FOR ANALYSIS

1. Why does Sherri Luna bang Jerry's head against the ground? Why does he ask her to do it again?

2. Why does Ricky let people punch him in the stomach? What about the "blotches" left by the punches parallels the hickey Sherri leaves on Jerry's neck?

3. A *winter count* is a story or oral history used by certain Native American tribes to mark individual years in tribal history by retelling an event from that year that is memorable or significant. Why do you think the incident retold in this essay is significant enough to mark its year?

MAKING CONNECTIONS

1. Compare the juxtaposition of violence and attraction in "Winter Count, 1964" to the juxtaposition of sex and parental love in Kinnell's "After Making Love We Hear Footsteps" (p. 953). What do these perhaps unexpected combinations have in common? How do they work in each piece of writing?

2. The children (including the **narrator**) "stared and stared" at Sherri Luna and Jerry Kruger's love dance. Compare this moment to the children staring in Bambara's "The Lesson"(p. 110). What are the children in each seeing? What does their seeing mean? What are they learning about?

WRITING TOPICS

1. In what other ways do people (of all ages) manifest the combination of desire for and fear of physical intimacy? Reflect on ways in which you and people you have observed or read about deal (or don't deal) with this tension.

2. "'Ka-chunk,' went Jerry's head" (para. 6). Write a short essay in which you relate an incident or a moment, using the vivid transcription of sound.

GRACE TALUSAN (B. 1972)

MY FATHER'S NOOSE 2007

When my father was a boy, his mother hung him.

Enter Tondo, a Manila slum, and stand in the kitchen of his childhood home. Look up. The crusty knot is still there, tied around the light fixture.

I imagine my father, Totoy, at ten. He hasn't graduated yet to long pants and shoes; his shorts and T-shirt are faded and soft from the wear of three older brothers.

Totoy has done something to make his mother angrier than she's ever been. And now, Totoy balances on a stack of vegetable crates, his neck connected to the ceiling. He's wearing one rubber slipper, and after slapping him on the ears, his mother has tucked the other slipper under the bowtie of her apron. If Totoy becomes dizzy and loses balance, or if Inang kicks the crates away, he might save himself by curling his fingers around the rope and pulling against the noose as if it were the mouth on a drawstring bag.

But his mother plants his palms to his hips and she looks up at him. She 5 doesn't say a word, but Totoy hears, "Don't try to save yourself. Don't you dare."

He moves only his eyes and from this height, he notices his mother is balding. Her gray hair is loosely bunned and there are triangles of white flesh between the comb tracks. Her body is thick and intimidating, fleshy roll layered onto fat, souvenirs from eleven pregnancies. Totoy is number seven.

When she's angry, she makes noise and breaks things and stares until you look away. One by one, Totoy's sibling return from school and work, take a step into the kitchen, and right back out without a word.

With a pestle, she pounds garlic in the mortar bowl. She raises the butcher knife to her shoulder and chops heads from fish. She'll fry the bodies for dinner and save the heads and tails for soup the next day.

What does Totoy think as he stands there watching his mother prepare dinner? Does he believe he will taste that dinner? Perhaps his mother will remove the crates and watch him suffocate and kick until the knot is as tight as it will go; allow his siblings to play tetherball with his body; or keep him tied there, hanging from the kitchen.

His siblings are hiding, staying far away from the kitchen. Even if his father 10 could be found—perhaps he is playing pool in a neighborhood bar or perhaps he is earning money by taking a passenger from the market to their home on the sidecar of his tricycle—Totoy's father wouldn't save him. Mother knows best, and she tells him, "I'm doing this because you're my son. You need to learn right from wrong."

Totoy doesn't know this yet: he will survive. Fifteen years later, he will have me, a daughter. But he will never forgive his mother, and half a century later, he won't attend her funeral. Totoy will try his best not to abuse his children. But he's his mother's son. He will.

FOR ANALYSIS

1. What circumstances of Totoy's mother's life help to explain (if not justify) her actions? Do you judge her less harshly because of what you know about her life?

2. Why does Totoy's mother say she does this to him? Does it work? If so, how? If not, why not?

3. Part of the power of this brief essay comes from the way it ends. How does the ending extend the meaning of the event described?

MAKING CONNECTIONS

1. Compare "My Father's Noose" to one or more of the poems in "Connecting Poems: Remembering Fathers." How do the two (or three) works address the ways in which love expresses itself? How do they show how love can look similar to hate?

2. Though about quite different situations, Talusan's essay and Hayden's poem "Winter Sundays" (p. 944) both recognize the hard work parents do to care for their children, the love that motivates that work, and the toll that work sometimes takes on those who do it. How do the selections differ? What do the children in each poem learn from their experiences?

WRITING TOPICS

1. How would Totoy's mother justify her actions? Do you think she could put together a convincing argument for the necessity of her actions? What might she include in such an argument?

2. Write a brief arresting essay (or story) in which you use some of Talusan's techniques (such as a shocking opening or an ending with a twist).

Love and hate are two of the most powerful emotions people feel and, as a result, are two of the most common literary subjects. Those who take the human experience as their subject in ways other than literary—for example, scientists and social scientists—reach different conclusions about the nature, causes, effects, and interconnections of love and hate. As you tackle these two essays, read not only to understand their sometimes complicated arguments but also to think about how their approaches demystify their subjects.

HELEN FISHER (B. 1945)

DUMPED! 2004

Emptiness, hopelessness, fear, fury: almost everyone endures the agony of romantic rejection at some point in their lives. Why do we suffer so? Sorrow and anger are metabolically expensive and time consuming. Why didn't humanity evolve a way to shrug off romantic loss and easily renew the quest to find a suitable reproductive partner?

I have been studying romantic love for ten years or so and have come to see it as an evolutionary adaptation. The ability to fall in love evolved because those who focused their courtship attention on a preferred partner saved time and energy and improved their chances of survival and reproduction.

Unfortunately, the same applies to love's darker side. We humans are soft wired to suffer terribly when we are rejected by someone we adore—for good evolutionary reasons.

Back in 1996 I decided to use a technique called functional MRI to study the brains of men and women who had just fallen madly in love. I and several collaborators, including neuroscientist Lucy Brown of the Albert Einstein College of Medicine in New York and psychologist Arthur Aron of the State University of New York at Stony Brook, asked our subjects, a group of seven men and ten women, to look at a photograph of their beloved projected on a screen just outside the brain scanner. We also showed each participant an emotionally neutral picture—a photograph of an acquaintance for whom they had no positive or negative feelings. In between looking at these photos, we asked each to perform a "distraction task" to wash the mind clean of all emotion.

The resulting scans told us many things about the brain in love. . . . Most significantly, when subjects were looking at their sweetheart, their brain showed increased activity in two regions: the right ventral tegmental area (VTA) in the midbrain, and parts of the caudate nucleus, a large c-shaped region near the centre. The VTA is rich in cells that produce and distribute the powerful stimulant dopamine to many areas of the brain, including the caudate nucleus. It is part of the brain's network that controls general arousal, focused attention, and motivation to acquire rewards. The regions of the caudate nucleus that became active are rich in dopamine receptors and are also associated with attention and motivation to acquire rewards.

The fact that intense, early stage romantic passion is associated with areas rich in dopamine suggested to us that romantic love is not, in fact, an emotion but primarily a motivational state designed to make us pursue a preferred partner. Indeed, romantic love appears to be a drive as powerful as hunger. No wonder people around the world live—and die—for love.

But we weren't interested in just the lovey dovey side of romance. We wanted to understand every aspect. So in 2001 we began scanning the brains of people who were suffering the trauma of a recent rejection in love.

The study is till in progress, but we suspect we will find continued activity in the VTA and associated parts of the caudate nucleus, largely because lovers keep loving long after they have been spurned. I think we will find much more than that, however. Being rejected in love is among the most painful experiences a human being can endure, so many other brain regions may be involved as well.

Even before the results come in, there is a lot we can say about the biology of rejection which suggests that it is an evolved response with specific functions. Psychiatrists have long divided romantic rejection into two phases: "protest" and "resignation/despair." During the protest phase, deserted lovers become obsessed with winning back the object of their affections. They agonise over what went wrong and how to rekindle the flame. They make dramatic, often humiliating, appearances at their lover's home or workplace, then storm out, only to return to berate or plead anew. They phone, e-mail, and write letters. They revisit mutual haunts and mutual friends. And alas, as the adversity intensifies, so does the romantic passion. This phenomenon is so common in the psychological literature (and in life) that they coined a term for it—frustration attraction. When romantic love is thwarted, the lover just loves harder.

What brain systems might underlie these odd behaviours? Psychiatrists 10 Thomas Lewis, Fari Amini, and Richard Lannon, all of the University of California, San Francisco, have argued that protest is a basic mammalian response to the rupturing of any social tie. They believe it is associated with dopamine, as well as with the closely related neurotransmitter norepinephrine. Elevated levels of both these chemicals lead to heightened alertness and stimulate the forlorn animal to call for help and search for its abandoner—generally its mother.

The rising level of dopamine may help explain the biology of frustration attraction. Since our research suggests that the dopamine system is activated during early stage romantic love, one would think that as dopamine activity increased during protest the rejected lover would feel even greater passion. And another brain mechanism kicks in during the protest phase that could add to this frustration attraction—the stress system. In the short term, stress triggers the production of dopamine and norepinephrine and suppresses serotonin activity, that heady combination of neurotransmitters that I maintain in my book, *Why We Love*, is associated with romantic love.

But frustration attraction may be due to other brain activities as well. Neuroscientist Wolfram Schultz at the University of Fribourg in Switzerland reported in 2000 that when an expected reward, such as love, is delayed, "reward-expecting" neurons prolong their activities.... These returns do not make or distribute dopamine, but they are central components of the brain's reward system, the system associated with focused attention and motivation—the very behaviours that characterise romantic love.

What irony! As the beloved slips away, the brain networks and chemicals that most likely create the potent feelings of love increase.

The protest phase of rejection may also trigger activity in the brain's panic system. Neuroscientist Jaak Panksepp of Bowling Green State University in Ohio believes that this brain network generates the well-known "separation anxiety" response in infant mammals abandoned by their mother. When their mother leaves, infants become troubled. They express their alarm with a pounding heart, sucking gestures, and distress calls.

Yet another brain system often becomes active as one protests against the 15 departure of a lover: anger. Even when the departing lover severs the relationship with honesty and compassion, and honours social and parental obligations, many rejected lovers swing violently from heartbreak to fury. Psychologist Reid Meloy of the University of California, San Diego, calls this reaction "abandonment rage." I use a different term: "love hatred." Whatever you call it, it's a curious reaction. Hate and rage don't generally entice a lover to return. Why does love turn to hate?

At first I assumed that hate was the opposite of love. But it isn't. The opposite of love is indifference. Moreover, it occurred to me that love and anger might be linked in the brain, and indeed they are. The basic rage network is closely connected to centres in the prefrontal cortex that anticipate rewards, including the reward of winning a beloved. In fact, experiments in animals have shown how intimately these reward and rage circuits are intertwined. Stimulate a cat's reward circuits and it feels intense pleasure. Withdraw the stimulation and it bites. This common response to unfulfilled expectations is known as the "frustration aggression hypothesis."

So romantic love and love hatred are probably well connected in the brain. And when the drive to love is thwarted, the brain turns passion into fury.

Why did our ancestors evolve brain links that enable us to hate the one we cherish? Rage is not good for your health: it elevates blood pressure, places stress on the heart, and suppresses the immune system. So love hatred must have evolved to solve some crucial reproductive problems. Among these, I now believe that it developed to enable jilted lovers to extricate themselves from dead-end love affairs and start again.

Abandonment rage also motivates people to flight for the welfare of their offspring. This certainly occurs in divorce proceedings: men and women who are otherwise well adjusted turn vicious to get the best deal for their children.

In the book *Why We Hate . . .*, science writer Rush Dozier tells of a judge who regularly presides over child custody cases and trials of violent criminals, and reports that he is much more worried about his personal safety during the custody cases. He and other judges have even installed panic buttons in their chambers in case arguing spouses become violent.

Sadly, abandonment rage does not necessarily extinguish love. In a study of 20 124 dating couples, psychologists Bruce Ellis of the University of Canterbury in New Zealand and Neil Malamuth of the University of California, Los Angeles, found that romantic love and feelings of anger are independent, and can operate simultaneously. Hence, you can be terribly angry but still be very much in love.

Eventually, however, the jilted lover gives up. Then he or she must deal with new forms of torture: resignation and despair. Drugged by the potent liquor of sorrow, they cry, lie in bed, stare into space, drink too much, or hole up and watch TV. Feelings of protest and anger or the desire for reconciliation sometimes resurface, but mostly they just feel deep melancholy. In 1991, sociologists at the University of California, Los Angeles, assessed 114 people who had been rejected by a sweetheart within the previous eight weeks. More than 40 percent of them were clinically depressed. Of these, 12 percent were suffering moderate to severe depression. Some people even kill themselves, and some die of a broken heart. Psychiatrist Norman Rosenthal of Georgetown University in Washington, D.C., has reported that broken-hearted lovers can expire from heart attacks or strokes caused by their depression.

Resignation and despair are well documented in other mammalian species. When infant mammals are abandoned by their mother, first they protest and panic. Later they slump into what psychologistis call the "despair response."

Despair has been associated with several different networks in the brain. One is the reward system. As the abandoned partner realises that the expected reward will never come, the dopamine making cells in the midbrain scale down their activity. And diminishing levels of dopamine produce lethargy, despondency, and depression. The stress system also plays a part. As the stress of abandonment wears on, it suppresses the activity of dopamine and other potent neurotransmitters, contributing to feelings of depression.

Like abandonment rage, the despair response seems counterproductive. Why waste time and energy moping? Some scientists now believe that depression evolved millions of years ago as a coping mechanism. Theories on this subject abound. One I particularly like has been proposed by anthropologist Edward Hagen of Humboldt University in Berlin, biologists Paul Watson and Paul Andrews of the University of New Mexico in Albuquerque, and psychiatrist Andy Thomson of the University of Virginia in Charlottesville. They argue that the high metabolic and social cost of depression is actually its benefit: depression is an honest, believable signal to others that something is desperately wrong. It is a cry for help which compels stressed people to request support in times of intense need.

Imagine a young woman living in a Palaeolithic tribe whose mate openly 25 mated with another woman. First she protested, grew angry, and tried to persuade her partner to give up his lover. She also appealed to her friends and kin for help. Unable to influence her mate or relatives with words or tantrums, however, she became depressed. Eventually her despondency motivated her family to drive out her unfaithful partner and console her until she could recover her vitality, find a new mate, and start contributing food and childcare again.

Depression is evolutionarily advantageous for another reason: It gives you insight. Depressed people suffer what psychologist Jeffrey Zeig of the Milton H. Erickson Foundation in Phoenix, Arizona, calls a "failure of denial," allowing them to make honest assessments of themselves and others. Severe depression can push a person to face unpalatable truths and make difficult decisions that ultimately promote their survival and reproductive success.

Not everyone suffers to the same degree, of course. Still, we human beings are intricately wired to suffer when we have been rejected by a loved one, and for good evolutionary reasons. I believe romantic love is one of three primary mating drives. The sex drive evolved to enable our ancestors to seek intercourse with any remotely appropriate individual. Romantic love developed to enable our forebears to focus their attention on preferred partners, thereby conserving precious mating time and energy. And long-term attachment evolved to motivate mates to rear their babies as a team. So falling in love is one of the most important (and powerful) things we do: it profoundly affects our social and genetic future.

As result, we are built to suffer terribly when love fails—first to protest the departure and try to win the beloved back, and later to give up utterly, dust ourselves off, and redirect our energy to fall in love again. We are likely to find evidence of any combination of these myriad motivations and emotions as we examine the rejected brain in love.

FOR ANALYSIS

1. Fisher asks, "Why do we suffer so?" (para. 1). What is her answer?

2. Fisher also asks, "Why does love turn to hate?" (para. 15). What is her answer to this question?

3. Many of the connected phenomena Fisher addresses seem counterproductive or unhealthy; in each case she explains that there is some advantage gained. Why does she need to find a hidden advantage to ostensibly damaging behaviors?

WRITING TOPICS

1. Fisher draws on studies from a number of different fields. What fields does she borrow from? Does the breadth of her reading and references strengthen or weaken her argument?

2. Do you agree that romantic love is not an emotion but, as Fisher argues, "a motivational state" (para. 6)? Why or why not?

LAURA KIPNIS   (B. 1956)

AGAINST LOVE   2001

Love is, as we know, a mysterious and controlling force. It has vast power over our thoughts and life decisions. It demands our loyalty, and we, in turn, freely comply. Saying no to love isn't simply heresy; it is tragedy—the failure to achieve what is most essentially human. So deeply internalized is our obedience to this most capricious despot that artists create passionate odes to its cruelty, and audiences seem never to tire of the most deeply unoriginal mass spectacles devoted to rehearsing the litany of its torments, fixating their very beings on the narrowest glimmer of its fleeting satisfactions.

Yet despite near total compliance, a buzz of social nervousness attends the subject. If a society's lexicon of romantic pathologies reveals its particular anxieties, high on our own list would be diagnoses like "inability to settle down" or "immaturity," leveled at those who stray from the norms of domestic coupledom either by refusing entry in the first place or, once installed, pursuing various escape routes: excess independence, ambivalence, "straying," divorce. For the modern lover, "maturity" isn't a depressing signal of impending decrepitude but a sterling achievement, the sine qua non of a lover's qualifications to love and be loved.

This injunction to achieve maturity—synonymous in contemporary usage with thirty-year mortgages, spreading waistlines, and monogamy—obviously finds its raison d'être in modern love's central anxiety, that structuring social contradiction the size of the San Andreas Fault: namely, the expectation that romance and sexual attraction can last a lifetime of coupled togetherness despite much hard evidence to the contrary.

Ever optimistic, heady with love's utopianism, most of us eventually pledge ourselves to unions that will, if successful, far outlast the desire that impelled them into being. The prevailing cultural wisdom is that even if sexual desire tends to be a short-lived phenomenon, "mature love" will kick in to save the day when desire flags. The issue that remains unaddressed is whether cutting off other possibilities of romance and sexual attraction for the more muted pleasures of mature love isn't similar to voluntarily amputating a healthy limb: a lot of anesthesia is required and the phantom pain never entirely abates. But if it behooves a society to convince its citizenry that wanting change means personal failure or wanting to start over is shameful or simply wanting more satisfaction than what you have is an illicit thing, clearly grisly acts of self-mutilation will be required.

There hasn't always been quite such optimism about love's longevity. For the Greeks, inventors of democracy and a people not amenable to being pushed around by despots, love was a disordering and thus preferably brief experience. During the reign of courtly love, love was illicit and usually fatal. Passion meant suffering: the happy ending didn't yet exist in the cultural imagination. As far as togetherness as an eternal ideal, the twelfth-century advice manual

5

1085

"De Amore et Amor is Remedio" ("On Love and the Remedies of Love") warned that too many opportunities to see or chat with the beloved would certainly decrease love.

The innovation of happy love didn't even enter the vocabulary of romance until the seventeenth century. Before the eighteenth century—when the family was primarily an economic unit of production rather than a hothouse of Oedipal tensions—marriages were business arrangements between families; participants had little to say on the matter. Some historians consider romantic love a learned behavior that really only took off in the late eighteenth century along with the new fashion for reading novels, though even then affection between a husband and wife was considered to be in questionable taste.

Historians disagree, of course. Some tell the story of love as an eternal and unchanging essence; others, as a progress narrative over stifling social conventions. (Sometimes both stories are told at once; consistency isn't required.) But has modern love really set us free? Fond as we are of projecting our own emotional quandaries back through history, construing vivid costume dramas featuring medieval peasants or biblical courtesans sharing their feelings with the post-Freudian savvy of lifelong analysands, our amatory predecessors clearly didn't share all our particular aspirations about their romantic lives.

We, by contrast, feel like failures when love dies. We believe it could be otherwise. Since the cultural expectation is that a state of coupled permanence is achievable, uncoupling is experienced as crisis and inadequacy—even though such failures are more the norm than the exception.

As love has increasingly become the center of all emotional expression in the popular imagination, anxiety about obtaining it in sufficient quantities—and for sufficient duration—suffuses the population. Everyone knows that as the demands and expectations on couples escalated, so did divorce rates. And given the current divorce statistics (roughly 50 percent of all marriages end in divorce), all indications are that whomever you love today—your beacon of hope, the center of all your optimism—has a good chance of becoming your worst nightmare tomorrow. (Of course, that 50 percent are those who actually leave their unhappy marriages and not a particularly good indication of the happiness level or nightmare potential of those who remain.) Lawrence Stone, a historian of marriage, suggests—rather jocularly, you can't help thinking— that today's rising divorce rates are just a modern technique for achieving what was once taken care of far more efficiently by early mortality.

Love may or may not be a universal emotion, but clearly the social forms it 10 takes are infinitely malleable. It is our culture alone that has dedicated itself to allying the turbulence of romance and the rationality of the long-term couple, convinced that both love and sex are obtainable from one person over the course of decades, that desire will manage to sustain itself for thirty or forty or fifty years and that the supposed fate of social stability is tied to sustaining a fleeting experience beyond its given life span.

Of course, the parties involved must "work" at keeping passion alive (and we all know how much fun that is), the presumption being that even after living in close proximity to someone for a historically unprecedented length of time, you will still muster the requisite desire to achieve sexual congress on a regular basis. (Should passion fizzle out, just give up sex. Lack of desire for a mate is never an adequate rationale for "looking elsewhere.") And it is true, many couples do manage to perform enough psychic retooling to reshape the anarchy of desire to the confines of the marriage bed, plugging away at the task year after year (once a week, same time, same position) like diligent assembly-line workers, aided by the occasional fantasy or two to help get the old motor to turn over, or keep running, or complete the trip. And so we have the erotic life of a nation of workaholics: if sex seems like work, clearly you're not working hard enough at it.

But passion must not be allowed to die! The fear—or knowledge—that it does shapes us into particularly conflicted psychological beings, perpetually in search of prescriptions and professional interventions, regardless of cost or consequence. Which does have its economic upside, at least. Whole new sectors of the economy have been spawned, with massive social investment in new technologies from Viagra to couples' porn: capitalism's Lourdes for dying marriages.

There are assorted low-tech solutions to desire's dilemmas too. Take advice. In fact, take more and more advice. Between print, airwaves and the therapy industry, if there were any way to quantify the G.N.P. in romantic counsel, it would be a staggering number. Desperate to be cured of love's temporality, a love-struck populace has molded itself into an advanced race of advice receptacles, like some new form of miracle sponge that can instantly absorb many times its own body weight in wetness.

Inexplicably, however, a rebellious breakaway faction keeps trying to leap over the wall and emancipate themselves, not from love itself—unthinkable!—but from love's domestic confinements. The escape routes are well trodden—love affairs, midlife crises—though strewn with the left-behind luggage of those who encountered unforeseen obstacles along the way (panic, guilt, self-engineered exposures) and beat self-abashed retreats to their domestic gulags, even after pledging body and soul to newfound loves in the balmy utopias of nondomesticated romances. Will all the adulterers in the audience please stand up? You know who you are. Don't be embarrassed! Adulterers aren't just "playing around." These are our home-grown closet social theorists, because adultery is not just a referendum on the sustainability of monogamy; it is a veiled philosophical discussion about the social contract itself. The question on the table is this: "How much renunciation of desire does society demand of us, versus the degree of gratification it provides?" Clearly, the adulterer's answer, following a long line of venerable social critics, would be, "Too much."

But what exactly is it about the actual lived experience of modern domestic 15 love that would make flight such a compelling option for so many? Let us briefly examine those material daily life conditions.

Fundamentally, to achieve love and qualify for entry into that realm of salvation and transcendence known as the couple (the secular equivalent of entering a state of divine grace), you must be a lovable person. And what precisely does being lovable entail? According to the tenets of modern love, it requires an advanced working knowledge of the intricacies of mutuality.

Mutuality means recognizing that your partner has needs and being prepared to meet them. This presumes, of course, that the majority of those needs can and should be met by one person. (Question this, and you question the very foundations of the institution. So don't.) These needs of ours run deep, a tangled underground morass of ancient, gnarled roots, looking to ensnarl any hapless soul who might accidentally trod upon their outer radices.

Still, meeting those needs is the most effective way to become the object of another's desire, thus attaining intimacy, which is required to achieve the state known as psychological maturity. (Despite how closely it reproduces the affective conditions of our childhoods, since trading compliance for love is the earliest social lesson learned; we learn it in our cribs.)

You, in return, will have your own needs met by your partner in matters large and small. In practice, many of these matters turn out to be quite small. Frequently, it is the tensions and disagreements over the minutiae of daily living that stand between couples and their requisite intimacy. Taking out the garbage, tone of voice, a forgotten errand—these are the rocky shoals upon which intimacy so often founders.

Mutuality requires communication, since in order to be met, these needs 20 must be expressed. (No one's a mind reader, which is not to say that many of us don't expect this quality in a mate. Who wants to keep having to tell someone what you need?) What you need is for your mate to understand you—your desires, your contradictions, your unique sensitivities, what irks you. (In practice, that means what about your mate irks you.) You, in turn, must learn to understand the mate's needs. This means being willing to hear what about yourself irks your mate. Hearing is not a simple physiological act performed with the ears, as you will learn. You may think you know how to hear, but that doesn't mean that you know how to listen.

With two individuals required to coexist in enclosed spaces for extended periods of time, domesticity requires substantial quantities of compromise and adaptation simply to avoid mayhem. Yet with the post-Romantic ideal of unconstrained individuality informing our most fundamental ideas of the self, this can prove a perilous process. Both parties must be willing to jettison whatever aspects of individuality might prove irritating while being simultaneously allowed to retain enough individuality to feel their autonomy is not being sacrificed, even as it is being surgically excised.

Having mastered mutuality, you may now proceed to advanced intimacy. Advanced intimacy involves inviting your partner "in" to your most interior self. Whatever and wherever our "inside" is, the widespread—if somewhat metaphysical—belief in its existence (and the related belief that whatever is in there is dying to get out) has assumed a quasi-medical status. Leeches once served a similar purpose. Now we "express our feelings" in lieu of our fluids because everyone knows that those who don't are far more prone to cancer, ulcers, or various dire ailments.

With love as our culture's patent medicine, prescribed for every ill (now even touted as a necessary precondition for that other great American obsession, longevity), we willingly subject ourselves to any number of arcane procedures in its quest. "Opening up" is required for relationship health, so lovers fashion themselves after doctors wielding long probes to penetrate the tender regions. Try to think of yourself as one big orifice: now stop clenching and relax. If the procedure proves uncomfortable, it just shows you're not open enough. Psychotherapy may be required before sufficient dilation can be achieved: the world's most expensive lubricant.

Needless to say, this opening-up can leave you feeling quite vulnerable, lying there psychically spread-eagled and shivering on the examining table of your relationship. (A favored suspicion is that your partner, knowing exactly where your vulnerabilities are, deliberately kicks you there—one reason this opening-up business may not always feel as pleasant as advertised.) And as anyone who has spent much time in—or just in earshot of—a typical couple knows, the "expression of needs" is often the Trojan horse of intimate warfare, since expressing needs means, by definition, that one's partner has thus far failed to meet them.

In any long-term couple, this lexicon of needs becomes codified over time 25 into a highly evolved private language with its own rules. Let's call this couple grammar. Close observation reveals this as a language composed of one recurring unit of speech: the interdiction—highly nuanced, mutually imposed commands and strictures extending into the most minute areas of household affairs, social life, finances, speech, hygiene, allowable idiosyncrasies and so on. From bathroom to bedroom, car to kitchen, no aspect of coupled life is not subject to scrutiny, negotiation, and codes of conduct.

A sample from an inexhaustible list, culled from interviews with numerous members of couples of various ages, races, and sexual orientations.

You can't leave the house without saying where you're going. You can't not say what time you'll return. You can't go out when the other person feels like staying at home. You can't be a slob. You can't do less than 50 percent of the work around the house, even if the other person wants to do 100 percent more cleaning than you find necessary or even reasonable. You can't leave the dishes for later, load them the way that seems best to you, drink straight from the carton, or make crumbs. You can't leave the bathroom door open—it's offensive. You can't leave the bathroom door closed—your partner needs to get in. You can't not shave your underarms or legs. You can't gain weight. You can't watch soap operas. You can't watch infomercials or the pregame show or Martha Stewart. You can't eat what you want—goodbye Marshmallow Fluff; hello tofu meatballs. You can't spend too much time on the computer. And stay out of those chat rooms. You can't take risks, unless they are agreed-upon risks, which somewhat limits the concept of "risk." You can't make major purchases alone, or spend money on things the other person considers excesses. You can't blow money just because you're in a bad mood, and you can't be in a bad mood without being required to explain it. You can't begin a sentence with

"You always. . . . " You can't begin a sentence with "I never. . . . " You can't be simplistic, even when things are simple. You can't say what you really think of that outfit or color combination or cowboy hat. You can't be cynical about things the other person is sincere about. You can't drink without the other person counting your drinks. You can't have the wrong laugh. You can't bum cigarettes when you're out because it embarrasses your mate, even though you've explained the unspoken fraternity between smokers. You can't tailgate, honk, or listen to talk radio in the car. And so on. The specifics don't matter. What matters is that the operative word is *can't*.

Thus is love obtained.

Certainly, domesticity offers innumerable rewards: companionship, child-rearing convenience, reassuring predictability, and many other benefits too varied to list. But if love has power over us, domesticity is its enforcement wing: the iron dust mop in the velvet glove. The historian Michel Foucault has argued that modern power made its mark on the world by inventing new types of enclosures and institutions, places like factories, schools, barracks, prisons, and asylums, where individuals could be located, supervised, processed and subjected to inspection, order, and the clock. What current social institution is more enclosed than modern intimacy? What offers greater regulation of movement and time, or more precise surveillance of body and thought, to a greater number of individuals?

Of course, it is your choice—as if any of us could really choose not to desire 30 love or not to feel like hopeless losers should we fail at it. We moderns are beings yearning to be filled, yearning to be overtaken by love's mysterious power. We prostrate ourselves at love's portals, like social strivers waiting at the rope line outside some exclusive club hoping to gain admission and thereby confirm our essential worth. A life without love lacks an organizing narrative. A life without love seems so barren, and it might almost make you consider how empty the rest of the world is, as if love were vital plasma and everything else just tap water.

Exchanging obedience for love comes naturally—after all, we all were once children whose survival depended on the caprices of love. And there you have the template for future intimacies. If you love me, you'll do what I want—or need, or demand—and I'll love you in return. We all become household dictators, petty tyrants of the private sphere, who are, in our turn, dictated to.

And why has modern love developed in such a way as to maximize submission and minimize freedom, with so little argument about it? No doubt a citizenry schooled in renouncing desire instead of imagining there could be something more would be, in many respects, advantageous. After all, wanting more is the basis for utopian thinking, a path toward dangerous social demands, even toward imagining the possibilities for altogether different social arrangements. But if the most elegant forms of social control are those that came packaged in the guise of individual needs and satisfactions, so wedded to the individual psyche that any opposing impulse registers as the anxiety of unlovability, who needs a soldier on every corner? We are more than happy to police ourselves and those we love and call it living happily ever after. Perhaps a secular society needed another metaphysical entity to subjugate itself to after the death of God, and love was available for the job. But isn't it a little depressing to think we are somehow incapable of inventing forms of emotional life based on anything other than subjugation?

Steve: When we got together, we immediately merged our finances. Chuck owned a lovely home in Sausalito, and to my total astonishment, he made me joint tenant with him. We have always maintained one checking account, and all of our investments and everything are in both our names. That is about as formal as a gay couple can get. And I think, like a lot of couples, it has helped us get through rough spots in life. When your lives are totally intertwined, it makes more sense to resolve issues than to start cutting things apart most of the time.

"At this point, after thirty years, Chuck and I have very few rules in our relationship. We don't have a rule, for instance, that you can never go out on the other one. We realized from time to time the opportunity would present itself, and we also realized that if we turned down every opportunity that presented itself to us, eventually we might begin to resent each other. So we said, O.K., you can go ahead and do it, but never make a date that leaves me sitting at home while you are out with someone else. And we have never done that. From time to time we have had affairs with other people, or moments of sexual release, but they were recreational."

Chuck: "Jealousy probably breaks up more gay people than anything in the   35 world. I guess that goes for all couples. And jealousy is caused by a lack of trust. The one who lacks trust the most and is accusing the other of cheating, he's usually the one who is cheating.

Jealousy is based on guilt, an awful lot. But if you are absolutely convinced that the person you are with is totally open to you, that nothing is hidden, there won't be problems, ever. I know that Brad Pitt could not walk in this house and take Steve away from me. I am absolutely convinced of that.

I have total confidence in that. In my case, it is Michael York, but I go way back. And when you know that, sex is really an unimportant aspect, in terms of the deep emotions of your relationship. There is a movie called *Relax . . . It's Just Sex* —I love that title. It is only sex; it has no deep-seated meaning. It may seem to be a part of romance—certainly it jump-starts it—but as the years go by, it becomes more of a bonus to the relationship. There are no earthquakes that can happen as a result of sex."

FOR ANALYSIS

1. According to Kipnis, are long-term relationships about love or submission?

2. How much importance does this essay attach to sex? How much to domesticity?

3. How does Kipnis connect what she sees as the necessary renunciation of sexual desire to the existence of an orderly citizenry?

WRITING TOPICS

1. Do you agree with the assumption Kipnis works from—what she calls "love's temporality" (para. 13)? Reflect, from experience and/or observation, on the question of whether love always fades.

2. How would you describe the author's **tone**? Is it appropriate for the subject matter? How did you react to it? Do you think it strengthens or weakens her argument?

MAKING CONNECTIONS

1. Kipnis and Fisher approach the subject of romantic love from two very different angles. How would you characterize their angles of approach? How do these approaches lead to their very different conclusions?

2. For both of these writers, romantic love is not what is depicted in poetry and song—true, pure, selfless, an end in itself, the most important thing in human experience. Can you imagine a way in which love could be what one or the other of these writers say it is—something explained by other phenomena—and at the same time could also be an emotionally true thing? Are these views mutually exclusive?

3. Which of these arguments about romantic love do you find more convincing? Why?

FURTHER QUESTIONS
FOR THINKING AND WRITING

1. How do the works in this section support the contention that love and hate are closely related emotions? **Writing Topic:** Discuss the relationship between love and hate in Carver's "What We Talk About When We Talk About Love" and Shakespeare's *Othello*.

2. What images are characteristically associated with love in the prose and poetry of this section? What images are associated with hate? **Writing Topic:** Compare the image patterns in Shakespeare's Sonnets 18 and 130 or the image patterns in Donne's "A Valediction: Forbidding Mourning" and Marlowe's "The Passionate Shepherd to His Love."

3. The Greeks have three words that can be translated by the English word *love: eros, agape,* and *philia.* Describe the differences among these three types of love. **Writing Topic:** Find a story or poem that is representative of each type of love. In analyzing each work, discuss the extent to which the primary notion of love being addressed or celebrated is tempered by the other two types.

4. Blake's "A Poison Tree," Peacock's "Say You Love Me," Kizer's "Bitch," and Plath's "Daddy" all seem to describe aspects of hate. Distinguish among the different varieties of hatred expressed in each poem. **Writing Topic:** Compare and contrast the source of the speaker's hatred in two of these poems.

5. Which works in this section treat love and/or hate in a way that corresponds most closely with your own experience or conception of those emotional states? Which contradict your experience? **Writing Topic:** For each case, isolate the elements in the work that provoke your response, and discuss them in terms of their "truth" or "falsity."

The Presence of Death

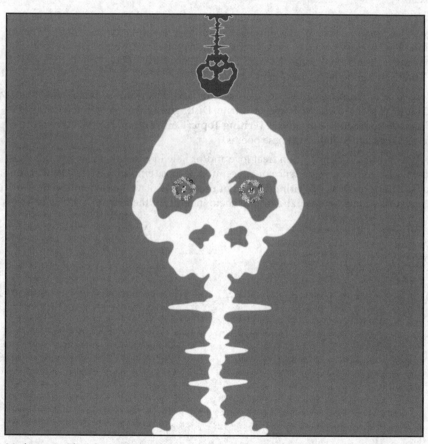

Mushroom Bomb Pink, 2001, by Takashi Murakami (Japanese, b. 1962). Offset lithograph 500 × 500 mm. Edition of 300. © 2001 Takashi Murakami/Kaikai Kiki Co., Ltd. All Rights Reserved.

The inevitability of death is not implied in the biblical story of creation; it required an act of disobedience before an angry God passed a sentence of hard labor and mortality on humankind: "In the sweat of your face you shall eat bread till you return to the ground, for out of it you were taken; you are dust and to dust you shall return." These words, written down some 2,800 years ago, preserve one ancient explanation for a persistently enigmatic condition of life. Though we cannot know what death is like, from earliest times men and women have attempted to characterize death, to cultivate beliefs about it. The mystery and certainty of death, in every age, make it an important theme for literary art.

Beliefs about the nature of death vary widely. The ancient Jews of the Pentateuch reveal no conception of immortality. Ancient Buddhist writings describe death as a mere translation from one painful life to another in an ongoing process of atonement that only the purest can avoid. The Christians came to conceive of a soul, separate from the body, which at the body's death is freed for a better (or worse) disembodied eternal life. More recently, attitudes about death reflect the great intellectual revolutions that affected all thought. For example, the Darwinian revolution replaced humans, the greatest glory of God's creation, with upright primates whose days are likely to be numbered by the flux between the fire and ice of geological history; and the Freudian revolution robbed men and women of their proudest certainty—the conviction that they possessed a dependable and controlling rational mind. In the context of Western tradition, these ideas serve to diminish us, to mock our self-importance. And, inevitably, these shifts lead us to alter our conception of death.

But despite the impact of intellectual history, death remains invested with a special awe—perhaps because it infallibly mediates between all human differences. For many, death, like birth and marriage, is the occasion for a solemn, reaffirming ritual. Although for Christians death holds promise of a better life hereafter, the belief in immortality does not eliminate sadness and regret. For those for whom there is no immortality, death is nonetheless a ceremonial affair, full of awe, for nothing human is so purely defined, so utterly important, as a life ended. Furthermore, both the religious and the secular see death in moral terms. For both, the killer is hateful. For both, there are some deaths that are deserved, some deaths that human weakness makes inevitable, some deaths that are outrageously unfair. For both, there are courageous deaths that exalt the community and cowardly deaths too embarrassing to recognize.

The speaker in Robert Frost's "Stopping by Woods on a Snowy Evening" gazes into the dark woods filling up with snow, momentarily drawn toward the peace it represents. But Frost's is a secular poem, and the speaker turns back to life. In much religious poetry—John Donne's sonnet "Death, Be Not Proud" is an outstanding example—death is celebrated as a release from a burdensome existence into the eternal happiness of the afterlife.

The view that establishes death as the great leveler, bringing citizens and emperors to the selfsame dust, is apparent in such poems as Percy Bysshe Shelley's "Ozymandias" and A. E. Housman's "To an Athlete Dying Young." This leveling view of death leads easily to the tradition wherein life itself is made absurd by the fact of death. You may remember that Macbeth finally declares that life is "a tale / Told by an idiot, full of sound and fury, / Signifying nothing." And the contemplation of suicide, which the pain and absurdity of life would seem to commend, provokes responses such as Edwin Arlington Robinson's ironic "Richard Cory." Some rage against death—Dylan Thomas in "Do Not Go Gentle into That Good Night"; others caution a quiet resignation—Frost in "After Apple-Picking" and Catherine Davis in "After a Time," her answer to Thomas. Much fine poetry on death is elegiac—it speaks the melancholy response of the living to the fact of death in poems such as A. E. Housman's "To an Athlete Dying Young" and Theodore Roethke's "Elegy for Jane."

In short, literary treatments of death display immense diversity. In Leo Tolstoy's "The Death of Iván Ilých," dying leads to a redemptive awareness. Leslie Marmon Silko's "The Man to Send Rain Clouds" explores sacrificial death as a means to control nature. In Dylan Thomas's "Do Not Go Gentle into That Good Night," death is an adversary, a thief that must be resisted. In Victor Hernandez Cruz's "Problems with Hurricanes" the comic lightens the weight of death. The inevitability of death and the way one confronts it paradoxically lend to life its meaning and its value.

QUESTIONS FOR THINKING AND WRITING

As you read the selections in this section, consider the following questions. You may want to write out your thoughts informally in a journal as a way of preparing to respond to the selections, or you may wish to make one of these questions the basis for a formal essay.

1. Has a close relative or friend of yours died? Was the person young or old, vigorous or feeble? How did you feel? How might the circumstances of death alter one's feelings toward death or toward the person who died?

2. Do you believe that some essential part of you will survive the death of your body? On what do you base the belief? How does it alter your feelings about the death of people close to you? How does it alter your own behavior?

3. Are there any circumstances that justify suicide? Explain. If you believe that some suicides are justifiable, would it also be justifiable to help someone end his or her life? Explain.

4. Are there any circumstances that justify killing someone? Explain.

5. Imagine as best you can the circumstances of your own death. Describe them.

FICTION

EDGAR ALLAN POE (1809–1849)

THE CASK OF AMONTILLADO 1846

The thousand injuries of Fortunato I had borne as I best could, but when he ventured upon insult, I vowed revenge. You, who so well know the nature of my soul, will not suppose, however, that I gave utterance to a threat. At *length* I would be avenged; this was a point definitely settled   but the very definitiveness with which it was resolved precluded the idea of risk. I must not only punish, but punish with impunity. A wrong is unredressed when retribution overtakes its redresser. It is equally unredressed when the avenger fails to make himself felt as such to him who has done the wrong.

It must be understood that neither by word nor deed had I given Fortunato cause to doubt my good will. I continued, as was my wont, to smile in his face, and he did not perceive that my smile *now* was at the thought of his immolation.

He had a weak point—this Fortunato—although in other regards he was a man to be respected and even feared. He prided himself on his connoisseurship in wine. Few Italians have the true virtuoso spirit. For the most part their enthusiasm is adopted to suit the time and opportunity to practise imposture upon the British and Austrian *millionnaires*. In painting and gemmary Fortunato, like his countrymen, was a quack, but in the matter of old wines he was sincere. In this respect I did not differ from him materially;—I was skillful in the Italian vintages myself, and bought largely whenever I could.

It was about dusk, one evening during the supreme madness of the carnival season, that I encountered my friend. He accosted me with excessive warmth, for he had been drinking much. The man wore motley. He had on a tight-fitting parti-striped dress, and his head was surmounted by the conical cap and bells. I was so pleased to see him, that I thought I should never have done wringing his hand.

I said to him—"My dear Fortunato, you are luckily met. How remarkably well you are looking to-day! But I have received a pipe[1] of what passes for Amontillado, and I have my doubts." 5

[1] Large wine cask.

"How?" said he, "Amontillado? A pipe? Impossible! And in the middle of the carnival!"

"I have my doubts," I replied; "and I was silly enough to pay the full Amontillado price without consulting you in the matter. You were not to be found, and I was fearful of losing a bargain."

"Amontillado!"

"I have my doubts."

"Amontillado!"   10

"And I must satisfy them."

"Amontillado!"

"As you are engaged, I am on my way to Luchesi. If any one has a critical turn, it is he. He will tell me—"

"Luchesi cannot tell Amontillado from Sherry."

"And yet some fools will have it that his taste is a match for your own."   15

"Come, let us go."

"Whither?"

"To your vaults."

"My friend, no; I will not impose upon your good nature. I perceive you have an engagement. Luchesi—"

"I have no engagement;—come."   20

"My friend, no. It is not the engagement, but the severe cold with which I perceive you are afflicted. The vaults are insufferably damp. They are encrusted with nitre."

"Let us go, nevertheless. The cold is merely nothing. Amontillado! You have been imposed upon; and as for Luchesi, he cannot distinguish Sherry from Amontillado."

Thus speaking, Fortunato possessed himself of my arm. Putting on a mask of black silk, and drawing a *roquelaure*[2] closely about my person, I suffered him to hurry me to my palazzo.

There were no attendants at home; they had absconded to make merry in honor of the time. I had told them that I should not return until the morning, and had given them explicit orders not to stir from the house. These orders were sufficient, I well knew, to insure their immediate disappearance, one and all, as soon as my back was turned.

I took from their sconces two flambeaux, and giving one to Fortunato,   25
bowed him through several suites of rooms to the archway that led into the vaults. I passed down a long and winding staircase, requesting him to be cautious as he followed. We came at length to the foot of the descent, and stood together on the damp ground of the catacombs of the Montresors.

The gait of my friend was unsteady, and the bells upon his cap jingled as he strode.

"The pipe," said he.

---

[2] Short cloak.

"It is farther on," said I; "but observe the white web-work which gleams from these cavern walls."

He turned towards me, and looked into my eyes with two filmy orbs that distilled the rheum of intoxication.

"Nitre?" he asked, at length. 30

"Nitre," I replied. "How long have you had that cough?"

"Ugh! ugh! ugh!—ugh! ugh! ugh!—ugh! ugh! ugh!—ugh! ugh! ugh!—ugh! ugh! ugh!"

My poor friend found it impossible to reply for many minutes.

"It is nothing," he said, at last.

"Come," I said, with decision, "we will go back; your health is precious. You 35 are rich, respected, admired, beloved; you are happy, as once I was. You are a man to be missed. For me it is no matter. We will go back; you will be ill, and I cannot be responsible. Besides, there is Luchesi—"

"Enough," he said; "the cough is a mere nothing: it will not kill me. I shall not die of a cough."

"True—true," I replied; "and, indeed, I had no intention of alarming you unnecessarily—but you should use all proper caution. A draught of this Medoc will defend us from the damps."

Here I knocked off the neck of a bottle which I drew from a long row of its fellows that lay upon the mould.

"Drink," I said, presenting him the wine.

He raised it to his lips with a leer. He paused and nodded to me familiarly, 40 while his bells jingled.

"I drink," he said, "to the buried that repose around us."

"And I to your long life."

He again took my arm, and we proceeded.

"These vaults," he said, "are extensive."

"The Montresors," I replied, "were a great and numerous family." 45

"I forget your arms."

"A huge human foot d'or, in a field azure; the foot crushes a serpent rampant whose fangs are imbedded in the heel."

"And the motto?"

"*Nemo me impune lacessit.*"[3]

"Good!" he said. 50

The wine sparkled in his eyes and the bells jingled. My own fancy grew warm with the Medoc. We had passed through walls of piled bones, with casks and puncheons intermingling, into the inmost recesses of the catacombs. I paused again, and this time I made bold to seize Fortunato by an arm above the elbow.

"The nitre!" I said; "see, it increases. It hangs like moss upon the vaults. We are below the river's bed. The drops of moisture trickle among the bones. Come, we will go back ere it is too late. Your cough—"

---

[3] No one provokes me with impunity (the motto of Scotland).

"It is nothing," he said; "let us go on. But first, another draught of the Medoc."

I broke and reached him a flagon of De Grâve. He emptied it at a breath. His eyes flashed with a fierce light. He laughed and threw the bottle upwards with a gesticulation I did not understand.

I looked at him in surprise. He repeated the movement—a grotesque one.   55

"You do not comprehend?" he said.

"Not I," I replied.

"Then you are not of the brotherhood."

"How?"

"You are not of the masons."[4]   60

"Yes, yes," I said; "yes, yes."

"You? Impossible! A mason?"

"A mason," I replied.

"A sign," he said.

"It is this," I answered, producing a trowel from beneath the folds of my   65
roquelaure.

"You jest," he exclaimed, recoiling a few paces. "But let us proceed to the Amontillado."

"Be it so," I said, replacing the tool beneath the cloak, and again offering him my arm. He leaned upon it heavily. We continued our route in search of the Amontillado. We passed through a range of low arches, descended, passed on, and descending again, arrived at a deep crypt, in which the foulness of the air caused our flambeaux rather to glow than flame.

At the most remote end of the crypt there appeared another less spacious. Its walls had been lined with human remains piled to the vault overhead, in the fashion of the great catacombs of Paris. Three sides of this interior crypt were still ornamented in this manner. From the fourth the bones had been thrown down, and lay promiscuously upon the earth, forming at one point a mound of some size. Within the wall thus exposed by the displacing of the bones, we perceived a still interior recess, in depth about four feet, in width three, in height six or seven. It seemed to have been constructed for no especial use within itself, but formed merely the interval between two of the colossal supports of the roof of the catacombs, and was backed by one of their circumscribing walls of solid granite.

It was in vain that Fortunato, uplifting his dull torch, endeavored to pry into the depths of the recess. Its termination the feeble light did not enable us to see.

"Proceed," I said; "herein is the Amontillado. As for Luchesi—"   70

"He is an ignoramus," interrupted my friend, as he stepped unsteadily forward, while I followed immediately at his heels. In an instant he had reached the extremity of the niche, and finding his progress arrested by the rock, stood stupidly bewildered. A moment more and I had fettered him to the granite.

[4] A member of the Freemasons, an international secretive mutual aid society.

In its surface were two iron staples, distant from each other about two feet, horizontally. From one of these depended a short chain, from the other a padlock. Throwing the links about his waist, it was but the work of a few seconds to secure it. He was too much astounded to resist. Withdrawing the key I stepped back from the recess.

"Pass your hand," I said, "over the wall; you cannot help feeling the nitre. Indeed it is *very* damp. Once more let me *implore* you to return. No? Then I must positively leave you. But I must first render you all the little attentions in my power."

"The Amontillado!" ejaculated my friend, not yet recovered from his astonishment.

"True," I replied; "the Amontillado."

As I said these words I busied myself among the pile of bones of which I 75 have before spoken. Throwing them aside, I soon uncovered a quantity of building-stone and mortar. With these materials and with the aid of my trowel, I began vigorously to wall up the entrance of the niche.

I had scarcely laid the first tier of the masonry when I discovered that the intoxication of Fortunato had in a great measure worn off. The earliest indication I had of this was a low moaning cry from the depth of the recess. It was *not* the cry of a drunken man. There was then a long and obstinate silence. I laid the second tier, and the third, and the fourth; and then I heard the furious vibrations of the chain. The noise lasted for several minutes, during which, that I might hearken to it with the more satisfaction, I ceased my labors and sat down upon the bones. When at last the clanking subsided, I resumed the trowel, and finished without interruption the fifth, the sixth, and the seventh tier. The wall was now nearly upon a level with my breast. I again paused, and holding the flambeaux over the masonwork, threw a few feeble rays upon the figure within.

A succession of loud and shrill screams, bursting suddenly from the throat of the chained form, seemed to thrust me violently back. For a brief moment I hesitated—I trembled. Unsheathing my rapier, I began to grope with it about the recess; but the thought of an instant reassured me. I placed my hand upon the solid fabric of the catacombs, and felt satisfied. I reapproached the wall. I replied to the yells of him who clamored. I re-echoed—I aided—I surpassed them in volume and in strength. I did this, and the clamorer grew still.

It was now midnight, and my task was drawing to a close. I had completed the eighth, the ninth, and the tenth tier. I had finished a portion of the last and the eleventh; there remained but a single stone to be fitted and plastered in. I struggled with its weight; I placed it partially in its destined position. But now there came from out the niche a low laugh that erected the hairs upon my head. It was succeeded by a sad voice, which I had difficulty in recognizing as that of the noble Fortunato. The voice said—

"Ha! ha! ha!—he! he! he!—a very good joke indeed—an excellent jest. We will have many a rich laugh about it at the palazzo—he! he! he!—over our wine—he! he! he!"

"The Amontillado!" I said.   80

"He! he! he!—he! he! he!—yes, the Amontillado. But is it not getting late? Will not they be awaiting us at the palazzo, the Lady Fortunato and the rest? Let us be gone."

"Yes," I said, "let us be gone."

"For the love of God, Montresor!"

"Yes," I said, "for the love of God!"

But to these words I hearkened in vain for a reply. I grew impatient. I called   85 aloud;

"Fortunato!"

No answer. I called again;

"Fortunato!"

No answer still, I thrust a torch through the remaining aperture and let it fall within. There came forth in return only a jingling of the bells. My heart grew sick—on account of the dampness of the catacombs. I hastened to make an end of my labor. I forced the last stone into its position; I plastered it up. Against the new masonry I reerected the old rampart of bones. For the half of a century no mortal has disturbed them. *In pace requiescat!*[5]

FOR ANALYSIS

1. We are not told how Fortunato insulted Montresor. Would the story be more effective if we knew? Explain.

2. Are there any clues that suggest when and to whom Montresor tells his tale? Explain.

3. How is Montresor able to lure Fortunato into the catacombs?

4. Describe the qualities that Montresor insists on as the characteristics of a successful vengeance.

5. Describe the **style** of this story, particularly the speech of the characters. What effect does the archaic flavor contribute to the tale?

MAKING CONNECTIONS

Compare this story with Jackson's "The Lottery" (p. 339), which also ends with an unexpected and horrible murder. What similarities do you find? What differences?

WRITING TOPICS

1. In an essay, imagine and describe the circumstances and the nature of Fortunato's insult.

2. Choose a short section of the story—say, three or four paragraphs—and carefully analyze the language line by line (particularly as it differs from ordinary colloquial English). How does the unusual language contribute to the story's effect?

---

[5] May he rest in peace.

THE DEATH OF IVÁN ILÝCH[1]   1886

Chapter I

During an interval in the Melvínski trial in the large building of the Law Courts the members and public prosecutor met in Iván Egórovich Shébek's private room, where the conversation turned on the celebrated Krasóvski case. Fëdor Vasílievich warmly maintained that it was not subject to their jurisdiction, Iván Egórovich maintained the contrary, while Peter Ivánovich, not having entered into the discussion at the start, took no part in it but looked through the *Gazette* which had just been handed in.

"Gentlemen," he said, "Iván Ilých has died!"

"You don't say so!"

"Here, read it yourself," replied Peter Ivánovich, handing Fëdor Vasílievich the paper still damp from the press. Surrounded by a black border were the words: "Praskóvya Fëdorovna Goloviná, with profound sorrow, informs relatives and friends of the demise of her beloved husband Iván Ilých Golovín, Member of the Court of Justice, which occurred on February the 4th of this year 1882. The funeral will take place on Friday at one o'clock in the afternoon."

Iván Ilých had been a colleague of the gentlemen present and was liked by   5 them all. He had been ill for some weeks with an illness said to be incurable. His post had been kept open for him, but there had been conjectures that in case of his death Alexéev might receive his appointment, and that either Vínnikov or Shtábel would succeed Alexéev. So on receiving the news of Iván Ilých's death the first thought of each of the gentlemen in that private room was of the changes and promotions it might occasion among themselves or their acquaintances.

"I shall be sure to get Shtábel's place or Vínnikov's," thought Fëdor Vasílievich. "I was promised that long ago, and the promotion means an extra eight hundred rubles a year for me besides the allowance."

"Now I must apply for my brother-in-law's transfer from Kalúga," thought Peter Ivánovich. "My wife will be very glad, and then she won't be able to say that I never do anything for her relations."

"I thought he would never leave his bed again," said Peter Ivánovich aloud. "It's very sad."

"But what really was the matter with him?"

"The doctors couldn't say—at least they could, but each of them said some-   10 thing different. When last I saw him I thought he was getting better."

[1] Translated by Aylmer Maude.

"And I haven't been to see him since the holidays. I always meant to go."

"Had he any property?"

"I think his wife had a little—but something quite trifling."

"We shall have to go to see her, but they live so terribly far away."

"Far away from you, you mean. Everything's far away from your place." 15

"You see, he never can forgive my living on the other side of the river," said Peter Ivánovich, smiling at Shébek. Then, still talking of the distances between different parts of the city, they returned to the Court.

Besides considerations as to the possible transfers and promotions likely to result from Iván Ilých's death, the mere fact of the death of a near acquaintance aroused, as usual, in all who heard of it the complacent feeling that, "it is he who is dead and not I."

Each one thought or felt, "Well, he's dead but I'm alive!" But the more intimate of Iván Ilých's acquaintances, his so-called friends, could not help thinking also that they would now have to fulfill the very tiresome demands of propriety by attending the funeral service and paying a visit of condolence to the widow.

Fëdor Vasílievich and Peter Ivánovich had been his nearest acquaintances. Peter Ivánovich had studied law with Iván Ilých and had considered himself to be under obligations to him.

Having told his wife at dinner-time of Iván Ilých's death, and of his conjec- 20 ture that it might be possible to get her brother transferred to their circuit, Peter Ivánovich sacrificed his usual nap, put on his evening clothes, and drove to Iván Ilých's house.

At the entrance stood a carriage and two cabs. Leaning against the wall in the hall downstairs near the cloak-stand was a coffin-lid covered with cloth of gold, ornamented with gold cord and tassels, that had been polished up with metal powder. Two ladies in black were taking off their fur cloaks. Peter Ivánovich recognized one of them as Iván Ilých's sister, but the other was a stranger to him. His colleague Schwartz was just coming downstairs, but on seeing Peter Ivánovich enter he stopped and winked at him, as if to say: "Iván Ilých has made a mess of things—not like you and me."

Schwartz's face with his Piccadilly whiskers, and his slim figure in evening dress, had as usual an air of elegant solemnity which contrasted with the playfulness of his character and had a special piquancy here, or so it seemed to Peter Ivánovich.

Peter Ivánovich allowed the ladies to precede him and slowly followed them upstairs. Schwartz did not come down but remained where he was, and Peter Ivánovich understood that he wanted to arrange where they should play bridge that evening. The ladies went upstairs to the widow's room, and Schwartz with seriously compressed lips but a playful look in his eyes, indicated by a twist of his eyebrows the room to the right where the body lay.

Peter Ivánovich, like everyone else on such occasions, entered feeling uncertain what he would have to do. All he knew was that at such times it is always safe to cross oneself. But he was not quite sure whether one should make obeisances while doing so. He therefore adopted a middle course. On entering the room he began crossing himself and made a slight movement resembling a bow. At the same time, as far as the motion of his head and arm allowed, he surveyed the room. Two young men—apparently nephews, one of whom was a high-school pupil—were leaving the room, crossing themselves as they did so. An old woman was standing motionless, and a lady with strangely arched eyebrows was saying something to her in a whisper. A vigorous, resolute Church Reader, in a frock-coat, was reading something in a loud voice with an expression that precluded any contradiction. The butler's assistant, Gerásim, stepping lightly in front of Peter Ivánovich, was strewing something on the floor. Noticing this, Peter Ivánovich was immediately aware of a faint odour of a decomposing body.

The last time he had called on Iván Ilých, Peter Ivánovich had seen Gerásim   25 in the study. Iván Ilých had been particularly fond of him and he was performing the duty of a sick nurse.

Peter Ivánovich continued to make the sign of the cross slightly inclining his head in an intermediate direction between the coffin, the Reader, and the icons on the table in a corner of the room. Afterwards, when it seemed to him that this movement of his arm in crossing himself had gone on too long, he stopped and began to look at the corpse.

The dead man lay, as dead men always lie, in a specially heavy way, his rigid limbs sunk in the soft cushions of the coffin, with the head forever bowed on the pillow. His yellow waxen brow with bald patches over his sunken temples was thrust up in the way peculiar to the dead, the protruding nose seeming to press on the upper lip. He was much changed and had grown even thinner since Peter Ivánovich had last seen him, but, as is always the case with the dead, his face was handsomer and above all more dignified than when he was alive. The expression on the face said that what was necessary had been accomplished, and accomplished rightly. Besides this there was in that expression a reproach and a warning to the living. This warning seemed to Peter Ivánovich out of place, or at least not applicable to him. He felt a certain discomfort and so he hurriedly crossed himself once more and turned and went out of the door—too hurriedly and too regardless of propriety, as he himself was aware.

Schwartz was waiting for him in the adjoining room with legs spread wide apart and both hands toying with his top-hat behind his back. The mere sight of that playful, well-groomed, and elegant figure refreshed Peter Ivánovich. He felt that Schwartz was above all these happenings and would not surrender to any depressing influences. His very look said that this incident of a church service for Iván Ilých could not be a sufficient reason for infringing the order of the session—in other words, that it would certainly not prevent his unwrapping a new pack of cards and shuffling them that evening while a footman placed four fresh candles on the table: in fact, there was no reason for supposing that this incident would hinder their spending the evening agreeably. Indeed he said this in a whisper as Peter Ivánovich passed him, proposing that they should meet for a game at Fëdor Vasílievich's. But apparently Peter Ivánovich was not destined to play bridge that evening. Praskóvya Fëdorovna (a short, fat woman who despite all efforts to the contrary had continued to broaden steadily from her shoulders downwards and who had the same extraordinarily arched eyebrows as the lady who had been standing by the coffin), dressed all in black, her head covered with lace, came out of her own room with some other ladies, conducted them to the room where the dead body lay, and said: "The service will begin immediately. Please go in."

Schwartz, making an indefinite bow, stood still, evidently neither accepting nor declining this invitation. Praskóvya Fëdorovna recognizing Peter Ivánovich, sighed, went close up to him, took his hand, and said: "I know you were a true friend to Iván Ilých . . ." and looked at him awaiting some suitable response. And Peter Ivánovich knew that, just as it had been the right thing to cross himself in that room, so what he had to do here was to press her hand, sigh, and say, "Believe me . . ." So he did all this and as he did it felt that the desired result had been achieved: that both he and she were touched.

"Come with me. I want to speak to you before it begins," said the widow. 30 "Give me your arm."

Peter Ivánovich gave her his arm and they went to the inner rooms, passing Schwartz who winked at Peter Ivánovich compassionately.

"That does for our bridge! Don't object if we find another player. Perhaps you can cut in when you do escape," said his playful look.

Peter Ivánovich sighed still more deeply and despondently, and Praskóvya Fëdorovna pressed his arm gratefully. When they reached the drawing-room, upholstered in pink cretonne and lighted by a dim lamp, they sat down at the table—she on a sofa and Peter Ivánovich on a low pouffe, the springs of which yielded spasmodically under his weight. Praskóvya Fëdorovna had been on the point of warning him to take another seat, but felt that such a warning was out of keeping with her present condition and so changed her mind. As he sat down on the pouffe Peter Ivánovich recalled how Iván Ilých had arranged this room and had consulted him regarding this pink cretonne with green leaves. The whole room was full of furniture and knick-knacks, and on her way to the sofa the lace of the widow's black shawl caught on the carved edge of the table. Peter Ivánovich rose to detach it, and the springs of the pouffe, relieved of his weight, rose also and gave him a push. The widow began detaching her shawl herself, and Peter Ivánovich again sat down, suppressing the rebellious springs of the pouffe under him. But the widow had not quite freed herself and Peter Ivánovich got up again, and again the pouffe rebelled and even creaked. When this was all over she took out a clean cambric handkerchief and began to weep. The episode with the shawl and the struggle with the pouffe had cooled Peter Ivánovich's emotions and he sat there with a sullen look on his face. This awkward situation was interrupted by Sokolóv, Iván Ilých's butler, who came to report that the plot in the cemetery that Praskóvya Fëdorovna had chosen would cost two hundred rubles. She stopped weeping and, looking at Peter Ivánovich with the air of a victim, remarked in French that it was very hard for her. Peter Ivánovich made a silent gesture signifying his full conviction that it must indeed be so.

"Please smoke," she said in a magnanimous yet crushed voice, and turned to discuss with Sokolóv the price of the plot for the grave.

Peter Ivánovich while lighting his cigarette heard her inquiring very circum- 35 stantially into the price of different plots in the cemetery and finally decide which she would take. When that was done she gave instructions about engaging the choir. Sokolóv then left the room.

"I look after everything myself," she told Peter Ivánovich, shifting the albums that lay on the table; and noticing that the table was endangered by his cigarette-ash, she immediately passed him an ashtray, saying as she did so: "I consider it an affectation to say that my grief prevents my attending to practical affairs. On the contrary, if anything can—I won't say console me, but—distract me, it is seeing to everything concerning him." She again took out her handkerchief as if preparing to cry, but suddenly, as if mastering her feeling, she shook herself and began to speak calmly. "But there is something I want to talk to you about."

Peter Ivánovich bowed, keeping control of the springs of the pouffe, which immediately began quivering under him.

"He suffered terribly the last few days."

"Did he?" said Peter Ivánovich.

"Oh, terribly! He screamed unceasingly, not for minutes but for hours. For the 40 last three days he screamed incessantly. It was unendurable. I cannot understand how I bore it; you could hear him three rooms off. Oh, what I have suffered!"

"Is it possible that he was conscious all that time?" asked Peter Ivánovich.

"Yes," she whispered. "To the last moment. He took leave of us a quarter of an hour before he died, and asked us to take Volódya away."

The thought of the sufferings of this man he had known so intimately, first as a merry little boy, then as a school-mate, and later as a grown-up colleague, suddenly struck Peter Ivánovich with horror, despite an unpleasant consciousness of his own and this woman's dissimulation. He again saw that brow, and that nose pressing down on the lip, and felt afraid for himself.

"Three days of frightful suffering and then death! Why, that might suddenly, at any time, happen to me," he thought, and for a moment felt terrified. But—he did not himself know how—the customary reflection at once occurred to him that this had happened to Iván Ilých and not to him, and that it should not and could not happen to him, and that to think that it could would be yielding to depression which he ought not to do, as Schwartz's expression plainly showed. After which reflection Peter Ivánovich felt reassured, and began to ask with interest about the details of Iván Ilých's death, as though death was an accident natural to Iván Ilých but certainly not to himself.

After many details of the really dreadful physical sufferings Iván Ilých 45 had endured (which details he learnt only from the effect those sufferings had produced on Praskóvya Fëdorovna's nerves) the widow apparently found it necessary to get to business.

"Oh, Peter Ivánovich, how hard it is! How terribly, terribly hard!" and she again began to weep.

Peter Ivánovich sighed and waited for her to finish blowing her nose. When she had done so he said, "Believe me . . ." and she again began talking and brought out what was evidently her chief concern with him—namely, to question him as to how she could obtain a grant of money from the government on the occasion of her husband's death. She made it appear that she was asking Peter Ivánovich's advice about her pension, but he soon saw that she already knew about that to the minutest detail, more even than he did himself. She knew how much could be got out of the government in consequence of her husband's death, but wanted to find out whether she could not possibly extract something more. Peter Ivánovich tried to think of some means of doing so, but after reflecting for a while and, out of propriety, condemning the government for its niggardliness, he said he thought that nothing more could be got. Then she sighed and evidently began to devise means of getting rid of her visitor. Noticing this, he put out his cigarette, rose, pressed her hand, and went out into the anteroom.

In the dining-room where the clock stood that Iván Ilých had liked so much and had bought at an antique shop, Peter Ivánovich met a priest and a few acquaintances who had come to attend the service, and he recognized Iván Ilých's daughter, a handsome young woman. She was in black and her slim figure appeared slimmer than ever. She had a gloomy, determined, almost angry expression, and bowed to Peter Ivánovich as though he were in some way to blame. Behind her, with the same offended look, stood a wealthy young man, an examining magistrate, whom Peter Ivánovich also knew and who was her fiancé, as he had heard. He bowed mournfully to them and was about to pass into the death-chamber, when from under the stairs appeared the figure of Iván Ilých's school-boy son, who was extremely like his father. He seemed a little Iván Ilých, such as Peter Ivánovich remembered when they studied law together. His tear-stained eyes had in them the look that is seen in the eyes of boys of thirteen or fourteen who are not pure-minded. When he saw Peter Ivánovich he scowled morosely and shamefacedly. Peter Ivánovich nodded to him and entered the death-chamber. The service began: candles, groans, incense, tears, and sobs. Peter Ivánovich stood looking gloomily down at his feet. He did not look once at the dead man, did not yield to any depressing influence, and was one of the first to leave the room. There was no one in the anteroom, but Gerásim darted out of the dead man's room, rummaged with his strong hands among the fur coats to find Peter Ivánovich's and helped him on with it.

"Well, friend Gerásim," said Peter Ivánovich, so as to say something. "It's a sad affair, isn't it?"

"It's God's will. We shall all come to it some day," said Gerásim, displaying 50 his teeth—the even, white teeth of a healthy peasant—and, like a man in the thick of urgent work, he briskly opened the front door, called the coachman, helped Peter Ivánovich into the sledge, and sprang back to the porch as if in readiness for what he had to do next.

Peter Ivánovich found the fresh air particularly pleasant after the smell of incense, the dead body, and carbolic acid.

"Where to, sir?" asked the coachman.

"It's not too late even now. . . . I'll call round on Fëdor Vasílievich."

He accordingly drove there and found them just finishing the first rubber, so that it was quite convenient for him to cut in.

Chapter II

Iván Ilých's life had been most simple and most ordinary and therefore most terrible. 55

He had been a member of the Court of Justice, and died at the age of forty-five. His father had been an official who after serving in various ministries and departments in Petersburg had made the sort of career which brings men to positions from which by reason of their long service they cannot be dismissed, though they are obviously unfit to hold any responsible position, and for whom therefore posts are specially created, which though fictitious carry salaries of from six to ten thousand rubles that are not fictitious, and in receipt of which they live on to a great age.

Such was the Privy Councillor and superfluous member of various superfluous institutions, Ilyá Epímovich Golovín.

He had three sons, of whom Iván Ilých was the second. The eldest son was following in his father's footsteps only in another department, and was already approaching that stage in the service at which a similar sinecure would be reached. The third son was a failure. He had ruined his prospects in a number of positions and was now serving in the railway department. His father and brothers, and still more their wives, not merely disliked meeting him, but avoided remembering his existence unless compelled to do so. His sister had married Baron Greff, a Petersburg official of her father's type. Iván Ilých was *le phénix de la famille*[2] as people said. He was neither as cold and formal as his elder brother nor as wild as the younger, but was a happy mean between them—an intelligent, polished, lively and agreeable man. He had studied with his younger brother at the School of Law, but the latter had failed to complete the course and was expelled when he was in the fifth class. Iván Ilých finished the course well. Even when he was at the School of Law he was just what he remained for the rest of his life: a capable, cheerful, good-natured, and sociable man, though strict in the fulfilment of what he considered to be his duty: and he considered his duty to be what was so considered by those in authority. Neither as a boy nor as a man was he a toady, but from early youth was by nature attracted to people of high station as a fly is drawn to the light, assimilating their ways and views of life and establishing friendly relations with them. All the enthusiasms of childhood and youth passed without leaving much trace on him; he succumbed to sensuality, to vanity, and latterly among the highest classes to liberalism, but always within limits which his instinct unfailingly indicated to him as correct.

---

[2] The phoenix of the family, here meaning "rare bird" or "prodigy."

At school he had done things which had formerly seemed to him very horrid and made him feel disgusted with himself when he did them; but when later on he saw that such actions were done by people of good position and that they did not regard them as wrong, he was able not exactly to regard them as right, but to forget about them entirely or not be at all troubled at remembering them.

Having graduated from the School of Law and qualified for the tenth rank of the civil service, and having received money from his father for his equipment, Iván Ilých ordered himself clothes at Scharmer's, the fashionable tailor, hung a medallion inscribed *respice finem*[3] on his watch-chain, took leave of his professor and the prince who was patron of the school, had a farewell dinner with his comrades at Donon's first-class restaurant, and with his new and fashionable portmanteau, linen, clothes, shaving and other toilet appliances, and a travelling rug, all purchased at the best shops, he set off for one of the provinces where, through his father's influence, he had been attached to the Governor as an official for special service.

In the province Iván Ilých soon arranged as easy and agreeable a position for himself as he had had at the School of Law. He performed his official tasks, made his career, and at the same time amused himself pleasantly and decorously. Occasionally he paid official visits to country districts, where he behaved with dignity both to his superiors and inferiors, and performed the duties entrusted to him, which related chiefly to the sectarians,[4] with an exactness and incorruptible honesty of which he could not but feel proud.

In official matters, despite his youth and taste for frivolous gaiety, he was exceedingly reserved, punctilious, and even severe; but in society he was often amusing and witty, and always good-natured, correct in his manner, and *bon enfant*, as the governor and his wife—with whom he was like one of the family—used to say of him.

In the provinces he had an affair with a lady who made advances to the elegant young lawyer, and there was also a milliner; and there were carousals with aides-de-camp who visited the district, and after-supper visits to a certain outlying street of doubtful reputation; and there was too some obsequiousness to his chief and even to his chief's wife, but all this was done with such a tone of good breeding that no hard names could be applied to it. It all came under the heading of the French saying: "Il faut que jeunesse se passe."[5] It was all done with clean hands, in clean linen, with French phrases, and above all among people of the best society and consequently with the approval of people of rank.

So Iván Ilých served for five years and then came a change in his official life. The new and reformed judicial institutions were introduced, and new men were needed. Iván Ilých became such a new man. He was offered the post of

[3] Regard the end.
[4] A large sect, whose members were placed under many legal restrictions, which broke away from the Orthodox Church in the seventeenth century.
[5] Youth must have its fling.

Examining Magistrate, and he accepted it though the post was in another province and obliged him to give up the connections he had formed and to make new ones. His friends met to give him a send-off; they had a group-photograph taken and presented him with a silver cigarette-case, and he set off to his new post.

As examining magistrate Iván Ilých was just as *comme il faut*[6] and decorous 65 a man, inspiring general respect and capable of separating his official duties from his private life, as he had been when acting as an official on special service. His duties now as examining magistrate were far more interesting and attractive than before. In his former position it had been pleasant to wear an undress uniform made by Scharmer, and to pass through the crowd of petitioners and officials who were timorously awaiting an audience with the governor, and who envied him as with free and easy gait he went straight into his chief's private room to have a cup of tea and a cigarette with him. But not many people had then been directly dependent on him—only police officials and the sectarians when he went on special missions—and he liked to treat them politely, almost as comrades, as if he were letting them feel that he who had the power to crush them was treating them in this simple, friendly way. There were then but few such people. But now, as an examining magistrate, Iván Ilých felt that everyone without exception, even the most important and self-satisfied, was in his power, and that he need only write a few words on a sheet of paper with a certain heading, and this or that important, self-satisfied person would be brought before him in the role of an accused person or a witness, and if he did not choose to allow him to sit down, would have to stand before him and answer his questions. Iván Ilých never abused his power; he tried on the contrary to soften its expression, but the consciousness of it and of the possibility of softening its effect, supplied the chief interest and attraction of his office. In his work itself, especially in his examinations, he very soon acquired a method of eliminating all considerations irrelevant to the legal aspect of the case, and reducing even the most complicated case to a form in which it would be presented on paper only in its externals, completely excluding his personal opinion of the matter, while above all observing every prescribed formality. The work was new and Iván Ilých was one of the first men to apply the new Code of 1864.[7]

On taking up the post of examining magistrate in a new town, he made new acquaintances and connections, placed himself on a new footing, and assumed a somewhat different tone. He took up an attitude of rather dignified aloofness towards the provincial authorities, but picked out the best circle of legal gentlemen and wealthy gentry living in the town and assumed a tone of slight dissatisfaction with the government, of moderate liberalism, and of enlightened citizenship. At the same time, without at all altering the elegance of his toilet, he ceased shaving his chin and allowed his beard to grow as it pleased.

[6] Proper.
[7] Judicial procedures were reformed after the emancipation of the serfs in 1861.

Iván Ilých settled down very pleasantly in this new town. The society there, which inclined towards opposition to the Governor, was friendly, his salary was larger, and he began to play *vint*,[8] which he found added not a little to the pleasure of life, for he had a capacity for cards, played good-humouredly, and calculated rapidly and astutely, so that he usually won.

After living there for two years he met his future wife, Praskóvya Fëdorovna Míkhel, who was the most attractive, clever, and brilliant girl of the set in which he moved, and among other amusements and relaxations from his labours as examining magistrate, Iván Ilých established light and playful relations with her.

While he had been an official on special service he had been accustomed to dance, but now as an examining magistrate it was exceptional for him to do so. If he danced now, he did it as if to show that though he served under the reformed order of things, and had reached the fifth official rank, yet when it came to dancing he could do it better than most people. So at the end of an evening he sometimes danced with Praskóvya Fëdorovna, and it was chiefly during these dances that he captivated her. She fell in love with him. Iván Ilých had at first no definite intention of marrying, but when the girl fell in love with him he said to himself: "Really, why shouldn't I marry?"

Praskóvya Fëdorovna came of a good family, was not bad looking and had some little property. Iván Ilých might have aspired to a more brilliant match, but even this was good. He had his salary, and she, he hoped, would have an equal income. She was well connected, and was a sweet, pretty, and thoroughly correct young woman. To say that Iván Ilých married because he fell in love with Praskóvya Fëdorovna and found that she sympathized with his views of life would be as incorrect as to say that he married because his social circle approved of the match. He was swayed by both these considerations: the marriage gave him personal satisfaction, and at the same time it was considered the right thing by the most highly placed of his associates.

So Iván Ilých got married.

The preparations for marriage and the beginning of married life, with its conjugal caresses, the new furniture, new crockery, and new linen, were very pleasant until his wife became pregnant—so that Iván Ilých had begun to think that marriage would not impair the easy, agreeable, gay and always decorous character of his life, approved of by society and regarded by himself as natural, but would even improve it. But from the first months of his wife's pregnancy, something new, unpleasant, depressing, and unseemly, and from which there was no way of escape, unexpectedly showed itself.

His wife, without any reason—*de gaieté de coeur*[9] as Iván Ilých expressed it to himself—began to disturb the pleasure and propriety of their life. She began to be jealous without any cause, expected him to devote his whole attention to her, found fault with everything, and made coarse and ill-mannered scenes.

[8] A card game similar to bridge.
[9] Of a joyous heart. Iván uses the expression ironically.

At first Iván Ilých hoped to escape from the unpleasantness of this state of affairs by the same easy and decorous relation to life that had served him heretofore: he tried to ignore his wife's disagreeable moods, continued to live in his usual easy and pleasant way, invited friends to his house for a game of cards, and also tried going out to his club or spending his evenings with friends. But one day his wife began upbraiding him so vigorously, using such coarse words, and continued to abuse him every time he did not fulfil her demands, so resolutely and with such evident determination not to give way till he submitted—that is, till he stayed at home and was bored just as she was—that he became alarmed. He now realized that matrimony—at any rate with Praskóvya Fëdorovna—was not always conducive to the pleasures and amenities of life but on the contrary often infringed both comfort and propriety, and that he must therefore entrench himself against such infringement. And Iván Ilých began to seek for means of doing so. His official duties were the one thing that imposed upon Praskóvya Fëdorovna, and by means of his official work and the duties attached to it he began struggling with his wife to secure his own independence.

With the birth of their child, the attempts to feed it and the various failures 75 in doing so, and with the real and imaginary illnesses of mother and child, in which Iván Ilých's sympathy was demanded but about which he understood nothing, the need of securing for himself an existence outside his family life became still more imperative.

As his wife grew more irritable and exacting and Iván Ilých transferred the centre of gravity of his life more and more to his official work, so did he grow to like his work better and became more ambitious than before.

Very soon, within a year of his wedding, Iván Ilých had realized that marriage, though it may add some comforts to life, is in fact a very intricate and difficult affair towards which in order to perform one's duty, that is, to lead a decorous life approved of by society, one must adopt a definite attitude just as towards one's official duties.

And Iván Ilých evolved such an attitude towards married life. He only required of it those conveniences—dinner at home, housewife, and bed—which it could give him, and above all that propriety of external forms required by public opinion. For the rest he looked for lighthearted pleasure and propriety, and was very thankful when he found them, but if he met with antagonism and querulousness he at once retired into his separate fenced-off world of official duties, where he found satisfaction.

Iván Ilých was esteemed a good official, and after three years was made Assistant Public Prosecutor. His new duties, their importance, the possibility of indicting and imprisoning anyone he chose, the publicity his speeches received, and the success he had in all these things, made his work still more attractive.

More children came. His wife became more and more querulous and ill- 80 tempered, but the attitude Iván Ilých had adopted towards his home life rendered him almost impervious to her grumbling.

After seven years' service in that town he was transferred to another province as Public Prosecutor. They moved, but were short of money and his wife did not like the place they moved to. Though the salary was higher the cost of living was greater, besides which two of their children died and family life became still more unpleasant for him.

Praskóvya Fëdorovna blamed her husband for every inconvenience they encountered in their new home. Most of the conversations between husband and wife, especially as to the children's education, led to topics which recalled former disputes, and those disputes were apt to flare up again at any moment. There remained only those rare periods of amorousness which still came to them at times but did not last long. These were islets at which they anchored for a while and then again set out upon that ocean of veiled hostility which showed itself in their aloofness from one another. This aloofness might have grieved Iván Ilých had he considered that it ought not to exist, but he now regarded the position as normal, and even made it the goal at which he aimed in family life. His aim was to free himself more and more from those unpleasantnesses and to give them a semblance of harmlessness and propriety. He attained this by spending less and less time with his family, and when obliged to be at home he tried to safeguard his position by the presence of outsiders. The chief thing however was that he had his official duties. The whole interest of his life now centered in the official world and that interest absorbed him. The consciousness of his power, being able to ruin anybody he wished to ruin, the importance, even the external dignity of his entry into court, or meetings with his subordinates, his success with superiors and inferiors, and above all his masterly handling of cases, of which he was conscious—all this gave him pleasure and filled his life, together with chats with his colleagues, dinners, and bridge. So that on the whole Iván Ilých's life continued to flow as he considered it should do—pleasantly and properly.

So things continued for another seven years. His eldest daughter was already sixteen, another child had died, and only one son was left, a schoolboy and a subject of dissension. Iván Ilých wanted to put him in the School of Law, but to spite him Praskóvya Fëdorovna entered him at the High School. The daughter had been educated at home and had turned out well: the boy did not learn badly either.

Chapter III

So Iván Ilých lived for seventeen years after his marriage. He was already a Public Prosecutor of long standing, and had declined several proposed transfers while awaiting a more desirable post, when an unanticipated and unpleasant occurrence quite upset the peaceful course of his life. He was expecting to be offered the post of presiding judge in a University town, but Happe somehow came to the front and obtained the appointment instead. Iván Ilých became irritable, reproached Happe, and quarreled both with him and with his immediate superiors—who became colder to him and again passed him over when other appointments were made.

This was in 1880, the hardest year of Iván Ilých's life. It was then that it 85 became evident on the one hand that his salary was insufficient for them to live on, and on the other that he had been forgotten, and not only this, but that what was for him the greatest and most cruel injustice appeared to others a quite ordinary occurrence. Even his father did not consider it his duty to help him. Iván Ilých felt himself abandoned by everyone, and that they regarded his position with a salary of 3,500 rubles as quite normal and even fortunate. He alone knew that with the consciousness of the injustices done him, with his wife's incessant nagging, and with the debts he had contracted by living beyond his means, his position was far from normal.

In order to save money that summer he obtained leave of absence and went with his wife to live in the country at her brother's place.

In the country, without his work, he experienced *ennui* for the first time in his life, and not only *ennui* but intolerable depression, and he decided that it was impossible to go on living like that, and that it was necessary to take energetic measures.

Having passed a sleepless night pacing up and down the veranda, he decided to go to Petersburg and bestir himself, in order to punish those who had failed to appreciate him and to get transferred to another ministry.

Next day, despite many protests from his wife and her brother, he started for Petersburg with the sole object of obtaining a post with a salary of five thousand rubles a year. He was no longer bent on any particular department, or tendency, or kind of activity. All he now wanted was an appointment to another post with a salary of five thousand rubles, either in the administration, in the banks, with the railways, in one of the Empress Márya's Institutions,[10] or even in the customs—but it had to carry with it a salary of five thousand rubles and be in a ministry other than that in which they had failed to appreciate him.

And this quest of Iván Ilých's was crowned with remarkable and unexpected 90 success. At Kursk an acquaintance of his, F. I. Ilyín, got into the first-class carriage, sat down beside Iván Ilých, and told him of a telegram just received by the Governor of Kursk announcing that a change was about to take place in the ministry: Peter Ivánovich was to be superseded by Iván Semënovich.

The proposed change, apart from its significance for Russia, had a special significance for Iván Ilých, because by bringing forward a new man, Peter Petróvich, and consequently his friend Zachár Ivánovich, it was highly favourable for Iván Ilých, since Zachár Ivánovich was a friend and colleague of his.

In Moscow this news was confirmed, and on reaching Petersburg Iván Ilých found Zachár Ivánovich and received a definite promise of an appointment in his former Department of Justice.

A week later he telegraphed to his wife: "Zachár in Miller's place. I shall receive appointment on presentation of report."

Thanks to this change of personnel, Iván Ilých had unexpectedly obtained an appointment in his former ministry which placed him two stages above his

---

[10] A charitable organization founded in the late eighteenth century by the empress Márya.

former colleagues besides giving him five thousand rubles salary and three thousand five hundred rubles for expenses connected with his removal. All his ill humour towards his former enemies and the whole department vanished, and Iván Ilých was completely happy.

He returned to the country more cheerful and contented than he had been 95 for a long time. Praskóvya Fёdorovna also cheered up and a truce was arranged between them. Iván Ilých told of how he had been fêted by everybody in Petersburg, how all those who had been his enemies were put to shame and now fawned on him, how envious they were of his appointment, and how much everybody in Petersburg had liked him.

Praskóvya Fёdorovna listened to all this and appeared to believe it. She did not contradict anything, but only made plans for their life in the town to which they were going. Iván Ilých saw with delight that these plans were his plans, that he and his wife agreed, and that, after a stumble, his life was regaining its due and natural character of pleasant lightheartedness and decorum.

Iván Ilých had come back for a short time only, for he had to take up his new duties on the 10th of September. Moreover, he needed time to settle into the new place, to move all his belongings from the province, and to buy and order many additional things: in a word, to make such arrangements as he had resolved on, which were almost exactly what Praskóvya Fёdorovna too had decided on.

Now that everything had happened so fortunately, and that he and his wife were at one in their aims and moreover saw so little of one another, they got on together better than they had done since the first years of marriage. Iván Ilých had thought of taking his family away with him at once, but the insistence of his wife's brother and her sister-in-law, who had suddenly become particularly amiable and friendly to him and his family, induced him to depart alone.

So he departed, and the cheerful state of mind induced by his success and by the harmony between his wife and himself, the one intensifying the other, did not leave him. He found a delightful house, just the thing both he and his wife had dreamt of. Spacious, lofty reception rooms in the old style, a convenient and dignified study, rooms for his wife and daughter, a study for his son—it might have been specially built for them. Iván Ilých himself superintended the arrangements, chose the wallpapers, supplemented the furniture (preferably with antiques which he considered particularly *comme il faut*), and supervised the upholstering. Everything progressed and progressed and approached the ideal he had set himself: even when things were only half completed they exceeded his expectations. He saw what a refined and elegant character, free from vulgarity, it would all have when it was ready. On falling asleep he pictured to himself how the reception-room would look. Looking at the yet unfinished drawing-room he could see the fireplace, the screen, the what-not, the little chairs dotted here and there, the dishes and plates on the walls, and the bronzes, as they would be when everything was in place. He was pleased by the thought of how his wife and daughter, who shared his taste in this matter, would be impressed by it. They were certainly not expecting as much. He had been particularly successful in finding, and buying cheaply, antiques which gave a particularly aristocratic character to the whole place. But in his letters he intentionally understated everything in order to be able to surprise them. All this so absorbed him that his new duties—though he liked his official work—interested him less than he had expected. Sometimes he even had moments of absent-mindedness during the Court Sessions, and would consider whether he should have straight or curved cornices for his curtains. He was so interested in it all that he often did things himself, rearranging the furniture, or rehanging the curtains. Once when mounting a step-ladder to show the upholsterer, who did not understand, how he wanted the hangings draped, he made a false step and slipped, but being a strong and agile man he clung on and only knocked his side against the knob of the window frame. The bruised place was painful but the pain soon passed, and he felt particularly bright and well just then. He wrote: "I feel fifteen years younger." He thought he would have everything ready by September, but it dragged on till mid-October. But the result was charming not only in his eyes but to everyone who saw it.

In reality it was just what is usually seen in the houses of people of moderate 100 means who want to appear rich, and therefore succeed only in resembling others like themselves: there were damasks, dark wood, plants, rugs, and dull and polished bronzes—all the things people of a certain class have in order to resemble other people of that class. His house was so like the others that it would never have been noticed, but to him it all seemed to be quite exceptional. He was very happy when he met his family at the station and brought them to the newly furnished house all lit up, where a footman in a white tie opened the door into the hall decorated with plants, and when they went on into the drawing room and the study uttering exclamations of delight. He conducted them everywhere, drank in their praises eagerly, and beamed with pleasure. At tea that evening, when Praskóvya Fëdorovna among other things asked him about his fall, he laughed and showed them how he had gone flying and had frightened the upholsterer.

"It's a good thing I'm a bit of an athlete. Another man might have been killed, but I merely knocked myself, just here; it hurts when it's touched, but it's passing off already—it's only a bruise."

So they began living in their new home—in which, as always happens, when they got thoroughly settled in they found they were just one room short—and with the increased income, which as always was just a little (some five hundred rubles) too little, but it was all very nice.

Things went particularly well at first, before everything was finally arranged and while something had still to be done: this thing bought, that thing ordered, another thing moved, and something else adjusted. Though there were some disputes between husband and wife, they were both so well satisfied and had so much to do that it all passed off without any serious quarrels. When nothing was left to arrange it became rather dull and something seemed to be lacking, but they were then making acquaintances, forming habits, and life was growing fuller.

Iván Ilých spent his mornings at the law court and came home to dinner, and at first he was generally in a good humour, though he occasionally became irritable just on account of his house. (Every spot on the tablecloth or the upholstery, and every broken window-blind string, irritated him. He had devoted so much trouble to arranging it all that every disturbance of it distressed him.) But on the whole his life ran its course as he believed life should do: easily, pleasantly, and decorously.

He got up at nine, drank his coffee, read the paper, and then put on his undress uniform and went to the law courts. There the harness in which he worked had already been stretched to fit him and he donned it without a hitch: petitioners, inquiries at the chancery, the chancery itself, and the sittings public and administrative. In all this the thing was to exclude everything fresh and vital, which always disturbs the regular course of official business, and to admit only official relations with people, and then only on official grounds. A man would come, for instance, wanting some information. Iván Ilých, as one in whose sphere the matter did not lie, would have nothing to do with him: but if the man had some business with him in his official capacity, something that could be expressed on officially stamped paper, he would do everything, positively everything he could within the limits of such relations, and in doing so would maintain the semblance of friendly human relations, that is, would observe the courtesies of life. As soon as the official relations ended, so did everything else. Iván Ilých possessed this capacity to separate his real life from the official side of affairs and not mix the two, in the highest degree, and by long practice and natural aptitude had brought it to such a pitch that sometimes, in the manner of a virtuoso, he would even allow himself to let the human and official relations mingle. He let himself do this just because he felt that he could at any time he chose resume the strictly official attitude again and drop the human relation. And he did it all easily, pleasantly, correctly, and even artistically. In the intervals between the sessions he smoked, drank tea, chatted a little about politics, a little about general topics, a little about cards, but most of all about official appointments. Tired, but with the feelings of a virtuoso—one of the first violins who has played his part in an orchestra with precision—he would return home to find that his wife and daughter had been out paying calls, or had a visitor, and that his son had been to school, had done his homework with his tutor, and was duly learning what is taught at High Schools. Everything was as it should be. After dinner, if they had no visitors, Iván Ilých sometimes read a book that was being much discussed at the time, and in the evening settled down to work, that is, read official papers, compared the depositions of witnesses, and noted paragraphs of the Code applying to them. This was neither dull nor amusing. It was dull when he might have been playing bridge, but if no bridge was available it was at any rate better than doing nothing or sitting with his wife. Iván Ilých's chief pleasure was giving little dinners to which he invited men and women of good social position, and just as his drawing-room resembled all other drawing-rooms so did his enjoyable little parties resemble all other such parties.

Once they even gave a dance. Iván Ilých enjoyed it and everything went off well, except that it led to a violent quarrel with his wife about the cakes and sweets. Praskóvya Fëdorovna had made her own plans, but Iván Ilých insisted on getting everything from an expensive confectioner and ordered too many cakes, and the quarrel occurred because some of those cakes were left over and the confectioner's bill came to forty-five rubles. It was a great and disagreeable quarrel. Praskóvya Fëdorovna called him "a fool and an imbecile," and he clutched at his head and made angry allusions to divorce.

But the dance itself had been enjoyable. The best people were there, and Iván Ilých had danced with Princess Trúfonova, a sister of the distinguished founder of the Society "Bear My Burden."

The pleasures connected with his work were pleasures of ambition; his social pleasures were those of vanity; but Iván Ilých's greatest pleasure was playing bridge. He acknowledged that whatever disagreeable incident happened in his life, the pleasure that beamed like a ray of light above everything else was to sit down to bridge with good players, not noisy partners, and of course to four-handed bridge (with five players it was annoying to have to stand out, though one pretended not to mind), to play a clever and serious game (when the cards allowed it) and then to have supper and drink a glass of wine. After a game of bridge, especially if he had won a little (to win a large sum was unpleasant), Iván Ilých went to bed in specially good humour.

So they lived. They formed a circle of acquaintances among the best people and were visited by people of importance and by young folk. In their views as to their acquaintances, husband, wife and daughter were entirely agreed, and tacitly and unanimously kept at arm's length and shook off the various shabby friends and relations who, with much show of affection, gushed into the drawing-room with its Japanese plates on the walls. Soon these shabby friends ceased to obtrude themselves and only the best people remained in the Golovíns' set.

Young men made up to Lisa, and Petríshchev, an examining magistrate and Dmítri Ivanovich Petríshchev's son and sole heir, began to be so attentive to her that Iván Ilých had already spoken to Praskóvya Fëdorovna about it, and considered whether they should not arrange a party for them or get up some private theatricals.

So they lived, and all went well, without change, and life flowed pleasantly.

Chapter IV

They were all in good health. It could not be called ill health if Iván Ilých sometimes said that he had a queer taste in his mouth and felt some discomfort in his left side.

But this discomfort increased and, though not exactly painful, grew into a sense of pressure in his side accompanied by ill humour. And his irritability became worse and worse and began to mar the agreeable, easy, and correct life that had established itself in the Golovín family. Quarrels between husband

and wife became more and more frequent, and soon the ease and amenity disappeared and even the decorum was barely maintained. Scenes again became frequent, and very few of those islets remained on which husband and wife could meet without explosion. Praskóvya Fëdorovna now had good reason to say that her husband's temper was trying. With characteristic exaggeration she said he had always had a dreadful temper, and that it had needed all her good nature to put up with it for twenty years. It was true that now the quarrels were started by him. His bursts of temper always came just before dinner, often just as he began to eat his soup. Sometimes he noticed that a plate or dish was chipped, or the food was not right, or his son put his elbow on the table, or his daughter's hair was not done as he liked it, and for all this he blamed Praskóvya Fëdorovna. At first she retorted and said disagreeable things to him, but once or twice he fell into such a rage at the beginning of dinner that she realized it was due to some physical derangement brought on by taking food, and so she restrained herself and did not answer, but only hurried to get the dinner over. She regarded this self-restraint as highly praiseworthy. Having come to the conclusion that her husband had a dreadful temper and made her life miserable, she began to feel sorry for herself, and the more she pitied herself the more she hated her husband. She began to wish he would die; yet she did not want him to die because then his salary would cease. And this irritated her against him still more. She considered herself dreadfully unhappy just because not even his death could save her, and though she concealed her exasperation, that hidden exasperation of hers increased his irritation also.

After one scene in which Iván Ilých had been particularly unfair and after which he had said in explanation that he certainly was irritable but that it was due to his not being well, she said that if he was ill it should be attended to, and insisted on his going to see a celebrated doctor.

He went. Everything took place as he had expected and as it always does. 115 There was the usual waiting and the important air assumed by the doctor, with which he was so familiar (resembling that which he himself assumed in court), and the sounding and listening, and the questions which called for answers that were foregone conclusions and were evidently unnecessary, and the look of importance which implied that "if only you put yourself in our hands we will arrange everything—we know indubitably how it has to be done, always in the same way for everybody alike." It was all just as it was in the law courts. The doctor put on just the same air towards him as he himself put on towards an accused person.

The doctor said that so-and-so indicated that there was so-and-so inside the patient, but if the investigation of so-and-so did not confirm this, then he must assume that and that. If he assumed that and that, then . . . and so on. To Iván Ilých only one question was important: was his case serious or not? But the doctor ignored that inappropriate question. From his point of view it was not the one under consideration, the real question was to decide between a floating kidney, chronic catarrh, or appendicitis. It was not a question of Iván Ilých's life or death, but one between a floating kidney and appendicitis. And that question the doctor solved brilliantly, as it seemed to Iván Ilých, in favour of the appendix, with the reservation that should an examination of the urine give fresh indications the matter would be reconsidered. All this was just what Iván Ilých had himself brilliantly accomplished a thousand times in dealing with men on trial. The doctor summed up just as brilliantly, looking over his spectacles triumphantly and even gaily at the accused. From the doctor's summing up Iván Ilých concluded that things were bad, but that for the doctor, and perhaps for everybody else, it was a matter of indifference, though for him it was bad. And this conclusion struck him painfully, arousing in him a great feeling of pity for himself and of bitterness towards the doctor's indifference to a matter of such importance.

He said nothing of this, but rose, placed the doctor's fee on the table, and remarked with a sigh: "We sick people probably often put inappropriate questions. But tell me, in general, is this complaint dangerous, or not? . . ."

The doctor looked at him sternly over his spectacles with one eye, as if to say: "Prisoner, if you will not keep to the questions put to you, I shall be obliged to have you removed from the court."

"I have already told you what I consider necessary and proper. The analysis may show something more." And the doctor bowed.

Iván Ilých went out slowly, seated himself disconsolately in his sledge, and   120 drove home. All the way home he was going over what the doctor had said, trying to translate those complicated, obscure, scientific phrases into plain language and find in them an answer to the question: "Is my condition bad? Is it very bad? Or is there as yet nothing much wrong?" And it seemed to him that the meaning of what the doctor had said was that it was very bad. Everything in the streets seemed depressing. The cabmen, the houses, the passers-by, and the shops, were dismal. His ache, this dull gnawing ache that never ceased for a moment, seemed to have acquired a new and more serious significance from the doctor's dubious remarks. Iván Ilých now watched it with a new and oppressive feeling.

He reached home and began to tell his wife about it. She listened, but in the middle of his account his daughter came in with her hat on, ready to go out with her mother. She sat down reluctantly to listen to this tedious story, but could not stand it long, and her mother too did not hear him to the end.

"Well, I am very glad," she said. "Mind now to take your medicine regularly. Give me the prescription and I'll send Gerásim to the chemist's." And she went to get ready to go out.

While she was in the room Iván Ilých had hardly taken time to breathe, but he sighed deeply when she left it.

"Well," he thought, "perhaps it isn't so bad after all."

He began taking his medicine and following the doctor's directions, which   125 had been altered after the examination of the urine. But then it happened that there was a contradiction between the indications drawn from the examination of the urine and the symptoms that showed themselves. It turned out that what was happening differed from what the doctor had told him, and that he had either forgotten, or blundered, or hidden something from him. He could not, however, be blamed for that, and Iván Ilých still obeyed his orders implicitly and at first derived some comfort from doing so.

From the time of his visit to the doctor, Iván Ilých's chief occupation was the exact fulfilment of the doctor's instructions regarding hygiene and the taking of medicine, and the observation of his pain and his excretions. His chief interests came to be people's ailments and people's health. When sickness, deaths, or recoveries were mentioned in his presence, especially when the illness resembled his own, he listened with agitation which he tried to hide, asked questions, and applied what he heard to his own case.

The pain did not grow less, but Iván Ilých made efforts to force himself to think that he was better. And he could do this so long as nothing agitated him. But as soon as he had any unpleasantness with his wife, any lack of success in his official work, or held bad cards at bridge, he was at once acutely sensible of his disease. He had formerly borne such mischances, hoping soon to adjust what was wrong, to master it and attain success, or make a grand slam. But now every mischance upset him and plunged him into despair. He would say to himself: "There now, just as I was beginning to get better and the medicine had begun to take effect, comes this accursed misfortune, or unpleasantness. . . ." And he was furious with the mishap, or with the people who were causing the unpleasantness and killing him, for he felt that this fury was killing him but could not restrain it. One would have thought that it should have been clear to him that this exasperation with circumstances and people aggravated his illness, and that he ought therefore to ignore unpleasant occurrences. But he drew the very opposite conclusion: he said that he needed peace, and he watched for everything that might disturb it and became irritable at the slightest infringement of it. His condition was rendered worse by the fact that he read medical books and consulted doctors. The progress of his disease was so gradual that he could deceive himself when comparing one day with another—the difference was so slight. But when he consulted the doctors it seemed to him that he was getting worse, and even very rapidly. Yet despite this he was continually consulting them.

That month he went to see another celebrity, who told him almost the same as the first had done but put his questions rather differently, and the interview with this celebrity only increased Iván Ilých's doubts and fears. A friend of a friend of his, a very good doctor, diagnosed his illness again quite differently from the others, and though he predicted recovery, his questions and suppositions bewildered Iván Ilých still more and increased his doubts. A homeopathist diagnosed the disease in yet another way, and prescribed medicine which Iván Ilých took secretly for a week. But after a week, not feeling any improvement and having lost confidence both in the former doctor's treatment and in this one's, he became still more despondent. One day a lady acquaintance mentioned a cure effected by a wonder-working icon. Iván Ilých caught himself listening attentively and beginning to believe that it had occurred. This incident alarmed him. "Has my mind really weakened to such an extent?" he asked himself. "Nonsense! It's all rubbish. I mustn't give way to nervous fears but having chosen a doctor must keep strictly to his treatment. That is what I will do. Now it's all settled. I won't think about it, but will follow the treatment seriously till summer, and then we shall see. From now there must be no more of this wavering!" This was easy to say but impossible to carry out. The pain in his side oppressed him and seemed to grow worse and more incessant, while the taste in his mouth grew stranger and stranger. It seemed to him that his breath had a disgusting smell, and he was conscious of a loss of appetite and strength. There was no deceiving himself: something terrible, new, and more important than anything before in his life, was taking place within him of which he alone was aware. Those about him did not understand or would not understand it, but thought everything in the world was going on as usual. That tormented Iván Ilých more than anything. He saw that his household, especially his wife and daughter who were in a perfect whirl of visiting, did not understand anything of it and were annoyed that he was so depressed and so exacting, as if he were to blame for it. Though they tried to disguise it he saw that he was an obstacle in their path, and that his wife had adopted a definite line in regard to his illness and kept to it regardless of anything he said or did. Her attitude was this: "You know," she would say to her friends, "Iván Ilých can't do as other people do, and keep to the treatment prescribed for him. One day he'll take his drops and keep strictly to his diet and go to bed in good time, but the next day unless I watch him he'll suddenly forget his medicine, eat sturgeon—which is forbidden—and sit up playing cards till one o'clock in the morning."

"Oh, come, when was that?" Iván Ilých would ask in vexation. "Only once at Peter Ivánovich's."

"And yesterday with Shébek."   130

"Well, even if I hadn't stayed up, this pain would have kept me awake."

"Be that as it may you'll never get well like that, but will always make us wretched."

Praskóvya Fëdorovna's attitude to Iván Ilých's illness, as she expressed it both to others and to him, was that it was his own fault and was another of the annoyances he caused her. Iván Ilých felt that this opinion escaped her involuntarily—but that did not make it easier for him.

At the law courts too, Iván Ilých noticed, or thought he noticed, a strange attitude towards himself. It sometimes seemed to him that people were watching him inquisitively as a man whose place might soon be vacant. Then again, his friends would suddenly begin to chaff him in a friendly way about his low spirits, as if the awful, horrible, and unheard-of thing that was going on within him, incessantly gnawing at him and irresistibly drawing him away, was a very agreeable subject for jests. Schwartz in particular irritated him by his jocularity, vivacity, and *savoir-faire*, which reminded him of what he himself had been ten years ago.

Friends came to make up a set and they sat down to cards. They dealt, bend-   135
ing the new cards to soften them, and he sorted the diamonds in his hand and

found he had seven. His partner said "No trumps" and supported him with two diamonds. What more could be wished for? It ought to be jolly and lively. They would make a grand slam. But suddenly Iván Ilých was conscious of that gnawing pain, that taste in his mouth, and it seemed ridiculous that in such circumstances he should be pleased to make a grand slam.

He looked at his partner Mikháil Mikháylovich, who rapped the table with his strong hand and instead of snatching up the tricks pushed the cards courteously and indulgently towards Iván Ilých that he might have the pleasure of gathering them up without the trouble of stretching out his hand for them. "Does he think I am too weak to stretch out my arm?" thought Iván Ilých, and forgetting what he was doing he over-trumped his partner, missing the grand slam by three tricks. And what was most awful of all was that he saw how upset Mikháil Mikháylovich was about it but did not himself care. And it was dreadful to realize why he did not care.

They all saw that he was suffering and said: "We can stop if you are tired. Take a rest." Lie down? No, he was not at all tired, and he finished the rubber. All were gloomy and silent. Iván Ilých felt that he had diffused this gloom over them and could not dispel it. They had supper and went away, and Iván Ilých was left alone with the consciousness that his life was poisoned and was poisoning the lives of others, and that this poison did not weaken but penetrated more and more deeply into his whole being.

With this consciousness, and with physical pain besides the terror, he must go to bed, often to lie awake the greater part of the night. Next morning he had to get up again, dress, go to the law courts, speak, and write; or if he did not go out, spend at home those twenty-four hours a day each of which was a torture. And he had to live thus all alone on the brink of an abyss, with no one who understood or pitied him.

Chapter V

So one month passed and then another. Just before the New Year his brother-in-law came to town and stayed at their house. Iván Ilých was at the law courts and Praskóvya Fëdorovna had gone shopping. When Iván Ilých came home and entered his study he found his brother-in-law there—a healthy, florid man—unpacking his portmanteau himself. He raised his head on hearing Iván Ilých's footsteps and looked up at him for a moment without a word. That stare told Iván Ilých everything. His brother-in-law opened his mouth to utter an exclamation of surprise but checked himself, and that action confirmed it all.

"I have changed, eh?"

"Yes, there is a change."

140

And after that, try as he would to get his brother-in-law to return to the subject of his looks, the latter would say nothing about it. Praskóvya Fëdorovna came home and her brother went out to her. Iván Ilých locked the door and began to examine himself in the glass, first full face, then in profile. He took up a portrait of himself taken with his wife, and compared it with what he saw in the glass. The change in him was immense. Then he bared his arms to the elbow, looked at them, drew the sleeves down again, sat down on an ottoman, and grew blacker than night.

"No, no, this won't do!" he said to himself, and jumped up, went to the table, took up some law papers and began to read them, but could not continue. He unlocked the door and went into the reception-room. The door leading to the drawing room was shut. He approached it on tiptoe and listened.

"No, you are exaggerating!" Praskóvya Fëdorovna was saying.

"Exaggerating! Don't you see it? Why, he's a dead man! Look at his eyes— 145 there's no light in them. But what is it that is wrong with him?"

"No one knows. Nikoláevich (that was another doctor) said something, but I don't know what. And Leshchetítsky (this was the celebrated specialist) said quite the contrary . . ."

Iván Ilých walked away, went to his own room, lay down, and began musing: "The kidney, a floating kidney." He recalled all the doctors had told him of how it detached itself and swayed about. And by an effort of imagination he tried to catch that kidney and arrest it and support it. So little was needed for this, it seemed to him. "No, I'll go to see Peter Ivánovich again." (That was the friend whose friend was a doctor.) He rang, ordered the carriage, and got ready to go.

"Where are you going, Jean?" asked his wife, with a specially sad and exceptionally kind look.

This exceptionally kind look irritated him. He looked morosely at her.

"I must go to see Peter Ivánovich."   150

He went to see Peter Ivánovich, and together they went to see his friend, the doctor. He was in, and Iván Ilých had a long talk with him.

Reviewing the anatomical and physiological details of what in the doctor's opinion was going on inside him, he understood it all.

There was something, a small thing, in the vermiform appendix. It might all come right. Only stimulate the energy of one organ and check the activity of another, then absorption would take place and everything would come right. He got home rather late for dinner, ate his dinner, and conversed cheerfully, but could not for a long time bring himself to go back to work in his room. At last, however, he went to his study and did what was necessary, but the consciousness that he had put something aside—an important, intimate matter which he would revert to when his work was done—never left him. When he had finished his work he remembered that this intimate matter was the thought of his vermiform appendix. But he did not give himself up to it, and went to the drawing-room for tea. There were callers there, including the examining magistrate who was a desirable match for his daughter, and they were conversing, playing the piano and singing. Iván Ilých, as Praskóvya Fëdorovna remarked, spent that evening more cheerfully than usual, but he never for a moment forgot that he had postponed the important matter of the appendix. At eleven o'clock he said good-night and went to his bedroom. Since his illness he had slept alone in a small room next to his study.

He undressed and took up a novel by Zola, but instead of reading it he fell into thought, and in his imagination that desired improvement in the vermiform appendix occurred. There was the absorption and evacuation and the reestablishment of normal activity. "Yes, that's it!" he said to himself. "One need only assist nature, that's all." He remembered his medicine, rose, took it, and lay down on his back watching for the beneficent action of the medicine and for it to lessen the pain. "I need only take it regularly and avoid all injurious influences. I am already feeling better, much better." He began touching his side: it was not painful to the touch. "There, I really don't feel it. It's much better already." He put out the light and turned on his side . . . "The appendix is getting better, absorption is occurring." Suddenly he felt the old, familiar, dull, gnawing pain, stubborn and serious. There was the same familiar loathsome taste in his mouth. His heart sank and he felt dazed. "My God! My God!" he muttered. "Again, again! and it will never cease." And suddenly the matter presented itself in a quite different aspect. "Vermiform appendix! Kidney!" he said to himself. "It's not a question of appendix or kidney, but of life and . . . death. Yes, life was there and now it is going, going and I cannot stop it. Yes. Why deceive myself? Isn't it obvious to everyone but me that I'm dying, and that it's only a question of weeks, days . . . it may happen this moment. There was light and now there is darkness. I was here and now I'm going there! Where?" A chill came over him, his breathing ceased, and he felt only the throbbing of his heart.

"When I am not, what will there be? There will be nothing. Then where shall I be when I am no more? Can this be dying? No, I don't want to!" He jumped up and tried to light the candle, felt for it with trembling hands, dropped candle and candlestick on the floor, and fell back on his pillow.

"What's the use? It makes no difference," he said to himself, staring with 155 wide-open eyes into the darkness. "Death. Yes, death. And none of them know or wish to know it, and they have no pity for me. Now they are playing." (He heard through the door the distant sound of a song and its accompaniment.) "It's all the same to them, but they will die too! Fools! I first, and they later, but it will be the same for them. And now they are merry . . . the beasts!"

Anger choked him and he was agonizingly, unbearably miserable. "It is impossible that all men have been doomed to suffer this awful horror!" He raised himself.

"Something must be wrong. I must calm myself—must think it all over from the beginning." And he again began thinking. "Yes, the beginning of my illness: I knocked my side, but I was still quite well that day and the next. It hurt a little, then rather more. I saw the doctors, then followed despondency and anguish, more doctors, and I drew nearer to the abyss. My strength grew less and I kept coming nearer and nearer, and now I have wasted away and there is no light in my eyes. I think of the appendix—but this is death! I think of mending the appendix, and all the while here is death! Can it really be death?" Again terror seized him and he gasped for breath. He leant down and began feeling for the matches, pressing with his elbow on the stand beside the bed. It was in his way and hurt him, he grew furious with it, pressed on it still harder, and upset it. Breathless and in despair he fell on his back, expecting death to come immediately.

Meanwhile the visitors were leaving. Praskóvya Fëdorovna was seeing them off. She heard something fall and came in.

"What has happened?"

"Nothing. I knocked it over accidentally." 160

She went out and returned with a candle. He lay there panting heavily, like a man who has run a thousand yards, and stared upwards at her with a fixed look.

"What is it, Jean?"

"No . . . o . . . thing. I upset it." ("Why speak of it? She won't understand," he thought.)

And in truth she did not understand. She picked up the stand, lit his candle, and hurried away to see another visitor off. When she came back he still lay on his back, looking upwards.

"What is it? Do you feel worse?" 165

"Yes."

She shook her head and sat down.

"Do you know, Jean, I think we must ask Leshchetítsky to come and see you here."

This meant calling in the famous specialist, regardless of expense. He smiled malignantly and said "No." She remained a little longer and then went up to him and kissed his forehead.

While she was kissing him he hated her from the bottom of his soul and 170 with difficulty refrained from pushing her away.

"Good-night. Please God you'll sleep."

"Yes."

Chapter VI

Iván Ilých saw that he was dying, and he was in continual despair.

In the depth of his heart he knew he was dying, but not only was he not accustomed to the thought, he simply did not and could not grasp it.

The syllogism he had learnt from Kiezewetter's Logic:[11] "Caius is a man, 175 men are mortal, therefore Caius is mortal," had always seemed to him correct as applied to Caius, but certainly not as applied to himself. That Caius—man in the abstract—was mortal, was perfectly correct, but he was not Caius, not an abstract man, but a creature quite, quite separate from all others. He had been little Ványa, with a mamma and a papa; with Mitya and Volódya, and the toys, a coachman and a nurse, afterwards with Kátenka and with all the joys, griefs, and delights of childhood, boyhood, and youth. What did Caius know

[11] Karl Kiezewetter (1766–1819), author of an outline of logic widely used in Russian schools at the time.

of the smell of that striped leather ball Ványa had been so fond of? Had Caius kissed his mother's hand like that, and did the silk of her dress rustle so for Caius? Had he rioted like that at school when the pastry was bad? Had Caius been in love like that? Could Caius preside at a session as he did? "Caius really was mortal, and it was right for him to die; but for me, little Ványa, Iván Ilých, with all my thoughts and emotions, it's altogether a different matter. It cannot be that I ought to die. That would be too terrible."

Such was his feeling.

"If I had to die like Caius I should have known it was so. An inner voice would have told me so, but there was nothing of the sort in me and I and all my friends felt that our case was quite different from that of Caius. And now here it is!" he said to himself. "It can't be. It's impossible! But here it is. How is this? How is one to understand it?"

He could not understand it, and tried to drive this false, incorrect, morbid thought away and to replace it by other proper and healthy thoughts. But that thought, and not the thought only but the reality itself, seemed to come and confront him.

And to replace that thought he called up a succession of others, hoping to find in them some support. He tried to get back into the former current of thoughts that had once screened the thought of death from him. But strange to say, all that had formerly shut off, hidden, and destroyed, his consciousness of death, no longer had that effect. Iván Ilých now spent most of his time in attempting to re-establish that old current. He would say to himself: "I will take up my duties again—after all I used to live by them." And banishing all doubts he would go to the law courts, enter into conversation with his colleagues, and sit carelessly as was his wont, scanning the crowd with a thoughtful look and leaning both his emaciated arms on the arms of his oak chair; bending over as usual to a colleague and drawing his papers nearer he would interchange whispers with him, and then suddenly raising his eyes and sitting erect would pronounce certain words and open the proceedings. But suddenly in the midst of those proceedings the pain in his side, regardless of the stage the proceedings had reached, would begin its own gnawing work. Iván Ilých would turn his attention to it and try to drive the thought of it away, but without success. *It* would come and stand before him and look at him, and he would be petrified and the light would die out of his eyes, and he would again begin asking himself whether *It* alone was true. And his colleagues and subordinates would see with surprise and distress that he, the brilliant and subtle judge, was becoming confused and making mistakes. He would shake himself, try to pull himself together, manage somehow to bring the sitting to a close, and return home with the sorrowful consciousness that his judicial labours could not as formerly hide from him what he wanted them to hide, and could not deliver him from *It*. And what was worst of all was that *It* drew his attention to itself not in order to make him take some action but only that he should look at *It*, look it straight in the face: look at it and without doing anything, suffer inexpressibly.

And to save himself from this condition Iván Ilých looked for consolations— 180
new screens—and new screens were found and for a while seemed to save him,
but then they immediately fell to pieces or rather became transparent, as if *It*
penetrated them and nothing could veil *It*.

In these latter days he would go into the drawing-room he had arranged—
that drawing-room where he had fallen and for the sake of which (how bitterly
ridiculous it seemed) he had sacrificed his life—for he knew that his illness
originated with that knock. He would enter and see that something had
scratched the polished table. He would look for the cause of this and find that
it was the bronze ornamentation of an album, that had got bent. He would
take up the expensive album which he had lovingly arranged, and feel vexed
with his daughter and her friends for their untidiness—for the album was torn
here and there and some of the photographs turned upside down. He would
put it carefully in order and bend the ornamentation back into position. Then
it would occur to him to place all those things in another corner of the room,
near the plants. He could call the footman, but his daughter or wife would
come to help him. They would not agree, and his wife would contradict him,
and he would dispute and grow angry. But that was all right, for then he did
not think about *It*. *It* was invisible.

But then, when he was moving something himself, his wife would say: "Let
the servants do it. You will hurt yourself again." And suddenly *It* would flash
through the screen and he would see it. It was just a flash, and he hoped it would
disappear, but he would involuntarily pay attention to his side. "It sits there as
before, gnawing just the same!" And he could no longer forget *It*, but could distinctly see it looking at him from behind the flowers. "What is it all for?"

"It really is so! I lost my life over that curtain as I might have done when
storming a fort. Is that possible? How terrible and how stupid. It can't be true!
It can't, but it is."

He would go to his study, lie down, and again be alone with *It*: face to face
with *It*. And nothing could be done with *It* except to look at it and shudder.

Chapter VII

How it happened it is impossible to say because it came about step by step, 185
unnoticed, but in the third month of Iván Ilých's illness, his wife, his daughter,
his son, his acquaintances, the doctors, the servants, and above all he himself,
were aware that the whole interest he had for other people was whether he
would soon vacate his place, and at last release the living from the discomfort
caused by his presence and be himself released from his sufferings.

He slept less and less. He was given opium and hypodermic injections of
morphine, but this did not relieve him. The dull depression he experienced in
a somnolent condition at first gave him a little relief, but only as something
new, afterwards it became as distressing as the pain itself or even more so.

Special foods were prepared for him by the doctors' orders, but all those
foods became increasingly distasteful and disgusting to him.

For his excretions also special arrangements had to be made, and this was a torment to him every time—a torment from the uncleanliness, the unseemliness, and the smell, and from knowing that another person had to take part in it.

But just through this most unpleasant matter Iván Ilých obtained comfort. Gerásim, the butler's young assistant, always came in to carry the things out. Gerásim was a clean, fresh peasant lad, grown stout on town food and always cheerful and bright. At first the sight of him, in his clean Russian peasant costume, engaged on that disgusting task embarrassed Iván Ilých.

Once when he got up from the commode too weak to draw up his trousers, 190 he dropped into a soft armchair and looked with horror at his bare, enfeebled thighs with the muscles so sharply marked on them.

Gerásim with a firm light tread, his heavy boots emitting a pleasant smell of tar and fresh winter air, came in wearing a clean Hessian apron, the sleeves of his print shirt tucked up over his strong bare young arms; and refraining from looking at his sick master out of consideration for his feelings, and restraining the joy of life that beamed from his face, he went up to the commode.

"Gerásim!" said Iván Ilých in a weak voice.

Gerásim started, evidently afraid he might have committed some blunder, and with a rapid movement turned his fresh, kind, simple young face which just showed the first downy signs of a beard.

"Yes, sir?"

"That must be very unpleasant for you. You must forgive me. I am helpless." 195

"Oh, why, sir," and Gerásim's eyes beamed and he showed his glistening white teeth, "what's a little trouble? It's a case of illness with you, sir."

And his deft strong hands did their accustomed task, and he went out of the room stepping lightly. Five minutes later he as lightly returned.

Iván Ilých was still sitting in the same position in the armchair.

"Gerásim," he said when the latter had replaced the freshly-washed utensil. "Please come here and help me." Gerásim went up to him. "Lift me up. It is hard for me to get up, and I have sent Dmítri away."

Gerásim went up to him, grasped his master with his strong arms deftly but 200 gently, in the same way that he stepped—lifted him, supported him with one hand, and with the other drew up his trousers and would have set him down again, but Iván Ilých asked to be led to the sofa. Gerásim, without an effort and without apparent pressure, led him, almost lifting him, to the sofa and placed him on it.

"Thank you. How easily and well you do it all!"

Gerásim smiled again and turned to leave the room. But Iván Ilých felt his presence such a comfort that he did not want to let him go.

"One thing more, please move up that chair. No, the other one—under my feet. It is easier for me when my feet are raised."

Gerásim brought the chair, set it down gently in place, and raised Iván Ilých's legs on to it. It seemed to Iván Ilých that he felt better while Gerásim was holding up his legs.

"It's better when my legs are higher," he said. "Place that cushion under 205 them."

Gerásim did so. He again lifted the legs and placed them, and again Iván Ilých felt better while Gerásim held his legs. When he set them down Iván Ilých fancied he felt worse.

"Gerásim," he said. "Are you busy now?"

"Not at all, sir," said Gerásim, who had learnt from the townsfolk how to speak to gentlefolk.

"What have you still to do?"

"What have I to do? I've done everything except chopping the logs for 210 tomorrow."

"Then hold my legs up a bit higher, can you?"

"Of course I can. Why not?" And Gerásim raised his master's legs higher and Iván Ilých thought that in that position he did not feel any pain at all.

"And how about the logs?"

"Don't trouble about that, sir. There's plenty of time."

Iván Ilých told Gerásim to sit down and hold his legs, and began to talk to 215 him. And strange to say it seemed to him that he felt better while Gerásim held his legs up.

After that Iván Ilých would sometimes call Gerásim and get him to hold his legs on his shoulders, and he liked talking to him. Gerásim did it all easily, willingly, simply, and with a good nature that touched Iván Ilých. Health, strength, and vitality in other people were offensive to him, but Gerásim's strength and vitality did not mortify but soothed him.

What tormented Iván Ilých most was the deception, the lie, which for some reason they all accepted, that he was not dying but was simply ill, and that he only need keep quiet and undergo a treatment and then something very good would result. He however knew that do what they would nothing would come of it, only still more agonizing suffering and death. This deception tortured him—their not wishing to admit what they all knew and what he knew, but wanting to lie to him concerning his terrible condition, and wishing and forcing him to participate in that lie. Those lies— lies enacted over him on the eve of his death and destined to degrade this awful, solemn act to the level of their visitings, their curtains, their sturgeon for dinner—were a terrible agony for Iván Ilých. And strangely enough, many times when they were going through their antics over him he had been within a hairbreadth of calling out to them: "Stop lying! You know and I know that I am dying. Then at least stop lying about it!" But he had never had the spirit to do it. The awful, terrible act of his dying was, he could see, reduced by those about him to the level of a casual, unpleasant, and almost indecorous incident (as if someone entered a drawing-room diffusing an unpleasant odour) and this was done by that very decorum which he had served all his life long. He saw that no one felt for him, because no one even wished to grasp his position. Only Gerásim recognized it and pitied him. And so Iván Ilých felt at ease only with him. He felt comforted when Gerásim supported his legs (sometimes all night long) and refused to go to bed, saying, "Don't you worry, Iván Ilých. I'll get sleep enough later on," or when he suddenly became familiar and exclaimed: "If you weren't sick it would be another matter, but as it is, why should I grudge a little trouble?" Gerásim alone did not lie; everything showed that he alone understood the facts of the case and did not consider it necessary to disguise them, but simply felt sorry for his emaciated and enfeebled master. Once when Iván Ilých was sending him away he even said straight out: "We shall all of us die, so why should I grudge a little trouble?"—expressing the fact that he did not think his work burdensome, because he was doing it for a dying man and hoped someone would do the same for him when his time came.

Apart from this lying, or because of it, what most tormented Iván Ilých was that no one pitied him as he wished to be pitied. At certain moments after prolonged suffering he wished most of all (though he would have been ashamed to confess it) for someone to pity him as a sick child is pitied. He longed to be petted and comforted. He knew he was an important functionary, that he had a beard turning grey, and that therefore what he longed for was impossible, but still he longed for it. And in Gerásim's attitude towards him there was something akin to what he wished for, and so that attitude comforted him. Iván Ilých wanted to weep, wanted to be petted and cried over, and then his colleague Shébek would come, and instead of weeping and being petted, Iván Ilých would assume a serious, severe, and profound air, and by force of habit would express his opinion on a decision of the Court of Cassation and would stubbornly insist on that view. This falsity around him and within him did more than anything else to poison his last days.

Chapter VIII

It was morning. He knew it was morning because Gerásim had gone, and Peter the footman had come and put out the candles, drawn back one of the curtains, and begun quietly to tidy up. Whether it was morning or evening, Friday or Sunday, made no difference, it was all just the same: the gnawing, unmitigated, agonizing pain, never ceasing for an instant, the consciousness of life inexorably waning but not yet extinguished, that approach of that ever dreaded and hateful Death which was the only reality, and always the same falsity. What were days, weeks, hours, in such a case?

"Will you have some tea, sir?"   220

"He wants things to be regular, and wishes the gentlefolk to drink tea in the morning," thought Iván Ilých, and only said "No."

"Wouldn't you like to move onto the sofa, sir?"

"He wants to tidy up the room, and I'm in the way. I am uncleanliness and disorder," he thought, and said only:

"No, leave me alone."

The man went on bustling about. Iván Ilých stretched out his hand. Peter   225
came up, ready to help.

"What is it, sir?"

"My watch."

Peter took the watch which was close at hand and gave it to his master.

"Half-past eight. Are they up?"

"No, sir, except Vladímir Ivánich" (the son) "who has gone to school. Pra- 230
skóvya Fëdorovna ordered me to wake her if you asked for her. Shall I do so?"

"No, there's no need to." "Perhaps I'd better have some tea," he thought, and
added aloud: "Yes, bring me some tea."

Peter went to the door but Iván Ilých dreaded being left alone. "How can I
keep him here? Oh yes, my medicine." "Peter, give me my medicine." "Why
not? Perhaps it may still do me some good." He took a spoonful and swallowed
it. "No, it won't help. It's all tomfoolery, all deception," he decided as soon as
he became aware of the familiar, sickly, hopeless taste. "No, I can't believe in it
any longer. But the pain, why this pain? If it would only cease just for a moment!" And he moaned. Peter turned towards him. "It's all right. Go and fetch
me some tea."

Peter went out. Left alone Iván Ilých groaned not so much with pain, terrible
though that was, as from mental anguish. Always and for ever the same, always
these endless days and nights. If only it would come quicker! If only *what* would
come quicker? Death, darkness? . . . No, no! Anything rather than death!

When Peter returned with the tea on a tray, Iván Ilých stared at him for a
time in perplexity, not realizing who and what he was. Peter was disconcerted
by that look and his embarrassment brought Iván Ilých to himself.

"Oh, tea! All right, put it down. Only help me to wash and put on a clean shirt." 235

And Iván Ilých began to wash. With pauses for rest, he washed his hands and
then his face, cleaned his teeth, brushed his hair, and looked in the glass. He
was terrified by what he saw, especially by the limp way in which his hair clung
to his pallid forehead.

While his shirt was being changed he knew that he would be still more
frightened at the sight of his body, so he avoided looking at it. Finally he was
ready. He drew on a dressing-gown, wrapped himself in a plaid, and sat down
in the armchair to take his tea. For a moment he felt refreshed, but as soon as
he began to drink the tea he was again aware of the same taste, and the pain
also returned. He finished it with an effort, and then lay down stretching out
his legs, and dismissed Peter.

Always the same. Now a spark of hope flashes up, then a sea of despair rages,
and always pain; always pain, always despair, and always the same. When alone he
had a dreadful and distressing desire to call someone, but he knew beforehand
that with others present it would be still worse. "Another dose of morphine—to
lose consciousness. I will tell him, the doctor, that he must think of something
else. It's impossible, impossible, to go on like this."

An hour and another pass like that. But now there is a ring at the door bell.
Perhaps it's the doctor? It is. He comes in fresh, hearty, plump, and cheerful,
with that look on his face that seems to say: "There now, you're in a panic
about something, but we'll arrange it all for you directly!" The doctor knows
this expression is out of place here, but he has put it on once for all and can't

take it off—like a man who has put on a frock-coat in the morning to pay a round of calls.

The doctor rubs his hands vigorously and reassuringly. 240

"Brr! How cold it is! There's such a sharp frost; just let me warm myself!" he says, as if it were only a matter of waiting till he was warm, and then he would put everything right.

"Well now, how are you?"

Iván Ilých feels that the doctor would like to say: "Well, how are our affairs?" but that even he feels that this would not do, and says instead: "What sort of a night have you had?"

Iván Ilých looks at him as much as to say: "Are you really never ashamed of lying?" But the doctor does not wish to understand this question, and Iván Ilých says: "Just as terrible as ever. The pain never leaves me and never subsides. If only something . . ."

"Yes, you sick people are always like that. . . . There, now I think I am warm 245 enough. Even Praskóvya Fëdorovna, who is so particular, could find no fault with my temperature. Well, now I can say good-morning," and the doctor presses his patient's hand.

Then, dropping his former playfulness, he begins with a most serious face to examine the patient, feeling his pulse and taking his temperature, and then begins the sounding and auscultation.

Iván Ilých knows quite well and definitely that all this is nonsense and pure deception, but when the doctor, getting down on his knee, leans over him, putting his ear first higher then lower, and performs various gymnastic movements over him with a significant expression on his face, Iván Ilých submits to it all as he used to submit to the speeches of the lawyers, though he knew very well that they were all lying and why they were lying.

The doctor, kneeling on the sofa, is still sounding him when Praskóvya Fëdorovna's silk dress rustles at the door and she is heard scolding Peter for not having let her know of the doctor's arrival.

She comes in, kisses her husband, and at once proceeds to prove that she has been up a long time already, and only owing to a misunderstanding failed to be there when the doctor arrived.

Iván Ilých looks at her, scans her all over, sets against her the whiteness and 250 plumpness and cleanness of her hands and neck, the gloss of her hair, and the sparkle of her vivacious eyes. He hates her with his whole soul. And the thrill of hatred he feels for her makes him suffer from her touch.

Her attitude towards him and his disease is still the same. Just as the doctor had adopted a certain relation to his patient which he could not abandon, so had she formed one towards him—that he was not doing something he ought to do and was himself to blame, and that she reproached him lovingly for this—and she could not now change that attitude.

"You see he doesn't listen to me and doesn't take his medicine at the proper time. And above all he lies in a position that is no doubt bad for him—with his legs up."

She described how he made Gerásim hold his legs up.

The doctor smiled with a contemptuous affability that said: "What's to be done? These sick people do have foolish fancies of that kind, but we must forgive them."

When the examination was over the doctor looked at his watch, and then 255 Praskóvya Fëdorovna announced to Iván Ilých that it was of course as he pleased, but she had sent to-day for a celebrated specialist who would examine him and have a consultation with Michael Danílovich (their regular doctor).

"Please don't raise any objections. I am doing this for my own sake," she said ironically, letting it be felt that she was doing it all for his sake and only said this to leave him no right to refuse. He remained silent, knitting his brows. He felt that he was so surrounded and involved in a mesh of falsity that it was hard to unravel anything.

Everything she did for him was entirely for her own sake, and she told him she was doing for herself what she actually was doing for herself, as if that was so incredible that he must understand the opposite.

At half-past eleven the celebrated specialist arrived. Again the sounding began and the significant conversations in his presence and in another room, about the kidneys and the appendix, and the questions and answers, with such an air of importance that again, instead of the real question of life and death which now alone confronted him, the question arose of the kidney and appendix which were not behaving as they ought to and would now be attacked by Michael Danílovich and the specialist and forced to amend their ways.

The celebrated specialist took leave of him with a serious though not hopeless look, and in reply to the timid question Iván Ilých, with eyes glistening with fear and hope, put to him as to whether there was a chance of recovery, said that he could not vouch for it but there was a possibility. The look of hope with which Iván Ilých watched the doctor out was so pathetic that Praskóvya Fëdorovna, seeing it, even wept as she left the room to hand the doctor his fee.

The gleam of hope kindled by the doctor's encouragement did not last long. 260 The same room, the same pictures, curtains, wall-paper, medicine bottles, were all there, and the same aching suffering body, and Iván Ilých began to moan. They gave him a subcutaneous injection and he sank into oblivion.

It was twilight when he came to. They brought him his dinner and he swallowed some beef tea with difficulty, and then everything was the same again and night was coming on.

After dinner, at seven o'clock, Praskóvya Fëdorovna came into the room in evening dress, her full bosom pushed up by her corset, and with traces of powder on her face. She had reminded him in the morning that they were going to the theater. Sarah Bernhardt was visiting the town and they had a box, which he had insisted on their taking. Now he had forgotten about it and her toilet offended him, but he concealed his vexation when he remembered that he had himself insisted on their securing a box and going because it would be an instructive and aesthetic pleasure for the children.

Praskóvya Fëdorovna came in, self-satisfied but yet with a rather guilty air. She sat down and asked how he was, but, as he saw, only for the sake of asking and not in order to learn about it, knowing that there was nothing to learn—and then went on to what she really wanted to say: that she would not on any account have gone but that the box had been taken and Helen and their daughter were going, as well as Petríshchev (the examining magistrate, their daughter's fiancé) and that it was out of the question to let them go alone; but that she would have much preferred to sit with him for a while; and he must be sure to follow the doctor's orders while she was away.

"Oh, and Fëdor Petróvich" (the fiancé) "would like to come in. May he? And Lisa?"

"All right."

Their daughter came in in full evening dress, her fresh young flesh exposed (making a show of that very flesh which in his own case caused so much suffering), strong, healthy, evidently in love, and impatient with illness, suffering, and death, because they interfered with her happiness.

Fëdor Petróvich came in too, in evening dress, his hair curled *á la Capoul,* a tight stiff collar round his long sinewy neck, an enormous white shirt-front and narrow black trousers tightly stretched over his strong thighs. He had one white glove tightly drawn on, and was holding his opera hat in his hand.

Following him the schoolboy crept in unnoticed, in a new uniform, poor little fellow, and wearing gloves. Terribly dark shadows showed under his eyes, the meaning of which Iván Ilých knew well.

His son had always seemed pathetic to him, and now it was dreadful to see the boy's frightened look of pity. It seemed to Iván Ilých that Vásya was the only one besides Gerásim who understood and pitied him.

They all sat down and again asked how he was. A silence followed. Lisa asked her mother about the opera-glasses, and there was an altercation between mother and daughter as to who had taken them and where they had been put. This occasioned some unpleasantness.

Fëdor Petróvich inquired of Iván Ilých whether he had ever seen Sarah Bernhardt. Iván Ilých did not at first catch the question, but then replied: "No, have you seen her before?"

"Yes, in *Adrienne Lecouvreur.*"[12]

Praskóvya Fëdorovna mentioned some roles in which Sarah Bernhardt was particularly good. Her daughter disagreed. Conversation sprang up as to the elegance and realism of her acting—the sort of conversation that is always repeated and is always the same.

In the midst of the conversation Fëdor Petróvich glanced at Iván Ilých and became silent. The others also looked at him and grew silent. Iván Ilých was staring with glittering eyes straight before him, evidently indignant with them. This had to be rectified, but it was impossible to do so. The silence had to be

265

270

---

[12] A play by the French dramatist Eugène Scribe (1791–1861).

broken, but for a time no one dared to break it and they all became afraid that the conventional deception would suddenly become obvious and the truth become plain to all. Lisa was the first to pluck up courage and break that silence, but by trying to hide what everybody was feeling, she betrayed it.

"Well, if we are going it's time to start," she said, looking at her watch, a pres- 275 ent from her father, and with a faint and significant smile at Fëdor Petróvich relating to something known only to them. She got up with a rustle of her dress.

They all rose, said good-night, and went away.

When they had gone it seemed to Iván Ilých that he felt better; the falsity had gone with them. But the pain remained—that same pain and that same fear that made everything monotonously alike, nothing harder and nothing easier. Everything was worse.

Again minute followed minute and hour followed hour. Everything remained the same and there was no cessation. And the inevitable end of it all became more and more terrible.

"Yes, send Gerásim here," he replied to a question Peter asked.

Chapter IX

His wife returned late at night. She came in on tiptoe, but he heard her, opened 280 his eyes, and made haste to close them again. She wished to send Gerásim away and to sit with him herself, but he opened his eyes and said: "No, go away."

"Are you in great pain?"

"Always the same."

"Take some opium."

He agreed and took some. She went away.

Till about three in the morning he was in a state of stupefied misery. It 285 seemed to him that he and his pain were being thrust into a narrow, deep black sack, but though they were pushed further and further in they could not be pushed to the bottom. And this, terrible enough in itself, was accompanied by suffering. He was frightened yet wanted to fall through the sack, he struggled but yet co-operated. And suddenly he broke through, fell, and regained consciousness. Gerásim was sitting at the foot of the bed dozing quietly and patiently, while he himself lay with his emaciated stockinged legs resting on Gerásim's shoulders; the same shaded candle was there and the same unceasing pain.

"Go away, Gerásim," he whispered.

"It's all right, sir. I'll stay a while."

"No. Go away."

He removed his legs from Gerásim's shoulders, turned sideways onto his arm, and felt sorry for himself. He only waited till Gerásim had gone into the next room and then restrained himself no longer but wept like a child. He wept on account of his helplessness, his terrible loneliness, the cruelty of man, the cruelty of God, and the absence of God.

"Why hast Thou done all this? Why hast Thou brought me here? Why, why 290 dost Thou torment me so terribly?"

He did not expect an answer and yet wept because there was no answer and could be none. The pain again grew more acute, but he did not stir and did not call. He said to himself: "Go on! Strike me! But what is it for? What have I done to Thee? What is it for?"

Then he grew quiet and not only ceased weeping but even held his breath and became all attention. It was as though he were listening not to an audible voice but to the voice of his soul, to the current of thoughts arising within him.

"What is it you want?" was the first clear conception capable of expression in words, that he heard.

"What do you want? What do you want?" he repeated to himself.

"What do I want? To live and not to suffer," he answered.   295

And again he listened with such concentrated attention that even his pain did not distract him.

"To live? How?" asked his inner voice.

"Why, to live as I used to—well and pleasantly."

"As you lived before, well and pleasantly?" the voice repeated.

And in imagination he began to recall the best moments of his pleasant life. 300 But strange to say none of those best moments of his pleasant life now seemed at all what they had then seemed—none of them except the first recollections of childhood. There, in childhood, there had been something really pleasant with which it would be possible to live if it could return. But the child who had experienced that happiness existed no longer, it was like a reminiscence of somebody else.

As soon as the period began which had produced the present Iván Ilých, all that had then seemed joys now melted before his sight and turned into something trivial and often nasty.

And the further he departed from childhood and the nearer he came to the present the more worthless and doubtful were the joys. This began with the School of Law. A little that was really good was still found there—there was lightheartedness, friendship, and hope. But in the upper classes there had already been fewer of such good moments. Then during the first years of his official career, when he was in the service of the Governor, some pleasant moments again occurred: they were the memories of love for a woman. Then all became confused and there was still less of what was good; later on again there was still less that was good, and the further he went the less there was. His marriage, a mere accident, then the disenchantment that followed it, his wife's bad breath and the sensuality and hypocrisy: then that deadly official life and those preoccupations about money, a year of it, and two, and ten, and twenty, and always the same thing. And the longer it lasted the more deadly it became. "It is as if I had been going downhill while I imagined I was going up. And that is really what it was. I was going up in public opinion, but to the same extent life was ebbing away from me. And now it is all done and there is only death."

"Then what does it mean? Why? It can't be that life is so senseless and horrible. But if it really has been so horrible and senseless, why must I die and die in agony? There is something wrong!"

"Maybe I did not live as I ought to have done," it suddenly occurred to him. "But how could that be, when I did everything properly?" he replied, and immediately dismissed from his mind this, the sole solution of all the riddles of life and death, as something quite impossible.

"Then what do you want now? To live? Live how? Live as you lived in the law courts when the usher proclaimed 'The judge is coming!' " "The judge is coming, the judge!" he repeated to himself. "Here he is, the judge. But I am not guilty!" he exclaimed angrily. "What is it for?" And he ceased crying, but turning his face to the wall continued to ponder on the same question: Why, and for what purpose, is there all this horror? But however much he pondered he found no answer. And whenever the thought occurred to him, as it often did, that it all resulted from his not having lived as he ought to have done, he at once recalled the correctness of his whole life and dismissed so strange an idea.

Chapter X

Another fortnight passed. Iván Ilých now no longer left his sofa. He would not lie in bed but lay on the sofa, facing the wall nearly all the time. He suffered ever the same unceasing agonies and in his loneliness pondered always on the same insoluble question: "What is this? Can it be that it is Death?" And the inner voice answered: "Yes, it is Death."

"Why these sufferings?" And the voice answered, "For no reason—they just are so." Beyond and besides this there was nothing.

From the very beginning of his illness, ever since he had first been to see the doctor, Iván Ilých's life had been divided between two contrary and alternating moods: now it was despair and the expectation of this uncomprehended and terrible death, and now hope and an intently interested observation of the functioning of his organs. Now before his eyes there was only a kidney or an intestine that temporarily evaded its duty, and now only that incomprehensible and dreadful death from which it was impossible to escape.

These two states of mind had alternated from the very beginning of his illness, but the further it progressed the more doubtful and fantastic became the conception of the kidney, and the more real the sense of impending death.

He had but to call to mind what he had been three months before and what he was now, to call to mind with what regularity he had been going downhill, for every possibility of hope to be shattered.

Latterly during that loneliness in which he found himself as he lay facing the back of the sofa, a loneliness in the midst of a populous town and surrounded by numerous acquaintances and relations but that yet could not have been more complete anywhere—either at the bottom of the sea or under the earth—during that terrible loneliness Iván Ilých had lived only in memories of the past. Pictures of his past rose before him one after another. They always began with what was nearest in time and then went back to what was most remote—to his childhood—and rested there. If he thought of the stewed prunes that had been offered him that day, his mind went back to the raw shrivelled French plums of his childhood, their peculiar flavor and the flow of saliva when he sucked their stones, and along with the memory of that taste came a whole series of memories of those days: his nurse, his brother, and their toys. "No, I mustn't think of that. . . . It is too painful," Iván Ilých said to himself, and brought himself back to the present—to the button on the back of the sofa and the creases in its morocco. "Morocco is expensive, but it does not wear well: there had been a quarrel about it. It was a different kind of quarrel and a different kind of morocco that time when we tore father's portfolio and were punished, and mamma brought us some tarts. . . ." And again his thoughts dwelt on his childhood, and again it was painful and he tried to banish them and fix his mind on something else.

Then again together with that chain of memories another series passed through his mind—of how his illness had progressed and grown worse. There also the further back he looked the more life there had been. There had been more of what was good in life and more of life itself. The two merged together. "Just as the pain went on getting worse and worse so my life grew worse and worse," he thought. "There is one bright spot there at the back, at the beginning of life, and afterwards all becomes blacker and blacker and proceeds more and more rapidly—in inverse ratio to the square of the distance from death," thought Iván Ilých. And the example of a stone falling downwards with increasing velocity entered his mind. Life, a series of increasing sufferings, flies, further and further towards its end—the most terrible suffering. "I am flying. . . ." He shuddered, shifted himself, and tried to resist, but was already aware that resistance was impossible, and again with eyes weary of gazing but unable to cease seeing what was before them, he stared at the back of the sofa and waited—awaiting that dreadful fall and shock and destruction.

"Resistance is impossible!" he said to himself. "If I could only understand what it is all for! But that too is impossible. An explanation would be possible if it could be said that I have not lived as I ought to. But it is impossible to say that," and he remembered all the legality, correctitude, and propriety of his life. "That at any rate can certainly not be admitted," he thought, and his lips smiled ironically as if someone could see that smile and be taken in by it. "There is no explanation! Agony, death. . . . What for?"

Chapter XI

Another two weeks went by in this way and during that fortnight an event occurred that Iván Ilých and his wife had desired. Petríshchev formally proposed. It happened in the evening. The next day Praskóvya Fëdorovna came into her husband's room considering how best to inform him of it, but that very night there had been a fresh change for the worse in his condition. She found him still lying on the sofa but in a different position. He lay on his back, groaning and staring fixedly straight in front of him.

She began to remind him of his medicines, but he turned his eyes towards her with such a look that she did not finish what she was saying; so great an animosity, to her in particular, did that look express. 315

"For Christ's sake, let me die in peace!" he said.

She would have gone away, but just then their daughter came in and went up to say good morning. He looked at her as he had done at his wife, and in reply to her inquiry about his health said dryly that he would soon free them all of himself. They were both silent and after sitting with him for a while went away.

"Is it our fault?" Lisa said to her mother. "It's as if we were to blame! I am sorry for papa, but why should we be tortured?"

The doctor came at his usual time. Iván Ilých answered "Yes" and "No," never taking his angry eyes from him, and at last said: "You know you can do nothing for me, so leave me alone."

"We can ease your sufferings." 320

"You can't even do that. Let me be."

The doctor went into the drawing-room and told Praskóvya Fëdorovna that the case was very serious and that the only resource left was opium to allay her husband's sufferings, which must be terrible.

It was true, as the doctor said, that Iván Ilých's physical sufferings were terrible, but worse than the physical sufferings were his mental sufferings which were his chief torture.

His mental sufferings were due to the fact that that night, as he looked at Gerásim's sleepy, good-natured face with its prominent cheek-bones, the question suddenly occurred to him: "What if my whole life has really been wrong?"

It occurred to him that what had appeared perfectly impossible before, namely that he had not spent his life as he should have done, might after all be true. It occurred to him that his scarcely perceptible attempts to struggle against what was considered good by the most highly placed people, those scarcely noticeable impulses which he had immediately suppressed, might have been the real thing, and all the rest false. And his professional duties and the whole arrangement of his life and of his family, and all his social and official interests, might all have been false. He tried to defend all those things to himself and suddenly felt the weakness of what he was defending. There was nothing to defend. 325

"But if that is so," he said to himself, "and I am leaving this life with the consciousness that I have lost all that was given me and it is impossible to rectify it—what then?"

He lay on his back and began to pass his life in review in quite a new way. In the morning when he saw first his footman, then his wife, then his daughter, and then the doctor, their every word and movement confirmed to him the awful truth that had been revealed to him during the night. In them he saw himself—all that for which he had lived—and saw clearly that it was not real at all, but a terrible and huge deception which had hidden both life and death.

This consciousness intensified his physical suffering tenfold. He groaned and tossed about, and pulled at his clothing which choked and stifled him. And he hated them on that account.

He was given a large dose of opium and became unconscious, but at noon his sufferings began again. He drove everybody away and tossed from side to side.

His wife came to him and said:

"Jean, my dear, do this for me. It can't do any harm and often helps. Healthy 330
people often do it."

He opened his eyes wide.

"What? Take communion? Why? It's unnecessary! However. . . ."

She began to cry.

"Yes, do, my dear. I'll send for our priest. He is such a nice man."

"All right. Very well," he muttered. 335

When the priest came and heard his confession, Iván Ilých was softened and seemed to feel a relief from his doubts and consequently from his sufferings, and for a moment there came a ray of hope. He again began to think of the vermiform appendix and the possibility of correcting it. He received the sacrament with tears in his eyes.

When they laid him down again afterwards he felt a moment's ease, and the hope that he might live awoke in him again. He began to think of the operation that had been suggested to him. "To live! I want to live!" he said to himself.

His wife came in to congratulate him after his communion, and when uttering the usual conventional words she added:

"You feel better, don't you?"

Without looking at her he said "Yes." 340

Her dress, her figure, the expression of her face, the tone of her voice, all revealed the same thing. "This is wrong, it is not as it should be. All you have lived for and still live for is falsehood and deception, hiding life and death from you." And as soon as he admitted that thought, his hatred and his agonizing physical suffering again sprang up, and with that suffering a consciousness of the unavoidable, approaching end. And to this was added a new sensation of grinding shooting pain and a feeling of suffocation.

The expression of his face when he uttered that "yes" was dreadful. Having uttered it, he looked her straight in the eyes, turned on his face with a rapidity extraordinary in his weak state and shouted:

"Go away! Go away and leave me alone!"

Chapter XII

From that moment the screaming began that continued for three days, and was so terrible that one could not hear it through two closed doors without horror. At the moment he answered his wife he realized that he was lost, that there was no return, that the end had come, the very end, and his doubts were still unsolved and remained doubts.

"Oh! Oh! Oh!" he cried in various intonations. He had begun by screaming 345 "I won't!" and continued screaming on the letter "o."

For three whole days, during which time did not exist for him, he struggled in that black sack into which he was being thrust by an invisible, resistless force. He struggled as a man condemned to death struggles in the hands of the executioner, knowing that he cannot save himself. And every moment he felt that despite all his efforts he was drawing nearer and nearer to what terrified him. He felt that his agony was due to his being thrust into that black hole and still more to his not being able to get right into it. He was hindered from getting into it by his conviction that his life had been a good one. That very justification of his life held him fast and prevented his moving forward, and it caused him most torment of all.

Suddenly some force struck him in the chest and side, making it still harder to breathe, and he fell through the hole and there at the bottom was a light. What had happened to him was like the sensation one sometimes experiences in a railway carriage when one thinks one is going backwards while one is really going forwards and suddenly becomes aware of the real direction.

"Yes, it was all not the right thing," he said to himself, "but that's no matter. It can be done. But what *is* the right thing?" he asked himself, and suddenly grew quiet.

This occurred at the end of the third day, two hours before his death. Just then his schoolboy son had crept softly in and gone up to the bedside. The dying man was still screaming desperately and waving his arms. His hand fell on the boy's head, and the boy caught it, pressed it to his lips, and began to cry.

At that very moment Iván Ilých fell through and caught sight of the light, 350 and it was revealed to him that though his life had not been what it should have been, this could still be rectified. He asked himself, "What *is* the right thing?" and grew still, listening. Then he felt that someone was kissing his hand. He opened his eyes, looked at his son, and felt sorry for him. His wife came up to him and he glanced at her. She was gazing at him open-mouthed, with undried tears on her nose and cheek and a despairing look on her face. He felt sorry for her too.

"Yes, I am making them wretched," he thought. "They are sorry, but it will be better for them when I die." He wished to say this but had not the strength to utter it. "Besides, why speak? I must act," he thought. With a look at his wife he indicated his son and said: "Take him away . . . sorry for him . . . sorry for you too. . . ." He tried to add, "forgive me," but said "forego" and waved his hand, knowing that He whose understanding mattered would understand.

And suddenly it grew clear to him that what had been oppressing him and would not leave him was all dropping away at once from two sides, from ten sides, and from all sides. He was sorry for them, he must act so as not to hurt them: release them and free himself from these sufferings. "How good and how simple!" he thought. "And the pain?" he asked himself. "What has become of it? Where are you, pain?"

He turned his attention to it.

"Yes, here it is. Well, what of it? Let the pain be."

"And death . . . where is it?"

355

He sought his former accustomed fear of death and did not find it. "Where is it? What death?" There was no fear because there was no death.

In place of death there was light.

"So that's what it is!" he suddenly exclaimed aloud. "What joy!"

To him all this happened in a single instant, and the meaning of that instant did not change. For those present his agony continued for another two hours. Something rattled in his throat, his emaciated body twitched, then the gasping and rattle became less and less frequent.

"It is finished!" said someone near him.

He heard these words and repeated them in his soul.

360

"Death is finished," he said to himself. "It is no more!"

He drew in a breath, stopped in the midst of a sigh, stretched out, and died.

FOR ANALYSIS

1. Discuss the evidence that Ilých's death is a moral judgment—that is, a punishment for his life.

2. Discuss "The Death of Iván Ilých" from Paul's perspective revealed in 1 Corinthians 13 (p. 1063). What accounts for the change in Ilých's attitude toward his approaching death?

3. Discuss the fact that Gerásim, Ilých's peasant servant, is more sympathetic to his condition than Ilých's family is.

4. Suggest a reason for Tolstoy's decision to begin the story immediately after Ilých's death and then move back to recount the significant episodes of his life.

MAKING CONNECTIONS

Compare the significance of death to the characters in this story with the significance of death to the characters in one or both of the following works: Porter's "The Jilting of Granny Weatherall" (p. 1168) and Silko's "The Man to Send Rain Clouds" (p. 1164).

WRITING TOPICS

1. At the conclusion of the story, Ilých achieves peace and understanding, and the questions that have been torturing him are resolved. He realizes that "though his life had not been what it should have been, this could still be rectified" (para. 350). What does this mean?

2. In an essay, compare and contrast the attitudes of various characters to Ilých's mortal illness. How do his colleagues respond? His wife? His children? His servant Gerásim?

SPUNK   1927

I

A giant of a brown-skinned man sauntered up the one street of the village and out into the palmetto thickets with a small pretty woman clinging lovingly to his arm.

"Looka theah, folkses!" cried Elijah Mosley, slapping his leg gleefully. "Theah they go, big as life an' brassy as tacks."

All the loungers in the store tried to walk to the door with an air of nonchalance but with small success.

"Now pee-eople!" Walter Thomas gasped. "Will you look at 'em!"

"But that's one thing Ah likes about Spunk Banks—he ain't skeered of 5 nothin' on God's green footstool—*nothin'!* He rides that log down at saw-mill jus' like he struts 'round wid another man's wife—jus' don't give a kitty. When Tes' Miller got cut to giblets on that circle saw, Spunk steps right up and starts ridin'. The rest of us was skeered to go near it."

A round-shouldered figure in overalls much too large came nervously in the door and the talking ceased. The men looked at each other and winked.

"Gimme some soda-water. Sass'prilla Ah reckon," the newcomer ordered, and stood far down the counter near the open pickled pig-feet tub to drink it.

Elijah nudged Walter and turned with mock gravity to the new-comer.

"Say, Joe, how's everything up yo' way? How's yo' wife?"

Joe started and all but dropped the bottle he was holding. He swallowed sev- 10 eral times painfully and his lips trembled.

"Aw 'Lige, you oughtn't to do nothin' like that," Walter grumbled. Elijah ignored him.

"She jus' passed heah a few minutes ago goin' thata way," with a wave of his hand in the direction of the woods.

Now Joe knew his wife had passed that way. He knew that the men lounging in the general store had seen her, moreover, he knew that the men knew *he* knew. He stood there silent for a long moment staring blankly, with his Adam's apple twitching nervously up and down his throat. One could actually *see* the pain he was suffering, his eyes, his face, his hands, and even the dejected slump of his shoulders. He set the bottle down upon the counter. He didn't bang it, just eased it out of his hand silently and fiddled with his suspender buckle.

"Well, Ah'm goin' after her to-day. Ah'm goin' an' fetch her back. Spunk's done gone too fur."

He reached deep down into his trouser pocket and drew out a hollow 15 ground razor, large and shiny, and passed his moistened thumb back and forth over the edge.

"Talkin' like a man, Joe. 'Course that's' *yo'* fambly affairs, but Ah like to see grit in anybody."

Joe Kanty laid down a nickel and stumbled out into the street.

Dusk crept in from the woods. Ike Clarke lit the swinging oil lamp that was almost immediately surrounded by candle-flies. The men laughed boisterously behind Joe's back as they watched him shamble woodward.

"You oughtn't to said whut you said to him, 'Lige—look how it worked him up," Walter chided.

"And Ah hope it did work him up. Tain't even decent for a man to take and 20 take like he do."

"Spunk will sho' kill him."

"Aw, Ah doan know. You never kin tell. He might turn him up an' spank him fur gettin' in the way, but Spunk wouldn't shoot no unarmed man. Dat razor he carried outa heah ain't gonna run Spunk down an' cut him, an' Joe ain't got the nerve to go to Spunk with it knowing he totes that Army .45. He makes that break outa heah to bluff us. He's gonna hide that razor behind the first palmetto root an' sneak back home to bed. Don't tell me nothin' 'bout that rabbit-foot colored man. Didn't he meet Spunk an' Lena face to face one day las week an' mumble sumthin' to Spunk 'bout lettin' his wife alone?"

"What did Spunk say?" Walter broke in. "Ah like him fine but tain't right the way he carries on wid Lena Kanty, jus' 'cause Joe's timid 'bout fightin'."

"You wrong theah, Walter. Tain't 'cause Joe's timid at all, it's 'cause Spunk wants Lena. If Joe was a passle of wile cats Spunk would tackle the job just the same. He'd go after *anything* he wanted the same way. As Ah wuz sayin' a minute ago, he tole Joe right to his face that Lena was his. 'Call her and see if she'll come. A woman knows her boss an' she answers when he calls.' 'Lena, ain't I yo' husband?' Joe sorter whines out. Lena looked at him real disgusted but she don't answer and she don't move outa her tracks. Then Spunk reaches out an' takes hold of her arm an' says: 'Lena, youse mine. From now on Ah works for you an' fights for you an' Ah never wants you to look to nobody for a crumb of bread, a stitch of close or a shingle to go over yo' head, but *me* long as Ah live. Ah'll git the lumber foh owah house to-morrow. Go home an git yo' things together!'

"'Thass mah house,' Lena speaks up. 'Papa gimme that.' 25

"'Well,' says Spunk, 'doan give up whut's yours, but when youse inside doan forgit youse mine, an' let no other man git outa his place wid you!'

"Lena looked up at him with her eyes so full of love that they wuz runnin' over, an' Spunk seen it an' Joe seen it too, and his lip started to tremblin' and his Adam's apple was galloping up and down his neck like a race horse. Ah bet he's wore out half a dozen Adam's apples since Spunk's been on the job with Lena. That's all he'll do. He'll be back heah after while swallowin' an' workin' his lips like he wants to say somethin' an' can't."

"But didn't he do *nothin'* to stop 'em?"

"Nope, not a frazzlin' thing—jus' stood there. Spunk took Lena's arm and walked off jus' like nothin' ain't happened and he stood there gazin' after them till they was outa sight. Now you know a woman don't want no man like that. I'm jus' waitin' to see whut he's goin' to say when he gits back."

II

But Joe Kanty never came back, never. The men in the store heard the sharp 30 report of a pistol somewhere distant in the palmetto thicket and soon Spunk came walking leisurely, with his big black Stetson set at the same rakish angle and Lena clinging to his arm, came walking right into the general store. Lena wept in a frightened manner.

"Well" Spunk announced calmly, "Joe came out there wid a meat axe an' made me kill him."

He sent Lena home and led the men back to Joe—crumpled and limp with his right hand still clutching his razor.

"See mah back? Mah close cut clear through. He sneaked up an' tried to kill me from the back, but Ah got him, an' got him good, first shot," Spunk said.

The men glared at Elijah, accusingly.

"Take him up an' plant him in Stony Lonesome," Spunk said in a careless 35 voice. "Ah didn't wanna shoot him but he made me do it. He's a dirty coward, jumpin' on a man from behind."

Spunk turned on his heel and sauntered away to where he knew his love wept in fear for him and no man stopped him. At the general store later on, they all talked of locking him up until the sheriff should come from Orlando, but no one did anything but talk.

A clear case of self-defense, the trial was a short one, and Spunk walked out of the court house to freedom again. He could work again, ride the dangerous log-carriage that fed the singing, snarling, biting circle-saw; he could stroll the soft dark lanes with his guitar. He was free to roam the woods again; he was free to return to Lena. He did all of these things.

III

"Whut you reckon, Walt?" Elijah asked one night later. "Spunk's gittin' ready to marry Lena!"

"Naw! Why, Joe ain't had time to git cold yit. Nohow Ah didn't figger Spunk was the marryin' kind."

"Well, he is," rejoined Elijah. "He done moved most of Lena's things—and 40 her along wid 'em—over to the Bradley house. He's buying it. Jus' like Ah told yo' all right in heah the night Joe was kilt. Spunk's crazy 'bout Lena. He don't want folks to keep on talkin' 'bout her—thass reason he's rushin' so. Funny thing 'bout that bob-cat, wan't it?"

"What bob-cat, 'Lige? Ah ain't heered 'bout none."

"Ain't cher? Well, night befo' las' as they was goin' to bed, a big black bob-cat, black all over, you hear me, *black*, walked round and round that house and howled like forty, an' when Spunk got his gun an' went to the winder to shoot it, he says it stood right still an' looked him in the eye, an' howled right at him. The thing got Spunk so nervoused up he couldn't shoot. But Spunk says twan't no bob-cat nohow. He says it was Joe done sneaked back from Hell!"

"Humph!" sniffed Walter, "he oughter be nervous after what he done. Ah reckon Joe come back to dare him to marry Lena, or to come out an' fight. Ah bet he'll be back time and again, too. Know what Ah think? Joe wuz a braver man than Spunk."

There was a general shout of derision from the group.

"Thass a fact," went on Walter. "Lookit whut he done; took a razor an' went 45 out to fight a man he knowed toted a gun an' wuz a crack shot, too; 'nother thing Joe wuz skeered of Spunk, skeered plumb stiff! But he went jes' the same. It took him a long time to get his nerve up. Tain't nothin' for Spunk to fight when he ain't skeered of nothin'. Now, Joe's done come back to have it out wid the man that's got all he ever had. Y'all know Joe ain't never had nothin' nor wanted nothin' besides Lena. It musta been a h'ant cause ain't nobody never seen no black bob-cat."

"'Nother thing," cut in one of the men, "Spunk was cussin' a blue streak to-day 'cause he 'lowed dat saw wuz wobblin'—almos' got 'im once. The machin-ist come, looked it over an said it wuz alright. Spunk musta been leanin t'wards it some. Den he claimed somebody pushed 'im but twan't nobody close to 'im. Ah wuz glad when knockin' off time came. I'm skeered of dat man when he gits hot. He'd beat you full of button holes as quick as he's look atcher."

IV

The men gathered the next evening in a different mood, no laughter. No badi-nage this time.

"Look, 'Lige, you goin' to set up wid Spunk?"

"Naw, Ah reckon not, Walter. Tell yuh the truth, Ah'm a li'l bit skittish. Spunk died too wicket—died cussin' he did. You know he thought he was done outa life."

"Good Lawd, who'd he think done it?" 50

"Joe."

"Joe Kanty? How come?"

"Walter, Ah b'leeve Ah will walk up thata way an' set. Lena would like it Ah reckon."

"But whut did he say, 'Lige?"

Elijah did not answer until they had left the lighted store and were strolling 55 down the dark street.

"Ah wuz loadin' a wagon wid scantlin' right near the saw when Spunk fell on the carriage but 'fore Ah could git to him the saw got him in the body—awful sight. Me an' Skint Miller got him off but it was too late. Anybody could see that. The fust thing he said wuz: 'He pushed me, 'Lige—the dirty hound pushed me in the back!'—he was spittin' blood at ev'ry breath. We laid him on the sawdust pile with his face to the East so's he could die easy. He helt mah han' till the last, Walter, and said: 'It was Joe, 'Lige . . . the dirty sneak shoved me . . . he didn't dare come to mah face . . . but Ah'll git the son-of-a-wood louse soon's Ah get there an' make hell too hot for him . . . Ah felt him shove me . . . !' Thass how he died."

"If spirits kin fight, there's a powerful tussle goin' on somewhere ovah Jordan 'cause Ah b'leeve Joe's ready for Spunk an' ain't skeered any more—yas, Ah b'leeve Joe pushed 'im mahself."

They had arrived at the house. Lena's lamentations were deep and loud. She had filled the room with magnolia blossoms that gave off a heavy sweet odor. The keepers of the wake tipped about whispering in frightened tones. Everyone in the village was there, even old Jeff Kanty, Joe's father, who a few hours before would have been afraid to come within ten feet of him, stood leering triumphantly down upon the fallen giant as if his fingers had been the teeth of steel that laid him low.

The cooling board consisted of three sixteen-inch boards on saw horses, a dingy sheet was his shroud.

The women ate heartily of the funeral baked meats and wondered who 60 would be Lena's next. The men whispered coarse conjectures between guzzles of whiskey.

FOR ANALYSIS

1. What is *spunk*? Which **characters** could be said to have it? Who has the most in the end?

2. How do the townspeople think about life after death? What does the story have to say about it?

3. How is Lena portrayed at the end of the story? Is she a grief-stricken victim? Is she to blame? Will she live out her life as a widow or move on to another man?

MAKING CONNECTIONS

1. Compare "Spunk" to Brooks's "We Real Cool" (p. 418) and Hughes's "Mother to Son" (p. 176) in terms of language use. What are the similarities? What are the differences?

2. Both Hurston's story and Hawthorne's "Young Goodman Brown" (p. 81) feature supernatural events that may or may not actually occur. How does each story present these events in ways that leave the question of whether they happened open? Why is this openness important to both stories?

WRITING TOPICS

1. Describe the workings of narration and **point of view** in this story. How does the story get told? Who does the telling? What effect do these choices have?

2. The southern black dialect used in this story has been received in a variety of ways both positive and negative. Why do you think Hurston chose to tell the story this way? What might have been some of the objections to her use of this dialect? What do you think of her choice?

TIM O'BRIEN   (B. 1946)

THE THINGS THEY CARRIED   1986

First Lieutenant Jimmy Cross carried letters from a girl named Martha, a junior at Mount Sebastian College in New Jersey. They were not love letters, but Lieutenant Cross was hoping, so he kept them folded in plastic at the bottom of his rucksack. In the late afternoon, after a day's march, he would dig his foxhole, wash his hands under a canteen, unwrap the letters, hold them with the tips of his fingers, and spend the last hour of light pretending. He would imagine romantic camping trips into the White Mountains in New Hampshire. He would sometimes taste the envelope flaps, knowing her tongue had been there. More than anything, he wanted Martha to love him as he loved her, but the letters were mostly chatty, elusive on the matter of love. She was a virgin, he was almost sure. She was an English major at Mount Sebastian, and she wrote beautifully about her professors and roommates and midterm exams, about her respect for Chaucer and her great affection for Virginia Woolf. She often quoted lines of poetry; she never mentioned the war, except to say, Jimmy, take care of yourself. The letters weighed ten ounces. They were signed "Love, Martha," but Lieutenant Cross understood that "Love" was only a way of signing and did not mean what he sometimes pretended it meant. At dusk, he would carefully return the letters to his rucksack. Slowly, a bit distracted, he would get up and move among his men, checking the perimeter, then at full dark he would return to his hole and watch the night and wonder if Martha was a virgin.

The things they carried were largely determined by necessity. Among the necessities or near necessities were P-38 can openers, pocket knives, heat tabs, wrist watches, dog tags, mosquito repellent, chewing gum, candy, cigarettes, salt tablets, packets of Kool-Aid, lighters, matches, sewing kits, Military Payment Certificates, C rations, and two or three canteens of water. Together, these items weighed between fifteen and twenty pounds, depending upon a man's habits or rate of metabolism. Henry Dobbins, who was a big man, carried extra rations; he was especially fond of canned peaches in heavy syrup over pound cake. Dave Jensen, who practiced field hygiene, carried a toothbrush, dental floss, and several hotel-size bars of soap he'd stolen on R&R[1] in Sydney, Australia. Ted Lavender, who was scared, carried tranquilizers until he was shot in the head outside the village of Than Khe in mid-April. By necessity, and because it was SOP,[2] they all carried steel helmets that weighed five pounds including the liner and camouflage cover. They carried the standard

[1] Rest and recreation.
[2] Standard operating procedure.

fatigue jackets and trousers. Very few carried underwear. On their feet they carried jungle boots—2.1 pounds—and Dave Jensen carried three pairs of socks and a can of Dr. Scholl's foot powder as a precaution against trench foot. Until he was shot, Ted Lavender carried six or seven ounces of premium dope, which for him was a necessity. Mitchell Sanders, the RTO, carried condoms. Norman Bowker carried a diary. Rat Kiley carried comic books. Kiowa, a devout Baptist, carried an illustrated New Testament that had been presented to him by his father, who taught Sunday school in Oklahoma City, Oklahoma. As a hedge against bad times, however, Kiowa also carried his grandmother's distrust of the white man, his grandfather's old hunting hatchet. Necessity dictated. Because the land was mined and booby-trapped, it was SOP for each man to carry a steel-centered, nylon-covered flak jacket, which weighed 6.7 pounds, but which on hot days seemed much heavier. Because you could die so quickly, each man carried at least one large compress bandage, usually in the helmet band for easy access. Because the nights were cold, and because the monsoons were wet, each carried a green plastic poncho that could be used as a raincoat or ground sheet or makeshift tent. With its quilted liner, the poncho weighed almost two pounds, but it was worth every ounce. In April, for instance, when Ted Lavender was shot, they used his poncho to wrap him up, then to carry him across the paddy, then to lift him into the chopper that took him away.

They were called legs or grunts.

To carry something was to "hump" it, as when Lieutenant Jimmy Cross humped his love for Martha up the hills and through the swamps. In its intransitive form, "to hump" meant "to walk," or "to march," but it implied burdens far beyond the intransitive.

Almost everyone humped photographs. In his wallet, Lieutenant Cross carried two photographs of Martha. The first was a Kodachrome snapshot signed "Love," though he knew better. She stood against a brick wall. Her eyes were gray and neutral, her lips slightly open as she stared straight-on at the camera. At night, sometimes, Lieutenant Cross wondered who had taken the picture, because he knew she had boyfriends, because he loved her so much, and because he could see the shadow of the picture taker spreading out against the brick wall. The second photograph had been clipped from the 1968 Mount Sebastian yearbook. It was an action shot—women's volleyball—and Martha was bent horizontal to the floor, reaching, the palms of her hands in sharp focus, the tongue taut, the expression frank and competitive. There was no visible sweat. She wore white gym shorts. Her legs, he thought, were almost certainly the legs of a virgin, dry and without hair, the left knee cocked and carrying her entire weight, which was just over one hundred pounds. Lieutenant Cross remembered touching that left knee. A dark theater, he remembered, and the movie was *Bonnie and Clyde*, and Martha wore a tweed skirt, and during the final scene, when he touched her knee, she turned and looked at him in a sad, sober way that made him pull his hand back, but he would always remember the feel of the tweed skirt and the knee beneath it and the sound of the gunfire that killed Bonnie and Clyde, how embarrassing it was, how slow and oppressive. He remembered kissing her good night at the dorm door. Right then, he thought, he should've done something brave. He should've carried her up the stairs to her room and tied her to the bed and touched that left knee all night long. He should've risked it. Whenever he looked at the photographs, he thought of new things he should've done.

What they carried was partly a function of rank, partly of field specialty.

As a first lieutenant and platoon leader, Jimmy Cross carried a compass, maps, code books, binoculars, and a .45-caliber pistol that weighed 2.9 pounds fully loaded. He carried a strobe light and the responsibility for the lives of his men.

As an RTO, Mitchell Sanders carried the PRC-25 radio, a killer, twenty-six pounds with its battery.

As a medic, Rat Kiley carried a canvas satchel filled with morphine and plasma and malaria tablets and surgical tape and comic books and all the things a medic must carry, including M&M's for especially bad wounds, for a total weight of nearly twenty pounds.

As a big man, therefore a machine gunner, Henry Dobbins carried the M-60, which weighed twenty-three pounds unloaded, but which was almost always loaded. In addition, Dobbins carried between ten and fifteen pounds of ammunition draped in belts across his chest and shoulders.

As PFCs or Spec 4s, most of them were common grunts and carried the standard M-16 gas-operated assault rifle. The weapon weighed 7.5 pounds unloaded, 8.2 pounds with its full twenty-round magazine. Depending on numerous factors, such as topography and psychology, the riflemen carried anywhere from twelve to twenty magazines, usually in cloth bandoliers, adding on another 8.4 pounds at minimum, fourteen pounds at maximum. When it was available, they also carried M-16 maintenance gear—rods and steel brushes and swabs and tubes of LSA oil—all of which weighed about a pound. Among the grunts, some carried the M-79 grenade launcher, 5.9 pounds unloaded, a reasonably light weapon except for the ammunition, which was heavy. A single round weighed ten ounces. The typical load was twenty-five rounds. But Ted Lavender, who was scared, carried thirty-four rounds when he was shot and killed outside Than Khe, and he went down under an exceptional burden, more than twenty pounds of ammunition, plus the flak jacket and helmet and rations and water and toilet paper and tranquilizers and all the rest, plus the unweighed fear. He was dead weight. There was no twitching or flopping. Kiowa, who saw it happen, said it was like watching a rock fall, or a big sandbag or something—just boom, then down—not like the movies where the dead guy rolls around and does fancy spins and goes ass over teakettle— not like that, Kiowa said, the poor bastard just flat-fuck fell. Boom. Down. Nothing else. It was a bright morning in mid-April. Lieutenant Cross felt the pain. He blamed himself. They stripped off Lavender's canteens and ammo, all the heavy things, and Rat Kiley said the obvious, the guy's dead, and Mitchell Sanders used his radio to report one U.S. KIA and to request a chopper. Then they wrapped Lavender in his poncho. They carried him out to a dry paddy, established security, and sat smoking the dead man's dope until the chopper came. Lieutenant Cross kept to himself. He pictured Martha's smooth young face, thinking he loved her more than anything, more than his men, and now Ted Lavender was dead because he loved her so much and could not stop thinking about her. When the dust-off arrived, they carried Lavender aboard. Afterward they burned Than Khe. They marched until dusk, then dug their holes, and that night Kiowa kept explaining how you had to be there, how fast it was, how the poor guy just dropped like so much concrete. Boom-down, he said. Like cement.

In addition to the three standard weapons—the M-60, M-16, and M-79— they carried whatever presented itself, or whatever seemed appropriate as a means of killing or staying alive. They carried catch-as-catch-can. At various times, in various situations, they carried M-14s and CAR-15s and Swedish Ks and grease guns and captured AK-47s and Chi-Coms and RPGs and Simonov carbines and black-market Uzis and .38-caliber Smith & Wesson handguns and 66 mm LAWs and shotguns and silencers and blackjacks and bayonets and C-4 plastic explosives. Lee Strunk carried a slingshot; a weapon of last resort, he called it. Mitchell Sanders carried brass knuckles. Kiowa carried his grandfather's feathered hatchet. Every third or fourth man carried a Claymore antipersonnel mine—3.5 pounds with its firing device. They all carried fragmentation grenades—fourteen ounces each. They all carried at least one M-18 colored smoke grenade—twenty-four ounces. Some carried CS or tear-gas grenades. Some carried white-phosphorus grenades. They carried all they could bear, and then some, including a silent awe for the terrible power of the things they carried.

In the first week of April, before Lavender died, Lieutenant Jimmy Cross received a good-luck charm from Martha. It was a simple pebble, an ounce at most. Smooth to the touch, it was a milky-white color with flecks of orange and violet, oval-shaped, like a miniature egg. In the accompanying letter, Martha wrote that she had found the pebble on the Jersey shoreline, precisely where the land touched water at high tide, where things came together but also separated. It was this separate-but-together quality, she wrote, that had inspired her to pick up the pebble and to carry it in her breast pocket for several days, where it seemed weightless, and then to send it through the mail, by air, as a token of her truest feelings for him. Lieutenant Cross found this romantic. But he wondered what her truest feelings were, exactly, and what she meant by separate-but-together. He wondered how the tides and waves had come into play on that afternoon along the Jersey shoreline when Martha saw the pebble and bent down to rescue it from geology. He imagined bare feet. Martha was a poet, with the poet's sensibilities, and her feet would be brown and bare, the toenails unpainted, the eyes chilly and somber like the ocean in

March, and though it was painful, he wondered who had been with her that afternoon. He imagined a pair of shadows moving along the strip of sand where things came together but also separated. It was phantom jealousy, he knew, but he couldn't help himself. He loved her so much. On the march, through the hot days of early April, he carried the pebble in his mouth, turning it with his tongue, tasting sea salts and moisture. His mind wandered. He had difficulty keeping his attention on the war. On occasion he would yell at his men to spread out the column, to keep their eyes open, but then he would slip away into daydreams, just pretending, walking barefoot along the Jersey shore, with Martha, carrying nothing. He would feel himself rising. Sun and waves and gentle winds, all love and lightness.

What they carried varied by mission.

When a mission took them to the mountains, they carried mosquito net- 15
ting, machetes, canvas tarps, and extra bug juice.

If a mission seemed especially hazardous, or if it involved a place they knew to be bad, they carried everything they could. In certain heavily mined AOs, where the land was dense with Toe Poppers and Bouncing Betties, they took turns humping a twenty-eight-pound mine detector. With its headphones and big sensing plate, the equipment was a stress on the lower back and shoulders, awkward to handle, often useless because of the shrapnel in the earth, but they carried it anyway, partly for safety, partly for the illusion of safety.

On ambush, or other night missions, they carried peculiar little odds and ends. Kiowa always took along his New Testament and a pair of moccasins for silence. Dave Jensen carried night-sight vitamins high in carotin. Lee Strunk carried his slingshot; ammo, he claimed, would never be a problem. Rat Kiley carried brandy and M&M's. Until he was shot, Ted Lavender carried the starlight scope, which weighed 6.3 pounds with its aluminum carrying case. Henry Dobbins carried his girlfriend's pantyhose wrapped around his neck as a comforter. They all carried ghosts. When dark came, they would move out single file across the meadows and paddies to their ambush coordinates, where they would quietly set up the Claymores and lie down and spend the night waiting.

Other missions were more complicated and required special equipment. In mid-April, it was their mission to search out and destroy the elaborate tunnel complexes in the Than Khe area south of Chu Lai. To blow the tunnels, they carried one-pound blocks of pentrite high explosives, four blocks to a man, sixty-eight pounds in all. They carried wiring, detonators, and battery-powered clackers. Dave Jensen carried earplugs. Most often, before blowing the tunnels, they were ordered by higher command to search them, which was considered bad news, but by and large they just shrugged and carried out orders. Because he was a big man, Henry Dobbins was excused from tunnel duty. The others would draw numbers. Before Lavender died there were seventeen men in the platoon, and whoever drew the number seventeen would strip off his gear and crawl in head first with a flashlight and Lieutenant Cross's .45-caliber pistol.

The rest of them would fan out as security. They would sit down or kneel, not facing the hole, listening to the ground beneath them, imagining cobwebs and ghosts, whatever was down there—the tunnel walls squeezing in—how the flashlight seemed impossibly heavy in the hand and how it was tunnel vision in the very strictest sense, compression in all ways, even time, and how you had to wiggle in—ass and elbows—a swallowed-up feeling—and how you found yourself worrying about odd things—will your flashlight go dead? Do rats carry rabies? If you screamed, how far would the sound carry? Would your buddies hear it? Would they have the courage to drag you out? In some respects, though not many, the waiting was worse than the tunnel itself. Imagination was a killer.

On April 16, when Lee Strunk drew the number seventeen, he laughed and muttered something and went down quickly. The morning was hot and very still. Not good, Kiowa said. He looked at the tunnel opening, then out across a dry paddy toward the village of Than Khe. Nothing moved. No clouds or birds or people. As they waited, the men smoked and drank Kool-Aid, not talking much, feeling sympathy for Lee Strunk but also feeling the luck of the draw. You win some, you lose some, said Mitchell Sanders, and sometimes you settle for a rain check. It was a tired line and no one laughed.

Henry Dobbins ate a tropical chocolate bar. Ted Lavender popped a tran- 20 quilizer and went off to pee.

After five minutes, Lieutenant Jimmy Cross moved to the tunnel, leaned down, and examined the darkness. Trouble, he thought—a cave-in maybe. And then suddenly, without willing it, he was thinking about Martha. The stresses and fractures, the quick collapse, the two of them buried alive under all that weight. Dense, crushing love. Kneeling, watching the hole, he tried to concentrate on Lee Strunk and the war, all the dangers, but his love was too much for him, he felt paralyzed, he wanted to sleep inside her lungs and breathe her blood and be smothered. He wanted her to be a virgin and not a virgin, all at once. He wanted to know her. Intimate secrets—why poetry? Why so sad? Why the grayness in her eyes? Why so alone? Not lonely, just alone—riding her bike across campus or sitting off by herself in the cafeteria. Even dancing, she danced alone—and it was the aloneness that filled him with love. He remembered telling her that one evening. How she nodded and looked away. And how, later, when he kissed her, she received the kiss without returning it, her eyes wide open, not afraid, not a virgin's eyes, just flat and uninvolved.

Lieutenant Cross gazed at the tunnel. But he was not there. He was buried with Martha under the white sand at the Jersey shore. They were pressed together, and the pebble in his mouth was her tongue. He was smiling. Vaguely, he was aware of how quiet the day was, the sullen paddies, yet he could not bring himself to worry about matters of security. He was beyond that. He was just a kid at war, in love. He was twenty-two years old. He couldn't help it.

A few moments later Lee Strunk crawled out of the tunnel. He came up grinning, filthy but alive. Lieutenant Cross nodded and closed his eyes while the others clapped Strunk on the back and made jokes about rising from the dead.

Worms, Rat Kiley said. Right out of the grave. Fuckin' zombie.

The men laughed. They all felt great relief. 25

Spook City, said Mitchell Sanders.

Lee Strunk made a funny ghost sound, a kind of moaning, yet very happy, and right then, when Strunk made that high happy moaning sound, when he went *Ahhooooo*, right then Ted Lavender was shot in the head on his way back from peeing. He lay with his mouth open. The teeth were broken. There was a swollen black bruise under his left eye. The cheekbone was gone. Oh shit, Rat Kiley said, the guy's dead. The guy's dead, he kept saying, which seemed profound—the guy's dead. I mean really.

The things they carried were determined to some extent by superstition. Lieutenant Cross carried his good-luck pebble. Dave Jensen carried a rabbit's foot. Norman Bowker, otherwise a very gentle person, carried a thumb that had been presented to him as a gift by Mitchell Sanders. The thumb was dark brown, rubbery to the touch, and weighed four ounces at most. It had been cut from a VC[3] corpse, a boy of fifteen or sixteen. They'd found him at the bottom of an irrigation ditch, badly burned, flies in his mouth and eyes. The boy wore black shorts and sandals. At the time of his death he had been carrying a pouch of rice, a rifle, and three magazines of ammunition.

You want my opinion, Mitchell Sanders said, there's a definite moral here.

He put his hand on the dead boy's wrist. He was quiet for a time, as if count- 30 ing a pulse, then he patted the stomach, almost affectionately, and used Kiowa's hunting hatchet to remove the thumb.

Henry Dobbins asked what the moral was.

Moral?

You know. *Moral.*

Sanders wrapped the thumb in toilet paper and handed it across to Norman Bowker. There was no blood. Smiling, he kicked the boy's head, watched the flies scatter, and said, It's like with that old TV show—Paladin. Have gun, will travel.

Henry Dobbins thought about it. 35

Yeah, well, he finally said. I don't see no moral.

There it *is*, man.

Fuck off.

They carried USO stationery and pencils and pens. They carried Sterno, safety pins, trip flares, signal flares, spools of wire, razor blades, chewing tobacco, liberated joss sticks and statuettes of the smiling Buddha, candles, grease pencils, *The Stars and Stripes*,[4] fingernail clippers, Psy Ops leaflets, bush hats, bolos, and much more. Twice a week, when the resupply choppers came in, they carried hot chow in green Mermite cans and large canvas bags filled with

---

[3] Vietcong.

[4] The military's officially sanctioned overseas newspaper.

iced beer and soda pop. They carried plastic water containers, each with a two-gallon capacity. Mitchell Sanders carried a set of starched tiger fatigues for special occasions. Henry Dobbins carried Black Flag insecticide. Dave Jensen carried empty sandbags that could be filled at night for added protection. Lee Strunk carried tanning lotion. Some things they carried in common. Taking turns, they carried the big PRC-77 scrambler radio, which weighed thirty pounds with its battery. They shared the weight of memory. They took up what others could no longer bear. Often, they carried each other, the wounded or weak. They carried infections. They carried chess sets, basketballs, Vietnamese-English dictionaries, insignia of rank, Bronze Stars and Purple Hearts, plastic cards imprinted with the Code of Conduct. They carried diseases, among them malaria and dysentery. They carried lice and ringworm and leeches and paddy algae and various rots and molds. They carried the land itself—Vietnam, the place, the soil—a powdery orange-red dust that covered their boots and fatigues and faces. They carried the sky. The whole atmosphere, they carried it, the humidity, the monsoons, the stink of fungus and decay, all of it, they carried gravity. They moved like mules. By daylight they took sniper fire, at night they were mortared, but it was not battle, it was just the endless march, village to village, without purpose, nothing won or lost. They marched for the sake of the march. They plodded along slowly, dumbly, leaning forward against the heat, unthinking, all blood and bone, simple grunts, soldiering with their legs, toiling up the hills and down into the paddies and across the rivers and up again and down, just humping, one step and then the next and then another, but no volition, no will, because it was automatic, it was anatomy, and the war was entirely a matter of posture and carriage, the hump was everything, a kind of inertia, a kind of emptiness, a dullness of desire and intellect and conscience and hope and human sensibility. Their principles were in their feet. Their calculations were biological. They had no sense of strategy or mission. They searched the villages without knowing what to look for, not caring, kicking over jars of rice, frisking children and old men, blowing tunnels, sometimes setting fires and sometimes not, then forming up and moving on to the next village, then other villages, where it would always be the same. They carried their own lives. The pressures were enormous. In the heat of early afternoon, they would remove their helmets and flak jackets, walking bare, which was dangerous but which helped ease the strain. They would often discard things along the route of march. Purely for comfort, they would throw away rations, blow their Claymores and grenades, no matter, because by nightfall the resupply choppers would arrive with more of the same, then a day or two later still more, fresh watermelons and crates of ammunition and sunglasses and woolen sweaters—the resources were stunning—sparklers for the Fourth of July, colored eggs for Easter. It was the great American war chest— the fruits of science, the smokestacks, the canneries, the arsenals at Hartford, the Minnesota forests, the vast fields of corn and wheat—they carried like freight trains; they carried it on their backs and shoulders—and for all the ambiguities of Vietnam, all the mysteries and unknowns, there was at least the single abiding certainty that they would never be at a loss for things to carry.

After the chopper took Lavender away, Lieutenant Jimmy Cross led his men 40 into the village of Than Khe. They burned everything. They shot chickens and dogs, they trashed the village well, they called in artillery and watched the wreckage, then they marched for several hours through the hot afternoon, and then at dusk, while Kiowa explained how Lavender died, Lieutenant Cross found himself trembling.

He tried not to cry. With his entrenching tool, which weighed five pounds, he began digging a hole in the earth.

He felt shame. He hated himself. He had loved Martha more than his men, and as a consequence Lavender was now dead, and this was something he would have to carry like a stone in his stomach for the rest of the war.

All he could do was dig. He used his entrenching tool like an ax, slashing, feeling both love and hate, and then later, when it was full dark, he sat at the bottom of his foxhole and wept. It went on for a long while. In part, he was grieving for Ted Lavender, but mostly it was for Martha, and for himself, because she belonged to another world, which was not quite real, and because she was a junior at Mount Sebastian College in New Jersey, a poet and a virgin and uninvolved, and because he realized she did not love him and never would.

Like cement, Kiowa whispered in the dark. I swear to God—boom-down. Not a word.

I've heard this, said Norman Bowker.   45

A pisser, you know? Still zipping himself up. Zapped while zipping.

All right, fine. That's enough.

Yeah, but you had to see it, the guy just—

I *heard*, man. Cement. So why not shut the fuck *up*?

Kiowa shook his head sadly and glanced over at the hole where Lieutenant 50 Jimmy Cross sat watching the night. The air was thick and wet. A warm, dense fog had settled over the paddies and there was the stillness that precedes rain.

After a time Kiowa sighed.

One thing for sure, he said. The Lieutenant's in some deep hurt. I mean that crying jag—the way he was carrying on—it wasn't fake or anything, it was real heavy-duty hurt. The man cares.

Sure, Norman Bowker said.

Say what you want, the man does care.

We all got problems.   55

Not Lavender.

No, I guess not, Bowker said. Do me a favor, though.

Shut up?

That's a smart Indian. Shut up.

Shrugging, Kiowa pulled off his boots. He wanted to say more, just to 60 lighten up his sleep, but instead he opened his New Testament and arranged it beneath his head as a pillow. The fog made things seem hollow and unattached. He tried not to think about Ted Lavender, but then he was thinking how fast it was, no drama, down and dead, and how it was hard to feel anything except surprise. It seemed un-Christian. He wished he could find some great sadness, or even anger, but the emotion wasn't there and he couldn't make it happen. Mostly he felt pleased to be alive. He liked the smell of the New Testament under his cheek, the leather and ink and paper and glue, whatever the chemicals were. He liked hearing the sounds of night. Even his fatigue, it felt fine, the stiff muscles and the prickly awareness of his own body, a floating feeling. He enjoyed not being dead. Lying there, Kiowa admired Lieutenant Jimmy Cross's capacity for grief. He wanted to share the man's pain, he wanted to care as Jimmy Cross cared. And yet when he closed his eyes, all he could think was Boom-down, and all he could feel was the pleasure of having his boots off and the fog curling in around him and the damp soil and the Bible smells and the plush comfort of night.

After a moment Norman Bowker sat up in the dark.

What the hell, he said. You want to talk, *talk*. Tell it to me.

Forget it.

No, man, go on. One thing I hate, it's a silent Indian.

For the most part they carried themselves with poise, a kind of dignity. Now and then, however, there were times of panic, when they squealed or wanted to squeal but couldn't, when they twitched and made moaning sounds and covered their heads and said Dear Jesus and flopped around on the earth and fired their weapons blindly and cringed and sobbed and begged for the noise to stop and went wild and made stupid promises to themselves and to God and to their mothers and fathers, hoping not to die. In different ways, it happened to all of them. Afterward, when the firing ended, they would blink and peek up. They would touch their bodies, feeling shame, then quickly hiding it. They would force themselves to stand. As if in slow motion, frame by frame, the world would take on the old logic—absolute silence, then the wind, then sunlight, then voices. It was the burden of being alive. Awkwardly, the men would reassemble themselves, first in private, then in groups, becoming soldiers again. They would repair the leaks in their eyes. They would check for casualties, call in dust-offs, light cigarettes, try to smile, clear their throats and spit and begin cleaning their weapons. After a time someone would shake his head and say, No lie, I almost shit my pants, and someone else would laugh, which meant it was bad, yes, but the guy had obviously not shit his pants, it wasn't that bad, and in any case nobody would ever do such a thing and then go ahead and talk about it. They would squint into the dense, oppressive sunlight. For a few moments, perhaps, they would fall silent, lighting a joint and tracking its passage from man to man, inhaling, holding in the humiliation. Scary stuff, one of them might say. But then someone else would grin or flick his eyebrows and say, Roger-dodger, almost cut me a new asshole, *almost.*

There were numerous such poses. Some carried themselves with a sort of wistful resignation, others with pride or stiff soldierly discipline or good humor or macho zeal. They were afraid of dying but they were even more afraid to show it.

They found jokes to tell.

They used a hard vocabulary to contain the terrible softness. *Greased,* they'd say. *Offed, lit up, zapped while zipping.* It wasn't cruelty, just stage presence. They were actors and the war came at them in 3-D. When someone died, it wasn't quite dying, because in a curious way it seemed scripted, and because they had their lines mostly memorized, irony mixed with tragedy, and because they called it by other names, as if to encyst and destroy the reality of death itself. They kicked corpses. They cut off thumbs. They talked grunt lingo. They told stories about Ted Lavender's supply of tranquilizers, how the poor guy didn't feel a thing, how incredibly tranquil he was.

There's a moral here, said Mitchell Sanders.

They were waiting for Lavender's chopper, smoking the dead man's dope.   70

The moral's pretty obvious, Sanders said, and winked. Stay away from drugs. No joke, they'll ruin your day every time.

Cute, said Henry Dobbins.

Mind-blower, get it? Talk about wiggy—nothing left, just blood and brains.

They made themselves laugh.

There it is, they'd say, over and over, as if the repetition itself were an act of   75 poise, a balance between crazy and almost crazy, knowing without going. There it is, which meant be cool, let it ride, because oh yeah, man, you can't change what can't be changed, there it is, there it absolutely and positively and fucking well *is.*

They were tough.

They carried all the emotional baggage of men who might die. Grief, terror, love, longing—these were intangibles, but the intangibles had their own mass and specific gravity, they had tangible weight. They carried shameful memories. They carried the common secret of cowardice barely restrained, the instinct to run or freeze or hide, and in many respects this was the heaviest burden of all, for it could never be put down, it required perfect balance and perfect posture. They carried their reputations. They carried the soldier's greatest fear, which was the fear of blushing. Men killed, and died, because they were embarrassed not to. It was what had brought them to the war in the first place, nothing positive, no dreams of glory or honor, just to avoid the blush of dishonor. They died so as not to die of embarrassment. They crawled into tunnels and walked point and advanced under fire. Each morning, despite the unknowns, they made their legs move. They endured. They kept humping. They did not submit to the obvious alternative, which was simply to close the eyes and fall. So easy, really. Go limp and tumble to the ground and let the muscles unwind and not speak and not budge until your buddies picked you up and lifted you into the chopper that would roar and dip its nose and carry you off to the world. A mere matter of falling, yet no one ever fell. It was not courage, exactly; the object was not valor. Rather, they were too frightened to be cowards.

By and large they carried these things inside, maintaining the masks of composure. They sneered at sick call. They spoke bitterly about guys who had found release by shooting off their own toes or fingers. Pussies, they'd say. Candyasses. It was fierce, mocking talk, with only a trace of envy or awe, but even so, the image played itself out behind their eyes.

They imagined the muzzle against flesh. They imagined the quick, sweet pain, then the evacuation to Japan, then a hospital with warm beds and cute geisha nurses.

They dreamed of freedom birds. 80

At night, on guard, staring into the dark, they were carried away by jumbo jets. They felt the rush of takeoff. *Gone!* they yelled. And then velocity, wings and engines, a smiling stewardess—but it was more than a plane, it was a real bird, a big sleek silver bird with feathers and talons and high screeching. They were flying. The weights fell off, there was nothing to bear. They laughed and held on tight, feeling the cold slap of wind and altitude, soaring, thinking *It's over, I'm gone!*—they were naked, they were light and free—it was all lightness, bright and fast and buoyant, light as light, a helium buzz in the brain, a giddy bubbling in the lungs as they were taken up over the clouds and the war, beyond duty, beyond gravity and mortification and global entanglements—*Sin loi!* they yelled, *I'm sorry, motherfuckers, but I'm out of it, I'm goofed, I'm on a space cruise, I'm gone!*—and it was a restful, disencumbered sensation, just riding the light waves, sailing that big silver freedom bird over the mountains and oceans, over America, over the farms and great sleeping cities and cemeteries and highways and the golden arches of McDonald's. It was flight, a kind of fleeing, a kind of falling, falling higher and higher, spinning off the edge of the earth and beyond the sun and through the vast, silent vacuum where there were no burdens and where everything weighed exactly nothing. *Gone!* they screamed, *I'm sorry but I'm gone!* And so at night, not quite dreaming, they gave themselves over to lightness, they were carried, they were purely borne.

On the morning after Ted Lavender died, First Lieutenant Jimmy Cross crouched at the bottom of his foxhole and burned Martha's letters. Then he burned the two photographs. There was a steady rain falling, which made it difficult, but he used heat tabs and Sterno to build a small fire, screening it with his body, holding the photographs over the tight blue flame with the tips of his fingers.

He realized it was only a gesture. Stupid, he thought. Sentimental, too, but mostly just stupid.

Lavender was dead. You couldn't burn the blame.

Besides, the letters were in his head. And even now, without photographs, 85 Lieutenant Cross could see Martha playing volleyball in her white gym shorts and yellow T-shirt. He could see her moving in the rain.

When the fire died out, Lieutenant Cross pulled his poncho over his shoulders and ate breakfast from a can.

There was no great mystery, he decided.

In those burned letters Martha had never mentioned the war, except to say, Jimmy, take care of yourself. She wasn't involved. She signed the letters "Love," but it wasn't love, and all the fine lines and technicalities did not matter.

The morning came up wet and blurry. Everything seemed part of everything else, the fog and Martha and the deepening rain.

It was a war, after all.   90

Half smiling, Lieutenant Jimmy Cross took out his maps. He shook his head hard, as if to clear it, then bent forward and began planning the day's march. In ten minutes, or maybe twenty, he would rouse the men and they would pack up and head west, where the maps showed the country to be green and inviting. They would do what they had always done. The rain might add some weight, but otherwise it would be one more day layered upon all the other days.

He was realistic about it. There was that new hardness in his stomach.

No more fantasies, he told himself.

Henceforth, when he thought about Martha, it would be only to think that she belonged elsewhere. He would shut down the daydreams. This was not Mount Sebastian, it was another world, where there were no pretty poems or midterm exams, a place where men died because of carelessness and gross stupidity. Kiowa was right. Boom-down, and you were dead, never partly dead.

Briefly, in the rain, Lieutenant Cross saw Martha's gray eyes gazing back 95
at him.

He understood.

It was very sad, he thought. The things men carried inside. The things men did or felt they had to do.

He almost nodded at her, but didn't.

Instead he went back to his maps. He was now determined to perform his duties firmly and without negligence. It wouldn't help Lavender, he knew that, but from this point on he would comport himself as a soldier. He would dispose of his good-luck pebble. Swallow it, maybe, or use Lee Strunk's slingshot, or just drop it along the trail. On the march he would impose strict field discipline. He would be careful to send out flank security, to prevent straggling or bunching up, to keep his troops moving at the proper pace and at the proper interval. He would insist on clean weapons. He would confiscate the remainder of Lavender's dope. Later in the day, perhaps, he would call the men together and speak to them plainly. He would accept the blame for what had happened to Ted Lavender. He would be a man about it. He would look them in the eyes, keeping his chin level, and he would issue the new SOPs in a calm, impersonal tone of voice, an officer's voice, leaving no room for argument or discussion. Commencing immediately, he'd tell them, they would no longer abandon equipment along the route of march. They would police up their acts. They would get their shit together, and keep it together, and maintain it neatly and in good working order.

He would not tolerate laxity. He would show strength, distancing himself.   100

Among the men there would be grumbling, of course, and maybe worse, because their days would seem longer and their loads heavier, but Lieutenant Cross reminded himself that his obligation was not to be loved but to lead. He would dispense with love; it was not now a factor. And if anyone quarreled or complained, he would simply tighten his lips and arrange his shoulders in the correct command posture. He might give a curt little nod. Or he might not. He might just shrug and say Carry on, then they would saddle up and form into a column and move out toward the villages of Than Khe.

FOR ANALYSIS

1. What are the various meanings of "Things" in the title?

2. What is the narrator's attitude toward war? Does his attitude differ from the attitudes of the soldiers he is describing? Explain.

3. How do Lieutenant Cross's thoughts about Martha fit into the overall thematic pattern of the story?

4. What is the attitude of the men toward the enemy?

5. How effective do you find the cataloging of things as a way to tell this story? Explain.

MAKING CONNECTIONS

Compare and contrast O'Brien's perspective on war with Owen's in "Dulce et Decorum Est" (p. 435). Which do you find to be a more effective antiwar statement? Explain.

WRITING TOPICS

1. Discuss the meaning of heroism in this story.

2. Write an essay showing how Lieutenant Cross's thoughts and feelings about Martha reflect the changes he undergoes in the course of the narrative.

LESLIE MARMON SILKO   (B. 1948)

THE MAN TO SEND RAIN CLOUDS   (1981)

They found him under a big cottonwood tree. His Levi jacket and pants were faded light blue so that he had been easy to find. The big cottonwood tree stood apart from a small grove of winterbare cottonwoods which grew in the wide, sandy arroyo. He had been dead for a day or more, and the sheep had wandered and scattered up and down the arroyo. Leon and his brother-in-law, Ken, gathered the sheep and left them in the pen at the sheep camp before they returned to the cottonwood tree. Leon waited under the tree while Ken drove the truck through the deep sand to the edge of the arroyo. He squinted up at the sun and unzipped his jacket—it sure was hot for this time of year. But high and northwest the blue mountains were still in snow. Ken came sliding down the low, crumbling bank about fifty yards down, and he was bringing the red blanket.

Before they wrapped the old man, Leon took a piece of string out of his pocket and tied a small gray feather in the old man's long white hair. Ken gave him the paint. Across the brown wrinkled forehead he drew a streak of white and along the high cheekbones he drew a strip of blue paint. He paused and watched Ken throw pinches of corn meal and pollen into the wind that fluttered the small gray feather. Then Leon painted with yellow under the old man's broad nose, and finally, when he had painted green across the chin, he smiled.

"Send us rain clouds, Grandfather." They laid the bundle in the back of the pickup and covered it with a heavy tarp before they started back to the pueblo.

They turned off the highway onto the sandy pueblo road. Not long after they passed the store and post office they saw Father Paul's car coming toward them. When he recognized their faces he slowed his car and waved them to stop. The young priest rolled down the car window.

"Did you find old Teofilo?" he asked loudly.   5

Leon stopped the truck. "Good morning, Father. We were just out to the sheep camp. Everything is O.K. now."

"Thank God for that. Teofilo is a very old man. You really shouldn't allow him to stay at the sheep camp alone."

"No, he won't do that any more now."

"Well, I'm glad you understand. I hope I'll be seeing you at Mass this week— we missed you last Sunday. See if you can get old Teofilo to come with you." The priest smiled and waved at them as they drove away.

Louise and Teresa were waiting. The table was set for lunch, and the coffee 10 was boiling on the black iron stove. Leon looked at Louise and then at Teresa.

"We found him under a cottonwood tree in the big arroyo near sheep camp. I guess he sat down to rest in the shade and never got up again." Leon walked toward the old man's bed. The red plaid shawl had been shaken and spread carefully over the bed, and a new brown flannel shirt and pair of stiff new Levi's were arranged neatly beside the pillow. Louise held the screen door open while Leon and Ken carried in the red blanket. He looked small and shriveled, and after they dressed him in the new shirt and pants he seemed more shrunken.

It was noontime now because the church bells rang the Angelus. They ate the beans with hot bread, and nobody said anything until after Teresa poured the coffee.

Ken stood up and put on his jacket. "I'll see about the gravediggers. Only the top layer of soil is frozen. I think it can be ready before dark."

Leon nodded his head and finished his coffee. After Ken had been gone for a while, the neighbors and clanspeople came quietly to embrace Teofilo's family and to leave food on the table because the gravediggers would come to eat when they were finished.

The sky in the west was full of pale yellow light. Louise stood outside with   15
her hands in the pockets of Leon's green army jacket that was too big for her. The funeral was over, and the old men had taken their candles and medicine bags and were gone. She waited until the body was laid into the pickup before she said anything to Leon. She touched his arm, and he noticed that her hands were still dusty from the corn meal that she had sprinkled around the old man. When she spoke, Leon could not hear her.

"What did you say? I didn't hear you."

"I said that I had been thinking about something."

"About what?"

"About the priest sprinkling holy water for Grandpa. So he won't be thirsty."

Leon stared at the new moccasins that Teofilo had made for the ceremonial   20
dances in the summer. They were nearly hidden by the red blanket. It was getting colder, and the wind pushed gray dust down the narrow pueblo road. The sun was approaching the long mesa where it disappeared during the winter. Louise stood there shivering and watching his face. Then he zipped up his jacket and opened the truck door. "I'll see if he's there."

Ken stopped the pickup at the church, and Leon got out; and then Ken drove down the hill to the graveyard where people were waiting. Leon knocked at the old carved door with its symbols of the Lamb. While he waited he looked up at the twin bells from the king of Spain with the last sunlight pouring around them in their tower.

The priest opened the door and smiled when he saw who it was. "Come in! What brings you here this evening?"

The priest walked toward the kitchen, and Leon stood with his cap in his hand, playing with the earflaps and examining the living room—the brown sofa, the green armchair, and the brass lamp that hung down from the ceiling by links of chain. The priest dragged a chair out of the kitchen and offered it to Leon.

"No thank you, Father. I only came to ask you if you would bring your holy water to the graveyard."

The priest turned away from Leon and looked out the window at the patio 25 full of shadows and the dining-room windows of the nuns' cloister across the patio. The curtains were heavy, and the light from within faintly penetrated; it was impossible to see the nuns inside eating supper. "Why didn't you tell me he was dead? I could have brought the Last Rites anyway."

Leon smiled. "It wasn't necessary, Father."

The priest stared down at his scuffed brown loafers and the worn hem of his cassock. "For a Christian burial it was necessary."

His voice was distant, and Leon thought that his blue eyes looked tired.

"It's O.K. Father, we just want him to have plenty of water."

The priest sank down into the green chair and picked up a glossy missionary 30 magazine. He turned the colored pages full of lepers and pagans without looking at them.

"You know I can't do that, Leon. There should have been the Last Rites and a funeral Mass at the very least."

Leon put on his green cap and pulled the flaps down over his ears. "It's getting late, Father. I've got to go."

When Leon opened the door Father Paul stood up and said, "Wait." He left the room and came back wearing a long brown overcoat. He followed Leon out the door and across the dim churchyard to the adobe steps in front of the church. They both stooped to fit through the low adobe entrance. And when they started down the hill to the graveyard only half of the sun was visible above the mesa.

The priest approached the grave slowly, wondering how they had managed to dig into the frozen ground, and then he remembered that this was New Mexico, and saw the pile of cold loose sand beside the hole. The people stood close to each other with little clouds of steam puffing from their faces. The priest looked at them and saw a pile of jackets, gloves, and scarves in the yellow, dry tumbleweeds that grew in the graveyard. He looked at the red blanket, not sure that Teofilo was so small, wondering if it wasn't some perverse Indian trick—something they did in March to ensure a good harvest—wondering if maybe old Teofilo was actually at sheep camp corraling the sheep for the night. But there he was, facing into a cold dry wind and squinting at the last sunlight, ready to bury a red wool blanket while the faces of his parishioners were in shadow with the last warmth of the sun on their backs.

His fingers were stiff, and it took him a long time to twist the lid off the holy 35 water. Drops of water fell on the red blanket and soaked into dark icy spots. He sprinkled the grave and the water disappeared almost before it touched the dim, cold sand; it reminded him of something—he tried to remember what it was, because he thought if he could remember he might understand this.

He sprinkled more water; he shook the container until it was empty, and the water fell through the light from sundown like August rain that fell while the sun was still shining, almost disappearing before it touched the wilted squash flowers.

The wind pulled at the priest's brown Franciscan robe and swirled away the corn meal and pollen that had been sprinkled on the blanket. They lowered the bundle into the ground, and they didn't bother to untie the stiff pieces of new rope that were tied around the ends of the blanket. The sun was gone, and over on the highway the eastbound lane was full of headlights. The priest walked away slowly. Leon watched him climb the hill, and when he had disappeared within the tall, thick walls, Leon turned to look up at the high blue mountains in the deep snow that reflected a faint red light from the west. He felt good because it was finished, and he was happy about the sprinkling of the holy water; now the old man could send them big thunderclouds for sure.

FOR ANALYSIS

1. Why do Leon and Ken not tell Father Paul that Teofilo is dead? Why do they later ask Father Paul to bring holy water to the funeral?

2. Two rituals associated with death—the Native American and the Roman Catholic— seem to conflict. Why does Teofilo's family seek the priest's help? Why does Father Paul agree to help them?

3. Although the story is mostly told from the point of view of an **omniscient narrator**, at one point we share two characters' thoughts. What effect does this shift generate?

4. Why do you think Silko included the detail (in the last paragraph) about the auto-mobile lights on the highway?

5. Why does Leon feel good at the end of the story?

MAKING CONNECTIONS

1. Compare this story with Jackson's "The Lottery" (p. 369). What similarities do you find? What differences?

2. Contrast the narrative **style** of this story with the style of Poe's "The Cask of Amontillado" (p. 1097) and Tolstoy's "The Death of Iván Ilých" (p. 1103). Some writers use unusual language and sentence structure; some insist on close realistic detail; some use understatement and leave much unsaid. How would you describe the style of this story? Defend your response.

WRITING TOPIC

"The Man to Send Rain Clouds" remains silent about the characters' spirituality: there is no narrator commenting on whether their rituals and beliefs are effective or true. How did you respond to the different points of view on death and the natural world presented in the story? How might the characters respond to your points of view about the world? Where did you get them?

The two stories in this unit show that the old saying that everybody dies alone is not always true. Even though in one story the moment of death is solitary, the preparations for dying are undertaken among companions, and in that same story the aftermath is very unsolitary. As you read these unusual and emotionally affecting stories, consider the difficulties entailed in writing about something you and your readers can never have experienced—death itself—and also the possibilities such an absence of experience opens up.

KATHERINE ANNE PORTER   (1890–1980)

THE JILTING OF
GRANNY WEATHERALL   1930

She flicked her wrist neatly out of Doctor Harry's pudgy careful fingers and pulled the sheet up to her chin. The brat ought to be in knee breeches. Doctoring around the country with spectacles on his nose! "Get along now, take your schoolbooks and go. There's nothing wrong with me."

Doctor Harry spread a warm paw like a cushion on her forehead where the forked green vein danced and made her eyelids twitch. "Now, now, be a good girl, and we'll have you up in no time."

"That's no way to speak to a woman nearly eighty years old just because she's down. I'd have you respect your elders, young man."

"Well, Missy, excuse me." Doctor Harry patted her cheek. "But I've got to warn you, haven't I? You're a marvel, but you must be careful or you're going to be good and sorry."

"Don't tell me what I'm going to be. I'm on my feet now, morally speaking.   5
It's Cornelia. I had to go to bed to get rid of her."

Her bones felt loose, and floated around in her skin, and Doctor Harry floated like a balloon around the foot of the bed. He floated and pulled down his waistcoat and swung his glasses on a cord. "Well, stay where you are, it certainly can't hurt you."

"Get along and doctor your sick," said Granny Weatherall. "Leave a well woman alone. I'll call for you when I want you. . . . Where were you forty years ago when I pulled through milk-leg and double pneumonia? You weren't even born. Don't let Cornelia lead you on," she shouted, because Doctor Harry appeared to float up to the ceiling and out. "I pay my own bills, and I don't throw my money away on nonsense!"

She meant to wave good-by, but it was too much trouble. Her eyes closed of themselves, it was like a dark curtain drawn around the bed. The pillow rose and floated under her, pleasant as a hammock in a light wind. She listened to the leaves rustling outside the window. No, somebody was swishing newspapers: no, Cornelia and Doctor Harry were whispering together. She leaped broad awake, thinking they whispered in her ear.

"She was never like this, *never* like this!" "Well, what can we expect?" "Yes, eighty years old. . . ."

Well, and what if she was? She still had ears. It was like Cornelia to whisper 10 around doors. She always kept things secret in such a public way. She was always being tactful and kind. Cornelia was dutiful; that was the trouble with her. Dutiful and good: "So good and dutiful," said Granny, "that I'd like to spank her." She saw herself spanking Cornelia and making a fine job of it.

"What'd you say, Mother?"

Granny felt her face tying up in hard knots.

"Can't a body think, I'd like to know?"

"I thought you might want something."

"I do. I want a lot of things. First off, go away and don't whisper." 15

She lay and drowsed, hoping in her sleep that the children would keep out and let her rest a minute. It had been a long day. Not that she was tired. It was always pleasant to snatch a minute now and then. There was always so much to be done, let me see: tomorrow.

Tomorrow was far away and there was nothing to trouble about. Things were finished somehow when the time came; thank God there was always a little margin over for peace: then a person could spread out the plan of life and tuck in the edges orderly. It was good to have everything clean and folded away, with the hair brushes and tonic bottles sitting straight on the white embroidered linen: the day started without fuss and the pantry shelves laid out with rows of jelly glasses and brown jugs and white stone-china jars with blue whirligigs and words painted on them: coffee, tea, sugar, ginger, cinnamon, allspice: and the bronze clock with the lion on top nicely dusted off. The dust that lion could collect in twenty-four hours! The box in the attic with all those letters tied up, well she'd have to go through that tomorrow. All those letters—George's letters and John's letters and her letters to them both—lying around for the children to find afterwards made her uneasy. Yes, that would be tomorrow's business. No use to let them know how silly she had been once.

While she was rummaging around she found death in her mind and it felt clammy and unfamiliar. She had spent so much time preparing for death there was no need for bringing it up again. Let it take care of itself now. When she was sixty she had felt very old, finished, and went around making farewell trips to see her children and grandchildren, with a secret in her mind: this is the very last of your mother, children! Then she made her will and came down with a long fever. That was all just a notion like a lot of other things, but it was lucky too, for she had once for all got over the idea of dying for a long time. Now she couldn't be worried. She hoped she had better sense now. Her father had lived to be one hundred and two years old and had drunk a noggin of strong hot toddy on his last birthday. He told the reporters it was his daily habit, and he owed his long life to that. He had made quite a scandal and was very pleased about it. She believed she'd just plague Cornelia a little.

"Cornelia! Cornelia!" No footsteps, but a sudden hand on her cheek. "Bless you, where have you been?"

"Here, mother."

"Well, Cornelia, I want a noggin of hot toddy." 20

"Are you cold, darling?"

"I'm chilly, Cornelia. Lying in bed stops the circulation. I must have told you that a thousand times."

Well, she could just hear Cornelia telling her husband that Mother was getting childish and they'd have to humor her. The thing that most annoyed her was that Cornelia thought she was deaf, dumb, and blind. Little hasty glances and tiny gestures tossed around her and over her head saying, "Don't cross her, let her have her way, she's eighty years old," and she sitting there as if she lived in a thin glass cage. Sometimes Granny almost made up her mind to pack up and move back to her own house where nobody could remind her every minute that she was old. Wait, wait, Cornelia, till your own children whisper behind your back!

In her day she had kept a better house and had got more work done. She 25 wasn't too old yet for Lydia to be driving eighty miles for advice when one of the children jumped the track, and Jimmy still dropped in and talked things over: "Now, Mammy, you've a good business head, I want to know what you think of this? . . ." Old Cornelia couldn't change the furniture around without asking. Little things, little things! They had been so sweet when they were little. Granny wished the old days were back again with the children young and everything to be done over. It had been a hard pull, but not too much for her. When she thought of all the food she had cooked, and all the clothes she had cut and sewed, and all the gardens she had made—well, the children showed it. There they were, made out of her, and they couldn't get away from that. Sometimes she wanted to see John again and point to them and say, Well, I didn't do so badly, did I? But that would have to wait. That was for tomorrow. She used to think of him as a man, but now all the children were older than their father, and he would be a child beside her if she saw him now. It seemed strange and there was something wrong in the idea. Why, he couldn't possibly recognize her. She had fenced in a hundred acres once, digging the post holes herself and clamping the wires with just a negro boy to help. That changed a woman. John would be looking for a young woman with the peaked Spanish comb in her hair and the painted fan. Digging post holes changed a woman. Riding country roads in the winter when women had their babies was another thing: sitting up nights with sick horses and sick negroes and sick children and hardly ever losing one. John, I hardly ever lost one of them! John would see that in a minute, that would be something he could understand, she wouldn't have to explain anything!

It made her feel like rolling up her sleeves and putting the whole place to rights again. No matter if Cornelia was determined to be everywhere at once, there were a great many things left undone in this place. She would start tomorrow and do them. It was good to be strong enough for everything, even if all you made melted and changed and slipped under your hands, so that by the time you finished you almost forgot what you were working for. What was it I set out to do? she asked herself intently, but she could not remember. A fog rose over the valley, she saw it marching across the creek swallowing the trees and moving up the hill like an army of ghosts. Soon it would be at the near edge of the orchard, and then it was time to go in and light the lamps. Come in, children, don't stay out in the night air.

Lighting the lamps had been beautiful. The children huddled up to her and breathed like little calves waiting at the bars in the twilight. Their eyes followed the match and watched the flame rise and settle in a blue curve, then they moved away from her. The lamp was lit, they didn't have to be scared and hang on to mother any more. Never, never, never more. God, for all my life I thank Thee. Without Thee, my God, I could never have done it. Hail, Mary, full of grace.

I want you to pick all the fruit this year and see that nothing is wasted. There's always someone who can use it. Don't let good things rot for want of using. You waste life when you waste good food. Don't let things get lost. It's bitter to lose things. Now, don't let me get to thinking, not when I am tired and taking a little nap before supper. . . .

The pillow rose about her shoulders and pressed against her heart and the memory was being squeezed out of it: oh, push down the pillow, somebody: it would smother her if she tried to hold it. Such a fresh breeze blowing and such a green day with no threats in it. But he had not come, just the same. What does a woman do when she has put on the white veil and set out the white cake for a man and he doesn't come? She tried to remember. No, I swear he never harmed me but in that. He never harmed me but in that . . . and what if he did? There was the day, the day, but a whirl of dark smoke rose and covered it, crept up and over into the bright field where everything was planted so carefully in orderly rows. That was hell, she knew hell when she saw it. For sixty years she had prayed against remembering him and against losing her soul in the deep pit of hell, and now the two things were mingled in one and the thought of him was a smoky cloud from hell that moved and crept in her head when she had just got rid of Doctor Harry and was trying to rest a minute. Wounded vanity, Ellen, said a sharp voice in the top of her mind. Don't let your wounded vanity get the upper hand of you. Plenty of girls get jilted. You were jilted, weren't you? Then stand up to it. Her eyelids wavered and let in streamers of blue-gray light like tissue paper over her eyes. She must get up and pull the shades down or she'd never sleep. She was in bed again and the shades were not down. How could that happen? Better turn over, hide from the light, sleeping in the light gave you nightmares. "Mother, how do you feel now?" and a stinging wetness on her forehead. But I don't like having my face washed in cold water!

Hapsy? George? Lydia? Jimmy? No, Cornelia, and her features were swollen 30
and full of little puddles. "They're coming, darling, they'll all be here soon." Go
wash your face, child, you look funny.

Instead of obeying, Cornelia knelt down and put her head on the pillow. She
seemed to be talking but there was no sound. "Well, are you tongue-tied?
Whose birthday is it? Are you going to give a party?"

Cornelia's mouth moved urgently in strange shapes. "Don't do that, you
bother me, daughter."

"Oh, no, Mother, Oh, no. . . . "

Nonsense. It was strange about children. They disputed your every word.
"No what, Cornelia?"

"Here's Doctor Harry." 35

"I won't see that boy again. He just left five minutes ago."

"That was this morning, Mother. It's night now. Here's the nurse."

"This is Doctor Harry, Mrs. Weatherall. I never saw you look so young and
happy!"

"Ah, I'll never be young again—but I'd be happy if they'd let me lie in peace
and get rested."

She thought she spoke up loudly, but no one answered. A warm weight on 40
her forehead, a warm bracelet on her wrist, and a breeze went on whispering,
trying to tell her something. A shuffle of leaves in the everlasting hand of God.
He blew on them and they danced and rattled. "Mother, don't mind, we're
going to give you a little hypodermic." "Look here, daughter, how do ants get in
this bed? I saw sugar ants yesterday." Did you send for Hapsy too?

It was Hapsy she really wanted. She had to go a long way back through a great
many rooms to find Hapsy standing with a baby on her arm. She seemed to herself to be Hapsy also, and the baby on Hapsy's arm was Hapsy and himself and
herself, all at once, and there was no surprise in the meeting. Then Hapsy
melted from within and turned flimsy as gray gauze and the baby was a gauzy
shadow, and Hapsy came up close and said, "I thought you'd never come," and
looked at her very searchingly and said, "You haven't changed a bit!" They
leaned forward to kiss, when Cornelia began whispering from a long way off,
"Oh, is there anything you want to tell me? Is there anything I can do for you?"

Yes, she had changed her mind after sixty years and she would like to see
George. I want you to find George. Find him and be sure to tell him I forgot
him. I want him to know I had my husband just the same and my children and
my house like any other woman. A good house too and a good husband that I
loved and fine children out of him. Better than I hoped for even. Tell him I was
given back everything he took away and more. Oh, no, oh, God, no, there was
something else besides the house and the man and the children. Oh, surely
they were not all? What was it? Something not given back. . . . Her breath
crowded down under her ribs and grew into a monstrous frightening shape
with cutting edges; it bored up into her head, and the agony was unbelievable.
Yes, John, get the doctor now, no more talk, my time has come.

When this one was born it should be the last. The last. It should have been born first, for it was the one she had truly wanted. Everything came in good time. Nothing left out, left over. She was strong. In three days she would be as well as ever. Better. A woman needed milk in her to have her full health.

"Mother, do you hear me?"

"I've been telling you—"

"Mother, Father Connolly's here."

"I went to Holy Communion only last week. Tell him I'm not so sinful as all that."

"Father just wants to speak to you."

He could speak as much as he pleased. It was like him to drop in and inquire about her soul as if it were a teething baby, and then stay on for a cup of tea and a round of cards and gossip. He always had a funny story of some sort, usually about an Irishman who made his little mistakes and confessed them, and the point lay in some absurd thing he would blurt out in the confessional showing his struggles between naive piety and original sin. Granny felt easy about her soul. Cornelia, where are your manners? Give Father Connolly a chair. She had her secret comfortable understanding with a few favorite saints who cleared a straight road to God for her. All as surely signed and sealed as the papers for the new Forty Acres. Forever . . . heirs and assigns forever. Since the day the wedding cake was not cut, but thrown out and wasted. The whole bottom dropped out of the world, and there she was blind and sweating with nothing under her feet and the walls falling away. His hand had caught her under the breast, she had not fallen, there was the freshly polished floor with the green rug on it, just as before. He had cursed like a sailor's parrot and said, "I'll kill him for you." Don't lay a hand on him, for my sake leave something to God. "Now, Ellen, you must believe what I tell you. . . . "

So there was nothing, nothing to worry about any more, except sometimes in the night one of the children screamed in a nightmare, and they both hustled out shaking and hunting for the matches and calling, "There, wait a minute, here we are!" John, get the doctor now, Hapsy's time has come. But there was Hapsy standing by the bed in a white cap. "Cornelia, tell Hapsy to take off her cap, I can't see her plain."

Her eyes opened very wide and the room stood out like a picture she had seen somewhere. Dark colors with the shadows rising towards the ceiling in long angles. The tall black dresser gleamed with nothing on it but John's picture, enlarged from a little one, with John's eyes very black when they should have been blue. You never saw him, so how do you know how he looked? But the man insisted the copy was perfect, it was very rich and handsome. For a picture, yes, but it's not my husband. The table by the bed had a linen cover and a candle and a crucifix. The light was blue from Cornelia's silk lampshades. No sort of light at all, just frippery. You had to live forty years with kerosene lamps to appreciate honest electricity. She felt very strong and she saw Doctor Harry with a rosy nimbus around him.

"You look like a saint, Doctor Harry, and I vow that's as near as you'll ever come to it."

"She's saying something."

"I heard you, Cornelia. What's all this carrying on?"

"Father Connolly's saying—"

Cornelia's voice staggered and bumped like a cart in a bad road. It rounded corners and turned back again and arrived nowhere. Granny stepped up in the cart very lightly and reached for the reins, but a man sat beside her and she knew him by his hands, driving the cart. She did not look in his face, for she knew without seeing, but looked instead down the road where the trees leaned over and bowed to each other and a thousand birds were singing a Mass. She felt like singing too, but she put her hand in the bosom of her dress and pulled out a rosary, and Father Connolly murmured Latin in a very solemn voice and tickled her feet. My God, will you stop that nonsense? I'm a married woman. What if he did run away and leave me to face the priest by myself? I found another a whole world better. I wouldn't have exchanged my husband for anybody except St. Michael himself, and you may tell him that for me with a thank you in the bargain.

Light flashed on her closed eyelids, and a deep roaring shook her. Cornelia, is that lightning? I hear thunder. There's going to be a storm. Close all the windows. Call the children in. . . . "Mother, here we are, all of us." "Is that you, Hapsy?" "Oh, no, I'm Lydia. We drove as fast as we could." Their faces drifted above her, drifted away. The rosary fell out of her hands and Lydia put it back. Jimmy tried to help, their hands fumbled together, and Granny closed two fingers around Jimmy's thumb. Beads wouldn't do, it must be something alive. She was so amazed her thoughts ran round and round. So, my dear Lord, this is my death and I wasn't even thinking about it. My children have come to see me die. But I can't, it's not time. Oh, I always hated surprises. I wanted to give Cornelia the amethyst set—Cornelia, you're to have the amethyst set, but Hapsy's to wear it when she wants, and, Doctor Harry, do shut up. Nobody sent for you. Oh, my dear Lord, do wait a minute. I meant to do something about the Forty Acres, Jimmy doesn't need it and Lydia will later on, with that worthless husband of hers. I meant to finish the altar cloth and send six bottles of wine to Sister Borgia for her dyspepsia. I want to send six bottles of wine to Sister Borgia, Father Connolly, now don't let me forget.

Cornelia's voice made short turns and tilted over and crashed. "Oh, Mother, oh, Mother, oh, Mother. . . ."

"I'm not going, Cornelia. I'm taken by surprise. I can't go."

You'll see Hapsy again. What about her? "I thought you'd never come." Granny made a long journey outward, looking for Hapsy. What if I don't find her? What then? Her heart sank down and down, there was no bottom to death, she couldn't come to the end of it. The blue light from Cornelia's lampshade drew into a tiny point in the center of her brain, it flickered and winked like an eye, quietly it fluttered and dwindled. Granny lay curled down within herself, amazed and watchful, staring at the point of light that was herself; her body was now only a deeper mass of shadow in an endless darkness and this darkness would curl around the light and swallow it up. God, give a sign!

For the second time there was no sign. Again no bridegroom and the priest in the house. She could not remember any other sorrow because this grief wiped them all away. Oh, no, there's nothing more cruel than this—I'll never forgive it. She stretched herself with a deep breath and blew out the light.

FOR ANALYSIS

1. Characterize Granny Weatherall. What facts about her life does the story provide?

2. Why, after sixty years, does the jilting by George loom so large in Granny's mind? Should we accept her own strong statements that the pain of the jilting was more than compensated for by the happiness she ultimately found with her husband, her children, and her grandchildren? Defend your response.

3. Who is Hapsy? Why do you think she is not present?

4. Why doesn't the author present Granny's final thoughts in an orderly and sequential way?

5. Granny is revealed to us not only through her direct thoughts but also through the many images that float through her mind—the "fog" (para. 26), the "breeze blowing" (para. 29), "a whirl of dark smoke" (para. 29), and others. What do these images reveal about Granny?

WRITING TOPIC

The final paragraph echoes Christ's parable of the bridegroom (Matthew 25:1–3). If you are not familiar with this parable, find a copy of the New Testament in print or online and read it. Why does Granny connect this final, deep religious grief with the grief she felt when George jilted her? What does this biblical **allusion** add to the story?

HELENA MARIA VIRAMONTES (B. 1954)

THE MOTHS 1985

I was fourteen years old when Abuelita requested my help. And it seemed only fair. Abuelita had pulled me through the rages of scarlet fever by placing, removing, and replacing potato slices on the temples of my forehead; she had seen me through several whippings, an arm broken by a dare jump off Tío Enrique's toolshed, puberty, and my first lie. Really, I told Amá, it was only fair.

Not that I was her favorite granddaughter or anything special. I wasn't even pretty or nice like my older sisters and I just couldn't do the girl things they could do. My hands were too big to handle the fineries of crocheting or embroidery and I always pricked my fingers or knotted my colored threads time and time again while my sisters laughed and called me bull hands with their cute waterlike voices. So I began keeping a piece of jagged brick in my sock to bash my sisters or anyone who called me bull hands. Once, while we all sat in the bedroom, I hit Teresa on the forehead, right above her eyebrow and she ran to Amá with her mouth open, her hand over her eye while blood seeped between her fingers. I was used to the whippings by then.

I wasn't respectful either. I even went so far as to doubt the power of Abuelita's slices, the slices she said absorbed my fever. "You're still alive, aren't you?" Abuelita snapped back, her pasty gray eye beaming at me and burning holes in my suspicions. Regretful that I had let secret questions drop out of my mouth, I couldn't look into her eyes. My hands began to fan out, grow like a liar's nose until they hung by my side like low weights. Abuelita made a balm out of dried moth wings and Vicks and rubbed my hands, shaped them back to size and it was the strangest feeling. Like bones melting. Like sun shining through the darkness of your eyelids. I didn't mind helping Abuelita after that, so Amá would always send me over to her.

In the early afternoon Amá would push her hair back, hand me my sweater and shoes, and tell me to go to Mama Luna's. This was to avoid another fight and another whipping, I knew. I would deliver one last direct shot on Marisela's arm and jump out of our house, the slam of the screen door burying her cries of anger, and I'd gladly go help Abuelita plant her wild lilies or jasmine or heliotrope or cilantro or hierbabuena in red Hills Brothers coffee cans. Abuelita would wait for me at the top step of her porch holding a hammer and nail and empty coffee cans. And although we hardly spoke, hardly looked at each other as we worked over root transplants, I always felt her gray eye on me. It made me feel, in a strange sort of way, safe and guarded and not alone. Like God was supposed to make you feel.

On Abuelita's porch, I would puncture holes in the bottom of the coffee cans 5 with a nail and a precise hit of a hammer. This completed, my job was to fill them with red clay mud from beneath her rose bushes, packing it softly, then making a perfect hole, four fingers round, to nest a sprouting avocado pit, or the spidery sweet potatoes that Abuelita rooted in mayonnaise jars with toothpicks and daily water, or prickly chayotes that produced vines that twisted and wound all over her porch pillars, crawling to the roof, up and over the roof, and down the other side, making her small brick house look like it was cradled within the vines that grew pear-shaped squashes ready for the pick, ready to be steamed with onions and cheese and butter. The roots would burst out of the rusted coffee cans and search for a place to connect. I would then feed the seedlings with water.

But this was a different kind of help, Amá said, because Abuelita was dying. Looking into her gray eye, then into her brown one, the doctor said it was just a matter of days. And so it seemed only fair that these hands she had melted and formed found use in rubbing her caving body with alcohol and marihuana, rubbing her arms and legs, turning her face to the window so that she could watch the Bird of Paradise blooming or smell the scent of clove in the air.

I toweled her face frequently and held her hand for hours. Her gray wiry hair hung over the mattress. Since I could remember, she'd kept her long hair in braids. Her mouth was vacant and when she slept, her eyelids never closed all the way. Up close, you could see her gray eye beaming out the window, staring hard as if to remember everything. I never kissed her. I left the window open when I went to the market.

Across the street from Jay's Market there was a chapel. I never knew its denomination, but I went in just the same to search for candles. I sat down on one of the pews because there were none. After I cleaned my fingernails, I looked up at the high ceiling. I had forgotten the vastness of these places, the coolness of the marble pillars and the frozen statues with blank eyes. I was alone. I knew why I had never returned.

That was one of Apá's biggest complaints. He would pound his hands on the table, rocking the sugar dish or spilling a cup of coffee and scream that if I didn't go to mass every Sunday to save my goddamn sinning soul, then I had no reason to go out of the house, period. Punto final. He would grab my arm and dig his nails into me to make sure I understood the importance of catechism. Did he make himself clear? Then he strategically directed his anger at Amá for her lousy ways of bringing up daughters, being disrespectful and unbelieving, and my older sisters would pull me aside and tell me if I didn't get to mass right this minute, they were all going to kick the holy shit out of me. Why am I so selfish? Can't you see what it's doing to Amá, you idiot? So I would wash my feet and stuff them in my black Easter shoes that shone with Vaseline, grab a missal and veil, and wave good-bye to Amá.

I would walk slowly down Lorena to First to Evergreen, counting the cracks on the cement. On Evergreen I would turn left and walk to Abuelita's. I liked her porch because it was shielded by the vines of the chayotes and I could get a good look at the people and car traffic on Evergreen without them knowing. I would jump up the porch steps, knock on the screen door as I wiped my feet and call Abuelita? mi Abuelita? As I opened the door and stuck my head in, I would catch the gagging scent of toasting chile on the placa. When I entered the sala, she would greet me from the kitchen, wringing her hands in her apron. I'd sit at the corner of the table to keep from being in her way. The chiles made my eyes water. Am I crying? No, Mama Luna, I'm sure not crying. I don't like going to mass, but my eyes watered anyway, the tears dropping on the tablecloth like candle wax. Abuelita lifted the burnt chiles from the fire and sprinkled water on them until the skins began to separate. Placing them in front of me, she turned to check the menudo. I peeled the skins off and put the flimsy, limp looking green and yellow chiles in the molcajete and began to crush and crush and twist and crush the heart out of the tomato, the clove of garlic, the stupid chiles that made me cry, crushed them until they turned into liquid under my bull hand. With a wooden spoon, I scraped hard to destroy the guilt, and my tears were gone. I put the bowl of chile next to a vase filled with freshly cut roses. Abuelita touched my hand and pointed to the bowl of menudo that steamed in front of me. I spooned some chile into the menudo and rolled a corn tortilla thin with the palms of my hands. As I ate, a fine Sunday breeze entered the kitchen and a rose petal calmly feathered down to the table.

I left the chapel without blessing myself and walked to Jay's. Most of the 10 time Jay didn't have much of anything. The tomatoes were always soft and the cans of Campbell soups had rusted spots on them. There was dust on the tops of cereal boxes. I picked up what I needed: rubbing alcohol, five cans of chicken broth, a big bottle of Pine Sol. At first Jay got mad because I thought I had forgotten the money. But it was there all the time, in my back pocket.

When I returned from the market, I heard Amá crying in Abuelita's kitchen. She looked up at me with puffy eyes. I placed the bags of groceries on the table and began putting the cans of soup away. Amá sobbed quietly. I never kissed her. After a while, I patted her on the back for comfort. Finally: "¿Y mi Amá?" she asked in a whisper, then choked again and cried into her apron.

Abuelita fell off the bed twice yesterday, I said, knowing that I shouldn't have said it and wondering why I wanted to say it because it only made Amá cry harder. I guess I became angry and just so tired of the quarrels and beatings and unanswered prayers and my hands just there hanging helplessly by my side. Amá looked at me again, confused, angry, and her eyes were filled with sorrow. I went outside and sat on the porch swing and watched the people pass. I sat there until she left. I dozed off repeating the words to myself like rosary prayers: when do you stop giving when do you start giving when do you. . . . and when my hands fell from my lap, I awoke to catch them. The sun was setting, an orange glow, and I knew Abuelita was hungry.

There comes a time when the sun is defiant. Just about the time when moods change, inevitable seasons of a day, transitions from one color to another, that hour or minute or second when the sun is finally defeated, finally sinks into the realization that it cannot with all its power to heal or burn, exist forever, there comes an illumination where the sun and earth meet, a final burst of burning red orange fury reminding us that although endings are inevitable, they are necessary for rebirths, and when that time came, just when I switched on the light in the kitchen to open Abuelita's can of soup, it was probably then that she died.

The room smelled of Pine Sol and vomit and Abuelita had defecated the remains of her cancerous stomach. She had turned to the window and tried to speak, but her mouth remained open and speechless. I heard you, Abuelita, I said, stroking her cheek, I heard you. I opened the windows of the house and let the soup simmer and overboil on the stove. I turned the stove off and poured the soup down the sink. From the cabinet I got a tin basin, filled it with luke-warm water and carried it carefully to the room. I went to the linen closet and took out some modest bleached white towels. With the sacredness of a priest preparing his vestments, I unfolded the towels one by one on my shoulders. I removed the sheets and blankets from her bed and peeled off her thick flannel nightgown. I toweled her puzzled face, stretching out the wrinkles, removing the coils of her neck, toweled her shoulders and breasts. Then I changed the water. I returned to towel the creases of her stretch-marked stomach, her sporadic vaginal hairs, and her sagging thighs. I removed the lint from between her toes and noticed a mapped birthmark on the fold of her buttock. The scars on her back which were as thin as the life lines on the palms of her hands made me realize how little I really knew of Abuelita. I covered her with a thin blanket and went into the bathroom. I washed my hands, and turned on the tub faucets and watched the water pour into the tub with vitality and steam. When it was full, I turned off the water and undressed. Then, I went to get Abuelita.

She was not as heavy as I thought and when I carried her in my arms, her body fell into a V, and yet my legs were tired, shaky, and I felt as if the distance between the bedroom and bathroom was miles and years away. Amá, where are you? 15

I stepped into the bathtub one leg first, then the other. I bent my knees slowly to descend into the water slowly so I wouldn't scald her skin. There, there, Abuelita, I said, cradling her, smoothing her as we descended, I heard you. Her hair fell back and spread across the water like eagle's wings. The water in the tub overflowed and poured onto the tile of the floor. Then the moths came. Small, gray ones that came from her soul and out through her mouth fluttering to light, circling the single dull light bulb of the bathroom. Dying is lonely and I wanted to go to where the moths were, stay with her and plant chayotes whose vines would crawl up her fingers and into the clouds; I wanted to rest my head on her chest with her stroking my hair, telling me about the moths that lay within the soul and slowly eat the spirit up; I wanted to return to the waters of the womb with her so that we would never be alone again. I wanted. I wanted my Amá. I removed a few strands of hair from Abuelita's face and held her small light head within the hollow of my neck. The bathroom was filled with moths, and for the first time in a long time I cried, rocking us, crying for her, for me, for Amá, the sobs emerging from the depths of anguish, the misery of feeling half born, sobbing until finally the sobs rippled into circles and circles of sadness and relief. There, there, I said to Abuelita, rocking us gently, there, there.

FOR ANALYSIS

1. Why do you think the observation that the narrator does not kiss people is repeated?

2. Why is it important that the old person with whom the narrator connects is a woman and not a man?

3. In what ways is the grandmother's death important to the narrator? Why, when the narrator holds her body at the end of the story, does she say that she rocks "us"?

WRITING TOPICS

1. Reread "The Moths" and keep a reading log, tracking your emotions as you go. Then reflect on what elements of the story made you feel these ways.

2. Does the story read significantly differently if you do or don't believe that the moths at the end actually exist? How so? What do you choose to believe?

MAKING CONNECTIONS

1. Compare the relationships between the two elderly women and their caregivers in this unit. How are they similar? How are they different?

2. How does telling the story of an older woman's death from her **point of view** differ from telling it from the younger woman's point of view? What effects does each have? Why do you think the authors chose to tell their stories the way they did?

3. How does representing the moment of death change when that moment is unnarrated—when it occurs, as it does in "The Moths," offstage and out of sight of the **narrator**? Does it make it more or less emotionally affecting?

POETRY

ANONYMOUS

EDWARD

1

"Why does your brand° sae° drap wi' bluid,   *sword/so*
    Edward, Edward,
Why does your brand sae drap wi' bluid,
    And why sae sad gang° ye, O?"   *go*
"O I ha'e killed my hawk sae guid,
    Mither, mither,
O I ha'e killed my hawk sae guid,
    And I had nae mair but he, O."

2

"Your hawke's bluid was never sae reid,°   *red*
    Edward, Edward,   10
Your hawke's bluid was never sae reid,
    My dear son I tell thee, O."
"O I ha'e killed my reid-roan steed,
    Mither, mither,
O I ha'e killed my reid-roan steed,
    That erst was sae fair and free, O."

3

"Your steed was auld, and ye ha'e gat mair,
    Edward, Edward,
Your steed was auld, and ye ha'e gat mair,
    Some other dule° ye drie,° O."   *grief/suffer* 20
"O I ha'e killed my fader dear,
    Mither, mither,
O I ha'e killed my fader dear,
    Alas, and wae° is me, O!"   *woe*

1181

4

"And whatten penance wul ye drie for that,
    Edward, Edward?
And whatten penance wul ye drie for that,
    My dear son, now tell me, O?"
"I'll set my feet in yonder boat,
    Mither, mither,
I'll set my feet in yonder boat,   30
    And I'll fare over the sea, O."

5

"And what wul ye do wi' your towers and your ha',
    Edward, Edward?
And what wul ye do wi' your towers and your ha',
    That were sae fair to see, O?"
"I'll let them stand tul they down fa',
    Mither, mither,
I'll let them stand tul they down fa',
    For here never mair maun° I be, O."   must 40

6

"And what wul ye leave to your bairns° and your wife,   children
    Edward, Edward?
And what wul ye leave to your bairns and your wife,
    Whan ye gang over the sea, O?"
"The warlde's° room, let them beg thrae° life,   world's/through
    Mither, mither,
The warlde's room, let them beg thrae life,
    For them never mair wul I see, O."

7

"And what wul ye leave to your ain mither dear,
    Edward, Edward?   50
And what wul ye leave to your ain mither dear,
    My dear son, now tell me, O?"
"The curse of hell frae° me sall° ye bear,   from/shall
    Mither, mither,
The curse of hell frae me sall ye bear,
    Sic° counsels ye gave to me, O."   such

FOR ANALYSIS

1. Why does the mother reject Edward's answers to her first two questions?

2. Does the poem provide any clues to the murderer's motive?

3. Edward has murdered his father and then bitterly turns away from his mother, wife, and children. What basis is there in the poem for nevertheless sympathizing with Edward?

WRITING TOPIC

What effects are achieved through the question-and-answer technique and the repetition of lines?

WILLIAM SHAKESPEARE (1564–1616)

SONNET 1609

73

That time of year thou mayst in me behold
When yellow leaves, or none, or few, do hang
Upon those boughs which shake against the cold,
Bare ruined choirs, where late the sweet birds sang.
In me thou see'st the twilight of such day
As after sunset fadeth in the west;
Which by and by black night doth take away,
Death's second self, that seals up all in rest.
In me thou see'st the glowing of such fire,
That on the ashes of his youth doth lie,   10
As the deathbed whereon it must expire,
Consumed with that which it was nourished by.
This thou perceiv'st, which makes thy love more strong,
To love that well which thou must leave ere long.

FEAR NO MORE
THE HEAT O' THE SUN 1623

Fear no more the heat o' the sun,[1]
   Nor the furious winter's rages;
Thou thy worldly task hast done,
   Home art gone, and ta'en thy wages:

Fear No More the Heat o' the Sun
[1] From *Cymbeline*, act IV, scene 2.

Golden lads and girls all must,
As chimney-sweepers, come to dust.

Fear no more the frown o' the great;
   Thou art past the tyrant's stroke;
Care no more to clothe and eat;
   To thee the reed is as the oak:
The scepter, learning, physic,° must[2]   10
All follow this, and come to dust.   medicine

Fear no more the lightning flash,
   Nor the all-dreaded thunder stone;[3]
Fear not slander, censure rash;
   Thou hast finished joy and moan:
All lovers young, all lovers must
Consign to° thee, and come to dust.   agree with

No exorciser harm thee!
Nor no witchcraft charm thee!
Ghost unlaid forbear thee!   20
Nothing ill come near thee!
Quiet consummation have;
And renownèd be thy grave!

JOHN DONNE   (1572–1631)

DEATH, BE NOT PROUD   1633

Death be not proud, though some have callèd thee
Mighty and dreadful, for thou art not so;
For those whom thou think'st thou dost overthrow
Die not, poor Death, nor yet canst thou kill me.
From rest and sleep, which but thy pictures be,
Much pleasure; then from thee much more must flow,
And soonest our best men with thee do go,
Rest of their bones, and soul's delivery.
Thou art slave to fate, chance, kings, and desperate men,
And dost with poison, war, and sickness dwell,   10
And poppy or charms can make us sleep as well

Fear No More the Heat o' the Sun
  [2] I.e., kings, scholars, and physicians.
  [3] It was believed that thunder was caused by falling meteorites.

And better than thy stroke; why swell'st thou then?
One short sleep past, we wake eternally
And death shall be no more; Death, thou shalt die.

PERCY BYSSHE SHELLEY   (1792–1822)

OZYMANDIAS[1]   1818

I met a traveller from an antique land
Who said: Two vast and trunkless legs of stone
Stand in the desert . . . Near them, on the sand,
Half sunk, a shattered visage lies, whose frown,
And wrinkled lip, and sneer of cold command,
Tell that its sculptor well those passions read
Which yet survive, stamped on these lifeless things,
The hand that mocked them, and the heart that fed:
And on the pedestal these words appear:
"My name is Ozymandias, king of kings: 10
Look on my works, ye Mighty, and despair!"
Nothing beside remains. Round the decay
Of that colossal wreck, boundless and bare
The lone and level sands stretch far away.

JOHN KEATS   (1795–1821)

ODE ON A GRECIAN URN   1820

I

Thou still unravished bride of quietness,
    Thou foster child of silence and slow time,
Sylvan historian, who canst thus express
    A flowery tale more sweetly than our rhyme:
What leaf-fringed legend haunts about thy shape
    Of deities or mortals, or of both,
        In Tempe or the dales of Arcady?[1]
    What men or gods are these? What maidens loath?

Ozymandias
    [1] Egyptian monarch of the thirteenth century B.C., said to have erected a huge statue of himself.

Ode on a Grecian Urn
    [1] Tempe and Arcady are valleys in Greece famous for their beauty. In ancient times, Tempe was
regarded as sacred to Apollo.

What mad pursuit? What struggle to escape?
    What pipes and timbrels? What wild ecstasy?   10

II

Heard melodies are sweet, but those unheard
    Are sweeter; therefore, ye soft pipes, play on;
Not to the sensual ear, but, more endeared,
    Pipe to the spirit ditties of no tone:
Fair youth, beneath the trees, thou canst not leave
    Thy song, nor ever can those trees be bare;
      Bold Lover, never, never canst thou kiss,
Though winning near the goal—yet, do not grieve;
    She cannot fade, though thou hast not thy bliss,
      Forever wilt thou love, and she be fair!   20

III

Ah, happy, happy boughs! that cannot shed
    Your leaves, nor ever bid the Spring adieu;
And, happy melodist, unwearièd,
    Forever piping songs forever new;
More happy love! more happy, happy love!
    Forever warm and still to be enjoyed,
      Forever panting, and forever young;
All breathing human passion far above,[2]
    That leaves a heart high-sorrowful and cloyed,
      A burning forehead, and a parching tongue.   30

IV

Who are these coming to the sacrifice?
    To what green altar, O mysterious priest,
Lead'st thou that heifer lowing at the skies,
    And all her silken flanks with garlands dressed?
What little town by river or sea shore,
    Or mountain-built with peaceful citadel,
      Is emptied of this folk, this pious morn?
And, little town, thy streets forevermore
    Will silent be; and not a soul to tell
      Why thou art desolate, can e'er return.   40

---

[2] I.e., far above all breathing human passion.

V

O Attic[3] shape! Fair attitude! with brede
   Of marble men and maidens overwrought,
With forest branches and the trodden weed;
   Thou, silent form, dost tease us out of thought
As doth eternity: Cold Pastoral!
   When old age shall this generation waste,
      Thou shalt remain, in midst of other woe
   Than ours, a friend to man, to whom thou say'st,
"Beauty is truth, truth beauty,—that is all
     Ye know on earth, and all ye need to know."   50

FOR ANALYSIS

1. Describe the scene the poet sees depicted on the urn. Describe the scene the poet imagines as a consequence of the scene on the urn.

2. Why are the boughs, the piper, and the lovers happy in stanza III?

3. Explain the assertion of stanza II: "Heard melodies are sweet, but those unheard / Are sweeter."

4. Does the poem support the assertion of the last two lines? What do they mean?

WRITING TOPIC

Discuss Keats's view of the connection between art and life. With this in mind, consider the meaning of the phrase "Cold Pastoral!" (l. 45).

EMILY DICKINSON   (1830–1886)

AFTER GREAT PAIN, A FORMAL FEELING COMES   CA 1862

After great pain, a formal feeling comes—
The Nerves sit ceremonious, like Tombs—
The stiff Heart questions was it He, that bore,
And Yesterday, or Centuries before?

The Feet, mechanical, go round—
Of Ground, or Air, or Ought—
A Wooden way

Ode on a Grecian Urn
  [3] Athenian, thus simple and graceful.

Regardless grown,
A Quartz contentment, like a stone—

This is the Hour of Lead—
Remembered, if outlived,   10
As Freezing persons, recollect the Snow—
First—Chill—then Stupor—then the letting go—

FOR ANALYSIS

Is this poem about physical or psychic pain? Explain.

WRITING TOPIC

What is the meaning of "stiff Heart" (l. 3) and "Quartz contentment" (l. 9)? What part
do they play in the larger pattern of **images** in this poem?

I HEARD A FLY BUZZ— WHEN I DIED   CA. 1862

I heard a Fly buzz—when I died—
The Stillness in the Room
Was like the Stillness in the Air—
Between the Heaves of Storm—

The Eyes around—had wrung them dry—
And Breaths were gathering firm
For that last Onset—when the King
Be witnessed—in the Room—

I willed my Keepsakes—Signed away
What portion of me be   10
Assignable—and then it was
There interposed a Fly—

With Blue—uncertain stumbling Buzz—
Between the light—and me—
And then the Windows failed—and then
I could not see to see—

APPARENTLY WITH NO SURPRISE   CA. 1884

Apparently with no surprise
To any happy Flower,
The Frost beheads it at its play
In accidental power.
The blond Assassin passes on,
The Sun proceeds unmoved
To measure off another Day
For an Approving God.

BECAUSE I COULD NOT STOP FOR DEATH   CA. 1863, 1890

Because I could not stop for Death—
He kindly stopped for me—
The Carriage held but just Ourselves—
And Immortality.

We slowly drove—He knew no haste
And I had put away
My labor and my leisure too,
For his Civility—

We passed the School, where Children strove
At Recess—in the Ring—   10
We passed the Fields of Gazing Grain—
We passed the Setting Sun—

Or rather—He passed Us—
The Dews drew quivering and chill—
For only Gossamer, my Gown—
My Tippet—only Tulle—

We paused before a House that seemed
A Swelling of the Ground—
The Roof was scarcely visible—
The Cornice—in the Ground—   20

Since then—'tis Centuries—and yet
Feels shorter than the Day
I first surmised the Horses' Heads
Were toward Eternity—

A. E. HOUSMAN   (1859–1936)

TO AN ATHLETE DYING YOUNG   1896

The time you won your town the race
We chaired you through the market place;
Man and boy stood cheering by,
And home we brought you shoulder-high.

Today, the road all runners come,
Shoulder-high we bring you home,
And set you at your threshold down,
Townsman of a stiller town.

Smart lad, to slip betimes away
From fields where glory does not stay,   10
And early though the laurel grows
It withers quicker than the rose.

Eyes the shady night has shut
Cannot see the record cut,
And silence sounds no worse than cheers
After earth has stopped the ears:

Now you will not swell the rout
Of lads that wore their honors out,
Runners whom renown outran
And the name died before the man.   20

So set, before its echoes fade,
The fleet foot on the sill of shade,
And hold to the low lintel up
The still-defended challenge cup.

And round that early-laureled head
Will flock to gaze the strengthless dead
And find unwithered on its curls
The garland briefer than a girl's.

WILLIAM BUTLER YEATS (1865–1939)

SAILING TO BYZANTIUM[1] 1927

1

That is no country for old men. The young
In one another's arms, birds in the trees
—Those dying generations—at their song,
The salmon-falls, the mackerel-crowded seas,
Fish, flesh, or fowl, commend all summer long
Whatever is begotten, born, and dies.
Caught in that sensual music all neglect
Monuments of unaging intellect.

2

An aged man is but a paltry thing,
A tattered coat upon a stick, unless   10
Soul clap its hands and sing, and louder sing
For every tatter in its mortal dress,
Nor is there singing school but studying
Monuments of its own magnificence;
And therefore I have sailed the seas and come
To the holy city of Byzantium.

3

O sages standing in God's holy fire
As in the gold mosaic of a wall,
Come from the holy fire, perne in a gyre,[2]
And be the singing-masters of my soul.   20
Consume my heart away; sick with desire
And fastened to a dying animal
It knows not what it is; and gather me
Into the artifice of eternity.

---

[1] Capital of the ancient Eastern Roman Empire, Byzantium (modern Istanbul) is celebrated for its great art, including mosaics (in ll. 17–18, Yeats addresses the figures in one of these mosaics). In *A Vision*, Yeats cites Byzantium as possibly the only civilization that had achieved what he called "Unity of Being"—a state where "religious, aesthetic, and practical life were one."

[2] I.e., whirl in a spiral motion. Yeats associated this motion with the cycles of history and the fate of the individual. Here he entreats the sages represented in the mosaic to take him out of the natural world described in the first stanza and into the eternal world of art.

4

Once out of nature I shall never take
My bodily form from any natural thing,
But such a form as Grecian goldsmiths make
Of hammered gold and gold enameling
To keep a drowsy Emperor awake;[3]
Or set upon a golden bough to sing   30
To lords and ladies of Byzantium
Of what is past, or passing, or to come.

FOR ANALYSIS

1. This poem incorporates a series of contrasts, among them "that" country and Byzantium, and the real birds of the first stanza and the artificial bird of the final stanza. What others do you find?

2. What are the meanings of "generations" (l. 3)?

3. For what is the poet "sick with desire" (l. 21)?

4. In what sense is eternity an "artifice" (l. 24)?

WRITING TOPIC

In what ways are the **images** of bird and song used throughout this poem?

EDWIN ARLINGTON ROBINSON   (1869–1935)

RICHARD CORY   1897

Whenever Richard Cory went down town,
We people on the pavement looked at him:
He was a gentleman from sole to crown,
Clean favored, and imperially slim.

And he was always quietly arrayed,
And he was always human when he talked;
But still he fluttered pulses when he said,
"Good-morning," and he glittered when he walked.

Sailing to Byzantium
[3] "I have read somewhere," Yeats wrote, "that in the Emperor's palace at Byzantium was a tree made of gold and silver, and artificial birds that sang." The poet wishes to become an artificial bird (a work of art) in contrast to the real birds of the first stanza.

And he was rich—yes, richer than a king—
And admirably schooled in every grace: 10
In fine, we thought that he was everything
To make us wish that we were in his place.

So on we worked, and waited for the light,
And went without the meat, and cursed the bread;
And Richard Cory, one calm summer night,
Went home and put a bullet through his head.

ROBERT FROST   (1874–1963)

AFTER APPLE-PICKING   1914

My long two-pointed ladder's sticking through a tree
Toward heaven still,
And there's a barrel that I didn't fill
Beside it, and there may be two or three
Apples I didn't pick upon some bough.
But I am done with apple-picking now.
Essence of winter sleep is on the night,
The scent of apples: I am drowsing off.
I cannot rub the strangeness from my sight
I got from looking through a pane of glass   10
I skimmed this morning from the drinking trough
And held against the world of hoary grass.
It melted, and I let it fall and break.
But I was well
Upon my way to sleep before it fell,
And I could tell
What form my dreaming was about to take.
Magnified apples appear and disappear,
Stem end and blossom end,
And every fleck of russet showing clear.   20
My instep arch not only keeps the ache,
It keeps the pressure of a ladder-round.
I feel the ladder sway as the boughs bend.
And I keep hearing from the cellar bin
The rumbling sound
Of load on load of apples coming in.
For I have had too much
Of apple-picking: I am overtired

Of the great harvest I myself desired.
There were ten thousand thousand fruit to touch, 30
Cherish in hand, lift down, and not let fall.
For all
That struck the earth,
No matter if not bruised or spiked with stubble,
Went surely to the cider-apple heap
As of no worth.
One can see what will trouble
This sleep of mine, whatever sleep it is.
Were he not gone,
The woodchuck could say whether it's like his 40
Long sleep, as I describe its coming on,
Or just some human sleep.

FOR ANALYSIS

1. What does apple-picking symbolize?

2. At the end of the poem, why is the speaker uncertain about what kind of sleep is coming on him?

'OUT, OUT—'[1] 1916

The buzz-saw snarled and rattled in the yard
And made dust and dropped stove-length sticks of wood,
Sweet-scented stuff when the breeze drew across it.
And from there those that lifted eyes could count
Five mountain ranges one behind the other
Under the sunset far into Vermont.
And the saw snarled and rattled, snarled and rattled,
As it ran light, or had to bear a load.
And nothing happened: day was all but done.
Call it a day, I wish they might have said 10
To please the boy by giving him the half hour
That a boy counts so much when saved from work.
His sister stood beside them in her apron
To tell them 'Supper.' At the word, the saw,
As if to prove saws knew what supper meant,

'Out, Out —'
  [1] The title is taken from the famous speech of Macbeth upon hearing that his wife has died (*Macbeth*, act V, scene 5).

Leaped out at the boy's hand, or seemed to leap—
He must have given the hand. However it was,
Neither refused the meeting. But the hand!
The boy's first outcry was a rueful laugh,
As he swung toward them holding up the hand   20
Half in appeal, but half as if to keep
The life from spilling. Then the boy saw all—
Since he was old enough to know, big boy
Doing a man's work, though a child at heart—
He saw all spoiled. 'Don't let him cut my hand off—
The doctor, when he comes. Don't let him, sister!'
So. But the hand was gone already.
The doctor put him in the dark of ether.
He lay and puffed his lips out with his breath.
And then—the watcher at his pulse took fright.   30
No one believed. They listened at his heart.
Little—less—nothing!—and that ended it.
No more to build on there. And they, since they
Were not the one dead, turned to their affairs.

NOTHING GOLD CAN STAY   1923

Nature's first green is gold,
Her hardest hue to hold.
Her early leaf's a flower;
But only so an hour.
Then leaf subsides to leaf.
So Eden sank to grief,
So dawn goes down to day.
Nothing gold can stay.

FOR ANALYSIS

1. Does this poem protest or accept the transitoriness of things?

2. Why does Frost use the word *subsides* in line 5 rather than a word like *expands* or *grows*?

3. How are "Nature's first green" (l. 1), "Eden" (l. 6), and "dawn" (l. 7) linked together?

STOPPING BY WOODS
ON A SNOWY EVENING   1923

Whose woods these are I think I know.
His house is in the village though;
He will not see me stopping here
To watch his woods fill up with snow.

My little horse must think it queer
To stop without a farmhouse near
Between the woods and frozen lake
The darkest evening of the year.

He gives his harness bells a shake
To ask if there is some mistake.   10
The only other sound's the sweep
Of easy wind and downy flake.

The woods are lovely, dark and deep,
But I have promises to keep,
And miles to go before I sleep,
And miles to go before I sleep.

FOR ANALYSIS

1. What does the description of the horse tell us about the speaker?

2. What function does the repetition in the last two lines of the poem serve?

3. Why does the speaker refer to the owner of the woods in the opening stanza?

DESIGN   1936

I found a dimpled spider, fat and white,
On a white heal-all, holding up a moth
Like a white piece of rigid satin cloth—
Assorted characters of death and blight
Mixed ready to begin the morning right,
Like the ingredients of a witches' broth—
A snow-drop spider, a flower like a froth,
And dead wings carried like a paper kite.

What had that flower to do with being white,
The wayside blue and innocent heal-all?   10

What brought the kindred spider to that height,
Then steered the white moth thither in the night?
What but design of darkness to appall?—
If design govern in a thing so small.

WRITING TOPIC

Compare this poem with Dickinson's "Apparently with no surprise" (p. 1189).

PABLO NERUDA (1904–1973)

THE DEAD WOMAN 1972

If suddenly you do not exist,
if suddenly you are not living,
I shall go on living.

I do not dare,
I do not dare to write it,
if you die.

I shall go on living.

Because where a man has no voice,
there, my voice.

Where blacks are beaten,   10
I can not be dead.
When my brothers go to jail
I shall go with them.

When victory,
not my victory
but the great victory
arrives,
even though I am mute I must speak:
I shall see it come even though I am blind.

No, forgive me.   20
If you are not living,
if you, beloved, my love,
if you
have died,

all the leaves will fall on my breast,
it will rain upon my soul night and day,
the snow will burn my heart,
I shall walk with cold and fire and death and snow,
my feet will want to march toward where you sleep,
but   30
I shall go on living,
because you wanted me to be, above all things,
untamable,
and, love, because you know that I am not just one man
but all men.

THEODORE ROETHKE   (1908–1963)

ELEGY FOR JANE   1958

MY STUDENT, THROWN BY A HORSE

I remember the neckcurls, limp and damp as tendrils;
And her quick look, a sidelong pickerel smile;
And how, once startled into talk, the light syllables leaped for her,
And she balanced in the delight of her thought,
A wren, happy, tail into the wind,
Her song trembling the twigs and small branches.
The shade sang with her;
The leaves, their whispers turned to kissing;
And the mold sang in the bleached valleys under the rose.

Oh, when she was sad, she cast herself down into such a pure depth,   10
Even a father could not find her:
Scraping her cheek against straw;
Stirring the clearest water.

My sparrow, you are not here,
Waiting like a fern, making a spiny shadow.
The sides of wet stones cannot console me,
Nor the moss, wound with the last light.

If only I could nudge you from this sleep,
My maimed darling, my skittery pigeon.
Over this damp grave I speak the words of my love: 20
I, with no rights in this matter,
Neither father nor lover.

CASE STUDY

POEMS ABOUT PAINTINGS

The works in this section offer a unique opportunity to reflect on the ways meaning can be conveyed through different media. Most of the poems here are linked with the paintings that inspired them; others appear with paintings thematically similar in their treatment of death. While all these groupings offer an opportunity for rich examination, the ones featuring poems inspired by a particular painting open up even more complex areas for analysis: not only can the painting and the poem be considered independently of each other, but the poem can also be analyzed as a reading of the painting—an interpretation in words of a visual object.

As you enter into a dialogue between the works of art and the poems, jot down your reactions to each painting in some detail before reading the accompanying poem. After you have read a poem, compare your reactions to the poet's. Did reading the poem clarify or in any other way alter your response to the painting? Are the poems successful or even comprehensible without reference to the paintings? How are the works alike or different? With paired works, why does the poet choose to emphasize certain details of a painting and ignore others? What accounts for the order in which the poet deals with the details of the painting? Is the poet attempting an accurate and neutral description of the painting or making some judgment about it?

If you wish to look beyond the individual work, you might consider researching one of the poets and investigating why he or she was so moved by the painting as to write about it. Or you might examine the historical context of both the poem and the painting for any illuminating connections.

W. H. AUDEN   (1907–1973)

MUSÉE DES BEAUX ARTS   1940

About suffering they were never wrong,
The Old Masters: how well they understood
Its human position; how it takes place
While someone else is eating or opening a window or just walking dully along;
How, when the aged are reverently, passionately waiting
For the miraculous birth, there always must be
Children who did not specially want it to happen, skating
On a pond at the edge of the wood:
They never forgot

That even the dreadful martyrdom must run its course   10
Anyhow in a corner, some untidy spot
Where the dogs go on with their doggy life and the torturer's horse
Scratches its innocent behind on a tree.

In Brueghel's *Icarus*,[1] for instance: how everything turns away
Quite leisurely from the disaster; the plowman may
Have heard the splash, the forsaken cry,
But for him it was not an important failure; the sun shone
As it had to on the white legs disappearing into the green
Water; and the expensive delicate ship that must have seen
Something amazing, a boy falling out of the sky,   20
Had somewhere to get to and sailed calmly on.

Landscape with the Fall of Icarus, ca. 1560, by Pieter Brueghel the Elder

---

[1] This poem describes and comments on Pieter Brueghel's painting *Landscape with the Fall of Icarus* (reproduced above). According to myth, Daedalus and his son Icarus made wings, whose feathers they attached with wax, to escape Crete. Icarus flew so near the sun that the wax melted and he fell into the sea.

FOR ANALYSIS

1. Look up the story of Icarus in an encyclopedia or other reference work. What aspects of the human condition or human nature does the story embody? How does Brueghel interpret the story? What other interpretations are possible? Compare Sexton's interpretation of the legend in her poem "To a Friend Whose Work Has Come to Triumph," which can be found in her volume *All My Pretty Ones* (1962).

2. Does the poem offer an accurate interpretation of the painting? Explain.

3. Which details of the painting does the poem describe? Does the poet omit details you found important?

LAWRENCE FERLINGHETTI (B. 1919)

IN GOYA'S GREATEST SCENES 1958

In Goya's greatest scenes[1] we seem to see
                  the people of the world
   exactly at the moment when
      they first attained the title of
           'suffering humanity'
    They writhe upon the page
         in a veritable rage
            of adversity
   Heaped up
       groaning with babies and bayonets   10
            under cement skies
   in an abstract landscape of blasted trees
    bent statues bats wings and beaks
       slippery gibbets
    cadavers and carnivorous cocks
and all the final hollering monsters
    of the
       'imagination of disaster'
   they are so bloody real
        it is as if they really still existed   20

  And they do

[1] Francisco José de Goya (1746–1828), famous Spanish artist, celebrated for his representations of "suffering humanity."

Only the landscape is changed
They still are ranged along the roads
plagued by legionaires
false windmills and demented roosters

They are the same people
only further from home
on freeways fifty lanes wide
on a concrete continent
spaced with bland billboards   30
illustrating imbecile illusions of happiness
The scene shows fewer tumbrils[2]
but more maimed citizens
in painted cars
and they have strange license plates
and engines
that devour America

The Third of May, 1808, Madrid, 1814, by Francisco de Goya

[2] Carts in which prisoners were conducted to the place of execution.

FOR ANALYSIS

1. While *The Third of May, 1808, Madrid* commemorates the uprising of the Spanish people against the invading forces of Napoleon, it has come to be seen as a powerful and universal statement against the brutalities of war. Goya also created a series of eighty-five etchings entitled *The Disasters of War* (1810–1820), which shows how individuals are transformed into "suffering humanity" when they are savaged by war. Compare the painting and some of the etchings as views of the disasters of war. Does the use of color in the painting and of black and white in the etchings cause different responses in the viewer? Explain.

2. Goya represents suffering and death in their most elemental, physical sense. Do you find Ferlinghetti's transformation of suffering and death from the literal to the metaphoric in the second half of his poem successful? Explain.

ANNE SEXTON   (1928-1974)

THE STARRY NIGHT   1961

That does not keep me from having a terrible need of—shall I say the word—religion. Then I go out at night to paint the stars.

> —Vincent van Gogh in a letter to his brother

The town does not exist
except where one black-haired tree slips
up like a drowned woman into the hot sky.
The town is silent. The night boils with eleven stars
Oh starry starry night! This is how
I want to die

It moves. They are all alive.
Even the moon bulges in its orange irons
to push children, like a god from its eye.
The old unseen serpent swallows up the stars.   10
Oh starry starry night! This is how
I want to die:

into that rushing beast of the night,
sucked up by that great dragon, to split
from my life with no flag,
no belly,
no cry.

The Starry Night, 1889, by Vincent van Gogh (1853–1890). Oil on canvas, 29″ × 36¼″. Acquired through the Lillie P. Bliss Bequest. (472.1941). The Museum of Modern Art, New York, NY, U.S.A. Digital image © The Museum of Modern Art/Licensed by SCALA/Art Resource, NY. Reproduced with permission.

FOR ANALYSIS

1. In what ways does your reaction to the painting agree with Sexton's? In what ways does it differ? Does her poem open your eyes to elements of the painting you had not initially seen? Explain.

2. The first two stanzas of the poem end with the refrain "This is how / I want to die." What does "This" refer to? In what sense might *The Starry Night* be described as a painting about death?

3. Around the time of this painting, van Gogh was much preoccupied with cypress trees. He wrote his brother, "The tree is as beautiful of line and proportion as an Egyptian obelisk. And the green has such a quality of distinction. It is a splash of black in a sunny landscape, but it is one of the most interesting black notes, and the most difficult to hit off exactly that I can imagine." How is Sexton's reference to the cypress tree in the opening lines of her poem related to her overall reading of the painting?

4. Describe the difference in brushstrokes van Gogh uses for the sky and those he uses for the village. How is this difference related to the painting's theme?

5. *The Starry Night* was painted in the town of Saint-Rémy. Later in the same year, van Gogh did another painting, this one in the town of Arles, to which he gave the same title. Look up this later painting, and compare the differences in the painter's handling of light, both natural and artificial.

6. Some of van Gogh's paintings have been described as mystical. Which of his two *Starry Night* paintings does the term best fit? Explain. What similarities and differences do you find between the depiction of the village and the sky in the two works?

DONALD FINKEL   (1929–2006)

THE GREAT WAVE: HOKUSAI   1959

But we will take the problem in its most obscure manifestation, and suppose that our spectator is an average Englishman. A trained observer, carefully hidden behind a screen, might notice a dilation in his eyes, even an intake of his breath, perhaps a grunt.
                                        —Herbert Read, *The Meaning of Art*

It is because the sea is blue,
Because Fuji is blue, because the bent blue
Men have white faces, like the snow
On Fuji, like the crest of the wave in the sky the color of their
Boats. It is because the air
Is full of writing, because the wave is still: that nothing
Will harm these frail strangers,
That high over Fuji in an earthcolored sky the fingers
Will not fall; and the blue men
Lean on the sea like snow, and the wave like a mountain leans   10
Against the sky.

        In the painter's sea
All fishermen are safe. All anger bends under his unity.
But the innocent bystander, he merely
'Walks round a corner, thinking of nothing': hidden
Behind a screen we hear his cry.
He stands half in and half out of the world; he is the men,
But he cannot see below Fuji
The shore the color of sky; he is the wave, he stretches
His claws against strangers. He is   20
Not safe, not even from himself. His world is flat.
He fishes a sea full of serpents, he rides his boat
Blindly from wave to wave toward Ararat.

The Great Wave Off Kanagawa, 1831–1833, by Katsushika Hokusai

FOR ANALYSIS

1. The "average Englishman" or indeed any other eyewitness to the actual scene depicted in this print would reasonably assume that the men in the boats are in imminent danger of being drowned by the enormous, menacing wave about to crash down upon them. Yet that is not how the poet interprets the scene. On what basis does he declare "that nothing / Will harm these frail strangers" (ll. 6–7) and that "in the painter's sea / All fishermen are safe" (ll. 12–13)?

2. What does Finkel mean when he says, "In the painter's sea / All fishermen are safe. All anger bends under his unity" (ll. 12–13)? How has the artist's representation of nature changed its reality—that is, eliminated the danger and imposed unity?

3. What does the "innocent bystander" not understand that the poet does? Why is the bystander not safe from himself? In contrast to the world represented by the artist, what kind of world does the bystander inhabit? Why is his sea "full of serpents" (l. 22), and why is his boat headed for Ararat (l. 23)?

4. Finkel's epigraph is taken from a passage in section 1, paragraph 17, of Herbert Read's *The Meaning of Art* (1968). Read the passage, which defines "the problem," and explain why Finkel uses it to introduce his poem.

5. Compare Finkel's poem with Keats's "Ode on a Grecian Urn" (p. 1185), and discuss the similarities and differences in the way they interpret the visual work that has inspired them to poetry.

MARY OLIVER (B. 1935)

WHEN DEATH COMES 1992

When death comes
like the hungry bear in autumn;
when death comes and takes all the bright coins from his purse

to buy me, and snaps the purse shut;
when death comes
like the measle-pox;

when death comes
like an iceberg between the shoulder blades,

I want to step through the door full of curiosity, wondering:
what is it going to be like, that cottage of darkness?   10

And therefore I look upon everything
as a brotherhood and a sisterhood,
and I look upon time as no more than an idea,
and I consider eternity as another possibility,

and I think of each life as a flower, as common
as a field daisy, and as singular,

and each name a comfortable music in the mouth,
tending, as all music does, toward silence,

and each body a lion of courage, and something
precious to the earth.   20

When it's over, I want to say: all my life
I was a bride married to amazement.
I was the bridegroom, taking the world into my arms.

When it's over, I don't want to wonder
if I have made of my life something particular, and real.
I don't want to find myself sighing and frightened,
or full of argument.

I don't want to end up simply having visited this world.

FOR ANALYSIS

1. This poem turns on a series of **images**. Describe each image associated with approaching death, evaluating its effectiveness and appropriateness.

2. What is the "cottage of darkness" (l. 10)?

3. What images are associated with life and experience? Are they effective? Explain.

4. What is wrong with "simply having visited this world" (l. 28)?

WRITING TOPIC

Lines 24–27 express the poet's attitude toward life as its end approaches. In an essay, explain how a life that is "particular, and real" leads naturally to a death that does not generate either sighing and fear, or argument.

SEAMUS HEANEY (B. 1939)

MID-TERM BREAK 1966

I sat all morning in the college sick bay
Counting bells knelling classes to a close.
At two o'clock our neighbors drove me home.

In the porch I met my father crying—
He had always taken funerals in his stride—
And Big Jim Evans saying it was a hard blow.

The baby cooed and laughed and rocked the pram
When I came in, and I was embarrassed
By old men standing up to shake my hand

And tell me they were "sorry for my trouble,"   10
Whispers informed strangers I was the eldest,
Away at school, as my mother held my hand

In hers and coughed out angry tearless sighs.
At ten o'clock the ambulance arrived
With the corpse, stanched and bandaged by the nurses.

Next morning I went up into the room. Snowdrops
And candles soothed the bedside; I saw him
For the first time in six weeks. Paler now,

Wearing a poppy bruise on his left temple,
He lay in the four foot box as in his cot.   20
No gaudy scars, the bumper knocked him clear.

A four foot box, a foot for every year.

FOR ANALYSIS

1. Although it contains little rhyme, this poem is remarkably musical. Identify the **assonance** and **alliteration** that permeate the poem.

2. What event does the poem describe?

3. How is the poem's title relevant?

WRITING TOPIC

Describe the family and the society revealed in this short poem.

JANICE MIRIKITANI   (B. 1942)

SUICIDE NOTE   1987

> . . . *An Asian-American college student was reported to have jumped to her death from her dormitory window. Her body was found two days later under a deep cover of snow. Her suicide note contained an apology to her parents for having received less than a perfect four-point grade average.* . . .

How many notes written . . .
ink smeared like birdprints in snow.

      not good enough   not pretty enough   not smart enough
dear mother and father.
I apologize
for disappointing you.
I've worked very hard,
            not good enough
harder, perhaps to please you.
If only I were a son, shoulders broad   10
as the sunset threading through pine,
I would see the light in my mother's
eyes, or the golden pride reflected
in my father's dream
of my wide, male hands worthy of work
and comfort.
I would swagger through life

muscled and bold and assured,
drawing praises to me
like currents in the bed of wind, virile   20
with confidence.
  not good enough   not strong enough   not good enough

I apologize.
Tasks do not come easily.
Each failure, a glacier.
Each disapproval, a bootprint.
Each disappointment,
ice above my river.
So I have worked hard.
     not good enough   30
My sacrifice I will drop
bone by bone, perched
on the ledge of my womanhood,
fragile as wings.
     not strong enough
It is snowing steadily
surely not good weather
for flying—this sparrow
sillied and dizzied by the wind
on the edge.   40
     not smart enough
I make this ledge my altar
to offer penance.
This air will not hold me,
the snow burdens my crippled wings,
my tears drop like bitter cloth
softly into the gutter below.
  not good enough   not strong enough   not smart enough
     Choices thin as shaved
     ice. Notes shredded   50
     drift like snow

on my broken body,
cover me like whispers
of sorries
sorries.
Perhaps when they find me
they will bury
my bird bones beneath
a sturdy pine
and scatter my feathers like   60

unspoken song
over this white and cold and silent
breast of earth.

FOR ANALYSIS

1. Would the speaker kill herself if she were male? Explain.

2. Why does the speaker kill herself? What assumptions about self-worth underlie her act?

3. What function does the bird **imagery** (beginning at l. 31) serve? Do you find these images effective? Explain.

4. Contrast the images associated with the imagined "son" she might have been with the images the speaker uses to display herself.

WRITING TOPICS

1. Argue that this poem should be placed in the thematic section "Culture and Identity" rather than in "The Presence of Death."

2. Is suicide ever justified? Explain.

JANE KENYON   (1947–1995)

LET EVENING COME   1996

Let the light of late afternoon
shine through chinks in the barn, moving
up the bales as the sun moves down.

Let the cricket take up chafing
as a woman takes up her needles
and her yarn. Let evening come.

Let dew collect on the hoe abandoned
in long grass. Let the stars appear
and the moon disclose her silver horn.

Let the fox go back to its sandy den.   10
Let the wind die down. Let the shed
go black inside. Let evening come.

To the bottle in the ditch, to the scoop
in the oats, to air in the lung
let evening come.

Let it come, as it will, and don't
be afraid. God does not leave us
comfortless, so let evening come.

FOR ANALYSIS

1. What does evening signify in this poem?

2. Why do you think Kenyon includes "air in the lung" (l. 14) as one of the things that evening should be allowed to come to?

3. How would you characterize the sounds and **rhythms** of this poem? How do they serve the subject?

WRITING TOPICS

1. "Let Evening Come" was published shortly after the death of its author. Reflect on how knowing this might change your reading experience or interpretation of the poem. Does it change your sense of what the poem is about? Does it change its emotional **tone**? Should it? Should knowing something about the life of a writer change how you read that writer's work?

2. Do you have an opinion on the poem's assertion that "God does not leave us / comfortless" (ll. 17–18)? What does it mean? Does your agreement or disagreement with that assertion change how you feel about the poem?

VICTOR HERNANDEZ CRUZ (B. 1949)

PROBLEMS WITH HURRICANES   1991

A campesino looked at the air
And told me:
With hurricanes it's not the wind
or the noise or the water.
I'll tell you he said:
it's the mangoes, avocados
Green plantains and bananas
flying into town like projectiles.

How would your family
feel if they had to tell
The generations that you
got killed by a flying
Banana.

Death by drowning has honor
If the wind picked you up

10

and slammed you
Against a mountain boulder
This would not carry shame
But
to suffer a mango smashing   20
Your skull
or a plantain hitting your
Temple at 70 miles per hour
is the ultimate disgrace.

The campesino takes off his hat—
As a sign of respect
towards the fury of the wind
and says:
Don't worry about the noise
Don't worry about the water   30
Don't worry about the wind—
If you are going out
beware of mangoes
And all such beautiful
sweet things.

MARY RUEFLE   (B. 1952)

STOPWATCH   2001

So your daughter had a white dress, and once you saw
a polar bear, yellow against the snow.
I do not think there are any sights in paradise,
except a woman on her hands and knees
washing the road between two cities
who has the impression she is wasting her time
while the earth is doing something differently.
When soap falls from her bucket the moon almost
glows. I believe everything you've ever done encroaches
on your being. Draw a wheat field with a reed pen   10
in brown ink, and afterwards your hands are straw.
Why were the martyrs eye-bitten, hand-bandaged, boiled alive?
I have sixty seconds to answer that. Let's go back
to the beginning of their lives and do a study
of death in its infancy: a baby in a bowl, bath time,
skin as blushed and firm as perfect fruit.

A painter can't look too closely at his model.
He'll be devoured like the bones of a churchmouse
in the jaws of an owl. When I look up
at the wish-washed sky, the crosshatched breath   20
of my boomerang comes back: why do we waste our time
while as faucet continually drips, a clock
with as little accuracy as the moon?
The last thing the martyrs saw was an eraser
of sorts, chalk drifting downwards out of felt. Star
pupils! They thought the perfection of a day
required years. In this manner they all passed.

JANE HIRSHFIELD   (B. 1953)

SALT HEART   1997

I was tired,
half sleeping in the sun.
A single bee
delved the lavender nearby,
and beyond the fence,
a trowel's shoulder knocked a white stone.
Soon, the ringing stopped.
And from somewhere,
a quiet voice said the one word.
Surely a command,   10
though it seemed more a question,
a wondering perhaps—"What about joy?"
So long it had been forgotten,
even the thought raised surprise.
But however briefly, there,
in the untuned devotions of bee
and the lavender fragrance,
the murmur of better and worse was unimportant.
From next door, the sound of raking,
and neither courage nor cowardice mattered.   20
Failure—uncountable failure—did not matter.
Soon enough that gate swung closed,
the world turned back to heart-salt
of wanting, heart-salts of will and grief.
My friend would continue dying, at last
only exhausted, even his wrists thinned with pain.

The river Suffering would take what it
wished of him, then go. And I would stay
and drink on, as the living do, until the rest
would enter into that water—the lavender swept in,   30
the bee, the swallowed labors of my neighbor.
The ordinary moment swept in, whatever it drowsily holds.
I begin to believe the only sin is distance, refusal.
All others stemming from this. Then, come.
Rivers, come. Irrevocable futures, come. Come even joy.
Even now, even here, and though it vanish like him.

FOR ANALYSIS

1. In line 23, the speaker asserts that "the world turned back to heart-salt." From what does the world turn back? Why? What does the figurative expression "heart-salt" mean?

2. Contrast the countryside setting created in lines 1–19 with the images that dominate the rest of the poem. How do they differ? What do you understand by "the river Suffering" (l. 27)?

3. The speaker asserts, "I begin to believe the only sin is distance, refusal" (l. 33). What does she mean?

4. To whom does the last word in the poem ("him") refer? What does he have to do with "joy"?

WRITING TOPIC

Explain how the poet creates an appealing real-world setting that is obliterated by the power of abstract reflection. Does the poet believe that memory and awareness can destroy the attractiveness of nature? Do you?

DEAN YOUNG (B. 1955)

ELEGY ON A TOY PIANO   2005

FOR KENNETH KOCH

You don't need a pony
to connect you to the unseeable
or an airplane to connect you to the sky.

Necessary it is to love to live
and there are many manuals
but in all important ways
one is on one's own.

You need not cut off your hand.
No need to eat a bouquet.
Your head becomes a peach pit.   10
Your tongue a honeycomb.

Necessary it is to live to love,
to charge into the burning tower
then charge back out
and necessary it is to die.
Even for the trees, even for the pony
connecting you to what can't be grasped.

The injured gazelle falls behind the
herd. One last wild enjambment.

Because of the sores in his mouth,   20
the great poet struggles with a dumpling.
His work has enlarged the world
but the world is about to stop including him.
He is the tower the world runs out of.

When something becomes ash,
there's nothing you can do to turn it back.
About this, even diamonds do not lie.

FOR ANALYSIS

1. What is an **elegy**? What might it mean to play one on a toy piano?

2. What is the pony doing in this poem?

3. Why do you think Young might have chosen to include lines 11, 20, and 21? What effect do they have?

WRITING TOPICS

1. Reflect on this poem in terms of genre. What kind of **tone** and **imagery** does one expect from elegy? In what ways does this poem seem like one? In what ways does it not? Is it acceptable to be playful in an elegy?

2. The towers and ash are generally taken as references to the destruction of the Twin Towers of the World Trade Center on September 11, 2001. Kenneth Koch was a poet and a friend of Young's (and an important influence on him); he died of leukemia the summer after 9/11. Reflect on the effect knowing these things has on your reading of the poem.

CONNECTING POEMS:
NIGHT THOUGHTS

The poems in this unit all deal with death as an immediate, personal thing, as the faceless opponent who steals away our loved ones and, eventually, us too. They confront the darkest moments when, in Philip Larkin's words, we "see what's really always there," that is, the inevitability of the end of life. As you read, note the ways these poets wring a kind of beauty out of an aspect of human experience not often thought to inspire such a reaction.

DYLAN THOMAS   (1914–1953)

DO NOT GO GENTLE INTO
THAT GOOD NIGHT   1952

Do not go gentle into that good night,
Old age should burn and rave at close of day;
Rage, rage against the dying of the light.

Though wise men at their end know dark is right,
Because their words had forked no lightning they
Do not go gentle into that good night.

Good men, the last wave by, crying how bright
Their frail deeds might have danced in a green bay,
Rage, rage against the dying of the light.

Wild men who caught and sang the sun in flight,   10
And learn, too late, they grieved it on its way,
Do not go gentle into that good night.

Grave men, near death, who see with blinding sight
Blind eyes could blaze like meteors and be gay,
Rage, rage against the dying of the light.

And you, my father, there on the sad height,
Curse, bless, me now with your fierce tears, I pray.
Do not go gentle into that good night.
Rage, rage against the dying of the light.

FOR ANALYSIS

1. What do wise, good, wild, and grave men have in common?
2. Why does the poet use the adjective *gentle* rather than the adverb *gently* in the title?
3. What is the "sad height" (l. 16)?

WRITING TOPIC

This poem is a **villanelle**, which means that it contains only two rhymes and that the first and third lines alternate as the third lines in each stanza following and form a final couplet. Why do you think Thomas chose this form for his poem? How does it relate to the poem's subject and its treatment of that subject?

PHILIP LARKIN (1922–1985)

AUBADE[1] 1977

I work all day, and get half drunk at night.
Waking at four to soundless dark, I stare.
In time the curtain-edges will grow light.
Till then I see what's really always there:
Unresting death, a whole day nearer now;
Making all thought impossible but how
And where and when I shall myself die.
Arid interrogation: yet the dread
Of dying, and being dead,
Flashes afresh to hold and horrify.   10

The mind blanks at the glare. Not in remorse
—The good not done, the love not given, time
Torn off unused—nor wretchedly because
An only life can take so long to climb
Clear of its wrong beginnings, and may never;
But at the total emptiness for ever,
The sure extinction that we travel to
And shall be lost in always. Not to be here,
Not to be anywhere,
And soon; nothing more terrible, nothing more true.   20

This is a special way of being afraid
No trick dispels. Religion used to try,

Aubade
[1] An aubade is a morning song.

That vast moth-eaten musical brocade
Created to pretend we never die,
And specious stuff that says *No rational being*
Can fear a thing it will not feel, not seeing
That this is what we fear—no sight, no sound.
No touch or taste to smell, nothing to think with.
Nothing to love or link with,
The anaesthetic from which none come round.   30

And so it stays just on the edge of vision,
A small unfocused blur, a standing chill
That slows each impulse down to indecision.
Most things may never happen: this one will.
And realisation of it rages out
In furnace-fear when we are caught without
People or drink. Courage is no good:
It means not scaring others. Being brave
Lets no one off the grave.
Death is no different whined at than withstood.   40

Slowly light strengthens, and the room takes shape.
It stands plain as a wardrobe, what we know,
Have always known, know that we can't escape,
Yet can't accept. One side will have to go.
Meanwhile telephones crouch, getting ready to ring
In locked-up offices, and all the uncaring
Intricate rented world begins to rouse.
The sky is white as clay, with no sun.
Work has to be done.
Postmen like doctors go from house to house.   50

FOR ANALYSIS

1. Why does the poem describe the whole world as "rented" (l. 47)?

2. What is it about the poem's subject that the speaker seems to fear most?

3. An **aubade** is traditionally a love poem in which approaching dawn forces lovers to part. Why might Larkin have chosen this form for his poem? Does he want night to linger? Morning never to come?

WRITING TOPIC

Make a list of all the instances in the poem in which the negative is used. Reflect on what they are used for and what they mean for the poem. Why might they be ultimately significant, given the subject?

CATHERINE DAVIS   (1924–2002)

AFTER A TIME   1961?

After a time, all losses are the same.
One more thing lost is one thing less to lose;
And we go stripped at last the way we came.

Though we shall probe, time and again, our shame,
Who lack the wit to keep or to refuse,
After a time, all losses are the same.

No wit, no luck can beat a losing game;
Good fortune is a reassuring ruse:
And we go stripped at last the way we came.

Rage as we will for what we think to claim,   10
Nothing so much as this bare thought subdues:
After a time, all losses are the same.

The sense of treachery—the want, the blame—
Goes in the end, whether or not we choose,
And we go stripped at last the way we came.

So we, who would go raging, will go tame
When what we have we can no longer use:
After a time, all losses are the same;
And we go stripped at last the way we came.

FOR ANALYSIS

1. What is this poem's **tone**? How might the fourth stanza help you describe it?

2. What kind of losses is the poem talking about?

WRITING TOPIC

This poem is free of concrete **images** and situations. Reflect on how it might be different if the poet had included some. What might be gained? What lost?

MAKING CONNECTIONS

1. Compare the emotions evoked by death in these three poems. Do they express a
single emotion or a mix of emotions?

2. These poems adopt traditional forms: two are **villanelles,** and one is an **aubade.**
How does the use of a traditional poetic form serve each poem? Do the poems use
these forms in the same ways?

1220

3. What death means to the speakers in these poems is not the same and neither are the "night thoughts" they have in response. How does each of these speakers ultimately deal with death? Which of these responses is most satisfying/least unsatisfying? How do you think about death?

CONNECTING POEMS: MEMORIALS

The poems in this unit explore different aspects of public mourning—the stories we tell about the dead, how those stories change over time, and how the shape of the story depends on the teller. As you read these poems, think about the way that each represents the dead and at the same time reflects on the ways in which the dead tend to be represented.

ROBERT LOWELL   (1917–1977)

FOR THE UNION DEAD   1964

"RELINQUUNT OMNIA SERVARE REM PUBLICAN."

The old South Boston Aquarium stands
in a Sahara of snow now. Its broken windows are boarded.
The bronze weathervane cod has lost half its scales.
The airy tanks are dry.

Once my nose crawled like a snail on the glass;
my hand tingled
to burst the bubbles
drifting from the noses of the cowed, compliant fish.

My hand draws back. I often sigh still
for the dark downward and vegetating kingdom   10
of the fish and reptile. One morning last March,
I pressed against the new barbed and galvanized

fence on the Boston Common. Behind their cage,
yellow dinosaur steamshovels were grunting
as they cropped up tons of mush and grass
to gouge their underworld garage.

Parking spaces luxuriate like civic
sandpiles in the heart of Boston.
A girdle of orange, Puritan-pumpkin colored girders
braces the tingling Statehouse,   20

shaking over the excavations, as it faces Colonel Shaw
and his bell-cheeked Negro infantry
on St. Gaudens' shaking Civil War relief,
propped by a plank splint against the garage's earthquake.

Two months after marching through Boston,
half the regiment was dead;
at the dedication,
William James could almost hear the bronze Negroes breathe.

Their monument sticks like a fishbone
in the city's throat.   30
Its Colonel is as lean
as a compass-needle.

He has an angry wrenlike vigilance,
a greyhound's gentle tautness;
he seems to wince at pleasure,
and suffocate for privacy.

He is out of bounds now. He rejoices in man's lovely,
peculiar power to choose life and die—
when he leads his black soldiers to death,
he cannot bend his back.   40

On a thousand small town New England greens,
the old white churches hold their air
of sparse, sincere rebellion; frayed flags
quilt the graveyards of the Grand Army of the Republic.

The stone statues of the abstract Union Soldier
grow slimmer and younger each year—
wasp-waisted, they doze over muskets
and muse through their sideburns . . .

Shaw's father wanted no monument
except the ditch,   50
where his son's body was thrown
and lost with his "niggers."

The ditch is nearer.
There are no statues for the last war here;
on Boylston Street, a commercial photograph
shows Hiroshima boiling

over a Mosler Safe, the "Rock of Ages"
that survived the blast. Space is nearer.
When I crouch to my television set,
the drained faces of Negro school-children rise like balloons.   60

Colonel Shaw
is riding on his bubble,
he waits
for the blessèd break.

The Aquarium is gone. Everywhere,
giant finned cars nose forward like fish;
a savage servility
slides by on grease.

FOR ANALYSIS

1. Are the "Union Dead" of the title the main subjects of this poem? Is Colonel Shaw,
who led an all black regiment in battle against Confederate forces? If not them, what is
the poem's subject? Who or what are the poem's heroes? Who or what are its villains?

2. What function does the Latin epigraph serve in this poem?

3. What war is the "last war" (l. 54)? How does it compare, in the poem, to the previous American wars referred or alluded to by Lowell?

WRITING TOPICS

1. Trace Lowell's ideas about the relation of the present to the past in "For the Union
Dead." How does he view Boston's and, by extension, America's history? Do things
stay the same? Have they changed? If so, for better or for worse?

2. The poem can be seen as a response to Allen Tate's 1928 "Ode to the Confederate
Dead." Read Tate's poem and reflect on how Lowell's poem might be a response to it.

LUCILLE CLIFTON   (B. 1936)

AT THE CEMETERY, WALNUT
GROVE PLANTATION, SOUTH
CAROLINA, 1989   1991

among the rocks
at walnut grove
your silence drumming
in my bones,
tell me your names.

nobody mentioned slaves
and yet the curious tools
shine with your fingerprints.
nobody mentioned slaves
but somebody did this work
who had no guide, no stone,
who moulders under rock.   10

tell me your names,
tell me your bashful names
and I will testify.

the inventory lists ten slaves
but only men were recognized.

among the rocks
at walnut grove
some of these honored dead   20
were dark
some of these dark
were slaves
some of these slaves
were women
some of them did this
honored work.
tell me your names
foremothers, brothers,
tell me your dishonored names.   30
here lies
here lies
here lies
here lies
hear

FOR ANALYSIS

1. What does the "silence" in line 3 represent?

2. Why does the speaker want to know the names?

3. What does *lies* mean at the end of the poem? Does it have one meaning or two? What do you think Clifton means when she changes *here* to *hear* in the last line?

WRITING TOPIC

History is often thought of as facts about the past, but it is really a narrative created by people who may leave things out, intentionally or unintentionally. Can you think of another example of history in which a long-accepted story turned out to be a lie? What does it mean when "history" does not tell the true story or the complete story?

YUSEF KOMUNYAKAA (B. 1947)

FACING IT 1988

My black face fades,
hiding inside the black granite.
I said I wouldn't,
dammit: No tears.
I'm stone. I'm flesh.
My clouded reflection eyes me
like a bird of prey, the profile of night
slanted against morning. I turn
this way—the stone lets me go.
I turn that way—I'm inside   10
the Vietnam Veterans Memorial
again, depending on the light
to make a difference.
I go down the 58,022 names,
half-expecting to find
my own in letters like smoke.
I touch the name Andrew Johnson;
I see the booby trap's white flash.
Names shimmer on a woman's blouse
but when she walks away   20
the names stay on the wall.
Brushstrokes flash, a red bird's
wings cutting across my stare.
The sky. A plane in the sky.
A white vet's image floats
closer to me, then his pale eyes
look through mine. I'm a window.
He's lost his right arm
inside the stone. In the black mirror
a woman's trying to erase names: 30
No, she's brushing a boy's hair.

FOR ANALYSIS

1. What is the speaker in "Facing It" facing? Is it one thing? More than one thing? If more than one, does "facing" mean the same thing for each "it"?

2. In what ways does the poem refer to the war itself? Does it include direct representation of the violence or the participants? Indirect representation? Why do you think Komunyakaa chose to refer to it in these ways?

WRITING TOPIC

The Vietnam Veterans Memorial was controversial when it first opened. (If you are not familiar with the memorial, refer to a picture of it.) How does "Facing It" engage how the memorial is experienced by people? What might it have to say to those who criticize the memorial as unpatriotic or disrespectful?

KEVIN YOUNG   (B. 1970)

FOR THE CONFEDERATE DEAD   2007

I go with the team also.
            —Whitman

These are the last days
my television says. Tornadoes, more
rain, overcast, a chance

of sun but I do not
trust weathermen,
never have. In my fridge only

the milk makes sense—
expires. No one, much less
my parents, can tell me why

my middle name is Lowell,   10
and from my table
across from the Confederate

Monument to the dead (that pale
finger bone) a plaque
declares war—not Civil,

or Between
the States, but for Southern
Independence. In this café, below sea-

and eye-level a mural runs
the wall, flaking, a plantation
scene most do not see—   20

it's too much
around the knees, height
of a child. In its fields Negroes bend

to pick the endless white.
In livery a few drive carriages
like slaves, whipping the horses, faces

blank and peeling. The old hotel
lobby this once was no longer
welcomes guests—maroon ledger,   30

bellboys gone but
for this. Like an inheritance
the owner found it

stripping hundred years
(at least) of paint
and plaster. More leaves each day.

In my movie there are no
horses, no heroes,
only draftees fleeing

into the pines, some few   10
who survive, gravely
wounded, lying

burrowed beneath the dead—
silent until the enemy
bayonets what is believed

to be the last
of the breathing. It is getting later.
We prepare

for wars no longer
there. The weather   50
inevitable, unusual—

more this time of year
than anyone ever seed. The earth
shudders, the air—

if I did not know
better, I would think
we were living all along

a fault. How late
it has gotten . . .
Forget the weatherman   60

whose maps move, blink,
but stay crossed
with lines none has seen. Race

instead against the almost
rain, digging beside the monument
(that giant anchor)

till we strike
water, sweat
fighting the sleepwalking air.

FOR ANALYSIS

1. What name appears on the monument for the war usually referred to as the Civil War? What does it mean that this name is used and not another?

2. What does the weather signify in this poem?

3. Why do you think the speaker emphasizes the age and condition of the hotel in which he sits?

WRITING TOPIC

A line from Whitman's 1881 *Song of Myself,* the epigraph is about racial intermingling and bonding: the speaker, seeing a black man described as strong and beautiful driving a carriage pulled by a team of horses, says that he joins him. Why do you think Young chose this epigraph for the poem? In what ways does it connect to the poem?

MAKING CONNECTIONS

1. Lowell's "For the Union Dead" is in part a response to Tate's "Ode to the Confederate Dead"; Young's "For the Confederate Dead" can be seen as a response to Lowell's "For the Union Dead." How do these poems interconnect? How do Lowell's and Young's write about history through literary history?

2. These poems about memorializing death are also all about race. How do these two themes connect in these poems?

3. In all of these poems, memorials are silent but also speak eloquently. How do they speak? What do they say?

CONNECTING POEMS: ANIMAL FATES

The poems in this unit focus on the decisions people make when faced with causing the death of animals, and the feelings people feel when they make them. These poems also reflect on how the animals might feel. As you read, note how the ethical dilemmas are not just set off against this sense of animals as individuals, with personalities, but are also informed by it.

ELIZABETH BISHOP   (1911–1979)

THE FISH   1946

I caught a tremendous fish
and held him beside the boat
half out of water, with my hook
fast in a corner of his mouth.
He didn't fight.
He hadn't fought at all.
He hung a grunting weight,
battered and venerable
and homely. Here and there
his brown skin hung in strips   10
like ancient wallpaper,
and its pattern of darker brown
was like wallpaper:
shapes like full-blown roses
stained and lost through age.
He was speckled and barnacles,
fine rosettes of lime,
and infested
with tiny white sea-lice,
and underneath two or three   20
rags of green weed hung down.
While his gills were breathing in
the terrible oxygen
—the frightening gills,
fresh and crisp with blood,
that can cut so badly—
I thought of the coarse white flesh
packed in like feathers,

the big bones and the little bones,
the dramatic reds and blacks
of his shiny entrails,   30
and the pink swim-bladder
like a big peony.
I looked into his eyes
which were far larger than mine
but shallower, and yellowed,
the irises backed and packed
with tarnished tinfoil
seen through the lenses
of old scratched isinglass.   40
They shifted a little, but not
to return my stare.
—It was more like the tipping
of an object toward the light.
I admired his sullen face,
the mechanism of his jaw,
and then I saw
that from his lower lip
—if you could call it a lip—
grim, wet, and weaponlike,   50
hung five old pieces of fish-line,
or four and a wire leader
with the swivel still attached,
with all their five big hooks
grown firmly in his mouth.
A green line, frayed at the end
where he broke it, two heavier lines,
and a fine black thread
still crimped from the strain and snap
when it broke and he got away.   60
Like medals with their ribbons
frayed and wavering,
a five-haired beard of wisdom
trailing from his aching jaw.
I stared and stared
and victory filled up
the little rented boat,
from the pool of bilge
where oil had spread a rainbow
around the rusted engine   70
to the bailer rusted orange,
the sun-cracked thwarts,
the oarlocks on their strings,

the gunnels—until everything
was rainbow, rainbow, rainbow!
And I let the fish go.

FOR ANALYSIS

1. What is the nature of the speaker's "victory" (l. 66)?

2. Where does the poem turn—that is, where does the poem shift its attention to something that changes what it is about and what it means?

WRITING TOPIC

"The Fish" is packed with details. List the details Bishop includes, breaking them down into the groups in which they appear (for example, those describing the fish's skin, those describing the boat). Then reflect on how the poem uses these details. How do they create pictures, set moods, imply thoughts and feelings?

WILLIAM STAFFORD   (1914–1995)

TRAVELING THROUGH THE DARK   1962

Traveling through the dark I found a deer
dead on the edge of the Wilson River road.
It is usually best to roll them into the canyon:
that road is narrow; to swerve might make more dead.

By glow of the tail-light I stumbled back of the car
and stood by the heap, a doe, a recent killing;
she had stiffened already, almost cold.
I dragged her off; she was large in the belly.

My fingers touching her side brought me the reason—
her side was warm; her fawn lay there waiting,   10
alive, still, never to be born.
Beside that mountain road I hesitated.

The car aimed ahead its lowered parking lights;
under the hood purred the steady engine.
I stood in the glare of the warm exhaust turning red;
around our group I could hear the wilderness listen.

I thought hard for us all—my only swerving—,
then pushed her over the edge into the river.

FOR ANALYSIS

1. Why is it best to clear the dead deer off the road? Why does the speaker hesitate?

2. How is the speaker's car described? Why do you think Stafford describes it this way?

3. Stafford uses versions of the word *swerve* twice. Why do you think he uses them?

WRITING TOPIC

Stafford chose not to explain how the deer came to be dead, perhaps in part because it is obvious that cars kill deer on this road often. Why else might he not have mentioned it? What could this poem be saying about this unnamed cause?

MAXINE KUMIN   (B. 1925)

WOODCHUCKS   1972

Gassing the woodchucks didn't turn out right.
The knockout bomb from the Feed and Grain Exchange
was featured as merciful, quick at the bone
and the case we had against them was airtight
both exits shoehorned shut with puddingstone,
but they had a sub-sub-basement out of range.

Next morning they turned up again, no worse
for the cyanide than we for our cigarettes
and state-store Scotch, all of us up to scratch.
They brought down the marigolds as a matter of course   10
and then took over the vegetable patch
nipping the broccoli shoots, beheading the carrots.

The food from our mouths, I said, righteously thrilling
to the feel of the .22, the bullets' neat noses.
I, a lapsed pacifist fallen from grace
puffed with Darwinian pieties for killing,
now drew a bead on the littlest woodchuck's face.
He died down in the everbearing roses.

Ten minutes later I dropped the mother. She
flipflopped in the air and fell, her needle teeth   20
still hooked in a leaf of early Swiss chard.
Another baby next. O one-two-three
the murderer inside me rose up hard,
the hawkeye killer came on stage forthwith.

There's one chuck left. Old wily fellow, he keeps
me cocked and ready day after day after day.
All night I hunt his humped-up form. I dream
I sight along the barrel in my sleep.
If only they'd all consented to die unseen
gassed underground the quiet Nazi way.   30

FOR ANALYSIS

1. Why does the speaker choose to kill the woodchucks with gas first?

2. How would you describe Kumin's language in "Woodchucks"? Is it uniform or does it vary? What are its effects on how you feel as you read?

WRITING TOPIC

While reading this poem, with whom did you identify—the speaker or the wood-chucks? Reflect on your own feelings in this light: Are your feelings as mixed as the speaker's?

MAKING CONNECTIONS

1. How do these poems create moments in which the speakers think of animals as individual beings? How do they create personal (or emotional) connections with animals?

2. Each of these poems confronts humans with a dilemma about killing animals. How does each resolve its dilemma? How does each poem present the decision that is made? Do any of them judge?

3. While these poems share a subject, they handle it differently. How does **tone** vary from poem to poem in this unit?

DRAMA

ARTHUR MILLER   (1915-2005)

DEATH OF A SALESMAN   1949

CERTAIN PRIVATE CONVERSATIONS IN TWO ACTS

AND A REQUIEM

CAST

Willy Loman	Uncle Ben
Linda	Howard Wagner
Biff	Jenny
Happy	Stanley
Bernard	Miss Forsythe
The Woman	Letta
Charley	

Scene: *The action takes place in Willy Loman's house and yard and in various places he visits in the New York and Boston of today.*

Throughout the play, in the stage directions, left and right mean stage left and stage right.

ACT I

A melody is heard, played upon a flute. It is small and fine, telling of grass and trees and the horizon. The curtain rises.

Before us is the Salesman's house. We are aware of towering, angular shapes behind it, surrounding it on all sides. Only the blue light of the sky falls upon the house and forestage; the surrounding area shows an angry glow of orange. As more light appears, we see a solid vault of apartment houses around the small, fragile-seeming home. An air of the dream clings to the place, a dream rising out of reality. The kitchen at center seems actual enough, for there is a kitchen table with three chairs, and a refrigerator. But no other fixtures are seen. At the back of the kitchen there is a draped entrance, which leads to the living-room. To the right of the kitchen, on a level raised two feet, is a bedroom furnished only with a brass bedstead and a straight chair. On a shelf over the bed a silver athletic trophy stands. A window opens onto the apartment house at the side.

Behind the kitchen, on a level raised six and a half feet, is the boys' bedroom, at present barely visible. Two beds are dimly seen, and at the back of the room a dormer window. (This bedroom is above the unseen living-room.) At the left a stairway curves up to it from the kitchen.

The entire setting is wholly or, in some places, partially transparent. The roof-line of the house is one-dimensional; under and over it we see the apartment buildings. Before the house lies an apron, curving beyond the forestage into the orchestra. This forward area serves as the backyard as well as the locale of all Willy's imaginings and of his city scenes. Whenever the action is in the present the actors observe the imaginary wall-lines, entering the house only through its door at the left. But in the scenes of the past these boundaries are broken, and characters enter or leave a room by stepping "through" a wall onto the forestage.

From the right, Willy Loman, the Salesman, enters, carrying two large sample cases. The flute plays on. He hears but is not aware of it. He is past sixty years of age, dressed quietly. Even as he crosses the stage to the doorway of the house, his exhaustion is apparent. He unlocks the door, comes into the kitchen, and thankfully lets his burden down, feeling the soreness of his palms. A word-sigh escapes his lips—it might be "Oh, boy, oh, boy." He closes the door, then carries his cases out into the living-room, through the draped kitchen doorway.

Linda, his wife, has stirred in her bed at the right. She gets out and puts on a robe, listening. Most often jovial, she has developed an iron repression of her exceptions to Willy's behavior—she more than loves him, she admires him, as though his mercurial nature, his temper, his massive dreams and little cruelties, served her only as sharp reminders of the turbulent longings within him, longings which she shares but lacks the temperament to utter and follow to their end.

Linda (hearing Willy outside the bedroom, calls with some trepidation). Willy!
Willy. It's all right. I came back.
Linda. Why? What happened? (Slight pause.) Did something happen, Willy?
Willy. No, nothing happened.
Linda. You didn't smash the car, did you?
Willy (with casual irritation). I said nothing happened. Didn't you hear me?
Linda. Don't you feel well?
Willy. I'm tired to the death. (The flute has faded away. He sits on the bed beside her, a little numb.) I couldn't make it. I just couldn't make it, Linda.
Linda (very carefully, delicately). Where were you all day? You look terrible.
Willy. I got as far as a little above Yonkers. I stopped for a cup of coffee. Maybe it was the coffee.
Linda. What?
Willy (after a pause). I suddenly couldn't drive any more. The car kept going off onto the shoulder, y'know?
Linda (helpfully). Oh. Maybe it was the steering again. I don't think Angelo knows the Studebaker.

Willy. No, it's me, it's me. Suddenly I realize I'm goin' sixty miles an hour and I don't remember the last five minutes. I'm—I can't seem to—keep my mind to it.

Linda. Maybe it's your glasses. You never went for your new glasses.

Willy. No, I see everything. I came back ten miles an hour. It took me nearly four hours from Yonkers.

Linda *(resigned).* Well, you'll just have to take a rest, Willy, you can't continue this way.

Willy. I just got back from Florida.

Linda. But you didn't rest your mind. Your mind is overactive, and the mind is what counts, dear.

Willy. I'll start out in the morning. Maybe I'll feel better in the morning. *(She is taking off his shoes.)* These goddam arch supports are killing me.

Linda. Take an aspirin. Should I get you an aspirin? It'll soothe you.

Willy *(with wonder).* I was driving along, you understand? And I was fine. I was even observing the scenery. You can imagine, me looking at scenery, on the road every week of my life. But it's so beautiful up there, Linda, the trees are so thick, and the sun is warm. I opened the windshield and just let the warm air bathe over me. And then all of a sudden I'm goin' off the road! I'm tellin' ya, I absolutely forgot I was driving. If I'd've gone the other way over the white line I might've killed somebody. So I went on again—and five minutes later I'm dreamin' again, and I nearly—*(He presses two fingers against his eyes.)* I have such thoughts, I have such strange thoughts.

Linda. Willy, dear. Talk to them again. There's no reason why you can't work in New York.

Willy. They don't need me in New York. I'm the New England man. I'm vital in New England.

Linda. But you're sixty years old. They can't expect you to keep traveling every week.

Willy. I'll have to send a wire to Portland. I'm supposed to see Brown and Morrison tomorrow morning at ten o'clock to show the line. Goddammit, I could sell them! *(He starts putting on his jacket.)*

Linda *(taking the jacket from him).* Why don't you go down to the place tomorrow and tell Howard you've simply got to work in New York? You're too accommodating, dear.

Willy. If old man Wagner was alive I'd a been in charge of New York now! That man was a prince, he was a masterful man. But that boy of his, that Howard, he don't appreciate. When I went north the first time, the Wagner Company didn't know where New England was!

Linda. Why don't you tell those things to Howard, dear?

Willy *(encouraged).* I will, I definitely will. Is there any cheese?

Linda. I'll make you a sandwich.

Willy. No, go to sleep. I'll take some milk. I'll be up right away. The boys in?

Linda. They're sleeping. Happy took Biff on a date tonight.

Willy *(interested).* That so?

Linda. It was so nice to see them shaving together, one behind the other, in the bathroom. And going out together. You notice? The whole house smells of shaving lotion.

Willy. Figure it out. Work a lifetime to pay off a house. You finally own it, and there's nobody to live in it.

Linda. Well, dear, life is a casting off. It's always that way.

Willy. No, no, some people—some people accomplish something. Did Biff say anything after I went this morning?

Linda. You shouldn't have criticized him, Willy, especially after he just got off the train. You mustn't lose your temper with him.

Willy. When the hell did I lose my temper? I simply asked him if he was making any money. Is that a criticism?

Linda. But, dear, how could he make any money?

Willy (*worried and angered*). There's such an undercurrent in him. He became a moody man. Did he apologize when I left this morning?

Linda. He was crestfallen, Willy. You know how he admires you. I think if he finds himself, then you'll both be happier and not fight any more.

Willy. How can he find himself on a farm? Is that a life? A farmhand? In the beginning, when he was young, I thought, well, a young man, it's good for him to tramp around, take a lot of different jobs. But it's more than ten years now and he has yet to make thirty-five dollars a week!

Linda. He's finding himself, Willy.

Willy. Not finding yourself at the age of thirty-four is a disgrace!

Linda. Shh!

Willy. The trouble is he's lazy, goddammit!

Linda. Willy, please!

Willy. Biff is a lazy bum!

Linda. They're sleeping. Get something to eat. Go on down.

Willy. Why did he come home? I would like to know what brought him home.

Linda. I don't know. I think he's still lost, Willy. I think he's very lost.

Willy. Biff Loman is lost. In the greatest country in the world a young man with such—personal attractiveness, gets lost. And such a hard worker. There's one thing about Biff—he's not lazy.

Linda. Never.

Willy (*with pity and resolve*). I'll see him in the morning; I'll have a nice talk with him. I'll get him a job selling. He could be big in no time. My God! Remember how they used to follow him around in high school? When he smiled at one of them their faces lit up. When he walked down the street . . . (*He loses himself in reminiscences.*)

Linda (*trying to bring him out of it*). Willy, dear, I got a new kind of American-type cheese today. It's whipped.

Willy. Why do you get American when I like Swiss?

Linda. I just thought you'd like a change—

Willy. I don't want a change! I want Swiss cheese. Why am I always being contradicted?

Linda (*with a covering laugh*). I thought it would be a surprise.

Willy. Why don't you open a window in here, for God's sake?

Linda (*with infinite patience*). They're all open, dear.

Willy. The way they boxed us in here. Bricks and windows, windows and bricks.

Linda. We should've bought the land next door.

Willy. The street is lined with cars. There's not a breath of fresh air in the neighborhood. The grass don't grow any more, you can't raise a carrot in the backyard. They should've had a law against apartment houses. Remember those two beautiful elm trees out there? When I and Biff hung the swing between them?

Linda. Yeah, like being a million miles from the city.

Willy. They should've arrested the builder for cutting those down. They massacred the neighborhood. *(Lost.)* More and more I think of those days, Linda. This time of year it was lilac and wisteria. And then the peonies would come out, and the daffodils. What fragrance in this room!

Linda. Well, after all, people had to move somewhere.

Willy. No, there's more people now.

Linda. I don't think there's more people. I think—

Willy. There's more people! That's what's ruining this country! Population is getting out of control. The competition is maddening! Smell the stink from that apartment house! And another one on the other side . . . How can they whip cheese?

On Willy's last line, Biff and Happy raise themselves up in their beds, listening.

Linda. Go down, try it. And be quiet.

Willy *(turning to Linda, guiltily).* You're not worried about me, are you, sweetheart?

Biff. What's the matter?

Happy. Listen!

Linda. You've got too much on the ball to worry about.

Willy. You're my foundation and my support, Linda.

Linda. Just try to relax, dear. You make mountains out of molehills.

Willy. I won't fight with him any more. If he wants to go back to Texas, let him go.

Linda. He'll find his way.

Willy. Sure. Certain men just don't get started till later in life. Like Thomas Edison, I think. Or B. F. Goodrich. One of them was deaf. *(He starts for the bedroom doorway.)* I'll put my money on Biff.

Linda. And Willy—if it's warm Sunday we'll drive in the country. And we'll open the windshield, and take lunch.

Willy. No, the windshields don't open on the new cars.

Linda. But you opened it today.

Willy. Me? I didn't. *(He stops.)* Now isn't that peculiar! Isn't that a remarkable— *(He breaks off in amazement and fright as the flute is heard distantly.)*

Linda. What, darling?

Willy. That is the most remarkable thing.

Linda. What, dear?

Willy. I was thinking of the Chevy. *(Slight pause.)* Nineteen twenty-eight . . . when I had that red Chevy—*(Breaks off.)* That funny? I coulda sworn I was driving that Chevy today.

Linda. Well, that's nothing. Something must've reminded you.

Willy. Remarkable. Ts. Remember those days? The way Biff used to simonize that car? The dealer refused to believe there was eighty thousand miles on it. *(He shakes his head.)* Heh! *(To Linda.)* Close your eyes, I'll be right up. *(He walks out of the bedroom.)*

Happy *(to Biff).* Jesus, maybe he smashed up the car again!

Linda *(calling after Willy).* Be careful on the stairs, dear! The cheese is on the middle shelf! *(She turns, goes over to the bed, takes his jacket, and goes out of the bedroom.)*

Light has risen on the boys' room. Unseen, Willy is heard talking to himself, "Eighty thousand miles," and a little laugh. Biff gets out of bed, comes downstage a bit, and stands attentively. Biff is two years older than his brother Happy, well built, but in these days bears a worn air and seems less self-assured. He has succeeded less, and his dreams are stronger and less acceptable than Happy's. Happy is tall, powerfully made. Sexuality is like a visible color on him, or a scent that many women have discovered. He, like his brother, is lost, but in a different way, for he has never allowed himself to turn his face toward defeat and is thus more confused and hard-skinned, although seemingly more content.

Happy *(getting out of bed).* He's going to get his license taken away if he keeps that up. I'm getting nervous about him, y'know, Biff?

Biff. His eyes are going.

Happy. No, I've driven with him. He sees all right. He just doesn't keep his mind on it. I drove into the city with him last week. He stops at a green light and then it turns red and he goes. *(He laughs.)*

Biff. Maybe he's color-blind.

Happy. Pop? Why he's got the finest eye for color in the business. You know that.

Biff *(sitting down on his bed).* I'm going to sleep.

Happy. You're not still sour on Dad, are you, Biff?

Biff. He's all right, I guess.

Willy *(underneath them, in the living-room).* Yes, sir, eighty thousand miles— eighty two thousand!

Biff. You smoking?

Happy *(holding out a pack of cigarettes).* Want one?

Biff *(taking a cigarette).* I can never sleep when I smell it.

Willy. What a simonizing job, heh!

Happy *(with deep sentiment).* Funny, Biff, y'know? Us sleeping in here again? The old beds. *(He pats his bed affectionately.)* All the talk that went across those two beds, huh? Our whole lives.

Biff. Yeah. Lotta dreams and plans.

Happy *(with a deep and masculine laugh).* About five hundred women would like to know what was said in this room.

They share a soft laugh.

Biff. Remember that big Betsy something—what the hell was her name—over on Bushwick Avenue?

Happy *(combing his hair).* With the collie dog!

Biff. That's the one. I got you in there, remember?

Happy. Yeah, that was my first time—I think. Boy, there was a pig! *(They laugh, almost crudely.)* You taught me everything I know about women. Don't forget that.

Biff. I bet you forgot how bashful you used to be. Especially with girls.

Happy. Oh, I still am, Biff.

Biff. Oh, go on.

Happy. I just control it, that's all. I think I got less bashful and you got more so. What happened, Biff? Where's the old humor, the old confidence? *(He shakes Biff's knee. Biff gets up and moves restlessly about the room.)* What's the matter?

Biff. Why does Dad mock me all the time?

Happy. He's not mocking you, he—

Biff. Everything I say there's a twist of mockery on his face. I can't get near him.

Happy. He just wants you to make good, that's all. I wanted to talk to you about Dad for a long time, Biff. Something's—happening to him. He—talks to himself.

Biff. I noticed that this morning. But he always mumbled.

Happy. But not so noticeable. It got so embarrassing I sent him to Florida. And you know something? Most of the time he's talking to you.

Biff. What's he say about me?

Happy. I can't make it out.

Biff. What's he say about me?

Happy. I think the fact that you're not settled, that you're still kind of up in the air . . .

Biff. There's one or two other things depressing him, Happy.

Happy. What do you mean?

Biff. Never mind. Just don't lay it all to me.

Happy. But I think if you just got started—I mean—is there any future for you out there?

Biff. I tell ya, Hap, I don't know what the future is. I don't know—what I'm supposed to want.

Happy. What do you mean?

Biff. Well, I spent six or seven years after high school trying to work myself up. Shipping clerk, salesman, business of one kind or another. And it's a measly manner of existence. To get on that subway on the hot mornings in summer. To devote your whole life to keeping stock, or making phone calls, or selling or buying. To suffer fifty weeks of the year for the sake of a two-week vacation, when all you really desire is to be outdoors, with your shirt off. And always to have to get ahead of the next fella. And still—that's how you build a future.

Happy. Well, you really enjoy it on a farm? Are you content out there?

Biff *(with rising agitation).* Hap, I've had twenty or thirty different kinds of jobs since I left home before the war, and it always turns out the same. I just realized it lately. In Nebraska when I herded cattle, and the Dakotas, and Arizona, and now in Texas. It's why I came home now, I guess, because I realized it. This farm I work on, it's spring there now, see? And they've got about fifteen new colts. There's nothing more inspiring or—beautiful than the sight of a mare and a new colt. And it's cool there now, see? Texas is cool now, and it's spring. And whenever spring comes to where I am, I suddenly get the feeling, my God, I'm not gettin' anywhere! What the hell am I doing, playing around with horses, twenty-eight dollars a week! I'm thirty-four years old, I oughta be makin' my future. That's when I come running home. And now, I get here, and I don't know what to do with myself. *(After a pause.)* I've always made a point of not wasting my life, and every time I come back here I know that all I've done is to waste my life.

Happy. You're a poet, you know that, Biff? You're a—you're an idealist!

Biff. No, I'm mixed up very bad. Maybe I oughta get married. Maybe I oughta get stuck into something. Maybe that's my trouble. I'm like a boy. I'm not married. I'm not in business, I just—I'm like a boy. Are you content, Hap? You're a success, aren't you? Are you content?

Happy. Hell, no!

Biff. Why? You're making money, aren't you?

Happy *(moving about with energy, expressiveness).* All I can do now is wait for the merchandise manager to die. And suppose I get to be merchandise manager? He's a good friend of mine, and he just built a terrific estate on Long Island. And he lived there about two months and sold it, and now he's building another one. He can't enjoy it once it's finished. And I know that's just what I would do. I don't know what the hell I'm workin' for. Sometimes I sit in my apartment—all alone. And I think of the rent I'm paying. And it's crazy. But then, it's what I always wanted. My own apartment, a car, and plenty of women. And still, goddammit, I'm lonely.

Biff *(with enthusiasm).* Listen, why don't you come out West with me?

Happy. You and I, heh?

Biff. Sure, maybe we could buy a ranch. Raise cattle, use our muscles. Men built like we are should be working out in the open.

Happy *(avidly).* The Loman Brothers, heh?

Biff *(with vast affection).* Sure, we'd be known all over the counties!

Happy *(enthralled).* That's what I dream about, Biff. Sometimes I want to just rip my clothes off in the middle of the store and outbox that goddam merchandise manager. I mean I can outbox, outrun, and outlift anybody in that store, and I have to take orders from those common, petty sons-of-bitches till I can't stand it any more.

Biff. I'm tellin' you, kid, if you were with me I'd be happy out there.

Happy *(enthused).* See, Biff, everybody around me is so false that I'm constantly lowering my ideals . . .

Biff. Baby, together we'd stand up for one another, we'd have someone to trust.

Happy. If I were around you—

Biff. Hap, the trouble is we weren't brought up to grub for money. I don't know how to do it.

Happy. Neither can I!

Biff. Then let's go!

Happy. The only thing is—what can you make out there?

Biff. But look at your friend. Builds an estate and then hasn't the peace of mind to live in it.

Happy. Yeah, but when he walks into the store the waves part in front of him. That's fifty-two thousand dollars a year coming through the revolving door, and I got more in my pinky finger than he's got in his head.

Biff. Yeah, but you just said—

Happy. I gotta show some of those pompous, self-important executives over there that Hap Loman can make the grade. I want to walk into the store the way he walks in. Then I'll go with you, Biff. We'll be together yet, I swear. But take those two we had tonight. Now weren't they gorgeous creatures?

Biff. Yeah, yeah, most gorgeous I've had in years.

Happy. I get that any time I want, Biff. Whenever I feel disgusted. The trouble is, it gets like bowling or something. I just keep knockin' them over and it doesn't mean anything. You still run around a lot?

Biff. Naa. I'd like to find a girl—steady, somebody with substance.

Happy. That's what I long for.

Biff. Go on! You'd never come home.

Happy. I would! Somebody with character, with resistance! Like Mom, y'know? You're gonna call me a bastard when I tell you this. That girl Charlotte I was with tonight is engaged to be married in five weeks. *(He tries on his new hat.)*

Biff. No kiddin'!

Happy. Sure, the guy's in line for the vice-presidency of the store. I don't know what gets into me, maybe I just have an overdeveloped sense of competition or something, but I went and ruined her, and furthermore I can't get rid of her. And he's the third executive I've done that to. Isn't that a crummy characteristic? And to top it all, I go to their weddings! *(Indignantly, but laughing.)* Like I'm not supposed to take bribes. Manufacturers offer me a hundred-dollar bill now and then to throw an order their way. You know how honest I am, but it's like this girl, see. I hate myself for it. Because I don't want the girl, and, still, I take it and—I love it!

Biff. Let's go to sleep.

Happy. I guess we didn't settle anything, heh?

Biff. I just got one idea that I think I'm going to try.

Happy. What's that?

Biff. Remember Bill Oliver?

Happy. Sure, Oliver is very big now. You want to work for him again?

Biff. No, but when I quit he said something to me. He put his arm on my shoulder, and he said, "Biff, if you ever need anything, come to me."

Happy. I remember that. That sounds good.

Biff. I think I'll go to see him. If I could get ten thousand or even seven or eight thousand dollars I could buy a beautiful ranch.

Happy. I bet he'd back you. 'Cause he thought highly of you, Biff. I mean, they all do. You're well liked, Biff. That's why I say to come back here, and we both have the apartment. And I'm tellin' you, Biff, any babe you want . . .

Biff. No, with a ranch I could do the work I like and still be something. I just wonder though. I wonder if Oliver still thinks I stole that carton of basketballs.

Happy. Oh, he probably forgot that long ago. It's almost ten years. You're too sensitive. Anyway, he didn't really fire you.

Biff. Well, I think he was going to. I think that's why I quit. I was never sure whether he knew or not. I know he thought the world of me, though. I was the only one he'd let lock up the place.

Willy (*below*). You gonna wash the engine, Biff?

Happy. Shh!

Biff looks at Happy, who is gazing down, listening. Willy is mumbling in the parlor.

Happy. You hear that?

They listen. Willy laughs warmly.

Biff (*growing angry*). Doesn't he know Mom can hear that?

Willy. Don't get your sweater dirty, Biff!

A look of pain crosses Biff's face.

Happy. Isn't that terrible? Don't leave again, will you? You'll find a job here. You gotta stick around. I don't know what to do about him, it's getting embarrassing.

Willy. What a simonizing job!

Biff. Mom's hearing that!

Willy. No kiddin', Biff, you got a date? Wonderful!

Happy. Go on to sleep. But talk to him in the morning, will you?

Biff (*reluctantly getting into bed*). With her in the house. Brother!

Happy (*getting into bed*). I wish you'd have a good talk with him,

The light on their room begins to fade.

Biff (*to himself in bed*). That selfish, stupid . . .

Happy. Sh . . . Sleep, Biff.

Their light is out. Well before they have finished speaking, Willy's form is dimly seen below in the darkened kitchen. He opens the refrigerator, searches in there, and takes out a bottle of milk. The apartment houses are fading out, and the entire house and surroundings become covered with leaves. Music insinuates itself as the leaves appear.

Willy. Just wanna be careful with those girls, Biff, that's all. Don't make any promises. No promises of any kind. Because a girl, y'know, they always believe what you tell 'em, and you're very young, Biff, you're too young to be talking seriously to girls.

Light rises on the kitchen. Willy, talking, shuts the refrigerator door and comes downstage to the kitchen table. He pours milk into a glass. He is totally immersed in himself, smiling faintly.

Willy. Too young entirely, Biff. You want to watch your schooling first. Then when you're all set, there'll be plenty of girls for a boy like you. (*He smiles broadly at a kitchen chair.*) That so? The girls pay for you? (*He laughs.*) Boy, you must really be makin' a hit.

Willy is gradually addressing—physically—a point offstage, speaking through the wall of the kitchen, and his voice has been rising in volume to that of a normal conversation.

Willy. I been wondering why you polish the car so careful. Ha! Don't leave the hubcaps, boys. Get the chamois to the hubcaps. Happy, use newspaper on the windows, it's the easiest thing. Show him how to do it, Biff! You see, Happy? Pad it up, use it like a pad. That's it, that's it, good work. You're doin' all right, Hap. (*He pauses, then nods in approbation for a few seconds, then looks upward.*) Biff, first thing we gotta do when we get time is clip that big branch over the house. Afraid it's gonna fall in a storm and hit the roof. Tell you what. We get a rope and sling her around, and then we climb up there with a couple of saws and take her down. Soon as you finish the car, boys, I wanna see ya. I got a surprise for you, boys.
Biff (*offstage*). Whatta ya got, Dad?
Willy. No, you finish first. Never leave a job till you're finished—remember that. (*Looking toward the "big trees."*) Biff, up in Albany I saw a beautiful hammock. I think I'll buy it next trip, and we'll hang it right between those two elms. Wouldn't that be something? Just swingin' there under those branches. Boy, that would be . . .

Young Biff and Young Happy appear from the direction Willy was addressing. Happy carries rags and a pail of water. Biff, wearing a sweater with a block "S," carries a football.

Biff (*pointing in the direction of the car offstage*). How's that, Pop, professional?
Willy. Terrific. Terrific job, boys. Good work, Biff.
Happy. Where's the surprise, Pop?
Willy. In the back seat of the car.
Happy. Boy! (*He runs off.*)
Biff. What is it, Dad? Tell me, what'd you buy?
Willy (*laughing, cuffs him*). Never mind, something I want you to have.
Biff (*turns and starts off*). What is it, Hap?
Happy (*offstage*). It's a punching bag!
Biff. Oh, Pop!
Willy. It's got Gene Tunney's signature on it!

Happy runs onstage with a punching bag.

Biff. Gee, how'd you know we wanted a punching bag?

Willy. Well, it's the finest thing for the timing.

Happy (*lies down on his back and pedals with his feet*). I'm losing weight, you notice, Pop?

Willy (*to Happy*). Jumping rope is good too.

Biff. Did you see the new football I got?

Willy (*examining the ball*). Where'd you get a new ball?

Biff. The coach told me to practice my passing.

Willy. That so? And he gave you the ball, heh?

Biff. Well, I borrowed it from the locker room. (*He laughs confidentially.*)

Willy (*laughing with him at the theft*). I want you to return that.

Happy. I told you he wouldn't like it!

Biff (*angrily*). Well, I'm bringing it back!

Willy (*stopping the incipient argument, to Happy*). Sure, he's gotta practice with a regulation ball, doesn't he? (*To Biff.*) Coach'll probably congratulate you on your initiative!

Biff. Oh, he keeps congratulating my initiative all the time, Pop.

Willy. That's because he likes you. If somebody else took that ball there'd be an uproar. So what's the report, boys, what's the report?

Biff. Where'd you go this time, Dad? Gee we were lonesome for you.

Willy (*pleased, puts an arm around each boy and they come down to the apron*). Lonesome, heh?

Biff. Missed you every minute.

Willy. Don't say? Tell you a secret, boys. Don't breathe it to a soul. Someday I'll have my own business, and I'll never have to leave home any more.

Happy. Like Uncle Charley, heh?

Willy. Bigger than Uncle Charley! Because Charley is not—liked. He's liked, but he's not—well liked.

Biff. Where'd you go this time, Dad?

Willy. Well, I got on the road, and I went north to Providence. Met the Mayor.

Biff. The Mayor of Providence!

Willy. He was sitting in the hotel lobby.

Biff. What'd he say?

Willy. He said, "Morning!" And I said, "You got a fine city here, Mayor." And then he had coffee with me. And then I went to Waterbury. Waterbury is a fine city. Big clock city, the famous Waterbury clock. Sold a nice bill there. And then Boston—Boston is the cradle of the Revolution. A fine city. And a couple of other towns in Mass., and on to Portland and Bangor and straight home!

Biff. Gee, I'd love to go with you sometime, Dad.

Willy. Soon as summer comes.

Happy. Promise?

Willy. You and Hap and I, and I'll show you all the towns. America is full of beautiful towns and fine, upstanding people. And they know me, boys, they know me up and down New England. The finest people. And when I bring you fellas up, there'll be open sesame for all of us, 'cause one thing, boys: I have friends. I can park my car in any street in New England, and the cops protect it like their own. This summer, heh?

Biff and Happy (together). Yeah! You bet!

Willy. We'll take our bathing suits.

Happy. We'll carry your bags, Pop!

Willy. Oh, won't that be something! Me comin' into the Boston stores with you boys carryin' my bags. What a sensation!

Biff is prancing around, practicing passing the ball.

Willy. You nervous, Biff, about the game?

Biff. Not if you're gonna be there.

Willy. What do they say about you in school, now that they made you captain?

Happy. There's a crowd of girls behind him every time the classes change.

Biff (taking Willy's hand). This Saturday, Pop, this Saturday—just for you, I'm going to break through for a touchdown.

Happy. You're supposed to pass.

Biff. I'm takin' one play for Pop. You watch me, Pop, and when I take off my helmet, that means I'm breakin' out. Then you watch me crash through that line!

Willy (kisses Biff). Oh, wait'll I tell this in Boston!

Bernard enters in knickers. He is younger than Biff, earnest and loyal, a worried boy.

Bernard. Biff, where are you? You're supposed to study with me today.

Willy. Hey, looka Bernard. What're you lookin' so anemic about, Bernard?

Bernard. He's gotta study, Uncle Willy. He's got Regents next week.

Happy (tauntingly, spinning Bernard around). Let's box, Bernard!

Bernard. Biff! (He gets away from Happy.) Listen, Biff, I heard Mr. Birnbaum say that if you don't start studyin' math, he's gonna flunk you, and you won't graduate. I heard him!

Willy. You better study with him, Biff. Go ahead now.

Bernard. I heard him!

Biff. Oh, Pop, you didn't see my sneakers! (He holds up a foot for Willy to look at.)

Willy. Hey, that's a beautiful job of printing!

Bernard (wiping his glasses). Just because he printed University of Virginia on his sneakers doesn't mean they've got to graduate him, Uncle Willy!

Willy (angrily). What're you talking about? With scholarships to three universities they're gonna flunk him?

Bernard. But I heard Mr. Birnbaum say—

Willy. Don't be a pest, Bernard! (To his boys.) What an anemic!

Bernard. Okay, I'm waiting for you in my house, Biff.

Bernard goes off. The Lomans laugh.

Willy. Bernard is not well liked, is he?

Biff. He's liked, but he's not well liked.

Happy. That's right, Pop.

Willy. That's just what I mean. Bernard can get the best marks in school, y'understand, but when he gets out in the business world, y'understand, you are going to be five times ahead of him. That's why I thank Almighty God you're both built like Adonises.[1] Because the man who makes an appearance in the business world, the man who creates personal interest, is the man who gets ahead. Be liked and you will never want. You take me, for instance. I never have to wait in line to see a buyer. "Willy Loman is here!" That's all they have to know, and I go right through.

Biff. Did you knock them dead, Pop?

Willy. Knocked 'em cold in Providence, slaughtered 'em in Boston.

Happy *(on his back, pedaling again).* I'm losing weight, you notice, Pop?

Linda enters, as of old, a ribbon in her hair, carrying a basket of washing.

Linda *(with youthful energy).* Hello, dear!

Willy. Sweetheart!

Linda. How'd the Chevy run?

Willy. Chevrolet, Linda, is the greatest car ever built. *(To the boys.)* Since when do you let your mother carry wash up the stairs?

Biff. Grab hold there, boy!

Happy. Where to, Mom?

Linda. Hang them up on the line. And you better go down to your friends, Biff. The cellar is full of boys. They don't know what to do with themselves.

Biff. Ah, when Pop comes home they can wait!

Willy *(laughs appreciatively).* You better go down and tell them what to do, Biff.

Biff. I think I'll have them sweep out the furnace room.

Willy. Good work, Biff.

Biff *(goes through wall-line of kitchen to doorway at back and calls down).* Fellas! Everybody sweep out the furnace room! I'll be right down!

Voices. All right! Okay, Biff.

Biff. George and Sam and Frank, come out back! We're hangin' up the wash! Come on, Hap, on the double! *(He and Happy carry out the basket.)*

Linda. The way they obey him!

Willy. Well, that's training, the training. I'm tellin' you, I was sellin' thousands and thousands, but I had to come home.

Linda. Oh, the whole block'll be at that game. Did you sell anything?

Willy. I did five hundred gross in Providence and seven hundred gross in Boston.

Linda. No! Wait a minute, I've got a pencil. *(She pulls pencil and paper out of her apron pocket.)* That makes your commission . . . Two hundred—my God! Two hundred and twelve dollars!

---

[1] In Greek mythology, Adonis was a young man known for his good looks and favored by Aphrodite, goddess of love and beauty.

Willy. Well, I didn't figure it yet, but . . .

Linda. How much did you do?

Willy. Well, I—I did—about a hundred and eighty gross in Providence. Well, no—it came to—roughly two hundred gross on the whole trip.

Linda (*without hesitation*). Two hundred gross. That's . . . (*She figures.*)

Willy. The trouble was that three of the stores were half closed for inventory in Boston. Otherwise I woulda broke records.

Linda. Well, it makes seventy dollars and some pennies. That's very good.

Willy. What do we owe?

Linda. Well, on the first there's sixteen dollars on the refrigerator—

Willy. Why sixteen?

Linda. Well, the fan belt broke, so it was a dollar eighty.

Willy. But it's brand new.

Linda. Well, the man said that's the way it is. Till they work themselves in, y'know.

They move through the wall-line into the kitchen.

Willy. I hope we didn't get stuck on that machine.

Linda. They got the biggest ads of any of them!

Willy. I know, it's a fine machine. What else?

Linda. Well, there's nine-sixty for the washing machine. And for the vacuum cleaner there's three and a half due on the fifteenth. Then the roof, you got twenty-one dollars remaining.

Willy. It don't leak, does it?

Linda. No, they did a wonderful job. Then you owe Frank for the carburetor.

Willy. I'm not going to pay that man! That goddam Chevrolet, they ought to prohibit the manufacture of that car!

Linda. Well, you owe him three and a half. And odds and ends, comes to around a hundred and twenty dollars by the fifteenth.

Willy. A hundred and twenty dollars! My God, if business don't pick up I don't know what I'm gonna do!

Linda. Well, next week you'll do better.

Willy. Oh, I'll knock 'em dead next week. I'll go to Hartford. I'm very well liked in Hartford. You know, the trouble is, Linda, people don't seem to take to me.

They move onto the forestage.

Linda. Oh, don't be foolish.

Willy. I know it when I walk in. They seem to laugh at me.

Linda. Why? Why would they laugh at you? Don't talk that way, Willy.

Willy moves to the edge of the stage. Linda goes into the kitchen and starts to darn stockings.

Willy. I don't know the reason for it, but they just pass me by. I'm not noticed.

Linda. But you're doing wonderful, dear. You're making seventy to a hundred dollars a week.

Willy. But I gotta be at it ten, twelve hours a day. Other men—I don't know—they do it easier. I don't know why—I can't stop myself—I talk too much. A man oughta come in with a few words. One thing about Charley. He's a man of few words, and they respect him.

Linda. You don't talk too much, you're just lively.

Willy (*smiling*). Well, I figure, what the hell, life is short, a couple of jokes. (*To himself.*) I joke too much! (*The smile goes.*)

Linda. Why? You're—

Willy. I'm fat. I'm very—foolish to look at, Linda. I didn't tell you, but Christmas time I happened to be calling on F. H. Stewarts, and a salesman I know, as I was going in to see the buyer I heard him say something about—walrus. And I—I cracked him right across the face. I won't take that. I simply will not take that. But they do laugh at me. I know that.

Linda. Darling . . .

Willy. I gotta overcome it. I know I gotta overcome it. I'm not dressing to advantage, maybe.

Linda. Willy, darling, you're the handsomest man in the world—

Willy. Oh, no, Linda.

Linda. To me you are. (*Slight pause.*) The handsomest.

From the darkness is heard the laughter of a woman. Willy doesn't turn to it, but it continues through Linda's lines.

Linda. And the boys, Willy. Few men are idolized by their children the way you are.

Music is heard as behind a scrim, to the left of the house, The Woman, dimly seen, is dressing.

Willy (*with great feeling*). You're the best there is, Linda, you're a pal, you know that? On the road—on the road I want to grab you sometimes and just kiss the life outa you.

The laughter is loud now, and he moves into a brightening area at the left, where The Woman has come from behind the scrim and is standing, putting on her hat, looking into a "mirror" and laughing.

Willy. 'Cause I get so lonely—especially when business is bad and there's nobody to talk to. I get the feeling that I'll never sell anything again, that I won't make a living for you, or a business, a business for the boys. (*He talks through The Woman's subsiding laughter; The Woman primps at the "mirror."*) There's so much I want to make for—

The Woman. Me? You didn't make me, Willy. I picked you.

Willy (*pleased*). You picked me?

The Woman (*who is quite proper-looking, Willy's age*). I did. I've been sitting at that desk watching all the salesmen go by, day in, day out. But you've got such a sense of humor, and we do have such a good time together, don't we?

Willy. Sure, sure. (*He takes her in his arms.*) Why do you have to go now?

The Woman. It's two o'clock . . .

Willy. No, come on in! (*He pulls her.*)

The Woman. . . . my sisters'll be scandalized. When'll you be back?

Willy. Oh, two weeks about. Will you come up again?

The Woman. Sure thing. You do make me laugh. It's good for me. (*She squeezes his arm, kisses him.*) And I think you're a wonderful man.

Willy. You picked me, heh?

The Woman. Sure. Because you're so sweet. And such a kidder.

Willy. Well, I'll see you next time I'm in Boston.

The Woman. I'll put you right through to the buyers.

Willy (*slapping her bottom*). Right. Well, bottoms up!

The Woman (*slaps him gently and laughs*). You just kill me, Willy. (*He suddenly grabs her and kisses her roughly.*) You kill me. And thanks for the stockings. I love a lot of stockings. Well, good night.

Willy. Good night. And keep your pores open!

The Woman. Oh, Willy!

The Woman bursts out laughing, and Linda's laughter blends in. The Woman disappears into the dark. Now the area at the kitchen table brightens. Linda is sitting where she was at the kitchen table, but now is mending a pair of her silk stockings.

Linda. You are, Willy. The handsomest man. You've got no reason to feel that—

Willy (*coming out of The Woman's dimming area and going over to Linda*). I'll make it all up to you, Linda, I'll—

Linda. There's nothing to make up, dear. You're doing fine, better than—

Willy (*noticing her mending*). What's that?

Linda. Just mending my stockings. They're so expensive—

Willy (*angrily, taking them from her*). I won't have you mending stockings in this house! Now throw them out!

Linda puts the stockings in her pocket.

Bernard (*entering on the run*). Where is he? If he doesn't study!

Willy (*moving to the forestage, with great agitation*). You'll give him the answers!

Bernard. I do, but I can't on a Regents! That's a state exam! They're liable to arrest me!

Willy. Where is he? I'll whip him, I'll whip him!

Linda. And he'd better give back that football, Willy, it's not nice.

Willy. Biff! Where is he? Why is he taking everything?

Linda. He's too rough with the girls, Willy. All the mothers are afraid of him!

Willy. I'll whip him!

Bernard. He's driving the car without a license!

The Woman's laugh is heard.

Willy. Shut up!

Linda. All the mothers—

Willy. Shut up!

Bernard *(backing quietly away and out).* Mr. Birnbaum says he's stuck up.

Willy. Get outa here!

Bernard. If he doesn't buckle down he'll flunk math! *(He goes off.)*

Linda. He's right, Willy, you've gotta—

Willy *(exploding at her).* There's nothing the matter with him! You want him to be a worm like Bernard? He's got spirit, personality . . .

As he speaks, Linda, almost in tears, exits into the living-room. Willy is alone in the kitchen, wilting and staring. The leaves are gone. It is night again, and the apartment houses look down from behind.

Willy. Loaded with it. Loaded! What is he stealing? He's giving it back, isn't he? Why is he stealing? What did I tell him? I never in my life told him anything but decent things.

Happy in pajamas has come down the stairs; Willy suddenly becomes aware of Happy's presence.

Happy. Let's go now, come on.

Willy *(sitting down at the kitchen table).* Huh! Why did she have to wax the floors herself? Every time she waxes the floors she keels over. She knows that!

Happy. Shh! Take it easy. What brought you back tonight?

Willy. I got an awful scare. Nearly hit a kid in Yonkers. God! Why didn't I go to Alaska with my brother Ben that time! Ben! That man was a genius, that man was success incarnate! What a mistake! He begged me to go.

Happy. Well, there's no use in—

Willy. You guys! There was a man started with the clothes on his back and ended up with diamond mines!

Happy. Boy, someday I'd like to know how he did it.

Willy. What's the mystery? The man knew what he wanted and went out and got it! Walked into a jungle, and comes out, the age of twenty-one, and he's rich! The world is an oyster, but you don't crack it open on a mattress!

Happy. Pop, I told you I'm gonna retire you for life.

Willy. You'll retire me for life on seventy goddam dollars a week? And your women and your car and your apartment, and you'll retire me for life! Christ's sake, I couldn't get past Yonkers today! Where are you guys, where are you? The woods are burning! I can't drive a car!

Charley has appeared in the doorway. He is a large man, slow of speech, laconic, immovable. In all he says, despite what he says, there is pity, and, now, trepidation. He has a robe over pajamas, slippers on his feet. He enters the kitchen.

Charley. Everything all right?

Happy. Yeah, Charley, everything's . . .

Willy. What's the matter?

Charley. I heard some noise. I thought something happened. Can't we do something about the walls? You sneeze in here, and in my house hats blow off.

Happy. Let's go to bed, Dad. Come on.

Charley signals to Happy to go.

Willy. You go ahead, I'm not tired at the moment.

Happy *(to Willy)*. Take it easy, huh? *(He exits.)*

Willy. What're you doin' up?

Charley *(sitting down at the kitchen table opposite Willy)*. Couldn't sleep good. I had a heartburn.

Willy. Well, you don't know how to eat.

Charley. I eat with my mouth.

Willy. No, you're ignorant. You gotta know about vitamins and things like that.

Charley. Come on, let's shoot. Tire you out a little.

Willy *(hesitantly)*. All right. You got cards?

Charley *(taking a deck from his pocket)*. Yeah, I got them. Someplace. What is it with those vitamins?

Willy *(dealing)*. They build up your bones. Chemistry.

Charley. Yeah, but there's no bones in a heartburn.

Willy. What are you talkin' about? Do you know the first thing about it?

Charley. Don't get insulted.

Willy. Don't talk about something you don't know anything about.

They are playing. Pause.

Charley. What're you doin' home?

Willy. A little trouble with the car.

Charley. Oh. *(Pause.)* I'd like to take a trip to California.

Willy. Don't say.

Charley. You want a job?

Willy. I got a job, I told you that. *(After a slight pause.)* What the hell are you offering me a job for?

Charley. Don't get insulted.

Willy. Don't insult me.

Charley. I don't see no sense in it. You don't have to go on this way.

Willy. I got a good job. *(Slight pause.)* What do you keep comin' in here for?

Charley. You want me to go?

Willy (*after a pause, withering*). I can't understand it. He's going back to Texas again. What the hell is that?

Charley. Let him go.

Willy. I got nothin' to give him, Charley, I'm clean, I'm clean.

Charley. He won't starve. None a them starve. Forget about him.

Willy. Then what have I got to remember?

Charley. You take it too hard. To hell with it. When a deposit bottle is broken you don't get your nickel back.

Willy. That's easy enough for you to say.

Charley. That ain't easy for me to say.

Willy. Did you see the ceiling I put up in the living-room?

Charley. Yeah, that's a piece of work. To put up a ceiling is a mystery to me. How do you do it?

Willy. What's the difference?

Charley. Well, talk about it.

Willy. You gonna put up a ceiling?

Charley. How could I put up a ceiling?

Willy. Then what the hell are you bothering me for?

Charley. You're insulted again.

Willy. A man who can't handle tools is not a man. You're disgusting.

Charley. Don't call me disgusting, Willy.

Uncle Ben, carrying a valise and an umbrella, enters the forestage from around the right corner of the house. He is a stolid man, in his sixties, with a mustache and an authoritative air. He is utterly certain of his destiny, and there is an aura of far places about him. He enters exactly as Willy speaks.

Willy. I'm getting awfully tired, Ben.

Ben's music is heard. Ben looks around at everything.

Charley. Good, keep playing; you'll sleep better. Did you call me Ben?

Ben looks at his watch.

Willy. That's funny. For a second there you reminded me of my brother Ben.

Ben. I only have a few minutes. (*He strolls, inspecting the place. Willy and Charley continue playing.*)

Charley. You never heard from him again, heh? Since that time?

Willy. Didn't Linda tell you? Couple of weeks ago we got a letter from his wife in Africa. He died.

Charley. That so.

Ben (*chuckling*). So this is Brooklyn, eh?

Charley. Maybe you're in for some of his money.

Willy. Naa, he had seven sons. There's just one opportunity I had with that man . . .

Ben. I must make a train, William. There are several properties I'm looking at in Alaska.

Willy. Sure, sure! If I'd gone with him to Alaska that time, everything would've been totally different.

Charley. Go on, you'd froze to death up there.

Willy. What're you talking about?

Ben. Opportunity is tremendous in Alaska, William. Surprised you're not up there.

Willy. Sure, tremendous.

Charley. Heh?

Willy. There was the only man I ever met who knew the answers.

Charley. Who?

Ben. How are you all?

Willy (taking a pot, smiling). Fine, fine.

Charley. Pretty sharp tonight.

Ben. Is mother living with you?

Willy. No, she died a long time ago.

Charley. Who?

Ben. That's too bad. Fine specimen of a lady, Mother.

Willy (to Charley). Heh?

Ben. I'd hoped to see the old girl.

Charley. Who died?

Ben. Heard anything from Father, have you?

Willy (unnerved). What do you mean, who died?

Charley (taking a pot). What're you talkin' about?

Ben (looking at his watch). William, it's half-past eight!

Willy (as though to dispel his confusion he angrily stops Charley's hand). That's my build!

Charley. I put the ace—

Willy. If you don't know how to play the game I'm not gonna throw my money away on you!

Charley (rising). It was my ace, for God's sake!

Willy. I'm through, I'm through!

Ben. When did Mother die?

Willy. Long ago. Since the beginning you never knew how to play cards.

Charley (picks up the cards and goes to the door). All right! Next time I'll bring a deck with five aces.

Willy. I don't play that kind of game!

Charley (turning to him). You ought to be ashamed of yourself!

Willy. Yeah?

Charley. Yeah! (He goes out.)

Willy (slamming the door after him). Ignoramus!

Ben (as Willy comes toward him through the wall-line of the kitchen). So you're William.

Willy (shaking Ben's hand). Ben! I've been waiting for you so long! What's the answer? How did you do it?

Ben. Oh, there's a story in that.

Linda enters the forestage, as of old, carrying the wash basket.

Linda. Is this Ben?

Ben *(gallantly).* How do you do, my dear.

Linda. Where've you been all these years? Willy's always wondered why you—

Willy *(pulling Ben away from her impatiently).* Where is Dad? Didn't you follow him? How did you get started?

Ben. Well, I don't know how much you remember.

Willy. Well, I was just a baby, of course, only three or four years old—

Ben. Three years and eleven months.

Willy. What a memory, Ben!

Ben. I have many enterprises, William, and I have never kept books.

Willy. I remember I was sitting under the wagon in—was it Nebraska?

Ben. It was South Dakota, and I gave you a bunch of wild flowers.

Willy. I remember you walking away down some open road.

Ben *(laughing).* I was going to find Father in Alaska.

Willy. Where is he?

Ben. At that age I had a very faulty view of geography, William. I discovered after a few days that I was heading due south, so instead of Alaska, I ended up in Africa.

Linda. Africa!

Willy. The Gold Coast!

Ben. Principally diamond mines.

Linda. Diamond mines!

Ben. Yes, my dear. But I've only a few minutes—

Willy. No! Boys! Boys! *(Young Biff and Happy appear.)* Listen to this. This is your Uncle Ben, a great man! Tell my boys, Ben!

Ben. Why, boys, when I was seventeen I walked into the jungle, and when I was twenty-one I walked out. *(He laughs.)* And by God I was rich.

Willy *(to the boys).* You see what I been talking about? The greatest things can happen!

Ben *(glancing at his watch).* I have an appointment in Ketchikan Tuesday week.

Willy. No, Ben! Please tell about Dad. I want my boys to hear. I want them to know the kind of stock they spring from. All I remember is a man with a big beard, and I was in Mamma's lap, sitting around a fire, and some kind of high music.

Ben. His flute. He played the flute.

Willy. Sure, the flute, that's right!

New music is heard, a high, rollicking tune.

Ben. Father was a very great and a very wild-hearted man. We would start in Boston, and he'd toss the whole family into the wagon, and then he'd drive the team right across the country; through Ohio, and Indiana, Michigan, Illinois, and all the Western states. And we'd stop in the towns and sell the flutes that he'd made on the way. Great inventor, Father. With one gadget he made more in a week than a man like you could make in a lifetime.

Willy. That's just the way I'm bringing them up, Ben—rugged, well liked, all-around.

Ben. Yeah? *(To Biff.)* Hit that, boy—hard as you can. *(He pounds his stomach.)*

Biff. Oh, no, sir!

Ben *(taking boxing stance).* Come on, get to me. *(He laughs.)*

Willy. Go to it, Biff! Go ahead, show him!

Biff. Okay! *(He cocks his fists and starts in.)*

Linda *(to Willy).* Why must he fight, dear?

Ben *(sparring with Biff).* Good boy! Good boy!

Willy. How's that, Ben, heh?

Happy. Give him the left, Biff!

Linda. Why are you fighting?

Ben. Good boy! *(Suddenly comes in, trips Biff, and stands over him, the point of his umbrella poised over Biff's eye.)*

Linda. Look out, Biff!

Biff. Gee!

Ben *(patting Biff's knee).* Never fight fair with a stranger, boy. You'll never get out of the jungle that way. *(Taking Linda's hand and bowing):* It was an honor and a pleasure to meet you, Linda.

Linda *(withdrawing her hand coldly, frightened).* Have a nice—trip.

Ben *(to Willy).* And good luck with your—what do you do?

Willy. Selling.

Ben. Yes. Well . . . *(He raises his hand in farewell to all.)*

Willy. No, Ben, I don't want you to think . . . *(He takes Ben's arm to show him.)* It's Brooklyn, I know, but we hunt too.

Ben. Really, now.

Willy. Oh, sure, there's snakes and rabbits and—that's why I moved out here. Why, Biff can fell any one of these trees in no time! Boys! Go right over to where they're building the apartment house and get some sand. We're gonna rebuild the entire front stoop now! Watch this, Ben!

Biff. Yes, sir! On the double, Hap!

Happy *(as he and Biff run off).* I lost weight, Pop, you notice?

Charley enters in knickers, even before the boys are gone.

Charley. Listen, if they steal any more from that building the watchman'll put the cops on them!

Linda *(to Willy).* Don't let Biff . . .

Ben laughs lustily.

Willy. You shoulda seen the lumber they brought home last week. At least a dozen six-by-tens worth all kinds a money.

Charley. Listen, if that watchman—

Willy. I gave them hell, understand. But I got a couple of fearless characters there.

Charley. Willy, the jails are full of fearless characters.

Ben (*clapping Willy on the back, with a laugh at Charley*). And the stock exchange, friend!

Willy (*joining in Ben's laughter*). Where are the rest of your pants?

Charley. My wife bought them.

Willy. Now all you need is a golf club and you can go upstairs and go to sleep. (*To Ben.*) Great athlete! Between him and his son Bernard they can't hammer a nail!

Bernard (*rushing in*). The watchman's chasing Biff!

Willy (*angrily*). Shut up! He's not stealing anything!

Linda (*alarmed, hurrying off left*). Where is he? Biff, dear! (*She exits.*)

Willy (*moving toward the left, away from Ben*). There's nothing wrong. What's the matter with you?

Ben. Nervy boy. Good!

Willy (*laughing*). Oh, nerves of iron, that Biff!

Charley. Don't know what it is. My New England man comes back and he's bleedin', they murdered him up there.

Willy. It's contacts, Charley, I got important contacts!

Charley (*sarcastically*). Glad to hear it, Willy. Come in later, we'll shoot a little casino. I'll take some of your Portland money. (*He laughs at Willy and exits.*)

Willy (*turning to Ben*). Business is bad, it's murderous. But not for me, of course.

Ben. I'll stop by on my way back to Africa.

Willy (*longingly*). Can't you stay a few days? You're just what I need, Ben, because I—I have a fine position here, but I—well, Dad left when I was such a baby and I never had a chance to talk to him and I still feel—kind of temporary about myself.

Ben. I'll be late for my train.

They are at opposite ends of the stage.

Willy. Ben, my boys—can't we talk? They'd go into the jaws of hell for me, see, but I—

Ben. William, you're being first-rate with your boys. Outstanding, manly chaps!

Willy (*hanging on to his words*). Oh, Ben, that's good to hear! Because sometimes I'm afraid that I'm not teaching them the right kind of—Ben, how should I teach them?

Ben (*giving great weight to each word, and with a certain vicious audacity*). William, when I walked into the jungle, I was seventeen. When I walked out I was twenty-one. And, by God, I was rich! (*He goes off into darkness around the right corner of the house.*)

Willy. . . . was rich! That's just the spirit I want to imbue them with! To walk into a jungle! I was right! I was right! I was right!

Ben is gone, but Willy is still speaking to him as Linda, in nightgown and robe, enters the kitchen, glances around for Willy, then goes to the door of the house, looks out, and sees him. Comes down to his left. He looks at her.

Linda. Willy, dear? Willy?

Willy. I was right!

Linda. Did you have some cheese? *(He can't answer.)* It's very late, darling. Come to bed, heh?

Willy *(looking straight up)*. Gotta break your neck to see a star in this yard.

Linda. You coming in?

Willy. Whatever happened to that diamond watch fob? Remember? When Ben came from Africa that time? Didn't he give me a watch fob with a diamond in it?

Linda. You pawned it, dear. Twelve, thirteen years ago. For Biff's radio correspondence course.

Willy. Gee, that was a beautiful thing. I'll take a walk.

Linda. But you're in your slippers.

Willy *(starting to go around the house at the left)*. I was right! I was! *(Half to Linda, as he goes, shaking his head.)* What a man! There was a man worth talking to. I was right!

Linda *(calling after Willy)*. But in your slippers, Willy!

Willy is almost gone when Biff, in his pajamas, comes down the stairs and enters the kitchen.

Biff. What is he doing out there?

Linda. Sh!

Biff. God Almighty, Mom, how long has he been doing this?

Linda. Don't, he'll hear you.

Biff. What the hell is the matter with him?

Linda. It'll pass by morning.

Biff. Shouldn't we do anything?

Linda. Oh, my dear, you should do a lot of things, but there's nothing to do, so go to sleep.

Happy comes down the stairs and sits on the steps.

Happy. I never heard him so loud, Mom.

Linda. Well, come around more often; you'll hear him. *(She sits down at the table and mends the lining of Willy's jacket.)*

Biff. Why didn't you ever write me about this, Mom?

Linda. How would I write to you? For over three months you had no address.

Biff. I was on the move. But you know I thought of you all the time. You know that, don't you, pal?

Linda. I know, dear, I know. But he likes to have a letter. Just to know that there's still a possibility for better things.

Biff. He's not like this all the time, is he?

Linda. It's when you come home he's always the worst.

Biff. When I come home?

Linda. When you write you're coming, he's all smiles, and talks about the future, and—he's just wonderful. And then the closer you seem to come, the more shaky he gets, and then, by the time you get here, he's arguing, and he seems angry at you. I think it's just that maybe he can't bring himself to—to open up to you. Why are you so hateful to each other? Why is that?

Biff (*evasively*). I'm not hateful, Mom.

Linda. But you no sooner come in the door than you're fighting!

Biff. I don't know why. I mean to change. I'm tryin', Mom, you understand?

Linda. Are you home to stay now?

Biff. I don't know. I want to look around, see what's doin'.

Linda. Biff, you can't look around all your life, can you?

Biff. I just can't take hold, Mom. I can't take hold of some kind of a life.

Linda. Biff, a man is not a bird, to come and go with the springtime.

Biff. Your hair . . . (*He touches her hair.*) Your hair got so gray.

Linda. Oh, it's been gray since you were in high school. I just stopped dyeing it, that's all.

Biff. Dye it again, will ya? I don't want my pal looking old. (*He smiles.*)

Linda. You're such a boy! You think you can go away for a year and . . . You've got to get it into your head now that one day you'll knock on this door and there'll be strange people here—

Biff. What are you talking about? You're not even sixty, Mom.

Linda. But what about your father?

Biff (*lamely*). Well, I meant him too.

Happy. He admires Pop.

Linda. Biff, dear, if you don't have any feeling for him, then you can't have any feeling for me.

Biff. Sure I can, Mom.

Linda. No. You can't just come to see me, because I love him. (*With a threat, but only a threat, of tears.*) He's the dearest man in the world to me, and I won't have anyone making him feel unwanted and low and blue. You've got to make up your mind now, darling, there's no leeway any more. Either he's your father and you pay him that respect, or else you're not to come here. I know he's not easy to get along with—nobody knows that better than me—but . . .

Willy (*from the left, with a laugh*). Hey, hey, Biffo!

Biff (*starting to go out after Willy*). What the hell is the matter with him? (*Happy stops him.*)

Linda. Don't—don't go near him!

Biff. Stop making excuses for him! He always, always wiped the floor with you. Never had an ounce of respect for you.

Happy. He's always had respect for—

Biff. What the hell do you know about it?

Happy (*surlily*). Just don't call him crazy!

Biff. He's got no character—Charley wouldn't do this. Not in his own house—spewing out that vomit from his mind.

Happy. Charley never had to cope with what he's got to.

Biff. People are worse off than Willy Loman. Believe me, I've seen them!

Linda. Then make Charley your father, Biff. You can't do that, can you? I don't say he's a great man. Willy Loman never made a lot of money. His name was never in the paper. He's not the finest character that ever lived. But he's a human being, and a terrible thing is happening to him. So attention must be paid. He's not to be allowed to fall into his grave like an old dog. Attention, attention must be finally paid to such a person. You called him crazy—

Biff. I didn't mean—

Linda. No, a lot of people think he's lost his—balance. But you don't have to be very smart to know what his trouble is. The man is exhausted.

Happy. Sure!

Linda. A small man can be just as exhausted as a great man. He works for a company thirty-six years this March, opens up unheard-of territories to their trademark, and now in his old age they take his salary away.

Happy (*indignantly*). I didn't know that, Mom.

Linda. You never asked, my dear! Now that you get your spending money someplace else you don't trouble your mind with him.

Happy. But I gave you money last—

Linda. Christmas time, fifty dollars! To fix the hot water it cost ninety-seven fifty! For five weeks he's been on straight commission, like a beginner, an unknown!

Biff. Those ungrateful bastards!

Linda. Are they any worse than his sons? When he brought them business, when he was young, they were glad to see him. But now his old friends, the old buyers that loved him so and always found some order to hand him in a pinch—they're all dead, retired. He used to be able to make six, seven calls a day in Boston. Now he takes his valises out of the car and puts them back and takes them out again and he's exhausted. Instead of walking he talks now. He drives seven hundred miles, and when he gets there no one knows him any more, no one welcomes him. And what goes through a man's mind, driving seven hundred miles home without having earned a cent? Why shouldn't he talk to himself? Why? When he has to go to Charley and borrow fifty dollars a week and pretend to me that it's his pay? How long can that go on? How long? You see what I'm sitting here and waiting for? And you tell me he has no character? The man who never worked a day but for your benefit? When does he get the medal for that? Is this his reward—to turn around at the age of sixty-three and find his sons, who he loved better than his life, one a philandering bum—

Happy. Mom!

Linda. That's all you are, my baby! (*To Biff.*) And you! What happened to the love you had for him? You were such pals! How you used to talk to him on the phone every night! How lonely he was till he could come home to you!

Biff. All right, Mom. I'll live here in my room, and I'll get a job. I'll keep away from him, that's all.

Linda. No, Biff. You can't stay here and fight all the time.

Biff. He threw me out of this house, remember that.

Linda. Why did he do that? I never knew why.

Biff. Because I know he's a fake and he doesn't like anybody around who knows!

Linda. Why a fake? In what way? What do you mean?

Biff. Just don't lay it all at my feet. It's between me and him—that's all I have to say. I'll chip in from now on. He'll settle for half my pay check. He'll be all right. I'm going to bed. *(He starts for the stairs.)*

Linda. He won't be all right.

Biff *(turning on the stairs, furiously)*. I hate this city and I'll stay here. Now what do you want?

Linda. He's dying, Biff.

Happy turns quickly to her, shocked.

Biff *(after a pause)*. Why is he dying?

Linda. He's been trying to kill himself.

Biff *(with great horror)*. How?

Linda. I live from day to day.

Biff. What're you talking about?

Linda. Remember I wrote you that he smashed up the car again? In February?

Biff. Well?

Linda. The insurance inspector came. He said that they have evidence. That all these accidents in the last year—weren't—weren't—accidents.

Happy. How can they tell that? That's a lie.

Linda. It seems there's a woman . . . *(She takes a breath as)*:

{ **Biff** *(sharply but contained)*. What woman?
{ **Linda** *(simultaneously)*. . . . and this woman . . .

Linda. What?

Biff. Nothing. Go ahead.

Linda. What did you say?

Biff. Nothing. I just said what woman?

Happy. What about her?

Linda. Well, it seems she was walking down the road and saw his car. She says that he wasn't driving fast at all, and that he didn't skid. She says he came to that little bridge, and then deliberately smashed into the railing, and it was only the shallowness of the water that saved him.

Biff. Oh, no, he probably just fell asleep again.

Linda. I don't think he fell asleep.

Biff. Why not?

Linda. Last month . . . *(With great difficulty.)* Oh, boys, it's so hard to say a thing like this! He's just a big stupid man to you, but I tell you there's more good in him than in many other people. *(She chokes, wipes her eyes.)* I was looking for a fuse. The lights blew out, and I went down the cellar. And behind the fuse box—it happened to fall out—was a length of rubber pipe—just short.

Happy. No kidding?

Linda. There's a little attachment on the end of it. I knew right away. And sure enough, on the bottom of the water heater there's a new little nipple on the gas pipe.

Happy *(angrily).* That—jerk.

Biff. Did you have it taken off?

Linda. I'm—I'm ashamed to. How can I mention it to him? Every day I go down and take away that little rubber pipe. But, when he comes home, I put it back where it was. How can I insult him that way? I don't know what to do. I live from day to day, boys. I tell you, I know every thought in his mind. It sounds so old-fashioned and silly, but I tell you he put his whole life into you and you've turned your backs on him. *(She is bent over in chair, weeping, her face in her hands.)* Biff, I swear to God! Biff, his life is in your hands!

Happy *(to Biff).* How do you like that damned fool!

Biff *(kissing her).* All right, pal, all right. It's all settled now. I've been remiss. I know that, Mom. But now I'll stay, and I swear to you, I'll apply myself. *(Kneeling in front of her, in a fever of self-reproach.)* It's just—you see, Mom, I don't fit in business. Not that I won't try. I'll try, and I'll make good.

Happy. Sure you will. The trouble with you in business was you never tried to please people.

Biff. I know, I—

Happy. Like when you worked for Harrison's. Bob Harrison said you were tops, and then you go and do some damn fool thing like whistling whole songs in the elevator like a comedian.

Biff *(against Happy).* So what? I like to whistle sometimes.

Happy. You don't raise a guy to a responsible job who whistles in the elevator!

Linda. Well, don't argue about it now.

Happy. Like when you'd go off and swim in the middle of the day instead of taking the line around.

Biff *(his resentment rising).* Well, don't you run off? You take off sometimes, don't you? On a nice summer day?

Happy. Yeah, but I cover myself!

Linda. Boys!

Happy. If I'm going to take a fade the boss can call any number where I'm supposed to be and they'll swear to him that I just left. I'll tell you something that I hate to say, Biff, but in the business world some of them think you're crazy.

Biff *(angered).* Screw the business world!

Happy. All right, screw it! Great, but cover yourself!

Linda. Hap, Hap!

Biff. I don't care what they think! They've laughed at Dad for years, and you know why? Because we don't belong in this nuthouse of a city! We should be mixing cement on some open plain, or—or carpenters. A carpenter is allowed to whistle!

Willy walks in from the entrance of the house, at left.

Willy. Even your grandfather was better than a carpenter. (*Pause. They watch him.*) You never grew up. Bernard does not whistle in the elevator, I assure you.

Biff (*as though to laugh Willy out of it*). Yeah, but you do, Pop.

Willy. I never in my life whistled in an elevator! And who in the business world thinks I'm crazy?

Biff. I didn't mean it like that, Pop. Now don't make a whole thing out of it, will ya?

Willy. Go back to the West! Be a carpenter, a cowboy, enjoy yourself!

Linda. Willy, he was just saying—

Willy. I heard what he said!

Happy (*trying to quiet Willy*). Hey, Pop, come on now . . .

Willy (*continuing over Happy's line*). They laugh at me, heh? Go to Filene's, go to the Hub, go to Slattery's, Boston. Call out the name Willy Loman and see what happens! Big shot!

Biff. All right, Pop.

Willy. Big!

Biff. All right!

Willy. Why do you always insult me?

Biff. I didn't say a word. (*To Linda.*) Did I say a word?

Linda. He didn't say anything, Willy.

Willy (*going to the doorway of the living-room*). All right, good night, good night.

Linda. Willy, dear, he just decided . . .

Willy (*to Biff*). If you get tired hanging around tomorrow, paint the ceiling I put up in the living-room.

Biff. I'm leaving early tomorrow.

Happy. He's going to see Bill Oliver, Pop.

Willy (*interestedly*). Oliver? For what?

Biff (*with reserve, but trying, trying*). He always said he'd stake me. I'd like to go into business, so maybe I can take him up on it.

Linda. Isn't that wonderful?

Willy. Don't interrupt. What's wonderful about it? There's fifty men in the City of New York who'd stake him. (*To Biff.*) Sporting goods?

Biff. I guess so. I know something about it and—

Willy. He knows something about it! You know sporting goods better than Spalding, for God's sake! How much is he giving you?

Biff. I don't know, I didn't even see him yet, but—

Willy. Then what're you talkin' about?

Biff (*getting angry*). Well, all I said was I'm gonna see him, that's all!

Willy (*turning away*). Ah, you're counting your chickens again.

Biff (*starting left for the stairs*). Oh, Jesus, I'm going to sleep!

Willy (*calling after him*). Don't curse in this house!

Biff (*turning*). Since when did you get so clean?

Happy (*trying to stop them*). Wait a . . .

Willy. Don't use that language to me! I won't have it!

Happy (*grabbing Biff, shouts*). Wait a minute! I got an idea. I got a feasible idea. Come here, Biff, let's talk this over now, let's talk some sense here. When I was

down in Florida last time, I thought of a great idea to sell sporting goods. It just
came back to me. You and I, Biff—we have a line, the Loman Line. We train a
couple of weeks, and put on a couple of exhibitions, see?

Willy. That's an idea!

Happy. Wait! We form two basketball teams, see? Two water-polo teams. We play
each other. It's a million dollars' worth of publicity. Two brothers, see? The
Loman Brothers. Displays in the Royal Palms—all the hotels. And banners over
the ring and the basketball court: "Loman Brothers." Baby, we could sell sporting
goods!

Willy. That is a one-million-dollar idea!

Linda. Marvelous!

Biff. I'm in great shape as far as that's concerned.

Happy. And the beauty of it is, Biff, it wouldn't be like a business. We'd be out
playin' ball again . . .

Biff *(enthused).* Yeah, that's . . .

Willy. Million-dollar . . .

Happy. And you wouldn't get fed up with it, Biff. It'd be the family again. There'd
be the old honor, and comradeship, and if you wanted to go off for a swim or
somethin'—well, you'd do it! Without some smart cooky gettin' up ahead of you!

Willy. Lick the world! You guys together could absolutely lick the civilized world.

Biff. I'll see Oliver tomorrow. Hap, if we could work that out . . .

Linda. Maybe things are beginning to—

Willy *(wildly enthused, to Linda).* Stop interrupting! *(To Biff.)* But don't wear
sport jacket and slacks when you see Oliver.

Biff. No, I'll—

Willy. A business suit, and talk as little as possible, and don't crack any jokes.

Biff. He did like me. Always liked me.

Linda. He loved you!

Willy *(to Linda).* Will you stop! *(To Biff.)* Walk in very serious. You are not applying for a boy's job. Money is to pass. Be quiet, fine, and serious. Everybody likes
a kidder, but nobody lends him money.

Happy. I'll try to get some myself, Biff. I'm sure I can.

Willy. I see great things for you kids, I think your troubles are over. But remember,
start big and you'll end big. Ask for fifteen. How much you gonna ask for?

Biff. Gee, I don't know—

Willy. And don't say "Gee." "Gee" is a boy's word. A man walking in for fifteen
thousand dollars does not say "Gee!"

Biff. Ten, I think, would be top though.

Willy. Don't be so modest. You always started too low. Walk in with a big laugh.
Don't look worried. Start off with a couple of your good stories to lighten things
up. It's not what you say, it's how you say it—because personality always wins
the day.

Linda. Oliver always thought the highest of him—

Willy. Will you let me talk?

Biff. Don't yell at her, Pop, will ya?

Willy (*angrily*). I was talking, wasn't I?

Biff. I don't like you yelling at her all the time, and I'm tellin' you, that's all.

Willy. What're you, takin' over this house?

Linda. Willy—

Willy (*turning on her*). Don't take his side all the time, goddammit!

Biff (*furiously*). Stop yelling at her!

Willy (*suddenly pulling on his cheek, beaten down, guilt ridden*). Give my best to Bill Oliver—he may remember me. (*He exits through the living-room doorway.*)

Linda (*her voice subdued*). What'd you have to start that for? (*Biff turns away.*) You see how sweet he was as soon as you talked hopefully? (*She goes over to Biff.*) Come up and say good night to him. Don't let him go to bed that way.

Happy. Come on, Biff, let's buck him up.

Linda. Please, dear. Just say good night. It takes so little to make him happy. Come. (*She goes through the living-room doorway, calling upstairs from within the living-room.*) Your pajamas are hanging in the bathroom, Willy!

Happy (*looking toward where Linda went out*). What a woman! They broke the mold when they made her. You know that, Biff?

Biff. He's off salary. My God, working on commission!

Happy. Well, let's face it: he's no hot-shot selling man. Except that sometimes, you have to admit, he's a sweet personality.

Biff (*deciding*). Lend me ten bucks, will ya? I want to buy some new ties.

Happy. I'll take you to a place I know. Beautiful stuff. Wear one of my striped shirts tomorrow.

Biff. She got gray. Mom got awful old. Gee, I'm gonna go in to Oliver tomorrow and knock him for a—

Happy. Come on up. Tell that to Dad. Let's give him a whirl. Come on.

Biff (*steamed up*). You know, with ten thousand bucks, boy!

Happy (*as they go into the living-room*). That's the talk, Biff, that's the first time I've heard the old confidence out of you! (*From within the living-room, fading off.*) You're gonna live with me, kid, and any babe you want just say the word . . . (*The last lines are hardly heard. They are mounting the stairs to their parents' bedroom.*)

Linda (*entering her bedroom and addressing Willy, who is in the bathroom. She is straightening the bed for him*). Can you do anything about the shower? It drips.

Willy (*from the bathroom*). All of a sudden everything falls to pieces! Goddam plumbing, oughta be sued, those people. I hardly finished putting it in and the thing . . . (*His words rumble off.*)

Linda. I'm just wondering if Oliver will remember him. You think he might?

Willy (*coming out of the bathroom in his pajamas*). Remember him? What's the matter with you, you crazy? If he'd've stayed with Oliver he'd be on top by now! Wait'll Oliver gets a look at him. You don't know the average caliber any more. The average young man today— (*he is getting into bed*)—is got a caliber of zero. Greatest thing in the world for him was to bum around.

Biff and Happy enter the bedroom. Slight pause.

Willy (*stops short, looking at Biff*). Glad to hear it, boy.

Happy. He wanted to say good night to you, sport.

Willy (*to Biff*). Yeah. Knock him dead, boy. What'd you want to tell me?

Biff. Just take it easy, Pop. Good night. (*He turns to go.*)

Willy (*unable to resist*). And if anything falls off the desk while you're talking to him—like a package or something—don't you pick it up. They have office boys for that.

Linda. I'll make a big breakfast—

Willy. Will you let me finish? (*To Biff.*) Tell him you were in the business in the West. Not farm work.

Biff. All right, Dad.

Linda. I think everything—

Willy (*going right through her speech*). And don't undersell yourself. No less than fifteen thousand dollars.

Biff (*unable to bear him*). Okay. Good night, Mom. (*He starts moving.*)

Willy. Because you got a greatness in you, Biff, remember that. You got all kinds a greatness . . . (*He lies back, exhausted. Biff walks out.*)

Linda (*calling after Biff*). Sleep well, darling!

Happy. I'm gonna get married, Mom. I wanted to tell you.

Linda. Go to sleep, dear.

Happy (*going*). I just wanted to tell you.

Willy. Keep up the good work. (*Happy exits.*) God . . . remember that Ebbets Field game? The championship of the city?

Linda. Just rest. Should I sing to you?

Willy. Yeah. Sing to me. (*Linda hums a soft lullaby.*) When that team came out—he was the tallest, remember?

Linda. Oh, yes. And in gold.

Biff enters the darkened kitchen, takes a cigarette, and leaves the house. He comes downstage into a golden pool of light. He smokes, staring at the night.

Willy. Like a young god. Hercules—something like that. And the sun, the sun all around him. Remember how he waved to me? Right up from the field, with the representatives of three colleges standing by? And the buyers I brought, and the cheers when he came out—Loman, Loman, Loman! God Almighty, he'll be great yet. A star like that, magnificent, can never really fade away!

The light on Willy is fading. The gas heater begins to glow through the kitchen wall, near the stairs, a blue flame beneath red coils.

Linda (*timidly*). Willy dear, what has he got against you?

Willy. I'm so tired. Don't talk any more.

Biff slowly returns to the kitchen. He stops, stares toward the heater.

Linda. Will you ask Howard to let you work in New York?
Willy. First thing in the morning. Everything'll be all right.

Biff reaches behind the heater and draws out a length of rubber tubing. He is horrified and turns his head toward Willy's room, still dimly lit, from which the strains of Linda's desperate but monotonous humming rise.

Willy (*staring through the window into the moonlight*). Gee, look at the moon moving between the buildings!

Biff wraps the tubing around his hand and quickly goes up the stairs.

Curtain

ACT II

Music is heard, gay and bright. The curtain rises as the music fades away. Willy, in shirt sleeves, is sitting at the kitchen table, sipping coffee, his hat in his lap. Linda is filling his cup when she can.

Willy. Wonderful coffee. Meal in itself.
Linda. Can I make you some eggs?
Willy. No. Take a breath.
Linda. You look so rested, dear.
Willy. I slept like a dead one. First time in months. Imagine, sleeping till ten on a Tuesday morning. Boys left nice and early, heh?
Linda. They were out of here by eight o'clock.
Willy. Good work!
Linda. It was so thrilling to see them leaving together. I can't get over the shaving lotion in this house!
Willy (*smiling*). Mmm—
Linda. Biff was very changed this morning. His whole attitude seemed to be hopeful. He couldn't wait to get downtown to see Oliver.
Willy. He's heading for a change. There's no question, there simply are certain men that take longer to get—solidified. How did he dress?
Linda. His blue suit. He's so handsome in that suit. He could be a—anything in that suit!

Willy gets up from the table. Linda holds his jacket for him.

Willy. There's no question, no question at all. Gee, on the way home tonight I'd like to buy some seeds.
Linda (*laughing*). That'd be wonderful. But not enough sun gets back there. Nothing'll grow any more.

Willy. You wait, kid, before it's all over we're gonna get a little place out in the country, and I'll raise some vegetables, a couple of chickens . . .

Linda. You'll do it yet, dear.

Willy walks out of his jacket. Linda follows him.

Willy. And they'll get married, and come for a weekend. I'd build a little guest house. 'Cause I got so many fine tools, all I'd need would be a little lumber and some peace of mind.

Linda (*joyfully*). I sewed the lining . . .

Willy. I could build two guest houses, so they'd both come. Did he decide how much he's going to ask Oliver for?

Linda (*getting him into the jacket*). He didn't mention it, but I imagine ten or fifteen thousand. You going to talk to Howard today?

Willy. Yeah. I'll put it to him straight and simple. He'll just have to take me off the road.

Linda. And Willy, don't forget to ask for a little advance, because we've got the insurance premium. It's the grace period now.

Willy. That's a hundred . . . ?

Linda. A hundred and eight, sixty-eight. Because we're a little short again.

Willy. Why are we short?

Linda. Well, you had the motor job on the car . . .

Willy. That goddam Studebaker!

Linda. And you got one more payment on the refrigerator . . .

Willy. But it just broke again!

Linda. Well, it's old, dear.

Willy. I told you we should've bought a well-advertised machine. Charley bought a General Electric and it's twenty years old and it's still good, that son-of-a-bitch.

Linda. But, Willy—

Willy. Whoever heard of a Hastings refrigerator? Once in my life I would like to own something outright before it's broken! I'm always in a race with the junkyard! I just finished paying for the car and it's on its last legs. The refrigerator consumes belts like a goddam maniac. They time those things. They time them so when you finally paid for them, they're used up.

Linda (*buttoning up his jacket as he unbuttons it*). All told, about two hundred dollars would carry us, dear. But that includes the last payment on the mortgage. After this payment, Willy, the house belongs to us.

Willy. It's twenty-five years!

Linda. Biff was nine years old when we bought it.

Willy. Well, that's a great thing. To weather a twenty-five year mortgage is—

Linda. It's an accomplishment.

Willy. All the cement, the lumber, the reconstruction I put in this house! There ain't a crack to be found in it any more.

Linda. Well, it served its purpose.

Willy. What purpose? Some stranger'll come along, move in, and that's that. If only Biff would take this house, and raise a family . . . *(He starts to go.)* Good-by, I'm late.

Linda *(suddenly remembering).* Oh, I forgot! You're supposed to meet them for dinner.

Willy. Me?

Linda. At Frank's Chop House on Forty-eighth near Sixth Avenue.

Willy. Is that so! How about you?

Linda. No, just the three of you. They're gonna blow you to a big meal!

Willy. Don't say! Who thought of that?

Linda. Biff came to me this morning, Willy, and he said, "Tell Dad, we want to blow him to a big meal." Be there six o'clock. You and your two boys are going to have dinner.

Willy. Gee whiz! That's really somethin'. I'm gonna knock Howard for a loop, kid. I'll get an advance, and I'll come home with a New York job. Goddammit, now I'm gonna do it!

Linda. Oh, that's the spirit, Willy!

Willy. I will never get behind a wheel the rest of my life!

Linda. It's changing, Willy, I can feel it changing!

Willy. Beyond a question. G'by, I'm late. *(He starts to go again.)*

Linda *(calling after him as she runs to the kitchen table for a handkerchief).* You got your glasses?

Willy *(feels for them, then comes back in).* Yeah, yeah, got my glasses.

Linda *(giving him the handkerchief).* And a handkerchief.

Willy. Yeah, handkerchief.

Linda. And your saccharine?

Willy. Yeah, my saccharine.

Linda. Be careful on the subway stairs.

She kisses him, and a silk stocking is seen hanging from her hand. Willy notices it.

Willy. Will you stop mending stockings? At least while I'm in the house. It gets me nervous. I can't tell you. Please.

Linda hides the stocking in her hand as she follows Willy across the forestage in front of the house.

Linda. Remember, Frank's Chop House.

Willy *(passing the apron).* Maybe beets would grow out there.

Linda *(laughing).* But you tried so many times.

Willy. Yeah. Well, don't work hard today. *(He disappears around the right corner of the house.)*

Linda. Be careful!

As Willy vanishes, Linda waves to him. Suddenly the phone rings. She runs across the stage and into the kitchen and lifts it.

Linda. Hello? Oh, Biff! I'm so glad you called, I just . . . Yes, sure, I just told him. Yes, he'll be there for dinner at six o'clock, I didn't forget. Listen, I was just dying to tell you. You know that little rubber pipe I told you about? That he connected to the gas heater? I finally decided to go down the cellar this morning and take it away and destroy it. But it's gone! Imagine? He took it away himself, it isn't there! *(She listens.)* When? Oh, then you took it. Oh—nothing, it's just that I'd hoped he'd taken it away himself. Oh, I'm not worried, darling, because this morning he left in such high spirits, it was like the old days! I'm not afraid any more. Did Mr. Oliver see you? . . . Well, you wait there then. And make a nice impression on him, darling. Just don't perspire too much before you see him. And have a nice time with Dad. He may have big news too! . . . That's right, a New York job. And be sweet to him tonight, dear. Be loving to him. Because he's only a little boat looking for a harbor. *(She is trembling with sorrow and joy.)* Oh, that's wonderful, Biff, you'll save his life. Thanks, darling. Just put your arm around him when he comes into the restaurant. Give him a smile. That's the boy . . . Good-by, dear. . . . You got your comb? . . . That's fine. Good-by, Biff dear.

In the middle of her speech, Howard Wagner, thirty-six, wheels in a small typewriter table on which is a wire-recording machine and proceeds to plug it in. This is on the left forestage. Light slowly fades on Linda as it rises on Howard. Howard is intent on threading the machine and only glances over his shoulder as Willy appears.

Willy. Pst! Pst!

Howard. Hello, Willy, come in.

Willy. Like to have a little talk with you, Howard.

Howard. Sorry to keep you waiting. I'll be with you in a minute.

Willy. What's that, Howard?

Howard. Didn't you ever see one of these? Wire recorder.

Willy. Oh. Can we talk a minute?

Howard. Records things. Just got delivery yesterday. Been driving me crazy, the most terrific machine I ever saw in my life. I was up all night with it.

Willy. What do you do with it?

Howard. I bought it for dictation, but you can do anything with it. Listen to this. I had it home last night. Listen to what I picked up. The first one is my daughter. Get this. *(He flicks the switch and "Roll Out the Barrel" is heard being whistled.)* Listen to that kid whistle.

Willy. That is lifelike, isn't it?

Howard. Seven years old. Get that tone.

Willy. Ts, ts. Like to ask a little favor if you . . .

The whistling breaks off, and the voice of Howard's daughter is heard.

His Daughter. "Now you, Daddy."

Howard. She's crazy for me! *(Again the same song is whistled.)* That's me! Ha! *(He winks.)*

Willy. You're very good!

The whistling breaks off again. The machine runs silent for a moment.

Howard. Sh! Get this now, this is my son.

His Son. "The capital of Alabama is Montgomery; the capital of Arizona is Phoenix; the capital of Arkansas is Little Rock; the capital of California is Sacramento . . ." *(and on, and on).*

Howard *(holding up five fingers).* Five years old, Willy!

Willy. He'll make an announcer some day!

His Son *(continuing).* "The capital . . ."

Howard. Get that—alphabetical order! *(The machine breaks off suddenly.)* Wait a minute. The maid kicked the plug out.

Willy. It certainly is a—

Howard. Sh, for God's sake!

His Son. "It's nine o'clock, Bulova watch time. So I have to go to sleep."

Willy. That really is—

Howard. Wait a minute! The next is my wife.

They wait.

Howard's Voice. "Go on, say something." *(Pause.)* "Well, you gonna talk?"

His Wife. "I can't think of anything."

Howard's Voice. "Well, talk—it's turning."

His Wife *(shyly, beaten).* "Hello." *(Silence.)* "Oh, Howard, I can't talk into this . . ."

Howard *(snapping the machine off).* That was my wife.

Willy. That is a wonderful machine. Can we—

Howard. I tell you, Willy, I'm gonna take my camera, and my bandsaw, and all my hobbies, and out they go. This is the most fascinating relaxation I ever found.

Willy. I think I'll get one myself.

Howard. Sure, they're only a hundred and a half. You can't do without it. Supposing you wanna hear Jack Benny, see? But you can't be at home at that hour. So you tell the maid to turn the radio on when Jack Benny comes on, and this automatically goes on with the radio . . .

Willy. And when you come home you . . .

Howard. You can come home twelve o'clock, one o'clock, any time you like, and you get yourself a Coke and sit yourself down, throw the switch, and there's Jack Benny's program in the middle of the night!

Willy. I'm definitely going to get one. Because lots of time I'm on the road, and I think to myself, what I must be missing on the radio!

Howard. Don't you have a radio in the car?

Willy. Well, yeah, but who ever thinks of turning it on?

Howard. Say, aren't you supposed to be in Boston?

Willy. That's what I want to talk to you about, Howard. You got a minute? *(He draws a chair in from the wing.)*

Howard. What happened? What're you doing here?

Willy. Well . . .

Howard. You didn't crack up again, did you?

Willy. Oh, no. No . . .

Howard. Geez, you had me worried there for a minute. What's the trouble?

Willy. Well, tell you the truth, Howard. I've come to the decision that I'd rather not travel any more.

Howard. Not travel! Well, what'll you do?

Willy. Remember, Christmas time, when you had the party here? You said you'd try to think of some spot for me here in town.

Howard. With us?

Willy. Well, sure.

Howard. Oh, yeah, yeah. I remember. Well, I couldn't think of anything for you, Willy.

Willy. I tell ya, Howard. The kids are all grown up, y'know. I don't need much any more. If I could take home—well, sixty-five dollars a week, I could swing it.

Howard. Yeah, but Willy, see I—

Willy. I tell ya why, Howard. Speaking frankly and between the two of us, y'know—I'm just a little tired.

Howard. Oh, I could understand that, Willy. But you're a road man, Willy, and we do a road business. We've only got a half-dozen salesmen on the floor here.

Willy. God knows, Howard, I never asked a favor of any man. But I was with the firm when your father used to carry you in here in his arms.

Howard. I know that, Willy, but—

Willy. Your father came to me the day you were born and asked me what I thought of the name of Howard, may he rest in peace.

Howard. I appreciate that, Willy, but there just is no spot here for you. If I had a spot I'd slam you right in, but I just don't have a single solitary spot.

He looks for his lighter. Willy has picked it up and gives it to him. Pause.

Willy *(with increasing anger).* Howard, all I need to set my table is fifty dollars a week.

Howard. But where am I going to put you, kid?

Willy. Look, it isn't a question of whether I can sell merchandise, is it?

Howard. No, but it's a business, kid, and everybody's gotta pull his own weight.

Willy *(desperately).* Just let me tell you a story, Howard—

Howard. 'Cause you gotta admit, business is business.

Willy *(angrily).* Business is definitely business, but just listen for a minute. You don't understand this. When I was a boy—eighteen, nineteen—I was already on the road. And there was a question in my mind as to whether selling had a future for me. Because in those days I had a yearning to go to Alaska. See, there were three gold strikes in one month in Alaska, and I felt like going out. Just for the ride, you might say.

Howard *(barely interested).* Don't say.

Willy. Oh, yeah, my father lived many years in Alaska. He was an adventurous man. We've got quite a little streak of self-reliance in our family. I thought I'd go out with my older brother and try to locate him, and maybe settle in the North with the old man. And I was almost decided to go, when I met a salesman in the Parker House. His name was Dave Singleman. And he was eighty-four years old, and he'd drummed merchandise in thirty-one states. And old Dave, he'd go up to his room, y'understand, put on his green velvet slippers—I'll never forget— and pick up his phone and call the buyers, and without ever leaving his room, at the age of eighty-four, he made his living. And when I saw that, I realized that selling was the greatest career a man could want. 'Cause what could be more satisfying than to be able to go, at the age of eighty-four, into twenty or thirty different cities, and pick up a phone, and be remembered and loved and helped by so many different people? Do you know? when he died—and by the way he died the death of a salesman, in his green velvet slippers in the smoker of the New York, New Haven, and Hartford, going into Boston—when he died, hundreds of salesmen and buyers were at his funeral. Things were sad on a lotta trains for months after that. *(He stands up. Howard has not looked at him.)* In those days there was personality in it, Howard. There was respect, and comradeship, and gratitude in it. Today, it's all cut and dried, and there's no chance for bringing friendship to bear—or personality. You see what I mean? They don't know me any more.

Howard *(moving away, to the right).* That's just the thing, Willy.

Willy. If I had forty dollars a week—that's all I'd need. Forty dollars, Howard.

Howard. Kid, I can't take blood from a stone, I—

Willy *(desperation is on him now).* Howard, the year Al Smith[2] was nominated, your father came to me and—

Howard *(starting to go off).* I've got to see some people, kid.

Willy *(stopping him).* I'm talking about your father! There were promises made across this desk! You mustn't tell me you've got people to see I put thirty-four years into this firm, Howard, and now I can't pay my insurance! You can't eat the orange and throw the peel away—a man is not a piece of fruit! *(After a pause.)* Now pay attention. Your father—in 1928 I had a big year. I averaged a hundred and seventy dollars a week in commissions.

Howard *(impatiently).* Now, Willy, you never averaged—

Willy *(banging his hand on the desk).* I averaged a hundred and seventy dollars a week in the year of 1928! And your father came to me or rather, I was in the office here—it was right over this desk—and he put his hand on my shoulder—

Howard *(getting up).* You'll have to excuse me, Willy, I gotta see some people. Pull yourself together. *(Going out.)* I'll be back in a little while.

On Howard's exit, the light on his chair grows very bright and strange.

---

[2] The Democratic candidate for president in 1928; he lost to Herbert Hoover.

Willy. Pull myself together! What the hell did I say to him? My God, I was yelling at him! How could I! *(Willy breaks off, staring at the light, which occupies the chair, animating it. He approaches this chair, standing across the desk from it.)* Frank, Frank, don't you remember what you told me that time? How you put your hand on my shoulder, and Frank . . . *(He leans on the desk and as he speaks the dead man's name he accidentally switches on the recorder, and instantly):*

Howard's Son. ". . . of New York is Albany. The capital of Ohio is Cincinnati, the capital of Rhode Island is . . ." *(The recitation continues.)*

Willy *(leaping away with fright, shouting).* Ha! Howard! Howard! Howard!

Howard *(rushing in).* What happened?

Willy *(pointing at the machine, which continues nasally, childishly, with the capital cities).* Shut it off! Shut it off!

Howard *(pulling the plug out).* Look, Willy . . .

Willy *(pressing his hands to his eyes).* I gotta get myself some coffee. I'll get some coffee . . .

Willy starts to walk out. Howard stops him.

Howard *(rolling up the cord).* Willy, look . . .

Willy. I'll go to Boston.

Howard. Willy, you can't go to Boston for us.

Willy. Why can't I go?

Howard. I don't want you to represent us. I've been meaning to tell you for a long time now.

Willy. Howard, are you firing me?

Howard. I think you need a good long rest, Willy.

Willy. Howard—

Howard. And when you feel better, come back, and we'll see if we can work something out.

Willy. But I gotta earn money, Howard. I'm in no position to—

Howard. Where are your sons? Why don't your sons give you a hand?

Willy. They're working on a very big deal.

Howard. This is no time for false pride, Willy. You go to your sons and you tell them that you're tired. You've got two great boys, haven't you?

Willy. Oh, no question, no question, but in the meantime . . .

Howard. Then that's that, heh?

Willy. All right, I'll go to Boston tomorrow.

Howard. No, no.

Willy. I can't throw myself on my sons. I'm not a cripple!

Howard. Look, kid, I'm busy this morning.

Willy *(grasping Howard's arm).* Howard, you've got to let me go to Boston!

Howard *(hard, keeping himself under control).* I've got a line of people to see this morning. Sit down, take five minutes, and pull yourself together, and then go home, will ya? I need the office, Willy. *(He starts to go, turns, remembering the recorder, starts to push off the table holding the recorder.)* Oh, yeah. Whenever you can this week, stop by and drop off the samples. You'll feel better, Willy, and then come back and we'll talk. Pull yourself together, kid, there's people outside.

Howard exits, pushing the table off left. Willy stares into space, exhausted. Now the music is heard—Ben's music—first distantly, then closer, closer. As Willy speaks, Ben enters from the right. He carries valise and umbrella.

Willy. Oh, Ben, how did you do it? What is the answer? Did you wind up the Alaska deal already?

Ben. Doesn't take much time if you know what you're doing. Just a short business trip. Boarding ship in an hour. Wanted to say good-by.

Willy. Ben, I've got to talk to you.

Ben *(glancing at his watch).* Haven't the time, William.

Willy *(crossing the apron to Ben).* Ben, nothing's working out. I don't know what to do.

Ben. Now, look here, William. I've bought timberland in Alaska and I need a man to look after things for me.

Willy. God, timberland! Me and my boys in those grand outdoors!

Ben. You've a new continent at your doorstep, William. Get out of these cities, they're full of talk and time payments and courts of law. Screw on your fists and you can fight for a fortune up there.

Willy. Yes, yes! Linda, Linda!

Linda enters as of old, with the wash.

Linda. Oh, you're back?

Ben. I haven't much time.

Willy. No, wait! Linda, he's got a proposition for me in Alaska.

Linda. But you've got—*(To Ben.)* He's got a beautiful job here.

Willy. But in Alaska, kid, I could—

Linda. You're doing well enough, Willy!

Ben *(to Linda).* Enough for what, my dear?

Linda *(frightened of Ben and angry at him).* Don't say those things to him! Enough to be happy right here, right now. *(To Willy, while Ben laughs.)* Why must everybody conquer the world? You're well liked, and the boys love you, and someday— *(to Ben)*—why, old man Wagner told him just the other day that if he keeps it up he'll be a member of the firm, didn't he, Willy?

Willy. Sure, sure. I am building something with this firm, Ben, and if a man is building something he must be on the right track, mustn't he?

Ben. What are you building? Lay your hand on it. Where is it?

Willy *(hesitantly).* That's true, Linda, there's nothing.

Linda. Why? *(To Ben.)* There's a man eighty-four years old—

Willy. That's right, Ben, that's right. When I look at that man I say, what is there to worry about?

Ben. Bah!

Willy. It's true, Ben. All he has to do is go into any city, pick up the phone, and he's making his living and you know why?

Ben *(picking up his valise).* I've got to go.

Willy *(holding Ben back).* Look at this boy!

Biff, in his high school sweater, enters carrying suitcase. Happy carries Biff's shoulder guards, gold helmet, and football pants.

Willy. Without a penny to his name, three great universities are begging for him, and from there the sky's the limit, because it's not what you do, Ben. It's who you know and the smile on your face! It's contacts, Ben, contacts! The whole wealth of Alaska passes over the lunch table at the Commodore Hotel, and that's the wonder, the wonder of this country, that a man can end with diamonds here on the basis of being liked! *(He turns to Biff.)* And that's why when you get out on that field today it's important. Because thousands of people will be rooting for you and loving you. *(To Ben, who has again begun to leave.)* And Ben! when he walks into a business office his name will sound out like a bell and all the doors will open to him! I've seen it, Ben, I've seen it a thousand times! You can't feel it with your hand like timber, but it's there!

Ben. Good-by, William.

Willy. Ben, am I right? Don't you think I'm right? I value your advice.

Ben. There's a new continent at your doorstep, William. You could walk out rich. Rich! *(He is gone.)*

Willy. We'll do it here, Ben! You hear me? We're gonna do it here!

Young Bernard rushes in. The gay music of the Boys is heard.

Bernard. Oh, gee, I was afraid you left already!

Willy. Why? What time is it?

Bernard. It's half-past one!

Willy. Well, come on, everybody! Ebbets Field next stop! Where's the pennants? *(He rushes through the wall-line of the kitchen and out into the living-room.)*

Linda *(to Biff).* Did you pack fresh underwear?

Biff *(who has been limbering up).* I want to go!

Bernard. Biff, I'm carrying your helmet, ain't I?

Happy. I'm carrying the helmet.

Bernard. How am I going to get in the locker room?

Linda. Let him carry the shoulder guards. *(She puts her coat and hat on in the kitchen.)*

Bernard. Can I, Biff? 'Cause I told everybody I'm going to be in the locker room.

Happy. In Ebbets Field it's the clubhouse.

Bernard. I meant the clubhouse. Biff!

Happy. Biff!

Biff *(grandly, after a slight pause).* Let him carry the shoulder guards.

Happy *(as he gives Bernard the shoulder guards).* Stay close to us now.

Willy rushes in with the pennants.

Willy *(handing them out).* Everybody wave when Biff comes out on the field. *(Happy and Bernard run off.)* You set now, boy?

The music has died away.

Biff. Ready to go, Pop. Every muscle is ready.

Willy *(at the edge of the apron).* You realize what this means?

Biff. That's right, Pop.

Willy *(feeling Biff's muscles).* You're comin' home this afternoon captain of the All-Scholastic Championship Team of the City of New York.

Biff. I got it, Pop. And remember, pal, when I take off my helmet, that touchdown is for you.

Willy. Let's go! *(He is starting out, with his arm around Biff, when Charley enters, as of old, in knickers.)* I got no room for you, Charley.

Charley. Room? For what?

Willy. In the car.

Charley. You goin' for a ride? I wanted to shoot some casino.

Willy *(furiously).* Casino! *(Incredulously.)* Don't you realize what today is?

Linda. Oh, he knows, Willy. He's just kidding you.

Willy. That's nothing to kid about!

Charley. No, Linda, what's goin' on?

Linda. He's playing in Ebbets Field.

Charley. Baseball in this weather?

Willy. Don't talk to him. Come on, come on! *(He is pushing them out.)*

Charley. Wait a minute, didn't you hear the news?

Willy. What?

Charley. Don't you listen to the radio? Ebbets Field just blew up.

Willy. You go to hell! *(Charley laughs. Pushing them out.)* Come on, come on! We're late.

Charley *(as they go).* Knock a homer, Biff, knock a homer!

Willy *(the last to leave, turning to Charley).* I don't think that was funny, Charley. This is the greatest day of his life.

Charley. Willy, when are you going to grow up?

Willy. Yeah, heh? When this game is over, Charley, you'll be laughing out of the other side of your face. They'll be calling him another Red Grange. Twenty-five thousand a year.

Charley *(kidding).* Is that so?

Willy. Yeah, that's so.

Charley. Well, then, I'm sorry, Willy. But tell me something.

Willy. What?

Charley. Who is Red Grange?
Willy. Put up your hands. Goddam you, put up your hands!

Charley, chuckling, shakes his head and walks away, around the left corner of the stage. Willy follows him. The music rises to a mocking frenzy.

Willy. Who the hell do you think you are, better than everybody else? You don't know everything, you big, ignorant, stupid . . . Put up your hands!

Light rises, on the right side of the forestage, on a small table in the reception room of Charley's office. Traffic sounds are heard. Bernard, now mature, sits whistling to himself. A pair of tennis rackets and an overnight bag are on the floor beside him.

Willy (*offstage*). What are you walking away for? Don't walk away! If you're going to say something say it to my face! I know you laugh at me behind my back. You'll laugh out of the other side of your goddam face after this game. Touchdown! Touchdown! Eighty thousand people! Touchdown! Right between the goal posts.

Bernard is a quiet, earnest, but self-assured young man. Willy's voice is coming from right upstage now. Bernard lowers his feet off the table and listens. Jenny, his father's secretary, enters.

Jenny (*distressed*). Say, Bernard, will you go out in the hall?
Bernard. What is that noise? Who is it?
Jenny. Mr. Loman. He just got off the elevator.
Bernard (*getting up*). Who's he arguing with?
Jenny. Nobody. There's nobody with him. I can't deal with him any more, and your father gets all upset every time he comes. I've got a lot of typing to do, and your father's waiting to sign it. Will you see him?
Willy (*entering*). Touchdown! Touch— (*He sees Jenny.*) Jenny, Jenny, good to see you. How're ya? Workin'? Or still honest?
Jenny. Fine. How've you been feeling?
Willy. Not much any more, Jenny. Ha, ha! (*He is surprised to see the rackets.*)
Bernard. Hello, Uncle Willy.
Willy (*almost shocked*). Bernard! Well, look who's here! (*He comes quickly, guiltily, to Bernard and warmly shakes his hand.*)
Bernard. How are you? Good to see you.
Willy. What are you doing here?
Bernard. Oh, just stopped by to see Pop. Get off my feet till my train leaves. I'm going to Washington in a few minutes.
Willy. Is he in?
Bernard. Yes, he's in his office with the accountant. Sit down.
Willy (*sitting down*). What're you going to do in Washington?
Bernard. Oh, just a case I've got there, Willy.
Willy. That so? (*Indicating the rackets.*) You going to play tennis there?

Bernard. I'm staying with a friend who's got a court.

Willy. Don't say. His own tennis court. Must be fine people, I bet.

Bernard. They are, very nice. Dad tells me Biff's in town.

Willy (*with a big smile*). Yeah, Biff's in. Working on a very big deal, Bernard.

Bernard. What's Biff doing?

Willy. Well, he's been doing very big things in the West. But he decided to establish himself here. Very big. We're having dinner. Did I hear your wife had a boy?

Bernard. That's right. Our second.

Willy. Two boys! What do you know!

Bernard. What kind of a deal has Biff got?

Willy. Well, Bill Oliver—very big sporting-goods man—he wants Biff very badly. Called him in from the West. Long distance, carte blanche, special deliveries. Your friends have their own private tennis court?

Bernard. You still with the old firm, Willy?

Willy (*after a pause*). I'm—I'm overjoyed to see how you made the grade, Bernard, overjoyed. It's an encouraging thing to see a young man really—really—Looks very good for Biff—very—(*He breaks off, then.*) Bernard—(*He is so full of emotion, he breaks off again.*)

Bernard. What is it, Willy?

Willy (*small and alone*). What—what's the secret?

Bernard. What secret?

Willy. How—how did you? Why didn't he ever catch on?

Bernard. I wouldn't know that, Willy.

Willy (*confidentially, desperately*). You were his friend, his boyhood friend. There's something I don't understand about it. His life ended after that Ebbets Field game. From the age of seventeen nothing good ever happened to him.

Bernard. He never trained himself for anything.

Willy. But he did, he did. After high school he took so many correspondence courses. Radio mechanics; television; God knows what, and never made the slightest mark.

Bernard (*taking off his glasses*). Willy, do you want to talk candidly?

Willy (*rising, faces Bernard*). I regard you as a very brilliant man, Bernard. I value your advice.

Bernard. Oh, the hell with the advice, Willy. I couldn't advise you. There's just one thing I've always wanted to ask you. When he was supposed to graduate, and the math teacher flunked him—

Willy. Oh, that son-of-a-bitch ruined his life.

Bernard. Yeah, but, Willy, all he had to do was go to summer school and make up that subject.

Willy. That's right, that's right.

Bernard. Did you tell him not to go to summer school?

Willy. Me? I begged him to go. I ordered him to go!

Bernard. Then why wouldn't he go?

Willy. Why? Why! Bernard, that question has been trailing me like a ghost for the last fifteen years. He flunked the subject, and laid down and died like a hammer hit him!

Bernard. Take it easy, kid.

Willy. Let me talk to you—I got nobody to talk to. Bernard, Bernard, was it my fault? Y'see? It keeps going around in my mind, maybe I did something to him. I got nothing to give him.

Bernard. Don't take it so hard.

Willy. Why did he lay down? What is the story there? You were his friend!

Bernard. Willy, I remember, it was June, and our grades came out. And he'd flunked math.

Willy. That son-of-a-bitch!

Bernard. No, it wasn't right then. Biff just got very angry, I remember, and he was ready to enroll in summer school.

Willy (surprised). He was?

Bernard. He wasn't beaten by it at all. But then, Willy, he disappeared from the block for almost a month. And I got the idea that he'd gone up to New England to see you. Did he have a talk with you then?

Willy stares in silence.

Bernard. Willy?

Willy (with a strong edge of resentment in his voice). Yeah, he came to Boston. What about it?

Bernard. Well, just that when he came back—I'll never forget this, it always mystifies me. Because I'd thought so well of Biff, even though he'd always taken advantage of me. I loved him, Willy, y'know? And he came back after that month and took his sneakers—remember those sneakers with "University of Virginia" printed on them? He was so proud of those, wore them every day. And he took them down in the cellar, and burned them up in the furnace. We had a fist fight. It lasted at least half an hour. Just the two of us, punching each other down the cellar, and crying right through it. I've often thought of how strange it was that I knew he'd given up his life. What happened in Boston, Willy?

Willy looks at him as at an intruder.

Bernard. I just bring it up because you asked me.

Willy (angrily). Nothing. What do you mean, "What happened?" What's that got to do with anything?

Bernard. Well, don't get sore.

Willy. What are you trying to do, blame it on me? If a boy lays down is that my fault?

Bernard. Now, Willy, don't get—

Willy. Well, don't—don't talk to me that way! What does that mean, "What happened?"

Charley enters. He is in his vest, and he carries a bottle of bourbon.

Charley. Hey, you're going to miss that train. (*He waves the bottle.*)

Bernard. Yeah, I'm going. (*He takes the bottle.*) Thanks, Pop. (*He picks up his rackets and bag.*) Good-by, Willy, and don't worry about it. You know. "If at first you don't succeed . . ."

Willy. Yes, I believe in that.

Bernard. But sometimes, Willy, it's better for a man just to walk away.

Willy. Walk away?

Bernard. That's right.

Willy. But if you can't walk away?

Bernard (*after a slight pause*). I guess that's when it's tough. (*Extending his hand.*) Good-by, Willy.

Willy (*shaking Bernard's hand*). Good-by, boy.

Charley (*an arm on Bernard's shoulder*). How do you like this kid? Gonna argue a case in front of the Supreme Court.

Bernard (*protesting*). Pop!

Willy (*genuinely shocked, pained, and happy*). No! The Supreme Court!

Bernard. I gotta run. 'By, Dad!

Charley. Knock 'em dead, Bernard!

Bernard goes off.

Willy (*as Charley takes out his wallet*). The Supreme Court! And he didn't even mention it!

Charley (*counting out money on the desk*). He don't have to—he's gonna do it.

Willy. And you never told him what to do, did you? You never took any interest in him.

Charley. My salvation is that I never took any interest in any thing. There's some money—fifty dollars. I got an accountant inside.

Willy. Charley, look . . . (*With difficulty.*) I got my insurance to pay. If you can manage it—I need a hundred and ten dollars.

Charley doesn't reply for a moment; merely stops moving.

Willy. I'd draw it from my bank but Linda would know, and I . . .

Charley. Sit down, Willy.

Willy (*moving toward the chair*). I'm keeping an account of everything, remember. I'll pay every penny back. (*He sits.*)

Charley. Now listen to me, Willy.

Willy. I want you to know I appreciate . . .

Charley (*sitting down on the table*). Willy, what're you doin'? What the hell is goin' on in your head?

Willy. Why? I'm simply . . .

Charley. I offered you a job. You can make fifty dollars a week. And I won't send you on the road.

Willy. I've got a job.

Charley. Without pay? What kind of a job is a job without pay? *(He rises.)* Now, look, kid, enough is enough. I'm no genius but I know when I'm being insulted.

Willy. Insulted!

Charley. Why don't you want to work for me?

Willy. What's the matter with you? I've got a job.

Charley. Then what're you walkin' in here every week for?

Willy *(getting up).* Well, if you don't want me to walk in here—

Charley. I am offering you a job.

Willy. I don't want your goddam job!

Charley. When the hell are you going to grow up?

Willy *(furiously).* You big ignoramus, if you say that to me again I'll rap you one! I don't care how big you are! *(He's ready to fight.)*

Pause.

Charley *(kindly, going to him).* How much do you need, Willy?

Willy. Charley, I'm strapped. I'm strapped. I don't know what to do. I was just fired.

Charley. Howard fired you?

Willy. That snotnose. Imagine that? I named him. I named him Howard.

Charley. Willy, when're you gonna realize that them things don't mean anything? You named him Howard, but you can't sell that. The only thing you got in this world is what you can sell. And the funny thing is that you're a salesman, and you don't know that.

Willy. I've always tried to think otherwise, I guess. I always felt that if a man was impressive, and well liked, that nothing—

Charley. Why must everybody like you? Who liked J. P. Morgan? Was he impressive? In a Turkish bath he'd look like a butcher. But with his pockets on he was very well liked. Now listen, Willy, I know you don't like me, and nobody can say I'm in love with you, but I'll give you a job because—just for the hell of it, put it that way. Now what do you say?

Willy. I—I just can't work for you, Charley.

Charley. What're you, jealous of me?

Willy. I can't work for you, that's all, don't ask me why.

Charley *(angered, takes out more bills).* You been jealous of me all your life, you damned fool! Here, pay your insurance. *(He puts the money in Willy's hand.)*

Willy. I'm keeping strict accounts.

Charley. I've got some work to do. Take care of yourself. And pay your insurance.

Willy *(moving to the right).* Funny, y'know? After all the highways, and the trains, and the appointments, and the years, you end up worth more dead than alive.

Charley. Willy, nobody's worth nothin' dead. *(After a slight pause.)* Did you hear what I said?

Willy stands still, dreaming.

Charley. Willy!

Willy. Apologize to Bernard for me when you see him. I didn't mean to argue with him. He's a fine boy. They're all fine boys, and they'll end up big—all of them. Someday they'll all play tennis together. Wish me luck, Charley. He saw Bill Oliver today.

Charley. Good luck.

Willy (*on the verge of tears*). Charley, you're the only friend I got. Isn't that a remarkable thing? (*He goes out.*)

Charley. Jesus!

Charley stares after him a moment and follows. All light blacks out. Suddenly raucous music is heard, and a red glow rises behind the screen at right. Stanley, a young waiter, appears, carrying a table, followed by Happy, who is carrying two chairs.

Stanley (*putting the table down*). That's all right, Mr. Loman, I can handle it myself. (*He turns and takes the chairs from Happy and places them at the table.*)

Happy (*glancing around*). Oh, this is better.

Stanley. Sure, in the front there you're in the middle of all kinds a noise. Whenever you got a party, Mr. Loman, you just tell me and I'll put you back here. Y'know, there's a lotta people they don't like it private, because when they go out they like to see a lotta action around them because they're sick and tired to stay in the house by theirself. But I know you, you ain't from Hackensack. You know what I mean?

Happy (*sitting down*). So how's it coming, Stanley?

Stanley. Ah, it's a dog's life. I only wish during the war they'd a took me in the Army. I coulda been dead by now.

Happy. My brother's back, Stanley.

Stanley. Oh, he come back, heh? From the Far West.

Happy. Yeah, big cattle man, my brother, so treat him right. And my father's coming too.

Stanley. Oh, your father too!

Happy. You got a couple of nice lobsters?

Stanley. Hundred per cent, big.

Happy. I want them with the claws.

Stanley. Don't worry, I don't give you no mice. (*Happy laughs.*) How about some wine? It'll put a head on the meal.

Happy. No. You remember, Stanley, that recipe I brought you from overseas? With the champagne in it?

Stanley. Oh, yeah, sure. I still got it tacked up yet in the kitchen. But that'll have to cost a buck apiece anyways.

Happy. That's all right.

Stanley. What'd you, hit a number or somethin'?

Happy. No, it's a little celebration. My brother is—I think he pulled off a big deal today. I think we're going into business together.

Stanley. Great! That's the best for you. Because a family business, you know what I mean?—that's the best.

Happy. That's what I think.

Stanley. 'Cause what's the difference? Somebody steals? It's in the family. Know what I mean? *(Sotto voce.*[3]*)* Like this bartender here. The boss is goin' crazy what kinda leak he's got in the cash register. You put it in but it don't come out.

Happy *(raising his head).* Sh!

Stanley. What?

Happy. You notice I wasn't lookin' right or left, was I?

Stanley. No.

Happy. And my eyes are closed.

Stanley. So what's the—?

Happy. Strudel's comin'.

Stanley *(catching on, looks around).* Ah, no, there's no—

He breaks off as a furred, lavishly dressed girl enters and sits at the next table. Both follow her with their eyes.

Stanley. Geez, how'd ya know?

Happy. I got radar or something. *(Staring directly at her profile.)* Oooooooo . . . Stanley.

Stanley. I think that's for you, Mr. Loman.

Happy. Look at that mouth. Oh, God. And the binoculars.

Stanley. Geez, you got a life, Mr. Loman.

Happy. Wait on her.

Stanley *(going to the girl's table).* Would you like a menu, ma'am?

Girl. I'm expecting someone, but I'd like a—

Happy. Why don't you bring her—excuse me, miss, do you mind? I sell champagne, and I'd like you to try my brand. Bring her a champagne, Stanley.

Girl. That's awfully nice of you.

Happy. Don't mention it. It's all company money. *(He laughs.)*

Girl. That's a charming product to be selling, isn't it?

Happy. Oh, gets to be like everything else. Selling is selling, y'know.

Girl. I suppose.

Happy. You don't happen to sell, do you?

Girl. No, I don't sell.

Happy. Would you object to a compliment from a stranger? You ought to be on a magazine cover.

Girl *(looking at him a little archly).* I have been.

Stanley comes in with a glass of champagne.

Happy. What'd I say before, Stanley? You see? She's a cover girl.

Stanley. Oh, I could see, I could see.

Happy *(to the Girl).* What magazine?

---

[3] "Softly" in Italian.

Girl. Oh, a lot of them. *(She takes the drink.)* Thank you.

Happy. You know what they say in France, don't you? "Champagne is the drink of the complexion"—Hya, Biff!

Biff has entered and sits with Happy.

Biff. Hello, kid. Sorry I'm late.

Happy. I just got here. Uh, Miss—?

Girl. Forsythe.

Happy. Miss Forsythe, this is my brother.

Biff. Is Dad here?

Happy. His name is Biff. You might've heard of him. Great football player.

Girl. Really? What team?

Happy. Are you familiar with football?

Girl. No, I'm afraid I'm not.

Happy. Biff is quarterback with the New York Giants.

Girl. Well, that is nice, isn't it? *(She drinks.)*

Happy. Good health.

Girl. I'm happy to meet you.

Happy. That's my name. Hap. It's really Harold, but at West Point they called me Happy.

Girl *(now really impressed)*. Oh, I see. How do you do? *(She turns her profile.)*

Biff. Isn't Dad coming?

Happy. You want her?

Biff. Oh, I could never make that.

Happy. I remember the time that idea would never come into your head. Where's the old confidence, Biff?

Biff. I just saw Oliver—

Happy. Wait a minute. I've got to see that old confidence again. Do you want her? She's on call.

Biff. Oh, no. *(He turns to look at the Girl.)*

Happy. I'm telling you. Watch this. *(Turning to the Girl.)* Honey? *(She turns to him.)* Are you busy?

Girl. Well, I am . . . but I could make a phone call.

Happy. Do that, will you, honey? And see if you can get a friend. We'll be here for a while. Biff is one of the greatest football players in the country.

Girl *(standing up)*. Well, I'm certainly happy to meet you.

Happy. Come back soon.

Girl. I'll try.

Happy. Don't try, honey, try hard.

The Girl exits. Stanley follows, shaking his head in bewildered admiration.

Happy. Isn't that a shame now? A beautiful girl like that? That's why I can't get married. There's not a good woman in a thousand. New York is loaded with them, kid!

Biff. Hap, look—

Happy. I told you she was on call!

Biff *(strangely unnerved).* Cut it out, will ya? I want to say something to you.

Happy. Did you see Oliver?

Biff. I saw him all right. Now look, I want to tell Dad a couple of things and I want you to help me.

Happy. What? Is he going to back you?

Biff. Are you crazy? You're out of your goddam head, you know that?

Happy. Why? What happened?

Biff *(breathlessly).* I did a terrible thing today, Hap. It's been the strangest day I ever went through. I'm all numb, I swear.

Happy. You mean he wouldn't see you?

Biff. Well, I waited six hours for him, see? All day. Kept sending my name in. Even tried to date his secretary so she'd get me to him, but no soap.

Happy. Because you're not showin' the old confidence, Biff. He remembered you, didn't he?

Biff *(stopping Happy with a gesture).* Finally, about five o'clock, he comes out. Didn't remember who I was or anything. I felt like such an idiot, Hap.

Happy. Did you tell him my Florida idea?

Biff. He walked away. I saw him for one minute. I got so mad I could've torn the walls down! How the hell did I ever get the idea I was a salesman there? I even believed myself that I'd been a salesman for him! And then he gave me one look and—I realized what a ridiculous lie my whole life has been! We've been talking in a dream for fifteen years. I was a shipping clerk.

Happy. What'd you do?

Biff *(with great tension and wonder).* Well, he left, see. And the secretary went out. I was all alone in the waiting-room. I don't know what came over me, Hap. The next thing I know I'm in his office—paneled walls, everything. I can't explain it. I—Hap, I took his fountain pen.

Happy. Geez, did he catch you?

Biff. I ran out. I ran down all eleven flights. I ran and ran and ran.

Happy. That was an awful dumb—what'd you do that for?

Biff *(agonized).* I don't know, I just—wanted to take something, I don't know. You gotta help me, Hap, I'm gonna tell Pop.

Happy. You crazy? What for?

Biff. Hap, he's got to understand that I'm not the man somebody lends that kind of money to. He thinks I've been spiting him all these years and it's eating him up.

Happy. That's just it. You tell him something nice.

Biff. I can't.

Happy. Say you got a lunch date with Oliver tomorrow.

Biff. So what do I do tomorrow?

Happy. You leave the house tomorrow and come back at night and say Oliver is thinking it over. And he thinks it over for a couple of weeks, and gradually it fades away and nobody's the worse.

Biff. But it'll go on forever!

Happy. Dad is never so happy as when he's looking forward to something!

Willy enters.

Happy. Hello, scout!

Willy. Gee, I haven't been here in years!

Stanley has followed Willy in and sets a chair for him. Stanley starts off but Happy stops him.

Happy. Stanley!

Stanley stands by, waiting for an order.

Biff *(going to Willy with guilt, as to an invalid).* Sit down, Pop. You want a drink?

Willy. Sure, I don't mind.

Biff. Let's get a load on.

Willy. You look worried.

Biff. N-no. *(To Stanley.)* Scotch all around. Make it doubles.

Stanley. Doubles, right. *(He goes.)*

Willy. You had a couple already, didn't you?

Biff. Just a couple, yeah.

Willy. Well, what happened, boy? *(Nodding affirmatively, with a smile.)* Everything go all right?

Biff *(takes a breath, then reaches out and grasps Willy's hand).* Pal . . . *(He is smiling bravely, and Willy is smiling too.)* I had an experience today.

Happy. Terrific, Pop.

Willy. That so? What happened?

Biff *(high, slightly alcoholic, above the earth).* I'm going to tell you everything from first to last. It's been a strange day. *(Silence. He looks around, composes himself as best he can, but his breath keeps breaking the rhythm of his voice.)* I had to wait quite a while for him, and—

Willy. Oliver.

Biff. Yeah, Oliver. All day, as a matter of cold fact. And a lot of— instances—facts, Pop, facts about my life came back to me. Who was it, Pop? Who ever said I was a salesman with Oliver?

Willy. Well, you were.

Biff. No, Dad, I was a shipping clerk.

Willy. But you were practically—

Biff *(with determination).* Dad, I don't know who said it first, but I was never a salesman for Bill Oliver.

Willy. What're you talking about?

Biff. Let's hold on to the facts tonight, Pop. We're not going to get anywhere bullin' around. I was a shipping clerk.

Willy (*angrily*). All right, now listen to me—

Biff. Why don't you let me finish?

Willy. I'm not interested in stories about the past or any crap of that kind because the woods are burning, boys, you understand? There's a big blaze going on all around. I was fired today.

Biff (*shocked*). How could you be?

Willy. I was fired, and I'm looking for a little good news to tell your mother, because the woman has waited and the woman has suffered. The gist of it is that I haven't got a story left in my head, Biff. So don't give me a lecture about facts and aspects. I am not interested. Now what've you got to say to me?

Stanley enters with three drinks. They wait until he leaves.

Willy. Did you see Oliver?

Biff. Jesus, Dad!

Willy. You mean you didn't go up there?

Happy. Sure he went up there.

Biff. I did. I—saw him. How could they fire you?

Willy (*on the edge of his chair*). What kind of a welcome did he give you?

Biff. He won't even let you work on commission?

Willy. I'm out! (*Driving.*) So tell me, he gave you a warm welcome?

Happy. Sure, Pop, sure!

Biff (*driven*). Well, it was kind of—

Willy. I was wondering if he'd remember you. (*To Happy.*) Imagine, man doesn't see him for ten, twelve years and gives him that kind of a welcome!

Happy. Damn right!

Biff (*trying to return to the offensive*). Pop, look—

Willy. You know why he remembered you, don't you? Because you impressed him in those days.

Biff. Let's talk quietly and get this down to the facts, huh?

Willy (*as though Biff had been interrupting*). Well, what happened? It's great news, Biff. Did he take you into his office or'd you talk in the waiting-room?

Biff. Well, he came in, see, and—

Willy (*with a big smile*). What'd he say? Betcha he threw his arm around you.

Biff. Well, he kinda—

Willy. He's a fine man. (*To Happy.*) Very hard man to see, y'know.

Happy (*agreeing*). Oh, I know.

Willy (*to Biff*). Is that where you had the drinks?

Biff. Yeah, he gave me a couple of—no, no!

Happy (*cutting in*). He told him my Florida idea.

Willy. Don't interrupt. (*To Biff.*) How'd he react to the Florida idea?

Biff. Dad, will you give me a minute to explain?

Willy. I've been waiting for you to explain since I sat down here! What happened? He took you into his office and what?

Biff. Well—I talked. And—and he listened, see.

Willy. Famous for the way he listens, y'know. What was his answer?

Biff. His answer was—*(He breaks off, suddenly angry.)* Dad, you're not letting me tell you what I want to tell you!

Willy *(accusing, angered)*. You didn't see him, did you?

Biff. I did see him!

Willy. What'd you insult him or something? You insulted him, didn't you?

Biff. Listen, will you let me out of it, will you just let me out of it!

Happy. What the hell!

Willy. Tell me what happened!

Biff *(to Happy)*. I can't talk to him!

A single trumpet note jars the ear. The light of green leaves stains the house, which holds the air of night and a dream. Young Bernard enters and knocks on the door of the house.

Young Bernard *(frantically)*. Mrs. Loman, Mrs. Loman!

Happy. Tell him what happened!

Biff *(to Happy)*. Shut up and leave me alone!

Willy. No, no! You had to go and flunk math!

Biff. What math? What're you talking about?

Young Bernard. Mrs. Loman, Mrs. Loman!

Linda appears in the house, as of old.

Willy *(wildly)*. Math, math, math!

Biff. Take it easy, Pop!

Young Bernard. Mrs. Loman!

Willy *(furiously)*. If you hadn't flunked you'd've been set by now!

Biff. Now, look, I'm gonna tell you what happened, and you're going to listen to me.

Young Bernard. Mrs. Loman!

Biff. I waited six hours—

Happy. What the hell are you saying?

Biff. I kept sending in my name but he wouldn't see me. So finally he . . . *(He continues unheard as light fades low on the restaurant.)*

Young Bernard. Biff flunked math!

Linda. No!

Young Bernard. Birnbaum flunked him! They won't graduate him!

Linda. But they have to. He's gotta go to the university. Where is he? Biff! Biff!

Young Bernard. No, he left. He went to Grand Central.

Linda. Grand— You mean he went to Boston!

Young Bernard. Is Uncle Willy in Boston?

Linda. Oh, maybe Willy can talk to the teacher. Oh, the poor, poor boy!

Light on house area snaps out.

Biff (*at the table, now audible, holding up a gold fountain pen*). . . . so I'm washed
up with Oliver, you understand? Are you listening to me?

Willy (*at a loss*). Yeah, sure. If you hadn't flunked—

Biff. Flunked what? What're you talking about?

Willy. Don't blame everything on me! I didn't flunk math—you did! What pen?

Happy. That was awful dumb, Biff, a pen like that is worth—

Willy (*seeing the pen for the first time*). You took Oliver's pen?

Biff (*weakening*). Dad, I just explained it to you.

Willy. You stole Bill Oliver's fountain pen!

Biff. I didn't exactly steal it! That's just what I've been explaining to you!

Happy. He had it in his hand and just then Oliver walked in, so he got nervous
and stuck it in his pocket!

Willy. My God, Biff!

Biff. I never intended to do it, Dad!

Operator's Voice. Standish Arms, good evening!

Willy (*shouting*). I'm not in my room!

Biff (*frightened*). Dad, what's the matter? (*He and Happy stand up.*)

Operator. Ringing Mr. Loman for you!

Willy. I'm not there, stop it!

Biff (*horrified, gets down on one knee before Willy*). Dad, I'll make good, I'll make
good. (*Willy tries to get to his feet. Biff holds him down.*) Sit down now.

Willy. No, you're no good, you're no good for anything.

Biff. I am, Dad, I'll find something else, you understand? Now don't worry about
anything. (*He holds up Willy's face.*) Talk to me, Dad.

Operator. Mr. Loman does not answer. Shall I page him?

Willy (*attempting to stand, as though to rush and silence the Operator*). No, no, no!

Happy. He'll strike something, Pop.

Willy. No, no . . .

Biff (*desperately, standing over Willy*). Pop, listen! Listen to me! I'm telling you
something good. Oliver talked to his partner about the Florida idea. You listening? He—he talked to his partner, and he came to me . . . I'm going to be
all right, you hear? Dad, listen to me, he said it was just a question of the
amount!

Willy. Then you . . . got it?

Happy. He's gonna be terrific, Pop!

Willy (*trying to stand*). Then you got it, haven't you? You got it! You got it!

Biff (*agonized, holds Willy down*). No, no. Look, Pop. I'm supposed to have lunch
with them tomorrow. I'm just telling you this so you'll know that I can still make
an impression, Pop. And I'll make good somewhere, but I can't go tomorrow, see?

Willy. Why not? You simply—

Biff. But the pen, Pop!

Willy. You give it to him and tell him it was an oversight!

Happy. Sure, have lunch tomorrow!

Biff. I can't say that—

Willy. You were doing a crossword puzzle and accidentally used his pen!

Biff. Listen, kid, I took those balls years ago, now I walk in with his fountain pen? That clinches it, don't you see? I can't face him like that! I'll try elsewhere.

Page's Voice. Paging Mr. Loman!

Willy. Don't you want to be anything?

Biff. Pop, how can I go back?

Willy. You don't want to be anything, is that what's behind it?

Biff (*now angry at Willy for not crediting his sympathy*). Don't take it that way! You think it was easy walking into that office after what I'd done to him? A team of horses couldn't have dragged me back to Bill Oliver!

Willy. Then why'd you go?

Biff. Why did I go? Why did I go! Look at you! Look at what's become of you!

Off left, The Woman laughs.

Willy. Biff, you're going to lunch tomorrow, or—

Biff. I can't go. I've got no appointment!

Happy. Biff, for . . . !

Willy. Are you spiting me?

Biff. Don't take it that way! Goddammit!

Willy (*strikes Biff and falters away from the table*). You rotten little louse! Are you spiting me?

The Woman. Someone's at the door, Willy!

Biff. I'm no good, can't you see what I am?

Happy (*separating them*). Hey, you're in a restaurant! Now cut it out, both of you! (*The girls enter.*) Hello, girls, sit down.

The Woman laughs, off left.

Miss Forsythe. I guess we might as well. This is Letta.

The Woman. Willy, are you going to wake up?

Biff (*ignoring Willy*). How're ya, miss, sit down. What do you drink?

Miss Forsythe. Letta might not be able to stay long.

Letta. I gotta get up very early tomorrow. I got jury duty I'm so excited! Were you fellows ever on a jury?

Biff. No, but I been in front of them! (*The girls laugh.*) This is my father.

Letta. Isn't he cute? Sit down with us, Pop.

Happy. Sit him down, Biff!

Biff (*going to him*). Come on, slugger, drink us under the table. To hell with it! Come on, sit down, pal.

On Biff's last insistence, Willy is about to sit.

The Woman (*now urgently*). Willy, are you going to answer the door!

The Woman's call pulls Willy back. He starts right, befuddled.

Biff. Hey, where are you going?

Willy. Open the door.

Biff. The door?

Willy. The washroom . . . the door . . . where's the door?

Biff *(leading Willy to the left).* Just go straight down.

Willy moves left.

The Woman. Willy, Willy, are you going to get up, get up, get up, get up?

Willy exits left.

Letta. I think it's sweet you bring your daddy along.

Miss Forsythe. Oh, he isn't really your father!

Biff *(at left, turning to her resentfully).* Miss Forsythe, you've just seen a prince walk by. A fine, troubled prince. A hard-working, unappreciated prince. A pal, you understand? A good companion. Always for his boys.

Letta. That's so sweet.

Happy. Well, girls, what's the program? We're wasting time. Come on, Biff. Gather round. Where would you like to go?

Biff. Why don't you do something for him?

Happy. Me!

Biff. Don't you give a damn for him, Hap?

Happy. What're you talking about? I'm the one who—

Biff. I sense it, you don't give a good goddamn about him. *(He takes the rolled-up hose from his pocket and puts it on the table in front of Happy.)* Look what I found in the cellar, for Christ's sake. How can you bear to let it go on?

Happy. Me? Who goes away? Who runs off and—

Biff. Yeah, but he doesn't mean anything to you. You could help him—I can't! Don't you understand what I'm talking about? He's going to kill himself, don't you know that?

Happy. Don't I know it! Me!

Biff. Hap, help him! Jesus . . . help him . . . Help me, help me, I can't bear to look at his face! *(Ready to weep, he hurries out, up right.)*

Happy *(starting after him).* Where are you going?

Miss Forsythe. What's he so mad about?

Happy. Come on, girls, we'll catch up with him.

Miss Forsythe *(as Happy pushes her out).* Say, I don't like that temper of his!

Happy. He's just a little overstrung, he'll be all right!

Willy *(off left, as The Woman laughs).* Don't answer! Don't answer!

Letta. Don't you want to tell your father—

Happy. No, that's not my father. He's just a guy. Come on, we'll catch Biff, and, honey, we're going to paint this town! Stanley, where's the check! Hey, Stanley!

They exit. Stanley looks toward left.

Stanley (*calling to Happy indignantly*). Mr. Loman! Mr. Loman!

Stanley picks up a chair and follows them off. Knocking is heard off left. The Woman enters, laughing. Willy follows her. She is in a black slip; he is buttoning his shirt. Raw, sensuous music accompanies their speech.

Willy. Will you stop laughing? Will you stop?

The Woman. Aren't you going to answer the door? He'll wake the whole hotel.

Willy. I'm not expecting anybody.

The Woman. Whyn't you have another drink, honey, and stop being so damn self-centered?

Willy. I'm so lonely.

The Woman. You know you ruined me, Willy? From now on, whenever you come to the office, I'll see that you go right through to the buyers. No waiting at my desk any more, Willy. You ruined me.

Willy. That's nice of you to say that.

The Woman. Gee, you are self-centered! Why so sad? You are the saddest, self-centeredest soul I ever did see-saw. (*She laughs. He kisses her.*) Come on inside, drummer boy. It's silly to be dressing in the middle of the night. (*As knocking is heard.*) Aren't you going to answer the door?

Willy. They're knocking on the wrong door.

The Woman. But I felt the knocking. And he heard us talking in here. Maybe the hotel's on fire!

Willy (*his terror rising*). It's a mistake.

The Woman. Then tell him to go away!

Willy. There's nobody there.

The Woman. It's getting on my nerves, Willy. There's somebody standing out there and it's getting on my nerves!

Willy (*pushing her away from him*). All right, stay in the bathroom here, and don't come out. I think there's a law in Massachusetts about it, so don't come out. It may be that new room clerk. He looked very mean. So don't come out. It's a mistake, there's no fire.

The knocking is heard again. He takes a few steps away from her, and she vanishes into the wing. The light follows him, and now he is facing Young Biff, who carries a suitcase. Biff steps toward him. The music is gone.

Biff. Why didn't you answer?

Willy. Biff! What are you doing in Boston?

Biff. Why didn't you answer? I've been knocking for five minutes, I called you on the phone—

Willy. I just heard you. I was in the bathroom and had the door shut. Did anything happen home?

Biff. Dad—I let you down.

Willy. What do you mean?

Biff. Dad . . .

Willy. Biffo, what's this about? *(Putting his arm around Biff.)* Come on, let's go downstairs and get you a malted.

Biff. Dad, I flunked math.

Willy. Not for the term?

Biff. The term. I haven't got enough credits to graduate.

Willy. You mean to say Bernard wouldn't give you the answers?

Biff. He did, he tried, but I only got a sixty-one.

Willy. And they wouldn't give you four points?

Biff. Birnbaum refused absolutely. I begged him, Pop, but he won't give me those points. You gotta talk to him before they close the school. Because if he saw the kind of man you are, and you just talked to him in your way, I'm sure he'd come through for me. The class came right before practice, see, and I didn't go enough. Would you talk to him? He'd like you, Pop. You know the way you could talk.

Willy. You're on. We'll drive right back.

Biff. Oh, Dad, good work! I'm sure he'll change it for you!

Willy. Go downstairs and tell the clerk I'm checkin' out. Go right down.

Biff. Yes, sir! See, the reason he hates me, Pop—one day he was late for class so I got up at the blackboard and imitated him. I crossed my eyes and talked with a lithp.

Willy *(laughing).* You did? The kids like it?

Biff. They nearly died laughing!

Willy. Yeah? What'd you do?

Biff. The thquare root of thixthy twee is . . . *(Willy bursts out laughing; Biff joins him.)* And in the middle of it he walked in!

Willy laughs and The Woman joins in offstage.

Willy *(without hesitation).* Hurry downstairs and—

Biff. Somebody in there?

Willy. No, that was next door.

The Woman laughs offstage.

Biff. Somebody got in your bathroom!

Willy. No, it's the next room, there's a party—

The Woman *(enters, laughing. She lisps this):* Can I come in? There's something in the bathtub, Willy, and it's moving!

Willy looks at Biff, who is staring open-mouthed and horrified at The Woman.

Willy. Ah—you better go back to your room. They must be finished painting by now. They're painting her room so I let her take a shower here. Go back, go back . . . *(He pushes her.)*

The Woman *(resisting)*. But I've got to get dressed, Willy, I can't—

Willy. Get out of here! Go back, go back . . . *(Suddenly striving for the ordinary)*: This is Miss Francis, Biff, she's a buyer. They're painting her room. Go back, Miss Francis, go back . . .

The Woman. But my clothes, I can't go out naked in the hall!

Willy *(pushing her offstage)*. Get outa here! Go back, go back!

Biff slowly sits down on his suitcase as the argument continues offstage.

The Woman. Where's my stockings? You promised me stockings, Willy!

Willy. I have no stockings here!

The Woman. You had two boxes of size nine sheers for me, and I want them!

Willy. Here, for God's sake, will you get outa here!

The Woman *(enters holding a box of stockings)*. I just hope there's nobody in the hall. That's all I hope. *(To Biff.)* Are you football or baseball?

Biff. Football.

The Woman *(angry, humiliated)*. That's me too. G'night. *(She snatches her clothes from Willy, and walks out.)*

Willy *(after a pause)*. Well, better get going. I want to get to the school first thing in the morning. Get my suits out of the closet. I'll get my valise. *(Biff doesn't move.)* What's the matter? *(Biff remains motionless, tears falling.)* She's a buyer. Buys for J. H. Simmons. She lives down the hall—they're painting. You don't imagine— *(He breaks off. After a pause.)* Now listen, pal, she's just a buyer. She sees merchandise in her room and they have to keep it looking just so . . . *(Pause. Assuming command.)* All right, get my suits. *(Biff doesn't move.)* Now stop crying and do as I say. I gave you an order. Biff, I gave you an order! Is that what you do when I give you an order? How dare you cry! *(Putting his arm around Biff.)* Now look, Biff, when you grow up you'll understand about these things. You mustn't—you mustn't overemphasize a thing like this. I'll see Birnbaum first thing in the morning.

Biff. Never mind.

Willy *(getting down beside Biff)*. Never mind! He's going to give you those points. I'll see to it.

Biff. He wouldn't listen to you.

Willy. He certainly will listen to me. You need those points for the U. of Virginia.

Biff. I'm not going there.

Willy. Heh? If I can't get him to change that mark you'll make it up in summer school. You've got all summer to—

Biff *(his weeping breaking from him)*. Dad . . .

Willy *(infected by it)*. Oh, my boy . . .

Biff. Dad . . .

Willy. She's nothing to me, Biff. I was lonely, I was terribly lonely.

Biff. You—you gave her Mama's stockings! *(His tears break through and he rises to go.)*

Willy *(grabbing for Biff)*. I gave you an order!

Biff. Don't touch me, you—liar!

Willy. Apologize for that!

Biff. You fake! You phony little fake! You fake! (*Overcome, he turns quickly and weeping fully goes out with his suitcase. Willy is left on the floor on his knees.*)

Willy. I gave you an order! Biff, come back here or I'll beat you! Come back here! I'll whip you!

Stanley comes quickly in from the right and stands in front of Willy.

Willy (*shouts at Stanley*). I gave you an order . . .

Stanley. Hey, let's pick it up, pick it up, Mr. Loman. (*He helps Willy to his feet.*) Your boys left with the chippies. They said they'll see you home.

A second waiter watches some distance away.

Willy. But we were supposed to have dinner together.

Music is heard, Willy's theme.

Stanley. Can you make it?

Willy. I'll—sure, I can make it. (*Suddenly concerned about his clothes.*) Do I—I look all right?

Stanley. Sure, you look all right. (*He flicks a speck off Willy's lapel.*)

Willy. Here—here's a dollar.

Stanley. Oh, your son paid me. It's all right.

Willy (*putting it in Stanley's hand*). No, take it. You're a good boy.

Stanley. Oh, no, you don't have to . . .

Willy. Here—here's some more, I don't need it any more. (*After a slight pause.*) Tell me—is there a seed store in the neighborhood?

Stanley. Seeds? You mean like to plant?

As Willy turns, Stanley slips the money back into his jacket pocket.

Willy. Yes. Carrots, peas . . .

Stanley. Well, there's hardware stores on Sixth Avenue, but it may be too late now.

Willy (*anxiously*). Oh, I'd better hurry. I've got to get some seeds. (*He starts off to the right.*) I've got to get some seeds, right away. Nothing's planted. I don't have a thing in the ground.

Willy hurries out as the light goes down. Stanley moves over to the right after him, watches him off. The other waiter has been staring at Willy.

Stanley (*to the waiter*). Well, whatta you looking at?

The waiter picks up the chairs and moves off right. Stanley takes the table and follows him. The light fades on this area. There is a long pause, the sound of the flute coming over. The light gradually rises on the kitchen, which is empty. Happy appears at the door of the house, followed by Biff. Happy is carrying a large bunch of long-stemmed roses. He enters the kitchen, looks around for Linda. Not seeing her, he turns to Biff, who is just outside the house door, and makes a gesture with his hands, indicating "Not here, I guess." He looks into the living-room and freezes. Inside, Linda, unseen, is seated, Willy's coat on her lap. She rises ominously and quietly and moves toward Happy, who backs up into the kitchen, afraid.

Happy. Hey, what're you doing up? *(Linda says nothing but moves toward him implacably.)* Where's Pop? *(He keeps backing to the right, and now Linda is in full view in the doorway to the living-room.)* Is he sleeping?

Linda. Where were you?

Happy *(trying to laugh it off).* We met two girls, Mom, very fine types. Here, we brought you some flowers. *(Offering them to her.)* Put them in your room, Ma.

She knocks them to the floor at Biff's feet. He has now come inside and closed the door behind him. She stares at Biff, silent.

Happy. Now what'd you do that for? Mom, I want you to have some flowers—

Linda *(cutting Happy off, violently to Biff).* Don't you care whether he lives or dies?

Happy *(going to the stairs).* Come upstairs, Biff.

Biff *(with a flare of disgust, to Happy).* Go away from me! *(To Linda.)* What do you mean, lives or dies? Nobody's dying around here, pal.

Linda. Get out of my sight! Get out of here!

Biff. I wanna see the boss.

Linda. You're not going near him!

Biff. Where is he? *(He moves into the living-room and Linda follows.)*

Linda *(shouting after Biff).* You invite him for dinner. He looks forward to it all day—*(Biff appears in his parents' bedroom, looks around, and exits.)*—and then you desert him there. There's no stranger you'd do that to!

Happy. Why? He had a swell time with us. Listen, when I—*(Linda comes back into the kitchen)*—desert him I hope I don't outlive the day!

Linda. Get out of here!

Happy. Now look, Mom . . .

Linda. Did you have to go to women tonight? You and your lousy rotten whores!

Biff re-enters the kitchen.

Happy. Mom, all we did was follow Biff around trying to cheer him up! *(To Biff.)* Boy, what a night you gave me!

Linda. Get out of here, both of you, and don't come back! I don't want you tormenting him any more. Go on now, get your things together! *(To Biff.)* You can sleep in his apartment. *(She starts to pick up the flowers and stops herself.)* Pick up this stuff, I'm not your maid any more. Pick it up, you bum, you!

Happy turns his back to her in refusal. Biff slowly moves over and gets down on his knees, picking up the flowers.

Linda. You're a pair of animals! Not one, not another living soul would have had the cruelty to walk out on that man in a restaurant!

Biff *(not looking at her).* Is that what he said?

Linda. He didn't have to say anything. He was so humiliated he nearly limped when he came in.

Happy. But, Mom, he had a great time with us—

Biff *(cutting him off violently).* Shut up!

Without another word, Happy goes upstairs.

Linda. You! You didn't even go in to see if he was all right!

Biff *(still on the floor in front of Linda, the flowers in his hand; with self-loathing).* No. Didn't. Didn't do a damned thing. How do you like that, heh? Left him babbling in a toilet.

Linda. You louse. You . . .

Biff. Now you hit it on the nose! *(He gets up, throws the flowers in the wastebasket.)* The scum of the earth, and you're looking at him!

Linda. Get out of here!

Biff. I gotta talk to the boss, Mom. Where is he?

Linda. You're not going near him. Get out of this house!

Biff *(with absolute assurance, determination).* No. We're gonna have an abrupt conversation, him and me.

Linda. You're not talking to him!

Hammering is heard from outside the house, off right. Biff turns toward the noise.

Linda *(suddenly pleading).* Will you please leave him alone?

Biff. What's he doing out there?

Linda. He's planting the garden!

Biff *(quietly).* Now? Oh, my God!

Biff moves outside, Linda following. The light dies down on them and comes up on the center of the apron as Willy walks into it. He is carrying a flashlight, a hoe, and a handful of seed packets. He raps the top of the hoe sharply to fix it firmly, and then moves to the left, measuring off the distance with his foot. He holds the flashlight to look at the seed packets, reading off the instructions. He is in the blue of night.

Willy. Carrots . . . quarter-inch apart. Rows . . . one-foot rows. *(He measures it off.)* One foot. *(He puts down a package and measures off.)* Beets. *(He puts down another package and measures again.)* Lettuce. *(He reads the package, puts it down.)* One foot—*(He breaks off as Ben appears at the right and moves slowly down to him.)* What a proposition, ts, ts. Terrific, terrific. 'Cause she's suffered,

Ben, the woman has suffered. You understand me? A man can't go out the way he came in, Ben, a man has got to add up to something. You can't, you can't— *(Ben moves toward him as though to interrupt.)* You gotta consider, now. Don't answer so quick. Remember, it's a guaranteed twenty-thousand-dollar proposition. Now look, Ben, I want you to go through the ins and outs of this thing with me. I've got nobody to talk to, Ben, and the woman has suffered, you hear me?

Ben *(standing still, considering).* What's the proposition?

Willy. It's twenty thousand dollars on the barrelhead. Guaranteed, gilt-edged, you understand?

Ben. You don't want to make a fool of yourself. They might not honor the policy.

Willy. How can they dare refuse? Didn't I work like a coolie to meet every premium on the nose? And now they don't pay off? Impossible!

Ben. It's called a cowardly thing, William.

Willy. Why? Does it take more guts to stand here the rest of my life ringing up a zero?

Ben *(yielding).* That's a point, William. *(He moves, thinking, turns.)* And twenty thousand—that *is* something one can feel with the hand, it is there.

Willy *(now assured, with rising power).* Oh, Ben, that's the whole beauty of it! I see it like a diamond, shining in the dark, hard and rough, that I can pick up and touch in my hand. Not like—like an appointment! This would not be another damned-fool appointment, Ben, and it changes all the aspects. Because he thinks I'm nothing, see, and so he spites me. But the funeral—*(Straightening up.)* Ben, that funeral will be massive! They'll come from Maine, Massachusetts, Vermont, New Hampshire! All the old-timers with the strange license plates— that boy will be thunder-struck, Ben, because he never realized—I am known! Rhode Island, New York, New Jersey—I am known, Ben, and he'll see it with his eyes once and for all. He'll see what I am, Ben! He's in for a shock, that boy!

Ben *(coming to the edge of the garden).* He'll call you a coward.

Willy *(suddenly fearful).* No, that would be terrible.

Ben. Yes. And a damned fool.

Willy. No, no, he mustn't, I won't have that! *(He is broken and desperate.)*

Ben. He'll hate you William.

The gay music of the Boys is heard.

Willy. Oh, Ben, how do we get back to all the great times? Used to be so full of light, and comradeship, the sleigh-riding in winter, and the ruddiness on his cheeks. And always some kind of good news coming up, always something nice coming up ahead. And never even let me carry the valises in the house, and simonizing, simonizing that little red car! Why, why can't I give him something and not have him hate me?

Ben. Let me think about it. *(He glances at his watch.)* I still have a little time. Remarkable proposition, but you've got to be sure you're not making a fool of yourself.

Ben drifts off upstage and goes out of sight. Biff comes down from the left.

Willy (*suddenly conscious of Biff, turns and looks up at him, then begins picking up the packages of seeds in confusion*). Where the hell is that seed? (*Indignantly.*) You can't see nothing out here! They boxed in the whole goddamn neighborhood!

Biff. There are people all around here. Don't you realize that?

Willy. I'm busy. Don't bother me.

Biff (*taking the hoe from Willy*). I'm saying good-by to you, Pop. (*Willy looks at him, silent, unable to move.*) I'm not coming back any more.

Willy. You're not going to see Oliver tomorrow?

Biff. I've got no appointment, Dad.

Willy. He put his arm around you, and you've got no appointment?

Biff. Pop, get this now, will you? Every time I've left it's been a fight that sent me out of here. Today I realized something about myself and I tried to explain it to you and I—I think I'm just not smart enough to make any sense out of it for you. To hell with whose fault it is or anything like that. (*He takes Willy's arm.*) Let's just wrap it up, heh? Come on in, we'll tell Mom. (*He gently tries to pull Willy to left.*)

Willy (*frozen, immobile, with guilt in his voice*). No, I don't want to see her.

Biff. Come on! (*He pulls again, and Willy tries to pull away.*)

Willy (*highly nervous*). No, no, I don't want to see her.

Biff (*tries to look into Willy's face, as if to find the answer there*). Why don't you want to see her?

Willy (*more harshly now*). Don't bother me, will you?

Biff. What do you mean, you don't want to see her? You don't want them calling you yellow, do you? This isn't your fault; it's me, I'm a bum. Now come inside! (*Willy strains to get away.*) Did you hear what I said to you?

Willy pulls away and quickly goes by himself into the house. Biff follows.

Linda (*to Willy*). Did you plant, dear?

Biff (*at the door, to Linda*). All right, we had it out. I'm going and I'm not writing any more.

Linda (*going to Willy in the kitchen*). I think that's the best way, dear. 'Cause there's no use drawing it out, you'll just never get along.

Willy doesn't respond.

Biff. People ask where I am and what I'm doing, you don't know, and you don't care. That way it'll be off your mind and you can start brightening up again. All right? That clears it, doesn't it? (*Willy is silent, and Biff goes to him.*) You gonna wish me luck, scout? (*He extends his hand.*) What do you say?

Linda. Shake his hand, Willy.

Willy (*turning to her, seething with hurt*). There's no necessity to mention the pen at all, y'know.

Biff (*gently*). I've got no appointment, Dad.

Willy (*erupting fiercely*). He put his arm around . . . ?

Biff. Dad, you're never going to see what I am, so what's the use of arguing? If I strike oil I'll send you a check. Meantime forget I'm alive.

Willy *(to Linda)*. Spite, see?

Biff. Shake hands, Dad.

Willy. Not my hand.

Biff. I was hoping not to go this way.

Willy. Well, this is the way you're going. Good-by.

Biff looks at him a moment, then turns sharply and goes to the stairs.

Willy *(stops him with)*. May you rot in hell if you leave this house!

Biff *(turning)*. Exactly what is it that you want from me?

Willy. I want you to know, on the train, in the mountains, in the valleys, wherever you go, that you cut down your life for spite!

Biff. No, no.

Willy. Spite, spite, is the word of your undoing! And when you're down and out, remember what did it. When you're rotting somewhere beside the railroad tracks, remember, and don't you dare blame it on me!

Biff. I'm not blaming it on you!

Willy. I won't take the rap for this, you hear?

Happy comes down the stairs and stands on the bottom step, watching.

Biff. That's just what I'm telling you!

Willy *(sinking into a chair at the table, with full accusation)*. You're trying to put a knife in me—don't think I don't know what you're doing!

Biff. All right, phony! Then let's lay it on the line. *(He whips the rubber tube out of his pocket and puts it on the table.)*

Happy. You crazy—

Linda. Biff! *(She moves to grab the hose, but Biff holds it down with his hand.)*

Biff. Leave it there! Don't move it!

Willy *(not looking at it)*. What is that?

Biff. You know goddam well what that is.

Willy *(caged, wanting to escape)*. I never saw that.

Biff. You saw it. The mice didn't bring it into the cellar! What is this supposed to do, make a hero out of you? This supposed to make me sorry for you?

Willy. Never heard of it.

Biff. There'll be no pity for you, you hear it? No pity!

Willy *(to Linda)*. You hear the spite!

Biff. No, you're going to hear the truth—what you are and what I am!

Linda. Stop it!

Willy. Spite!

Happy *(coming down toward Biff)*. You cut it now!

Biff *(to Happy)*. The man don't know who we are! The man is gonna know! *(To Willy.)* We never told the truth for ten minutes in this house!

Happy. We always told the truth!

Biff *(turning on him).* You big blow, are you the assistant buyer? You're one of the two assistants to the assistant, aren't you?

Happy. Well, I'm practically—

Biff. You're practically full of it! We all are! And I'm through with it. *(To Willy.)* Now hear this, Willy, this is me.

Willy. I know you!

Biff. You know why I had no address for three months? I stole a suit in Kansas City and I was in jail. *(To Linda, who is sobbing.)* Stop crying. I'm through with it.

Linda turns away from them, her hands covering her face.

Willy. I suppose that's my fault!

Biff. I stole myself out of every good job since high school!

Willy. And whose fault is that?

Biff. And I never got anywhere because you blew me so full of hot air I could never stand taking orders from anybody! That's whose fault it is!

Willy. I hear that!

Linda. Don't, Biff!

Biff. It's goddam time you heard that! I had to be boss big shot in two weeks, and I'm through with it!

Willy. Then hang yourself! For spite, hang yourself!

Biff. No! Nobody's hanging himself, Willy! I ran down eleven flights with a pen in my hand today. And suddenly I stopped, you hear me? And in the middle of that office building, do you hear this? I stopped in the middle of that building and I saw—the sky. I saw the things that I love in this world. The work and the food and time to sit and smoke. And I looked at the pen and said to myself, what the hell am I grabbing this for? Why am I trying to become what I don't want to be? What am I doing in an office, making a contemptuous, begging fool of myself, when all I want is out there, waiting for me the minute I say I know who I am! Why can't I say that, Willy? *(He tries to make Willy face him, but Willy pulls away and moves to the left.)*

Willy *(with hatred, threateningly).* The door of your life is wide open!

Biff. Pop! I'm a dime a dozen, and so are you!

Willy *(turning on him now in an uncontrolled outburst).* I am not a dime a dozen! I am Willy Loman, and you are Biff Loman!

Biff starts for Willy, but is blocked by Happy. In his fury, Biff seems on the verge of attacking his father.

Biff. I am not a leader of men, Willy, and neither are you. You were never anything but a hard-working drummer who landed in the ash can like all the rest of them! I'm one dollar an hour, Willy! I tried seven states and couldn't raise it. A buck an hour! Do you gather my meaning? I'm not bringing home any prizes any more, and you're going to stop waiting for me to bring them home!

Willy *(directly to Biff)*. You vengeful, spiteful mutt!

Biff breaks from Happy. Willy, in fright, starts up the stairs. Biff grabs him.

Biff *(at the peak of his fury)*. Pop, I'm nothing! I'm nothing, Pop. Can't you understand that? There's no spite in it any more. I'm just what I am, that's all.

Biff's fury has spent itself, and he breaks down, sobbing, holding on to Willy, who dumbly fumbles for Biff's face.

Willy *(astonished)*. What're you doing? What're you doing? *(To Linda.)* Why is he crying?
Biff *(crying, broken)*. Will you let me go, for Christ's sake? Will you take that phony dream and burn it before something happens? *(Struggling to contain himself, he pulls away and moves to the stairs.)* I'll go in the morning. Put him—put him to bed. *(Exhausted, Biff moves up the stairs to his room.)*
Willy *(after a long pause, astonished, elevated)*. Isn't that—isn't that remarkable? Biff—he likes me!
Linda. He loves you, Willy!
Happy *(deeply moved)*. Always did, Pop.
Willy. Oh, Biff! *(Staring wildly.)* He cried! Cried to me. *(He is choking with his love, and now cries out his promise.)* That boy—that boy is going to be magnificent!

Ben appears in the light just outside the kitchen.

Ben. Yes, outstanding, with twenty thousand behind him.
Linda *(sensing the racing of his mind, fearfully, carefully)*. Now come to bed, Willy. It's all settled now.
Willy *(finding it difficult not to rush out of the house)*. Yes, we'll sleep. Come on. Go to sleep, Hap.
Ben. And it does take a great kind of a man to crack the jungle.

In accents of dread, Ben's idyllic music starts up.

Happy *(his arm around Linda)*. I'm getting married, Pop, don't forget it. I'm changing everything. I'm gonna run that department before the year is up. You'll see, Mom. *(He kisses her.)*
Ben. The jungle is dark but full of diamonds, Willy.

Willy turns, moves, listening to Ben.

Linda. Be good. You're both good boys, just act that way, that's all.
Happy. 'Night, Pop. *(He goes upstairs.)*
Linda *(to Willy)*. Come, dear.
Ben *(with greater force)*. One must go in to fetch a diamond out.

Willy (*to Linda, as he moves slowly along the edge of the kitchen, toward the door*). I just want to get settled down, Linda. Let me sit alone for a little.

Linda (*almost uttering her fear*). I want you upstairs.

Willy (*taking her in his arms*). In a few minutes, Linda. I couldn't sleep right now. Go on, you look awful tired. (*He kisses her.*)

Ben. Not like an appointment at all. A diamond is rough and hard to the touch.

Willy. Go on now. I'll be right up.

Linda. I think this is the only way, Willy.

Willy. Sure, it's the best thing.

Ben. Best thing!

Willy. The only way. Everything is gonna be—go on, kid, get to bed. You look so tired.

Linda. Come right up.

Willy. Two minutes.

Linda goes into the living-room, then reappears in her bedroom. Willy moves just outside the kitchen door.

Willy. Loves me. (*Wonderingly.*) Always loved me. Isn't that a remarkable thing? Ben, he'll worship me for it!

Ben (*with promise*). It's dark there, but full of diamonds.

Willy. Can you imagine that magnificence with twenty thousand dollars in his pocket?

Linda (*calling from her room*). Willy! Come up!

Willy (*calling into the kitchen*). Yes! Yes. Coming! It's very smart, you realize that, don't you, sweetheart? Even Ben sees it. I gotta go, baby. 'By! 'By! (*Going over to Ben, almost dancing.*) Imagine? When the mail comes he'll be ahead of Bernard again!

Ben. A perfect proposition all around.

Willy. Did you see how he cried to me? Oh, if I could kiss him, Ben!

Ben. Time, William, time!

Willy. Oh, Ben, I always knew one way or another we were gonna make it, Biff and I!

Ben (*looking at his watch*). The boat. We'll be late. (*He moves slowly off into the darkness.*)

Willy (*elegiacally, turning to the house*). Now when you kick off, boy, I want a seventy-yard boot, and get right down the field under the ball, and when you hit, hit low and hit hard, because it's important, boy. (*He swings around and faces the audience.*) There's all kinds of important people in the stands, and the first thing you know . . . (*Suddenly realizing he is alone.*) Ben! Ben, where do I . . . ? (*He makes a sudden movement of search.*) Ben, how do I . . . ?

Linda (*calling*). Willy, you coming up?

Willy (*uttering a gasp of fear, whirling about as if to quiet her*). Sh! (*He turns around as if to find his way; sounds, faces, voices, seem to be swarming in upon him and he flicks at them, crying.*) Sh! Sh! (*Suddenly music, faint and high, stops him.*

It rises in intensity, almost to an unbearable scream. He goes up and down on his toes, and rushes off around the house.) Shhh!

Linda. Willy?

There is no answer. Linda waits. Biff gets up off his bed. He is still in his clothes. Happy sits up. Biff stands listening.

Linda *(with real fear)*. Willy, answer me! Willy!

There is the sound of a car starting and moving away at full speed.

Linda. No!
Biff *(rushing down the stairs)*. Pop!

As the car speeds off, the music crashes down in a frenzy of sound, which becomes the soft pulsation of a single cello string. Biff slowly returns to his bedroom. He and Happy gravely don their jackets. Linda slowly walks out of her room. The music has developed into a dead march. The leaves of day are appearing over everything. Charley and Bernard, somberly dressed, appear and knock on the kitchen door. Biff and Happy slowly descend the stairs to the kitchen as Charley and Bernard enter. All stop a moment when Linda, in clothes of mourning, bearing a little bunch of roses, comes through the draped doorway into the kitchen. She goes to Charley and takes his arm. Now all move toward the audience, through the wall-line of the kitchen. At the limit of the apron, Linda lays down the flowers, kneels, and sits back on her heels. All stare down at the grave.

REQUIEM

Charley. It's getting dark, Linda.

Linda doesn't react. She stares at the grave.

Biff. How about it, Mom? Better get some rest, heh? They'll be closing the gate soon.

Linda makes no move. Pause.

Happy *(deeply angered)*. He had no right to do that. There was no necessity for it. We would've helped him.
Charley *(grunting)*. Hmmm.
Biff. Come along, Mom.
Linda. Why didn't anybody come?
Charley. It was a very nice funeral.

Linda. But where are all the people he knew? Maybe they blame him.

Charley. Naa. It's a rough world, Linda. They wouldn't blame him.

Linda. I can't understand it. At this time especially. First time in thirty-five years we were just about free and clear. He only needed a little salary. He was even finished with the dentist.

Charley. No man only needs a little salary.

Linda. I can't understand it.

Biff. There were a lot of nice days. When he'd come home from a trip; or on Sundays, making the stoop; finishing the cellar; putting on the new porch; when he built the extra bathroom; and put up the garage. You know something, Charley, there's more of him in that front stoop than in all the sales he ever made.

Charley. Yeah. He was a happy man with a batch of cement.

Linda. He was so wonderful with his hands.

Biff. He had the wrong dreams. All, all, wrong.

Happy (*almost ready to fight Biff*). Don't say that!

Biff. He never knew who he was.

Charley (*stopping Happy's movement and reply. To Biff*). Nobody dast blame this man. You don't understand: Willy was a salesman. And for a salesman, there is no rock bottom to the life. He don't put a bolt to a nut, he don't tell you the law or give you medicine. He's a man way out there in the blue, riding on a smile and a shoeshine. And when they start not smiling back—that's an earthquake. And then you get yourself a couple of spots on your hat, and you're finished. Nobody dast blame this man. A salesman is got to dream, boy. It comes with the territory.

Biff. Charley, the man didn't know who he was.

Happy (*infuriated*). Don't say that!

Biff. Why don't you come with me, Happy?

Happy. I'm not licked that easily. I'm staying right in this city, and I'm gonna beat this racket! (*He looks at Biff, his chin set.*) The Loman Brothers!

Biff. I know who I am, kid.

Happy. All right, boy. I'm gonna show you and everybody else that Willy Loman did not die in vain. He had a good dream. It's the only dream you can have—to come out number-one man. He fought it out here, and this is where I'm gonna win it for him.

Biff (*with a hopeless glance at Happy, bends toward his mother*). Let's go, Mom.

Linda. I'll be with you in a minute. Go on, Charley. (*He hesitates.*) I want to, just for a minute. I never had a chance to say good-by.

Charley moves away, followed by Happy. Biff remains a slight distance up and left of Linda. She sits there, summoning herself. The flute begins, not far away, playing behind her speech.

Linda. Forgive me, dear. I can't cry. I don't know what it is, but I can't cry. I don't understand it. Why did you ever do that? Help me. Willy, I can't cry. It seems to me that you're just on another trip. I keep expecting you. Willy, dear, I can't cry.

Why did you do it? I search and search and I search, and I can't understand it, Willy. I made the last payment on the house today. Today, dear. And there'll be nobody home. *(A sob rises in her throat.)* We're free and clear. *(Sobbing more fully, released.)* We're free. *(Biff comes slowly toward her.)* We're free . . . We're free . . .

Biff lifts her to her feet and moves out up right with her in his arms. Linda sobs quietly. Bernard and Charley come together and follow them, followed by Happy. Only the music of the flute is left on the darkening stage as over the house the hard towers of the apartment buildings rise into sharp focus, and

The Curtain Falls

FOR ANALYSIS

1. What is Linda's role in the tragedy of Willy? Do you admire her?

2. In what ways are Biff and Happy similar? In what ways different? Is Biff, as Willy asserts, a failure? Explain.

3. Which of the brothers is most likely to become another Willy Loman? Explain.

4. What does Ben represent to Willy? Are we meant to see Ben as Willy sees him? Explain.

5. The play contains many references to the outdoors, the West, working with one's hands. What purpose do these references serve?

6. The last paragraph of the first stage direction describes Linda. Comment on the parts of the stage direction that cannot be translated into dramatic action. Why do you suppose Miller wrote of Linda as he did?

7. What else could be said to die at the end of *Death of a Salesman*, besides the salesman himself? Does the American Dream die? Does hope die?

MAKING CONNECTIONS

1. Use the following comment by Miller as the basis for a comparison of this play with Sophocles' *Oedipus Rex* (p. 183): "I think the tragic feeling is evoked in us when we are in the presence of a character who is ready to lay down his life, if need be, to secure one thing—his sense of personal dignity."

2. Compare *Death of a Salesman* to the selections in "Connecting Poems: Working Mothers." How is the meaning of work different for the women in those poems than for the men in this play?

WRITING TOPICS

1. In an essay, either support or refute the assertion that Willy is a victim of the American Dream.

2. Argue for or against the view that Biff's treatment of Willy is justified.

DEATH KNOCKS   1968

The play takes place in the bedroom of Nat Ackerman's two-story house, somewhere in Kew Gardens.[1] *The carpeting is wall-to-wall. There is a big double bed and a large vanity. The room is elaborately furnished and curtained, and on the walls there are several paintings and a not really attractive barometer. Soft theme music as the curtain rises. Nat Ackerman, a bald, paunchy fifty-seven-year-old dress manufacturer, is lying on the bed finishing off tomorrow's* Daily News.[2] *He wears a bathrobe and slippers, and reads by a bed light clipped to the white headboard of the bed. The time is near midnight. Suddenly we hear a noise, and Nat sits up and looks at the window.*

Nat. What the hell is that?

(Climbing awkwardly through the window is a sombre, caped figure. The intruder wears a black hood and skintight black clothes. The hood covers his head but not his face, which is middle-aged and stark white. He is something like Nat in appearance. He huffs audibly and then trips over the windowsill and falls into the room.)

Death *(for it is no one else).* Jesus Christ. I nearly broke my neck.
Nat *(watching with bewilderment).* Who are you?
Death. Death.
Nat. Who?
Death. Death. Listen—can I sit down? I nearly broke my neck. I'm shaking like a
  leaf.
Nat. Who *are* you?
Death. *Death.* You got a glass of water?
Nat. Death? What do you mean, Death?
Death. What is wrong with you? You see the black costume and the whitened face?
Nat. Yeah.
Death. Is it Halloween?
Nat. No.
Death. Then I'm Death. Now can I get a glass of water—or a Fresca?
Nat. If this is some joke—
Death. What kind of joke? You're fifty-seven? Nat Ackerman? One eighteen Pacific
  Street? Unless I blew it—where's that call sheet? *(He fumbles through pocket, finally
  producing a card with an address on it. It seems to check.)*
Nat. What do you want with me?

---

[1] A middle-class neighborhood in the New York City borough of Queens.   [2] The *Daily News* is a tabloid newspaper; the morning edition used to be distributed at about 10 P.M. the previous night.

Death. What do I want? What do you think I want?

Nat. You must be kidding. I'm in perfect health.

Death *(unimpressed)*. Uh-huh. *(Looking around)* This is a nice place. You do it yourself?

Nat. We had a decorator, but we worked with her.

Death *(looking at picture on the wall)*. I love those kids with the big eyes.

Nat. I don't want to go yet.

Death. *You* don't want to go? Please don't start in. As it is, I'm nauseous from the climb.

Nat. What climb?

Death. I climbed up the drainpipe. I was trying to make a dramatic entrance. I see the big windows and you're awake reading. I figure it's worth a shot. I'll climb up and enter with a little—you know . . . *(Snaps fingers)* Meanwhile, I get my heel caught on some vines, the drainpipe breaks, and I'm hanging by a thread. Then my cape begins to tear. Look, let's just go. It's been a rough night.

Nat. You broke my drainpipe?

Death. Broke. It didn't break. It's a little bent. Didn't you hear anything? I slammed into the ground.

Nat. I was reading.

Death. You must have really been engrossed. *(Lifting newspaper Nat was reading)* "NAB COEDS IN POT ORGY." Can I borrow this?

Nat. I'm not finished.

Death. Er—I don't know how to put this to you, pal. . . .

Nat. Why didn't you just ring downstairs?

Death. I'm telling you, I could have, but how does it look? This way I get a little drama going. Something. Did you read "Faust"?

Nat. What?

Death. And what if you had company? You're sitting there with important people. I'm Death—I should ring the bell and traipse right in the front? Where's your thinking?

Nat. Listen, Mister, it's very late.

Death. Yeah. Well, you want to go?

Nat. Go where?

Death. Death. It. The Thing. The Happy Hunting Grounds. *(Looking at his own knee)* Y'know, that's a pretty bad cut. My first job, I'm liable to get gangrene yet.

Nat. Now, wait a minute. I need time. I'm not ready to go.

Death. I'm sorry. I can't help you. I'd like to, but it's the moment.

Nat. How can it be the moment? I just merged with Modiste Originals.

Death. What's the difference, a couple of bucks more or less.

Nat. Sure, what do you care? You guys probably have all your expenses paid.

Death. You want to come along now?

Nat *(studying him)*. I'm sorry, but I cannot believe you're Death.

Death. Why? What'd you expect—Rock Hudson?

Nat. No, it's not that.

Death. I'm sorry if I disappointed you.

Nat. Don't get upset. I don't know, I always thought you'd be . . . uh . . . taller.

Death. I'm five seven. It's average for my weight.

Nat. You look a little like me.

Death. Who should I look like? I'm your death.

Nat. Give me some time. Another day.

Death. I can't. What do you want me to say?

Nat. One more day. Twenty-four hours.

Death. What do you need it for? The radio said rain tomorrow.

Nat. Can't we work out something?

Death. Like what?

Nat. You play chess?

Death. No, I don't.

Nat. I once saw a picture of you playing chess.

Death. Couldn't be me, because I don't play chess. Gin rummy, maybe.

Nat. You play gin rummy?

Death. Do I play gin rummy? Is Paris a city?

Nat. You're good, huh?

Death. Very good.

Nat. I'll tell you what I'll do—

Death. Don't make any deals with me.

Nat. I'll play you gin rummy. If you win, I'll go immediately. If I win, give me some more time. A little bit—one more day.

Death. Who's got time to play gin rummy?

Nat. Come on. If you're so good.

Death. Although I feel like a game . . .

Nat. Come on. Be a sport. We'll shoot for a half hour.

Death. I really shouldn't.

Nat. I got the cards right here. Don't make a production.

Death. All right, come on. We'll play a little. It'll relax me.

Nat (*getting cards, pad, and pencil*). You won't regret this.

Death. Don't give me a sales talk. Get the cards and give me a Fresca and put out something. For God's sake, a stranger drops in, you don't have potato chips or pretzels.

Nat. There's M&M's downstairs in a dish.

Death. M&M's. What if the President came? He'd get M&M's too?

Nat. You're not the President.

Death. Deal.

(*Nat deals, turns up a five.*)

Nat. You want to play a tenth of a cent a point to make it interesting?

Death. It's not interesting enough for you?

Nat. I play better when money's at stake.

Death. Whatever you say, Newt.

Nat. Nat, Nat Ackerman. You don't know my name?

Death. Newt, Nat—I got such a headache.

Nat. You want that five?

Death. No.

Nat. So pick.

Death (*surveying his hand as he picks*). Jesus, I got nothing here.

Nat. What's it like?

Death. What's what like?

(*Throughout the following, they pick and discard.*)

Nat. Death.

Death. What should it be like? You lay there.

Nat. Is there anything after?

Death. Aha, you're saving twos.

Nat. I'm asking. Is there anything after?

Death (*absently*). You'll see.

Nat. Oh, then I will actually see something?

Death. Well, maybe I shouldn't have put it that way. Throw.

Nat. To get an answer from you is a big deal.

Death. I'm playing cards.

Nat. All right, play, play.

Death. Meanwhile, I'm giving you one card after another.

Nat. Don't look through the discards.

Death. I'm not looking. I'm straightening them up. What was the knock card?

Nat. Four. You ready to knock already?

Death. Who said I'm ready to knock. All I asked was what was the knock card.

Nat. And all I asked was is there anything for me to look forward to.

Death. Play.

Nat. Can't you tell me anything? Where do we go?

Death. We? To tell you the truth, *you* fall in a crumpled heap on the floor.

Nat. Oh, I can't wait for that! Is it going to hurt?

Death. Be over in a second.

Nat. Terrific. (*Sighs*) I needed this. A man merges with Modiste Originals . . .

Death. How's four points?

Nat. You're knocking?

Death. Four points is good?

Nat. No, I got two.

Death. You're kidding.

Nat. No, you lose.

Death. Holy Christ, and I thought you were saving sixes.

Nat. No. Your deal. Twenty points and two boxes. Shoot. (*Death deals.*) I must fall on the floor, eh? I can't be standing over the sofa when it happens?

Death. No. Play.

Nat. Why not?

Death. Because you fall on the floor! Leave me alone. I'm trying to concentrate.

Nat. Why must it be on the floor? That's all I'm saying! Why can't the whole thing happen and I'll stand next to the sofa?

Death. I'll try my best. Now can we play?

Nat. That's all I'm saying. You remind me of Moe Lefkowitz. He's also stubborn.

Death. I remind you of Moe Lefkowitz. I'm one of the most terrifying figures you could possibly imagine, and him I remind of Moe Lefkowitz. What is he, a furrier?

Nat. You should be such a furrier. He's good for eighty thousand a year. Passementeries. He's got his own factory. Two points.

Death. What?

Nat. Two points. I'm knocking. What have you got?

Death. My hand is like a basketball score.

Nat. And it's spades.

Death. If you didn't talk so much.

(They redeal and play on.)

Nat. What'd you mean before when you said this was your first job?

Death. What does it sound like?

Nat. What are you telling me—that nobody ever went before?

Death. Sure they went. But I didn't take them.

Nat. So who did?

Death. Others.

Nat. There's others?

Death. Sure. Each one has his own personal way of going.

Nat. I never knew that.

Death. Why should you know? Who are you?

Nat. What do you mean who am I? Why—I'm nothing?

Death. Not nothing. You're a dress manufacturer. Where do you come to knowledge of the eternal mysteries?

Nat. What are you talking about? I make a beautiful dollar. I sent two kids through college. One is in advertising, the other's married. I got my own home. I drive a Chrysler. My wife has whatever she wants. Maids, mink coat, vacations. Right now she's at the Eden Roc. Fifty dollars a day because she wants to be near her sister. I'm supposed to join her next week, so what do you think I am—some guy off the street?

Death. All right. Don't be so touchy.

Nat. Who's touchy?

Death. How would you like it if I got insulted quickly?

Nat. Did I insult you?

Death. You didn't say you were disappointed in me?

Nat. What do you expect? You want me to throw you a block party?

Death. I'm not talking about that. I mean me personally. I'm too short, I'm this, I'm that.

Nat. I said you looked like me. It's like a reflection.

Death. All right, deal, deal.

(*They continue to play as music steals in and the lights dim until all is in total darkness. The lights slowly come up again, and now it is later and their game is over. Nat tallies.*)

Nat. Sixty-eight . . . one-fifty . . . Well, you lose.

Death (*dejectedly looking through the deck*). I knew I shouldn't have thrown that nine. Damn it.

Nat. So I'll see you tomorrow.

Death. What do you mean you'll see me tomorrow?

Nat. I won the extra day. Leave me alone.

Death. You were serious?

Nat. We made a deal.

Death. Yeah, but—

Nat. Don't "but" me. I won twenty-four hours. Come back tomorrow.

Death. I didn't know we were actually playing for time.

Nat. That's too bad about you. You should pay attention.

Death. Where am I going to go for twenty-four hours?

Nat. What's the difference? The main thing is I won an extra day.

Death. What do you want me to do—walk the streets?

Nat. Check into a hotel and go to a movie. Take a *schvitz.*[3] Don't make a federal case.

Death. Add the score again.

Nat. Plus you owe me twenty-eight dollars.

Death. *What?*

Nat. That's right, Buster. Here it is—read it.

Death (*going through pockets*). I have a few singles—not twenty-eight dollars.

Nat. I'll take a check.

Death. From what account?

Nat. Look who I'm dealing with.

Death. Sue me. Where do I keep my checking account?

Nat. All right, gimme what you got and we'll call it square.

Death. Listen, I need that money.

Nat. Why should you need money?

Death. What are you talking about? You're going to the Beyond.

Nat. So?

Death. So—you know how far that is?

Nat. So?

Death. So where's gas? Where's tolls?

Nat. We're going by car!

Death. You'll find out. (*Agitatedly*) Look—I'll be back tomorrow, and you'll give me a chance to win the money back. Otherwise I'm in definite trouble.

---

[3] Steam bath.

Nat. Anything you want. Double or nothing we'll play. I'm liable to win an extra week or a month. The way you play, maybe years.

Death. Meantime I'm stranded.

Nat. See you tomorrow.

Death *(being edged to the doorway).* Where's a good hotel? What am I talking about hotel, I got no money. I'll go sit in Bickford's.[4] *(He picks up the* News.*)*

Nat. Out. Out. That's my paper. *(He takes it back.)*

Death *(exiting).* I couldn't just take him and go. I had to get involved in rummy.

Nat *(calling after him).* And be careful going downstairs. On one of the steps the rug is loose.

(And, on cue, we hear a terrific crash. Nat sighs, then crosses to the bedside table and makes a phone call.)

Nat. Hello, Moe? Me. Listen, I don't know if somebody's playing a joke, or what, but Death was just here. We played a little gin . . . No, *Death.* In person. Or somebody who claims to be Death. But, Moe, he's such a *schlep!*[5]

Curtain

FOR ANALYSIS

1. Consider the stage direction that opens the play. What sort of household is described?

2. The stage direction describes Nat Ackerman as a dress manufacturer. If you were directing the play, how might you convey that information to your audience? Why do you suppose Allen included the information in a stage direction?

3. Reread the stage directions and identify any others that are literary rather than dramatic tools.

4. Describe the speech patterns of the characters. How do they contribute to the play's effect?

MAKING CONNECTIONS

Compare Allen's handling of the theme of death with Miller's in *Death of a Salesman*.

WRITING TOPIC

Either read—or rent a video of—Ingmar Bergman's *The Seventh Seal*. In an essay, describe the effect of Allen's central **allusion** to *The Seventh Seal* in *Death Knocks*.

---

[4] Bickford's was a chain of inexpensive all-night cafeterias in New York City.   [5] Boring jerk.

NONFICTION

JOHN DONNE (1572–1631)

MEDITATION XVII, FROM DEVOTIONS UPON EMERGENT OCCASIONS 1623

Nunc lento sonitu dicunt morieris.
Now this bell tolling softly for another says to me, Thou must die.

Perchance he for whom this bell tolls may be so ill as that he knows not it tolls for him; and perchance I may think myself so much better than I am, as that they who are about me and see my state may have caused it to toll for me, and I know not that. The church is catholic, universal, so are all her actions; all that she does belongs to all. When she baptizes a child, that action 5 concerns me; for that child is thereby connected to that head which is my head too, and ingrafted into that body whereof I am a member. And when she buries a man, that action concerns me: all mankind is of one author and is one volume; when one man dies, one chapter is not torn out of the book, but translated into a better language; and every chapter must be so translated. God 10 employs several translators; some pieces are translated by age, some by sickness, some by war, some by justice; but God's hand is in every translation, and his hand shall bind up all our scattered leaves again for that library where every book shall lie open to one another. As therefore the bell that rings to a sermon calls not upon the preacher only, but upon the congregation to come, so this 15 bell calls us all; but how much more me, who am brought so near the door by this sickness. There was a contention as far as a suit[1] (in which piety and dignity, religion and estimation, were mingled) which of the religious orders should ring to prayers first in the morning; and it was determined that they should ring first that rose earliest. If we understand aright the dignity of this 20 bell that tolls for our evening prayer, we would be glad to make it ours by rising

---

[1] An argument settled by a lawsuit.

early, in that application, that it might be ours as well as his whose indeed it is. The bell doth toll for him that thinks it doth, and though it intermit again, yet from that minute that that occasion wrought upon him, he is united to God. Who casts not up his eye to the sun when it rises? but who takes off his eye 25 from a comet when that breaks out? Who bends not his ear to any bell which upon any occasion rings? but who can remove it from that bell which is passing a piece of himself out of this world? No man is an island, entire of itself; every man is a piece of the continent, a part of the main. If a clod be washed away by the sea, Europe is the less, as well as if a promontory were, as well as if 30 a manor of thy friend's or of thine own were. Any man's death diminishes me, because I am involved in mankind; and therefore never send to know for whom the bell tolls; it tolls for thee. Neither can we call this a begging of misery or a borrowing of misery, as though we were not miserable enough of ourselves but must fetch in more from the next house, in taking upon us the 35 misery of our neighbors. Truly it were an excusable covetousness if we did; for affliction is a treasure, and scarce any man hath enough of it. No man hath affliction enough that is not matured and ripened by it, and made fit for God by that affliction. If a man carry treasure in bullion, or in a wedge of gold, and have none coined into current moneys, his treasure will not defray him as he 40 travels. Tribulation is treasure in the nature of it, but it is not current money in the use of it, except we get nearer and nearer our home, heaven, by it. Another man may be sick too, and sick to death, and this affliction may lie in his bowels as gold in a mine and be of no use to him; but this bell that tells me of his affliction digs out and applies that gold to me, if by this consideration of 45 another's danger I take mine own into contemplation and so secure myself by making my recourse to my God, who is our only security.

FOR ANALYSIS

1. What does Donne mean when he says that the death bell "tolls for thee" (l. 33)?

2. Toward the end of his meditation, Donne states that "tribulation is treasure" (l. 41). What does he mean? What will that treasure purchase?

3. Donne is justly admired for his use of **figurative language**. What extended **metaphors** does he use to characterize humankind and death?

MAKING CONNECTIONS

Read this meditation with Donne's "Death, Be Not Proud" (p. 1184). What attitude does each have toward death? How does each offer alternatives to fear of death and sadness about death?

WRITING TOPICS

1. What does Donne mean by "affliction is a treasure" (l. 37)? Do you agree? Explain.

2. Identify and analyze the **figurative language** Donne uses to illuminate the human condition and his attitude toward death.

TOI DERRICOTTE   (B. 1941)

BEGINNING DIALOGUES   2007

O n the way, he said, "When you visit the cemetery, you do it for yourself. They don't know you're there." But maybe some part of me believes she will know, that she's brought many good things to me after her death, that she's taking care. Maybe I visit her grave because she would have visited the grave of her mother, because she taught me to send thank-you notes and be a good girl. Maybe I'm going to find signs of whether she's still there; maybe she hasn't blown open the ground, and we'll find an angel lounging on her gravestone, saying, "She's not here. Go and find her elsewhere."

I don't seem to suffer the pains of anguish that many women whose mothers have died feel. Last night, a group about my age, all in that midlife past midlife, late fifties or early sixties, ate dinner and talked about our mothers' deaths. It's not a new conversation; women whose mothers have died always talk about it. They did even when I was in my twenties. Yet here no one is hearing these stories with expectancy; everyone has faced that which at one time was unthinkable. It's as if we're all in the same club, as if we have all finally arrived, as if we could all look back at those women on the other side and know we are totally new.

One woman talked about that inconsolable stabbing in the heart when she realized she wouldn't buy a Christmas present for her mother again this year. I've wondered about it, about perhaps having grieved the separation between my mother and me in my early childhood, for, in a way, I truly do not miss her like that, do not feel that irreversible moment of no return, as I did when she would go into the bathroom and shut the door, the ache that breaks the heart and has no answer. I felt the goneness of her then, as if the center of me was gone, and I tried to bring it back by peering through the crack at the bottom of the door, trying to see anything, even her feet.

I said this to the women who talked last night about their mothers. One woman, who said that her mother had died a few days after she was born, had always struck me before as cold, contained, and now, as she spoke, I noticed she was squeezing the fleshy part of her cheek, near her mouth, making a little fat bubble of flesh between her ring and baby fingers. I have seen that before, a kind of clumsy, unconscious pinching of the self, and it makes me feel great pity. Her fingers seemed squat, doing an act whose purpose I couldn't imagine—perhaps a partial holding to signify that she could not hold the whole of what she needed held. Now, clumsily, here was her body (was it her clumsy body that had killed her mother, ungracefully slipping out?)—her liveliness covered by a dreary cape, her hair dreary, her face unmade, as if who would care?—speaking about her mother's death (we had never heard of this, though we had known her for years!)

1317

without tears, just those two fingers clenching and opening, pinching a clump of cheek, letting go and clenching again, moving slightly, as if she couldn't find the right spot, and since the cheek is larger than what those two fingers can grasp, and since the two fingers form a small vise and take in only a slot of flesh, it seemed she was stopping the flesh from moving, clamping it in place. It seemed inadequate, incomplete, and ill chosen; in literature, the small thing signifies the whole of something we can imagine from the reference to the small thing, but here, the small reference did not convey. It was a clumsy effort, as a child might pinch the breast. Or perhaps it was an effort to make another mouth, to pucker the face, as the lips of the child might pucker for its mother's breast.

At my mother's grave, I tried to imagine what I should do. My partner had 5 taken my picture at the grave and a picture of the inscription. He was sitting in the car. How long should I stay? My mind didn't know what to settle on. No particular feeling or idea carried me. I became lost in nothing. Just me, stuttering over an immensity that I couldn't absorb, the way I used to feel guilty for not feeling enough happiness at Christmas, after my mother's great efforts. I guess I felt that I was incompetent, too broken to hold. I sang her favorite song: "This little light of mine, I'm gonna let it shine." I wanted to give her a promise; I wanted to change my life because of her, just the way I did before.

I am struck by my own inability to feel grief. It feels like a refusal to face an end. I know I have great trouble facing boundaries, my own and others'. So, instead, perhaps there is this magical thinking built on my own inadequacy to face the truth: I say I get messages from my mother, that she is still in my life, and now, perhaps even more, she is reaching me, since her destruction is out of my way.

Once, when I called a friend to say I couldn't go on teaching at the prestigious workshop I was visiting because I could not stand the torturing voices in my head, twenty-four hours a day, saying I was no good, stupid, not as smart as the others, not as respected or loved, that I had no value, that I was there only because I was black, that I had done or said the wrong thing, that I was not really a poet, my friend said, "Why not ask the torturing voices from where they get their information?" I did, and without hesitation they answered, "From your mother."

Things had changed by then, so I flipped back, "You haven't got the latest information!"

Just a few months before she died, my mother turned the universe of an unloved daughter around with one sentence. Instead of screaming at me when I asked her not to come to one of my readings because I might read things that would make her uncomfortable, she said, "Oh, dear, would you be uncomfortable? I don't want you to be uncomfortable, so I won't come."

I've written a lot about messages from her—I won't repeat them here—just 10 to say my conversation with my mother isn't over, and I think it isn't over for her, either.

In the manuscript of my mother's book, I read about the women in her childhood—her mother, aunts, and grandmother—who helped each other beyond the bounds of the imaginable. Because of their hard labor, our family succeeded. I read this manuscript, which she put into my hands to publish only two days before her death, and I think that, although my mother began writing after I did, after I was published, she was a writer before she began writing. Though she is dead, our stories are in dialogue: my writing has been against her writing, as if there was a war between us. It is more than our writing that is in dialogue; it is our lives.

When I was seven, she told me how, when she left the house of the rich white people her mother worked for, the white kids were waiting to beat her up on her way to school, and as soon as she crossed the line to the black part of town, the black kids were there to beat her up too. Why would she tell me that story? Why would a mother tell a seven-year-old such a sad story, such a defeating one? I thought it was her way of saying, "Trust no one but your mother," a way of binding me to her by making me fear.

It's a question—what she said and did that I didn't understand, what she did to hurt me. It is not over; it is still a riddle being solved. I do not need to be held, and so, therefore, isn't my mother free too? Is that why she told me those stories? Was I to be the mother who freed her?

My partner and I have just spent a delightful weekend together, a sunny, windy fall weekend with the trees half shredded, the bright blue sky both miraculous and unavoidable through the nude branches and their silence. On the drive home, my mind comes to how my life has changed since my mother's death: slowly, I have been loosed from those heavy, nearly inconsolable fears like Houdini's chains, lock by lock, as if some magician part of me occasionally appears, from some unseen and undetectable room, with one more chain gone. Finally, I am gloriously undrowned.

Everyone says that I changed for the better, as if, when my mother's slight body, not even one hundred pounds, slipped into the earth, the whole world suddenly belonged to me. The first year I stopped jogging. People said it was grief, but whatever grief felt like—except for the first few days after her death, especially the burial day, heavy lodestar—it was too indistinct for me to grab on to. Two years later, I bought a house and found a man in my life, like a spectacular hat pin in just the right hat. The simple explanation would have been my mother's narcissism—the way she pushed me toward independence, screaming, "You're weighing me down," and yet, when I was sixteen and came in late one night, slamming the door, she was behind it in the shadows, like a burglar, and her hand went around my neck while she screamed, "I'll kill you!" Who hasn't wanted to kill the one she loved? 15

But there was so much unaccounted for, so much in my mother's past that I couldn't fix, not ever, or make up for. Maybe my mother never had such a weekend of happiness with a man as I have just had, though a former lover of hers once told me, when I asked about the affair, how much she had loved to make love to him. Perhaps he told me because he loved me and thought I should know that aspect of my mother, because knowing might help me put a necessary piece in the puzzle. Perhaps he had sympathy for me—in spite of the fact he had loved my mother—and didn't feel the need to protect her. Perhaps he thought it was better to give a daughter that important piece than to keep still about a dead woman. And perhaps he was bragging a bit when he said it.

My mother had slept alone, in another room, in another bed, for eighteen years of her marriage, until my parents divorced. I never saw her kiss my father, and the only touch was the time I heard him smash her against the table. My mother always gave abundantly with one hand and pushed you away with the other. The mystery of a beautiful woman. Perhaps in some reciprocal way, my unhappy, angry, guilt-producing mother had also been a planter, had been planting the seeds of my happiness with an invisible hand, the hand I didn't see. She left me enough money to buy a house. She told me all my life she loved me, as if she completely forgot the hundred slights, humiliations, threats, and insinuations. Of course she loved me; why would I think otherwise? She loved me more than anything. Sometimes she'd scream, as if my doubts were another evil, another proof of my unworthiness. How exasperating my complaints must have been when, all along, she was planting seeds with that invisible hand.

The women of that generation, my mother and aunts, counted their blessings: Chinese food and beer on Friday nights after work, and fried chicken breasts, twice-baked potatoes, and broccoli for early Sunday afternoon dinners. And there were parties with bounteous tables; polished glasses and silver, a chandelier, every bauble; ammonia-shiny; and heat's seven coolnesses, the little cups of rice turned over and decorated, each small, white breast with a nipple of parsley. Polished floors, shopping trips, lunch at Hudson's—these were the good things, the punctuation marks that held back despondency, that danced away despair. No hardship was unredeemable to women who had one endless belief: bread on the water always comes home. It wasn't until I was in my sixties that I realized it did, but not necessarily to the ones who cast it. I am eating bread from hands that are no longer there. I cannot reach back to touch their actual bodies. It is good that they are gone.

My mother helps me. She sends me signs: her African violet bloomed for the first time on my windowsill three years after her death, on the first day of her death month. She says, "Remember me. My miracles are still there for you, still becoming apparent as you have eyes to see." I love my mother now in ways I could not have loved her when she was alive, fierce, terrifying, unpredictable, mad, shame-inducing, self-involved, relentless, and determined by any means necessary. When she was a child, to get what she wanted from her mother, she would hold her breath until she was blue and pass out. Even if she had to inflict the greatest pain—making me see her suffer, making me fear her death and that I had caused it—she would do it without thinking; without hesitation. That worst threat was always between us—that she could take herself away, that she could hurt herself in my eyes—and it was out of my control to stop it. She was the hostage of an insane government, her own body. And so I revoked my love: I took away, as much as I could, the only real currency between us. I would not count on her to save me from her death. And therefore I saved myself by cutting the part of my heart that was in her heart; I cut it off as if snipping a pigtail. It is only now, when I am at a safe distance, that my heart begins to grow again, as if a surgeon has inserted a little gray balloon to open it up to blood. There begins to be an invisible cell, a chamber, a thumping like the thump inside the embryo shell, tissues paper thin, of hardly any substance, except that, somewhere in it, it still knows what it is, what it will grow up to be used for.

FOR ANALYSIS

1. Why is Derricotte unable to feel grief?

2. What is the nature of the messages the author says she gets from her mother?

3. How does her mother now help her?

MAKING CONNECTIONS

In paragraph 15, Derricotte writes, "Who hasn't wanted to kill the one she loved?" Compare the violence in "Beginning Dialogues" to that in Talusan's "My Father's Noose" (p. 1078). Is it of a similar nature? Does it spring from similar sources? Does it have similar effects?

WRITING TOPICS

1. "Beginning Dialogues" is not structured as a seamless, flowing argument or narrative. Describe how it is structured instead, and consider how this structure works for this subject. Can you envision this essay written in a more traditional fashion? Would it have been better, worse, or just different?

2. Reflect on your reactions to the essay. When Derricotte writes that she does not feel grief, that she is better off since her mother has died, that it is good that her mother is gone, how do you feel? What does that tell you about your expectations for how people should feel in this kind of situation?

MAUREEN STANTON   (B. 1960)

WATER   1995

I see that old woman every now and then at the Y, the one who is not a lunch meat lover. She swims, as I do. She swims in a pair of black shorts and a black shirt. She is ashamed to show her loose, curdled flesh in front of the old men in the hot tub, with their big bellies and skinny legs, red faced, eyeing the teen-age girls splashing each other.

She's been coming here every day for seventeen years. She swims a half-mile, I heard her tell someone. Her swimming is more like walking and treading than swimming, so slow I pass her three times before she reaches the end of the pool. Underwater, blurry and dark, she is like a manatee, slow and graceful, as if her ancestors dwelled in the water, like the water is her voice.

I, on the other hand, am fast. I am faster than any of the other swimmers. My arms are long and they easily pull the water to me. My legs are pure muscle and they push me along. I glide through the water like a slippery fish. The water flows in and out of my mouth, like a filter separating air from water, like gills, and I feel like a fish. I am a fish.

I do a turn at the end of each length, a near, tucked somersault, efficient and powerful, propelled by my fins. I submerge and glide, scissor kick and go deeper, rise for air. I swim back and forth, one end to the other like the neon tetras in my tank at home. And each time I pass over a bobby pin at the bottom of the pool, or a Band-Aid, a rubber band. It makes me feel lonely. I stare down at the one-inch-square, dirty blue and white tiles at the bottom of the pool. Some are missing. It reminds me of when I was a child, scared of driving through Callahan Tunnel in Boston because little squares of tiles had fallen out. Water dripped from the celling, and I imagined more tiles popping off from the pressure and then water from Boston Harbor bursting through, rushing in, drowning us. Like a tidal wave.

I was never afraid of the ocean until I thought I could swim so well that I   5
owned it, until once in California when I was a fearless teen-ager I swam out to some pelicans and couldn't get back in. No matter how hard I swam 1 still was being dragged farther and farther out to sea. I panicked. I put my face In the water and paddled my arms as hard as I could, and finally stepped down and touched soft sand on the ocean floor. I was never the same in the ocean. Never again let myself be seaweed and let the waves tumble me about until my bathing suit is full of sand, and weak and chilled fall onto the warmth of my towel to let the sun bake me.

On top of the water I am fast, like a water bug. But underneath, to myself, swimming, everything is in slow motion, dreamy. Underwater I am honest. I am left with myself. My lungs, my heart, my thoughts. When I swim I fantasize.

I invent my life. Scenes are acted out in my mind. I am confident. I am witty. I am sleek and smart, and sophisticated. I am a poet of the sea. I am a painter, an athlete, a walker, a hermit on a mountain. I am dreaming. Fish water water water. I talked in my sleep once, and my friend told me I said that. Fish water water water. It has become my mantra.

After our laps, we sit in the hot tub. I and the old woman and others I don't know. Once she said to anyone, "We're blessed, ain't we?" And no one answered her. They just stared at each other. I stare too. It's because we are afraid. We are exposed. We come waddling out of the locker room. Fat hangs off our arms and legs and necks. Nipples and penises are outlined in wet bathing suits. Makeup is washed away. Hair is flattened. Baldness shows. People look like they were just born, wet and slick and ugly. They are honest.

There is a man I see often at the Y. He has broad shoulders and takes bold strokes. He has distinguished, graying hair and looks like a corporate executive. I thought he was, until one day I recognized a man in the airport and placed him as the corporate executive swimmer at the Y. His uniform pulled his shoulders down, he seemed too tall for his job, barely fit under the electronic metal detector, as he took a woman's belongings and put them in a Tupperware container, asked her to pass through again. And after that, when I saw him at the Y, I thought he could see right through me, because I can see through him. I know him now, know he is not a corporate executive, but a man who stands in the airport all day, watching people come and go, looking inside their bags and purses. But still he swims fast with strong, powerful arms that make him seem like a giant, like a great white.

There was another man who I only saw in the hot tub once. He struck up a conversation like he was lighting a cigar and puffing until he got it going, asking me if I ever listened to the radio, liked that new jazz station. I said no.

"I'm tired of listening to country, all they ever do is cry about a broken 10 heart. I know enough about that, my wife left me two weeks ago after eighteen years. She was twenty years younger than me."

"That's too bad," I said. I am not good at small talk.

"How old do you think I look?" he asked, I thought he looked sixty so I said, "Fifty-five?"

He said proudly, "Sixty-one."

"Nice talking to you," he said and shook my hand like we were in a business meeting, and he stepped out of the hot tub in his bathing trunks and I felt like I was acting in a movie.

It happens a lot to me, on buses and in supermarkets. Once a woman at the 15 grocery store told me about her life, taking all the time she wanted to ring up my items, hesitating, holding my canned ham in her hand, shaking it at me when she wanted to make a point, throwing my tomatoes into the bag because she was angry about her boyfriend cheating on her and leaving her. I said, "Maybe you could start over," and she said, "Nah, too many broken promises, too many shattered dreams." And she gave me my change and picked up the tabloid she was reading with Sarah Ferguson and Lady Diana on the cover.

I take a shower after sitting in the hot tub, and the old woman is there too. Her belly falls below her pubic area so you can't see her hair there, and her skin is gathered together, stretched out from so much use, years and years of movement. Her legs are like logs, her ankles and knees are lost. She puts her dripping clothes into the new machine in the women's locker room which dries them out through centrifugal force. She turns to a lady behind her. "Ain't that wonderful?"

After her shower, she asks someone to rub lotion on her back. Her wide, white, curved back. She asks anyone who happens to be around. I've seen her. A kind stranger softens her back with lotion and she talks.

"My son and his wife are coming over today so I am making my special casserole with tomatoes and green peppers and rice and cheese."

And the other woman said. "I have a wonderful casserole that I make with peas and noodles and deli loaf."

"Oh, I'm not a lunch meat lover," the old woman says. It sounded to me like 20 a sad poem. They talk about leftovers, what keeps, what doesn't, as the stranger kneads the old woman's back. She closes her eyes and says, "You don't know how much I appreciate that."

One day I see the woman who is not a lunch meat lover with a gadget, a towel thing with handles that lets her rub her own back, which she uses when no one is around. Some days I want to see her, with her short cropped hair, that yarn yellow of blondes when they get old, not gray or silver but like the color of her teeth. Other days I don't want to see her, cheerful and happy because we have a bathing suit dryer or a hot tub.

She looks at me and I glance away. But our eyes touch, enough for her to ask me if I would mind rubbing lotion on her back. Slowly, I put some cold lotion in my hand and touch her soft, ashy skin and she begins to talk. She says she used to be a dancer and worked on Broadway and then taught dance lessons.

"You like to swim," I said to her.

"Oh, that's not swimming," she said. "That's ballet."

I rub the lotion into her skin, and add more, basting, and coating and mov- 25 ing my hand all over her back without taking it off, like her back was a Ouija board and my hand, moving mysteriously, would reveal something to me. I start to cry, silently, tears streaming down my face, and she reaches around and touches my arm and says, "There, there."

FOR ANALYSIS

1. How is the author feeling in the moments she narrates in this essay? How does she generally feel while in the pool? How does that differ from when she is out of the pool?

2. Why is it important that the woman "who is not a lunch meat lover" is old? How does the author feel about aging?

3. Why does the author cry at the end of the essay?

MAKING CONNECTIONS

Compare "Water" to the selections in "Connecting Stories: Companions to the End." How does the relationship between Stanton and the old woman compare to the relationships in those stories?

WRITING TOPICS

1. Midway through "Water," Stanton tells a story about an incident at the beach when she was a teenager. Reflect on how that anecdote works in the larger essay and on the use of anecdotes generally. How does "Water" incorporate its anecdotes? To what end does it employ them? Does it manage to sew them into a neat pattern? Does it lay them across each other more randomly or only apparently so?

2. How does Stanton capture the feeling of loneliness in her essay? What kinds of literary techniques does she use to imply the **theme,** to evoke the feeling, to illustrate its effects?

JILL CHRISTMAN   (B. 1969)

THE SLOTH   2002

There is a nothingness of temperature, a point on the body's mercury where our blood feels neither hot nor cold. I remember a morning swim on the black sand eastern coast of Costa Rica four months after my twenty-two-year-old fiancé was killed in a car accident. Walking into the water, disembodied by grief, I felt no barriers between my skin, the air, and the water.

Later, standing under a trickle of water in the wooden outdoor shower, I heard a rustle, almost soundless, and looking up, expecting something small, I saw my first three-toed sloth. Mottled and filthy, he hung by his meat-hook claws not five feet above my head in the cecropia tree. He peered down at me, his flattened head turned backwards on his neck. Here is a fact: a sloth cannot regulate the temperature of his blood. He must live near the equator.

I thought I knew slow, but this guy, this guy was *slow*. The sound I heard was his wiry-haired blond elbow, brushed green with living algae, stirring a leaf as he reached for the next branch. Pressing my wet palms onto the rough wooden walls, I watched the sloth move in the shadows of the canopy. Still reaching. And then still reaching.

What else is this slow? Those famous creatures of slow—the snail, the tortoise—they move faster. Much. This slow seemed impossible, not real, like a trick of my sad head. Dripping and naked in the jungle, I thought, *That sloth is as slow as grief.* We were numb to the speed of the world. We were one temperature.

FOR ANALYSIS

1. What emotion other than grief is present in this essay?

2. How does the author approach the subject of her grief? What are the effects of writing about it in this way? Would representing it and discussing it more directly have been more or less effective for you?

MAKING CONNECTIONS

Read "The Sloth" with any or all of the selections in "Connecting Poems: Animal Fates." How does Christman's use of the sloth compare to the way these other writers use animals in their work?

WRITING TOPIC

Write about a time when you felt something strongly. Is there an animal you could have compared yourself to? How?

These two essays explore the ways we think about the past—the way we remember it, the way we long for it, the way we create it out of whole cloth. Known as great stylists, E. B. White and David Sedaris focus in rich descriptive detail on the surface of things but always manage to touch on bigger issues below that surface. As you read, keep an eye out for the ways in which these writers confront important issues and deep emotions while using a light, stylish hand.

E. B. WHITE   (1899–1985)

ONCE MORE TO THE LAKE   1941

One summer, along about 1904, my father rented a camp on a lake in Maine and took us all there for the month of August. We all got ringworm from some kittens and had to rub Pond's Extract on our arms and legs night and morning, and my father rolled over in a canoe with all his clothes on; but outside of that the vacation was a success and from then on none of us ever thought there was any place in the world like that lake in Maine. We returned summer after summer—always on August 1st for one month. I have since become a saltwater man, but sometimes in summer there are days when the restlessness of the tides and the fearful cold of the sea water and the incessant wind which blows across the afternoon and into the evening make me wish for the placidity of a lake in the woods. A few weeks ago this feeling got so strong I bought myself a couple of bass hooks and a spinner and returned to the lake where we used to go, for a week's fishing and to revisit old haunts.

I took along my son, who had never had any fresh water up his nose and who had seen lily pads only from train windows. On the journey over to the lake I began to wonder what it would be like. I wondered how time would have marred this unique, this holy spot—the coves and streams, the hills that the sun set behind, the camps and the paths behind the camps. I was sure that the tarred road would have found it out and I wondered in what other ways it would be desolated. It is strange how much you can remember about places like that once you allow your mind to return into the grooves which lead back. You remember one thing, and that suddenly reminds you of another thing. I guess I remembered clearest of all the early mornings, when the lake was cool and motionless, remembered how the bedroom smelled of the lumber it was made of and of the wet woods whose scent entered through the screen. The partitions in the camp were thin and did not extend clear to the top of the rooms, and as I was always the first up I would dress softly so as not to wake the others, and sneak out into the sweet outdoors and start out in the canoe, keeping close along the shore in the long shadows of the pines. I remembered being very careful never to rub my paddle against the gunwale for fear of disturbing the stillness of the cathedral.

The lake had never been what you would call a wild lake. There were cottages sprinkled around the shores, and it was in farming country although the shores of the lake were quite heavily wooded. Some of the cottages were owned by nearby farmers, and you would live at the shore and eat your meals at the farmhouse. That's what our family did. But although it wasn't wild, it was a fairly large and undisturbed lake and there were places in it which, to a child at least, seemed infinitely remote and primeval.

I was right about the tar: it led to within half a mile of the shore. But when I got back there, with my boy, and we settled into a camp near a farmhouse and into the kind of summertime I had known, I could tell that it was going to be pretty much the same as it had been before—I knew it, lying in bed the first morning, smelling the bedroom, and hearing the boy sneak quietly out and go off along the shore in a boat. I began to sustain the illusion that he was I, and therefore, by simple transposition, that I was my father. This sensation persisted, kept cropping up all the time we were there. It was not an entirely new feeling, but in this setting it grew much stronger. I seemed to be living a dual existence. I would be in the middle of some simple act, I would be picking up a bait box or laying down a table fork, or I would be saying something, and suddenly it would be not I but my father who was saying the words or making the gesture. It gave me a creepy sensation.

We went fishing the first morning. I felt the same damp moss covering the 5 worms in the bait can, and saw the dragonfly alight on the tip of my rod as it hovered a few inches from the surface of the water. It was the arrival of this fly that convinced me beyond any doubt that everything was as it always had been, that the years were a mirage and there had been no years. The small waves were the same, chucking the rowboat under the chin as we shed at anchor, and the boat was the same boat, the same color green and the ribs broken in the same places, and under the floor-boards the same freshwater leavings and débris—the dead helgramite, the wisps of moss, the rusty discarded fishhook, the dried blood from yesterday's catch. We stared silently at the tips of our rods, at the dragonflies that came and went. I lowered the tip of mine into the water, tentatively, pensively dislodging the fly, which darted two feet away, poised, darted two feet back, and came to rest again a little farther up the rod. There had been no years between the ducking of this dragonfly and the other one—the one that was part of memory. I looked at the boy, who was silently watching his fly, and it was my hands that held his rod, my eyes watching. I felt dizzy and didn't know which rod I was at the end of.

We caught two bass, hauling them in briskly as though they were mackerel, pulling them over the side of the boat in a businesslike manner without any landing net, and stunning them with a blow on the back of the head. When we got back for a swim before lunch, the lake was exactly where we had left it, the same number of inches from the dock, and there was only the merest suggestion of a breeze. This seemed an utterly enchanted sea, this lake you could leave to its own devices for a few hours and come back to, and find that it had not stirred, this constant and trustworthy body of water. In the shallows, the dark, water-soaked sticks and twigs, smooth and old, were undulating in clusters on the bottom against the clean ribbed sand, and the track of the mussel was plain. A school of minnows swam by, each minnow with its small, individual shadow, doubling the attendance, so clear and sharp in the sunlight. Some of the other campers were in swimming, along the shore, one of them with a cake of soap, and the water felt thin and clear and insubstantial. Over the years there had been this person with the cake of soap, this cultist, and here he was. There had been no years.

Up to the farmhouse to dinner through the teeming, dusty field, the road under our sneakers was only a two-track road. The middle track was missing, the one with the marks of the hooves and the splotches of dried, flaky manure. There had always been three tracks to choose from in choosing which track to walk in; now the choice was narrowed down to two. For a moment I missed terribly the middle alternative. But the way led past the tennis court, and something about the way it lay there in the sun reassured me; the tape had loosened along the backline, the alleys were green with plantains and other weeds, and the net (installed in June and removed in September) sagged in the dry noon, and the whole place steamed with midday heat and hunger and emptiness. There was a choice of pie for dessert, and one was blueberry and one was apple, and the waitresses were the same country girls, there having been no passage of time, only the illusion of it as in a dropped curtain—the waitresses were still fifteen; their hair had been washed, that was the only difference—they had been to the movies and seen the pretty girls with the clean hair.

Summertime, oh summertime, pattern of life indelible, the fade proof lake, the woods unshatterable, the pasture with the sweetfern and the juniper forever and ever, summer without end; this was the background, and the life along the shore was the design, the cottages with their innocent and tranquil design, their tiny docks with the flagpole and the American flag floating against the white clouds in the blue sky, the little paths over the roots of the trees leading from camp to camp and the paths leading back to the outhouses and the can of lime for sprinkling, and at the souvenir counters at the store the miniature birch-bark canoes and the post cards that showed things looking a little better than they looked. This was the American family at play, escaping the city heat, wondering whether the newcomers at the camp at the head of the cove were "common" or "nice," wondering whether it was true that the people who drove up for Sunday dinner at the farmhouse were turned away because there wasn't enough chicken.

It seemed to me, as I kept remembering all this, that those times and those summers had been infinitely precious and worth saving. There had been jollity and peace and goodness. The arriving (at the beginning of August) had been so big a business in itself, at the railway station the farm wagon drawn up, the first smell of the pineladen air, the first glimpse of the smiling farmer, and the great importance of the trunks and your father's enormous authority in such matters, and the feel of the wagon under you for the long ten-mile haul, and at the top of the last long hill catching the first view of the lake after eleven months of not seeing this cherished body of water. The shouts and cries of the other campers when they saw you, and the trunks to be unpacked, to give up their rich burden. (Arriving was less exciting nowadays, when you sneaked up in your car and parked it under a tree near the camp and took out the bags and in five minutes it was all over, no fuss, no loud wonderful fuss about trunks.)

Peace and goodness and jollity. The only thing that was wrong now, really, was   10
the sound of the place, an unfamiliar nervous sound of the outboard motors. This was the note that jarred, the one thing that would sometimes break the illusion and set the years moving. In those other summertimes, all motors were inboard; and when they were at a little distance, the noise they made was a sedative, an ingredient of summer sleep. They were one-cylinder and two-cylinder engines, and some were make-and-break and some were jump-spark, but they all made a sleepy sound across the lake. The one-lungers throbbed and muttered, and the twin-cylinder ones purred and purred, and that was a quiet sound too. But now the campers all had outboards. In the daytime, in the hot mornings, these motors made a petulant, irritable sound; at night, in the still evening when the afterglow lit the water, they whined about one's ears like mosquitoes. My boy loved our rented outboard, and his great desire was to achieve singlehanded mastery over it, and authority, and he soon learned the trick of choking it a little (but not too much), and the adjustment of the needle valve. Watching him I would remember the things you could do with the old one-cylinder engine with the heavy flywheel, how you could have it eating out of your hand if you got really close to it spiritually. Motor boats in those days didn't have clutches, and you would make a landing by shutting off the motor at the proper time and coasting in with a dead rudder. But there was a way of reversing them, if you learned the trick, by cutting the switch and putting it on again exactly on the final dying revolution of the flywheel, so that it would kick back against compression and begin reversing. Approaching a dock in a strong following breeze, it was difficult to slow up sufficiently by the ordinary coasting method, and if a boy felt he had complete mastery over his motor, he was tempted to keep it running beyond its time and then reverse it a few feet from the dock. It took a cool nerve, because if you threw the switch a twentieth of a second too soon you could catch the flywheel when it still had speed enough to go up past center, and the boat would leap ahead, charging bull-fashion at the dock.

We had a good week at the camp. The bass were biting well and the sun shone endlessly, day after day. We would be tired at night and lie down in the accumulated heat of the little bedrooms after the long hot day and the breeze would stir almost imperceptibly outside and the smell of the swamp drift in through the rusty screens. Sleep would come easily and in the morning the red squirrel would be on the roof, tapping out his gay routine. I kept remembering everything, lying in bed in the mornings—the small steamboat that had a long rounded stern like the lip of a Ubangi, and how quietly she ran on the moonlight sails, when the older boys played their mandolins and the girls sang and we ate doughnuts dipped in sugar, and how sweet the music was on the water in the shining night, and what it had felt like to think about girls then. After breakfast we would go up to the store and the things were in the same place—the minnows in a bottle, the plugs and spinners disarranged and pawed over by the youngsters from the boys' camp, the fig newtons and the Beeman's gum. Outside, the road was tarred and cars stood in front of the store. Inside, all was just as it had always been, except there was more Coca-Cola and not so much Moxie and root beer and birch beer and sarsaparilla. We would walk out with a bottle of pop apiece and sometimes the pop would backfire up our noses and hurt. We explored the streams, quietly, where the turtles slid off the sunny logs and dug their way into the soft bottom; and we lay on the town wharf and fed worms to the tame bass. Everywhere we went I had trouble making out which was I, the one walking at my side, the one walking in my pants.

One afternoon while we were there at that lake a thunderstorm came up. It was like the revival of an old melodrama that I had seen long ago with childish awe. The second-act climax of the drama of the electrical disturbance over a lake in America had not changed in any important respect. This was the big scene, still the big scene. The whole thing was so familiar, the first feeling of oppression and heat and a general air around camp of not wanting to go very far away. In mid-afternoon (it was all the same) a curious darkening of the sky, and a lull in everything that had made life tick; and then the way the boats suddenly swung the other way at their moorings with the coming of a breeze out of the new quarter, and the premonitory rumble. Then the kettle drum, then the snare, then the bass drum and cymbals, then crackling light against the dark, and the gods grinning and licking their chops in the hills. Afterward the calm, the rain steadily rustling in the calm lake, the return of light and hope and spirits, and the campers running out in joy and relief to go swimming in the rain, their bright cries perpetuating the deathless joke about how they were getting simply drenched, and the children screaming with delight at the new sensation of bathing in the rain, and the joke about getting drenched linking the generations in a strong indestructible chain. And the comedian who waded in carrying an umbrella.

When the others went swimming my son said he was going in too. He pulled his dripping trunks from the line where they had hung all through the shower, and wrung them out. Languidly, and with no thought of going in, I watched him, his hard little body, skinny and bare, saw him wince slightly as he pulled up around his vitals the small, soggy, icy garment. As he buckled the swollen belt suddenly my groin felt the chill of death.

FOR ANALYSIS

1. How is the lake the same as it was in the past? How has it changed?

2. Why is it important that White brings his son along on this trip?

3. What does the trip remind White of? What does that reminiscence make him aware of?

WRITING TOPICS

1. Note the kinds of details White selects in painting his portrait of the lake. Reflect on his choices: Why is the lake "fade-proof," the woods "unshatterable"?

2. Write a short narrative of a trip you took or a visit you made that brought you back to when you were younger. Try to include as much descriptive detail as you can, and try to make that detail work to express the feelings you had.

DAVID SEDARIS (B. 1956)

THIS OLD HOUSE 2007

When it came to decorating her home, my mother was nothing if not practical. She learned early on that children will destroy whatever you put in front of them, so for most of my youth our furniture was chosen for its durability rather than for its beauty. The one exception was the dining-room set, which my parents bought shortly after they were married. Should a guest eye the buffet for longer than a second, my mother would notice and jump in to prompt a compliment. "You like it?" she'd ask. "It's Scandinavian!" This, we learned, was the name of a region—a cold and forsaken place where people stayed indoors and plotted the death of knobs.

The buffet, like the table, was an exercise in elegant simplicity. The set was made of teak, and had been finished with tung oil. This brought out the character of the wood, allowing it, at certain times of day, to practically glow. Nothing was more beautiful than our dining room, especially after my father covered the walls with cork. It wasn't the kind you use on bulletin boards but something coarse and dark, the color of damp pine mulch. Light the candles beneath the chafing dish, lay the table with the charcoal-textured dinnerware we hardly ever used, and you had yourself a real picture.

This dining room, I liked to think, was what my family was all about. Throughout my childhood, it brought me great pleasure, but then I turned sixteen and decided that I didn't like it anymore. What happened was a television show, a weekly drama about a close-knit family in Depression-era Virginia. The family didn't have a blender or a country-club membership, but they did have one another—that and a really great house, an old one, built in the twenties or something. All their bedrooms had slanted clapboard walls and oil lamps that bathed everything in fragile golden light. I wouldn't have used the word *romantic*, but that's how I thought of it.

"You think those prewar years were cozy?" my father once asked. "Try getting up at 5 A.M. to sell newspapers on the snow-covered streets. That's what I did and it stunk to high heaven."

"Well," I told him, "I'm just sorry that you weren't able to appreciate it."   5

Like anyone nostalgic for a time he didn't live through, I chose to weed out the little inconveniences: polio, say, or the thought of eating stewed squirrel.

The world was simply grander back then, somehow more civilized, and nicer to look at. Wasn't it crushing to live in a house no older than our cat?

"No," my father said. "Not at all."

My mother felt the same: "Boxed in by neighbors, having to walk through my parents' bedroom in order to reach the kitchen. If you think that was fun, you never saw your grandfather with his teeth out."

They were more than willing to leave their pasts behind them, and reacted strongly when my sister Gretchen and I began dragging it home. "The *Andrews* Sisters?" my father groaned. "What the hell do you want to listen to them for?"

When I started buying clothes from Goodwill, he really went off, and for 10 good reason, probably. The suspenders and knickers were bad enough, but when I added a top hat he planted himself in the doorway and physically prevented me from leaving the house. "It doesn't make sense," I remember him saying. "That hat with those pants, worn with the damn platform shoes . . ." His speech temporarily left him, and he found himself waving his hands, no doubt wishing that they held magic wands. "You're just . . . a mess is what you are."

The way I saw it, the problem wasn't my outfit but my context. Sure I looked out of place beside a Scandinavian buffet, but put me in the proper environment and I'd undoubtedly fit right in.

"The environment you're looking for is called a psychiatric hospital," my father said. "Now give me the damn hat before I burn it off."

I longed for a home where history was respected—and, four years later, I finally found one. This was in Chapel Hill, North Carolina. I'd gone there to visit an old friend from high school—and because I was between jobs, and had no real obligations, I decided to stay for a while and maybe look for some dishwashing work. The restaurant that hired me was a local institution, all dark wood and windowpanes the size of playing cards. The food was O.K., but what the place was really known for was the classical music that the man in charge, someone named Byron, pumped into the dining room. Anyone else might have thrown in a compilation tape, but he took his responsibilities very seriously, and planned each meal as if it were an evening at Tanglewood. I hoped that dish washing might lead to a job in the dining room, busing tables, and, eventually, waiting on them, but I kept these aspirations to myself. Dressed as I was, in jodhpurs and a smoking jacket, I should have been grateful that I was hired at all.

After getting my first paycheck, I scouted out a place to live. My two requirements were that it be cheap and close to where I worked, and on both counts I succeeded. I couldn't have dreamed that it would also be old and untouched, an actual boarding house. The owner was adjusting her "Room for Rent" sign as I passed, and our eyes locked in an expression that said, "Hark, stranger, you are one of me!" Both of us looked like figures from a scratchy newsreel: me the unemployed factory worker in tortoiseshell safety glasses and a tweed overcoat two sizes too large, and her, the feisty widow lady, taking in boarders in order to make ends meet. "Excuse me," I called, "but is that hat from the forties?"

The woman put her hands to her head and adjusted what looked like a fistful 15
of cherries spilling from a velveteen saucer. "Why, yes it is," she said. "How canny
of you to notice." I'll say that her name was Rosemary Dowd, and, as she introduced herself, I tried to guess her age. What foxed me was her makeup, which
was on the heavy side, and involved a great deal of peach-colored powder. From
a distance, her hair looked white, but now I could see that it was streaked with
yellow, almost randomly, like snow that had been peed on. If she seemed somewhat mannish, it was the fault of her clothing rather than her features. Both her
jacket and her blouse were kitted out with shoulder pads, and when they were
worn together she could barely fit through the door. This might be a problem for
others, but Rosemary didn't get out much. And why would she want to?

I hadn't even crossed the threshold when I agreed to take the room. What
sold me was the look of the place. Some might have found it shabby—
"a dump," my father would eventually call it—but, unless you ate them, a few
thousand paint chips never hurt anyone. The same could be said for the groaning front porch and the occasional missing shingle. It was easy to imagine that
the house, set as it was, on the lip of a student parking lot, had dropped from
the sky, like Dorothy's in *The Wizard of Oz*, but with a second story. Then there
was the inside, which was even better. The front door opened into a living
room, or, as Rosemary called it, "the parlor." The word was old-fashioned, but
fitting. Velvet curtains framed the windows. The walls were papered in a faint,
floral pattern, and doilies were everywhere, laid flat on tabletops and sagging
like cobwebs from the backs of overstuffed chairs. My eyes moved from one
thing to another, and, like my mother with her dining-room set, Rosemary
took note of where they landed. "I see you like my davenport," she said, and,
"You don't find lamps like that anymore. It's a genuine Stephanie."

It came as no surprise that she bought and sold antiques, or "dabbled" in
them, as she said. Every available surface was crowded with objects: green-glass
candy dishes, framed photographs of movie stars, cigarette boxes with mono-
grammed lids. An umbrella leaned against an open steamer trunk, and, when I
observed that its handle was Bakelite, my new landlady unpinned her saucer of
cherries and predicted that the two of us were going to get along famously.

And for many months we did. Rosemary lived on the ground floor, in a set
of closed-off rooms she referred to as her chambers. The door that led to them
opened onto the parlor, and when I stood outside I could sometimes hear her
television. This seemed to me a kind of betrayal, like putting a pool table inside
the Great Pyramid, but she assured me that the set was an old one—"My
'Model Tee Vee,'" she called it.

My room was upstairs, and in letters home I described it as "hunky-dory."
How else to capture my peeling, buckled wallpaper, and the way that it
brought everything together. The bed, the desk, the brass-plated floor lamp: it
was all there waiting for me, and though certain pieces had seen better days—
the guest chair, for instance, was missing its seat—at least everything was uni-
formly old. From my window I could see the parking lot and, beyond that, the
busy road leading to the restaurant. It pleased Rosemary that I worked in such

a venerable place. "It suits you," she said. "And don't feel bad about washing dishes. I think even Gable did it for a while."

"Did he?"   20

I felt so clever, catching all her references. The other boarder didn't even know who Charlie Chan was, and the guy was half Korean! I'd see him in the hall from time to time—a chemistry major, I think he was. There was a third room as well, but owing to some water damage Rosemary was having a hard time renting it. "Not that I care so much," she told me. "In my business, it's more about quality than quantity."

I moved in at the beginning of January, and throughout that winter my life felt like a beautiful dream. I'd come home at the end of the day and Rosemary would be sitting in the parlor, both of us fully costumed. "Aha!" she'd say. "Just the young man I was looking for." Then she'd pull out some new treasure she'd bought at an estate sale and explain what made it so valuable: "On most of the later Fire King loaf pans, the trademark helmet is etched rather than embossed."

The idea was that we were different, not like the rest of America, with its Fuzzbusters and shopping malls and rotating showerheads. "If it's not new and shiny, they don't want anything to do with it," Rosemary would complain. "Give them the Liberty Bell and they'd bitch about the crack. That's how folks are nowadays. I've seen it."

There was a radio station in Raleigh that broadcast old programs, and sometimes at night, when the reception was good, we'd sit on the davenport and listen to Jack Benny or *Fibber McGee and Molly*. Rosemary might mend a worn Wac uniform with her old-timey sewing kit, while I'd stare into the fireplace and wish that it still worked. Maybe we'd leaf through some old *Look* magazines. Maybe the wind would rattle the windows and we'd draw a quilt over our laps and savor the heady scent of mothballs.

I hoped that our lives would continue this way forever, but inevitably the past   25 came knocking. Not the good kind that was collectible but the bad kind that had arthritis. One afternoon in early April, I returned home from work to find a lost-looking white-haired woman sitting in the parlor. Her fingers were stiff and gnarled, so rather than shake hands I offered a little salute. "Sister Sykes" was how she introduced herself. I thought that was maybe what they called her in church, but then Rosemary walked out of her chambers and told me through gritted teeth that this was a professional name.

"Mother here was a psychic," she explained. "Had herself a tarot deck and a crystal ball and told people whatever stupid malarkey they wanted to hear."

"That I did," Sister Sykes said, chuckling.

You'd think that someone who occasionally wore a turban herself would like having a psychic as a mom, but Rosemary was over it. "If she'd forecast thirty years ago that I'd wind up having to take care of her, I would have put my head in the oven and killed myself," she told me.

When June rolled around, the chemistry student graduated, and his room was rented to a young man I'll call Chaz, who worked on a road-construction crew. "You know those guys that hold the flags?" he said. "Well, that's me. That's what I do."

His face, like his name, was chiselled and memorable, and, after deciding 30 that he was too handsome, I began to examine him for flaws. The split lower lip only added to his appeal, so I moved on to his hair, which had clearly been blow-dried, and to the strand of turquoise pebbles visible through his unbuttoned shirt.

"What are you looking at?" he asked, and before I had a chance to blush he started telling me about his ex-girlfriend. They'd lived together for six months, in a little apartment behind Fowler's grocery store, but then she cheated on him with someone named Robby, an asshole who went to U.N.C. and majored in fucking up other people's lives. "You're not one of those college snobs, are you?" he asked.

I probably should have said "No," rather than "Not presently."

"What did you study?" he asked. "Bank robbing?"

"Excuse me?"

"Your clothes," he said. "You and that lady downstairs look like those people 35 from *Bonnie and Clyde,* not the stars but the other ones. The ones who fuck everything up."

"Yes, well, we're individuals."

"Individual freaks," he said, and then he laughed, suggesting that there were no hard feelings. "Anyway, I don't have time to stand around and jaw. A friend and me are hitting the bars."

He'd do this every time: start a conversation and end it abruptly, as if it had been me who was running his mouth. Before Chaz moved in, the upstairs was fairly quiet. Now I heard the sound of his radio through the wall, a rock station that made it all the harder to pretend I was living in gentler times. When he was bored, he'd knock on my door and demand that I give him a cigarette. Then he'd stand there and smoke it, complaining that my room was too clean, my sketches were too sketchy, my old-fashioned bathrobe was too old-fashioned. "Well, enough of this," he'd say. "I have my own life to lead." Three or four times a night this would happen.

As Chaz changed life on the second floor, Sister Sykes changed it on the first. I went to check my mail one morning and found Rosemary dressed just like anyone else her age: no hat or costume jewelry, just a pair of slacks and a ho-hum blouse with unpadded shoulders. She wasn't wearing makeup, either, and had neglected to curl her hair. "What can I tell you?" she said. "That kind of daz-zle takes time, and I just don't seem to have any lately." The parlor, which had always been just so, had gone downhill as well. Now there were cans of iced-tea mix sitting on the Victrola, and boxed pots and pans parked in the corner where the credenza used to be. There was no more listening to Jack Benny, because that was Sister Sykes's bath time. "The queen bee," Rosemary called her.

Later that summer, just after the Fourth of July, I came downstairs and 40 found a pair of scuffed white suitcases beside the front door. I hoped that someone was on his way out—Chaz, specifically—but it appeared that the luggage was coming rather than going. "Meet my daughter," Rosemary said, this with the same grudging tone she'd used to introduce her mother. The young woman—I'll call her Ava—took a rope of hair from the side of her head and stuck it in her mouth. She was a skinny thing, and very pale, dressed in jeans and a Western-style shirt. "In her own little world," Sister Sykes said.

Rosemary told me later that her daughter had just been released from a mental institution, and though I tried to act surprised, I don't think I was very convincing. It was like she was on acid almost, the way she'd sit and examine something long after it had lost its mystery: an ashtray, a dried-up moth, Chaz's blow-dryer in the upstairs bathroom—everything got equal attention, including my room. There were no lockable doors on the second floor. The keys had been lost years earlier, so Ava just wandered in whenever she felt like it. I'd come home after a full day of work—my clothes smelling of wet garbage, my shoes squishy with dishwater—and find her sitting on my bed, or standing like a zombie behind my door.

"You scared me," I'd say, and she'd stare into my face until I turned away.

The situation at Rosemary's sank to a new low when Chaz lost his job. "I was overqualified," he told me, but, as the days passed, his story became more elaborate, and he felt an ever-increasing urge to share it with me. He started knocking more often, not caring that it was 6 A.M. or well after midnight. "And another thing . . ." he'd say, stringing ten separate conversations into one. He got into a fight that left him with a black eye. He threw his radio out the window and then scattered the broken pieces throughout the parking lot.

Late one evening, he came to my door, and when I opened it he grabbed me around the waist and lifted me off the floor. This might sound innocent, but his was not a celebratory gesture. We hadn't won a game or been granted a stay of execution, and carefree people don't call you a "hand puppet of the Dark Lord" when they pick you up without your consent. I knew then that there was something seriously wrong with the guy, but I couldn't put a name to it. I guess I thought that Chaz was too good looking to be crazy.

When he started slipping notes under my door, I decided it was time to 45 update my thinking. "Now I'm going to *die* and come back on the same day," one of them read. It wasn't just the messages but the writing itself that spooked me, the letters all jittery and butting up against one another. Some of his notes included diagrams, and flames rendered in red ink. When he started leaving them for Rosemary, she called him down to the parlor and told him he had to leave. For a minute or two, he seemed to take it well, but then he thought better of it and threatened to return as a vapor.

"Did he say 'viper'?" Sister Sykes asked.

Chaz's parents came a week later, and asked if any of us had seen him. "He's a schizophrenic, you see, but sometimes he goes off his medication."

I'd thought that Rosemary would be sympathetic, but she was sick to death of mental illness, just as she was sick of old people, and of having to take in boarders to make ends meet. "If he was screwy you should have told me before he moved in," she said to Chaz's father. "I can't have people like that running through my house. What with these antiques, it's just not safe." The man's eyes wandered around the parlor, and through them I saw what he did: a dirty room full of junk. It had never been anything more than that, but for some reason—the heat, maybe, or the couple's heavy, almost contagious sense of despair—every gouge and smudge jumped violently into focus. More depressing still was the thought that I belonged here, that I fit in.

For years, the university had been trying to buy Rosemary's property. Representatives would come to the door, and her accounts of these meetings seemed torn from a late-night movie: "So I said to him, 'But don't you see? This isn't just a house. It's my home, sir. My home.'"

They didn't want the building, of course, just the land. With every passing semester, it became more valuable, and she was smart to hold out for as long as she did. I don't know what their final offer was, but Rosemary accepted it. She signed the papers with a vintage fountain pen, and was still holding it when she came to give me the news. This was in August, and I was lying on my floor, making a sweat angel. A part of me was sad that the house was being sold, but another, bigger part—the part that loved air-conditioning—was more than ready to move on. It was pretty clear that as far as the restaurant was concerned I was never going to advance beyond dishwashing. Then, too, it was hard to live in a college town and not go to college. The students I saw out my window were a constant reminder that I was just spinning my wheels, and I was beginning to imagine how I would feel in another ten years, when they started looking like kids to me.

A few days before I left, Ava and I sat together on the front porch. It had just begun to rain when she turned and asked, "Did I ever tell you about my daddy?"

This was more than I'd ever heard her say, and before continuing she took off her shoes and socks and set them on the floor beside her. Then she drew a hank of hair into her mouth, and told me that her father had died of a heart attack. "Said he didn't feel well and an hour later he just plunked over."

I asked a few follow-up questions, and learned that he had died on November 19, 1963. Three days after that, the funeral was held, and while riding from the church to the cemetery Ava looked out the window and noticed that everyone she passed was crying. "Old people, college students, even the colored men at the gas station—the soul brothers, or whatever we're supposed to call them now."

It was such an outmoded term, I just had to use it myself. "How did the soul brothers know your father?"

"That's just it," she said. "No one told us until after the burial that Kennedy had been shot. It happened when we were in the church, so that's what everyone was so upset about. The President, not my father."

She then put her socks back on and walked into the parlor, leaving both me and her shoes behind.

When I'd tell people about this later, they'd say, "Oh, come on," because it was all too much, really. An arthritic psychic, a ramshackle house, and either two or four crazy people, depending on your tolerance for hats. Harder to swallow is that each of us was such a cliché. It was as if you'd taken a Carson McCullers novel, mixed it with a Tennessee Williams play, and dumped all the sets and characters into a single box. I didn't even add that Sister Sykes used to own a squirrel monkey, as it only amounted to overkill. Even the outside world seems suspect here: the leafy college town, the restaurant with its classical music.

I never presumed that Kennedy's death was responsible for Ava's breakdown. Plenty of people endure startling coincidences with no lasting aftereffects, so I imagine that her troubles started years earlier. As for Chaz, I later learned that it was fairly common for schizophrenics to go off their medication. I'd think it strange that the boarding house attracted both him and me, but that's what cheap places do—draw in people with no money. An apartment of my own was unthinkable at that time of my life, and, even if I'd found an affordable one, it wouldn't have satisfied my fundamental need: to live in a communal past, or what I imagined the past to be like—a world full of antiques. What I could never fathom, and still can't, really, is that at one point all those things were new—the wheezing Victrola, the hulking davenport. How were they any different from the eight-track tape player, or my parents' Scandinavian dining-room set? Given enough time, I guess, anything can look good. All it has to do is survive.

FOR ANALYSIS

1. According to Sedaris, what makes him and Rosemary different from "the rest of America" (para. 23)? Do they like to feel this way?

2. Is Sedaris the essayist still nostalgic about the past?

3. How does Sedaris use humor? Does it distract from the more serious points? Provide a rest from them? Lead into them?

WRITING TOPICS

1. *Nostalgia* is defined as a longing for familiar surroundings, often from the past. What does it mean to be nostalgic for a time one didn't live through and so couldn't have ever been familiar with?

2. Sedaris's work is known by many through his readings on the radio. Reflect on the **style** of "This Old House." Do you think it would read well? What about the way Sedaris writes this essay might make it a good piece to listen to?

MAKING CONNECTIONS

1. What are the similarities and differences between White's memories of his past and Sedaris's attraction to the past?

2. How does death figure in both White's and Sedaris's essays? How does thinking about the past unavoidably entail thinking about death?

3. Compare the styles of White and Sedaris. Both are famous for having distinctive, well-crafted ways in which they write. How would you characterize these styles? Do you like one more? Why?

FURTHER QUESTIONS
FOR THINKING AND WRITING

1. Although Housman's "To an Athlete Dying Young," Neruda's "The Dead Woman," and Roethke's "Elegy for Jane" employ different poetic forms, they all embody a poetic mode called **elegy**. Define *elegy* in terms of the characteristic **tone** of these poems. Compare the elegiac tone of these poems. **Writing Topic:** Compare the elegiac tone of one of these poems with the tone of Owen's "Dulce et Decorum Est" or Thomas's "Do Not Go Gentle into That Good Night."

2. What **figurative language** in the prose and poetry of this section is commonly associated with death? With dying? Contrast the characteristic **imagery** of this section with the characteristic imagery of love poetry. **Writing Topic:** Compare the imagery in Shakespeare's Sonnet 18 (p. 909) with the imagery in Sonnet 73.

3. In Tolstoy's "The Death of Iván Ilých" and Donne's **sonnet** "Death, Be Not Proud," death and dying are considered from a religious viewpoint. **Writing Topic:** Discuss whether these works develop a similar attitude toward death or whether the attitudes they develop differ.

4. State the argument against resignation to death made in Thomas's "Do Not Go Gentle into That Good Night." State the argument of Davis's reply, "After a Time." **Writing Topic:** Using these positions as the basis of your discussion, select for analysis two works that support Thomas's argument and two works that support Davis's.

5. Viramontes, a Mexican American, and Silko, an American Indian, both treat death as a ritualistic event. How are their stories similar? How do they differ? **Writing Topic:** Contrast the ritualistic elements in these stories with the religious elements in Tolstoy's "The Death of Iván Ilých."

6. Which works in this section treat death and dying in a way that corresponds most closely to your own attitude toward mortality? Which contradict your attitude? **Writing Topic:** Choose two works, each of which affects you differently, and discuss the elements responsible for your response.

APPENDICES

GLOSSARY OF CRITICAL APPROACHES

INTRODUCTION

This glossary attempts to define, briefly and in general terms, some major critical approaches to literature. Because literary criticism has to do with the *value* of literature—not with its history—judgments tend to be subjective, and disagreements frequent and even acrimonious. The truth of a work of art is very different from the truth of a mathematical formula. Certainly one's attitudes toward war, religion, sex, and politics are irrelevant to the truth of a formula but quite relevant to one's judgment of a literary work.

Most critical approaches can, in a general sense, be placed into one of three categories:

1. those that focus exclusively on the work itself, including the internal connections between its various parts and elements

2. those that approach a work with certain preconceived assumptions against which the work is evaluated

3. those that reject any "pure" approach and instead encourage an eclecticism that draws from whatever sources seem best suited to the work and the predilections of the critic.

Most of us are likely to find the third approach most congenial.

Yet any examination of the broad range of literary criticism reveals that groups of critics (and all readers are ultimately critics) share certain assumptions about literature. These assumptions govern the way critics approach a work, the elements they tend to look for and emphasize, the details they find significant or insignificant, and finally, the overall value they place on the work.

We do not suggest that one approach is more valid than another or that the lines dividing the various approaches are always clear and distinct. Readers will perhaps discover one approach more congenial to their temperament, more "true" to their sense of the world, than another. More likely, they will find themselves using more than one approach in dealing with a single work. Many of the diverse approaches described here actually overlap, and even those critics who champion a single abstract theory often draw on a variety of useful approaches when they write about a particular work.

Formalist critics assume that a literary text remains independent of the writer who created it. The function of the critic, then, is to discover how the author has deployed language to create (or perhaps failed to create) a formal and aesthetically satisfying structure. The influential American formalists of the 1940s and 1950s (the New Critics) were fond of describing literary texts as "autonomous," meaning that political, historical, biographical, and other considerations were always secondary if not irrelevant to any discussion of their merits.

Furthermore, formalist critics argue that the various elements of a "great" work interweave to create a seamless whole that embodies "universal" values. Unsurprisingly, the "universal" values formalist critics praise, on close analysis, tend to parallel the moral, political, and cultural ideals of the critics' social class. This tendency becomes even more problematic and complex in dealing with the literature of formerly colonized people.

But the formalist point of view, cherishing the artwork's structure, spawned its own antithesis—a group of theorists called *deconstructionists*. These writers argued that language itself was too shifty to support the expectations of formalist criticism. One reader might read a sentence literally, while another might read it ironically. Hence, their "understanding" of the text would be diametrically opposed.

The deconstructionists believe that intelligent readers cannot be expected to ignore those responses that interfere with some "correct" or "desirable" reading of the piece. Given what they see as the notoriously ambiguous and unstable nature of language, deconstructionist critics argue that a literary text can never have a fixed meaning.

While the formalists and deconstructionists wrestle over the philosophy of language and its implications for the nature of literary texts, other critics pursue quite different primary interests. The term *ethical criticism* describes a variety of approaches, all of which argue that literature, like any other human activity, connects to the real world and, consequently, influences real people. If that is so, our appraisal of a work must take into account the ethical and moral values it embodies. Though it sounds simple enough, in reality the task is difficult and often quite controversial. Ethical criticism is the very opposite of the "art for art's sake" approach, best represented by formalist criticism. The formalist critic tries to isolate the work in a timeless world of universal aesthetic considerations; the ethical critic insists on making judgments about whether a work serves values that are "good" or encourages values that are "bad."

Other critical approaches analyze literary works from still other perspectives. *Reader-response* critics assert that a work of art is created as much by its audience as by the artist. For these critics, art has no significant abstract existence: a reader's experience of the work gives birth to it and contributes crucially to its power and value. Further, since each reader embodies a unique set of experiences and values, each reader's response to the work will in some respects be uniquely personal. *Psychoanalytic* criticism, similar to reader-response, is nevertheless distinctive in its application of psychoanalytic principles to works of art. Those principles, originally derived from the work of Sigmund Freud (1856–1939), now often reflect the views of more recent theorists such as Jacques Lacan (1901–1981). There is, finally, the recently emergent approach called *new historical* criticism, which brings historical knowledge to bear on the analysis of literary works in new and sophisticated ways. The result is a some-times dizzying proliferation of analyses that argue for the relationship between literature and life.

The glossary that follows reveals the widely diverse and often contradictory views expressed by professional theorists and critics.

Deconstruction This approach grew out of the work of certain twentieth-century European philosophers, notably Jacques Derrida (1930–2004), whose study of language led to the conclusion that since we can know only through the medium of language, and language is unstable and ambiguous, it is impossible to talk about truth and knowledge and meaning in any absolute sense. Verbal structures, these critics maintained, inevitably contained within themselves oppositions. Derrida asserted that in the Western world, language leads us to think in terms of opposites (for example, soul/body, man/woman, master/slave) that imply what he called "a violent hierarchy," with one of the terms (the first) always being superior to the other (the second). The aim of deconstruction is to show that this hierarchy of values cannot be permanent and absolute.

Readers therefore cannot be expected to ignore the oppositions and contradictions in a text just because they do not contribute to some "correct" or "desirable" reading of the piece that might uphold a particular political, social, or cultural view.

Formalism assures us that the successful artist is the master of language and that he or she consciously deploys all its resources to achieve a rich and unified work. Sensitive readers can aspire to a complete understanding of a work undistorted by their own idiosyncrasies, subjective states, or ideological biases.

Rejecting the formalist assumption about authorial control and conscious design, deconstruction attempts to show that by its very nature, language is constantly "saying" more than the writer can control or even know. Thus, a close study of any text (literary or otherwise) will reveal contradictory and irreconcilable elements.

Deconstructionist critics do not necessarily reject the validity of feminist, Marxist, formalist, and other critical approaches. In fact, they often draw on the insights furnished by them. But the deconstructionist critic says that any discourse or critical approach that fails to recognize the inherently shifting and unstable nature of language is bound to produce only a partial if not misleading interpretation. For example, in his study *America the Scrivener: Deconstruction and the Subject of Literary Studies* (1990), Gregory S. Jay finds Emily Grierson, the protagonist of William Faulkner's story "A Rose for Emily" (p. 622), a "puzzle" and warns against simplistic interpretations:

> As feminist subject, her story speaks of a revolutionary subversion of patriarchy; as herself, a figure of racial and class power, Emily also enacts the love affair of patriarchy with its own past, despite all the signs of decline and degradation. She is a split subject, crossed by rival discourses. What the text forces us to think, then, is the complex and ironic alliances between modes of possession and subjection, desire and ownership, identity and position.

Like Marxism and feminism, deconstruction defines itself both as a critical theory of literature and as a philosophy of human values. Hence, it is applicable not only to literature but also to an understanding of the power relations among humans and the societies they create. In insisting that we recognize the way language embodies and supports class, gender, and other biases, deconstruction challenges both the ethnocentrism of political structures and the idea of "universal values" in literary works.

Ethical Criticism   Ethical criticism may range from a casual appraisal of a work's moral content to the more rigorous and systematic analysis driven by a coherent set of stated beliefs and assumptions. A *religious* critic (committed to certain moral positions) might attack a work (regardless of its artfulness or brilliance) because it does not condemn adultery. A *feminist* critic might focus on the way literary works devalue women; a *black* critic, on the way they stereotype blacks; a *Marxist* critic, on the way they support class divisions; and a *new historicist* critic, on the way a dominant class interprets history to protect its own interests. But all of them agree that literary works invite ethical judgments. Most of them also agree that literary works must be judged as another means by which a society both defines and perpetuates its political institutions and cultural values. The feminist critic, the black critic, and the Marxist critic would also agree that the political institutions and cultural values of most Western societies have been carefully designed to serve the interests of a dominant class: white, male, and wealthy.

Ethical criticism takes us out of the comparatively calm, academic world of aesthetic values into the larger world of moral judgments. If a literary work's capacity to promote good or bad behavior becomes the criterion for judging its value, then surely some people will try to suppress works they perceive as morally threatening. It is here that ethical criticism encounters its most vexing and dangerous problem: censorship. The literary critic Wayne Booth, who advocates ethical criticism in his book *The Company We Keep: An Ethics of Fiction* (1988), concedes the danger but notes that teaching itself is a form of censorship in that "we impose our ethical choices on our students when we choose our reading lists."

Feminist Criticism   Feminist critics hold that literature is merely one of many expressions of a patriarchal society with a vested interest in keeping women subordinate to men. Thus literature, in the way it portrays gender roles, helps to condition women to accept as normal a society that directs them to become nurses rather than doctors, secretaries rather than attorneys or corporate executives, sex symbols rather than thinkers, elementary school teachers rather than university professors. Beyond this general critique of patriarchy, feminists differ in their detailed analyses. Some have re-examined history to show that a literary canon created by males has slighted and ignored female authors. Others, studying canonical works from a feminist perspective, have come up with fresh readings that challenge conventional interpretations, focusing on how women are empowered in literary texts or through writing literary texts. Some, believing that language itself allows men to impose their power, use literary analyses to expose the gender bias of language. Why, they ask, is the English language so rich in words to describe a quarrelsome, abusive woman (*shrew, harridan, termagant*) but so lacking in comparable terms for men? Some feminists believe that the male bias of language, far deeper than mere words, is actually structural. The constellation of qualities connoted by *masculine* and *feminine,* they say, reveals how deeply the positive (male) and negative (female) values are embedded in the language.

While a psychoanalytic critic might use Freud's Oedipal theories to explain Emily's relationship to Homer Barron in William Faulkner's "A Rose for Emily" (p. 622), the feminist critic Judith Fetterley maintains that the explanation is to be found in the fact that a patriarchal culture instills in us the notion "that men and women are made for each other" and that " 'masculinity' and 'femininity' are the natural reflection of that divinely ordained complement." In a society where there is "a massive differentiation of everything according to sex, one sees that in reality a sexist culture is one in which men and women are not simply incompatible but murderously so. . . . Emily murders Homer Barron because she must at any cost get a man" (*The Resisting Reader: A Feminist Approach to American Fiction,* 1978).

Formalist Criticism   Like deconstruction, formalism focuses on the ambiguous and multilayered nature of language but does so to achieve the precisely opposite effect. Formalism assures us that the successful artist is the master of language and consciously deploys all its resources to achieve a rich and unified work. Careful readers can aspire to a complete understanding of a work undistorted by their own idiosyncrasies or subjective states or ideological biases. The formalist rejects the central tenet of the reader-response critic—that a work comes into existence, so to speak, through the interaction of the reader with the work. For the formalist, the work exists independent of any particular reader. The work is a structured and formal aesthetic object comprising such elements as symbol, image, and sound patterns. Political, biographical, or historical considerations not embodied in the work itself are irrelevant.

The formalist sees literature as a sort of Platonic ideal form—immutable and objective. Works close to that ideal are praised for their aesthetic energy and their universality (a characteristic of the greatest literature). Works that do not exhibit this prized formal coherence are dispraised and often dismissed as neither universal nor important. Because formalism focuses on the internal structure of literature above all else, it rejects didactic works—those intended to teach or convey moral observations. During the 1940s and 1950s, when the New Critics (as the formalists were called) dominated academic literary criticism, social protest writing was generally dismissed as subliterary because it lacked the "universality" of great literature. What was important in a work of art was not that it might change people's behavior but that its parts coalesced into a beautiful whole. Consider the following comment by two formalist critics (Caroline Gordon and Allen Tate, *The House of Fiction*, 1950) on Nathaniel Hawthorne's "Young Goodman Brown" (p. 81):

> *The dramatic impact would have been stronger if Hawthorne had let the incidents tell their own story: Goodman Brown's behavior to his neighbors and finally to his wife show us that he is a changed man. Since fiction is a kind of shorthand of human behavior and one moment may represent years in a man's life, we would have concluded that the change was to last his entire life. But Hawthorne's weakness for moralizing and his insufficient technical equipment betray him into the anticlimax of the last paragraph.*

African American writers and critics, for example, complained that the criterion of universality was merely a way of protecting white, conservative social and political dominance. The New Critics dismissed African American literature that sought to deal with racism and the struggle for equality as mere didacticism or agitprop, not to be compared with the great white literary productions that achieved universal import. In a major work of New Criticism published in 1952, the influential critic R. P. Blackmur dismissed *Native Son*, a powerful and now classic novel about white racism, as "one of those books in which everything is undertaken with seriousness except the writing."

Marxist Criticism   The Marxist critic sees literature as one activity among many to be studied and judged in terms of a larger and all-encompassing ideology derived from the economic and political doctrines of Karl Marx (1818–1883). Marxism offers a comprehensive theory about the nature of humans and the way in which a few of them manage to seize control of the means of production and thereby exploit the masses of working people. But Marxism is about more than analysis. As Karl Marx himself said, "It is not enough to analyze society; we must also change it."

The Marxist critic analyzes literary works to show how, wittingly or unwittingly, they support the dominant social class or how they, in some way, contribute to the struggle against oppression and exploitation. And since the Marxist critic views literature as just one among the variety of human activities that reflect power relations and class divisions, he or she is likely to be more interested in what a work says than in its formal structure.

The Marxist argues that one cannot properly understand a literary work unless one understands how it reflects the relationship between economic production and social class. Further, this relationship cannot be explored adequately without examining a range of questions that other critical approaches, notably formalism, deem irrelevant. How does the work relate to the profit-driven enterprise of publishing? What does the author's biography reveal about his or her class biases? Does the work accurately portray the class divisions of society? Does the work expose the economic bases of oppression and advance the cause of liberation?

And since Marxist critics see their duty—indeed, the duty of all responsible and humane people—as not merely to describe the world but to change it, they judge literature by the contribution it makes to bringing about revolution or in some way enlightening its readers about oppression and the necessity for class struggle.

For example, a Marxist critic's analysis of Matthew Arnold's poem "Dover Beach" (p. 920) might see it not as a brilliantly structured pattern of images and sounds but as the predictable end product of a dehumanizing capitalist economy in which a small class of oligarchs is willing, at whatever cost, to protect its wealth and power. The Marxist critic, as a materialist who believes that humans make their own history, would find Arnold's reference to "the eternal note of sadness" (l. 14) a mystic evasion of the real sources of his alienation and pain: Arnold's misery can be clearly and unmystically explained by his fearful responses to the socioeconomic conditions of his time.

Arnold's refusal to face this fact leads him to the conclusion typical of a bourgeois artist-intellectual who cannot discern the truth. But the cure for Arnold's pain, the Marxist would argue, cannot be found in a love relationship because relations between people are determined crucially by socioeconomic conditions. The cure for the pain he describes so well will be found in the world of action, in the struggle to create a society that is just and humane. "Dover Beach," the Marxist critic would conclude, is both a brilliant evocation of the alienation and misery caused by a capitalist economy and a testimony to the inability of a bourgeois intellectual to understand what is responsible for his feelings.

New Historical Criticism There is nothing "new" about historians drawing on literary works as significant documents to support and illuminate historical analysis; nor is there anything "new" about literary critics drawing on history to illuminate literary works. For the historian, Sophocles' *Oedipus Rex* (p. 183) tells us much about the conflict between the old-time religion and the new secularism in fifth-century B.C. Athens. The literary critic of *Othello* (p. 958) goes to the historian to understand the way in which Shakespeare and his contemporaries viewed black Africans. But until recently, the provinces of the historian and of the literary critics were pretty much mutually exclusive.

The new historians (influenced by modern theories of language and literature) began to question the very idea of history as it had been practiced. The historians of the past tended, for the most part, to think of history in terms of overarching themes and theses, and attempted to understand it in terms of some perceived *Zeitgeist,* or "spirit of the times." This kind of history was often linked to nationalism. Hence (for one example), nineteenth-century Americans created the idea of manifest destiny and then used it to explain and justify eastern settlers' movement west and their attendant atrocities against the Native Americans who resided there. When the Nazis came to power in Germany, they developed the idea that true Germans were descended from a superior Aryan race and then used that idea to deprive "inferior races" of civil rights, of property, and finally, of life.

More abstractly, the purpose of writing history was to articulate and reinforce the values and beliefs that gave a culture unity. By that means, some new historians note, history became the story (and the ideas and beliefs and culture) of the rich, the powerful, the privileged, the victorious. The new historians see history not as the search for some grand, unifying thesis but as the articulation of the various kinds of discourse that compete with, contradict, overlap, and modify one another in the constant struggle for dominance. Indeed, the new historians, influenced by deconstructionist views of language, came to question the very idea of historical truth.

The new historians also reject the traditional division between history and other disciplines, appropriating to historical studies many kinds of texts—including literary texts—that traditional historians left to others. These critics assert that without an understanding of the historical context that produced it, no work of literature can really be understood; therefore, in their eyes, literature belongs as much to the historian as to the literary critic. Such critics aim at what they call a "thick" description of a literary work, one that applies to a text as much information as can be gathered about every aspect of the author, his work, and his times. While its practitioners generally share the fundamental ideas outlined here, they can differ widely in the tools and methodologies they use to analyze a literary text. That is to say, a new historian may also be a Marxist, feminist, or deconstructionist.

Postcolonial Criticism   Postcolonial criticism belongs to the larger field of postcolonial studies, which evolved in the wake of the liberation of many nations from the domination of the European powers of the nineteenth century. It is distinguished not so much by any singular approach as by its subject: the examination of postcolonial writings that explore the way in which the colonizers imposed their culture and values on native peoples and thus distorted or suppressed their past.

One prominent purpose of postcolonial criticism is to explain and expose the mechanisms the colonizer used—from brute force to subtle psychological techniques—to gain and maintain control. It becomes, in effect, a new lens through which the literature of the colonizing culture can be examined in order to expose its biased judgments about the society it has dominated, its distortions of native culture as compared with the colonizing culture. This kind of analysis will lead the critic away from narrowly defined literary concerns to examine the colonized culture's past, including its precolonial past. Thus postcolonial critics (and historians), by uncovering the past, may give their newly liberated compatriots the means of re-creating an identity and may give its imaginative writers the material for a national literature.

Because postcolonial criticism is a relatively new field, it is still developing its distinctive areas of interest and techniques of analysis. By its nature it is eclectic, drawing on any other literary approach (as well as academic discipline) that seems relevant to a critic's purpose.

Psychoanalytic Criticism   Psychoanalytic criticism always proceeds from a set of principles that describes the inner life of men and women. Though differing psychological theorists argue for diverse views, all analysts and all psychoanalytic critics assume that the development of the psyche is analogous to the development of the body. Doctors can provide charts indicating physical growth stages; analysts can supply similar charts indicating stages in the growth of the psyche. Sigmund Freud, for all practical purposes, invented psychoanalysis by creating a theoretical model for the (mostly male) human psyche.

The Oedipus complex is a significant element in that model. Freud contends that everyone moves through a childhood stage of erotic attachment to the parent of the opposite sex and an accompanying hostility and aggression against the parent of the same sex, who is seen as a rival. Such feelings, part of the natural biography of the psyche, pass or are effectively controlled in most cases. But sometimes the child grown to adulthood is still strongly gripped by the Oedipal mode, which then may result in neurotic or even psychotic behavior. Freud did not invent the Oedipus complex—he simply described it. It was always there, especially noticeable in the work of great literary artists who, in every era, demonstrate a special insight into the human condition.

Along with Oedipal feelings, the psyche inevitably embodies aggressive feelings—the urge to attack those who exercise authority, who deny us our primal desires. For the young, the authority figure is frequently a parent. Adults must deal with police, government officials, the boss. As far back as the Hebrew Bible story of the tower of Babel and the old Greek myths in which the giant Titans, led by Cronus, overthrow their father, and Zeus and the Olympians subsequently overthrow Cronus, there is evidence of the rebellion against the parent-authority figure. Freud views that aggressive hostility as another component of the developing psyche. But, in the interest of civilization, society has developed ways to control that aggressiveness.

Freud saw us as divided selves. An unconscious *id* struggles to gratify aggressive and erotic primal urges, while a *superego* (roughly what society calls *conscience*), by producing guilt feelings, struggles to control the id. The *ego* (the self) is defined by the struggle. Thus the Freudian psychoanalytic critic is constantly aware that authors and their characters suffer and resuffer a primal tension that results from the conflict between psychic aggressions and social obligations.

Freud has been succeeded by a number of psychological theorists who present quite different models of the psyche, and recent literary theory has responded to these post-Freudian views. Among the most important are Carl Gustav Jung (1875–1961), who argued that there exists a collective (as well as a racial and individual) unconscious. Residing there are archetypes—original patterns—that emerge into our consciousness in the form of shadowy images that persistently appear and reappear in such literary themes as the search for the father, death and resurrection, the quest, and the double.

The psychoanalytic critic understands literature in terms of the psychic models that Freud and others defined. Originally, such critics tended to analyze literature in an attempt to identify the author's neuroses. More recently, psychoanalytic critics have argued that the patterns they discover in works allow us to tap into and, perhaps, resolve our own neuroses.

Reader-Response Criticism   Reader-response criticism (also called *transactional theory*) emerged in the 1970s as one of the many challenges to formalist principles. Reader-response critics focus on the interaction between the work and the reader, holding that, in a sense, a work exists only when it is experienced by the reader. If the work exists only in the mind of the reader, the reader becomes an active participant in the creative process rather than a passive receptacle for an autonomous work. The creation of a work thus becomes a dynamic enterprise between the reader and the text, each acting on the other. The study of the affective power of a work becomes not a fallacy, as formalism holds, but the central focus of criticism. The task of the critic is to investigate this dynamic relationship between reader and text in order to discover how it works.

We know that various readers respond differently to the same text. In fact, the same reader might respond to the text quite differently at a different time. The reader-response critic wants to know why. In what ways do such conditions as age, gender, upbringing, and race account for differing responses? Does the reader's mood at the time of reading make a difference? If you accept the principles of reader-response criticism, the inevitable conclusion— *reductio ad absurdum,* its critics would say—is that there is no limit to the possible readings of any text. Consequently, many reader-response critics qualify the intense subjectivity of their approach by admitting that an "informed" or "educated" reader is likely to produce a more "valid" reading than an "uninformed" or "uneducated" one.

Gaps or blanks in literary texts provide particular opportunities to readers. Every narrative work omits, for example, periods of time that the reader must fill in. In Nathaniel Hawthorne's "Young Goodman Brown" (p. 81), the author omits all the years of Brown's life between his emergence from the forest and his death. The reader is free to imagine that history. The filling in of these blanks enables readers to participate in "creating" a text and reinforces the arguments of reader-response theorists.

Biographical Notes on the Authors

CHINUA ACHEBE (b. 1930)   Born in Ogidi, Nigeria, Achebe attended University College, Ibadan (1948–1953), and London University, where he earned a B.A. (1953). After spending some years working in broadcasting in his native country, Achebe began a distinguished academic career as professor of English at Anambra State University of Technology in Enugu. His acclaim as a writer led to many academic appointments and honors, including visiting professorships at the University of Massachusetts at Amherst, the University of Connecticut, and the University of California at Los Angeles. His numerous literary awards include the Commonwealth Poetry Prize (1972) and the Man Booker International Prize for fiction (2007). Although Achebe's native language is Ibo, he writes in English, a language he learned in his youth. Achebe's novels include *Things Fall Apart* (1958), *Arrow of God* (1964), and *Anthills of the Savannah* (1988). He has also published volumes of poetry, short stories, and essays, including the poetry and text for *Another Africa* (1998), a picture book. A collection of autobiographical essays called *Reflections of a British Protected Child* is forthcoming.

ANNA AKHMATOVA (1889–1966)   Akhmatova was born Anna Andreevna Gorenko in Odessa, Ukraine. She started writing poems as a very young woman; her father's disapproval led her to assume a pen name. Her first collection of poems, *Evening*, was published in 1912; her second collection, *Rosary*, appeared in 1914. Her work was banned under Stalin from 1925 to 1940, but she had become so popular with the Russian people that they shared her work illicitly. Although Akhmatova and her family suffered at the hands of the Bolsheviks, she remained in Russia rather than flee like many of her contemporaries. After Stalin's death in 1953, she was celebrated as a symbol of survival of the repression. Several volumes of her poems were collected and published beginning in the late 1950s. A well-respected figure, she was visited at her villa by the likes of Joseph Brodsky and Robert Frost. Akhmatova died in St. Petersburg in 1966. What is perhaps her greatest poem, *Requiem*, about the suffering of the Russian people under Stalin, was not published in its entirety in the Soviet Union until 1987.

SHERMAN ALEXIE (b. 1966)   A Spokane/Coeur d'Alene Indian, Sherman Alexie was born on the Spokane Indian Reservation in Wellpinit, Washington. In 1981, he left the reservation school and enrolled in a predominantly white high school, where, according to Alexie, he "kept [his] mouth shut and became a good white Indian." He enrolled at Gonzaga University in Spokane and began to discover his love for literature and his talent for writing. After two years at Gonzaga, he transferred to Washington State University in Pullman, where he began to write seriously. A year after he received his degree, he published two collections of poetry, *The Business of Fancydancing* (1992) and *I Would Steal Horses* (1992), followed the next year by another poetry collection, *First Indian on the Moon* (1993). Alexie then turned to prose, publishing a volume of loosely related stories dealing with life on the reservation, *The Lone Ranger and Tonto Fistfight in Heaven* (1993). One of the stories in this collection, "This Is What It Means to Say Phoenix, Arizona," provided the basis for the film *Smoke Signals* (1998), which Alexie produced and for which he wrote the screenplay. He went on to write two more films: *The Business of Fancydancing* (2002), which he also directed, and *49?* (2003). He has published two other collections of short stories, *The Toughest Indian in the World* (2000) and *Ten Little Indians* (2003), along with a number of collections of poetry, including *Dangerous Astronomy* (2005). Alexie has also penned several novels, among them *Reservation Blues* (1995), *Indian Killer* (1996), and *Flight* (2007). His novel for young adults, *The Absolutely True Diary of a Part-Time Indian* (2007), won the National Book Award for Young People's Literature. About the criticism he has received from members of his reservation, who find his portrayals of Native Americans and reservation life demeaning, Alexie replied, "I write what I know, and I don't try to mythologize myself, which is what some seem to want, and which some Indian women and men writers are doing, this Earth Mother and Shaman Man thing, trying to create these 'authentic, traditional' Indians. We don't live our lives that way."

WOODY ALLEN (b. 1935)   After being dismissed from both City College of New York and New York University, this precocious and prototypical New Yorker became a television comedy writer at the age of eighteen. He wrote two successful Broadway plays; his first screenplay, *What's New Pussycat?*, appeared in 1965. A dozen years in show business gave him the confidence to set out on his own, and he began performing as a stand-up comic. Soon after, he embarked on the filmmaking—writing, performing, directing, and producing—career for which he is famous. His talents, and those of the actors and technical group he has brought together as a kind of filmmaking repertory company, account for his reputation as an innovative contributor to cinema history. (His 1977 film, *Annie Hall*, won four Academy Awards, and Allen has received lifetime achievement awards from the Venice Film Festival [1995], the Directors Guild of America [1996], and the Cannes Film Festival [2002].) In his spare time, he plays the clarinet in a Dixieland jazz group at a New York nightspot, and continues to write occasional pieces such as *Death Knocks*. His recent films include *Match Point* (2005), *Vicky Cristina Barcelona* (2008), and *Whatever Works* (2009).

JULIA ALVAREZ (b. 1950)   Alvarez was born in New York City to Dominican parents. Her family moved to the Dominican Republic when she was three months old and remained there until she was ten, when her father's involvement in a political uprising forced them to flee to the United States. Her struggle to assimilate into American culture and forge an identity informs much of her work. She published a volume of poetry, *Homecoming* (1984), before writing three novels that brought her great acclaim: *How the García Girls Lost Their Accents* (1991), *In the Time of the Butterflies* (1994), and *¡Yo!* (1997). She went on to publish more poetry, a children's book, and several novels. Among the places Alvarez has taught are the University of Vermont, George Washington College, and the University of Illinois, Urbana; she is now a writer-in-residence at Middlebury College. Some of her most recent publications are a novel, *Saving the World* (2006); a work of nonfiction, *Once upon a Quinceañera: Coming of Age in the USA* (2007); and a novel for children about migrant workers, *Return to Sender* (2009). Alvarez has said, "When I'm asked what made me into a writer, I point to the watershed experience of coming to this country. Not understanding the language, I had to pay close attention to each word. . . . I also discovered the welcoming world of the imagination and books. There, I sunk my new roots."

ARISTOTLE (384–322 B.C.) Aristotle was born in the north of Greece, near Macedonia, which, under Alexander the Great, was to become a dominant power in the region. At seventeen, he became Plato's student at the famous Academy in Athens, and remained there until Plato died in 348 B.C. After serving as a tutor to the young Alexander in Macedonia, he returned to Athens and founded his own school, the Lyceum, where he and his students studied zoology, botany, biology, physics, ethics, logic, music, mathematics, and, of course, literary criticism. His *Poetics* is the first Western effort to create a systematic literary theory. When Alexander died, the Athenians demonstrated so violent a resentment against all things Macedonian that Aristotle left Athens. He died a year later. His intellect and wide-ranging curiosity made him the predominant Greek philosopher, and his influence is still apparent in the modern world.

MATTHEW ARNOLD (1822–1888) Born in Middlesex, England, Arnold attended Rugby School, where his father was headmaster, and studied classics at Oxford University. Following his graduation in 1844, he became a fellow at Oxford and a master at Rugby. In 1851, he was appointed inspector of schools in England and was sent by the government to observe educational systems in Europe. He remained in that post for some thirty-five years. As a poet, Arnold took inspiration from Greek tragedies, Keats, and Wordsworth. His collections include *Empedocles on Etna and Other Poems* (1852). An eminent social and literary critic in his later years, Arnold lectured in the United States in 1883 and 1886. His essay "The Function of Criticism" sheds light on his transition from poet to critic. Much of his work is collected in *Complete Prose Works* (11 volumes, 1960–1977).

HANAN MIKHA'IL 'ASHRAWI (b. 1946) 'Ashrawi was born to a wealthy Christian Palestinian family just two years before Israel became a country—an event the Palestinians call *al-nakba* (the disaster). She grew up in Ramallah, a West Bank town outside Jerusalem. She was a student of literature at the American University in Beirut, Lebanon, when the 1967 Six Days' War broke out. When the fighting ended, her hometown, along with significant additional territory west of the river Jordan was occupied by Israel, and for six years the occupying forces refused to allow Palestinians, absent during the war, to return to the West Bank. During that period, 'Ashrawi traveled and continued her studies, earning a Ph.D. from the University of Virginia in medieval and comparative literature. She returned to Palestine in 1973, where she established and chaired the department of English at Birzeit University in the West Bank, rose to the position of dean of the faculty of arts, and remained a faculty member through 1995. She produced several works on literary theory and on contemporary Palestinian literature. She served on numerous commissions on education and politics in the region and is recognized as an eloquent spokesperson for Palestinian civil, economic, and political rights. Her publications include *Intifada to Independence* (1989) and her autobiography, *This Side of Peace: A Personal Account* (1995).

W. H. AUDEN (1907–1973)   A poet, playwright, translator, librettist, critic, and editor, Wystan Hugh Auden was born in York, England, son of a medical officer and a nurse. He attended Oxford University from 1925 to 1928, then taught, traveled, and moved from faculty to faculty of several universities in the United States (he became a naturalized citizen in 1946). He won the Pulitzer Prize in 1948 for his collection *The Age of Anxiety*, an expression he coined to describe the 1930s. While his early writing exhibited Marxist sympathies and reflected the excitement of new Freudian psychoanalytic thought, he later embraced Christianity and produced sharply honed verse in the rhyme and meter of traditional forms.

JIMMY SANTIAGO BACA (b. 1952)   Born in Santa Fe, New Mexico, to Mexican and Apache Indian parents, Baca was abandoned by his mother and father, raised by his grandmother for a time, and eventually sent to an orphanage. At age thirteen, he was a runaway living on the streets; by age twenty-one, he was a convict sentenced to five years in a maximum security prison. Before he was released, Baca had three of his poems published in *Mother Jones* magazine. In 1979, he got out of jail, earned his GED, and published his first collection of poems, *Immigrants in Our Own Land*. He followed that with a novel, a film script, a memoir, and more than a dozen volumes of poetry. Baca has won numerous awards, including the Pushcart Prize and the American Book Award for Poetry. He currently devotes much of his time to conducting writing workshops at prisons, shelters, community centers, educational institutions, housing projects, and on reservations. His latest publications include two collections of poetry: *Spring Poems Along the Rio Grande* (2007) and *Rita and Julia* (2008).

JAMES BALDWIN (1924–1987)   Born in New York City, the son of a Harlem minister, Baldwin began preaching as a young teenager. Some years later, he experienced a religious crisis, left the church, and moved to New York City's bohemian Greenwich Village, where he began his career as a writer, supporting himself with menial jobs and publishing occasional articles in journals such as the *Nation* and *Commentary*. By the end of the 1940s, Baldwin's anger over the treatment of African Americans led him into exile in France. There, Baldwin completed his acclaimed first novel, *Go Tell It on the Mountain* (1953), a work focusing on a minister's son for which he drew heavily on his own childhood. His next work, *Notes of a Native Son* (1955), a collection of personal, literary, and social essays, secured Baldwin's reputation as a major American writer. Two later collections of essays, *Nobody Knows My Name* (1961) and *The Fire Next Time* (1963), established Baldwin as one of the most powerful voices of the turbulent civil rights movement of the 1960s. But as riots, bombings, and other violence grew more frequent, Baldwin grew increasingly pessimistic over the prospect that white America could ever overcome its racism. That pessimism was deepened by two traumatic events: the 1964 bombing of the Sixteenth Avenue Baptist Church in Birmingham, Alabama, that killed four young girls attending a Sunday-school class and the assassination of the Reverend Martin Luther King Jr. in 1968. Baldwin began making periodic trips to France, settling there permanently in 1974.

TONI CADE BAMBARA (1939–1995)   Born in New York City, Bambara was educated there as well as in Italy and Paris. Early in her career she worked as an investigator for the New York State Department of Social Welfare, but she later devoted herself to teaching and writing. One of the best representatives of a group of African American writers who emerged in the 1960s, Bambara was a consistent civil rights activist, both politically and culturally involved in African American life. Much of her writing focuses on African American women, particularly as they confront experiences that force them to new awareness. She authored several collections of short stories, including *Gorilla, My Love* (1972) and *The Sea Birds Are Still Alive: Collected Stories* (1977), and two novels, *The Salt Eaters* (1980) and *If Blessing Comes* (1987). She also edited a groundbreaking collection of African American women's writing, *The Black Woman: An Anthology* (1970). Two works, *Deep Sightings and Rescue Missions: Fiction, Essays, and Conversations* (1996) and the novel *These Bones Are Not My Child* (1999), were published posthumously.

APHRA BEHN (1640–1689)   Behn was born near Canterbury, England, but little else can be confirmed about her early life. She formed friendships with playwrights of her time and began writing in 1670, making her one of the first British women to adopt writing as a profession. Behn is credited with having written at least three novels, two collections of short stories, one collection of poems, and seventeen plays. Among her most popular works are her novels *Love-Letters between a Nobleman and His Sister* (1684) and *Oroonoko* (1688) and her play *The Rover* (Part 1, 1677; Part 2, 1681). Behn, who is thought to have been bisexual, is recognized as having given a bold and early voice to women's rights and female sexuality.

AIMEE BENDER (b. 1969)   Bender attended the University of California at San Diego and taught elementary school in San Francisco for three years before getting her M.F.A. from the University of California at Irvine. She cites Oscar Wilde, Hans Christian Andersen, and the Brothers Grimm as influences on her writing. Her first collection of short stories, *The Girl in the Flammable Skirt* (1998), was a *New York Times* notable book of the year. Bender then published a novel, *An Invisible Sign of My Own* (2000), and another collection of short stories, *Willful Creatures* (2005). Her work has also appeared in magazines such as *Granta, GQ,* and *Harper's,* among others. She won the Pushcart Prize twice. Bender currently lives in Los Angeles and teaches creative writing at the University of Southern California. Her writing has been described as contemporary fairy tales, and she has said about fiction, "There are no rules. You're absolutely free."

BRUCE BENNETT (b. 1940)   Bennett was born in Philadelphia, Pennsylvania, and began writing poems when he was eight years old. He attended Harvard University as an undergraduate and graduate student, receiving a Ph.D. in English (1967). From 1967 to 1970 he taught at Oberlin College, where he co-founded *Field: Contemporary Poetry and Poetics.* In 1971 he co-founded and co-edited the literary journal *Ploughshares.* In that year he married Renaissance art historian Bonnie Apgar; the couple lived in Florence, Italy, for two years, and return there often. Since 1973, Bennett has taught English and directed creative writing at Wells College in Aurora, New York, where, in 1993, he also became director of the Wells College Book Arts Center. He has published numerous books and chapbooks, including *Navigating the Distances* (1999), which was selected by *Booklist* as "one of the Top Ten Poetry Books of 1999." His recent publications include *Will Nobody Stop the Poet?* (2006) and *Examined Life* (2006). Bennett writes in a variety of forms and moods, and regards storytelling as a key element of his work. He believes poetry should be accessible, a part of everyone's life, and approvingly quotes William Carlos Williams: "If it ain't pleasure, it ain't a poem." Through public readings and visits to schools, he encourages young people to write poems. X. J. Kennedy has called Bennett a "master fabulist and satirist" and a "parodist *par excellence*," who "often compresses realms of wisdom into tight, economical packages."

ELIZABETH BISHOP (1911–1979)   Bishop was born in Worcester, Massachusetts. Her father died before she was a year old; four years later, when her mother suffered a mental breakdown, Bishop was taken to live with her grandmother in Nova Scotia. Although her mother lived until 1934, Bishop saw her for the last time in 1916, a visit recalled in one of her rare autobiographical stories, "In the Village." Bishop planned to enter Cornell Medical School after graduating from Vassar, but was persuaded by poet Marianne Moore to become a writer. For the next fifteen years, she was a virtual nomad, traveling in Canada, Europe, and North and South America. In 1951, she finally settled in Rio de Janeiro, where she lived for almost twenty years. During the final decade of her life, Bishop continued to travel, but she resumed living in the United States and taught frequently at Harvard University. She was an austere writer, publishing only four slim volumes of poetry: *North and South* (1946); *A Cold Spring* (1955), which won the Pulitzer Prize; *Questions of Travel* (1965); and *Geography III* (1976), which won the National Book Critics Circle Award. *The Complete Poems, 1927–1979* (1984) was published after her death, as was a collection of her prose. Despite her modest output, she has earned an enduring place of respect among twentieth-century poets.

WILLIAM BLAKE (1757–1827) Born in London to an obscure family, Blake was educated at home until he was ten and then enrolled in a drawing school, advancing ultimately to a formal apprenticeship as an engraver. At an early age, Blake exhibited talent as both an artist and a poet. Throughout his life, he read widely among modern philosophers and poets and experienced mystical visions that provided him with the inspiration for many of his poems. Blake devised a process he called illuminated printing, which involved the preparation of drawings and decorative frames to complement his poems. He published *Songs of Innocence* (1789) and *Songs of Experience* (1794) in this fashion. These books, as well as the many subsequent works he wrote and illustrated, earned him a reputation as one of the most important artists of his day. Many of Blake's works assert his conviction that the established church and state hinder rather than nurture human freedom and the sense of divine love.

ANNE BRADSTREET (1612–1672) The first notable poet in American literature, Bradstreet was born in England, where her father, a Puritan, managed the business affairs of the estate of the earl of Lincoln. Unlike most women of her time, Bradstreet received a good deal of formal education. At age sixteen, she married Simon Bradstreet, a graduate of Cambridge University, who, like her father, was a Puritan. Two years later, Anne Bradstreet, her husband, and her parents set sail for the Massachusetts Bay Colony, where her father and husband became governors. Anne and Simon Bradstreet settled on a farm near Andover, on the Merrimac River, where the primitive conditions of life left her unhappy and unsatisfied for a period. Ultimately, she reconciled to this new life and her role as a wife, giving birth to eight children. But despite the demands of domestic life in a frontier village, she read a great deal and wrote poetry, which she circulated among family and friends. One of her relatives, who preserved copies of her poems without her knowledge, took them to England, where they were published in 1650 under the title *The Tenth Muse Lately Sprung Up in America . . . By a Gentlewoman of Those Parts.* The first volume of poetry by an English colonist, it was to be the only volume of Bradstreet's poetry published during her lifetime. But she continued to write new poems and to revise her older ones. These later poems were included in the second edition of *The Tenth Muse,* published posthumously in 1678.

KATE BRAVERMAN (b. 1950)   Braverman grew up in Los Angeles. She was a runaway, a teenage mother, and a drug addict. She managed to earn degrees from the University of California at Berkeley and Sonoma State University, but it wasn't until she was thirty-five and living in her car with her daughter that she achieved sobriety. Braverman claims that her first novel, *Lithium for Medea* (1979), is also the first novel written in English that features a "heroin-addicted heroine." She is the author of three other novels, four books of poetry, two collections of short stories, and, most recently, *Frantic Transmissions to and from Los Angeles: An Accidental Memoir* (2006). She has won numerous awards, including the Pushcart Prize in 2007. She currently lives in San Francisco and often performs her poetry to live music.

JOHN BREHM (b. 1955)   Brehm was born in Lincoln, Nebraska, and educated at the University of Nebraska and Cornell University. His poems have appeared in *Poetry*, the *Gettysburg Review*, the *Southern Review*, *Barrow Street*, *Prairie Schooner*, *The Best American Poetry*, and many other journals. He has taught at Cornell University, Emerson College, and Portland State University, and he currently works as a freelance writer in Brooklyn. He is the author of *Sea of Faith*, which won the University of Wisconsin Press Brittingham Prize in 2004, and a chapbook, *The Way Water Moves* (2002). He is associate editor of *The Oxford Book of American Poetry* (2005).

GWENDOLYN BROOKS (1917–2000)   Brooks, who was born in Topeka, Kansas, attended public schools in Chicago and graduated from Wilson Junior College in 1936. She received early recognition for her talent when she attended a poetry workshop at Chicago's Southside Community Art Center. Shortly after, she published her first book of poems, *A Street in Bronzeville* (1945). She quickly established her reputation as a major poet with *Annie Allen* (1949), which received the Pulitzer Prize for Poetry, making Brooks the first African American to receive this distinction. Her many honors include her designation as poet laureate of Illinois (1968) and as poetry consultant to Congress (1985–1986). Although her poetry always focused on the hardships and joys of being poor and black, she steadily moved away from the apolitical integrationist views of her early years. By the 1960s, she had become a passionate advocate of African American consciousness and activism. In addition to reworking traditional forms such as the ballad and sonnet, Brooks achieved greater power in many poems by juxtaposing formal speech with black vernacular. Her other collections of poems include *The Bean Eaters* (1960), *In the Mecca* (1968), *To Disembark* (1981), and *Children Coming Home* (1992). She also published a novel, *Maude Martha* (1953), and an autobiography, *Report from Part One* (1972). Her final volume of poetry, *Montgomery and Other Poems*, was published posthumously in 2003. Its title is taken from the Alabama city that one critic describes as "one of those iconic sites of the Civil Rights Movement, in large part because of the yearlong bus boycotts from 1955 to 1956."

ROBERT BROWNING (1812–1889) Born in London, Browning attended a private school and was later tutored at home. After one year as a student of Greek at the University of London, he moved with his family to Hatcham, where he studied, wrote poetry, and practiced writing for the theater. In 1845, he began exchanging poems and letters with the already famous poet Elizabeth Barrett; they eloped in 1846. They moved to Italy, where Browning completed most of his work. When Elizabeth died in 1861, he returned to England and began to establish his own reputation. He is noted especially for his fine dramatic monologues in which a wide range of characters reveal the complexity of human belief and passion. His many volumes of poetry include *Dramatis Personae* (1864) and *The Ring and the Book* (1868–1869).

ROBERT BURNS (1759–1796) Born in Scotland to a family of poor tenant farmers, Burns was working in the fields with his father by age twelve. During these early years, the family moved often, in fruitless attempts to improve their lot. Although Burns received formal education only intermittently, he read widely on his own. After the death of his father, Burns and his brother worked vainly to make their farm pay, an effort Burns was able to abandon when his first volume of poetry, *Poems, Chiefly in the Scottish Dialect* (1786) brought him overnight fame. One result of this fame was his appointment as an excise officer, a position that gave him some financial security while he continued to write poetry. Burns's humble origins instilled in him a lifelong sympathy for the poor and downtrodden, the rebels and iconoclasts, as well as a disdain for religion, particularly Calvinism and what he considered the hypocrisy of its "devout" ministers.

SCOTT CAIRNS (b. 1954) Born in Tacoma, Washington, Cairns earned degrees from Washington University, Hollins College, Bowling Green State University, and the University of Utah. He has taught at Kansas State University, Westminster College, the University of North Texas, and Old Dominion University and is currently the director of the Creative Writing Program and the Center for the Literary Arts at the University of Missouri. His six collections of poetry include *The Theology of Doubt* (1985), *The Translation of Babel* (1990), *Figures for the Ghost* (1994), *Recovered Body* (1998), *Philokalia* (2002), and *Compass of Affection: Poems New and Selected* (2006). He was named a Guggenheim fellow in 2006. His most recent book is a spiritual memoir, *Short Trip to the Edge: Where Earth Meets Heaven—a Pilgrimage* (2007). Although Cairn's work is religious in nature, he has said, "I'm not much interested in reducing my vocation as a poet to something like propagandist. I write poems to find things out, not to communicate some previously ossified conclusion."

RAYMOND CARVER (1938–1988) Carver was born in Clatskanie, Oregon, the son of a sawmill worker and a mother who did odd jobs. He graduated from high school at age eighteen, and was married and the father of two children before he was twenty. The following years were difficult as he struggled to develop a writing career while supporting a family. While at Chico State College (now California State University at Chico), Carver took a creative writing course that profoundly affected him. He went on to earn a B.A. (1963) from Humboldt State College in Eureka and spent the following year studying writing at the University of Iowa. As he became known, he began to lecture on English and creative writing at various universities, including the University of Iowa's Writers' Workshop. He taught at Goddard College in Vermont and was professor of English at Syracuse University from 1980 to 1983. In 1983, he received the Mildred and Harold Strauss Living Award, which allowed him to devote the next five years to writing. His first collection of short stories, *Will You Please Be Quiet, Please?* (1976), was nominated for the National Book Award. Other short-story collections include *What We Talk About When We Talk About Love* (1981) and *Cathedral* (1984). He also published five volumes of poems, among them *Near Klamath* (1968), *Ultramarine* (1986), and *A New Path to the Waterfall* (1989); *No Heroics, Please* (1992) was published posthumously. During the last ten years of his life, Carver lived with the poet and short-story writer Tess Gallagher, whom he married shortly before his death.

MARILYN CHIN (b. 1955) Chin emigrated with her family from Hong Kong, grew up in Portland, Oregon, and earned degrees from the University of Massachusetts and the University of Iowa. She is the author of three volumes of poetry: *Dwarf Bamboo* (1987), *The Phoenix Gone, the Terrace Empty* (1994), and *Rhapsody in Plain Yellow* (2002). She has received two grants from the National Endowment for the Arts as well as a Stegner Fellowship, the PEN/Josephine Miles Award, four Pushcart Prizes, and a Fulbright scholarship. She is codirector of the M.F.A. program at San Diego State University. About her work, Chin says, "My poetry both laments and celebrates my 'hyphenated' identity. . . . I am an American poet, a hyphenated American poet, to be precise; and what is American about my poetry is my muse's indomitable conviction to hammer the rich virtues and contradictions of my adopted country into a fusionist's delight."

KATE CHOPIN (1851–1904) Born Kate O'Flaherty in St. Louis, Missouri, Chopin was raised by her mother, grandmother, and great grandmother, all widows, after her father's death when she was four. In 1870, following her graduation from Sacred Heart Convent, she married Oscar Chopin and moved to New Orleans, where she became a housewife and eventually had six children. After her husband's death in 1882, she returned to her mother's home in St. Louis and began her career as a writer. Her first novel, *At Fault* (1890), and her stories, collected in *Bayou Folk* (1894) and *A Night in Acadie* (1897), gained her a reputation as a vivid chronicler of the lives of Creoles and Acadians (Cajuns) in Louisiana. Many of these stories explore a female protagonist's attempts to achieve self-fulfillment. Her novel *The Awakening* (1899) is probably her most ambitious exploration of this theme. It is the story of a woman whose awakening to her passion and inner self leads her to adultery and suicide. The storm of controversy with which this work was met virtually ended Chopin's literary career.

JILL CHRISTMAN (b. 1969) Christman earned her M.F.A. at the University of Alabama and is currently a professor at Ball State University, where she teaches courses in creative nonfiction. Her memoir, *Darkroom: A Family Exposure* (2002), which chronicles her difficult childhood and a string of family tragedies, won the Associated Writing Programs Award for Creative Nonfiction. More recently, Christman's essays have appeared in journals such as *Brevity, Harpur Palate,* and *Mississippi Review.* She lives with her husband and daughter in Muncie, Indiana.

SANDRA CISNEROS (b. 1954) Cisneros, the daughter of a Mexican father and a Mexican American mother, grew up in poor neighborhoods of Chicago, where she attended public schools. The only daughter among seven children, Cisneros recalled that because her brothers attempted to control her and expected her to assume a traditional female role, she grew up feeling as if she had "seven fathers." The family's frequent moves, many of them between the United States and Mexico to visit a grandmother, left Cisneros feeling alone and displaced. She found refuge both in reading and in writing poems and stories. In the late 1970s, Cisneros's writing talent earned her admission to the University of Iowa's Writers' Workshop. There, Cisneros observed, "Everyone seemed to have some communal knowledge which I did not have. . . . My classmates were from the best schools in the country. They had been bred as fine hothouse flowers. I was a yellow weed among the city's cracks." This realization led Cisneros to focus her writing on the conflicts and yearnings of her own life and culture. Her writings include four volumes of poetry—*Bad Boys* (1980), *The Rodrigo Poems* (1985), *My Wicked, Wicked Ways* (1987), and *Loose Woman* (1994)—and three volumes of fiction—*The House on Mango Street* (1983), *Woman Hollering Creek and Other Stories* (1991), and *Carmelo* (2002). She is also the author of a bilingual children's book, *Hairs = Pelitos* (1994). She received a prestigious MacArthur Fellowship in 1995. Her most recent work, *Vintage Cisneros* (2004), includes excerpts from her novels as well as previously published poems and short stories.

LUCILLE CLIFTON (b. 1936) Born in Depew, New York, Clifton attended Howard University (1953–1955) and Fredonia State Teachers College. She worked as a claims clerk in the New York State Division of Employment, Buffalo (1958–1960), and as literature assistant in the Office of Education in Washington, D.C. (1960–1971). In 1969, she received the YM-YWHA Poetry Center Discovery Award, and her first collection, *Good Times,* was selected as one of the ten best books of 1969 by the *New York Times.* From 1971 to 1974 she was poet-in-residence at Coppin State College in Baltimore, and in 1979 she was named poet laureate of the state of Maryland. She has written many collections for children and a free-verse chronicle of five generations of her family, *Generations: A Memoir* (1976). Her most recent publication is *Mercy: Poems* (2004). In 2007, Clifton was awarded the Ruth Lilly Poetry Prize, a prestigious honor given to living U.S. poets "whose lifetime accomplishments warrant extraordinary recognition." Noted for celebrating ordinary people and everyday things, Clifton has said, "I am a black woman poet, and I sound like one."

JOSHUA CLOVER (b. 1962)   Clover was born in Berkeley, California; he grew up there and just outside of Boston. He graduated from Boston University and the University of Iowa's Writers' Workshop and is currently a professor at the University of California at Davis. Clover has been a regular contributor to the *New York Times Sunday Book Review,* the *Village Voice,* the *Nation,* and *Spin* magazine. He has won two Pushcart Prizes and received a grant from the National Endowment for the Arts. His two volumes of poetry are *Madonna anno domini* (1997), which won the Academy of American Poets' Walt Whitman Award, and *The Totality for Kids* (2006). His most recent book, a cultural study titled *1989: Bob Dylan Didn't Have This to Sing About,* is set to be published in 2009.

JUDITH ORTIZ COFER (b. 1952)   Cofer was born in Hormigueros, Puerto Rico. She earned a B.A. (1974) from Augusta College and an M.A. (1977) from Florida Atlantic University and briefly attended Oxford University. She began her teaching career as a bilingual instructor in Florida public schools and taught at a number of schools, including the University of Miami and the University of Georgia. Her first volume of poems, *Latin Women Pray,* appeared in 1981, and she has since published poetry collections, essays, and a novel. Her recent work includes several multigenre collections of stories, poems, and essays about coming of age in the barrio, including *The Year of Our Revolution: New and Selected Stories and Poems* (1998) and *Woman in Front of the Sun: On Becoming a Writer* (2000). More recently, she published a novel, *Call Me Maria* (2004), and a collection of poetry, *A Love Story Beginning in Spanish* (2005). Cofer points out that her family is an important source for her writing. "The place of birth itself becomes a metaphor for the things we must all leave behind; the assimilation of a new culture is the coming into maturity by accepting the terms necessary for survival."

BILLY COLLINS (b. 1941)   Collins was born in New York City and earned a B.A. (1963) from the College of the Holy Cross and a Ph.D. (1971) from the University of California at Riverside. He has been teaching at the City University of New York since 1971. *Pokerface,* the first of his several books of poetry, was published in 1977. Collins's later work attracted so much attention that his early poetry books became economically valuable. Consequently, the University of Pittsburgh Press, publisher of *The Art of Drowning* (1995) and *Picnic, Lightning* (1998), at first withheld permission from Random House to reprint earlier poems in Collins's *Sailing around the Room: New and Selected Poems* (2000). The matter was settled, and Random House published his next collection of poems, *Nine Horses* (2002). The struggle between Random House and the University of Pittsburgh Press over the rights to Collins's work made him sufficiently notorious. He has since published *The Trouble with Poetry and Other Poems* (2005) and *Ballistics: Poems* (2008). He has won several poetry prizes as well as fellowships from the New York Foundation for the Arts, the National Endowment for the Arts, and the Guggenheim Foundation. Collins was the poet laureate of the United States from 2001 to 2003 and the poet laureate for New York State from 2004 to 2006. In 2005, he was the first recipient of the Mark Twain Prize for Humor in Poetry. He commented to one journalist: "I think my work has to do with a sense that we are attempting, all the time, to create a logical, rational path through the day. To the left and right there are an amazing set of distractions that we usually can't afford to follow. But the poet is willing to stop anywhere."

VICTOR HERNANDEZ CRUZ (b. 1949)   Cruz was born in Aguas Buenas, Puerto Rico, and immigrated with his family to New York City in 1954. He recalls, "My family life was full of music, guitars and conga drums, maracas and songs. . . . Even when it was five below zero in New York [my mother] sang warm tropical ballads." By 1966, he had already completed a collection of verse, *Papa Got His Gun, and Other Poems,* and in 1969 published *Snaps.* He has edited *Umbra* magazine in New York, lectured at the University of California, Berkeley, and taught at San Francisco State University. Cruz says he writes in three languages: Spanish, English, and Bilingual. "From the mixture a totally new language emerges, an intense collision, not just of words, but of attitudes." His other works include *Mainland* (1973), *Tropicalizations* (1976), *Red Beans: Poems* (1991), *Panoramas* (1997), *Maraca: New and Selected Poems, 1965–2000* (2001), and, most recently, *The Mountain in the Sea* (2006). Cruz is also co-editor of the poetry anthology *Paper Dance: 55 Latino Poets* (2008).

COUNTEE CULLEN (1903–1946)   Born Countee L. Porter in New York City, Cullen was adopted by the Reverend and Mrs. Cullen in 1918 and raised in Harlem. He was extraordinarily precocious, and by 1920 his poems had been published in *Poetry,* the *Nation,* and *Harper's.* He published his famous poem "Heritage" in 1925, the year he graduated from New York University. After earning an M.A. in English from Harvard in 1926, he taught French in a junior high school and was assistant editor of the National Urban League's *Opportunity: Journal of Negro Life.* Cullen, along with Langston Hughes and Jean Toomer, was a central figure in the Harlem Renaissance of the 1920s. He received a Guggenheim Fellowship in 1929. In addition to five volumes of poetry, he published a novel, *One Way to Heaven* (1932), which deals with the interaction between upper- and lower-class African Americans in Harlem in the 1920s.

E. E. CUMMINGS (1894–1962)   Born in Cambridge, Massachusetts, Edward Estlin Cummings attended Harvard University (B.A., 1915; M.A., 1916), served as a volunteer ambulance driver in France during World War I, was imprisoned for three months in a French detention camp, served in the United States Army (1918–1919), and then studied art and painting in Paris (1920–1924). His prose narrative *The Enormous Room* (1922), a recollection of his imprisonment, brought instant acclaim. Several volumes of poetry followed. His experiments with punctuation, line division, and capitalization make his work immediately recognizable. In a letter to young poets published in a high school newspaper,

Cummings said, "[N]othing is quite so easy as using words like somebody else. We all of us do exactly this nearly all the time—and whenever we do it, we're not poets."

CATHERINE DAVIS (1924–2002) Davis studied poetry with Allen Tate at the University of Minnesota and with J. V. Cunningham at the University of Chicago before going to Stanford University on a Stegner Creative Writing Fellowship in 1950. She studied with Yvor Winters, worked for the Stanford University Press as a copy editor, and won several poetry prizes. Winters praised her work in *Forms of Discovery* (1967), and included seven of her poems in *Quest for Reality* (1969). In 1953, Winters wrote to Louise Bogan, *New Yorker* poetry editor, asking her help in finding editorial work for Davis in New York: she "grew up in extreme poverty and in pretty rough surroundings and has had a hard life all the way." Davis lived in New York in the early 1950s and moved to Alexandria, Virginia, in the late 1950s to work in Washington and study at George Washington University. During this time she purchased a handpress and self-published two pamphlets of her work: *The Leaves: Lyrics and Epigrams* (1960) and *Second Beginnings and Other Poems* (1961). She also published widely in periodicals such as *Poetry, Paris Review,* and *Southern Review* and in the anthology *The New Poets of England and America* (1957). In the early 1960s, she studied at the Creative Writing Workshop, University of Iowa, where she published another fine press book, *Under This Lintel* (1962) while working in the University of Iowa Typographic Laboratory under the distinguished printer Harry Duncan. She taught at various schools throughout the country and spent her later years teaching at the University of Massachusetts–Boston. She died after suffering from Alzheimer's disease for two years. In a 1973 *Southern Review* essay, Helen Pinkerton Trimpi wrote that Davis's contribution to the classical epigram is "her adaptation of it to her own subject matter: physical, mental, and moral destitution."

TOI DERRICOTTE (b. 1941) Derricotte was born in Hamtramck, Michigan. She earned degrees from Wayne State University and New York University and is now a professor of English at the University of Pittsburgh. She is the author of four books of poetry: *The Empress of the Death House* (1978), *Natural Birth* (1983), *Captivity* (1989), and *Tender* (1997). Her memoir, *The Black Notebooks: An Interior Journey* (1997), chronicles her African American family's experience as one of the first to move into an all-white suburb in New Jersey. In fact, racism is one of the central themes in her work; Derricotte is a light-skinned black woman who often "passes" for white. She has said, "My skin causes certain problems continuously, problems that open the issue of racism over and over like a wound."

EMILY DICKINSON (1830–1886) Dickinson, one of three children, was born in Amherst, Massachusetts. Her father was a prominent lawyer. Except for one year away at a nearby college and a trip with her sister to Washington, D.C., to visit her father when he was serving in Congress, she lived out her life, unmarried, in her parents' home. During her trip to Washington, she met the Reverend Charles Wadsworth, a married man, whom she came to characterize as her "dearest earthly friend." Little is known of this relationship except that Dickinson's feelings for Wadsworth were strong. In 1862 Wadsworth moved to San Francisco, an event that coincided with a period of Dickinson's intense poetic creativity. Also in that year, she initiated a literary correspondence with the critic T. W. Higginson, to whom she sent some of her poems for his opinion. Higginson, although he recognized her talent, was puzzled by her startling originality and urged her to write more conventionally. Unable to do so, she concluded, we may surmise, that her poems would not be published in her lifetime. In fact, only seven of her poems were published while she was alive, none of them with her consent. After her death, the extraordinary richness of her imaginative life came to light with the discovery of her more than one thousand poems.

JOAN DIDION (b. 1934)   A fifth-generation Californian, Didion was born in Sacramento and raised in the great central plain of California, an area she often describes nostalgically in her work. As an undergraduate English major at the University of California, Berkeley, she won an essay prize sponsored by *Vogue* magazine. As a result, *Vogue* hired her, and for eight years she lived in New York City, while she rose to associate features editor. She published her first novel, *Run River*, in 1963 and in the same year married the writer John Gregory Dunne. In 1964 the couple returned to California, where they remained for twenty-five years. Although Didion wrote four more novels, her reputation rests on her essays collected as *Slouching towards Bethlehem* (1968) and *The White Album* (1979). In addition to her work as a columnist, essayist, and fiction writer, she has collaborated with her husband on a number of screenplays. She has focused her trenchant powers of observation in two documentary, book-length studies: *Salvador* (1983) and *Miami* (1987). Her reputation as a prose stylist is reflected in a comment by one critic who asserts that "nobody writes better English prose than Joan Didion. Try to rearrange one of her sentences, and you've realized that the sentence was inevitable, a hologram." Among her recent publications are a novel, *The Last Thing He Wanted* (1996), and *Where I Was From* (2004), a meditation on her native state of California. Her latest book, *The Year of Magical Thinking* (2005), is a memoir recounting the year after her husband's death in 2003, during which her only daughter suffered a serious illness. Didion's daughter subsequently died in 2005, at age thirty-nine. The memoir won the National Book Award for nonfiction in 2005 and became a one-woman play on Broadway. In 2007, Didion won the National Book Foundation's annual Medal for Distinguished Contribution to American Letters and the Evelyn F. Burkey Award from the Writers Guild of America.

STEPHEN DOBYNS (b. 1941)   Dobyns was born in Orange, New Jersey, and grew up in New Jersey, Michigan, Virginia, and Pennsylvania. He attended Wayne State University and the University of Iowa and worked as a reporter for the *Detroit News*. He has taught at a number of institutions, including Sarah Lawrence College, Warren Wilson College, the University of Iowa, Syracuse University, and Boston University. He is the author of ten books of poetry, among them *Velocities: New and Selected Poems, 1966–1992* (1994); *The Porcupine's Kisses* (2002); and *Mystery, So Long* (2005). He has also written ten novels in his Charlie Bradshaw detective series, as well as ten other novels, most recently *The Church of Dead Girls* (1997) and *Boy in the Water* (1999). His other works include a collection of essays, *Best Words, Best Order* (1996), and a collection of short stories, *Eating Naked* (2000). He has won numerous awards as well as fellowships from the National Endowment for the Arts and the Guggenheim Foundation. He lives in Boston with his wife and three children.

E. L. DOCTOROW (b. 1931)   Doctorow was born and raised in New York City, where he attended the Bronx High School of Science. After earning an A.B. degree with honors at Kenyon College, Ohio, he returned to new York for a year of graduate studies and then served in the U.S. Army. On his return to New York, he worked as senior editor for New American Library from 1959 to 1964. During this period, he also worked as a script reader for Columbia Pictures, a job which he said required him "to suffer one lousy Western after another, and it occurred to me that I could lie about the West in a much more interesting way than any of these people were lying." The result was his first novel, *Welcome to Hard Times* (1961), a dark, symbolic novel about the West. Among his subsequent novels are *The Book of Daniel* (1971), a fictionalized account of the lives of Julius and Ethel Rosenberg, executed for conspiracy to commit treason during the Cold War (adapted in 1983 into the film *Daniel*, directed by Sidney Lumet). This novel was followed by *Ragtime* (1975), a sprawling historical novel about early twentieth-century America (adapted in 1981 into the film *Ragtime*, directed by Milos Forman). *Ragtime* was named by the editorial board of the Modern Library as one of the 100 best English-language novels of the twentieth century. Doctorow's most recent novel, *The March* (2005), won the PEN/Faulkner Award and the National Book Critics Circle Award. He then published *Creationists: Selected Essays 1993–2006*. He has received numerous awards and prizes, among them the National Book Award and the National Humanities Medal. Since 1982, Doctorow has taught at New York University, where he holds the Lewis and Loretta Brennan Glucksman Chair of English and American Letters.

JOHN DONNE (1572–1631)   Born in London into a prosperous Roman Catholic family of tradespeople, at a time when England was staunchly anti-Catholic, Donne was forced to leave Oxford University without a degree because of his religion. He studied law and at the same time read widely in theology in an attempt to decide whether the Roman or the Anglican Church was the true Catholic Church, a decision he was not able to make for many years. In the meantime, he became known as a witty man of the world and the author of original, often dense, erotic poems. Donne left his law studies, participated in two naval expeditions, and then became secretary to a powerful noble, a job he lost when he was briefly sent to prison for secretly marrying his patron's niece. In 1615, at the age of forty-two, Donne accepted ordination in the Anglican Church. He quickly earned a reputation as one of the greatest preachers of his time. He was dean of St. Paul's from 1621 until his death. In his later years, Donne repudiated the poetry of his youth.

MARK DOTY (b. 1953)   Doty was born in Maryville, Tennessee, and earned degrees from Drake University in Des Moines, Iowa, and Goddard College in Plainfield, Vermont. He was a graduate-level creative writing professor at the University of Houston before joining the faculty at Rutgers University. His poetry has appeared in numerous publications, among them the *Atlantic Monthly, Ploughshares, Poetry,* and the *New Yorker.* Doty has published several collections of poems, most recently *Source* (2001), *School of the Arts* (2005), *Theories and Apparitions* (2008), and *Fire to Fire: New and Selected Poems* (2008), which won the National Book Award for Poetry. He is also the author of *Still Life with Oysters and Lemon: On Objects and Intimacy* (2001) and three memoirs: *Heaven's Coast* (1996), *Firebird* (1999), and *Dog Years* (2007), which made the *New York Times* best-seller list. Doty has received fellowships from the Guggenheim Foundation and the National Endowment for the Arts. He is the only American to win the T. S. Eliot Prize for poetry.

RITA DOVE (b. 1952)   Dove was born in Akron, Ohio, the daughter of an African American research chemist who broke the color barrier in the tire industry. She began writing and staging plays at an early age. In 1970, she was named a Presidential Scholar, an annual award given to the top 100 high-school graduates in the country. She attended Miami University in Ohio on a National Merit Scholarship, graduating Phi Beta Kappa in 1973. After completing a Fulbright fellowship at the University of Tubingen, Germany, she returned to the United States and earned an M.F.A. at the University of Iowa's Writers' Workshop. Her earliest poems appeared in two chapbooks, followed by her first volume of poems, *The Yellow House on the Corner* (1980). Since then, she has published more than a half dozen volumes of poetry, including the Pulitzer Prize–winning *Thomas and Beulah* (1987). In recognition of her poetic achievement, she was appointed poet laureate of the United States in 1993. *On the Bus with Rosa Parks* (1999), inspired by a bus trip the author shared with the celebrated heroine of the civil rights movement, was nominated for a National Book Critics Circle Award. Her most recent volumes are *American Smooth* (2004) and *Sonata Mulattica* (2009). Dove is also the author of a collection of short stories, *Fifth Sunday* (1990); a novel, *Through the Ivory Gate* (1992); and a play, *The Darker Face of the Earth* (1997). Among her many other honors, she has received the National Association for the Advancement of Colored People's Great American Artist Award (2003) and the Duke Ellington Lifetime Achievement Award (2001). She is Commonwealth Professor of Creative Writing at the University of Virginia.

BRIAN DOYLE (b. 1956)   Doyle, the son of a journalist and a teacher, was born in New York City and graduated from the University of Notre Dame. He was an editor at *U.S. Catholic* magazine and a writer at *Boston College Magazine* before becoming the editor of *Portland Magazine* at the University of Portland. He is the author of several books, among them *Credo: Essays on Grace, Altar Boys, Bees, Kneeling, Saints, the Mass, Priests, Strong Women, Epiphanies, a Wake, and the Haunting Thin Energetic Dusty Figure of Jesus the Christ* (1999); *The Wet Engine: Exploring the Mad Wild Miracle of the Heart* (2005); and *Epiphanies and Elegies: Very Short Stories* (2006). His work has also appeared in anthologies, such as *The Best Spiritual Writing* and *The Best American Essays*, and a number of periodicals, among them *Atlantic Monthly, American Scholar, Harper's, Gourmet,* and the *London Times*. Doyle served as editor of the Best Catholic Writing series from Loyola Press from 2004 to 2006. He lives with his wife and three children.

PAUL LAURENCE DUNBAR (1872–1906)   The son of former slaves, Dunbar was born in Dayton, Ohio, where he graduated from Dayton High School (1891) and worked for two years as an elevator operator. In 1894, he worked in Chicago at the World's Columbian Exhibition. His first verse collection, *Oak and Ivy,* was published in 1893. William Dean Howells—an eminent editor, author, and critic—encouraged him to write and had him join a lecture bureau in 1896. Dunbar read his own works in the United States and traveled to England in 1897. While Dunbar maintained that African American poetry was not much different from white poetry—and wrote many poems in standard English—he often wrote poems in black dialect that seemed to cater to the racial stereotypes of his white audience. He died of tuberculosis in 1906. His complete works appear in *The Dunbar Reader* (1975).

STEVE EARLE (b. 1955)   Earle was born in Fort Monroe, Virginia, the son of an air traffic controller, and grew up in Schertz, Texas, where he attended school. At fourteen, he left home for Houston to live with an uncle, who encouraged Earle's guitar playing. By the time he graduated from high school, Earle was launched on a career in music. At age nineteen, he was in Nashville, playing in rockabilly bands and trying to get well-known artists to record his songs. From 1975 to 1978, he was a staff writer for a music division of RCA. His first album, *Guitar Town* (1986), was an instant critical and commercial success, garnering him two Grammy nominations. But after his fourth album, *Shut Up and Die Like an Aviator* (1991), MCA refused to renew his contract because of his severe drug addiction. In 1994, he was arrested and sent to prison for narcotics possession and later paroled after successfully completing a drug rehabilitation program. He resumed his career with *The Hard Way* (1996), an album he said he "almost died in the process of making." The albums that have followed show an artist who has moved steadily away from country music and into hard rock, and they reveal Earle's growing sense of social and political outrage. His album *The Revolution Starts Now* (2004) is comprised wholly of protest songs. It won a Grammy for best contemporary folk album. In the liner notes, Earle writes that the album grew out of his sense of urgency in responding to what was happening both at home and abroad: "The prisoner scandal had just broken and the Bush administration, still reeling from the 9/11 commission hearings, was circling the wagons. The Democrats, for their part, were carefully (sometimes, in my opinion, too carefully) trying to sort out how best to press the advantage. Meanwhile, back here in Tennessee, me and my boys had a deadline to meet." Most recently, Earle released his Grammy-winning album *Washington Square Serenade* (2007), produced an album for Joan Baez, appeared as a recovering drug addict in several episodes of HBO's series *The Wire*, and hosted a show on Sirius Satellite Radio.

T. S. ELIOT (1888–1965)   Thomas Stearns Eliot was born in St. Louis, Missouri. His father was president of the Hydraulic Press Brick Company, and his mother was a teacher, social worker, and writer. Educated in private academies, Eliot earned two philosophy degrees at Harvard University (B.A., 1909; M.A., 1910). After graduate study in Paris and England, he worked for eight years as a clerk in Lloyd's Bank in London and became a naturalized British citizen in 1927. He was editor, then director, of Faber & Gwyer Publishers (later Faber & Faber) from 1925 to 1965 and spent time in the United States as a visiting lecturer and scholar. Admirers and detractors alike agree that Eliot was the most imposing and influential poet writing between the world wars. His poems "The Love Song of J. Alfred Prufrock" (1917) and *The Waste Land* (1922) are among his earliest and most famous. Acknowledging his dependence on a preexisting cultural tradition, Eliot explained: "The existing order is complete before the new work arrives; for order to persist after the supervention of novelty, the whole existing order must be altered." Eliot also wrote plays, including *Murder in the Cathedral* (1935) and *The Cocktail Party* (1950). The long-running Broadway musical *Cats* is based on his 1939 verse collection, *Old Possum's Book of Practical Cats*. He won the Nobel Prize for Literature in 1948.

HARLAN ELLISON (b. 1934)   Born in Cleveland, Ohio, Ellison published his first story when he was thirteen. He left Ohio State University after two years and worked at a variety of odd jobs while establishing himself as a writer. In a career spanning over fifty years, he has written or edited sixty-five books and more than seventeen hundred stories, essays, reviews, articles, motion picture scripts, and teleplays. He has won the Hugo Award ten and a half times, the Nebula Award four times, the Edgar Allan Poe Award of the Mystery Writers of America twice, the Bram Stoker Award of Horror Writers of America twice, the World Fantasy Award, the British Fantasy Award, and the Silver Pen for journalism from P.E.N. He is the only scenarist in Hollywood ever to have won the Writers Guild of America award for Most Outstanding Teleplay four times for solo work. His latest books are *Troublemakers* (2001), a collection for young adults, and *The Essential Ellison: A 50-Year Retrospective Revised & Expanded* (2001). He has also written numerous short stories for various science fiction and fantasy magazines, most recently "Loose Cannon, or Rubber Duckies from Space" (2004) and "Prologue to the Endeavor: Luck Be a Lady Tonight" (2006). In celebration of Ellison's seventy-fifth birthday, documentarian Erik Nelson produced a feature-length film that looks at the life and work of Ellison. The documentary, *Dreams with Sharp Feeth*, was released on DVD in May 2009. Ellison currently lives with his wife, Susan, in the Los Angeles area.

RALPH ELLISON (1914–1994)   Ellison was born in Oklahoma City, Oklahoma. He studied music, specifically trumpet and piano, and sculpture before embarking on a writing career. In New York City, encouraged by his friend and fellow writer Richard Wright, Ellison began writing book reviews, essays, and short stories. He also earned money as a freelance photographer. His first novel, *Invisible Man* (1952), for which he is best known, won the National Book Award in 1953. He published two collections of essays, *Shadow and Act* (1964) and *Going to the Territory* (1986). He taught at Bard College, Rutgers, University the University of Chicago, and New York University before dying of pancreatic cancer in 1994. His short stories were collected and published posthumously in *Flying Home and Other Stories* (1996). Ellison wrote more than 2,000 pages for a second novel, *Juneteenth*, over the span of forty years; it was edited down to 368 pages and published five years after his death, in 1999.

LOUISE ERDRICH (b. 1954)   Erdrich was born in Little Falls, Minnesota, and grew up in North Dakota. Her father was German American and her mother was French and Anishinaabe; Erdrich is a member of the Native American Anishinaabe nation. She earned degrees from Dartmouth College and Johns Hopkins University. Before fully embarking on her writing career, she worked as a lifeguard, waitress, prison poetry teacher, construction flagger, and newspaper editor. She began by publishing poems and short fiction and won the Nelson Algren Prize for her short story "The World's Greatest Fisherman" in 1982. Her first novel, *Love Medicine* (1984), won the National Book Critics Circle Award. She went on to write more than ten other novels, notably *The Beet Queen* (1986), *Tracks* (1988), *The Antelope Wife* (1998), and *The Painted Drum* (2005). In addition to having written five novels for adolescents and three works of nonfiction, Erdrich has published three books of poetry: *Jacklight* (1984), *Baptism of Desire* (1989), and *Original Fire: Selected and New Poems* (2003). Her most recent works are a novel, *The Plague of Doves* (2008), and *The Red Convertible: Collected and New Stories 1978–2008* (2009). She has won several awards including an O. Henry Award, a Pushcart Prize, and a Guggenheim Fellowship. Erdrich owns a bookstore in Minneapolis, Minnesota, and hosts annual writing workshops on the Turtle Mountain Indian Reservation in North Dakota.

WILLIAM FAULKNER (1897–1962)   Faulkner was born in New Albany, Mississippi, and lived most of his life in Oxford, the seat of the University of Mississippi. Although he did not graduate from high school, he attended the university as a special student from 1919 to 1921. During this period, he also worked as a janitor, a bank clerk, and a postmaster. His southern forebears had held slaves, served during the Civil War, endured the deprivations of Reconstruction, fought duels, and even wrote the occasional romance of the old South. Faulkner mined these generous layers of history in his work. He created the mythical Yoknapatawpha County in northern Mississippi and traced the destinies of its inhabitants from the colonial era to the middle of the twentieth century in such novels as *The Sound and the Fury* (1929), *Light in August* (1932), and *Absalom, Absalom!* (1936). Further, Faulkner described the decline of the pre–Civil War aristocratic families and the rise of mean-spirited money-grubbers in a trilogy: *The Hamlet* (1940), *The Town* (1957), and *The Mansion* (1959). Recognition came late, and Faulkner fought a constant battle to keep afloat financially. During the 1940s, he wrote screenplays in Hollywood, but his achievements brought him the Nobel Prize in 1950.

FRANCIS FERGUSSON (1904–1986)   Fergusson was born in Albuquerque, New Mexico. He attended Harvard University and was a Rhodes Scholar at Queen's College of Oxford University. Fergusson is best known for being a theater critic, although he was at one time the associate director of the American Laboratory Theatre in New York City. He also taught literature and drama at several institutions, including Bennington College, Princeton University, Rutgers University, and Indiana University at Bloomington. He twice translated Sophocles' *Electra* (1938 and 1965), wrote a play with music titled *The King and the Duke: A Melodramatic Farce from Huckleberry Finn* (1952), and produced a volume of poetry, *Poems, 1929–1961* (1962). His numerous books of criticism include *The Idea of a Theater: A Study of Ten Plays* (1949), *Dante's Drama of the Mind: A Modern Reading of the "Purgatorio"* (1953), *The Human Image in Dramatic Literature* (1957), *Shakespeare: The Pattern in His Carpet* (1970), and *Literary Landmarks: Essays on the Theory and Practice of Literature* (1976).

LAWRENCE FERLINGHETTI (b. 1919)   Born Lawrence Ferling, this irreverent writer assumed his original family name in 1954. He earned a B.A. in journalism from the University of North Carolina in 1941, served as lieutenant commander in the U.S. Naval Reserve during World War II, and then received graduate degrees from Columbia and the University of Paris. He worked briefly as a translator of French before rising to prominence in the San Francisco–based Beat literary movement of the 1950s, composed of a group of writers who felt strongly that art should be accessible to all, not just to a small group of intellectuals. Ferlinghetti received great praise from many readers and some critics for his attempts to incorporate American vernacular speech and the rhythms of modern jazz into his writings, while he was roundly attacked by defenders of the status quo. Ferlinghetti has been a prolific writer in all genres. In addition, he co-founded the San Francisco bookstore City Lights and two publishing enterprises, City Lights Books and the Pocket Book Series. In 1998 Ferlinghetti was named San Francisco's first poet laureate.

He won the Robert Frost Memorial Medal, the Author's Guild Lifetime Achievement Award, and was elected to the American Academy of Arts and Letters in 2003. In 2005, he received the National Book Foundation's first Literarian Award for outstanding service to the American literary community. He has published two novels, many plays, and over two dozen volumes of poetry including *Americus, Book I* (2004) and *Poetry as Insurgent Art* (2007). His early work, *A Coney Island of the Mind* (1958), remains his most popular and best-selling poetry collection.

ANNIE FINCH (b. 1956)   Finch was born in New Rochelle, New York, and earned degrees from Yale University, the University of Houston, and Stanford University. She taught at the University of Northern Iowa and Miami University of Ohio before assuming her current role as director of the M.F.A. program at the University of Southern Maine. Among her several books of poetry are *The Encyclopedia of Scotland* (1982), *Eve* (1997), *Calendars* (2003), and *Annie Finch's Greatest Hits* (2007). She has also written two opera librettos, translated the poems of French Renaissance poet Louise Labé, and edited several anthologies of poetry and essays. About the influence of other poets on her own work, Finch has said, "I love the way bits of poems I've read, maybe years ago, will find their way subtly, secretly, into the poems I write and surprise me when I find them there. And I love to consciously invoke or copy the form or some other aspect of poems I've read in my own work; it's a wonderful way to pay tribute."

DONALD FINKEL (b. 1929)   Donald Finkel was born in New York City, the son of an attorney. He earned a B.S. (1952) and an M.A. (1953) from Columbia University. In 1956 he married the writer Constance Urdang. Shortly thereafter, Finkel began a university teaching career at the University of Iowa and in 1960 moved to Washington University in St. Louis where he became poet-in-residence. His interest in Antarctica and exploration produced *Endurance: An Antarctic Idyll* and *Going Under* (1978). The first describes the shipwreck and rescue of Ernest Shackleton's 1914 expedition. The second examines two men who explored Kentucky's Mammoth Cave. His many books, including *Selected Shorter Poems* (1987), *A Splintered Mirror: Chinese Poetry from the Democracy Movement* (1991), and *A Question of Seeing: Poems* (1998), have earned him abundant awards and honors, among them a Guggenheim Fellowship (1967), nomination for a National Book Award (1970), and two nominations for the National Book Critics Circle Award (1975, 1981). His most recent volume is *Not So the Chairs: Selected and New Poems* (2003).

HELEN FISHER (b. 1945)   Fisher earned her doctorate degree from the University of Colorado in 1975. She worked as a research associate at the American Museum of Natural History in New York before joining the Department of Anthropology at Rutgers University. She is considered an expert in human brain evolution as it relates to gender, love, mate choice, and sexuality. Articles by Fisher have appeared in numerous journals and magazines, among them *Journal of Comparative Neurology, Journal of Neurophysiology, Journal of Sex and Marital Therapy, American Journal of Physical Anthropology, New York Times Book Review, Psychology Today,* and *Scientific American.* She is the author of four books: *The Sex Contract: The Evolution of Human Behavior* (1982); *Anatomy of Love: The Natural History of Monogamy, Adultery and Divorce* (1992); *The First Sex: The Natural Talents of Women and How They Are Changing the World* (1999); and *Why We Love: The Nature and Chemistry of Romantic Love* (2004). She is currently writing a book about falling in love and the reasons behind choosing one mate over another.

CAROLYN FORCHÉ (b. 1950) Born in Detroit, Forché earned a B.A. in international relations and creative writing at Michigan State University in 1972. After graduate study at Bowling Green State University in 1975, she taught at a number of schools, including the University of Arkansas, Vassar College, Columbia University, and George Mason University. She won the Yale Series of Younger Poets Award in 1976 for her first collection, *Gathering the Tribes.* Other honors include a Guggenheim Fellowship and the Lamont Award (1981). Forché was a journalist for Amnesty International in El Salvador in 1983 and Beirut correspondent for the National Public Radio program *All Things Considered.* Her works include the collections of poetry *The Country between Us* (1981) and *The Angel of History* (1994), both embodying her passionate preoccupation with the dehumanizing effects of political repression. Among her most recent publications are a book of poems, *Blue Hour* (2003), and a memoir, *The Horse on Our Balcony* (2009). She currently teaches and directs the creative writing center at Skidmore College.

SIGMUND FREUD (1856–1939) Sigismund Schlomo Freud, widely accepted as the father of psychoanalysis, was born in Freiberg, Moravia, and raised in Leipzig and Vienna. After attending medical school, he started his own practice in which he focused on neurology. After experimenting with hypnosis as a treatment, he abandoned it in favor of encouraging patients to talk through their issues, the inception of psychotherapy as we know it. Freud is renowned for his pioneering theories about the unconscious mind, repressed memories, psychosexual development, the Oedipus complex, the libido, and the ego, superego, and id. His first book, *The Interpretation of Dreams* (1900), earned him great recognition and remains one of his most widely read works. He wrote a large number of groundbreaking works, contributed to psychological journals, and penned volumes of correspondence. After the Nazi occupation of Austria in 1938, Freud and his family fled to London where, after many years of heavy cigar smoking, he died of oral cancer.

ROBERT FROST (1874–1963) Frost was born in San Francisco but from the age of ten lived in New England. He attended Dartmouth College briefly, became a teacher, but soon decided to resume his formal training and enrolled at Harvard University. He left Harvard after two years without a degree and for several years supported himself and his growing family by tending a farm his grandfather bought for him. When he was not farming, he read and wrote intensively, though he received little recognition. Discouraged by his lack of success, he sold the farm and moved his family to England, where he published his first volumes of poetry, *A Boy's Will* (1913) and *North of Boston* (1914). After three years in England, Frost returned to the United States a recognized poet. Later volumes, notably *Mountain Interval* (1916), *New Hampshire* (1923), *West-Running Brook* (1928), and *A Further Range* (1936), won Frost numerous awards, including two Pulitzer Prizes, and wide popularity. By the time he delivered his poem "The Gift Outright" at the inauguration of President John F. Kennedy in 1961, Frost had achieved the status of unofficial poet laureate of the United States, widely revered and beloved for his folksy manner and seemingly artless, accessible poems.

TESS GALLAGHER (b. 1943)   Gallagher was born in Port Angeles, Washington, the eldest of five children of a logger and longshoreman. She earned degrees from the University of Washington in Seattle and the University of Iowa. She has been married three times, most recently to writer Raymond Carver. She has taught at a number of institutions, among them St. Lawrence University; the University of Montana; Missoula; the University of Arizona, Tucson; Syracuse University; and Willamette University. Her many awards include an Elliston award, multiple grants from the National Endowment for the Arts, and a Guggenheim Fellowship. Gallagher has written two collections of short stories, *The Lover of Horses* (1986) and *At the Owl Woman Saloon* (1996), as well as two collections of essays, *A Concert of Tenses* (1983) and *Soul Barnacles* (2003). She has penned more than ten volumes of poetry, including *Instructions to the Double* (1976), *Moon Crossing Bridge* (1992), *I Stop Writing the Poem* (1992), and *Dear Ghosts,* (2006).

RICHARD GARCIA (b. 1941)   Garcia was born in San Francisco, California, and earned his M.F.A. in creative writing at Warren Wilson College in Asheville, North Carolina. He is the author of four volumes of poetry: *Selected Poems* (1972), *The Flying Garcias* (1991), *Rancho Notorious* (2001), and *The Persistence of Objects* (2006). In addition, his poems have appeared in a number of periodicals, including *Ploughshares, Antioch Review, Blue Moon Review, Slope,* and *Diode.* He is also the author of a bilingual book for children titled *My Aunt Otilia's Spirits* (1978). Among Garcia's awards are a Pushcart Prize and a fellowship from the National Endowment for the Arts. He has served as the poet-in-residence at the Long Beach Museum of Art and at the Children's Hospital Los Angeles. Before assuming his current role as faculty member in the M.F.A. program at Antioch University in Los Angeles, he taught at the University of Southern California and at numerous writing festivals, conferences, and workshops. He lives with his wife and dog on James Island in South Carolina.

DEBORAH GARRISON (b. 1965)   Garrison was born in Ann Arbor, Michigan; she earned degrees from Brown University and New York University. She worked for the *New Yorker* magazine, as part of the editorial staff and as the senior nonfiction editor, for over fifteen years before taking on her current roles as poetry editor at Alfred A. Knopf and senior editor at Pantheon Books. Her poems have appeared in a number of periodicals, among them *Elle*, the *New Yorker*, the *New York Times*, and *Slate*. Her first book of poetry, *A Working Girl Can't Win, and Other Poems* (1998), is considered a poetry best seller. Her second volume of poetry is *The Second Child* (2007). Garrison lives with her husband and three children in Montclair, New Jersey. About her work, both as a poetry editor and a writer, she has said, "There's a real yearning for authenticity. It's just such a pure thing. Poetry isn't being optioned to the movies for $3 million. Poetry is immune to all that stuff. It's a haven."

CHARLOTTE PERKINS GILMAN (1860–1935)   Charlotte Perkins Gilman was born in Hartford, Connecticut. Shortly after her birth, her father deserted the family. Left with two children to support and scant help from their father, her mother was unable to provide her children with a secure and stable childhood. Gilman attended the Rhode Island School of Design for a time and went on to work as a commercial artist and teacher. In 1884 she married Charles Stetson, an artist. Following the birth of her only child the next year, Gilman was immobilized by a deep depression. At the urging of her husband, she became the patient of S. Weir Mitchell, a physician celebrated for his treatment of female nervous disorders. Gilman found the treatment intolerable and finally abandoned it. In 1888, convinced that her marriage threatened her sanity, she moved with her daughter to California and began her productive career as writer and feminist. In 1900, after her divorce, she married her first cousin George Houghton Gilman, enjoying a happy relationship that lasted until his sudden death thirty-four years later. Among Gilman's many works are *Women and Economics* (1899), *The Home: Its Work and Influence* (1903), and *The Man-Made World* (1911), whose thesis is that war and injustice will be eliminated only when women assume a larger role in national and international affairs. Gilman's fiction includes the novels *Moving the Mountain* (1911), *Herland* (1915), and *With Her in Ourland* (1916). Her autobiography, *The Living of Charlotte Perkins Gilman*, was published posthumously in 1935, the year she committed suicide to avoid suffering the final stages of breast cancer.

NIKKI GIOVANNI (b. 1943)   Born Yolande Cornelia Giovanni Jr. in Knoxville, Tennessee, daughter of a probation officer and a social worker, Giovanni graduated with honors from Fisk University in 1967. She attended the University of Pennsylvania School of Social Work and Columbia School of the Arts, was assistant professor of black studies at Queens College (1968), and associate professor of English at Rutgers University (1968–1970). She is currently Distinguished Professor of English at Virginia Tech. Giovanni's early work reflects her social activism as an African American college student in the

1960s, while her later works focus on the individual struggle for fulfillment rather than the collective struggle for black empowerment. Her books include *Black Feeling, Black Talk, Black Judgment* (1970), *My House* (1972), and *The Women and the Men* (1975). Among her most recent publications are *Quilting the Black-Eyed Pea: Poems and Not Quite Poems* (2002), *Acolytes* (2007), and *Hip Hop Speaks to Children* (2008). She was nominated for a Grammy in 2004 for her spoken-word album, *The Nikki Giovanni Poetry Collection*.

SUSAN GLASPELL (1882–1948) Born and raised in Davenport, Iowa, Glaspell began her career as a novelist and author of sentimental short stories for popular magazines. By 1915, she had turned her energies to the theater, becoming one of the founders of the Provincetown Players, a group devoted to experimental drama. In 1916, Glaspell moved with the company, now called the Playwright's Theatre, to Greenwich Village in New York, where for two seasons—as writer, director, and actor—she played an important role in a group that came to have a major influence on the development of American drama. *Trifles* was written to be performed with a group of one-act plays by Eugene O'Neill at the company's summer playhouse on Cape Cod. Among her longer plays that embody a feminist perspective are *The Verge* (1921) and *Allison's House* (1931), a Pulitzer Prize–winning drama based on the life of Emily Dickinson. Among more than forty short stories, some twenty plays, and ten novels, Glaspell's best works deal with the theme of the new woman, presenting a protagonist who embodies the American pioneer spirit of independence and freedom.

LOUISE GLÜCK (b. 1943) Glück was born in New York City and raised on Long Island. She attended Sarah Lawrence College and Columbia University and has taught at over a dozen institutions, among them the University of Iowa, Columbia University, the University of California at Berkeley, and Harvard University; she is currently a faculty member at Boston University and a writer in residence at Yale University. Her numerous awards include an Academy of American Poets Prize, a National Book Critics Circle Award, a Pulitzer Prize, and most recently the Wallace Stevens Award in 2008. She is also the recipient of fellowships from the Guggenheim Foundation, the Rockefeller Foundation, and the National Endowment for the Arts. Glück was the poet laureate of the United States from 2003 to 2004. She is the author of one nonfiction book, *Proofs and Theories: Essays on Poetry* (1994), and a dozen volumes of poetry, including *Firstborn* (1968), *The Triumph of Achilles* (1985), *Ararat* (1990), *The Wild Iris* (1992), *Vita Nova* (1999), and *Averno* (2006), her latest.

MARILYN HACKER (b. 1942) Hacker, the only child of two chemists, was born and raised in the Bronx and graduated from the Bronx High School of Science at age fifteen. She immediately enrolled at New York University, dropped out, got married, and worked as an editor for a time, before returning to NYU to earn a bachelor's degree in Romance languages. Hacker's poems appeared in *Epoch, London Magazine, Ambit,* and *New American Review* before her first book of poetry, *Presentation Piece,* was published in 1974 and won the National Book Award. Among her numerous other volumes of poetry are *Separations* (1976), *Taking Notice* (1980), *Winter Numbers: Poems* (1995), *Desesperanto: Poems 1999–2002* (2003), and *Essays on Departure: New and Selected Poems* (2006). She has served as editor of the *Kenyon Review* and taught at the City College of New York. Hacker is known for her use of traditional poetic forms, including the sonnet and villanelle, to explore subjects such as feminism, anti-Semitism, AIDS, suffering, lesbianism, and her own battle with breast cancer.

MARK HALLIDAY (b. 1949) Halliday earned bachelor's and master's degrees from Brown University before earning a doctorate in English literature from Brandeis University. He taught at Wellesley College, the University of Pennsylvania, Western Michigan University, and Indiana University before joining the faculty at Ohio University. His is the author of five volumes of poems: *Little Star* (1987), *Tasker Street* (1992), *Selfwolf* (1999), *Jab* (2002), and *Keep This Forever* (2008). He was awarded the Rome Prize of the American Academy of Arts and Letters in 2001 and a fellowship from the Guggenheim Foundation in 2006. About the colloquial style of his poetry, Halliday has said, "I love the analogy between a poem and a speech that you might actually hear in real life. . . . People do, over a few beers, let's say, if they're having trouble in their marriage or they're trying to change their lives, they do go from anecdote to meditation to comic speculation and then back to the beer, back to a joke— the movement of thought has those different levels. I love poems that show a speaker living through those moves."

LORRAINE HANSBERRY (1930–1965) Lorraine Hansberry was born into a prosperous, middle-class African American family on the south side of Chicago. When she was seven, her family went to court over an attempt to deny them the right to buy a home in a restricted white neighborhood. Their lawsuit challenging the restrictive covenant was finally decided in their favor by the U.S. Supreme Court. Hansberry later recalled, "Both of my parents were strong-minded, civic-minded, exceptionally race-minded people who made enormous sacrifices on behalf of the struggle for civil rights throughout their lifetimes." After graduating from the segregated public school system of Chicago, she attended the University of Wisconsin and studied at the Art Institute of Chicago and abroad. She soon gave up her artistic plans and moved to New York City to pursue a writing career. She also became politically active in liberal causes. During a protest demonstration at New York University, she met Robert Nemiroff, a white writer and political activist. They married in 1953. Encouraged by her husband, Hansberry finally completed *A Raisin in the Sun,* a play she had been working on for some time. It opened in 1959, becoming the first play written by a black woman to be produced on Broadway. An immediate success, the play won the New York Drama Critics' Circle Award. A film version, for which she wrote the screenplay, was released in 1961. Her next play, *The Sign* *in Sidney Brustein's Window* (1964), met with less success. She was working on another play, *Les Blancs,* when she died of cancer (the play was produced in 1970). Although Nemiroff and Hansberry divorced in 1964, he was appointed her literary executor and assembled, from his former wife's writings and words, a dramatic autobiography titled *To Be Young, Gifted, and Black* (1969).

THOMAS HARDY (1840–1928) Hardy was born near Dorchester in southeastern England (on which he based the Wessex of many of his novels and poems). Hardy worked for the ecclesiastical architect John Hicks from 1856 to 1861. He then moved to London to practice architecture and took evening classes at King's College for six years. In 1867, he gave up architecture to become a full-time writer, and after writing short stories and poems, he found success as a novelist. *The Mayor of Casterbridge* (1886) and *Tess of the d'Urbervilles* (1891) reveal Hardy's concern for victims of circumstance and his appeal to humanitarian sympathy in readers. After his novel *Jude the Obscure* (1896) was strongly criticized, Hardy set aside prose fiction and returned to poetry—a genre in which he was most prolific and successful after he reached the age of seventy.

MICHAEL S. HARPER (b. 1938) Born in Brooklyn, New York, Harper earned degrees from what is now California State University, Los Angeles, before earning an M.F.A. from the University of Iowa. He has been a professor at Brown University since 1970. He is the author of ten books of poetry, among them *Dear John, Dear Coltrane* (1970), *History Is Your Own Heartbeat* (1971), *Images of Kin* (1977), and, most recently, *Selected Poems* (2002). His poems have also appeared in a number of periodicals, including *Black Scholar, Black World, Chicago Review, Negro American Literature Forum, Negro Digest,* and *Poetry* magazine. Among his many awards are a Black Academy of Arts and Letters award; a National Institute of Arts and Letters award; a Guggenheim Fellowship; a National Endowment for the Arts creative writing award, and a Melville-Crane Award from the Poetry Society of America. Harper served as poet laureate of Rhode Island from 1988 to 1993.

NATHANIEL HAWTHORNE (1804–1864) The son of a merchant sea captain who died in a distant port when Nathaniel was four, Hawthorne grew up in genteel poverty in Massachusetts and Maine. His earliest American ancestor, the magistrate William Hathorne, ordered the whipping of a Quaker woman in Salem. William's son John was one of the three judges at the Salem witch trials of 1692. Aware of his family's role in colonial America, Hawthorne returned to Salem after graduating from Bowdoin College (where future president Franklin Pierce was a friend and classmate), determined to be a writer. He recalled and destroyed copies of his first novel, the mediocre *Fanshawe* (1828). His short stories, often set in Puritan America, revealed a moral complexity that had not troubled his righteous ancestors William and John. His success as an author allowed him to marry Sophia Peabody in 1842 (after a four-year engagement). Though his stories were critically praised, they did not earn much money, and in 1846, he used his political connections with the Democratic Party to obtain a job at the Salem custom house. His dismissal in 1849 (when the Democrats lost) produced both anger and resolve. The result was a great American novel, *The Scarlet Letter* (1850), which made him famous and improved his fortune. Although he was friendly with Emerson and his circle of optimistic transcendentalists (some of whom established the utopian socialist community at Brook Farm), Hawthorne's vision of the human condition was considerably darker. Herman Melville dedicated *Moby-Dick* to Hawthorne and characterized him as a man who could say "No" in thunder.

ROBERT HAYDEN (1913–1980)   Born in Detroit, Hayden studied at Wayne State University and the University of Michigan (M.A., 1944). In 1946, he joined the faculty of Fisk University. He left Fisk in 1968 for a professorship at the University of Michigan, where he remained until his death. He produced some ten volumes of poetry but did not receive the acclaim many thought he deserved until late in life, with the publication of *Words in the Mourning Time: Poems* (1971). In the 1960s, he aroused some hostility from African Americans who wanted him to express more militancy. But Hayden did not want to be part of what he called a "kind of literary ghetto." He considered his own work "a form of prayer—a prayer for illumination, perfection."

SEAMUS HEANEY (b. 1939)   Heaney, the eldest of nine children, was born on his family's farm near Belfast in County Derry, Northern Ireland. He attended local schools; earned a degree in English with first-class honors from Queen's University, Belfast; and received a teacher's certificate in English from St. Joseph's College in Belfast. He published his first writings while a student at St. Joseph's and began a career as a teacher. His first volume of poetry, *Death of a Naturalist* (1966), won several prizes and launched Heaney's distinguished career as a poet. He has produced several volumes of essays, most recently *Finders Keepers: Selected Prose 1971–2001* (2002). Among his numerous volumes of poetry are *The Spirit Level* (1996), *Opened Ground: Poems 1966–1996* (1998), *The Riverbank Field* (2007), and *Articulations* (2008). His 2006 volume, *District and Circle,* won the T. S. Eliot Prize. Other recent publications include *Beowulf: A New Verse Translation* (2002) and *The Burial at Thebes: A Version of Sophocles' Antigone* (2004). He has taught at Oxford University, the University of California at Berkeley, and Harvard University. An immensely popular poet, he enjoys the support of a host of "Heaneyboppers" who attend his readings. Several modern critics characterize him as "the most important Irish poet since Yeats." When asked "about his abiding interest in memorializing the people of his life, he replied, 'The elegiac Heaney? There's nothing else.'" In 1995, Heaney was awarded the Nobel Prize for Literature.

ERNEST HEMINGWAY (1899–1961)   Born in Oak Park, Illinois, Hemingway became a cub reporter after high school. After World War I—during which he was seriously wounded while serving as an ambulance driver—he lived in Paris, a member of a lively and productive expatriate community characterized by Gertrude Stein as "a lost generation." He lived an active life, not only as a writer but as a war correspondent, big-game hunter, and fisherman. In such novels as *The Sun Also Rises* (1926), *A Farewell to Arms* (1929), and *For Whom the Bell Tolls* (1940), his fictional characters exhibit a passion for courage and integrity, for grace under pressure. Hemingway's spare, unembellished style reinforced his central theme that one must confront danger and live honorably. He won the Nobel Prize for Literature in 1954. In 1961, unable to write because treatment for mental instability affected his memory, he killed himself with the shotgun he had so often used when hunting.

GEORGE HERBERT (1593–1633) Herbert was born in Montgomery, Wales, to a wealthy and important family; his mother was a friend and patron of John Donne. He attended Trinity College, Cambridge, with the aim of becoming a priest; his scholarship gained him the attention of King James I, and Herbert became orator of Cambridge University and a member of Parliament. Herbert remained a courtier until the king's death in 1625. It was then that he decided to return to the church; he was a compassionate and well-respected priest in Bemerton, a rural parish in Wiltshire, for three years until he died of tuberculosis at age thirty-nine. Having written religious poetry throughout his life, Herbert first shared his collected poems, *The Temple: Sacred Poems and Private Ejaculations*, on his deathbed. *The Temple* was published and reprinted twelve more times in less than fifty years and some of the poems were adapted into hymns.

JUAN FELIPE HERRERA (b. 1948) Herrera was born in Fowler, California, to Mexican migrant farmworkers. He earned a bachelor's degree in social anthropology at the University of California at Los Angeles, a master's degree in social anthropology from Stanford University, and an M.F.A. from the University of Iowa. He taught at California State University at Fresno before assuming his current role as the Tomás Rivera Endowed Chair in the Creative Writing Department at the University of California, Riverside. Herrera describes himself as an educator, poet, writer, artist, performer, and musician. In addition to writing children's books, novels for young adults, prose, and short stories, he is the author of more than a dozen volumes of poetry. Among his most recent publications are *Cinnamon Girl: Letters Found Inside a Cereal Box* (2005), *Downtown Boy* (2005), and *187 Reasons Mexicanos Can't Cross the Border: Undocuments 1971–2007* (2007).

ROBERT HERRICK (1591–1674) Born in London, Herrick was apprenticed to his uncle, a goldsmith, for ten years until at age twenty-two he was sent to Cambridge University in recognition of his academic talents. Little is known of the decade following his graduation from Cambridge, although it seems certain that he associated with a circle of literary artists. In 1629, he was appointed vicar at Dean Prior, Devonshire, a rural parish that the sophisticated and cosmopolitan Herrick looked upon as a kind of exile. Yet, he was fascinated by the pagan elements of local songs and dances, and often drew upon pre-Christian writers for inspiration. His chief work, *Hesperides* (1648), is a collection of some twelve hundred poems—mostly written in Devonshire—about local scenery, customs, and people.

JANE HIRSHFIELD (b. 1953) Hirshfield, who was born in New York City, attended Princeton University, where she earned an A.B. magna cum laude in 1973. Following graduation, she spent a year on a farm and then, as she described it, "hopped into [my] red Dodge van hung with tie-dyed curtains and slowly headed west." She settled in northern California, where she has lived ever since. She has been a lecturer in creative writing at the University of San Francisco as well as a visiting professor at the University of California, Berkeley. Among her volumes of poetry are *Of Gravity and Angels* (1988), *The Lives of the Heart* (1997) and *Given Sugar, Given Salt* (2001). Her most recent publication, *After* (2006), was named one of the best books of the year by the *Washington Post*. She has received many awards, among them a Guggenheim Fellowship (1985) and a Rockefeller Foundation fellowship at the Bellagio Center (1995). A Zen Buddhist, she has published a translation of Japanese verse, *The Ink Dark Moon* (1988), and a collection of essays, *Nine Gates: Entering the Mind of Poetry* (1997), that draw upon her religious beliefs. Hirshfield describes the relationship between her beliefs and her poetry as indirect, based upon her "hope that the experience of that practice underlies and informs it as a whole."

TONY HOAGLAND (b. 1953) Tony Hoagland was born in Fort Bragg, North Carolina, and educated at the University of Iowa and the University of Arizona. He has taught at many universities, including Kalamazoo College, Michigan, Warren Wilson College, and Colby College. He now teaches in the creative writing program at the University of Houston. His poems and critical writings have appeared in such publications as *Ploughshares*, *American Poetry Review*, and the *Pushcart Prize Anthology* (1991). Hoagland's first three collections of poems were chapbooks: *A Change in Plans* (1985), *Talking to Stay Warm* (1986), and *History of Desire* (1990). His first full-length volume of poetry, *Sweet Ruin* (1992), won the Brittingham Prize in poetry as well as the Zacharas Award from Emerson College. His most recent books of poetry are *Donkey Gospel* (1998), *What Narcissism Means to Me* (2003), and *Hard Rain* (2005). In 2005, he won the Poetry Foundation's Mark Twain Award and the Folger Shakespeare Library's O. B. Hardison Jr. Poetry Prize, which honors excellence in teaching as well as in writing. In 2006, Hoagland published *Real Sofistikashun: Essays on Poetry and Craft*, which explores "how poems behave and how they are made."

LINDA HOGAN (b. 1947) Hogan was born in Denver, Colorado, and grew up in Colorado and Oklahoma. Her family's association with the military meant that they moved often; as a result, Hogan did not, as a young woman, feel a particularly strong affiliation to her Native American Chickasaw tribe. She earned her master's degree from the University of Colorado at Boulder and worked as a nurse's aide, dental assistant, waitress, homemaker, and secretary, among other things. She was working with children with orthopedic disabilities when she began writing professionally. She has penned six volumes of poetry: *Calling Myself Home* (1979), *Daughters, I Love You* (1981), *Eclipse* (1983), *Seeing through the Sun* (1985), *Savings* (1988), and *The Book of Medicines* (1993). She is also the author of numerous novels, plays, essays, screenplays, a documentary, and a memoir. Her work frequently explores feminist, environmental, and Native American themes.

M. CARL HOLMAN (1919–1988) Holman was born in Minter City, Mississippi, and grew up in St. Louis, Missouri. He graduated magna cum laude from Lincoln University and earned a master's degree from the University of Chicago and a master of fine arts from Yale University, which he attended on a creative writing scholarship. He taught as an English professor at Hampton University, Lincoln University, and Clark College. For a while, he edited the Atlanta *Inquirer*, a weekly publication that reported on civil rights activities in the South. In 1962, he moved to Washington, D.C., to become an information officer at the U.S. Civil Rights Commission, becoming its deputy director in 1966. From 1971 to 1988, he served as director of the Urban Coalition, an organization formed after the riots of 1967 for the purpose of forging partnerships between industry and government to promote inner-city development.

GERARD MANLEY HOPKINS (1844–1889) Raised in London, Hopkins won a scholarship to Balliol College, Oxford University, where he studied classical literature. He converted to Roman Catholicism in 1866 and two years later entered the Jesuit novitiate. In 1877, he was ordained a Jesuit priest and served in missions in London, Liverpool, Oxford, and Glasgow until 1882. From 1884 to his death in 1889, he was professor of Greek at University College, Dublin. A technically innovative poet, Hopkins saw only three of his poems published during his lifetime. He gained posthumous recognition in 1918 when a friend, the poet laureate Robert Bridges, published Hopkins's complete works. His early poems celebrate the beauty of God's world, but later works reflect his poor health and depression.

A. E. HOUSMAN (1859–1936) Born in Fockbury, England, and an outstanding student, Alfred Edward Housman nonetheless failed his final examinations at Oxford University in 1881 (possibly due to emotional chaos caused by his love for a male classmate). Working as a clerk in the patent office in London, he pursued classical studies on his own, earned an M.A., and was appointed chair of Latin at University College, London. In 1910, he became professor of Latin at Cambridge, where he remained until his death in 1936. As a poet, Housman was concerned primarily with the fleetingness of love and the decay of youth. After his first collection, *A Shropshire Lad,* was rejected by several publishers, Housman published it at his own expense in 1896. It gained popularity during World War I, and his 1922 collection, *Last Poems*, was well received. In his lecture "The Name and Nature of Poetry" (1933), Housman argued that poetry should appeal to emotions rather than intellect. *More Poems* (1936) was published posthumously.

LANGSTON HUGHES (1902–1967) Hughes was born in Joplin, Missouri. His father was a businessman and lawyer; his mother, a teacher. Hughes attended Columbia University, graduated from Lincoln University in 1929, traveled throughout the world, and held many odd jobs as a young man. While Hughes had a long and prolific career as a writer in all genres, he is still remembered as the central figure of the Harlem Renaissance of the 1920s, a movement that committed itself to the examination and celebration of black life in America and its African heritage. He was the Madrid correspondent for the Baltimore *Afro-American* (1937) and a columnist for the Chicago *Defender* (1943–1967) and the New York *Post* (1962–1967). His poems of racial affirmation and protest are often infused with the rhythms of blues and jazz music. He wrote over two dozen plays (many musicalized) and founded the Suitcase Theater (Harlem, 1938), the New Negro Theater (Los Angeles, 1939), and the Skyloft Players (Chicago, 1941). His works include *The Weary Blues* (1926), *Montage of a Dream Deferred* (1951), and *The Panther and the Lash: Poems of Our Times* (1969).

ZORA NEALE HURSTON (1891–1960) Born in Eatonville, Florida, an African American town, Hurston enjoyed a happy early childhood in a town that spared her from racism and with a mother who instilled a strong sense of self-worth in her. With the death of her mother, she was sent off to boarding school but was forced to give up her formal education when her father remarried and refused to give her further financial help. She supported herself with odd jobs, managing to earn a high school diploma and enter Howard University in Washington, D.C. Unable to support herself as a full-time student, Hurston quit college after five years, having earned only a year and a half of college credits. She moved to Harlem, determined to pursue a writing career. In New York, she was hired as a personal secretary by the novelist Fannie Hurst, who arranged a scholarship for her at Barnard College. There, she studied with the famous anthropologist Franz Boas and became interested in black folk traditions. She earned her degree from Barnard in 1927 and received a fellowship to study the oral traditions of her hometown. She wrote her first novel, *Jonah's Gourd Vine* (1934), while doing fieldwork in Eatonville. *Mules and Men* (1935), based on the material her fieldwork had produced, was attacked by African American intellectuals and writers for its refusal to acknowledge and confront racism. Nevertheless, Hurston was awarded a Guggenheim Fellowship to study voodoo in the Caribbean, which gave her the material for her second and most celebrated novel, *Their Eyes Were Watching God* (1937). During the last two decades of her life, she continued to write novels, plays, and an autobiography, *Dust Tracks on the Road* (1942), but drew increasing criticism from the African American press for her refusal to publicly condemn segregation. In 1950, she was the subject of a *Miami Herald* news story that carried the headline: "Famous Negro Author Working as a Maid Here 'Just to Live a Little.' " She claimed that she needed a break from writing and that she was busy making plans for writing projects and for a national magazine devoted to domestics. Her last years were troubled by poor health, emotional fatigue, and lack of money. She died of a stroke, penniless, in a welfare home in Fort Pierce, Florida.

DAVID HENRY HWANG (b. 1957) Hwang was born in Los Angeles, California, earned a degree from Stanford University, and attended the Yale University School of Drama for one year. His first play, *F. O. B.* (for "fresh off the boat") won an Obie for best new American Off-Broadway play of 1980. Hwang has written a number of plays, musicals, operas, and screenplays but is best known for *M. Butterfly,* for which he won a Tony Award in 1988 and received a Pulitzer Prize nomination in 1989. His other awards include fellowships from the Guggenheim Foundation and the National Endowment for the Arts; an Obie for best playwriting in 1997 and a Tony award nomination for best Broadway play in 1998 for *Golden Child;* and a Tony award nomination for his adaptation of the musical *Flower Drum Song* in 2003. Although Hwang once called his Chinese American heritage "a minor detail, like having red hair," cultural conflict and Asian themes are hallmarks of his most acclaimed works.

HENRIK IBSEN (1828–1906) Ibsen was born in Skien, Norway (a seaport about a hundred miles south of Oslo), the son of a wealthy merchant. When Ibsen was eight, his father's business failed, and at fifteen he was apprenticed to an apothecary in the tiny town of Grimstad. He hated this profession. To solace himself, he read poetry and theology and began to write. When he was twenty-two, he became a student in Christiania (now Oslo) and published his first play. In 1851, his diligent, though unremarkable, writing earned him an appointment as theater-poet to a new theater in Bergen, where he remained until 1857, learning both the business and the art of drama. He wrote several plays based on Scandinavian folklore, held positions at two theaters in Christiania, and married. When he was thirty-six, he applied to the government for a poet's pension—a stipend that would have permitted him to devote himself to writing. The stipend was refused. Enraged, he left Norway and, though he was granted the stipend two years later, spent the next twenty-seven years in Italy and Germany, where he wrote the realistic social dramas that established his reputation as the founder of modern theater. Such plays as *Ghosts* (1881), *An Enemy of the People* (1882), and *A Doll's House* (1878) inevitably generated controversy as Ibsen explored venereal disease, the stupidity and greed of the "compact majority," and the position of women in society. In 1891, he returned to live in Christiania, where he was recognized and honored as one of Norway's (and Europe's) finest writers.

SHIRLEY JACKSON (1919–1965) Born in San Francisco, Jackson moved with her family to Rochester, New York, in her teens. An episode of severe depression (a recurrent problem during her life) forced her out of the University of Rochester, but she later graduated from Syracuse University. She married the eminent critic Stanley Edgar Hyman, had four children, and kept to a rigid writing schedule. Although her major work tends toward the ominous, she contributed humorous pieces on the problems of housekeeping and raising children to popular magazines. These were collected in *Life among the Savages* (1953) and *Raising Demons* (1957). She wrote four novels, and her short stories are collected in three volumes: *The Lottery* (1949), *The Magic of Shirley Jackson* (1966), and *Come Along with Me* (1968).

HA JIN (b. 1956) Jin is the pen name of Jīn Xuéfēi. Born in Liaoning, China, he grew up under the communist regime and was enlisted in the People's Liberation Army for six years. He earned two degrees in China before completing his doctorate at Brandeis University near Boston. Jin taught at Emory University and currently teaches at Boston University, where he is a professor in the English department. He has written three books of poetry: *Between Silences* (1990), *Facing Shadows* (1996), and *Wreckage* (2001). He is also the author of three books of short stories and five novels, most recently *The Crazed* (2002), *War Trash* (2004), and *A Free Life* (2007). He is the recipient of numerous awards, including the Flannery O'Connor Prize for Short Fiction, a PEN/Hemingway Award, two PEN/Faulkner Awards, a National Book Award, and fellowships from the Guggenheim Foundation and the American Academy of Arts and Sciences. His latest work is a collection of essays titled *The Writer as Migrant* (2008). Jin, who writes entirely in English about thorny Chinese-related themes, has said, "When a writer adopts another language there are a lot of motivations: necessity, ambition, estrangement. Estrangement is a big part of it. . . . It creates a kind of distance. In a way, it enables me to write more objectively."

BEN JONSON (1572–1637) Jonson was born in Westminster, England, and after leaving school, began earning his living (in the manner of his stepfather) as a bricklayer. Though he never attended college, he taught himself enough to be considered learned. He soon abandoned construction work and earned his reputation as one of the preeminent playwrights of his period. A contemporary of Shakespeare, he also wrote poetry and translations of classical Roman authors for his English Renaissance audience.

JUNE JORDAN (1936–2002) Jordan was born in Harlem, New York, and attended Barnard College (1953–1955) and the University of Chicago (1955–1956). A poet, novelist, and writer of children's books, she taught widely at university campuses, including the City College of the City University of New York (1966–1968) and Connecticut College (1969–1974), where she both taught English and served as director of Search for Education, Elevation and Knowledge (SEEK). She was later professor of English at the State University of New York, Stony Brook. In addition to many appointments as visiting professor, she served as chancellor's distinguished lecturer, University of California at Berkeley (1986). Her numerous honors include the Prix de Rome in Environmental Design (1970–1971), the Nancy Bloch Award (1971) for her reader *The Voice of the Children*, and the achievement award from the National Association of Black Journalists (1984). Her many books include *His Own Where* (1971), *Dry Victories* (1972), and *Kimako's Story* (1981), all for juvenile and young adult readers. Her collections of poetry include *Things That I Do in the Dark* (1977), *Living Room: New Poems, 1980–1984* (1985), *Naming Our Destiny: New and Selected Poems* (1989), *Poetic Justice* (1991), *Haruko: Love Poems* (1994), and *Kissing God Goodbye: Poems 1991–1997* (1997). Jordan is also the author of *Technical Difficulties: African-American Notes on the State of the Union* (1992) and *Affirmative Acts: Political Essays* (1998). *Some of Us Did Not Die: New and Selected Essays* (2002) was published shortly after her death.

JAMES JOYCE (1882–1941)   Though educated in Jesuit schools, Joyce came to reject Catholicism; and though an expatriate living in Paris, Trieste, and Zurich for most of his adult life, he wrote almost exclusively about his native Dublin. Joyce's rebelliousness, which surfaced during his university career, generated a revolution in modern literature. His novels *Ulysses* (1922) and *Finnegan's Wake* (1939) introduced radically new narrative techniques. "Araby"—from his first collection of short stories, *Dubliners* (1914)—is one of a series of sharply realized vignettes based on Joyce's experiences in Ireland, the homeland he later characterized as "a sow that eats its own farrow." Joyce lived precariously on earnings as a language teacher and modest contributions from wealthy patrons. That support Joyce justified: he was one of the most influential novelists of the twentieth century. Because *Ulysses* dealt frankly with sexuality and used coarse language, the U.S. Post Office charged that the novel was obscene and forbade its importation. A celebrated 1933 court decision lifted the ban in the United States.

FRANZ KAFKA (1883–1924)   Born into a middle-class, German-speaking Jewish family in Prague, Kafka earned a law degree in 1906 and worked as a claims investigator for an insurance company for most of his adult life. He remained in constant conflict with his domineering father, who belittled his literary aims. He became engaged to a woman in 1912 but broke with her after five years. In 1917, he contracted the tuberculosis that was to kill him at forty-one. Despite the deadening monotony of his job and his personal anguish, he created a remarkable and original body of work during his short life, including the masterful novels *The Trial* (1925) and *The Castle* (1926). His starkly realistic stories and novels take place in nightmarish dreamworlds where stifling bureaucracy chokes his protagonists and diminishes their dignity and their lives. A fierce perfectionist, Kafka published little during his life and left written instructions to his friend and executor, Max Brod, to destroy his unpublished manuscripts. Fortunately, Brod could not bring himself to comply.

JOHN KEATS (1795–1821)   Keats was born in London, the eldest son of a stablekeeper who died in an accident in 1804. His mother died of tuberculosis shortly after remarrying, and the grandmother who raised Keats and his siblings died in 1814. At eighteen, Keats wrote his first poem, "Imitation of Spenser," inspired by Edmund Spenser's long narrative poem *The Faerie Queene.* The thirty-three poems he wrote while training to be a surgeon were published in a collection in 1817, and Keats then gave up medicine for writing. After more traumatic losses in 1818, including the departure of one brother for the United States and the death of his other brother of tuberculosis, Keats wrote his second collection, *Lamia, Isabella, The Eve of St. Agnes, and Other Poems* (1820). Ill with tuberculosis himself, Keats was sent to Rome to recover. He died at twenty-six, but despite his short career, he is a major figure of the romantic period.

JANE KENYON (1947–1995)   Kenyon was born in Ann Arbor, Michigan, and attended the University of Michigan, where she received a B.A. (1970) and M.A. (1972). While at Michigan, she studied under Donald Hall, the eminent poet and teacher, whom she married in the year she received her master's. The couple moved to Eagle Pond Farm in rural New Hampshire, living a quiet life that Kenyon celebrated in many of her early poems. They became well known not only through her poems but also through the books Hall wrote about life on their farm. In her last poems, Kenyon wrote about her struggle with leukemia, which claimed her life at age forty-eight. At the time of her death, she was New Hampshire's poet laureate. During her lifetime, she published four collections of poems, *From Room to Room* (1978), *The Boat of Quiet Hours* (1986), *Let Evening Come* (1990), and *Constance* (1993). Since her death, two additional volumes have been published, *Otherwise: New and Selected Poems* (1996) and *A Hundred White Daffodils: Essays, Interviews, the Akhmatova Translations, Newspaper Columns, and One Poem* (1999). In 1998, on the third anniversary of Kenyon's death, Donald Hall published *Without: Poems,* a volume *Publishers Weekly* called "a heartbreaking portrait of a marriage that has not quite ended."

JAMAICA KINCAID (b. 1949)   Kincaid was born Elaine Potter Richardson in St. Johns, Antigua, in the West Indies, then a British colony. At age seventeen, she left home to become an au pair in New York. Determined to make something of her life, Kincaid took night classes and ultimately earned a high school diploma. She went on to take classes at the New School for Social Research in New York, and attended college in New Hampshire on a scholarship. When she returned to New York, she changed her name to Jamaica Kincaid and began writing. Of her life up to this point, Kincaid told a reporter: "Everyone thought I had a way with words, but it came out as a sharp tongue. No one expected anything from me at all. Had I just sunk in the cracks it would not have been noted. I would have been lucky to be a secretary somewhere." Her first publication, a collection of short stories titled *At the Bottom of* *the River* (1983), earned her wide critical praise and recognition as a new voice in American fiction. That was followed by three novels, including *The Autobiography of My Mother* (1995). *My Brother* (1997) deals with the death of her brother from AIDS. Her most recent publication is *Among Flowers: A Walk in the Himalaya* (2005). The recipient of many literary honors, Kincaid served as a staff writer for the *New Yorker* (1976–1995) and visiting professor at Harvard University.

MARTIN LUTHER KING JR. (1929–1968)   King was born in Atlanta, Georgia, where his father was pastor of the Ebenezer Baptist Church. He attended public schools (skipping the ninth and twelfth grades) and entered Morehouse College in Atlanta. He was ordained as a Baptist minister just before his graduation in 1948. He then enrolled in Crozer Theological Seminary in Pennsylvania and after earning a divinity degree there, attended graduate school at Boston University, where he earned a Ph.D. in theology in 1955. At Boston University, he met Coretta Scott; they were married in 1953. King's rise to national and international prominence began in Montgomery, Alabama, in 1955. In that year, Rosa Parks, an African American woman, was arrested for refusing to obey a city ordinance that required African Americans to sit or stand at the back of municipal buses. The African American citizens of the city (one of the most thoroughly segregated in the South) organized a bus boycott in protest and asked King to serve as their leader. Thousands boycotted the buses for more than a year, and despite segregationist violence against them, King grounded their protests in his deeply held belief in nonviolence. In 1956, the U.S. Supreme Court ordered Montgomery to provide integrated seating on public buses. In the following year, King and other African American ministers founded the Southern Christian Leadership Conference (SCLC) to carry forward the nonviolent struggle against segregation and legal discrimination. As protests grew, so did the unhappiness of King and his associates with the unwillingness of the president and Congress to support civil rights. The SCLC, therefore, organized massive demonstrations in Montgomery (King wrote "Letter from Birmingham Jail" during these demonstrations). With the civil rights movement now in the headlines almost every day, President Kennedy proposed to Congress a far-reaching civil rights bill. On August 28, 1963, over 200,000 blacks and whites gathered at the Lincoln Memorial in Washington, D.C., where King delivered his now famous speech, "I Have a Dream." In the following year, Congress passed the Civil Rights Act of 1964, prohibiting racial discrimination in public places and calling for equal opportunity in education and employment. In that year, King received the Nobel Peace Prize. In 1965, King and others organized a march to protest the blatant denial of African Americans' voting rights in Selma, Alabama, where the march began. Before the protesters were able to reach Birmingham, the state capital, they were attacked by police with tear gas and clubs. This outrage, viewed live on national television, led President Johnson to ask Congress for a bill that would eliminate all barriers to voting rights. Congress responded by passing the landmark Voting

Rights Act of 1965. King remained committed to nonviolence, but his conviction that economic inequality—not just race—was one of the root causes of injustice led him to begin organizing a Poor People's Campaign that would unite all poor people in the struggle for justice. These views also led him to criticize the role played by the United States in the Vietnam War. The Poor People's Campaign took King to Memphis, Tennessee, to support a strike of African American sanitation workers, where on April 4, 1968, he was shot and killed while standing on the balcony of his hotel room. Riots immediately erupted in scores of cities across the nation. A few months later, Congress enacted the Civil Rights Act of 1968, banning discrimination in the sale and rental of housing. King is the author of *Stride toward Freedom* (1958), dealing with the Montgomery bus boycott; *Strength to Love* (1953), a collection of sermons; and *Why We Can't Wait* (1964), a discussion of his general views on civil rights.

MAXINE HONG KINGSTON (b. 1940)   Kingston was born in Stockton, California. She earned a bachelor's degree from the University of California, Berkeley (1962), and a teaching certificate (1965). After teaching English and mathematics at a California high school, she moved to Hawaii and taught language arts and English as a second language at a number of schools. She became a visiting associate professor of English at the University of Hawaii after winning the National Book Critics Circle Award for *The Woman Warrior: Memoirs of a Girlhood among Ghosts* (1976). In that volume, she fashioned a new sort of genre—essays with substantial fictive elements. Her next book, *China Men* (1980), further developed that form. Her most recent works include *Hawaii One Summer* (1998), *To Be the Poet* (2002), and *The Fifth Book of Peace* (2003). An early critic characterized Kingston's work as the blending of "myth, legend, history, and autobiography into a genre of her own invention." Another argued that though Kingston's works are classified as nonfiction, "in a deeper sense, they are fiction at its best—novels, fairytales, epic poems." In 1993, Kingston founded the Veteran's Writing Group; she compiled and edited a collection of the writings in *Veterans of War, Veterans of Peace* (2006).

GALWAY KINNELL (b. 1927)   Born in Providence, Rhode Island, Kinnell graduated summa cum laude from Princeton University, served in the navy during World War II, and returned to earn a master's degree from the University of Rochester. He traveled extensively and lectured in France and Iran before returning again to the United States. In 1963, he was a field worker for the Congress of Racial Equality (CORE) and his involvement in the American civil rights movement informed what is perhaps his most famous collection of poetry, *Body Rags* (1968). Another of his prominent works, *The Book of Nightmares* (1971), is a book-length poem about the Vietnam War. He is the author of more than twenty additional volumes of poetry, the most recent being *Strong Is Your Hold* (2006). Kinnell taught at a large number of institutions, earned numerous awards, and served as chancellor of the Academy of American Poets from 2001 to 2007 before retiring to his home in Vermont.

LAURA KIPNIS (b. 1956)   Kipnis earned degrees from the San Francisco Art Institute and the Nova Scotia College of Art and Design. As a video artist, she produced a number of short works that were shown at the American Film Institute, the Museum of Modern Art in New York, and the Whitney Museum, among other locations. She went on to become a professor of media studies at Northwestern University. She writes on a wide range of topics from American politics and pop culture to sexuality, adultery, and pornography. Her four books are *Ecstasy Unlimited: On Sex, Capital, Gender, and Aesthetics* (1993), *Bound and Gagged: Pornography and the Politics of Fantasy in America* (1996), *Against Love: A Polemic* (2003), and *The Female Thing: Dirt, Sex, Envy, Vulnerability* (2006). She is also a regular contributor to periodicals such as *Slate,* the *Nation,* the *Village Voice, Harper's,* and the *New York Times Magazine.* Kipnis has received fellowships from the Guggenheim and Rockefeller foundations and the National Endowment for the Arts.

CAROLYN KIZER (b. 1925)   Kizer was born in Spokane, Washington. Her father was a lawyer, her mother a biologist and professor. After graduating from Sarah Lawrence College in 1945, Kizer pursued graduate study at Columbia University and the University of Washington. From 1959 to 1965, she was editor of *Poetry Northwest* (which she founded in 1959 in Seattle) and spent 1964 and 1965 as a State Department specialist in Pakistan, where she taught at a women's college and translated poems from Urdu into English. She chose to leave early, after the U.S. decision to bomb North Vietnam in 1965. Later, she joined archaeological tours in Afghanistan and Iran. She has worked as director of literary programs for the National Endowment for the Arts in Washington, D.C.; has taught at several universities; and was poet-in-residence at the University of North Carolina and Ohio University. Her volumes of poetry include *Yin* (1984), which won a Pulitzer Prize the following year; *Mermaids in the Basement: Poems for Women* (1984); *The Nearness of You* (1986); *Harping On: Poems 1985–1995* (1996); *Pro Femina: A Poem* (2000); and *Cool, Calm & Collected: Poems 1960–2000* (2001). She has also published two collections of essays— *Proses: On Poems and Poets* (1993) and *Picking and Choosing: Essays on Prose* (1995)—and edited *100 Great Poems by Women: A Golden Ecco Anthology* (1995).

ETHERIDGE KNIGHT (1931–1991)   Knight was born in Corinth, Mississippi, attended two years of public high school in Kentucky, and served in the U.S. Army from 1948 to 1951. After being convicted on a robbery charge and sentenced in 1960 to twenty years in Indiana State Prison, he discovered poetry; his first collection is entitled *Poems from Prison* (1968). Knight was paroled after eight years. From 1968 to 1971 he was poet-in-residence at several universities. An important African American voice in the 1960s and 1970s, Knight rejected the American and European aesthetic tradition, arguing that "the red of this esthetic rose got its color from the blood of black slaves, exterminated Indians, napalmed Vietnamese children." His collection *Belly Song* *and Other Poems* was nominated for the National Book Award and the Pulitzer Prize in 1973. His awards include National Endowment for the Arts and Guggenheim grants and the 1987 American Book Award for *The Essential Etheridge Knight* (1986).

YUSEF KOMUNYAKAA (b. 1947) Born and raised in Bogalusa, Louisiana, James Willie Brown Jr. later took the surname of his great-grandparents who had come from Trinidad on a slave ship. His work often explores themes related to his life in the American south, the civil rights movement in America, and his tour of duty as a soldier during the Vietnam War. He began composing poetry even before he earned degrees from the University of Colorado, Colorado State University, and the University of California at Irvine. He taught at the University of New Orleans, Indiana University at Bloomington, and Princeton University before assuming his current role as a professor in the Creative Writing Program at New York University. He is the author of over a dozen books of poetry but gained attention for *Copacetic* (1984), *I Apologize for the Eyes in My Head* (1986), and *Dien Cai Dau* (1988). He is best known for *Neon Vernacular: New and Selected Poems* (1993), for which he won the Kingsley Tufts Poetry Award and a Pulitzer Prize. He also received the 2001 Ruth Lilly Poetry Prize, a prestigious honor given to living U.S. poets "whose lifetime accomplishments warrant extraordinary recognition."

MAXINE KUMIN (b. 1925) Born Maxine Winokur, Kumin attended Radcliffe College (B.A., 1946; M.A., 1948) and has lectured at many universities, including Princeton, Tufts, and Brandeis. She is the author of several collections of poetry, including *Up Country* (1972), for which she won a Pulitzer Prize, and *Nurture* (1989), *Looking for Luck: Poems* (1992), and *Connecting the Dots: Poems* (1996). She has also published several novels, collections of essays and short stories, and more than twenty children's books—several of them in collaboration with the poet Anne Sexton. Her most recent poetry collections are *Bringing Together: Uncollected Early Poems, 1958–1988* (2003); *Jack and Other New Poems* (2005); and *Still to Mow* (2007).

HARI KUNZRU (b. 1969) Kunzru was born in London to a Kashmiri Indian doctor and an English nurse. He grew up in Essex and earned degrees from Oxford University and the University of Warwick in Coventry, England. He worked as a journalist for a number of periodicals and as a decorator, disc jockey, juggler, promotions coordinator, telemarketer, van driver, and waiter. It was while working as a satellite-television host that he began writing his first novel, *The Impressionist* (2002), about a character who, like Kunzru himself, is a biracial Indian Englishman. The book was widely praised and a best seller, short-listed for a number of awards and named one of the best novels of 2002 by *Publishers Weekly*. His second novel, *Transmission* (2004), was a *New York Times* notable book of the year. He followed that with a collection of short stories, *Noise* (2005), and *My Revolutions: A Novel* (2007).

JHUMPA LAHIRI (b. 1967) Lahiri was born to Bengalese parents in London and was raised in Rhode Island before she earned multiple degrees from Barnard College and Boston University. Her time spent visiting extended family in Calcutta, India, and her immigrant identity informs her work. Her first book, a collection of stories titled *Interpreter of Maladies* (1999) won the Pulitzer Prize, the PEN/Hemingway Award, and was the *New Yorker* Debut of the Year. Her second work, the novel *The Namesake* (2003), was a *New York Times* notable book and was selected as one of the best books of the year by a number of publications, including *USA Today* and *Entertainment Weekly*. She has also received an O. Henry Award and a Guggenheim Fellowship and was named one of the twenty best young writers in America by *New Yorker* magazine. Her most recent work, a collection of stories, is *Unaccustomed Earth* (2008).

PHILIP LARKIN (1922–1985) Born in Coventry, Larkin attended St. John's College, Oxford University (B.A., 1943; M.A., 1947). He was appointed librarian at the University of Hull in 1955, wrote jazz feature articles for the London *Daily Telegraph* from 1961 to 1971, and won numerous poetry awards, including the Queens Gold Medal (1965) and the Benson Medal (1975). His first collection, *The North Ship* (1945), was not well received, but he gained recognition after publication of *The Less Deceived* (1960). Larkin once said, "Form holds little interest for me. Content is everything."

EVELYN LAU (b. 1971) Lau was born in Vancouver, Canada, to Chinese Canadian parents. Driven by an unhappy family life, she ran away from home and wound up living on the streets of Vancouver working as a prostitute to support her drug addiction. During these turbulent early years, Lau kept a diary, and she published poems in Canadian and American journals even before she ran away. Throughout the years of living on the edge, during which she made a number of suicide attempts and was confined in a psychiatric ward, Lau continued to write. With the help of a sympathetic psychiatrist and her commitment to writing, she managed to pull herself out of the chaos and turn herself into a professional and very successful writer. Her first published work was an autobiographical account of her early years, *Runaway: Diary of a Street Kid* (1989). An immediate success, it was filmed as *The Diary of Evelyn Lau* and aired on the Canadian Broadcasting Corporation in 1994. *Runaway* was followed by three volumes of poems, *You Are Not Who You Claim* (1990); *Oedipal Dreams,* nominated for the prestigious Governor General's Award for poetry (1993); and *In the House of Slaves* (1993). Lau is also the author of a novel, *Other Women* (1995), and a collection of short stories, *Choose Me* (1999). Her most recent publications are *Inside Out: Reflections on a Life So Far* (2001) and *Treble* (2005). Asked by an interviewer if she had acquired her "beautiful, clear" writing style in school, Lau replied, "Nope. All self-taught. In my teens I took some one-day writers' workshops and things like that. But I've never gone properly back to school."

LI-YOUNG LEE (b. 1957)   Lee was born in Jakarta, Indonesia, to Chinese parents. While there, his father was imprisoned for his religious beliefs, and further anti-Chinese sentiment caused the entire family to flee the country. They traveled in exile for six years before finally settling in the United States. Lee earned a degree from the University of Pittsburgh and attended the University of Arizona and the State University of New York College at Brockport for brief periods. He began writing in earnest in college and is the author of four books of poetry: *Rose* (1986), *The City in Which I Love You* (1990), *Book of My Nights* (2001), and *Behind My Eyes* (2008). He also penned a memoir, *The Winged Seed: A Remembrance* (1995), in which he recounts his family's troubled history and his turbulent youth. Lee has received awards from the Lannan and Whiting foundations, as well as fellowships from the Guggenheim Foundation and the National Endowment for the Arts.

URSULA K. LE GUIN (b. 1929)   The daughter of distinguished University of California at Berkeley anthropologists, Le Guin graduated from Radcliffe College and earned an M.A. from Columbia University. She enjoyed early success writing for science-fiction and fantasy magazines (a genre often stigmatized as subliterary popular fiction), but she quickly established a reputation that places her in the tradition of earlier writers who used fantastic circumstances to shape their understanding of the human condition, such as Jonathan Swift, Edgar Allan Poe, and H. G. Wells. A prolific writer of fantasy fiction, Le Guin's latest works include *The Other Wind* (2001), *Tales from Earthsea* (2001), and the *Annals of the Western Shore* trilogy (2004–2007). Her most recent novel is *Lavinia* (2008). Among her collections of short stories are *The Birthday of the World* (2002) and *Changing Planes* (2003). Her new book of poetry is *Incredible Good Fortune* (2006).

JONATHAN LETHEM (b. 1964)   Born in metropolitan New York, Lethem attended Bennington College in Vermont, dropped out during sophomore year, hitchhiked across the country, and landed in California, where he worked as a clerk in a bookstore for over a decade. He published his first short story in 1989. A prolific writer of novels, short stories, and essays, Lethem is widely considered by some to be a science-fiction author, while others think his work much harder to categorize. A profile about Lethem in *Publishers Weekly* noted that his writing "exists somewhere in the previously uncharted interstices between science fiction, western, and coming-of-age novels." His notable novels include *Gun, with Occasional Music,* his first book, published in 1994; *Motherless Brooklyn* (1999), which won a National Book Critics Circle Award; and *The Fortress of Solitude,* which was a New York Times best seller. His work has appeared in numerous periodicals, among them *Entertainment Weekly, Esquire, GQ, Harper's,* the *New York Times,* the *New Yorker, Rolling Stone, Salon,* and the *Village Voice.*

DENISE LEVERTOV (1923–1997)   Levertov was born in Ilford, Essex, England and educated entirely at home. She published her first poem when she was just seventeen years old and her first book of poetry, *Double Image,* six years later in 1946. She immigrated to the United States in 1948 and became a naturalized citizen in 1955. Levertov was a prolific writer producing over twenty volumes of poetry in addition to works of prose and translations; she also edited several anthologies and served as the poetry editor of the *Nation*. She taught at Brandeis University, MIT, Tufts University, the University of Washington, and Stanford University and was awarded the Shelley Memorial Award and the Robert Frost Medal. Among Levertov's collections of poems—which often explored themes related to political activism, feminism, and religion—are *Here and Now* (1956), *The Sorrow Dance* (1967), *Relearning the Alphabet* (1970), *Life in the Forest* (1978), *A Door in the Hive* (1989), and *The Sands of the Well* (1996).

PHILIP LEVINE (b. 1928) The son of Russian Jewish immigrants, Levine was born in Detroit, Michigan, into a household where debates and discussions about radical politics instilled in him a political sensibility and an abiding sympathy for the poor and the powerless. After receiving his B.A. from Wayne State University (1950), he returned to Detroit and worked at various industrial jobs in the auto industry before enrolling in the University of Iowa in 1955, where he received his M.F.A. (1957). He earned his living teaching poetry, primarily at California State University at Fresno and Tufts University in Massachusetts, and is now retired. Since his first collection of poems, *On the Edge* (1961), Levine has published more than twenty volumes of poetry, many of them exhibiting his radical political consciousness. Among them are *They Feed They Lion* (1972); *Ashes* (1979); *What Work Is* (1991), which received the National Book Award; and *The Simple Truth* (1995), for which he received the Pulitzer Prize. His most recent volumes of poetry are *The Mercy: Poems* (2000) and *Breath* (2004). In 1997, Levine was elected to the American Academy of Arts and Letters. He has summed up his aspirations as an artist with the remark, "My hope is to write poetry for people for whom there are no poems."

ELLEN LEVY Levy earned a degree in history from Yale University and an M.F.A. from the Ohio State University. She is currently an assistant professor in the Creative Writing Program at the University of Missouri. Her essays, articles, and works of fiction have appeared in anthologies as well as a number of periodicals, among them *Gettysburg Review, Missouri Review,* the *Nation, North American Review, Orion, Out, Paris Review,* and *Salmagundi*. She also edited the anthology *Tasting Life Twice: Literary Lesbian Fiction by New American Writers* (1995). Levy was named one of the "Twenty-Five Nonfiction Writers to Watch" in the new millennium by *Writer's Digest*.

STUART LISHAN (b. 1955) Lishan is currently an associate professor of English at the Ohio State University, where he teaches courses in creative writing, poetry, and literature. An author of both poetry and fiction, his work has appeared in numerous periodicals, including *American Literary Review, Antioch Review, Arts & Letters, Barrow Street, Kenyon Review,* and *Smartish Pace*. His chapbook manuscript, *Body Tapestries,* was a finalist in the 2000 Walt Whitman award competition and was published in the e-journal *Mudlark* in 2001. About "Winter Count, 1964," Lishan has said that he was inspired by "the deep need for intimacy among these kids, for physical contact, and the hostility and fear of it, as well. I love the edge and dramatic tension that creates. Basically, these kids don't know what to do with these desires. This piece explores that territory."

AUDRE LORDE (1934–1992)   Born to middle-class West Indian immigrant parents in New York City, Lorde grew up in Harlem and attended the National University of Mexico (1954), Hunter College (B.A., 1959), and Columbia University (M.L.S., 1961). Her marriage in 1962, which produced two children, ended in divorce in 1970. During these early years, she worked as a librarian, but in 1968 her growing reputation as a writer led to her appointment as lecturer in creative writing at City College in New York. The following year, she was named lecturer in the education department at Herbert H. Lehman College. In 1970 she joined the English department at John Jay College of Criminal Justice, and in 1980 returned to Hunter College as professor of English. Besides teaching, Lorde raised a son and a daughter in an interracial lesbian relationship and was involved in political organizing of other black feminists and lesbians. In the early 1980s, Lorde helped to start Kitchen Table: Women of Color Press, and in 1991, she was named New York State Poet. Lorde is probably best known for her prose writings, among them two collections of essays, *Sister Outsider* (1984) and *Burst of Light* (1988), and the autobiographical *Zami: The Cancer Journals* (1980), a chronicle of her struggle with the breast cancer that ultimately claimed her life. Her poetry publications include *The First Cities* (1968), *The Black Unicorn* (1978), and *Undersong: Chosen Poems Old and New* (1993). Near the end of her life, Lorde made her home on St. Croix, U.S. Virgin Islands, and adopted the African name *Gamba Adisa* (Warrior—She Who Makes Her Meaning Known).

ROBERT LOWELL (1917–1977)   Born into a prominent Boston family, Lowell attended Harvard University, transferred to Kenyon College in Ohio, and engaged in some graduate studies at Louisiana State University. He was politically active—jailed for being a conscientious objector during World War II, engaged in protests against the Vietnam War, and involved in the American civil rights movement. In addition to suffering three failed marriages, he was an alcoholic and a manic depressive, for which he was institutionalized several times. Lowell was a playwright and a translator but is known for his volumes of poetry, of which there were many. Among his best-known works are *Land of Unlikeness* (1944), *Lord Weary's Castle* (1946), *Life Studies* (1959), *Imitations* (1961), *For the Union Dead* (1964), *Notebooks, 1967–1968* (1969), and *The Dolphin* (1973). His countless awards included two Pulitzer Prizes, a Guggenheim Fellowship, a National Book Award, a Copernicus Award from the Academy of American Poets, a National Medal for Literature, and a National Book Critics Circle Award. Lowell also served as poet laureate of the United States from 1947 to 1948.

D. W. Lucas (1905–1985) Lucas was born in London (his father was a teacher); earned an honors B.A. (1927) from King's College, Cambridge; and remained at his alma mater to become a fellow, lecturer, and director of studies in classics. He wrote two critical works, *The Greek Tragic Poets* (1950) and *A Commentary on Aristotle's "Poetics"* (1968). In addition, he translated the plays of Euripides and was a regular contributor to both the *Encyclopaedia Britannica* and the *Oxford Classical Dictionary.*

Katharyn Howd Machan (b. 1952) Machan grew up in Woodbury, Connecticut, and Pleasantville, New York. She studied creative writing and literature at the College of Saint Rose and at the University of Iowa, taught college for five years, then returned to graduate school for a Ph.D. in interpretation (performance studies) at Northwestern University. She is on the faculty of the Writing Program of Ithaca College, New York. For eight years she coordinated the Ithaca Community Poets and directed the national Feminist Women's Writing Workshops. Since 1967, more than 1,200 of her poems have appeared in numerous magazines (such as *Yankee, Nimrod, South Coast Poetry Journal, Hollins Critic, Seneca Review,* and *Louisiana Literature*) and literature anthologies. She has published more than twenty-five collections of poetry; the most recent include *Sleeping with the Dead* (2004), *Redwing: Voices from 1888* (2005), and *Flags* (2007).

Christopher Marlowe (1564–1593) Born in Canterbury, Marlowe was educated at Cambridge University, where he embarked on a career of writing and political activity, eventually giving up his original intention of entering the priesthood. He was arrested in 1593 on a charge of atheism, but before he could be brought to trial he was murdered in a brawl apparently involving a wealthy family that had reason to want him silenced. Marlowe's literary reputation rests primarily on his plays, powerful in their own right and the most significant precursors of Shakespeare's poetic dramas. The most important are *Tamburlaine, Parts I and II* (ca. 1587–1588; published 1590), *The Jew of Malta* (1589; published 1633), and *The Tragical History of the Life and Death of Dr. Faustus* (1592; published 1604).

Andrew Marvell (1621–1678) Born in Yorkshire and educated at Cambridge University, Marvell received an inheritance on his father's death that allowed him to spend four years traveling the Continent. Though not a Puritan himself, Marvell supported the Puritans' cause during the civil war and held a number of posts during the Puritan regime, including that of assistant to the blind John Milton, Oliver Cromwell's Latin secretary. In 1659, a year before the Restoration, Marvell was elected to Parliament, where he served until his death. Soon after the Restoration, Marvell expressed strong disagreements with the government in a series of outspoken and anonymously printed satires. It was for these satires, rather than for his many love poems, that he was primarily known in his own day.

KATHERINE MCALPINE (b. 1948)   Katherine McAlpine grew up in western New Jersey. She studied voice with Leon Kurzer of the Vienna Opera and worked for a number of years as a singer and voice teacher. She now lives in Maine, where she works as a freelance writer. Her poetry has appeared in a wide variety of magazines and in several anthologies, and she is co-editor of *The Muse Strikes Back: A Poetic Response by Women to Men* (1997). She was a 1992 winner of the *Nation*'s Discovery Award and the Judith's Room Award for emerging women poets. Her latest chapbook of poetry is *Past and Present* (2004).

CLAUDE MCKAY (1890–1948)   Born in Sunny Ville, Jamaica, McKay had already completed two volumes of poetry before coming to the United States in 1912 at the age of twenty-three (the two volumes earned him awards, which paid his way). The racism he encountered as a black immigrant brought a militant tone to his writing. His popular poem "If We Must Die" (1919) helped to initiate the Harlem Renaissance of the 1920s. Between 1922 and 1934 he lived in Great Britain, Russia, Germany, France, Spain, and Morocco. His writings include four volumes of poems, many essays, an autobiography (*A Long Way from Home* [1937]), a novel (*Home to Harlem* [1928]), and a sociological study of Harlem. His conversion to Roman Catholicism in the 1940s struck his audience as an ideological retreat. McKay wrote in a letter to a friend: "[T]o have a religion is very much like falling in love with a woman. You love her for her . . . beauty, which cannot be defined."

DAVID MEANS (b. 1961)   Means was born in Kalamazoo, Michigan. He earned a bachelor's degree from the College of Wooster in Ohio in 1984 and an M.F.A. from Columbia University two years later. He is the author of three collections of short stories: *A Quick Kiss of Redemption* (1991), *Assorted Fire Events* (2000), and *The Secret Goldfish* (2004). His work has also appeared in several periodicals, including *Esquire, Harper's,* the *New Yorker,* and *Paris Review.* He is the recipient of a Los Angeles Times Book Prize, an O. Henry Prize, and a Pushcart Prize. Means currently teaches writing at Vassar College in Poughkeepsie, New York. About short stories, Means has said, "A story is just a blip, a ping. Where the story ends is a risk the writer takes; the reader feels that risk too. . . . And it's a wondrous work of art; it stands perfect and complete. That's the mystery of a good story."

PETER MEINKE (b. 1932)   Born in Brooklyn, New York, the son of a salesman, Meinke served in the U.S. Army from 1955 to 1957, attended Hamilton College (B.A., 1955) and the University of Michigan (M.A., 1961), and earned his Ph.D. at the University of Minnesota (1965). He taught English at a New Jersey high school, Hamline University, Presbyterian College (now Eckerd College), and Old Dominion University, where he held the Darden Chair in Creative Writing. His reviews, poems, and stories have appeared in periodicals such as the *Atlantic,* the *New Yorker,* and the *New Republic.* The latest of his published books include *Zinc Fingers: Poems A to Z* (2000), *The Contracted*

World: New & More Selected Poems (2006), and *Unheard Music: Stories* (2007). His collection of stories, *The Piano Tuner*, won the 1986 Flannery O'Connor Award. He has also been the recipient of a National Endowment for the Arts Fellowship in poetry.

HERMAN MELVILLE (1819–1891)   The death of his merchant father when Melville was twelve shattered the economic security of his family. The financial panic of 1837 reduced the Melvilles to the edge of poverty, and at age nineteen, Melville went to sea. Economic conditions on his return were still grim, and after a frustrating stint as a country schoolteacher, he again went to sea—this time on a four-year whaling voyage. He deserted the whaler in the South Pacific, lived for some time with cannibals, made his way to Tahiti and Hawaii, and finally joined the navy for a return voyage. He mined his experiences for two successful South Sea adventure books, *Typee* (1846) and *Omoo* (1847). On the strength of these successes he married, but his next novel, *Mardi* (1849), was too heavy-handed an allegory to succeed. Driven by the obligation to support his growing family, Melville returned to sea-adventure stories, with moderate success. But neither his masterpiece, *Moby-Dick* (1851), nor his subsequent short stories and novels found much of an audience, and in 1886, he accepted an appointment as customs inspector in Manhattan, a job he held until retirement. He continued to write, mostly poetry, and lived to see himself forgotten as an author. *Billy Budd,* found among his papers after his death and published in 1924, led to a revival of interest in Melville, now recognized as one of America's greatest writers.

LOUIS MENAND (b. 1952)   Menand was born in Syracuse, New York, and raised in Boston. He graduated from Pomona College in Claremont, California, before attending Harvard Law School for one year and going on to earn his doctorate degree from Columbia University. He taught at Princeton University and the City University of New York before joining the faculty at Harvard. Menand, who is both an academic and a journalist and considered a preeminent critic and historian of American culture, has worked for the *New Republic* and the *New Yorker*. His writing has also appeared in countless other periodicals, among them *Harper's, New York Review of Books*, the *New York Times*, and *Slate*. His first book, *Discovering Modernism: T. S. Eliot and His Context*, was published in 1987. His second book, *The Metaphysical Club: A Story of Ideas in America* (2001), won a Pulitzer Prize in history. His most recent book, *American Studies* (2002), is a collection of essays about individuals who have made an impact on American culture.

ROBERT MEZEY (b. 1935)   Born in Philadelphia, Mezey attended Kenyon College and served a troubled hitch in the U.S. Army before earning his B.A. from the University of Iowa in 1959. He worked as a probation officer, advertising copywriter, and social worker; did graduate study at Stanford University; and began teaching English at Case Western Reserve University in 1963. After a year as poet-in-residence at Franklin and Marshall College, he joined the English department of California State University at Fresno, spent three years at the University of Utah, and settled in 1976 at Pomona College in Claremont, California. Mezey won the Lamont Award for *The Lovemaker* in 1960 and has published many other poetry collections. In addition, he co-edited *Naked Poetry* (1969) and was one of several translators for *Poems from the Hebrew* (1973). His recent work includes *Collected Poems: 1952–1999* (2000), for which he was awarded the 2002 Poet's Prize.

ARTHUR MILLER (1915–2005)   Raised in New York City, the son of a schoolteacher and clothing manufacturer, Arthur Miller studied playwriting at the University of Michigan. Although he wrote radio scripts and plays, during World War II he made his living as a steamfitter. His first Broadway play in 1944 was a failure, but *All My Sons* (1947), about a corrupt defense contractor, was named best play of the year. The 1949 production of *Death of a Salesman* (which won the Pulitzer Prize) was an immense success and established Miller's reputation. The infamous loyalty hearings conducted by Senator Joseph McCarthy contributed to the substance of *The Crucible* (1953), an investigation into the Salem witchcraft trials. Miller adapted *The Crucible* for the film version (1996), which was directed by Nicholas Hytner. His play *After the Fall* (1964) is a thinly veiled account of his five-year marriage to Marilyn Monroe. In 1956, Miller was cited for contempt by the House Un-American Activities Committee when, after testifying fully about his own political activities, he refused to name others. His plays invariably turn on moral issues and continue to illustrate the comment he made to an interviewer after the success of *All My Sons:* "I don't see how you can write anything decent without using as your basis the question of right or wrong." His dedication to individual conscience and suspicion of government repression led him to adapt Ibsen's *An Enemy of the People* for the Broadway stage in 1951. His most recent play, *Broken Glass* (1994), focuses on the aftermath of Kristallnacht, the night in 1938 in Nazi Germany when thousands of Jewish shops and synagogues were destroyed. Miller is also the author of an autobiography, *Timebends* (1987), and a collection of stories, *Homely Girl, A Life: And Other Stories* (1995). His last play, *The Man Who Had All the Luck,* appeared in 2004.

KATHERINE MIN (b. 1959)   Min was born in Champaign, Illinois, and earned degrees at Amherst College in Massachusetts and Columbia University. She taught at Plymouth State University in New Hampshire before joining the faculty at the University of North Carolina at Asheville. Her work has appeared in a number of periodicals, including *Ploughshares, Threepenny Review,* and *TriQuarterly;* her story "The Brick" was featured on National Public Radio. Among her awards are a grant from the National Endowment for the Arts and a Pushcart Prize for "Courting a Monk." She earned praise for her debut novel, *Secondhand World* (2006), in which she called on her own experiences to write about a family of Korean American immigrants. She is working on her second novel, to be titled *The Suicide Sonata*. About her work, Min has said, "I love words and how you can play around with them, burnishing them until they glow. Also, people mystify and fascinate me, and writing is a way of trying to figure them out."

SUSAN MINOT (b. 1956) Minot was born in Manchester, Massachusetts, and attended Boston University before earning degrees from Brown University and Columbia University. In addition to being a writer, she has worked as a waitress, bookstore clerk, editorial assistant, and professor. Her first short stories appeared in *Grand Street* and the *New Yorker;* her work has also been included in *Paris Review, Atlantic Monthly, Mademoiselle,* and *GQ,* among other periodicals. Her debut novel, *Monkeys* (1986), earned her wide acclaim and a French literary prize, the *Prix Femina Étranger.* Her other awards include an O. Henry Prize and a Pushcart Prize. Minot is the author of three other novels, *Folly* (1993), *Evening* (1998), and *Rapture* (2002); a collection of short fiction, *Lust and Other Stories* (1989); two screenplays, *Stealing Beauty* (1996) and *Evening* (with Michael Cunningham, 2007); and a volume of poetry, *Poems 4 A.M.* (2003).

JANICE MIRIKITANI (b. 1942) Mirikitani, a third-generation Japanese American, was born in Stockton, California, a year after the Japanese attack on Pearl Harbor, which drew the United States into World War II. She was not yet two when she and her family, like thousands of other American citizens of Japanese descent, were rounded up and sent to an internment camp as security risks. After the war, her parents divorced; her mother's remarriage took her back to northern California, and there she endured years of sexual abuse. Despite these difficult years, Mirikitani graduated from the University of California at Los Angeles (cum laude, 1962). In the midst of pursuing a master's degree at San Francisco State University, she was drawn to the civil rights movement. She quit school, divorced her husband, and devoted a decade to raising her daughter Tianne and collaborating with other writers in Third World Communications, a literary collective. During this time, she began working at San Francisco's Glide Memorial United Methodist Church in the Tenderloin District. In 1982, she married the church's minister, Cecil Williams. The church has been the focus of Mirikitani's many community activities, and she currently serves as executive director of its foundation. She and her husband were awarded the Chancellor's Medal of Honor, University of California (1988). Among her other awards and honors are the American Book Lifetime Achievement Award for Literature (1996) and appointment as San Francisco's poet laureate (2000). She is the author of four collections of poems, most recently *Love Works* (2002).

LADY MARY WORTLEY MONTAGU (1689–1762) The eldest child of the Earl of Kingston and Lady Mary Fielding (who died young), she was raised by her paternal grandmother in Yorkshire. Fascinated by literature, the teenaged

Mary used a Latin grammar and dictionary from the family library to teach herself enough Latin to read Ovid. Her father was so pleased he had her tutored in Italian; she later added French and Turkish to her polyglot repertoire. Her ability to quote Horace in Latin attracted the attention of Edward Wortley Montagu, one of the few eighteenth-century gentlemen who believed that women should be educated as men were. He began a correspondence with the sixteen-year-old Mary that culminated seven years later in their elopement. She was an early advocate of inoculation against smallpox, and her two children were among the first to be vaccinated in England. Her wit and talent nourished lively friendships with some of the leading writers of the time: Joseph Addison, Richard Steele, William Congreve, Alexander Pope, and John Gay. Her published Turkish correspondence established her reputation as a remarkable letter writer in an age that celebrated the literary correspondence of such writers as Thomas Gray, William Cowper, and Horace Walpole. But her contemporaries also admired her poetry for its candor and for its vigorous expression of women's viewpoints. When her marriage faded, she pursued a paramour, Francesco Algarotti, to Italy in 1739. But that liaison also failed, and at the request of her embarrassed family, she remained a wanderer in Europe, supported by her estranged husband. She died shortly after returning to London. The novelist E. M. Forster asserted that the quality of her poetry secured her a place as an aristocrat, not in an "aristocracy of power, based upon rank and influence, but an aristocracy of the sensitive, the considerate, and the plucky."

LISEL MUELLER (b. 1924)   Born in Hamburg, Germany, to parents who were both teachers, Mueller moved to the United States in 1939 and became a citizen in 1945. Shortly before earning a B.A. from the University of Evansville (1944), she married. Later, she bore two children, pursued graduate studies at Indiana University, and held a number of positions, among them receptionist, caseworker, and library assistant. She served as an instructor in poetry writing at Elmhurst College (1969–1972) and later as an instructor in the Master of Fine Arts Writing Program at Goddard College, Vermont. She has received numerous awards, including the Robert M. Ferguson Memorial Award for her first book of poems, *Dependencies* (1965), the Pulitzer Prize for Poetry (1997) for *Alive Together: New and Selected Poems,* and a National Book Award for *The Need to Hold Still* (1980). Commenting on the nature of her verse in *The Private Life* (1976), one critic noted that "she goes after our secrets, this poet; often she finds them." In 2002, Mueller was awarded the Ruth Lilly Poetry Prize, a prestigious honor given to living U.S. poets "whose lifetime accomplishments warrant extraordinary recognition."

BHARATI MUKHERJEE (b. 1940)   Born in Calcutta, India, Mukherjee attended the University of Calcutta (B.A., 1959), the University of Baroda (M.A., 1961), and the University of Iowa, where she earned an M.F.A. (1963) and a Ph.D. (1969). In 1963 she married Clark Blaise, a Canadian writer and professor, and joined the faculty at McGill University in Montreal. In 1973,

Mukherjee and her husband visited India and kept separate diaries of the trip, published as *Days and Nights in Calcutta* (1977). The diaries reveal marked differences in their responses: Mukherjee found her home environs, especially the status of women, worse than she remembered, while Blaise, after an initial revulsion at the squalor and poverty, found India a fascinating and attractive culture compared to the West. Mukherjee "left Canada after fifteen years due to the persistent effects of racial prejudice against people of my national origin." Her fiction frequently explores the tensions inevitable in intercultural relationships. Her first novel, *The Tiger's Daughter* (1972), deals with the disappointment of an expatriate's return to India. In her second novel, *Wife* (1975), a psychologically abused woman finally kills her husband. *The Middleman and Other Stories* (1988) won the National Book Critics' Award. *Desirable Daughters* (2003) and *The Tree Bride* (2004) are the first two novels in a projected trilogy dealing with Indian expatriates in America. Mukherjee currently teaches at the University of California at Berkeley.

TASLIMA NASRIN (b. 1962)   Born and educated in Mymensingh, Bangladesh, Nasrin began writing poetry in her childhood, her earliest works appearing in a literary journal edited by her eldest brother. Following in the footsteps of her father, a doctor, she earned a degree in medicine from Mymensingh Medical College and for a few years practiced as a government doctor. Her study of modern science, Nasrin has written, "made me a rationalist." While practicing medicine, she continued her writing, publishing poems and novels. These works, along with the essays she penned as a syndicated columnist in Bangladesh, earned her a number of important literary prizes in 1992 and 1993. However, her rationalism and her feminism, as well as her 1993 novel *Shame*, enraged Islamic fundamentalists. Forced into hiding by death threats, Nasrin fled to Europe in 1994; she returned to India in 2007 only to flee again after facing further threats and physical violence. She entered India once again in 2008 and lives in hiding under tight security. Nasrin has won several humanitarian awards, among them the UNESCO-Madanjeet Singh Prize for the promotion of tolerance and nonviolence in 2004 and the Simone de Beauvoir feminist award in recognition of her writing on women's rights in 2008. In an essay titled "Women's Rights," Nasrin writes, "My poetry, my prose, my entire output expresses the deprivation of women who have been exploited for centuries." She has written a multivolume autobiography which includes *Meyebela, My Bengali Girlhood: A Memoir of Growing Up Female in a Muslim World* (2002) and *Ka* (*Speak Up*, 2003), which was banned in Bangladesh. Among her other publications are an essay collection, *Narir Kono Desh Nei* (*A Woman Has No Country*, 2007), and several volumes of poetry, most recently *Bondini* (*Prisoner*, 2008).

PABLO NERUDA (1904–1973)   Neruda was born in Parral, Chile, the son of a railroad worker. Shortly after leaving college, he joined the Chilean foreign service to begin a distinguished career as consul and ambassador at a variety of posts around the world, including Burma, Ceylon, Indonesia, Siam, Cambodia, Spain, France, and Mexico. He was elected to the Chilean senate as a communist. But when he published letters attacking the policies of Gabriel González Videla, the president of Chile, he was forced into exile. He returned to Chile after the victory of anti-Videla forces and rejoined the foreign service. His vast literary output won many prizes and honors. And, although American readers found it difficult to separate his poetry from his politics, he was, at his prime, generally considered to be the greatest poet writing in Spanish. One critic pointed out that Neruda "never bothered his head about the state of poetry. He has just gone on exuding it as he draws breath." In an essay on impure poetry, Neruda wrote: "Let [this] be the poetry we search for: worn with the hand's obligations, as by acids, steeped in sweat and in smoke, smelling of lilies and urine, spattered diversely by the trades that we love by, inside the law or beyond it. A poetry impure as the clothing we wear, or our bodies, soup-stained, soiled with our shameful behavior, our wrinkles and vigils and dreams, observations and prophecies, declarations of loathing and love, idylls and beasts, the shocks of encounter, political loyalties, denials and doubts, affirmation and taxes." *Five Decades, a Selection: Poems, 1925–1970* appeared in 1974. He was awarded the Nobel Prize for Literature in 1971.

JOHN FREDERICK NIMS (1913–1999) Nims was born in Muskegon, Michigan, and earned degrees from De Paul University, the University of Notre Dame, and the University of Chicago. He taught at a number of institutions, including the University of Toronto; the University of Illinois, Urbana; Harvard University; and Williams College. He wrote two works of nonfiction, namely *Western Wind: An Introduction to Poetry* (1974) and *A Local Habitation: Essays on Poetry* (1985). In addition to serving as the editor of *Poetry* magazine from 1978 to 1984, Nims was a talented poet in his own right. He was the author of more than eight collections of poems, including *The Iron Pastoral* (1947), *Of Flesh and Bone* (1967), *The Kiss: A Jambalaya* (1982), and *The Six-Cornered Snowflake* (1990). He was also known as an astute translator, publishing translations of the poetry of Sappho and St. John of the Cross, as well as *Andromache*, a Greek tragedy. His work appeared in a number of periodicals, such as *American Scholar, Atlantic, Harper's, Kenyon Review, Mademoiselle,* and *New Republic.* Among Nims's many awards were fellowships from the Academy of American Poets, the Guggenheim Foundation, and the University of Illinois Institute of the Humanities, as well as grants from the American Academy of Arts and Letters and the National Foundation for the Arts and Humanities.

JOYCE CAROL OATES (b. 1938) Born in Lockport, New York, Oates majored in English at Syracuse University (B.A., 1960) as a scholarship student and earned an M.A. in English (1961) from the University of Wisconsin. While still an undergraduate, she won the *Mademoiselle* college fiction award (1959), beginning an enormously prolific career as a writer and editor. She publishes an average of two books a year, to date well over fifty volumes including novels, short-story collections, poetry, drama, and critical essays. Her numerous awards and honors include the 1970 fiction National Book Award for her novel *Them* (1969). She taught at the universities of Detroit and Windsor (Canada) before joining the faculty at Princeton University, where she is the Roger S. Berlind Distinguished Professor. Among her many recent publications are the short-story collection *Wild Nights!* (2008) and the novels *The Gravedigger's Daughter* (2007) and *My Sister, My Love* (2008).

TIM O'BRIEN (b. 1946)   O'Brien was born in Austin, Minnesota; attended public schools; and received a B.A. summa cum laude from Macalester College. Immediately following graduation, he was drafted into the U.S. Army (1968–1970), earning a Purple Heart. On his return to civilian life, he pursued graduate work at Harvard University and worked as a national affairs reporter for the *Washington Post*. His first novel, *If I Die in a Combat Zone, Box Me Up and Ship Me Home* (1973), is a semi-fictionalized account of his own Vietnam experiences. Many of O'Brien's novels either are set in Vietnam or focus on characters haunted by the war: *Northern Lights* (1975); *Going after Cacciato* (1978), which won a National Book Award; *The Nuclear Age* (1985); *The Things They Carried* (1990); and *In the Lake of the Woods* (1994). In an interview, O'Brien explained that his preoccupation with the Vietnam War was part of his need to write with "passion." Writing "good" stories, he went on to say, "requires a sense of passion, and my passion as a human being and as a writer intersect in Vietnam, not in the physical stuff but in the issues of Vietnam—of courage, rectitude, enlightenment, holiness, trying to do the right thing in the world." O'Brien wrote a comic novel, *Tomcat in Love* (1998), about a womanizing professor's midlife crisis, before returning to his earlier themes in his most recent book, *July, July* (2002).

FLANNERY O'CONNOR (1925–1964)   O'Connor, afflicted with lupus erythematosus, spent most of her tragically short life in Milledgeville, Georgia. She began writing while a student at Georgia State College for Women in her hometown, and in 1947 earned an M.F.A. from the University of Iowa. Back in Milledgeville, she lived on a farm with her mother, raised peacocks, and endured the indignity of constant treatment for her progressive and incurable disease. She traveled and lectured when she could. She wrote two novels, *Wise Blood* (1952) and *The Violent Bear It Away* (1960), and two collections of stories, *A Good Man Is Hard to Find* (1955) and *Everything That Rises Must Converge* (1965). She was deeply religious and wrote numerous book reviews for Catholic newspapers. Her southern gothic tales often force readers to confront physical deformity, spiritual depravity, and the violence they often engender.

SHARON OLDS (b. 1942)   Born in San Francisco, Olds attended Stanford University (B.A., 1964) and Columbia University (Ph.D., 1972). She joined the faculty of Theodor Herzl Institute in 1976 and has given readings at many colleges. She is currently teaching at the Graduate Creative Writing Program at

New York University. She won the Madeline Sadin Award from the *New York Quarterly* in 1978 for "The Death of Marilyn Monroe." Often compared to confessional poets Sylvia Plath and Anne Sexton, Olds published her first collection, *Satan Says*, in 1980, and won both the National Book Critics' Circle Award and the Lamont Award for *The Dead and the Living* in 1983. She was poet laureate of New York State from 1998 to 2000. Her most recent volumes of poetry are *The Unswept Room* (2002) and *Strike Sparks: Selected Poems, 1980–2002* (2004).

MARY OLIVER (b. 1935)   Mary Oliver was born in Cleveland, Ohio. She spent one year at Ohio State University and a second year at Vassar. Her distinctive poetic talent led to an appointment as the chair of the writing department of the Fine Arts Workshop in Provincetown, Massachusetts (1972–1973). Though she never graduated from college, she was awarded the Mather Visiting Professorship at Case Western Reserve University for 1980 and 1982, and among her many awards and honors, she received a National Endowment for the Arts Fellowship (1972–1973) and a Guggenheim Fellowship (1980–1981). The first of her several volumes of poems, *No Voyage and Other Poems*, appeared in 1963. Other books include *New and Selected Poems* (1992), *A Poetry Handbook* (1995), and *Blue Pastures* (1995), a collection of prose nature writing. Her most recent volumes are *Thirst: Poems* (2006); *Our World* (2007), which includes poetry and prose with photographs by her partner, Molly Malone Cook; and *Red Bird* (2008).

GEORGE ORWELL (1903–1950)   Born Eric Blair in India, the son of a minor British colonial officer, Orwell was raised in England. His education at good grammar schools, culminating with a stay at Eton College, introduced him to what he later called the snobbish world of England's middle and upper classes. Denied a university scholarship, he joined the Indian Imperial Police in 1922 and served in Burma until he resigned in 1927, disgusted with the injustice of British imperialism in India and Burma. He was determined to be a writer and, living at the edge of poverty, deliberately mingled with social outcasts and impoverished laborers. These experiences produced *Down and Out in Paris and London* (1933). Although he was a socialist, his experiences while fighting alongside the leftists during the Spanish Civil War disillusioned him, and he embodied his distaste for any totalitarian system in *Animal Farm* (1945)—a satirical attack on the leadership of the Soviet Union. In his pessimistic novel *1984* (1949), he imagined a social order shaped by a propagandistic perversion of language, in which the government, an extension of "Big Brother," uses two-way television to control the citizenry. Orwell succumbed to tuberculosis at the age of forty-seven, but not before he produced six novels, three documentary works, over seven hundred newspaper articles and reviews, and a volume of essays.

WILFRED OWEN (1893–1918)   Born in the Shropshire countryside of England, Owen began writing verse before he matriculated at London University, where he was known as a quiet and contemplative student. After some years of teaching English in France, Owen returned to England and joined the army. Wounded in 1917, he was killed in action leading an attack a few days before the armistice was declared in 1918. Owen's poems, published only after his death, along with his letters from the front to his mother, are perhaps the most powerful and vivid accounts of the horror of war to emerge from World War I.

Z. Z. PACKER (b. 1973)   Packer, who was born in Chicago, swapped her Swahili given name, *Zuwena*, for her family nickname, *ZZ*, early in her adolescence. She grew up in Atlanta and Louisville. Her first published short story appeared in *Seventeen* magazine during her senior year at Yale University. She went on to teach high-school English in Baltimore, Maryland, before earning graduate degrees at Johns Hopkins University and the University of Iowa's Writers' Workshop. Packer's first collection of short stories, *Drinking Coffee Elsewhere* (2003), earned her great critical acclaim. Her work has appeared in numerous anthologies, journals, and magazines, including *Harper's* and the *New Yorker*. She is the recipient of fellowships from Stanford University, and Yale University and awards from the Whiting Foundation and the Rona Jaffee Foundation. Packer is currently writing a novel about buffalo soldiers and teaching at Stanford University and the University of Iowa.

DOROTHY PARKER (1893–1967)   Parker was born in West End, New Jersey, to a Scottish Presbyterian mother and a Jewish father as "a late unexpected arrival in a loveless family." She was educated in private schools and moved in 1911 to New York, where she lived in a boardinghouse and earned her living by playing piano at a dancing school. In 1915, one of the verses she sent around was accepted by *Vogue* magazine, and the editor later hired her to write captions for fashion illustrations. Her native wit captivated the editor, and he persuaded her to join *Vanity Fair* as drama critic, although she was fired when she wrote unfavorable reviews of several plays. She became the first woman among the regulars of the Algonquin Round Table—a group of writers who met regularly at the Algonquin Hotel in New York City that included Alexander Woollcott, George S. Kaufman, Robert Benchley, and Edna Ferber, among others. A master of irony and scathing wit, Parker, despite a troubled personal life that led to suicide attempts, flourished as a humorist, poet, short-story writer, playwright, and screenwriter.

SUZAN-LORI PARKS (b. 1963)   Parks was born in Fort Knox, Kentucky. The daughter of an army colonel, she moved frequently and attended school in Germany. After earning a degree from Mount Holyoke College, where she began writing plays, and studying at the Yale University School of Drama, she moved to London to study acting. Her first play, *Betting on the Dust Commander,* was produced in New York City in 1987. Her second play, *Imperceptible Metabolites in the Third Kingdom,* won an Obie for being one of the best new American Off-Broadway plays of 1989. Among her ten other plays are *Venus* (1996), *In the Blood* (1999), and *Topdog/Underdog* (2001), winner of a Pulitzer

Prize. Parks is also the author of three plays for radio; a novel, *Getting Mother's Body* (2003); and three screenplays, namely *Girl 6* (1996), *Their Eyes Were Watching God* (2005), and *The Great Debaters* (2007). Her numerous awards include a Whiting Writer's Award, a Guggenheim Fellowship, and grants from the Rockefeller Foundation, the National Endowment for the Arts, and the MacArthur Foundation. Parks has taught at Yale University, the University of Michigan, and the Pratt Institute for the Arts; she is now director of the California Institute of the Arts in Valencia.

PAUL (d. ca. C.E. 64)   Paul was born Saul in Tarsus of Cilicia (located near the Mediterranean Sea in south-central Turkey, near Syria). He was an important Jerusalem Pharisee who, according to the Acts of the Apostles (Chapter 9), vigorously attacked (both intellectually and physically) those who proclaimed the deity of Jesus. The same source provides an account of Saul's conversion. Traveling to Damascus to arrest followers of Jesus, he experienced an intense light that blinded him and heard a voice that declared, "I am Jesus, whom you are persecuting." In Tarsus, his blindness was cured by Ananias, a follower of Jesus, and Paul became, arguably, the most important disciple of Jesus in the early church: his letters (and those attributed to him) constitute a quarter of the New Testament. His attempts to preach the new Way in the synagogues of the region were rebuffed, sometimes violently, and Paul was frequently jailed. He became the apostle to the Gentiles, traveling throughout the Mediterranean region to establish churches. His epistles to those young and fragile congregations helped formulate the political, legal, and spiritual institutions of the early church. His final arrest brought him to Rome to answer charges, and after two years of imprisonment, he died about C.E. 64.

MOLLY PEACOCK (b. 1947)   Born in Buffalo, New York, Peacock was educated at the State University of New York at Binghamton and at Johns Hopkins University, where she received an M.A. with honors in 1977. From 1970 to 1973, she was the director of academic advising at Binghamton. She was appointed honorary fellow at Johns Hopkins in 1977 and, in the following year, poet-in-residence at the Delaware State Arts Council in Wilmington. Since 1979, she has directed the Wilmington Writing Workshops. She has published in many magazines, including the *Southern Review,* the *Ohio Review,* and the *Massachusetts Review.* She has published several books of poems including *And Live Apart* (1980); *Raw Heaven* (1984); *Take Heart* (1989), which deals with her father's alcoholism and the mental and physical abuse she endured while growing up; and *Original Love* (1995). She was also co-editor of *Poetry in Motion: 100 Poems from the Subways and Buses* (1996), a collection of the popular poems displayed on placards in New York City's subways and buses. *Paradise, Piece by Piece* (1998), which she calls a "hybrid memoir," blends real and invented characters and explains why she decided not to have children. Her most recent books are *Cornucopia: New and Selected Poems 1975–2002* (2002) and *The Second Blush* (2008).

MARGE PIERCY (b. 1936) Born in Detroit, Marge Piercy was the first of her family to attend college. In 1957, she graduated from the University of Michigan (where she won prizes for poetry and fiction) and earned an M.A. from Northwestern University (1958). She was active in social and political causes and fought for equal treatment of women and minorities while opposing the Vietnam War. She supported herself with odd jobs in Chicago as she pursued a writing career, but her first novel was not published until after her 1969 move to Wellfleet, Massachusetts, where she still lives. She is an extraordinarily prolific writer. Among her more than a dozen novels are *He, She and It* (1991), *The Longings of Women* (1994), and *City of Darkness, City of Lights* (1996). Her many volumes of poetry include *My Mother's Body* (1985), *Available Light* (1988), *The Earth Shines Secretly: A Book of Days* (1990), and *Mars and Her Children* (1992). She has also written plays and several volumes of nonfiction and has edited the anthology *Early Ripening: American Women's Poetry Now* (1987). In the introduction to a volume of selected poems, *Circles on the Water* (1982), Piercy asserted that she wanted her poems to be "useful." "What I mean by useful is simply that readers will find poems that speak to and for them, will take those poems into their lives and say them to each other and put them up on the bathroom wall and remember bits and pieces of them in stressful or quiet moments. . . . To find ourselves spoken for in art gives dignity to our pain, our anger, our lust, our losses." Most recently, she has published two novels, *The Third Child* (2003) and *Sex Wars* (2005), and two collections of poetry, *Colors Passing through Us* (2003) and *The Crooked Inheritance* (2006).

SYLVIA PLATH (1932–1963) Plath was born in Boston, Massachusetts, where her parents taught at Boston University. She graduated summa cum laude in English from Smith College (1955); earned an M.A. as a Fulbright scholar at Newnham College, Cambridge (1955–1957); and married British poet Ted Hughes (1956). Plath's poetry reveals the anger and anxiety that would eventually lead to her suicide. Her view that all relationships were in some way destructive and predatory surely darkened her life. Yet in 1963, during the month between the publication of her only novel, *The Bell Jar* (about a suicidal college student), and her death, Plath was extraordinarily productive; she produced finished poems every day. Her *Collected Poems* was published in 1981.

PO CHU-I (772–846) Po was born in T'ai-yuan, a city in Shansi Province, and later resided in Ch'ang-an, the provincial capital. There he passed the examinations that allowed him to enter and rise through the ranks of the Chinese civil service, holding various positions from palace librarian through provincial governor. But his satirical streak frequently irritated his superiors, and from time to time, he was demoted and banished from the seat of power. But as students of his work assert, he was "dedicated to the idea that poetry should have a moral and social purpose." Po pointed out that the poetry of his time had devolved into "playing with the wind and the moon, the flowers and the grass," when it should have addressed the pervasive corruption and militarism of oppressive officials, as well as the superstition that kept the people politically docile. Suffering from partial paralysis, he retired to a monastery in 832. He is immensely popular in China because of his caustic and plain-spoken verse that muses not only on the rapacity of officials but also on his own human weakness.

EDGAR ALLAN POE (1809–1849) Poe, the son of traveling actors, was born in Boston, Massachusetts. Within a year, his alcoholic father deserted his mother and their three infant children. When his mother died of tuberculosis in Richmond, Virginia, three-year-old Edgar was adopted by John Allan and his wife. Allan, a prosperous businessman, spent time in England, where Poe began his education at private schools. Back in the United States, Allan forced Poe to leave the University of Virginia in 1826, when Poe incurred gambling debts he could not pay. He served in the U.S. Army from 1827 to 1829, eventually attaining the rank of sergeant major. Poe next attended West Point, hoping for further military advancement. Shortly thereafter, Mrs. Allan died of tuberculosis. Poe angrily confronted his foster father about his extramarital affairs; for this candor he was disowned. Believing that Allan would never reinstate him as heir, Poe deliberately violated rules to provoke his dismissal from the academy. In 1835, Poe began his career as editor, columnist, and reviewer, earning a living he could not make as a writer of stories and poems. He married his thirteen-year-old cousin, Virginia Clemm, in 1836, and lived with her and her mother during a period marked by illness and poverty. Virginia died of tuberculosis in 1847. Poe died, delirious, under mysterious circumstances, in 1849. He perfected the gothic horror story ("Fall of the House of Usher") and originated the modern detective story ("The Gold Bug," "The Murders in the Rue Morgue"). Poe's work fascinated the French poet Baudelaire, who translated it into French.

DEBORAH POPE (b. ?) Born in Cincinnati, Ohio, Pope graduated from Denison University and then attended the University of Wisconsin, where she earned a Ph.D. At present, she teaches at Duke University, where she co-founded the Duke Writers Conference. Using her Ph.D. thesis as a basis, she published a study in criticism, *Separate Vision: Isolation in Contemporary Women's Poetry* (1984). In 1990, she co-edited *Ties That Bind: Essays on Mothering and Patriarchy*. Her first volume of poetry, *Frantic Heart* (1992), was followed by several others, including *Falling Out of the Sky* (1999). Doubtless, some of her poems are generated by the pain and joy of a home life that includes two young sons. In an interview, she summed up her enthusiasm for teaching: "There is nothing like the joy and exhilaration that comes to me . . . when [students] have been able to bring some kind of formless chaotic experience into a balance in language."

KATHERINE ANNE PORTER (1890–1980) Born in Texas and educated mostly at small convent schools, Porter traveled widely in her early years, living for some time in Mexico and, more briefly, in Germany. She gained a reputation primarily as a writer of finely crafted stories, gathered in *The Collected Stories of Katherine Anne Porter* (1965). She published one novel, *Ship of Fools*, in 1962. Porter's output of fiction was small, and she earned her livelihood mostly as a reporter, lecturer, scriptwriter, speaker, and writer-in-residence. Her achievement in fiction was recognized by a National Book Award and Pulitzer Prize for Fiction, both in 1966. Her final work, *The Never-Ending Wrong* (1977), is a memoir about her involvement in the celebrated Sacco-Vanzetti case.

WYATT PRUNTY (b. 1947)   Prunty was born in Humboldt, Tennessee. After earning a B.A. from the University of the South in Sewanee, he went on to earn an M.A. from Johns Hopkins University and a Ph.D. (1979) from Louisiana State University. His poetry chapbook, *Domestic of the Outer Banks*, was published in 1980. Several volumes followed, among them *Since the Noon Mail Stopped* (1997) and *Unarmed and Dangerous* (2000). His poetry has been anthologized in *Anthology of Magazine Verse and Yearbook of American Poetry* for both 1979 and 1980. He was awarded a poetry prize by *Sewanee Review* (1969) and has been a fellow at the Bread Loaf Writers' Conference. He has taught in the graduate program of the Johns Hopkins Writing Seminars, where he was Elliott Coleman Professor of Poetry. Currently, he serves as Carlton Professor of English at the University of the South, where he teaches poetry, and where he founded and now directs the Sewanee Writers' Conference. His most recent work is a collection of poetry and fiction, *The Lover's Guide to Trapping* (2009).

SIR WALTER RALEIGH (1554–1618)   Born in Devonshire, England, into the landed gentry, Raleigh attended Oxford University but dropped out after a year to fight for the Huguenot cause in France. He returned to England, began the study of law, but again was drawn to a life of adventure and exploration. Through the influence of friends he came to the attention of Elizabeth I, after which his career flourished: he was knighted, given a number of lucrative commercial monopolies, made a member of Parliament, and, in 1587, named captain of the Yeomen of the Guard. During these years, he invested in various colonies in North America, but all his settlements failed. He was briefly imprisoned in the Tower of London for offending the queen but was soon back in favor and in command of an unsuccessful expedition to Guiana (now Venezuela) in 1595. In 1603, he was again imprisoned in the tower, this time on a probably trumped-up charge of treason, where he remained until 1616, spending part of his time writing *A History of the World* (1614). After his release, he undertook yet another expedition to Guiana but again returned empty-handed. As a consequence of more political intrigue, James I ordered him executed. Although Raleigh epitomized the great merchant adventurers of Elizabethan England, he was also a gifted poet.

DUDLEY RANDALL (1914–2000)   Born in Washington, D.C., Randall worked during the Depression in the foundry of the Ford Motor Company in Dearborn, Michigan, and then as a carrier and clerk for the U.S. Post Office in

Detroit. He served in the U.S. Army Signal Corps (1942–1946) and graduated from Wayne State University (B.A., 1949) and the University of Michigan (M.A.L.S., 1951). He was a librarian at several universities and founded the Broadside Press in 1965 "so black people could speak to and for their people." Randall told *Negro Digest,* "Precision and accuracy are necessary for both white and black writers. . . . 'A black aesthetic' should not be an excuse for sloppy writing." He urges African American writers to reject what was false in white poetry but not to forsake universal concerns in favor of a racial agenda. His works include *On Getting a Natural* (1969) and *A Litany of Friends: New and Selected Poems* (1981). He edited *For Malcolm: Poems on the Life and Death of Malcolm X* (1969) and *The Black Poets* (1971), an extensive anthology of poetry, from slave songs to the present.

HENRY REED (1914–1986)   Reed was born in Birmingham, England; earned a B.A. from the University of Birmingham (1937); worked as a teacher and free-lance writer (1937–1941); and served in the British Army (1941–1942). His early poetry dealt with political events before and during World War II. "Naming of Parts" was based on his frustrating experience in cadet training. His collection of poetry, *A Map of Verona* (1946), revealed a formal, reverent, but also humorous and ironic voice. Another collection of poetry, *Lessons of War,* was published in 1970. Reed began writing radio plays in 1947 and generated as many as four scripts a year. His best-known satirical work is the *Hilda Tablet* series, a 1960s BBC Radio production that parodied British society of the 1930s.

ADRIENNE RICH (b. 1929)   Born to a middle-class family, Rich was educated by her parents until she entered public school in the fourth grade. She graduated Phi Beta Kappa from Radcliffe College in 1951, the same year her first book of poems, *A Change of World,* appeared. That volume, chosen by W. H. Auden for the Yale Series of Younger Poets Award, and her next, *The Diamond Cutters and Other Poems* (1955), earned her a reputation as an elegant, controlled stylist. In the 1960s, however, Rich began a dramatic shift away from her earlier mode as she took up political and feminist themes and stylistic experimentation in such works as *Snapshots of a Daughter-in-Law* (1963), *The Necessities of Life* (1966), *Leaflets* (1969), and *The Will to Change* (1971). In *Diving into the Wreck* (1973) and *The Dream of a Common Language* (1978), she continued to experiment with form and to deal with the experiences and aspirations of women from a feminist perspective. In addition to her poetry, Rich has published many essays on poetry, feminism, motherhood, and lesbianism. She has also won numerous awards, most recently the National Book Foundation's Medal for Distinguished Contribution to American Letters in 2006. Her recent collections include *Telephone Ringing in the Labyrinth: Poems: 2004–2006* (2007) and *A Human Eye: Essays on Art in Society, 1997–2008* (2009).

EDWIN ARLINGTON ROBINSON (1869–1935)   Robinson grew up in Gardiner, Maine; attended Harvard University; returned to Gardiner as a freelance writer;

and then settled in New York City in 1896. His various odd jobs included a one-year stint as subway-construction inspector. President Theodore Roosevelt, a fan of his poetry, had him appointed to the United States Customs House in New York, where he worked from 1905 to 1909. Robinson wrote about people rather than nature, particularly New England characters remembered from his early years. Describing his first volume of poems, *The Torrent and the Night Before* (1896), he told a friend there was not "a single red-breasted robin in the whole collection." Popular throughout his career, Robinson won three Pulitzer Prizes (1921, 1924, and 1927).

THEODORE ROETHKE (1908–1963) Born in Saginaw, Michigan, Roethke was the son of a greenhouse owner; greenhouses figure prominently in the imagery of his poems. He graduated magna cum laude from the University of Michigan in 1929, where he also earned an M.A. in 1936 after graduate study at Harvard University. He taught at several universities, coached two varsity tennis teams, and settled at the University of Washington in 1947. Intensely introspective and demanding of himself, Roethke was renowned as a great teacher, though he was sometimes incapacitated by bipolar disorder. His collection *The Waking: Poems 1933–1953* won the Pulitzer Prize in 1954. Other awards include Guggenheim Fellowships in 1945 and 1950, and a National Book Award and the Bollingen Prize in 1959 for *Words for the Wind* (1958).

MARY RUEFLE (b. 1952) Ruefle, the daughter of a military officer, was born near Pittsburgh and moved frequently throughout the United States and Europe during her childhood. She earned a degree from Bennington College and currently teaches in the M.F.A. program at Vermont College. She is also a visiting faculty member at the University of Iowa's Writers' Workshop. In addition to being widely published in journals and anthologies, Ruefle has received fellowships from the Guggenheim Foundation and the National Endowment for the Arts, as well as awards from the American Academy of Arts and Letters and the Whiting Foundation. She is the author of ten volumes of poetry, among them *Memling's Veil* (1982), *The Adamant* (1989), *A Little White Shadow* (2006), and *Indeed I Was Pleased with the World* (2007). Her latest work, *The Most of It* (2008), is her first published book of prose.

MURIEL RUKEYSER (1913–1980) Born in New York City, Rukeyser attended Vassar College and Columbia University, then spent a short time at Roosevelt Aviation School, which no doubt helped shape her first published volume of poetry, *Theory of Flight* (1935). In the early 1930s, she joined Elizabeth Bishop, Mary McCarthy, and Eleanor Clark in founding a literary magazine that challenged the policies of the *Vassar Review*. (The two magazines later merged.) A social activist, Rukeyser witnessed the Scottsboro trials (where she was one of the reporters arrested by authorities) in 1933. She visited suffering tunnel workers in West Virginia in 1936 and went to Hanoi to protest U.S. involvement in the Vietnam War. She gave poetry readings across the United

States and received several awards, including a Guggenheim Fellowship and the Copernicus Award. *Waterlily Fire: Poems 1935–1962* appeared in 1962, and later work was collected in *Twenty-Nine Poems* (1970). *The Collected Poems of Muriel Rukeyser* appeared in 1978. Her only novel, *The Orgy,* appeared in 1965.

SALMAN RUSHDIE (b. 1947)   Rushdie was born in Bombay into a family of Indian Muslims just two months before Indian independence and four months before South Asia was partitioned into a principally Muslim Pakistan and Hindu India. That process resulted in the murder of hundreds of thousands of people in the fighting that accompanied the vast migration of Hindus to the south and Muslims to the north. Some years later, Rushdie's upper-middle-class family sent him first to a British-style private school in Bombay and then to the elite Rugby School in England. There, Rushdie told an interviewer, he was miserable: "I was suddenly an Indian . . . and at the schoolboy level that was no fun." His Islamic family finally moved from Bombay to Karachi, Pakistan, while Rushdie completed an M.A. with honors in history at Cambridge University (1968). But shortly after his return to Pakistan, the government prohibited the performance of a television play he had produced and the publication of an article he had written about Pakistan. This numbing experience of official censorship convinced him to return to Britain in late 1968. There he supported himself as an actor and freelance advertising copywriter until he began his successful career as a writer. His second novel, *Midnight's Children* (1981), won three awards, including the prestigious Booker Prize, and was honored as the best Booker Prize novel in in the prize's forty-year history. But his eminence seriously affected the conduct of his life when his novel *The Satanic Verses* (1988) profoundly offended Muslim sensibilities in some quarters and resulted in a *fatwa* issued by the Iranian ayatollah Khomeini, who offered one million dollars to the person who would execute Rushdie for blasphemy. Though Iran renounced the *fatwa* in 1998, in some Islamic quarters Rushdie remains a marked man. In 2007, Rushdie was knighted by the queen of England causing another outcry among Muslims; Al Qaeda called the knighthood "an insult to Islam" and threatened to retaliate. He has been elected to many prestigious positions in the world of letters, including the Royal Society of Literature, and he served as president of the PEN American Center. His most recent novels are *Shalimar the Clown* (2005) and *The Enchantress of Florence* (2008). Bharati Mukherjee once characterized Rushdie as "up there with Joyce and Solzhenitsyn, an educated, implacable, remorseless dissenter from deep inside the family." And Rushdie characterized himself as one who has "spent my entire life as a writer in opposition, and had indeed conceived the writer's role as including the function as antagonist to the state."

KAY RYAN (b. 1945)   Ryan was born in San Jose and grew up in central and southern California. She attended Antelope Valley College in Lancaster, California, before earning two degrees from UCLA. For over thirty-five years, she was a part-time instructor of English at the College of Marin. Ryan is the author of six volumes of poetry: *Dragon Acts to Dragon Ends* (1983), *Strangely Marked Metal* (1985), *Flamingo Watching* (1994), *Elephant Rocks* (1997), *Say Uncle* (2000), and *The Niagara River* (2005). Her poems have also appeared in a number of periodicals, including *American Scholar, Atlantic,* the *New Yorker, Paris Review,* and *Poetry* magazine. Among her many awards are fellowships from the Guggenheim Foundation and the National Endowment for the Arts and the 2004 Ruth Lilly Poetry Prize, a prestigious honor given to living U.S. poets "whose lifetime accomplishments warrant extraordinary recognition." In autumn of 2008, Ryan began a one-year term as poet laureate of the United States.

TOMAŽ ŠALAMUN (b. 1941) Šalamun was born in Zagreb, Croatia, and spent his childhood in Koper, Slovenia. He studied art history at the University of Ljubljana in Slovenia, earning a master's degree and working as a museum curator. In the early 1970s, he turned his attention to writing and for two years attended the University of Iowa's Writers' Workshop. Šalamun has written more than thirty volumes of poetry in Slovenian and his work has also been translated into nearly a dozen other languages. More than ten collections of his poems are available in English, including *The Selected Poems of Tomaž Šalamun* (1988), *The Shepherd, the Hunter* (1992), *The Four Questions of Melancholy* (1997), and *The Book for My Brother* (2006). His poems and articles have also appeared in a large number of periodicals, among them *Harvard Review, Mississippi Review, New Republic, Paris Review,* and *Ploughshares.* Šalamun lives in Ljubljana, Slovenia. His latest volume of poetry to be translated into English is *Woods and Chalices* (2008).

SAPPHO (ca. 610–ca. 580 B.C.) Almost nothing certain is known of the finest woman lyric poet of the ancient world. Sappho was born to an aristocratic family and had three brothers, one of whom was a court cupbearer, a position limited to the sons of good families. She is associated with the island of Lesbos, set in the Aegean Sea. She married and had a daughter. For over two thousand years, her reputation depended on fragments of her work quoted by other ancient authors. However, in the late nineteenth century a cache of papyrus and vellum codices, dating from the second to the sixth centuries A.D. and containing authentic transcriptions of a few of her lyrical poems, was discovered in Egypt. Unlike other ancient Greek poets, she wrote in ordinary Greek rather than in an exalted literary dialect; her lyrics, despite their simple language, conveyed women's concerns with intense emotion.

DAVID SEDARIS (b. 1956) Sedaris was born in Binghamton, New York, and raised in Raleigh, North Carolina. He attended Kent State University before working odd jobs and eventually earning a degree from the School of the Art Institute of Chicago. Sedaris garnered fame when he began reading essays based on his diary on National Public Radio, first on *Morning Edition* and then, at the behest of host Ira Glass, as a regular contributor to *This American*

Life. His first book of humorous stories and autobiographical essays, *Barrel Fever,* was published in 1994. All five of his other collections—*Naked* (1997), *Holidays on Ice* (1997), *Me Talk Pretty One Day* (2000), *Dress Your Family in Corduroy and Denim* (2004), and *When You Are Engulfed in Flames* (2008)— have appeared on the *New York Times* best-seller list. He has also contributed regularly to the *New Yorker* and *Esquire* magazines; has coauthored several plays with his sister Amy; and has been nominated for two Grammys for audio recordings of his own work.

ANNE SEXTON (1928–1974)   Born in Newton, Massachusetts, Sexton attended Garland Junior College and Boston University, where she studied under Robert Lowell. She worked for a year as a fashion model in Boston and later wrote her first poetry collection, *To Bedlam and Part Way Back* (1960), while recovering from a nervous breakdown. Writing a poem almost every day was successful therapy for her. From 1961 to 1963, Sexton was a scholar at the Radcliffe Institute for Independent Study. A confessional poet, Sexton acknowledged her debt to W. D. Snodgrass, whose collection of poetry, *Heart's Needle* (1959), influenced her profoundly. Her second collection, *All My Pretty Ones* (1962), includes a quote from a letter by Franz Kafka that expresses her own literary philosophy: "A book should serve as the axe for the frozen sea within us." *Live or Die* (1967), her third collection of poems, won a Pulitzer Prize. She committed suicide in 1974.

WILLIAM SHAKESPEARE (1564–1616)   Shakespeare was born at Stratford-on-Avon in April 1564. His father became an important public figure, rising to the position of high bailiff (equivalent to mayor) of Stratford. Although we know practically nothing of Shakespeare's personal life, we may assume that he received a decent grammar school education in literature, logic, and Latin (though not in mathematics or natural science). When he was eighteen, he married Anne Hathaway, eight years his senior; six months later their son was born. Two years later, Anne bore twins. We do not know how the young Shakespeare supported his family, and we do not hear of him again until 1592, when a rival London playwright sarcastically refers to him as an "upstart crow." Shakespeare seems to have prospered in the London theater world. He probably began as an actor and earned enough as author and part owner of his company's theaters to acquire property. His sonnets, which were written during the 1590s, reveal rich and varied interests. Some are addressed to an attractive young man (whom the poet urges to marry); others to the mysterious dark lady; still others suggest a love triangle of two men and a woman. His dramas include historical plays based on English dynastic struggles; comedies, both festive and dark; romances such as *Pericles* (1608) and *Cymbeline* (1611) that cover decades in the lives of their characters; and the great tragedies *Hamlet* (1602), *Othello* (1604), *King Lear* (1605), and *Macbeth* (1606). About 1611, at age forty-seven, he retired to the second largest house in Stratford. He died in 1616, leaving behind a body of work that still stands as a pinnacle in world literature.

PERCY BYSSHE SHELLEY (1792–1822) Born near Horsham, England, Shelley was the son of a wealthy landowner who sat in Parliament. At University College, Oxford University, he befriended Thomas Jefferson Hogg. Both became interested in radical philosophy and quickly became inseparable. After one year at Oxford they were both expelled for writing and circulating a pamphlet entitled "The Necessity of Atheism." Shelley married Harriet Westbrook soon after leaving Oxford. Though they had two children, the marriage was unsuccessful, and in 1814, Shelley left Harriet for Mary Wollstonecraft Godwin, the author of *Frankenstein*. After Harriet's apparent suicide, Shelley and Godwin were married. Escaping legal problems in England, he settled in Pisa, Italy, in 1820, and died in a sailing accident before his thirtieth birthday. A playwright and essayist as well as a romantic poet, Shelley is admired for his dramatic poem "Prometheus Unbound" (1820).

GARY SHTEYNGART (b. 1972) Shteyngart was born in Leningrad (now St. Petersburg), Russia, and immigrated to the United States with his family when he was seven years old. Raised in Queens, New York, he studied politics at Oberlin College in Ohio. Shteyngart, who felt out of place in America, then traveled to Prague, where he garnered the experiences that would inform his first novel. He returned to New York and wrote the book on the sly while working for nonprofit organizations. He sent the manuscript along with his M.F.A. application to Hunter College of the City University of New York; a professor there passed it on to an editor. Shteyngart earned his M.F.A. in creative writing from Hunter and numerous awards for his debut novel, *The Russian Debutante's Handbook* (2002). He wrote a second novel, *Absurdistan* (2006). His writing has also appeared in a number of periodicals, including the *New Yorker*, the *New York Times*, *Slate*, and *Travel and Leisure*. He lives in Manhattan and teaches at Columbia University and Princeton University.

LESLIE MARMON SILKO (b. 1948) Born in Albuquerque, New Mexico, Silko grew up on the Laguna Pueblo Reservation. She was educated in Bureau of Indian Affairs schools and at the University of New Mexico, where she graduated with highest honors. After three semesters in the American Indian Law program, Silko decided to devote her talents to writing about Native Americans. Her short stories quickly earned her a reputation; in 1974, she published a volume of poems, *Laguna Woman*. Her novel *Ceremony* (1977) was widely acclaimed and revived interest in her earlier short stories. *Storyteller* (1981) is a semiautobiographical collection of stories and poems. In 1991 the novel *Almanac of the Dead* appeared, and a collection of essays on contemporary Native American life, *Yellow Woman and a Beauty of the Spirit*, followed in 1996. Silko has taught at the University of Arizona and the University of New Mexico, but with a large award from the prestigious MacArthur Foundation, she has been, in her words, "a little less beholden to the everyday world." Her work includes the novel *Gardens in the Dunes* (1999). *Conversations with Leslie Marmon Silko* was published in 2000.

STEVIE SMITH (1902–1971) Born Florence Margaret Smith in Hull, England, Stevie Smith was a secretary at Newnes Publishing Company in London from 1923 to 1953 and occasionally worked as a writer and broadcaster for the BBC. Though she began publishing verse, which she often illustrated herself, in the 1930s, Smith did not reach a wide audience until 1962—with the publication of *Selected Poems* and her appearance in the Penguin Modern Poets series. She is noted for her eccentricity and mischievous humor, often involving an acerbic twist on nursery rhymes, common songs, or hymns. Force-fed with what she considered lifeless language in the New English Bible, she often aimed satirical barbs at religion. Smith won the Queen's Gold Medal for poetry in 1969, two years before her death. She published three novels in addition to her eight volumes of poetry.

CATHY SONG (b. 1955) Song was born in Honolulu of Korean and Chinese ancestry. A precocious writer, by age nine she was keeping a journal of her family's activities. After graduating from high school, she moved to Boston, where she attended Wellesley College (B.A., 1977) and Boston University (M.F.A., 1981). She then returned to Honolulu. Two years later, her first volume of poetry, *Picture Bride* (1983), was published to great acclaim. It received the prestigious Yale Series Younger Poets Award and was nominated for a National Book Critics Circle Award. The title poem deals with Song's grandmother, who left Korea at age twenty-three to marry an older man, whom she knew only through an exchange of photographs. She has since published four other volumes of poetry: *Frameless Windows, Squares of Light* (1988), *School Figures* (1994), *The Land of Bliss* (2001), and *Cloud Moving Hands* (2007). In 1993, she won the Poetry Society of America's Shelly Memorial Award. In the following year, the United States Information Agency's Arts America program invited her to travel and lecture in South Korea and Hong Kong. Commenting on her mixed cultural heritage, Song told an interviewer, "Being a woman and an Asian American has only helped my work as an artist. You have to be on the periphery, on the outside looking in, marginalized in some way, to gain a different perspective, a perspective which only provokes your art because there is no way you can possibly accept the party line."

SOPHOCLES (496?–406 B.C.) Born into a wealthy family at Colonus, a village just outside Athens, Sophocles distinguished himself early in life as a performer, musician, and athlete. Our knowledge of him is based on a very few ancient laudatory notices, but he certainly had a brilliant career as one of the three great Greek classical tragedians (the other two are Aeschylus, an older contemporary, and Euripides, a younger contemporary). He won the drama competition associated with the Dionysian festival (entries consisted of a tragic trilogy and a farce) at least twenty times, far more often than his two principal rivals. However, *Oedipus Rex,* his most famous tragedy, and the three other plays it was grouped with, took second place (ca. 429 B.C.). He lived during the golden age of Athens, when architecture, philosophy, and the arts flourished under Pericles.

In 440 B.C., Sophocles was elected as one of the ten *strategoi* (military commanders), an indication of his stature in Athens. But his long life ended in sadder times, when the Peloponnesian War (431–404 B.C.), between the Athenian empire and an alliance led by Sparta, darkened the region. Though Sophocles wrote some 123 plays, only seven have survived; nonetheless, these few works establish him as the greatest of the ancient Western tragedians.

GARY SOTO (b. 1952)   Soto was born in Fresno, California, to working-class Mexican American parents. He grew up in the San Joaquin Valley and worked as a migrant laborer in California's rich agricultural regions. Uncertain of his abilities, he began his academic career at Fresno City College, moving on to California State University at Fresno and the University of California at Irvine, where he earned an M.F.A. (1976). In 1975, he married Carolyn Oda, a woman of Japanese ancestry. Although his work earned him recognition as early as 1975 (an Academy of American Poets Prize), his first book of poems—*The Elements of San Joaquin*, portraying grim pictures of Mexican American life in California's central valley—didn't appear until 1977. In 1985, he joined the faculty at the University of California at Berkeley, where he taught in both the English and Chicano studies departments. He gave up teaching in 1993 to become a full-time writer but returned to teaching in 2003, at the University of California at Riverside. His prolific output of poetry, memoirs, essays, and fiction continues unabated and has earned him numerous prizes, including an American Book Award from the Before Columbus Foundation for *Living up the Street* (1985). Soto's novel, *Buried Onions* (1999), deals with the struggle and discomfort of a teenage boy's life in Fresno, California. *Nickel and Dime* (2000) is a fictional exploration of the interlocking lives of three Mexican American men in California. His latest publications are a novel for teenagers, *Accidental Love* (2006), and a collection of stories for adolescents, *Facts of Life: Stories* (2008). He is set to publish a new collection of poetry called *Human Nature* and is working on a collection of love poems for preteens. One critic points out that Soto has transcended the social commentary of his early work and shifted to "a more personal, less politically motivated poetry." Another argues that "Gary Soto has become not an important Chicano poet but an important American poet."

WOLE SOYINKA (b. 1934)   One of the most prolific and versatile writers of our time, and the first African to receive the Nobel Prize for Literature (1986), Soyinka was born in Akinwande, Nigeria, to Yoruba parents. After attending Nigerian schools, including the University of Obada, he moved to England, where he earned a B.A. (1958) in English literature. For the next few years, he worked at the Royal Court Theatre in London, where his first works were performed. He returned to Nigeria in 1960, teaching drama in several universities and working on the creation of a Nigerian national theater. Because of his political opposition to the governing military dictatorship during the Nigerian civil war, he was twice arrested and jailed during the 1960s. Following his release almost two years after his second arrest, he went into voluntary exile in England, where he lectured and continued to write. This pattern of exile and return continued, depending on the political situation in his home country. He again went into exile in 1994, declaring, "Some people think the Nobel Prize makes you bulletproof. I never had that illusion." Following the death of the military dictator Sani Abacha in 1998, Soyinka returned to Nigeria, where he now lives and teaches. Among his many plays are *The Lion and Jewel* (1959), *The Strong Breed* (1963), *The Trials of Brother Jero* (1964), *A Scourge of Hyacinths* (1992), and *King Baabu* (2001). *The Man Died* (1972) is an account of his first arrest and imprisonment. His volumes of poetry include *Mandela's Earth and Other Poems* (1988), *Early Poems* (1997), *Outsiders* (1999), and *Samarkand and Other Markets I Have Known* (2002). *The Burden of Memory, the Muse of Forgiveness* (1999) comprises Soyinka's reflections on the politics, government, and literature of Africa. His latest publications include his nonfiction work *Climate of Fear: The Quest for Dignity in a Dehumanized World* (2005) and his memoirs, *You Must Set Forth at Dawn* (2006).

WILLIAM STAFFORD (1914–1993)   Born in Hutchinson, Kansas, Stafford earned his bachelor's and master's degrees from the University of Kansas and his doctorate from the University of Iowa. Drafted during the Second World War, he declared himself pacifist and conscientious objector and spent several years doing forestry and soil-conservation work instead. He taught at a small number of institutions around the country before settling on Lewis & Clark College and the Pacific Northwest. Stafford did not publish a collection of poetry until he was forty-eight years old; his first volume, *Traveling through the Dark* (1962), won the National Book Award in 1963. An astonishingly prolific writer, he kept a journal for fifty years and composed almost twenty-two thousand poems, three thousand of which were published in nearly sixty volumes of poetry. Among his many titles are *The Rescued Year* (1966), *Stories That Could Be True: New and Collected Poems* (1977), *Writing the Australian Crawl: Views on the Writer's Vocation* (1978), and *An Oregon Message* (1987). Stafford also contributed to numerous periodicals; authored a memoir, essays, reviews, and a children's book; and edited and translated the works of others. His many awards include a Guggenheim Fellowship, a grant from the National Endowment for the Arts, a Shelley Memorial Award, and a Western States Lifetime Achievement Award in Poetry.

MAUREEN STANTON (b. 1960)   Stanton earned degrees from the University of Massachusetts–Amherst and Ohio State University. She has had nearly thirty different jobs, among them hotdog vendor, gas-station attendant, cashier, clerk, janitor, assembly-line worker, nursing-home aide, surveyor, secretary, bartender, waitress, switchboard operator, sales representative, and painter at a nuclear power plant. She now teaches creative nonfiction writing at the University of Missouri. Her essays have appeared in a number of publications, including *American Literary Review, Creative Nonfiction, Fourth Genre, Iowa Review,* and the *Sun*. Stanton has received a number of awards, including a literature fellowship from the National Endowment for the Arts in 2006 and a Pushcart Prize in 2007.

WALLACE STEVENS (1879–1955)   Born in Reading, Pennsylvania, Stevens graduated from Harvard University in 1900, worked for a year as a reporter for the New York *Herald Tribune,* graduated from New York University Law School in 1903, and practiced law in New York for twelve years. From 1916 to 1955, Stevens worked for the Hartford Accident and Indemnity Company, where he was appointed vice president in 1934. He was in his forties when he published his first book of poetry, *Harmonium, Ideas of Order* (1923). Stevens argued that poetry is a "supreme fiction" that shapes chaos and provides order to both nature and human relationships. He illuminates his philosophy in *Ideas of Order* (1935) and *Notes toward a Supreme Fiction* (1942). His *Collected Poems* (1954) won the Pulitzer Prize and established him as a major American poet.

RUTH STONE (b. 1915)   Born in Roanoke, Virginia, Stone grew up in Indianapolis and attended the University of Illinois and Harvard University. Her first book of poetry, *In an Iridescent Time,* was published in 1958. Shortly thereafter, her husband's suicide left her with three young children to care for. She embarked on a career as a teacher of writing, moving often from job to job. Her second volume of poetry, *Topography and Other Poems,* appeared in 1971, more than a decade after her first collection. Since 1990, she has been professor of English and creative writing at the State University of New York, Binghamton. One critic has characterized Stone as "a major talent" who has suffered from an "odd neglect." Her most recent work, *In the Next Galaxy,* won the National Book Award for poetry and the Wallace Stevens Award in 2002. She became the poet laureate of Vermont in 2007. Her latest volumes of poetry are *In the Dark* (2004) and *What Love Comes To* (2008).

VIRGIL SUÁREZ (b. 1962)   Suárez was born in Havana, Cuba, and immigrated to the United States with his family when he was eight years old. He earned his M.F.A. from Louisiana State University and currently teaches creative writing at Florida State University, Tallahassee. His debut novel, *Latin Jazz* (1989), which relays a family's struggles in Cuba under Fidel Castro and in Los Angeles as immigrants, earned him widespread attention. His other novels are *The Cutter* (1991), *Havana Thursdays* (1995), and *Going Under: A Cuban-American Fable* (1996). He is the author of nearly a dozen volumes of poetry, including *Banyan,* winner of the Latino Literature Hall of Fame Poetry Prize for Best Book of Poetry in 2001, and, more recently, *Guide to the Blue Tongue* (2002), *Landscapes & Dreams* (2003), and *90 Miles* (2005). His poems, short stories, and essays have been published in a number of periodicals, including the *Kenyon Review,* the *Southern Review, Poetry London,* and *Ploughshares.* Suárez is the recipient of a fellowship from the National Endowment for the Arts, as well as a number of other awards.

JONATHAN SWIFT (1667–1745)   Born in Dublin, Ireland, of English parents, Swift moved to England following his graduation from Trinity College, Dublin. In 1695, he was ordained minister of the Anglican Church of Ireland and five years later became a parish priest in Laracor, Ireland. The conduct of church business took Swift to England frequently, where his wit and skill in defense of Tory politics made him many influential friends. He was rewarded for his efforts in 1713, when Queen Anne appointed him dean of St. Patrick's Cathedral in Dublin. The accession of George I to the throne in the following year, followed by the Tory's loss of the government to Whig control, ended the political power of Swift and his friends. He spent the rest of his life as dean of St. Patrick's, writing during this period his most celebrated satirical narrative, *Gulliver's Travels* (1726), and his most savage essay, "A Modest Proposal" (1729). Among his many other works are *A Tale of a Tub* and *The Battle of the Books* (both 1704), and many poems.

WISLAWA SZYMBORSKA (b. 1923)   Born in Pozna, Poland, Szymborska was eight when her family moved to Krakow, where she has lived ever since. After earning a degree from the University of Krakow, she worked as an editor on literary publications and as a newspaper columnist. Her attempt to publish a volume of poems in 1949 was thwarted by Communist censors. Her first collection was finally published in 1952, and a second appeared in 1954. She later renounced these first two collections, which conformed to the socialist realism dogma of the Stalinist era. Her first collection to appear in English, *Sounds, Feelings, Thoughts: Seventy Poems,* appeared in 1981. By this time, Poland was under martial law, and she had to assume a pseudonym and publish her works in exile. Through it all, her fame in her native country remained undiminished. With the fall of the Soviet Union, Szymborska became more popular than ever. Little known outside Poland, she gained worldwide recognition when she was awarded the Nobel Prize for Literature in 1996. Among her other works available in English translation are *People on a Bridge* (1986, trans. 1990) and an anthology from earlier collections, *The End and the Beginning* (1993). Her most recent volumes in English are *Miracle Fair: Selected Poems* (2001), *Nonrequired Reading: Prose Pieces* (2002), and *Monologue of a Dog* (2005).

GRACE TALUSAN (b. 1972)   At age three, Talusan emigrated with her family from the Philippines to the United States. She was raised near Boston and earned degrees from Tufts University and the University of California at Irvine. Talusan taught at the University of Oregon and now teaches at Tufts. Her work, both fiction and memoir, has appeared in a number of periodicals, including *Asiaweek, Brevity,* the *Boston Globe, Creative Nonfiction,* the *Del Sol Review,* and the *San Diego Reader.*

AMY TAN (b. 1952)   Tan's parents emigrated from China to Oakland, California, before she was born, and she grew up in a rather traditional Chinese household. She earned a B.A. (1973) and an M.A. (1974) from San Jose State

University and spent an additional two years in postgraduate study at the University of California at Berkeley. Her shift from a premed program to English and linguistics caused a serious break with her mother, and they didn't speak for two years. She was a writer from the outset and earned her living for several years as a medical and freelance technical writer. But her interest in fiction led her to the Squaw Valley Community of Writers, and shortly after returning from a trip to China, she published her first novel, *The Joy Luck Club* (1989), consisting of sixteen interwoven stories that reveal the struggles of four Chinese mothers with their sometimes rebellious daughters. Four more novels followed: *The Kitchen God's Wife* (1991), *The Hundred Secret Senses* (1995), *The Year of No Flood* (1995), and *The Bonesetter's Daughter* (2001). Her most recent publications are *The Opposite of Fate* (2003), a collection of essays, and *Saving Fish from Drowning* (2005), a novel.

ALFRED, LORD TENNYSON (1809–1892) Tennyson was born in Lincolnshire and attended Trinity College, Cambridge (1828–1831), where he won the Chancellor's Medal for poetry in 1829. His 1842 collection, *Poems,* was not well received, but he gained prominence and the queen's favor with the 1850 publication of *In Memoriam,* an elegy written over seventeen years and inspired by the untimely death of his friend Arthur Hallam in 1833. That same year he married Emily Sellwood, after what had been a fourteen-year engagement. In 1850, he was named poet laureate of England after Wordsworth's death. His works include *Maud and Other Poems* (1855) and *Idylls of the King* (1859), based on the legendary exploits of King Arthur and the knights of the Round Table.

DYLAN THOMAS (1914–1953) Born in Swansea, Wales, Thomas decided to pursue a writing career directly after grammar school. At age twenty, he published his first collection, *Eighteen Poems* (1934), but his lack of a university degree deprived him of most opportunities to earn a living as a writer in England. Consequently, his early life (as well as the lives of his wife and children) was darkened by a poverty compounded by his free spending and heavy drinking. A self-proclaimed romanticist, Thomas called his poetry a "record of [his] struggle from darkness towards some measure of light." *The Map of Love* appeared in 1939 and *Deaths and Entrances* in 1946. Later, as a radio playwright and screenwriter, Thomas delighted in the sounds of words, sometimes at the expense of sense. *Under Milk Wood* (produced in 1953) is filled with his private, onomatopoetic language. He suffered from alcoholism and lung ailments and died in a New York hospital in 1953. Earlier that year, he noted in his *Collected Poems:* "These poems, with all their crudities, doubts and confusions are written for the love of man and in Praise of God, and I'd be a damn fool if they weren't."

LEO TOLSTOY (1828–1910) Born in Russia into a family of aristocratic landowners, Tolstoy cut short his university education and joined the army, serving among the primitive Cossacks, who became the subject of his first novel, *The Cossacks* (1863). Tolstoy left the army and traveled abroad, but was disappointed by Western materialism and returned home. After a brief period in St. Petersburg, he became bored with the life of literary celebrity and returned to his family estate. There he wrote his two greatest novels, *War and Peace* (1869) and *Anna Karenina* (1877). Around 1876, Tolstoy experienced a spiritual crisis that ultimately led him to reject his former beliefs, way of life, and literary works. Henceforth, he adopted the simple life of the Russian peasants, rejecting orthodoxy in favor of a rational Christianity that disavowed private property, class divisions, secular and institutional religious authority, as well as all art (including his own) that failed to teach the simple principles he espoused.

JOHN UPDIKE (1932–2009)   Updike was born in Shillington, Pennsylvania, and graduated from Harvard University before attending the Ruskin School of Drawing and Fine Arts in Oxford. In England, he made the acquaintance of E. B. White, who offered Updike a job at the *New Yorker*. After two years at the magazine, he left to pursue his writing. His first book of poetry, *The Carpentered Hen and Other Tame Creatures,* was published in 1958. Updike was a prolific short-story writer, poet, novelist, and critic, having written over sixty books, among them *A & P* (short stories, 1961), *Self-Consciousness: Memoirs* (1989), *Collected Poems 1953–1993* (1993), *Still Looking: Essays on American Art* (2005), and the novels *The Poorhouse Fair* (1959), *Rabbit, Run* (1960), *The Centaur* (1963), *The Witches of Eastwick* (1984), and *In the Beauty of the Lilies* (1996). His recent works include *Terrorist* (2006), *Due Considerations: Essays and Criticism* (2007), and *The Widows of Eastwick* (2008). Until he lost his battle with cancer in 2009, he was a regular contributor to the *New Yorker* and the *New York Review of Books*. His countless awards include a Guggenheim Fellowship, a National Book Award, an O. Henry Award, a Fulbright Fellowship, a Pulitzer Prize, a National Book Critics Circle Award, a PEN/Faulkner Award, a National Medal of Arts, and a Caldecott Medal. Updike said that it was his aim to "give the mundane its beautiful due."

HELEN MARIA VIRAMONTES (b. 1954)   Viramontes was one of nine children born to a construction worker and a homemaker in East Los Angeles, California. She earned degrees from Immaculate Heart College and the University of California at Irvine and currently teaches at Cornell University. Her work has appeared in a number of anthologies; in addition, she co-edited *Chicana Creativity and Criticism: Charting New Frontiers in American Literature* (1988) and *Chicana (w)rites: On Word and Film* (1995). She received a first prize for fiction from *Statement Magazine* and a fellowship from the National Endowment for the Arts. Viramontes, who writes about Chicano culture and women, is the author of thee books: *The Moths and Other Stories* (1985), *Under the Feet of Jesus* (1995), and *Their Dogs Came with Them* (2007), which took her seventeen years to complete.

ALICE WALKER (b. 1944)   Born in Eatonton, Georgia, the eighth child of sharecroppers, Walker was educated at Spelman College and Sarah Lawrence College. She has been deeply involved in the civil rights movement, working to register voters in Georgia and on behalf of welfare rights and Head Start in Mississippi. She also worked for the Welfare Department of New York City. She has taught at Wellesley College and Yale University and been an editor of *Ms.* Her nonfiction works include a biography for children, *Langston Hughes: American Poet* (1973); numerous contributions to anthologies about African American writers; and a collection of essays, *In Search of Our Mothers' Gardens: Womanist Prose* (1983). Her novels, all dealing with the African American experience, include *The Third Life of Grange Copeland* (1973); *Meridian* (1976); *The Color Purple* (1982), which won both the Pulitzer Prize and the National Book Award; *The Temple of My Familiar* (1989); and *Possessing the Secret of Joy* (1992). Her short stories are collected in three volumes, *In Love and Trouble: Stories of Black Women* (1973), *You Can't Keep a Good Woman Down* (1981), and *The Way Forward Is with a Broken Heart* (2000). Her recent publications include *We Are the Ones We Have Been Waiting For: Light in a Time of Darkness* (2006), a collection of essays, and *Devil's My Enemy* (2008), a novel.

DAVID FOSTER WALLACE (1962–2008)   Wallace, the son of college professors, was born in Ithaca, New York, and grew up in the cities of Champaign and Urbana in Illinois. He attended Amherst College in Massachusetts where he majored in English and philosophy, with a focus on modal logic and mathematics. He turned down an opportunity to study philosophy at Harvard and instead earned his M.F.A. from the University of Arizona; he then went on to teach at Pomona College in Claremont, California. His first novel, *The Broom of the System*, was published in 1987. His second novel, *Infinite Jest* (1996), earned him praise from both critics and readers. Among his short-fiction collections are *Girl with Curious Hair* (1989), *Brief Interviews with Hideous Men* (1999), and *Oblivion: Stories* (2004). His nonfiction work includes *A Supposedly Fun Thing I'll Never Do Again* (1997), *Everything and More: A Compact History of Infinity* (2003), and *Consider the Lobster* (2005). His work also appeared in a great number of periodicals, including the *Boston Globe*, the *Los Angeles Times*, the *Nation*, the *New Yorker*, the *New York Times*, and *Time* magazine. Among his numerous honors were a writer's award from the Whiting Foundation, a fellowship from the National Endowment for the Arts, and a grant from the MacArthur Foundation. Wallace, who was widely considered one of the best young writers in the United States, battled depression for many years before committing suicide on September 12, 2008.

PHILLIS WHEATLEY (1754?–1784)   Wheatley was abducted from her home in Africa by slave traders and brought to Boston. There, according to an advertisement on August 3, 1761, in the *Boston Evening Post*, "A parcel of likely Negroes, imported from Africa" was offered "cheap for cash." One of them, a seven- or eight-year-old child, was bought as a house servant for Susannah

Wheatley, the wife of a prosperous Boston tailor. The Wheatley family, impressed by the young African's quickness of intellect, taught her English and Christianity as well as Latin, ancient history, and classical literature. As Phillis Wheatley's formidable talents developed, the family allowed her time to study and to write. Her early poems, the first of them published when she was a young teenager, appeared in local broadside sheets sold on the streets of Boston. In 1773, her fame as a poet now growing, she was taken to London by the Wheatleys, where thirty-nine of her poems were published as *Poems on Various Subjects Religious and Moral.* The book was an instant success. Phillis Wheatley was widely honored and lionized. The "Sable Muse," as the English dubbed her, received a visit from Benjamin Franklin, America's colonial agent in Britain; the Lord Mayor of London honored her with a gift; and even Voltaire praised her poems. As arrangements were being made to present her to George III, she was recalled to America to tend to her ailing mistress. In the following years, upon the deaths of the Wheatleys, she gained her freedom; married another freed slave, John Peters; and bore three children, all of whom died in childhood. During her final years, which were marked by failing health and the burdens of menial work, she did not publish any poems. Her attempt to revive her fortunes by advertising a three-hundred-page volume titled "Poems & Letters on various subjects dedicated to the Right Hon. Benjamin Franklin, Esq." failed to attract enough subscribers. She died, obscure and destitute, when she was about thirty.

E. B. WHITE (1899–1985) Elwyn Brooks White was born in Mount Vernon, New York, a suburb of Manhattan. He served in the U.S. Army before earning a degree from Cornell University and then worked as a journalist at the *Seattle Times* and *Seattle Post-Intelligencer* and in advertising, jobs he loathed. In 1925, White submitted his first article to the *New Yorker;* he joined the staff two years later and contributed to the magazine for nearly sixty years. He was also a columnist for *Harper's* magazine from 1938 to 1943. Although White wrote poetry and published letters, he is perhaps best known for his essays, which varied widely in subject matter but always incorporated his amiable wit. He also took to writing children's literature for a beloved niece, and his books—*Stuart Little* (1945), *Charlotte's Web* (1952), and *Trumpet of the Swan* (1970)—became unqualified classics. Among White's countless awards are a Newbery Honor, a gold medal from the National Institute of Arts and Letters, a Laura Ingalls Wilder Award for "a lasting contribution to children's literature," a National Medal for Literature, and a Pulitzer Prize special citation for the body of his work. He spent most of his life at his home in Maine, where he died at age eighty-six.

WALT WHITMAN (1819–1892) One of nine children, Whitman was born in Huntington, Long Island, in New York, and grew up in Brooklyn, where his father worked as a carpenter. At age eleven, after five years of public school, Whitman took a job as a printer's assistant. He learned the printing trade and, before his twentieth birthday, became editor of the *Long Islander,* a Huntington newspaper. He edited several newspapers in the New York area and one in New Orleans before leaving the newspaper business in 1848. He then lived with his parents, worked as a part-time carpenter, and began writing *Leaves of Grass,* which he first published at his own expense in 1855. After the Civil War (during which he was a devoted volunteer, ministering to the wounded), Whitman was fired from his job in the Department of the Interior by Secretary James Harlan, who considered *Leaves of Grass* obscene. Soon, however, he was rehired in the attorney general's office, where he remained until 1874. In 1881, after many editions, *Leaves of Grass* finally found a publisher willing to print it uncensored. Translations were enthusiastically received in Europe, but Whitman remained relatively unappreciated in the United States; not until after his death would a large audience come to admire his original and innovative expression of American individualism.

DAVID WILES (b. 1951)   Wiles earned a master's degree at the University of Cambridge and a doctorate from the University of Bristol in England. Although he began his career as a scholar of Shakespeare, he turned his attention to studying Greek theater. He is currently a professor of theater at Royal Holloway, a college in the University of London, where he has taught courses on Greek theater, playwriting, and performance space. He is the author of eight books about theater, most recently *Greek Theatre Performance: An Introduction* (2000), *A Short History of Western Performance Space* (2003), and *Mask and Performance in Greek Tragedy: From Ancient Festival to Modern Experimentation* (2007). In addition, Wiles has published articles in theatrical journals; organized Greek mask demonstrations in Los Angeles and Moscow; and directed productions, most recently an adaptation of Euripides' *Helen.*

OSCAR WILLIAMS (1900–1964)   Williams was born in Brooklyn, New York, and worked at various advertising agencies between 1921 and 1937. His first book of poetry, *The Golden Darkness,* won the Yale Series of Younger Poets Award in 1921. Although his own poetic productivity was modest, he carved himself a special niche as an editor and anthologizer. Since his anthologies were frequently used as textbooks in university courses, he exercised significant influence on the mainstream of Western poetry from the 1940s until his death.

VIRGINIA WOOLF (1882–1941)   Born in London, where she spent most of her life, Woolf, because of her frail health and her father's Victorian attitudes about the proper role of women, received little formal education (none at the university level). Nevertheless, the advantages of an upper-class family (her father, Sir Leslie Stephen, was a distinguished scholar and man of letters who hired tutors for her) and an extraordinarily powerful and inquiring mind allowed Woolf to educate herself. She began keeping a regular diary in her early teens. After moderate success with her first novels, the publication of *To the Lighthouse* (1927) and *Orlando* (1929) established her as a major novelist.

While Woolf's reputation rests primarily on her novels, which helped revolutionize fictional technique, she was also a distinguished literary and social critic. A strong supporter of women's rights, she expressed her views on the subject in a series of lectures published as *A Room of One's Own* (1929) and in a collection of essays, *Three Guineas* (1938). Her reputation grew with the publication of her letters and diaries following her suicide by drowning.

WILLIAM WORDSWORTH (1770–1850)   Born in Cockermouth in the Lake District of England, Wordsworth was educated at Cambridge University. During a summer tour in France in 1790, Wordsworth had an affair with Annette Vallon that resulted in the birth of a daughter. The tour also made Wordsworth an ardent defender of the French Revolution of 1789 and kindled his sympathies for the plight of the common person. Wordsworth's acquaintance with Samuel Taylor Coleridge in 1795 began a close friendship that led to the collaborative publication of *Lyrical Ballads* in 1798. Wordsworth supplied a celebrated preface to the second edition in 1800, in which he announced himself a nature poet of pantheistic leanings, committed to democratic equality and the language of common people. He finished *The Prelude* in 1805, but it was not published until after his death. As he grew older, Wordsworth grew increasingly conservative, and though he continued to write prolifically, little that he wrote during the last decades of his life attained the heights of his earlier work. In 1843, he was appointed poet laureate.

LADY MARY WROTH (1587–1651 or 1653)   Wroth's mother was a wealthy heiress from Wales and Sir Walter Raleigh's first cousin; her father was appointed the first Earl of Leicester by King James I. In 1604, it was arranged that Mary would marry Sir Robert Wroth, who turned out to be an alcoholic, a philanderer, and a compulsive gambler. Although Lady Wroth became a fixture in Queen Anne's court and was a close friend, and perhaps lover, of playwright, poet, and actor Ben Jonson, her husband's death in 1614 saddled her with considerable debt. Perhaps in an attempt to earn money to satisfy her creditors, she published *The Countess of Montgomeries Urania* (1621). Credited as the first substantial work of fiction written by an Englishwoman, it included sonnets interspersed throughout the romantic prose. The work, however, was highly controversial as royal society believed that it bore a striking resemblance to real life and revealed the court's secrets; King James ordered that it be withdrawn. Among her other works, all unpublished, are *The Second Part of the Countesse of Montgomerys Urania*, a few poems, and an unfinished play titled *Love's Victory*. Scholars believe that her financial circumstances and the scandal surrounding *Urania* led to Wroth's departure from royal societal circles; thus, very little about her later life, including the exact date of her death, is known.

WILLIAM BUTLER YEATS (1865–1939)   Yeats was born in Ireland and educated in both Ireland and London. Much of his poetry and many of his plays reflect his fascination with the history of Ireland—particularly the myths and legends of its ancient, pagan past—as well as his interest in the occult. As Yeats matured, he turned increasingly to contemporary subjects, expressing his nationalism in poems about the Irish struggle for independence from England. In 1891, he became one of the founders of an Irish literary society in London (the Rhymers' Club) and of another in Dublin the following year. Already a recognized poet, Yeats helped to establish the Irish National Theater in 1899; its first production was his play *The Countess Cathleen* (written in 1892). His contribution to Irish cultural and political nationalism led to his appointment as a senator when the Irish Free State was formed in 1922. Yeats's preeminence as a poet was recognized in 1923, when he received the Nobel Prize for Literature. Among his works are *The Wanderings of Oisin and Other Poems* (1889), *The Wind among the Reeds* (1899), *The Green Helmet and Other Poems* (1910), *Responsibilities: Poems and a Play* (1914), *The Tower* (1928), and *Last Poems and Two Plays* (1939).

YEVGENY YEVTUSHENKO (b. 1933)   Son of two geologists, Yevtushenko was born in Siberia. He attended Gorky Literary Institute from 1951 to 1954 and worked on a geological expedition while establishing himself as an influential Soviet poet. During the 1950s, his books were published regularly, and he was allowed to travel abroad. In 1960, he gave readings in Europe and the United States but was criticized by Russians for linking them with anti-Semitism in his poem "Babi Yar," the name of a ravine near Kiev where 96,000 Jews were killed by Nazis during World War II. Although considering himself a "loyal revolutionary Soviet citizen," he elicited official disapproval by opposing the 1968 occupation of Czechoslovakia (a performance of his play *Bratsk Power Station* [1967] was cancelled as a result) and for sending a telegram to then-Premier Brezhnev expressing concern for Aleksandr Solzhenitsyn after his arrest in 1974. His works include *A Precocious Autobiography* (1963); *From Desire to Desire* (1976); *Fatal Half Measures: The Culture of Democracy in the Soviet Union* (1991), an analysis of recent Russian history; and *Don't Die before You're Dead* (1995), an autobiographical novel.

DEAN YOUNG (b. 1955)   Young was born in Columbia, Pennsylvania, and currently lives in Berkeley, California. He teaches at the University of Iowa's Writers' Workshop and in the M.F.A. program at Warren Wilson College. He has been the recipient of fellowships from the Guggenheim Foundation, the National Endowment for the Arts, and Stanford University. He is the author of eight books of poetry, most recently *Skid* (2002), *Elegy on Toy Piano* (2005), *Embryoyo* (2007), and *Primitive Mentor* (2008). About his poems, Young has said, "I think they're very much about misunderstanding. . . . I wrote my first book to be understood, to be accepted. . . . And I realized that the poems in the first book weren't by me—they were instilled in my head. And that not being understood, not being accepted, was my subject." His forthcoming volume of poetry is titled *The Art of Recklessness*.

KEVIN YOUNG (b. 1970)   Young was born in Lincoln, Nebraska, and earned degrees from Harvard University and Brown University. He was a Stegner Fellow at Stanford University in the interim. Before taking on his current position as the Atticus Haygood Professor of English and Creative Writing at Emory University, he taught at the University of Georgia and Indiana University. He has edited two collections in the Everyman's Library, *Blues Poems* (2003) and *Jazz Poems* (2006), and has published six volumes of his own poetry: *Most Way Home* (1998), *To Repel Ghosts: Five Sides in B Minor* (2002), *Jelly Roll: A Blues* (2003), *Black Maria: Poems Produced and Directed* (2005), *For the Confederate Dead* (2007), and *Dear Darkness* (2008). His work has also appeared in a number of periodicals, including the *New Yorker,* the *Paris Review, Ploughshares,* and *Poetry* magazine. Young has been the recipient of fellowships from the Guggenheim Foundation and the National Endowment for the Arts.

TAWFIQ ZAYYAD (1932–1994)   Zayyad was educated in Nazareth and Moscow. He joined Rakah, a Communist organization, and worked through that group to enhance the rights of Palestinian Arabs in Israel. For several years he was mayor of Nazareth. He translated a number of Russian works into Arabic and published several volumes of poetry, including *Warmly I Shake Your Hands* (1966), a book that is regarded as a landmark in the history of the Palestinian struggle against Israel. Some of his poems have been set to music and have entered into the popular Palestinian literature of struggle.

GLOSSARY OF LITERARY TERMS

Abstract language Language that describes ideas, concepts, or qualities, rather than particular or specific persons, places, or things. *Beauty, courage, love* are abstract terms, as opposed to such concrete terms as *man, stone, woman*. George Washington, the Rosetta stone, and Helen of Troy are particular concrete terms. Characteristically, literature uses *concrete* language to animate *abstract* ideas and principles. When Robert Frost, in "Provide, Provide" describes the pain of impoverished and lonely old age, he doesn't speak of an old, no longer beautiful female. He writes: "The witch that came (the withered hag) / To wash the steps with pail and rag, / Was once the beauty Abishag."

Alexandrine In poetry, a line containing six iambic feet (iambic hexameter). Alexander Pope, in "An Essay on Criticism," reveals his distaste for the forms in a couplet: "A needless Alexandrine ends the song, / That, like a wounded snake, drags its slow length along." *See* Meter.

Allegory A narrative in verse or prose, in which abstract qualities (*death, pride, greed,* for example) are personified as characters. In Nathaniel Hawthorne's story "Young Goodman Brown" (p. 81), Brown's wife personifies faith and the old man in the forest personifies Satan.

Alliteration The repetition of the same consonant sounds, usually at the beginning of words in close proximity. The *w* sounds in these lines from Robert Frost's "Provide, Provide" alliterate: "The witch that came (the withered hag) / To wash the steps with pail and rag, / Was once the beauty Abishag."

Allusion A reference in a literary work to something outside the work, usually to some famous person, place, thing, event, or other literary work.

Ambiguity A phrase, statement, or situation that may be understood in two or more ways. In literature, ambiguity is used to enrich meaning or achieve irony by forcing readers to consider alternative possibilities. When the duke in Robert Browning's "My Last Duchess" (p. 142) says that he "gave commands; / Then all smiles stopped together. There she stands / As if alive," the reader cannot know exactly what those commands were or whether the last words refer to the commands (as a result of which she is no longer alive) or merely refer to the skill of the painter (the painting is extraordinarily lifelike).

Analogy A comparison that uses a known thing or concept to explain something unfamiliar. *See* Metaphor; Simile.

Anapest A three-syllable metrical foot consisting of two unaccented syllables followed by an accented syllable. *See* Meter.

Antagonist A character in a story, play, or narrative poem who stands in opposition to the hero (*see* Protagonist). The conflict between antagonist and protagonist often generates the action or plot of the story.

Antistrophe *See* Strophe.

Apostrophe A direct address to a person who is absent or to an abstract or inanimate entity. In one of his sonnets (p. 1184), John Donne admonishes: "Death, be not proud!" And in "Lines Composed a Few Miles above Tintern Abbey," Wordsworth speaks to a river in Wales: "How oft, in spirit, have I turned to thee, / O sylvan Wye! thou wanderer through the woods."

1431

Archaism   The literary use of obsolete language. When Keats, in "Ode on a Grecian Urn" (p. 1185), writes: "with brede / Of marble men and maidens overwrought," he uses an archaic word for *braid* and intends an obsolete definition, "worked all over" (that is, "ornamented"), for *overwrought*.

Archetype   Themes, images, and narrative patterns that are universal and thus embody some enduring aspects of human experience. Some of these themes are the death and rebirth of the hero, the underground journey, and the search for the father.

Assonance   The repetition of vowel sounds in a line, stanza, or sentence: *road nowhere*. By using assonance that occurs at the end of words—*my, pie*—or a combination of assonance and consonance (the repetition of final consonant sounds—*fish, wish*), poets create rhyme. Some poets use assonantial and consonantial off rhymes (*see* Near rhyme). W. H. Auden, in a celebrated verse from "Five Songs," writes: "That night when joy began / Our narrowest veins to flush, / We waited for the flash / Of morning's levelled gun." *Flush* and *gun* are assonantial, *flush* and *flash* are consonantial (and, of course, alliterative).

Atmosphere   The general feeling or mood created in the reader by a work. *See* Mood.

Aubade   A love song or lyric to be performed at sunrise. Philip Larkin's "Aubade" (p. 1218) uses the form ironically in a somber contemplation of mortality.

Ballad   A narrative poem, originally of folk origin, usually focusing on a climactic episode and told without comment. The most common ballad form consists of quatrains of alternating four- and three-stress iambic lines, with the second and fourth lines rhyming. Often, the ballad will employ a *refrain*—that is, the last line of each stanza will be identical or similar. "Bonny Barbara Allan" (p. 908) is a traditional ballad. Dudley Randall's "Ballad of Birmingham" (p. 416) is a twentieth-century example of the ballad tradition.

Blank verse   Lines of unrhymed iambic pentameter. Shakespeare's dramatic poetry is written principally in blank verse. *See* Meter.

Caesura   A strong pause within a line of poetry. Note the caesuras indicated by a double vertical line (‖) in these lines from Robert Browning's "My Last Duchess" (p. 142): "That's my last Duchess painted on the wall, / Looking as if she were alive, ‖ I call / That piece a wonder, now: ‖ Frà Pandolf's hands / Worked busily a day, ‖ and there she stands."

Carpe diem   Latin, meaning "seize the day." A work, usually a lyric poem, in which the speaker calls the attention of the auditor (often a young woman) to the shortness of youth and life and then urges the auditor to enjoy life while there is time. Andrew Marvell's "To His Coy Mistress" (p. 950) is among the best of the *carpe diem* tradition in English. The opening stanza of a famous Robert Herrick poem nicely illustrates *carpe diem* principles: "Gather ye rosebuds while ye may, / Old Time is still a-flying / And this same flower that smiles today, / Tomorrow will be dying."

Catharsis   A key concept in the *Poetics* of Aristotle that attempts to explain why representations of suffering and death in drama paradoxically leave the audience feeling relieved rather than depressed. According to Aristotle, the fall of a tragic hero arouses in the viewer feelings of "pity" and "terror"—pity because the hero is an individual of great moral worth and terror because the viewer identifies with and, consequently, feels vulnerable to the hero's tragic fate. Ideally, the circumstances within the drama allow viewers to experience a catharsis that purges those feelings of pity and terror and leaves them emotionally purified.

Central intelligence   *See* Point of view.

Character   A person or figure in a literary work, sometimes classified as either *flat* (quickly describable) or *round* (more developed, complex). *See* Protagonist *and* Antagonist.

Characterization   The means of presenting and developing a character, shown through the author's description, the character's actions or thoughts, or other characters' actions or thoughts.

Chorus   Originally, a group of masked dancers who chanted lyric hymns at religious festivals in ancient Greece. In the plays of Sophocles, the chorus, while circling around the altar to Dionysius, chants the odes that separate the episodes. These odes, in some respects, represented an audience's reaction to, and comment on, the action in the episodes. In Elizabethan drama, and even, on occasion, in modern drama, the chorus appears, usually as a single person who comments on the action.

Comedy   In drama, the representation of situations that are designed to delight and amuse and that end happily. Comedy often deals with ordinary people in their human condition, while tragedy deals with the ideal and heroic and, until recently, embodied only the high born as tragic heroes. *Compare* Tragedy.

Conceit   A figure of speech that establishes an elaborate parallel between unlike things. The *Petrarchan conceit* (named for the fourteenth-century Italian writer of love lyrics) was often imitated by Elizabethan sonneteers until the device became so hackneyed that Shakespeare mocked the tendency in Sonnet 130 (p. 911): "My mistress' eyes are nothing like the sun; / Coral is far more red than her lips' red; / If snow be white, why then her breasts are dun; / If hairs be wires, black wires grow on her head." The *metaphysical conceit* employs strange, even bizarre, comparisons to heighten the wit of the poem. Perhaps the most famous metaphysical conceit is John Donne's elaborate and extended parallel of a drawing compass to the souls of the couple in "A Valediction: Forbidding Mourning" (p. 914).

Concrete language   *See* Abstract language.

Conflict   The struggle of a protagonist, or main character, with forces that threaten to destroy him or her. The struggle creates suspense and is usually resolved at the end of the narrative. The force opposing the main character may be another person—the antagonist—or society (as in Harlan Ellison's "'Repent, Harlequin!' Said the Ticktockman," p. 372), or natural forces (as in Katherine Anne Porter's "The Jilting of Granny Weatherall," p. 1168). A fourth type of conflict reflects the struggle of opposing tendencies within an individual (as in Tolstoy's "The Death of Iván Ilých," p. 1103).

Connotation   The associative and suggestive meanings of a word, in contrast to its literal or *denotative* meaning. One might speak of an *elected official*, a relatively neutral term without connotative implications. Others might call the same person a *politician*, a more negative term; still others might call him or her a *statesman*, a more laudatory term. *Compare* Denotation.

Consonance   Repetition of the final consonant sounds in stressed syllables. In the second poem of W. H. Auden's "Five Songs," lines 1 and 4 illustrate consonance, as do lines 2 and 3. "That night when joy began / Our narrowest veins to flush, / We waited for the flash / Of morning's levelled gun."

Couplet   A pair of rhymed lines—for example, these from A. E. Housman's "Terence, This Is Stupid Stuff" (p. 146). "Why, if 'tis dancing you would be, / There's brisker pipes than poetry."

Dactyl   A three-syllable metrical foot consisting of an accented syllable followed by two unaccented syllables. *See* Meter.

Denotation   The literal dictionary definition of a word, without associative and suggestive meanings. *See* Connotation.

Denouement   The final revelations that occur after the main conflict is resolved; literally, the "untying" of the plot following the climax.

Deus ex machina Latin for "god from a machine." Difficulties were sometimes resolved in ancient Greek and Roman plays by a god, who was lowered to the stage by means of machinery. The term is now used to indicate unconvincing or improbable coincidences that are used to advance or resolve a plot.

Dialect A variety of a language distinguished by its pronunciation, vocabulary, rhetoric, and grammar. When used in dialogue, dialect reveals a character's membership in certain groups or communities.

Dialogue The exchange of words between characters in a drama or narrative.

Diction The choice of words in a work of literature and hence an element of style crucial to the work's effectiveness. The diction of a story told from the point of view of an inner-city child (as in Toni Cade Bambara's "The Lesson," p. 110) will differ markedly from a similar story told from the point of view of a mature and educated adult, like the narrator of James Joyce's "Araby" (p. 92).

Didactic A term applied to works with the primary and avowed purpose of persuading the reader that some philosophical, religious, or moral doctrine is true.

Dimeter A line of poetry consisting of two metrical feet. *See* Meter.

Distance The property that separates an author or a narrator from the actions of the characters he or she creates, thus allowing a disinterested, or aloof, narration of events. Similarly, distance allows the reader or audience to view the characters and events in a narrative dispassionately.

Dramatic irony *See* Irony.

Dramatic monologue A type of poem in which the speaker addresses another person (or persons) whose presence is known only from the speaker's words. During the course of the monologue, the speaker (often unintentionally) reveals his or her own character. Such poems are dramatic because the speaker interacts with another character at a specific time and place; they are monologues because the entire poem is uttered by the speaker. Robert Browning's "My Last Duchess" (p. 142), Matthew Arnold's "Dover Beach" (p. 920), and T. S. Eliot's "The Love Song of J. Alfred Prufrock" (p. 646) are dramatic monologues.

Elegy Usually, a poem that laments the death of a particular person. The term often is used to describe meditative poems on the subject of human mortality. A. E. Housman's "To an Athlete Dying Young" (p. 190) and Theodore Roethke's "Elegy for Jane" (p. 1198) are elegies.

End-rhyme *See* Rhyme.

End-stopped line A line of verse that embodies a complete logical and grammatical unit. A line of verse that does not constitute a complete syntactic unit is called *run-on*. For example, in the opening lines of Robert Browning's "My Last Duchess" (p. 142): "That's my last Duchess painted on the wall, / Looking as if she were alive. I call / That piece a wonder, now . . . ," the opening line is end-stopped while the second line is run-on, because the direct object of *call* runs on to the third line.

English sonnet Also called *Shakespearean sonnet. See* Sonnet.

Enjambment The use of run-on lines. *See* End-stopped line.

Epigraph In literature, a short quotation or observation related to the theme and placed at the head of the work. T. S. Eliot's "The Love Song of J. Alfred Prufrock" (p. 646) has an epigraph.

Epiphany In literature, a showing forth, or sudden manifestation. James Joyce used the term to indicate a sudden illumination that enables a character (and, presumably, the reader) to understand his situation. The narrator of Joyce's "Araby" (p. 92) experiences an epiphany toward the end of the story, as does Leo Tolstoy's Iván Ilých (p. 1103).

Epode *See* Strophe.

Euphony Language embodying sounds pleasing to the ear.

Exposition Information supplied to readers and audiences that enables them to understand narrative action. Often, exposition establishes what has occurred before the narrative begins, or informs the audience about relationships among principal characters. The absence of exposition from some modern literature, particularly modern drama, contributes to the unsettling feelings sometimes experienced by the audience.

Farce A type of comedy, usually satiric, that relies on exaggerated character types, ridiculous situations, and often horseplay.

Feminine rhyme A two-syllable rhyme in which the second syllable is unstressed, as in the second and fourth lines of these verses from James Fenton's "God, A Poem": "A nasty surprise in a sandwich, / A drawing-pin caught in your sock, / The limpest of shakes from a hand which / You'd thought would be firm as a rock."

Figurative language A general term covering the many ways in which language is used nonliterally. *See* Hyperbole, Irony, Metaphor, Metonymy, Paradox, Simile, Symbol, Synecdoche, Understatement.

First-person narrator *See* Point of view.

Foot *See* Meter.

Free verse Poetry, usually unrhymed, that does not adhere to the metrical regularity of traditional verse. Although free verse is not metrically regular, it is nonetheless clearly more rhythmic than prose and makes use of other aspects of poetic discourse to achieve its effects.

Heroic couplet Iambic pentameter lines that rhyme *aa, bb, cc,* and so on. Usually, heroic couplets are *closed*—that is, the couplet's end coincides with a major syntactic unit so that the line is end stopped. These lines from Alexander Pope's "Essay on Man" illustrate the form: "And, spite of pride, in erring reason's spite, / One truth is clear; Whatever is, IS RIGHT."

Hexameter A line of verse consisting of six metrical feet. *See* Meter.

Hubris In Greek tragedy, arrogance resulting from excessive pride.

Hyperbole Figurative language that embodies overstatement or exaggeration. The boast of the speaker in Robert Burns's "A Red, Red Rose" (p. 920) is hyperbolic: "And I will luve thee still, my dear, / Til a' the seas gang dry."

Iamb A metrical foot consisting of an unstressed syllable followed by a stressed syllable. *See* Meter.

Imagery Language that embodies an appeal to a physical sense, usually sight, although the words may invoke sound, smell, taste, and touch as well. The term is often applied to all figurative language. *Images* illustrate a concept, thing, or process by appealing to the senses.

Internal rhyme *See* Rhyme.

Irony Figurative language in which the intended meaning differs from the literal meaning. *Verbal irony* includes overstatement (hyperbole), understatement, and opposite statement. The following lines from Robert Burns's "A Red, Red Rose" (p. 920) embody overstatement: "As fair art thou, my bonnie lass, / So deep in luve am I; / And I will luve thee still, my dear, / Til a' the seas gang dry." These lines from Andrew Marvell's "To His Coy Mistress" (p. 950) understate: "The grave's a fine and private place, / But none, I think, do there embrace." W. H. Auden's ironic conclusion to "The Unknown Citizen" (p. 415) reveals opposite statement: "Was he free? Was he happy? The question is absurd: / Had anything been wrong, we should certainly have heard." *Dramatic irony* occurs when a reader or an audience knows things a character does not and, consequently, hears things differently. For example, in Shakespeare's *Othello* (p. 958), the audience knows that Iago is Othello's enemy, but Othello doesn't. Hence, the audience's understanding of Iago's speeches to Othello differs markedly from Othello's.

Italian sonnet Also called *Petrarchan sonnet. See* Sonnet.

Lyric Originally, a song accompanied by lyre music. Now, a relatively short poem expressing the thought or feeling of a single speaker. Almost all the nondramatic poetry in this anthology is lyric poetry.

Metaphor A figurative expression consisting of two elements in which one element is provided with special attributes by being equated with a second, unlike element. In Theodore Roethke's "Elegy for Jane" (p. 1198), for example, the speaker addresses his dead student: "If only I could nudge you from this sleep, / My maimed darling, my skittery pigeon." Here, Jane is characterized metaphorically as a "skittery pigeon," and all the reader's experience of a nervous pigeon's movement becomes attached to Jane. *See* Simile.

Meter Refers to recurrent patterns of accented and unaccented syllables in verse. A metrical unit is called a *foot,* and there are four basic accented patterns. An *iamb,* or *iambic foot,* consists of an unaccented syllable followed by an accented syllable (bĕfóre, tŏdáy). A *trochee,* or *trochaic foot,* consists of an accented syllable followed by an unaccented syllable (fúnnў, phántŏm). An *anapest,* or *anapestic foot,* consists of two unaccented syllables followed by an accented syllable (in the line "If év ‖ erўthĭng háp ‖ pĕns thăt cán't ‖ bĕ dóne," the second and third metrical feet are anapests). A *dactyl,* or *dactylic foot,* consists of a stressed syllable followed by two unstressed syllables (sýllăblĕ, métrĭcăl). One common variant, consisting of two stressed syllables, is called a *spondee,* or *spondaic foot* (dáybréak, moónshíne).

Lines are classified according to the number of metrical feet they contain (an iambic hexameter line is an *alexandrine*):

one foot	monometer
two feet	dimeter
three feet	trimeter
four feet	tetrameter
five feet	pentameter
six feet	hexameter

Here are some examples of various metrical patterns:

Tŏ eách ‖ hĭs súff ‖ erĭngs: áll ‖ ăre mén,	*iambic tetrameter*
Cŏndemnéd ‖ aliké ‖ tŏ groán;	*iambic trimeter*
Ónce ŭp ‖ ón ă ‖ mídnĭght ‖ dréarў, ‖ whíle Ĭ ‖	
póndĕred ‖ wéak ănd ‖ wéarў	*trochaic octameter*
Thĕ Ăssýr ‖ iăn căme dówn ‖ likĕ ă wólf ‖ ŏn thĕ fóld	*anapestic tetrameter*
Iš thís ‖ thĕ rég ‖ iŏn, thís ‖ thĕ soíl, ‖ thĕ clíme,	*iambic pentameter*
Fóllŏw ĭt ‖ úttĕrlў,	*dactylic dimeter*
Hópe bĕ ‖ yónd hópe:	*dimeter line—trochee and spondee*

Metonymy A figure of speech in which a word stands for a closely related idea. In the expression "The pen is mightier than the sword," *pen* and *sword* are metonyms for written ideas and physical force.

Monologue A long, uninterrupted speech by a character.

Mood The atmosphere or general feeling of a work. *See* Atmosphere.

Muses   The nine daughters of Zeus and Mnemosyne (memory) who preside over various humanities. Although there are some variations, generally they may be assigned as follows: Calliope, epic poetry; Clio, history; Erato, lyric poetry; Euterpe, music; Melpomene, tragedy; Polyhymnia, sacred poetry; Terpsichore, dance; Thalia, comedy; and Urania, astronomy.

Narrator   The speaker of the story, not to be confused with the author. For kinds of narrators, *see* Point of view.

Near rhyme   Also called *off rhyme*, *slant rhyme*, or *oblique rhyme*. Usually the occurrence of consonance where rhyme is expected, as in *pearl*, *alcohol*, or *heaven*, *given*. *See* Rhyme.

Octave   An eight-line stanza. More often, the opening eight-line section of an Italian sonnet, rhymed *abbaabba*, followed by the sestet that concludes the poem. *See* Sonnet.

Ode   Usually, a long, serious poem on exalted subjects, often in the form of an address. Keats's "Ode on a Grecian Urn" (p. 1185) is representative. In Greek dramatic poetry, odes consisting of three parts—the *strophe*, the *antistrophe*, and the *epode*—were sung by the chorus between the episodes of the play. *See* Strophe.

Off rhyme   *See* Near rhyme.

Omniscient narrator   *See* Point of view.

Onomatopoeia   Language that sounds like what it means. Words like *buzz*, *bark*, and *hiss* are onomatopoetic. Also, sound patterns that reinforce the meaning may be designated onomatopoetic. Alexander Pope illustrates such onomatopoeia in this passage from "An Essay on Criticism":

> 'Tis not enough no harshness gives offense,
> The sound must seem an echo to the sense:
> Soft is the strain when Zephyr gently blows,
> And the smooth stream in smoother numbers flows;
> But when loud surges lash the sounding shore,
> The hoarse, rough verse should like the torrent roar:
> When Ajax strives some rock's vast weight to throw,
> The line too labors, and the words move slow;
> Not so, when swift Camilla scours the plain,
> Flies o'er the unbending corn, and skims along the main.

Opposite statement   *See* Irony.

Ottava rima   An eight-line, iambic pentameter stanza rhymed *ababacc*. Originating with the Italian poet Boccaccio, the form was made popular in English poetry by Milton, Keats, and Byron, among others.

Oxymoron   Literally, "acutely silly." A figure of speech in which contradictory ideas are combined to create a condensed paradox: *thunderous silence*, *sweet sorrow*, *wise fool*.

Paean   In classical Greek drama, a hymn of praise, usually honoring Apollo. Now, any lyric that joyously celebrates its subject.

Paradox   A statement that seems self-contradictory or absurd but is, somehow, valid. The conclusion of Donne's "Death, Be Not Proud" (p. 1184) illustrates: "One short sleep past, we wake eternally / And death shall be no more; Death, thou shalt die." In Holy Sonnet 14, Donne, speaking of his relationship with God, writes: "Take me to You, imprison me, for I, / Except You enthrall me, never shall be free, / Nor ever chaste, except You ravish me."

Parody   An imitation of a work using the original's form or content as a model, meant to criticize or create a humorous effect.

Pastoral   *Pastor* is Latin for "shepherd," and the pastoral is a poetic form invented by ancient Roman writers that deals with the complexities of the human condition as if they exist in a world peopled by idealized rustic shepherds. Pastoral poetry suggests that country life is superior to urban life. In the hands of such English poets as Marlowe and Milton, the pastoral embodies highly conventionalized and artificial language and situations. Christopher Marlowe's "The Passionate Shepherd to His Love" (p. 949) is a famous example, as is Sir Walter Raleigh's mocking response, "The Nymph's Reply to the Shepherd" (p. 948).

Pentameter   A line containing five metrical feet. *See* Meter.

Persona   Literally, "actor's mask." The term is applied to a first-person narrator in fiction or poetry. The persona's views may differ from the author's.

Personification   The attribution of human qualities to nonhuman things, such as animals, aspects of nature, or even ideas and processes. When Donne exclaims in "Death, Be Not Proud" (p. 1184), "Death, thou shalt die," he uses personification.

Petrarchan sonnet   Also called *Italian sonnet. See* Sonnet.

Plot   A series of events in a story or drama that bear a significant relationship to each other. E. M. Forster illuminates the definition: "'The King died, and then the Queen died,' is a story. 'The King died, and then the Queen died of grief,' is a plot."

Poetic license   Variation from standard word order to satisfy the demands of rhyme and meter.

Point of view   The person or intelligence a writer of fiction creates to tell the story to the reader. The major techniques are: (1) *first person,* where the story is told by someone (often, though not necessarily, the principal character) who identifies himself or herself as "I," as in James Joyce's "Araby" (p. 92); (2) *third person,* where the story is told by someone (not identified as "I") who is not a participant in the action and who refers to the characters by name or as "he," "she," and "they," as in Harlan Ellison's "'Repent, Harlequin!' Said the Ticktockman" (p. 372); (3) *omniscient,* a variation on the third person, where the narrator knows everything about the characters and events, can move about in time and place as well as from character to character at will, and can, whenever he or she wishes, enter the mind of any character, as in Tolstoy's "The Death of Iván Ilých" (p. 1103); (4) *central intelligence,* another variation on the third person, where narrative elements are limited to what a single character sees, thinks, and hears, as in Toni Cade Bambara's "The Lesson" (p. 110). *See also* Unreliable narrator.

Prose   Ordinary written or spoken expression, resembling everyday language or speech.

Prosody   The study of the elements of versification, such as *rhyme, meter, stanzaic patterns,* and so on.

Protagonist   Originally, the first actor in a Greek drama. In Greek, *agon* means "contest." Hence, the protagonist is the hero, the main character in a narrative, in conflict either with his or her situation or with another character. *See* Antagonist.

Quatrain   A four-line stanza.

Refrain   The repetition within a poem of a group of words, often at the end of ballad stanzas.

Rhyme   The repetition of the final stressed vowel sound and any sounds following (*cat, rat; debate, relate; pelican, belly can*) produces perfect rhyme. When the last stressed syllable rhymes, the rhyme is called masculine (*cat, rat*). Two-syllable rhymes with unstressed last syllables are called feminine (*ending, bending*). When rhyming words appear at the end of lines, the poem is *end-rhymed.* When rhyming words appear within one line, the line contains *internal rhyme.* When the correspondence in sounds is imperfect (*heaven, given; began, gun*), *off rhyme, slant rhyme,* or *near rhyme* is produced.

Rhythm   The quality created by the relationship between stressed and unstressed syllables. A regular pattern of alternation between stressed and unstressed syllables produces *meter*. Irregular alternation of stressed and unstressed syllables produces *free verse*. Compare the rhythm of the following verses from Robert Frost's "Stopping by Woods on a Snowy Evening" (p. 1196) and Walt Whitman's "Out of the Cradle Endlessly Rocking":

> Whose woods these are I think I know.
> His house is in the village though;
> He will not see me stopping here
> To watch his woods fill up with snow.

> Out of the cradle endlessly rocking,
> Out of the mocking-bird's throat, the musical shuttle,
> Out of the Ninth-month midnight,
> Over the sterile sands and the fields beyond, where the child leaving his bed
>   wander'd alone, bareheaded, barefoot,
> Down from the shower'd halo.

Run-on line   *See* End-stopped line.

Satire   Writing in a comic mode that holds a subject up to scorn and ridicule, often with the purpose of correcting human vice and folly. Harlan Ellison's "'Repent, Harlequin!' Said the Ticktockman" (p. 372) satirizes a society obsessed with time and order.

Scansion   The analysis of patterns of stressed and unstressed syllables to establish the metrical or rhythmical pattern of a poem.

Sestet   The six-line resolution of a Petrarchan sonnet. *See* Sonnet.

Setting   The place, time, and social context in which a work occurs. Often the setting contributes significantly to the story; for example, the tawdry gloom at the fair in James Joyce's "Araby" (p. 92) destroys the narrator's expectations.

Shakespearean sonnet   Also called *English sonnet. See* Sonnet.

Simile   Similar to metaphor, the simile is a comparison of unlike things introduced by the words *like* or *as*. For example, Robert Burns, in "A Red, Red Rose" (p. 920), exclaims, "O My Luve's like a red, red rose," and Shakespeare mocks extravagant similes when he admits in Sonnet 130, "My mistress' eyes are nothing like the sun" (p. 911).

Slant rhyme   *See* Rhyme.

Soliloquy   A dramatic convention in which an actor, alone on the stage, speaks his or her thoughts aloud. Iago's speech that closes act I of Shakespeare's *Othello* (p. 958) is a soliloquy, as is Othello's speech in act III, scene 3, lines 258–279.

Sonnet   A lyric poem of fourteen lines, usually of iambic pentameter. The two major types are the Petrarchan (or Italian) and Shakespearean (or English). The Petrarchan sonnet is divided into an octave (the first eight lines, rhymed *abbaabba*) and sestet (the final six lines, usually rhymed *cdecde* or *cdcdcd*). The Shakespearean sonnet consists of three quatrains and a concluding couplet, rhymed *abab cdcd efef gg*. In general, the sonnet establishes some issue in the octave or three quatrains and then resolves it in the sestet or final couplet. Robert Frost's "Design" (p. 1196) is a Petrarchan sonnet; several Shakespearean sonnets appear in the text.

Spondee   A metrical foot consisting of two stressed syllables, usually a variation within a metrical line. *See* Meter.

Stanza   The grouping of a fixed number of verse lines in a recurring metrical and rhyme pattern. Keats's "Ode on a Grecian Urn" (p. 1185), for example, employs ten-line stanzas rhymed *ababcdecde*.

Stream-of-consciousness technique   The narrative technique that attempts to reproduce the full and uninterrupted flow of a character's mental process, in which ideas, memories, and sense impressions may intermingle without logical transitions. Writers using this technique sometimes abandon conventional rules of syntax and punctuation.

Strophe   In Greek tragedy, the unit of verse the chorus chanted as it moved to the left in a dance rhythm. The chorus sang the *antistrophe* as it moved to the right and the *epode* while standing still.

Style   The way an author expresses his or her matter. Style embodies, and depends upon, all the choices an author makes—the diction, syntax, figurative language, and sound patterns of the piece.

Subplot   A second plot, usually involving minor characters. The subplot is subordinate to the principal plot but is often resolved by events that figure in the main plot. For example, Iago's manipulation of Roderigo in Shakespeare's *Othello* (p. 958) is a subplot that enters the main plot and figures prominently in the play's climax.

Symbol   An object, an action, or a person that represents more than itself. The urn in Keats's "Ode on a Grecian Urn" (p. 1185) symbolizes the cold immortality of art. The symbolism arises from the *context. Public* symbols, in contrast to these *contextual symbols,* are objects, actions, or persons that history, myth, or legend has invested with meaning—the cross, Helen of Troy, a national flag.

Synecdoche   A figure of speech in which a part is used to signify the whole. In "Elegy Written in a Country Churchyard," Thomas Gray writes of "Some heart once pregnant with celestial fire; / Hands that the rod of empire might have swayed." That heart, and those hands, of course, refer to whole persons who are figuratively represented by significant parts.

Synesthesia   An image that uses a second sensory impression to modify the primary sense impression. When one speaks of a "cool green," for example, the primary *visual* evocation of green is combined with the *tactile* sensation of coolness. Keats, in "Ode to a Nightingale," asks for a drink of wine "Tasting of Flora and the country green, / Dance, and Provençal song, and sunburnt mirth!" Here, the *taste* of wine is synesthetically extended to the sight of flowers and meadows, the movement of dance, the sound of song, and the heat of the sun.

Tetrameter   A verse line containing four metrical feet. *See* Meter.

Theme   The statement or underlying idea of a literary work, advanced through the concrete elements of character, action, and setting. The theme of Harlan Ellison's "'Repent, Harlequin!' Said the Ticktockman" (p. 372), in which an ordinary person defies an oppressive system, might be that to struggle against dehumanizing authority is obligatory.

Third-person narrator   A voice telling a story who refers to characters by name or as "he," "she," or "they." *See* Point of view.

Tone   The attitude embodied in the language a writer chooses. The tone authors take in a work toward readers, the subject matter, or themselves might be sad, joyful, ironic, solemn, playful. Notice, for example, the somber tone of Matthew Arnold's "Dover Beach" (p. 920).

Tragedy   The dramatic representation of serious and important actions that culminate in catastrophe for the protagonist, or chief actor, in the play. Aristotle saw tragedy as the fall of a noble figure from a high position and happiness to defeat and misery as a result of *hamartia,* some misjudgment or frailty of character. *Compare* Comedy.

Trimeter   A verse line consisting of three metrical feet. *See* Meter.

Triplet   A sequence of three verse lines that rhyme.

Trochee   A metrical foot consisting of a stressed syllable followed by an unstressed syllable. *See* Meter.

Understatement   A figure of speech that represents something as less important than it really is—hence, a form of irony. When in Robert Browning's "My Last Duchess" (p. 142) the duke asserts, "This grew; I gave commands; / Then all smiles stopped together," the words ironically understate what was likely an order for his wife's execution.

Unreliable narrator   The speaker or voice of a work who is not able to accurately or objectively report events, as in Charlotte Perkins Gilman's "The Yellow Wallpaper" (p. 547).

Verse   A stanza of a poem. More generally, verse can be used interchangeably with the term *poetry*.

Villanelle   A French verse form of nineteen lines (of any length) divided into six stanzas— five tercets and a final quatrain—employing two rhymes and two refrains. The refrains consist of lines 1 (repeated as lines 6, 12, and 18) and 3 (repeated as lines 9, 15, and 19). Dylan Thomas's "Do Not Go Gentle into That Good Night" (p. 1217) and Catherine Davis's response "After a Time" (p. 1220) are villanelles.

Acknowledgments

Chinua Achebe. "Marriage is a Private Affair." From *Girls at War and Other Stories.* Copyright © 1972, 1973 by Chinua Achebe. Used by permission of Doubleday, a division of Random House, Inc. and Harold Ober Associates.

Anna Akhmatova. "Requiem." From *Anna Akhmatova, Poems,* edited and translated by Lyn Coffin. Copyright © 1983. Used by permission of W. W. Norton & Company, Inc.

Sherman Alexie. "This Is What It Means to Say Phoenix, Arizona." From *The Lone Ranger and Tonto Fistfight in Heaven.* Copyright © 1993 by Sherman Alexie. Used by permission of Grove/Atlantic, Inc. Scenes 37–42, 59. From *Smoke Signals* by Sherman Alexie. Copyright © 1998 by Sherman Alexie. Reprinted with permission of the author.

Woody Allen. "Death Knocks." From *Getting Even* by Woody Allen. Copyright © 1966, 1967, 1968, 1969, 1970, 1971 by Woody Allen. Used by permission of Random House, Inc.

Julia Alvarez. "Women's Work." Copyright © 1994 by Julia Alvarez. Originally appeared in *The New York Times,* September 5, 1994. By permission of Susan Bergholz Services, New York, NY. All rights reserved.

Anonymous. "Edward." From *The Earliest English Poems,* translated by Michael Alexander (Penguin 1966). Copyright © 1966, 1977, 1991 by Michael Alexander. Reprinted with the permission of Penguin Books, Ltd.

Hanan Mikha'il 'Ashrawi. Excerpt from "Diary of an Almost Four-Year Old" and "Night Patrol." From *Anthology of Modern Palestinian Literature* edited by Salma Khadra Jayyusi. Copyright © 1992 by Columbia University Press. Reprinted with the permission of the publisher.

W. H. Auden. "Musée des Beaux Arts" and "The Unknown Citizen." From *Collected Poems* by W. H. Auden. Copyright © 1940 and copyright renewed 1968 by W. H. Auden. Used by permission of Random House, Inc.

Jimmy Santiago Baca. "Tire Shop." Reprinted by permission of the author.

James Baldwin. "Sonny's Blues." Copyright © 1957 by James Baldwin. Originally published in *Partisan Review.* Copyright renewed. Collected in *Going to Meet The Man,* published by Vintage Books. Reprinted by arrangement with the James Baldwin Estate.

Toni Cade Bambara. "The Lesson." From *Gorilla, My Love* by Toni Cade Bambara. Copyright © 1972 by Toni Cade Bambara. Used by permission of Random House, Inc.

Aimee Bender. "Tiger Mending." From *Best American Nonrequired Reading 2005* by Dave Eggers. Copyright © 2005 by Aimee Bender. Reprinted by permission of the author.

Bruce Bennett. "The True Story of Snow White." From *Navigating the Distance: Poems New and Old Selected* by Bruce Bennett. Copyright © 1999 by Bruce Bennett. Reprinted with permission of the author.

The Birmingham News. "A Call for Unity from Alabama Clergymen." From *The Birmingham News,* April 13, 1963. Reprinted by permission.

Elizabeth Bishop. "One Art" and "The Fish." From *The Complete Poems 1927–1979* by Elizabeth Bishop. Copyright © 1979, 1983 by Alice Helen Methfessel. Reprinted by permission of Farrar, Straus and Giroux, LLC.

Anne Bradstreet. "To My Dear and Loving Husband." From *The Works of Anne Bradstreet,* edited by Jeannine Hensley, Cambridge, MA: The Belknap Press of Harvard University Press. Copyright © 1976 by the President and Fellows of Harvard College. Reprinted by permission of the publisher.

Kate Braverman. "Tall Tales from the Mekong Delta." From *Squandering the Blue* by Kate Braverman. Copyright © 1990 by Kate Braverman. Used by permission of Random House, Inc.

John Brehm. "At the Poetry Reading." From *Poetry,* June 1998. Reprinted with permission of the author.

Gwendolyn Brooks. "We Real Cool." From *Blacks* by Gwendolyn Brooks. Copyright © 1991 by Gwendolyn Brooks Blakely. Reprinted by consent of Brooks Permissions.

John Frederick. "Love Poem." From *Grace Period* by Gary Miranda. Copyright © 1983 Princeton University Press. Reprinted by permission of Princeton University Press.

Sigmund Freud. "Oedipus Complex" (editor's title). Copyright © The Institute of Psychoanalysis and The Hogarth Press for permission to quote from Volume 4 of *The Standard Edition of the Complete Psychological Works of Sigmund Freud* translated and edited by James Strachey. Reprinted by permission of Basic Books, a division of the Perseus Books Group, and Random House Group, Ltd.

Robert Frost. "A Semi-Revolution," "Design," "Fire and Ice," "Nothing Gold Can Stay," "Out, Out –," "Stopping by Woods on a Snowy Evening," and "The Road Not Taken." From *The Poetry of Robert Frost*, edited by Edward Connery Lathem. Copyright © 1916, 1923, 1930, 1939, 1969 by Henry Holt and Company. Copyright © 1936, 1942, 1944, 1951, 1958 by Robert Frost. Copyright © 1964, 1970 by Lesley Frost Ballantine. Reprinted with the permission of Henry Holt and Company, LLC.

Tess Gallagher. "I Stop Writing the Poem." From *Moon Crossing Bridge* by Tess Gallagher. Copyright © 1992 by Tess Gallagher. Reprinted by permission of Graywolf Press. www.graywolfpress.com.

Richard Garcia. "Why I Left Church." From *The Flying Garcias*, by Richard Garcia. Copyright © 1993. Reprinted by permission of the University of Pittsburgh Press.

Deborah Garrison. "Sestina for the Working Mother." From *The Second Child: Poems* by Deborah Garrison. Copyright © 2007 by Deborah Garrison. Reprinted by permission of Alfred A. Knopf, Inc., a division of Random House, Inc. Used by permission of Alfred A. Knopf, Inc., a division of Random House, Inc.

Nikki Giovanni. "Dreams." From *The Women and the Men* by Nikki Giovanni. Copyright © 1970, 1974, 1975 by Nikki Giovanni. Reprinted by permission of HarperCollins Publishers.

Louise Glück. "The School Children." From *The First Four Books of Poems*. Copyright © 1975, 1985 by Louise Glück. Reprinted with the permission of HarperCollins Publishers, Inc.

Marilyn Hacker. "Conte." From *Taking Notice* by Marilyn Hacker. Copyright © 1976, 1978, 1979, 1980 by Marilyn Hacker. Reprinted by permission of Frances Collin, Literary Agent.

Mark Halliday. "Seventh Avenue." From *Tasker Street* by Mark Halliday. Copyright © 1992 by Mark Halliday. Published by the University of Massachusetts Press. Reprinted by permission of the publisher.

Lorraine Hansberry. "A Raisin in the Sun." Copyright © 1958 by Robert Nemiroff, as an unpublished work. Copyright © 1959, 1966, 1984 by Robert Nemiroff. Used by permission of Random House, Inc.

Michael S. Harper. "Discovery." From *Men of Our Time: An Anthology of Male Poetry in Contemporary America*, University of Georgia Press, 1992. Reprinted with permission.

Robert Hayden. "Those Winter Sundays." From *Collected Poems of Robert Hayden* by Robert Hayden, edited by Frederick Glaysher. Used by permission of Liveright Publishing Corporation.

Seamus Heaney. "Mid-term Break." From *Opened Ground: Selected Poems 1966–1996* by Seamus Heaney. Copyright © 1998 by Seamus Heaney. "Valediction." From *Poems 1965–1975*. Copyright © 1980 by Seamus Heaney. Reprinted by permission of Farrar, Straus and Giroux, LLC. and Faber and Faber Ltd.

———. "Valediction." From *Poems 1965–1975*. Copyright © 1980 by Seamus Heaney. Reprinted by permission of Farrar, Straus and Giroux, LLC. and Faber and Faber Ltd.

Ernest Hemingway. "Hills Like White Elephants." From *The Short Stories of Ernest Hemingway* by Ernest Hemingway. Copyright © 1927 by Charles Scribner's Sons. Copyright renewed 1955 by Ernest Hemingway. Reprinted with permission of Scribner, an imprint of Simon & Schuster Adult Publishing Group.

Juan Felipe Herrera. "187 Reasons Why Mexicanos Can't Cross the Border." From *187 Reasons Why Mexicanos Can't Cross the Border: Undocuments* by Juan Felipe Herrera. Copyright © 2007. Reprinted by permission.

Jane Hirshfield. "Salt Heart." From *The Lives of the Heart* by Jane Hirshfield. Copyright © 1997 by Jane Hirshfield. Reprinted by permission of HarperCollins Publishers.

Tony Hoagland. "The Dog Years." From *Many Mountains Moving* (Summer 1998). Copyright © 1998 by Tony Hoagland. Reprinted with the permission of the author.

Linda Hogan. "Heritage." Reprinted by permission.

Carl M. Holman. "Mr. Z." Reprinted with permission of Mariella A. Holman.

Langston Hughes. "Harlem," "I, Too," and "Mother to Son." From *The Collected Poems of Langston Hughes*. Copyright © 1994 by the Estate of Langston Hughes. Reprinted by permission of Alfred A. Knopf, Inc., a division of Random House Inc. Used by permission of Alfred A. Knopf, a division of Random House, Inc.

Evelyn Lau. "Solipsim." From *In the House of Slaves* by Evelyn Lau. Copyright © 1994 (Coach House Press, 1994). Reprinted by permission of the author.

Li-Young Lee. "Eating Alone." From *Rose* by Li-Young Lee. Copyright © 1986 by Li-Young Lee. Reprinted with the permission of BOA Editions, Ltd. www.boaeditions.org

Ursula K. Le Guin. "The Ones Who Walk Away from Omelas." From *The Wind's Twelve Quarters*. Originally published in *New Dimensions 3*. Copyright © 1973, 2001 by Ursula K. Le Guin. Reprinted by permission of the author and the author's agent, the Virginia Kidd Agency, Inc.

Jonathan Lethem. "Super Goat Man." Originally published in *The New Yorker*, April 5, 2004. Copyright © 2004 by Jonathan Lethem. Reprinted by permission.

Denise Levertov. "The Ache of Marriage" and "O Taste and See." From *Poems 1960–1967*. Copyright © 1964, 1966 by Denise Levertov. Reprinted with the permission of New Directions Publishing Corporation.

Philip Levine. "What Work Is." From *What Work Is* by Philip Levine. Copyright © 1992 by Philip Levine. Used by permission of Alfred A. Knopf, Inc., a division of Random House, Inc.

Ellen Levy. "Mastering the Art of French Cooking." Previously published in *Salmagundi* and *The Best American Essays 2005*. Reprinted by permission of the author.

Stuart Lishan. "Winter Count, 1964." Reprinted by permission of the author.

Audre Lorde. "Power" and "Hanging Fire." From *The Black Unicorn* by Audre Lorde. Copyright © 1978 by Audre Lorde. Used by permission of W. W. Norton & Company, Inc.

Robert Lowell. "For the Union Dead." From *Collected Poems*. Copyright © 2003 by Harriet Lowell and Sheridan Lowell. Reprinted by permission of Farrar, Straus and Giroux, LLC.

D. W. Lucus. "The Drama of Oedipus." From *The Greek Tragic Poets* by D. W. Lucus. Copyright © 1950 by Routledge and Kegan Paul Ltd. Reprinted with permission of International Thomson Publishing Services, Ltd.

Katharyn Howd Machan. "Hazel Tells Laverne." From *Light Year 1985* by Katharyn Howd Machan. Reprinted with the permission of the author.

Katherine McAlpine. "Plus C'est la Même Chose." Originally published in *The Nation*. Copyright © 1994 by Katherine McAlpine. Reprinted with permission of the author.

David Means. "The Secret Goldfish." From *The Secret Goldfish: Stories* by David Means. Copyright © 2004 by David Means. Reprinted by permission of HarperCollins Publishers.

Peter Meinke. "Advice to My Son." From *Liquid Paper: New and Selected Poems* by Peter Meinke. Copyright © 1991. Reprinted by permission of the University of Pittsburgh Press.

Louis Menand. "The Graduates." Originally published in *The New Yorker*, May 21, 2007. Copyright © 2007 by Louis Menand. Reprinted by permission.

Robert Mezzey. "My Mother." From *The Door Standing Open* (London: Oxford University Press, 1970). Reprinted with permission of the author.

Arthur Miller. "Death of a Salesman" and "Tragedy and the Common Man." From *The Theatre Essays of Arthur Miller* by Arthur Miller, edited by Robert A. Martin. Copyright © 1949 and renewed 1977 by Arthur Miller. "Tragedy and the Common Man." Used by permission of Viking Penguin, a division of Penguin Group (USA) Inc.

Katherine Min. "Courting a Monk." Originally published in *TriQuarterly*, Winter 2006. Copyright © 2006 by Katherine Min. Reprinted by permission of the author.

Susan Minot. "My Husband's Back." Originally appeared in *The New Yorker*, August 22, 2005. Reprinted by permission of Georges Borchardt, Inc., on behalf of the author.

Janice Mirikitani. "Suicide Note." From *Shredding Silence* by Janice Mirikitani. Copyright © 1987 by Janice Mirikitani. Reprinted with the permission of Celestial Arts, Berkley California. www.tenspeed.com.

Lisel Mueller. "Happy and Unhappy Families." From *Alive Together* by Lisell Mueller. Copyright © 1996 by Lisel Mueller. Reprinted with the permission of Louisiana State University Press.

Bharati Mukherjee. "Two Ways to Belong in America." From *The New York Times*, September 22, 1996. Copyright © 1996 *The New York Times*. Reprinted by permission.

Taslima Nasrin. "Things Cheaply Had." From *The New Yorker*, October 9, 1995. Translated from the Bengali by Carolyne Wright, with Mohammad Nurul Huda and the author. Copyright © 1995 by Carolyne Wright. Reprinted with the permission of Carolyne Wright.

Pablo Neruda. "The Dead Woman." From *The Captain's Verses* by Pablo Neruda. Copyright © 1972 by Pablo Neruda and Donald D. Walsh. Reprinted with permission of New Directions Publishing Corporation.

Amy Tan. "Two Kinds." From *The Joy Luck Club* by Amy Tan. Copyright © 1989 by Amy Tan. Used by permission of G. P. Putnam's Sons, a division of Penguin Group (USA) Inc.

Dylan Thomas. "Do Not Go Gentle into That Good Night." From *Collected Poems of Dylan Thomas* by Dylan Thomas. Copyright © 1952 by Dylan Thomas. Reprinted with permission of New Directions Publishing Corporation and David Higham Associates, Ltd.

———. "Fern Hill." From *The Poems of Dylan Thomas* by Dylan Thomas. Copyright © 1945 by the Trustees for the copyrights of Dylan Thomas. Reprinted with permission of New Directions Publishing Corporation and David Higham Associates, Ltd.

Leo Tolstoy. "The Death of Iván Ilých." From *The Death of Iván Ilých and Other Stories*, translated by Louise and Aylmer Maude. Reprinted with the permission of Oxford University Press.

John Updike. "A&P." From *Pigeon Feathers and Other Stories* by John Updike. Copyright © 1962 and renewed 1990 by John Updike. Used by permission of Alfred A. Knopf, Inc., a division of Random House, Inc.

Helena Maria Viramontes. "The Moths." From *The Moths and Other Stories* by Helena Maria Viramontes. Copyright ©1985 Arte Público Press–University of Houston. Reprinted by permission from the publisher.

Alice Walker. "Everyday Use." From *In Love and Trouble: Stories of Black Women* by Alice Walker. Copyright © 1973 by Alice Walker. Reprinted by permission of Houghton Mifflin Harcourt Publishing Company.

David Foster Wallace. "Plain old untrendy troubles and emotions." From *The Guardian*, September 20, 2008 (Adapted from the commencement speech the author gave to a graduating class at Kenyon College, Ohio).

E. B. White. "Once More to the Lake." From *One Man's Meat* by E. B. White. Text copyright © 1941 by E. B. White, renewed. Reprinted by permission of Tilbury House Publishers, Gardiner, Maine.

David Wiles. "On Oedipus the King as a Political Play." From *Greek Theater Performance: An Introduction* by David Wiles. Copyright © David Wiles. Reprinted with the permission of Cambridge University Press.

Oscar Williams. "A Total Revolution." From *That's All That Matters* by Oscar Williams. Reprinted with permission.

Virginia Woolf. "What if Shakespeare Had Had a Sister?" Originally titled "Shakespeare's Sister" from *A Room of One's Own* by Virginia Woolf. Copyright © 1929 by Houghton Mifflin Harcourt Publishing Company, renewed 1957 by Leonard Woolf. Reprinted by permission of the publisher.

W. B. Yeats. "Leda and the Swan," "Sailing to Byzantium," "Easter 1916," and "The Second Coming." From *The Collected Works of W. B. Yeats, Volume I: The Poems, Revised*, edited by Richard J. Finneran. Copyright © 1928 by The Macmillan Company, renewed 1956 by Georgie Yeats. Reprinted with the permission of Scribner, a division of Simon & Schuster, Inc. All rights reserved.

———. "The Great Day." From *The Collected Works of W. B. Yeats, Volume I: The Poems, Revised*, edited by Richard J. Finneran. Copyright © 1940 by Georgie Yeats. Copyright © 1968 by Bertha Georgie Yeats, Michael Butler Yeats and Anne Yeats. Reprinted with the permission of Scribner, a division of Simon & Schuster, Inc. All rights reserved.

Yevgeny Yevtushenko. "I Would Like." From *Yevgeny Yevtushenko: The Collected Poems 1952–1990*, edited by Albert C. Todd. Copyright © 1991 by Henry Holt and Company, LLC. Reprinted with the permission of Lilia Todd.

Dean Young. "Elegy On Toy Piano." From *Elegy On Toy Piano* by Dean Young. Copyright © 2005. Reprinted by permission of the University of Pittsburgh Press.

Kevin Young. "For the Confederate Dead." From *For the Confederate Dead* by Kevin Young. Copyright © 2007 by Kevin Young. Reprinted by permission of Alfred A. Knopf, Inc., a division of Random House, Inc.

———. "Negative." From *To Repel Ghost: The Remix* by Kevin Young. Copyright © 2005 by Kevin Young. Reprinted by permission of Alfred A. Knopf, Inc., a division of Random House, Inc.

Tawfiq Zayyad. "Here We Shall Stay." From *Anthology of Modern Palestinian Literature*, edited by Salma Khadra Jayyusi. Copyright © 1992 by Columbia University Press. Reprinted with the permission of the publisher.

Art Credits

p. 24. The Dionysius Theatre in Athens. © Bettmann/CORBIS.

p. 25. Interior of the Swan Theatre, London, 1596. © Culver Pictures, Inc.

p. 26. Hypothetical reconstruction of the interior of the Globe Theatre in the days of Shakespeare. © Bettmann/CORBIS.

p. 26. A seventeenth-century French box stage. © Bettmann/CORBIS.

p. 78. *Pedro*, 1974, by Fernando Botero. Courtesy El Museo de Antioquia, Medellin, Colombia. Reproduced with permission.

p. 288. *Untitled*, 1985, by Keith Haring. © Keith Haring Foundation. Used by permission.

p. 544. *This Is Harlem* (detail), 1943, by Jacob Lawrence. © 2009 The Jacob and Gwendolyn Lawrence Foundation, Seattle/Artists Rights Society (ARS), New York. Image courtesy Hirshhorn Museum and Sculpture Garden.

p. 802. *Two Lovers*, 1630, by Safavid, Riza 'Abbasi (ca. 1565-1635), Isfahan, Iran. Tempera and gilt paint on paper; 7 1/8 x 4 11/16 in. (18.1 x 11.9 cm). The Metropolitan Museum of Art, Purchase, Francis M. Weld Gift, 1950. (50.164). Image © The Metropolitan Museum of Art. Reproduced with permission.

p. 1094. *Mushroom Bomb Pink*, 2001, by Takashi Murakami (Japanese, b. 1962). Offset lithograph, 500 x 500 mm. Edition of 300. © 2001 Takashi Murakami/Kaikai Kiki Co., Ltd. All Rights Reserved.

p. 1200. *Landscape with the Fall of Icarus*, ca. 1560, by Pieter Brueghel the Elder. Musée d'Art Ancien, Musées Royaux des Beaux-Arts, Brussels, Belgium. Photo credit: Scala/Art Resource, NY. Reproduced with permission.

p. 1202. *The Third of May, 1808*, by Francisco de Goya y Lucientes. Painted in 1814. Oil on canvas, 266 x 345 cm. Museo del Prado, Madrid, Spain. Photo credit: Erich Lessing/Art Resource, NY. Reproduced with permission.

p. 1204. *The Starry Night*, 1889, by Vincent van Gogh (1853-1890). Oil on canvas, 29″ x 36 ¼″. Acquired through the Lillie P. Bliss Bequest. (472.1941). The Museum of Modern Art, New York, NY, U.S.A. Digital image © The Museum of Modern Art/Licensed by SCALA/Art Resource, NY. Reproduced with permission.

p. 1206. *The Great Wave off Kanagawa* (from a series of "Thirty-six Views of Mount Fuji"), Edo period (1615-1868), ca. 1831-33, Katsushika Hokusai (Japanese, 1760-1849); Published by Eijudo, polychrome ink and color on paper; 10 1/8 x 14 15/16 in. (25.7 x 37.9 cm) (Oban size). The Metropolitan Museum of Art, H. O. Havemeyer Collection. Bequest of Mrs. H. O. Havemeyer, 1929, (JP 1847). Image © The Metropolitan Museum of Art. Reproduced with permission.